PERFORMING ARTS BOOKS IN PRINT

AN ANNOTATED BIBLIOGRAPHY

PERFORMING ARTS/

AN ANNOTATED BIBLIOGRAPHY / BY

DRAMA BOOK SPECIALISTS

BOOKS IN PRINT

RALPH NEWMAN SCHOOLCRAFT

ISBN: 0-910482-27-6
Library of Congress Catalog Card Number: 72-78909

Library of Congress Cataloging in Publication Data

Schoolcraft, Ralph Newman.
Performing arts books in print: an annotated bibliography.
1. Performing arts--Bibliography. I. Title.
Z6935.S34 016.7902 72-78909
ISBN 0-910482-27-6

INTRODUCTION

PERFORMING ARTS BOOKS IN PRINT: AN ANNOTATED BIBLIOGRAPHY is a thoroughly revised, rewritten, and up-dated edition of THEATRE BOOKS IN PRINT, originally published in 1963 and revised in 1966. Since the second edition of that work was published, many of the titles listed in that edition have gone out-of-print; many new works have been published; and new categories of books on the performing arts have been established.

This first edition of PERFORMING ARTS BOOKS IN PRINT was undertaken to provide an up-to-date annotated guide presenting descriptive information on all books concerned with the performing arts, including the literature of the theatre, drama, motion pictures, television, radio, and the mass media. Although there are diverse sources for much of the material, no single source lists and annotates books that are currently in print in the many areas of the performing arts.

Some limits had to be placed on the types of books that would be admitted to the bibliography. The listings are restricted to books that are now available in the United States. With few exceptions the books are in English; books in other languages are noted only when they treat an aspect of theatre not fully covered by works in English. No plays or collections of plays are included except those of Shakespeare, or those scholarly editions which provide, in addition to a text, an extensive study of the background, the style, the playwright's intention, etc. While books on musical theatre are listed, works that deal with music theory and composition are not; neither are books on the playing of musical instruments. In the selection of works on acting, some titles in the area of public speaking are included, but all works on debate, rhetoric, and forensics are omitted. The editor could not hope to provide complete coverage of works on the mass media, but trusts his selection of recent studies in the fields of advertising, the work of Marshall McLuhan, and the popular arts will be of help to theatre scholars.

The system of classification used in the first two editions of THEATRE BOOKS IN PRINT is followed here. PERFORMING ARTS BOOKS IN PRINT is divided into two major sections. The first section of the work includes works in print which were published prior to December 31, 1970; the second section, beginning on page 511, lists and annotates books published during the calendar year 1971, as well as those volumes published prior to that time which were not previously known to the editor.

Each section of the volume is broken down into four major parts: Books on Theatre and Drama; Books on the Technical Arts of the Theatre; Books on Motion Pictures, Television, and Radio; and Books on the Mass Media and The Popular Arts. These parts are subdivided into smaller units arranged according to a geographical area, historical period, important playwright, subdivision of a particular genre, or, as in the case of technical works, by skill.

There are approximately 12,000 entries. Each entry includes: author, title, publisher, year of publication, pagination, and price. Following this bibliographic information is an annotation of approximately sixty-five words explaining the contents of the book without attempting to be a critical evaluation. Each book listed has been examined and its overall theme and major premise have been taken into account in placing it in a particular category. Where no author's or editor's name appears on the book, the work has been given the designation "Anonymous."

No task as wide in scope as the completion of this bibliography can be achieved without the help, advice, criticism, and encouragement of many people. First of all, the classification system established in THEATRE BOOKS IN PRINT by A. E. Santaniello, was of such value that, had no such system existed, the editor would have abandoned the project many times before its completion. He is deeply grateful for the original scholarship provided by Mr. Santaniello. The counsel and encouragement of Mr. Arthur Seelen of The Drama Book Shop, and the assistance of his staff in researching new books, must also be acknowledged here. The editor is also grateful to Mr. Allen F. Collins of The Drama Book Shop and to Mr. Ralph Pine of Drama Book Specialists/Publishers for their confidence in the editor's abilities.

Credit must also be given to the many people who at one time or another assisted the editor in the preparation of the manuscript and the proofreading of the galleys: the Misses Betty Chambers, Carolyn Krigbaum, and Linda Lawrence, and the Messrs Robert Packard, Steve Schwarz, and Robert Trenour among them. Their help in trying circumstances was greatly appreciated. No listing of credits would be complete without citing the one person most responsible for the completion of this work. Miss Antoinette Pirrera's patience, good humor, and attention to detail in deciphering the editor's codes, in reading his writing, correcting his spelling, and, particularly, in the final design, layout, and paste-up of the work must be acknowledged with thanks.

The difficulties encountered in the compiling and editing of the bibliography were many and varied. The sheer volume of entries makes it inevitable that errors will appear, but the editor endeavored to be as accurate as possible. If there are omissions of specific books, misspellings of names, or mistakes in bibliographic information, the editor apologizes. Although this bibliography is offered as an improvement over the previous works available, there is no doubt that it, too, can be improved. It is the editor's hope that its flaws will be discovered so they can be corrected in future editions.

The facilities of The Drama Book Shop were used extensively for research by the editor and his staff. All books listed in PERFORMING ARTS BOOKS IN PRINT: AN ANNOTATED BIBLIOGRAPHY are available from The Drama Book Shop, 150 West 52 Street, New York, New York 10019.

Ralph Newman Schoolcraft

April, 1973

To enable purchasers of PERFORMING ARTS BOOKS IN PRINT to research new publications in their field in one convenient source, a quarterly compilation of new books is now available on a subscription basis.

Published four times a year, ANNOTATED BIBLIOGRAPHY OF NEW PUBLICATIONS IN THE PERFORMING ARTS is edited by Ralph Newman Schoolcraft. All books in the performing arts fields are catalogued in the Annotated Bibliography as soon as they become generally available in the United States and England. This paper bound bibliography is consistent in size, format, and specific categories with PERFORMING ARTS BOOKS IN PRINT.

Subscriptions are available on a prepaid basis. The cost of a one year subscription is $2.50. Please write directly to: ANNOTATED BIBLIOGRAPHY, 150 West 52 Street, New York, New York 10019.

TABLE OF CONTENTS

NATIONAL THEATRES

PART TWO: BOOKS ON TECHNICAL ARTS

PART THREE: BOOKS ON MOTION PICTURES, TELEVISION, AND RADIO

PART ONE

BOOKS ON THEATRE AND DRAMA

PART ONE: BOOKS ON THEATRE AND DRAMA

GENERAL REFERENCE WORKS

BIBLIOGRAPHIES

ADELMAN, IRVING and RITA DWORKIN — Compilers
Modern Drama: A Checklist of Critical Literature on 20th Century Plays
Scarecrow, 1967. 370pp. $10.00. This is a selective survey of the critical literature of the twentieth century drama. The compilers have arranged their list alphabetically by author. Title of work, where it first appeared, publisher, and date of publication are all given where possible.

BAKER, BLANCH M.
Dramatic Bibliography
Blom, 1968. 320pp. $17.50. Originally published in 1933, and now reissued, this bibliography contains over 4,000 annotated entries covering books on all aspects of English and American theatre published between the last decades of the nineteenth century and 1933. Author Index. Analytical Subject Index.

BAKER, BLANCH M.
Theatre and Allied Arts
Blom, 1967. 536pp. $17.50. A reissue of the 1952 publication, this is a guide to books dealing with the history, criticism, and technic of the drama and theatre and related arts and crafts. The guide is divided into three main parts: (1) Drama, Theatre and Actors; (2) Stagecraft and Allied Arts; (3) Miscellaneous Reference Material. Author and Subject Indices.

BELKNAP, S. Y. — Compiler
Guide to the Performing Arts: 1963
Scarecrow, 1963. 515pp. $12.00. A guide to articles on theatre, drama, dance and music. The articles and reviews appeared during the calendar year of the volume in both American and foreign periodicals.

BELKNAP, S. Y. — Compiler
Guide to the Performing Arts: 1964
Scarecrow, 1964. 447pp. $12.00. A guide to articles on theatre, drama, dance and music. The articles and reviews appeared during the calendar year of the volume in both American and foreign periodicals.

BELKNAP, S. Y. — Compiler
Guide to the Performing Arts: 1965
Scarecrow, 1965. 422pp. $13.50. A guide to articles on theatre, drama, dance and music. The articles and reviews appeared during the calendar year of the volume in both American and foreign periodicals.

BELKNAP, S. Y. — Compiler
Guide to the Performing Arts: 1966
Scarecrow, 1966. 307pp. $11.00. A guide to articles on theatre, drama, dance and music. The articles and reviews appeared during the calendar year of the volume in both American and foreign periodicals.

BELKNAP, S. Y. — Compiler
Guide to the Performing Arts: 1967
Scarecrow, 1969. 514pp. $17.50. A guide to articles on theatre, drama, dance and music. The articles and reviews appeared during the calendar year of the volume in both American and foreign periodicals.

BIDDULPH, HELEN R. and JULIA H. MAILER — Compilers
Bibliography of Books, Pamphlets and Magazines Relating to Community Theatre
A.E.T.A., 1966. 21pp. $ .75. This bibliography suggests some possible sources of information on various theatre subjects related to community theatre. Pamphlet is mimeographed and stapled.

BOSTON PUBLIC LIBRARY
A Catalogue of the Allen A. Brown Collection of Books Relating to the Stage in the Public Library of the City of Boston
Kraus, 1970. 952pp. $35.00. Originally published in 1919 and now reissued, this is a catalogue of books in the Boston Library concerning the history of the stage. Arranged in dictionary form, the catalogue contains authors, titles, and subjects in a single alphabet. Information includes place of publication, publisher, date, and number of pages.

BROCKETT, OSCAR G. and SAMUEL L. BECKER, DONALD C. BRYANT
A Bibliographical Guide to Research in Speech and Dramatic Art
Scott, Foresman, 1963. 118pp. $3.50. The aim of this book is to list the important aids and reference tools in the field and to place these aids in the general context of relevant material in other works of reference.

BUSFIELD, ROGER M.
Theatre Arts Publications Available in the United States 1953 — 1957: A Five Year Bibliography
A.E.T.A., 1964. 188pp. $5.00. This bibliography reflects the availability of theatre arts periodicals in the United States. Author Index.

CHESHIRE, DAVID
Theatre
Shoe String, 1967. 131pp. $4.95. This is a study of literature about the theatre. Divided into six sections: general reference works; histories; dramatic criticism; biographies; theories; and current periodicals. Mr. Cheshire examines principal or significant works, analyzes and discusses their contents to provide a composite critical survey. Index.

COLEMAN, ARTHUR and GARY TYLER
Drama Criticism: Volume I

Swallow, 1966. 457pp. $7.50. A bibliography of criticism on American and British drama appearing in periodicals and books published from 1940 to 1964. Over 1,000 periodicals and 1,500 books were researched to provide the material in the two sections of the volume: "Plays by Shakespeare" and "Plays Other Than Shakespeare's." A Bibliography lists sources in which criticism was found and an Appendix lists periodicals containing criticism.

COLEMAN, EDWARD D. – Compiler
The Jew in English Drama
New York Public Library, 1970. 265pp. $12.00. An annotated bibliography, originally published in 1943 and now reprinted. Among works in the volume are bibliographies, general works, collections, individual plays from the earliest times to 1938, and an index of authors and an index of titles. Also included in the volume are an essay by Edgar Rosenberg entitled "The Jew In Western Drama" and a check list of titles.

CORNYN, STAN
A Selective Index to Theatre Magazine
Scarecrow, 1964. 289pp. $7.00. A selective guide to the articles, authors, subjects, and dramatic works in Theatre Magazine from 1901 to 1931. There are approximately 45,000 references.

DUKORE, BERNARD F.
A Bibliography of Theatre Arts Publications in English: 1963
A.E.T.A., 1965. 82pp. Paper $3.00. Compiled by the Bibliography Project of the AETA, this listing is first by author, then by subject in three main categories: time, country, and subject area.

HUNTER, FREDERICK J. – Editor
A Guide to the Theatre and Drama Collections at the University of Texas
University of Texas, 1967. 85pp. $5.00. Paper $2.00. This volume catalogues some of the materials in the theatre and drama collections at the University of Texas. Illustrated with photographs and other material from the collections.

LITTO, FREDRIC M.
American Dissertations on the Drama and the Theatre
Kent State University, 1969. 519pp. $16.50. This bibliography brings together references to all doctoral dissertations on subjects related to theatre, drama, and the performing arts completed in all academic departments of American universities. Author Index. Key Word-in-Context Index. Subject Index.

LOWE, ROBERT W.
A Bibliographical Account of English Theatrical Literature
Gale Research, 1966. 384pp. $14.00. Originally published in 1888 and now reissued, this bibliography deals with theatrical literature rather than plays. A short summary of the content of the work, author, publisher, and date are given.

MELNITZ, WILLIAM
Theatre Arts Publications in the United States 1947–1952: A Five Year Bibliography
A.E.T.A., 1959. 91pp. Paper $3.00. The 4,063 titles included in this bibliography are all of books and articles on the theatre and related media that appeared in the United States and Canada during the period 1947–1952.

PRITNER, CALVIN LEE – General Editor
A Selected and Annotated Bibliography for the Secondary School Theatre Teacher and Student
A.E.T.A., 1968. 70pp. Paper $1.95. This mimeographed pamphlet is an annotated list of in print reference works on the theatre. Included are works on theatre history, books on technical aspects such as acting and directing, and books on children's theatre, radio, television, and film.

REARDON, WILLIAM R. and THOMAS D. PAWLEY – Editors
The Black Teacher and the Dramatic Arts: A Dialogue, Bibliography, and Anthology
See Page 246

VEINSTEIN, ANDRE – Editor
Performing Arts Libraries and Museums of the World: Second Edition
Editions du Centre National de la Recherche Scientifique, 1967. 801pp. $20.75. Originally published in 1960, this bilingual second edition, revised and enlarged by Cecile Giteau, is a census of all the known performing arts collections, libraries, and museums throughout the world. The general characteristics of the collection, the nature of the documents, hours and admission procedures, and assistance given to the reader are noted. Index of Names. Subject Index.

WELKER, DAVID
Educational Theatre Journal: A Ten Year Index 1948–1958
A.E.T.A., 1959. 84pp. Paper $3.00. Each article that has appeared in the Journal in the period is listed by author, title, and subject.

DICTIONARIES

BARNET, SYLVAN and MORTON BERMAN, WILLIAM BURTO – Editors
Aspects of the Drama: A Handbook
See Page 10

BOWMAN, WALTER P. and ROBERT H. BALL – Editors
Theatre Language: A Dictionary of Terms in English

Theatre Arts, 1961. 428pp. $7.95. Definitions of over 3,000 terms and phrases selected from every era from the Middle Ages to the present. Technical and standard non-technical terms, jargon, cant, and slang are defined and cross-referenced.

EAGLE, DOROTHY
The Concise Oxford Dictionary of English Literature
Oxford, 1970. 628pp. $8.00. Paper $2.95. This abridgment of Harvey's "Oxford Companion to English Literature" was first published in 1939. It has been revised by Miss Eagle, and reset in the light of the fourth edition of the parent volume, and includes in abbreviated form all Harvey's principal entries on authors and their works and on mythological and his torical subjects relating to English literature. Brief notes refer the reader to sources for more than a thousand characters from books and plays. Included are short articles on general literary topics and terms. These have been revised to take account of development or research during the last thirty years.

GRANVILLE, WILFRED
A Dictionary of Theatrical Terms
Andre Deutsch, 1952. 206pp. $5.75. This alphabetized glossary of theatrical terms, published in England, covers technical and colloquial terms, slang and jargon, and gives definitions, derivations, and information as to usage.

RAE, KENNETH and RICHARD SOUTHERN – Editors
An International Vocabulary of Technical Theatre Terms in Eight Languages
Theatre Arts, 1960. 139pp. $5.25. The technical vocabulary of the theatre in American English, Dutch, English, French, German, Italian, Spanish and Swedish. Complete indices and marginal space for notations are included.

ENCYCLOPEDIAS

GASSNER, JOHN and EDWARD QUINN – Editors
The Reader's Encyclopedia of World Drama
Crowell, 1969. 1,030pp. $15.00. A single volume reference work that covers the drama as literature from its ritual origins to the present on all five continents. The entries by ninety-five specialists fall into four general categories: national drama, playwrights, plays, genres. All entries of substantial length include bibliographic references. An appendix of basic documents in dramatic theory is included. About 350 photographs and drawings illustrate the text.

GAYE, FREDA – Editor
Who's Who in the Theatre: 14th Edition
Pitman, 1967. 1,720pp. $25.00. A biographical record of the contemporary stage. Included are biographical summaries of theatrical personalities, playbills of the London and Stratford theatres, and many other features related to the British theatre.

HALL, LILLIAN ARVILLA
Catalogue of Dramatic Portraits in the Theatre Collection of the Harvard College Library
Harvard University. Volume One: 1930. 438pp. Volume Two: 1931. 427pp. Volume Three: 1932. 456pp. Volume Four: 1934. 357pp. Four Volume Set: $24.00. These volumes provide a descriptive index to the engraved dramatic portraits in the Collection. The prints, about 40,000, considered in this index are portraits of individuals, chiefly British and American, whose names are associated with theatre history. Dates of birth and death are noted where possible and each engraving is described as to type, measurement, creator, source, and style of composition. Sold in four volume set only.

HARTNOLL, PHYLLIS – Editor
The Oxford Companion to the Theatre: Third Edition
Oxford, 1967. 1,088pp. & plates, $15.00. Originally published in 1957 and now reissued with much new material. This volume covers the history of theatre in all countries and in all its aspects from acoustics and architecture, through costume, lighting, make-up, and scenery. A new section of forty pages of illustrations has been added.

MELCHINGER, SIEGFRIED
The Concise Encyclopedia of Modern Drama
Horizon, 1964. 269pp. $15.00. Translated by George Wellwarth and edited by Henry Popkin, with a Foreword by Eric Bentley, this volume includes critical biographies of more than 800 dramatists from Shaw to the new American and British artists. Analyses of plays and discussions of main trends, extensive glossary, important documents by leading playwrights, and a chronology of opening nights are provided. Illustrated with over 150 photographs.

RIGDON, WALTER – Editor
The Biographical Encyclopaedia and Who's Who of the American Theatre
J.H. Heineman, 1965. 1,101pp. $82.50. This reference book contains biographies of important persons connected with every aspect of American theatre, a list of New York productions from 1900 through May 1964, lists of premieres of American plays abroad since 1946, production records of theatre groups, a biographical Bibliography, and a Discography.

PLAY GUIDES AND INDICES

BERGQUIST, G. WILLIAM – Editor
Three Centuries of English and American Plays: A Checklist
Hafner, 1963. 281pp. $30.00. An index to English

plays from 1515 to 1800 and to American plays from 1714 to 1830. It lists approximately 5,500 plays giving the earliest extant edition available and later significant editions of every important play published during the periods covered. Illustrated.

CARTMELL, VAN H. – Editor
Plot Outlines of 100 Famous Plays
Doubleday, 1962. 416pp. Paper $1.45. Synopses of five ancient Greek and Roman plays, thirty-nine English, nineteen American, six Russian, and twenty-three from other countries.

COLLEY, D. I.
Handlist of Plays
Manchester Public Library, 1965. Unpaged. Paper $2.75. Over 2,600 titles in the play collection of the Manchester Public Libraries, London, England, are listed by author, whether drama or comedy, number of characters and sets.

CORRIGAN, BEATRICE
Catalogue of Italian Plays: 1500–1700
See Page 212

EDYVEAN, ALFRED R.
Religious Drama Project Play List
A.E.T.A., Undated. 24pp. Paper $100. This mimeographed list of plays suitable for religious drama projects includes author, title, cast requirements, type of play, publisher, and length of play.

FIDELL, ESTELLE A. and DOROTHY MARGARET PEAKE – Editors
Play Index: 1953–1960
Wilson, 1963. 404pp. $15.00. This volume indexes 4,592 plays in 1,735 volumes published during the period 1953–1960. Entries are indexed under author, title, and subject. Information includes, author, title, description phrase, number of acts and scenes, size of cast, and number of sets required, as well as publisher and date. Complete information on collections is provided as is a directory of publishers and a section designed to locate plays by number of players in the cast.

FIDELL, ESTELLE A. – Editor
Play Index: 1961–1967
Wilson, 1968. 464pp. $22.00. An index to 4,793 plays, both individual works and collections, published from 1961 to 1967. Entries are indexed by author, title, and subject. List of Collections Indexed. Directory of Publishers and Distributors. One section is designed to locate plays by numbers of players in the cast.

HAZLITT, W. CAREW – Editor
A Manual of Old English Plays
Franklin, 1966. 284pp. $25.00. Originally published in 1892, the bibliography of English plays, listed by title, extends to the end of the seventeenth century. Information given includes, where possible, author, date of first performance, and date of first publication. Also included are a List of Collected Works of Dramatic Authors and Collections of Old English Plays. Index of Names, Theatres, Theatrical Companies, and City Guilds.

HILL, FRANK PIERCE
American Plays Printed: 1714–1830
Blom, 1968. 152pp. $12.50. Originally published in 1934, this is the most complete listing of plays written and published by American authors, foreign authors living in America, and American authors living abroad during the period covered. The author has provided alphabetical lists by author and by title and a chronological list by title.

IRELAND, NORMA OLIN
Index to Full Length Plays: 1944–1964
Faxon, 1965. 296pp. $10.00. A twenty year selective coverage of full length plays published in English. Approximately 979 authors, 1,962 subjects and 1,187 titles are included.

IRELAND, NORMA OLIN
An Index to Monologs and Dialogs
Faxon, 1949. 171pp. $7.50. A listing of material published prior to 1948.

IRELAND, NORMA OLIN
Index to Monologs and Dialogs: Supplement
Faxon, 1959. 160pp. $8.00. A list of material published between 1948 and 1958.

IRELAND, NORMA OLIN
An Index to Skits and Stunts
Faxon, 1958. 348pp. $9.50. The author has indexed 148 collections by author, title, and subject. The main entry is under title. Authors are listed when possible and number of characters necessary is given. Included are monologs and dialogs, burlesque, chorus materials, and minstrels.

JOHNSON, ALBERT
Best Church Plays
Pilgrim, 1968. 180pp. Paper $3.95. A bibliography of religious drama which features alphabetical listings, subject matter listings, and addresses of publishers, authors and agents. Pertinent information on content, age group, number and sexes of characters, running times, scenes, props, and prices is given for each play.

LASS, ABRAHAM H. and MILTON LEVIN – Editors
A Student's Guide to 50 American Plays
Washington Square Press, 1969. 316pp. Paper $ .75. A guide to fifty American plays with plot outlines, character and setting descriptions, critical evaluations, and author's biographies. A special introduction on "How to Read a Play" is included. Index of Titles, Authors, and Main Characters.

LOGASA, HANNAH and WINIFRED VER NOOY – Editors
An Index to One-Act Plays
Faxon, 1924. 327pp. $9.00. This index contains over 5,000 titles of one-act plays written in English, or translated into English, published from 1900 to 1923. Author, number of characters, background, and location of published play are given.

LOGASA, HANNAH and WINIFRED VER NOOY – Editors
An Index to One-Act Plays: Supplement 1924–1931
Faxon, 1932. 432pp. $9.00. This supplement contains over 7,000 titles. The arrangements and information follow the order of the previous volume.

LOGASA, HANNAH and WINIFRED VER NOOY – Editors
An Index to One-Act Plays: Second Supplement 1932–1940
Faxon, 1941. 556pp. $9.00. Over 8,000 titles are listed in this volume. The subjects of the plays are analyzed fully and subject headings have been increased in number in order to increase the usefulness of the book.

LOGASA, HANNAH – Editor
An Index to One-Act Plays: Third Supplement 1941–1948
Faxon, 1950. 318pp. $9.00. This volume includes about 4,000 plays with information and arrangement, following the order of the previous volumes.

LOGASA, HANNAH – Editor
An Index to One-Act Plays: Fourth Supplement 1948–1957
Faxon, 1958. 245pp. $9.00. There are over 2,000 plays listed in this index. The arrangements and information follow the order of the previous volumes.

LOGASA, HANNAH – Editor
An Index to One-Act Plays for Stage, Radio, and Television: Fifth Supplement 1956–1964
Faxon, 1966. 260pp. $10.50. A bibliography of 1,000 one-act plays. They are indexed by title, author, and subject and there is a list of collections with the various titles that appear in them.

MERSAND, JOSEPH
Index to Plays with Suggestions for Teaching
Scarecrow, 1966. 114pp. $5.00. This Index has been compiled to enable teachers of modern plays to make a selection of various authorities in developing his own techniques of teaching. The lists include both one act and longer plays and radio and television plays to be found in collections designed to be used in schools. The lists are annotated to include title, author, anthology in which the play may be found, publisher, date of publication, and biographical information on the author as well as study aids on the play.

MURPHY, DONN B.
A Director's Guide to Good Theatre
National Contemporary Theatre Conference, 1968. 84pp. Paper $3.50. A guide to play selection for the director in school situations. It includes title, author, a short summary, production details, and publisher for short and full length plays of various types.

NICOLL, ALLARDYCE
A History of English Drama Vol. Six: Alphabetical Catalogue of the Plays
See Page 147

OTTEMILLER, JOHN H.
Index to Plays in Collections
Scarecrow, 1964. 370pp. $12.50. This volume lists more than 2,500 plays appearing in collections published in England and the United States from 1900 through 1962. Plays are listed by author and title.

PLAY LIST REVISION COMMITTEE OF THE SECONDARY SCHOOL THEATRE CONFERENCE
Plays Recommended for High Schools
A.E.T.A.,1967. 8pp. Paper $ .50. This mimeographed list of plays suitable for high schools includes title, author, publisher, type of play, and cast requirements.

RODEN, ROBERT F.
Later American Plays: 1831–1900
Franklin, 1900. 136pp. $12.50. A compilation of the titles of plays, by American authors, published and performed in America during the period indicated in the title of the volume. It includes title, author, type of play, production details, and producer. Indices.

SALEM, JAMES M.
Drury's Guide to Best Plays
Scarecrow, 1969. 512pp. $17.50. A second edition of the bibliography originally authored in 1953 by Francis K. W. Drury and now revised and re-edited by Mr. Salem. Plays are listed by author with date of first performance or publication, translator – if any, publisher, a short resume of the plot, cast information, and royalty information – if available. Various indices group the plays by subjects, award winners, plays for amateur groups, plays for high school groups, and plays requiring no scenery. Index of Authors and Adaptors. Index of Titles.

SHANK, THEODORE – Editor
A Digest of 500 Plays: Plot Outlines and Production Notes
Collier, 1963. 475pp. $5.95. Paper $1.95. Individual commentary on plays from the ancient theatre to the present, with date of composition, foreign title when appropriate, and an interpretive description of the plot. Included are production notes defining the casting and set requirements and the staging problems. Information on available translations, texts, royalty requirements, and publishers is also provided.

SHARP, HAROLD S. and MARJORIE Z. SHARP
Index to Characters in the Performing Arts. Part I: Non-Musical Plays
Scarecrow, 1966. 1,533pp. $39.50. An alphabetical listing which identifies 30,000 characters with the play in which they appear, tells something about the character, indicates the author of the play, and shows the year in which the play was written, produced, copyrighted or published. Some 3,600 plays by 1,400 authors are included with a time range from the late fifth century to the 1964–1965 Broadway season. This is a two volume set.

SHIPLEY, JOSEPH T.
A Guide to Great Plays
Public Affairs Press, 1956. 867pp. $12.00. Alphabetical listing of 660 masterpieces of world drama, with plot summaries, information on the lives of playwrights, on significant productions, and on leading interpreters of roles. Opinions of critics are included.

SOBEL, BERNARD
The New Theatre Handbook and Digest of Plays
Crown, 1959. 749pp. $5.95. A revision of the 1940 edition, this volume contains synopses of over 1,000 plays, glossaries of theatre terms, bibliographies of works on plays and playwrights, biographies, and information on productions and producers, amateur and professional groups, and leading actors and actresses.

SPRINCHORN, EVERT – Editor
20th Century Plays in Synopsis
Crowell, 1966. 492pp. $6.95. Act-by-act synopses of 133 representative dramas by modern playwrights from Strindberg to Albee. Many of the plays summarized are not generally available here and several have never been translated into English. This volume also contains biographical information on playwrights.

STRATMAN, CARL J.
Bibliography of English Printed Tragedy: 1565–1900
Southern Illinois University, 1966, 843pp. $15.00. A listing of over 1,700 titles of English tragedies first published between 1565 and 1900. There are 6,852 numbered entries arranged in alphabetical order according to author. Each entry gives author, title, imprint, pagination, library symbols, and necessary notes or commentaries.

STRATMAN, CARL J.
Dramatic Play Lists: 1591–1963
New York Public Library, 1966. 44pp. Paper $2.25. This study is devoted to an enumeration and evaluation of printed play lists, arranged chronologically. It attempts to include every significant work which relates to the category of play lists. The full title of each work, the publisher, pagination, scope of the work, number of plays in each work, the relative merits, and the editions are given. Index.

THOMPSON, LAWRENCE S.
A Bibliography of Spanish Plays on Microcards
Shoe String, 1968. 490pp. $16.00. A bibliography of more than 6,000 Spanish, Spanish American, and Catalonian dramas, from the sixteenth century to the present, which have been published in microcard editions from 1957 through 1966. The majority of the plays belong to the dramatic production of Spain's nineteenth century but a significant number of titles from the Golden Age and modern Spain are included.

THOMSON, RUTH G.
Index to Full-Length Plays: 1895–1925
Faxon, 1956. 172pp. $9.50. Plays in English are listed, with cast requirement, type of play, and set and costume requirements.

THOMSON, RUTH G.
Index to Full-Length Plays: 1926–1944
Faxon, 1946. 306pp. $8.00. This index lists 1,340 titles, representing 879 authors. Subject Index.

WEST, DOROTHY H. and DOROTHY M. PEAKE
Play Index: 1949–1952
Wilson, 1953. 239pp. $10.00. An author, title, and subject index to 2,616 plays. Included are cast analyses, and annotation on type and production requirements.

WEST, DOROTHY H. and DOROTHY M. PEAKE
Play Index: 1953–1960
Wilson, 1963. 401pp. $13.00. An index to 4,592 plays in 1,735 volumes in the same arrangement as the companion volume listed above.

ANNUALS

CHAPMAN, JOHN – Editor
The Best Plays Series
Dodd, Mead, $10.00 per volume. The first volumes in this series were edited by Burns Mantle. See that listing for description. See also succeeding editor listings: Louis Kronenberger, Henry Hewes, and Otis L. Guernsey.
Best Plays of 1947–1948. 494pp.
Best Plays of 1948–1949, 486pp.
Best Plays of 1949–1950. 437pp.
Best Plays of 1950–1951. 429pp.
Best Plays of 1951–1952. 387pp.

GUERNSEY, OTIS L. – Editor
The Best Plays Series
Dodd, Mead. $10.00 per volume. The first volumes in this series were edited by Burns Mantle. See that listing for description. See also suceeding editor listings: John Chapman, Louis Kronenberger, and Henry Hewes.
The Best Plays of 1964–1965. 434pp.

The Best Plays of 1965–1966. 508pp.
The Best Plays of 1966–1967. 498pp.
The Best Plays of 1967–1968. 495pp.
The Best Plays of 1968–1969. 526pp.
The Best Plays of 1969–1970. 476pp.

HEWES, HENRY – Editor
The Best Plays Series
Dodd, Mead. $10.00 per volume. The first volumes in this series were edited by Burns Mantle. See that listing for description. See also succeeding editor listings: John Chapman, Louis Kronenberger, and Otis L. Guernsey.
The Best Plays of 1961–1962. 413pp.
The Best Plays of 1962–1963. 432pp.
The Best Plays of 1963–1964. 467pp.

KRONENBERGER, LOUIS – Editor
The Best Plays Series
Dodd, Mead. $10.00 per volume. The first volumes in this series were edited by Burns Mantle. See that listing for description. See also succeeding editor listings: John Chapman, Henry Hewes, and Otis L. Guernsey.
The Best Plays of 1952–1953. 374pp.
The Best Plays of 1953–1954. 433pp.
The Best Plays of 1954–1955. 490pp.
The Best Plays of 1955–1956. 472pp.
The Best Plays of 1956–1957. 446pp.
The Best Plays of 1957–1958. 402pp.
The Best Plays of 1958–1959. 405pp.
The Best Plays of 1959–1960. 435pp.
The Best Plays of 1960–1961. 436pp.

MANTLE, BURNS – Editor
The Best Plays Series
Dodd, Mead. $10.00 per volume. Each volume includes, by excerpt and summary, the ten most representative plays of the Broadway season. In addition, it lists the full casts for each production of the year plus other statistics. There are also the usual statistical summary of the season; a complete listing of all Broadway and off-Broadway productions; Shakespeare festivals; important premieres of plays in the United States and Europe; birth statistics of prominent actors; a necrology; information on the London and European seasons are included in later volumes as are annual awards. In later volumes one of the ten best plays is presented by means of a photographic summary. Volumes of later years include drawings by caricaturist Al Hirschfeld. (See also John Chapman, Louis Kronenberger, Henry Hewes, and Otis L. Guernsey.)
The Best Plays of 1919–1920. 474pp.
The Best Plays of 1920–1921. 471pp.
The Best Plays of 1921–1922. 574pp.
The Best Plays of 1922–1923. 610pp.
The Best Plays of 1923–1924. 471pp.
The Best Plays of 1924–1925. 635pp.
The Best Plays of 1925–1926. 637pp.
The Best Plays of 1926–1927. 563pp.
The Best Plays of 1927–1928. 588pp.
The Best Plays of 1928–1929. 537pp.
The Best Plays of 1929–1930. 584pp.
The Best Plays of 1930–1931. 570pp.
The Best Plays of 1931–1932. 559pp.
The Best Plays of 1932–1933. 545pp.
The Best Plays of 1933–1934. 574pp.
The Best Plays of 1934–1935. 529pp.
The Best Plays of 1935–1936. 561pp.
The Best Plays of 1936–1937. 549pp.
The Best Plays of 1937–1938. 527pp.
The Best Plays of 1938–1939. 545pp.
The Best Plays of 1939–1940. 524pp.
The Best Plays of 1940–1941. 482pp.
The Best Plays of 1941–1942. 508pp.
The Best Plays of 1942–1943. 543pp.
The Best Plays of 1943–1944. 548pp.
The Best Plays of 1944–1945. 501pp.
The Best Plays of 1945–1946. 515pp.
The Best Plays of 1946–1947. 555pp.

MERRYN, ANTHONY – Editor
The Stage Year Book
Carson & Comerford. $7.95 per volume. Complete statistical record of the London season. Production, casts, and other statistics of London theatre, opera, and ballet productions. Festivals, ice shows, television productions, and British company repertories on tours are included. Reference section lists theatres, managements, music publishers, press representatives, etc. Essays on various aspects of the season are also provided. Illustrated. Index.
The Stage Year Book: 1968. 474pp.
The Stage Year Book: 1969. 464pp.

WILLIS, JOHN – Editor
Theatre World
Crown. $8.95 per volume. A pictorial and statistical record of all Broadway and off-Broadway productions, plus professional repertory companies, Lincoln Center, New York Shakespeare Festival, and national touring company productions. Biographies of actors and an obituary section are included as are lists of award winning productions and actors. Illustrated with hundreds of photographs. Index.
Volume 23: 1966–1967. 286pp.
Volume 24: 1967–1968. 272pp.
Volume 25: 1968–1969. 272pp.
Volume 26: 1969–1970. 288pp.

PHILOSOPHY OF THEATRE

THEORIES OF DRAMATIC ART

ALTENBERND, LYNN and LESLIE L. LEWIS
A Handbook for the Study of Drama
Macmillan, 1966. 85pp. Paper $1.25. The authors cover the nature and elements of drama, traditional types of plays, and the nature of modern plays. They try to indicate the connection between theatres and societies.

ALTSHULER, THELMA and RICHARD JANARO
Responses to Drama: An Introduction to Plays and Movies
Houghton Mifflin, 1967. 351pp. Paper $3.50. It is the purpose of this book to assist playgoers, film viewers, and readers in the making of critical evaluations of dramatic experiences. Illustrated. Glossary. Selected Bibliography. Index.

BARNET, SYLVAN and MORTON BERMAN, WILLIAM BURTO – Editors
Aspects of the Drama: A Handbook
Little, Brown, 1962. 270pp. $4.00. A Handbook consisting of two sections: a collection of essays that examines basic issues of dramatic art and theatre development; and a dictionary (with Bibliography) of dramatic terms.

BARRY, JACKSON G.
Dramatic Structure: The Shaping of Experience
University of California, 1970. 261pp. $9.75. The author shows how dramatic structure is derived and how it is used in the shaping of a play. He probes the origins of the dramatic form as an expression of experience and an image of man's interaction in time. Appendices. Notes. Index.

BATE, W. JACKSON
The Burden of the Past and the English Poet
Harvard, 1970. 141pp. $5.95. An investigation of the responses of English writers to the predicament of achieving anything new. The author concentrates especially on the period between 1660 and 1830 as the first modern period to face the problem on a large scale. He analyzes the eighteenth century and the Romantic writers' discussion of the problem and their efforts to solve it. Index.

BATE, WALTER J.
Criticism: The Major Texts
Harcourt, 1952. 610pp. $11.50. This is an anthology of the essential contributions of thirty-eight critics from classical antiquity to the present day. Among the critics represented are: Aristotle, Ben Jonson, William Hazlitt, and Edmund Wilson. Index.

BECKERMAN, BERNARD
Dynamics of Drama: Theory and Method of Analysis
Knopf, 1970. 272pp. Paper $4.50. The author proposes a theory of dramatic form and illustrates a method of descriptive analysis. He clarifies the relationship between theatre and drama and details the central element of drama, examing how it is structured, how it can be modified and varied, how it exerts its power in the presence of an audience, and how it can be organized into different modes.

BELASCO, DAVID
The Theatre Through Its Stage Door
Blom, 1969. 246pp. $12.50. Edited by Louis V. Defoe and originally published in 1919. Now reissued in a facsimile edition, this volume is a compendium of the theatrical producer/playwright/actor's theories, views, and practices in the making of his theatrical productions, in the training and development of actors, and in the regulation and direction of the elements which enter into the mounting and unfolding of works of dramatic art. Illustrated with photographs.

BENTLEY, ERIC
The Life of the Drama
Atheneum, 1964. 371pp. Paper $2.95. This is Mr. Bentley's comprehensive study of drama. Part One discusses plot, character, dialogue, thought, and enactment. Part Two considers such types of plays as melodrama, farce, tragedy, comedy, and tragi-comedy. Index.

BENTLEY, ERIC – Editor
The Theory of the Modern Stage
Penguin, 1968. 493pp. Paper $2.45. The essays in this anthology comprise an introduction to modern theatre and drama. Among the theatrical theorists who reveal the ideas underlying their productions and point to the possibilities of the modern theatre are: Adolphe Appia, Antonin Artaud, Bertolt Brecht, E. Gordon Craig, Pirandello, Shaw, Stanislavsky, and Romain Rolland. Index of Authors and Works.

BROWN, IVOR
What Is a Play?
Dufour, 1970. 160pp. $3.95. In this study of the nature of drama, Mr. Brown discusses such topics as the changing styles of acting in relation to the changing purposes of the dramatist and the special problems of writing for television. Illustrated. Index.

BROWN, JOHN RUSSELL
Drama
Heinemann, 1968. 105pp. Paper $1.75. Professor Brown examines the role of the theatre in relation to the other arts. He reviews plays and theatres, actors, design, television drama, and dramatic criticism and examines the possible future developments of the theatre and the part it could play in modern society. Suggestions for Further Reading.

BROWN, JOHN RUSSELL
Effective Theatre
Heinemann, 1969. 250pp. $9.50. This volume is the author's own view of the theatre: What it is, how it works, and what it achieves. There are chapters on actors, on training and criticism, theatre organization and design, styles of performance and the development of theatrical forms. The main emphasis is on the present day although theatrical history is referred to wherever it is relevant to a particular topic. Sixteen pages of plates illustrate theatres, actors, stage settings, and stage design. Suggestions for Further Reading.

CALDERWOOD, JAMES and HAROLD E. TOLIVER – Editors
Perspectives on Drama
Oxford, 1968. 453pp. Paper $3.25. This is a collection of essays on dramatic theory. The editors attempt to assemble some sort of coherent image out of a great many ways of looking at the literary and theatrical aspects of drama.

CAMERON, KENNETH M. and THEODORE J. C. HOFFMAN
The Theatrical Response
Macmillan, 1969. 429pp. $10.50. This text is designed to develop the student's response to theatre both as literature and performance. The authors concentrate on seven plays as they examine the elements in the creation of performance — acting, directing, and design — and the function of criticism. The plays studied are: "Oedipus Rex," "Everyman," "Hamlet," "Phaedra," "The Miser," "Death of a Salesman," and "Endgame." Illustrated with photographs, drawings, and diagrams. Appendix of Technical Practice. Glossary. Bibliography. Index.

CLARK, BARRETT H.
European Theories of the Drama
Crown, 1965. 628pp. $7.50. This fully annotated collection of writing on drama from Aristotle to the present has been established as one of the great standard reference works in its field. Commentaries, biographies, and bibliographies are included on all entries. This edition of the work originally published in 1945 has been completely revised by Henry Popkin and brings the work up to date with material on Ibsen, Strindberg, Chekhov, and representatives of important modern movements in drama, and such schools as realism, problem drama, poetic and folk drama, epic theatre, and theatre of the absurd. Bibliography. Index.

CORRIGAN, ROBERT W. and JAMES L. ROSENBERG – Editors
The Context and Craft of Drama
Chandler, 1964. 466pp. Paper $5.50. An anthology of essays on the nature, language, structure, and criticism of drama, as well as studies of the function of the playwright, actor, director, designer, and critic.

DICKINSON, HUGH
Myth on the Modern Stage
University of Illinois, 1969. 359pp. $8.50. The use of classical mythology by playwrights conspicuous for their modernity is described and analyzed in this interpretive study of the theatre of Anouilh, Cocteau, Eliot, Gide, Giraudoux, Ionesco, Jeffers, O'Neill, Sartre, and Williams. Bibliography. Index.

EDMAN, IRWIN
Arts and the Man
Norton, 1949. 154pp. Paper $1.85. A revised and enlarged edition of the book published in 1928 as "The World, the Arts and the Artist." The book is a consideration of the arts out of which the aesthetic reflection arises.

ELLIS–FERMOR, UNA
The Frontiers of Drama
Methuen, 1964. 162pp. $4.50. Paper – 1967. $2.25. A second edition of the work published in 1945, with a new introduction by Allardyce Nicoll and a bibliography by Harold Brooks. The book is a study of the relation between content and form in drama — the conflict between the ultimate reconciliation of certain kinds of material and the demands of dramatic form and technique.

FERGUSSON, FRANCIS
The Human Image in Dramatic Literature
Peter Smith, 1957. 217pp. $3.00. A collection of essays whose major concern is with the establishment and projection in literature and the theatre of a genuine and complex image of man. Included are essays on the American theatre since World War I, on Brecht, Joyce, Wilder, T.S. Eliot, Lorca, on Boleslavsky's theory of acting, and on several of Shakespeare's plays. A final essay explores methods and attitudes of criticism.

FERGUSSON, FRANCIS
The Idea of a Theatre
Princeton, 1968. 240pp. $8.50. Paper $1.95. Originally published in 1949 and now reissued, this is a study of ten plays which illustrate the art of drama in its changing perspective. The plays studied are: "Oedipus Rex," "Berenice," "Tristan und Isolde," "Hamlet," "Ghosts," "The Cherry Orchard," "Six Characters in Search of an Author," "Infernal Machine," "Noah," and "Murder in the Cathedral."

FREEDMAN, MORRIS
The Moral Impulse
Southern Illinois University, 1967. 136pp. $4.95. This study of modern drama from Ibsen to the present gives critical attention to drama as a form of literature. The author calls the trend of probing the depths of human relationships "the moral impulse" and he discusses drama from this angle. Among the dramatists discussed are Iben, Shaw, Strindberg, Chekhov, O'Casey, Lorca, and Brecht. Index.

FRYE, NORTHROP
Anatomy of Criticism
Atheneum, 1970. 383pp. Paper $3.50. Originally published in 1957 and now reprinted, this an attempt to give "a synoptic view of the scope, theory, principles, and techniques of literary criticism." The four essays deal with historical, ethical, archetypal, and rhetorical criticism. Notes. Glossary. Index.

FRYE, NORTHROP and L. C. KNIGHTS, et al
Myth and Symbol: Critical Approaches and Applications
University of Nebraska, 1963. 196pp. Paper $1.95. Fifteen essays that analyze the use of symbolism and myth in various literary forms. Among the studies are considerations of "King Lear," "All's Well," and such playwrights as Brecht and Chekhov.

GLICKSBERG, CHARLES I.
The Self in Modern Literature
Pennsylvania State University, 1963. 218pp. $7.50. The author maintains that modern literature represents a continuous effort at self-revelation and shows this effort to be the basic impulse in the works of Strindberg, Ibsen, Kafka, Gide, Beckett, and others. Index.

GRANVILLE-BARKER, HARLEY
On Dramatic Method
Hill & Wang, 1956. 191pp. Paper $1.35. An investigation of the basic laws of dramatic art. Such authors as Aeschylus, Shakespeare, and Ibsen are studied in terms of the theatre of their day and their dramatic theories are shown to derive from use rather than authority.

GRENE, DAVID
Reality and the Heroic Pattern
University of Chicago, 1967. 169pp. $5.00. Paper $1.95. In this study of the last plays of Ibsen, Shakespeare, and Sophocles, the author sees the plays as forming a kind of series with common features of plot and treatment and similar theme. Selected Bibliography. Notes.

HAMBURGER, KATE
From Sophocles to Sartre
Ungar, 1969. 186pp. $6.50. In this study, Dr. Hamburger offers a new thesis to explain why playwrights through the centuries have returned to the heroes and heroines of Greek drama to find subjects for their theatre. She defines the figures and not the themes as the subject of her study. The author is concerned with the modern reinterpretations by contemporary playwrights, among them Anouilh, Braun, Giraudoux, Hauptmann, Sartre, and Wilder. Index.

HARDISON, O. B.
Christian Rite and Christian Drama in the Middle Ages
Johns Hopkins, 1966. 328pp. $7.50. Paper—1969. $2.45. This is a collection of essays on the origins and early history of modern drama. The author reassesses the knowledge available concerning the early history of medieval drama, examines the relation of drama to ritual, the nature of dramatic form, and the development of representational techniques. A chronology of early liturgical plays of the tenth through the thirteenth centuries is included. Index.

HATLEN, THEODORE W.
Orientation to the Theatre
Appleton, 1962. 286pp. Paper $4.50. A study of dramatic structure, its techniques, and the various forms of dramatic composition, all within the context of the cultural milieu.

HATTERER, LAWRENCE J.
The Artist in Society
Grove, 1966. 188pp. Paper $1.95. Dr. Hatterer formulates important generalizations about the creative process and the psychological problems of the artist.

HAUGER, GEORGE
Theatre – General and Particular
M. Joseph, 1966. 213pp. $5.00. This book takes a very broad view of theatre and deals with problems related to opera and ballet as well as the play. The book begins by asking the question: "What is the essential nature of this activity called theatre?" Other chapters deal with particular aspects of theatre such as financing.

HOGAN, ROBERT and SVEN ERIC MOLIN – Editors
Drama: The Major Genres
Dodd, Mead, 1962. 652pp. Paper $6.95. This anthology contains the following plays: "Antigone," "King Lear," "The House of Bernarda Alba," "The Silent Woman," "Tartuffe," "The Six of Calais," "The Three Sisters," "The Plough and the Stars," "Yegor Bulychov and the Others," "The American," and "Bus Stop." Also included are historical introductions, selections from criticism, critical essays, and discussion questions on each play.

HONIG, EDWIN
Dark Conceit: The Making of Allegory
Oxford, 1958. 210pp. Paper $1.65. This book examines the changing conceptions of allegory to the present, examines the typical construction of allegorical narrative, and studies the three essential verbal modes in allegory.

HUNNINGHER, BENJAMIN
The Origin of the Theatre.
Hill & Wang, 1961. 114pp. $3.75. Paper $1.35. An essay which questions the assumption that the festivals of the Christian Church in the Middle Ages gave rise to the modern theatre. The author suggests that theatre originated with the adaptation by the Church of surviving pagan rites and pantomimes. Illustrated.

INGLIS, FRED
An Essential Discipline
Barnes & Noble, 1968. 272pp. $6.50. Paper $3.50. This book describes the techniques and procedures of criticism. The author states his own moral and critical position and goes on to outline the student's approach to a poem, a novel, or a play. Index.

JELLICOE, ANN
Some Unconscious Influences in the Theatre
Cambridge, 1967. 36pp. Paper $ .95. Miss Jellicoe considers some of the ways in which a dramatist imposes his truth upon an audience in the theatre and the audience's conscious and unconscious reactions to this stimulus.

JOHNSON, ALBERT
Drama: Technique and Philosophy
Judson, 1963. 282pp. $6.95. A textbook for drama students designed to equip them with the essential technical knowledge necessary for work in the theatre, as well as with a philosophy of acting and participating in the life of the theatre.

JOURDAIN, ELEANOR F.
Dramatic Theory and Practice in France 1690 – 1808
Blom, 1968. 240pp. $12.50. Originally published in 1921, this volume traces the development and shows the relation between stage practices and the theories of Voltaire, Diderot, Rousseau, and Marie-Joseph Chenier. Miss Jourdain studies the experiments of the eighteenth century in an attempt to find the roots of nineteenth century French Romantic drama.

KERNODLE, GEORGE R.
Invitation to the Theatre
Harcourt, 1967. 677pp. $11.00. This introductory textbook considers all major forms of the theatre and shows how playwrights both past and present shaped their plays in different ways to express different aspects of their times and their attitudes toward life. It also describes the ways in which the director, actor, and the designer work together to create a production. Illustrated. Index.

KIRBY, E. T. – Editor
Total Theatre
Dutton, 1969. 280pp. $6.95. Paper $2.45. A critical anthology in which the editor contends that the theatre is the place of intersection of all the arts and that there must be an effective interplay among the various elements or a significant synthesis of them.

LEECH, CLIFFORD
The Dramatist's Experience and Other Essays
Barnes & Noble, 1970. 248pp. $8.50. Professor Leech expounds his belief that, in its proper condition, criticism should be "agnostic, existentialist, republican." The essays discuss phenomena which either recur in literature or are associated with a particular place and period. Index.

MANHEIM, LEONARD and ELEANOR MANHEIM
Hidden Patterns: Studies in Psychoanalytic Literary Criticism
Macmillan, 1966. 310pp. $6.95. Outstanding psychologists and literary critics discuss the psychoanalytic interpretation of literary themes and character motivations. Among the contributions are Freud on Shakespeare, Mark Kanzer on the Oedipus trilogy, and Richard Hovey on "The Cocktail Party." Index.

MANN, THOMAS
Last Essays
Knopf, 1959. 218pp. $4.95. Thomas Mann's last essays include "On Schiller," "Fantasy on Goethe," and "Chekhov." Included is a listing of Mann's principal works.

MARK, MILTON
The Enjoyment of Drama
Appleton, 1961. 167pp. $2.50. A revised edition of the book first published in 1940, with chapters on the purpose and aim of drama, the nature of a play, "Conflict: The Essence of Drama," the structure of a play, tragedy, comedy, literary movements and the drama, and on judging a play. Bibliography.

MINER, EARL
The Japanese Tradition in British and American Literature
Princeton, 1966. 312pp. Paper $2.95. Originally published in 1958, this is a general historical survey of the effect of Japanese literature on British and American authors. One of the chapters deals with the Kabuki and No as dramatic criteria and there is a chapter on Yeats and the No plays. Bibliographical Essay. Notes. Index.

NICOLL, ALLARDYCE
The Theatre and Dramatic Theory
Barnes & Noble, 1962. 221pp. $3.75. A study of the theoretical approach to drama which developed from the sentimental movement of two centuries ago and which still dominates the modern theatre. The author analyzes the nature of drama, the types of dramatic compositions, and the limitations and potential virtues of the modern audience.

NICOLL, ALLARDYCE
The Theory of Drama
Blom, 1966. 262pp. $8.50. A reissue of the 1931 publication in which Professor Nicoll presents in systematic form a discussion of each characteristic of the dramatic art, showing the evolution of various types of drama from Ancient Greece to the theatre of Ibsen and Shaw. Also examined are the various critical theories of drama that have dominated each age and the "rules" of comedy, tragedy, melodrama, and farce. Suggestions for Reading. Index.

ORTEGA Y GASSET, JOSE
The Dehumanization of Art

Princeton, 1968. 204pp. Paper $2.45. Originally published in Spain in 1925 and now translated and issued in the U.S., this is a collection of essays by the twentieth century Spanish philosopher. In the title essay the author attempts to ascertain the meaning of the new intents of art in music, painting, poetry, and the theatre. There is also an essay on the novel, on point of view in the arts, and one on Goethe.

PETERKIEWICZ, JERZY
The Other Side of Silence
Oxford, 1970. 128pp. $5.00. The author is concerned with the crisis of the poet who finds himself at the limits of language and the alternatives open to him—activism, the cult of experience, actual or poetical suicide—and their meaning for poetry. Poetic drama throughout the ages is discussed as an aspect of this problem. Index.

SELDEN, SAMUEL
Man in His Theatre
University of North Carolina, 1957. 113pp. $3.00. A practicing playwright analyzes the nature of drama. The origins of drama are seen in man's protoplasmic inheritance and are traced through primitive worship, early rituals of the seasons, and early myth.

SELDEN, SAMUEL
Theatre Double Game
University of North Carolina, 1969. 123pp. $6.00. The author shows how playwrights, actors, and directors serve the playgoer as creators and guides to his part in the performance as the primary player in the playhouse. Mr. Selden shows how theatre at its best illumines, excites, and fulfills its spectators and how the skilled theatre artist creates this kind of experience in the playhouse.

SHANK, THEODORE
The Art of Dramatic Art
Dickenson, 1969. 206pp. $7.95. This is an introductory theatre text in which the author attempts to present a coherent way of comprehending dramatic art without reliance on the other arts. The approach develops a theory of dramatic art as a single fine art distinct from literature and the other arts. This theory provides a basis for understanding the creative process of the art and works of dramatic art from all periods. Bibliography.

SORELL, WALTER
The Duality of Vision: Genius and Versatility in the Arts
Bobbs—Merrill, 1970. 360pp. $15.00. Mr. Sorell analyzes the phenonenon of creative versatility. After examining the nature of creativity and versatility in general, the author discusses outstanding examples of multiple creative talent down the centuries. He singles out prominent artists and discusses their social and cultural background, analyzes the psychological factors which influenced them and compares the artists' accomplishments in various media. The chapter on performing artists discusses actors as painters and dramatists, and dancers as writers, choreographers and painters. Illustrated with almost 150 drawings and plates. Notes. Bibliography. Index.

STEIN, WALTER
Criticism as Dialogue
Cambridge, 1969. 253pp. $7.50. Mr. Stein argues that there is, and must be, a specifically Christian attitude toward tragedy. In his restatement of the "radical Christian humanist" philosophy, he aims to test his standpoint in dialogue with liberal humanist or Marxist approaches to literature. The central chapter on Chekhov and "King Lear" develops Mr. Stein's position and he also discusses Eliot's "The Cocktail Party" and the work of Beckett. Index.

STUART, DONALD CLIVE
The Development of Dramatic Art
Dover, 1960. 679pp. Paper $3.50. A study of dramatic art with emphasis on the social pressures which brought about changes, on the origins of styles, and on the influences for change in each period. The author analyzes changes in such structural matters as exposition, plot devices, stock situations, point of attack, and characterization.

STYAN, JOHN LOUIS
The Elements of Drama
Cambridge, 1960. 306pp. $5.50. Paper $1.95. A study in three parts of dramatic theory. The author analyzes the elements which build events on the stage, the way these elements are organized, and the value judgments the playgoer makes. Included is a Reading List and a list of references. Indices.

TUNISON, JOSEPH S.
Dramatic Traditions of the Dark Ages
Franklin, 1970. 350pp. $15.75. Originally published in 1907 and now reprinted, this is a study of the process of the transfer of theatrical aptitudes from the East to the West, and from ancient to modern times. The author analyzes the quarrels between the church and the theatre, the dramatic impulses in religion, ancient Eastern influences on Western theatre, and traditions of Ancient and Mediaeval Italy that were passed on. Index.

VAN LAAN, THOMAS F.
The Idiom of Drama
Cornell University, 1970. 374pp. $15.00. The devices and strategems that dramatists employ to elicit audience response are defined and illustrated in this contribution to dramatic theory. Examples are drawn primarily from Aeschylus' "Oresteia," Shakespeare's "Hamlet," and Ibsen's "Rosmersholm." The author combines a schematic theory of dramatic structure and interpretation with a detailed analysis of the plays to show how dramatic action works and how dramatic effects are achieved. Index.

WEALES, GERALD
A Play and Its Parts
Basic Books, 1964. 165pp. $5.50. The author elucidates the playwright's craft, the art of creating characters, the language and dress of the stage, and the technique of directing. Illustrated with references to such productions as Guthrie's "The Three Sisters" and Kazan's "After the Fall."

WEISSMAN, PHILIP
Creativity in the Theatre: A Psychological Study
Basic Books, 1965. 276pp. $8.50. Paper—Dell, 1966. 275pp. $1.95. The author, a practicing psychoanlyst, attempts to find what there is in the makeup, milieu, artistic endowment, childhood development and design of unconscious drives that link the actor, dramatist, director, and critic to his creative contribution to the theatre. There are studies of such theatre personalities as Stanislavski, John Wilkes Booth, Shaw, O'Neill, and Williams. The critical contributions that psychoanalysis can make to modern theatre are investigated. Bibliography. Index.

WILLIAMS, RAYMOND
Drama in Performance
Watts, 1968. 198pp. $3.50. Originally published in 1954 and now revised and expanded, the central theme of this study is the changing relationship between dramatic forms and methods of performance in the history of European drama. Analyses of plays in performance, including "Antigone," "Antony and Cleopatra," and "Family Reunion," form the central part of the book. Illustrated. Selected Bibliography. Index.

WRIGHT, EDWARD A. and LENTHIEL H. DOWNS
A Primer for Playgoers: Second Edition
Prentice–Hall, 1969. 335pp. $8.95. Originally published in 1958 and now reissued in an expanded edition, this text covers all of the aspects of a live theatre production — writing, direction, acting, technical elements, and design. An analysis of fourteen plays illustrates the distinction between reading and seeing a play. The questions for discussion and bibliographies follow each section. Glossary of Theatre Terms. Index.

THEORIES OF COMEDY AND TRAGEDY

ABEL, LIONEL – Editor
Moderns on Tragedy
Fawcett, 1967. 416pp. Paper $ .95. Major essays by playwrights, critics, and philosophers about the nature of tragedy from the time of the Greeks through the twentieth century. Among the writers included are: Jean Giraudoux, W. H. Auden, Paul Goodman, H. D. F. Kitto, G. Wilson Knight, Friedrich Nietzsche, and Francis Fergusson.

BENSON, CARL and TAYLOR LITTLETON
The Idea of Tragedy
Scott, Foresman, 1966. 370pp. Paper $4.75. The authors divide their book into two parts: Idea and Tragedy. In the first section they attempt to define tragedy and in the second they discuss six of the great tragedies of the theatre.

BERGSON, HENRI and GEORGE MEREDITH
Comedy
Doubleday, 1956. 260pp. Paper $1.45. This volume includes two classic essays on the nature of comedy: "An Essay on Comedy" by George Meredith and "Laughter" by Henri Bergson. Wylie Sypher has contributed an introduction to the volume and an essay, "The Meaning of Comedy," in which he discusses the new sense of the comic in modern drama, the ancient rites of comedy, and the social meaning of comedy.

BLISTEIN, ELMER
Comedy in Action
Duke University, 1964. 143pp. $4.00. Concerned with comedy as revealed on the stage and screen, this book ranges over the whole field of comic characters and situations. Comic theories of the past are examined, and a new theory—the drive for respectability as an aspect of the comic character—is proposed. Bibliography. Index.

BRERETON, GEOFFREY
Principles of Tragedy
University of Miami, 1969. 285pp. $7.95. Dr. Brereton seeks to establish the basis for a definition of tragedy. Various theories are examined and tested on representative works by Sophocles, Shakespeare, Racine, Ibsen, Beckett, and others, and the findings are developed. Index.

CALARCO, N. JOSEPH
Tragic Being: Apollo and Dionysus in Western Drama
University of Minnesota, 1968. 202pp. $6.00. This is a study of tragedy in Western drama from classic to modern times. The author examines twelve plays by nine playwrights to explore the order hidden beneath tragedy's visible circle of action and suffering and the value which that order assigns to human existence. Bibliography. Index.

CORRIGAN, ROBERT W. – Editor
Tragedy: Vision and Form
Chandler, 1965. 474pp. Paper $6.50. Essays on the characteristics and effects of tragedy by such critics and philosophers as Karl Jaspers, Susanne Langer, George Boas, D. D. Raphael, Eric Bentley, Robert Heilman, and William Arrowsmith.

COURTNEY, W. L.
The Idea of Tragedy in Ancient and Modern Drama
Russell & Russell, 1967. 132pp. $7.50. Originally published in 1900 and now reissued, this study

begins with the premise that tragic drama has its birth in the popular mind and not in the intellectual nature of man. The study consists of three lectures originally delivered in England and the volume includes a Prefatory Note by Arthur Wing Pinero.

COX, SAMUEL S.
Why We Laugh
Bloom, 1969. 387pp. $12.50. A new edition of the 1880 publication of Cox's study. This Civil War politician believed that wit was the indispensable ingredient of the political address. In his analysis, he turned to the actual reports of his fellow Congressmen for his illustrations.

ELLIOTT, ROBERT C.
The Power of Satire: Magic, Ritual, Art
Princeton, 1960. 300pp. Paper $2.95. The author studies satire from primitive magic and incantation to its use by such modern writers as Wyndham Lewis, Shakespeare, Moliere, and Johathan Swift. Mr. Elliott attempts to reveal the place of the satirist in society. Index.

FEIBLEMAN, JAMES K.
In Praise of Comedy
Horizon, 1970. 284pp. Paper $2.95. Originally published in 1939 and now reissued, this is a philosophical inquiry into the meanings and nature of the comic. The author includes a survey of the history of comedy, some classic theories of comedy, and criticism of modern theories of comedy. Index.

FEINBERG, LEONARD
The Satirist: His Temperament, Motivation, and Influence
Iowa State University, 1963. 370pp. $4.95. Paper—Citadel, 1965. 370pp. $2.25. An analysis of satiric writings and writers which discusses the personality of the satirist, the reasons he writes in this mode, and the relation of his work to other creative arts and to society. Among the satirists examined are Voltaire, Swift, Mark Twain, Lewis Carroll, Bernard Shaw, James Thurber, and W.H. Auden.

FRYE, PROSSER HALL
Romance and Tragedy
University of Nebraska, 1961. 372pp. Paper $1.25. A study of classic and romantic elements in the great tragedies of European literature. The playwrights discussed are the Greek tragic playwrights, Racine, Corneille, Shakespeare, and Calderon.

GUTHKE, KARL S.
Modern Tragicomedy
Random House, 1966. 205pp. Paper $3.00. The author intends to furnish a background for the study and enjoyment of tragicomic drama. He concentrates on the theoretical problems of the genre and the meaning and significance of modern tragicomedy. Notes. Bibliography. Index of Authors and Plays.

HATHORN, RICHMOND Y.
Tragedy, Myth, and Mystery
Indiana University, 1962. 282pp. $6.75. Paper $2.65. The author examines "Oresteia," "Antigone," "Oedipus Rex," "Hippolytus," "Bacchae," "Hamlet," "King Lear," and "Murder in the Cathedral" to show how each is based on a myth that symbolizes man's mysterious place in the universe. Index.

HENN, T.R.
The Harvest of Tragedy
Barnes & Noble, 1966. 304pp. $6.00. Paper $2.50. A reprint of the 1956 edition of the study in which the author discusses Shakespeare, Racine, Ibsen, Shaw, Synge, Eliot, Yeats, Lorca, and Anouilh. Mr. Henn analyzes the psychological implications of the tragic form each writer used. The author suggests a synthesis in terms of the Christian tradition as stated by Niebuhr and his school. Bibliography. Index.

HERRICK, MARVIN T.
Comic Theory in the Sixteenth Century
University of Illinois, 1964. 248pp. Paper $1.75. This study indicates that Terence and the Terentian commentators furnished the principal matter for the discussion of comedy in the sixteenth century, and that the study of Terence laid the foundations of Renaissance theories of comedy. Bibliography. Index.

HERRICK, MARVIN T.
Tragicomedy: Its Origin and Development in Italy, France, and England
University of Illinois, 1962. 331pp. Paper $1.95. A study of the mixed drama that flourished during the second half of the sixteenth century and the first half of the seventeenth. The classical background is studied and the contributions of Terence and of Giraldi Cinthio are analyzed. French tragicomedy from Garnier to Corneille and English works from Beaumont and Fletcher through Davenant are studied.

HOY, CYRUS
The Hyacinth Room: An Investigation into the Nature of Comedy, Tragedy, and Tragicomedy
Knopf, 1964. 318pp. $5.95. The author contends that the fundamental basis of all valid dramatic literature is the conflict between man's heavenly aspirations and his worldly involvements. The elements of this conflict seen in each type of drama and the qualities that distinguish treatment in each genre are examined. Among the dramatists studied are Euripides, Shakespeare, Ibsen, Chekhov, and Beckett. Index.

JACQUOT, JEAN — Editor
Le Theatre Tragique
Editions du Centre National de La Recherche Scientifique, 1965. 540pp. $14.25. A collection of articles on tragic theatre from the Greek and Roman periods to the Renaissance to today. The text is in the French language. Illustrated. Index.

JASPERS, KARL
Tragedy Is Not Enough
Archon, 1969. 123pp. $5.00. A consideration of tragic knowledge and the meaning of tragedy. The volume includes an Introduction by Karl W. Deutsch and a postscript on the sources of Jaspers' style by Harold A. T. Reiche. Notes. Bibliography. Index.

KAUFMANN, WALTER
Tragedy & Philosophy
Doubleday, 1968. 388pp. $6.95. Paper—1969. 460pp. $1.95. Professor Kaufmann's central aim is to develop an approach to tragedy and thus illuminate Greek tragedy and tragedy in our time. He takes issues with traditional ideas about both tragedy and philosophy and applies his ideas to Greek literature, Shakespeare, and contemporary drama. Bibliography. Index.

KERNAN, ALVIN B.
The Plot of Satire
Yale, 1966. 227pp. $8.75. The author suggests a new definition of satire and attempts to clear away a great deal of the imprecision in commonly accepted notions of the genre. He studies "Volpone," "The Dunciad," and Byron's "Don Juan" among others. Index.

KERR, WALTER
Tragedy and Comedy
Simon & Schuster, 1967. 350pp. $5.95. Paper—1968. 355pp. $2.45. Mr. Kerr discusses the development and meaning of tragedy and comedy. He analyzes the masterpieces of the past—from Aristophanes to Chekhov and the new theatre of Beckett, Osborne, Albee, and others—in the light of criteria traditionally applied only to the classics. Included is a list of sources quoted and references.

KROOK, DOROTHEA
Elements of Tragedy
Yale, 1969. 279pp. $6.75. This volume uses examples from a wide range of familiar dramas to isolate four elements fundamental to the universal tragic pattern: an act or situation of shame or horror which precipitates a spectacle of intense human suffering followed by a deeper knowledge of man's condition issuing in a final reaffirmation of the value of human life. Mrs. Krook tests the validity of her scheme by examining plays by Sophocles, Shakespeare, Ibsen, Chekhov, and Thomas Middleton. Notes. Index.

LAUTER, PAUL—Editor
Theories of Comedy
Doubleday, 1964. 529pp. Paper $1.95. In this anthology Plato, Minturno, Jonson, Moliere, Hazlitt, Emerson, Schiller, Freud, Santayana, Frye and others examine comedy and the comic from every critical perspective: analysis of comic plot and character; statements on the social and moral function of comedy; inquiries into the nature of the ridiculous and the role of laughter; and the psychology of comedy.

LEASKA, MITCHELL A.
The Voice of Tragedy
Speller, 1963. 313pp. $6.00. This study considers the main philosophical attitudes toward tragedy and examines the human processes which shaped those attitudes from the time of the Greeks. Tragic attitudes in major playwrights are examined in detail and are related to the distinctive values of Western culture.

LEECH, CLIFFORD
Tragedy
Methuen, 1969. 92pp. $2.85. Paper $1.45. Professor Leech considers the significance of the term "tragedy" as it has been used from classical times to the present day. He gives examples of tragic writing from a wide variety of dramatic literatures and relates theoretical writings on tragedy and the tragedies that have been contemporaneous with them. Special stress is laid on the tragedies of the Greeks, of the Renaissance writers, and of Harold Pinter and Tom Stoppard. Select Bibliography. Index.

LUCAS, F. L.
Tragedy: Serious Drama in Relation to Aristotle's "Poetics"
Collier, 1962. 160pp. Paper $1.25. Originally published in 1958 and now revised, this study begins with an investigation of Aristotle's definition of tragedy, then examines the problems raised by the "Poetics" and considers its relation not only to Greek tragedy but to the plays of Shakespeare, Racine, Ibsen, and the modern dramatists.

MANDEL, OSCAR
A Definition of Tragedy
New York University, 1961. 178pp. $6.00. Paper $1.95. After a survey of trends from Aristotle to the present in the definition of the term "tragedy," the author proposes a definition of the term. Dr. Mandel maintains that the tragic idea is permanent rather than historical or national. He analyzes the character of the hero, the question of free will, tragic guilt, consciousness, and recognition to provide an understanding of tragedy. In a final chapter he explores the sources of tragic literature in the world of actual experience. List of References. Index.

MATTHEWS, HONOR
The Primal Curse: The Myth of Cain and Abel in the Theatre
Schocken, 1967. 221pp. $5.95. Miss Matthews traces The Cain-Abel myth in drama from Shakespeare and Chapman to Beckett, Camus, and Pinter. She shows how it has informed not only characterization and plotting but also visual stage imagery and theatrical style. Miss Matthews provides an extended study of dramatists concerned with the myth. Index.

MEREDITH, GEORGE and HENRI BERGSON
Comedy
See Under: **BERGSON, HENRI**

MONRO, D.H.
Argument of Laughter
University of Notre Dame, 1963. 264pp. Paper $1.95. First published in 1951 and now reissued, this is an analysis of humor. Professor Monro theorizes that humor falls into four main classes; these he summarizes from his own critical point of view. Index.

MULLER, HERBERT J.
The Spirit of Tragedy
Washington Square Press, 1965. 320pp. Paper $ .75. In this reprint of the study first published in 1956, the author investigates the peculiar Western impulse that has given rise to tragedy in our literature. The philosophical and cultural implications of tragedy are discussed and major playwrights are analyzed.

MYERS, HENRY ALONZO
Tragedy: A View of Life
Cornell University, 1965. 210pp. Paper $1.95. Originally published in 1956, this is a study of tragedy. Myers studies the great tragic playwrights from Sophocles to O'Neill as well as poetry and novels and the lives of the great. Index.

NIETZSCHE, FRIEDRICH
The Birth of Tragedy and The Case of Wagner
Vintage, 1967. 223pp. Paper $1.65. Translated with commentary by Walter Kaufmann, these two books by Nietzsche deal with art and culture and the problems of the modern age. Bibliography. Index.

O'CONNOR, WILLIAM VAN and MARY ALLEN O'CONNOR
Climates of Tragedy
Russell & Russell, 1965. 155pp. $7.75. The chief aim of the authors has been "to present a theory of philosophical patterns in which the tragic spirit conceivably may have inhered." The authors discuss Periclean Greece and Elizabethan England and analyze several of the great tragic dramas.

OLSON, ELDER
The Theory of Comedy
Indiana University, 1968. 145pp. $4.50. Paper $1.95. In the first chapters of this volume, Mr. Olson reviews the critical literature of comedy and presents his "poetics of comedy." He offers definitions of comic terms, analyzes the components of comedy and defines its major forms. In succeeding chapters he examines the masterpieces of comic dramatic literature from the Greeks through Moliere, Shakespeare, Shaw, and the twentieth century dramatists. Index.

OLSON, ELDER
Tragedy and the Theory of Drama
Wayne State University, 1961. 269pp. $6.95. Paper $2.95. An inquiry into dramatic principles from the point of view of the working dramatist. The problems the dramatist faces, the technical means of their solution, and the philosophical principles governing the choice of different solutions are considered. There are detailed expositions of "Agamemnon," "King Lear," and "Phedre," and a chapter on modern drama.

POTTS, L.J.
Comedy
Putnam, 1966. 174pp. Paper $1.45. A survey of the various forms and styles of comic writing from ancient times to the present day. The author includes discussions on Aristophanes, Cervantes, Shakespeare, Jonson, Moliere, Dryden, Congreve, and Shaw. Bibliography. Index.

PRIESTLEY, J.B.
The English Comic Characters
Dutton, 1966. 242pp. Paper $1.35. First published in 1925, this is a collection of literary criticism on the characters created by Shakespeare, Dickens, Fielding, Sterne, Austen, and Peacock.

PRIOR, MOODY E.
The Language of Tragedy
Indiana University, 1966. 430pp. Paper $2.95. First published in 1947, this volume examines the language of tragic drama. The author attempts to discover the relationship between the language of plays written in verse and the dramatic nature of the form. Index.

RAPHAEL, D.D.
The Paradox of Tragedy
Indiana University, 1960. 112pp. $3.00. Paper $1.45. The author rejects the Aristotelian concept of catharsis and defines tragedy as a conflict between two forms of the sublime in which the sublimity of human nature is exalted above that of overwhelming power.

RISTINE, FRANK H.
English Tragicomedy: Its Origin and History
Russell & Russell, 1963. 247pp. $7.50. A reprint of the original edition published in 1910, this study discusses the origins of tragicomedy in Greek and Roman drama, traces early developments on the continent, and shows the evolution of the type in England from 1564 through 1700. List of plays of the type in England. Bibliography.

SEDGEWICK, G.G.
Of Irony, Especially in Drama
University of Toronto, 1948. 127pp. $5.00. Paper $2.25. A study of the development of the various meanings of irony from Socrates through Bacon, Schlegel, Thirlwell, and Moulton. Greek tragedy and the works of Shakespeare and Ibsen are analyzed and there is a detailed exposition of irony in "Othello." Index.

SEWALL, RICHARD B.
The Vision of Tragedy
Yale, 1959. 178pp. $6.75. Paper $1.45. An analysis of the nature of tragedy. The author takes his examples from such works as "The Book of Job" and

Faulkner's "Absalom, Absalom!" Dominant themes, meanings, and images are examined in "Oedipus," "Dr. Faustus," "King Lear," and other literature.

SHARPE, ROBERT BOIES
Irony in the Drama: An Essay on Impersonation, Shock, and Catharsis
University of North Carolina, 1959. 222pp. $6.00. The author maintains that irony is the center of every effective drama and that irony—a perception of incongruity and paradox as well as a dramatic device—comes from impersonation, the distinguishing feature of true drama. The artistic value of shock as catharsis is also studied.

STEINER, GEORGE
The Death of Tragedy
Hill & Wang, 1963. 355pp. Paper $1.95. The author contends that tragedy in Western literature ended with Racine. He examines the reasons why playwrights since Racine have not been able to capture the essence of tragic conflict.

STYAN, J. L.
The Dark Comedy: The Development of Modern Comic Tragedy
Cambridge, 1968. 311pp. $7.50. Paper $2.95. Originally published in 1962, this is the Second Edition of Professor Styan's analysis of the comedy–tragedy of the last sixty years, from Ibsen to Beckett and Pinter. He has brought his book up to date in relation to recent plays and theatrical developments and added detailed analyses of "Mother Courage" and "Waiting for Godot." Reading List. Index.

WILLIAMS, RAYMOND
Modern Tragedy
Stanford University, 1966. 208pp. $5.50. Paper—1967. $2.25. Essays on the idea of tragedy, in life and in the drama, and on modern tragic writing from Ibsen to Williams. The author's own play, "Koba," in which tragic action is directly embodied, is included. Index.

WIMSATT, W. K. – Editor
The Idea of Comedy
Prentice–Hall, 1969. 320pp. Paper $4.50. Twenty-six critical essays in prose and verse on the nature of stage comedy as presented in selected English critical writing from the beginnings of the classical tradition with Ben Jonson to its approximate end 250 years later with George Meredith. The editor provides a general historical introduction, introduction for each author, essays on the psychology of laughter, and the modern world of the comic. Index.

WORCESTER, DAVID
The Art of Satire
Russell & Russell, 1960. 191pp. $7.00. This is an analysis of the protean nature of irony. The problems met in trying to classify and define the various forms of satire are discussed and the natural evolution of satiric forms is traced with emphasis on rhetorical analysis rather than chronological history. Index.

WORLD THEATRE

COMPREHENSIVE REFERENCE WORKS

Histories and Critiques

ALLEN, JOHN
Masters of Modern Drama
Citadel, 1968. 189pp. Paper $2.25. Originally published in 1962, this is a survey of the lives and work of European dramatists. Among the playwrights studied are Plautus and Terence, Goldoni, Greban, Lope de Vega, Goethe, Schiller, Strindberg, Pirandello, Claudel, and Brecht. Illustrated with photographs. Index.

BAUR-HEINHOLD, MARGARETE
The Baroque Theatre
McGraw, 1967. 292pp. $22.00. The author has brought together all the elements of the seventeenth and eighteenth centuries to show the living forms of the baroque theatre in their endless variety. A large portion of the book is devoted to the major works of theatre architecture but there is also a discussion of the development of the theatre as a visual and living spectacle: the plays, ballets, and opera, the costumes and scenery, the playbills, the music, the actors and the direction of the productions. Included are a large number of reproductions of contemporary illustrations, color and black-and-white plates, and a series of photographs by Helga Schmidt-Glassner. Chronological Tables of Drama and Opera have been compiled by Veronika Baur. Bibliography. Index.

BROCKETT, OSCAR G.
History of the Theatre
Allyn and Bacon, 1968. 741pp. $15.35. A chronological narrative of the theatre from the Egyptian passion play to the recent "happenings." The author encompasses playwriting, directing, producing, costume, make-up, theatre architecture, management, audiences, and criticism. He relates major changes in the theatre to significant political and cultural developments and recognizes the importance of the Oriental theatre. Over 300 illustrations clarify the text. Bibliographies. Index.

BROCKETT, OSCAR G.
The Theatre: An Introduction
Holt, Rinehart, 1969. 596pp. $12.95. Originally published in 1964 and now reissued in a revised and redesigned second edition, this is a survey of the historical development of Western dramatic literature and the art and craft of the theatre. Part I deals with the theatre as an art form, the audience and the critic, and dramatic structure, form and style. Part II is a survey of the theatre of the past. Part III surveys the modern theatre; and Part IV is concerned with the theatre arts in America today with the emphasis on the modern professional theatre. Profusely illustrated. Bibliography. Index.

BURTON, E. J.
The Student's Guide to World Theatre
Jenkins, 1962. 207pp. $5.00. Paper $2.95. A survey of drama from the first mimes and dances of early man through to the fully developed practice of Eastern and Western contemporary theatre. There are sections on the Chinese opera, the No plays and the Sanskrit drama in Sakuntala. Drawings. Discography. Bibliography. Index.

CHENEY, SHELDON
The Theatre: Three Thousand Years of Drama, Acting, and Stagecraft
McKay, 1967. 592pp. $11.50. A revised, enlarged edition of the comprehensive study of theatre arts, originally published in 1929, with considerations of the origin and development of drama, the great playhouses, styles in staging, dramatists, the art of playwriting, poetry in the theatre, and the actors and producers. Illustrated. Index.

CLARKE, R. F.
The Growth and Nature of Drama
Cambridge, 1965. 70pp. Paper $1.75. This brief history for beginners in theatre selects certain important periods in the history of drama and describes them in simple terms. Illustrated.

COCHRANE, JENNIFER – Editor
The Theatre
Macdonald, 1970. 61pp. $1.75. Published in England, this is a history of the theatre for young people. Written in the form of a dictionary, the entries describe all facets of the theatre from acting to technical terms. Illustrated with drawings and photographs in black and white and color.

CREIZANACH, WILHELM
Geschichte des Neueren Dramas
Blom, 1965. Volume 1 – 628pp. Volume 2 – 581pp. Volume 3 – 637pp. $65.00. A history of European drama from its medieval origins to the Renaissance. This reprint edition is based upon the revised Halle editions of 1911/18/23. This classic work of scholarship is particularly useful for such little explored areas as the Central European drama. The text is, however, in the German language. Sold as a three volume set.

DRIVER, TOM F.
Romantic Quest and Modern Query
Delacorte, 1970. 493pp. $7.50. The author traces through the nineteenth and twentieth centuries the history of the modern theatre. He highlights the works of the great dramatists—among them Goethe and Kleist, Ibsen and Strindberg, Chekhov, Shaw and Pirandello, Brecht and Genet. Selected Bibliography. Indices.

FREEDLEY, GEORGE and JOHN A. REEVES
A History of the Theatre
Crown, 1968. 1,008pp. $10.00. Recognized as the standard book on the subject since its first publication in 1941, this is a completely revised and augmented third edition. Special new additono include full treatments of the Yiddish and Hebrew theatres, Korean drama, and the theatre in Canada, Rumania, and South America. Illustrated with portraits, settings and costumes by noted designers of the past and the present, and playbills, scripts, etc. Bibliography. Index.

FULLER, EDMUND
A Pageant of the Theatre
Crowell, 1965. 295pp. $4.95. This survey of theatre throughout history recreates actual performances, offers glimpses of back-stage activity, and describes the lives of actors and playwrights. Excerpts from the literature of the theatre are included.

GASCOIGNE, BAMBER
World Theatre: An Illustrated History
Little, Brown, 1968. 335pp. $15.00. A history of the theatre told from the vantage point of actual theatre illustrations: sketches, drawings, engravings, paintings, and diagrams. This collection provides a graphic account of changing theatre techniques in text and 290 black and white illustrations and thirty-two color plates. Notes on the illustrations. Bibliography. Index.

GASSNER, JOHN
Masters of the Drama
Dover, 1954. 890pp. $8.50. Originally published in 1940, this third edition of the history of world drama has been revised and enlarged. In addition to providing a detailed account of the work of virtually every important dramatist and the drama of every period and nation, a comprehensive chapter on post-World War II drama has been added. Illustrated. Bibliography. Appendices. Notes. Index.

GASSNER, JOHN and RALPH G. ALLEN – Editors
Theatre and Drama in the Making
Volume One: From Antiquity through the Eighteenth Century
Houghton Mifflin, 1964. 518pp. Paper $7.35. An annotated anthology designed to provide the student with an introduction to the methods and materials of research in theatre history and drama criticism. Primary and secondary source materials are included. Selected Bibliography. List of Research Topics.

GASSNER, JOHN and RALPH G. ALLEN – Editors
Theatre and Drama in the Making
Volume Two: The Nineteenth and Twentieth Centuries
Houghton Mifflin, 1964. 526pp. Paper $7.35. The second volume in the annotated anthology listed directly above.

HARTNOLL, PHYLLIS
The Concise History of Theatre
Abrams, 1968. 288pp. Paper $3.95. This is an illustrated history of the theatre that embraces acting, direction, stagecraft, theatre architecture, and design, and also includes a survey of the evolution of dramatic literature. The book is illustrated in color and black and white. Bibliography. Index.

HEWITT, BARNARD
History of the Theatre from 1800 to the Present
Random House, 1970. 210pp. Paper $4.95. A survey of the principal developments in Western theatre in the context of economic, political, and social change. Professor Hewitt focuses on stylistic innovations, developments in set and scene design, and approaches to theatrical production citing significant plays and playwrights, actors, managers, designers, directors, critics, and theorists. Illustrated. Bibliography. Index.

HUNT, HUGH
The Live Theatre: An Introduction to the History and Practice of the Stage
Oxford, 1962. 196pp. $5.75. A history of the theatre told in terms of the changing traditions of producing, directing, and acting.

LEACROFT, HELEN and RICHARD LEACROFT
The Theatre
Roy, 1958. 74pp. $3.25. An illustrated guide to the history of the theatre for the young reader.

MacDONALD, J.W. and J.C.W. SAXTON – Editors
Four Stages
St. Martin's, 1966. 398pp. $4.00. This historical survey is designed to acquaint the reader with the broad development of world drama. A running narrative, linking four plays which have been selected to represent some of the major movements in dramatic literature from the time of the Greeks to the present, attempts to place the dramas in their social and historical contexts and to show how one dramatic form developed out of another. The plays presented are: "Oedipus Rex" by Sophocles, "Doctor Faustus" by Christopher Marlowe, "Pillars of Society" by Henrik Ibsen, and "All My Sons" by Arthur Miller.

MacGOWAN, KENNETH and WILLIAM MELNITZ
Golden Ages of the Theatre
Prentice–Hall, 1959. 166pp. Paper $1.95. This volume is based on the authors' "The Living Stage." It deals briefly with the main currents in playgoing and acting in the last 2,500 years. Illustrated.

MacGOWAN, KENNETH and WILLIAM MELNITZ
The Living Stage: A History of the World Theatre
Prentice–Hall, 1955. 543pp. $13.95. A study of changing trends in acting and producing, in the physical characteristics of playhouses, in types of plays, and in staging throughout the history of drama. The

changing political, social, economic, and religious background is examined. Over 250 illustrations, with chronological tables for reference, are included. Bibliography.

McKECHNIE, SAMUEL
Popular Entertainments Through the Ages
Blom, 1969. 257pp. $12.50. Originally published in 1931 and now reissued, this is a history of the popular theatre in all its forms—from Roman circus through the Bartholomew Fair, Commedia dell'Arte, and Punch and Judy. Commentary on the folklore of entertainment through the centuries is provided. Illustrated.

MALE. DAVID
The Story of the Theatre
Dufour, 1960. 80pp. $2.95. This book for the young reader traces the history of the theatre from ancient Greece to modern television drama. Illustrated.

MILLETT, FRED B. and GERALD EADES BENTLEY
The Art of the Drama
Appleton, 1935. 253pp. $5.50. A discussion of the historical aspects of the drama, of the nature of the theatre and audience in each period, and of the types of drama characteristic of each. The major types of drama are studied, along with the particular problems of technique and the solutions found for them in each type and in each period.

NAGLER, A.M.
A Source Book in Theatrical History
Dover, 1959. 611pp. Paper $3.00. A reprint of the author's "Sources of Theatrical History." More than 300 basic documents and other primary materials are collected to present a history of the theatre over the last 2,500 years. Illustrated.

NICOLL, ALLARDYCE
World Drama: From Aeschylus to Anouilh
Harcourt, Brace, 1949. 1,000pp. $9.75. A survey of the history of drama with chapters on Greek theatre, religious drama of the Middle Ages, drama in Renaissance England, Italy, and Spain, French classical theatre, realism, and psychological drama and expressionism in the modern theatre. A concluding essay discusses the possibility of a dramatic revival in the modern era. Illustrated.

PRIESTLEY, J.B.
The Wonderful World of the Theatre
Doubleday, 1959. 69pp. $3.50. A folio-sized book which describes, through colored reproductions of contemporary illustrations, the history of the theatre.

ROBERTS, VERA MOWRY
On Stage: A History of the Theatre
Harper & Row, 1962. 534pp. $13.35. A comprehensive study covering all periods of the drama. Each chapter considers the theatre in the social framework of the age. The producers, actors, designers, playwrights, and audiences are also studied. Illustrated. List of Plays. Suggested Study Guide. Glossary. Bibliography.

ROBINSON, RUTH
The Theatre
Oliver & Boyd, 1968. 64pp. $3.50. A history of the theatre written for children. The author traces the theatre from the Church plays of the Middle Ages to today. Illustrated with drawings by Philip Gough. Index.

SAMACHSON, DOROTHY and JOSEPH SAMACHSON
The Dramatic Story of the Theatre
Abelard, 1956. 168pp. $4.50. An account of the evolution of the theatre from ancient Greece to the 1930's. The material is presented in terms of significant moments in theatrical history when a particular style or type of drama was perfected. Illustrated.

SAQUET, LABEEBEE J.H.
The Evolution of the Theatre
Carlton Press, 1968. 107pp. $3.50. This is a general introduction to the theatre. Included are such varied subjects as the early theatre, opera, recent developments, radio, television, make-up, lighting, and motion pictures. Index.

SOUTHERN, RICHARD
The Seven Ages of the Theatre
Hill & Wang, 1961. 312pp. $5.95. Paper $2.45. The long pageant of theatre history is presented in terms of significant phases. Among the periods considered are the age of the great religious festivals, the rise of the professional player, the beginnings of the organized stage, and the roofed playhouse with scenery.

SPEAIGHT, ROBERT
The Christian Theatre
See Page 327

VARGAS, LUIS
Guidebook to the Drama
Dover, 1961. 220pp. Paper $2.00. A simplified account of the development of the drama of the West.

WHITING, FRANK M.
An Introduction to the Theatre
Harper & Row, 1969. 401pp. $15.00. Originally published in 1954 and now reissued in a revised third edition. The author attempts to offer a comprehensive view of theatre so that the beginning student may examine the whole before studying the detailed arts and crafts that combine into stage art. Part One is concerned with plays and playwrights. Part Two considers acting and directing. Part Three considers the architects, designers, and technicians and Part Four is a short chapter on the theatre as a profession. Illustrated with photographs, charts and diagrams. Selected Bibliography. Index.

WILLIAMS, C. J.
Theatres and Audiences: A Background to Dramatic Texts
Longman, 1970. 122pp. Paper $3.50. A guide to theatres and audiences from the ancient world to modern times. The theatrical conventions of each era are detailed. Illustrated with drawings. Glossary. Time Chart. Index.

Collections of Essays and Books on Various Periods

GUTHRIE, TYRONE
In Various Directions
Macmillan, 1965. 221pp. $4.95. A collection of portraits, tributes, and discussions ranging from the theatre of antiquity to the popular entertainments of today. Illustrations of Guthrie productions.

HOLMSTROM, KIRSTEN GRAM
Monodrama, Attitudes, Tableaux Vivants
Almqvist, 1967. 278pp. Paper $16.50. This is a study of the trends of theatrical fashions from 1770 to 1815. The three art forms of monodrama, attitudes, and tableaux vivants are described and analyzed with regard to their stylistic characteristics and the artistic milieux in which they operated. Illustrated. Bibliography. Index.

KAUFMANN, WALTER
From Shakespeare to Existentialism
See Page 137

LUCAS, F. L.
The Drama of Chekhov, Synge, Yeats, and Pirandello
Cassell, 1963. 452pp. $12.00. A companion volume to the author's study, "Ibsen and Strindberg," 1962, this book treats of four major playwrights born between 1860 and 1871. The major plays of each are examined. Bibliography. Index.

MILLER, ANNA
The Independent Theatre in Europe
Blom, 1966. 435pp. $12.50. Originally published in 1931, this is a reissue of the study of some of the most important of the European independent theatres from 1887 to the 1930's. Those in France, Germany, Russia, Ireland, England, the Intimate Theatre of Stockholm, and the National Theatre at Bergen in Ibsen's day are studied. Bibliography. Index.

MUIR, KENNETH
Last Periods of Shakespeare, Racine, Ibsen
Wayne State University, 1961. 117pp. $5.00. Four lectures discussing the quality of the plays written by the three playwrights in their final creative periods. An introductory essay considers the final achievements of a group of other artists including Sophocles, Euripides, and Strindberg.

ROEBURT, JOHN
The Wicked and the Banned
Macfadden, 1963. 157pp. Paper $ .60. A study of censorship of books, motion pictures, television, and the theatre, with a brief review of noteworthy law cases that set precedents in the field of censorship.

SCHECHNER, RICHARD
Public Domain: Essays on the Theatre
Bobbs-Merrill, 1969. 244pp. $6.95. Paper—Avon, 1970. 252pp. $1.65. This is a collection of essays, all of which have been revised, which originally appeared in "The Tulane Drama Review" and other periodicals. The essays range in subject from classical theatre to absurdist theatre to the ritualized communal theatre of the 1960's as influenced by Artaud, Grotowski, Chaikin, Beck, and Schechner himself. Index.

SLOTE, BERNICE – Editor
Literature and Society: Nineteen Essays by Germaine Bree and Others
University of Nebraska, 1964. 269pp. Paper $1.95. Essays selected and grouped to illustrate some of the ways in which literature has social relevance. Among the essays on theatre are "King and Church in Classical Tragedy," "A Note on Iago's Name," "Major Barbara: Shaw's Challenge to Liberalism," "The Role of Society in the Theatre of the Absurd," and essays on Clifford Odets, Hugo von Hofmannsthal, and the Corpus Christi plays.

STOLL, ELMER EDGAR
Poets and Playwrights
See Page 52

STOLL, ELMER EDGAR
Shakespeare and Other Masters
See Page 103

MODERN THEATRE (Dating from Henrik Ibsen)

Histories and Critiques

ABEL, LIONEL
Metatheatre: A New View of Dramatic Form
Hill & Wang, 1963. 146pp. $3.95. Paper $1.45. An analysis of modern theatre in terms of a new concept of dramatic form—the self-conscious awareness of dramatic devices and theatricality. The origins of this concept are traced back to Sophocles, Shakespeare, Calderon, and Racine, and its predominance in modern authors such as Brecht, Beckett, Genet, Gelber, and others is examined.

BAXTER, K. M.
Contemporary Theatre and the Christian Faith
See Page 325

BELLI, ANGELA
Ancient Greek Myths and Modern Drama: A Study in Continuity
New York University, 1969. 201pp. $5.95. Paper $2.50. The author investigates the motives that prompt modern dramatists to reinterpret the ancient legends, the methods used in creating new plays, and the ways in which the different treatments vary from their source and from one another. Dr. Belli considers the works of Cocteau, O'Neill, Sartre, Montherlant, Maxwell Anderson, and Tennessee Williams, among others.

BROWN, JOHN MASON
Upstage: The American Theatre in Performance
Kennikat, 1969. 276pp. $13.50. Originally published in 1930 and now reissued in a facsimile edition, this is a collection of discussions of the American theatre and some of the participants in it including playwrights, actors, scenic artists, directors, critics, and audiences.

BRUSTEIN, ROBERT
The Theatre of Revolt: An Approach to the Modern Drama
Little, Brown, 1964. 435pp. $7.50. Studies of Ibsen, Strindberg, Chekhov, Shaw, Brecht, Pirandello, O'Neill, and Genet which examine the nature of the revolt from convention found in each. The author maintains there is a unity of approach in these playwrights in that they all rebelled against the fashionable pieties of their day and against accepted notions of decorum in art and literature.

CHIARI, J.
Landmarks of Contemporary Drama
Herbert Jenkins, 1965. 223pp. $5.00. This study examines the theatre of the absurd, the theatre of cruelty and violence, the problem of tragedy in our times and the effect of naturalism and social realism on recent Shakespearean productions. Major British, American, French, and German dramatists are studied. Index.

CLARK, BARRETT H. and GEORGE FREEDLEY–Editors
History of Modern Drama
Appleton, 1947. 832pp. $9.50. Twenty four theatre historians describe the development of drama from Ibsen to the present. Reading List. Bibliography.

COHN, RUBY
Currents in Contemporary Drama
Indiana University, 1969. 276pp. $5.95. Paper $2.95. Miss Cohn synthesizes several of the most important themes of the drama as they have been developed since World War II in the English, French, and German theatres. She examines contemporary drama as an expression of Artaud's theory of the "theatre of cruelty." Among the playwrights observed are T.S. Eliot, John Osborne, Harold Pinter, Arthur Miller, Tennessee Williams, Edward Albee, Bertolt Brecht, Max Frisch, and Peter Weiss. Bibliography. Notes. Index.

CRAIG, EDWARD GORDON
The Theatre Advancing
Blom, 1968, 290pp. $12.50. First printed in 1947, and long unavailable, this collection of essays by the English actor, stage designer, producer, and writer is now reprinted.

DONOGHUE, DENIS
The Third Voice
Princeton, 1959. 286pp. $5.75. Paper $1.95. A study of modern verse drama in England and America with a detailed analysis of the work of T. S. Eliot.

DORIAN, FREDERICK
Commitment to Culture: Art Patronage in Europe–Its Significance for America
University of Pittsburgh, 1964. 520pp. $10.00. A report of investigations into the subsidy of performing arts in Europe. The history of art patronage is described and related to the political, social, and economic traditions of Europe. The possibility for such patronage on a public and official level in the United States is considered.

DOWNS, HAROLD
Appraising a Play
Jenkins, 1955. 96pp. $2.00. The author attempts to explain how to assess the values of a play in terms of the theatre and of life. The volume is intended for the casual playgoer. Index.

EELLS, RICHARD
The Corporation and the Arts
Interbook, 1967. 365pp. $7.95. This is a detailed examination of the growing relationship between the world of art and the corporate world of business. Professor Eells stresses those arts that contribute to the strength of the total social environment in which private enterprise can be successfully carried on. Index.

ELLMANN, RICHARD
Eminent Domain
Oxford, 1970. 161pp. Paper $1.75. Originally published in 1967 and now reissued, this study presents the relationships among the six great founders of modern literature: Yeats, Wilde, Joyce, Pound, Eliot, and Auden. Notes. Index.

ESSLIN, MARTIN
The Theatre of the Absurd
Doubleday, 1969. 424pp. Paper $1.95. Originally published in 1961 and now reissued in a revised and updated edition, this is an analysis of the work of the major playwrights of the "theatre of the absurd." Playwrights discussed include Beckett, Adamov, Ionesco, Genet, and many others. Bibliography. Index.

FRASER, G.S. – Editor
The Modern Writer and His World
Penguin, 1964. 427pp. Paper $1.45. This collection of essays relates the main movements and innovators in all fields of literature since 1880. Many chapters have been widely revised since its original edition in 1953.

GASCOIGNE, BAMBER
Twentieth Century Drama
Barnes & Noble, 1966. 216pp. Paper $1.75. This book presents an observation of the continuing development of drama in the twentieth century. The author studies the variety of subject matter in each decade from the twenties to the fifties, evaluates the attempts of modern playwrights in poetic drama, and examines the use of symbol and imagery. Index.

GASSNER, JOHN
Directions in Modern Theatre and Drama
Holt, Rinehart, 1965. 457pp. $11.95. This is an enlarged edition of Gassner's 1956 book, "Form and Idea in Modern Theatre," on trends in playwriting and production styles. The author considers the modern drama in terms of its changing forms and aims and suggests how the theatre might resolve some of its confusion to attain more artistically significant expression. New material on contemporary playwrights and theatre developments is included. Chronology. Index.

GASSNER, JOHN
Theatre at the Crossroads
Holt, Rinehart, 1960. 327pp. $5.95. In this investigation the author contends that mid-century theatre is in a state of serious crisis, the result of an impasse between realism and avant-garde experiments in illusion and fantasy.

GASSNER, JOHN
The Theatre in Our Times: A Survey of the Men, Materials, and Movements in the Modern Theatre
Crown, 1954. 609pp. $5.95. Paper $2.95. A collection of essays on theatre history, dramatic criticism, and dramatic theory that provide a survey of the major dramatic works and trends in modern drama. There is a concluding section on motion pictures.

GASSNER, JOHN
The World of Contemporary Drama
American Library Association, 1965. 31pp. Paper $ .60. A reading guide to contemporary drama from Ibsen and Chekhov up to the plays of 1964. A Reading List is included.

GILSON, ETIENNE
Forms and Substances in the Arts
Scribner, 1966. 282pp. $4.95. Translated from the French by Salvator Attanasio, this study analyzes the basic materials afforded the artist in the fields of architecture, sculpture, painting, music, the dance, poetry, and the theatre. The author discusses the possibilities of artistic form and the means of transformation and creation. Index.

GINGRICH, ARNOLD
Business and the Arts: An Answer to Tomorrow
Eriksson, 1969. 146pp. $4.95. An examination into one of the cultural and artistic developments of today: the involvement and support of the arts by business and industrial corporations. Mr. Gingrich explores the reasons for the involvement and the methods by which business might help support the various arts. He also looks at the future of the new business-arts cooperation. David Rockefeller has contributed a Foreword. Illustrated with photographs. Selected Bibliography. Index.

GORELIK, MORDECAI
New Theatres for Old
Dutton, 1962. 553pp. Paper $2.45. An account of the rise and fall of stage and screen techniques in the modern era. Playwrights, actors, directors, and stage designers are studied against a background of social and political change. Illustrated. Glossary.

GROSSVOGEL, DAVID I.
Four Playwrights and a Postscript: Brecht, Ionesco, Beckett, Genet
Cornell, 1962. 209pp. $5.50. Paper $1.95. A discussion of each playwright in terms of his essential dramatic problems: For Brecht, the difficulty of "witnessing;" for Ionesco, that of living; for Beckett, that of dying; and for Genet, that of defining. Paperbound edition is titled "The Blasphemers: The Theatre of Brecht, Ionesco, Beckett, Genet."

HAMBURGER, KATE
From Sophocles to Sartre
See Page 12

HANSEN, AL
A Primer of Happenings & Time/Space Art
Something Else Press, 1965. 145pp. $4.50. Paper $2.25. Mr. Hansen attempts to deal in a concise way with all the aspects of the happening and its related forms and analogues. Illustrated. Index.

JAMES, HENRY
The Scenic Art: Notes on Acting and the Drama 1872 – 1901
Hill & Wang, 1957. 384pp. Paper $1.35. Edited by Allan Wade, this is a collection of thirty-two essays on the English, French, and American theatre.

JOSEPH, STEPHEN
Theatre in the Round
Barrie & Rockliffe, 1967. 179pp. $6.50. Mr. Joseph is the director of the only professional "in the round" theatre which is open to the public in England. He dissects all elements which go into this form of theatre,

dealing with buildings, plays, acting, production, and he delivers accounts of his own experiences in Britain and in America. Illustrated with drawings, sketches, diagrams, and photographs. Bibliography. Index.

KAHN, DR. SAMUEL
Psychodrama Explained
Philosophical Library, 1964. 77pp. $3.00. This book deals in part with the origin and development of Psychodrama, describing its functions and practices and how they relate to other forms of psychotherapy.

KAPROW, ALLAN
Assemblage, Environments & Happenings
Abrams, 1966. 341pp. $25.00. Paper $9.95. This book is an introduction to some recent developments in the arts. It concentrates on the background, the theory, and some of the implications of these developments. Lavishly illustrated with photographs of these new arts.

KENNER, HUGH
Flaubert, Joyce and Beckett: The Stoic Comedians
Beacon Press, 1962. 107pp. $3.95. The author illustrates how three artists exploit the devices of our "typographic culture"—a culture in which "the language of the printed word has become, like the language of mathematics, voiceless." Illustrated with drawings by Guy Davenport.

KIRBY, MICHAEL
The Art of Time: Essays on the Avant-Garde
Dutton, 1969. 255pp. $5.95. Paper $1.95. In this series of essays Mr. Kirby proposes a theory of aesthetics based on and derived from the thought of the avant-garde. The author also devotes attention to the most recent developments in theatre including naturalistic theatre, objective dance, the use of film in theatre, and environmental theatre.

KIRBY, MICHAEL
Happenings: An Illustrated Anthology
Dutton, 1965. 288pp. $6.95. Paper $1.95. This collection contains a comprehensive introduction to the new form of the happening, working scripts of fourteen happenings, descriptions of the productions, with comments by the artists, and a collection of seventy-nine photographs illustrating each production. The scripts and productions are by Jim Dine, Red Grooms, Allan Kaprow, Claes Oldenburg, and Robert Whitman.

KITCHIN, LAURENCE
Drama in the Sixties: Form and Interpretation
Faber & Faber, 1966. 226pp. $7.50. Mr. Kitchin examines theory and practice of today's creative theatre. He considers the value of the international style that has become popular and the difficulties of directors faced with "the contrary claims of screen techniques and the original Shakespearean text." Bibliography. Illustrated. Index.

KOSTELANETZ, RICHARD
The Theatre of Mixed Means
Dial, 1968. 311pp. $6.50. An introduction to happenings, kinetic environments, and other mixed means performances. Nine members of the avant-garde movement, including John Cage, Ann Halprin, Robert Rauschenberg, Allan Kaprow, and Claes Oldenburg, discuss their purposes and processes. Illustrated. Bibliography. Index.

KOTT, JAN
Theatre Notebook: 1947–67
Doubleday, 1968. 268pp. $5.95. Paper $2.95. Mr. Kott, a contemporary Polish critic, covers the whole field of modern drama from Polish, Soviet, and Chinese theatre, to the theatre of the absurd in the East and West, the Spoleto and Edinburgh Festivals, puppeteers and mimes, the impact of Oedipus translated into prose.

KRUTCH, JOSEPH WOOD
"Modernism" in Modern Drama: A Definition and an Estimate
Russell & Russell, 1962. 138pp. $7.00. Paper—Cornell University, 1966. 138pp. $1.45. In this reprint of the 1953 edition, the author writes essays on Ibsen, Strindberg, Shaw, Pirandello, and Synge. He discusses those tendencies in their works which seem to contain elements of a threatening moral and intellectual crisis. A concluding chapter considers the influence of their work and ideas on American drama.

LUMLEY, FREDERICK
New Trends in Twentieth Century Drama
Oxford, 1967. 398pp. $8.50. Originally published in 1956 as "Trends in Twentieth Century Drama," this is a complete revised version of the comprehensive survey of the theatre since Ibsen and Shaw. The author places in perspective the many new important playwrights from all over the world. The book is concerned with the whole of the theatre and not with just one of its "schools." Among those considered are Osborne, Pinter, Arden, Shaffer, Albee, Durrenmatt, Frisch, and Weiss. Selected Book List. Index.

PEACOCK, RONALD
The Art of Drama
Routledge & Kegan Paul, 1957. 263pp. $6.00. This study is concerned with modern drama and the manner in which new forms in verse drama, in surrealistic fantasy, and in the revival of myth are linked with the movement of much modern art away from realism and toward symbolism.

PHELPS, WILLIAM LYON
The Twentieth Century Theatre
Kennikat, 1968. 147pp. $8.00. Originally published in 1918 and now reissued, this volume is an observation of the English and American stage from 1900 to 1918. Index.

PRONKO, LEONARD C.
Theatre East and West
See Page 116

ROOSE-EVANS, JAMES
Experimental Theatre from Stanislavsky to Today
Universe, 1970. 160pp. $6.95. Mr. Roose-Evans traces the major experiments that, over the past hundred years, have extended the range of theatre as art. He gives concise accounts of the work of such key figures as Stanislavsky, Meyerhold, Craig, Appia, Artaud, Piscator, and Brecht, as well as discussing the current experiments in America today. Illustrated. Bibliography. Index.

SAINT-DENIS, MICHEL
Theatre: The Rediscovery of Style
Theatre Arts, 1969. 110pp. Paper $2.85. Originally published in 1960 and now reprinted, this book is adapted from a series of lectures the author gave in New York under the general title, "Classical Theatre and Modern Realism." An essay on the French theatre completes the volume. Illustrated.

SMITH, MICHAEL
Theatre Trip
Bobbs-Merrill, 1969. 178pp. $7.50. The critic for "Village Voice" takes a look at what he considers the depressed state of the American theatre and goes abroad to exorcise his disenchantment through contact with Julian Beck's and Judith Malina's Living Theatre, the Polish Laboratory Theatre, and the Berliner Ensemble. Smith's observations and criticism run concurrently with his personal diary. Illustrated.

STYAN, J. L.
The Dramatic Experience: A Guide to the Reading of Plays
Cambridge, 1965. 154pp. $4.95. The author analyzes the different aspects of creative play reading, investigates the difference between reading drama and reading other types of literature, and explores the nature of dramatic effects.

TREWIN, J.C.
Verse Drama Since 1800
Cambridge, 1956. 27pp. Paper $ .75. A brief essay surveying the history of verse drama from 1800 to 1955 with a bibliography of plays and critical studies published during those years.

VALENCY, MAURICE
The Flower and the Castle: An Introduction to Modern Drama
Macmillan, 1963. 460pp. $8.95. Paper—Grosset & Dunlap, 1966. 460pp. $2.95. A study of the nature and scope of that radical transformation of the art of the drama at the end of the nineteenth century which created the modern theatre. Special attention is given to the germinal work of Ibsen and Strindberg. Bibliography. Index.

WEBB, KAYE—Editor
An Experience of Critics and The Approach to Dramatic Criticism
Oxford, 1953. 62pp. $2.25. Christopher Fry and eight drama critics analyze the position of the critic in the theatre today: the influences on him and his influence on the theatre. The critics are Ivor Brown, W. A. Darlington, Alan Dent, Harold Hobson, Philip Hope-Wallace, Eric Keowan, J. C. Trewin, and T. C. Worsley.

WHITMAN, ROBERT F.
The Play-Reader's Handbook
Bobbs-Merrill, 1966. 216pp. Paper $2.25. Mr. Whitman has written a handbook on how to read a play. His purpose is to suggest how reality can best be brought forth on a stage or on the printed page. There are many suggestions for further reading. Bibliography. Index.

WILLIAMS, RAYMOND
Drama from Ibsen to Brecht
Oxford, 1969. 352pp. $6.50. Originally published in 1952 as "Drama from Ibsen to Eliot" and now fully revised and expanded to include playwrights such as Brecht, Beckett, O'Neill, Miller, Lorca, O'Casey, Whiting, Arden, Pinter, and Osborne. It is a discussion of drama as literature and a re-evaluation of modern naturalist drama. Notes. Index.

WRIGHT, EDWARD A.
A Primer for Playgoers: An Introduction to the Understanding and Appreciation of Cinema-Stage-Television.
Prentice—Hall, 1958. 270pp. $10.00. A book for the beginning playgoer which presents the critical basis for the development of a standard of good judgement applicable to any form of dramatic entertainment. Glossary of theatre terms and a series of questions for discussion groups are included.

WRIGHT, EDWARD A.
Understanding Today's Theatre: Cinema, Stage, Television
Prentice—Hall, 1959. 178pp. Paper $1.95. An abridged version of the author's "A Primer for Playgoers." This book is primarily addressed to the playgoer with little or no background in drama history. Chapters consider the technique of playwriting, acting, directing, scene design, and dramatic criticism.

Collections of Essays

ADLER, RENATA
Toward a Radical Middle
Random House, 1969. 259pp. $7.95. A collection of fourteen pieces of reporting and criticism on various facets of our culture and society by the "New Yorker"

critic. Among the subjects are the lyrics and sounds of contemporary popular music, book reviews, and literary essays on such figures as Genet, and mixed media and art and technology in the theatre.

ATKINSON, BROOKS
Brief Chronicles
Putman, 1966. 255pp. $5.95. A collection of informal essays by "The New York Times" critic-at-large. Mr. Atkinson's observations run the gamut from Con Edison to William Shakespeare. Index.

BAKEWELL, MICHAEL and ERIC EWENS
From the Fifties
British Broadcasting Co., 1961. 96pp. Paper $1.50. A series of short critiques and histories of contemporary plays from England and Europe which were first produced during the fifties. Among the major writers represented are: John Arden, Jean Anouilh, Bertold Brecht, Samuel Beckett, T.S. Eliot, Eugene Ionesco, Harold Pinter, and John Whiting. Illustrated with photographs.

BEHRMAN, S.N.
The Suspended Drawing Room
Stein & Day, 1965. 253pp. $6.00. A collection of profiles of Bernard Shaw, Gabriel Pascal, Robert E. Sherwood, Ferenc Molnar, and Harold Ross.

BENTLEY, ERIC
In Search of Theatre
Vintage, 1959. 385pp. Paper $1.85. The chapters in this volume deal with playwrights, actors, producers, critics, and audiences in Italy, France, Switzerland, Ireland, England, Austria, Germany, and the United States. Major modern playwrights are examined in detail. Illustrated.

BENTLEY, ERIC
The Playwright as Thinker: A Study of Drama in Modern Times
Harcourt, Brace, 1955. 328pp. Paper $2.45. A collection of essays on the various traditions of modern drama, on modern tragedy and on comedy. Emphasis is placed mainly on Wagner, Ibsen, Strindberg, Sartre, and Brecht. Index.

BENTLEY, ERIC
The Theatre of Commitment and Other Essays
Atheneum, 1967. 241pp. $5.00. In his title essay, Mr. Bentley speaks for the problems of political engagement in the theatre, as exemplified in the work of Brecht, Weiss, and Hochhuth in particular. This essay is supported by a group of pieces dealing with the most important general problems of the theatre. Index.

BOGARD, TRAVIS and WILLIAM I. OLIVER – Editors
Modern Drama: Essays in Criticism
Oxford, 1965. 393pp. Paper $2.50. Twenty critics discuss modern playwrights from Chekhov through Anouilh, Genet, and Durrenmatt. Among the contributors are Eric Bentley, John Gassner, Hubert Heffner, Thomas Parkinson, Francis Fergusson, Henry Raleigh, Sartre, and William Arrowsmith.

BROWN, JOHN MASON
Dramatis Personnae: A Retrospective Show
Viking, 1963. 563pp. $7.50. Paper $2.25. Sixty selections from eleven of Mr. Brown's books, with several uncollected articles, new headnotes, and a new introduction. Included is the complete text of "The Modern Theatre in Revolt," long out-of-print. Shaw and O'Neill are treated in detail.

BRUSTEIN, ROBERT
The Third Theatre
Knopf, 1969. 294pp. $6.95. Paper $2.95. A collection of essays and articles by the Dean of the Yale School of Drama. Mr. Brustein begins with a history of the off-off-Broadway theatre, particularly of the Living Theatre group, and discusses the place of politics in the theatre today. The second section of the volume includes reviews originally published in "The New Republic." The third section is a group of non-theatre essays, reviews, and interviews.

CLURMAN, HAROLD
The Naked Image
Macmillan, 1966. 312pp. $6.50. A collection of Clurman's observations on today's theatre. Most of the reviews and essays first appeared in such publications as "The Nation," "Show," and "The New York Times." Index.

COE, RICHARD N. and R.F. JACKSON, LAWRENCE RYAN, ROSS CHAMBERS, and PETER DAVISON
Aspects of Drama and the Theatre
Methuen, 1965. 197pp. Paper $1.75. Five lectures delivered in the University of Sydney between 1961 and 1963. The first three lectures deal with "meaning" including political and philosophical in the work of Ionesco, Sartre, and Brecht. There is an evaluation of Antonin Artaud and a study of the influence on English drama of the techniques of music hall, pantomime, radio and television.

CORRIGAN, ROBERT W. – Editor
Theatre in the Twentieth Century: Playwright, Actor, and Critic on the Modern Theatre.
Grove, 1963. 320pp. Paper $1.95. An anthology of essays on modern theatre by such representative figures as Miller, Ionesco, Durrenmatt, Brecht, Fry, Betti, von Hofsmannsthal, Sartre, John Gassner, Eric Bentley, and Freud.

CRAIG, EDWARD GORDON
The Theatre Advancing
Blom, 1964. 290pp. $12.50. A reprint of the essays first published in 1947. Among the essays are "A Plea for Two Theatres," "A Durable Theatre," "The Modern Theatre and Another," "The Open

Air," "Theatrical Reform," "A Note on Masks," "Shakespeare's Collaborators," "The True Hamlet," "Church and Stage: Rome." There is a section of articles on such actresses as Ellen Terry, Sacha Yacco, and Duse.

ESSLIN, MARTIN
Reflections: Essays on Modern Theatre
Doubleday, 1969. 229pp. $5.95. Paper—1971. 226pp. $1.95. This is a collection of essays which were originally published in various periodicals. They cover the entire range of modern theatre from Ibsen and Pirandello to Brecht, Ionesco, Beckett, and Weiss. Violence in modern drama, nudity, the theatre of the absurd, epic theatre, and the happening are all considered as is the role of live theatre in the age of the mass media. Index.

FREEDMAN, MORRIS—Editor
Essays in the Modern Drama
Heath, 1964. 374pp. Paper $4.50. The four sections of this anthology have essays on modern dramatic figures, on the relation between the new drama and society, on poetic drama, and on the experimental and avant-garde drama.

GASSNER, JOHN
Dramatic Soundings
Crown, 1968. 716pp. $7.50. Glenn Loney has introduced and edited this posthumous collection of more than sixty essays from John Gassner's thirty year career as one of America's most respected drama critics. The major sections span the world of the stage from Aeschylus to Albee and investigate the esthetics and practices of drama. The 1930's and the 1960's receive particularly complete treatment. Index.

GASSNER, JOHN—Editor
Ideas in the Drama
Columbia, 1964. 174pp. $5.50. A collection of essays by various authors. Among the subjects are: Shaw on Ibsen, ideas in the plays of O'Neill, Brecht and the drama of ideas, Sartre and the drama of ensnarement, and ideas in the Greek theatre.

GIBBS, WOLCOTT
More in Sorrow
Houghton Mifflin, 1964. 308pp. Paper $1.95. Originally published in 1958, this is a collection of thirty-five pieces by the "New Yorker" theatre critic.

GILMAN, RICHARD
The Confusion of Realms
Vintage, 1970. 273pp. Paper $1.95. Originally published in 1969 and now reissued, this volume contains fifteen essays dealing with drama, fiction, films, and other things mostly in contemporary America. Among the subjects are Norman Mailer, Marshall McLuhan, Susan Sontag, The Living Theatre, and black writing.

GOTTFRIED, MARTIN
Opening Nights
Putnam, 1969. 384pp. $6.95. A collection of the reviews and theatre pieces of the critic for "Women's Wear Daily" from 1963 to 1969. The pieces range geographically from New York to Europe to the resident theatre companies throughout the United States. Index.

GREEN, PAUL
Dramatic Heritage
Samuel French, 1953. 177pp. $2.50. A collection of essays and short papers on life and the theatre. Among the topics covered are symphonic drama, folk art, the mysticism of Bernard Shaw, Paul Claudel, Kabuki Theatre, "The Common Glory," and the Indian theatre.

HIGGINS, DICK
Jefferson's Birthday
Something Else Press, 1964. 271pp. This book consists of all the things Mr. Higgins wrote, composed or invented in one year. He is a member of the new pop art establishment, a composer of happenings, events, musical and time/space work. Also included in this volume is "Postface" an essay in which he expands on the theory that art is bound up in the situation where it is produced and where it is experienced. Illustrated.

KERR, WALTER
Pieces at Eight
Dutton, 1968. 244pp. Paper $1.55. First published in 1957, this is a collection of fifty-six of Mr. Kerr's theatre essays which were originally printed in "The New York Herald Tribune" and other publications.

KERR, WALTER
The Theatre in Spite of Itself
Simon & Schuster, 1963. 319pp. $5.00. Articles and drama reviews on a variety of aspects of American theatre by the critic for "The New York Herald Tribune." The current crisis in commercial theatre receives special treatment.

KERR, WALTER
Thirty Plays Hath November
Simon & Schuster, 1969. 343pp. $6.50. Paper—1970. $2.95. A collection of Mr. Kerr's writings and comments on plays, playwrights, actors, directors, and the state of the contemporary stage. The volume is divided into twelve sections with a theme linking the essays in each section. Index.

KOTT, JAN
Shakespeare, Our Contemporary
See Page 50

KRAUS, TED—Editor
1970 Theatre Trends
Critical Digest, 1970. 92pp. Paper $2.00. A work-

book of research projects in current theatre trends within the various aspects of contemporary theatre: Broadway, Off-Broadway, Off-Off-Broadway, resident theatre, college and community theatre, the theatre in London, and the theatre of the future. Background articles present pro/con arguments on diverse subjects, reports on theatre conferences and festivals, and commentary on theatre trends.

KRIEGER, MURRAY – Editor
Northrop Frye in Modern Criticism
Columbia, 1966. 203pp. $5.50. A selection of essays and papers delivered to the English Institute in 1965 on Northrop Frye, the author of "The Anatomy of Criticism." Mr. Krieger comments and indicates the relations between Frye and contemporary criticism and Mr. Frye contributes some remarks in answer to the views advanced by the writers included. There is a checklist of writings by and about Mr. Frye.

LAHR, JOHN
Up Against the Fourth Wall
Grove, 1970. 305pp. $7.50. Paper $2.95. A collection of essays, originally published in "Evergreen Review" from 1968 to 1970. The theatre critic writes of the modern theatre of the past decade, analyzing the plays and playwrights and chronicling the emergence of the theatre groups which have formulated radical innovations of concept and technique. Index.

LUNACHARSKY, ANATOLY
On Literature and Art
New Era Books, 1965. 379pp. $3.95. A collection of critical articles by the Russian critic, divided into three sections: Lunacharsky as theoretician and ideologist, as a critic of Russian art, and as a critic of foreign art. Included are articles on Bacon and the characters of Shakespeare's plays, and on George Bernard Shaw. Illustrated.

MILLER, JAMES E., JR. and PAUL D. HERRING
The Arts and the Public
University of Chicago, 1967. 266pp. $8.75. This is a collection of papers originally given at a conference held at the University of Chicago in October, 1966. Some of the questions debated are: "What can the critic expect to learn from the artist?" "What is the role of the reviewer in increasing public understanding of the arts?" "Is academic criticism inaccessible to the general public?" Contributors include Saul Bellow, Robert W. Corrigan, Wright Morris, Alan Schneider, and Anthony West.

MORGAN, GEOFFREY – Editor
Contemporary Theatre
Alan Ross, 1968. 202pp. Paper $2.75. Published in England, this is a selection of reviews of productions from the London theatre season of 1966/1967. The author takes contrasting extracts from the leading critics to build a coherent picture of how individual plays were received.

NEWQUIST, ROY – Editor
Counterpoint
Simon & Schuster, 1968. 653pp. Paper $2.95. Originally published in 1964 and now reissued, this is an anthology of comments on life and living, writers and writing, by sixty-three leading authors, critics, and playwrights. Among the contributors are: Truman Capote, Jules Feiffer and Tyrone Guthrie.

OPPENHEIMER, GEORGE – Editor
The Passionate Playgoer: A Personal Scrapbook
Viking, 1962. 623pp. Paper $1.95. A collection of over 1,000 articles by more than ninety contributors on various aspects of modern theatre.

RAHV, PHILIP
The Myth and the Powerhouse
Farrar, 1965. 243pp. $4.95. A new volume of criticism and essays on literature and ideas by one of the founding editors of "Partisan Review." There are sixteen essays dealing with Gogol, Chekhov, Dostoevski, Eliot, Hemingway, Saul Bellow, Norman Mailer, and many others.

SCOTT, NATHAN A. – Editor
Man in the Modern Theatre
John Knox, 1965. 100pp. Paper $1.00. Four essays on playwrights who have examined the theme of modern man's anxiety before the threat of meaninglessness. The essays are on T. S. Eliot, O'Neill, Brecht, and Beckett. Bibliography.

SMITH, MICHAEL
Theatre Journal: Winter 1967
University of Missouri, 1968. 50pp. Paper $1.50. A journal of theatre-going for the first three months of 1968 which records and reviews the productions seen during that time period by the author. It records an era of experimentation, particularly off-off-Broadway, and the author's conclusion that this era is ended.

SONTAG, SUSAN
Against Interpretation
Farrar, Straus, 1966. 304pp. $4.95. Paper – Delta, 1967. 304pp. $1.95. Also Paper – Dell, 1969. 304pp. $ .95. A selection of Miss Sontag's critical writings between 1961 and 1965. The author presents the argument that the critic's task is not to show the "meaning" of the work but to demonstrate how it is what it is.

SULLIVAN, FRANK
Frank Sullivan Through the Looking Glass
Doubleday, 1970. 267pp. $5.95. Edited by George Oppenheimer with an introduction by Marc Connelly, this is a collection of the essays and letters of the writer for "The New Yorker" magazine. The pieces provide glimpses of Sullivan's friends, among them Edna Ferber, Russel Crouse, Howard Lindsay, Helen Hayes, Thornton Wilder, and Groucho Marx.

TYNAN, KENNETH
Tynan, Right and Left
Atheneum, 1967. 479pp. $8.95. A collection of the writings of the director, producer, and drama critic. The writings focus on theatre, movies, books, cities, and the lives of other people. Index.

VOS, NELVIN
The Drama of Comedy
See Page 327

WHITING, JOHN
John Whiting on Theatre
Secker & Warburg, 1966. 109pp. Paper $1.95. A collection of writings of the English playwright and critic. He discusses Sartre, satire, Wesker, Osborne, the critics, acting, "The Cherry Orchard," Coward, and Brecht among other things.

WICKHAM, GLYNNE
Drama in a World of Science and Three Other Lectures
University of Toronto, 1962. 92pp. $3.75. Four lectures on the place of drama in the modern world. Included are studies of the post-war revolution in British drama, studies of poets and playwrights, and a study on the problems of teaching drama in college classes.

GREEK AND ROMAN THEATRE

REFERENCE WORKS AND GENERAL HISTORIES

ALLEN, JAMES T.
Stage Antiquities of the Greeks and Romans and Their Influence
Cooper Square, 1963. 206pp. $3.50. A reprint of the 1926 edition, this study considers the Greek and Roman dramatic festivals, the essential features of the theatre in Greece and the developments in later Roman drama, stage properities and machines, the use of the chorus and spectacle, actors and styles of acting, costumes, and the influence of the classic theatre. Illustrated.

ARNOTT, PETER D.
Greek Scenic Conventions of the Fifth Century B.C.
Oxford, 1962. 147pp. $5.50. In this study the author expresses radically different ideas about the stage and its decoration. Particular problems discussed include stage machinery, furnishings, country settings, and stage spectacle. There are comments on Euripides' trend toward stage illusion. Illustrated.

ARNOTT, PETER D.
An Introduction to the Greek Theatre
Indiana University, 1963. 240pp. Paper $2.45. A reprint of the 1959 study of the background against which the plays were written, of the theatre and its equipment, and of the audience. "Agamemnon," "Medea," "Cyclops," and "The Birds" are studied in detail. Roman comedy is also considered and there is an analysis of "Menaechmi." Problems of translation and production are analyzed. Illustrated.

ARNOTT, PETER D.
An Introduction to the Greek World
Funk & Wagnalls, 1968. 238pp. Paper $2.95. Originally published in 1967 and now reissued, this is a study of the Classical era with background material on the day to day life of the people. A section on "The Greek Theatre and Its Plays" is included. Illustrated. Index.

AYLEN, LEO
Greek Tragedy and the Modern World
Methuen, 1964. 376pp. $8.50. Each of the works of the Greek dramatists are examined in order to determine what their attitude toward life consisted of. Those modern dramatists who have attempted to present aspects of this attitude in contemporary terms are examined. Among the dramatists considered are Buchner, Ibsen, Strindberg, Miller, Cocteau, Giraudoux, Anouilh, Sartre, Gheon, and T.S. Eliot. Bibliography. Index.

BEARE, W.
The Roman Stage: A Short History of Latin Drama in the Time of the Republic
Barnes & Noble, 1964. 397pp. $8.50. Paper $5.00. A third revised edition of the study first published in 1950, completed in accordance with the author's original plan by Professor N. G. L. Hammond. New chapters on the Roman theatre and the origins of its dramas are included. Appendices. Notes and Sources. Illustrated. Bibliography. Index.

BELLI, ANGELA
Ancient Greek Myths and Modern Drama: A Study in Continuity
See Page 24

BERVE, HELMUT and GOTTFRIED GRUBEN
Greek Temples, Theatres and Shrines
Abrams, 1963. 508pp. $20.00. The first part of this folio-sized book, written by Professor Berve, considers such questions as the origin, nature, and ritual content of Greek religious ceremonies, festivals, and pageants. The use of shrines and theatres for religious ceremonies is studied in detail. Part Two, by Professor Gruben, presents detailed architectural reconstructions of the temples and shrines, showing how they developed, were constructed and used. Illustrated with 160 ground plans and architectural sections. There is a section of 212 full page photographs illustrating in detail the text. In addition there is a section of thirty-six photographs in color. Glossary. Bibliography. Index.

BIEBER, MARGARET
The History of the Greek and Roman Theatre
Princeton, 1961. 343pp. $20.00. A completely revised and enlarged second edition of the 1939 publication, this study of the development of the ancient theatre and stage production makes use of all the available literary, epigraphical, architectural, and figurative sources. 865 illustrations.

BOWRA, C.M.
Ancient Greek Literature
Oxford, 1960. 256pp. Paper $1.75. This reprint of the study first published in 1933 presents the complete text of that edition. The qualities that made Greek literature supreme in epic poetry, drama, oratory, history, and philosophy are examined in detail. Index.

BOWRA, C.M.
The Greek Experience
New American Library, 1957. 223pp. Paper $ .95. This survey of classical culture sums up the Greek achievement from its dawn in the epics of Homer to its decay after the fall of Athens in 404 B.C. Illustrated with photographs. Index.

BOWRA, C.M.
Landmarks in Greek Literature

World, 1966. 284pp. $8.95. Paper $3.95. A descriptive and critical history of the most important works in Greek literature from the known beginnings to the Alexandrian poets of the third century B.C. Notes. Suggestions for Further Reading. Index.

BROADHEAD, H.D.
Tragica: Elucidations of Passages in Greek Tragedy
University of Canterbury, 1968. 179pp. $8.75. Dr. Broadhead discusses 120 passages from Greek tragedy in which he suspects the text has been corrupted. The result of each discussion is usually a practical and constructive suggestion which is dramatically possible. In some cases these suggestions may materially affect the understanding of the play under discussion. An appendix gives notes on passages not discussed at length and refers to a number of already published articles.

CAMPBELL, LEWIS
Tragic Drama in Aeschylus, Sophocles, and Shakespeare
Russell & Russell, 1965. 280pp. $8.50. First published in 1904 and now reissued, this is an analysis of tragic fable, action, characterization, ideas, construction, and diction in the three playwrights. The parallels between the usage of Shakespeare and the ancient writers are examined in detail. Index.

CERAM, C.W.
Archaeology
Odyssey, 1964. 46pp. $ .95. A brief history of the methods and discoveries of archaeology. Color drawings by Peter Spier.

DALE, A.M.
The Lyric Metres of Greek Drama: Second Edition
Cambridge, 1968. 228pp. $9.50. Miss Dale has corrected errors in the first edition, published in 1948, and taken into account works published in the intervening years for this second edition. The author instructs the reader's ear to respond to the characteristic rhythms of Greek lyric and the laws which control them without losing sight of the poetry. Index.

D'ALTON, J.F.
Roman Literary Theory and Criticism: A Study in Tendencies
Russell & Russell, 1962. 608pp. $12.50. The author attempts to illustrate the main tendencies in the work of the Roman critics. He shows the interrelation of Greek and Roman literary theory and discusses aspects of the problem of style, the supremacy of rhetoric and the two poets, Cicero and Horace. Index.

DE ROMILLY, JACQUELINE
Time in Greek Tragedy
Cornell, 1968. 180pp. $5.95. Mme. de Romilly studies the concept of time as it was presented by the classic Greek tragedians. Her findings show the uses of time in the works of Aeschylus, Sophocles, and Euripides, the changes in views of time from one generation to the next, and the lessons of time as taught by its effects upon the lives of the tragic heroes. Index to Passages in Greek Tragedies.

DICKINSON, G. LOWES
The Greek View of Life
Collier, 1961. 159pp. Paper $ .95. First published in 1869, this reprinted study of Greek civilization covers four main topics: Greek attitudes toward religion, toward the state, toward the individual, and toward art. The philosophy of Plato is seen as the unifying concept in the civilization of ancient Greece.

DRIVER, TOM F.
The Sense of History in Greek and Shakespearean Drama
Columbia, 1961. 231pp. $7.00. Paper $2.25. An analysis of the conception of historical process in Greek culture and in the Judaeo-Christian religious tradition. Plays studied in detail are "The Persians," "Oresteia," "Oedipus Tyrannus," "Alcestis," "Richard III," "Hamlet," "Macbeth," and "The Winter's Tale." Bibliography. Index.

DUCKWORTH, GEORGE E.
The Nature of Roman Comedy: A Study in Popular Entertainment
Princeton, 1952. 499pp. $13.95. This study considers the background and history of Roman comedy, the staging and production of plays, the nature of the comedies, with special attention to stage conventions, the structure of plots, suspense and irony, characterization, and moral tone. Brief plot summaries of each of the twenty-six comedies are given.

ELSE, GERALD F.
The Origin and Early Form of Greek Tragedy
Harvard, 1965. 127pp. $4.50. The author maintains that tragedy did not have its origins in primitive religious ritual nor in the choral performances as described by Aristotle, but rather arose in sixth century Athens and, in particular, from the poetry of Solon. Index.

FEDER, LILLIAN
Handbook of Classical Literature
Crowell, 1964. 448pp. $7.95. Paper—1970. $3.45. The 950 entries in this book give information on the writers and literature of the classical world. Long works are synopsized, and major philosophical treatises are summarized. Illustrated with four maps.

FINLEY, JOHN H.
Four Stages of Greek Thought
Stanford University, 1968. 114pp. $3.95. Paper $1.95. Reprinted from the original publication in 1955, this is a literary approach to the masterpieces of Greek literature from Homer to Aeschylus and Sophocles, Euripides and Thucydides to Plato. Notes.

FLICKINGER, ROY C.
The Greek Theatre and Its Drama
University of Chicago, 1968. 385pp. $10.00. A reprint of the fourth edition, 1936, of the study originally published in 1918. The author analyzes the peculiar conventions of Greek drama in terms of the cultural and intellectual environment. The technical aspects of ancient drama are emphasized and ancient practice is elucidated by parallels from medieval and modern drama. Illustrated. Index of Passages. General Index.

GLEN, R.S.
The Two Muses
St. Martin's, 1968. 230pp. $3.25. This book aims to provide an introduction to fifth century Athens by way of the drama. Euripides' "Medea" and Aristophanes' "Clouds" are studied as specimens of tragedy and comedy. Illustrated with photographs. Chronology. List of books for Further Reading. Index.

HADAS, MOSES
A History of Greek Literature
Columbia, 1962. 307pp. $7.50. Paper $1.95. This is a reprint of the 1950 edition of the author's re-creation of the cultural environment of ancient Greece and investigation of the major types of literature produced from Homer to the novelist Lucian. The tragedies and comedies are examined in detail.

HAIGH, A.E.
The Tragic Drama of the Greeks
Dover, 1968. 499pp. Paper $3.50. An unabridged republication of the basic reference on the history and development of Greek tragedy as originally published in 1896. The author discusses in detail the life and work of Aeschylus, Sophocles, and Euripides. Illustrated. Appendices. Index.

HAMILTON, EDITH
The Ever Present Past
Norton, 1964. 189pp. $4.50. Paper $1.75. A collection of essays, reviews, and addresses on Plato, Greek drama, "Faust," the theatre of Corneille and Racine, the nature of comedy in Moliere and Shakespeare, modern poetry, Faulkner, and Dylan Thomas.

HAMILTON, EDITH
The Greek Way
Random House, no date, 347pp. $2.45. Paper—Norton, 1964. 212pp. $ .95. A reprint of the 1942 edition, this is an interpretation of the meaning of Greek literature, philosophy, and art, with an evaluation of their influence on world history and their importance for modern man.

HAMILTON, EDITH
The Roman Way
Norton, 1932. 281pp. $4.50. A study of Roman life and civilization as seen through the works of her leading writers and political figures. A companion volume to the author's "The Greek Way," this volume points out the contrasts between the two civilizations. Chronological Table.

HANDLEY, E.W.
Menander and Plautus: A Study in Comparison
H.K. Lewis, 1969. 25pp. Paper $1.25. This short study was originally delivered as a lecture at University College, London, In 1968.

HANSON, JOHN ARTHUR
Roman Theatre—Temples
Princeton, 1959. 112pp. $8.50. A study of the archaeological evidence for the religious significance of the Roman theatre of the late Republic and early and late Empire. The study reveals that an important architectural factor was the combination of temples and shrines and the "cavea" of the theatre. A detailed study of the first monumental Roman theatre, that of Pompey in the Campus Martius, is given. Illustrated with charts, diagrams and photographs.

HARRISON, JANE
Themis
World, 1969. 559pp. Paper $3.95. A new edition of the work originally published in 1912. Drawing on the insights of social psychologists and historical studies of the turn of the century, Miss Harrison offers a view of the social origins of Greek religion. This revised edition contains additional chapters by Gilbert Murray and F.M. Cornford. Illustrated. Index.

HARRISON, JANE
Prolegomena to the Study of Greek Religion
World, 1959. 682pp. Paper $3.25. Originally published in 1903 and reissued in 1959, this is a study of various aspects of Greek religion which may be useful to students of the work of the Greek playwrights. Profusely illustrated with examples of Grecian art. Index.

HARSH, PHILIP WHALEY
A Handbook of Classical Drama
Stanford, 1944. 526pp. $12.00. Paper $3.45. A comprehensive reference work consisting of introductions to the various types of classical drama, sketches of the lives of the dramatists, summaries and analyses of each of the extant Greek and Roman plays. The cultural background and the methods and aims of each playwright are considered. Bibliography.

HATHORN, RICHMOND Y.
Crowell's Handbook of Classical Drama
Crowell, 1967. 350pp. $7.95. A modern guide to the Greek and Roman theatre with biographies of their authors. Alphabetically arranged, the volume contains detailed entries on all of the known classical plays and playwrights, on the form and language of the plays, on relevant theatrical conventions, persons and places mentioned in the plays, and the large number of terms used in classical drama.

JEBB, R.C.
The Attic Orators from Antiphon to Isaeos
Russell & Russell, 1962. Two volume set. $17.50. First published in 1875 and now reissued, the object of these volumes is to trace the course of Athenian oratory from its beginnings as an art to the days of its decline. The artistic development of Attic orators is sketched as a whole and particular treatment is given to Antiphon, Andokides, Lysias, Isokrates, and Isaeos. Sold as a two volume set only.

KITTO, H.D.F.
Greek Tragedy: A Literary Study
Barnes & Noble, 1966. 401pp. $8.50. A detailed investigation of the form and language of Greek tragedy. Since its first publication in 1939, this book has been recognized as one of the most important modern studies of the Greek drama. This revised edition contains translations of quotations from the plays left in the original language in the earlier edition, and a glossary of terms.

KITTO, H.D.F.
The Greeks
Penguin, 1951. 256pp. Paper $1.25. A study of the character and history of ancient Greece. Chapters on the formation of the country, Homer, the Polis, Classical Greece, warfare, the decline of the Polis, myth and religion, and Greek thought.

KITTO, H.D.F.
Poiesis: Structure and Thought
University of California, 1966. 407pp. $7.50. Professor Kitto explores the attempts that scholars have made to understand Greek literature. He examines and analyzes Aeschylus' "Persae," Sophocles' "Trachiniae" and "Tyrannus," and the "Odyssey," and provides a chapter on Pindar and Plato and another on Shakespeare's "Coriolanus." Index.

LATTIMORE, RICHMOND
The Poetry of Greek Tragedy
Johns Hopkins, 1958. 157pp. $4.00. Paper—Harper, 1966. 157pp. $1.45. A study of the specific contribution the verse form makes to the dramatic effectiveness of Greek tragedy. The author analyzes the poetry in the following plays: "The Suppliant Maidens," "The Persians," "Seven Against Thebes," "Ajax," "Oedipus the King," "Helen," "Medea," and "The Bacchae."

LATTIMORE, RICHMOND
Story Patterns in Greek Tragedy
University of Michigan, 1964. 106pp. $4.00. Paper $1.95. The author examines the story patterns to discover what the most important characteristics of Greek tragedy are, what stories were actually used, and what tradition required, permitted, or forbade a playwright to use. Each major story pattern is defined and its roots traced to the folklore and myth of ancient Greece. Bibliography. Index.

LESKY, ALBIN
Greek Tragedy
Barnes & Noble, 1965. 230pp. $8.95. Paper—1967. 229pp. $4.00. The first English translation of one of the most important general surveys of Greek tragedy. Of particular value are the bibliographies and notes.

LESKY, ALBIN
A History of Greek Literature
Crowell, 1966. 921pp. $15.00. First published in German in 1958 and extensively revised for this English reprinting, this book is a comprehensive survey of the entire range of Greek literature from the Homeric epics to the early Christian era. Bibliography. Index.

LUCAS, D.W.
The Greek Tragic Poets: Second Edition
Norton, 1964. 274pp. Paper $1.75. The second edition of the book first published in 1950 has been extensively rewritten in the light of new knowledge. The discussion of Aeschylus and the "Supplices" is largely new. The section on religious background and tragic origins is also new.

McDANIEL, WALTON B.
Roman Private Life and Its Survival
Cooper Square, 1963. 203pp. $3.50. This is a reprint of the 1924 study of the private life of the upper classes in Rome. Among the items considered are marriage contracts, house planning, slave ownership, dining, clothing, amusements, attitudes towards literature and writers. Bibliography.

MERIVALE, PATRICIA
Pan the Goat—God: His Myth in Modern Times
Harvard, 1969. 286pp. $10.00. The author examines the development of the various basic concepts of Pan from classical mythology and chronicles his appearances in modern literature, especially in English writing. Use of the myth in the theatre is mentioned casually. Illustrated. Index.

MOULTON, RICHARD GREEN
Ancient Classical Drama
Russell & Russell, 1968. 480pp. $15.00. Originally published in 1890, revised in 1898, and now reissued, this history of the classical drama traces the rise of new literary species or transitional tendencies in the development of the drama. General Index. Index of Plays.

MURRAY, GILBERT
Greek Studies
Oxford, 1946. 231pp. $5.50. A collection of eleven lectures on various aspects of Greek literature and art.

MURRAY, GILBERT
A History of Ancient Greek Literature
Ungar, 1966. 420pp. $6.50. An authoritative account

of a great literary tradition presenting all the writers from primitive to folkloric times, to the highly sophisticated Golden Age of Greece, to the centuries of decline and eventual amalgamation with Roman literature. Index.

NORWOOD, GILBERT
Greek Comedy
Hill & Wang, 1963. 413pp. Paper $1.95. A reprint of the study published in 1931 in which the author discusses the literary history of comedy, the productions of plays, their metre and rhythm, and the works of Aristophanes, Menander, Epicharmus, Cratinus, the school of Crates, and Eupolis.

NORWOOD, GILBERT
Greek Tragedy
Hill & Wang, 1960. 394pp. Paper $1.75. A study of the literary history of the tragedies, with chapters on the productions of the plays, their metre and rhythm, and the individual styles and contributions of each tragic playwright.

NORWOOD, GILBERT
Plautus and Terence
Cooper Square, 1963. 212pp. $3.50. In this reprint of the 1931 study special attention is given to Plautus' "Mercator," which Mr. Norwood regards as the playwright's greatest achievement. The other nineteen plays are described briefly. The discussion of Terence involves a consideration of style, moralization, characterization, plot structure, and philosophy. List of English plays influenced by these playwrights is included. Bibliography.

OATES, WHITNEY J.—Editor
From Sophocles to Picasso: The Present-Day Vitality of the Classical Tradition
University of Indiana, 1962. 208pp. $4.50. Seven contributions which examine the influence of classical tradition on contemporary painting, drama, music, culture, and politics. The writers are Herbert Muller, H. D. F. Kitto, Otto Brendel, E. A. Havelock, Stephen Greene, Roger Sessions, and Whitney J. Oates.

PICKARD–CAMBRIDGE, A.W.
Dithyramb Tragedy and Comedy
Oxford, 1962. 334pp. $9.50. A standard work on the origin and early development of the drama. This revised, second edition by T. B. L. Webster includes an account of the new papyrus fragments of Epicharmus and an expanded section of illustrations based on a wider range of archaeological material.

PICKARD–CAMBRIDGE, A.W.
The Dramatic Festivals of Athens
Oxford, 1968. 358pp. $17.50. Originally published in 1953 and now revised by John Gould and D.M. Lewis, this study details the development and organization of the Athenian dramatic festivals, actors and acting, costume, the chorus, dancing and music, and the audience and its tastes and behavior. The fully revised second edition has new illustrations added. Bibliography. Concordance. Indices.

PICKARD–CAMBRIDGE, A.W.
The Theatre of Dionysus in Athens
Oxford, 1956. 288pp. $12.50. A history of the theatre from its earliest days to the time of the Roman Empire based on extant remains and evidence from literature and inscriptions.

REID, DORIS FIELDING—Editor
A Treasury of Edith Hamilton
Norton, 1969. 143pp. $5.00. A selection of Miss Hamilton's writings grouped under a variety of subjects. Subjects include: tragedy and comedy, classicism and romanticism, religion, freedom, education, and mind and spirit.

REINHOLD, MEYER
Barron's Simplified Approach to Ten Greek Tragedies
Barron, 1965. 169pp. Paper $ .95. Historical and literary background with commentary on ten Greek plays: "Prometheus Bound," "Agamemnon," "Oedipus the King," "Antigone," "Medea," "Bacchae," "Hippolytus," "Iphigenia in Tauris," and both Sophocles' and Euripides' "Electra." Bibliography.

REINHOLD, MEYER
Classical Drama: Greek and Roman
Barron, 1959. 342pp. $5.00. Paper $1.95. A survey in outline form of the dramatic literature of the classical era. The volume includes a brief historical outline of the period, details of staging, and scene-by-scene analyses of all the extant dramas. Bibliography.

REINHOLD, MEYER
Essentials of Greek and Roman Classics: A Guide to the Humanities
Barron, 1962. 391pp. $4.50. Paper $1.95. A study guide consisting of a concise survey of the significant cultural and historical developments, brief biographies, list of extant works, summaries of complete works, and analyses of thought and style. An Appendix treats mythological concepts. Glossary. Selected Bibliography.

REINHOLD, MEYER
Simplified Approach to Plato and Aristotle
Barron, 1964. 90pp. Paper $ .95. Detailed analyses and summaries of the philosophical concepts of Plato and Aristotle. Included are biographies of the philosophers, historical background, and a bibliography.

RIDGEWAY, WILLIAM
The Origin of Tragedy
Blom, 1966. 228pp. $12.50. A reprint of the 1910 edition, in this study the author advances the theory that tragedy originated in the worship of the dead. He investigates the origin of tragedy with special reference to the Greek tragedians. Index.

ROSENMEYER, THOMAS G.
The Masks of Tragedy: Essays on Six Greek Dramas
University of Texas, 1963. 248pp. $5.00. In these studies the author's concern is with the tragic ideas the playwrights designed to release certain massive responses in the large theatre audience. Parallels are drawn between the writings of the philosophers and the tragedians. The six plays studied are Aeschylus' "Prometheus" and "Seven Against Thebes," Sophocles' "Ajax," and Euripides' "Bacchae," "Alcestis," and "Ion."

SCHLESINGER, ALFRED CARY
Boundaries of Dionysus: Athenian Foundations for the Theory of Tragedy
Harvard, 1963. 145pp. $4.25. The author examines the dramatic logic of high tragedy, the nature of the characters shown in the various types of dramas, the intellectual content of the tragedies, and the civic function of drama. The essential nature of the tragic spirit is shown from an examination of the many different forms the drama assumed. Index.

SHEPPARD, JOHN T.
Aeschylus and Sophocles: Their Work and Influence
Cooper Square, 1963. 204pp. $3.50. A reprint of the 1927 study in which the author assesses the unique contribution of Aeschylus and Sophocles and shows their influence on their contemporaries. He establishes the links between them and such later writers as Horace, Dante, Marlowe, Racine, and Shakespeare.

SIFAKIS, G.M.
Studies in the History of Hellenistic Drama
Oxford, 1967. 200pp. $10.75. Dr. Sifakis disputes the widespread belief that Greek drama made little progress after Menander. He discusses important innovations such as a new role for the chorus, a special kind of dramatic music, and a new technique in writing tragedy based upon evidence from Delos and Delphi. Bibliography. Index of Scholars. Index of Ancient Authors and Inscriptions. General Index.

SNELL, BRUNO
Scenes from Greek Drama
University of California, 1964. 143pp. $6.00. This study attempts to reconstruct several lost Greek dramas from the fragments, utilizing textual evidence and drawing on the emotional attitudes inherent in these fragments and in related known plays.

VAN AKEN, A.R.A.
The Encyclopedia of Classical Mythology
Prentice–Hall, 1965. 155pp. Paper $2.45. A complete guide to classical myth and legend. The Encyclopedia emphasizes the influence of mythology on art and literature. Illustrated.

VON HILDEBRAND, ALICE – Editor
Greek Culture: The Adventure of the Human Spirit
Braziller, 1966. 382pp. $6.95. Dr. von Hildebrand has brought together the great writers and art works of ancient Greece. The major themes of Greek experience are here exemplified from the works of literature, philosophy, and the arts. Among the authors discussed are Homer, Sophocles, Aristophanes, Aeschylus, Euripides, Plato, Aristotle and Herodotus.

WALTER, WILLIAM
The Plays of Euripides, Aeschylus, and Aristophanes
Monarch, 1966. 105pp. Paper $1.00. A critical guide to Greek drama. Complete background, plot discussion, theme development, character analysis, and critical commentary are all included as are review questions and answers and a guide to research.

WATT, LAUCHLAN MACLEAN
Attic and Elizabethan Tragedy
Kennikat, 1968. 356pp. $13.50. Originally published in 1908 and now reissued, this is a study and comparison of Greek and Elizabethan tragic drama. All of the great Greek playwrights are studied and analyzed and there are individual chapters on many of Shakespeare's plays. Index.

WEBSTER, T.B.L.
The Greek Chorus
Barnes & Noble, 1970. 223pp. $10.50. The primary concern of this study is the history of the dance in Greek chorus. The author describes the visual appearance of the chorus as exemplified on Greek vases and reliefs from the eighth to the fourth century B.C. and discusses the choral performances them-selves, with references to literary sources. The author explains how the chorus was based on tradition, when and where innovations were made, and to what extent different types of chorus influenced one another. Illustrated with photographs. Glossary of Metrical Terms. Index.

WEBSTER, T.B.L.
Greek Theatre Production
Methuen, 1970. 214pp. & plates. $8.50. Originally published in 1956 and now reissued in a revised edition. Scenery, staging and costume are the three main topics. They are treated chronologically within geographical areas. A final chapter traces the history of staging, scenery and costumes from the earliest times. A catalogue lists over 250 of the most important monuments and there is a section of twenty-four half-tone plates. Index.

ZIMMERMAN, J.E.
Dictionary of Classical Mythology
Bantam, 1966. 300pp. Paper $ .95. Originally published in 1964, this guide contains over 2,000 entries with simple, complete explanations of classical myths, heroes, authors, works, place names, and symbols. A Bibliography lists recommended translations of Greek and Roman prose and poetry as well as other source works on mythology.

STUDIES OF PLAYWRIGHTS

Aeschylus

CAMPBELL, LEWIS
Tragic Drama in Aeschylus, Sophocles, and Shakespeare
See Page 33

DAWE, R.D.
The Collation and Investigation of Manuscripts of Aeschylus
Cambridge, 1964. 352pp. $16.50. Dr. Dawe has collated sixteen manuscripts of the Byzantine triad of plays (''Prometheus,'' ''Persians,'' and ''Seven Against Thebes'') and offers an''apparatus criticus'' for each play. The study shows that no surviving manuscript is free from interpolation and emendation and that all existing stemmata are therefore invalid.

GARVIE, A.F.
Aeschylus' Supplices: Play and Trilogy
Cambridge, 1969. 279pp. $11.50. Mr.Garvie studies the fragment of ''Supplices'' to analyze the style, dramatic structure, and historical background of the play. He considers to what extent the lost plays can be reconstructed in the light of evidence for the theory that the ''Supplices'' once formed part of a trilogy. Bibliography. Indices.

HAVELOCK, E.A.
Prometheus
University of Washington, 1968. 218pp. $6.95. Originally published in 1951 as ''The Crucifixion of Modern Man'' and now reissued, this is a commentary on Aeschylus' ''Prometheus Bound'' and a study of the role of the intellectual in modern society. The author's translation of the play is also provided as is an Appendix on ''The Theology of the 'Prometheus Bound'.'' Subject Indices.

HERINGTON, C.J.
The Author of the ''Prometheus Bound''
University of Texas, 1970. 135pp. $6.50. This monograph attempts to answer the questions of when ''Prometheus Bound'' was written and whether the play is by Aeschylus. The author surveys the general questions of the authenticity problem and catalogues in detail the stylistic, metrical, and thematic features of the play. Appendices. Bibliography.

MURRAY, GILBERT
Aeschylus: The Creator of Tragedy
Oxford, 1962. 242pp. $7.00. Originally published in 1940 and now reprinted, this is a study of how Aeschylus created a new style of drama, starting with what Aristotle described as ''little myths and ridiculous language.'' The poet's stage technique, themes, his war plays, the ''Oresteia,'' and the fragments are examined. An Appendix gives a complete scenario for the ''Agamemnon.''

MURRAY, ROBERT DUFF
The Motif of Io in Aeschylus' ''Suppliants''
Princeton, 1958. 104pp. $2.50. Professor Murray examines the techniques used by Aeschylus to integrate and manipulate the motif of Io in his poetic structure. His interpretation of ''Suppliants'' provides a new approach to Aeschylean tragedy.

PODLECKI, ANTHONY J.
The Political Background of Aeschylean Tragedy
University of Michigan, 1966. 188pp. $7.50. This book examines the seven extant plays of Aeschylus against the background of their period in Greek history. Notes. Index.

THOMSON, GEORGE
Aeschylus and Athens
Grosset & Dunlap, 1968. 374pp. $6.95. Paper $3.45. A reprint of the 1940 study in the social origins of drama. The author contends that the plays of Aeschylus contain fundamental problems which could never be solved within the accepted limits of conventional literary criticism or classical scholarship. He inquires into the origins and development of Athenian democracy to study the plays and what they meant to the audiences for which they were written. Diagrams and illustrations. Chronological Table. Index.

Aristophanes

EHRENBERG, VICTOR
The People of Aristophanes: A Sociology of Old Attic Comedy
Schocken, 1962. 387pp. $2.95. Drawing upon Old Attic comedy and the plays of Aristophanes, the author recreates the life of the Athenian people of all social classes. Social structure, the family, religion, and politics are examined. Illustrated.

LITTLEFIELD, DAVID J.—Editor
The Frogs: Twentieth Century Interpretations
Prentice—Hall, 1968. 118pp. $3.95. Paper $1.25. A collection of critical essays by eighteen distingushed critics who examine Aristophanes' comedy and offer modern views of the work. Among the authors are Gilbert Murray, Bruno Snell, and Henry David Thoreau. Chronology of Important Dates. Bibliography.

LORD, LOUIS E.
Aristophanes: His Plays and His Influence
Cooper Square, 1963. 183pp. $3.50. Originally published in 1925 and now reprinted, this is a study of the background and attitudes of society out of which Aristophanes' comedies arose and of the particular

character of his plays. Special attention is given to his influence on later Greek and Roman playwrights, and on the comedy of the Renaissance in England, France and Germany. Bibliography.

MURRAY, GILBERT
Aristophanes: A Study
Oxford, 1965. 268pp. $7.50. A reprint of the edition first published in 1933, this study discusses each play under its major theme, considers the sources and background, and examines the transformation of comedy under Menander. Index.

STRAUSS, LEO
Socrates and Aristophanes
Basic Books, 1966. 321pp. $10.00. This book derives from Professor Strauss' concern with Socrates as the founder of political philosophy. The earliest known document dealing with Socrates is Aristophanes' comedy,"The Clouds." This comedy is important not only for the light it casts on Socrates but also because it leads to the basic stratum of the poet's thought. The book also deals with others of Aristophanes' plays. Index.

WHITMAN, CEDRIC H.
Aristophanes and the Comic Hero
Harvard, 1964. 333pp. $7.95. In this analysis of the comic hero, the author makes use of the modern Greek concept of "Poneria," which best describes the devious and delightful wickedness by which the hero comes out on top. Attention is focused on Aristophanes as poet, dramatic artist, and myth-maker, rather than as social critic and reformer. Appendix on modern Greek shadow theatre.

Aristotle

ARISTOTLE
Aristotle on the Art of Poetry
Oxford, 1967. 95pp. Paper $1.60. This is the Ingram Bywater translation of Aristotle's "Poetics" originally published in 1920 and now reissued. Preface to the volume is by Gilbert Murray.

ARISTOTLE
Aristotle: Poetics
Oxford, 1968. 313pp. $10.00. This volume includes the Oxford classical text of the "Poetics" in Greek, plus commentary on the text by D. W. Lucas. The introduction and appendices, which include detailed studies of Catharsis, Homartia, and Peripeteia, are written so as to be intelligible to those who know no Greek. Mr. Lucas tries to give within a reasonable compass an explanation which takes account of the wealth of discussion devoted to Aristotle's literary theory. Index.

ARISTOTLE
Aristotle's Poetics
Regnery, 1961. 172pp. Paper $1.25. This translation, by Kenneth Telford, offers copious footnotes which explain many things to which Aristotle refers, a complete index of terms, and an analysis of the "Poetics."

ARISTOTLE
Aristotle's Poetics
Hill & Wang, 1961. 118pp. $3.50. Paper $1.25. Translated by S. H. Butcher, this volume includes an introductory essay by Francis Fergusson which uses the example of Sophocles' "Oedipus Rex" to point out that Aristotle's essay is not a strict rule book for the playwright. He than analyzes the "Poetics" and shows that its ideas are applicable to so modern a playwright as Brecht.

ARISTOTLE
Aristotle's Theory of Poetry and Fine Art
Dover, 1951. 421pp. Paper $2.25. Originally published in 1907 and now reissued. This is the S. H. Butcher translation of Artistotle's "Poetics," with the complete Greek text on facing pages. Mr. Butcher provides a 300-page exposition and interpretation of the work. An introductory essay by John Gassner discusses the validity of Aristotle's ideas today and their application to contemporary literature. Bibliography. Indices.

ARISTOTLE
On the Art of Poetry with a Supplement on Music
Bobbs-Merrill, 1956. 51pp. Paper $ .85. Edited, with an introduction by Milton C. Nahm, this is a translation by S. H. Butcher of Aristotle's work.

ARISTOTLE
Poetics
University of Michigan, 1967. 124pp. $4.50. Paper—1970. $1.95. Professor Gerald F. Else aims, in this new translation, to provide a "way in" to Aristotle's process of thinking about literature. He has made a special effort to present the work in the English idiom. An introduction relates the "Poetics" to Plato's attack on the poets and places the treatise in the context of Aristotle's works as a whole. Notes. Select Bibliography. Index.

ARISTOTLE
The Poetics of Aristotle
University of North Carolina, 1942. 70pp. Paper $ .95. Translated by Preston H. Epps, this is an attempt to put before the reader, in clear English, what Aristotle actually said rather than what may have been meant by what he said. Index to Literary Works. Index to Proper Names.

ARISTOTLE
The Rhetoric and The Poetics of Aristotle
Modern Library, 1954. 289pp. $2.45. The complete

text of the works, in the authoritative Oxford translations by W. Rhys Roberts and Ingram Bywater, with an introduction and notes by the editor, Friedrich Solmsen of Cornell University.

COOPER, LANE
Aristotle on the Art of Poetry
Cornell, 1947. 100pp. Paper $1.75. Originally published in 1913 and revised in 1947, this is an introduction to Aristotle's "Poetics" with explanations, comments, and illustrations. Index.

COOPER, LANE
The Poetics of Aristotle: Its Meaning and Influence
Cooper Square 1963. 157pp. Paper $3.50. An account of the general character of the work, its scope and antecedents, and its style and composition, with a survey of its influence on theories of drama and art throughout history. Bibliography.

COOPER, LANE and ALFRED GUDEMAN
A Bibliography of the Poetics of Aristotle
Yale, 1928. 193pp. Paper $2.50. Originally published in 1928, this is a listing of texts, translations, commentaries, articles, and illusions on the "Poetics" from 1481 to 1927. Index.

EDEL, ABRAHAM
Aristotle
Dell, 1967. 493pp. Paper $ .95. A biography and selections from the works of Aristotle. An Appendix on "The Works and Their Contents" is included. Selected Bibliography.

ELSE, GERALD F.
Aristotle's Poetics: The Argument
Harvard, 1967. 670pp. $18.50. Originally published in 1957, corrected in 1963 and now reissued, this study offers a detailed analysis of Aristotle's argument in "The Poetics." Dr. Else presents a great many new interpretations, some on small points of detail, some bearing on the major concepts which went to form the doctrine of "classicism." Each section of the analysis is preceded by the corresponding section of Greek text, with an English translation. Bibliography. Indices.

JONES, JOHN
On Aristotle and Greek Tragedy
Oxford, 1962. 285pp. $5.75. Paper—1968. 284pp. $1.75. A re-examination of the "Poetics" to determine what Aristotle actually intended as opposed to what the neo-classicists said he intended. The "Oresteia," Sophocles' "Electra," "Ajax," "Antigone," and the "Oedipus" plays, and Euripides' "Electra" are analyzed in terms of the author's reading of the Aristotle text. Index.

KIERNAN, THOMAS P.
Aristotle Dictionary
Philosophical Library, 1962. 524pp. $7.50. This book presents in alphabetical arrangement precise definitions of all the basic concepts in the philosopher's work, with source references. An introduction gives detailed analyses of all the major works and a foreword by Theodore E. James is provided.

LLOYD, G.E.R.
Aristotle: The Growth & Structure of His Thought
Cambridge, 1968. 324pp. Paper $2.45. Dr. Lloyd divides his book into two parts. The first tells the story of Aristotle's intellectual development as far as it can be reconstructed; the second presents the fundamentals of his thought in the main fields of inquiry which interested him. The final chapter considers the unity and coherence of Aristotle's philosophy and records briefly his later influence on European thought. Index.

LUCAS, F.L.
Tragedy: Serious Drama in Relation to Aristotle's Poetics
See Page 17

MURE, G.R.G.
Aristotle
Oxford, 1964. 280pp. Paper $1.65. In this reprint of the study published in 1932 the author summarizes the development of Aristotle's thought and its position in the development of Western philosophy. The historical context is fully developed and textual problems are considered. Bibliography. Index.

OLSON, ELDER—Editor
Aristotle's Poetics and English Literature: A Collection of Critical Essays
University of Chicago, 1965. 236pp. $7.95. Paper $2.45. A collection designed to illustrate the influence of "The Poetics" on the literary criticism of men of letters in English. The essays are by such men as John Henry Newman, James Harris, Thomas Taylor, John Gassner, Kenneth Burke, Francis Fergusson, and Reuben A. Brower.

ROSS, SIR DAVID
Aristotle
Barnes & Noble, 1964. 300pp. $7.00. Paper $1.95. A reprint of the study first published in 1923. The author gives an account of the main features of Aristotle's philosophy as it stands before us, without criticism or evaluation. Chronology of commentators on the philosopher. Bibliography. Index.

Ennius

JOCELYN, H.D.
The Tragedies of Ennius
Cambridge, 1967. 473pp. $21.25. Dr. Jocelyn has collected the fragments of the twenty-two tragedies of Ennius and edited them with an introduction and

commentary. The introduction discusses the early history of Roman public spectacles, the physical conditions of the theatre in the third and second centuries, the general character of the Latin plays, and the fate of these scripts in later antiquity. Bibliography. Indices.

Euripides

BATES, WILLIAM NICKERSON
Euripides: A Student of Human Nature
A.S. Barnes, 1961. 315pp. Paper $1.95. This reprint of the 1930 edition includes chapters on the life and work of Euripides, with a detailed analysis of the plays and a survey of the fragments of lost works. Illustrated.

CONACHER, D.J.
Euripidean Drama: Myth, Theme and Structure
University of Toronto, 1967. 355pp. $8.50. A study of Euripides' dramatic technique and his use of traditional myth as a basis for inventing new forms in which to cast his perceptions of the sources of human tragedy. All the extant Euripidean drama is examined in this book. Bibliography.

GRUBE, G.M.A.
The Drama of Euripides
Barnes & Noble, 1961. 456pp. $7.50. Reprinted with minor corrections from the 1941 edition, this is a discussion of the plays with emphasis on dramatic structure and development.

LUCAS, F.L.
Euripides and His Influence
Cooper Square, 1963. 188pp. $3.50. This volume is a reprint of the 1923 edition and includes a brief biography of the playwright, with a detailed account of his influence on antiquity, on the drama of the middle ages and on the Renaissance, and on the neo-classic and later drama. Introduction by R.W. Livingstone. Bibliography.

MURRAY, GILBERT
Euripides and His Age
Oxford, 1965. 132pp. Paper $1.85. First published in 1918 and now reissued with a new introduction by H.D.F. Kitto which evaluates Murray's contribution to the study of Greek drama.

RITCHIE, WILLIAM
The Authenticity of the Rhesus of Euripides
Cambridge, 1964. 384pp. $8.50. In contradiction to the prevailing critical opinion, the author demonstrates that the "Rhesus" is the earliest extant work of Euripides. The play is considered in terms of its dramatic structure, its vocabulary, syntax, versification, lyrics and style. Comparison is made with other plays by the author. Bibliography.

SEGAL, ERICH – Editor
Euripides: A Collection of Critical Essays
Prentice–Hall, 1968. 177pp. $4.95. Paper $1.95. The contributors to this collection of essays see Euripides as an innovator whose works brought serious drama a step forward by departing from the classical form of tragedy. Chronology. Bibliography.

SUTHERLAND, DONALD and HAZEL E. BARNES
Hippolytus in Drama and Myth: "The Hippolytus of Euripides" – A New Translation by Donald Sutherland. "The Hippolytus of Drama and Myth" – A Study by Hazel E. Barnes
University of Nebraska, 1960. 123pp. Paper $1.65. The essay considers the tragedy to stem from the emotional involvement of three individuals whose acts are not wholly determined by their own rational natures.

WEBSTER, T.B.L.
The Tragedies of Euripides
Methuen, 1967. 316pp. $14.00. Professor Webster places Euripides' plays in chronological order to study the different principles which guided the playwright. He discusses the relation of Euripides to Aeschylus and Sophocles, describes the sixty-six tragedies in four chronological groups, reconstructs the lost plays, and defines the quality of the poetry and the relation between Euripides' uses of myth and the various contemporary attitudes toward myth. Index.

WILSON, JOHN R. – Editor
Twentieth Century Interpretations of Euripides' "Alcestis"
Prentice–Hall, 1968. 122pp. $4.95. Paper $1.25. A collection of critical essays by fifteen authorities. The essays analyze themes, style, genre, structural elements, artistic influences, and historical background. A chronology of important dates and a selected bibliography are included.

ZUNTZ, G.
An Inquiry into the Transmission of the Plays of Euripides
Cambridge, 1965. 295pp. $12.50. A detailed examination of the Byzantine manuscripts "L" and "P" which preserve most of the plays. The relation between the two is examined and the interpolator of "L" (Triclinius) is studied to determine the extent of his interference with the text, and the final evaluation of the Triclinian "Corpus Euripideum." Papyrus II and the Helena excerpt are examined. Illustrated with photographs of the manuscript. Index.

Herodas

KNOX, A.D. – Editor
Herodas: The Mimes and Fragments

Cambridge, 1966. 465pp. $16.25. Originally published in 1922 and now reissued, this is a collection of the fifteen mimes (dramatic scenes in popular life) written for Alexandria in 270—250 B.C. The original notes by Walter Headlam are included in the volume. Indices.

Menander

HANDLEY, E.W.—Editor
The Dyskolos of Menander
Harvard, 1965. 323pp. $12.00. A new critical text of the play discovered in the 1950's restored for continuous reading, and equipped with a select "apparatus criticus" to show how the text has been constituted. The long introduction considers the life of the playwright, then relates the play to its time and conventions. The text of the play is in Greek; the extensive footnotes and glossary, however, are in the English language.

Plautus

SEGAL, ERICH
Roman Laughter: The Comedy of Plautus
Harvard, 1968. 229pp. $6.95. This is a study on Plautus and his theatrical art. Mr. Segal pursues the question of the contemporary appeal of the comedies and argues that the essence of Plautus' art lies in his farcical inversion of the values and decorum of everyday Roman society. Notes. Index to Passages. General Index.

Seneca

CUNLIFFE, JOHN W.
The Influence of Seneca on Elizabethan Tragedy
See Page 153

Sophocles

ADAMS, S.M.
Sophocles the Playwright
University of Toronto, 1962. 182pp. Paper $5.50. A study of the general nature of each play, with special emphasis on the dramatic unity achieved by the theme of the controlling power of the gods and their participation in the affairs of man.

BATES, WILLIAM NICKERSON
Sophocles: Poet and Dramatist
A.S. Barnes, 1961. 291pp. Paper $1.95. This reprint of the original 1940 edition includes a discussion of the playwright's life and works, with an examination of each of the extant plays and satyr dramas, and a consideration of the lost plays. Bibliography of the Sophocles' Papyri. Illustrated with reproductions of ancient art. Index.

BERKOWITZ, LUCI and THEODORE F. BRUNNER—Editors
Oedipus Tyrannus
Norton, 1970. 261pp. Paper $2.35. A new translation of Sophocles' drama. The text is accompanied by background materials and essays including selections from ancient authors, essays in criticism by such authors and authorities as Aristotle, C.M. Bowra, Albin Lesky, John Jones, Francis Fergusson, and H.D.F. Kitto. Writings on the Oedipus myth are included under the topic, "Religion and Psychology." Selected Bibliography.

BOWRA, C.M.
Sophoclean Tragedy
Oxford, 1960. 384pp. $8.00. Paper—1965. $2.50. A reprint of the original edition just published in 1944, this is a discussion of the meaning of the central themes of the plays. Each play is considered in a separate chapter.

CAMERON, ALISTER
The Identity of Oedipus the King
New York University, 1968. 165pp. $9.00. Five essays on Sophocles' "Oedipus Tyrannus." Professor Cameron examines Sophocles' sources and the way they were transformed in the play to show the essential aim of Greek tragedy as it sought to capture the nature of man and his relation to the universe. Bibliography. Index.

CAMPBELL, LEWIS
Tragic Drama in Aeschylus, Sophocles, and Shakespeare
See Page 33

COOK, ALBERT
Oedipus Rex: A Mirror for Greek Drama
Wadsworth, 1963. 178pp. Paper $3.00. This handbook provides the student with a full introduction to the history of the play, beginning with the "Poetics" of Aristotle. Major critical statements on the fable on which the play is based, and on the play itself, are quoted and examined. The text of the play is given in full. There are also questions for review.

EHRENBERG, VICTOR
Sophocles and Pericles
Humanities, 1954. 187pp. $7.50. A study of the relationship between the two greatest men of Athens. The men are seen to reflect essential trends in Athenian thought and belief. Chapters consider tragedy and history, written laws and common law, Sophoclean rulers, Pericles as ruler, and administration and politics. Illustrated. Index.

GOHEEN, ROBERT F.
The Imagery of Sophocles' Antigone: A Study of Poetic Language and Structure
Princeton, 1951. 171pp. $4.75. A study of the workings of dominant images or master tropes in the play. Six groups of recurring images are analyzed: money and merchandising; warfare and military activity; animals and control of animals; the sea and sailing; marriage; sickness and disease.

KALLICH, MARTIN and ANDREW MacLEISH, GERTRUDE SCHOENBOHM – Editors
Oedipus: Myth and Drama
Odyssey, 1968. 404pp. Paper $3.50. A collection of three variations on the Oedipus myth by Sophocles, John Dryden and Nathaniel Lee, and von Hoffmannstahl. Also included are sections on "Literary Criticism," and "Modern Anthropological and Psychological Interpretations of the Oedipus Myth." Suggestions for Papers and Discussions. Bibliography.

KNOX, BERNARD
The Heroic Temper: Studies in Sophoclean Tragedy
University of California, 1964. 210pp. $6.00. The first two chapters describe the recurring type of tragic hero and situation found in all but one of the extant Sophoclean plays. There are close examinations of "Antigone," "Philoctetes," and "Oedipus at Colonus."

KNOX, BERNARD
Oedipus at Thebes
Yale, 1957. 280pp. $8.75. Paper – 1966. $1.95. A close analysis of the vocabulary and imagery of "Oedipus Rex." The nature of the hero, his relation to Athens, to his fellow man, and to God are considered. Bibliography.

O'BRIEN, MICHAEL J. – Editor
Twentieth Century Interpretations of "Oedipus Rex"
Prentice–Hall, 1968. 199pp. $3.95. Paper $1.25. A collection of twenty-six critical essays reflecting the diversity of opinion on Sophocles' tragedy. Included are a Chronology and a Selected Bibliography.

WALDOCK, A. J. A.
Sophocles the Dramatist
Cambridge, 1966. 234pp. Paper $2.25. In this reprint of the 1951 publication, Professor Waldock's intention is to provide an introduction to the plays of Sophocles. He gives a chapter to each one and also explains his general approach in a first section which is a compendium of critical theory. Index.

WEBSTER, T. B. L.
An Introduction to Sophocles
Methuen, 1969. 220pp. $7.00. A new edition of the study first published in 1936. Additions and corrections bring the volume up to date. The author includes a chapter on the life of Sophocles and the chronology of his plays, gives accounts of the playwright's thought, characters, plots, songs, and style. A new appendix on the early plays has been added. Notes. Appendices. Indices.

WOODARD, THOMAS – Editor
Sophocles: A Collection of Critical Essays
Prentice–Hall, 1965. 179pp. $4.95. Paper $1.95. Essays by Nietzsche, Spengler, Robert Murray, Bernard Knox, Charles Segal, Freud, Virginia Woolf, and Cedric Whitman. Bibliography.

Terence

NORWOOD, GILBERT
The Art of Terence
Russell & Russell, 1965. 156pp. $7.50. This reprint of the 1923 study includes a defense of the greatness of the playwright Terence. The author examines the six plays in detail and shows what elements in the plays and in their theatrical histories have obscured their greatness from modern readers. Index.

SHAKESPEARE

REFERENCE WORKS

Bibliographies

BATE, JOHN
How to Find Out About Shakespeare
Pergamon Press, 1968. 161pp. $3.50. Paper $2.25. This is a guide to the study of the plays and poetry of Shakespeare. The author discusses books about Shakespeare's life and work, about the theatre of Shakespeare's time, criticism of the works, and commentaries on individual plays. He seeks to provide as briefly as possible the author's intentions in writing the work cited. Index of Works Cited.

BERMAN, RONALD
A Reader's Guide to Shakespeare's Plays: A Discursive Bibliography
Scott, Foresman, 1965. 151pp. Paper $2.50. A critical bibliography of over 3,000 books of fundamental importance to an understanding of the plays.

EBISCH, WALTHER and LEVIN L. SCHUCKING
A Shakespeare Bibliography
Blom, 1968. 294pp. $17.50. Originally published in 1930 and now reissued, this standard reference aid lists over 3,800 items. It is divided into two sections, "General Bibliography" and "The Works of Shakespeare." Among the subjects covered are: Elizabethan Literature, Shakepeare's Life, Shakespeare's Personality, Sources, Literary Influences and Cultural Relations, The Art of Shakespeare, Shakespeare's Stage and the Production of His Plays, Shakespeare's Influence, and the Shakespeare-Bacon Controversy. Index.

EBISCH, WALTHER and LEVIN L. SCHUCKING
Supplement for the Years 1930–1935 to a Shakespeare Bibliography
Blom, 1964. 104pp. $10.00. Originally published in 1936 and now reissued, this is a corrected edition. The method and arrangements of "A Shakespeare Bibliography" are followed. See that entry directly above.

FORD, HERBERT L.
Shakespeare: 1700–1740
Blom, 1969. 140pp. $12.50. Originally published in 1935 and now reissued, this is a collation of editions from Rowe to Theobald, and of printings of separate plays in the period, with an account of the Tonson-Walker controversy.

JAGGARD, WILLIAM
Shakespeare Bibliography: A Dictionary of Every Known Issue of the Writings of the Poet and of Recorded Opinion Thereon in the English Language
Ungar, 1959. 729pp. $17.50. A cumulative catalogue with over 36,000 separate entries, annotated and indexed, of the world's twelve largest Shakespeare libraries. Illustrated with forty-eight plates.

PAYNE, WAVENEY R. N.
A Shakespeare Bibliography
DBS Publications, 1969. 93pp. Paper $2.25. This is a selection of Shakespearean literature that is currently available with a preference given to more recent English books. Among the categories are reference works, the text, literary criticism, philosophy and knowledge of Shakespeare, groups of the plays, history and production, and bibliographies. Index.

SHATTUCK, CHARLES H.
The Shakespeare Promptbooks: A Descriptive Catalogue
University of Illinois, 1965. 553pp. $15.00. This comprehensive catalogue describes and gives library locations of more than 2,200 copies of plays marked for stage use by professionals from the 1620's to 1961. The value and use of the promptbooks are analyzed, and there are guides to symbols and abbreviations in older books. The books are listed chronologically under each play and numbered serially. Index.

SMITH, GORDON ROSS
A Classified Shakespeare Bibliography: 1936 – 1958
Pennsylvania State University, 1963. 784pp. $40.00. This comprehensive cross-referenced bibliography lists over 20,000 books, articles and reviews. Classes are generally continued from the Ebisch and Schucking work: "A Shakespeare Bibliography."

VELZ, JOHN W.
Shakespeare and the Classical Tradition: A Critical Guide to Commentary, 1660 – 1960
University of Minnesota, 1967. 459pp. $22.50. This is an annotated critical bibliography of books, articles, notes, and other materials concerning Shakespeare's classicism or lack of it. It contains 2,817 entries listing the relevant criticism and scholarship in English, French, and German. The entries are organized in sections according to groups of Shakespeare's works and are arranged alphabetically by author within each section. There are also sections listing the bibliographies consulted and modern editions of the classical works which scholars believe Shakespeare may have read. Subject Index. Author Index.

WELLS, STANLEY
Shakespeare: A Reading Guide
Oxford, 1969. 44pp. Paper $1.95. This pamphlet provides a selection of Shakespearean literature currently available. Among the categories provided are bibliographies, biographies, editions, textual studies, and general criticism.

Concordances, Dictionaries, Glossaries

ABBOTT, E.A.
A Shakespearean Grammar
Dover, 1966. 511pp. Paper $2.75. An unabridged republication of the 1870 edition of the guide to special difficulties of Shakespearean syntax, grammar, and prosody. The author covers every idiomatic usage that modern readers will encounter in Shakespeare. Notes and Questions. Verbal Index. Index to Quotes.

BARTLETT, JOHN
A Complete Concordance of Shakespeare
St. Martin's 1960. 1,910pp. $40.00. First published in 1894 and now reissued, this is an index to phrases, words, and passages in the dramatic works, with a supplement on the poems.

FOSTER, JOHN
A Shakespeare Word-Book
Russell & Russell, 1969. 735pp. $23.50. Originally published in 1908, this is a glossary of the forms and usages of words employed by Shakespeare.

HOWARD-HILL, T.H.—Editor
The Oxford Shakespeare Concordance
Oxford. $10.50 per volume. The text for each Concordance is the one chosen by Dr. Alice Walker for the Oxford Old Spelling Shakespeare. Each Concordance takes account of every word in the text and represents their occurrence by frequency counts, line numbers, and reference lines, or a selection of these according to the interest of the particular word. The introduction to each volume records the facsimile copy of the text from which the Concordance was prepared, a table of Folio through line numbers and Globe edition act and scene numbers, a list of the misprints corrected in the text, and an account of the order of printing, and the proofreading. Volumes in the series are listed below.
All's Well That Ends Well. 1969. 302pp.
As You Like It. 1969. 274pp.
The Comedy of Errors. 1969. 284pp.
Henry VI—Part I. 1970. 294pp.
Henry VI—Part 2. 1970. 339pp.
King John. 1970. 270pp.
Love's Labour's Lost. 1970. 302pp.
Measure for Measure. 1969. 189pp.
The Merchant of Venice. 1969. 287pp.
The Merry Wives of Windsor. 1969. 234pp.
A Midsummer Night's Dream. 1970. 227pp.
Much Ado About Nothing. 1970. 290pp.
The Taming of the Shrew. 1969. 268pp.
The Tempest. 1969. 234pp.
Twelfth Night. 1969. 260pp.
The Two Gentlemen of Verona. 1969. 209pp.
The Winter's Tale. 1969. 333pp.

KOKERITZ, HELGE
Shakespeare's Names: A Pronouncing Dictionary
Yale, 1959. 100pp. $3.25. Approximately 1,800 names, each provided with phonetic transcription (in the broad form of the International Phonetic Association Alphabet) showing the modern and the Shakespearean pronunciation. Phonological and etymological notes support the pronunciations given and metrical and dialectal variants of the names are indicated.

KOKERITZ, HELGE
Shakespeare's Pronunciation
Yale, 1953. 521pp. $13.50. A study of Elizabethan English as revealed in the works of the dramatist. The work is based on evidence of his rhymes, spellings, homonymic puns, and versification, compared with the statements of contemporary orthoepists and interpreted in the light of recent theories concerning the phonological characteristics of the sixteenth century. The Appendix gives a rhyme dictionary, lists of syncopated words and words stressed differently today.

ONIONS, C.T.
A Shakespeare Glossary
Oxford, 1958. 264pp. $5.00. First published in 1911, this second edition of the work contains definitions and illustrations of obsolete, archaic, and difficult words. List of Shakespearian Editors, Commentators and Critics. List of Authors and Works Cited.

SCHMIDT, ALEXANDER
Shakespeare Lexicon
Blom, 1967. 1,484pp. $45.00. This is a complete dictionary, originally published in 1901 and now reissued, of all the English words, phrases, and constructions in the works of Shakespeare. Two volume set.

STOKES, FRANCIS GRIFFIN
A Dictionary of the Characters and Proper Names in the Works of Shakespeare
Dover, 1970. 360pp. Paper $3.75. An unabridged, slightly corrected republication of the original 1924 edition, this is a dictionary of dramatis personae and every proper name that occurs in the First Folio, "Pericles," and the Poems. Entries include the work or works in which they appear, their authentic biographies, summaries of their dramatic action in the plays, and the dramatist's indebtedness to other sources. An Appendix provides genealogical tables of important families figuring in the plays.

VIETOR, WILHELM
A Shakespeare Phonology: With a Rime Index to the Poems as a Pronouncing Vocabulary
Ungar, 1963. 290pp. $5.50. Based on Elizabethan and Jacobean authorities as well as on the linguistic findings of later authorities, this reprint of the original 1906 edition presents an accurate record of how Shakespeare sounded to his contemporaries.

Outlines of Plays

BAKER, ARTHUR E.
A Shakespeare Commentary
Unger, 1958. Volume One: 482pp. Volume Two: 482pp. Two volume set: $19.50. Originally published in 1938, this is a source book covering many of Shakespeare's plays. The author provides pertinent information concerning date of composition and particulars of publication, with sources of plots and detailed outlines, as well as notes on characters, and archaic words, etc. Brief comments from critics and authorities are also included.

McSPADDEN, J. WALKER
Shakespearean Synopses
Crowell, 1961. 210pp. $2.95. Originally published in 1951 and now reissued in a revised edition, this volume includes synopses of every play with index to characters, an introduction on the Elizabethan stage and other background material.

McSPADDEN, J. WALKER
Shakespeare's Plays in Digest Form
Crowell, 1961. 210pp. Paper $1.25. Originally published in 1951 as "Shakespearean Synopses," this volume includes synopses of every play, with index to characters, and background material.

MAGILL, LEWIS M. and NELSON A. AULT
Synopses of Shakespeare's Complete Plays
Littlefield, Adams, 1965. 192pp. Paper $1.50. These synopses have been written for students and the general reader. Sketches of the principal characters of each play are included as well as background material.

VANDIVER, EDWARD P.
Highlights of Shakespeare's Plays
Barron, 1964. 454pp. $5.00. Paper $2.25. A selection of passages from twenty-three plays with commentary, notes, and detailed explications. A condensed presentation of the substance of twenty-three tragedies, histories, and comedies by means of plot summaries to bridge obscure or ponderous passages. The balance of the play is given in full with the abridgments inserted for continuous reading. Illustrated with photographs taken at Stratford, Ontario. Explanations, comments, emphasis on famous quotations are provided.

WATT, HOMER and KARL J. HOLZKNECHT, RAYMOND ROSS – Editors
Outlines of Shakespeare's Plays
Barnes & Noble, 1968. 212pp. Paper $1.50. A reprint of the book first published in 1934, this volume contains act-by-act synopses of all the plays. The introduction provides background material on the author and the works. Bibliography.

Quotation and Quiz Books

CRAWFORD, NORMAN
Shakespeare and the Bible
Carlton Press, 1967. 91pp. $2.75. This anthology of quotations, under thirty-five chapter headings, juxtaposes Biblical and Shakespearean passages to illustrate the author's chapter themes.

GARVIN, WILLIAM
You Said It, Shakespeare!
Eriksson, 1969. 79pp. $3.95. Quotations from Shakespeare's works are applied to contemporary life to produce a comic affect. Illustrated with drawings.

GROSS, FANNIE
Shakespeare Quiz Book
Crowell, 1959. 215pp. $2.95. Over 2,000 questions and answers on all the plays are arranged by subject and play.

GROSS, FANNIE
The Shakespearean Review Book
Apollo, 1959. 215pp. Paper $1.25. Over 2,000 questions cover every important detail of plot, character, and dialogue.

KAISER, BEZA BOYNTON
Shakespearean Oracles
Faxon, 1923. 142pp. $2.25. A collection of the most quotable short sayings from the plays, designed for the public speaker and writer.

STEVENSON, BURTON
The Home Book of Shakespeare Quotations
Scribners, 1965. 2,055pp. $20.00. A reprinting of the 1937 concordance and glossary of words and phrases in the plays and poems. The volume includes some 90,000 separate quotations arranged by topic. All quotations are centered on a key word and grouped together so that the reader may find at a glance the quotation bearing on any one of a great variety of subjects. Index.

STEVENSON, BURTON
The Standard Book of Shakespeare Quotations
Funk & Wagnalls, 1953. 766pp. $7.50. Alphabetical arrangement, by subject, of almost 9,000 quotations, with complete references. Obscure words and phrases are glossed and historical backgrounds are given.

VIETOR, WILHELM
A Shakespeare Reader: In the Old Spelling with a Phonetic Transcription
Ungar, 1963. 178pp. $5.00. Reprinted from the 1906 edition, this is a selection of familiar passages from the plays and poems, presented in their original spelling, with phonetic transcriptions on the facing pages.

Annuals

MUIR, KENNETH – Editor
Shakespeare Survey
Cambridge. $10.75 per volume. A continuation of the yearly volumes originally edited by Allardyce Nicoll. Each volume deals with Shakespearean discoveries, history, criticism, and productions all over the world and is made up of articles by a number of contributors. Each volume is illustrated and each contains an Index. No volume is limited to one theme but the main theme of each of the available volumes is listed below. (See also the entry under: **Nicoll, Allardyce.**)

Survey #19. Macbeth. 1966. 171pp.
Survey #20. Shakespearean and Other Tragedy. 1967. 188pp.
Survey #21. Othello. 1968. 219pp.
Survey #22. Aspects of Shakespearean Comedy. 1969. 193pp.
Survey #23. Shakespeare's Language. 1970. 192pp.

NICOLL, ALLARDYCE – Editor
Shakespeare Survey
Cambridge. $10.75 per volume. A series of annual volumes dealing with Shakespearean discoveries, history, criticism, and productions all over the world. Each volume is made up of articles by a number of contributors; each is illustrated; and each has an index. No volume is limited to one theme, but the main themes of each of the volumes is listed below. (See also **Kenneth Muir** entry directly above.)

Survey # 1. Shakespeare and the Stage. 1948. 144pp.
Survey # 2. Shakespearean Production. 1949. 164pp.
Survey # 3. The Man and the Writer. 1950. 167pp.
Survey # 4. Interpretations. 1951. 176pp.
Survey # 5. Textual Criticism. 1952. 164pp.
Survey # 6. The Histories. 1953. 185pp.
Survey # 7. Style and Language. 1954. 168pp.
Survey # 8. The Comedies. 1955. 172pp.
Survey # 9. Hamlet. 1956. 168pp.
Survey #10. The Roman Plays. 1957. 171pp.
Survey #11. The Last Plays (With an Index to Surveys #1–10.) 1958. 223pp.
Survey #12. The Elizabethan Theatre. 1959. 164pp.
Survey #13. King Lear. 1960. 182pp.
Survey #14. Shakespeare and his Contemporaries. 1961. 180pp.
Survey #15. Poems and Music in the Plays. 1962. 195pp.
Survey #16. Shakespeare in the Modern World. 1963. 189pp.
Survey $17. Shakespeare in His Own Age. 1964. 277pp.
Survey #18. Shakespeare Then Til Now. 1965. 205pp.

BIOGRAPHIES AND GENERAL SURVEYS

AKRIGG, G. P. V.
Shakespeare and The Earl of Southampton
Harvard, 1968. 280pp. $6.00. Mr. Akrigg investigates the relationship between Shakespeare and the Earl of Southampton. He begins with a biography of Southampton—the first to make use of the Earl's family archives— and deals in the second part of the book with the view that the Earl was the "Mr. W.H." to whom Shakespeare's sonnets were dedicated. Illustrated. Index.

ALEXANDER, PETER
Shakespeare's Life and Art
New York University, 1962. 247pp. $8.00. Paper $1.95. An analysis of the facts known about Shakespeare's career, with a summary of the unfavorable judgment created by early biographers. An order among the plays is established to reveal the gradual development of the poet.

BENTLEY, GERALD EADES
Shakespeare: A Biographical Handbook
Yale, 1961. 256pp. $8.75. Paper $1.95. A presentation of the hundred or more surviving documents pertaining to the playwright in the context of similar records. The evidence of the documents is seen against the background of Elizabethan customs and prejudices.

BOYDELL, JOHN – Compiler
A Collection of Prints Illustrating the Dramatic Works of Shakespeare
Blom, 1968. 200 plates. $45.00. Originally published in 1803 and now reissued, these 200 engravings are acknowledged to be one of the treasures of Shakesspearean illustration. Among the great eighteenth century English painters who are associated with the work are: Reynolds, Benjamin West, Romney, Opie, Northcote, Fuseli, Hamilton, and Wheatley.

BROWN, IVOR
How Shakespeare Spent the Day
Hill & Wang, 1963. 237pp. $5.00. Paper—1965. $1.65. Without speculating on biographical theory or aesthetic criticism, the author reconstructs the day-to-day life of the dramatist as he struggled to make a living in the competitive theatre of his time. Such questions as length of rehearsals, identity and function of the director, touring, earning capacity of the dramatist, the dramatist's health and welfare, and the final years in retirement are among the issues discussed. Index.

BROWN, IVOR
Shakespeare in His Time
Thomas Nelson, 1960. 238pp. $6.00. A study of Elizabethan and Jacobean England and its way of life

which utilizes the evidence of the plays, pamphlets, and chronicles of the epoch, especially Shakespeare's own work. Illustrated.

BROWN, IVOR
William Shakespeare
Morgan-Grampion, 1968. 92pp. $3.50. A biographical study of Shakespeare illustrated in color and black and white with material from contemporary sources, photographs from twentieth century stage and film productions. A selected book list is included.

BROWN, IVOR
The Women in Shakespeare's Life
Coward—McCann, 1969. 224pp. $5.95. The author studies Shakespeare's life and the women who figured in it. He examines the status of women in Stratford and London, and the lives of the playwright's mother, wife, and daughters. List of Books Consulted. Index.

BURGESS, ANTHONY
Shakespeare
Knopf, 1970. 272pp. $17.50. This biography of Shakespeare portrays not only the artist and the man but also the world in which he lived and worked. Lavishly illustrated with forty-three color plates and other photographs, and contemporary works of art in the text. List of Books. Index.

BURTON, H.M.
Shakespeare and His Plays
Roy, 1958. 66pp. $2.95. This brief survey emphasizes two points: Shakespeare as practical man of the theatre and the essential feature of the plays as written to be acted.

CAMPBELL, LEWIS
Tragic Drama in Aeschylus, Sophocles, and Shakespeare
See Page 33

CAMPBELL, OSCAR JAMES and EDWARD G. QUINN – Editors
The Reader's Encyclopedia of Shakespeare
Crowell, 1966. 1,014pp. $15.00. This encyclopedia brings together more than 2,700 entries on Shakespeare and his works. It includes all the basic information on Shakespeare, his plays and his poems. The book is divided into seven main categories: the man, his works, characters in the plays, production, scholarship and criticism, and documents. Illustrated.

CHAMBERS, E.K.
A Short Life of William Shakespeare, with the Sources
Oxford, 1933. 260pp. $2.50. A one volume edition, abridged by Charles Williams from the two volume "William Shakespeare: A Study of Facts and Problems." Only the material of importance to specialists is eliminated. All the important facts and documents on the plays and the life of the playwright are preserved.

CHAMBERS, E.K.
Sources for a Biography of Shakespeare
Oxford, 1970. 80pp. $4.50. First published in 1946 and out of print since 1950, this volume is now reprinted. The author discusses the study of Shakespeare's life and the original documents on which such a study may be based. Bibliographical Note. Index.

CHAMBERS, E.K.
William Shakespeare
Oxford, 1930. Volume One: 576pp. Volume Two: 488pp. $14.00. Volume One considers Shakespeare's origins, the Quartos and the First Folio, plays in the printing house, the problem of authenticity, the problem of chronology, and the plays of the First Folio. Volume Two contains notes on records, lists of dates, the pedigree of Shakespeare and Arden, all the principal records, contemporary allusions, the Shakespeare-Mythos, list of performances, the name Shakespeare, a table of Quartos, metrical tables, lists of books, and subject index of the two volumes. Illustrated. Sold as a two volume set. (Also see: **Beatrice White-Editor.** "An Index to 'William Shakespeare'.")

CHUTE, MARCHETTE
An Introduction to Shakespeare
Dutton, 1951. 123pp. $3.25. A brief survey of Shakespeare and his theatre.

CHUTE, MARCHETTE
Shakespeare of London
Dutton, 1949. 397pp. $7.95. Paper $1.85. An account, based entirely on contemporary documents, of the life and times of Shakespeare.

CROCE, BENEDETTO
Ariosto, Shakespeare and Corneille
Russell & Russell, 1966. 440pp. $10.00. A reprint of the 1920 edition of three critical essays by the Italian philosopher-critic. Translated by Douglas Ainslie. Index.

DUTHIE, G.I.
Shakespeare
Hillary, 1963. 207pp. Paper $3.00. A reprint of the 1956 publication, this is an analysis of a select number of plays in the light of such questions as the theatrical conventions of the day, the validity of a psychological approach to the plays, and the religious, moral, and political ideas of the playwright. Index.

ECCLES, MARK
Shakespeare in Warwickshire
University of Wisconsin, 1961. 192pp. $4.50. Paper $1.75. A study of Shakespeare's relation to his birthplace, his family, and his friends, with chapters on the Arden family, Shakespeare's father, the Stratford school, Anne Hathaway, New Place, and the last years. Illustrated with four plates and two maps. Notes. Index.

EVANS, GARETH LLOYD
Shakespeare I: 1564–1592
Oliver & Boyd, 1969. 120pp. $3.95. Paper $1.95. The author follows, chronologically, the progress of Shakespeare's life from his youth in Stratford through his earlier plays. The volume examines: "Henry VI, Parts I, II, and III," "Richard III," "Titus Andronicus," "The Two Gentlemen of Verona," "The Comedy of Errors," "Love's Labour's Lost," and "The Taming of the Shrew."

EVANS, GARETH LLOYD
Shakespeare II: 1587–1598
Oliver & Boyd, 1969. 120pp. $3.95. Paper $1.95. This is a study of the theatre context of Shakespeare's early days in London and the plays in which he began to acquire and display mastery over his craft and art. The plays discussed are "Richard II," "King John," "Henry IV, Parts I and II," "Henry V," "The Merry Wives of Windsor," "A Midsummer Night's Dream," "Romeo and Juliet," and "The Merchant of Venice."

FLEMING, JOAN
Shakespeare's Country in Colour
Batsford, 1960. 95pp. $3.95. This is a collection of twenty-five color photographs showing the villages, churches, ancient houses, and landscape around Stratford. The author has provided an introductory text and notes on the illustrations.

FORD, BORIS – Editor
The Age of Shakespeare
Penguin, 1960. 480pp. Paper $1.45. In Addition to material on other writers and literature of the era, this study contains five essays on Shakespeare by Derek Traversi, J. C. Maxwell, L. C. Knights, and Kenneth Muir. The essays discuss "King Lear," the middle plays, and changing interpretations, among other subjects.

FRYE, ROLAND MUSHAT
Shakespeare's Life and Times: A Pictorial Record
Princeton, 1967. 126pp. $10.00. In text and 114 illustrations, many of them taken from sixteenth and seventeenth century originals, this biography provides a view of Shakespeare from birth and boyhood in Stratford, through his career in London, and back to Stratford in retirement. Two authentic portraits are included among the illustrations of the houses in which he lived, the theatres in which he worked, and the actors and people who knew him, worked with him, and wrote about him. Bibliographical Note. Index.

GRACE, WILLIAM
Approaching Shakespeare
Basic Books, 1964. 248pp. $5.95. This survey of the playwright has chapters on the tragic image of the plays, on comedy and the law of disproportion, on the poetry of the plays, on ideas in Shakespeare, and on the laws of the drama as found in the plays. Bibliography. Index.

GRANVILLE–BARKER, HARLEY and G. B. HARRISON
A Companion to Shakespeare Studies
Cambridge, 1955. 408pp. $8.50. Paper – Doubleday, 1960. 408pp. $1.75. A collection of essays on all aspects of Shakespearean scholarship. Among the topics covered are biographical studies, the theatre, the poetry of the plays, the spoken English of Shakespeare's time, the texts of the plays, and Shakespearean criticism. Illustrated.

GROSE, K. H. and B. T. OXLEY
Shakespeare
Evans, 1965. 160pp. Paper $2.00. Chapters on the life, times, theatre, craft, and moral vision of the playwright. Bibliography. Index.

HAINES, CHARLES
William Shakespeare and His Plays
Watts, 1968. 181pp. $2.95. This is a study of the life of Shakespeare and the production of his plays during his lifetime. Bibliography. Index.

HALLIDAY, FRANK E.
The Enjoyment of Shakespeare.
Duckworth, 1959. 116pp. $2.50. A short life of the playwright, with the description of an imaginary visit to the Globe Theatre. Shakespeare's use of prose and verse to achieve different dramatic effects is also considered.

HALLIDAY, FRANK E.
The Life of Shakespeare
A. S. Barnes, 1961. 248pp. $5.00. Paper – Penguin, 1963. 299pp. $1.25. Using the materials of recent research, in particular the work of Leslie Hotson and T. W. Baldwin, Mr. Halliday has written a comprehensive biography of the poet. Appendices give the family line of Shakespeare, and the interrelationship of the families of Combe, Lane, Nash, Shakespeare, and Quiney. Bibliography. Index.

HALLIDAY, FRANK E.
Shakespeare: A Pictorial Biography
Viking, 1959. 147pp. $6.50. A life of the playwright illustrated with facsimile reproductions of Elizabethan and Jacobean records and with photographs of Stratford.

HALLIDAY, FRANK E.
Shakespeare in His Age
A. S. Barnes, 1956. 362pp. $6.00. The author studies the political, social, and religious background of the age; examines the poet's political and cultural inheritance; and gives a year-by-year rundown of the important events in his life. Illustrated. Index.

HARBAGE, ALFRED
Conceptions of Shakespeare
Harvard, 1966. 164pp. $4.95. Paper – Schocken, 1968. 164pp. $1.95. This study examines the impact of

Shakespeare and his works on biographers, critics, actors, directors, theatregoers, and moral philosophers in the dramatist's own era and thereafter. The author tries to distinguish between what is known about Shakespeare and what is said about him. Notes. Index.

HARRIS, FRANK
The Man Shakespeare
Horizon, 1969. 422pp. $10.00. Paper $3.45. Originally published in 1909 and now reprinted, this is a study of the biographical aspects of Shakespeare's plays.

HARRISON, G. B.
Introducing Shakespeare
Penguin, 1966. 232pp. Paper $1.75. A new and revised edition of the 1939 publication. Dr. Harrison deals with the legend and the life of Shakespeare and shows the methods, discoveries and conclusions of modern inquiry. He explores the Elizabethan playhouse and includes a chapter on Shakespeare's company. Illustrated. Index.

HOLLAND, NORMAN
Psychoanalysis and Shakespeare
McGraw–Hill, 1966. 412pp. $9.95. This study begins with a statement of the psychoanalytic theory of literature, then summarizes and evaluates the major psychoanalytic comments on the plays and the personality of the playwright. How various theories developed out of particular plays and how the theories helped to clarify (or confuse) the works are discussed. Index.

HOLZKNECHT, KARL J.
The Background of Shakespeare's Plays
Van Nostrand, 1950. 482pp. $15.25. A biographical and critical handbook to the works describing the more important social and cultural aspects of the playwright's era, the traditions of his theatre, the language and style of the plays, the sources, themes, and printings. Illustrated. Bibliography. Index.

ISAACS, J.
Shakespeare's Earliest Years in the Theatre
Oxford, 1953. 20pp. Paper $ .85 A brief analysis of the so-called "missing years" (1584–1594) in the life of Shakespeare.

IYENGAR, K. R. SRINIVASA
Shakespeare: His World and His Art
Asia Publishing House, 1964. 711pp. $15.75. This full-length biography by the noted Indian scholar and critic presents an examination of the life and works of the poet, with discussion of the major themes dramatized during his lifetime.

JOSEPH, HARRIET
Shakespeare's Son-In-Law: John Hall, Man and Physician
Shoe String, 1964. 328pp. $9.00. In this study of Hall and his medical practice, Mrs. Joseph has uncovered details relative to Shakespeare and his time. There is a facsimile reproduction of Hall's case book (the second edition of "Select Observations on English Bodies") and notes on his medical diagnoses. Bibliography. Index.

JUSSERAND, J. J.
A Literary History of the English People
Blom, 1968. Volume One: 545pp. Volume Two: 551pp. Volume Three: 629pp. $37.50. Originally published in 1895–1909, and now reissued in a facsimile edition, this three volume study extends from the origins of the English people through the age of Elizabeth. Among the fields covered are the origins of theatre in England, Shakespeare's predecessors, a personal and literary biography of Shakespeare, Shakespeare's dramatic work, and the contemporaries and successors of Shakespeare. Index. Sold only as a three volume set.

KER, W. P. and A. S. NAPIER – Editors
An English Miscellany
See Page 146

KLEIN, DAVID
Milestones to Shakespeare
See Page 146

KOTT, JAN
Shakespeare, Our Contemporary
Doubleday, 1964. 241pp. $4.50. Paper $1.45. This study examines those aspects of Shakespeare's imagination that seem to bear a direct relation to the plays of such playwrights as Beckett, Ionesco, Genet, and other exponents of the Theatre of the Absurd. The violence, political cynicism, existential despair, and idealogical intolerance in such plays as "King Lear," "Hamlet," Richard III," "Tempest, and "A Midsummer Night's Dream" are related to the political and moral climate of our time.

LAMBORN, E. A. G. and G. B. HARRISON
Shakespeare: The Man and His Stage
Oxford, 1923. 128pp. $1.75. A brief scholarly account of the playwright. Illustrated.

LEE, SIDNEY
A Life of William Shakespeare
Dover, 1968. 792pp. Paper $3.75. An unabridged republication of the 1931 edition of a biography of Shakespeare which was first published in 1898. The author combines accounts of all the existing records of Shakespeare's activities and evaluations of the various legends with a historical study of each of the plays and poems, including the apocryphal works. Illustrated. Appendices. Index.

LUDOWYK, E. F. C.
Understanding Shakespeare
Cambridge, 1962. 266pp. $3.75. Paper $1.95. A

general introduction to the life and times of the playwright with detailed studies of six plays: "Richard II," "Merchant of Venice," "Henry V," "Julius Caesar," "Twelfth Night," and "Macbeth."

MASEFIELD, JOHN
William Shakespeare
Fawcett, 1964. 191pp. Paper $ .60. This general introduction presents a survey of the life, followed by a play-by-play analysis and chapters on the reputation of the poet since his death.

MERCHANT, W. MOELWYN
Shakespeare and the Artist
Oxford, 1959. 254pp. $18.50. A consecutive history of Shakespearean illustrations and decor, indicating the comparative importance of artist and theatre designer in each age. Over 250 half-tone plates and line engravings are examined in detail.

MORYSON, FYNES
Shakespeare's Europe
Blom, 1967. 521pp. $17.50. This is a survey of the condition of Europe at the end of the sixteenth century, edited and with an account of Fynes Moryson's career by Charles Hughes. Moryson was a traveller-author of the sixteenth century and his "Itinerary," of which this is unpublished chapters, was first published in 1617. This reprint contains a specially compiled index. Illustrated.

MURRY, J. MIDDLETON
Keats and Shakespeare: A Study of Keats' Poetic Life from 1816 to 1820
Oxford, 1958. 248pp. $8.75. A reprint of the original edition of 1925, this is a study of Keats' sudden flowering as a poet and of the influence of Shakespeare on that maturing of genius.

MURRY, J. MIDDLETON
Shakespeare
Johnathan Cape, 1965. 448pp. Paper $3.85. A reprinting of the study first published in 1936, of which the "Times Literary Supplement" said: "From beginning to end...rich in ideas and observations which will notably help the plain man to see more of the beauty and the meaning in the plays." Index.

NEILSON, WILLIAM ALLAN and ASHLEY HORACE THORNDIKE
The Facts About Shakespeare
Macmillan, 1961. 262pp. Paper $2.25. A revised edition of the book first published in 1941, this is a compact summary of scholarship in the field of Shakespearean biography and textual criticism.

NICOLL, ALLARDYCE
Shakespeare
Methuen, 1961. 181pp. $2.25. A reprint of the 1952 edition, this is a brief introduction to Shakespearean studies dealing with existing knowledge of the background and with textual problems. The playwright's growth as a dramatist is analyzed and critical opinions are evaluated.

NOBLE, IRIS
William Shakespeare
Messner, 1961. 190pp. $3.50. Written for the young reader, this is an account of the life and work of the playwright. The author recreates the incidents and emotions which inspired the plays and she condenses the most famous scenes.

NORMAN, CHARLES
The Playmaker of Avon
McKay, 1949. 155pp. Paper $1.45. Suitable for young readers, this is a short account of the life and works of Shakespeare.

NORMAN, CHARLES
So Worthy a Friend: William Shakespeare
Collier, 1961. 319pp. Paper $1.50. The author puts the facts about Shakespeare's life in an orderly sequence and studies those poems and plays which have some definite relation to the biography.

PARROTT, THOMAS MARC
William Shakespeare: A Handbook
Scribner, 1955. 266pp. Paper $1.65. A revised edition of the work first published in 1934, this is a narrative, interpretative account of Shakespeare's life as a playwright and actor. Illustrated with a chronological table.

QUENNELL, PETER
Shakespeare: A Biography
World, 1963. 352pp. $6.95. Paper—Avon, 1963. 384pp. $ .75. An account of Shakespeare's life and literary development as seen against the historical and social history of his day. Detailed portraits are given of Southampton and of Shakespeare's relation with him, as well as of Raleigh, the Cecils, and, in particular, Essex. Bibliography. Index.

RALEIGH, WALTER
Shakespeare
St. Martin's, 1961. 232pp. $3.25. A study of the playwright and his relation to his era with critical examinations of the major themes of the plays.

REESE, M. M.
Shakespeare: His World and His Work
St. Martin's, 1953. 589pp. $12.00. A comprehensive history of the playwright with chapters on his youth, his predecessors in drama, the condition of the theatre in his time, and his own contribution to drama. Illustrated with drawings.

REESE, M. M.
William Shakespeare
St. Martin's, 1963. 64pp. $2.95. Written especially for young people, this is an introduction to the life

and work of the playwright. The author describes the world in which the poet lived and the problems he faced as a leading member and director of a professional acting company. The second part of the book deals with the plays. Illustrations by David Chalmers with a section of photographs of productions. Glossary. End maps. Index.

RIBNER, IRVING
William Shakespeare: An Introduction to His Life, Times, and Theatre
Blaisdell, 1969. 280pp. Paper $1.95. Written to accompany the "Kittredge Shakespeare Series" of texts of the plays, this volume provides the necessary background material of the playwright's life and times. Professor Ribner summarizes the biographical information on Shakespeare and presents a guide to the body of critical commentary on his works. Illustrated with drawings. Select Bibliography. Index.

ROLFE, WILLIAM
Shakespeare As a Boy
Ungar, 1965. 250pp. $4.50. First published in 1896 and now reprinted, this is a recreation of the world of the young in the time Shakespeare was growing up. The author shows how the games, lessons, stories, entertainment, and neighborhood of his youth were woven into the fabric of Shakespeare's plays. Illustrated with contemporary materials.

ROSIGNOLI, MARIA PIA
The Life and Times of Shakespeare
Hamlyn, 1968. 75pp. $3.50. This is the record of every known aspect of Shakespeare's life and times. More than 100 pictures in color and black and white have been chosen, including photographs of the places he knew, portraits of the people who influenced him, and reproductions of contemporary paintings, maps and manuscripts.

ROWSE, A. L.
William Shakespeare: A Biography
Harper, 1964. 484pp. $8.95. Paper—Pocket Books, 1965. 484pp. $ .95. A leading historian of the Elizabethan age examines the record of Shakespeare's life and the aesthetic merits of his work. Emphasis is placed on the influence of the early years on his work. Illustrated. Index.

SCHOENBAUM, S.
Shakespeare's Lives
Oxford, 1970. 838pp. $15.00. Professor Schoenbaum has consulted letters, diaries, and personal papers in widely scattered collections which cover four centuries to bring into a clear light what is actually known about Shakespeare. How the documents were found, accounts of forged papers, portraits of the playwright in plays and novels are considered. Extensive quotations from the various sources are suppled. Twenty-five illustrations include portraits, genuine and suppositious, of Shakespeare. Notes. Index.

SISSON, ROSEMARY ANNE
The Young Shakespeare
Roy, 1959. 160pp. $3.00. Written for the young reader, this is a portrait of Shakespeare as a youth.

SMART, JOHN S.
Shakespeare: Truth and Tradition
Oxford, 1966. 193pp. Paper $3.75. In this reprint of the 1928 study the author interprets the historical documents and surveys Shakespeare's social and professional background to put his Stratford and London career in true perspective. Index.

SPENCER, HAZELTON
The Art and Life of William Shakespeare
Barnes & Noble, 1970. 495pp. $13.95. Originally published in 1940 and now reissued, this study reviews the life and career of the dramatist with chapters on the stage, the companies and theatres, and acting in his day. Each of the plays is critically analyzed. Illustrated. Notes. Bibliography. Index.

SPRAGUE, ARTHUR COLBY
Shakespeare and the Audience: A Study in the Technique of Exposition
Russell & Russell, 1966. 325pp. $9.00. First published in 1935 and now reprinted, this study considers the time and spatial dimension of a Shakespearean play, the Elizabethan stage conventions, the initial and concluding scenes, preparation, suspense, testimony, chorus characters, villains and heroes, and motivation. Index.

STOLL, ELMER EDGAR
Poets and Playwrights: Shakespeare, Jonson, Spenser, Milton
Russell & Russell, 1965. 304pp. $9.00. Paper—University of Minnesota, 1967. 282pp. $2.95. First published in 1930 and now reissued, this volume includes essays on plays by Shakespeare, comparisons of Shakespeare and other authors, Ben Jonson and the relation between old drama and new, and the theatre building in the Elizabethan age and in modern times.

SULLIVAN, WALTER
Shakespeare: His Times and His Problems
Paulist Press, 1968. 118pp. Paper $ .95. This is an introduction to the life of Shakespeare and to the works he produced. Chronology of the world events integrated with the events on the English stage during Shakespeare's lifetime.

WAIN, JOHN
The Living World of Shakespeare: A Playgoer's Guide
St. Martin's 1964. 239pp. $5.95. Paper—Penguin, 1966. 268pp. $1.25. The novelist/critic/ poet examines the plays in order to discover for the modern theatre-goer the basis of Shakespeare's greatness, his literary roots, and the timeliness of his themes to modern life.

WEBSTER, MARGARET
Shakespeare Without Tears
Fawcett, 1942. 240pp. Paper $ .60. A study of Shakespeare as a playwright for the living stage and as a craftsman for the theatre written by a producer of his plays.

WHITAKER, VIRGIL K.
Shakespeare's Use of Learning: An Inquiry into the Growth of His Mind and Art
Huntington Library, 1953. 366pp. $7.50. A study of Shakespeare's acquisition and use of contemporary learning and of the effect of his knowledge on his development as a dramatist. The author states his belief that Shakespeare "selected and adapted his material to produce the effects that he wanted. As we watch this process of choice and alteration, we have a unique opportunity to see his mind at work." Bibliography. Index.

WHITE, ANNE TERRY
Will Shakespeare and the Globe Theatre
Random House, 1955. 182pp. $1.95. Suitable for the young reader, this is a reconstruction of Shakespeare's life. Illustrated by C. Walter Hodges.

WHITE, BEATRICE – Editor
An Index to "The Elizabethan Stage" and "William Shakespeare" by Sir Edmund Chambers
Blom, 1964. 161pp. $7.50. A reprint of the original 1934 edition, this index is based on the works themselves although it makes use of the existing indices which it attempts to enlarge upon uniform lines.

WILSON, JOHN DOVER
The Essential Shakespeare
Cambridge, 1952. 148pp. $2.95. Paper – 1960. $1.25. The author places Shakespeare in the setting of Elizabethan England and he is shown to have taken an interest in the course of history – especially as it affected his patrons. Dr. Wilson argues that the plays manifest this interest and that they reflect Shakespeare's own personal development from youth and vitality in the comedies, through tension in the tragedies, to final peace of mind.

ZUKOFSKY, LOUIS and CELIA ZUKOFSKY
Bottom: On Shakespeare
University of Texas, 1963. Two volumes: $20.00. The author describes his book as follows: "To me Bottom is firstly, a long poem built on a theme for the variety of its recurrences. The theme is simply that Shakespeare's text throughout favors the clear physical eye against the erring brain, and that this theme has historical implications." He considers the forty-four items of the Shakespeare canon to be "one work, sometimes poor, sometimes good, sometimes great ....durable as one thing from itself never turning." The second volume contains music by Celia Zukofsky to the text of "Pericles." Sold as a slipcased two volume set.

SHAKESPEARE'S WORKS

General Studies of Shakespearean Comedy

BARBER, C. L.
Shakespeare's Festive Comedy: A Study of Dramatic Form and Its Relation to Social Custom
Meridian, 1963. 266pp. Paper $2.45. This is a reprint of the 1959 edition. The study shows the development of English comic drama. Emphasis is on the comedies of Shakespeare's early career.

BROWN, JOHN RUSSELL
Shakespeare and His Comedies
Barnes & Noble, 1962. 252pp. $6.50. Paper $3.50. A second edition of the book first published in 1957, this volume contains an extensive new chapter on "Pericles," "Cymbeline," "The Winter's Tale," and "The Tempest." These are studied as developments from the earlier comedies, informed by a similar idea, and presented by similar techniques.

CHAMPION, LARRY S.
The Evolution of Shakespeare's Comedy
Harvard, 1970. 241pp. $8.50. Mr. Champion concentrates on nine of Shakespeare's comedies to show that the playwright's comic vision expanded to include a complete reflection of human life. Notes. Index.

CHARLTON, H. B.
Shakespearean Comedy
Barnes & Noble, 1961. 303pp. $6.50. Paper $2.50. Originally published in 1938 and now reissued, this is a survey of Shakespeare's comedies undertaken with the object of seeing them as a progessive realization of the playwright's increasing grasp on the art and idea of comedy. Index.

EVANS, BERTRAND
Shakespeare's Comedies
Oxford, 1960. 337pp. $8.50. Paper – 1967. $2.50. The comedies and romances are examined individually in chronological order. The author shows how Shakespeare exploits the gaps between the awareness of the characters and that of the audience.

FRYE, NORTHROP
A Natural Perspective
Harcourt, 1965. 159pp. Paper $1.95. A collection of four essays concerned with principles of criticism and the enjoyment of Shakespeare's comedies.

GORDON, GEORGE STUART
Shakespearean Comedy and Other Studies
Oxford, 1944. 158pp. $3.00. This is a series of essays on the theory of comedy as practiced by Shakespeare, and on the clowns of the plays.

GUPTA, S. C. SEN
Shakespearean Comedy
Oxford, 1967. 281pp. Paper $5.95. Originally published in 1950 and now reissued, this study is an attempt to create a theory of the comedy of character. Gupta believes that Shakespeare's principal purpose was to portray character in all its complexity and depth and place the characters of his comedies in situations where they would learn the deeper secrets of their own hearts. Index.

LASCELLES, MARY
Shakespeare's Comic Insight.
Oxford, 1962. 18pp. Paper $1.50. Miss Lascelles decries the current fashion to separate the "comic" elements from the total fabric of the comedies and from the total reading of Shakespeare's world picture.

LAWRENCE, WILLIAM WITHERLE
Shakespeare's Problem Comedies
Ungar, 1960. 259pp. $5.00. A study of "All's Well that Ends Well," "Measure for Measure," "Troilus and Cressida," and "Cymbeline" that considers their relation to the medieval tradition of thought and to Shakespeare's other works. The literary and social changes in his day that are reflected in these plays are studied.

LEECH, CLIFFORD
Twelfth Night and Shakespearean Comedy
University of Toronto, 1965. 87pp. $3.50. Mr. Leech demonstrates that "Twelfth Night" is the key play in the sequence of the changing nature of Shakespeare's comic art from its early forms to the later developments where the tragic vision of the poet prevents the effect from being completely comic.

LERNER, LAURENCE – Editor
Shakespeare's Comedies: An Anthology of Modern Criticism
Penguin, 1967. 346pp. Paper $1.75. This anthology of criticism follows the pattern of the editor's previous volume, "Shakespeare's Tragedies." Mr. Lerner has collected some of the best of the modern Shakespearean criticism, mostly written in this century, and arranged it to throw light on nine of the comedies.

MUIR, KENNETH – Editor
Shakespeare: The Comedies
Prentice–Hall, 1965. 182pp. $4.95. Paper $1.95. Essays by various authorities including Harold Brooks, J. Middleton Murry, A. P. Rossiter, M. C. Bradbrook, and others.

PARROTT, THOMAS MARC
Shakespearean Comedy
Russell & Russell, 1962. 417pp. $15.00. Reprinted from the original 1949 edition, this is a chronological survey of all the plays which analyzes the comic elements found in each. The study considers the comedy of the plays in terms of its development from the medieval drama and in terms of the new learning of the Renaissance.

VYVYAN, JOHN
Shakespeare and Platonic Beauty
Chatto & Windus, 1961. 244pp. $5.25. Mr. Vyvyan traces among certain comedies the Platonic system of love as the force that produces order out of chaos. The heroines of "A Midsummer Night's Dream," "As You Like it," and "All's Well that Ends Well" are seen as embodiments of this Platonic force. "Troilus and Cressida" is seen as an example of tragedy resulting from breaking with this ideal.

WEIL, HERBERT – Editor
Discussions of Shakespeare's Romantic Comedy
Heath, 1966. 142pp. Paper $2.50. This volume is devoted to essays on Shakespeare's comedies. Among the authors are: Samuel Johnson, Charles Lamb, William Hazlitt, and G. B. Shaw.

WILSON, JOHN DOVER
Shakespeare's Happy Comedies
Northwestern University. 1963. 224pp. $4.50. Paper – Faber & Faber, 1962. 224pp. $2.95. Professor Wilson analyzes the comedies of Shakespeare's early career, beginning with "The Comedy of Errors" and reaching a climax with "Twelth Night." Index.

General Studies of Shakespearean Tragedy

ARTHOS, JOHN
The Art of Shakespeare
Barnes & Noble, 1964. 198pp. $6.00. The author shows that Shakespeare's tragedies reveal a continuing exploration of the relation of character to truth and that this idea is instrumental in determining the forms of the plays, the variety of techniques as well as of the subjects employed, and the tragic effect itself.

BATTENHOUSE, ROY W.
Shakespearean Tragedy: Its Art and Its Christian Premises
Indiana University, 1969. 466pp. $15.00. The author attempts to establish the relationship between Shakespeare's tragedies and Christian thought. Mr. Battenhouse infers a theory of tragedy implicit in the language and structure of Shakespeare's tragedies by close study of seven of the plays. He provides a hypothesis that the intellectual basis of Shakespeare's art was provided by Aristotelian principles modified and deepened by the Christian concepts of Augustine and Aquinas. Appendices. Notes. Index.

BRADLEY, A. C.
Shakespearean Tragedy: Hamlet, Othello, King Lear, Macbeth

Fawcett, 1965. 432pp. Paper $ .95. Lectures on the general nature and construction of Shakespearean tragedy.

CAMPBELL, LEWIS
Tragic Drama in Aeschylus, Sophocles, and Shakespeare
Russell & Russell, 1965. 280pp. $8.50. First published in 1904 and now reissued, this is an analysis of tragic fable, action, characterization, ideas, construction, and diction in the three playwrights. The parallels between the usage of Shakespeare and the ancient writers are examined in detail. Index.

CAMPBELL, LILY B.
Shakespeare's Tragic Heroes
Barnes & Noble, 1952. 295pp. $4.00. Paper $1.95 A study of "Othello," "Hamlet," "King Lear," and "Macbeth" which shows how the playwright analyzed in each case a dominating passion according to the medical and philosophical teaching of his time, especially the theories of the controlling passions.

COE, CHARLES N.
Demi–Devils: The Characters of Shakespeare's Villains
Twayne, 1963. 122pp. $4.00. A sequel to the author's "Shakespeare's Villains." Like that book, this study is written for the general student rather than the scholar and includes discussions of the major villains.

DICKEY, FRANKLIN M.
Not Wisely But Too Well: Shakespeare's Love Tragedies
Huntington Library, 1957. 205pp. $5.00. "Romeo and Juliet," "Troilus and Cressida," and "Antony and Cleopatra" are analyzed and the rhetoric of love is examined in its relation to theories of decorum and stage conventions. Attitudes toward love in "Venus and Adonis" and in "The Rape of Lucrece" are also studied.

FARNHAM, WILLARD
Shakespeare's Tragic Frontier
University of California, 1963. 289pp. Paper $1.95. A reprint of the 1950 edition, this is an examination of the paradox of nobility which stems from ignobleness as exemplified by the heroes of "Timon of Athens," "Macbeth," "Coriolanus," and "Antony and Cleopatra."

FRYE, NORTHROP
Fools of Time: Studies in Shakespearean Tragedy
University of Toronto, 1967. 121pp. $4.95. In Dr. Frye's view, three general types can be distinguished in Shakespearean tragedy: the tragedies of order, passion, and isolation. Frye analyzes various plays to show the impact of heroic energy on the human situation and the resulting destruction of the heroic but the survival of the human situation.

HARBAGE, ALFRED – Editor
Shakespeare: The Tragedies
Prentice–Hall, 1964. 189pp. $5.95. Paper $1.95. This volume includes essays by Donald Stauffer, Helen Gardner, G. Wilson Knight, Harry Levin, and others.

HARRISON, G. B.
Shakespeare's Tragedies
Oxford, 1969. 277pp. Paper $1.85. Originally published in 1952 and now reissued, Professor Harrison contends in this study that Shakespeare wrote plays to be performed on the Elizabethan stage and not as psychological, philosophical, or theological treatises. After an opening chapter on the nature of the tragic experience, each of the twelve tragedies is discussed as a stage play. Index.

HOBSON, ALAN
Shakespeare Looks at Man
Guild of Pastoral Psychology, 1967. 24pp. Paper $ .50. This lecture was delivered in England in 1967. The author looks at several of Shakespeare's plays, including "King Lear" and "Macbeth," to conclude that Shakespeare wrote very moral plays and that man, in Shakespeare's view, must learn from his experience but that such a learning process is slow and the change man can effect may often be catastrophic.

HOLLOWAY, JOHN
The Story of the Night: Studies in Shakespeare's Major Tragedies
University of Nebraska, 1961. 187pp. $3.50. Paper $1.25. These detailed studies of the tragedies draw on the history of Renaissance thought and on certain insights from the field of social anthropology.

JENKINS, HAROLD
The Catastrophe in Shakespearean Tragedy
Edinburgh University, 1969. 22pp. Paper $1.25. This lecture was originally delivered at Edinburgh University. Jenkins studies the tragic acts which bring some of Shakespeare's plays to their conclusions.

KNIGHT, G. WILSON
The Imperial Theme: Further Interpretations of Shakespeare's Tragedies, Including the Roman Plays
Methuen, 1958. 367pp. $7.00. Paper $3.50. A revision of the edition first published in 1931, this volume includes extensive analyses of "Julius Caesar," "Coriolanus," and "Antony and Cleopatra," with other essays on "Macbeth" and "Hamlet," and a note on "Richard II." In the foreword, the author surveys the advance of Shakespearean studies during the past three decades and relates his own unique method of analysis to the general body of criticism.

KNIGHT, G. WILSON
The Wheel of Fire: Interpretations of Shakespearean Tragedy, with Three New Essays
Barnes & Noble, 1956. 343pp. $7.00. Paper – World,

1957. 343pp. $1.85. A reissue of the first of Mr. Knight's four studies of Shakespeare, published originally in 1930. Emphasis in this study is on symbolic overtone and poetic atmosphere. T. S. Eliot has provided an Introduction.

LEECH, CLIFFORD
Shakespeare's Tragedies and Other Studies in Seventeenth Century Drama
Oxford, 1950. 232pp. $4.75. Essays on the nature of dramatic tension in tragedy, the Caroline audience, love as a dramatic theme in the seventeenth century drama, the links between English and Spanish playwrights of the era, and Shakespeare's "The Tempest" and "Timon of Athens."

LERNER, LAURENCE – Editor
Shakespeare's Tragedies: A Selection of Modern Criticism
Penguin, 1964. 317pp. Paper $1.25. Examples of all the modern schools of criticism, arranged according to the plays they deal with. Among the critics presented are M. M. Mahood, David Daiches, Bernard Shaw, A. C. Bradley, G. Wilson Knight, T. S. Eliot, Eric Bentley, W. H. Auden, and Alan S. Downer. Bibliography.

McFARLAND, THOMAS
Tragic Meaning in Shakespeare
Random House, 1966. 179pp. Paper $3.00. A study of "Othello," "King Lear," "Antony and Cleopatra," and "Hamlet" which uses the philosophy of existentialism to bring new light to Shakespeare's conception of character.

PROSER, MATTHEW N.
The Heroic Image in Five Shakespearean Tragedies
Princeton, 1965. 254pp. $7.00. The heroic self-image, the author maintains, has both private and public aspects. It is a gauge to the hero's personal aspirations, and at the same time suggests a public role, a persona, that gives impetus to his course of action. The heroes studied are Brutus, Macbeth, Othello, Coriolanus, and Antony. Index.

RIBNER, IRVING
Patterns in Shakespearean Tragedy
Barnes & Noble, 1970. 205pp. $6.50. Paper $3.00. The author provides an examination of the entire body of Shakespearean tragedy, the historical plays included, in terms of the cognitive function of tragedy, its value as a distinctive way of knowing, with emphasis upon the total play as a unified dramatic symbol. Index.

ROSEN, WILLIAM
Shakespeare and the Craft of Tragedy.
Harvard, 1960. 231pp. $5.25. This study concentrates on dramatic techniques and investigates how the playwright established the audience's point of view toward the protagonist.

SIEGEL, PAUL N.
Shakespearean Tragedy and the Elizabethan Compromise
New York University, 1957. 243pp. $6.75. A study of the defeat of the Spanish Armada showing, through the words of the playwright, how it affected the social structure on which the Elizabethan pattern of belief was founded. The compromise he describes is the balance of class forces that Elizabeth maintained for security and peace.

SPENCER, THEODORE
Shakespeare and the Nature of Man
Macmillan, 1961. 233pp. $6.00. Paper $1.95. A survey of the tradition of belief into which Shakespeare was born, and of the conflict between the medieval and the Renaissance concept of man. This conflict is seen as the basis of Shakespearean tragedy.

SPIVACK, BERNARD
Shakespeare and the Allegory of Evil: The History of a Metaphor in Relation to His Villains
Columbia, 1958. 508pp. $10.00. A study of the medieval allegorical figure of Vice from its origin on the morality stage to its disguised survival in Elizabethan drama.

STERNFELD, F.W.
Music in Shakespearean Tragedy
Routledge & Kegan Paul, 1963. 334pp. $9.00. A comparison of Shakespeare's practices with those of Marlowe, Jonson, Marston, and Chapman to demonstrate the greater and more integral use of music in Shakespeare's tragedies. Included are chapters on the tradition of vocal and instrumental music in tragedy, blank verse and song writing, instruments for music, and the songs in "King Lear." Forty-two musical examples in modern transcription. Illustrated. Index.

WHITE, BEATRICE – Editor
An Index to "The Elizabethan Stage" and "William Shakespeare" by Sir Edmund Chambers
Blom, 1964. 161pp. $7.50. A reprint of the original 1934 edition, this index is based on the works themselves, although it makes use of the existing indices which it attempts to enlarge upon uniform lines. Players' names are included.

WILSON, H.S.
On the Design of Shakespearean Tragedy
University of Toronto, 1957. 256pp. $6.00. Paper $2.25. Professor Wilson views Shakespeare's development as a tragic playwright as a continual striving towards a unified tragic interpretation of human life. Those plays which evoke Christian ideas of guilt and retribution are contrasted with those based on pagan naturalism. Wilson suggests that "King Lear" and "Antony and Cleopatra" represent Shakespeare's highest achievements. Appendices. Notes. Index.

Studies of Plays in Groups

ASIMOV, ISAAC
Asimov's Guide to Shakespeare
Doubleday, 1970. Two volumes: 1,565pp. $25.00. A scene-by-scene exploration of thirty-eight plays and two narrative poems in terms of their mythological, historical, and geographic roots. The author's aim is to provide the modern reader with a working knowledge of the topics which Shakespeare assumed his potential Elizabethan audience to be well versed in. Volume One deals with the Greek, Roman, and Italian Plays and Volume Two with the English plays. Dr. Asimov presents the historical facts surrounding each play and explores the literary and linguistic history of Shakespearean images. Maps, charts, and quotations supplement the text. Index in each volume. Slipcased.

BAKER, ARTHUR E.
A Shakespeare Commentary
Ungar, 1958. Volume One: 482pp. Volume Two: 482pp. $19.50. Twenty-two plays are studied in this reprint of the 1937 edition. Dates of composition and first publication, sources of plots, and plot outlines, lists of characters, place names, allusions, and glosses are provided. Appendices give extracts from sources. Also included is a fold-out genealogical table of the family of Edward II and of the Houses of York and Lancaster. Two volume set.

BOSWELL-STONE, W.G.
Shakespeare's Holinshed
Blom, 1966. 532pp. $12.50. A reprint of the 1896 study in which the chronicle and the historical plays are compared. Index.

BROOKE, NICHOLAS
Shakespeare's Early Tragedies
Methuen, 1968. 214pp. $6.75. Essays on six of Shakespeare's plays which show the varied kind of play and the themes which are grouped under the general term: tragedy. The essays develop an understanding of Shakespeare's use of stage picture in relation to the imagery of Elizabethan poetry and his experiments in using varied modes of speech in verse and prose to establish dramatic contrast. Bibliography. Index.

BROOKE, STOPFORD A.
Ten More Plays of Shakespeare
Barnes & Noble, 1963. 313pp. $6.00. A reprint of the 1913 edition, this is a detailed study of "Much Ado About Nothing," "Twelfth Night," "Julius Caesar," "Hamlet," "Measure for Measure," "Othello," "King Lear," "King John," "Henry IV, Parts 1 and 2," and "Henry V."

BROWN, JOHN RUSSELL
Shakespeare's Dramatic Style
Barnes & Noble, 1970. 208pp. $8.00. A study of the language and dramatic qualities of Shakespeare's greatest plays, particularly the plays Professor Brown considers representative: "Romeo and Juliet," "As You Like It," "Julius Caesar," "Twelfth Night," and "Macbeth." The author examines the problems of interpretation as seen from the point of view of actors and directors of Shakespearean productions. Passages from the representative plays are examined for their various meanings within the theatrical context. The book is of particular interest to those concerned with the plays in performance.

BROWN, JOHN RUSSELL and BERNARD HARRIS—Editors
Stratford-Upon-Avon Studies, Volume III: Early Shakespeare
St. Martin's, 1961. 232pp. $5.75. Paper—Schocken, 1966. 232pp. $1.95. A study of the first ten years of Shakespeare's career by ten critics. Central importance is given to "Romeo and Juliet," "Richard II," and "The Merchant of Venice." Among the contributors are R.A. Foakes, Norman Sanders, Harold Brooks, John Lawler, John Russell Brown, and Frank Kermode.

BUCKNILL, JOHN CHARLES
The Mad Folk of Shakespeare
Franklin, 1969. 333pp. $18.75. Originally published in 1867 and now reissued in a facsimile edition, this is a series of "psychological essays" on some of the characters in Shakespeare's plays who might be considered mentally abnormal: Macbeth, Hamlet, Lear, Ophelia, and others.

BURTON, PHILIP
The Sole Voice: Character Portraits from Shakespeare
Dial, 1970. 432pp. $8.95. Mr. Burton maintains that Shakespeare wrote for the stage and his characters should be studied in a dramaturgical rather than an academic frame of reference. In his analyses of twenty-one key characters, he imparts the interpretations and theories he has developed during his lifetime as actor, director, instructor, and playwright.

CAMPBELL, LILY B.
Shakespeare's Histories: Mirrors of Elizabethan Policy
Huntington Library, 1963. 346pp. $8.50. First published in 1947, this is a second printing of this study. The author examines principles and methods of sixteenth century historical writing in relation to the plays, which are interpreted in the light of history, historiography, and Elizabethan politics. Index.

CHAMBERS, E.K.
Shakespeare: A Survey
Hill & Wang, 1958. 325pp. Paper $1.95. First published between 1904 and 1908, these introductions to all the plays are concerned with a variety of subjects,

seen from various critical points of view, to provide the student with the information he requires when approaching Shakespeare for the first time.

CHARNEY, MAURICE – Editor
Discussions of Shakespeare's Roman Plays
Heath, 1964. 170pp. Paper $2.50. A collection of essays on the general nature of the Roman plays, by such writers as T. J. B. Spencer, Edward Dowden, Harold S. Wilson, L. C. Knights, and Derek A. Traversi.

CHARNEY, MAURICE
Shakespeare's Roman Plays
Harvard, 1961. 250pp. $6.75. In an intensive analysis of "Julius Caesar," "Antony and Cleopatra," and "Coriolanus," the author examines the plays chiefly through their imagery, but uses that word to cover all the non-verbal resources of theatre.

CRAIG, HARDIN
An Interpretation of Shakespeare
Lucas Brothers, 1948. 400pp. $4.50. A study of all the plays, stressing the originality of Shakespeare in the manner in which he changed, enlarged, and recreated the drama of his age. The point of view of the study is that of historical criticism. Attention is focused on the less well-known and more obscure plays.

DORIUS, R. J.
Discussions of Shakespeare's Histories: Richard II to Henry V.
Heath, 1964. 148pp. Paper $2.50. A collection of essays by A. P. Rossiter, Coleridge, Yeats, Harold Jenkins, Clifford Leech, A. C. Bradley, J. I. M. Stewart, E. E. Stoll, and Charles Williams.

ENRIGHT, D. J.
Shakespeare and the Students
Chatto & Windus, 1970. 206pp. $6.95. Paper $2.95. Scene-by-scene analyses of four of Shakespeare's works: "King Lear," "Antony and Cleopatra," "Macbeth," and "The Winter's Tale." The author points out that Shakespeare's characters demonstrate the reactions of real people to possible situations. Index.

EVANS, GARETH LLOYD
Shakespeare in the Limelight
Blackie, 1968. 150pp. $3.25. This work is intended to be a picture of the characteristic attitude to the works of Shakespeare in each century. The anthology of dramatic criticism contains comments from sources from the seventeenth century to the present day and the emphasis is on acting and interpretation. Index.

FERGUSSON, FRANCIS
Shakespeare: The Pattern in His Carpet
Delacorte, 1970. 331pp. $6.95. Dr. Fergusson seeks the poetic intention of each of Shakespeare's thirty-seven plays in order to bring out the recurrent themes. The plays are grouped chronologically, according to the main parts of Shakespeare's career, and within each part according to those themes that indicate the basic elements of the playwright's vision of life. Bibliographic Notes. Index.

GODDARD, HAROLD C.
The Meaning of Shakespeare
University of Chicago, 1951. 691pp. $12.00. Paper – 1960. Volume One. 394pp. $1.95. Volume Two. 300pp. $2.45. Originally published in 1951 and now reissued, these two volumes provide detailed examinations and explications of all the plays. Shakespeare's religious, moral, political, and social convictions are explained and the influence of these on the structure of the plays is considered. Index.

GUPTA, S. C. SEN
Shakespeare's Historical Plays
Oxford, 1964. 172pp. $5.75. The author maintains that it is a critical error to view the histories as political and didactic treatises rather than aesthetic creations. His study presents the histories as works of art portraying characters issuing in action, and shows that whatever ideas they may have emerge from the developing plot. Index.

HAMILTON, A. C.
The Early Shakespeare
Huntington Library, 1967. 237pp. $6.50. In twelve essays, Professor Hamilton studies Shakespeare's first plays and poems. He contends that the playwright explored the potentialities of tragedy, comedy, and poetry with subtlety and dramatic comprehension. Index.

HARBAGE, ALFRED
A Reader's Guide to William Shakespeare
Farrar, Straus, 1963. 498pp. $6.95. Paper $2.95. A general introduction to the reading of Shakespeare, beginning with an analysis of his diction, the metrical and non-metrical media, and the dramatic structure. The plays are grouped chronologically and the most important are discussed scene-by-scene.

HAWKES, TERENCE
Shakespeare and the Reason
Humanities, 1965. 207pp. $6.75. Subtitled "A Study of the Tragedies and the Problem Plays," this study suggests that in the age of Shakespeare, human reason embraced two opposed mental activities, rationalization and intuition. After defining these terms, Dr. Hawkes studies the plays in the light thrown on them by this hitherto unexplored aspect of the culture from which they spring. Index.

HUNTER, G. K.
Shakespeare: The Later Comedies
Longman, 1964. 64pp. Paper $1.25. A reprint with additions to the bibliography, of the 1962 essay in which Mr. Hunter seeks to define "the particular kind of excellence" in four of the comedies. List of Recordings. Selected Bibliography.

JAMES, D. G.
The Dream of Learning: An Essay on the Advancement of Learning, Hamlet, and King Lear
Oxford, 1961. 126pp. $4.50. A comparison of the mission Francis Bacon set himself in his writings, especially "The Advancement of Learning," and the humanistic achievement of Shakespeare in his tragedies.

KERMODE, FRANK
Shakespeare: The Final Plays
Longmans, 1963. 59pp. Paper $ .85. A study of the similarities and, particularly, the differences between the plays of Shakespeare's last creative period. Illustrated. Bibliography.

KIRSCH, JAMES
Shakespeare's Royal Self
Putnam, 1966. 422pp. $7.95. This is an analysis of "Hamlet," "King Lear," and "Macbeth" in which an eminent analytical psychologist examines each of the plays as he would the dream of a patient in the consulting room. The result is an analysis of the principal characters, their unconscious motivations, their relationships to other figures in the drama, and what they reveal about the playwright himself.

KNIGHT, G. WILSON
The Crown of Life: Essays in Interpretation of Shakespeare's Final Plays
Barnes & Noble, 1964. 336pp. $7.00. Paper—Methuen, 1965. 336pp. $3.50. Essays on "Pericles," "The Winter's Tale," "Cymbeline," "The Tempest," and "Henry VIII." The author contends that these plays do not show artistic regression but rather a definite advance beyond tragedy to an even more deeply considered reading of human destiny. This edition also includes a reprinting of the essay, "Myth and Miracle," the author's first Shakespearean study originally published in 1929.

KNIGHTS, L. C.
Shakespeare: The Histories
Longmans, 1962. 59pp. Paper $ .85. A brief study of the plays, with emphasis on the political concepts underlying them. Illustrated. Bibliography.

LAWRENCE, WILLIAM WITHERLE
Shakespeare's Problem Comedies
Ungar, 1960. 259pp. $5.00. Paper—Penguin, 1969. 222pp. $1.45. A reprint of the original 1931 edition, this volume includes detailed studies of "All's Well That Ends Well," "Measure for Measure," "Troilus and Cressida," and "Cymbeline" in which the author explores the inner meaning of these comedies in terms of the moral code, customs, and traditions of the playwright's time.

LEECH, CLIFFORD
Shakespeare: The Chronicles
Longmans, 1964. 48pp. Paper $1.25. A reprint of the 1962 essay with a revised bibliography. Professor Leech discusses Shakespeare's "open-textured" historical writing. List of Recordings, Selected Bibliography.

LEECH, CLIFFORD—Editor
Shakespeare: The Tragedies. A Collection of Critical Essays
University of Chicago, 1965. 256pp. $7.95. Paper $2.45. Essays by Dryden, Coleridge, A. C. Bradley, G. Wilson Knight, Wolfgang Clemen, D. A. Traversi, Robert Ornstein, Nicholas Brooke, A. P. Rossiter, and William Frost, among others.

LOKSE, OLAV
Outrageous Fortune
Humanities, 1960. 192pp. Paper $4.25. This is a critical study of Shakespeare's plays, "Hamlet" and "King Lear." Mr. Lokse makes comparisons between the previous versions and those of Shakespeare and gives the reader an insight into Shakespeare's problems and his skill in solving them. Bibliography. Index.

MacCALLUM, SIR MUNGO
Shakespeare's Roman Plays and Their Background
Russell & Russell, 1967. 666pp. $15.00. First published in 1910 and long out of print, this is a reissue of the study of "Antony and Cleopatra," "Coriolanus," and "Julius Caesar. There is a long introduction on Roman plays in the sixteenth century, Shakespeare's treatment of history, and the ancestry of Shakespeare's Roman plays. Index.

MARSH, D. R. C.
The Recurring Miracle
University of Nebraska, 1969. 197pp. Paper $1.95. Originally published in 1962 and now reprinted, this study is primarily concerned with "Cymbeline" which is examined in a detailed analysis after a brief review of the critical attitude toward Shakespeare's romances in general. Other chapters offer readings of "Pericles," "The Winter's Tale," and "The Tempest."

MASON, H. A.
Shakespeare's Tragedies of Love
Chatto & Windus, 1970. 290pp. $8.25. A study of "Romeo and Juliet," "Othello," "King Lear," and "Antony and Cleopatra." The author believes it should be possible to arrive at a general agreement about the main features of each play and he suggests lines of thought toward this end. Index.

MILWARD, PETER
An Introduction to Shakespeare's Plays
Kenkyusha, 1964. 171pp. $4.75. After an introduction to the intellectual, social, literary, and theatrical background of the times, the author studies the early life of Shakespeare and the sources of the plays. He discusses the plays in groups. Bibliography.

MUIR, KENNETH
Shakespeare: The Great Tragedies
Longmans, 1963. 46pp. Paper $ .85. A brief essay on "Hamlet," "Othello," "King Lear," and "Macbeth." Illustrated.

NOSWORTHY, J.M.
Shakespeare's Occasional Plays: Their Origin and Transmission
Edward Arnold, 1965. 238pp. $10.50. "The Merry Wives of Windsor," "Macbeth," "Troilus and Cressida," and possibly "Hamlet," were written for special occasions. This study examines the relevance of the "occasional" origin to the subsequent history of the plays, particularly their textual transmission. The author concludes that the revisions and abridgments in the plays were the work of Shakespeare himself, marred only by the blunders of scribes and compositors. Index.

ORNSTEIN, ROBERT – Editor
Discussions of Shakespeare's Problem Comedies
Heath, 1961. 111pp. Paper $2.25. A collection of essays illustrating the diversity of interpretation of the problem comedies in the past century and a half. The essayists include Coleridge, F. S. Boas, Una Ellis-Fermor, Robert Ornstein, Clifford Leech, A. Quiller-Couch, and M. C. Bradbrook.

PHIALAS, PETER G.
Shakespeare's Romantic Comedies
University of North Carolina, 1966. 314pp. $7.50. Paper $2.95. This study defines the nature and traces the development of some of the distinctive features of nine of Shakespeare's comedies. Notes. Index.

PRICE, GEORGE R.
Reading Shakespeare's Plays
Barron, 1962. 122pp. $4.00. Paper $1.25. A practical guide for college students through the major difficulties of unfamiliar dramatic conventions, diction, staging, social practice, and philosophical attitude in Shakespeare's plays.

PROSER, MATTHEW N.
The Heroic Image in Five Shakespearean Tragedies
Princeton, 1965. 254pp. Paper $2.95. The author examines five Shakespearean tragedies ("Julius Caesar," "Macbeth," "Othello," "Coriolanus," and "Antony and Cleopatra") in an attempt to show that the tragic issue of each of these plays lies in part in the "discrepancy between the main character's self-conception and his entire human reality." Bibliography. Index.

REESE, M.M.
The Cease of Majesty: A Study of Shakespeare's History Plays
St. Martin's, 1961. 305pp. $8.00. A re-evaluation of Shakespeare's attitude toward politics. The study demonstrates that the quest in these plays was for the ideal king and the ideal social relationship in which king and people were united by a conception of duty.

RICHMOND, H.M.
Shakespeare's Political Plays
Random House, 1967. 241pp. Paper $3.00. This is a study of eight of Shakespeare's plays which use historical facts to show a steadily evolving study of man as a political animal. The plays are: "Henry VI," "Richard III," "King John," "Richard II," "Henry IV," "Henry V," "Julius Caesar," and "Coriolanus." Index.

ROGERS, WILLIAM HUDSON
Shakespeare and English History
Littlefield, Adams, 1966. 149pp. Paper $2.50. This is a study of the ten history plays in which each of the plays is synopsized and characters and motivations are discussed in detail. The author introduces each of the plays with a lengthy description of the actual history of the period. Index.

SCHANZER, ERNEST
The Problem Plays of Shakespeare: A Study of Julius Caesar, Measure for Measure, Antony and Cleopatra
Schocken, 1963. 196pp. $4.95. Paper $1.95. This study breaks away from the traditional groupings of "All's Well," "Troilus and Cressida," and "Hamlet," as the problem plays. It redefines the term "problem play" as applied to the works and submits each of the plays to a careful examination. Such items as theme, structure, characterization, and relation to other plays are considered. Index.

SMITH, GORDON ROSS – Editor
Essays in Shakespeare
Pennsylvania State University, 1965. 249pp. $7.75. This collection of essays consists of examinations of six of Shakespeare's plays in various ways: evidence for dating, analyses of structure and language, the merits of successive dominant critical interpretations, interpretation of complimentary themes, and aspects of certain productions in America and Russia.

SPENCER, T.J.B.
Shakespeare: The Roman Plays
Longmans, 1966. 56pp. Paper $1.25. First published in 1963 and now reprinted with additions to the Bibliography, this is a brief essay on Roman history in the Elizabethan literary scene, with commentary on Shakespeare's use of that history. Illustrated. Selected Bibliography. List of Recordings.

SPRAGUE, ARTHUR COLBY
Shakespeare's Histories: Plays for the Stage
Society for Theatre Research, 1964. 165pp. $5.50. This study of eight of Shakespeare's plays is concerned with critical opinion of the plays and especially in how they have been acted by various actors.

Index of Shakespearean Plays. Index of Players and Producers.

TALBERT, ERNEST WILLIAM
Elizabethan Drama and Shakespeare's Early Plays: An Essay in Historical Criticism
University of North Carolina, 1963. 410pp. $9.50. Shakespeare's techniques and his intent in writing his early plays are considered in the light of the probable expectation of contemporary theatre-goers and their possible familiarity with current concepts, current representational methods, and current features of the stage. Thirteen of the plays are examined, in addition to plays of Robert Wilson, Greene, Peele, Kyd, Lyly, and Marlowe. Index.

THOMSON, W. H.
Shakespeare's Characters: A Historical Dictionary
John Sherratt, 1970. 320pp. $6.95. Originally published in 1951 and now reprinted, this study is designed to provide the background of historical fact to the characters and events of the historical plays of Shakespeare and in "Macbeth." Genealogical Tables. Frontispiece.

TILLYARD, E. M. W.
Shakespeare's Early Comedies
Chatto & Windus, 1965. 216pp. $5.00. A posthumously published volume, edited by Dr. Tillyard's son, this book examines four of the comedies: "The Comedy of Errors," "The Taming of the Shrew," "Two Gentlemen of Verona," and "Love's Labour's Lost." There is also a chapter on Shylock's spiritual stupidities.

TILLYARD, E. M. W.
Shakespeare's History Plays
Barnes & Noble, 1946. 336pp. $5.25. Paper—Penguin, 1969. 351pp. $2.75. Originally published in 1944 and now reprinted, this study sets Shakespeare's history plays against the general background of Elizabethan thought. Dr. Tillyard describes the religious, scientific, and political ideas current in Shakespeare's day and enumerates the historical and literary sources for the plays. He examines the individual plays in separate chapters. Notes. List of Books for Further Reading. Index.

TILLYARD, E. M. W.
Shakespeare's Last Plays
Barnes & Noble, 1958. 85pp. $2.75. A reprint of the first edition published in 1938, this is a brief survey of "Cymbeline," "The Winter's Tale," and "The Tempest" which analyzes the circumstances under which they were written and produced and the characteristics they share in common.

TILLYARD, E. M. W.
Shakespeare's Problem Plays
University of Toronto, 1964. 156pp. $4.25. Paper $1.75. A reprint of the 1950 first edition, this is a study of the relationship between "Hamlet," "Troilus and Cressida," "All's Well That Ends Well," and "Measure for Measure." Each play is seen to be concerned with dogma, with the problem of evil, with the contrast between youth and age, and with actual, as opposed to ideal, human nature.

TRAVERSI, DEREK
Shakespeare: From Richard II to Henry V
Stanford, 1957. 198pp. $6.00. An analysis of dramatic elements in the four histories of Shakespeare's mature period. The author shows the unity of concept which prevails in them.

TRAVERSI, DEREK
Shakespeare: The Early Comedies
Longmans, 1964. 60pp. Paper $1.25. A revised edition of the 1960 publication. The author considers five of the early comedies of Shakespeare. List of Recordings. Selected Bibliography.

TRAVERSI, DEREK
Shakespeare: The Roman Plays
Stanford, 1963. 288pp. $6.75. A discussion of the Roman chronicle plays, "Julius Caesar," "Antony and Cleopatra," and "Coriolanus," placing them in relation to each other and to the whole body of the dramatic works. The author's method is to follow the text in detail providing frequent extracts.

URE, PETER
Shakespeare: The Problem Plays
Longmans, 1961. 62pp. Paper $ .85. A discussion of the common elements that link together "All's Well That Ends Well," "Troilus and Cressida," and "Timon of Athens." Bibliography.

USHERWOOD, STEPHEN
Shakespeare Play by Play
Hill & Wang, 1967. 103pp. $5.95. This is an introduction to the plays of Shakespeare. It provides an outline of each of the plays, a short account of the literary origins and historical setting. Raymond Piper has provided illustrations which show the players in period costumes and in recent productions. A summary of Shakespeare's life is also included.

WAITH, EUGENE M. — Editor
Shakespeare: The Histories — A Collection of Critical Essays
Prentice–Hall, 1965. 185pp. $5.95. Paper $1.95. These essays consider the background of politics, history, and dramatic convention in each of the history plays. Essays by Lily B. Campbell, E. M. W. Tillyard, J. P. Brockbank, A. P. Rossiter, and J. Dover Wilson, among others. Chronology. Bibliography. Index.

WATT, LAUCHLAN MACLEAN
Attic and Elizabethan Tragedy
See Page 37

WILSON, F. P.
Marlowe and the Early Shakespeare
Oxford, 1953. 144pp. $3.00. Lectures on "Tamburlaine," "The Jew of Malta," "Doctor Faustus," "The Massacre of Paris," and "Edward II." One lecture considers the relationship between Marlowe's history plays and Shakespeare's early efforts.

WINNY, JAMES
The Player King: A Theme of Shakespeare's Histories
Chatto & Windus, 1968. 219pp. $5.50. This book deals chiefly with three of Shakespeare's history plays: "Richard II," "Henry IV," and "Henry V." Mr. Winny believes their common concern lies in the struggle to assume the supreme identity of king. Index.

Studies of Individual Plays

All's Well That Ends Well

PRICE, JOSEPH G.
The Unfortunate Comedy
University of Toronto, 1968. 197pp. $7.25. A study of "All's Well that Ends Well" in which the author seeks to provide a historical framework in which the director, critic, or student may examine the play. The bulk of the study is an account of the play's theatrical and critical history leading to the critical interpretation of the play in the final chapter. Illustrated. Notes. Bibliography. Index.

RANALD, MARGARET L.
Notes on All's Well That Ends Well
Monarch Press, 1966. 89pp. Paper $1.00. A study guide which provides an act-by-act discussion of the plot, theme development, character analysis, critical commentary, study questions and answers for review, and a guide to research. Bibliography.

Antony and Cleopatra

BROWN, JOHN RUSSELL – Editor
Antony and Cleopatra: A Casebook
Aurora, 1970. 224pp. Paper $2.50. This volume contains a selection of early criticism, reviews of the play in performance, and a section of twentieth-century criticism by A. C. Bradley, Maurice Charney, L. C. Knights, and others. Select Bibliography. Index.

CLIFF'S NOTES EDITORS
Antony and Cleopatra: Notes
Cliff's Notes, 1960. 38pp. Paper $1.00. Notes on the play including scene-by-scene synopsis and character sketches.

MILLS, LAURENS J.
The Tragedies of Shakespeare's Antony and Cleopatra
Indiana University, 1964. 66pp. Paper $4.00. This study of the play gives a separate analysis of each of the leading figures and has a note on the character of Enobarbus.

SHIPLEY, JOSEPH T.
Antony and Cleopatra: Analytic Notes and Review
Study Master, 1964. 72pp. Paper $1.00. A scene-by-scene analysis with critical commentary, summary of characters, suggested study topics, notes and questions for review, and a Bibliography.

WALSH, WILLIAM
Notes on Antony and Cleopatra
Monarch Press, 1964. 103pp. Paper $1.00. A study guide which provides an act-by-act summary of the play, character analyses, critical commentary, essay questions and answers for review, and a Bibliography.

As You Like It

HALIO, JAY L. – Editor
Twentieth Century Interpretations of As You Like It
Prentice–Hall, 1968. 120pp. $3.95. Paper $1.25. A collection of critical essays, ranging from a discussion of the play's satirical aspects to an analysis of historical sources. Among the fourteen contributors are H. B. Charlton, Helen Gardner, and John Russell Brown. Chronology. Selected Bibliography.

JAMIESON, MICHAEL
As You Like It: A Critical Study
Barron, 1965. 72pp. Paper $1.00. The author clarifies plot, characterization, symbolism, style. Critical literary appraisal is provided. List of Books for Further Reading. Index.

JONES, J.
A Simplified Approach to As You Like It
Barron, 1970. 160pp. Paper $ .95. Shakespearean comedy, characters, plot, and language explained in detail.

NAUMAN, JANET – Editor
As You Like It: Analytic Notes and Review
Study Master, 1964. 58pp. Paper $1.00. A scene-by-scene analysis with critical appraisal, summary of characters, suggested study topics, notes and questions for review, and a Bibliography.

PINEAS, RAINER
Notes on As You Like It
Monarch Press, 1964. 82pp. Paper $1.00. A study guide which provides an act-by-act summary of the play, character analyses, critical commentary, essay questions and answers for review, and a Bibliography.

ROBERTS, JAMES L. – Editor
As You Like It: Notes
Cliff's Notes, 1962. 54pp. Paper $1.00. Scene-by-scene summaries and commentaries on Shakespeare's play. Also included is material on the life of Shakespeare, the background and technique of the play, general questions for review, and a Selected Bibliography.

SCHOENBAUM, S.
As You Like It: Book Notes
Barnes & Noble, 1967. 83pp. Paper $1.00. Copy not available for perusal.

The Comedy of Errors

BALDWIN, T.W.
On the Compositional Genetics of The Comedy of Errors
University of Illinois, 1965. 422pp. $8.75. Professor Baldwin states that because of the nature of its origins, this play probably gives us the fullest illustration we shall ever have of Shakespeare's methods of composition. Besides examining the rhetorical methods and structure, this study also clarifies the political, religious, and geographical genetics of the play. The relation of the play to Plautus' "Menaechmi" is examined in detail. Index.

BLACKBURN, RUTH
Notes on Comedy of Errors
Monarch Press, 1966. 74pp. Paper $1.00. A study guide which provides an act-by-act discussion of the plot, theme development, character analysis, critical commentary, study questions and answers for review, and a guide to research. Bibliography.

SMITH, JOHN H.
The Comedy of Errors: Analytic Notes and Review
Study Master, 1966. 88pp. Paper $1.00. A scene-by-scene analysis with critical appraisal, summary of characters, suggested study topics, notes and questions for review, and an Annotated Bibliography. Index.

Coriolanus

CLIFF'S NOTES EDITORS
Coriolanus: Notes
Cliff's Notes, 1961. 103pp. Paper $1.00. Scene-by-scene summaries and commentaries on the play. Also provided is background information on the play, selected examination questions, and character analyses.

JOHNSON, EDWARD
Notes on Coriolanus
Monarch Press, 1965. 112pp. Paper $1.00. A study guide which provides an act-by-act discussion of the plot, character analyses, critical commentary, study questions and answers for review, and a guide to further study. Bibliography.

PHILLIPS, JAMES E. – Editor
Twentieth Century Interpretation of Coriolanus
Prentice–Hall, 1970. 120pp. $4.95. Paper $1.25. A collection of critical essays. Seventeen noted authors and critics, including Oscar James Campbell, Maurice Charney, Harley Granville-Barker, G. Wilson Knight, and A. P. Rossiter, examine the style, form, characters, and background of the play. Chronology. Selected Bibliography.

Hamlet

ALEXANDER, PETER
Hamlet, Father and Son
Oxford, 1955. 189pp. $3.50. A series of lectures on the relationship between commentators' opinions on the plays and actual productions and acting techniques. Special attention is given to the interpretation of "Hamlet" in the Sir Laurence Olivier film. The philosophical basis of the character of Hamlet is also studied.

BABCOCK, WESTON
Hamlet: A Tragedy of Errors
Purdue University, 1961. 134pp. Paper $1.75. A detailed analysis of the dramaturgy of the play. The play is considered scene-by scene to determine what a spectator uncoached by commentary would conclude at successive points of development.

BEVINGTON, DAVID – Editor
Twentieth Century Interpretations of Hamlet
Prentice–Hall, 1968. 120pp. $3.95. Paper $1.25. Eighteen distinguished critics examine Shakespeare's play, the use of irony and word-play, use of the Elizabethan stage, and the conflicts in the contemporary philosophy that informed the playwright's world view. Among the essayists are: T. S. Eliot, Harley Granville-Barker, and C. S. Lewis. Chronology of Important Dates. Bibliography.

BOWERS, FREDSON
Hamlet: Book Notes
Barnes & Noble, 1967. 87pp. Paper $1.00. Copy not available for perusal.

BRADDY, HALDEEN
Hamlet's Wounded Name
Texas Western College, 1964. 82pp. $5.00. The author presents a new approach to the involved and controversial problems of "Hamlet" criticism. For the first time the character is seen as a crafty schemer—the traditional Scandinavian trickster.

BRODWIN, LEONORA
Notes on Hamlet

Monarch Press, 1964. 153pp. Paper $1.00. A study guide which provides an act-by-act discussion of the plot, character analyses, critical commentary, essay questions and answers for review, and a Bibliography.

BROWN, JOHN RUSSELL and BERNARD HARRIS – Editors
Hamlet: A Reading and Playing Guide
Schocken, 1966. 212pp. Paper $1.95. This is an authoritative volume of readings on "Hamlet." Index.

BROWN, JOHN RUSSELL and BERNARD HARRIS – Editors
Stratford–Upon–Avon Studies: Volume V: Hamlet
Edward Arnold, 1963. 212pp. $5.75. A collection of essays on Shakespeare's play by renowned authorities. Among the contributors are Peter Ure, G. K. Hunter, R. A. Foakes, John Russell Brown, T. J. B. Spencer, Stanley Wells, and E. A. J. Honigmann. Index.

BUELL, WILLIAM ACKERMAN
The Hamlets of the Theatre
Astor–Honor, 1968. 175pp. $12.50. A history of the role as played by Burbage, Betterton, Garrick, Kemble, Kean, Forrest, Macready, Booth, up to Barrymore, Gielgud, Evans, and Burton. It offers contemporary critical opinion of the performers and an insight into the techniques and interpretation each actor brought to the role. Illustrated with photographs. Bibliography.

CHARNEY, MAURICE
Styles in Hamlet
Princeton, 1969. 333pp. $10.00. Professor Charney presents an analysis of three aspects of the style of "Hamlet": imagery, staging, and dramatic character. He attempts to show that a study of these qualities can bring us closer to an understanding of the play itself. Index.

CLIFF'S NOTES EDITORS
Hamlet: Notes
Cliff's Notes. Paper $1.00. Copy not available for perusal. Material assumed to be consistent with other volumes in the series. See: "Antony and Cleopatra: Notes" by Cliff's Notes Editors.

DAVIS, ARTHUR G.
Hamlet and the Eternal Problems of Man
St. John's University, 1964. 227pp. Paper $5.00. Mr. Davis takes the position that the character of Hamlet had an obligation to avenge the murder of his father above and beyond vengeance. He believes that the eternal problems of good and evil, hope and despair, are philosophical problems which exist in our own time as well as in Hamlet's time and that the character of Hamlet must be sought in terms of man himself.

DE MADARIAGA, SALVADOR
On Hamlet
Barnes & Noble, 1964. 145pp. $6.00. First published in 1948, this second edition deals with the criticism which the author's essay provoked when it first appeared. His conclusion, reached in the first edition, that no commentator had put forward a consistent interpretation of the chief character and therefore of the play remains intact. Bibliography.

ELLIOTT, G. R.
Scourge and Minister
A. M. S. Press, 1965. 208pp. $9.50. Originally published in 1951, this is a study of "Hamlet" as "tragedy, the play of revengefulness and justice." The author sees Hamlet as the tragedy of civilization and social man pursuing justice and mercy. Index.

HOLMES, MARTIN
The Guns of Elsinore: A New Approach to Hamlet
Barnes & Noble, 1964. 188pp. $5.50. The author reviews the evidence provided by contemporary sources and shows how a closer consideration of the contemporary gossip about Elsinore and its influence on English trade and commercial life can provide insights into "Hamlet."

HUBBARD, E. D. – Editor
Hamlet: Analytic Notes and Review
Study Master, 1963. 72pp. Paper $1.00. A scene-by-scene analysis with critical appraisal summary of characters, suggested study topics, notes and questions for review, and a Bibliography.

JONES, ERNEST
Hamlet and Oedipus
Doubleday, 1954. 194pp. Paper $1.25. This study begins with a comprehensive review of the "Hamlet" literature in all languages. In rejecting previous theories about the nature of the hero's malady, the author examines Hamlet as suffering from a psychoneurosis. This neurosis is related to the general psychological condition foreshadowed in the Oedipus legend.

JUMP, JOHN – Editor
Hamlet: A Casebook
Aurora, 1970. 221pp. Paper $2.50. A selection of critical essays including early criticism. Modern contributors include Ernest Jones, H. D. F. Kitto, T. S. Eliot, Jan Kott, and Helen Gardner, among others. Selected Bibliography. Index.

KNIGHTS, L. C.
Some Shakespearean Themes and An Approach To Hamlet
Stanford University, 1966. 259pp. $6.75. Paper $2.95. In a series of essays, Mr. Knights traces the emergence and development of the major themes of the plays of Shakespeare's maturity. In "An Approach to Hamlet," Mr. Knights continues his analysis of the major themes of "Hamlet."

LAMB, SIDNEY – Editor
Hamlet: Complete Study Edition
Cliff's Notes, 1965. 100pp. Paper $1.00. This edition

contains the complete text of Shakespeare's play with background information about the playwright and his work. A three-column arrangement has been provided with running commentary and glosses in separate columns adjacent to the text column. Illustrated with drawings. Bibliography.

LEAVENWORTH, RUSSELL E.
Interpreting Hamlet: Materials for Analysis
Chandler, 1960. 265pp. $3.95. Critical essays representing a sampling of various approaches that have been made to the play, ranging from Goethe and Coleridge to G. Wilson Knight, E. E. Stoll, Ernest Jones, and Francis Fergusson. Bibliography and suggestions to the student on writing and organizing the research paper.

LEVENSON, J. C. – Editor
Discussions of Hamlet
D. C. Heath, 1960. 113pp. Paper $2.25. This collection of essays on "Hamlet" range in time from the seventeenth century to the present. Among the contributors are: Dryden, Coleridge, A. C. Bradley, T. S. Eliot, E. E. Stoll, G. Wilson Knight, John Dover Wilson, and M. M. Mahood. An introductory essay is provided by the editor.

LEVIN, HARRY
The Question of Hamlet
Oxford, 1959. 178pp. $3.75. Paper – Viking, 1961. 178pp. $1.35. Three features of Elizabethan rhetoric are examined—interrogation, doubt, and irony—and the threads of thought, action, style, and symbolism that run through the play are studied. Three essays deal with the role of the Fool, the ethics of tragedy, and the Player's speech.

MALONE, KEMP
The Literary History of Hamlet
Humanities, 1964. 268pp. $5.75. The author attempts to furnish a literary history of "Hamlet" and the Hamlet saga, treating the origins of the hero and the tale and their developments in early tradition.

MUIR, KENNETH
Hamlet, A Critical Study
Barron, 1963. 62pp. Paper $1.00. In this study the author provides criticism, discussions of the action and characters and includes material on the "mystery" of the play.

PRICE, GEORGE R.
A Simplified Approach to Hamlet
Barron, 1964. 90pp. Paper $ .95. An approach to Shakespeare's play with detailed scene-by-scene analysis, comment on characterization, language, style, and staging, and a sampling of criticism. Notes.

PROSSER, ELEANOR
Hamlet and Revenge
Stanford University, 1967. 287pp. $7.50. Miss Prosser re-examines the Elizabethan attitudes toward revenge and then analyzes the convention of revenge in the plays of Shakespeare and his contemporaries. She presents a detailed explication of "Hamlet" that challenges traditional assumptions about many important elements of the play and supports her interpretation with a survey of "Hamlet" criticism and productions from the seventeenth century to the present. Index.

RAVEN, ANTON A.
A Hamlet Bibliography and Reference Guide: 1877 – 1935
Russell & Russell, 1966. 292pp. $9.50. This bibliography includes all writings published since 1876 about "Hamlet" which have appeared as books, sections of, or essays in, books, in periodicals, a list of the more important editions of the play since the publication of the Variorum, and reviews of criticisms of "Hamlet" up to 1935. The contents of these writings are summarized and conclusions of the authors are given. Index.

SACKS, CLAIRE and EDGAR WHAM – Editors
Hamlet: Enter Critic
Appleton, 1960. 298pp. $3.25. A selection of critical material about "Hamlet," arranged and designed to teach the student the techniques of research paper work.

SANFORD, WENDY COPPEDGE
Theatre as Metaphor in Hamlet
Harvard, 1967. 51pp. Paper $2.50. Mrs. Sanford discusses Shakespeare's use of the theatre as a metaphor to objectify on stage the internal movement and meaning of "Hamlet." She focuses upon Hamlet's roles as director, dramatist, and actor and seeks to show that "the nature of Hamlet's play-acting contains the inevitability of his death." Bibliography.

STOLL, ELMER EDGAR
Hamlet: An Historical and Comparative Study
Gordian Press, 1968. 76pp. $5.35. The author studies the technique, construction, situations, characters and sentiments of the play in the light of other plays in which similar constructions, situations, characters, and sentiments appear. Originally published in 1919 and now reissued, the volume also includes an Appendix noting how Shakespeare's play was influenced by Euripides.

TURING, JOHN
My Nephew Hamlet
Barnes, 1967. 144pp. $5.00. Mr. Turing has set himself the task of rescuing Hamlet's uncle, Claudius, from the odium of murderer and usurper. The narrative is written in the form of Claudius' journal. Illustrated with drawings.

WEINER, ALBERT B.
Hamlet: The First Quarto, 1603

Barron, 1962. 176pp. $3.95. Paper $1.95. A full analysis and carefully reasoned solution to the many problems raised by this little-known edition of the play. The edition is based on the most recent research and correlation with later printings.

WEITZ, MORRIS
Hamlet and the Philosophy of Literary Criticism
University of Chicago, 1964. 335pp. $8.00. Part One of this study consists of detailed examinations of the criticism of A. C. Bradley, Ernest Jones, G. Wilson Knight, T. S. Eliot, Francis Fergusson, and J. Dover Wilson. Part Two is an investigation of certain types of critical procedure that are frequently the unquestioned basis of the critical positions taken by various critics.

WILSON, JOHN DOVER
The Manuscript of Shakespeare's "Hamlet" and the Problems of Its Transmission
Cambridge, 1963. 437pp. $10.25. Originally published in 1934 and now reissued, this two volume set deals with the textual problems of the play. Volume One examines the problems of the texts of 1605 and 1623. Volume Two is concerned with the editorial problems and solutions. Professor Ian Duthie has added an introduction. J. C. Maxwell has provided a few additional notes and queries. Appendices. Indices.

WILSON, JOHN DOVER
What Happens in Hamlet
Cambridge, 1957. 357pp. $5.50. Paper—1961. $1.95. A study of the play which stresses the significance of each dramatic element in the complex structure of the tragedy. The background of Elizabethan belief and prejudice is also considered.

WORMHOUDT, ARTHUR
Hamlet's Mouse Trap: A Psychoanalytical Study of the Drama
Philosophical Library, 1956. 220pp. $3.50. This book studies the play against a background of ideas concerned with the nature of language. The author considers the auditory aspects of language, the manner in which the stream of sound and free visual images are linked together in words, and the manner in which truth is produced through words.

Henry IV

ANONYMOUS
King Henry IV, Part I: Complete Study Guide
Cliff's Notes, 1965. 75pp. Paper $1.00. This edition contains the complete text of Shakespeare's play with background information about the playwright and his work. A three-column arrangement has been provided with commentary and glosses in columns adjacent to the text. Illustrated with drawings.

BARASCH, FRANCES K.
Notes on Henry IV, Part II
Monarch Press, 1964. 96pp. Paper $1.00. A study guide which provides an Introduction on Shakepeare's life and work, an act-by-act discussion of the plot, character analyses, critical commentary, essay questions and answers for review, and a guide to research papers. Bibliography.

BECK, RICHARD J.
Henry IV: A Critical Approach
Barron, 1965. 72pp. Paper $1.00. The author clarifies plot, characterization, symbolism, and style. He provides critical literary appraisal on the play. Select Bibliography. Index.

BOWDEN, W. R.
Henry IV, Part I: Book Notes
Barnes & Noble, 1969. 89pp. Paper $1.00. Copy not available for perusal.

DORIUS, R. J.—Editor
Twentieth Century Interpretations of Henry IV—Part One
Prentice—Hall, 1970. 117pp. $4.95. Paper $1.95. A collection of critical essays by fourteen noted contributors utilizing various critical approaches to provide insights into the characters and events in Shakespeare's history play. Among the contributors are: C. L. Barber, A. C. Bradley, and Northrop Frye. Chronology of Important Dates. Selected Bibliography.

GREBANIER, BERNARD
A Simplified Approach to Henry IV, Part One
Barron, 1965. 102pp. Paper $ .95. A study of the history play with detailed scene-by-scene analysis and summary, analyses of characters, commentary on the action, characterization and language, dialogue and staging, together with historical background materials. Suggestions for Further Reading.

GRENNEN, JOSEPH E.
Notes on Henry IV, Part I
Monarch Press, 1964. 83pp. Paper $1.00. A study guide which provides an act-by-act discussion of the plot, character analyses, essay questions and answers for review, critical commentary, and a guide to research. Bibliography.

LOWERS, JAMES K.—Editor
King Henry IV, Part I: Notes
Cliff's Notes, 1960. 72pp. Paper $1.00. Scene-by-scene analysis and synopses, critical notes, character analysis and review questions on the play.

MARSH, D. R. C.
Shakespeare: Henry IV, Part One
Macmillan, 1967. 73pp. Paper $1.50. A critical commentary on Shakespeare's history plays in general, and on "Henry IV" in particular. A List of Books for Further Reading is included.

NAUMAN, JANET
Henry IV, Part One: Analytic Notes and Review
Study Master, 1964. 76pp. Paper $1.00. A scene-by-scene analysis with critical appraisal, summary of characters, suggested study topics, notes and questions for review, and a Bibliography.

ROBERTS, JAMES L. – Editor
King Henry IV, Part II: Notes
Cliff's Notes, 1963. 68pp. Paper $1.00. Scene-by-scene synopsis of the play with character sketches, and selected examination questions and answers.

WILSON, JOHN DOVER
The Fortunes of Falstaff
Cambridge, 1953. 143pp. $3.50. Paper $1.25. A new interpretation of Falstaff and Prince Hal which challenges the one developed by A. C. Bradley.

YOUNG, DAVID P. – Editor
Twentieth Century Interpretations of Henry IV, Part Two
Prentice–Hall, 1968. 117pp. $3.95. Paper $1.25. Outstanding critics reveal the growing esteem in which this play is held and bring into focus its many successful features. The play comes under the scrutiny of such contributors as Clifford Leech, A. C. Bradley, and E. M. W. Tillyard. Chronology of Important Dates. Selected Bibliography.

Henry V

BERMAN, RONALD – Editor
Twentieth Century Interpretations of Henry V
Prentice–Hall, 1968. 120pp. $3.95. Paper $1.25. This is a collection of critical essays demonstrating the wide range of critical debate over the English history play. Among the sixteen essayists are Una Ellis-Fermor, A. P. Rossiter, E. M. W. Tillyard, and Derek Traversi. Chronology of Important Dates. Selected Bibliography.

LIPPMAN, LAURA
Notes on Henry V
Monarch Press, 1964. 96pp. Paper $1.00. A study guide which provides an act-by-act discussion of the plot, character analyses, critical commentary, essay questions and answers for review, and a Bibliography.

NAUMAN, JANET
Henry V: Analytic Notes and Review
Study Master, 1965. 78pp. Paper $1.00. A scene-by-scene analysis with critical appraisal, summary of characters, suggested study topics, notes and questions for review, and an Annotated Bibliography. Index.

O'BRIEN, M. A.
Shakespeare: Henry V
Macmillan, 1967. 66pp. Paper $1.50. A critical commentary on Shakespeare's play. A list of books for further reading and a series of questions for discussion are included.

QUINN, MICHAEL – Editor
Henry V: A Casebook
Aurora, 1970. 252pp. Paper $2.50. A selection of critical essays. Brief extracts from eighteenth, nineteenth, and twentieth century critics are included as are longer essays by Mark Van Doren, Una Ellis-Fermor, Derek Traversi, and others. Select Bibliography. Index.

ROBERTS, JAMES L. – Editor
King Henry V: Notes
Cliff's Notes, 1961. 79pp. Paper $1.00. A scene-by-scene synopsis of the play with commentaries, character sketches, critical notes, and selected questions and answers for review.

Julius Caesar

ANONYMOUS
Julius Caesar: Complete Study Guide
Cliff's Notes, 1965. 64pp. Paper $1.00. This edition contains the complete text of Shakespeare's play with background information about the playwright and his work. A three-column arrangement has been provided with running commentary and glosses in separate columns adjacent to the text column. Illustrated with drawings.

CLIFF'S NOTES EDITORS
Julius Caesar: Notes
Cliff's Notes, 1960. 62pp. Paper $1.00. Scene-by-scene analysis of the play with character sketches and selected examination questions.

DEAN, LEONARD F. – Editor
Twentieth Century Interpretations of Julius Caesar
Prentice–Hall, 1968. 120pp. $3.95. Paper $1.25. A collection of critical essays which emphasize the endurance of Shakespeare's classic and place it in relation to his other plays. Contributors include: Harley Granville-Barker, Mark Van Doren, Northrop Frye, L. C. Knights, and sixteen others. Chronology. Selected Bibliography.

LITTMAN, ROBERT
Notes on Julius Caesar
Monarch Press, 1964. 93pp. Paper $1.00. A study guide, edited by Frances Barasch, which provides an act-by-act summary of the plot with analytic comment, analyses of the characters, critical commentary, essay questions and answers for review, and a guide to research. Bibliography.

MARKELS, JULIAN – Editor
Shakespeare's Julius Caesar

Scribner, 1961. 124pp. $3.50. The text of the play, with nine essays by such critics as Kenneth Burke, Coleridge, G. Wilson Knight, and Bernard Boyer. Suggested topics for research are given with instructions on writing the research paper.

PRICE, GEORGE R.
A Simplified Approach to Julius Caesar
Barron, 1964. 54pp. Paper $ .95. A volume in the critical series giving a summary of the plot, a commentary on the action and notes on criticism. Material on the date and sources of the play and the characters is also included.

RIBNER, IRVING
Julius Caesar: Book Notes
Barnes & Noble, 1967. 80pp. Paper $1.00. Copy not available for perusal.

TURNER, DAVID R.
Notes on William Shakespeare's Julius Caesar
Arco, 1969. 44pp. Paper $ .95. A complete summary and review of plot and characters. Also included is a brief biography of Shakespeare and a Selected Bibliography.

URE, PETER – Editor
Julius Caesar: A Casebook
Aurora, 1970. 264pp. Paper $2.50. A selection of critical essays. Besides extracts from earlier criticism, there are modern contributions by Harley Granville-Barker, G. Wilson Knight, John Dover Wilson, and others. Select Bibliography. Notes.

WARNER, JOHN F. – Editor
Julius Caesar: Analytic Notes and Review
Study Master, 1963. 72pp. Paper $1.00. A scene-by-scene analysis with critical appraisal, summary of characters, suggested study topics, notes and questions for review, and a Bibliography.

King Lear

ANONYMOUS
King Lear: Complete Study Guide
Cliff's Notes, 1964. 86pp. Paper $1.00. This edition contains the complete text of Shakespeare's play with background information about the playwright and his work. A three-column arrangement has been provided with running commentary and glosses in separate columns adjacent to the text column. Illustrated with drawings. Bibliography.

BONHEIM, HELMUT – Editor
The King Lear Perplex
Wadsworth, 1960. 195pp. Paper $3.35. A collection of seventy-one brief essays on the play ranging in time from Nahum Tate in 1687 to William Elton in 1960. Bibliography.

BROOKE, NICHOLAS
King Lear: A Critical Study
Barron, 1964. 63pp. Paper $1.00. This study begins with a consideration of poetic diction, characterization and major themes, then presents an act-by act analysis of the action.

BYRD, DAVID G. and EDWARD F. NOLAN
Simplified Approach to King Lear
Barron, 1968. 110pp. Paper $ .95. A study of the play with detailed scene-by-scene analysis and summary, analyses of characters, commentary on the action, characterization and language, dialogue and staging, together with historical background materials. Questions for review, discussion, and papers are included. Bibliography.

DANBY, JOHN F.
Shakespeare's Doctrine of Nature: A Study of King Lear
Faber & Faber, 1959. 234pp. $6.50. Paper – 1965. $2.95. A detailed study of the play as the prime instance of the doctrine of nature that influenced all the plays. The theme of nature is also treated in such plays as "Richard III," "King John," "Henry IV," "Hamlet," "Othello," and "Macbeth."

ECCLES, MARK
King Lear: Book Notes
Barnes & Noble, 1967. 75pp. Paper $1.00. Copy not available for perusal.

ELTON, WILLIAM R.
King Lear and the Gods
Huntington Library, 1966. 369pp. $8.50. Professor Elton studies "King Lear" in the light of the play's acknowledged sources and the changing religious climate of the Renaissance. He concludes that the popular modern view of the play as primarily a drama of meaningful suffering and redemption constitutes a serious misreading of the tragedy. Index.

FRASER, RUSSELL A.
Shakespeare's Poetics in Relation to King Lear
Vanderbilt University, 1966. 184pp. $5.00. Originally published in 1962 and now reissued, it is the author's purpose in this study to determine the degree, nature, and meaning of the involvement of poetic symbols in terms of the imagery of "King Lear." Illustrated. List of Works Consulted. Index.

GARDNER, HELEN
King Lear
Athlone, 1967. 28pp. Paper $1.50. Miss Gardner contends that there is an extraordinary unity of action, characterization, and language in "King Lear" and that it is the most universal and profound, the most deeply poetic of all of Shakespeare's plays.

HEILMAN, ROBERT B.
This Great Stage: Image and Structure in King Lear

University of Washington, 1963. 339pp. $5.95. Paper — 1965. $2.45. This study, a reprint of the 1948 edition, approaches the play through an analysis of its patterns of imagery which are seen to develop different aspects of the complex tragic statement. These patterns lead directly to questions of good and evil that underlie the plot.

JORGENSEN, PAUL A.
Lear's Self–Discovery
University of California, 1967. 154pp. $4.50. Mr. Jorgensen examines the self-discovery achieved by Shakespeare's King Lear, the meaning of self-discovery in the Renaissance and in the play, the process whereby self-discovery is achieved, and the dramatic and intellectual significance of the process. Index.

KERMODE, FRANK — Editor
King Lear: A Casebook
Aurora, 1970. 304pp. Paper $2.50. A selection of critical essays. Early comments and critiques are included as are modern contributions by George Orwell, Jan Kott, A. C. Bradley, and others. Select Bibliography. Index.

LEBOWITZ, REGINA — Editor
King Lear: Analytic Notes and Review
Study Master, 1965. 72pp. Paper $1.00. A scene-by-scene analysis with critical appraisal, summary of characters, suggested study topics, notes and questions for review, and a Bibliography.

LOTHIAN, JOHN M.
King Lear
Bell, 1966. 96pp. Paper $1.95. A reprint of the 1949 study in which Professor Lothian considers the means by which Shakespeare is able to transmute an old fairy tale into a masterpiece.

LOWERS, JAMES K. — Editor
King Lear: Notes
Cliff's Notes, 1968. 92pp. Paper $1.00. Scene-by-scene synopsis of the play with background material on the playwright and the play including review questions. Selected Bibliography.

MACK, MAYNARD
King Lear in Our Time
University of California, 1965. 126pp. $3.75. Professor Mack considers certain historical and analytical problems bearing on the stage production and central meaning of "King Lear." Beginning with Nahum Tate's edition of the play in 1681, he considers productions of the play through the years and up to the modern versions of Herbert Blau and Peter Brook. Index.

SCHUETTINGER, ROBERT
Notes on King Lear
Monarch Press, 1966. 124pp. Paper $1.00. A study guide which provides an act-by-act discussion of the plot with analytic comment, character analyses, critical commentary, essay questions and answers for review, and a guide to further research. Bibliography.

Macbeth

BARTHOLOMEUSZ, DENNIS
Macbeth and the Players
Cambridge, 1969. 302pp. $10.50. The major interpretations of Macbeth and Lady Macbeth from 1611 to the 1960's are reconstructed from old playbills, prompt books, newspaper and magazine reviews, personal interviews, and bibliographical sources. The performances are related to the overall history of productions of the play over 350 years. Illustrated. Bibliography. Index.

BROWN, JOHN RUSSELL
Macbeth: A Critical Study
Barron, 1964. 63pp. Paper $1.00. Material on the history, presentation, form, settings, timing and dramatic focus and an evaluation of the play are provided by the author.

CLIFF'S NOTES EDITORS
Macbeth: Notes
Cliff's Notes. Paper $1.00. Copy not available for perusal. Material assumed to be consistent with other volumes in the series. See: "Antony and Cleopatra: Notes" by Cliff's Notes Editors.

FERGUSSON, JAMES
The Man Behind Macbeth
Faber & Faber, 1969. 187pp. $8.95. Shakespearean scholars may not agree that the characters of Macbeth and Lady Macbeth were modelled on two much-hated figures of Shakespeare's own day, but in putting forward this theory, Sir James has brought to life two highly picturesque characters and some of the turbulent history unfamiliar to the general reader. Eight pages of half-tone illustrations. Index.

GEWIRTZ, ARTHUR
Notes on Macbeth
Monarch Press, 1965. 128pp. Paper $1.00. Revised and edited by Leonora Brodwin, this is a study guide which provides an act-by-act discussion of the plot with analytic comment, character analyses, critical commentary, essay questions and answers for review, and a guide to further research. Bibliography.

HALIO, JAY L. — Editor
Approaches to Macbeth
Wadsworth, 1966. 162pp. Paper $3.25. The editor presents an anthology of criticism of "Macbeth" and some of the major critical approaches to Shakespearean tragedy. Also included are suggestions for further reading.

HARVEY, JOHN
Shakespeare's Macbeth
Barnes & Noble, 1963. 59pp. Paper $1.25. This brief study stresses the kind of theatre and audience for which Shakespeare wrote and the way in which Shakespeare and his contemporaries looked at the world. The characters of the play, the plot and structure, and the poetry of the lines are examined.

HILL, KNOX C.
Interpreting Literature
University of Chicago, 1966. 194pp. $6.75. Paper $1.95. Professor Hill shows the reader how to recognize and solve various problems characteristic of the various forms of literature including history, fiction, philosophy, rhetoric, and drama. The chapter on drama includes a long analysis of Shakespeare's "Macbeth." Appendices. Index.

LAMB, SIDNEY – Editor
Macbeth: Complete Study Edition
Cliff's Notes, 1964. 70pp. Paper $1.00. This edition contains the complete text of Shakespeare's play with background information about the playwright and his work. A three-column arrangement has been provided with running commentary and glosses in separate columns adjacent to the text column. Illustrated with drawings. Bibliography.

McCUTCHAN, J. WILSON
Macbeth: Book Notes
Barnes & Noble, 1967. 77pp. Paper $1.00. Copy not available for perusal.

McCUTCHAN, J. WILSON
Macbeth: A Complete Guide to the Play
Barnes & Noble, 1963. 123pp. $2.50. Copy not available for perusal.

MUIR, KENNETH – Editor
Shakespeare Survey: Volume 19
Cambridge, 1966. 171pp. $10.75. The central theme of this volume is the study of "Macbeth." G. K. Hunter, R. B. Heilman, G. I. Duthie, W. A. Murray, and Kenneth Muir are among the contributors. There is also a summary of Shakespearean productions in the United Kingdom in 1965. Illustrated. Index.

PRICE, GEORGE R.
A Simplified Approach to Macbeth
Barron, 1966. 211pp. Paper $ .95. This approach includes material on sources and background, characterization, problems, and a sampling of critical excerpts by Samuel Johnson, DeQuincey, Coleridge, and others.

RAE, T. I.
Scotland in the Time of Shakespeare
Cornell University, 1965. 38pp. & plates. Paper $1.50. The author seeks to prove that during the life of Shakespeare the relationship between the English and the Scots was undergoing a complete transformation and that "Macbeth" was written partly as a flattering tribute of the new Scottish King of England.

ROGERS, H. L.
"Double Profit" in Macbeth
Cambridge, 1964. 65pp. Paper $1.95. A brief study of the idea of "doubleness" or equivocation in "Macbeth." Shakespeare's use of Holinshed is also studied and there is a discussion of the authenticity of "Macbeth III."

TURNER, DAVID R.
Notes on William Shakespeare's Macbeth
Arco, 1969. 52pp. Paper $ .95. A complete summary and review of plot and characters. Also included is a brief biography of Shakespeare and a Selected Bibliography.

WAIN, JOHN – Editor
Macbeth: A Casebook
Aurora, 1970. 301pp. Paper $2.50. A selection of critical essays. Extracts from earlier criticism are included as are modern contributions by A. C. Bradley, G. Wilson Knight, Helen Gardner, and others. Select Bibliography. Index.

WARNER, JOHN F. – Editor
Macbeth: Analytic Notes and Review
Study Master, 1964. 78pp. Paper $1.00. A scene-by-scene analysis with critical appraisal, summary of characters, suggested study topics, notes and questions for review, and a Bibliography.

Measure for Measure

BENNETT, JOSEPHINE WALTERS
Measure for Measure as Royal Entertainment
Columbia, 1966. 208pp. $6.00. Professor Bennett discusses the plot of the play, the art with which it is contrived, and devotes particular attention to the role of the Duke both as "playwright of the play within the play and as actor in that play." Index.

CLIFF'S NOTES EDITORS
Measure for Measure: Notes
Cliff's Notes. Paper $1.00. Copy not available for perusal. Material assumed to be consistent with other volumes in the series. See: "Antony and Cleopatra: Notes" by Cliff's Notes Editors.

GECKLE, GEORGE L. – Editor
Twentieth Century Interpretations of Measure for Measure
Prentice–Hall, 1970. 119pp. $4.95. Paper $1.25. A collection of critical essays by thirteen noted critics which offers a variety of approaches to the questions of morality, politics, and justice raised by the play.

Among the contributors are Francis Fergusson, G. Wilson Knight, Kenneth Muir, and E. M. W. Tillyard. Chronology. Selected Bibliography.

STEVENSON, DAVID
The Achievement of Shakespeare's Measure for Measure
Cornell University, 1966. 169pp. $7.50. Professor Stevenson considers this "problem comedy" to carry its meaning within its own dramatic design and offers an analysis of the major dramatic components of the play. He examines critical attitudes from Dryden to contemporary writers. Index.

TROUSDALE, MARION – Editor
Measure for Measure: Analytic Notes and Review
Study Master, 1964. 52pp. Paper $1.00. A scene-by-scene analysis with critical appraisal, summary of characters, suggested study topics, notes and questions for review, and a Bibliography.

VIOLI, UNICIO J.
Notes on Measure for Measure
Monarch Press, 1964. 94pp. Paper $1.00. A study guide providing an act-by-act discussion of the plot with analytic comment, character analyses, critical commentary, essay questions and answers for review, and a guide to research papers. Bibliography.

The Merchant of Venice

ANONYMOUS
Merchant of Venice: Complete Study Guide
Cliff's Notes, 1965. 70pp. Paper $1.00. This edition contains the complete text of Shakespeare's play with background information about the playwright and his work. A three-column arrangement has been provided with running commentary and glosses in separate columns adjacent to the text column. Illustrated with drawings.

BARNET, SYLVAN – Editor
Twentieth Century Interpretations of The Merchant of Venice
Prentice–Hall, 1970. 122pp. $4.95. Paper $1.25. A collection of critical essays by ten noted critics. Among the contributors are: C. L. Barber, Harley Granville-Barker, John Russell Brown, G. Wilson Knight, and W. H. Auden. Chronology. Selected Bibliography.

CLIFF'S NOTES EDITORS
Merchant of Venice: Notes
Cliff's Notes. Paper $1.00. Copy not available for perusal. Material assumed to be consistent with other volumes in the series. See: "Antony and Cleopatra: Notes" by Cliff's Notes Editors.

GREBANIER, BERNARD
The Truth About Shylock
Random House, 1962. 369pp. $5.95. This study places the controversial character in historical perspective and shows that Shakespeare did not set out to create a derogatory symbol of Jewish merchants.

LELYVELD, TOBY
Shylock on the Stage
Western Reserve University, 1960. 149pp. $4.95. A study of the role as it was played by leading actors of the British and American theatre from Shakespeare's time to the present.

LIPPMAN, LAURA
Notes on The Merchant of Venice
Monarch Press, 1964. 100pp. Paper $1.00. A study guide which provides an act-by-act discussion of the plot, character analyses, critical commentary, essay questions and answers for review, and a Bibliography.

McNEIR, WALDO F.
The Merchant of Venice: Book Notes
Barnes & Noble, 1967. 83pp. Paper $1.00. Copy not available for perusal.

MOODY, A. D.
The Merchant of Venice: A Critical Study
Barron, 1964. 64pp. Paper $1.00. The study clarifies plot, characterization, symbolism and style in the play. The author provides an Appendix on "The Jew of Malta" and "The Merchant of Venice." Note on Texts and Criticism. Index.

NOLAN, EDWARD F.
A Simplified Approach to The Merchant of Venice
Barron, 1971. 131pp. Paper $ .95. Detailed analyses and interpretations of the play with background and source material. Act-by-act summary of the action with commentary is provided. Significant criticism is excerpted and there are study questions for review and discussion. Suggestions for Further Reading.

SINSHEIMER, HERMANN
Shylock: The History of a Character
Blom, 1963. 147pp. $6.50. Paper – Citadel, 1964. $1.95. First published in 1947 and now reissued, this study analyzes "The Merchant of Venice" as Shakespeare wrote it and as critics have interpreted it.

STEIN, MORRIS – Editor
The Merchant of Venice: Analytic Notes and Review
Study Master, 1964. 66pp. Paper $1.00. A scene-by-scene analysis with critical appraisal, summary of characters, suggested study topics, notes and questions for review, and a Bibliography.

WILDERS, JOHN – Editor
The Merchant of Venice: A Casebook
Aurora, 1970. 249pp. Paper $2.50. A selection of critical essays. Extracts from early criticism are

included as are modern contributions by E. E. Stoll, Mark Van Doren, M. C. Bradbrook, and others. Selected Bibliography. Index.

The Merry Wives of Windsor

BRACY, WILLIAM
The Merry Wives of Windsor: The History and Transmission of Shakespeare's Text
University of Missouri, 1952. 154pp. $2.50. This study attempts to clear the ground of much untenable conjecture that has grown up around the "Bad Quartos" during the last three centuries and to give a detailed textual analysis of the Quarto and Folio texts. Bibliography. Index.

GREEN, WILLIAM
Shakespeare's Merry Wives of Windsor
Princeton, 1962. 239pp. $5.75. This study of the play employs historical methods to investigate the background and the many textual problems. Topical references are explained and the relation of the play to the rest of the works is examined.

A Midsummer Night's Dream

BLACK, MATTHEW
A Midsummer Night's Dream: Book Notes
Barnes & Noble, 1967. 88pp. Paper $1.00. Copy not available for perusal.

CLIFF'S NOTES EDITORS
A Midsummer Night's Dream: Notes
Cliff's Notes. Paper $1.00. Copy not available for perusal. Material assumed to be consistent with other volumes in the series. See: "Antony and Cleopatra: Notes" by Cliff's Notes Editors.

FENDER, STEPHEN
A Midsummer Night's Dream: A Critical Study
Barron, 1969. 80pp. Paper $1.00. Intensive analysis and evaluations of the action, language, sources and characters.

LEOFF, EVE
Notes on A Midsummer Night's Dream
Monarch Press, 1964. 87pp. Paper $1.00. A study guide providing act-by-act discussion of the plot, character analyses, critical commentary, essay questions and answers for review, and a Bibliography.

NOLAN, EDWARD F.
A Simplified Approach to A Midsummer Night's Dream
Barron, 1969. 192pp. Paper $ .95. Detailed synopsis of the action, explanation of the characters, the various sources and allusions.

TROUSDALE, MARION – Editor
A Midsummer Night's Dream: Analytic Notes and Review
Study Master, 1964. 47pp. Paper $1.00. A scene-by-scene analysis with critical appraisal, summary of characters, suggested study topics, notes and questions for review, and a Bibliography.

Much Ado About Nothing

DAVIS, WALTER R. – Editor
Twentieth Century Interpretations of Much Ado About Nothing
Prentice–Hall, 1969. 119pp. $4.95. Paper $1.25. A collection of critical essays by nineteen authorities including W. H. Auden, Francis Fergusson, and Northrop Frye. Professor Davis provides an Introduction. Chronology. Selected Bibliography.

GRENNEN, JOSEPH E.
Notes on Much Ado About Nothing
Monarch Press, 1964. 81pp. Paper $1.00. A study guide which provides act-by-act discussion of the plot, character analyses, critical commentary, essay questions and answers for review, and a Bibliography.

HENDERSON, ARCHIBALD
Much Ado About Nothing: Analytic Notes and Review
Study Master, 1966. 72pp. Paper $1.00. A scene-by-scene analysis with critical appraisal, summary of characters, suggested study topics, notes and questions for review, and an Annotated Bibliography. Index.

MULRYNE, J. R.
Much Ado About Nothing: A Critical Study
Barron, 1965. 63pp. Paper $1.00. This study clarifies plot, characterization, symbolism, and style in the play. The author also provides a List of Books for Further Reading. Index.

ROYSTER, SALIBELLE – Editor
Much Ado About Nothing: Notes
Cliff's Notes, 1963. 64pp. Paper $1.00. Scene-by-scene synopsis of the play with character sketches, and selected examination questions.

Othello

CHASSERIAU, THEODORE
Othello
Walker, 1969. 20pp. & plates, $50.00. A boxed set of fifteen facsimile etchings by the nineteenth century artist reproduced from the 1844 edition. The plates illustrate Shakespeare's play and are considered classics in the field of art. A short introduction to the plates is provided by Philip Hofer in a separate pamphlet of twenty pages.

DEAN, LEONARD F.
A Casebook on Othello
Crowell, 1961. 269pp. $3.25. An annotated text of the play with fourteen essays on its structure and meaning and two essays on the nature of tragedy.

GRACE, WILLIAM J.
Notes on Othello
Monarch Press, 1964. 123pp. Paper $1.00. A study guide which provides an act-by-act discussion of the plot with analytic comment, character analyses, critical commentary, essay questions and answers for review, and a guide to further research. Bibliography.

HEILMAN, ROBERT B.
Magic in the Web: Action and Language in Othello
University of Kentucky, 1956. 298pp. $5.00. A study of the dramatic function of action—physical activity, psychological movement, and intellectual operations —and of language—speech habits, image types, recurring language—in the play.

HUNTER, G.K
Othello and Colour Prejudice
Oxford, 1967. 26pp. Paper $1.50. Mr. Hunter suggests that Shakespeare's choice of Othello as a hero was a daring theatrical novelty. He seeks to explain what the purpose of this novelty might have been. Illustrated.

HYMAN, STANLEY EDGAR
Iago: Some Approaches to the Illusion of His Motivation
Atheneum, 1970. 180pp. $5.95. The author examines the character of Iago from five different critical points of view. His book is also a study of the play both in itself and as a vehicle of criticism through the centuries as he quotes from and comments on the criticism of the past. A long Appendix, complete with musical examples, on Verdi's "Othello" is also included. Index.

JORGENSEN, PAUL A.
Othello: Book Notes
Barnes & Noble, 1967. 64pp. Paper $1.00. Copy not available for perusal.

JORGENSEN, PAUL A.
Othello: A Complete Guide to the Play
Barnes & Noble, 1964. 124pp. $2.50. Copy not available for perusal.

LOWERS, JAMES K. – Editor
Othello: Complete Study Edition
Cliff's Notes. 1966. 89pp. Paper $1.00. This edition contains the complete text of Shakespeare's play with background information about the playwright and his work. A three-column arrangement has been provided with running commentary and glosses in separate columns adjacent to the text column. Illustrated with drawings. Bibliography.

MUIR, KENNETH – Editor
Shakespeare Survey: Volume 21
Cambridge, 1968. 210pp. $8.50. This volume of "Shakespeare Survey" is mainly devoted to the study of a single play: "Othello." It begins with an account by Dame Helen Gardner of critical attitudes to the play in the present century and includes eight other essays on the play. Also included are articles on various other subjects, a survey of the year's contributions to Shakespearean study, and an Index to Volumes 11–20 of the Survey. Illustrated.

NOLAN, EDWARD F.
A Simplified Approach to Othello
Barron, 1967. 90pp. Paper $ .95. An act-by-act summary of Shakespeare's play with character sketches, detailed analyses and interpretations, sources of the play, critical excerpts and a Bibliography.

ROBERTS, JAMES L. – Editor
Othello: Notes
Cliff's Notes, 1959. 82pp. Paper $1.00. A scene-by-scene synopsis of the play with commentaries, character studies, critical notes, and selected questions and answers for review.

STOLL, ELMER EDGAR
Othello: An Historical and Comparative Study
Gordian Press, 1967. 71pp. $5.35. Among the facets of the character of Othello pursued in this study, originally published in 1915 and now reissued, are the contradictions in that character, his jealousy, his trustfulness, his passion and stupidity. The author provides a postscript on Shakespeare's characterization in general.

WARNER, JOHN F. – Editor
Othello: Analytic Notes and Review
Study Master, 1963. 59pp. Paper $1.00. A scene-by-scene analysis with critical appraisal, summary of characters, suggested study topics, notes and questions for review, and a Bibliography.

Richard II

GREBANIER, BERNARD
A Simplified Approach to Richard II
Barron, 1967. 83pp. Paper $ .95. Detailed analyses and interpretations of Shakespeare's history play. Included are an act-by-act summary with commentary, sources and historical background, character sketches, selected critiques, and a Bibliography.

HUMPHREYS, A.R.
Richard II: A Critical Study
Barron, 1969. 64pp. Paper $1.00. Discussion of the history play with the significance of Shakespeare's characterization, action, and staging analyzed.

NAUMAN, JANET and LOUIS MARDER
Richard II: Analytic Notes and Review
Study Master, 1965. 72pp. Paper $1.00. A scene-by-scen analysis with critical appraisal, summary of characters, suggested study topics, notes and questions for review, and a Bibliography. Index.

ROBERTS, JAMES L. – Editor
Richard II: Notes
Cliff's Notes, 1960. 78pp. Paper $1.00. Scene-by-scene synopsis of the play with character sketches, and selected examination questions and answers.

SCANLAN, MARY H.
Notes on Richard II
Monarch Press, 1964. 96pp. Paper $1.00. A study guide providing an act-by-act discussion of the plot, character analyses, critical commentary, essay questions and answers for review, and a guide to research. Bibliography.

Richard III

CLEMEN, W.H.
A Commentary on Shakespeare's Richard III
Methuen, 1968. 247pp. $10.00. Originally published in 1957 and now translated into English for the first time, by Jean Bonheim, this scene-by-scene commentary on Shakespeare's play sets out to provide a detailed analysis of the meaning of the play while maintaining the structure of the play. List of Editions Consulted. List of Pre-Shakespearean Plays Used in the Commentary. Index of Names.

CLIFF'S NOTES EDITORS
Richard III: Notes
Cliff's Notes. Paper $1.00. Copy not available for perusal. Material assumed to be consistent with other volumes in the series. See: "Antony and Cleopatra: Notes" by Cliff's Notes Editors.

LORDI, ROBERT J. and JAMES E. ROBINSON
Richard III: Analytic Notes and Review
Study Master, 1966. 79pp. Paper $1.00. A scene-by-scene analysis with critical appraisal, summary of characters, suggested study topics, notes and questions for review, and an Annotated Bibliography. Index.

NUGENT, F.M.
Notes on Richard III
Monarch Press, 1964. 91pp. Paper $1.00. A study guide providing an act-by-act discussion of the plot, character analyses, critical commentary, essay questions and answers for review, and a Bibliography.

Romeo and Juliet

CLIFF'S NOTES EDITORS
Romeo and Juliet: Notes
Cliff's Notes, 1960. 59pp. Paper $1.00. This guide to the play includes scene-by-scene analysis of the plot with notes on the purpose of the scene and on the characters. Questions and answers for the student are provided. The consulting editor for the guide is James L. Roberts.

COLE, DOUGLAS – Editor
Twentieth Century Interpretations of Romeo and Juliet
Prentice–Hall, 1970. 117pp. $4.95. Paper $1.25. A collection of critical essays by sixteen critics. Among the essayists are: T. S. Eliot, Elmer Edgar Stoll, John Dover Wilson, and Harry Levin. Chronology. Selected Bibliography.

EVANS, ROBERT O.
The Osier Cage: Rhetorical Devices in Romeo and Juliet
University of Kentucky, 1966. 108pp. $4.00. This study offers a reading of "Romeo and Juliet" through a consideration of diction, a critical category neglected in modern times. Mr. Evans shows how Shakespeare, by a deft manipulation of the devices of rhetoric and diction, has reinforced characterization and bound the elements of the plot into a cohesive whole. Index.

HOSLEY, RICHARD
Romeo and Juliet: Book Notes
Barnes & Noble, 1968. 69pp. Paper $1.00. Copy not available for perusal.

JENKIN, LEONARD
Notes on Romeo and Juliet
Monarch Press, 1964. 96pp. Paper $1.00. A study guide which provides an act-by-act discussion of the plot with analytic comment, character analyses, critical commentary, essay questions and answers for review, and a guide to further research. Bibliography.

LAMB, SIDNEY – Editor
Romeo and Juliet: Complete Study Edition
Cliff's Notes, 1965. 80pp. Paper $1.00. This edition contains the complete text of Shakespeare's play with background information about the playwright and his work. A three-column arrangement has been provided with running commentary and glosses in separate columns adjacent to the text column. Illustrated with drawings. Bibliography.

NOLAN, EDWARD F.
A Simplified Approach to Romeo and Juliet
Barron, 1967. 117pp. Paper $ .95. Discussions of the date and background of the play, characters, Shakespeare's source and his treatment of it. Act-by-act summary of the play with running commentary

and selected critiques of the play are provided. Suggestions for Further Reading.

TROUSDALE, MARION and EUGENE B. VEST
Romeo and Juliet: Analytic Notes and Review
Study Master, 1965. 78pp. Paper $1.00. A scene by scene analysis with critical appraisal, summary of characters, suggested study topics, notes and questions for review, and a Bibliography. Index.

The Taming of the Shrew

RANALD, MARGARET L.
Notes on The Taming of the Shrew
Monarch Press, 1965. 118pp. Paper $1.00. A study guide providing act-by-act discussion of the plot, character analyses, critical commentary, essay questions and answers for review and a guide to further study. Bibliography.

ROYSTER, SALIBELLE – Editor
Taming of the Shrew: Notes
Cliff's Notes, 1964. 71pp. Paper $1.00. A scene-by-scene synopsis of the play with character sketches, and selected questions for review.

SANDERS, NORMAN
The Taming of the Shrew: Analytic Notes and Review
Study Master, 1967. 72pp. Paper $1.00. A scene-by-scene analysis with critical appraisal, summary of characters, suggested study topics, notes and questions for review, and a Bibliography. Index.

The Tempest

JAMES, D. G.
The Dream of Prospero
Oxford, 1967. 174pp. $6.50. The author contends that "The Tempest" is a work in which the old world of Europe and the new world of America came together in Shakespeare's imagination. Throughout the essay runs a comparison and contrast between Shakespeare and Francis Bacon.

KIMBALL, ARTHUR G.
A Simplified Approach to The Tempest
Barron, 1966. 95pp. Paper $ .95. Notes on dates and sources of the play, detailed scene-by-scene analyses with commentaries, excerpts from twenty-one famous critical essays, topics for review, discussion and critical papers, and suggestions for further reading are all provided in this volume.

LAMB, SIDNEY – Editor
The Tempest: Complete Study Edition
Cliff's Notes, 1965. 68pp. Paper $1.00. This edition contains the complete text of Shakespeare's play with background information about the playwright and his work. A three column arrangement has been provided with running commentary and glosses in separate columns adjacent to the text column. Illustrated with drawings. Bibliography.

LANGBAUM, ROBERT
The Modern Spirit
Oxford, 1970. 221pp. Paper $1.95. Ten essays in which Professor Langbaum relates individual works from the nineteenth and twentieth centuries to broad cultural movements. A concluding essay on Shakespeare's "The Tempest" takes the contemporary taste for Shakespeare's last plays as an appreciation of the mythical view of life. Notes. Index.

NUTTALL, A. D.
Two Concepts of Allegory
Routlege, 1967. 175pp. $8.50. This is a study of Shakespeare's "The Tempest" and the logic of allegorical expression. Mr. Nuttall's argument has the consequence of suggesting that allegory and metaphysics are in practice more closely allied than is commonly supposed. Bibliography. Index.

PALMER, D. J. – Editor
The Tempest: A Casebook
Aurora, 1970. 271pp. Paper $2.50. A selection of critical essays. Extracts from early criticism are included as are modern contributions by E. M. W. Tillyard, G. Wilson Knight, Jan Kott, and others. Select Bibliography. Index.

RANALD, RALPH A.
Notes on The Tempest
Monarch Press, 1964. 80pp. Paper $1.00. A study guide providing act-by-act discussion of the plot, character analyses, critical commentary, essay questions and answers for review and a Bibliography.

ROBERTS, JAMES L. – Editor
The Tempest: Notes
Cliff's Notes, 1960. 51pp. Paper $1.00. A scene-by-scene synopsis of the play with commentaries, critical notes, character sketches, and questions and answers for review.

SHIPLEY, JOSEPH T.
The Tempest: Analytic Notes and Review
Study Master, 1965. 74pp. Paper $1.00. A scene-by-scene analysis with critical appraisal, summary of characters, suggested study topics notes and questions for review, and an Annotated Bibliography.

SMITH, HALLETT – Editor
Twentieth Century Interpretations of The Tempest
Prentice–Hall, 1969. 114pp. $4.95. Paper $1.25. A collection of critical essays offering an appraisal of the philosophy behind the play, its dramatic structure and theatrical effects, its music and autobiographical content. Among the seventeen contributors

are Bonamy Dobree, Northrop Frye, G. Wilson Knight, and the Editor. Chronology. Selected Bibliography.

Timon of Athens

BUTLER, FRANCELIA
The Strange Critical Fortunes of Shakespeare's Timon of Athens
Iowa State University, 1966. 188pp. $4.50. An analysis of the structure, meaning, and literary and dramatic history of "Timon of Athens." The author contends that its meaning for contemporary audiences is more significant today than ever before. Illustrated. Bibliography. Index.

Troilus and Cressida

CAMPBELL, OSCAR JAMES
Comicall Satyre and Shakespeare's Troilus and Cressida
Huntington Library, 1959. 246pp. $5.50. A study which establishes the relation between this play and others of the period styled by Ben Johson as "comicall satyres." Five other plays of the type are analyzed and the author contends that these plays arose out of an effort to find an effective substitute for the satires ordered destroyed by an edict of the Bishops issued June 1, 1599.

KIMBROUGH, ROBERT
Shakespeare's Troilus and Cressida and Its Setting
Harvard, 1964. 208pp. $5.75. After a discussion of earlier criticism of the play, the author recreates the particular theatrical atmosphere within which the play was written in order to demonstrate that Shakespearean drama arises in part from the pressure the playwright felt as a writer for and shareholder in a highly competitive commercial venture. Index.

KIMBROUGH, ROBERT
Troilus and Cressida: Analytic Notes and Review
Study Master, 1966. 80pp. Paper $1.00. A scene-by-scene analysis with critical appraisal, summary of characters, suggested study topics, notes and questions for review, and an Annotated Bibliography. Index.

LOWERS, JAMES K. – Editor
Troilus and Cressida: Notes
Cliff's Notes, 1964. 85pp. Paper $1.00. A scene-by-scene synopsis of the play with comments, character analysis, and question and answer sections.

Twelfth Night

CARRINGTON, NORMAN T.
Notes on Shakespeare: Twelfth Night
James Brodie, 1965. 70pp. Paper $1.50. A brief survey of the play and its background.

CLIFF'S NOTES EDITORS
Twelfth Night: Notes
Cliff's Notes, 1960. 79pp. Paper $1.00. This guide to the play provides scene-by-scene analysis of the play. These analyses include synopsis of the plot, notes on the characters, and questions for the student. The editors have also included sections on character analysis, outline of the major characters, a note on the title of the play, notes on the dramatic structure and the prose and poetry, the songs, and the sources of interest.

GILBERT, SANDRA
Notes on Twelfth Night
Monarch Press, 1964. 94pp. Paper $1.00. A study guide to the play providing act-by-act discussion of the plot. The editor has also included sections of character analysis and critical commentary. Questions and answers for student review are provided. Also supplied are an Introduction on Shakespeare's life and works, a guide to research papers, and a Bibliography.

KING, WALTER N. – Editor
Twentieth Century Interpretations of Twelfth Night
Prentice–Hall, 1968. 114pp. $3.95. Paper $1.25. A collection of critical essays on Shakespeare's play which reveal the critical disagreement over the purpose and meaning of the play. Among the essayists are: C. L. Barber, Leslie Hotson, Clifford Leech, W. Moelwyn Merchant, and Mark Van Doren. Chronology of Important Dates. Bibliography.

LAMB, SIDNEY – Editor
Twelfth Night: Complete Study Edition
Cliff's Notes, 1965. 67pp. Paper $1.00. This edition contains the complete text of Shakespeare's play with background information about the playwright and his work. A three-column arrangement has been provided with running commentary and glosses in separate columns adjacent to the text column. Illustrated with drawings. Bibliography.

SHIPLEY, JOSEPH T. and WILLIAM E. COLES, JR.
Twelfth Night: Analytic Notes and Critical Commentary
Study Master, 1965. 84pp. Paper $1.00. This guide to the play includes a scene-by-scene analysis. Critical appraisal and a summary of the characters are also provided. The volume includes a section of suggested study topics and notes and questions for the student's review. Also provided are an Annotated Bibliography and an Index.

The Two Gentlemen of Verona

RANALD, MARGARET L.
Notes on Two Gentlemen of Verona
Monarch Press, 1966. 112pp. Paper $1.00. A study guide which provides an act-by-act discussion of the plot, character analyses, critical commentary, essay questions and answers for review, and a Bibliography.

The Winter's Tale

FOX, G. P.
The Winter's Tale
Blackwell, 1967. 63pp. Paper $1.50. This is an introduction, designed primarily for students, to Shakespeare's play. It contains questions on the text and suggestions for further reading.

MUIR, KENNETH – Editor
The Winter's Tale: A Casebook
Aurora, 1970. 243pp. Paper $2.50. A selection of critical essays including early criticism and modern contributions by such authorities as E. M. W. Tillyard, G. Wilson Knight, Derek Traversi, Northrop Frye, Louis Macneice and others. Select Bibliography. Index.

PYLE, FITZROY
The Winter's Tale: A Commentary on the Structure
Routledge & Kegan Paul, 1969. 195pp. $6.50. This is a scene-by-scene commentary on Shakespeare's play. The author examines the structure in relation to its source book and places special emphasis on the ending as a culmination of a dramatic structure whose beauty has not hitherto been fully recognized. Index.

RANALD, MARGARET L.
Notes on The Winter's Tale
Monarch Press, 1965. 122pp. Paper $1.00. A study guide which provides an act-by-act discussion of the plot with analytic comment, character analyses, critical commentary, essay questions and answers for review, and a guide to further research. Bibliography.

WILLIAMS, JOHN ANTHONY
The Natural Work of Art: The Experience of Romance in Shakespeare's The Winter's Tale
Harvard, 1967. 47pp. Paper $2.50. The author views Shakespearean romance as a poetic response to the metaphysical problems of "mutability" and man's place in nature. He rejects the notion that Shakespeare deliberately created a fantasy world as an escape from reality. Bibliography.

Studies of Songs, Sonnets, and Poems

BLACKMUR, R. P. et al
The Riddle of Shakespeare's Sonnets
Basic Books, 1962. 346pp. $10.50. This edition has the complete text of the Sonnets with essays by R. P. Blackmur, Leslie A. Fiedler, Northrop Frye, and Stephen Spender, among others, and the complete text of Oscar Wilde's "Portrait of Mr. W. H." Indices.

BOOTH, STEPHEN
An Essay on Shakespeare's Sonnets
Yale, 1969, 218pp. $7.50. Mr. Booth suggests that the source of pleasure in Shakespeare's Sonnets is in the line-to-line reading experience. He describes and illustrates the various patterning systems that coexist in the individual sonnets and then analyzes representative sonnets in terms of the reading experiences they evoke. Index of Sonnets.

HERRNSTEIN, BARBARA – Editor
Discussions of Shakespeare's Sonnets
Heath, 1964. 164pp. Paper $2.50. This collection of essays demonstrates the interpretations the Sonnets have undergone since the seventeenth century. The editor indicates that the more recent essays show a more rational approach to the poems than earlier ones.

HOTSON, LESLIE
Mr. W. H.
Knopf, 1964. 328pp. $6.95. Mr. Hotson identifies William Hatcliffe as the "Mr. W. H." of the Sonnets and shows how the specific details of the poems all correspond to the facts as he has uncovered them. Index.

HOTSON, LESLIE
Shakespeare's Sonnets Dated and Other Essays
Oxford, 1949. 244pp. $6.00. This work discusses the author's discovery of the year in which the Sonnets were written and shows that most scholars were from seven to fourteen years off. The other essays deal with a variety of similar literary discoveries, among them the identity of the host of the Mermaid Tavern.

HUBLER, EDWARD
The Sense of Shakespeare's Sonnets
Hill & Wang, 1962. 169pp. Paper $1.25. An analysis of the Sonnets as poems, with emphasis placed on an explication of their content.

KNIGHT, G. WILSON
The Mutual Flame: On Shakespeare's Sonnets and The Phoenix and the Turtle
Barnes & Noble, 1955. 233pp. $7.00. Studies of the themes and patterns of the Sonnets, and of their relation to the plays and the life of the poet. "Love's Martyr," the collection in which "The Phoenix" first

appeared, is analyzed and Shakespearean work is seen in some of the ostensibly non-Shakespearean parts.

KRIEGER, MURRAY
A Window to Criticism: Shakespeare's Sonnets and Modern Poetics
Princeton, 1964. 244pp. $5.75. The author attempts to move beyond the concept of the language of poetry as a closed system and tries to connect the "insular criticism of literature as literature with the mainland of man's concern as a social-historical being."

LANDRY, HILTON
Interpretations in Shakespeare's Sonnets
University of California, 1963. 185pp. $4.00. The author investigates a number of problems in interpretation of the most difficult Sonnets. The presence of ambiguity in the poetry is stressed and the author discounts the assumption that the poems fall into two series, one to the Fair Youth, and the other to the Dark Lady. The narrative content is called into question. Bibliography. Index.

LOWERS, JAMES K.—Editor
Shakespeare's Sonnets: Notes
Cliff's Notes, 1965. 65pp. Paper $1.00. Notes on the Sonnets with background material on sixteenth century sonnets, selected criticism, questions for review, and a Selected Bibliography.

NOBLE, RICHMOND
Shakespeare's Use of Song with the Text of the Principal Songs
Oxford, 1966. 160pp. $4.85. A reprint of the 1923 edition in which the author shows that the songs in Shakespeare's plays are not interchangeable but have definite dramatic value. There is comment on the methods and limitations of stage singing in the Elizabethan theatre and on the subject of interpreting Shakespeare in the light of the conditions under which he wrote. Index of Songs.

SENG, PETER J.
The Vocal Songs in the Plays of Shakespeare: A Critical History
Harvard, 1967. 314pp. $10.50. In this book, Peter Seng brings together the available information on the vocal songs in Shakespeare's plays. He presents the texts of seventy songs taken from the earliest authoritative editions of twenty-one plays, discusses important textual variants, and provides a history of the critical treatment of the songs since 1709. Bibliography. Index.

SHIPLEY, JOSEPH T.
Shakespeare's Sonnets: Analytic Notes and Critical Commentary
Study Master, 1964. 70pp. Paper $1.00. A guide to the Sonnets including notes on the publication, the order and arrangements, themes and motifs, and the sonnet form. Also included are critical appraisal, suggested study topics, and a Bibliography.

STIRLING, BRENTS
The Shakespeare Sonnet Order: Poems & Groups
University of California, 1968. 317pp. $10.00. Mr. Stirling believes that Shakespeare's Sonnets are badly disarranged in the Quarto of 1609. Past attempts to correct the Sonnet order have ended in frustration; however, he finds in the Quarto text two kinds of internal evidence that lead to a revised Sonnet order and that test that order. The author includes both text and commentary on the amended Sonnet order he proposes. Notes. General Index. Index of First Lines.

VIOLI, UNICIO J.
Notes on The Sonnets
Monarch Press, 1965. 158pp. Paper $1.00. A study guide to the Sonnets. The author provides an in-depth analysis of the form, meaning and style of Shakespeare's poetry by means of a discussion of the background, plot, theme development, character analysis, a guide to critical commentary, and a guide to further research. He also provides a review section of questions and answers for the student. Bibliography.

WILLEN, GERALD and VICTOR B. REED—Editors
A Casebook on Shakespeare's Sonnets
Crowell, 1964. 311pp. Paper $3.95. This volume presents a newly edited text of the Sonnets with essays focusing on them. Six full-length essays and eight explications are provided by such authorities as Robert Graves, L. C. Knights, Arthur Mizener, G. Wilson Knight, and Edward F. Nolan. Appendices include a Bibliography and an Index of Sonnets.

WILSON, J. DOVER
An Introduction to Shakespeare's Sonnets for Historians and Others
Cambridge, 1964. 109pp. $2.75. Paper—88pp. $1.25. Professor Wilson defends the case for the Earl of Pembroke as the young man for whom Shakespeare wrote his Sonnets. This introduction, written for the "New Shakespeare" edition, is a refutation of Dr. A. L. Rowse's theory of Southampton as the inspiration. Professor Wilson also examines the human relationships that are the subject of the poems.

WINNY, JAMES
The Master–Mistress: A Study of Shakespeare's Sonnets
Chatto & Windus, 1968. 216pp. $5.00. A reinterpretation of the Sonnets which sees them neither as fiction nor private autobiography. Mr. Winny draws attention to the element of dualism that runs through the work of the playwright and argues that the meaning of the Sonnets must be sought in this concern with dualistic figures. Index of Sonnets. Index of Names.

Editorial Problems

BALDWIN, T.W.
On Act and Scene Division in the Shakespeare First Folio
Southern Illinois University, 1965. 179pp. $5.50. Professor Baldwin demonstrates that the printers probably consulted some sort of manuscript when making act divisions for the Folio. There are significant indications that as printing proceeded editorial policy abandoned manuscripts and sought as nearly as possible the author's original version.

BOWERS, FREDSON
Textual and Literary Criticism
Cambridge, 1967. 186pp. Paper $1.65. Professor Bowers indicates the importance of textual criticism and how the literary critic uses such criticism. He discusses Whitman's "Leaves of Grass," textual criticism of Shakespeare, and the editing of early dramatic texts.

CRAIG, HARDIN
A New Look at Shakespeare's Quartos
Stanford University, 1961. 134pp. $3.50. An examination of the nature and origin of the early editions of an important group of plays, those for which there exist, besides the text in the First Folio, one or more versions in Quarto form.

GREG, W.W.
The Editorial Problem in Shakespeare: A Survey of the Foundations of the Text
Oxford, 1962. 210pp. $3.95. A third edition, with some corrections, of the six lectures delivered in 1939, in which the author summarizes our present knowledge regarding the bibliographical foundations of the texts of the plays. The essay, "On Editing Shakespeare," analyzes editorial principles along the lines begun by R. B. McKerro in his "Prolegomena for the Oxford Shakespeare." Index.

GREG, W.W.
The Shakespeare First Folio: Its Biographical and Textual History
Oxford, 1955. 496pp. $11.00. This study, planned as an introduction to a facsimile edition of the Folio, discusses the planning of the collection, the question of copyright, and the major editorial problems. There are considerations of the special problems of each play and a study of the actual mechanics of printing.

HINMAN, CHARLTON
The Printing and Proofreading of the First Folio of Shakespeare
Oxford, 1963. Volume One: 507pp. Volume Two: 560pp. $26.75. A systematic reconstruction of the printing of the first Folio in which the author, by detailed bibliographical analysis, shows how and when the various parts of the book were set and the way textual integrity was affected during the printing. The author maintains that changes must be made in current notions about the worth of the Folio text. Sold as a two volume set.

HONIGMAN, E.A.J.
The Stability of Shakespeare's Text
University of Nebraska, 1965. 212pp. $5.50. A study of the problem of a "final text" of the plays which examines the bibliographical background since Shakespeare's time, describing certain celebrated editorial problems and commenting on recent editors and editions. Index.

NICOLL, ALLARDYCE
Co-operation in Shakespearean Scholarship
Oxford, 1952. 18pp. Paper $1.00. A brief discussion of the problems facing scholars in the field of editing, with a suggestion that there be some general collaboration in the production of a new, definitive text.

POLLARD, ALFRED W.
Shakespeare Folios and Quartos
Cooper Square, 1970. 176pp. $11.50. A study in the bibliography of Shakespeare's plays, 1594–1685. The author presents the nature of the existing editions of Shakespeariana. The conditions of publishing in Shakespeare's day are studied in an introductory chapter. Illustrated with facsimiles of pages from the various editions. Appendices. Index.

SIMPSON, PERCY
Shakespearean Punctuation
Oxford, 1969. 107pp. $6.50. Originally published in 1911 and now reissued, after being long out of print, in a facsimile edition. The author attempts to prove there was a system of punctuation used by the early printers of Shakespeare's plays.

WALKER, ALICE
Textual Problems of the First Folio: Richard III, King Lear, Troilus and Cressida, 2 Henry IV, Hamlet, Othello
Cambridge, 1953. 170pp. $6.00. The author contends that Heminge and Condell provided the printer with playhouse manuscripts which were then corrected by collation with Quartos. Among problems discussed are: how many errors did the collator overlook, how can the present-day editor detect and amend them, how far can the compositor be taken to have reproduced his copy. Bibliography. Index.

WILSON, F.P.
Shakespeare and the New Bibliography
Oxford, 1970. 136pp. $6.95. Originally published in 1942, corrected and revised in 1948, and now reissued as revised and edited by Helen Gardner, this is a survey of the range of problems presented by the text of

Shakespeare. The author sums up the achievements of the school of bibliographical critics founded by Pollard, McKerrow, and Greg. Miss Gardner provides supplementary notes on the developments of the last twenty years. Index.

SHAKESPEARE'S CRAFTSMANSHIP

Shakespearean Techniques

ANDERSON, RUTH LEILA
Elizabethan Psychology and Shakespeare's Plays
Russell & Russell, 1966. 182pp. $7.50. A reprint of the 1927 edition. The author seeks to prove that Shakespeare was familiar with the psychological thinking of his age and that he made use of aspects of this thinking in his plays. Bibliography. Index.

ARMSTRONG, EDWARD A.
Shakespeare's Imagination: A Study of the Psychology of Association and Inspiration
University of Nebraska, 1963. 230pp. Paper $1.60. This is a revised edition of the 1946 analysis of the linked images in the plays and of what these "image clusters" tell us about the mentality of the playwright. The author contends that his method of cluster criticism can provide additional proof to authenticate doubtful works, especially "The Two Noble Kinsmen."

AUCHINCLOSS, LOUIS
Motiveless Malignity
Houghton, Mifflin, 1969. 158pp. $5.00. This is a personal commentary on the works of Shakespeare by the distinguished American novelist. The author studies Shakespeare's main characters not only as archetypal figures but also as characters created to beguile an audience. The apparent lack of motivation in the characters, Mr. Auchincloss believes, is a reflection of Shakespeare's sense of the perverse and irrational in human nature. The author also finds a new interpretation of the "Sonnets" and compares the plays of Shakespeare and Racine.

BALDWIN, T.W.
Shakespeare's Five-Act Structure: Shakespeare's Early Plays on the Background of Renaissance Theories of Five-Act Structure from 1470
University of Illinois, 1963. 848pp. $10.00. First published in 1947 and now reissued, this is a study of the concepts of five-act division in plays from earliest recorded times to Shakespeare's days. The author concludes that the early plays should be redated on the basis of an understanding of Shakespeare's relation to and reactions to the theories of act-division. Index.

BALDWIN, T.W.
William Shakespeare's Small Latine & Lesse Greeke
University of Illinois, 1956. Volume One: 753pp. Volume Two: 772pp. $12.50 A reprint of the edition first published in 1944, this is an investigation into Shakespeare's formal education and its influence on his work. Included is a history of the Stratford schools, the texts used, and the Latin curriculum of the Lower School. Volume Two covers the Uppper School, its rhetorical training, prose and verse composition, the study of the Latin poets, moral and history training, and the Greek curriculum. Sold as a two volume set.

BRADBROOK, M.C.
Shakespeare and Elizabethan Poetry
Chatto & Windus, 1961. 279pp. $4.25. Paper—Penguin, 1964. 254pp. $1.95. A reprint of the original edition of 1951. In this study the author seeks to relate Shakespeare's work to the poetry, critical works, and social attitudes of his age. The influence of medieval, classical, and popular literature and drama on the playwright is considered and there are examinations of a number of the plays. Notes. Index.

BRADBROOK, M.C.
Shakespeare, the Craftsman
Chatto & Windus, 1969. 187pp. $5.50. Miss Bradbrook's work traces the descent from the medieval tradition of Shakespeare's plays, shown to be written in response to some immediate demand such as a new actor, a new stage, or some other specific occasion. Illustrated. Notes. Index.

BULLOUGH, GEOFFREY
Shakespeare the Elizabethan
Oxford, 1964. 21pp. Paper $1.00. Mr. Bullough seeks to prove that Shakespeare embodied the spirit, mores, current beliefs, prejudices, and attitudes of his times.

CLARKE, CHARLES and MARY COWDEN CLARKE
The Shakespeare Key
Ungar, 1961. Two volumes: 810pp. $15.00. Originally published in 1879 and now reissued, this is an alphabetical arrangement of passages, with descriptive commentary, illustrating a number of facets of Shakespeare's style in language and in the composition of scenes and creation of characters. Sold as a two volume set.

CLEMEN, WOLFGANG
The Development of Shakespeare's Imagery
Harvard, 1951. 235pp. $6.00. Paper—Hill & Wang, 1962. 235pp. $1.45. The first survey of the imagery considered as an integral part of the development of Shakespeare's dramatic art. The author shows the progessive stages in the use of imagery and relates it to the structure, style, and subject matter of each play. Preface by J. Dover Wilson.

CLEMEN, WOLFGANG
Past and Future in Shakespeare's Drama
Oxford, 1966. 24pp. Paper $1.50. The annual Shake-

speare Lecture of the British Academy. The author analyzes Shakespeare's use of the past and the future in his plays.

CLEMEN, WOLFGANG
Shakespeare's Soliloquies
Folcroft, 1964. 27pp. Paper $5.25. In this brief pamphlet the author considers the great variety of soliloquies, shows how Shakespeare used them in a manner unlike other dramatists, and illustrates how they are made dramatically effective in the plays.

COGHILL, NEVILL
Shakespeare's Professional Skills
Cambridge, 1964. 224pp. $7.50. A study of Shakespeare's creative imagination and of the ways his sense of dramatic necessity directed his writing. The use of the soliloquy and the juxtaposition of scenes are studied in detail. Special emphasis is placed on "Hamlet," "Troilus and Cressida," "Othello," and "A Midsummer Night's Dream." A comparison is made of the Quarto (1622) and the First Folio versions of "Othello" to show how the playwright made revisions after the first performance.

COX, ROGER L.
Between Earth and Heaven: Shakespeare, Dostoevsky and the Meaning of Christian Tragedy
Holt, Rinehart, 1969. 252pp. $5.95. Professor Cox analyzes the Gospel narratives of the Passion as tragedy, making use of Freudian doctrine, in an attempt to throw fresh light on the major works of both Shakespeare and Dostoevsky. He contends that both writers derived many of their symbols and motifs from the Bible. Notes. Bibliography.

CRANE, MILTON
Shakespeare's Prose
University of Chicago, 1963. 220pp. Paper $1.50. In this reprint of the 1951 edition, Milton Crane analyzes the plays to show how Shakespeare used prose for dramatic contrast with verse and thus made conflict command the language of the plays. Appendices. Notes. Bibliography. Index.

CRUTTWELL, PATRICK
The Shakespearean Moment and Its Place in the Poetry of the Seventeenth Century
Random House, 1960. 244pp. Paper $1.45. Originally published in 1955 and now reissued, this is a study of the poetic revolution, headed by Shakespeare and Donne, which began in the 1590's. The author shows that this new language came out of a spirit of disillusionment, irony, and disrespect and was finally ended when the Puritan doctrine of predestination obliterated the tragic view of life and destroyed the poetic form.

DRIVER, TOM F.
The Sense of History in Greek and Shakespearean Drama
See Page 33

EDWARDS, PHILIP
Person and Office in Shakespeare's Plays
Oxford, 1970. 19pp. Paper $1.40. The annual Shakespeare Lecture of the British Academy. The nature of the individual and his relation with society are discussed.

EDWARDS, PHILIP
Shakespeare and the Confines of Art
Barnes & Noble, 1968. 170pp. $5.50. Professor Edwards attempts to see Shakespeare's work as a whole and to explain why his art developed as it did. By means of a selective study of certain of the comedies, tragedies, and Sonnets, the author suggests that Shakespeare was striving to create a fusion of comedy and tragedy. Index. Notes.

ELLIS–FERMOR, UNA and KENNETH MUIR
Shakespeare the Dramatist
Barnes & Noble, 1961. 188pp. $5.50. Kenneth Muir has collected and edited the unfinished book on Shakespeare and three other articles left uncollected at the time of Miss Ellis-Fermor's death. The work discusses Shakespeare's methods with regard to plot, diction, character, and imagery. There are comparisons of Shakespeare with Ibsen, and Corneille. Mr. Muir has written an appreciation of the author, an outline of the unfinished book, and a list of her writings.

EVANS, B. IFOR
The Language of Shakespeare's Plays: Third Edition
Methuen, 1964. 216pp. $6.00. Paper $2.95. A study of the function of verse in drama and of the developing way in which Shakespeare controlled the rhetorical and decorative elements of speech and language for dramatic purposes. For this edition a complete reassessment of the history plays has been made. Index.

FLUCHERE, HENRI
Shakespeare and the Elizabethans
Hill & Wang, 1956. 254pp. Paper $1.35. A conspectus of the drama as a whole with a special emphasis placed on the techniques of language and dramatic structure. Foreword by T. S. Eliot.

FRYE, ROLAND MUSHAT
Shakespeare and Christian Doctrine
Princeton, 1965. 314pp. Paper $2.95. In this reprint of the 1963 edition, the author maintains that Shakespeare's works are pervasively secular and that he used theological sources as he did any other. Mr. Frye presents the arguments for both secular and religious interpretation, deals with the major figures of sixteenth century religious thought, and provides a glossary of the theological terms used by Shakespeare.

GESNER, CAROL
Shakespeare and the Greek Romance: A Study of Origins

University Press of Kentucky, 1970. 216pp. $9.25. Greek romances are related to Elizabethan drama in this study. What is known of the Greek romance materials in Shakespeare's plays is collected in order to clarify some of the backgrounds of the playwright's composite art. Miss Gesner describes the Greek romance tradition as it may be observed historically and in Continental and English writings embodying such traditions. A bibliographic survey is also included. Notes. Bibliography. Index.

GOLDSMITH, ROBERT HILLIS
Wise Fools in Shakespeare
Michigan State University, 1955. 123pp. $5.50. A study of the popular and literary traditions of the wise Fool. Shakespeare's four Fools—Touchstone, Lavache, Feste, and Lear's Fool—are studied in detail and the characteristics that distinguish them are analyzed.

HALLIDAY, F.E.
The Poetry of Shakespeare's Plays
Barnes & Noble, 1964. 194pp. $4.25. Paper $1.50. This study of the poetry of the five major periods examines the words themselves, their rhythmical relationships, and the use of metaphor and imagery.

HARBAGE, ALFRED
As They Liked It
Peter Smith, 1947. 234pp. $4.25. An investigation into the effects the dramatist attained by confronting his audience with moral issues. The indirection of his moral presentation is stressed.

HARRISON, G.B.
Shakespeare at Work
University of Michigan, 1958. 325pp. Paper $1.95. A study of Shakespeare against the background of his time, his theatre, and the development of the drama. Attention is paid to his dramatic development during the years 1592–1603.

HOLLAND, NORMAN N.
The Shakespearean Imagination
Macmillan, 1964. 338pp. $7.50. Paper – Indiana University, 1968. 338pp. $2.95. Based on the author's television course, this study begins with a summary of the facts of the life of Shakespeare and discusses the influence of the age and the theatre on his works. Such basic issues are considered as how to read a play, why one play is better than another, great themes and symbols in the plays and their evolution, and the characters as living people. Thirteen plays are considered in detail. Illustrated. Index.

HOWSE, ERNEST MARSHALL
Spiritual Values in Shakespeare
Abingdon, 1955. 158pp. Paper $1.25. A study of "Hamlet," "Othello," "Macbeth," "King Lear," "Richard III," "Julius Caesar," "The Merchant of Venice," and "The Tempest." The moral problem which each play dramatizes is discussed in detail.

HULME, HILDA M.
Explorations in Shakespeare's Language: Some Problems of Lexical Meaning in the Dramatic Text
Barnes & Noble, 1963. 352pp. $7.00. This study of the language Shakespeare used gives special attention to the recognition of "quotation fragments" from the spoken language of his day: splinters of proverb idiom, oblique allusions within the half-secret less decent vocabulary of the time, and the Latin reference carried by English words. Bibliography. Index.

JOSEPH, SISTER MIRIAM
Shakespeare's Use of the Arts of Language
Hafner, 1966. 423pp. Paper $3.75. Originally published in 1947 and now reissued, this volume is intended to show how Shakespeare used the Renaissance theory of composition. Bibliography. Index.

KELLY, HENRY ANSGAR
Divine Providence in the England of Shakespeare's Histories
Harvard, 1970. 344pp. $13.50. The author's purpose is to study the processes involved in the supernatural references that appear in the historical treatments of the period covered by Shakespeare's double tetralogy (1398–1485). Professor Kelly analyzes and evaluates the use that Shakespeare himself made of this aspect of the historical writings of his day. He suggests that each of Shakespeare's history plays created its own ethos and mythos to eliminate the suportedly objective judgements of his sources and present such judgements as the opinions of the persons voicing them. Appendices. Bibliography. Index.

KENNEDY, MILTON BOONE
The Oration in Shakespeare
University of North Carolina, 1942. 270pp. $3.75. A study of Shakespeare's use of sophistic rhetoric which classifies and traces the origins of the rhetorical patterns in the orations and shows how they are integrated into the plays. Elizabethan oratory in general and school teaching of oratory are also examined. Bibliography. Index.

KIRSHBAUM, LEO
Character and Characterization in Shakespeare
Wayne State University, 1962. 168pp. Paper $2.25. The essays in this volume are concerned with some of the more puzzling persons in a number of plays, with special attention focused on their particular dramatic function.

KNIGHT, G. WILSON
The Shakespearian Tempest: With a Chart of Shakespeare's Dramatic Universe
Barnes & Noble, 1963. 332pp. $9.00. A revised, third edition of Mr. Knight's Shakespearean studies. The central symbols of tempest and music are traced

through the poems and the plays. The "chart" gives Shakespeare's various value and symbolic powers, and sums up Mr. Knight's work on the poet.

LANIER, SIDNEY
Shakespeare and His Forerunners
Johns Hopkins, 1945. 419pp. $12.50. A series of lectures given at the Peabody Institute in Baltimore and at Johns Hopkins University in 1878 and 1879. The Peabody Lectures present "the influence of Shakespeare's time on him and then of his influence on us." The Hopkins Lectures deal with English verse, especially Shakespeare's.

LEWIS, WYNDHAM
The Lion and the Fox
Barnes & Noble, Undated. 326pp. Paper $2.50. Originally published in 1927, this is a study of aspects of the heroic role in some of Shakespeare's plays. The author examines the political, historical, intellectual and social conditions in which Shakespeare's personality grew and traces these ideas to the literature of the European Renaissance.

MAHOOD, M.M.
Shakespeare's Wordplay
Barnes & Noble, 1957. 192pp. $6.00. Paper—Methuen, 1968. 192pp. $2.25. This is an analysis of the varied dramatic functions of the Shakespearean pun: the fusion of images which it achieves, its part in the revelation of character, its power to bring out the governing idea of each play. Index.

MOULTON, RICHARD G.
Shakespeare as a Dramatic Artist
Dover, 1966. 443pp. Paper $2.50. Professor Moulton deals with the plot structure of Shakespeare's plays. He analyzes several of the plays and discusses Shakespeare's skill at dramatic composition. Subject Index. Index of Scenes. Appendix.

MUIR, KENNETH
Shakespeare as Collaborator
Barnes & Noble, 1960. 164pp. $4.25. An analysis of the extent of Shakespeare's collaboration on "Edward III," "The Two Noble Kinsmen," "Pericles," and the lost "Cardenio." The author detects imagery and image clusters in each of these plays that go far to establish the presence of Shakespeare's hand.

MUIR, KENNETH—Editor
Shakespeare Survey #23
See Page 47

O'CONNOR, FRANK
Shakespeare's Progress
Collier, 1961. 192pp. Paper $1.50. A reprint of the 1960 study of the development of Shakespeare's genius. The author uses the poems and sonnets to develop theories about the authorship of the plays and suggests that Shakespeare did write "Edward III."

PARTRIDGE, A.C.
Orthography in Shakespeare and Elizabethan Drama
University of Nebraska, 1964. 200pp. $4.75. After an introduction on Shakespeare's orthography, there are three chapters on colloquial contractions in drama before 1600, based on a study of three manuscript plays: "John a Kent," "Thomas of Woodstock," and "Sir Thomas Moore." Shakespeare's orthography in the early quartos is studied and the editorial revisions and corruptions of the First Folio texts are examined in detail.

PARTRIDGE, ERIC
Shakespeare's Bawdy
Dutton, 1969. 223pp. Paper $1.75. A revised edition of the study first published in 1948. It is a documented examination of Shakespeare's sexual allusions from the literary, psychological, and lexicographical standpoints.

RABKIN, NORMAN
Shakespeare and the Common Understanding
Macmillan, 1967. 267pp. $6.95. Professor Rabkin provides a new conceptual framework for understanding Shakespeare's art. It defines Shakespeare's way of seeing as complementary—an approach to experience in which opposed commitments to the meaning of life coexist in a single harmonious vision. Index.

RIGHTER, ANNE
Shakespeare and the Idea of the Play
Barnes & Noble, 1962. 224pp. $6.50. Paper—Penguin, 1967. 200pp. $1.65. A study of the changing relation between actor and audience and the playwright's changing ideas of what the relation should be. Investigating Shakespeare's plays, the author analyzes the parody of participation, the vice of the morality plays, and the world as theatre in the plays. Index.

SCHUCKING, LEVIN L.
Character Problems in Shakespeare's Plays: A Guide to Better Understanding of the Dramatist
Peter Smith, 1959. 270pp. $5.75. A reprint of the 1922 edition, this is a study of character, expression, and action in the plays which emphasizes the influence on Shakespeare of contemporary ideas of psychology and conditions of acting, producing, and playwriting.

SEWELL, ARTHUR
Character and Society in Shakespeare
Oxford, 1951. 149pp. $4.50. A study of character creation in the plays from a moral, rather than a psychological, viewpoint. Character is seen as part of a creation of society.

SIMS, JAMES H.
Dramatic Uses of Biblical Allusions in Marlowe and Shakespeare
University of Florida, 1966. 82pp. Paper $2.00. A

monograph in which the author intends to show the many ways in which Marlowe and Shakespeare, in particular, used their audience's knowledge of the Bible to add depth and breadth to the characterizations in their plays. Bibliography.

SIPE, DOROTHY L.
Shakespeare's Metrics
Yale, 1968. 266pp. $11.50. Analysis of more than 13,000 lines of dramatic poetry provides evidence that Shakespeare's word choice was consistent with the accepted practices of his age and that he regularly wrote carefully constructed iambic verse with only minor variations. The important stylistic, phonological, and lexical implications of Shakespeare's adherence to iambic prosody conclude the study.

SMITH, ROBERT METCALF
Froissart and the English Chronicle Play
See Page 150

STEVENSON, DAVID
The Meditations of William Shakespeare
Vantage, 1965. 264pp. $3.95. The author shows that through the medium of anagrams Shakespeare has left the world a legacy of his private opinions. Posterity can discover these critical views of Elizabeth in the "Sonnets" where the poet hid his unkind views from the censors.

STYAN, J. L.
Shakespeare's Stagecraft
Cambridge, 1967. 244pp. $7.95. Paper $2.45. This is an introduction to the study of Shakespeare's dramatic craftsmanship in which Professor Styan stresses his opinion that the plays were written for acting in a theatre of a particular type. The plays are seen as a sequence of stage-effects, planned with great art to enrich, reinforce, and modify each other. Selected Bibliography. Index of Scenes, Proper Names, and Subjects.

TALBERT, ERNEST WILLIAM
The Problem of Order
University of North Carolina, 1962. 244pp. $7.25. Dr. Talbert's book begins with a discussion of the Elizabethan belief in kingship and the necessity for degree and order in the body politic. He studies "Richard II" and demonstrates how Shakespeare utilized current concepts and representational methods to interpret an important aspect of the political thought of the day and still escape censorship. Index.

THORNDIKE, ASHLEY H.
The Influence of Beaumont and Fletcher on Shakespeare
Russell & Russell, 1965. 176pp. $7.50. First published in 1901 and now reissued, this study presents a brief theatrical history of the period when the careers of the three dramatists came into contact. There are detailed discussions of "Henry VIII," "The Two Noble Kinsmen," "Cymbeline," "Philaster," "A Winter's Tale," and "The Tempest."

TRAVERSI, DEREK
An Approach to Shakespeare
Doubleday, 1956. 304pp. Paper $1.25. Through an examination of recurring words, phrases, and images, from the earliest to the last works, the author shows the gradual formation of a symbolic pattern which controls the development of character and action and provides a unity to the plays.

VAN DOREN, MARK
Shakespeare
Doubleday, 1949. 302pp. Paper $1.25. A study of dramatic technique, illustrated with passages from all the plays.

VICKERS, BRIAN
The Artistry of Shakespeare's Prose
Methuen, 1968. 452pp. $10.00. This is a detailed study of Shakespeare's use of prose in the plays. It begins by defining the different functions which Shakespeare gave to prose and verse and proceeds to analyze the recurrent stylistic devices in his prose. The general and particular application of prose is studied through all the plays in chronological order. Index.

VYVYAN, JOHN
The Shakespearean Ethic
Barnes & Noble, 1968. 208pp. $5.50. A reprint of the study first published in 1959. Mr. Vyvyan offers the viewpoint that Shakespeare was never ethically neutral and was deeply concerned with the idea of creative mercy. He shows the pattern of regeneration or damnation by pairing certain plays such as "Hamlet" and "Measure for Measure" and "Othello" and "The Winter's Tale." Index.

WEST, ROBERT H.
Shakespeare and the Outer Mystery
University of Kentucky, 1968. 205pp. $6.50. Mr. West explores the philosophical and supernatural elements in five Shakespearean dramas. He considers such questions as whether the plays are Christian, existential, optimistic, pessimistic, tragic, or absurd. The author concludes that Shakespeare used philosophy and morality to create a dramatic effect rather than to teach a moral or ideological lesson. Notes. Index.

WHITAKER, VIRGIL K.
The Mirror Up to Nature: The Technique of Shakespeare's Tragedies
Huntington Library, 1965. 332pp. $7.50. Emphasizing the need for interpreting Shakespeare's tragedies in traditional Christian terms, Professor Whitaker shows how the dramatist squared his plays with his moral and philosophic assumptions, relating particular action to universal principles of conduct. Index.

WHITAKER, VIRGIL K.
Shakespeare's Use of Learning: An Inquiry into the Growth of His Mind and Art
Huntington Library, 1953. 366pp. $7.50. A study of the playwright's acquisition and use of contemporary history, science, and philosophy. The plays are used to illustrate the author's contention that Shakespeare's genius as a playwright developed as his learning deepened.

WICKHAM, GLYNNE
Shakespeare's Dramatic Heritage
Routledge & Kegan Paul, 1969. 277pp. $8.50. Professor Wickham examines the religious drama of the Middle Ages in terms of dramatic literature as well as in terms of theatres, stages, and production conventions. He appraises the origins and development of drama as an art form within the liturgies of the Catholic Church and suggests that this drama and its structural patterns, characters, and stage conventions made a deep impression on the minds of Elizabethan playmakers. The use Shakespeare and his contemporaries made of these traditional and popular models is examined. Illustrated. Index.

Shakespearean Themes

BLOOM, ALLAN and HARRY V. JAFFA
Shakespeare's Politics
Basic Books, 1964. 150pp. $5.95. This study states that Shakespeare saw human problems largely in political terms. The author examines "The Merchant of Venice," "Othello," "Julius Caesar," and "King Lear," as examples of Shakespeare's political wisdom and understanding.

BRYANT, JOSEPH A.
Hippolyta's View: Some Christian Aspects of Shakespeare's Plays
University of Kentucky, 1960. 239pp. $6.50. An analysis of major plays in which the author contends Shakespeare presents a Christian view of life. Christian allusions and themes, especially the analagous relation between poetic and divine creativity are studied in "The Winter's Tale," "Cymbeline," "Antony and Cleopatra," "Macbeth," "Othello," "Hamlet," "Measure for Measure," and "Richard II."

BURCKHARDT, SIGURD
Shakespearean Meanings
Princeton, 1968. 317pp. $9.00. In this analysis of the language of Shakespeare's plays, the author does not discuss the plays as theatre but seeks to discover what Shakespeare meant. He extends his readings of the plays to the themes and meanings which he believes were crucial to Shakespeare in all that he wrote. Index.

BUSH, GEOFFREY
Shakespeare and the Natural Condition
Harvard, 1956. 135pp. $3.75. Lectures on Shakespeare's attitude toward nature in the plays, with special reference to "Hamlet," and "King Lear."

CUTTS, JOHN P.
The Shattered Glass: A Dramatic Pattern in Shakespeare's Early Plays
Wayne State University, 1968. 154pp. $5.95. This is an interpretive study of Shakespeare's early plays as structural units setting up their own terms, imagery, symbols, and criteria for criticism. Professor Cutts, in thirteen essays, traces the emergence of a shattered glass pattern by concentrating on mirror imagery, substance and shadow, and fragmentation and synthesis.

DRIVER, TOM F.
The Sense of History in Greek and Shakespearean Drama
See Page 33

EAGLETON, TERENCE
Shakespeare and Society: Critical Studies in Shakespearean Drama
Schocken, 1967. 208pp. $5.50. A critical study of Shakespeare's tragedies, problem plays, and late comedies which sets out to examine the relationship between man and society as Shakespeare conceived it. Separate chapters deal with "Troilus and Cressida," "Hamlet," "Measure for Measure," "Coriolanus," "Antony and Cleopatra," "Macbeth," "The Winter's Tale," "Timon of Athens," and "The Tempest."

FALCONER, ALEXANDER FREDERICK
Shakespeare and the Sea
Constable, 1964. 164pp. $6.95. This study examines the extent and accuracy of the playwright's knowledge of the sea and ships, nautical terms and naval customs. Special attention is paid to "Othello," "Hamlet," and "Antony and Cleopatra."

JAMESON, THOMAS H.
The Hidden Shakespeare
Funk & Wagnalls, 1967. 168pp. $4.95. Paper—1969. $2.95. Mr. Jameson contends that Shakespeare was a rebel against the tyranny of the Tudor establishment, that the poet's critical commentary on his times was subtle and masked but was present in his plays, particularly in "Henry V," despite the banning of books, the deleting of passages from plays, and the closing of the theatres. Index.

KAISER, WALTER
Praisers of Folly: Erasmus, Shakespeare, Rabelais
Harvard, 1963. 318pp. $10.00. Detailed analyses of three Fools—Erasmus' Stultitia, Rabelais' Panurge, and Shakespeare's Falstaff. The book examines certain trends of thought characteristic of the late

Renaissance and shows how writers reassessed the potentials of human nature. The proposition was advanced that the highest form of wisdom was a kind of folly or ignorance. Don Quixote is studied as the character who brought this trend to a close.

KAUFMANN, WALTER
From Shakespeare to Existentialism
Doubleday, 1960. 454pp. Paper $1.45. A study of the origins and development of existentialism and its relation to drama, poetry and religion. Chapters on Shakespeare, Goethe, Hegel, Kierkegaard, Nietzsche, Rilke, Freud, Jaspers, Heidegger, and Toynbee.

KEETON, GEORGE W.
Shakespeare's Legal and Political Background
Pitman, 1967. 417pp. $12.50. The author attempts to analyze the manner in which Shakespeare employed the language and content of the law in his plays and the connection between his treatment of legal problems and his treatment of legal ideas. Illustrated. Selected Bibliography. Index.

KNIGHT, G. WILSON
Shakespeare and Religion
Routledge & Kegan Paul, 1967. 374pp. $9.00. Paper —Simon & Schuster, 1968. 374pp. $2.95. This collection of essays is concerned primarily with the main elements of Shakespeare's spiritual content, the exploration of a truth beyond tragedy and death in the plays of his final period. Professor Knight argues that Shakespeare adds to the Christian tradition a visionary humanism. Index.

KNIGHTS, L.C.
Some Shakespearean Themes and An Approach to Hamlet
Stanford, 1966. 259pp. $6.75. Paper $2.95. In a series of essays, Mr. Knights traces the emergence and development of the major themes of the plays of Shakespeare's maturity. In "An Approach to Hamlet," Mr. Knights continues his analysis of the major themes of "Hamlet."

MATTHEWS, HONOR
Character and Symbol in Shakespeare's Plays
Chatto & Windus, 1969. 211pp. $7.50. A new edition of the study first published in 1962. Miss Matthews is concerned with certain elements of popular belief, both Christian and pagan, which were current in Elizabethan England and are reflected in Shakespeare's plays. She uses illustrations from the plays to show the hold this traditional material held over the imagination of the playwright. Index.

MENDL, R.W.S.
Revelation in Shakespeare
Calder, 1964. 223pp. $7.00. Paper $3.95. A study of the supernatural, religious, and spiritual elements in Shakespeare's art. In considering the subject from various elements, the author investigates ghosts, apparitions, or witchcraft which have a religious association; the avowedly religious elements, including the parts played by clerics, and prayers; and the ethical conceptions underlying the plays as a whole. Index.

PALMER, JOHN
Political and Comic Characters of Shakespeare
Macmillan, 1962. 483pp. Paper $5.50. A one-volume collection of two series of essays: the 1945 study of Brutus, Richard of Gloucester, Richard of Bordeaux, Henry of Monmouth, and Coriolanus; and the 1946 study of Berowne, Touchstone, Shylock, Bottom, Beatrice, and Benedick. Shakespeare's attitudes toward public figures and toward the craft of statesmanship is analyzed and his theories of the comic in human nature are examined.

SISSON, C.J.
Shakespeare's Tragic Justice
Methuen, 1963. 106pp. $4.50. A study of Shakespeare's treatment of one of the central problems of the sixteenth and seventeenth centuries. The book examines "King Lear," "Macbeth," "Othello," and "Hamlet," and shows how the final solution is obtained in "King Lear."

SMITH, MARION BODWELL
Dualities in Shakespeare
University of Toronto, 1966. 252pp. $6.50. The author discusses the contemporary climate of opinion in regard to the paradoxes of the human condition and the development of Shakespeare's attitudes towards them. Subsequent chapters discuss the ways in which concepts of duality operate in particular works. Index.

STAUFFER, DONALD A.
Shakespeare's World of Images: The Development of His Moral Ideas
Indiana University, 1966. 393pp. Paper $2.95. An analysis of the moral ideas of Shakespeare as revealed in the plays. The author analyzes the choice of subjects, modifications of sources, individual character studies, and many other subjects to show that Shakespeare's ultimate view of morality was a complex one based upon imagination as the prime source of man's moral action. Notes. Index.

STEVENSON, ROBERT
Shakespeare's Religious Frontier
Humanities, 1958. 97pp. Paper $2.75. A brief survey of Shakespeare's treatment of the clergy. Other essays on various subjects are included.

STIRLING, BRENTS
The Populace in Shakespeare
AMS Press, 1965. 203pp. $12.00. Originally published in 1949 and now reprinted, this is a study of Shakespeare as a historian of his age. The author analyzes Shakespeare's use of politics and the social conditions of the people of his time.

STOLL, ELMER EDGAR
Shakespeare Studies: Historical and Comparative in Method
Ungar, 1960. 502pp. $7.50. A reprint of the second edition of 1942 with additional corrections, this study is concerned with Shakespeare's themes, how he differed from other dramatists in presenting them, and how he made use of contemporary ideas and stage conventions. Among the items considered are how he achieved his comic effects, his attitude toward Jews, his ghosts and criminals, and his intention in the characterization of Falstaff.

STOLL, ELMER EDGAR
Shakespeare's Young Lovers
A. M. S. Press, 1966. 118pp. $10.75. Originally presented as a series of lectures at the University of Toronto in 1935 and now revised and issued in book form. The author discusses "Romeo and Juliet," the maidens of Shakespeare's prime, and the maidens in the dramatic romances.

TALBERT, ERNEST WILLIAM
The Problem of Order: Elizabethan Political Commonplaces and an Example of Shakespeare's Art
University of North Carolina, 1962. 244pp. $7.25. A study of the appearances and some of the contexts of political ideas current in Elizabethan England. The influence of Sir Thomas Smith, Richard Hooker, and Sir Philip Sidney on political thought is considered. Samuel Daniel's defense of his "Philotas" and Shakespeare's treatment of the deposition in "Richard II" are also examined.

WATKINS, W. B. C.
Shakespeare and Spenser
Princeton, 1966. 339pp. Paper $2.95. This work explores the themes and techniques which Shakespeare and Spenser had in common: the interdependence of the physical and the spiritual, the instability of human life, the nature of allegory, and the craft of language. Index.

WATSON, CURTIS BROWN
Shakespeare and the Renaissance Concept of Honor
Princeton, 1960. 471pp. $8.50. A study of the moral crisis that developed in the sixteenth century when the Christian influences of the Middle Ages clashed with the pagan moral philosophy that had been rediscovered in the Renaissance. This ambivalence in values is especially reflected in Shakespeare's treatment of honor.

WEST, ROBERT H.
Shakespeare and the Outer Mystery
University of Kentucky, 1968. 205pp. $6.50. Mr. West explores the philosophical and supernatural elements in five Shakespearean dramas: "Macbeth," "Hamlet," "Othello," "King Lear," and "The Tempest." He considers such questions as whether the plays are Christian, existential, optimistic, tragic, or absurd. He contends that Shakespeare used the philosophical and supernatural elements to create a dramatic effect rather than to teach a moral lesson. Notes. Index.

Shakespearean Sources

BOSWELL–STONE, W. G.
Shakespeare's Holinshed: The Chronicle and the Plays Compared
Dover, 1968. 532pp. Paper $2.95. In this reprint of the edition originally printed in 1907, Mr. Boswell-Stone has assembled everything in Holinshed that Shakespeare used, arranged it according to Shakespearean play, annotated it, and provided cross references to other works. Index.

BULLOUGH, GEOFFREY – Editor
Narrative and Dramatic Sources of Shakespeare – Volume One: Early Comedies
Columbia, 1957. 532pp. $13.50. The major sources used by Shakespeare for his plots and characters, along with works he might have consulted without directly borrowing from them. In an introduction to each play an attempt is made to suggest how Shakespeare treated the given sources, the date of his work, and the circumstances of its conception. This volume contains the sources for the early comedies, the poems, and "Romeo and Juliet."

BULLOUGH, GEOFFREY – Editor
Narrative and Dramatic Sources of Shakespeare – Volume Two: Comedies
Columbia, 1958. 543pp. $12.50. This volume provides the sources of the comedies from 1597–1603. Bibliography. Index.

BULLOUGH, GEOFFREY – Editor
Narrative and Dramatic Sources of Shakespeare – Volume Three: The Earlier English History Plays
Columbia, 1958. 512pp. $12.50. This volume contains the sources for the earlier English history plays, "Henry V," "Richard III," and "Richard II." Chronological Table. Bibliography. Index to the Introductions.

BULLOUGH, GEOFFREY – Editor
Narrative and Dramatic Sources of Shakespeare – Volume Four: Later English History Plays
Columbia, 1962. 534pp. $12.50. The fourth volume in the series contains the sources for "King John," "Henry IV," "Henry V," and "Henry VIII." Genealogical Table. Chronological Table. Bibliography. Index to the Introductions.

BULLOUGH, GEOFFREY – Editor
Narrative and Dramatic Sources of Shakespeare – Volume Five: The Roman Plays
Columbia, 1964. 577pp. $12.50. The sources and analogues for the Roman plays: "Julius Caesar,"

"Antony and Cleopatra," and "Coriolanus." Bibliography. Index to the Introductions.

BULLOUGH, GEOFFREY – Editor
Narrative and Dramatic Sources of Shakespeare – Volume Six: Other Classical Plays
Columbia, 1966. 578pp. $12.50. The main sources and analogues of "Titus Andronicus," "Troilus and Cressida," "Timon of Athens," and "Pericles." Appendix. Bibliography. Index to the Introductions.

GRIFFIN, ALICE – Editor
The Sources of Ten Shakespearean Plays
Crowell, 1966. 312pp. Paper $3.50. The author includes the texts of the prose and play sources of ten of Shakespeare's plays. Her aim is to assist the college student in the preparation of term papers on comparative studies of the plays and their sources. Study notes and "Topics for Research Papers" are included.

HAZLITT, W. CAREW – Editor
Shakespeare Jest–Books
Franklin, 1967. Volume I: 162pp. Volume II: 367pp. Volume III: 519pp. $35.00. First published in 1864, this is a reprint of the early and very rare jest-books supposed to have been used by Shakespeare. It is a collection of folk and humorous tales from the fifteenth, sixteenth, and seventeenth centuries. Sold as a three volume set.

HOSLEY, RICHARD
Shakespeare's Holinshed
Putnam, 1968. 346pp. $7.50. Paper $2.45. The "Chronicles of Holinshed" is an annotated modern edition covering all the material pertinent to a study of Shakespeare's plays. Glosses. Notes. Maps. Chronologies. Genealogies. Bibliography.

MUIR, KENNETH
Shakespeare's Sources – Volume One: Comedies and Tragedies
Barnes & Noble, 1961. 281pp. $6.75. This volume attempts to discover what the actual sources were, to consider the dramatic reasons why Shakespeare departed from them and to give examples of the way he made use of his general reading for particular scenes and speeches. This reprint of the 1957 edition has new appendices on plays with unknown sources, Shakespeare's use of Pliny, and the background of "Coriolanus." Index.

NICOLL, ALLARDYCE and JOSEPHINE NICOLL – Editors
Holinshed's Chronicle as Used in Shakespeare's Plays
Dutton, 1965. 233pp. $4.25. The editors regard "The Chronicles" as a Shakespearian source book and not as a history; thus, passages which have a bearing on the plays are presented in a new order according to the order of the First Folio. Introduction by the editors. Bibliographical Note.

SCHELLING, FELIX E.
Foreign Influences in Elizabethan Plays
See Page 541

SCOT, REGINALD
The Discoverie of Witchcraft
Southern Illinois University, 1964. 400pp. $22.50. A new edition of the classic study of witches, witchcraft, and demonology which Shakespeare consulted for "Macbeth" and "A Midsummer Night's Dream."

SMITH, CHARLES G.
Shakespeare's Proverb Lore: His Use of the Sententiae of Leonard Culman and Publilius Syrus
Harvard, 1963. 181pp. $6.25. The author demonstrates that Shakespeare's use of the "Sententiae" is more extensive than has been thought. He finds at least 166 parallels to proverbs in Culman's work, and 137 parallels in the works of Syrus. The body of this book consists of the lists of proverbs with central words in bold face type for quick reference. Indices.

SPENCER, T. J. B. – Editor
Elizabethan Love Stories
Penguin, 1968. 215pp. Paper $1.25. This anthology contains eight stories known to Shakespeare and used in the plots of his plays. Professor Spencer introduces and explains the links between the stories and the plays and includes a Glossary and a Bibliography.

SPENCER, T. J. B.
Shakespeare's Plutarch
Penguin, 1964. 365pp. Paper $1.95. This edition of Plutarch contains the lives of Julius Caesar, Brutus, Marcus Antonius, and Coriolanus in the Sir Thomas North translation. Parallel passages from the plays are given.

THALER, ALWIN
Shakespeare and Sir Philip Sidney: The Influence of "The Defense of Poesy"
Russell & Russell, 1967. 100pp. $8.00. Originally published in 1947 and now reissued, this is an analysis of Sidney's "The Defense of Poesy" and a study of Shakespeare's use of its major ideas. Notes. Index.

THOMSON, J. A. K.
Shakespeare and the Classics
Barnes & Noble, 1952. 254pp. $4.75. An investigation, by the noted scholar, of Shakespeare's indebtedness to the ancient classics. Professor Thomson suggests that the belief held about Shakespeare by his intimates that he had no scholarly acquaintance with Latin or Greek has not been seriously shaken. Second, because of his understanding of the tragic conception underlying Plutarch's "Life of Caesar," Shakespeare created a new kind of drama which owed much to the spirit of Greek tragedy.

Playhouses and Productions in Shakespeare's Time

ADAMS, JOHN CRANFORD
The Globe Playhouse
Barnes & Noble, 1961. 435pp. $8.50. An analysis of all the available evidence concerning the playhouse as a whole as well as each of its parts. A detailed analysis of the original production of "King Lear" is included. This edition includes the new discoveries made since the first edition of 1942. Illustrated. Appendices. Index.

ADAMS, JOSEPH QUINCY
Shakespearean Playhouses: A History of English Theatres from the Beginnings to the Restoration
Peter Smith, 1960. 473pp. $7.50. A record of the history of seventeen regular and five temporary or projected theatres based on an examination of original sources. Illustrated with end maps showing the locations of playhouses in London. A checklist of maps and views of London is included. Bibliography.

BALDWIN, T.W.
The Organization and Personnel of the Shakespearean Company
Russell & Russell, 1961. 464pp. $15.00. A reprint of the original 1927 edition, this is a study of the laws and customs governing the organization of an acting company in Shakespeare's time and of the particular company that acted his plays.

BECKERMAN, BERNARD
Shakespeare at the Globe: 1599–1609
Macmillan, 1962. 254pp. $5.95. Paper $1.95. A study of the actual staging of Shakespeare's plays with a discussion of the repertory system, acting techniques, and dramaturgy.

BENTLEY, GERALD EADES
Shakespeare and His Theatre
University of Nebraska, 1964. 128pp. $3.50. Paper $1.50. A collection of essays which deal with the character and personnel of Shakespeare's acting company, the Globe and Blackfriars Theatres, stage practices, and the conventions of the theatre.

BRADBROOK, M.C.
Elizabethan Stage Conditions
Cambridge, 1968. 149pp. $4.95. Paper $1.65. Originally published in 1932 and now reissued, this is a study of the place of Elizabethan stage conditions in the interpretation of Shakespeare's plays.

BRIDGES, ROBERT
The Influence of the Audience on Shakespeare's Drama
Haskell House, 1966. 29pp. Paper $6.50. Originally published in 1927 and now reissued in a facsimile edition, this is a short essay.

DAVIES, W. ROBERTSON
Shakespeare's Boy Actors
Russell & Russell, 1964. 207pp. $9.00. A reprint of the edition of 1939, this study considers the general background of the use of boys in women's roles in the Elizabethan theatre, discusses Puritan attacks on them, considers their training, competence, use in tragedy and comedy, special roles written for them, and audience reaction. Illustrated.

GRIFFIN, ALICE V.
Pageantry on the Shakespearean Stage
College and University Press, 1951. 242pp. Paper $1.95. A demonstration of the dramatic effectiveness of Shakespeare's scenes of spectacle. The original staging of these scenes is reconstructed and the relationship between street and stage pageantry is analyzed. Illustrated.

GURR, ANDREW
The Shakespearean Stage: 1574–1642
Cambridge, 1970. 192pp. $10.25. Paper $2.75. Professor Gurr studies the theatre conditions which supplied Shakespeare and his contemporaries with the venue for their plays. He provides details of the acting companies, their organization, development, finance, and personalities involved and describes the playhouses, evaluating the various interpretations of contemporary sketches and accounts. He also discusses the staging of the plays and provides extensive quotation from legal documents, contemporary memoirs, letters, and plays. Illustrated. Appendix. Select List of Plays. Notes. Index.

HARBAGE, ALFRED
Shakespeare and the Rival Traditions
Barnes & Noble, 1968. 393pp. $13.50. Paper $3.45. Originally published in 1952 and now reissued, this is a study of the facts about Elizabethan theatres and the content of Elizabethan plays as a means of defining Shakespeare's materials and intentions. The author concentrates on the organization of the Elizabethan theatrical industry and shows the duality of Elizabethan drama. Documentation. List of Works Cited. Index.

HARBAGE, ALFRED
Shakespeare's Audience
Columbia, 1961. 201pp. Paper $1.65. Drawing largely on the writings of the era, this study analyzes the tastes and moral prejudices of Shakespeare's audience and evaluates its capacity for aesthetic and intellectual judgement.

HODGES, C. WALTER
The Globe Restored: A Study of the Elizabethan Theatre

Oxford, 1968. 177pp. $10.50. An enlarged edition of the study first published in 1953 and widely accepted as one of the most comprehensive works of general reconstruction of the use and appearance of the playhouse in Shakespeare's London. The author has provided many reconstruction drawings of his own to supplement a wide collection of illustrations from historical sources. Select Bibliography. Index.

HODGES, C. WALTER
Shakespeare and the Players
Coward–McCann, 1970. 110pp. $4.00. Originaly published in 1949 and now reissued in a revised edition, this is an account, for the young reader, of the Elizabethan playhouse and play production. Illustrated with drawings by the author.

HODGES, C. WALTER
Shakespeare's Theatre
Putnam, 1964. 104pp. $7.25. The text, with full color illustrations by the author, shows how the idea of the theatre in Shakespeare's time developed gradually from pagan festivals and religious drama. A typical performance of "Julius Caesar" at the Globe is described in detail. Index.

HOLMES, MARTIN
Shakespeare's Public: Touchstone of His Genius
John Murray, 1964. 237pp. $6.75. In this study of the influence of the audience on the playwright's art, the author examines allusions, contemporary jokes, and recreations of contemporary persons in order to suggest clues to the dating of the plays and new insights into their meaning. Seventeen illustrations reproduce contemporary artwork from Holinshed and other sources. Appendices. Index.

JOSEPH, BERTRAM
Acting Shakespeare
See Page 412

LAWRENCE, WILLIAM J.
The Physical Conditions of the Elizabethan Public Playhouse
Cooper Square, 1968. 129pp. $5.25. Originally published in 1927, this is a study of the physical features of the theatres of Shakespeare's day. Among the theatres discussed are the Red Bull, the Swan, and the Globe. Illustrated.

LINTHICUM, M. CHANNING
Costume in the Drama of Shakespeare and His Contemporaries
Russell & Russell, 1963. 307pp. $9.00. A reprint of the 1936 edition, this study provides a survey of sixteenth and seventeenth century costumes: their colors, production, symbolism, and periods of fashion. There are illustrative quotations from the plays on the use of accessories and the wearing of the garments, as well as on the styles of dress. Illustrated. Bibliography.

LONG, JOHN H.
Shakespeare's Use of Music: A Study of the Music and Its Performance in the Original Productions of Seven Comedies
University of Florida, 1955. 214pp. $5.50. A study of the use of instrumental and vocal music as a dramatic device in seven of Shakespeare's plays.

LONG, JOHN H.
Shakespeare's Use of Music: The Final Comedies
University of Florida, 1961. 159pp. $5.50. Studies of eight comedies provide the basis for the author's observations.

NAGLER, A.M.
Shakespeare's Stage
Yale, 1958. 117pp. $4.50. Paper $1.45. An analysis of the theory behind the Elizabethan stage. The practical application of this theory is seen in the playhouses of London and its environs in Shakespeare's time. A production of "Romeo and Juliet" is reconstructed and the acting technique is analyzed. The indoor Blackfriars Theatre and a production of "The Tempest" at that theatre are also discussed.

NAYLOR, EDWARD WOODALL
Shakespeare and Music
Blom, 1965. 224pp. $7.50. First published in 1931, this volume lists and studies thirty-two plays which contain references to music. Over 300 stage directions about music are examined.

NEILSON, FRANCIS
Shakespeare and the Tempest
R. R. Smith, 1956. 181pp. $3.50. An actor-manager's view of the play from the standpoint of productions. The study is based on a consideration of Elizabethan customs and habits.

NEWCOMB, WILBURN W.
Lute Music of Shakespeare's Time
See Page 281

ODELL, GEORGE C.D.
Shakespeare: From Betterton to Irving
Blom, 1964. Volume One: 456pp. Volume Two: 498pp. $18.50 per set. Paper—Dover, 1966. Two Volumes—Each $3.00. A reprint of the 1920 edition, this study gives a history of Shakespeare on the London stage from his own time to the time of Henry Irving. All the major productions and all the various acting and producing techniques are examined. Special attention is given to the details of production—scenery, machines, costumes, etc.—as well as to the manner in which the plays were altered and rewritten. Illustrated with contemporary source material.

POEL, WILLIAM
Shakespeare in the Theatre
Blom, 1968. 247pp. $9.75. Originally published in 1913 and now reissued, this is a study of Shakespeare's

plays as played in the theatre during his lifetime and after. Index.

SHIRLEY, FRANCES A.
Shakespeare's Use of Off-Stage Sounds
University of Nebraska, 1963. 258pp. $5.00. A study of all the facts known about the mechanical devices used for sound, their locations, and the cueing. The sounds in Shakespeare are classified by type and the use is traced and examined. The integral part sound plays in "Julius Caesar," "Hamlet," and "Macbeth" is studied. Appendix.

SMITH, IRWIN
Shakespeare's Blackfriars Playhouse: Its History and Its Design
New York University, 1964. 577pp. $20.00. Paper $4.95. Based on architectural and archeological research, on clues found in stage directions, and on contemporary notices, this book recreates in text and drawings the second playhouse built within the precinct walls of the Blackfriars. The theatrical practices of the child actor companies and their influences on Shakespeare are studied. Twenty-six illustrations in the text and eight plates are included. Appendix. Bibliography. Index.

SMITH, IRWIN
Shakespeare's Globe Playhouse: A Modern Reconstruction in Text and Scale Drawings, Based on the Reconstruction of the Globe by John Cranford Adams
Scribner, 1956. 240pp. $10.00. A complete set of scale drawings taken from the Adams reconstruction, for study and for the guidance of model builders. Included are a collection of contemporary views and maps of the Bankside district, and a survey of the Globe stage and its influence on Shakespeare's dramaturgy.

SPENCER, HAZELTON
Shakespeare Improved: The Restoration Versions in Quarto and on the Stage
Ungar, 1963. 406pp. $7.00. A reprint of the original 1927 edition, this study considers the history of the theatres from the reopening in 1660 to the death of Betterton in 1710, and gives a record of the work of D'Avenant, Dryden, Tate, Shadwell, Otway, Cibber, D'Urfey, and other editors of Shakespeare. Lists of the theatres and companies of the period. Bibliography. Index.

SPRAGUE, ARTHUR COLBY
Shakespeare and the Actors: The Stage Business in His Plays (1660–1905)
Russell & Russell, 1963. 442pp. $15.00. A reprint of the 1944 edition, this is a study, based on contemporary accounts, newspaper articles, and extant prompt-copies, of the tradition of acting techniques used in the plays up to the death of Irving in 1905, and the advent of the directors who would determine the actor's business.

THORNDIKE, ASHLEY H.
Shakespeare's Theatre
Macmillan, 1958. 472pp. $6.95. A history of the stage in Shakespeare's time, with a discussion of the physical aspects of the stage, production methods, acting companies from Elizabeth to Charles I, the audience, the dramatists, and the Court theatres. Appendices list stage directions illustrating the use of the curtain and the inner stage. Illustrated. Bibliography.

WATKINS, RONALD
On Producing Shakespeare
Blom, 1964. 335pp. $12.50. This book examines such questions as what properties and scenic effects were used, what styles of acting were in vogue, and what devices were used to create special effects in Shakespeare's time. Illustrated with photographs and an extensive record of a modern production of "Macbeth."

WINTER, WILLIAM
Shakespeare on the Stage
Blom, 1969. 1,766pp. $37.50. Originally published in 1911, 1915, and 1916 and now reissued in facsimile editions, these three volumes provide stage histories of twenty of Shakespeare's plays with comment on the actors who appeared in them, their choice of texts, and reading of lines. Illustrated. Indices. Sold as a three volume set.

WRIGHT, LOUIS B. and HORIZON MAGAZINE – Editors
Shakespeare's England
Harper, 1964. 153pp. $5.95. A pictorial survey of Stratford, London, the theatres, the fashions of the times, the playing company, and the editions of the plays during Shakespeare's lifetime. The text analyzes the period and its influence on the dramatist. Illustrated. Index.

THE AUTHORSHIP CONTROVERSY

Studies and Critiques

BLUMENTHAL, WALTER HART
Paging Mr. Shakespeare: A Critical Challenge
University Publishers, 1961. 336pp. $6.00. The author maintains that there is no authenticity to the supposed documentary evidence that Shakespeare wrote his plays.

BROWNLEE, A.
William Shakespeare and Robert Burton
Crown Press, 1960. 337pp. $3.50. Mr. Brownlee attempts to show that Shakespeare collaborated on the great body of his work with Robert Burton, the author of "The Anatomy of Melancholy."

FORD, GERTRUDE C.
A Rose by Any Name
A. S. Barnes. 1964. 302pp. $6.50. Miss Ford analyzes Shakespeare's poetry and plays for the clues that will prove that Edward de Vere, Earl of Oxford, is the actual author of the works. Miss Ford's clues are presented in verse form together with annotations in the form of marginal notes giving the source of each clue, either internally in the works or in contemporary documents. Illustrated.

FRIEDMAN, WILLIAM F. and ELIZABETH S. FRIEDMAN
The Shakespearean Ciphers Examined: An Analysis of Cryptographic Systems Used as Evidence that Some Author Other than William Shakespeare Wrote the Plays Commonly Attributed to Him
Cambridge, 1957. 303pp. $5.50. The authors are both professional cryptographers who have spent many years in the service of the U. S. Government. They examine all the main systems of hidden messages that are supposed to reveal the true author of the plays. None of these systems meets the test for a true cipher.

GITTINGS, ROBERT
Shakespeare's Rival
Heinemann, 1965. 138pp. $4.50. An investigation into the possible identity of the "rival poet" of the "Sonnets." The author suggests that a certain topical Elizabethan satire refers to Shakespeare and names a rival writer, Gervase Markham, as the subject of an attack in "Love's Labour's Lost." Index.

HONEY, WILLIAM
The Shakespeare Epitaph Deciphered
Mitre Press, 1969. 237pp. $7.25. Mr. Honey seeks to prove that Christopher Marlowe wrote the "Sonnets" and other major works attributed to Shakespeare. His explorations correlate the known facts with his own research in this exposition. Illustrated with photographs of the Shakespeare signatures. Bibliography. Index.

McMICHAEL, GEORGE and EDGAR M. GLENN
Shakespeare and His Rivals
Odyssey, 1962. 262pp. Paper $3.00. Subtitled, "A Casebook on the Authorship Controversy," this book presents a selection of materials, arranged historically, on the controversy. The authors do not seek to prove a case but merely to give the historical evidence. Selected Bibliography.

MARTIN, MILWARD W.
Was Shakespeare Shakespeare?
Cooper Square, 1965. 155pp. $5.25. Mr. Martin reviews the documented evidence of the Shakespeare authorship controversy and claims that Shakespeare did indeed write the plays and poems. Illustrated with a frontispiece. Bibliographical Index. Subject Index.

OGBURN, CHARLTON and DOROTHY OGBURN
Shake–speare: The Man Behind the Name
Morrow, 1962. 282pp. $6.00. Paper—Apollo. $1.95. The authors maintain that the facts about Will Shakespeare of Stratford do not characterize him as the cultivated, well-educated, well-traveled, and well-behaved gentleman who must have written the plays. They believe that Edward de Vere, Earl of Oxford had the endowments, the background, the temperament to write the plays and impelling reasons for anonymity. Notes. Index.

POLLARD, A.W.
Shakespeare's Fight with the Pirates and Shakespeare's Hand in the Play of "Sir Thomas More"
Cambridge, 1967. 353pp. $9.50. "Shakespeare's Fight" is a collection of bibliographical lectures on the regulation of the book trade in the sixteenth century, authors, players, and pirates in Shakespeare's day, and the manuscripts and manuscript "improvers" of the time. Originally published in 1920 and now reprinted. "Shakespeare's Hand" is a study in which the contributors set out to strengthen the evidence of the existence of three pages written by Shakespeare in his own hand as part of the play, "Sir Thomas More."

VENTON, W.B.
The Analyses of Shakespeare's Sonnets Using the Cipher Code
Mitre Press, 1968. 39pp. $3.00. The author has analyzed the "Sonnets" using the cipher code and verified and confirmed the results by computer. These decodings lead Mr. Venton to believe that Shakespeare was really Edward Tudor VI.

WADSWORTH, FRANK W.
The Poacher from Stratford
University of California, 1969. 174pp. $9.50. Originally published in 1958, this is an account of the controversy over the authorship of Shakespeare's plays. Illustrated. Index.

WILLIAMS, DAVID RHYS
Shakespeare Thy Name is Marlowe
Vision, 1966. 94pp. $4.95. Dr. Williams presents the case for Christopher Marlowe as the author of Shakespeare's plays. Some evidence is derived from the plays and the sonnets in the First Folio and also from those writings first presented under Marlowe's own name. Illustrated. Index.

WINCHCOMBE, GEORGE and BERNARD WINCHCOMBE
Shakespeare's Ghost Writers
Michael Lancet, 1968. 285pp. $8.50. Paper—Thab, 1970. 285pp. $3.75. This work attempts to discover the authors of Shakespeare's masterpieces. The authors conclude that John Williams was the author of the Shakespeare works. Illustrated with forty plates. Appendices.

Studies of Plays of Doubtful Authorship

BALDWIN, T.W.
Shakespeare's Love's Labor's Won: New Evidence from the Account Book of an Elizabethan Bookseller
Southern Illinois University, 1957. 52pp. $5.00. Actual size collotype reproductions of three recently discovered manuscript leaves which offer evidence of the existence in 1603 of a play titled, "Love's Labor's Won."

BERTRAM, PAUL
Shakespeare and the Two Noble Kinsmen
Rutgers University, 1965. 306pp. $10.00. This book seeks to show that the play must have been entirely the work of Shakespeare, despite the appearance in 1634 of the first publication with a title page ascribing it to John Fletcher and Shakespeare. It offers a comprehensive and detailed examination of the relevant historical and textual evidence to prove this theory. Index.

BROOKE, C.F. TUCKER
The Shakespeare Apocrypha
Oxford, 1967. 456pp. $7.25. This collection of fourteen plays which have been ascribed to Shakespeare was first published in 1908 and is now reissued. A long introduction on the doubtful plays in general is included. Notes. Bibliography.

PARTRIDGE, A.C.
The Problem of Henry VIII Reopened: Some Linguistic Criteria for the Two Apparent Styles in the Play
Fernhill, 1949. 35pp. $2.50. From an analysis of vocabulary and syntax the author contends that "Henry VIII" was an unfinished play left by Shakespeare at his retirement in the hands of his company, and finished by Fletcher.

EIGHTEENTH CENTURY TO THE PRESENT

Productions

BALL, ROBERT HAMILTON
Shakespeare on Silent Film
Theatre Arts, 1968. 403pp. $12.50. In this history, the author traces in detail the fate of Shakespeare's plays on silent film from Herbert Beerbohm Tree's 1899 effort as "King John" until the establishment of sound in 1929. Excerpts from scenarios, from reviews and contemporary film journals are included. Reproductions of stills, frames from the films and photographs of leading actors illustrate the volume. Notes. Bibliography. Indices.

BOAS, GUY
Shakespeare and the Young Actor
See Page 409

BROWN, JOHN RUSSELL
Shakespeare's Plays in Performance
St. Martin, 1967. 244pp. $7.95. Paper—Penguin, 1969. 266pp. $1.75. This study deals with Shakespeare's plays in actual performance. Dr. Brown examines particular English productions from recent years to show how today's theatre directors and actors present the plays. Illustrated. Notes. Index.

BUELL, W.A.
The Hamlets of the Theatre
See Page 64

DUNN, ESTHER CLOUDMAN
Shakespeare in America
Blom, 1968. 310pp. $12.50. Originally published in 1939 and now reissued, this study is an account of the production of Shakespeare's plays in America. There are chapters on Shakespeare for Cherokees, the founding fathers and the bard, Shakespeare in the gold rush, and Shakespeare and the American scholar. Illustrated. Index.

GOODWIN, JOHN
Royal Shakespeare Theatre Company: 1960–1963
Theatre Arts, 1964. 243pp. $7.95. This record in pictures and text covers the formation and expansion of the Company and considers at length Peter Brook's production of "King Lear," Peter Hall's "Wars of the Roses" trilogy in 1963, and Clifford Williams' "Comedy of Errors." There are articles by Peter Hall and Robert Bolt and a selection of press reviews.

HACKETT, JAMES HENRY
Notes, Criticisms, and Correspondence Upon Shakespeare's Plays and Actors
Blom, 1968. 353pp. $12.50. Originally published in 1863 and now reissued, Hackett's work is distinguished by the acuteness of its observation on how Shakespeare was acted by major nineteenth century performers.

HARBAGE, ALFRED
Theatre for Shakespeare
University of Toronto, 1955. 118pp. $3.50. An analysis of the current lack of dramatic vitality in productions of Shakespeare's plays.

HOROWITZ, DAVID
Shakespeare: An Existential View
Hill & Wang, 1965. 134pp. $4.00. Paper—Tavistock, 1968. 134pp. $2.95. The author challenges the view of Shakespeare as a non-philosophic student of character and a non-philosophical artist. Mr. Horowitz attempts to reveal the playwright as a poet concerned with issues that have a bearing on the complexity of man's contemporary situation. Index.

HUDSON, A. K.
Shakespeare and the Classroom
Heinemann, 1963. 116pp. $3.50. A guide for teachers of Shakespeare which attempts to develop a technique for a "stage-centered" presentation of the plays in the classroom. Originally published in 1954 and revised for this edition, the volume includes a list of editions, books, recordings of plays, and filmed versions. Index.

KNIGHT, G. WILSON
Shakespearean Production with Special Reference to the Tragedies
Northwestern University, 1964. 323pp. $6.95. Paper — Routledge & Kegan Paul, 1968. 323pp. $3.95. Based on the author's "Principles of Shakespearean Production," originally published in 1936, this new edition contains much new material which reveals his developing thoughts on the problem of discovering the unifying principle in each play and using that principle as the center of the production. With new notes on filming Shakespeare, surveys of recent productions, and comments on open-stage productions. Illustrated with photographs. Index.

KOZINTSEV, GRIGORI
Shakespeare: Time and Conscience
Hill & Wang, 1966. 276pp. $5.95. The director of the prize-winning Soviet Film, "Hamlet," discusses Shakespeare's plays, the production and staging problems, and analyzes "King Lear" and "Hamlet." Appended is a collection of notes the director made during his production of the film. Illustrated with photographs from the film.

REDFIELD, WILLIAM
Letters from an Actor
Viking, 1967. 243pp. $5.75. Paper — 1969. $1.75. A series of letters describing the daily happenings and Mr. Redfield's reactions to them during the preparation of the Sir John Gielgud — Richard Burton production of "Hamlet."

ROSSI, ALFRED
Minneapolis Rehearsals
University of California, 1970. 230pp. $12.50. A study of the production of "Hamlet" directed by Tyrone Guthrie for the Minnesota Theatre Company in Minneapolis in 1963. Included in the volume are the personal log of the author in which he recorded daily rehearsals and other details of planning and preparation. The prompt script, prepared by Edward Payson Call, is completely annotated with directions. A selection of sketches of costume designs by Tanya Moiseiwitsch, photographs of rehearsals and production, and a selection of reviews of the production are also provided.

SAMARIN, ROMAN
Shakespeare in the Soviet Union
See Page 220

SHATTUCK, CHARLES H. — Editor
William Charles Macready's "King John"
University of Illinois, 1962. 184pp. $6.95. This is a facsimile prompt-book that recreates in detail the production of "King John" mounted at the Drury Lane Theatre in London, October, 1842. This is the transcription that George Ellis made for Kean and which Kean used in the autumn of 1846 for his production at New York City's Park Theatre. The editor examines and reports the details of and relationships between six other relevant prompt-books and three "acting editions" that were printed. Thirty-four plates include illustrations of Drury Lane Theatre and scene designs.

SPEAIGHT, ROBERT
William Poel and the Elizabethan Revival
Heinemann, 1954. 302pp. $4.00. A study of the late-Victorian theatre producer who laid the ground work for the modern techniques of Shakespearean productions. In this study, Poel's influence on modern production techniques is stressed, particularly his use of the platform stage. Illustrated. Index.

SPRAGUE, ARTHUR COLBY and J. C. TREWIN
Shakespeare's Plays Today
Sidgewick & Jackson, 1970. 147pp. $5.50. The authors trace the development of Shakespearean production, both in the U. S. and England, during this century. They discuss the differing attitudes of the theatre towards the plays themselves, and, looking back over more than fifty years of theatre-going, describe the changing fashions and conventions of visual presentation, actors' costumes, and interpretation of characters. Illustrated with photographs. Notes. Index of Persons. Index of Plays.

STERNE, RICHARD L.
John Gielgud Directs Richard Burton in "Hamlet"
Random House, 1968. 339pp. $6.95. Mr. Sterne tape-recorded the rehearsals of the Broadway production of "Hamlet" with the approval of Sir John Gielgud. These are transcriptions of those tapes and his journal. The volume also includes the prompt script of the production with the stage directions and emphases Sir John advised the cast to place on their speeches. There are also interviews with Sir John and Mr. Burton on their own personal and professional interpretations of the character of Hamlet and the play. Illustrated with rehearsal photographs.

TREWIN, J. C.
Shakespeare on the English Stage: 1900—1964 — A Survey of Production
Barrie and Rockliff, 1964. 328pp. $9.00. This survey gives special attention to London and Stratford-upon-Avon and traces the rise in the influence of the director and the development of a classical style of acting. Lists of every production in the period and photographs showing productions of every play in the canon. Bibliography. Index.

WATKINS, RONALD
On Producing Shakespeare
See Page 91

WEBSTER, MARGARET
Shakespeare Today
Dent, 1957. 318pp. $4.95. Long out of print in the U. S., this is an English edition of Miss Webster's study of Shakespeare's plays. She discusses modern productions of the plays, specifically those in which she has been involved as producer and/or director. Index.

WINTER, WILLIAM
Shakespeare on the Stage
See Page 91

Shakespeare's Reputation

BABCOCK, ROBERT WITBECK
The Genesis of Shakespeare Idolatry 1766–1799: A Study in English Criticism of the Late Eighteenth Century
Russell & Russell, 1964. 307pp. $9.00. A reprint of the original 1931 edition, this book deals with scholarly and popular interest in Shakespeare from Johnson's "Preface" of 1765 to the end of the century. The author discusses the new defense of the playwright against the traditional objections of the neoclassicists. Bibliography. Index.

BENTLEY, GERALD EADES
Shakespeare and Jonson: Their Reputations in the 17th Century Compared
University of Chicago, 1965. 307pp. $12.00. Published in two volumes in 1945 and now reissued in one volume, this study examines the allusions to the playwrights and each of their works and major characters, and tries to evaluate the relative importance of the allusions, decade by decade, in helping us to arrive at a final and fair picture of the relative popularity each held in the period.

COLLISON–MORLEY, LACY
Shakespeare in Italy
Blom, 1967. 180pp. $9.50. Originally published in 1916 and now reissued, this is a study of Shakespeare's influence on the Italian stage and the production and translations of his work in Italy from the sixteenth to the nineteenth centuries. Illustrated. Bibliography. Index.

DEELMAN, CHRISTIAN
The Great Shakespeare Jubilee
Viking, 1964. 326pp. $6.95. An account of the first Shakespeare Festival, held in 1769 under the general direction of David Garrick. The author makes use of much new material to describe the events, solemn and ribald, that turned the Festival into a fiasco. Illustrated. Index.

FROST, DAVID L.
The School of Shakespeare
Cambridge, 1968. 304pp. $9.50. This is a study of the influence of Shakespeare on English drama, 1600–1642. Dr. Frost's premise is that "the Jacobean dramatists make better sense if seen as working in Shakespeare's light." His discussions offer a new approach to Shakespeare's final plays. Select Bibliography. Index.

GIBIAN, G.
Tolstoy and Shakespeare
See Page 223

HALLIDAY, F.E.
The Cult of Shakespeare
Yoseloff, 1957. 218pp. $5.00. A survey of the reputation of Shakespeare from his death to the present. The excesses of "Bardolatry" are described. The liberties taken with his works by Davenant, Dryden, Garrick, Bowdler, and others are described in detail. Contemporary theories on producing the plays are also discussed. Illustrated.

HOGAN, CHARLES BEECHER
Shakespeare in the Theatre 1701–1800: A Record of Performances in London 1701–1750 – Volume One
Oxford, 1952. 517pp. $10.50. The first volume of a two-volume series giving lists of performances, arranged chronologically, with the benefits allowed to actors and the nightly receipts. This is followed by an alphabetical grouping of the plays performed with, as far as possible, the complete casts. Appendices outline the comparative popularity of the plays and give a brief history of the London stage. Indices list actors and characters in the plays.

HOGAN, CHARLES BEECHER
Shakespeare in the Theatre 1701–1800: A Record of Performances in London 1751–1800 – Volume Two
Oxford, 1957. 798pp. $16.00. This second volume completes the record of performances—somwhat over 7,000—between 1701 and 1800. Unlike the first volume, this volume is based on a virtually complete, day-to-day run of the playbills used in the theatres.

KNIGHT, G. WILSON
Byron and Shakespeare
See Page 182

LOUNSBURY, THOMAS R.
Shakespeare and Voltaire
Blom, 1968. 463pp. $12.50. Originally published in 1902 and now reissued, this study shows the effect Voltaire had on the taste of the public in France particularly as it affected the acceptance of Shakespeare's works.

LOUNSBURY, THOMAS R.
Shakespeare as a Dramatic Artist, with an Account of His Reputation at Various Periods

Ungar, 1965. 449pp. $7.50. A reprint of the 1901 first edition, this study examines the ways in which Shakespeare's admirers apologized for (while his detractors condemned) such items as the dramatic unities and disunities in the plays, the mingling of comedy and tragedy, bloodshed and violence, and minor dramatic conventions. The alterations made in the plays over the centuries are also studied.

MARDER, LOUIS
His Exits and His Entrances: The Story of Shakespeare's Reputation
John Murray, 1963. 386pp. $6.50. Mr. Marder discusses the conjectures concerning the life, identity, and appearance of Shakespeare. He discusses the metamorphoses Shakespearean acting has undergone and the liberties that actors, producers and directors have taken with the plays. Selected Bibliography. Index.

MURRAY, PATRICK
The Shakespearean Scene
Longmans, 1969. 182pp. $6.50. A survey of the modern attitudes and approaches towards Shakespeare and his work. It follows the major trends of criticism and scholarship and assesses the relative value of the various critical standpoints of the twentieth century. Methods of modern critics are compared with those of their predecessors and attention is drawn to some of the shortcomings of modern criticism. References. Bibliography. Index.

NOYES, ROBERT GALE
The Thespian Mirror
Brown University, 1952. 100pp. $5.50. References to Shakespeare in the eighteenth century novel are examined for testimony about the plays on the contemporary stage and about scholarly opinions on the playwright. Illustrated. Index.

PRAWER, SIEGBERT
Heine's Shakespeare: A Study in Contexts
Oxford, 1970. 40pp. Paper $2.25. A short study of the nineteenth century German poet and satirist, Heinrich Heine, and his dealings with Shakespeare's works.

SAMARIN, ROMAN
Shakespeare in the Soviet Union
See Page 220

SMITH, D. NICHOL – Editor
Eighteenth Century Essays on Shakespeare
Oxford, 1963. 340pp. $8.25. The purpose of this study is to give an account of Shakespeare's reputation during the eighteenth century. The nine essays here reprinted and revised were originally published in 1903. The essays represent the chief phases of Shakespearean study from the days of Dryden to those of Coleridge. The essayists include: Rowe, Dennis, Pope, Theobald, Hanmer, Warburton, Johnson, Farmer, and Morgann. Index.

SMITH, DAVID NICHOL
Shakespeare in the Eighteenth Century
Oxford, 1967. 91pp. $4.75. Originally published in 1928 and now reissued, this volume contains three lectures which comprise a study of Shakespeare's reputation in the eighteenth century and how the actors, critics, and scholars of that time contributed to the playwright's fame.

SPENCER, T. J. B.
The Tyranny of Shakespeare
Oxford, 1959. 19pp. Paper $1.00. A brief lecture on Shakespeare's dominance over the imagination of English writers and readers with an account of the short-lived critical reactions against him at various times.

STAVISKY, ARON Y.
Shakespeare and the Victorians: Roots of Modern Criticism
University of Oklahoma, 1969. 146pp. $4.95. The author of this study proposes that there were many serious and original aspects to Victorian Shakespearean criticism and that much of our present scholarship and critical approach is actually derived from research and study carried out in the nineteenth century. Illustrated. Selected Bibliography. Index.

WESTFALL, ALFRED VAN RENSSELAER
American Shakespearean Criticism: 1607–1865
Blom, 1968. 305pp. $12.50. The establishing of an American edition of Shakespearean texts is the theme of this study. Aesthetic criticism of Shakespeare is also examined along with such side-lights as American presidents as Shakespearean critics, the American Baconian school, and moral justifications of Shakespeare. Chronology of editions and criticism. Index.

WRIGHT, LOUIS B.
Shakespeare for Everyman
Simon & Schuster, 1964. 217pp. $4.95. Paper – Washington Square Press, $ .90. This study is based on papers given by Mr. Wright. The author evaluates for the layman the continuing vitality of interest in the playwright and suggests the reasons for it. Illustrated with material from the Folger Library.

Adaptations of Plays

ARMOUR, RICHARD
Twisted Tales from Shakespeare
New American Library, 1966. 128pp. Paper $ .75. A spoof of some of Shakespeare's plays and sonnets. Illustrated by Campbell Grant.

BARTON, JOHN with PETER HALL – Adaptors
The Wars of the Roses
B. B. C., 1970. 242pp. $9.25. Mr. Barton's adapta-

tion of four of Shakespeare's plays, "Henry VI, Parts I, II, III" and "Richard III" for the Royal Shakespeare Company. The trilogy is divided into the seventy-five scenes of the stage production and the text shows which is Shakespeare's original text and which was written for the adaptation by John Barton. There is an introduction by Peter Hall, an article by John Barton on how the adaptation came about, and Michael Bakewell discusses the television production. Sixteen pages of plates from the production are included.

BAZAGONEV, M. S.
Shakespeare in the Red
Arco, 1965. 77pp. $2.50. Paper $ .95. A retelling of five tales from Shakespeare with somewhat revised plots as Shakespeare would have written the plays "if he had enjoyed the freedom of Soviet writers."

BRENNECKE, ERNEST and HENRY BRENNECKE
Shakespeare in Germany: 1590–1700
University of Chicago, 1964. 302pp. $9.00. To surmount the English-German language barrier, Shakespeare's plays were reduced to scenes of wild violence or equally wild burlesque when performed in Germany. This book presents five translations of plays which illustrate the way the plays were corrupted by resourceful actors and dramatists.

BUCKMAN, IRENE
Twenty Tales from Shakespeare
Methuen, 1963. 228pp. $5.00. The plots of twenty plays, suited for the young, told in a direct, lucid style. Illustrated with photographs of famous performers in key roles.

CHUTE, MARCHETTE
Stories from Shakespeare
New American Library, 1962. 319pp. Paper $ .95. Miss Chute retells all the plays in narrative form following the sequence of action.

CHUTE, MARCHETTE and ERNESTINE PERRIE
The Worlds of Shakespeare
Dutton, 1963. 128pp. $3.95. Paper $1.25. A play in two acts for two players, one taking all the male roles, the other the female, constructed out of selections from twelve plays. The play presents a condensed view of the whole range of interest in the twelve plays.

CULLUM, ALBERT
Shake Hands with Shakespeare
Citation Press, 1968. 320pp. Paper $4.50. Adaptations of eight plays especially for performance by elementary school children: "Hamlet," "Macbeth," "Romeo and Juliet," "A Midsummer Night's Dream," "Julius Caesar," "The Comedy of Errors," "The Taming of the Shrew," "The Tempest." Mr. Callum explains how to emphasize the appropriate mood and theme of each play and supplies simple costuming and staging hints. Lists of vocabulary words. Illustrated with drawings.

DEUTSCH, BABETTE
The Reader's Shakespeare
Messner, 1946. 510pp. $5.00. The stories of sixteen of the most popular plays, retold by the American poet with historical and critical background.

GRACZYK, ED
The Rude Mechanicals
Anchorage Press, 1970. 46pp. Paper $1.50. This play for nine males and one female (all children) is freely adapted from Shakespeare's "A Midsummer Night's Dream." Illustrated. Acting edition.

JOHNSON, ALBERT
Shakespeare Vignettes: Adaptations for Acting
A. S. Barnes, 1970. 207pp. $6.75. Vignette versions of six of Shakespeare's plays, edited and arranged for classroom study and for stage and television performance. Each of the plays is adapted for a thirty minute production. The plays include: "The Merchant of Venice," "The Taming of the Shrew," "Romeo and Juliet," "Macbeth," "Hamlet," and "Othello." Appendices.

KERMAN, GERTRUDE LERNER
Shakespeare for Young Players: From Tens to Teens
Harvey House, 1964. 242pp. $6.95. Adaptations, using the original lines of "A Midsummer Night's Dream," "Romeo and Juliet," "Twelfth Night," "The Taming of the Shrew," "The Tempest," and "As You Like It." The scripts vary in length from twenty minutes to one hour. Staging suggestions are included. Illustrated. Index.

LAMB, CHARLES and MARY LAMB
Tales from Shakespeare
Crowell, 1942. 360pp. $3.75. This edition of the classic work is illustrated in color by Elinore Blaisdell. Adapted especially for children ages nine and up.

LAURENTS, ARTHUR and STEPHEN SONDHEIM
Romeo and Juliet and West Side Story
Dell, 1965. 254pp. Paper $ .75. This volume contains the complete text of Shakespeare's play with notes by John Bettenbender as well as the libretto of the musical production set in New York's upper west side in the present day. The book for the musical is by Mr. Laurents with lyrics, which are included, by Stephen Sondheim. Music for the production was written by Leonard Bernstein but is not provided in this volume. Norris Houghton has provided an introduction.

MacKAYE, PERCY
The Mystery of Hamlet, King of Denmark, or What We Will, A Tetralogy, in Prologue to the Tragicall Historie of Hamlet, Prince of Denmark, by William Shakespeare

Bond Wheelwright, 1950. 676pp. $6.50. Four plays in verse that are an imaginative reconstruction of life and events in Denmark during the thirty years before the birth of Hamlet.

MAMOULIAN, ROUBEN
Shakespeare's Hamlet: A New Version
Bobbs–Merrill, 1965. 263pp. $5.00. Paper $1.25. Mr. Mamoulian has eliminated Elizabethan archaisms of speech and substituted twentieth century equivalents to give the play new immediacy for its readers. A lengthy foreword is provided by the author.

MILLER, KATHERINE – Editor
Five Plays from Shakespeare
Houghton–Mifflin, 1964. 236pp. $6.00. The editor has shortened each of the following plays to a playing time of one hour each: "The Tempest," "Comedy of Errors," "A Midsummer Night's Dream," "Macbeth," and "Julius Caesar." Songs by Norman Carzden are included in the volume. Illustrated.

NESBIT, E.
The Children's Shakespeare
Random House, 1938. 117pp. $2.95. Eleven plays retold for young children, with drawings by Rolf Klep.

SERRAILLIER, IAN
The Enchanted Island: Stories from Shakespeare
Walck, 1964. 201pp. $5.00. These eleven stories are narratives derived from the plays, designed to appeal to a child's sensibilities and tastes. Color drawings by Peter Farmer.

SUMMERS, MONTAGUE – Editor
Shakespeare Adaptations
Blom, 1966. 390pp. $12.50. Originally published in 1922 and now reissued, this volume includes three typical seventeenth century adaptations of Shakespeare: Davenant and Dryden's "The Tempest," Duffet's "The Mock Tempest," and Tate's "The History of King Lear." An extensive introduction by the editor examines the adverse criticism made against these plays and explains why they held the stage for many years. Each play is fully annotated.

URWIN, G. G.
The Neglected Shakespeare
Blackie, 1969. 211pp. $3.50. This volume consists of scenes from some of Shakespeare's plays which are mostly neglected in the public schools. The author provides introductions to each extract which provide a working knowledge of the play, its theme, mood and style, and sketches the context of the extract printed.

VANDIVER, EDWARD P.
Highlights of Shakespeare's Plays
Barron, 1964. 454pp. Paper $1.95. A selection of passages from twenty-three plays with commentary, notes, and detailed explication.

ESSAYS ON VARIOUS SUBJECTS

ALEXANDER, PETER – Editor
Studies in Shakespeare: British Academy Lectures
Oxford, 1964. 246pp. Paper $1.95. These ten lectures, printed together for the first time are grouped in three sections: the first deals with Shakespeare in the theatre; the second deals with the texts of the plays; and the third considers Shakespeare in the modern theatre. Index.

ANDERSON, RUTH LEILA
Elizabethan Psychology and Shakespeare's Plays
Russell & Russell, 1966. 182pp. $10.00. Originally published in 1927, this is an attempt to determine the principles of Elizabethan psychology and their bearing on Shakespeare's plays. The author confines her work to treatises which might have been available to Shakespeare in English. Bibliography. Index.

ARAGON, LOUIS and PABLO PICASSO
Shakespeare
Abrams, 1965. 125pp. $35.00. A series of drawings by Picasso to celebrate the 400th anniversary of Shakespeare's birth. To accompany the drawings, Louis Aragon wrote a short essay, "Shakespeare, Hamlet, and Us." Also included is a short story, "Murmer," which is in the Surrealist vein. A limited and over-sized edition.

BERRY, FRANCIS
The Shakespeare Inset: Word and Picture
Theatre Arts, 1965. 173pp. $5.75. A study of the relationships between the language being heard from the stage and the picture being exhibited. The identity between sound and sight, language and spectacle, and the frequent divergence between what the audience hears and what it sees—the "insets" of the author's terminology—are examined. Index.

BLISTEIN, ELMER M. – Editor
The Drama of the Renaissance
Brown University, 1970. 199pp. $7.00. Ten essays dealing with the works of four playwrights: Shakespeare, Calderon, Gager, and the anonymous author of "La Venexiana." More than half the contributors have chosen to write about Shakespeare.

BLOOM, EDWARD A.
Shakespeare 1564–1964: A Collection of Modern Essays by Various Hands
Brown University, 1964. 226pp. $6.50. Among the essayists included in this collection are: Fredson Bowers, Nicholas Brooke, Hardin Craig, R. A. Foakes, Robert B. Heilman, Kenneth Muir, Irving Ribner, T. J. B. Spencer, E. M. W. Tillyard, and Brents Stirling. The subject plays are "Hamlet," "King Lear," "The Taming of the Shrew," and others.

BROWN, JOHN RUSSELL and BERNARD HARRIS—Editors
Later Shakespeare
St. Martin's 1967. 264pp. $5.75. A series of essays on the range of Shakespeare's late dramatic activity. The authors seek to observe the nature of specific, individual achievements within the fuller record of Shakespeare's later work. Index.

CALDERWOOD, JAMES L. and HAROLD E. TOLIVER—Editors
Essays in Shakespearean Criticism
Prentice–Hall, 1970. 590pp. $6.50. The editors have collected thirty-eight mid-twentieth century essays they believe clarify and illuminate "something" Shakespearean. Among the subjects are staging and acting conventions in Elizabethan times, essays on the structure and strategy of language in the Sonnets, and essays on individual plays. Among the contributors: J. L. Styan, Northrop Frye, Robert Heilman, and Francis Fergusson. Paper bound.

CARLISLE, CAROL JONES
Shakespeare from the Greenroom
University of North Carolina, 1969. 493pp. $15.75. This volume brings together, from sources from the eighteenth century to the present, criticisms of four of Shakespeare's plays by English-speaking actors. Each of the four major tragedies ("Hamlet," "Othello," "King Lear," and "Macbeth") is presented in a separate chapter with the actors' ideas about the structure, language, meaning, etc. of the play itself and the interpretation of its characters. The concluding chapter evaluates the actors' criticisms and points out some relationships between actor-critics and other critics of Shakespeare. Index.

CHAMBERS, E.K.
Shakespearean Gleanings
Folcroft, 1969. 147pp. $15.95. Originally published in 1944, this is a collection of essays on Shakespeare and Shakespearean subjects. Among the subjects are the "Sonnets," "A Midsummer Night's Dream," the date of "Hamlet," and the stage of the Globe Theatre.

CHAPMAN, GERALD W.—Editor
Essays on Shakespeare
Princeton, 1965. 176pp. $5.75. Essays by Robert Heilman, Northrop Frye, Harry Levin, and others with particular discussions of "Love's Labour's Lost," "Hamlet," and "King Lear."

COLERIDGE, SAMUEL TAYLOR
Shakespearean Criticism
Dutton, 1960. Volume One: 162pp. Volume Two: 183pp. Price per volume: $3.75. A recession of the Raysor text, 1930, with collation of part of the text with recently discovered manuscripts. Some omissions have been made of the non-Shakespearean criticism of the Raysor text.

DAVIS, HERBERT and HELEN GARDNER—Editors
Elizabethan and Jacobean Studies
Oxford, 1969. 355pp. $15.00. Originally published in 1959 and out of print since 1963, this is a republication of the volume of essays on various aspects of theatre in the Elizabethan and Jacobean period. Among the contributors are E. M. W. Tillyard, W. W. Greg, Nevill Coghill, Helen Gardner, and John Dover Wilson. Illustrated with five plates. Index.

DEAN, LEONARD F.—Editor
Shakespeare: Modern Essays in Criticism
Oxford, 1967. 476pp. Paper $2.95. This is a revised second edition of the book originally published in 1957. Twenty-eight articles written in recent years provide a representative cross-section of modern trends in criticism. Among the critics are Alfred Harbage, E. K. Chambers, E. E. Stoll, Wolfgang Clemen, Mark Van Doren, and Edward Hubler.

DYER, T.F. THISELTON
Folk-Lore of Shakespeare
Dover, 1966. 526pp. Paper $2.75. Just about every one of Shakespeare's plays is canvassed for references to Elizabethan folk-lore and allusions to folkloristic beliefs. These references are then explained in light of the particular element of folk-lore to which they pertain. An unabridged republication of the 1883 edition. Bibliography. Index.

EASTMAN, A.M. and G.B. HARRISON—Editors
Shakespeare's Critics from Jonson to Auden: A Medley of Judgements
University of Michigan, 1964. 346pp. $9.00. Paper $6.00. Criticism by 120 poets and writers over more than three and a half centuries, on both general and specific problems of interpretation. General topics such as themes, attitudes, style, and characterization are considered in Part One. Part Two has essays on individual plays.

EASTMAN, ARTHUR M.
A Short History of Shakespearean Criticism
Random House, 1968. 418pp. $7.95. The author presents the history of Shakespearean criticism as a gallery of critics from Shakespeare's day to the present time. He portrays the great critics in their own words, quoting passages from their works. Concentrating on our own century, half the book is devoted to contemporary critics. Index.

FORD, BORIS—Editor
The Age of Shakespeare
See Page 49

FRYE, NORTHROP
Fables of Identity
Harcourt, Brace, 1963. 265pp. Paper $3.45. A collection of Northrop Frye's critical essays. After a preface, the first four essays outline the theoretical assumptions on which the remaining twelve are based.

They are studies in poetic mythology and the author discusses various works and authors. Among the papers are one on Shakespeare's "Sonnets" and one on recognition in "The Winter's Tale."

GITTINGS, ROBERT – Editor
The Living Shakespeare
Heinemann, 1960. 154pp. $3.00. Fifteen lectures, based on talks given on the BBC, covering many aspects of Shakespeare's art. Among the contributors are Margaret Webster, Leslie Hotson, J. Dover Wilson, David Daiches, L. C. Knights, and C. J. Sissons.

GREBANIER, BERNARD
The Great Shakespeare Forgery
Norton, 1965. 308pp. $5.00. An account of the life of the late eighteenth century forger, William Henry Ireland, and of the social, literary, and personal reasons for his fabrications.

HALLIDAY, F. E.
Shakespeare and His Critics
Schocken, 1963. 336pp. Paper $1.95. A reprint of the 1958 edition. After an analysis of Shakespearean criticism and critics, the author presents the plays of the canon as they have been analyzed throughout the ages in a variety of different interpretations. Illustrations. Bibliography. Indices.

HARTING, JAMES EDMUND
The Birds of Shakespeare
Argonaut, 1965. 321pp. $10.00. In this reprint of the first edition (1871), all the allusions to birds in the corpus are collected and examined for aptness. Shakespeare's great knowledge of birds and his use of this knowledge is illustrated. Grundy Steiner has contributed an essay, "Of Men and Birds: Prolegomena to the Birds of Shakespeare."

HARTNOLL, PHYLLIS – Editor
Shakespeare in Music
St. Martin, 1964. 333pp. $10.00. This collection of four essays by eminent musicologists shows how great and enduring was the playwright's influence on many aspects of music. John Stevens writes on Shakespeare and the music of the Elizabethan stage; Charles Cudworth on song and part-song settings of the lyrics from 1660 to 1960; Winton Dean on Shakespeare and opera; and Roger Fiske on Shakespeare and the concert hall.

HAZLITT, WILLIAM
Characters of Shakespeare's Plays
Oxford, 1962. 276pp. $2.25. The famous essays, first published in 1817, in a new edition with an introduction by Sir Arthur Quiller-Couch.

HOROWITZ, DAVID
Shakespeare: An Existential View
Hill & Wang, 1965. 134pp. $4.00. Two essays: "Imagining the Real," and "The Bonds of Human Kindness." They each approach Shakespeare with "a view that proves itself in the reality of lived experience, not in the principles of metaphysical or theological discourse."

HOSLEY, RICHARD – Editor
Essays on Shakespeare and Elizabethan Drama in Honor of Hardin Craig
University of Missouri, 1962. 382pp. $9.50. Twenty-eight essays by leading British, Canadian, and American scholars. The majority of the essays are on Shakespeare and Marlowe.

HOWARTH, HERBERT
The Tiger's Heart
Chatto & Windus, 1970. 210pp. $6.25. Eight essays on Shakespearean subjects by the distinguished critic. Among the subjects are the effects of the burning of the books in 1599 on Shakespeare, the Viola-Olivia-Sebastian relationship, and how Malvolio borrows the voice of Ben Jonson. Notes. Index.

HUNTER, EDWIN R.
Shakespeare and Common Sense
Christopher Press, 1954. 312pp. $4.00. The author maintains that Shakespeare offered a philosophy of "common sense" as a palliative against sentiment and pretense. This common sense approach is also seen in the manner in which he treated complex issues in the most direct dramatic terms, particularly in common-sensical and folk-lore terms. Index.

JACKSON, B. A. W. – Editor
Manner and Meaning in Shakespeare
Irish University Press, 1970. 232pp. $8.50. A selection of thirteen lectures originally delivered at a Shakespeare Seminar at Stratford, Ontario during the summers of 1965–1967. The papers range in subject from the general problems of teaching and producing Shakespeare's works to a close examination of characterization and interpretation in specific plays. Among the contributors are: L. C. Knights, Arthur Colby Sprague, Muriel Bradbrook, John Russell Brown, and Bamber Gascoigne.

JAMES DAVID G.
The Dream of Learning: An Essay on the Advancement of Learning, Hamlet, and King Lear
Oxford, 1951. 126pp. $3.95. The author considers briefly the genius, performance, and significance of each of these works individually and in relation to one another. Bacon's "mission" in writing is compared with the achievement of Shakespeare in his two greatest tragedies and the significance of all three works, occurring as they do in the transitional period between Medieval and modern learning, is examined.

JEFFERSON, D. W. – Editor
The Morality of Art
Barnes & Noble, 1969. 237pp. $8.00. The essays

collected here in the honor of G. Wilson Knight by his colleagues and friends deal with topics within fields in which Wilson Knight's reputation has been made. There are studies of several of Shakespeare's plays, a description of a production of "Macbeth" based on Wilson Knight's "ideal production," and a study of Wilson Knight as an interpreter of Shakespeare. Illustrated. Select List of the published works of G. Wilson Knight. Index.

JOHNSON, SAMUEL
Johnson on Shakespeare
Yale, 1968. Two volume set: 1,100pp. $33.25. Volumes VII and VIII in the Yale edition of the works of Samuel Johnson. Edited by Arthur Sherbo, this is a fully annotated edition of Johnson's writings on Shakespeare. Relevant portions of Shakespeare's text and of the annotation and commentary by Johnson's editorial predecessors are reproduced. Illustrated. Indices.

JOHNSON, SAMUEL
Samuel Johnson on Shakespeare
Hill & Wang, 1960. 115pp. $3.50. Paper $1.50. Edited by W. K. Wimsatt, Jr., this volume includes the preface and notes from the 1765 edition of Jonson's work on Shakespeare. Also included are several other essays and works by Johnson. Notes. Bibliography.

JOSEPH, BERTRAM
Acting Shakespeare
See Page 412

KAUFMANN, WALTER
From Shakespeare to Existentialism
See Page 137

KER, W. P. and A. S. NAPIER – Editors
An English Miscellany
See Page 146

KERMODE, FRANK – Editor
Four Centuries of Shakespeare Criticism
Avon, 1965. 571pp. Paper $1.45. Arranged in four sections: general criticism; the comedies; the histories; the tragedies. This collection represents selections of scholarship from early critics to critics of the present day.

KETTLE, ARNOLD – Editor
Shakespeare in a Changing World
Lawrence and Wishart, 1964. 269pp. $6.50. Paper – International Publishers, $1.95. This collection of essays lays stress on the humanism of the playwright and on the value of the Marxist historical method for discovering the sources of that humanism. Among the essayists: Robert Weimann, Kenneth Muir, David Craig, and Charles Barber.

KNIGHT, G. WILSON
Byron and Shakespeare
Barnes & Noble, 1966. 381pp. $8.95. Professor Knight seeks to show how the life and thought of Byron reflect the main comedic and tragic experiences involved in the dramas of Shakespeare. The comparisons given seek to show that Shakespeare's dramas possess a relevance to the modern world. Index of Byronic Themes. Index of Names and Titles.

KNIGHTS, L. C.
Further Explorations: Essays in Criticism
Stanford University, 1965. 204pp. $5.00. Essays on such topics as Shakespeare's politics, personality and politics in "Julius Caesar," the social background of metaphysical poetry, "King Lear" as metaphor, and the question of character in Shakespeare's works.

LEECH, CLIFFORD
Shakespeare's Tragedies and Other Studies in Seventeenth Century Drama
Oxford, 1950. 232pp. $4.75. The essays on Shakespeare include studies of "Timon of Athens," "The Tempest," and "Othello" with general comments on the nature of the tragic conflict.

LEWINTER, OSWALD – Editor
Shakespeare in Europe
World, 1963. 382pp. Paper $2.25. Twenty-five major critics, over a period of 300 years, writing on all aspects of Shakespeare's art as seen from a Continental point of view. Included are essays by Voltaire, Lessing, Goethe, Schiller, Hegel, Stendahl, Grillparzer, Pushkin, Heine, Turgenev, von Hofmannsthal, and Barrault. Introduction. Bibliography. Index.

McKERROW, RONALD B.
Prolegomena for the Oxford Shakespeare
Oxford, 1969. 113pp. $6.00. Originally published in 1939, this is a reissue of the study in editorial methods as applied to Shakespeare's writings and especially to the Oxford edition of the writings.

McNEIR, WALDO F. and THELMA N. GREENFIELD – Editors
Pacific Coast Studies in Shakespeare
University of Oregon, 1966. 315pp. $7.50. The twenty essays which comprise this volume are a sampling of the variety of critical opinions and techniques found among Shakespearean scholars. The essays approach their subject from interpretive, bibliographic, linguistic, and comparative bases and touch upon nearly every phase of Shakespeare's work.

MATTHEWS, BRANDER and ASHLEY HORACE THORNDIKE – Editors
Shakespearean Studies
Russell & Russell, 1962. 452pp. $10.00. A reprint of the edition first published in 1916, this volume includes eighteen essays on a variety of subjects. It was prepared to honor the tercentenary of Shakespeare's death.

MIZENER, ARTHUR — Editor
Teaching Shakespeare
New American Library, 1969. 352pp. Paper $1.95. In a discussion that represents as closely as possible the actual teaching process, twelve of Shakespeare's plays are described in terms of plot, dramatic method, philosophic import, and place in the Shakespeare canon. Suggestions for discussion, specific questions, essay assignments, and comprehensive examinations are included for each play.

MUIR, KENNETH
Last Periods of Shakespeare, Racine, Ibsen
Wayne State University, 1961. 117pp. $5.00. Four lectures discussing the quality of the plays written by these playwrights in their final creative periods. An introductory essay considers the final achievements of a group of artists, among them Beethoven, Botticelli, Sophocles, Euripides, and Strindberg.

OLSON, CHARLES
Selected Writings
New Directions, 1966. 280pp. $7.95. Paper $2.45. Although this is primarily a collection of the poetry of Charles Olson, it also includes an essay on Shakespeare's use of verse in the later plays.

RABKIN, NORMAN — Editor
Approaches to Shakespeare
McGraw—Hill, 1964. 333pp. $5.95. Paper $2.95. This anthology of criticism attempts to isolate and discuss current issues in Shakespearean criticism by presenting a series of statements definitive of each of the major approaches being taken by important critics. Among these critics: A. C. Bradley, Francis Fergusson, Alfred Harbage, and F. W. Bateson.

RABKIN, NORMAN — Editor
Reinterpretations of Elizabethan Drama
Columbia, 1969. 205pp. $5.50. These six essays discuss the way audiences respond to the work of Shakespeare and his contemporaries in the theatre. These discussions, according to the editor, require a reassessment of the relation between the work of art and the subjective experience. Among the contributors are Jonas A. Barish, Max Bluestone, and John Russell Brown.

RALEIGH, SIR WALTER et.al. — Editors
Shakespeare's England: An Account of the Life and Manners of His Age
Oxford, 1962. Two volume set. $20.00. A reissue of the original 1916 edition, this volume contains a collection of essays on all aspects of life in Shakespeare's time. Among the contributors are Sir Walter Raleigh, George Unwin, C. T. Onions, Henry B. Wheatly, and others.

RALLI, AUGUSTUS
A History of Shakespearean Criticism
Humanities, 1932. $24.00. Volume One: 566pp. Volume Two: 582pp. This work traces the course of aesthetic opinion on Shakespeare from his own time to the end of 1925. The author has made a selection from the vast body of criticism with an exposition of each selection and a commentary. Sold as a two volume set.

RIDLER, ANNE — Editor
Shakespeare Criticism: 1919—1935
Oxford, 1936. 388pp. $2.75. An anthology of criticism and essays by fifteen acknowledged authorities. Among the contributors: E. E. Stoll, W. W. Greg, H. Granville—Barker, T. S. Eliot, H. B. Charlton, and G. Wilson Knight.

RIDLER, ANNE — Editor
Shakespeare Criticism: 1935—1960
Oxford, 1963. 401pp. $2.75. A sequel to the above book, this volume contains textual and imaginative essays by R. W. Chambers, J. Dover Wilson, Helen Gardner, G. Wilson Knight, W. H. Auden, and many others.

ROSSITER, A. P.
Angel with Horns and Other Shakespeare Lectures
Theatre Arts, 1961. 316pp. $6.85. A collection of fifteen lectures given at Stratford and Cambridge. Among the subjects are the history and problem plays and most of the great tragedies. Three lectures have a particular concern with tragi-comedy in its different guises. Index.

SCHUELLER, HERBERT — Editor
The Persistence of Shakespeare Idolatry
Wayne State University, 1964. 181pp. $5.00. A collection of essays by such authorities as Henri Peyre, Earl R. Wasserman, and Herman J. Weigand. Among the subjects are Shakespeare and modern French criticism, Dryden and the beginnings of Shakespeare, Shakespeare and German criticism. Mr. Weigand's "Hamlet's Consistent Inconsistency" is included as an appendix.

SHERBO, ARTHUR
Samuel Johnson: Editor of Shakespeare
University of Illinois, 1956. 181pp. Paper $3.00. A detailed examination of Johnson's 1765 edition of Shakespeare. The author considers the genesis and progress of the work. Also included is an essay on "The Adventurer."

SIEGEL, PAUL N.
His Infinite Variety: Major Shakespearean Criticism Since Johnson
Lippincott, 1964. 432pp. Paper $2.50. This anthology has essays on the poet's dramatic work in general and on the various genres in which he worked. Each section has an introduction which traces the trends in criticism from one period to the next.

SISSON, C. J.
Shakespeare

Longman, 1962, 50pp. Paper $ .85. A brief essay on the various critical and theatrical approaches to Shakespeare from the Elizabethan age to the present. Illustrated. Selected Bibliography.

SITWELL, EDITH
A Notebook on William Shakespeare
Beacon Press, 1961. 233pp. Paper $1.75. A series of random observations which make up a running commentary on a number of aspects of Shakespeare's art and themes.

SMITH, DAVID NICHOL – Editor
Shakespeare Criticism: A Selection – 1623–1840
Oxford, 1916. 371pp. $2.75. A collection of essays by such critics as Ben Jonson, Milton, Dryden, Pope, Lamb, DeQuincey, Hazlitt, Coleridge, and Carlyle.

SPENCER, T. J. B. – Editor
Shakespeare: A Celebration – 1564–1964
Penguin, 1964. 73pp. Paper $1.45. Among the authors and critics who have contributed essays to this anthology are C. J. Sisson, T. J. B. Spencer, Kenneth Muir, Laurence Kitchin, and Stanley Wells. Illustrated.

SPRAGUE, ARTHUR COLBY
The Doubling of Parts in Shakespeare's Plays
Society for Theatre Research, 1966. 35pp. Paper $2.50. Mr. Sprague asserts that in the eighteenth and nineteenth centuries the practice of doubling parts was often concealed from the audience and he gives numerous examples.

SPURGEON, CAROLINE F. E.
Keats's Shakespeare: A Descriptive Study
Oxford, 1966. 178pp. $8.00. This is a reprint of a book first published in 1928. The author had access to a copy of Shakespeare which bore markings by Keats and her book gives a fairly comprehensive description, and in part a reproduction, of the marks and notations. Illustrated.

STENDHAL
Racine and Shakespeare
See Page 123

STEWART, J. I. M.
Character and Motive in Shakespeare
Longman, 1965. 147pp. Paper $3.00. First published in 1949 and now reissued, this is a critical examination of the theories of the "realistic" school of Shakespearean criticism. Among the critics who belong to this school are Robert Bridges, Levin L. Schucking, and E. E. Stoll.

STOLL, ELMER EDGAR
From Shakespeare to Joyce
Ungar, 1964. 442pp. $7.95. First published in 1944 and now reissued, this collection of essays and studies presents the author's opinions on authors and critics, literature and life. Professor Stoll discusses Shakespeare's theatrical technique, his use of source material, and his characterization. There is consideration of the problem comedies, of motivation in "Hamlet," and essays on various of Shakespeare's characters. Index.

STOLL, ELMER EDGAR
Poets and Playwrights: Shakespeare, Jonson, Spenser, Milton
University of Minnesota, 1967. 282pp. Paper $2.95. This is a collection of nine essays originally published in 1930. Professor Stoll presents a consideration of the art of the poets and playwrights of the title. The longest essay, "Shakespeare and the Moderns," includes a review of Shakespeare as Professor Stoll conceives him. Index.

STOLL, ELMER EDGAR
Shakespeare and Other Masters
Russell & Russell, 1962. 430pp. $12.00. A reprint of the 1940 edition, this is a study of certain aspects of the art of Shakespeare, Homer, Sophocles, Moliere, and Racine. The work is a reaction against the overcareful textual criticism and ambiguity-hunting of modern critics.

SUTHERLAND, JAMES and JOEL HURSTFIELD – Editors
Shakespeare's World
St. Martin's, 1964. 199pp. $6.00. The essays in this volume are: "Shakespeare's World," "The Elizabethan People in the Age of Shakespeare," "Shakespeare's Tragedies," "Shakespeare's Treatment of Comedy," "The Uses of History," "Shakespeare's Language," "The Course of Shakespeare Criticism," and "The Close of an Epoch." Index.

TERRY, ELLEN
Four Lectures on Shakespeare
Blom, 1969. 201pp. $9.75. Originally published in 1932 and now reissued in a facimile edition, edited and with an introduction by Christopher St. John. The lectures were given in various places over the years 1911 to 1921 and the subjects include the children, the women, and the letters in Shakespeare's plays. Illustrated with a portrait of Miss Terry.

THALER, ALWIN
Shakespeare and Democracy
University of Tennessee, 1941. 312pp. $2.50. A collection of essays on such topics as Shakespeare and Whitman, the "lost" scenes of "Macbeth," the origin of Malvolio, the "country" plays and the strolling players, and various Elizabethan writers.

THALER, ALWIN and NORMAN SANDERS – Editors
Shakespearean Essays
University of Tennessee, 1964. 187pp. $3.50. Essays on various aspects of Shakespeare's tragic and comic art, by Kenneth Muir, Clifford Leech, Robert West, Norman Sanders, Mario Praz, and others.

TRAVERSI, DEREK
Shakespeare: The Last Phase
Stanford University, 1965. 272pp. $6.75. A study of the last plays which sees them as closely related to the great tragedies which preceded them. The apparent conventionality of their conception is revealed as a vehicle for a profoundly personal reading of life. This second edition of the book first published in 1955 contains a note by the author in which he modifies his views on the artistic failure of "Hamlet."

URE, PETER
W. B. Yeats and the Shakespearian Moment
Queen's University, 1969. 25pp. Paper $1.25. Professor Ure delivered this lecture in 1966 at Queen's University, Belfast, Ireland. It deals with W. B. Yeats' attitude toward Shakespeare as it is revealed in his criticism and in his work for the theatre. References.

WHITER, WALTER
A Specimen of a Commentary on Shakespeare
Methuen, 1967. 233pp. $14.95. Edited by Alan Over and Mary Bell, this is a revised and enlarged edition of the study originally published in 1794. In an age when the study of Shakespeare's characters was of prime interest and importance, Whiter developed a form of textual criticism closely linked to a study of the workings of the human mind and his book offers a psychological survey of the creative imagination illustrated by examples from Shakespeare's plays. Selected Bibliography. Index.

WILSON, F. P.
Shakespearian and Other Studies
Oxford, 1969. 345pp. $13.95. Edited by Helen Gardner, this is a collection of essays, articles and lectures on Shakespeare and related subjects. The volume includes long essays on "The English History Play" and "Shakespeare's Comedies."

SCHOLARLY EDITIONS OF PLAYS

Plays in Series

THE ALDUS SHAKESPEARE
Funk & Wagnall. Each volume—Paper $ .95. This series provides an annotated text of the play with, in each volume, a Preface by Israel Gollancz, an Introduction by C. H. Herford, and notes and comments by other Shakespearean authorities. Each volume also includes a Glossary.

Antony and Cleopatra	1967.	189pp.
As You Like It	1967.	144pp.
The Comedy of Errors	1968.	93pp.
Coriolanus	1968.	193pp.
Hamlet	1967.	220pp.
Julius Caesar	1967.	136pp.
King Lear	1967.	203pp.
King Richard II	1967.	167pp.
King Richard III	1967.	208pp.
Macbeth	1967.	142pp.
The Merchant of Venice	1968.	137pp.
The Merry Wives of Windsor	1967.	140pp.
A Midsummer Night's Dream	1967.	110pp.
Othello	1967.	176pp.
Romeo and Juliet	1968.	167pp.
The Sonnets	1968.	116pp.
The Taming of the Shrew	1967.	129pp.
The Tempest	1968.	119pp.
Twelfth Night	1967.	128pp.
The Winter's Tale	1968.	159pp.

THE ARDEN SHAKESPEARE
Barnes & Noble. Each volume $6.50. Paper $1.95. Originally published over sixty years ago, each of the volumes in this series has been revised and re-edited in the light of modern criticism and research. The text for the series is based on the Shakespeare Folio of 1623. The collation to the play's text records all the substantive emendations of the play's text made in the history of the play's editing. The Introduction and the Appendices by the editor investigate the text, its date, sources, stage history, and the nature of the plot. General Editors of the series are Dr. H. F. Brooks and Professor Harold Jenkins. The editor of each volume is listed below.

All's Well That Ends Well Edited by G. K. Hunter
1959. 216pp. $6.50. Paper—1967. 152pp. $1.95.

Antony and Cleopatra Edited by M. R. Ridley
1954. 285pp. $6.50. Paper—1965. 278pp. $1.95.

The Comedy of Errors Edited by R. A. Foakes
1962. 117pp. $6.50. Paper—1968. 117pp. $1.95.

Cymbeline Edited by J. M. Nosworthy
1955. 224pp. $6.50. Paper—1969. 216pp. $1.95.

Julius Caesar Edited by T. S. Dorsch
1955. 166pp. $6.50. Paper—1965. 166pp. $1.95.

King Henry IV – Part I Edited by A. R. Humphreys
1960. 203pp. $6.50. Paper—1966. 203pp. $1.95.

King Henry IV – Part II Edited by A. R. Humphreys
1966. 242pp. $6.50. Paper—1967. 242pp. $1.95.

King Henry V Edited by J. H. Walter
1954. 174pp. $6.50. Paper—1965. 174pp. $1.95.

King Henry VI – Part I Edited by A. S. Cairncross
1962. 172pp. $6.50. Paper—1969. 172pp. $1.95.

King Henry VI – Part II Edited by A. S. Cairncross
1957. 197pp. $6.50. Paper—1969. 197pp. $1.95.

King Henry VI – Part III Edited by A. S. Cairncross
1964. 187pp. $6.50. Paper—1969. 187pp. $1.95.

King Henry VIII Edited by R. A. Foakes
1957. 215pp. $6.50. Paper—1968. 215pp. $1.95.

King John Edited by A. J. Honigmann
1954. 176pp. $6.50. Paper—1967. 176pp. $1.95.

King Lear Edited by K. Muir
1952. 260pp. $6.50. Paper—1964. 260pp. $1.95.

King Richard II Edited by P. Ure
1956. 210pp. $6.50. Paper—1966. 210pp. $1.95.

Love's Labour's Lost Edited by R. W. David
1951. 196pp. $6.50. Paper—1968. 187pp. $1.95.

Macbeth Edited by K. Muir
1951. 205pp. $6.50. Paper—1964. 205pp. $1.95.

Measure for Measure Edited by J. W. Lever
1965. 304pp. $6.50. Paper – 1967. 203pp. $1.95.
The Merchant of Venice Edited by J. R. Brown
1955. 174pp. $6.50. Paper – 1964. 174pp. $1.95.
The Merry Wives of Windsor Edited by H. J. Oliver
1971. 149pp. $6.50.
Othello Edited by M. R. Ridley
1958. 246pp. $6.50. Paper – 1965. 246pp. $1.95.
Pericles Edited by F. D. Hoeniger
1963. 188pp. $6.50. Paper – 188pp. 1969. $1.95.
The Poems Edited by F. T. Prince
1960. 201pp. $6.50. Paper – 1969. 201pp. $1.95.
The Tempest Edited by Frank Kermode
1954. 174pp. $6.50. Paper – 1964. 174pp. $1.95.
Timon of Athens Edited by H. J. Oliver
1959. 155pp. $6.50. Paper – 1969. 155pp. $1.95.
Titus Andronicus Edited by J. C. Maxwell
1953. 138pp. $6.50. Paper – 1968. 132pp. $1.95.
The Two Gentlemen of Verona Edited by C. Leech
1969. 122pp. $6.50.
The Winter's Tale Edited by J. H. P. Pafford
1963. 225pp. $6.50. Paper – 1966. 225pp. $1.95.

THE BLACKFRIAR'S SHAKESPEARE

Wm. C. Brown. This series of texts of Shakespeare's plays is printed in an 8½ x 11 size. The edition includes an annotated text, a general introduction that discusses Shakespeare's life and time, and a critical introduction by the individual editor of the play. A feature of the series is a wide right-hand margin for note taking. The General Editor for the series is J. Leeds Barroll. All volumes are paperbound.

Antony and Cleopatra Edited by C. J. Gianakaris
1969. 89pp. $1.25.
Hamlet Edited by J. Leeds Barroll
1970. 101pp. $1.25.
Henry IV – Part II Edited by Herbert R. Coursen
1971. 83pp. $1.25.
Henry V Edited by Charles R. Forker
1971. 82pp. $1.25.
Henry VIII Edited by H. M. Richmond
1971. 80pp. $1.25.
Julius Caesar Edited by Rudolph E. Habenicht
1970. 74pp. $ .95.
King Lear Edited by W. R. Elton
1971. 91pp. $1.25.
Love's Labour's Lost Edited by James L. Calderwood
1970. 71pp. $1.25.
Macbeth Edited by R. W. Dent
1969. 61pp. $1.25.
The Merchant of Venice Edited by John Cutts
1970. 66pp. $ .95.
A Midsummer Night's Dream Edited by Sidney Homan
1970. 54pp. $ .95.
Much Ado About Nothing Edited by Barbara Lewalski
1970. 68pp. $ .95.
Othello Edited by J. Leeds Barroll
1971. 89pp. $1.25.
Richard II Edited by Norman Sanders
1971. 72pp. $1.25.
Romeo and Juliet Edited by Marvin Spevack
1970. 82pp. $1.25.
The Tempest Edited by Leonard Nathanson
1970. 56pp. $ .95.
Troilus and Cressida Edited by Scott Colley
1970. 85pp. $1.25.
Twelfth Night Edited by T. H. Howard–Hill
1970. 65pp. $ .95.
The Winter's Tale Edited by Dean Frye
1971. 89pp. $1.25.

THE CAMBRIDGE POCKET SHAKESPEARE

Cambridge University Press. Each volume – $1.45. This series provides the "New Shakespeare" text of the play. The General Editor of the series is John Dover Wilson. A Glossary is provided at the end of each volume. Editors of individual plays are listed below.

All's Well That Ends Well Edited by J. D. Wilson
1963. 113pp.
Antony and Cleopatra Edited by J. D. Wilson
1959. 141pp.
As You Like It Edited by Arthur Quiller–Couch and J. D. Wilson
1957. 102pp.
The Comedy of Errors Edited by Arthur Quiller–Couch and J. D. Wilson
1962. 73pp.
Coriolanus Edited by J. D. Wilson
1958. 159pp.
Cymbeline Edited by J. D. Wilson
1961. 149pp.
Hamlet Edited by Arthur Quiller–Couch and J. D. Wilson
1958. 169pp.
Julius Caesar Edited by J. D. Wilson
1957. 108pp.
King Henry IV – Part I Edited by J. D. Wilson
1958. 116pp.
King Henry IV – Part II Edited by J. D. Wilson
1958. 130pp.
King Henry V Edited by J. D. Wilson
1958. 126pp.
King Henry VI – Part I Edited by J. D. Wilson
1961. 114pp.
King Henry VI – Part II Edited by J. D. Wilson
1962 133pp.
King Henry VI – Part III Edited by J. D. Wilson
1962. 133pp.
King Henry VIII Edited by J. C. Maxwell
1962. 135pp.
King John Edited by J. D. Wilson
1958. 104pp.
King Lear Edited by J. D. Wilson
1961. 145pp.
King Richard II Edited by J. D. Wilson
1957. 112pp.
Love's Labour's Lost Edited by J. D. Wilson
1962. 121pp.
Macbeth Edited by J. D. Wilson
1963. 100pp.

Measure for Measure Edited by Arthur Quiller–Couch and J. D. Wilson
1958. 106pp.
The Merchant of Venice Edited by J. D. Wilson
1958. 97pp.
The Merry Wives of Windsor Edited by Arthur Quiller–Couch and J. D. Wilson
1965. 103pp.
A Midsummer Night's Dream Edited by Arthur Quiller–Couch and J. D. Wilson
1958. 83pp.
Much Ado About Nothing Edited by Arthur Quiller–Couch and J. D. Wilson
1969. 98pp.
Othello Edited by Alice Walker and J. D. Wilson
1957. 147pp.
Pericles Edited by J. C. Maxwell
1965. 103pp.
Romeo and Juliet Edited by J. D. Wilson and G. I. Duthie
1959. 139pp.
The Taming of the Shrew Edited by Arthur Quiller–Couch and J. D. Wilson
1965. 103pp.
The Tempest Edited by Arthur Quiller–Couch and J. D. Wilson
1959. 84pp.
Timon of Athens Edited by J. D. Wilson
1961. 103pp.
Titus Andronicus Edited by J. D. Wilson
1963. 104pp.
Troilus and Cressida Edited by Alice Walker and J. D. Wilson
1957. 146pp.
Twelfth Night Edited by Arthur Quiller–Couch and J. D. Wilson
1958. 100pp.
The Two Gentlemen of Verona Edited by J. D. Wilson
1958. 80pp.
The Winter's Tale Edited by J. D. Wilson
1959. 120pp.

THE FOLGER LIBRARY GENERAL READER'S SHAKESPEARE

Washington Square Press. In this series, the text of the play is set on right-hand pages with all notes placed on facing unpaged left-hand pages. An introduction to the play with essential information about the playwright and his stage is included as are Suggestions for Further Reading. Illustrated with material from the Folger Library collections. The editors of the series are Louis B. Wright and Virginia A. LaMar. All volumes are paperbound.

All's Well That Ends Well	1965.	116pp.	$ .45.
Antony and Cleopatra	1961.	143pp.	$ .50.
As You Like It	1959.	105pp.	$ .50.
The Comedy of Errors	1963.	77pp.	$ .50.
Coriolanus	1962.	145pp.	$ .50.
Cymbeline	1965.	139pp.	$ .45.
Hamlet	1957.	147pp.	$ .50.
Julius Caesar	1959.	95pp.	$ .60.
King Henry IV – Part I	1961.	115pp.	$ .60.
King Henry IV – Part II	1961.	126pp.	$ .50.
King Henry V	1960.	123pp.	$ .50.
King Henry VI – Part I	1966.	111pp.	$ .45.
King Henry VI – Part II	1966.	125pp.	$ .45.
King Henry VI – Part III	1967.	125pp.	$ .45.
King Henry VIII	1968.	131pp.	$ .45.
King John	1967.	100pp.	$ .45.
King Lear	1956.	125pp.	$ .60.
King Richard II	1962.	113pp.	$ .60.
King Richard III	1960.	148pp.	$ .60.
Love's Labour's Lost	1961.	107pp.	$ .45.
Macbeth	1959.	93pp.	$ .60.
Measure for Measure	1965.	112pp.	$ .50.
The Merchant of Venice	1957.	94pp.	$ .60.
The Merry Wives of Windsor	1964.	113pp.	$ .50.
A Midsummer Night's Dream	1958.	81pp.	$ .60.
Much Ado About Nothing	1964.	101pp.	$ .50.
Othello	1957.	127pp.	$ .60.
Pericles	1968.	99pp.	$ .45.
Romeo and Juliet	1959.	107pp.	$ .50.
The Sonnets	1967.	154pp.	$ .60.
The Taming of the Shrew	1963.	107pp.	$ .50.
The Tempest	1961.	88pp.	$ .50.
Timon of Athens	1967.	98pp.	$ .45.
Titus Andronicus	1968.	100pp.	$ .45.
Troilus and Cressida	1966.	137pp.	$ .45.
Twelfth Night	1960.	99pp.	$ .60.
The Two Gentlemen of Verona	1964.	86pp.	$ .45.
The Winter's Tale	1966.	121pp.	$ .50.

THE INVITATION TO SHAKESPEARE

Dell. Each volume – Paper $ .50. The complete text of Shakespeare's play, edited, introduced, and with facing page notes by Edmund Fuller. Prepared particularly for high school students by a high-school teacher. Plot summaries of each scene at the beginning of the scene are also included. The Introduction is addressed to the teacher. Selections from Shakespearean criticism are also provided.

As You Like It	1968.	280pp.
Hamlet	1967.	407pp.
Henry IV – Part I	1968	317pp.
Julius Caesar	1966.	272pp.
Macbeth	1967.	256pp.
The Merchant of Venice	1966.	268pp.
A Midsummer Night's Dream	1968.	223pp.
Romeo and Juliet	1968.	318pp.

THE KITTREDGE SHAKESPEARE

Xerox College Publishing. Each volume: Paper $ .95. Originally edited by George Lyman Kittredge, the reknowned Shakespeare scholar, and newly revised by Irving Ribner to bring the introductions and notes up to date and to add new explanatory notes.

All's Well That Ends Well	1968.	116pp.
Antony and Cleopatra	1966.	149pp.
As You Like It	1967.	109pp.
The Comedy of Errors	1966.	71pp.
Coriolanus	1967.	148pp.

Cymbeline	1969.	145pp.
Hamlet	1967.	179pp.
Julius Caesar	1966.	102pp.
King Henry IV – Part I	1966.	117pp.
King Henry IV – Part II	1966.	123pp.
King Henry VI – Part I	1969.	115pp.
King Henry VI – Part II	1969.	122pp.
King Henry VI – Part III	1969.	119pp.
King Henry VIII	1968.	128pp.
King John	1966.	100pp.
King Lear	Undated	147pp.
King Richard II	1966.	108pp.
King Richard III	1968.	150pp.
Love's Labour's Lost	1968.	112pp.
Macbeth	1966.	101pp.
Measure for Measure	1967.	112pp.
The Merchant of Venice	1966.	102pp.
The Merry Wives of Windsor	1969.	104pp.
A Midsummer Night's Dream	1966.	85pp.
Much Ado About Nothing	1967.	109pp.
Othello	1966.	141pp.
Pericles	1969.	99pp.
The Minor Poems	1969.	147pp.
Romeo and Juliet	1966.	126pp.
The Sonnets	1968.	163pp.
The Taming of the Shrew	1966.	104pp.
The Tempest	1967.	93pp.
Timon of Athens	1967.	104pp.
Titus Andronicus	1969.	100pp.
Troilus and Cressida	1967.	140pp.
Twelfth Night	1966.	104pp.
The Two Gentlemen of Verona	1969.	90pp.
The Two Noble Kinsmen	1969.	130pp.
The Winter's Tale	1967.	126pp.

THE LAUREL SHAKESPEARE

Dell. Each volume in this series includes the text of the play in a modern restoration of the original folios completed in late 1960 by Charles Jasper Sisson. Francis Fergusson, the General Editor, provides an Introduction to the dramatic and critical background of the work and an essay entitled, "Shakespeare and His Theatre." Glossary notes by H. H. Smith are provided. Also included are Suggestions for Further Reading. Each volume provides a modern commentary by an outstanding actor, director, critic, or other authority in a special aspect of the play. All volumes are paperbound.

All's Well That Ends Well Commentary by Dorothy Jeakins
1961. 221pp. $ .45.

Antony and Cleopatra Commentary by William Troy
1961. 254pp. $ .45.

As You Like It Commentary by Esme Church
1959. 192pp. $ .45.

The Comedy of Errors Commentary by Frederic McConnell
1965. 157pp. $ .35.

Coriolanus Commentary by Sir Tyrone Guthrie
1962. 255pp. $ .35.

Cymbeline Commentary by Elizabeth Drew
1964. 237pp. $ .45.

Hamlet Commentary by Maurice Evans
1958. 255pp. $ .45.

Julius Caesar Commentary by Philip Lawrence
1958. 188pp. $ .45.

King Henry IV – Part I Commentary by Sir Ralph Richardson
1959. 224pp. $ .45.

King Henry IV – Part II Commentary by Eric Berry
1962. 222pp. $ .35.

King Henry V Commentary by Joseph Papp
1962. 224pp. $ .35.

King Henry VI – Part I, II, and III Commentary by James Sandoe
1963. 510pp. $ .95.

King Henry VIII Commentary by Charles Jasper Sisson
1968. 222pp. $ .50.

King John Commentary by Douglas Seale
1963. 190pp. $ .35.

King Lear Commentary by Dudley Fitts
1961. 190pp. $ .45.

King Richard II Commentary by J. A. Bryant, Jr.
1961. 191pp. $ .35.

King Richard III Commentary by Stuart Vaughan
1958. 254pp. $ .40.

Love's Labour's Lost Commentary by J. V. Cunningham
1965. 191pp. $ .35.

Macbeth Commentary by Flora Robson
1959. 188pp. $ .45.

Measure for Measure Commentary by Robert H. Chapman
1962. 223pp. $ .35.

The Merchant of Venice Commentary by Morris Carnovsky
1958. 188pp. $ .45.

The Merry Wives of Windsor Commentary by Charles H. Shattuck
1966. 219pp. $ .45.

A Midsummer Night's Dream Commentary by Lincoln Kirstein
1960. 159pp. $ .45.

Much Ado About Nothing Commentary by Virgil Thomson
1960. 191pp. $ .35.

The Narrative Poetry of Shakespeare Introduction by Monroe K. Spears
1968. 252pp. $ .75.

Othello Commentary by John Houseman
1959. 252pp. $ .45.

Pericles Commentary by R. W. B. Lewis
1966. 189pp. $ .50.

Romeo and Juliet Commentary by W. H. Auden
1958. 223pp. $ .45.

The Sonnets Introduction by C. L. Barber
1960. 224pp. $ .45.

The Taming of the Shrew Commentary by Margaret Webster
1958. 190pp. $ .45.

The Tempest Commentary by Jean Rosenthal
1961. 190pp. $ .45.

Timon of Athens Commentary by Kenneth Burke
1963. 190pp. $ .35.

Titus Andronicus Commentary by Alan S. Downer
1967. 188pp. $ .50.

Troilus and Cressida Commentary by R. P. Blackmur
1966. 253pp. $ .50.

Twelfth Night Commentary by E. Martin Browne
1959. 191pp. $ .45.

The Two Gentlemen of Verona Commentary by Howard Nemerov
1964. 173pp. $ .35

The Winter's Tale Commentary by D. A. Traversi
1959. 224pp. $ .35.

THE LUDOWYK SHAKESPEARE

Cambridge. This edition contains the text of the New Shakespeare series with notes edited by E. F. C. Ludowyk. The series is to be used in conjunction with Ludowyk's introduction to Shakespearean study, "Understanding Shakespeare."

King Henry V	1966.	229pp.		$2.00.
Julius Caesar	1965.	185pp.		$2.00.
Macbeth	1964.	171pp.	Paper	$1.25.
The Merchant of Venice	1964.	185pp.	Paper	$1.25.
Richard II	1968.	205pp.		$2.00.
Twelfth Night	1963.	170pp.	Paper	$1.25.

THE NEW SHAKESPEARE

Cambridge. This edition provides a text of the play which takes account of the scholarship—bibliographical, historical, and linguistic—of the twentieth century. Each volume contains the text of the play, full notes, both textual and explanatory, an introduction by the editors, a stage history, and a glossary of difficult words and phrases. The series began to appear in 1921 and the publication dates below reflect the latest edition which includes additions or editorial changes from the first edition. The paperbound editions are photographic reprints of the original setting, unabridged and in its latest revision, with the type enlarged for greater clarity.

All's Well That Ends Well Edited by Sir Arthur Quiller–Couch and J. Dover Wilson
1955. 202pp. $5.50. Paper – 1968. 203pp. $ .95.

Antony and Cleopatra Edited by John Dover Wilson
1950. 262pp. $5.50. Paper – 1968. 262pp. $ .95.

As You Like It Edited by Sir Arthur Quiller–Couch and J. Dover Wilson
1965. 181pp. $5.50. Paper – 1968. 181pp. $ .95.

The Comedy of Errors Edited by J. Dover Wilson
1962. 125pp. $5.50. Paper – 1968. 125pp. $ .95.

Coriolanus Edited by J. Dover Wilson
1964. 274pp. $5.50. Paper – 1969. 274pp. $ .95.

Cymbeline Edited by J. C. Maxwell
1960. 246pp. $5.50. Paper – 1968. 246pp. $ .95.

Hamlet Edited by J. Dover Wilson
1934. 310pp. $5.50. Paper – 1968. 310pp. $ .95.

Julius Caesar Edited by J. Dover Wilson
1964. 219pp. $5.50. Paper – 1968. 219pp. $ .95.

King Henry IV – Part I Edited by J. Dover Wilson
1964. 210pp. $5.50. Paper – 1968. 210pp. $ .95.

King Henry IV – Part II Edited by J. Dover Wilson
1965. 231pp. $5.50. Paper – 1968. 231pp. $ .95.

King Henry V Edited by J. Dover Wilson
1964. 201pp. $5.50. Paper – 1968. 201pp. $ .95.

King Henry VI – Part I Edited by J. Dover Wilson
1965. 222pp. $5.50. Paper – 1968. 222pp. $ .95.

King Henry VI – Part II Edited by J. Dover Wilson
1965. 221pp. $5.50. Paper – 1968. 221pp. $ .95.

King Henry VI – Part III Edited by J. Dover Wilson
1965. 225pp. $5.50. Paper – 1968. 225pp. $ .95.

King Henry VIII Edited by J. C. Maxwell
1962. 251pp. $5.50. Paper – 1969. 251pp. $ .95.

King John Edited by J. Dover Wilson
1954. 208pp. $5.50. Paper – 1969. 208pp. $ .95.

King Lear Edited by G. I. Duthie and J. Dover Wilson
1968. 300pp. $5.50. Paper – 1968. 300pp. $ .95.

King Richard II Edited by J. Dover Wilson
1966. 250pp. $5.50. Paper – 1968. 250pp. $ .95.

King Richard III Edited by J. Dover Wilson
1968. 280pp. $5.50. Paper – 1968. 280pp. $ .95.

Love's Labour's Lost Edited by J. Dover Wilson
1962. 213pp. $5.50. Paper – 1969. 213pp. $ .95.

Macbeth Edited by J. Dover Wilson
1947. 186pp. $5.50. Paper – 1968. 186pp. $ .95.

Measure for Measure Edited by Sir Arthur Quiller–Couch and J. Dover Wilson
1965. 176pp. $5.50. Paper – 1969. 176pp. $ .95.

The Merchant of Venice Edited by Sir Arthur Quiller–Couch and J. Dover Wilson
1962. 194pp. $5.50. Paper – 1968. 194pp. $ .95.

The Merry Wives of Windsor Edited by Sir Arthur Quiller–Couch and J. Dover Wilson
1964. 149pp. $5.50. Paper – 1969. 149pp. $ .95.

A Midsummer Night's Dream Edited by Sir Arthur Quiller–Couch and J. Dover Wilson
1940. 176pp. $5.50. Paper –1968. 176pp. $ .95.

Much Ado About Nothing Edited by Sir Arthur Quiller–Couch and J. Dover Wilson
1962. 174pp. $5.50. Paper – 1969. 174pp. $ .95.

Othello Edited by John Dover Wilson and Alice Walker
1966. 246pp. $5.50. Paper – 1969. 246pp. $ .95.

Pericles Edited by J. C. Maxwell
1956. 211pp. $5.50. Paper – 1969. 211pp. $ .95.

The Poems Edited by J. C. Maxwell
1966. 258pp. $5.50. Paper – 1969. 258pp. $ .95.

Romeo and Juliet Edited by J. Dover Wilson and G. I. Duthie
1961. 249pp. $5.50. Paper – 1969. 249pp. $ .95.

The Sonnets Edited by J. Dover Wilson
1967. 273pp. $5.50. Paper – 1969. 273pp. $ .95.

The Taming of the Shrew Edited by Sir Arthur Quiller–Couch and J. Dover Wilson
1953. 194pp. $5.50. Paper – 1968. 194pp. $ .95.

The Tempest Edited by Sir Arthur Quiller–Couch and J. Dover Wilson
1965. 117pp. $5.50. Paper – 1969. 117pp. $ .95.

Timon of Athens Edited by J. C. Maxwell
1957. 189pp. $5.50. Paper – 1968. 189pp. $ .95.

Titus Andronicus Edited by J. Dover Wilson
1948. 171pp. $5.50. Paper – 1968. 171pp. $ .95.

Triolus and Cressida Edited by Alice Walker
1963. 254pp. $5.50. Paper – 1969. 254pp. $ .95.

Twelfth Night Edited by Sir Arthur Quiller–Couch and J. Dover Wilson
1964. 193pp. $5.50. Paper – 1968. 193pp. $ .95.

The Two Gentlemen of Verona Edited by Sir Arthur Quiller–Couch and J. Dover Wilson
1969. 110pp. $5.50. Paper – 1969. 110pp. $ .95.

The Winter's Tale Edited by Sir Arthur Quiller–Couch and J. Dover Wilson
1965. 206pp. $5.50. Paper – 1968. 206pp. $ .95.

THE NEW VARIORUM SHAKESPEARE

Dover. This series is an unabridged republication of the New Variorum editions edited by H. H. Furness. The editor has taken for his basic text the First Folio of 1623 and against this text has collated via footnotes every change, addition or omission, no matter how slight, from all the other Folios and Quartos. The footnotes further record all variant readings, suggested emendations, special interpretations, and important conclusions of every editor from Rowe to Grant White. Appendices contain critical essays by most of the major writers who have given Shakespeare their attention as well as reprints of source writings. Bibliographies. Lists of Editions. Indices. All volumes are paperbound.

As You Like It	1963.	452pp.	$2.75.
Hamlet – Volume One	1963.	473pp.	$2.75.
Hamlet – Volume Two	1963.	432pp.	$2.75.
King Lear	1963.	503pp.	$2.75.
Love's Labour's Lost	1964.	401pp.	$2.75.
Macbeth	1963.	566pp.	$4.00.
A Midsummer Night's Dream	1963.	357pp.	$2.75.
Much Ado About Nothing	1964.	420pp.	$3.00.
Othello	1963.	471pp.	$2.75.
Romeo and Juliet	1963.	480pp.	$2.75.
The Tempest	1964.	465pp.	$2.75.
Twelfth Night	1964.	434pp.	$2.75.
The Winter's Tale	1964.	432pp.	$2.75.

THE PELICAN SHAKESPEARE

Penguin. Each volume – Paper $ .95. Each volume in this series provides a fully annotated text of the play with an introduction by the editor and an essay on Shakespeare and his stage by the General Editor, Alfred Harbage.

All's Well That Ends Well Edited by Jonas A. Barish
1964. 143pp. $ .65.

Antony and Cleopatra Edited by Maynard Mack
1960. 160pp. $ .95.

As You Like It Edited by Ralph M. Sargent
1970. 121pp. $ .95.

The Comedy of Errors Edited by Paul A. Jorgensen
1964. 98pp. $ .50.

Coriolanus Edited by Harry Levin
1956. 164pp. $ .65.

Cymbeline Edited by Robert B. Heilman
1964. 176pp. $ .65.

Hamlet Edited by Willard Farnham
1969. 178pp. $ .75.

Julius Caesar Edited by S. F. Johnson
1960. 128pp. $ .95.

King Henry IV – Part I Edited by M. A. Shaaber
1970. 134pp. $ .85.

King Henry IV – Part II Edited by Allan Chester
1957. 147pp. $ .95.

King Henry V Edited by Alfred Harbage
1966. 153pp. $ .65.

King Henry VI – Part I Edited by David Bevington
1966. 131pp. $ .95.

King Henry VI – Parts II and III Edited by Robert K. Turner, Jr. and George Walton Williams
1967. 275pp. $1.25.

King Henry VIII Edited by F. David Hoeniger
1966. 153pp. $ .95.

King John Edited by Irving Ribner
1962. 128pp. $ .65.

King Lear Edited by Alfred Harbage
1970. 175pp. $ .95.

King Richard II Edited by Matthew W. Black
1957. 131pp. $ .95.

King Richard III Edited by G. Blakemore Evans
1969. 187pp. $1.15.

Love's Labour's Lost Edited by Alfred Harbage
1963. 138pp. $ .65.

Macbeth Edited by Alfred Harbage
1956. 115pp. $ .65.

Measure for Measure Edited by R. C. Bald
1970. 128pp. $ .85.

The Merchant of Venice Edited by Brents Stirling
1970. 124pp. $ .95.

The Merry Wives of Windsor Edited by Fredson Bowers
1963. 132pp. $ .65.

A Midsummer Night's Dream Edited by Madeleine Doran
1959. 119pp. $ .95.

Much Ado About Nothing Edited by Josephine Waters Bennett
1958. 126pp. $ .50.

Othello Edited by Gerald Eades Bentley
1970. 160pp. $ .85.

Pericles Edited by James G. McManaway
1967. 126pp. $ .95.

The Poems Edited by Richard Wilbur and Alfred Harbage
1966. 184pp. $ .95.

Romeo and Juliet Edited by John E. Hankins
1960. 150pp. $ .65.

The Sonnets Edited by Douglas Bush and Alfred Harbage
1970. 181pp. $1.25.

The Taming of the Shrew Edited by Richard Hosley
1970. 139pp. $ .95.

The Tempest Edited by Northrop Frye
1970. 108pp. $ .75.

Timon of Athens Edited by Charlton Hinman
1964. 128pp. $ .65.

Titus Andronicus Edited by Gustav Cross
1967. 127pp. $ .95.

Troilus and Cressida Edited by Virgil K. Whitaker
1958. 155pp. $ .95.

Twelfth Night Edited by Charles T. Prouty
1958. 121pp. $ .50.

The Two Gentlemen of Verona Edited by Berners A. W. Jackson
1964. 115pp. $ .65.

The Winter's Tale Edited by Baldwin Maxwell
1956. 140pp. $ .65.

THE SAMUEL FRENCH ACTING EDITION

Samuel French, Ltd. Each volume (Except as Noted): Paper $2.00. Published in England, this series is edited and annotated by George Skillan. This edition provides a fully annotated text of the play, a comprehensive analysis of the action, the words, the characters, sets, properties, and a light plot, and a set plan. Illustrations of costumes and scenery.

Antony and Cleopatra	1970.	182pp.	$4.00.
As You Like It	1944.	78pp.	
Hamlet	1964.	144pp.	
Julius Caesar	1937.	97pp.	
King Henry IV – Part I	Undated	75pp.	
King Henry IV – Part II	Undated	103pp.	
King Henry V	1938.	108pp.	
King Henry VIII	Undated	73pp.	
King Lear	1967.	216pp.	
King Richard II	1959.	141pp.	
King Richard III	1950.	116pp.	
Macbeth	Undated	110pp.	
The Merchant of Venice	1934.	77pp.	
The Merry Wives of Windsor	Undated	51pp.	
A Midsummer Night's Dream	Undated	58pp.	
Much Ado About Nothing	Undated	88pp.	
Othello	Undated	94pp.	
Romeo and Juliet	1947.	110pp.	
The Taming of the Shrew	Undated	79pp.	
The Tempest	1953.	74pp.	
Twelfth Night	Undated	91pp.	

THE SIGNET CLASSIC SHAKESPEARE

New American Library. Each volume contains a full text of the play with detailed footnotes at the bottom of each page. Introduction to the play by the editor, general discussion of Shakespeare's life by the General Editor, Sylvan Barnet, notes on the sources, and a collection of dramatic criticism from the past and present, as well as a Bibliography. All volumes are paperbound.

All's Well That Ends Well Edited by Sylvan Barnet
1965. 200pp. $ .50.

Antony and Cleopatra Edited by Barbara Everett
1964. 276pp. $ .75.

As You Like It Edited by Albert Gilman
1963. 237pp. $ .75.

The Comedy of Errors Edited by Harry Levin
1965. 176pp. $ .50.

Coriolanus Edited by Reuben Brower
1966. 304pp. $ .75.

Cymbeline Edited by Richard Hosley
1968. 239pp. $ .75.

Hamlet Edited by Edward Hubler
1963. 271pp. $ .75.

Julius Caesar Edited by Barbara Rosen and William Rosen
1963. 240pp. $ .75.

King Henry IV – Part I Edited by Maynard Mack
1965. 268pp. $ .50.

King Henry IV – Part II Edited by Norman N. Holland
1965. 240pp. $ .75.

King Henry V Edited by John Russell Brown
1965. 240pp. $ .50.

King Henry VI – Part I Edited by Lawrence V. Ryan
1967. 222pp. $ .50.

King Henry VI – Part II Edited by Arthur Freeman
1967. 224pp. $ .50.

King Henry VI – Part III Edited by Milton Crane
1968. 224pp. $ .75.

King Henry VIII Edited by S. Schoenbaum
1967. 239pp. $ .75.

King John Edited by William H. Matchett
1966. 224pp. $ .50.

King Lear Edited by Russell Fraser
1963. 287pp. $ .50.

King Richard II Edited by Kenneth Muir
1963. 255pp. $ .50.

King Richard III Edited by Mark Eccles
1964. 256pp. $ .50.

Love's Labour's Lost Edited by John Arthos
1965. 192pp. $ .50.

Macbeth Edited by Sylvan Barnet
1963. 247pp. $ .50.

Measure for Measure Edited by S. Nagarajan
1964. 240pp. $ .75.

The Merchant of Venice Edited by Kenneth Myrick
1965. 176pp. $ .50.

The Merry Wives of Windsor Edited by William Green
1965. 188pp. $ .50.

A Midsummer Night's Dream Edited by Wolfgang Clemen
1963. 186pp. $ .75.

Much Ado About Nothing Edited by David L. Stevenson
1964. 160pp. $ .50.

The Narrative Poems Edited by William Burto
1968. 223pp. $ .95.

Othello Edited by Alvin Kernan
1963. 270pp. $ .50.

Pericles Edited by Ernest Schanzer
1965. 208pp. $ .50.

Romeo and Juliet Edited by J. A. Bryant, Jr.
1964. 220pp. $ .50.

The Sonnets Edited by William Burto
1964. 240pp. $ .75.

The Taming of the Shrew Edited by Robert B. Heilman
1966. 223pp. $ .75.

The Tempest Edited by Robert Langbaum
1964. 224pp. $ .75.

Timon of Athens Edited by Maurice Charney
1965. 239pp. $ .50.

Titus Andronicus Edited by Sylvan Barnet
1964. 181pp. $ .50.

Troilus and Cressida Edited by Daniel Seltzer
1963. 288pp. $ .60.
Twelfth Night Edited by Herschel Baker
1965. 208pp. $ .75.
The Two Gentlemen of Verona Edited by Bertrand Evans
1964. 200pp. $ .50.
The Two Noble Kinsman Edited by Clifford Leech
1966. 268pp. $ .50.
The Winter's Tale Edited by Frank Kermode
1963. 223pp. $ .50.

THE YALE SHAKESPEARE

Yale University Press. Each volume in this series includes a complete text of the play, edited by a Shakespearean scholar. Among the features of the volumes are Appendices and notes. Some of the volumes include an Index and/or a facsimile page. Helge Kokeritz and Charles Prouty have included a special Preface to some of the volumes. None of the volumes were available for perusal so information may be incomplete.

All's Well That Ends Well Edited by Arthur E. Case
1926. 140pp. $4.00.
Antony and Cleopatra Edited by Peter G. Phialas
1955. 171pp. $4.00. Paper $ .95.
The Comedy of Errors Edited by R. D. French
1926. 96pp. $4.00.
Coriolanus Edited by Tucker Brooke
1924. 182pp. $4.00.
Hamlet Edited by Tucker Brooke and Jack Randall Crawford
1947. 222pp. $4.00. Paper $1.25.
Julius Caesar Edited by Alvin Kernan
1959. 125pp. Paper $1.25.
King Henry IV – Part I Edited by Tucker Brooke and Samuel B. Hemingway
1947. 169pp. $4.00. Paper $1.25.
King Henry V Edited by R. J. Dorius
1955. 166pp. Paper $ .95.
King Henry VI – Part II Edited by Tucker Brooke
1923. 166pp. $4.00.
King Henry VI – Part III Edited by Tucker Brooke
1923. 149pp. $4.00.
King Henry VIII Edited by John M. Berdan and Tucker Brooke
1925. 166pp. $4.00.
King John Edited by Stanley T. Williams
1927. 133pp. $4.00.
King Lear Edited by Tucker Brooke and William Lyon Phelps
1947. 202pp. $4.00. Paper $1.25.
King Richard II Edited by Robert T. Petersson
1957. 163pp. $4.00.
King Richard III Edited by Jack R. Crawford
1927. 207pp. $4.00.
Love's Labour's Lost Edited by Wilbur L. Cross and Tucker Brooke
1925. 153pp. $4.00.
Macbeth Edited by Eugene M. Waith
1954. 138pp. $4.00. Paper $1.25.
Measure for Measure Edited by David Harding
1954. 131pp. $4.00. Paper $1.25.
The Merchant of Venice Edited by A. D. Richardson III
1960. 123pp. $4.00. Paper $1.25.
The Merry Wives of Windsor Edited by George Van Santvoord
1922. 134pp. $4.00.
A Midsummer Night's Dream Edited by Willard Higley Durham
1918. 96pp. $4.00.
Much Ado About Nothing Edited by Tucker Brooke
1917. 138pp. $4.00.
Othello Edited by Tucker Brooke and Lawrence Mason
1947. 188pp. $4.00. Paper $1.25.
Pericles Edited by Alfred R. Bellinger
1925. 139pp. $4.00.
Romeo and Juliet Edited by Richard Hosley
1954. 174pp. $4.00. Paper $1.25.
The Sonnets Edited by Edward Bliss Reed
1923. 107pp. $4.00.
The Tempest Edited by David Horne
1955. 105pp. $4.00. Paper $ .95.
Timon of Athens Edited by Stanley T. Williams
1919. 141pp. $4.00.
Titus Andronicus Edited by A. M. Witherspoon
1926. 156pp. $4.00.
Troilus and Cressida Edited by Jackson J. Campbell
1956. 169pp. $4.00.
Twelfth Night Edited by William P. Holden
1954. 144pp. $4.00. Paper $ .95.
The Two Gentlemen of Verona Edited by Karl Young
1924. 105pp. $4.00.
Venus and Adonis, Lucrece, and The Minnor Poems Edited by Albert Feuillerat
1927. 198pp. $4.00.

One Volume Editions

ALEXANDER, PETER – Editor
William Shakespeare: The Complete Works
Random House, 1952. 1,376pp. $7.95. Thirty-seven plays, the poems and "The Sonnets" are included in this one volume edition. Also provided is a special transcript by Sir Walter Greg of Shakespeare's contribution to "Sir Thomas More." A biographical introduction, the preliminary matter to the First Folio, and a Glossary of nearly 2,500 entries complete the volume.

CRAIG, W. J. – Editor
The Oxford Shakespeare: Complete Works
Oxford, 1969. 1,166pp. $5.00. Originally published in 1906, this edition provides the thirty-seven plays, "The Sonnets," and the poems. The editor has included an Index of Characters, an Index of First Lines of Songs, and a twenty-three page Glossary.

CRAIG, W. J. – Editor
The Oxford Shakespeare: Oxford India Paper Edition
Oxford, 1965. 1,166pp. $12.00. Originally printed in this edition in 1954, this volume is printed on Oxford India Paper and contains the same material as the previously noted edition. Also provided in this volume are thirty-two illustrations of modern productions of the works by the Old Vic and other London theatres, Stratford-on-Avon productions, and productions from the Bristol Old Vic, and the Stratford, Ontario, Shakespeare Festival. Notes on the Sequence of the Plays. Glossary. Index of Characters.

HARBAGE, ALFRED – General Editor
The Complete Pelican Shakespeare
Penquin, 1969. 1,481pp. $15.00. Originally published in thirty-eight separate volumes between 1956 and 1967, and now brought together in a one volume edition for the first time. A general introduction gives an account of Shakespeare's life and art. The works are divided into five sections: Commedies, Histories, Tragedies, Romances, and Non-Dramatic Poetry. Each section is preceded by a Foreword and the poetry and all the plays are accompanied by individual introductions. There are full bibliographies and notes. Five new drawings by C. Walter Hodges are included as are nineteen pages of the First Folio in facsimile and a reproduction of Hollar's famous panorama of London in 1647.

HARRISON, GEORGE B. – Editor
Shakespeare: The Complete Works
Harcourt, 1968. 1,675pp. $14.95. Originally published in 1948, this volume provides annotated texts of the thirty-seven plays, "The Sonnets," and other poems. A long introduction by the editor provides material on the extant records of the life of Shakespeare, Elizabethan drama and playhouses, the study of the text, the development of Shakespeare's art, Shakespearean criticism and scholarship. Twenty-two pages of plates illustrate the volume. The editor has provided a series of Appendices which include topics needing larger annotation than a footnote. An annotated Reading List contains a selection of books of general interest, classical and modern Shakespearean criticism.

KITTREDGE, GEORGE LYMAN – Editor
The Complete Works of William Shakespeare
Crowell, 1966. 1,561pp. $15.00. This edition includes all the plays and poems ascribed to Shakespeare, in whole or in part, on satisfactory evidence. The text has been determined by a collation of the original editions. Introductions to the individual plays provide essential literary data and historical background and discuss the sources of the play and its relation to other works. A Glossary explains some 5,000 archaic and unusual terms. Also provided are over seven hundred photographs illustrating productions at the Old Vic and at the Royal Shakespeare Theatre at Stratford-on-Avon. Background articles by Michael Benthall and Edwin E. Willoughby complete the volume.

SISSON, CHARLES JASPER – Editor
William Shakespeare: The Complete Works
Harper & Row, 1960. 1,376pp. $10.00. Professor Sisson has edited from the Quartos and the First Folio all thirty-seven of the plays and has included "Sir Thomas More" as prepared by Harold Jenkins from the British Museum manuscript. Also included are five poems and "The Sonnets." An informative preface and an introduction for each play are provided. A biographical essay by Harold Jenkins and essays on the text, the editions, the language, the music, and other topics are provided by other Shakespearean authorities. The preliminary matter printed in the First Folio is provided in an Appendix. An Index of Characters is included as is a Glossary.

WRIGHT, WILLIAM ALDIS – Editor
The Complete Works of William Shakespeare
Doubleday, 1936. 1,527pp. $8.95. Originally published in a two-volume limited edition, this is a reissue of the edition with Rockwell Kent's forty illustrations. The text is that of the Cambridge edition and the Temple Notes are also included. The volume includes complete Indices and a Glossary plus a synopsis of each play, specially prepared for this edition. Historical data precede every play. Christopher Morley has written a Preface to the volume.

Collections of Plays

ALEXANDER, PETER – Editor
The Heritage Shakespeare
Heritage Press. $8.50. per volume. Three volume set: $25.00. Under the general editorship of Peter Alexander, who has provided an introduction to each play and a Glossary to each volume, this edition uses the text of the Collins Tudor Shakespeare series first published in 1951. The volume of comedies includes a preface by Tyrone Guthrie and reproduces the preliminary matter of the First Folio. The volume is illustrated by Edward Ardizzone. The volume of histories includes a preface by James G. McManaway and is illustrated with wood-engravings by John Farleigh. The volume of tragedies includes a preface by George Rylands and is illustrated by Agnes Miller Parker. Each volume is slip-cased separately.
The Heritage Shakespeare: Volume One. The Comedies. 1958. 1,120pp.
The Heritage Shakespeare: Volume Two. The Histories. 1958. 1,016pp.
The Heritage Shakespeare: Volume Three. The Tragedies. 1958. 1,362pp.

ANONYMOUS
The Portable Shakespeare
Viking, 1944. 800pp. $5.50. Paper $1.85. The complete texts of "Hamlet," "Macbeth," "Romeo and Juliet," "Julius Caesar," "A Midsummer Night's Dream," "As You Like It," and "The Tempest."

Famous passages from the other plays are included as are the complete Sonnets and Songs. Key-Word Index.

BROWNING. D. C. – Editor
Everyman's Library Works of Shakespeare
Dutton. $4.25 per volume. A three volume set of Shakespeare's works originally published in 1906. This edition includes D. C. Browning's prefatory notes. The text follows Clark and Wright's Cambridge Shakespeare text. Oliphant Smeaton has written a biographical introduction for this edition. Glossaries are provided in each volume.
Shakespeare's Comedies. 1966. 848pp.
Shakespeare's Histories and Poems. 1956. 888pp.
Shakespeare's Tragedies. 1968. 982pp.

FERGUSSON, FRANCIS – Editor
Shakespeare's Tragedies of Monarchy: Hamlet, Macbeth, and King Lear
Dell, 1962. 412pp. Paper $1.85. The texts of three of Shakespeare's tragedies edited and with introductions by Francis Fergusson. The text has been edited by Charles Jasper Sisson. A Preface and Introduction by Professor Fergusson provides information on the worlds of Shakespeare's theater and the world of the traditional monarchy. Suggestions for Further Reading. Glossary. Notes.

HOLLAND, NORMAN N. – General Editor
The American Shakespeare Festival Theatre Edition of Hamlet, Much Ado About Nothing, and Richard III
Avon, 1964. 702pp. Paper $ .95. Three prominent teachers of Shakespeare have provided authoritative texts of three of Shakespeare's plays. Professor Holland has prepared a general introduction considering Shakespeare's life and theater. Also included are expanded stage directions. A study guide for each play provides essays on plot and main characters, sources and early productions, questions for review, questions for discussion, lists of famous quotations, and a preparation for anyone contemplating a visit to a production of the play. Selected References.

MASEFIELD, JOHN – Introducer
The Great Illustrated Classics Series
Dodd, Mead. $4.50 per volume. Six volume set: $27.00. A general introduction to Shakespeare's plays and special introductions to each play have been provided by John Masefield, the seventeenth poet laureate of England. The texts of the plays is that of the New Clarendon Shakespeare, edited by W. J. Craig. A chronology of the life and works of Shakespeare is included as is a Glossary of unfamiliar words. Sixteen pages of Illustrations are included in each of the six volumes.
The Great Illustrated Classics Series. Three Comedies. 1965. 266pp. Includes: "A Midsummer Night's Dream," "As You Like It," "The Merchant of Venice."
The Great Illustrated Classics Series. Comedies II. 1967. 330pp. Includes "The Comedy of Errors," "The Two Gentlemen of Verona," "The Taming of the Shrew," "Much Ado About Nothing."
The Great Illustrated Classics Series. Three Histories. 1966. 331pp. Includes "Henry IV, Part I," "Henry IV, Part II," and "Henry V."
The Great Illustrated Classics Series. Histories II. 1968. 317pp. Includes "Henry VI, Part I," "Henry VI, Part II," "Henry VI, Part III,"
The Great Illustrated Classics Series. Three Tragedies. 1965. 325pp. Includes "Julius Caesar," "Hamlet," "Macbeth."
The Great Illustrated Classics Series. Tragedies II. 1966. 336pp. Includes "Romeo and Juliet," "Othello," "King Lear."

MODERN LIBRARY EDITORS
The Modern Library Complete Shakespeare
Modern Library. $2.95 per volume. Six volume set: $17.70. A six volume set of the complete Shakespeare. The first volume of each category includes texts of plays and the second volume includes texts as well as Notes and a Glossary.
The Comedies of Shakespeare: Volume One. No Date. 545pp. Includes "The Tempest," "The Two Gentlemen of Verona," "The Merry Wives of Windsor," "Measure for Measure," "The Comedy of Errors," "Much Ado About Nothing," "Love's Labour's Lost," "A Midsummer Night's Dream."
The Comedies of Shakespeare: Volume Two. No Date. 556pp. Includes: "The Merchant of Venice,""As You Like It," "The Taming of the Shrew," "All's Well That Ends Well," "Twelfth Night," "The Winter's Tale."
The Histories of Shakespeare: Volume One. No Date. 673pp. Includes: "King John," "Richard the Second," "Henry the Fourth," "Henry the Fifth," "Henry the Sixth."
The Histories and Poems of Shakespeare: Volume Two. No Date. 480pp. Includes: "Richard the Third," "Henry the Eighth," "The Sonnets," and "The Poetry."
The Tragedies of Shakespeare: Volume One. No Date. 579pp. Includes: "Troilus and Cressida," "Coriolanus," "Titus Andronicus," "Romeo and Juliet," "Timon of Athens," "Julius Caesar," "Macbeth."
The Tragedies of Shakespeare: Volume Two. No Date. 687pp. Includes: "Hamlet," "King Lear," "Othello," "Antony and Cleopatra," "Cymbeline," "Pericles."

WRIGHT, WILLIAM ALDIS – Editor
Four Great Comedies
Washington Square Press, 1948. 342pp. Paper $ .60. The Cambridge texts of "A Midsummer Night's Dream," "As You Like It," "Twelfth Night," and "The Tempest" are provided with a general introduction and introductions to each play by Mark Van Doren, synopses by J. Walker McSpadden, and illustrations by Frederick E. Banbery. Glossaries.

WRIGHT, WILLIAM ALDIS – Editor
Four Great Tragedies

Washington Square Press, 1968. 441pp. Paper $ .60. The texts of "Romeo and Juliet," "Macbeth," "Julius Caesar," and "Hamlet" are provided in the Cambridge text. J. Walker McSpadden has provided a summary of each plot and the texts are illustrated by Louis Glanzman. Introductions to each play have been written by Mark Van Doren. Glossary.

Single Editions of Works

BECKERMAN, BERNARD and JOSEPH PAPP—Editors
Love's Labour's Lost. Festival Shakespeare Edition
Macmillan, 1968. 228pp. $5.95. The text of the version used by the New York Shakespeare Festival production directed by Gerald Freedman in Central Park. The volume is illustrated with scenes from that 1965 production.

BECKERMAN, BERNARD and JOSEPH PAPP—Editors
Troilus and Cressida. Festival Shakespeare Edition
Macmillan, 1967. 212pp. $4.95. The text of the version used at the New York Shakespeare Festival in Central Park. Included is an essay on the direction of the play by Mr. Papp. Illustrated with photographs of the production.

BOCK, VERA
Love Poems and Sonnets of William Shakespeare
Doubleday, 1957. 160pp. $3.95. This edition is illustrated with eight full-color paintings by Miss Bock.

CAMPBELL, OSCAR JAMES—Editor
The Sonnets, Songs, and Poems of Shakespeare
Schocken, 1964. 378pp. $5.00. Paper $1.95. This edition provides an introduction, the text of the works, running commentary, glosses and notes. Illustrated with twenty-five woodcuts by Francesco Colonna originally published at Venice in 1499. Chronology of the life of Shakespeare. Bibliography.

DOWNER, ALAN S.—Editor
Oxberry's 1822 Edition of "King Richard III"
Society for Theatre Research, 1959. 168pp. $9.50. A facsimile edition of Shakespeare's tragedy with the descriptive notes recording Edmund Kean's performance as recorded by James H. Hackett. It is the most detailed account in existence of Kean's moves, business, and rhetorical delivery and gesture in a complete Shakespearean role, as recorded by another actor. Introduction and Notes by the editor. Illustrated. Bibliography. Paperbound.

HOY, CYRUS—Editor
Hamlet: A Critical Edition
Norton, 1963. 270pp. $5.00. Paper $2.00. This volume includes an authoritative text, intellectual background, extracts from the sources, plus essays in criticism by such critics as Samuel Johnson, Goethe, Schlegel, Coleridge, Hazlitt, T. S. Eliot, Edgar Stoll, G. Wilson Knight, John Dover Wilson, and others. Bibliography.

HUBLER, EDWARD—Editor
Shakespeare's Songs and Poems
McGraw–Hill, 1959. 534pp. Paper $3.95. The first annotated collection in a single volume of the songs and poems. An objective appraisal of the works is provided by the editor in a long critical essay.

INGRAM, W. G. and THEODORE REDPATH—Editors
Shakespeare's Sonnets
Barnes & Noble, 1965. 382pp. $7.50. Paper $3.00. The editors concentrate on a literary rather than a biographical interpretation of the Sonnets. The text is revised and rendered in modern spelling with detailed commentary on facing pages. Bibliography. Index.

JONES, HAROLD—Editor
Songs from Shakespeare
Faber & Faber, 1961. 61pp. $2.50. A collection of songs, illustrated in color by Mr. Jones, arranged to form the pattern of the round year, and conceived as the child's first introduction to Shakespeare.

KINES, TOM—Editor
Songs from Shakespeare's Plays and Popular Songs of Shakespeare's Time
Oak, 1964. 104pp. Paper $2.45. The words and music for seventy songs from Shakespeare's plays or contemporary with his time. Each song is chorded for guitar in the musical style of the Elizabethan era. Illustrated. Bibliography. Glossary.

PAPP, JOSEPH and TED CORNELL
William Shakespeare's Naked Hamlet
Macmillan, 1969. 187pp. $5.95. A production handbook for the controversial production of the play which was produced at the New York Shakespeare Festival Theatre. This volume includes the text, rock scores, photographs, a detailed commentary on the staging, text sources for each scene, and an introductory essay which probes the psychological background of the controversial interpretation. A preface recounts the violent critical and public reactions.

PROUDFOOT, G. R.—Editor
The Two Noble Kinsmen
University of Nebraska, 1970. 141pp. $4.75. Paper $2.00. A volume in the Regents Renaissance Drama series. This play has been ascribed to Shakespeare and John Fletcher. The volume includes an annotated text, an Introduction by the editor, and a Chronology.

SMITH, BARBARA HERRNSTEIN—Editor
The Sonnets: William Shakespeare
New York University, 1969. 290pp. $10.00. Paper—Avon, 1969. 290pp. $1.25. An annotated edition of

the Sonnets with a new indexing and critical commentary by the editor. Thematic Index. Index to Key Words. Index to First Lines.

TYNAN, KENNETH – Editor
Othello
Rupert Hart-Davis, 1966. 110pp. $6.95. This edition of the play is illustrated with color and black and white photographs from the rehearsals and the production of the National Theatre, England, which starred Sir Laurence Olivier. Introductory essay by Sir Laurence is included.

WEINER, ALBERT B.
Hamlet: The First Quarto – 1603
Barron, 1962. 176pp. $3.95. Paper $1.95. A full analysis and carefully reasoned solution to the many problems raised by this little-known edition of the play. The edition is based on the most recent research and correlation with later printings.

WILLIAMS, GEORGE WALTON – Editor
The Most Excellent and Lamentable Tragedie of Romeo and Juliet/A Critical Edition
Duke University, 1964. 170pp. $7.75. Mr. Williams bases the text of this edition on the Second Quarto. He includes a collation of all copies of the Second Quarto still available in the United States and in England. Original form and old spelling have been retained. A large section of Textual Notes provides the core of the book and an introduction to the major issues of textual analysis. Mr. Williams has mustered the evidence and arguments revolving around more than 150 disputed passages. Also provided are a selection of staging notes, a list of the emendations of accidentals and a historical collation of all editions published before 1700.

Facsimile Editions

ADAMS, JOSEPH QUINCEY – Introducer
Titus Andronicus: First Quarto, 1594
Cornell University, 1936. 41pp. $2.50. An edition of the play reproduced in facsimile from the edition in the Folger Library with an Introduction by Joseph Quincey Adams.

GREG, W. W. – Editor
Oxford Shakespeare Quartos
Oxford. $5.20 per volume. Quarto editions in collotype facsimiles. Books not available for examination. No other information available. See also: Hinman, Carlton – Editor.
The Merchant of Venice (Hayes Quarto, 1600). 1957.
The Merry Wives of Windsor (1602).
Pericles (1609). 1940.
Romeo and Juliet (Second Quarto, 1599).
Hamlet (First Quarto, 1603). 1940.
Troilus and Cressida (First Quarto, 1609).
Henry V (1600). 1957.
Love's Labour's Lost (1598). 1957.
Henry the Sixth, Part III (1595) (Richard Duke of York). 1955.
Richard III (1597). 1959.

HINMAN, CHARLTON – Editor
Oxford Shakespeare Quartos
Oxford. $5.20 per volume. Quarto editions in collotype facsimiles. Books not available for examination. No other information available. See also: Greg, W. W. – Editor.
King Lear (1608). 1939.
Hamlet (1604–05 – Second Quarto). 1940.
Richard II (1597). 1966.
Henry IV Part I (1598). 1966.

HINMAN, CHARLTON – Editor
The Norton Facsimile: The First Folio of Shakespeare
Norton, 1969. 928pp. $18.95. The First Folio of Shakespeare is reproduced in an accurate full-sized photographic facsimile. This volume shows the finally corrected state of every page of the Folio. Professor Hinman has written an Introduction in which he discusses the value and "authority" of the Folio version of each of the plays and explains the principles and problems involved in the preparation of the Facsimile and the printing of the original Folio.

KOKERITZ, HELGE and CHARLES TYLER PROUTY – Editors
Mr. William Shakespeare's Comedies, Histories, and Tragedies: A Facsimile Edition
Yale, 1954. 889pp. $32.00. A photographic facsimile of the First Folio of 1623 reproducing the copy in the possession of the Elizabethan Club of Yale University. Size of the original printed page has been reduced by approximately one-fifth for convenient handling but no retouching has been done. Two paginations are included: The original Folio numbering printed at the top and the new, continuous pagination at the bottom. Introduction by Mr. Prouty.

MARTZ, L. L. and E. M. WAITH – Editors
Shakespeare's Poems: A Facsimile of the Earliest Editions
Yale, 1964. 318pp. $13.50. Published in honor of the four hundredth anniversary of Shakespeare's birth, this facsimile edition incorporates all of his poems as they appear in the earliest editions now extant. The 155 plates are exact facsimiles of the rare originals dated from 1593 to 1609. Included are: "Venus and Adonis," "Lucrece," "The Passionate Pilgrim," "The Phoenix and the Turtle," "The Sonnets," and "A Lover's Complaint." A Preface includes textual notes.

NATIONAL THEATRES

AFRICA

CARTEY, WILFRED
Whispers from a Continent: The Literature of Contemporary Black Africa
Vintage, 1969. 397pp. Paper $2.45. This is an introduction to contemporary black African writing. Dr. Cartey discusses both novels and plays and elucidates the experience of the colonized and alienated black man. Among the authors discussed are Peter Abrahams, Leopold Senghor, Aime Cesaire, and Wole Soyinka. Index.

JONES, ELDRED
Othello's Countrymen: The African in English Renaissance Drama
Oxford, 1965. 158pp. $3.50. A study of the background of knowledge available to Renaissance playwrights through works published during the sixteenth and early seventeenth centuries on Africans and African explorations, and of how this knowledge was used in plays. Index.

LAURENCE, MARGARET
Long Drums and Cannons
Macmillan 1968. 209pp. $5.95. Miss Laurence is concerned with the work of Nigerian dramatists and novelists, during the years 1952—1966, who write in English. She provides detailed interpretative expositions of the plays and novels and gives a general picture of the sources and themes. She also indicates the probable lines of development in this area of contemporary writing. Lists of Works. General Bibliography. Index.

MPHAHLELE, EZEKIEL — Editor
African Writing Today
Penguin, 1967. 347pp. Paper $1.75. An anthology of recent African work in English, French, and Portuguese (translated into English) from Angola, Cameroun, Congo, Dahomey, Kenya, Nigeria, and South Africa, among other African nations. Included is an extract from the play, "The Swamp Dwellers," by Wole Soyinka.

VAN HEYNINGEN, C. and J.A. BERTHOUD
Uys Krige
Twayne, 1966. 159pp. $4.50. The authors appraise the work of the South African poet/playwright/short story writer. An account of Krige's life is included followed by critiques of individual works with plot summaries and a description of the work's emotional force and the means employed to achieve this force. An Appendix provides an excerpt from a lecture by Krige. Chronology. Bibliography. Index.

ASIA - GENERAL

BOWERS, FAUBION
Theatre in the East: A Survey of Asian Dance and Drama
Grove, 1960. 374pp. Paper $3.95. Originally published in 1956 and now reissued, this is a study of dance, drama, and related forms of theatre in the East. The countries covered include: India, Ceylon, Burma, Thailand, Cambodia, Laos, Malaya, Indonesia, China, Vietnam, and Japan, as well as the Phillipine Islands, Hong Kong, and Okinawa. Ancient as well as modern forms of theatre are included in the survey. The volume is illustrated with sixty-one photographs showing actors and dancers in performance. The author has provided a Bibliography and an Index.

BRANDON, JAMES R.
On Thrones of Gold: Three Javanese Shadow Plays
See Page 342

BRANDON, JAMES R.
Theatre in Southeast Asia
Harvard, 1967. 370pp. $12.50. Mr. Brandon considers the variety of the contemporary theatre in southeast Asia from four perspectives: its origins, its art, its role as a social institution, and its function as a medium of communication and propaganda. Illustrated. Glossary. Bibliography. Index.

GASTER, THEODOR H.
Thespis: Ritual, Myth and Drama in the Ancient Near East
Harper, 1966. 512pp. Paper $2.95. A reprint of the 1950 edition which attempts to explain in detail the pattern of ritual, myth and drama in the near East.

JACQUOT, JEAN — Editor
Les Theatres D'Asie
Editions du Centre National de la Recherche Scientifique, 1961. 308pp. $10.00. A series of articles and essays by eminent authorities on Asian theatre. The text is in the French language. Illustrated with drawings and photographs. Index.

PRONKO, LEONARD C.
Theatre East and West
University of California, 1967. 230pp. $7.50. Mr. Pronko discusses the whole range of Eastern theatre and examines the influence it has exerted on such contemporary playwrights as Artaud, Brecht, Copeau, Genet, and Beckett. Illustrated. Bibliography. Index.

WELLS, HENRY W.
The Classical Drama of the Orient
Taplinger, 1965. 347pp. $15.00. A comprehensive study of the aesthetic, ethical, and mythological facets of ancient Chinese and Japanese tragedy, comedy, and tragicomedy. There is a discussion of the

literary value of Chinese classical drama, and a critique of the growth, development, and aesthetic principles of Noh drama. Index.

AUSTRALIA

ARGYLE, BARRY
Patrick White
Oliver & Boyd, 1967. $2.95. Paper $1.95. Published in England, this is a critical interpretation of all of the Australian author's work: novels, plays, and short stories. An annotated Bibliography of White's works and of criticism on White's work is included in the volume.

PORTER, HAL
Stars of the Australian Stage and Screen
See Page 262

WILKES, G. A. – Editor
Ten Essays on Patrick White
Angus and Robertson, 1970. 181pp. $7.25. Ten essays, reprinted from the literary magazine, "Southerly," presenting a comprehensive study of the work of the Australian novelist, short story writer, and playwright. Four of the author's plays are discussed.

AUSTRIA

FRIEDMAN, MAURICE – Editor
Martin Buber and the Theater
See Page 325

MICHALSKI, JOHN
Ferdinand Raimund
Twayne, 1968. 142pp. $4.50. A critical study of the work of the nineteenth century Austrian playwright which draws upon critical consensus from Europe and America. Chronology. Notes and References. Selected Bibliography. Index.

WELLS, G. A.
The Plays of Grillparzer
Pergamon 1969. 173pp. $6.50. Paper $4.00. A comprehensive analysis of the plays of Franz Grillparzer. In this first study in English, the author covers the plays for the popular stage, the tragedies on Greek lengends, and the historical dramas. List of References. Index of Authors. Index of Plays.

BALI

McPHEE, COLIN
Music in Bali
See Page 281

BELGIUM

HALLS, W. D.
Maurice Maeterlinck: A Study of His Life and Thought
Oxford, 1960. 189pp. $7.25. The first comprehensive biographical and critical study of Maeterlinck in English, based mainly on unpublished and hitherto unknown material. It examines his work as poet, essayist, and dramatist and his contributions to the Belgian literary renaissance and to French Symbolism. A chronology of compositions is established. Illustrated.

BURMA

AUNG, MAUNG HTIN
Burmese Drama: A Study with Translations of Burmese Plays
Oxford, 1937. 266pp. $4.75. A study of the origins of Burmese drama and of the rise of court drama with detailed analyses of the works of U Kyin U and U Pon Nya. The so-called "decadent" period, and drama after the British annexation are considered. Twelve plays are given complete or in excerpt.

SEIN, KENNETH and JOSEPH A. WITHEY
The Great Po Sein: A Chronicle of the Burmese Theatre
Indiana University, 1965. 170pp. $4.95. An account of the development of the theatre in Burma over the last eighty years as mirrored in the work of the actor Po Sein and his family. There are descriptions of the puppet theatre, gambling plays, and the traditional productions which combine dancing, singing, and acting. Illustrated with photographs and line drawings. Glossary. Bibliography.

CANADA

EDWARDS, MURRAY D.
A Stage in Our Past
University of Toronto, 1968. 211pp. $12.50. A study of the early developments in Canadian theatre with a picture of the life and times of the Canada in which they took place from the 1790's to 1914. Dr. Edwards describes the primitive frontier society and the saloons and fire halls where plays were performed, the touring stars from England and the U. S., the touring companies of the Marks Brothers, the Canadian reaction to the first productions of Ibsen and Shaw. Contemporary photographs and posters illustrate the text. Bibliography. Index.

GRAHAM, FRANKLIN
Histrionic Montreal
Blom, 1969. 312pp. $18.75. Originally published in 1902 and reissued in a facsimile edition, this is a history of the theatre in Montreal from 1786. Biographical and critical notices of the plays and players are included. Illustrated. Index.

LEE, ALVIN A.
James Reaney
Twayne, 1968. 187pp. $4.50. The first critical interpretation of the works of the Canadian author and playwright. The poetry and dramatic writings are interpreted in terms of a developing antithetical symbolism composed of two visions. Chronology. Bibliography. Index.

MOORE, MAVOR – Editor
The Awkward Stage
Methuen, 1970. 244pp. $12.95. This report by the Province of Ontario Council for the Arts is a study in depth of all aspects of theatre in Ontario, with implications of national and international significance. It considers such subjects as the economics and administration of the theatre as well as its artistic and performing aspects. The state of permanent and touring facilities as well as the future role of dramatic education in schools and universities are also analyzed, and recommendations are made. Illustrated with drawings, photographs, charts and diagrams.

RABY, PETER – Editor
The Stratford Scene 1958–1968
Clarke Irwin, 1968. 256pp. $15.00. This volume recalls in text and pictures the outstanding performances of the last eleven years of the Stratford Festival in Canada. Each production of the 1967–68 season receives the attention of one writer intimately connected with the production – director, playwright, or actor. Company and cast lists are included. Almost 200 photographs illustrate the volume. Index.

CEYLON

DE ZOETE, BERYL
Dance and Magic Drama in Ceylon
Theatre Arts, 1953. 237pp. $4.50. A study of magic drama and other rituals performed in and around Kandy, the last royal city of Ceylon. Also studied are the exorcistic "balis" and "devol maduwas," and the "devil dances" of the south coast. Temple dancing, drumming, and religious processions are described. Illustrated.

CHINA

ARLINGTON, L.C.
The Chinese Drama: From the Earliest Times Until Today
Blom, 1966. 187pp. $32.50. A reissue of the 1930 guide to the Chinese theatre: its history, techniques, drama, and artists. The author has provided synopses of thirty classic plays. Hundreds of black and white plates plus eighteen plates in color are included. Bibliography.

HALSON, ELIZABETH
Peking Opera
Oxford, 1966. 92pp. $5.75. Designed to "stimulate the imagination of those interested in Oriental drama or to help the spectator... to understand a little of what lies behind this most attractive but complicated art." Illustrated.

OBRAZTSOV, SERGEI
The Chinese Puppet Theatre
See Page 583

PUSEY, JAMES R.
Wu Han: Attacking the Present Through the Past
Harvard, 1969. 84pp. Paper $4.50. This is a monograph on the Chinese historian and vice-mayor of Peking under the Communist regime. The author used his Chinese opera, "The Dismissal of Hai Jui," to attack Mao Tse-tung and his regime. Glossary. Bibliography. Index.

SCOTT, A.C.
An Introduction to the Chinese Theatre
Theatre Arts, 1959. 91pp. $2.95. Essays on the Chinese theatre, with summaries and analyses of twenty plays. Illustrated with photographs and drawings.

ZUNG, CECILIA L.
Secrets of the Chinese Drama
Blom, 1964. 299pp. $15.00. First published in 1937 and now reprinted, this is a complete guide to the Chinese drama. The author studies methods of acting, use of masks, costumes, etc., and the historical development of the theatre. Synopses of fifty classic plays and 240 illustrations. Index.

CZECHOSLOVAKIA

HARKINS, WILLIAM E.
Karel Capek
Columbia, 1962. 193pp. $6.50. The first full-length study in English, including a biography and a critical examination of the major works: "R. U. R.," "The War with the Newts," "The Markropolos Secret,"

"From the Insect World," and "An Ordinary Life." Many of the short stories are analyzed in detail.

KIMBALL, STANLEY BUCHHOLZ
Czech Nationalism: A Study of the National Theatre Movement, 1845–1883
University of Illinois, 1964. 186pp. $5.00. Paper $4.00. This study maintains that the movement to construct the National Theatre is one of the best single examples of the origin, growth, and development of the Czech national "reawakening" from its origins in the late eighteenth century to full maturity a century later. Bibliography. Index.

DENMARK

CAMPBELL, OSCAR JAMES
The Comedies of Holberg
Blom, 1968. 363pp. $12.50. Originally published in 1914 and now reissued in a facsimile edition, this is a study of the works of the eighteenth century Danish playwright, Ludvig Holberg. The author studies his life, his work, and his influences. Bibliography. Notes.

FRANCE

Pre-Classical Period

BROWN, HOWARD MAYER
Music in the French Secular Theatre 1400–1550
Harvard, 1963. 338pp. $12.00. A study of the chansons, dances, fanfares, and street cries used in early French drama. The author gives an account of each play and the performances, analyzes the whole scope of the chanson's influence on polyphonic settings in the plays, and gives a complete catalogue of all the songs mentioned in plays of the period with their settings.

BROWN, HOWARD MAYER
Theatrical Chansons of the Fifteenth and Early Sixteenth Centuries
Harvard, 1963. 188pp. Paper $6.00. An anthology of sixty chansons in polyphonic settings, most of them not available in modern editions. A brief introduction explains editorial procedures and discusses the problems of transcription.

FRANK, GRACE
The Medieval French Drama
Oxford, 1954. 296pp. $9.50. Written for both the student and the lay reader, this comprehensive history incorporates the latest results of scholarly research. The plays are evaluated as literature and the competence of the playwrights is considered.

WILEY, W. L.
The Early Public Theatre in France
Harvard, 1960. 326pp. $8.50. This study examines the plays and the competition among the playing companies from the beginnings of the professional theatre around 1580 to 1630. The sets, music, sound effects, and costumes are considered.

Classical Period: Histories and Critiques

BARNWELL, H. T.
The Tragic in French Tragedy
Queen's University, 1966. 23pp. $1.25. Professor Barnswell asks the question: "Was French tragedy in the seventeenth century tragic?" and explores the work of Racine and Corneille to answer the question.

JACQUOT, JEAN and MARCEL ODDON – Editors
Les Tragedies de Seneque et Le Theatre de La Renaissance
Editions du Centre National de La Recherche Scientifique, 1964. 320pp. $9.95. A series of articles and essays about the tragedies of Seneca and the theatre of the Renaissance. The text is in the French language. Index.

JEFFERY, BRIAN
French Renaissance Comedy 1552–1630
Oxford, 1969. 209pp. $7.50. The author provides a brief history of Renaissance comedy in France; examines the stages for which the plays were written; and, in the principal section, studies the conventions of plot, character, and speech out of which the plays were created. An Appendix provides synopses of the plays mentioned. Illustrated. Bibliography. Index.

JOURDAIN, ELEANOR F.
Dramatic Theory and Practice in France 1690–1808
See Page 13

KAISER, WALTER
Praisers of Folly: Erasmus, Shakespeare, Rabelais
See Page 85

LANCASTER, HENRY CARRINGTON
The French Tragi–Comedy: Its Origin and Development from 1552 to 1628
Gordian Press, 1966. 191pp. $8.00. Originally published in 1907 and now reissued, this study covers the origin and development of French tragi-comedy from 1552 to 1628. Appendices provide lists of non-French tragi-comedies written before 1582 and French tragi-comedies from 1552 to 1636. Bibliography.

LANCASTER, HENRY CARRINGTON
A History of French Dramatic Literature in the Seventeenth Century
Gordian Press, 1966. Nine Volume Set – $133.00. This nine volume history of French dramatic literature, now reprinted, was originally published from 1929 to 1942. The study covers the years from 1610 through 1700. Each volume covers a particular period with a conclusion, a list of extant plays and an Index. The final volume is a recapitulation of the entire period with a conclusion, a Subject Index, a Finding List of Plays, and a General Index. Each volume is available separately as listed below.

Part I.	Volume One.	The Pre-Classical Period: 1610–1634. 368pp. $16.75.
Part I.	Volume Two.	The Pre-Classical Period: 1610–1634. 423pp. $16.75.
Part II.	Volume One.	The Period of Corneille: 1635–1651. 371pp. $16.75.
Part II.	Volume Two.	The Period of Corneille: 1635–1651. 433pp. $18.75.
Part III.	Volume One.	The Period of Moliere: 1652–1672. 428pp. $16.75.
Part III.	Volume Two.	The Period of Moliere: 1652–1672. 468pp. $18.75.
Part IV.	Volume One.	The Period of Racine: 1673–1700. 482pp. $18.75.
Part IV.	Volume Two.	The Period of Racine: 1673–1700. 502pp. $18.75.

Part V. Recapitulation: 1610–1700. 235pp. $13.50

LOCKERT, LACY
Studies in French Classical Tragedy
Vanderbilt University, 1958. 529pp. $6.50. Studies in the major works of Racine and Moliere, as well as discussions of such neglected dramatists of the period as Tristan l'Hermite, Du Ryer, Rotrou, and Quinault. Excerpts from the plays are in French, with English verse translations. A chapter discusses the relationship between French and Elizabethan Classic drama.

LOUGH, JOHN
Paris Theatre Audiences in the Seventeenth and Eighteenth Centuries
Oxford, 1957. 293pp. $11.00. The author studies changes in the size and composition of theatre audiences and their effect on taste in drama throughout the seventeenth and eighteenth centuries in France. He argues that the changes are reflected in the drama of the time in its evolution from crudity to the works of the great classical writers. Illustrated. Bibliography. Index.

MAXWELL, IAN
French Farce and John Heywood
See Page 162

MONGREDIEN, GEORGE
Daily Life in the French Theatre at the Time of Moliere
Allen & Unwin, 1969. 216pp. $9.95. Translated from the French by Claire Eliane Engel, this book is a study of daily life in the theatre in France during the seventeenth century. Among the topics covered are: the church and the theatre, actors and public opinion, and the theatres in the Provinces. Illustrated. Index.

NICOLL, ALLARDYCE
The World of Harlequin
See Page 348

NIKLAUS, THELMA
Harlequin, or the Rise and Fall of a Bergamask Rogue
See Page 348

PROUTY, C. T.
George Gascoigne, Elizabethan Courtier, Soldier and Poet
Blom, 1966. 351pp. $12.50. A critical survey of the writings of the chief poet of Elizabeth's court. The first four chapters deal with the life of Gascoigne and the remainder of the volume is an examination of the sources, principles of composition and technique. Bibliography. Index.

SPINGARN, JOEL E.
History of Literary Criticism in the Renaissance
See Page 541

Classical Period: Studies of Playwrights

Corneille, Pierre

CROCE, BENEDETTO
Ariosto, Shakespeare and Corneille
Russell & Russell, 1966. 440pp. $10.00. A reprint, translated by Douglas Ainslie, of the 1920 edition of three critical essays by the Italian philosopher-critic. Index.

CURRIE, PETER
Polyeucte: A Critical Study
Barron, 1960. 64pp. $2.50. Paper $1.00. This brief study considers the background of the play, its structure and form, its characterizations, and the problem of the ending. Bibliography.

FOGEL, HERBERT
The Criticism of Cornelian Tragedy
Exposition, 1967. 139pp. $6.00. This is a study of critical writing from the seventeenth to the twentieth century. The author considers primarily two central themes of Corneille's theatre—the conflict between duty and passion and the glorification of will at the expense of the emotions. He traces the origin and development of the literary criticism devoted to these two topics. Bibliography.

HARRIS, EUGENIE
The Plays of Racine and Corneille
Monarch, 1966. 128pp. Paper $1.00. A critical guide to the plays of the seventeenth century French playwrights. Detailed summaries of eleven plays with a discussion of the playwrights' lives and works, an introduction to seventeenth century France, essay questions and answers for review and a Bibliography are all provided.

NELSON, ROBERT J.
Corneille: His Heroes and Their World
University of Pennsylvania, 1963, 332pp. $8.50. The author re-examines the entire output of thirty-two plays in an attempt to demonstrate that Corneille's vision is not tragic, despite the externals of composition. Bibliography.

NELSON, ROBERT J. – Editor
Corneille and Racine: Parallels and Contrasts
Prentice–Hall, 1966. 176pp. Paper $4.50. A collection of essays by various authors comparing the two French playwrights. Most of the essays are in the French language.

TURNELL, MARTIN
The Classical Moment: Studies of Corneille, Moliere and Racine
See Page 123

YARROW, P.J.
Corneille
St. Martin's, 1963. 325pp. $12.00. The three parts of this study consider the intellectual climate of Corneille's period, his career as a dramatist, and particular aspects of his tragedies. The relation between the comedies and the tragedies is studied and special attention is given to the elements of realism in the plays. Bibliography.

Garnier, Robert

JONDORF, GILLIAN
Robert Garnier and the Themes of Political Tragedy in the Sixteenth Century
Cambridge, 1969. 162pp. $6.00. The author is concerned with the French playwright's extension of the Senecan tradition of tragedy and his preoccupation with political themes. The playwright is studied as a sixteenth century writer attuned to the thought and art of his own time. Bibliography. Index.

Marivaux, Pierre Carlet de

TILLEY, ARTHUR
Three French Dramatists: Racine, Marivaux, Musset
See Page 123

Moliere (Jean–Baptiste Poquelin)

BULGAKOV, MIKHAIL
The Life of Monsieur de Moliere
Funk & Wagnalls, 1970. 260pp. $6.95. Translated from the Russian by Mirra Ginsburg, this is a portrait of the great seventeenth century French satirist by the Russian satirist. One of the principal themes of the biography is the relation of the artist to his art and to society, especially a repressive society. Moliere's career as playwright, producer, and actor is recounted. Frontispiece. List of Plays. Index.

CALANDRA, DENIS M.
Misanthrope and Bourgeois Gentleman: Notes
Cliff's Notes, 1967. 71pp. Paper $1.00. Included in this volume are scene-by scene summaries of the two plays by Moliere, critical evaluations of the plays, review questions, and a Selected Bibliography.

CHAPMAN, PERCY ADDISON
The Spirit of Moliere: An Interpretation
Russell & Russell, 1965. 250pp. $9.00. First published in 1940, this study traces the playwright's development in terms of the nature of comedy, the relationship between the playwright and his audience, and the inner struggle of the playwright to present his vision of the world. The study was edited by Jean-Albert Bede and the volume includes an Introduction by Christian Gauss. Bibliography.

FERNANDEZ, RAMON
Moliere: The Man Seen Through the Plays
Hill & Wang, 1958. 212pp. $3.75. Paper – 1960. $1.45. First published in France in 1929 as "La Vie de Moliere" and now translated by Wilson Follett and published in the U.S., this study attempts to read the unprovable actualities of Moliere's life and character from the proved actualities of the plays.

GOSSMAN, LIONEL
Men and Masks: A Study of Moliere
Johns Hopkins, 1964. 310pp. $6.50. Paper – 1969. $2.45. Mr. Gossman re-appraises Moliere's comedy in the light of historical experience and interprets it in terms of the conditions from which it emerged. By bringing the comedies into the mainstream of seventeenth century thought and literature the author shows that Moliere shared the same concerns as Racine and Descartes.

GREBANIER, BERNARD
Simplified Approach to Moliere
Barron, 1965. 195pp. Paper $ .95. An introductory chapter on Moliere's era and career, with discussions of all the major works. Bibliography.

GUICHARNAUD, JACQUES – Editor
Moliere: A Collection of Critical Essays
Prentice–Hall, 1964. 188pp. $4.95. Paper $1.95. Essays on Moliere the actor, on his theory of comedy,

and on individual plays. Such critics and authorities as Rene Bray, Gustave Lanson, Alfred Simon, Will G. Moore, Lionel Gossman, Jacques Copeau, Charles Dullin, and Jacques Audiberti have provided material. A Chronology of Important Dates is included as is a list of twentieth century performances of the works in France. Selected Bibliography.

HALL, H. GASTON
Tartuffe: A Critical Study
Barron, 1960. 63pp. $2.50. Paper $1.00. A study of the background of the play with a scene-by scene analysis.

KLIBBE, LAWRENCE
The Plays of Moliere
Monarch, 1965. 126pp. Paper $1.00. A critical guide to nine plays with introductions to the life, the age, and the theatre of Moliere. Contemporary evaluations are provided. Bibliography.

LAWRENCE, FRANCIS L.
Moliere: The Comedy of Unreason
Tulane University, 1968. 119pp. Paper $5.00. A study of Moliere's early plays in chronological order. Index of Writers and Editors.

MASTERS, BRIAN
A Student's Guide to Moliere
Heinemann, 1970. 92pp. Paper $1.95. In this study of Moliere, the author describes the playwright's background and early experience. The plays are studied and quotations used extensively to illustrate Moliere's ideas, characterization, and the objects of his satire. Chronology. Bibliography.

MOORE, WILL G.
Moliere: A New Criticism
Oxford, 1949. 152pp. $3.00. Paper—1968. 147pp. $1.35. A study based on an examination of the texts of the plays in terms of the theatrical conditions prevalent in Paris in the seventeenth century. The relation between Moliere and the English comic writers is considered. Index.

PALMER, JOHN
Moliere
Blom, 1970. 518pp. $12.50. A reissue of the 1930 publication with a new Index, this is a biography and survey of the work of Moliere. Illustrated. Bibliographical Note. Index.

ROBERTS, JAMES L.
Tartuffe and The Miser: Notes
Cliff's Notes 1968. 77pp. Paper $1.00. Notes on two plays by Moliere.

TURNELL, MARTIN
The Classical Moment: Studies of Corneille, Moliere and Racine.
See Page 123

Montchrestien, Antoine de

GRIFFITHS, RICHARD
The Dramatic Technique of Antoine de Montchrestien
Oxford, 1970. 236pp. $13.00. Subtitled, "Rhetoric and Style in French Renaissance Tragedy," this is a study of the aims, methods, and techniques of the tragedies of the sixteenth century. Mr. Griffiths examines the influence of Renaissance rhetoric upon composition and style and goes into other sources and methods of imitation. Appendices. Bibliography. Index.

Musset, Alfred de

TILLEY, ARTHUR
Three French Dramatists: Racine, Marivaux, Musset
See Page 123

Racine, Jean

BARTHES, ROLAND
On Racine
Hill & Wang, 1964. 172pp. $3.95. Paper $1.75. The first section of this book studies Racinian man as he is displayed within the context of the plays. The second section is a discussion of the Jean Vilar-Maria Casares production of "Phedre." The third section is a critique of the academic tradition of Racinian scholarship and criticism.

deMOURGES, ODETTE
Racine, or, The Triumph of Relevance
Cambridge, 1967. 171pp. $5.50. Paper $2.25. A critical introduction to the work of Racine, this study concentrates on the plays and attempts to say what they are and how they work on the mind of the spectator or reader. Selected Bibliography. Index.

FRANCE, PETER
Racine's Rhetoric
Oxford, 1965. 256pp. $7.50. This study attempts to show that the influence of rhetoric on literature should be neither neglected nor disparaged. Mr. France investigates the place of rhetoric in the tragedies of Racine and in those of Quinalt, Pradon, Campistron, and Corneille.

FREEMAN, BRYANT C. and ALAN BATSON
Concordance du Theatre et des Poesies de Jean Racine
Cornell University, 1968. Two volumes: 1,481pp. $20.00. This concordance to the complete dramatic and poetic works of Racine, with full variant readings, is based on the "Grands Ecrivains de la France" edition. An editor's preface is followed by a programmer's preface, both in the French language. A frequency list and an analytical table of the dramas are provided in Appendices. Sold as a two volume set.

GIRAUDOUX, JEAN
Racine
Folcroft, 1969. 36pp. $5.25. Originally published in 1938, this is a short study of the French playwright.

HARRIS, EUGENIE
The Plays of Racine and Corneille
See Page 121

KLIN, GEORGE and AMY L. MARSLAND
Phaedra and Andromache: Notes
Cliff's Notes, 1969. 86pp. Paper $1.00. Notes on two plays by Racine.

KNIGHT, R. C. – Editor
Racine: Modern Judgements
Macmillan, 1969. 239pp. $9.00. Paper – Aurora, 1970. 239pp. $2.50. A selection of criticism with an Introduction by the editor. Among the fourteen contributors are C. M. Bowra, Mr. Knight, and Jules Brody. Chronology. Select Bibliography. Index.

LAPP. JOHN C.
Aspects of Racinian Tragedy
University of Toronto, 1964. 196pp. $6.50. Paper $2.25. The essays in this volume consider the major themes and the dramatic conventions of the plays; use of symbolism; and the essential nature of Racinian tragedy. Index.

MOORE, WILL G.
Britannicus: A Critical Study
Barron, 1960. 48pp. Paper $1.00. A study of the sources and background of the play, its intellectual content and its form.

MUIR, KENNETH
Last Periods of Shakespeare, Racine, Ibsen
Wayne State University, 1961. 117pp. $5.00. Four lectures discussing the quality of the plays written by these playwrights in their final creative periods. An introductory essay considers the final achievements of a group of artists, among them Beethoven, Botticelli, Rilke, Sophocles, Euripides, and Strindberg.

NELSON, ROBERT J. – Editor
Corneille and Racine: Parallels and Contrasts
Prentice–Hall, 1966. 176pp. Paper $4.50. A collection of essays by various authors comparing the two French playwrights. Most of the essays are in French.

STENDHAL
Racine and Shakespeare
Crowell–Collier, 1962. 220pp. $3.95. A statement on the nature of romanticism in which Stendhal uses the two playwrights as two archetypes of literary genius. The work is an attack on the closet drama written by the French "classicists" of the day. Translated by Guy Daniels, with a Foreword by Andre Maurois.

TILLEY, ARTHUR
Three French Dramatists: Racine, Marivaux, Musset
Russell & Russell, 1967. 206pp. $10.00. A reissue of the 1933 study in which Mr. Tilley contends that the three French playwrights studied all have certain characteristics in common: they are chiefly concerned with the portrayal of passion and character; they all have a strong dramatic sense; and they all possess a style which is individual, distinctive, and charming.

TURNELL, MARTIN
The Classical Moment: Studies of Corneille, Moliere, and Racine
Hamish Hamilton, 1947. 253pp. $5.00. Paper – 1964. 255pp. $3.00. A study of the peculiar quality of the poetry of the classic French dramatists that makes them especially inaccessible to the English reader. The attention in the study is focused on Racine's work.

WEINBERG, BERNARD
The Art of Jean Racine
University of Chicago, 1963. 355pp. $9.00. Paper – 1969. $3.45. An analysis of all of Racine's tragedies in which the author demonstrates that the playwright succeeded in fulfilling the criteria of the dramatic aesthetic against which he measured his own art. Index.

Eighteenth and Nineteenth Centuries

ANTOINE, ANDRE
Andre Antoine's "Memories of the Theatre–Libre"
University of Miami, 1964. 239pp. $6.50. The first English edition of Antoine's "Souvenirs," as translated by Marvin A. Carlson and edited by H. D. Albright. First published in Paris in 1921, in this volume Antoine attacked the theatrical stereotypes of his day an inaugurated a pivotal movement in modern theatre history. A collection of rare photographs of Antoine and his fellow workers is included. Index of Names.

ARVIN, NEIL COLE
Eugene Scribe and the French Theatre: 1815–1860
Blom, 1967. 268pp. $12.50. First published in 1924 and now reissued, this is a study of the French dramatist who for nearly fifty years was the most popular dramatist in Europe. Professor Arvin contends that the plays were a perfect representation of the French bougeoisie of the Restoration. Index.

CARLSON, MARVIN
The Theatre of the French Revolution
Cornell University, 1966. 328pp. $14.50. This is a history of the French theatre from the fall of the Bastille to the rise of Napoleon. The author discusses the audiences, the actors, producers, authors, and theatre organizations. Illustrated. Selected Bibliography. Index.

GREENE, E.J.H.
Marivaux
University of Toronto, 1965. 368pp. $10.00. This critical study of the entire body of Marivaux's writings consists of an analysis of the individual works, in chronological order, showing the development of Marivaux's thinking, and the intimate relationships among the plays, novels, and essays. Bibliography. Index.

LESSING, G.E.
Hamburg Dramaturgy
See Page 137

LOUNSBURY, THOMAS R.
Shakespeare and Voltaire
See Page 95

McKEE, KENNETH N.
The Theatre of Marivaux
New York University, 1958. 277pp. $8.00. An introduction to the life of Marivaux (1688–1763), to the theatre of his time, and to his more than thirty romantic fantasies. The stage histories of the plays and their critical reception since they were first produced are considered. Jean-Louis Barrault has written an Appreciation.

MATTHEWS, BRANDER
French Dramatists of the Nineteenth Century
Blom, 1968. 321pp. $12.50. First published in 1901 and now reissued, this is a study of the careers of those French playwrights who set the style for comedy and tragedy throughout much of Europe. Among the authors discussed in separate chapters are Victor Hugo, Dumas—father and son, Scribe, Sardou, Labiche, and Emile Zola. The course of drama is traced throughout the century.

MILLER, HAROLD
Edmond Rostand's Cyrano de Bergerac
Monarch, 1966. 78pp. Paper $1.00. A critical guide to the play with detailed act-by-act summaries and analytic comment, character analysis, critical commentary, review questions and answers, and a Bibliography.

RATERMANIS, J.B. and W.R. IRWIN
The Comic Style of Beaumarchais
University of Washington, 1961. 140pp. $5.95. A detailed examination of "Le Barbier de Seville" and "Le Mariage de Figaro" that illustrates the interplay of character, action, and expression that is the unique style of Beaumarchais.

SKINNER, CORNELIA OTIS
Elegant Wits and Grand Horizontals
Houghton Mifflin, 1962. 262pp. $5.00. A panoramic account of the 1890's in Paris. The gilded society, courtesans and theatrical personalities are described. Illustrated.

WICKS, CHARLES BEAUMONT
The Parisian Stage
University of Alabama. An alphabetical list of plays and authors presented in Paris in the nineteenth century. The volumes in the series are as follows:
Volume One: 1800–1815. 1950. 102pp. Paper $2.00.
Volume Two: 1816–1830. 1953. 118pp. Paper $2.50.
Volume Three: 1831–1850. 1960. 287pp. Paper $4.00.
Volume Four: 1851–1875. 1967. 335pp. Paper $8.50.

WINTER, MARIAN HANNAH
The Theatre of Marvels
Blom, 1964. 208pp. $17.50. First published in France in 1962, this is a revised English language edition, with twenty-two additional pages of illustrations. This type of theatre was a combination of all the performing arts—music, ballet, mime, acting, and circus—and its importance in the nineteenth century is examined. Over 200 illustrations depict the spectacles produced in the theatres.

Twentieth Century: Histories and Critiques

BARRAULT, JEAN-LOUIS
The Theatre of Jean-Louis Barrault
Hill & Wang, 1959. 244pp. $5.00. Barrault reviews the accumulated experience of his career, especially that of his own company and theatre. Part One discusses the foundation and development of the Renaud-Barrault theatre; Part Two contains four essays on the craft of acting.

BISHOP, THOMAS
Pirandello and the French Theatre
New York University, 1960. $6.00. Paper $2.25.

A study of Pirandello's influence on the French theatre of the early 1900's and on the post-war generation. The author views the reception of the plays in Paris and considers the major themes of the playwright and the adaptation of these themes by French playwrights. Bibliography. Index.

FOWLIE, WALLACE
Dionysus in Paris: A Guide to Contemporary French Theatre
World, 1960. 314pp. Paper $2.95. A study of the theatres, directors, and actors of modern French theatre, with chapters on the major tragic dramatists, religious theatre, the theatre of ideas, and the experimental theatre. Illustrated.

GHEON, HENRI
The Art of the Theatre
Hill & Wang, 1961. 100pp. $3.50. Paper $1.25. Four lectures delivered in 1923 and now collected in book form. Michael Saint-Denis has contributed an Introduction to the volume.

GROSSVOGEL, DAVID I.
Twentieth Century French Drama
Columbia, 1961. 378pp. Paper $2.25. Originally published in 1958 as "The Self-Conscious Stage in Modern French Drama," and now reissued, this is a study of the work of Anouilh, Giraudoux, Ionesco, Cocteau, and Sartre. The author relates the theatre to an aesthetic of the stage which focuses attention on the interrelation of the spectator and the actor.

GUICHARNAUD, JACQUES and JUNE GUICHARNAUD
Modern French Theatre from Giraudoux to Genet
Yale, 1967. 383pp. $8.50. Paper $2.45. This is a thoroughly revised and expanded edition of the work originally published in 1961. It presents in review the revolutionary work of Giraudoux, Claudel, Montherlant, Ghelderode, Camus, Genet, Cocteau, Salacrou, Anouilh, Sartre, Ionesco, and Beckett. The appendices on directors and productions provide a survey of French theatrical activity during the past forty years. Selected Bibliography. Index.

HOBSON, HAROLD
The French Theatre Today
Blom, 1965. 232pp. $6.00. Mr. Hobson discusses various aspects of the French theatre and provides a survey of contemporary French playwriting and production. He discusses and quotes extensively from Sartre, Salacrou, Montherlant, and Anouilh. Index.

JACOBSEN, JOSEPHINE and WILLIAM R. MUELLER
Ionesco and Genet: Playwrights of Silence
Hill & Wang, 1968. 242pp. $5.95. Paper $1.95. This is a critical examination of Ionesco and Genet, two playwrights of the theatre of the absurd who share not only a desire to communicate but also pessimism over the possibility of communication. Bibliography. Index.

JACQUOT, JEAN — Editor
Le Theatre Moderne: Hommes et Tendances
Editions du Centre National de La Recherche Scientifique, 1965. 373pp. $7.75. A collection of articles and essays on the men and the trends of the modern theatre. The text is in French. Among the subjects covered are dramatics and economics in France since 1914, the decentralization of the stage in France, the recent work of Armand Salacrou, and the heroine in the theatre of Giraudoux. Index.

JACQUOT, JEAN — Editor
Realisme et Poesie au Theatre
Editions du Centre National de La Recherche Scientifique, 1960. 294pp. $13.00. A collection of articles and essays on realism and poetry in the French theatre. The text is in the French language. Index.

JONES, ROBERT EMMET
The Alienated Hero in Modern French Drama
University of Georgia, 1962. 137pp. Paper $2.75. A study of the spiritually alienated hero and heroine of French drama since the First World War. Among the authors whose plays are studied are: Francois de Curel, Montherlant, Lenormand, Giraudoux, Anouilh, and Sartre.

KNOWLES, DOROTHY
French Drama of the Inter-War Years: 1918–1939
Harrap, 1967. 334pp. $6.50. Dr. Knowles' book is an attempt to describe what happened in the French theatre between the two world wars and to point to the influence that the ideas then current had on subsequent developments. Illustrated. Index.

LEE, VERA
Quest for a Public
Schenkman, 1970. 209pp. $11.95. Dr. Lee considers all the factors involved in the growth of popular theatre in France since 1945. Illustrated. Appendices. Bibliography. Index.

PRONKO, LEONARD CABELL
Avant–Garde: The Experimental Theatre in France
University of California, 1962. 226pp. $4.75. Paper $1.50. An introduction to the major avant-garde plays of the period 1950–1960. The importance of the earlier playwrights—Jarry, Apollinaire, and Artaud—is stressed. The works of Tardieu, Vauthier, Pichette, Ghelderode, Audiberti, and Schehade are examined. The chief stage directors of avant-garde drama in France are listed.

SHATTUCK, ROGER
The Banquet Years
Random House, 1968. 397pp. Paper $2.45. A revised edition of the 1961 study of the origins of the avant-garde in France from 1885 to World War I. Each of the four most prominent men in the movement, Jarry, Rousseau, Satie, and Apollinaire, is given a section in the study. Illustrated. Bibliography. Index.

Twentieth Century: Studies of Playwrights

Anouilh, Jean

DELLA FAZIA, ALBA
Jean Anouilh
Twayne, 1969. 154pp. $4.95. Dr. della Frazia provides a study of Anouilh's style and dramatic techniques. Chronology. Notes and References. Selected Bibliography. Index.

HARVEY, JOHN
Anouilh: A Study in Theatrics
Yale, 1964. 191pp. $8.00. Paper $1.75. The thesis of this book is that the plays of Anouilh do not imitate reality, but rather transpose it by means of an open exploitation of the conventions and illusions of the stage. Chronology of plays and productions. Bibliography. Index.

PRONKO, LEONARD CABELL
The World of Jean Anouilh
University of California, 1961. 264pp. $6.00. Paper $2.25. Summaries and interpretations of the plays with a discussion of the major themes, the playwright's dramatic development and his aims. Bibliography.

THODY, PHILIP
Anouilh
Oliver & Boyd, 1968. 96pp. $2.95. Paper $1.75. In this critical study of Anouilh's dramatic works, Professor Thody tries to strike a balance between an analysis of his ideas and an examination of his dramatic technique. Details of the performances each play has had in France, Britain, and America are given. Bibliography.

Artaud, Antonin

ARTAUD, ANTONIN
Collected Works: Volume One
Calder & Boyars, 1968. 247pp. $10.50. Paper $3.95. Translated and with an introduction by Victor Corti, this volume contains the important correspondence with Riviere, together with many of Artaud's most significant miscellaneous writings, including poetry, drama, long and short texts.

ARTAUD, ANTONIN
The Theatre and Its Double
Calder & Boyars, 1970. 102pp. $5.00. Paper $1.95. Translated by Victor Corti, this is a collection of essays on the theatre. The volume contains both famous Manifestos of the Theatre of Cruelty, definitions of this theatre, the underlying impulses of performance, some suggestions on a physical training method for actors, an appreciation of the expressed values of Eastern dance drama, and an attempt by Artaud to apply Taoist principles of fullness and emptiness to the theatre.

KNAPP, BETTINA L.
Antonin Artaud: Man of Vision
David Lewis, 1969. 233pp. $6.95. The author has tried to trace Artaud's intellectual, philosophical, and psychological development through his own works. Misunderstood by most of his contemporaries, his ideas concerning the theatre, motion pictures, and the pictorial arts are now being rediscovered. Preface by Anais Nin. Notes. Bibliography. Index.

SELLIN, ERIC
The Dramatic Concepts of Antonin Artaud
University of Chicago, 1968. 190pp. $7.50. Professor Sellin explores Artaud's ideas and his dramaturgic concepts. He examines the three themes that recur constantly in Artaud's theatrical works and also discusses the degree to which Artaud put his concepts into practice. Bibliography. Index.

Beckett, Samuel

BARNARD, G. C.
Samuel Beckett: A New Approach
Dodd, Mead, 1970. 144pp. $4.50. A study of the novels and plays for the general reader. The author attempts to shed light on the schizophrenic condition of the main characters and the identity of all the heroes of the novels. Bibliography. Index of Names. Index of Subjects.

BECKETT, SAMUEL
Poems in English
Grove, 1961. 61pp. $2.75. Paper $1.45. The poems cover a twenty year period, from the dramatic monologue "Whoroscope" of 1930 to the bilingual "Quatre Poeme."

CALDER, JOHN – Editor
Beckett at Sixty: A Festschrift
Calder & Boyars, 1967. 100pp. $5.25. Reminiscences of and tributes to Samuel Beckett. Among the contributors are A. J. Leventhal, Maria Jolas, John Fletcher, Jack Macgowran, Alan Schneider, Harold Hobson, and Martin Esslin. Illustrated with photographs and drawings.

CHEVIGNY, BELL GALE – Editor
Twentieth Century Interpretations of "Endgame"
Prentice–Hall, 1969. 120pp. $4.95. Paper $1.95. A collection of critical essays on Samuel Beckett's play. Among the contributors are Hugh Kenner, Martin Esslin, and Alan Schneider. Chronology. Selected Bibliography.

COE, RICHARD N.
Samuel Beckett
Grove, 1970. 120pp. Paper $1.50. Originally published in 1964 and revised in 1968, this is a new edition of Professor Coe's study of Beckett's work. The emphasis is on the four major novels but the plays are also studied. Bibliography.

COHN, RUBY – Editor
Casebook on "Waiting for Godot"
Grove, 1967. 192pp. Paper $1.95. Professor Cohn has gathered together a broad selection of the most important critical commentaries, pro and con, on Beckett's play. The range of material extends from directors' comments to Marxian analysis and includes points of view from fellow writers to prisoners in San Quentin. Bibliography.

COHN, RUBY
Samuel Beckett: The Comic Gamut
Rutgers University, 1962. 340pp. $6.00. An extensive discussion of all Beckett's literary works, from his first prize-winning poem on Descartes, his early parodies and English novels, to the French trilogy, poems, plays, and radio scripts. There is a chapter on Beckett as self-translator.

ESSLIN, MARTIN – Editor
Samuel Beckett: A Collection of Critical Essays
Prentice–Hall, 1965. 182pp. $4.95. Paper $1.95. Essays by John Fletcher, Maurice Naudeau, Hugh Kenner, Jean-Jacques Mayoux, Alain Robbe-Grillet, Eva Metman, Ross Chambers and others.

FLETCHER, JOHN
Samuel Beckett's Art
Barnes & Noble, 1967. 154pp. $5.50. Dr. Fletcher deals with Beckett's methods rather than his message. He discusses Beckett's techniques of writing for stage and radio, his criticism and his poetry. There are chapters on the use of French, the influence of Sterne, Dante, Descartes, and of pre-Socratic thought. Chronology of Works. Index.

FRIEDMAN, MELVIN J. – Editor
Samuel Beckett Now
University of Chicago, 1970. 275pp. $7.95. Critical commentaries on the work of the novelist/playwright by eleven contributors. The editor has provided an Introduction and there is a checklist of criticism. Index.

HARVEY, LAWRENCE E.
Samuel Beckett: Poet and Critic
Princeton, 1970. 451pp. $12.50. A study of Beckett's earliest writings, his poems and criticisms from about 1929 to 1949. Professor Harvey combines detailed analysis of the poems with insights into the intellectual and physical world of Beckett, drawing on conversations with Beckett, unpublished manuscripts, and research in Ireland, England, and France. Index.

HASSAN, IHAB
The Literature of Silence: Henry Miller and Samuel Beckett
Knopf, 1967. 234pp. Paper $3.95. The author proposes that literature has adopted a new attitude toward itself and that silence is its metaphor and the result is anti-literature. Two figures, Miller and Beckett, are proposed as masters of anti-literature. Selected Bibliography. Index.

HAYMAN, RONALD
Samuel Beckett
Heinemann, 1968. 80pp. Paper $1.25. In this study of the playwright, Mr. Hayman discusses all of Beckett's plays including those written for radio and television. He shows how Beckett has abandoned the traditional features of drama to investigate the loneliness of individual consciousness. Illustrated. Bibliography. List of Productions.

HOFFMAN, FREDERICK J.
Samuel Beckett: The Language of Self
Southern Illinois University, 1962. 177pp. $4.50. Paper – Dutton, 1964. 177pp. $1.25. An analysis of the twentieth century views of the self, beginning with a study of the powerful doubts hindering self-esteem found in nineteenth century literature. Beckett is seen as the most representative modern expresser of self-doubt.

JACOBSEN, JOSEPHINE and WILLIAM R. MUELLER
The Testament of Samuel Beckett
Hill & Wang, 1964. 178pp. $3.95. Paper $1.65. The first part of this book examines Beckett's techniques —his poetic modes, epistemological sense, and comic approach. The second part considers this craftsmanship as a vehicle for his vision. Bibliography.

KENNER, HUGH
Samuel Beckett: A Critical Study
University of California, 1968. 226pp. Paper $2.25. A new edition, with a supplementary chapter, of the study first published in 1961. Professor Kenner concerns himself with the internal structures discoverable in Beckett's work rather than the moods and messages attributed to the man. The supplementary chapter concerns Beckett's most recent work which is still unknown in the U.S.

KERN, EDITH
Existential Thought and Fictional Technique: Kierkegaard, Sartre, Beckett
Yale, 1970. 262pp. $6.75. Miss Kern provides an introduction to the existential viewpoint through her analyses of the means Kierkegaard, Sartre, and Beckett developed to save their fiction from solipsism. She devotes particular attention to the problem of the author-hero. Selected Bibliography. Index. (Please note this is a work about the fiction of the writers although their dramatic works are mentioned briefly throughout.)

REID, ALEC
All I Can Manage, More Than I Could: An Approach to the Plays of Samuel Beckett
Dolmen Press, 1968. 94pp. $4.50. Paper $2.25. This work is designed primarily for the average theatre-goer who has no specialized literary or technical knowledge. The author argues that Beckett has devised a completely new kind of drama and that some adjustment will be needed in the normal attitudes and expectations of the audience if they are to get the most out of the plays. The second section of the book describes each play.

ROBINSON, MICHAEL
The Long Sonata of the Dead
Grove, 1970. 318pp. $7.50. Paper $2.45. This is a comprehensive study of Samuel Beckett's work. Each of the novels and plays is discussed separately and in detail. The author stresses throughout the volume the fundamental unity of all Beckett has written. Bibliography. Notes. Index.

SCOTT, NATHAN A.
Samuel Beckett
Bowes & Bowes, 1965. 141pp. $3.50. The author approaches Beckett with a theologian's concern for man's spiritual predicament in the modern world to which Beckett bears testimony. Professor Scott places Beckett in terms both of literary history and contemporary philosophy to assess the importance of the playwright. Selected Bibliography.

SIMPSON, ALAN
Beckett and Behan and a Theatre in Dublin
See Page 205

TANNER, JAMES T. F. and J. DON VANN
Samuel Beckett: A Checklist of Criticism
Kent State University, 1969. 85pp. $6.00. In five major headings, the authors list some of the criticism on Beckett and his works. Bibliographies, books about Beckett, chapters about Beckett, and reference to Beckett in books, articles, and reviews are included. Chronological Listing of Beckett's Major Books.

TINDALL, WILLIAM YORK
Samuel Beckett
Columbia, 1964. 48pp. Paper $1.00. A short critical study of the Irish playwright. Included is a Selected Bibliography of the principal works, critical works, and commentary.

WEBB, EUGENE
Samuel Beckett: A Study of His Novels
University of Washington, 1970. 192pp. $6.95. The author contends that Beckett's works of fiction constitute a single coherent presentation of his views of life, at once sombre and grotesquely humorous. Webb interprets Beckett's aesthetic intentions by examining his use of literary parody and his experiments with different forms. Notes. Bibliography. Index.

Bernanos, Georges

BLUMENTHAL, GERDA
The Poetic Imagination of Georges Bernanos: An Essay in Interpretation
Johns Hopkins, 1965. 154pp. $4.50. The author examines the poetic structure of the works and shows that it encompasses a vision at once cosmological, spiritual, and psychological. In all Bernanos' work man's quest for paradise is conceived poetically, as a gigantic contest of divorce and reconciliation between water and earth. Bibliography.

BUSH, WILLIAM
Georges Bernanos
Twayne, 1969. 171pp. $4.95. Professor Bush aims at presenting to non-French readers the contemporary relevance of Bernanos' work and thought, giving particular emphasis to the complex and personal genesis of the author's nine volumes of fiction. One chapter is devoted to "The Dialogues of the Carmelites," Bernanos' one play which was later set to music by Poulenc. Chronology. Notes and References. Annotated Bibliography. Index.

Camus, Albert

BREE, GERMAINE
Albert Camus
Columbia, 1964. 48pp. Paper $1.00. A brief survey of the author's career.

BREE, GERMAINE
Camus
Rutgers University, 1961. 281pp. $5.00. Paper—Harcourt, Brace, 1964. 280pp. $2.25. A revised edition of the 1959 study, this volume begins with a brief biographical sketch of the author which is then followed by an evaluation of Camus' work in all the fields of literature.

BREE, GERMAINE — Editor
Camus: A Collection of Critical Essays
Prentice—Hall, 1962. 182pp. $4.95. Paper $1.95. Among the contributors to this collection of essays are Jean-Paul Sartre, Roger Quillot, Thomas Hanna, and Serge Doubrovsky.

CAMUS, ALBERT
Lyrical and Critical Essays
Knopf, 1968. 365pp. $6.95. Paper — Vintage, 1970. 365pp. $1.95. Edited and with notes by Philip Thody, this is a collection of Camus' earliest published writings as well as some of his most important critical statements over the years. The book is divided into three sections: autobiographical writings, selections

from the critical writings, and a section of interviews in which the author speaks about his own writings.

CAMUS, ALBERT
Notebooks: 1935–1942
Knopf, 1963. 225pp. $5.00. Also Modern Library, 1965. 225pp. $2.45. Translated from the French with a preface by Philip Thody, this is the first of three volumes of Camus' notebooks in which he sketched out ideas for future work and jotted down his reflections on life and art.

CAMUS, ALBERT
Notebooks: 1942–1951
Knopf, 1965. 274pp. $5.00. Translated and annotated by Justin O'Brien, this volume was written at the height of Camus' career. It constitutes an involuntary self- portrait, revealing a conscience tormented by the need to find an ethic of human freedom in an absurd world.

CARRUTH, HAYDEN
After the Stranger: Imaginary Dialogues with Camus.
Macmillan, 1964. 180pp. $4.95. In this fictional and philosophical recreation of the world of Camus, characters from his works appear and engage the protagonist, an American artist who suffers the existential despair of alienation in an inquiry into the meaning of life. Camus himself appears and his conscience is probed.

CRUICKSHANK, JOHN
Albert Camus and the Literature of Revolt
Oxford, 1960. 249pp. Paper $1.65. In this reprint of the 1951 edition, the author offers a critical examination of the works in the context both of Camus' personal experience and of the intellectual background of his era.

DE LUPPE, ROBERT
Albert Camus
Funk & Wagnalls, 1968. 101pp. $3.95. Paper $1.95. Translated from the French by John Cumming and J. Hargreaves, this is an assessment of a writer and thinker whose allegories are recognized as perhaps the most accurate and poignant expressions of contemporary man's predicament. Camus' basic conceptions of absurdity, rebellion, and solidarity are traced through his plays and his fiction. Bibliography.

FOWLER, AUSTIN
The Major Works of Albert Camus
Monarch, 1965. 79pp. Paper $1.00. A critical commentary on two of the novels, "The Stranger" and "The Plague," and two of the essays, "The Myth of Sisyphus" and "The Rebel," of the French author. The introductory essay on the life of Camus mentions his theatre experience and plays.

FRIEDMAN, MAURICE
Problematic Rebel
University of Chicago, 1970. 523pp. Paper $3.95. Originally published in 1963 and now revised and reissued, this volume deals with the image of man as a rebel and the fundamental problem of modern man's image of himself. Dr. Friedman casts light upon this problem by extensive discussions of the work of Herman Melville, Doestoievsky, Franz Kafka, and Albert Camus including analysis of Camus' play, "Caligula." This is, however, not a work of theatre literature. Bibliography. Index.

KING, ADELE
Camus
Oliver & Boyd, 1964. 120pp. Paper $1.95. A brief biographical introduction, followed by chapters on the major works, with a report on the best published criticism and a Selected Bibliography.

MAQUET, ALBERT
Albert Camus: The Invincible Summer
Calder, 1958. 224pp. $4.25. The author provides a literary portrait of the French philosopher and playwright. He analyzes and discusses all of the novels, stories, plays, and essays. A complete bibliography of the writings in French and Italian about Camus and a supplementary bibliography of the major articles which have been written about Camus in English are provided.

O'BRIEN, CONOR CRUISE
Camus
Fontana, 1970. 94pp. Paper $1.25. Dr. O'Brien reinterprets Camus as a writer who represents the Western consciousness and conscience in its relation to the non-Western world. The three major novels are examined in a chapter apiece. Bibliographical Note.

PARKER, EMMETT
Albert Camus: The Artist in the Arena
University of Wisconsin, 1965. 245pp. $6.00. Paper $1.95. This systematic analysis of Camus' activity as a journalist focuses attention on Camus' understanding of the social, economic, and political problems of the day and how that understanding influenced his work as a whole. Index.

PETERSEN, CAROL
Albert Camus
Ungar, 1969. 122pp. $4.50. Paper $1.45. An introduction to the French writer. Full biographical information and synopses of each of Camus' works, exclusive of journalism, are included. Notes. Chronology. Bibliographic References.

RHEIN, PHILLIP H.
Albert Camus
Twayne, 1969. 148pp. $4.95. The purpose of this study is to analyze the gradual evolution of Camus' thought into an art and a philosophy that bears his particular seal. Chronology. Selected Bibliography. Index.

ROEMING, ROBERT F.—Compiler and Editor
Camus: A Bibliography
University of Wisconsin, 1968. 298pp. $6.50. This is a bibliography of writings by and about Albert Camus. Critical writings about the author are catalogued under the author's name, and then recorded in three supplementary indices, each organized by country of publication and language. The first index lists entries by author, the second by journal, and the third by date of publication. Materials from nearly forty countries are included.

SCOTT, NATHAN A.
Camus
Bowes & Bowes, 1962. 112pp. $3.50. Dr. Scott traces the development of the themes of the dignity of "l'humaine presence" and the "sacrament of the brother" throughout Camus' entire body of work. Selected Bibliography.

THODY, PHILIP
Albert Camus: A Study of His Work
Grove, 1959. 155pp. Paper $1.45. Detailed examinations of the novels, essays, and plays with a discussion of the major themes. Camus' ideas on suicide as a philosophical problem, on the history of revolt, and on the absurd nature of man are studied.

Claudel, Paul

BERCHAN, RICHARD
The Inner Stage
Michigan State University, 1966. 118pp. $3.50. An essay in the conflict of vocations in the early works of Paul Claudel. Mr. Berchan examines the various stages of this conflict as reflected in the literary production of the author up to 1905.

CHIARI, JOSEPH
The Poetical Drama of Paul Claudel
Gordian Press, 1969. 186pp. $10.00. Originally published in 1954 and now reissued, this is a study of the drama and poetry of Claudel. All fifteen of the plays are discussed and there are examinations of theology and love in Claudel's works and the poetry in the dramas. Bibliography.

CLAUDEL, PAUL
The Correspondence 1899–1926 Between Paul Claudel and Andre Gide
Beacon Press, 1964. 299pp. Paper $1.95. The introduction and notes to this volume, by Robert Mallet, trace the general course of the correspondence. The preface by the translator, John Russell, places the letters in historical perspective and shows how it reveals not only significant facts about French literature and these two writers, but also about French life at the turn of the century.

MATHESON, WILLIAM H.
Claudel and Aeschylus: A Study of Claudel's Translation of The Oresteia
University of Michigan, 231pp. $7.00. The author traces the sprititual and artistic development of Claudel and discusses his training in the classics, his early admiration for Mallarme, and the Aeschylean reminiscences in his plays. The manner in which Claudel assimilated Aeschylus and then recast him for the modern stage is examined in detail. Index.

WATERS, HAROLD A.
Paul Claudel
Twayne, 1970. 176pp. $5.50. An introductory study to the work of the French playwright. The author discusses the aspects of Claudel's life that are significant to the works, the important themes, and the individual genres of drama, poetry, and prose, and the individual works within each genre. Chronology. Notes and References. Selected Bibliography. Index.

Cocteau, Jean

BROWN, FREDERICK
An Impersonation of Angels
Viking, 1968. 438pp. $12.50. Each chapter in this biography of Jean Cocteau focuses on the man or men on whom Cocteau modeled himself during a given period. The author contends that Cocteau adopted the opinions, mannerisms, almost the personae of some of the most outstanding figures in twentieth century art, music, and letters in a search not only for beauty but for love and acceptance as well. Illustrated with photographs. Bibliography. Notes. Index.

COCTEAU, JEAN
The Difficulty of Being
Putnam, 1969. 160pp. $4.50. Translated by Elizabeth Sprigge, this work was regarded by Cocteau as the key to his work. It reveals his own interior struggles with his writings, his film and theatre work, and his personal relationships.

COCTEAU, JEAN
The Journals of Jean Cocteau
Indiana University, 1965. 250pp. Paper $1.95. Edited, translated, and introduced by Wallace Fowlie, these selections include a number of revelations by the author on his films, on his idea of the theatre, and on such personages as Picasso, Gide, Nijinsky, and Raymond Radiguet. Illustrated with sixteen drawings by Cocteau.

COCTEAU, JEAN
Maalesh: A Theatrical Tour in the Middle East
Peter Owen, 1956. 136pp. $3.95. This is a diary of a theatrical tour centering on Egypt and Turkey in which Cocteau recreates the colorful scenes and conveys the exoticism of the near Orient. Illustrated. Index.

COCTEAU, JEAN
My Contemporaries
Chilton, 1968. 146pp. $5.95. Edited and introduced by Margaret Crosland, this is a collection of personal reminiscences of some of the leading figures in the French cultural life during Cocteau's lifetime. Among the portraits presented are Apollinaire, Colette, Chaplin, Gide, Picasso, Piaf, Proust, Radiguet and others. Illustrated with Cocteau's drawings.

FOWLIE, WALLACE
Jean Cocteau: The History of A Poet's Age
Indiana University, 1965. 217pp. $5.00. A biography and a historical-critical study of Cocteau. It includes analyses of Cocteau's major works, their backgrounds and intent, and a chapter on the friendship between Cocteau and Picasso and their influences on each other. Illustrated. Index.

OXENHANDLER, NEAL
Scandal and Parade: The Theatre of Jean Cocteau
Rutgers University, 1957. 284pp. $7.50. All the major plays, certain of the minor ones, and a selection of the films are given scene-by-scene analysis. The cultural and historical background of Cocteau's work is discussed and the relation of the artist to existentialism is considered. Special attention is given to the use of ambiguity in the works. A chronology of the films and plays is added.

PHELPS, ROBERT
Professional Secrets
Farrar, Straus, 1970. 331pp. $8.50. An autobiography of Jean Cocteau drawn from his own writings by Mr. Phelps and translated by Richard Howard. Thirty of Cocteau's books as well as memoirs by friends and co-workers were used by the author to show Cocteau's life and past from his own point of view. Illustrated with photographs and reproductions of drawings and paintings.

SPRIGGE, ELIZABETH and JEAN-JACQUES KIHM
Jean Cocteau: The Man and the Mirror
Coward-McCann, 1968. 286pp. $5.95. An account of the career and achievement of Cocteau as a poet, dramatist, novelist, producer, actor, director, creator of ballets, and philosopher. This biography is illustrated with photographs and reproductions of Cocteau's own drawings. Bibliography. List of Works Consulted. Index.

STEEGMULLER, FRANCIS
Cocteau: A Biography
Atlantic—Little Brown, 1970. 583pp. $12.50. A biography of the man, his work, and of the age in which he flourished. Steegmuller's work is based upon years of research, hundreds of unpublished documents, and personal interviews with a wide spectrum of Cocteau's friends and acquaintances. The author has included fourteen Appendices and a comprehensive Bibliography. Illustrated with forty-five photographs. Index.

Genet, Jean

COE, RICHARD N.
The Vision of Jean Genet
Grove, 1968. 343pp. $7.50. Paper—1969. 343pp. $2.95. In this critical study, the first formal analysis of the evolution of the ideas, art, and imagery in Jean Genet's writing, Professor Coe seeks to illuminate the "vision" behind Genet's work which transforms brutality, war, murder, degradation, and abjection into art. Through careful dissection and analysis of the entire body of Genet's poetry, novels, and plays, and by relating his work to his contemporaries—Beckett, Robbe-Grillet, Ionesco, and others—Professor Coe presents a cohesive picture of Genet's vision. Bibliography. Index.

COE, RICHARD N.—Editor
The Theatre of Jean Genet: A Casebook
Grove, 1970. 250pp. Paper $3.95. In addition to criticism specifically related to each of Genet's five plays, this casebook includes essays on the psychogical, sociological, ethical and aesthetic aspects of Genet's concept of drama. Among the contributors are Sartre, Cocteau, de Beauvoir, Tynan, Brook, Barrault, Abel, and Blin. Bibliography.

DRIVER, TOM F.
Jean Genet
Columbia, 1966. 48pp. Paper $1.00. A short critical study of the French playwright. Bibliography.

GENET, JEAN
Funeral Rites
Grove, 1970. 256pp. Paper $1.50. Originally published in the U. S. in 1969 and now reissued, this is and autobiographical work of fiction which takes place in France during the Nazi occupation.

GENET, JEAN
Letters to Roger Blin
Grove, 1969. 72pp. Paper $1.95. Originally published in France in 1966 and published in the U. S. as translated by Richard Seaver, this volume is subtitled "Reflections on the Theater." It is a series of letters and notes to Roger Blin, who staged "The Screens" in Paris with the Barrault company. The book adds up to a compilation of Genet's conception of the theatre. Thirty-two pages of photographs from the Blin production.

GENET, JEAN
Our Lady of the Flowers
Grove, 1963. 318pp. $6.50. Paper—Bantam, 1968. 307pp. $1.25. This first novel, published in a limited edition in Lyons in 1943, is here presented in an English translation, unexpurgated, by Bernard Frechtman. There is a long introduction by Jean-Paul Sartre taken from his study "Saint Genet." The novel records the reveries of a prisoner and contains many of the same themes as the plays.

KNAPP, BETTINA L.
Jean Genet
Twayne, 1968. 172pp. $4.50. This is an assessment of the works of the French playwright and author. The first part of the volume deals with Genet's non-dramatic works and the second part is a discussion of his well-known plays. Chronology. Notes and References. Selected Bibliography. Index.

McMAHON, JOSEPH H.
The Imagination of Jean Genet
Yale, 1963. 273pp. $8.75. An analysis of Genet's writings—both novels and plays—which traces the development of his ideas from their first expression in "Our Lady of the Flowers" to their recent declaration in "The Balcony," "The Blacks," and "The Screens." The author evaluates the power and persuasiveness of Genet's work and provides detailed examinations of the plays and a Bibliography.

MORRIS, KELLY – Editor
Genet/Ionesco: The Theatre of the Double
Bantam, 1969. 244pp. Paper $1.25. An anthology of essays by and about the two playwrights. Among the contributors are Jean-Paul Sartre, Martin Esslin, Richard Schechner, Bettina Knapp, and Ionesco and Genet themselves. Chronology. Bibliography.

SARTRE, JEAN–PAUL
Saint Genet: Actor and Martyr
New American Library, 1964. 669pp. Paper $1.25. A reprint of the 1963 edition, translated by Bernard Frechtman, this is a comprehensive evaluation of the career and work of Genet. The author discusses the moral, social, religious, and aesthetic significances of the novels, the plays written before 1952, and the playwright's attitudes toward society, art, and conventional morality.

THODY, PHILIP
Jean Genet: A Study of His Novels and Plays
Stein & Day, 1969. 261pp. $6.95. Paper $2.45. In this study of Genet's novels and plays, Philip Thody establishes the relevance of Genet's ideas to his skill as a writer. Thody discusses the moral questions raised by the open publication of Genet's work and the philosophical significance of an author who has admitted to devoting his art to the exaltation of evil. The book contains details of all of the productions of Genet's plays in America, France, and England as well as a critical history of his prose works. Bibliography. Notes and References.

Gide, Andre

BREE, GERMAINE
Gide
Rutgers University, 1963. 302pp. $6.00. This study is a completely rewritten version of the author's "Andre Gide: l'Insaisissable Protee," originally published in France. Each of the author's major works is analyzed.

BRUGMANS, LINETTE F. – Editor
The Correspondence of Andre Gide and Edmund Grosse
New York University, 1959. 220pp. $8.00. Eighty-eight of the approximately 100 letters exchanged between Gide and the English critic and author. The editor has contributed several introductory chapters together with notes which provide a socio-historical setting and identify persons and locales mentioned.

CORDLE, THOMAS
Andre Gide
Twayne, 1969. 183pp. $4.95. The author provides individual analyses of twenty major works – novels, stories, plays, and lyrical essays. He examines recurrent motifs and strategies to locate the source of Gide's artistic power in his own radical discontent. Chronology. Notes and References. Selected Bibliography. Index.

DELAY, JEAN
The Youth of Andre Gide
University of Chicago, 1963. 498pp. $7.95. The author, a psychiatrist who knew Gide, reconstructs the author's first twenty-five years during which he resolved to put his personal problems into his work and devised a technique for doing so.

FOWLIE, WALLACE
Andre Gide: His Life and Art
Macmillan, 1965. 217pp. $4.95. Paper $1.95. The author maintains that Gide is the most persistently autobiographical writer in French history. All the major works are examined, and there are chapters on all periods of the author's life.

GIDE, ANDRE
The Correspondence 1899 – 1926 Between Paul Claudel and Andre Gide
See Page 130

GIDE, ANDRE
The Journals of Andre Gide:
Volume One – 1889 – 1924
Vintage, 1956. 368pp. Paper $1.65. Originally published in English in 1947 and 1948, as edited, translated, abridged and introduced by Justin O'Brien, these journals are a mixture of persons and places, the record of the writer's life. Index.

GIDE, ANDRE
The Journals of Andre Gide:
Volume Two – 1924 – 1949
Vintage, 1956. 380pp. Paper $1.95. Originally published in English between 1948 and 1951 as translated, edited, abridged, and introduced by Justin O'Brien, these are the continuation of the author's journals. Index.

GUERARD, ALBERT
Andre Gide
Harvard, 1969. 287pp. $6.95. Originally published in 1951 and now reissued with new introductory material and Appendix, this is a critique of Gide's personality and writings. The new appendix examines the terms of Gide's intraphysical conflicts, analyzes the stresses and strains of his marriage, and considers the psychosexual background of "L'Immoraliste." Introduction by Thomas Mann. Chronology. Notes. Index.

GUERARD, ALBERT
Andre Gide
Dutton, 1963. 263pp. Paper $1.35. A reprint of the 1951 edition, this is a critique of Gide's personality and writings, with chapters on his novels, his inner conflicts, and his influence. Emphasis is placed on Gide's importance as a psychological novelist who explored and exposed the conflict between the conscious and the unconscious life and who analyzed the various impulses to self-destruction. This edition does not include the Appendix mentioned above.

LITTLEJOHN, DAVID – Editor
Gide: A Collection of Critical Essays
Prentice–Hall, 1970. 177pp. $5.95. Paper $1.95. Essays by noted authors and critics probing Andre Gide's life and work to assess his effect on modern literature. Among the contributors are Jean-Paul Sartre, Francois Mauriac, Germain Bree, and Albert J. Guerard. Chronology of Important Dates. Selected Bibliography.

MALLET, ROBERT and JUNE GUICHARNAUD – Editors
Self-Portraits: The Gide-Valery Letters – 1890 – 1942
University of Chicago, 1965. 340pp. $12.00. Gide and Valery wrote to each other as friends who shared the same ideas, despite the differences in their temperaments. This record of their correspondence, translated and abridged, reveals how they praised and criticized each other and how the change in political and social events caused them to write to each other in a painfully frank manner. Index.

MAURIAC, CLAUDE
Conversations with Andre Gide
Braziller, 1965. 235pp. $5.00. Translated from the French by Michael Lebeck, this book details the friendship between Mauriac and Gide. It reveals the man behind the myth, and the human side of the celebrity.

PAINTER, GEORGE D.
Andre Gide: A Critical Biography
Atheneum, 1968. 148pp. $5.00. This study traces the conflicts of Gide's inner life and applies them to his works. The author uses the Nobel Prize winner's journals and letters to give an understanding of Gide's attempts to balance Protestant morality against homosexual tastes. A shorter version of this book was published in 1951. Illustrated with photographs. Bibliography. Index.

Giraudoux, Jean

COHEN, ROBERT
Giraudoux: Three Faces of Destiny
University of Chicago, 1968. 164pp. $10.00. Paper–1970. $2.45. The author begins with an analysis of the playwright's philosophical premises and then analyzes the twelve major plays, organizing them into three groups of four plays each. Mr. Cohen relates dramaturgical techniques to intellectual and emotional content and, in a concluding chapter, demonstrates that the famous Giraudoux "style" is a direct reflection of his philosophical premises and a precursor to existentialist theatre, the theatre of the absurd, and the theatre of cruelty. Bibliography of English translations of plays and non-dramatic works plus works consulted or cited in the study.

LE SAGE, LAURENT
Jean Giraudoux: His Life and Works
Pennsylvania State University, 1960. 238pp. $7.75. Part One of this study traces the main forces in the life and career of the playwright, situating and describing each work. Part Two analyzes the themes, motifs, attitudes, and styles of his writing. A final section reviews his changing reputation.

RAYMOND, AGNES G.
Jean Giraudoux: The Theatre of Victory and Defeat
University of Massachusetts, 1966. 196pp. Paper $2.50. A study of the work of Giraudoux in its historical context. The author offers the information that Giraudoux may have been the perpetrator of an extraordinary literary hoax. He also examines the recurrent theme of the "tiger-men." Appendices include a chronology of events in the life of Giraudoux and a record of the performances of Giraudoux plays given by Louis Jouvet from 1928 to 1945. Index.

Guitry, Sacha

HARDING, JAMES
Sacha Guitry: The Last Boulevardier
Scribner, 1968. 277pp. $6.95. A biography of the French actor, playwright, producer, and sculptor. It details the stream of plays in which he starred and directed and the five wives who appeared opposite him in succession. Guitry's thirty films are discussed and the new techniques he introduced are mentioned. Illustrated with photographs. List of Published Works. List of Plays. List of Films. Index.

Ionesco, Eugene

COE, RICHARD N.
Eugene Ionesco: A Study of His Work
Grove, 1970. 129pp. Paper $1.50. A revised edition of the study first published in 1961. Professor Coe discusses the background of the new theatre, Ionesco's use of banalities, platitudes, and cliches, and his awareness of death and despair. Bibliography.

IONESCO, EUGENE
Fragments of a Journal
Grove, 1968. 150pp. $5.00. Paper—1969. $1.95. Translated by Jean Stewart, this is a collection of thoughts, memories and dreams which Ionesco describes as "an exploration ... in search of myself." He explores history, politics, psychology, and aesthetics and the sources of his art are uncovered aes-the reader gains insight into the playwright's mind.

IONESCO, EUGENE
Notes and Counternotes: Writings on the Theatre
Grove, 1964. 271pp. Paper $2.45. Translated by Donald Watson, this collection of essays, interviews, exchanges, and polemics with dramatists and critics, and random observations is Ionesco's apologia and explanation of his theatre. He dismisses as useless the concept of "theatre of the absurd," and maintains that his only bond with the new dramatists is their mutual desire to return to the sources of the theatre itself.

MORRIS, KELLY—Editor
Genet/Ionesco: The Theatre of the Double
Bantam, 1969. 244pp. Paper $1.25. A critical anthology of essays, interviews, and translations about or by the two French playwrights. Among the contributors are Jean-Paul Sartre, Bettina Knapp, Martin Esslin, Richard Schechner, and Ionesco and Genet themselves. Chronology. Bibliography.

PRONKO, LEONARD C.
Eugene Ionesco
Columbia, 1965. 47pp. Paper $1.00. A short critical study of the work of the Rumanian playwright whose works have been critically acclaimed in both France and the U. S. Included is a Selected Bibliography of the works, critical works, and commentary.

Mallarme, Stephane

BLOCK, HASKELL M.
Mallarme and the Symbolist Drama
Wayne State University, 1963. 164pp. Paper $5.00. The first comprehensive account of Mallarme's dramatic theory and its impact on the symbolist drama. Early versions of the "Herodiade" and "l'Apres-midi d'une faune," originally written for the stage, are contrasted with later versions, and the revisions are shown to indicate Mallarme's movement toward a theatre of the mind, relying on all the resources of the arts of music, language, mime, and dance. Bibliography. Index.

FOWLIE, WALLACE
Mallarme
University of Chicago, 1962. 298pp. Paper $1.75. A critical study of Mallarme as a poet and as a forerunner of modern poetry and poetic judgment. Mallarme's influence on Gide, Claudel, Eliot, and Yeats is examined. Fourteen line drawings by Matisse. Bibliography. Index.

Montherlant, Henri de

BECKER, LUCILLE
Henry De Montherlant: A Critical Biography
Southern Illinois University, 1970. 137pp. $4.95. This study deals comprehensively with all of the contemporary French writer's work. The protagonists in Montherlant's plays are defeated by their illusions, Mrs. Becker argues, and she considers the plays to be the most enduring of Montherlant's works. Notes. Bibliography. Index.

CRUICKSHANK, JOHN
Montherlant
Oliver & Boyd, 1964. 126pp. Paper $1.95. An attempt to offer an overall account of French playwright and novelist Montherlant's work and the ideas lying behind it. Bibliography of works by the author and studies and articles about him.

JOHNSON, ROBERT B.
Henry De Montherlant
Twayne, 1968. 157pp. $4.50. A comprehensive study of the twentieth century playwright and novelist. Professor Johnson attempts a fresh appraisal of the works as seen apart from their creator and as a balanced critical judgment of those works. A Chronology of events during Montherlant's lifetime is included. Notes and References. Selected Bibliography of Primary and Secondary Sources. Index.

Romains, Jules

NORRISH, P. J.
Drama of the Group: A Study of Unanimism in the Plays of Jules Romains
Cambridge, 1958. 171pp. $5.50. An analysis of the concept of unanimism and its relation to earlier ideas in sociology and literature. Romain's plays of this type are examined.

Sartre, Jean–Paul

BELKIND, ALLEN
Jean-Paul Sartre: A Bibliographical Guide
Kent State University, 1970. 234pp. $10.00. This work is subtitled "Sartre and Existentialism in English." In it the author makes available a comprehensive listing of Sartre's plays, fiction and essays in English translation; books, articles, and reviews written in English about Sartre; and books in English on existentialism and other subjects which include discussions of Sartre up to 1968. A Foreword has been provided by Oreste F. Pucciani. Index.

CUMMING, ROBERT DENOON – Editor
The Philosophy of Jean-Paul Sartre
Modern Library, 1965. 494pp. $2.95. An anthology of selections from every major medium and period of Sartre's activity. The editor has alternated philosophical excerpts and literary pieces and has also provided a long introduction. Selective Bibliography.

DESAN, WILFRID
The Marxism of Jean-Paul Sartre
Doubleday, 1965. 320pp. $4.95. The author provides a study of the evolution of Sartre's social thought to its mature expression in the "Critique de la Raison Dialectique" published in France in 1960. He attempts an evaluation of Sartre's views and raises questions concerning the relationship of the individual to the group. Bibliography. Index.

GREENE, NORMAN N.
Jean-Paul Sartre: The Existentialist Ethic
University of Michigan, 1963. 213pp. $4.40. Paper $1.75. A study of Sartre's philosophy and its relation to the three great systems of orthodox thought against which it is usually measured: Catholicism, Liberalism, and Marxism.

KERN, EDITH
Existential Thought and Fictional Technique: Kierkegaard, Sartre, Beckett
See Page 127

KERN, EDITH – Editor
Sartre: A Collection of Critical Essays
Prentice–Hall, 1962. 180pp. $4.95. Paper $1.95. Essays by Jacques Guicharnaud, Henri Peyre, Hazel E. Barnes, and Kenneth Douglas.

McCALL, DOROTHY
The Theatre of Jean-Paul Sartre
Columbia, 1969. 195pp. $7.50. Mrs. McCall explores and clarifies the discrepancy between Sartre's "project" and the plays as they finally exist. She relies extensively on Sartre's nondramatic writings insofar as they elucidate what he is doing in the theatre. All nine of the published plays are discussed. Notes. Selected Bibliography. Index.

MANSER, ANTHONY
Sartre: A Philosophic Study
Oxford, 1966. 280pp. $7.75. Paper – 1967. $1.75. Mr. Manser gives a critical exposition of Sartre's thought. Chapters are devoted to the novels, the plays, and to Sartre's theory of literature. Bibliography. Index.

MASTERS, BRIAN
A Student's Guide to Sartre
Heinemann, 1970. 82pp. Paper $1.95. A study of the French novelist, playwright, philosopher, and political thinker. The author begins with an introductory account of existentialism and goes on to examine key Sartrean ideas and themes as revealed in the works. Bibliography.

MURDOCH, IRIS
Sartre: Romantic Rationalist
Yale, 1959. 115pp. Paper $1.25. A study of Sartre's place in the history of philosophy, political thought, and the novel. His concept of freedom is examined in detail.

RICHTER, LISELOTTE
Jean-Paul Sartre
Ungar, 1970. 118pp. $5.00. Paper $1.45. Translated from the German by Fred D. Wieck, this is an introduction to the French writer. The main currents of existentialist thought both as it influenced Sartre and as it was interpreted by him are discussed by the author. Notes. Chronology.

SARTRE, JEAN–PAUL
Being and Nothingness
Washington Square Press, 1966. 784pp. Paper $ .90. Jean-Paul Sartre offers a systematic presentation of his philosophy of being. Analyzing the human consciousness and the world it confronts, he explains his views on man's social responsibility, the doctrine of freedom, and the theory of existential psychoanalysis. Translated by Hazel E. Barnes. Index.

SARTRE, JEAN–PAUL
Search for a Method
Knopf, 1963. 181pp. $4.95. Paper – 1968. $1.65. An approach to the sociology and philosophy of history in which Sartre maintains that Marx's original theory of historical development is the most valuable working hypothesis for today. A summary of the main arguments of "Critique de la Raison Dialectique." Translation by Hazel Barnes.

SARTRE, JEAN–PAUL
Situations
Braziller, 1965. 371pp. $5.95. Paper – Fawcett, 1966. 371pp. $ .95. A collection of essays, translated by Benita Eisler, in which Sartre examines the lives and work of Gide, Camus, Giacometti, and Nathalie Sarraute, among others, to discover how they have attempted to discover their salvation.

SARTRE, JEAN–PAUL
The Words
Braziller, 1964. 255pp. $5.00. Paper — Fawcett, 1968. 160pp. $ .75. In this autobiographical sketch, an account of the writer's childhood, Sartre is exploring and evaluating his own discovery of literature and the use he has made of books.

SHEPARD, LESLIE
Jean-Paul Sartre's No Exit and The Flies
Monarch, 1965. 93pp. Paper $1.00. A critical guide to three plays, and some of the non-theatrical works of the French philosopher. Scene-by-scene summaries and critical comment are provided. Also included are essay questions and answers for review. Bibliography.

SUHL, BENJAMIN
Jean-Paul Sartre: The Philosopher as a Literary Critic
Columbia, 1970. 311pp. $9.95. A survey and appraisal of the literary criticism written by Sartre during the last thirty years. Professor Suhl includes descriptive presentation of the material including recent articles as yet unavailable in English. Bibliography. Index.

THODY, PHILIP
Jean-Paul Sartre: A Literary and Political Study
Hamish Hamilton, 1960. 269pp. $4.50. Paper $2.95. A consideration of Sartre's work from a philosophical and a literary point of view with a detailed examination of Sartre's aims and achievements.

GERMANY

Histories and Critiques

BERLAU, RUTH and BERTOLT BRECHT, CLAUS HUBALEK, PETER PALITZSCH, KATHE RULICKE — Editors
Theaterarbeit
DBS Publications, 1969. 473pp. $15.00. This is a study of six productions of the Berliner Ensemble. The book deals with the art of the theatre in all its phases and includes contributions by Brecht, Paul Dessau, Hanns Eisler, and Helene Weigel, among others. Includes a photographic chronicle of the Ensemble productions from 1949 to 1966/67 plus production information in an Appendix. 400 photographs and illustrations are included. Text is in German.

BRENNECKE, ERNEST and HENRY BRENNECKE
Shakespeare in Germany: 1590 — 1700
See Page 97

FUCHS, GEORG
Revolution in the Theatre: Conclusions Concerning the Munich Artists' Theatre
Cornell University, 1959. 22pp. $5.75. Written at the conclusion of the first season of the revolutionary new theatre established at Munich in 1907, this book describes the design of the stage, the auditorium, the performances, and the group of players. Condensed and adapted by Constance C. Kuhn. Illustrated.

GARTEN, H. F.
Modern German Drama
Grove, 1962. 272pp. Paper $2.45. A second revised edition of the 1959 publication, this is a comprehensive study which ranges from the rise of the realistic drama in the 1890's to the present. This edition contains expanded materials on the period from 1945, an expanded Bibliography, and a list of English translations. Index.

GROPIUS, WALTER — Editor
The Theatre of the Bauhaus
Wesleyan University, 1961. 109pp. $7.50. The first English language edition of this trail-blazing work of 1924 in which the theatrical aesthetic of the Bauhaus experimental theatre found its most complete verbal expression. Walter Gropius has written the introduction and there are essays by Oskar Schlemmer, Farkas Molnar, and Laszlo Moholy-Nagy.

HATFIELD, HENRY
Modern German Literature: The Major Figures in Contrast
St. Martin's, 1967. 167pp. $6.95. Paper — Indiana University, 1968. 167pp. $1.85. An account of the period from 1890 to 1956 in the history of German literature. It is intended as a critical survey and the author has elected to discuss a small number of writers in detail rather than attempt to catalogue the whole field. Of particular interest is the chapter "The Drama and Lyric After the First War" in which the author discusses Hauptmann, Hofmannsthal, Brecht, Zuckmayer, Rilke and Kraus. Bibliography. Index.

HEATON, Vernon
The Oberammergau Passion Play
See Page 326

HEITNER, ROBERT R.
German Tragedy in the Age of Enlightenment: A Study of the Development of Original Tragedies, 1724 — 1768
University of California, 1963. 467pp. $12.50. This comprehensive study is a history and critique of the forerunners of Goethe and Schiller. It provides a reference source for plots, themes, and roles for scores of plays, many of them inaccessible. Among topics discussed are the first Alexandrine tragedies and works by Gottshed, Schlegel, Lessing, and Gerstenberg. Index of Names, Titles, Subjects, and Motifs. Bibliography and chronological lists of tragedies, 1729—1768.

HELLER, ERICH
The Artist's Journey Into the Interior and Other Essays
Vintage, 1968. 240pp. Paper $1.65. Seven essays by the renowned critic of German literature. Among the

subjects are Schiller, Nietzsche, and the morality of the Faust legend. Index.

KAUFMANN, WALTER
From Shakespeare to Existentialism
Doubleday, 1960. 454pp. Paper $1.75. A study of the origins and development of existentialism and its relation to drama, poetry, and religion. Chapers on Shakespeare, Goethe, Hegel, Kierkegaard, Nietzsche, Rilke, Freud, Jaspers, Heidigger, and Toynbee.

KISTLER, MARK O.
Drama of the Storm and Stress
Twayne, 1969. 170pp. $4.95. Professor Kistler gives a detailed analysis of the major dramas of Lenz, Klinger, H. L. Wagner, Maler Muller, and J. A. Leisewitz. Chronology. Notes and References. Selected Bibliography. Index.

LESSING, G. E.
Hamburg Dramaturgy
Dover, 1962. 265pp. Paper $1.45. A reprint of the 1890 edition with a new introduction by Victor Lang. A collection of 104 articles by the eighteenth century playwright which constitutes an attack on the classical French theatre in an effort to restore Aristotelian tragedy. The playwright makes a comparative study of Greek and classical French dramatists and comments on the histrionic styles and techniques of the eighteenth century.

LEY–PISCATOR, MARIA
The Piscator Experiment: The Political Theatre
Southern Illinois University, 1970. 336pp. Paper $2.85. Originally published in England in 1967 and now released in the U. S., this is an explanation by Erwin Piscator's widow of her husband's productions of "total theatre," his politics, his acquaintance with the playwrights and performers of the Epic Theatre stage, especially Brecht. Bibliography. Index.

MANN, THOMAS
Last Essays
Knopf, 1959. 218pp. $4.95. Essays on Schiller, Goethe, Chekhov and Nietzsche. Translated from the German by Richard and Clara Winston and Tania and James Stern.

MIDDLETON, CHRISTOPHER – Editor
German Writing Today
Penguin, 1967. 238pp. Paper $1.45. This anthology contains, in translation, poetry, prose and drama written during the past fifteen years. Included is a play by Gunter Grass, a story by Peter Weiss, and contributions by Hans Arp, Ingeborg Bachmann, Helmut Heissenbuttel, and Karl Krolow.

NIETZSCHE, FRIEDRICH
The Birth of Tragedy and The Genealogy of Morals
Doubleday, 1956. 299pp. Paper $1.45. Translations by Francis Golffing of two famous works on the conflict between the moral and the aesthetic approach to life, and on the contrast between the Apollonian and the Dionysian spirits.

PURSCHKE, HANS R.
Liebenswerte Puppenwelt
See Page 342

SAYLER, OLIVER M. – Editor
Max Reinhardt and His Theatre
Blom, 1968. 381pp. $25.00. Originally published in 1924 and now reissued, this is a collection of essays that examines the work of the director from a variety of points of view. A complete chronology of Reinhardt productions, 199 photographs of productions, sketches of stage designs, and the complete Regie Book or production manual for "The Miracle," annotated by Norman Bel Geddes.

SHAW, LEROY R. – Editor
The German Theatre Today: A Symposium
University of Texas, 1963. 141pp. $4.50. The essays in this collection include: "American Drama and the German Stage," by Walther Karsch; "German Drama and the American Stage," by Francis Hodge; and "Epic Theatre is Lyric Theatre," by Eric Bentley. Introduction by the editor. Index.

SOKEL, WALTER H.
The Writer in Extremis: Expressionism in Twentieth Century German Literature
Stanford University, 1959. 251pp. $7.50. An examination of some of the philosophical assumptions underlying the practice of modern art and literature in twentieth century Germany. Bibliography. Index.

VAN ABBE, DEREK
Drama in Renaissance Germany and Switzerland
Melbourne University, 1961. 164pp. $7.50. A survey of the German drama of the early sixteenth century. The lack of truly successful drama is analyzed and the period is seen as one of transition in which devotional drama continued to be popular and in which the tradition of Medieval community plays was revived. List of plays performed 1500–1540.

WITKOWSKI, GEORG
The German Drama of the Nineteenth Century
Blom, 1968. 230pp. $12.50. Originally published in 1909 and now reissued, in this volume Professor Witkowski discusses the major trends of the German drama of the nineteenth century from the early middle class drama to the romantic drama of the 1820's and 1830's, the "Young Germany" ferment, and the impact of naturalism in the 1880's and 1890's. Among the playwrights discussed are Schlegel, Von Kleist, Grillparzer, Hebbel, Hauptmann, Raimund, Wienbarg, Freytag, and Blumenthal. Index.

ZOFF, OTTO
The German Theatre Today

Marquette University, 1960. 13pp. Paper $ .50. A brief account of the vitality of the German theatre today.

Studies of Playwrights

Barlach, Ernst

CHICK, EDSON M.
Ernst Barlach
Twayne, 1967. 154pp. $4.50. This study of the German sculptor, artist, and writer is the first book-length treatment of Barlach in English. Through a detailed analysis of the body of Barlach's writings and examination of the staging of his plays, Professor Chick demonstrates why he believes Barlach deserves to be ranked with Brecht as one of the two leading dramatists of the 1920's and 1930's in Germany. Selected Bibliography. Index.

Brecht, Bertolt

BRECHT, BERTOLT
Brecht on Theatre
Hill & Wang, 1964. 294pp. $6.50. Paper—1966. $2.45. Edited by John Willett, this volume presents for the first time in English Brecht's major critical writings on the theatre and on aesthetics. Here is his definition of the Epic Theatre, his theory of alienation-effects in directing, acting, and writing. Illustrated. Index.

BRECHT, BERTOLT
Manual of Piety (Die Hauspostille)
Grove, 1966. 312pp. $10.00. Paper—1967. $1.95. A bilingual edition, with translations by Eric Bentley, of Brecht's first book of poems. Notes by Hugo Schmidt place each poem in its historical and literary context.

BRECHT, BERTOLT
The Messingkauf Dialogues
Methuen, 1965. 112pp. $4.25. Paper—1967. $1.95. Abandoned more than twenty years ago by the author, and never previously published in English,'''The Dialogues'' are the longest of Brecht's discussions of the theatre. Here an actor, actress, dramaturg (literary adviser) and electrician argue with the extremely Brechtian philosopher who wants to exploit their art and their talent for his own purposes. Translated by John Willett.

BRECHT, BERTOLT
Selected Poems
Grove, 1959. 179pp. Paper $1.95. A reprint of the 1947 edition, this is a bilingual edition, with English translations and introduction by H. R. Hayes, of some of Brecht's poetry. Mr. Hayes evaluates Brecht's position among modern poets.

BRECHT, BERTOLT
Tales from the Calendar
Methuen, 1966. 124pp. Paper $2.75. Translated by Yvonne Kapp and Michael Hamburger, this is a compilation of stories, poems and anecdotes by Brecht. The volume contains most of the short stories that Brecht considered worth preserving.

DEMETZ, PETER—Editor
Brecht: A Collection of Critical Essays
Prentice-Hall, 1962. 186pp. $4.95. Paper $1.95. Essays on all aspects of Brecht's theatre by Eric Bentley, Walter Sokel, Hannah Arendt, and others. Included in this volume is Brecht's testimony before the House Un-American Activities Committee. Bibliography.

ESSLIN, MARTIN
Bertolt Brecht
Columbia, 1969. 48pp. Paper $1.00. A short essay on the work of the German playwright. Selected Bibliography.

ESSLIN, MARTIN
Brecht: The Man and His Work
Doubleday, 1961. 370pp. Paper $1.45. A critical examination of the man and his writings which shows how his commitment to his art always rose above his dedication to his Party. The relation between the freedom of artistic expression and the rigidity of Communistic ideology is studied in relation to the playwright.

EWEN, FREDERIC
Bertolt Brecht: His Life, His Art, and His Times
Citadel, 1967. 573pp. $10.00. Paper—1969. $3.95. A study of the German playwright. Each of Brecht's major works is examined in detail both as to technique and meaning. The meaning of epic theatre as Brecht conceived it is clarified and the theory of estrangement is analyzed by Dr. Ewen. Illustrated with photographs. Bibliography. Index.

HAAS, WILLY
Bert Brecht
Ungar, 1970. 121pp. $5.00. Paper $1.45. An introduction to the German dramatist. The author examines Brecht's stated aims in relation to the works themselves as well as to Brecht the man. Selected Bibliography. Chronology.

KENNEY, WILLIAM
The Plays of Bertolt Brecht
Monarch, 1965. 114pp. Paper $1.00. A critical guide to ten plays. Scene-by-scene analysis and criticism is provided for each of the plays and there are essays on the theatre of Brecht and the unity of Brecht's work. Bibliography.

LYONS, CHARLES R.
Bertolt Brecht: The Despair and the Polemic
Southern Illinois University, 1968. 165pp. $4.95.

Mr. Lyons' discussions bring together readings of Brecht's major plays, tracing the thematic concern and dramatic structure from the initial Expressionism of ''Baal'' to the sophisticated romance of ''Caucasian Chalk Circle.'' He details Brecht's projections of dismay, studies the epic theatre, and Marxist theories in the arts. Notes. Index.

SPALTER, MAX
Brecht's Tradition
John's Hopkins, 1967. 271pp. $6.95. A discussion of the literary tradition of Bertolt Brecht. Dr. Spalter studies the influence of a number of dramatists on Brecht's work and development and identifies the techniques he learned from his forerunners. Among the authors whose influence is studied are J. M. R. Lenz, Christian Dietrich Grabbe, Georg Buchner, and Frank Wedekind. Appendices include selected scenes in English translation from Lenz's ''The Tutor,'' Grabbe's ''Napoleon or the Hundred Days,'' and Kraus's ''The Last Days of Mankind.'' Selected Bibliography. Index.

SZCZESNY, GERHARD
The Case Against Bertolt Brecht
Ungar, 1968. 126pp. $5.00. Translated from the German by Alexander Gode, this is a study of the three versions of Brecht's ''Life of Galileo.'' The author examines the recorded life of Galileo to show how Brecht departed from known history. He contends that Brecht imputed to a scientist of the early seventeenth century the conflicts of conscience that only a contemporary atomic physicist could experience. Notes. Bibliographical References.

WEIDELI, WALTER
The Art of Bertolt Brecht
New York University, 1963. 145pp. $6.50. Paper $1.95. A study of Brecht's development as playwright and poet which traces the various influences that shaped his work. The major plays are examined and particular attention is given to an assessment of Brecht's role as a theatrical reformer, his ideas of the theatre as a social force, and to Brecht as a non-Aristotelian dramatist. This English translation of the French original is by Daniel Russell. Chronology. Bibliography.

WILLETT, JOHN
The Theatre of Bertolt Brecht
New Directions, 1968. 243pp. $10.00. Paper $3.50. Originally published in 1959 and now reissued in a revised edition, this is a study from eight aspects of all the writings of Brecht. Mr. Willett traces the development of Brecht's style, analyzes the theories which have influenced contemporary drama and relates them to the 1920's, the rise of Nazism, and the Comnunist orthodoxy of today. There is a discussion of each of the forty stage and radio works. Illustrated with over 100 photographs of various productions of the plays. Chronology. Bibliography. Index.

Buchner, Georg

LINDENBERGER, HERBERT
Georg Buchner
Southern Illinois University, 1964. 162pp. $4.50. Buchner's work has become an important part of the history of modern literature. He anticipated many of the themes and techniques of the ''theatre of the absurd,'' influenced Brecht and Ionesco, and had much to do with the shape of the modern theatre. This critical account offers detailed discussions of the four extant plays. Index.

Durrenmatt, Friedrich

PEPPARD, MURRAY B.
Friedrich Durrenmatt
Twayne, 1969. 156pp. $4.95. A full-length treatment of the writer as creative author and as critic. The stages of Durrenmatt's development forms the main concern of the volume. The important themes and motifs are carefully examined for their intrinsic merit and for their relationship to contemporary German drama. Chronology. Notes and References. Selected Bibliography. Index.

Frisch, Max

WEISSTEIN, ULRICH
Max Frisch
Twayne, 1967. 192pp. $4.50. This study is planned as an introduction to the Swiss playwright. It seeks to show the continuity of Frisch's writings and his artistic development from his earliest works to his contemporary concerns and style. Selected Bibliography. Index.

Goethe, Johann Wolfgang von

ATKINS, STUART
Goethe's Faust: A Literary Analysis
Harvard, 1958. 290pp. $7.50. A study of the drama as a self-contained unit. The compositional and symbolic elements, the action, character, themes, motifs, and stylistic features are elucidated with reference to their various interrelationships. Index.

BATES, PAUL A.
Faust: Sources, Works, Criticism
Harcourt, Brace, 1969. 218pp. Paper $3.50. This volume contains materials for a study of the Faust story as it originated and evolved. Part I contains the

sources of the story and theme; Part II includes a number of literary treatments including Marlowe's complete play and parts of Goethe's play; Part III contains critical documents on the Faust theme and interpretations and commentaries on the various treatments.

BRUFORD, W. H.
Culture and Society in Classical Weimar 1775 – 1806
Cambridge, 1962. 465pp. $11.50. Professor Bruford shows how the eighteenth century court of Weimar produced a set of ideals and an ideal of personal development. He describes the background of the court, the duties of Goethe as administrator of the court and the contributions of the great writers, lecturers, and journalists who were members of the court. His central chapter analyzes the formal writings of these men and Goethe's notion of culture. Illustrated. Selected Bibliography. Index.

EISSLER, K. R.
Goethe: A Psychoanalytic Study
Wayne State University, 1963. 1,538pp. $35.00. A biography and psychoanalytic study of Goethe's life. The author contends that Goethe cannot be classified under any of the headings of the textbook psychiatry or psychopathology; he is rather the representative of a special group that occupies a position parallel to the known classifications. Bibliography. Index. Two volume set.

FRIEDENTHAL, RICHARD
Goethe: His Life and Times
World, 1965. 561pp. $8.50. This full-scale study of Goethe's life, examines not only Goethe's creative output but all the many aspects of his many different careers. Illustrated. Annotated Bibliography. Index.

GOETHE, JOHANN WOLFGANG VON
The Autobiography of Goethe
Horizon, 1969. 869pp. $15.00. An illustrated edition of Goethe's autobiography as translated by John Oxenford. Gregor Sebba, Goethe scholar, has written an introduction.

GRAY, RONALD
Goethe: A Critical Introduction
Cambridge, 1967. 289pp. $7.50. Paper $2.75. A concise survey and criticism of Goethe's work for the general reader and the student. Comparative table of biographical dates. Bibliography. Index.

GRONICKA, ANDRE VON
The Russian Image of Goethe
University of Pennsylvania, 1968. 304pp. $6.50. This is a study of the interrelationship between German and Russian literature. The early Russian reaction to Goethe and his work, Goethe's translator and interpreter V. A. Zhukovski, the Russian romanticists, and Pushkin, Lermontov, and Herzen are all studied. Notes. Bibliography. Indices.

HATFIELD, HENRY
Goethe: A Critical Introduction
Harvard, 1964. 238pp. $5.50. Paper — Lippincott, 1963. $1.95. A study which traces the development of Goethe's art and thought through studies of the most important poems, all the novels, and several major dramas. An analysis of "Faust: Parts I and II" is given. Illustrated.

HOHENDORF, HORST
The Life and Times of Goethe
Curtis, 1967. 75pp. $3.95. This is the record of every known aspect of Goethe's life and times. More than 150 pictures, in color and black and white, have been chosen, including photographs of the places he knew, portraits of the people who influenced him, reproductions of contemporary paintings, maps and manuscripts. A chronology of Goethe's life is included.

HOPPER, VINCENT F.
A Simplified Approach to Goethe's Faust, Part One and Part Two
Barron, 1964. 57pp. Paper $ .95. This brief study considers the background of the poet, and the important events in his life. In addition to "Faust," six other major works and the lyric poetry are analyzed. Bibliography.

JANTZ, HAROLD
The Mothers in Faust: The Myth of Time and Creativity
Johns Hopkins, 1969. 96pp. $6.95. Professor Jantz examines the realm of the "mothers" in Goethe's "Faust" from an artistic-poetic perspective. He interprets the scene as poetry to clarify Goethe's intent not only in this scene but in the drama as a whole. Notes. Index.

KAUFMANN, WALTER
From Shakespeare to Existentialism
See Page 137

KING, ROLF and CALVIN BROWN, ERICH FUNKE — Editors
Goethe on Human Creativity and Other Goethe Essays
University of Georgia, 1963. 252pp. $5.00. Eight essays on various aspects of Goethe's life and work. Three of these essays are in German. The essays include: "Goethe the Man," By L. A. Willoughby, "Goethe und Werther," by Gerhard Fricke, "Goethe on Human Creativity," by Gregor Sebba, "Goethe's Mind," by A. Didier Graeffe, "Some Complimentary Notes to a Translation of the Gretchen Tragedy," by Carlo Rudino.

LANGE, VICTOR — Editor
Goethe: A Collection of Critical Essays
Prentice-Hall, 1968. 185pp. $4.95. Paper $1.95. The essays in this volume explore and clarify the achievements of the German playwright. Among the essayists are Ronald Peacock who discusses Goethe's version

of poetic drama and Mary Elizabeth Wilkinson who provides insights into the poet's conception of form. Chronology of Important Dates. Selected Bibliography.

LEPPMANN, WOLFGANG
The German Image of Goethe
Oxford, 1961. 220pp. $7.75. An account of the effect of Goethe on the literary, scientific, political, and musical mind and life of Germany from the 1770's to the present.

LUKACS, GEORG
Goethe and His Age
Grosset & Dunlap, 1968. 258pp. $6.95. Paper—1969. $2.45. This is a critical revaluation of Germany's poet/playwright, as translated from the German by Robert Anchor. A large portion of the book deals with studies of "Faust." Index.

MASON, EUDO C.
Goethe's Faust: Its Genesis and Purport
University of California, 1967. 423pp. $10.00. Professor Mason examines the antecedants of "Faust," the creative process by which it came into existence, and considers the literary and philosophical qualities of the tragedy. Selected Bibliography. Index.

MONTGOMERY, PAUL
Goethe's Faust
Monarch, 1966. 122pp. Paper $1.00. Revised and edited by James R. Lindroth and Colette Lindroth, this is a critical guide to the play. Detailed summary and comment on the play is provided as are character analysis, critical commentary, and an introduction on the playwright, his life and work. Essay questions and answers are provided for review. Bibliography.

PEACOCK, RONALD
Goethe's Major Plays
Barnes & Noble, 1966. 236pp. $6.95. A reprint of the 1959 edition in which the author places Goethe's plays in the context of drama in general and tries to assess the originality of Goethe's contribution to drama. Index.

RAPHAEL, ALICE
Goethe and the Philosopher's Stone: Symbolic Patterns in The Parable and The Second Part of Faust
Routledge and Kegan Paul, 1965. 273pp. $6.95. This study deals with Goethe's knowledge of ancient myths, mysteries, and Hellenistic religions, and traces the many alchemical references in "Faust." Goethe's life and work are interpreted in terms of Jung's psychology. Index.

ROLLAND, ROMAIN
Goethe and Beethoven
Blom, 1968. 254pp. $12.50. Originally published in 1931 and now reissued, this is a collection of four essays translated from the French by G. A. Pfister and E. S. Kemp. The essays are entitled: "Goethe and Beethoven," "Goethe's Silence," "Goethe the Musician" and "Bettina." Illustrated.

SCHWEITZER, ALBERT
Goethe: Five Studies
Beacon, 1961. 143pp. Paper $1.95. A portrayal of Goethe as the symbol and embodiment of a great ethical idea and as a faithful student of nature. Translated by Charles R. Joy.

STAHL, E. L.
Iphigenie auf Tauris: A Critical Study
Barron, 1961. 61pp. $2.50. Paper $1.00. An analysis of the background, historical significance, and dramatic structure of the play, with a Selected Bibliography.

VICKERY, JOHN B. and J'NAN SELLERY—Editors
Goethe's "Faust: Part One"—Essays in Criticism
Wadsworth, 1969. 183pp. Paper $3.95. A selection of recent critical essays on Goethe's play. The essays are divided into four general headings: introductory perspectives, structure and literary form, scenes and characters, and themes and motifs. A chronology of Goethe's life is also included. Suggestions for Further Study. Selective Bibliography.

Grabbe, Christian Dietrich

HORNSEY, A. W.
Idea and Reality in the Dramas of Christian Dietrich Grabbe
Pergamon, 1966. 120pp. $5.25. Paper $3.25. The author discusses Grabbe's artistic merit and his influence on current drama. He studies the German author's approach to tragic drama, and analyzes the themes and intentions of Grabbe's tragedies. Bibliography. Index.

Grass, Gunter

CUNLIFFE, W. GORDON
Gunter Grass
Twayne, 1969. 146pp. $4.95. The author tries to show how the German novelist and playwright, using biographical material, provides a chronicle of his times without losing sight of their cruel and pointless absurdity. Chronology. Selected Bibliography. Index.

TANK, KURT LOTHAR
Gunter Grass
Ungar, 1969. 127pp. $4.50. Paper $1.45. Translated by John Conway, this is an introduction to the German novelist/poet/ playwright whose use of the absurd has been praised. Chronology. Bibliography.

Hauptmann, Gerhart

KNIGHT, K. G. and F. NORMAN – Editors
Hauptmann: Centenary Lectures
London University – Institute of Germanic Studies, 1964. 167pp. $8.50. A collection of essays on Hauptmann and his works by such authorities as J. W. McFarlane, H. F. Garten, Mary Gilbert, and Ann C. Weaver. Index.

Hebbel, Friedrich

FLYGT, STEN G.
Friedrich Hebbel
Twayne, 1969. 174pp. $4.95. A comprehensive literary criticism and analysis of the works of the nineteenth century German playwright who has been identified as one of the forerunners of Ibsen. Extensive biographical material and a chronology of Hebbel's life are included. Selected Bibliography. Index.

PURDIE, EDNA
Friedrich Hebbel: A Study of His Life and Work
Oxford, 1969. 276pp. $10.50. First published in 1932 and long out of print, this is a new edition of the study of the German dramatist. Chronological list of dramas. Selected Bibliography. Index.

Hochhuth, Paul

BENTLEY, ERIC – Editor
The Storm Over the Deputy
Grove, 1964. 254pp. Paper $1.25. This collection of articles on Rolf Hochhuth's play has comments by Erwin Piscator, Pope Paul VI, Hannah Arendt, Harold Clurman, Karl Jaspers, Golo Mann, Lionel Abel, Susan Sontag, and the playwright.

Hofmannsthal, Hugo von

COGHLAN, BRIAN
Hofmannsthal's Festival Dramas
Cambridge, 1964. 370pp. $10.50. A study of "Jedermann," "Das Salzburger Grosse-Welttheater" and "Der Turm." The author examines the political-social background of Hofmannsthals's times and works and studies the influence of the Austrian-Hungarian empire on Hofmannsthal's concern with a sense of tradition and his desire to establish contact, through participation in a work of art, between the intellectuals and the Austrian people. Bibliography. Index.

Kaiser, Georg

KENWORTHY, B. J.
Georg Kaiser
Basil Blackwell, 1957. 217pp. $5.00. A biographical sketch of the German Expressionist playwright, with a detailed examination of his plays. The plays are arranged according to dominant theme, and are seen to fall into two groups: the plays that explore the problems of the material world; and the plays wherein the individual discovers his own individuality. Lists of first performances and translations. Bibliography.

Kleist, Heinrich von

DICKSON, KEITH A. – Editor
Amphitryon
Harrap. 1967. 168pp. $2.75. Edited by Keith A. Dickson, this is a German Language edition of Kleist's play, "Amphitryon." The bulk of the volume is, however, devoted to a study of the playwright and the play in English. Included are a biographical summary, Bibliography, Notes, Classical References and a Vocabulary List.

GEAREY, JOHN
Heinrich von Kleist: A Study in Tragedy and Anxiety
University of Pennsylvania, 1968. 202pp. $6.95. The author believes the German playwright was a man whose nature was constantly in opposition to itself. Chronology. Bibliography.

Lessing, Gotthold Ephraim

ALLISON, HENRY E.
Lessing and the Enlightenment
University of Michigan, 1966. 216pp. $7.50. Gotthold Lessing was the major figure of the Enlightenment in Germany. The author relates the philosophy of the playwright to the major issues of the Enlightenment. Notes. Index.

ROBERTSON, JOHN GEORGE
Lessing's Dramatic Theory: Being an Introduction to and Commentary on His "Hamburgische Dramaturgie"
Blom, 1965. 551pp. $15.00. This study of Lessing's record of theatre activity in Hamburg in the 1760's contains a vast selection of passages from the work as well as many selections from other works of the author and of his French, English and German contemporaries, together with extensive notes and commentaries. The "Dramaturgie" is recognized as one of the most profound examinations of tragedy ever written.

Schiller, Friedrich von

FREY, JOHN R. – Editor
Schiller 1759 – 1959: Commemorative American Studies
University of Illinois Press, 1959. 213pp. Paper $3.50. This volume includes ten essays on various aspects of Schiller's art, in commemoration of the bicentennial of his birth. Among the contributors who have written essays for the volume are: Henry Hartfield, F. W. Kaufmann, Helmut Rehder, Walter Silz, John R. Frey, and Harold Jantz.

GARLAND, H. B.
Schiller: The Dramatic Writer
Oxford, 1969. 301pp. $11.75. A study of style in the plays of the German author. Significant vocabulary is classified, syntax is examined, and the role of colloquial speech is made plain. Each of the plays is studied in a separate chapter. Bibliography.

MILLER, R. D.
Schiller and the Ideal of Freedom
Oxford, 1970. 130pp. $6.50. Originally published in 1959 and now reissued, this is a study of Schiller's philosophical works with chapters on Kant. An account of Schiller's theoretical writings on the drama throws light on his dramatic practice. Index.

WILLSON, A. LESLIE – Editor
A Schiller Symposium
University of Texas, 1961. 135pp. $4.00. A collection of essays in honor of the bicentenary of the playwright's birth. Material has been contributed by, among others, A. L. Willson, Helmut Rehder, Oskar Seidlin, Stephen Spender, Harold Jantz, and Hermann Wiegand.

Wagner, Richard

RAPHAEL, ROBERT
Richard Wagner
See Page 287

Wedekind, Frank

GITTLEMAN, SOL
Frank Wedekind
Twayne, 1969. 151pp. $4.95. A study of the German playwright who kept alive the theatrical traditions of the anti-Naturalistic, imaginative mythic aspects of the drama during the mid-twentieth century. Chronology. Notes and References. Selected Bibliography. Index.

Weiss, Peter

HILTON, IAN
Peter Weiss: A Search for Affinities
Oswald Wolff, 1970. 126pp. $4.25. A study of the German playwright with colected translations from his major writings. The author seeks to trace the various stages in Weiss's search for affinities. Frontispiece. Selected Bibliography.

Zuckmayer, Carl

ZUCKMAYER, CARL
A Part of Myself: Portrait of an Epoch
Harcourt, Brace, 1970. 425pp. $7.95. Translated from the German by Richard and Clara Winston, this is the contemporary German playwright's autobiography. The author tells of his life during the German cultural explosion of the 1920's, the rise of Hitler, his exile to America, and his triumphant return after World War II. Index.

GREAT BRITAIN
(Including England, Scotland, and Wales)

General Histories and Critiques

AGATE, JAMES – Editor
The English Dramatic Critics: An Anthology, 1660 – 1932
Hill & Wang, 1958. 370pp. Paper $1.45. A collection of pieces on drama and performers, primarily English, by such critics as Addison, Goldsmith, Lamb, Boswell, Hazlitt, Shaw, Ervine, Beerbohm, Agate, and others.

ALLEN, JOHN
Masters of British Drama
Citadel, 1968. 192pp. Paper $2.25. An introduction to the lives and works of the English drama. Mr. Allen writes of the development of the British theatre, providing biographical sketches of Marlowe, Shakespeare, Jonson, Dryden, Congreve, Sheridan, Pinero, Shaw, and O'Casey, as well as other great playwrights. Illustrated with photographs. Bibliography. Index.

ARUNDELL, DENNIS
The Story of Sadler's Wells
Theatre Arts, 1967. 306pp. $6.95. The first complete record of the theatre that is, with the exception of The Drury Lane, the oldest still active theatre in London. The author has uncovered much new material on the life of the theatre from the seventeenth century to the present. Illustrated.

BAKER, H. BARTON
History of the London Stage
Blom, 1969. 557pp. $12.50. Originally published in 1904 and now reissued in a facsimile edition, this is a history of the London stage. The principal dramatic events are covered with some account of the authors and actors for a period of some 330 years, from 1576 to 1903. Illustrated. Index.

BATES, KATHARINE LEE
The English Religious Drama
See Page 325

BATESON, F.W.
A Guide to English Literature
Doubleday, 1968. 261pp. Paper $1.45. This is the second revised edition of the study originally published in 1965. In addition to listings of principal works with commentaries, "inter-chapters" provide interpretations of the principal periods of English literature.

BELDEN, K.B.
The Story of the Westminster Theatre
Westminster Prods., 1965. 56pp. $3.00. The two hundred year history of the Westminster Theatre. Illustrated with photographs.

BORER, MARY CATHCART
Covent Garden
Abelard, 1967. 144pp. $6.00. The author traces in detail the history of Covent Garden Square from its earliest days through its present day center of theatre. The book includes photographs by A. F. Kersting and many contemporary engravings. Bibliography. Index.

BOULTON, WILLIAM BRIGGS
The Amusements of Old London
Blom, 1970. 562pp. $10.75. Sports, tea gardens, parks, and playhouses in London from the seventeenth to the nineteenth century are discussed in this volume originally published in 1901 and now reissued in a facsimile edition. Illustrated.

BRADBROOK, M.C.
English Dramatic Form: A History of Its Development
Chatto & Windus, 1965. 205pp. $6.00. The author here presents an historical survey of the Shakespearean age and of the revival of poetic drama with Yeats and its culmination in Beckett, Ionesco, Pinter, and Albee. Index.

BROADBENT, R.J.
Annals of the Liverpool Stage
Blom, 1969. 393pp. $15.75. Originally published in 1908 and reissued in a facsimile edition, this is a history of the theatre in Liverpool from the earliest period of the minstrels and jesters through the nineteenth century. Illustrated with twenty-four pages of reproductions of contemporary prints of theatres, concert halls, and actors. Index.

BRODY, ALAN
The English Mummers and Their Plays: Traces of Ancient Mystery
University of Pennsylvania, 1970. 201pp. $9.50. Dr. Brody examines the English folk-play. He attempts to separate the features which have accumulated over the years from the more basic structures and characters of these ceremonial plays. Photographs and many samples of the players' chapbooks are included. Appendices. Notes. Bibliography. Indices.

BURTON, E.J.
The British Theatre, 1100 – 1900
Herbert Jenkins, 1960. 271pp. $5.50. A history of the British theatre in which the characteristics of each period are examined, the plays listed, and original production methods described. Illustrated.

CAWTE, E.C. and ALEX HELM and N. PEACOCK
English Ritual Drama: A Geographical Index
Folk Lore Society, 1967. 132pp. $6.50. The authors deal with the dramatic elements in the three types of English folk play as acted by country "Mummers" in Great Britain. There are chapters devoted to the origin, distribution, and criteria of classification with examples of texts and a table of locations. Bibliography.

CHAMBERS, EDUMUND
The English Folk–Play
Oxford, 1969. 248pp. $8.00. Originally published in 1933 and out of print since 1949, this study is now reissued. The author analyzes the Mummers' play and its congeners and discusses the origin of the genre. Two illustrations. List of Texts. Index.

CLEMEN, WOLFGANG
English Tragedy Before Shakespeare
Barnes & Noble, 1967. 301pp. Paper $3.50. Originally published in Germany in 1955, this is a translation by T.S. Dorsch. The author relates the problems of form and style to the development of dramatic speech in pre-Shakespearean tragedy. This book offers a standard by which to assess this development and helps to illuminate the foundations on which Shakespeare built his drama. Bibliography. Index of Plays, Authors, and Subjects.

CLUNES, ALEC
The British Theatre
A. S. Barnes, 1964. 188pp. $12.00. After a brief survey of the origins and classic background of the theatre, the author examines in detail every period of British theatre. Illustrated with over 100 contemporary drawings and paintings.

DAY, MARTIN S.
History of English Literature to 1660
Doubleday, 1963. 467pp. Paper $1.95. A study of English literature from the ancient times of the Celtics and Romans through the age of Milton (1642–1660). Included are synopses and commentaries on

all major works, biographies of the major figures, and examinations of major literary trends. Index.

DAY, MARTIN S.
History of English Literature 1660—1837
Doubleday, 1963. 562pp. Paper $1.95. A study of English literature from the Restoration to the Romantic era. Included are synopses and commentaries on all major and many minor works, biographies of the major figures and a detailed examination of important literary trends. Drama during the period is covered in four separate chapters. Index.

DAY, MARTIN S.
History of English Literature 1837 to the Present
Doubleday, 1964. 442pp. Paper $1.95. A survey of English literature from the Victorian era to the outstanding figures on the present day scene. Included are synopses and commentaries on all major and many minor works and biographies of major and lesser figures. Drama during the nineteenth and twentieth centuries is covered in four separate chapters. Index.

DISHER, M. WILLSON
Clowns and Pantomimes
See Page 347

DONALDSON, FRANCES
The Actor Managers
Weidenfeld and Nicolson, 1970. 195pp. $6.50. Using material from memoirs, diaries, letters, reviews, and biographies, Lady Donaldson presents portraits of six theatrical innovators of the nineteenth and early twentieth centuries. The growth of the theatrical company and the influence on the theatre of these companies are explored through the contributions of the Bancrofts, Sir Henry Irving, Sir George Alexander, Johnston Forbes-Robertson, Herbert Beerbohm Tree, and Gerald du Maurier. Illustrated. Bibliography. Index.

DOOLEY, ROGER B.
Review Notes and Study Guide to Modern British and Irish Drama
Monarch, 1964. 102pp. Paper $1.00. A study guide to the playwrights of England and Ireland since the 1800's. Among the authors discussed are: Shaw, Wilde, Maugham, Coward, Synge, O'Casey, Carroll, Eliot, Osborne, Rattigan. Bibliographies.

DORAN, DR.
Annals of the English Stage from Thomas Betterton to Edmund Kean
AMS Press, 1968. 1,278pp. $31.00. Originally published in 1863 as "Their Majesties' Servants," revised and edited in 1897 by Robert W. Lowe, and now reprinted, this is a chronicle of the English theatre during the period 1670—1850. Dr. Doran gives an account of the careers of the important actors and actresses, managers, and authors of the period. Fifty copperplate portraits and eighty wood engravings are included. Indices. Sold as a three volume set.

DOWNER, ALAN S.
The British Drama: A Handbook and Brief Chronicle
Appleton, 1950. 397pp. $5.50. The basic facts of literary and stage history selected and arranged to focus attention on the development of the drama as a form of communication. Extensive treatment of the beginnings and later development of the panoramic drama, which the author considers the unique English form. Illustrated.

DUGGAN, GEORGE CHESTER
The Stage Irishman
Blom, 1970. 331pp. $12.50. Originally published in 1937 and now reissued in a facsimile edition, this is a study of the treatment of the Irishman in English drama from the beginnings to the nineteenth century. Eleven Appendices include a chronological list of plays. Illustrated. Index.

DUNCAN, BARRY
The St. James's Theatre: Its Strange and Complete History, 1835—1957
Barrie and Rockliff, 1964. 406pp. $10.75. A history of the theatre that housed Pinero's "The Second Mrs. Tanquery," the first and last of Oscar Wilde's plays, W. S. Gilbert's first play, and such performers as Charles Dickens, the Kendalls, and Lillie Langtry. Lists of persons and events connected with the theatre. Illustrated. Index.

EAGLE, DOROTHY
The Concise Oxford Dictionary of English Literature
See Page 5

EVANS, IFOR
A Short History of English Drama
Houghton, Mifflin, 1965. 216pp. Paper $2.50. First published in 1948 and revised and enlarged for this edition, this is a survey of drama in all periods, with emphasis on those plays that had the most notable success in each period. Index.

FINDLATER, RICHARD
Banned! A Review of Theatrical Censorship in Britain
Macgibbon, 1967. 238pp. $7.95. This is a survey of the Lord Chamberlain's office, the theatrical censor of England, past and present. The author offers a panoramic historical narrative describing theatrical censorship since Tudor times and especially the recent battles over sex, politics, and religion. Selected Bibliography. Index.

JONES, ELDRED
Othello's Countrymen: The African in English Renaissance Drama
Oxford, 1965. 158pp. $4.25. A study of the background of knowledge available to playwrights through works published during the sixteenth and seventeenth centuries on Africans and African explorations, and on how this knowledge was used in plays. Index.

JOSEPH, STEPHEN
The Story of the Playhouse in England
Barrie & Rockliff, 1963. 156pp. $5.25. Designed for the young reader, this book presents the story of the theatre from the Middle Ages to the present. Chapters on the modern film and on television. Illustrated. Bibliography. Index.

JUSSERAND, J. J.
A Literary History of the English People
Blom, 1968. Volume I — 545pp. Volume II — 551pp. Volume III — 629pp. $37.50. Originally published in 1895—1909, and now reissued in a facsimile edition, this three volume study extends from the origins of the English people through the age of Elizabeth. Among the fields covered are the origins of theatre in England, Shakespeare's predecessors, a personal and literary biography of Shakespeare, Shakespeare's dramatic work, and the contemporaries and successors of Shakespeare. Index. Three volume set.

KAUL, A. N.
The Action of English Comedy
Yale, 1970. 338pp. $8.75. Concentrating on a selected group of plays and novels from widely separated periods of English literature, Mr. Kaul investigates the conflict and resolution characteristic of a particular kind of comedy and describes the values it enforces. The author examines the works of Shakespeare, the Restoration dramatists, Sheridan, Fielding, Jane Austen, Henry James, and George Bernard Shaw. Index.

KENNEDY, DAVID
Entertainment
Batsford, 1969. 96pp. $4.50. This is a survey of entertainment in England from the miracle plays to Harold Pinter. Illustrated with over seventy photographs and reproductions of contemporary art. Index.

KER, W. P. and A. S. NAPIER — Editors
An English Miscellany
Blom, 1969. 500pp. $17.50. Originally published in 1901 and now reissued in a facsimile edition, this is a collection of essays by forty-nine scholars of English and Romance language in honor of the editor, F. J. Furnivall. A number of the essays deal with Shakespeare and the English drama. Illustrated.

KLEIN, DAVID
Milestones to Shakespeare
Twayne, 1970. 126pp. $5.00. A collection of essays providing a history of English drama and theatre from early Medieval times through the Elizabethan age. A look at theatre in Shakespeare's time including the acting profession, the playhouse and the audience, staging, and the development of Shakespeare as a playwright are among the topics provided. Bibliography. Index.

KNIGHT, G. WILSON
The Golden Labyrinth: A Study of British Drama
Norton, 1962. 402pp. $7.50. Paper 1964. $1.85. The author examines the development of the Ango-American theatrical ethos and tradition to convey the essential nature of drama.

LEATHERS, VICTOR
British Entertainers in France
University of Toronto, 1959. 179pp. $5.50. A compilation of contemporary reports concerning the visits to France of actors, pantomime dancers, and clowns from the first recorded visit in 1583.

LOWE, ROBERT W.
A Bibliographical Account of English Theatrical Literature
See Page 4

MANDER, RAYMOND and JOE MITCHENSON
The Lost Theatres of London
Taplinger, 1968. 576pp. $12.00. A record of the central London theatres which have been destroyed. Twenty-eight theatres are discussed and the authors provide complete information on architectural changes and the types of playbills offered, the fates of each theatre, and the managerial policies. Illustrated with 108 plates.

MELLING, JOHN KENNEDY
Discovering Lost Theatres
Shire, 1969. 70pp. Paper $1.00. In an introductory essay, the author shows how the theatre reflects tastes and trends and how theatres in England were torn down or converted to other uses. The main body of the work is a list of historic English theatres with brief histories. Illustrated.

MORLEY, MALCOLM
Margate and Its Theatres
Museum Press, 1966. 176pp. $5.75. This book concerns itself with the theatre in Margate, England from 1783 onwards and it contains a great deal of little-known information about famous players and managers of the provincial theatre in England. Illustrated. Index of Names and Plays.

NICOLL, ALLARDYCE
British Drama
Barnes & Noble, 1962. 365pp. $6.50. A fifth revised edition of this survey of drama. Emphasis is placed on the social and historical background and new material on the most recent developments has been added. Illustrated. Bibliography.

NICOLL, ALLARDYCE
English Drama: A Modern Viewpoint
Harrap, 1968. 184pp. $3.95. Professor Nicoll aims to select those plays from theatrical history that have relevance to what is happening on the stage today. The author contends that dramatic developments which seem new today often originated many centuries ago. Illustrated with drawings and photographs. Index.

NICOLL, ALLARDYCE
A History of English Drama: 1660–1900
Volume One: Restoration Drama, 1660–1700
Cambridge, 1965. 462pp. $15.75. The fourth edition, revised and expanded from the 1923 first edition. This volume covers the theatre, audiences, actors, staging, tragedies and comedies. Appendices give a history of the stage, and a hand-list of plays.
Volume Two: Early Eighteenth Century Drama
Cambridge, 1961. 466pp. $15.75. This third edition is revised and expanded from the 1925 first edition. It covers the same ground as Volume One. Appendices on the playhouses, 1700–1750, and a hand-list of plays including Italian operas, oratorios, and serenatas.
Volume Three: Late Eighteenth Century Drama, 1750–1800
Cambridge, 1961. 432pp. $15.75. This second edition, revised and expanded from the first edition of 1927, covers the same material as Volume One for the time period indicated in the title. Appendices include a hand-list of plays and operas, and the playhouses.
Volume Four: Early Nineteenth Century Drama, 1800–1850
Cambridge, 1955. 668pp. $15.75. This new edition is substantially the text of the original 1930 edition, with supplementary materials not found in the two previous editions. Chapters are included on the theatre, dramatic conditions of the age, the illegitimate and legitimate drama, with Appendices on theatre, 1800–1850.
Volume Five: Late Nineteenth Century Drama, 1850–1900
Cambridge, 1962. 901pp. $15.75. The final volume in the "History." Chapters on the theatre, contemporary dramatic conditions, and such figures as Boucicault, Taylor, Robertson, Byron, Gilbert, Jones, Pinero, Wilde, and Shaw.
Volume Six: Alphabetical Catalogue of the Plays
Cambridge, 1965. 565pp. $15.75. This reprint of the 1959 edition gives a comprehensive catalogue of the plays known to have been produced or printed in England from 1600 to 1900. It serves as a guide to the first five volumes and provides new material not in the hand-lists in the other volumes.

NICOLL, ALLARDYCE
The World of Harlequin
See Page 348

NIKLAUS, THELMA
Harlequin, or the Rise and Fall of a Bergamask Rogue
See Page 348

ROSENBERG, EDGAR
From Shylock to Svengali: Jewish Stereotypes in English Fiction
Stanford University, 1960. 388pp. $8.50. The first part of this study examines the portraits of Jews found in literature to the nineteenth century and discusses the central antithesis in these portraits. The second part examines the Shylock legend as it appears in the novels of the nineteenth century, especially in "Ivanhoe" and "Oliver Twist."

ROSTON, MURRAY
Bibical Drama in England from the Middle Ages to the Present Day
See Page 326

SAWYER, NEWELL W.
The Comedy of Manners from Sheridan to Maugham
Russell & Russell, 1969. 275pp. $12.00. Paper—A. S. Barnes, 1961. 275pp. $1.95. Originally published in 1931 and now reissued, this is a study of English comedy and of the society it mirrored during two centuries. Bibliography. Index.

SPEAIGHT, GEORGE
The History of the English Puppet Theatre
See Page 342

STRATMAN, CARL J.
British Dramatic Periodicals: 1720–1960
See Page 513

SUTHERLAND, JAMES
English Satire
Cambridge, 1958. 174pp. $4.50. Paper $1.45. An historical survey of satire in verse, prose, the novel, and the theatre covering each period from the Middle Ages to Shaw and Orwell.

SYMONDS, JOHN ADDINGTON
Shakespeare's Predecessors in the English Drama
Cooper Square, 1967. 551pp. $11.50. Originally published in 1884, this is a survey of the miracle and morality plays, the rise of comedy, tragedy, and similar subjects with discussion of several of the individual dramatists: Peele, Lyly, Greene, Nash, Lodge, and Marlowe. Index.

TAYLOR, ALISON
The Story of the English Stage
Pergamon, 1967. 94pp. $3.50. Written in a simple style for use by children, the author describes the development of the English theatre from the first mystery plays to the present day. Illustrated. Glossary. Bibliography. Index.

THALER, ALWIN
Shakespeare to Sheridan: A Book About the Theatre of Yesterday and Today
Blom, 1963. 339pp. Sold as a set of two volumes with:
WATSON, ERNEST BRADLEE
Sheridan to Robertson: A Study of the Nineteenth Century London Stage
Blom, 1963. 485pp. $25.00. These two volumes constitute a history of the stage and its practices from Shakespeare's time to the end of the nineteenth century. The two volumes were originally published in 1922 and 1926. Both volumes are illustrated and include Bibliographies and Indices.

THORNDIKE, ASHLEY, H.
English Comedy
Copper Square, 1965. 635pp. $11.50. Originally published in 1929 and now reissued, this is a survey of English comedy from the Medieval period to 1900. Notes. Index.

THORNDIKE, ASHLEY H.
English Tragedy
Cooper Square, 1965. 390pp. $8.95. Originally published in 1908, this study attempts to trace the course of English tragedy from approximately 1562 to the middle of the nineteenth century and to indicate the part which it has played in the history of both the theatre and literature. There is a brief Bibliography at the end of each chapter listing books of reference. Index.

TROUBRIDGE, ST. VINCENT
The Benefit System in the British Theatre
Society for Theatre Research, 1967. 172pp. Paper $10.00. This is a full length study of the benefit—the system whereby actors' salaries were augmented by the proceeds of special performances—which was prevalent for about two hundred years from the 1680's to the 1880's. The author studies the origin of the system, the types and terms of benefit, the decline of the system, and the actual performances. List of Books Quoted. Indices.

WATSON, ERNEST BRADLEE
Sheridan to Robertson: A Study of the Nineteenth Century London Stage
See Entry Under: **THALER, ALWIN**
Shakespeare to Sheridan

WATSON, GEORGE – Editor
Literary English Since Shakespeare
Oxford, 1970. 407pp. Paper $2.75. A collection of twenty-three essays concerning "those aspects of English which are fully characteristic of its genius as a language." There are considerations of Shakespeare's poetry, Johnson's dramatic prose, the language of the Victorians, styles of realism, and the current linguistic scene.

WITHINGTON, ROBERT
English Pageantry: An Historical Outline
Blom, 1963. Two Volumes. Volume One: 258pp. Volume Two: 435pp. $27.50. This two volume study, first published in 1918, deals with the elements of pageantry, the pageantic features of tournaments and early masques, the development of the "royal-entry" from 1300, and the growth of the Elizabethan pageantry. The second volume deals with the development of the Lord Mayor's show, various survivals and revivals of pageants, and the Parkerian pageant. Bibliography. Index. Illustrated. Sold as a set.

YATES, FRANCES A.
Theatre of the World
University of Chicago, 1969. 218pp. Paper $3.45. The English public theatre is studied as an adaptation of the Vitruvian ancient theatre. Dr. Yates shows that it is from within a Renaissance world of thought that the English public theatres made their appearance. She suggests new approaches to the problems of the ground plan of the Globe Theatre and outlines its stage. Illustrated. Index.

Chronological Periods: Beginnings to 1485

ANDERSON, MARY D.
Drama and Imagery in English Medieval Churches
Cambridge, 1963. 248pp. $9.50. The author shows that dramatic elements in the imagery of medieval churches, whether stained glass, wall paintings, or sculpture, were intended to convey the same traditional themes of religious teaching as the plays of the period. The side-by-side development of these two forms of instruction is described, and the author indicates how a study of church imagery can expand our knowledge of the plays. Illustrated. Bibliography. Index.

CAWLEY, A. C. – Editor
The Wakefield Pageants in the Towneley Cycle
Barnes & Noble, 1958. 187pp. $4.95. A critical edition of six complete pageants which form the major part of the Wakefield group. The text of the edition is transcribed from photographs of the manuscript preserved at the Huntington Library. Glossary. Index.

CHAMBERS, E. K.
The English Folk-Play
Russell & Russell, 1964. 248pp. $8.50. A reprint of the text first published in 1933, this is a study of the Mummers' play and its congeners, based on an examination of over 100 examples. The study considers the question of the origin of the folk-play, discussing parallels with Western European and Balkan examples. Index of Texts.

CHAMBERS, E. K.
The Medieval Stage
Oxford, 1954. Volume One: 419pp. Volume Two: 480pp. $17.00. A reprinting of the original edition of 1903, this is a comprehensive study which aims to state and define the pre-existing conditions which, by the later half of the sixteenth century, made the Elizabethan stage possible. The author describes the breakdown of the Graeco-Roman theatre and the rise of the wandering minstrels, studies folk and religious drama, and considers the "interludes."

CRAIG, HARDIN
English Religious Drama of the Middle Ages
Oxford, 1955. 430pp. $13.00. A survey of the whole

field of religious drama, with special attention given to the great cycles of mystery plays.

CUSHMAN, L.W.
The Devil and the Vice in English Dramatic Literature Before Shakespeare
Frank Cass, 1970. 148pp. $10.00. Originally published in 1900 and now reissued, this was the first investigation of the history and relationship of the devil and the Vice as dramatic figures. The serious drama of the period forms the basis of the study which shows that the Vice was a development of the devil-figure and the forerunner of the clown. Bibliography.

DAVIS, NORMAN – Editor
Non–Cycle Plays and Fragments
Oxford, 1970. 168pp. $11.50. An antholgoy of thirteen miscellaneous medieval plays, originally published in 1909 and now reissued with corrections from the manuscripts that survive, and a number of added short dramatic pieces. A new Glossary is provided and a rewritten Introduction which describes the textual authority for each piece and discusses verse technique and linguistic features of special interest. Illustrated with reproductions of fragments of the works. Bibliography.

DAVIS, R.T.
Medieval English Lyrics: A Critical Anthology
Northwestern University, 1963. 384pp. $7.00. Paper – 1964. $3.95. A critical and comprehensive anthology containing 187 shorter poems with adjusted spelling. Introduction. Notes. Index.

FARNHAM, WILLARD
The Medieval Heritage of Elizabethan Tragedy
Barnes & Noble, 1956. 487pp. $9.95. A revised edition of the 1936 study of the continuity of the whole body of tragedy from medieval story and miracle play to "Hamlet" and "King Lear." Illustrated.

GARDINER, HAROLD C.
Mysteries' End: An Investigation of the Last Days of the Medieval Religious Stage
Archon, 1967. 139pp. $5.25. Originally published in 1946 and now reissued, this study treats of the reasons for the discontinuance of medieval religious plays, especially in England. The author considers the Reformation distaste for the religious culture of the past to have been almost the sole cause for the plays' disappearance. Bibliography. Index.

HARDISON, O.B.
Christian Rite and Christian Drama in the Middle Ages
Johns Hopkins, 1966. 328pp. $7.50. Paper – 1969. $2.45. This is a collection of essays on the origin and early history of modern drama. The author reassesses the knowledge available concerning the early history of medieval drama, examines the relation of drama to ritual, and the development of representational techniques. A chronology of early liturgical plays of the tenth through the thirteenth centuries is included. Index.

HUNNINGHER, BENJAMIN
The Origin of the Theatre
See Page 12

KINGHORN, A.M.
Mediaeval Drama
Evans, 1968. 160pp. $3.95. Paper $1.95. Dr. Kinghorn introduces his subject through the liturgical plays and describes the nature of the various influences which helped to determine the character of the English stage-play before Shakespeare. Illustrated. Bibliography. Index.

LONGSWORTH, ROBERT
The Cornish Ordinalia
See Page 326

MILL, ANNA JEAN
Mediaeval Plays in Scotland
Blom, 1970. 356pp. $12.50. Originally published in 1924 and now reissued in a facsimile edition, this is a study of folk plays, minstrelsy, court revels, and municipal plays. Appendices of excerpts from local records, court records, and pageants and playfields are included. Index.

NORRIS, EDWIN – Editor
The Ancient Cornish Drama
Blom, 1968. 1,005pp. $37.50. The only anthology of Cornish drama with original texts and complete scholarly apparatus. Originally published in 1859 as edited and translated by Mr. Norris, this is a reissue. Two volume set.

PROSSER, ELEANOR
Drama and Religion in the English Mystery Plays: A Re–evaluation
Stanford University, 1961. 229pp. $6.00. A study of the mysteries in terms of the religious doctrine that the playwrights used to shape traditional materials into drama. The emphasis is on the doctrine of repentance. Intensive, line-by-line analyses are given of "Cain," "Joseph," "The Woman Taken in Adultery," "Magdalene," and "Thomas."

ROSSITER, A.P.
English Drama from Early Times to the Elizabethans
Barnes & Noble, 1960. 176pp. $5.25. Paper – 1967. 192pp. $1.95. A study of the background, origins, and development of the English drama. Detailed examinations are given of representative plays up to the foundation of the Tudor stage. Notes. Index.

SALTER, F.M.
Mediaeval Drama in Chester
Russell & Russell, 1968. 138pp. $10.00. Originally published in 1955, this is a series of lectures on the

Chester cycle of mystery plays which were performed by the guilds of the city during the thirteenth to the fifteenth centuries. Index.

SMITH, ROBERT METCALF
Froissart and the English Chronicle Play
Blom, 1965. 176pp. $10.00. First published in 1915 and now reissued, this is a study of Lord Berner's 1523-1525 translation of the Froissart "Chronicles" which were an important source for the dramatists of the period, particularly those writing plays about Edward III and Richard II. The last two chapters show the use made of Berner's translation by Samuel Daniel while writing his "Civil Wars," and, in view of this relationship, throw new light on the indebtedness of Shakespeare's "Richard II" to Daniel's epic. A Bibliography includes the listing of the principal works referred to in the study. Index.

WICKHAM, GLYNNE
Early English Stages: 1300 to 1660
Part I: 1300 to 1576
Columbia, 1959. 428pp. $15.00. A history of the development of dramatic spectacle and stage conventions in England. The aim of this study is to trace the indebtedness of the Elizabethan Court and the public theatres to their antecedents in the Middle Ages. This first volume is in three books: Book One studies indoor entertainments; Book Two considers open-air entertainments; Book Three analyzes Medieval dramatic theory and practice. Illustrated. Appendices. Notes. Book List. Index.

WICKHAM, GLYNNE
Shakespeare's Dramatic Heritage
See Page 85

WILLIAMS, ARNOLD
The Characterization of Pilate in the Towneley Plays
Michigan State University, 1950. 112pp. $2.50. A study of the ideas traditionally associated with Pilate as they are found in documents of the Middle Ages, and of how these ideas shaped the dramatic character in these plays.

WILLIAMS, ARNOLD
The Drama of Medieval England
Michigan State University, 1961. 186pp. $5.00. The development of drama from its beginnings in the liturgy to the cycle plays.

YOUNG, KARL
The Drama of the Medieval Church
Oxford, 1962. Volume One: 708pp. Volume Two: 612pp. $32.50. A revised reprinting of the original 1933 edition, the purpose of this work is to assemble, in their original form, the dramatic compositions which were employed by the Medieval Church in Western Europe as a part of public worship and which are regarded as the origins of modern drama. Illustrated. Two volume set.

Chronological Periods: Tudor, Elizabethan, and Stuart (1485-1660)

HISTORIES AND CRITIQUES

ADAMS, JOSEPH QUINCY – Editor
The Dramatic Records of Sir Henry Herbert, Master of the Revels 1623 – 1673
Blom, 1963. 155pp. $8.75. A reprint of the original edition published in 1917, these are the official records of the Office of the Revels during the period when it attained the height of its power and influence. The primary source is the reconstruction of the Office Book, 1622—1642, supplemented by miscellaneous documents for the periods 1622—1642 and 1660—1670. Index.

ANGLO, SYDNEY
Spectacle Pageantry and Early Tudor Policy
Oxford, 1969. 375pp. $18.00. An attempt to elucidate early Tudor spectacle and pageantry which together constitute a significant part of the historical materials through which the making of the Tudor achievement can be traced. Annotated analysis of contemporary entries covering festivals, masques, and tournaments from the accession of Henry VII to the coronation of Elizabeth I. Index.

ARMSTRONG, WILLIAM A.
The Elizabethan Private Theatres: Facts and Problems
Folcroft, 1969. 17pp. $3.95. Originally published in 1958 and now reissued, this is a short study of private theatres in the Elizabethan era. Illustrated.

ASHTON, JOHN – Editor
Humour, Wit and Satire of the Seventeenth Century
Dover, 1968. 454pp. Paper $2.75. Originally published in 1883, this collection of ballads, jests, light verse, riddles, and libels dates from the beginning of the seventeenth century to about 1670. Over one hundred verse and prose pieces comment on seventeenth century English life, offering a picture of the concerns, pastimes, and attitudes of the man-in-the-street. Bibliographical References to Sources. Compilation of Music. Illustrated. Index.

BAKER, HOWARD
Induction to Tragedy: A Study in a Development of Form in Gorboduc, The Spanish Tragedy, and Titus Andronicus
Russell & Russell, 1965. 247pp. $9.00. A reprint of the original edition of 1939, the intention of the author of this study is to show how Elizabethan tragedy, without changing importantly the kind of technical and moral material it had inherited from the Middle Ages and without being overly influenced by Seneca, achieved competence in more difficult versions of those materials. Index.

BENTLEY, GERALD EADES
The Jacobean and Caroline Stage: Dramatic Companies and Players
Oxford, 1966. 748pp. Two volume set: $25.00. Originally published in 1941 and reprinted with corrections, these two volumes continue the detailed history of the English stage begun in Sir Edmund Chambers' "The Medieval Stage" and "The Elizabethan Stage." This set of two volumes is concerned with dramatic companies and players.

BENTLEY, GERALD EADES
The Jacobean and Caroline Stage: Plays and Playwrights
Oxford, 1956. 1,456pp. Three volume set: $35.00. The continuation of Bentley's study of the English stage.

BENTLEY, GERALD EADES
The Jacobean and Caroline Stage: Theatres and Appendixes and Index
Oxford, 1968. 699pp. Two volume set: $22.50. The completion of Bentley's study of dramatic and theatrical affairs from the death of Shakespeare to the closing of the theatres. The final volume includes Appendixes and the General Index.

BENTLEY, GERALD EADES—Editor
The Seventeenth Century Stage: A Collection of Critical Essays
University of Chicago, 1968. 287pp. $12.50. Paper $2.95. This collection of essays, edited and introduced by G. E. Eades, concerns early seventeenth century theatres, acting styles, and production methods. Bibliography. Index.

BEVINGTON, DAVID M.
From Mankind to Marlowe: Growth of Structure in the Popular Drama of Tudor England
Harvard, 1962. 310pp. $8.50. The author establishes the canon of popular native plays, from "Mankind" (circa 1471) to the beginning of the London theatre (1574), analyzes the organization of the popular acting troupes, traces the development of structure in the moralities, and shows the principle of design inherent in a linear form and a blending of humor and tragedy.

BEVINGTON, DAVID M.
Tudor Drama and Politics
Harvard, 1968. 360pp. $12.00. The author studies topical meaning in sixteenth century English drama in terms of political issues in the playwriting of the Tudor age. He approaches Shakespeare as one of the leading participants but the emphasis is on the entire Tudor period. List of Works Cited. Index.

BLUESTONE, MAX and NORMAN RABKIN—Editors
Shakespeare's Contemporaries
Prentice—Hall, 1969. 411pp. Paper $6.00. Originally published in 1961 and now reissued in an enlarged and revised second edition, this is a collection of contemporary essays on twenty-nine Elizabethan and Stuart plays. The volume is an introduction to major non-Shakespearean plays of the English Renaissance in thirty-six essays. Bibliographies.

BOAS, FREDERICK S.
An Introduction to Stuart Drama
Oxford, 1946. 443pp. $6.50. A study of the chief playwrights whose work falls mainly or entirely between the accession of James I and the Restoration. Special attention is given to critical examination of plots and characterization.

BOAS, FREDERICK S.
An Introduction to Tudor Drama
Oxford, 1933. 176pp. $4.00. This study contains chapters on such early Tudor playwrights as Medwall, Heywood, and Rastell; chapters on tragedy at the Inns of Court; plays at the Universities; the children players; Lyly's court comedies; chronicle, history, and biographical plays; and the University wits and their experiments.

BOWERS, FREDSON THAYER
Elizabethan Revenge Tragedy: 1587—1642
Peter Smith, 1959. 288pp. $4.75. Paper—Princeton, 1966. 288pp. $2.95. A reprint of the 1940 study of the background, origin, and chronological development of revenge tragedy, presented in terms of the dramatic, literary, and ethical influences working on the dramatists of the era.

BRADBROOK, M. C.
Elizabethan Stage Conditions: A Study of Their Place in the Interpretation of Shakespeare's Plays
Cambridge, 1968. 149pp. $4.95. Paper $1.65. Originally published in 1932 and now reissued, this study begins with a survey of Shakespearean criticism from the eighteenth to the twentieth centuries. There follows a discussion of the stage in Shakespeare's time and its influence on his dramatic structure, the topical elements in the plays, and the influence of the stage on characterization, poetry, and textual criticism.

BRADBROOK, M. C.
The Growth and Structure of Elizabethan Comedy
Chatto & Windus, 1961. 246pp. $6.00. Miss Bradbrook traces the development of Elizabethan comedy and sets out to form a critical estimate of various forms, taking into account recent scholarly work on the Elizabethan theatre and audience, and on Elizabethan critical theory. Among the writers dealt with in the course of her survey are Lyly and Peele, Dekker, Heywood, Marston, Middleton, Chapman, and Fletcher. Chronological Table of Plays. Notes. Index.

BRADBROOK, M. C.
The Rise of the Common Player
Harvard, 1962. 320pp. $6.75. A study of the actor and his relation to society in Shakespeare's England.

Four representative figures—Laneham, Tarlton, Wilson, and Alleyn—are examined in detail. The author investigates the creation of a new audience, the actor's struggle for social status, and the Puritan attacks on the theatre of the day.

BRADBROOK, M.C.
Themes and Conventions of Elizabethan Tragedy
Cambridge, 1957. 275pp. $5.00. Paper—1960. 275pp. $1.75. A reprint of the work first published in 1935, this study was written in an attempt to discover how an Elizabethan would have approached a tragedy by Chapman, Tourneur, or Middleton. The author explores the conventions of the theatre, of acting, speech, reading, writing, and listening and shows how these conventions influenced the playwrights.

BRERETON, J. LE GAY
Writings on Elizabethan Drama
Cambridge, 1944. 115pp. $1.75. A collection, edited by R. G. Howarth, of essays on Marlowe, Francis Ingram, Marston, "Richard II," "Tamburlaine," and the Elizabethan playhouses. Illustrations of structural details of the playhouses. List of Brereton's Publications.

BROOKE, TUCKER
The Tudor Drama: A History of English National Drama to the Retirement of Shakespeare
Shoe String, 1964. 461pp. $11.50. A reprint of the work first published in 1911, this historical survey considers the scriptural and miracle drama, the early morality play, the Tudor interlude, the classical influences in comedy and tragedy, the heroic play, romantic comedy and pastoral comedy, and the nature of Elizabethan drama. Illustrated. Index.

BROWN, JOHN RUSSELL and BERNARD HARRIS—Editors
Elizabethan Theatre
Arnold, 1966. 248pp. $5.75. A collection of ten essays on the theatre in which Shakespeare worked. There are single chapters on Marlowe, Kyd, Lyly, and Jonson, the influence of Plautus and Terence, and Elizabethan tragic heroes by such authorities as T. W. Craik, Edward B. Partridge, and Jonas A. Barish. Illustrated. Index.

BROWN, JOHN RUSSELL and BERNARD HARRIS—Editors
Stratford—Upon—Avon Studies I: Jacobean Theatre
St. Martin's, 1960. 252pp. $5.75. Paper—Putnam, 1967. 253pp. $1.65. A collection of essays on the themes and achievements of such playwrights as Marston, Jonson, Fletcher, and Chapman. Among the contributors are Maynard Mack, William A. Armstrong, Arthur Brown, Peter Ure, and David William. Index.

BULLEN, A.H.
Elizabethans
Russell & Russell, 1962. 226pp. $8.50. A reprint of the original edition published in 1924, this is a collection of essays on such figures as Chapman, Dekker, Nicholas Brenton, Drayton, and Shakespeare.

BUXTON, JOHN
Elizabethan Taste
St. Martin's, 1963. 370pp. $7.95. A study of the aesthetic principles that guided the patrons of the arts in the period. The architecture, painting, sculpture, and music of the age are examined, and five of the most popular literary works of the age, by Spenser, Sidney, and Shakespeare, are analyzed. Illustrated. Index.

CHAMBERLAIN, JOHN
The Chamberlain Letters
Putnam, 1965. 370pp. $6.50. Paper—Capricorn, 1966. 370pp. $2.45. Edited by Elizabeth Thomson, these are a selection of the letters of John Chamberlain concerning life in Jacobean England from 1597 to 1626. They offer a discriminating portrait and commentary on the outstanding men and events of the time. Index of Proper Names.

CHAMBERS, E. K.
The Elizabethan Stage
Oxford, 1923. Volume One: 388pp. Volume Two: 577pp. Volume Three: 518pp. Volume Four: 467pp. $32.50. A definitive work which summarizes all the discoverable evidence on the various aspects of the subject. Volume One considers the Court and the control of the stage; Volume Two, the companies and the playhouses; Volume Three, staging at Court and in the theatres, plays and playwrights; Volume Four, anonymous works. Illustrated. Sold as a four volume set.
Also See: **WHITE, BEATRICE—Editor**
An Index to The Elizabethan Stage

CLARK, ELEANOR GRACE
Ralegh and Marlowe: A Study in Elizabethan Fustian
Russell & Russell, 1965. 488pp. $12.00. A reprint of the work first published in 1941. The first part of this study examines Elizabethan censorship practices and their effect upon playwrights and essayists. The topical references in plays and satires are considered. Part Two considers the relation between Marlowe and the group known as the Ralegh circle.

CLEMEN, WOLFGANG
English Tragedy Before Shakespeare: The Development of Dramatic Speech
Barnes & Noble, 1961. 301pp. $7.00. Paper—Methuen, 1967. 301pp. $3.50. A study of plays and playwrights between "Gorboduc" and Marlowe's "Edward II," with discussions of plot, characterization and exposition, versification and style. The author traces the change from oration and epic report to a style of speech closely bound up with character and situation. The foundations on which Shakespeare built are thus illuminated for the reader.

COWLING, G.H.
Music on the Shakespearean Stage
Russell & Russell, 1964. 116pp. $6.00. A reprint of the original edition published in 1913, this study discusses music in pre-Shakespearean drama, the stage and its music, musical instruments and their uses, incidental music, the musicians and the singers, the function of music in the drama, and some literary allusions to music in Elizabethan plays. Illustrated. Index.

CRAIG, HARDIN
The Enchanted Glass: The Renaissance Mind in English Literature
Oxford, 1960. 239pp. $6.00. The mental life and outlook of the Renaissance, and the books which shaped that outlook, presented as a background for an understanding of Elizabethan literature.

CREIZENACH, WILHELM
The English Drama in the Age of Shakespeare
Haskell House, 1964. 454pp. $16.00. Translated by Cecile Hugon, this volume contains a general account of the Elizabethan drama and the general conditions in which it flourished. First published in 1916 and revised and corrected for this edition by Professor Creizenach. Three illustrations. Index.

CUNLIFFE, JOHN W.
The Influence of Seneca on Elizabethan Tragedy
Shoe String, 1965. 155pp. $5.75. First published in 1893, this is an examination of the elements in Seneca that made him an appealing figure to the Elizabethan playwrights. Specific points of imitation in a variety of plays are examined in detail.

CUNNINGHAM, J.V.—Editor
The Renaissance in England
Harcourt, Brace, 1966. 274pp. Paper $2.45. An anthology which introduces the reader to the background of Renaissance England. Included are a little known dramatic scene attributed to Shakespeare and a selection from the court entertainments of Jonson. Bibliography.

CUNNINGHAM, JOHN E.
Elizabethan and Early Stuart Drama
Evans, 1965, 128pp. $3.95. Paper $2.65. This study examines the major playwrights of the era: Marlowe, Kyd, Jonson, Beaumont and Fletcher, and Webster. Bibliography. Index.

CURRY, JOHN V.
Deception in Elizabethan Comedy
Loyola University, 1955. 197pp. $3.50. This book examines the various types of knavery and knaves in the comedy of the period, with studies of the kinds of victims, the trick of the duper duped, the various means of deception, and the audience appeal of deception. Bibliography of dramatic texts and historical and critical works. Index.

DAVIS, JOE LEE
The Sons of Ben: Jonsonian Comedy in Caroline England
Wayne State University, 1967. 252pp. $8.95. A guidebook to the comedy of thirty-two disciples of Ben Jonson in the age of Charles I. Mr. Davis describes the menace and challenge of the age, the comic theory, and the heritage of comic practice. Bibliography. Index.

DEMARAY, JOHN G.
Milton and the Masque Tradition
Harvard, 1968. 188pp. $7.25. This study places Milton's early poetry against the background of the Renaissance court masque and entertainment. Mr. Demaray identifies and examines masque allusions in the early verse; he reveals the French ballet and English masque influence on "Comus;" and he recreates in detail the initial performances of the entertainment "Arcades" and the masque "Comus." Illustrated. Notes. Bibliography. Index.

DODD, A.H.
Life in Elizabethan England
Putnam, 1961. 176pp. $4.50. A description of the common day-to-day life of English men and women of all social classes and professions in the days of Elizabeth I. Life in the Court, in the country, in the home, church, schools, and the various professional entertainment companies is described. Illustrated. Index.

DORAN, MADELEINE
Endeavors of Art: A Study of Form in Elizabethan Drama
University of Wisconsin, 1964. 482pp. Paper $2.95. A reprint of the 1954 edition, this essay in historical criticism investigates the frame of artistic references within which the dramatists of the period worked. The ways in which the playwrights were limited as well as aided by their literary heritage, their rhetorical education, contemporary tastes, and the commonplaces of Renaissance aesthetics and poetics are examined in detail. Illustrated. Index.

ELIOT, T.S.
Essays on Elizabethan Drama
Harcourt, Brace, 1956. 178pp. Paper $ .95. Originally published in 1932, this is a collection of essays on Elizabethan playwrights.

ELLIS-FERMOR, UNA
The Jacobean Drama: An Interpretation
Methuen, 1961. 348pp. $6.00. Paper—Vintage, 1964. 348pp. $1.95. A reprint of the edition of 1958, this study traces the evolution of thought and mood from the end of Marlowe's career, through the works of Jonson, Marston, Chapman, Middleton, Tourneur, and Webster, to a culminating phase in the work of Shakespeare. The modifications made by Beaumont and Fletcher, Rowley, and Ford are also studied. Index.

FLEAY, FREDERICK GARD
A Biographical Chronicle of the English Drama, 1559 – 1642
Burt Franklin, 1962. Two volume set: 792pp. $33.25. A reprint of the edition first published in 1891, this volume is alphabetically arranged. The entries give biographies, lists of plays in order of production, names of theatres and companies, lists of university plays, and lists of translations.

FLEAY, FREDERICK GARD
A Chronicle History of the London Stage, 1559 – 1642
Burt Franklin, 1964. 424pp. $18.50. Originally published in 1890, this is a reprint of the author's history of the Shakespearean stage. It includes general introductions to the various periods, lists of Court performances, companies, theatres, and authors of the period. Indices.

FOAKES, R.A. and R.T. RICKERT – Editors
Henslowe's Diary
Cambridge, 1961. 368pp. $13.50. A new transcript of the whole relevant portion of the diary of the theatre owner and financier of companies of players. One of the primary sources of our knowledge of the stage from 1591 to 1604.

FORD, BORIS – Editor
The Age of Shakespeare
Penguin, 1960. 480pp. Paper $1.45. A survey of the poets, prose-writers, and dramatists of the English Renaissance. The social background is examined in detail. Five essays on Shakespeare are included.

GIBBONS, BRIAN
Jacobean City Comedy
Harvard, 1968. 223pp. $6.00. Beginning with a study of aspects of the social, economic, and political background in Jacobean England which are related to the plays of the time, the author then traces the chronological development of city comedy from Jonson's early satires through the work of Marston and Middleton to its climax in the masterpieces "Bartholomew Fair" and "The Devil is an Ass." Illustrated. Bibliography.

GILDERSLEEVE, VIRGINIA C.
Government Regulations of the Elizabethan Drama
Burt Franklin, 1962. 259pp. $11.50. A reprint of the edition first published in 1908, this is an account of the laws and regulations which affected the drama during the Elizabethan period. Chapters on national regulations, the Master of the Revels, local regulations in London from 1543 to 1642, and the Puritan attack on the theatre. Appendix on Royal Patents to Companies of Players.

GRAVES, THORNTON SHIRLEY
The Court and the London Theatres During the Reign of Elizabeth
Russell & Russell, 1967. 93pp. $7.00. This monograph was originally published in 1913 and is now reissued. The author discusses the structural elements of the Elizabethan theatre, the inn-yard and its relationship to the first London playhouses, and the indications of Court influence on general stage structure and the methods of presenting dramas during the reign of Elizabeth. Index of Authors and Titles.

GREEN, A. WIGFALL
The Inns of Court and Early English Drama
Blom, 1965. 198pp. $12.50. In this reprint of the 1931 study, the rise of the Inns, the English legal society's special groups, and their internal organizations are described, followed by a study of theatrical entertainments held in the Inns. The important "Revels" are described in detail and special attention is paid to the masques produced between 1526 and 1683.

GREG, WALTER W.
Dramatic Documents from the Elizabethan Playhouses
Oxford, 1969. Two volume set: 373pp. $40.00. First published in 1931 and long out of print, this is a new publication of documents used in the original productions of Elizabethan plays. The first volume of the two volume set is a commentary with illustrations and includes reference lists. The second volume includes reproductions and transcripts of eight plots, specimen pages from nine prompt books and facsimiles of the part of Orlando in Greene's play, "Orlando Furioso," which was apparently used by Edward Alleyn.

GREG, WALTER W.
Pastoral Poetry and Pastoral Drama: A Literary Inquiry, with Special Reference to the Pre-Restoration Stage in England
Russell & Russell, 1959. 464pp. $11.50. A reprint of the edition first published in 1905, this study considers the origin and nature of the pastoral in ancient Greek and Roman models and in the Medieval eclogues. Italian, Spanish, and French pastorals are examined. The dramatic origins of pastoral drama and the English masterpieces are given special attention and there is also a discussion of masques. Bibliography.

HARBAGE, ALFRED
Cavalier Drama: An Historical and Critical Supplement to the Study of the Elizabethan and Restoration Stage
Russell & Russell, 1964. 302pp. $12.50. A reprint of the edition first published in 1936, the purpose of this study is to discuss the trends in English drama during the Caroline and Commonwealth periods, with a view to illustrating the continuity of an English literary tradition. The author considers in detail the Cavalier usurpation of the stage which was a major factor in the theatre of the Restoration. Index.

HARBAGE, ALFRED
Shakespeare and The Rival Traditions
See Page 89

HARRISON, G. B.
Elizabethan Plays and Players
University of Michigan, 1956. 306pp. Paper $2.25. This survey of the Elizabethan era records the fortunes of the different companies and playhouses.

HARRISON, G. B.
A Second Jacobean Journal: Being a Record of Those Things Most Talked of During the Years 1607 – 1610
University of Michigan, 1958. 278pp. $5.50. The author has used authentic contemporary sources to recreate the day-to-day life of the Jacobean era.

HAZLITT, W. C. – Editor
The English Drama and Stage Under the Tudor and Stuart Princes: 1543 – 1664
Burt Franklin, 1964. 289pp. $35.00. A reprint of the 1869 publication of the documents and treatises which directly illustrate the early history of English dramatic poetry and the English stage. Included are documents and proclamations of Henry VIII, Edward VI, Queens Mary and Elizabeth, the Lord Mayor of London, and many others. Notes. Index.

HELTON, TINSLEY – Editor
The Renaissance: A Reconsideration of the Theories and Interpretations of the Age
University of Wisconsin, 1964. 160pp. Paper $1.65. A collection of six essays in which an eminent scholar summarizes and evaluates the scholarship in his respective discipline. Political history, intellectual history, the history of art, science, and literature are all studied. Bibliographies. Index.

HERNDL, GEORGE C.
The High Design: English Renaissance Tragedy and the Natural Law
University Press of Kentucky, 1970. 337pp. $10.50. Mr. Herndl analyzes the drama of Heywood, Webster, Tourneur, Beaumont and Fletcher, and Ford and examines the intellectual currents of the Jacobean era to show the difference between the spirit of the Jacobean plays and that of the older tradition. Notes. Index.

HILLEBRAND, HAROLD N.
The Child Actors: A Chapter in Elizabethan Stage History
Russell & Russell, 1964. 355pp. $9.00. This reprint of the 1926 study begins with a survey of children in plays between 1100 and 1570, then goes on to give a detailed portrait of the Chapel Royal before and during the reign of Elizabeth. In addition the author studies the children of St. Paul's from 1551 to 1590, the children at the Blackfriars from 1600 to 1609, and the Revels at Whitefriars. An Appendix lists names and plays. Bibliography. Index.

HOLMES, ELIZABETH
Aspects of Elizabethan Imagery
Russell & Russell, 1966. 134pp. $7.50. First published in 1929 and now reprinted, in this study the author contends that the beginning and some development of metaphysical poetry were to be found in the work of Elizabethan and Jacobean poets.

HOLMES, MARTIN
Elizabethan London
Praeger, 1969. 123pp. $5.95. A guidebook to and portrait of London during the reign of Elizabeth I. Twenty-nine illustrations are provided. Index.

JOHANSSON, BERTIL
Law and Lawyers in Elizabethan England
Almqvist & Wiksell, 1967. 65pp. Paper $4.50. This study concentrates on the numerous satirical allusions to law, lawyers and legal procedure in the works of the playwrights Ben Jonson and Thomas Middleton as well as in other contemporary sources. Bibliography.

JOHN, LISLE CECIL
The Elizabethan Sonnet Sequences: Studies in Conventional Conceits
Russell & Russell, 1964. 278pp. $13.50. A reprint of the 1938 edition, this book examines the relation of Elizabethan sonnet sequences to the convention of Petrarchan pattern. Appendix on the identity of "Stella," the date of Shakespeare's sonnets, and the English Petrarch. Bibliography. Index.

JOSEPH, SISTER MIRIAM
Rhetoric in Shakespeare's Time
Harcourt, Brace, 1962. 421pp. Paper $1.85. This handbook is designed to provide a general background to the methods of composition used by authors, without special reference to Shakespeare, in Renaissance Europe.

KAUFMANN, RALPH J. – Editor
Elizabethan Drama: Modern Essays in Criticism
Oxford, 1961. 372pp. Paper $2.50. A collection of essays that approach the poetic dramas of Shakespeare's contemporaries through a variety of critical methods. Language, imagery, staging, philosophical perspectives, and characterization are studied.

KERNAN, ALVIN
The Cankered Muse: Satire of the English Renaissance
Yale, 1959. 261pp. $8.75. The formal peculiarities of satire are defined on the basis of an examination of satiric works from Juvenal to Waugh. This definition is used to describe the mass of prose, poetry, and fiction that made up the satire of the English Renaissance. Index.

KERNODLE, GEORGE R.
From Art to Theatre: Form and Convention in the Renaissance
University of Chicago, 1964. 255pp. $12.50. In comparing the theatre with the other visual arts, the author shows that every Renaissance theatre derived its

form and many of its conventions from the traditions of art. The sixty-eight illustrations show the pattern of Renaissance theatres and the art backgrounds from which they developed. Bibliography. Index.

KLEIN, DAVID
The Elizabethan Dramatists as Critics
Philosophical Library, 1963. 420pp. $6.00. A systematic arrangement of the utterances of Elizabethan dramatists on the various aspects of dramatic writing. The author supports his contention that the playwrights were conscious artists, aware that they were creating a kind of romantic drama alien to the dictates of the Aristotelian code.

KNIGHTS, L.C.
Drama and Society in the Age of Jonson
Barnes & Noble, 1957. 347pp. $6.50. Paper—Norton, 1968. 347pp. $2.25. This is a study of the economic and social background of the early seventeenth century and of the Elizabethan-Jacobean culture. The author analyzes the work of Jonson, Dekker, Heywood, Middleton, and Massinger. Bibliography. Index.

KNIGHTS, L.C.
Explorations: Essays in Criticism, Mainly on the Literature of the Seventeenth Century
New York University, 1964. 219pp. Paper $1.95. A collection of essays on Shakespeare, Bacon, George Herbert, Congreve, Dryden, Henry James, and W. B. Yeats. Included are an analysis of the language and structure of "Macbeth" and a study of the frivolity of Restoration comedy.

LAWRENCE, W.J.
The Elizabethan Playhouse and Other Studies
Russell & Russell, 1963. Volume One: 263pp. Volume Two: 251pp. Two volume set: $18.00. The first volume of essays was first published in 1913 and considers the evolution and influence of the playhouse, music and song in the plays, the mounting of Carolan masques, curtains, early French players in England, and the Blackfriars. Volume Two, first published in 1912, deals with light and darkness in the theatre, windows, the system of admission, origins of the picture stage, and Louis XIV's scene painters.

LAWRENCE, W.J.
Pre-Restoration Stage Studies
Blom, 1967. 435pp. $12.50. A reissue of the 1927 publication, this collection of essays includes studies on the physical characteristics of the theatres, the practice of doubling, "Hamlet" as Shakespeare staged it, stage properties, the masque, and early prompt books. Index.

LAWRENCE, W.J.
Speeding Up Shakespeare: Studies of the Bygone Theatre and Drama
Blom, 1968. 220pp. $12.50. First published in 1937 and now reissued, this volume includes essays on such topics as Shakespearean dramaturgy, the "to be or not to be" soliloquy, the clown Dick Tarleton, and topical allusions to famous or notorious actors. Illustrated. Index.

LEA, K.M.
Italian Popular Comedy
See Page 213

LEECH, CLIFFORD
Shakespeare's Tragedies and Other Studies in Seventeenth Century Drama
Oxford, 1950. 232pp. $4.75. Essays on the nature of dramatic tension in tragedy, the Caroline audience, love as a dramatic theme in seventeenth century drama, the links between English and Spanish playwrights of the era, and Shakespeare's "The Tempest" and "Timon of Athens."

LIEVSAY, JOHN L.
The Sixteenth Century: Skelton Through Hooker
See Page 513

LONG, JOHN H.—Editor
Music in English Renaissance Drama
University of Kentucky, 1968. 184pp. $7.50. This volume contains seven essays in which distinguished scholars explore the use of music in dramatic works of the English Renaissance. The essays range in subject from the mystery cycles of the late sixteenth century to the Cavalier drama of the early seventeenth century. A Bibliography of the primary sources for the music of the early seventeenth century drama concludes the volume. Illustrated with musical examples. Index.

McDONALD, CHARLES OSBORNE
The Rhetoric of Tragedy: Form in Stuart Drama
University of Massachusetts, 1966. 360pp. $7.50. This study of the evolution of Renaissance English drama is concerned with the shaping influence of the tradition of classical sophistic rhetoric and the dialectical structure of thought which was the legacy of this rhetoric. The author considers in detailed formal analyses several major dramatic works by Shakespeare and his contemporaries and sucessors. Index.

McNEIR, WALDO F.
Studies in Comparative Literature
Louisiana State University, 1962. 311pp. $3.00. Essays on a variety of subjects concerned with the relationship between the cultures of various countries. Included are studies of English and Spanish tragedy of the Renaissance, an investigation of the Spanish source for Fletcher's "Love Cure," and a comparison of Marc Connelly's "The Green Pastures" and Goethe's "Faust."

MARGESON, J.M.R.
The Origins of English Tragedy
Oxford, 1967. 195pp. $8.50. The author makes an

assessment of the background of Elizabethan tragedy in order to show the importance of embryonic tragic situations, characters, and patterns of emotion in Medieval and Tudor Drama. He considers how these basic elements were later combined and shaped into effective dramatic forms by current ideas about the nature of tragic action. Bibliography. Index.

MASON, DOROTHY E.
Music in Elizabethan England
University Press of Virginia, 1958. 38pp. Paper $1.50. This brief pamphlet analyzes music as one of the influences on Elizabethan life. Illustrated with twenty pages of reproductions of period art and music.

MEHL, DIETER
The Elizabethan Dumb Show: The History of a Dramatic Convention
Harvard, 1966. 207pp. $8.75. This study traces the roots of the dumb show back to civic shows and pageants and shows its development up to the time of Beaumont and Fletcher. The author provides a list of plays containing dumb shows. Bibliography. Index.

MEYER, EDWARD
Machiavelli and the Elizabethan Drama
Burt Franklin, 180pp. 1967. $11.50. First published in 1897 and now reissued, this is an examination of the references to Machiavelli in the drama of the Elizabethan period. The author shows that the works of the Italian were almost never quoted directly or with any accuracy and that most references were drawn from the "Contre-Michiavel" of Gentillet.

MITCHELL, W. FRASER
English Pulpit Oratory from Andrewes to Tillotson: A Study of Its Literary Aspects
Russell & Russell, 1962. 516pp. $12.00. First published in 1931 and now reissued, this book examines the rhetorical and homiletical theory of the seventeenth century, then gives a detailed reading of the Anglo-Catholic preachers including Donne, other Anglicans in the period to 1660, the Cambridge Platonists, and the preachers of the Restoration.

MURRAY, JOHN TUCKER
English Dramatic Companies: 1558 – 1642
Russell & Russell, 1963. Volume One: 370pp. Volume Two: 434pp. Two volume set: $20.00. This is a reprint of the 1910 edition. Volume One covers the London dramatic companies of the period. It describes the makeup and activities of the important men's companies, and the children's companies. Volume Two describes the provincial companies, those under Royal patronage, and the lesser independent companies. Index.

NICOLL, ALLARDYCE
A History of English Drama. Volume One: Restoration Drama, 1660 – 1700
See Page 147

NICOLL, ALLARDYCE
Stuart Masques and the Renaissance Stage
Blom, 1963. 224pp. $17.50. A reprint of the 1938 edition, this is a study of the staging of the Stuart masques produced at Whitehall under the supervision of the Lords Chamberlain to James I and Charles I. Special attention is given to the work of Inigo Jones and his fellow "architects" and this work is examined in the light of contemporary Italian stage practice. Among items discussed are the theatres, the machines, and the scenery. Illustrated with contemporary prints and engravings.

ORAS, ANTS
Pause Patterns in Elizabethan and Jacobean Drama: An Experiment in Prosody
University of Florida, 1960. 90pp. $3.00. An examination of the incidents of internal pause in the verse line in virtually the entire field of Renaissance drama. Illustrated with graphs and statistical tables.

ORNSTEIN, ROBERT
The Moral Vision of Jacobean Tragedy
University of Wisconsin, 1965. 310pp. Paper $2.25. This reprint of the 1960 study examines the ethical viewpoints and artistic achievements of all the major dramatists of the period. The author examines the different meanings of the Machiavellian figures and the Italianate settings of Jacobean tragedy in an attempt to discover the reality behind the portraits of vice and depravity. Index.

ORR, DAVID
Italian Renaissance Drama in England Before 1625
University of North Carolina, 1970. 141pp. $9.00. This is an attempt to examine some of the significant primary and secondary material relating to the influence exercised by the formal drama of Italy on that of Elizabethan and Jacobean drama in England. Appendices include summaries of plots of Italian plays and brief discussions of scholarly arguments. Bibliography. Index.

PAINTER, WILLIAM
The Palace of Pleasure
Dover, 1966. Three volumes: 1,224pp. Paper $6.75 per set. An unaltered, unabridged republication of the 1890 edition, this three volume set includes the stories, biographical and bibliographical material, an annotated table of contents which includes the source, the origin, and parallel and derivative works, and an Index. Painter introduced into England the first translation of some of the best tales from the "Decameron," the "Heptameron," and other classical sources that influenced Elizabethan drama and provided the main source for many of the Elizabethan playwrights' dramas.

PARR, JOHNSTONE
Tamburlaine's Malady: Studies in Astrology in Elizabethan Drama

University of Alabama, 1953. 158pp. $3.50. Detailed explanations of the references to astrology in many obscure passages in the plays of Elizabethan and Jacobean playwrights including: Shakespeare, Marlowe, Lyly, Greene, Chapman, Webster, and Jonson. Bibliography of the astrological works know in England at the time. Index.

PARROTT, THOMAS MARC and ROBERT HAMILTON BALL
A Short View of Elizabethan Drama: Together with Some Account of Its Principal Playwrights and the Conditions Under Which It Was Produced
Scribner, 1958. 311pp. Paper $1.45. A revised edition of the book published in 1943, this is a study of the rise, development, and decline of drama from its origins in the liturgy of the Church to the closing of the theatres in 1642. Emphasis is on the major playwrights.

PEARSON, LU EMILY
Elizabethans at Home
Stanford, 1967. 630pp. Paper $3.75. The author attempts to make a synthesis for the student of the material which is available about Elizabethan domestic life. Illustrated. Bibliography. Index.

PROUTY, C. T.
George Gascoigne, Elizabethan Courtier, Soldier and Poet
See Page 120

RABKIN, NORMAN – Editor
Reinterpretations of Elizabethan Drama
See Page 102

REYHER, PAUL
Les Masques Anglais: Etude sur les Ballets et la Vie de Cour en Angle–Terre 1512 – 1640
Blom, 1964. 563pp. $27.50. A study of the evolution and major characteristics of the various kinds of masques that were popular in aristocratic theatrical circles, with a consideration of music, dance, scenery, and acting in the genre. First published in Paris in 1909, reprinted here with the text in French.

RIBNER, IRVING
The English History Play in the Age of Shakespeare
Methuen, 1965. 365pp. $8.50. A revised version of the 1957 publication, this is a comprehensive account of the English historical drama from its beginning to the closing of the theatres in 1642. The author relates this development to Renaissance historiography and Elizabethan political theory.

RIBNER, IRVING
Jacobean Tragedy: The Quest for Moral Order
Barnes & Noble, 1962. 179pp. $5.00. A companion volume to the author's "Patterns in Shakespearian Tragedy," this study deals with Chapman, Heywood, Tourneur, Webster, Middleton, and Ford. The plays of these men are seen as attempts to find some sort of moral order in the universe to replace the weakened religious sanctions.

RIBNER, IRVING
Tudor and Stuart Drama
Appleton, 1966. 72pp. Paper $1.50. A selected bibliography of books in the field of Tudor and Stuart drama. Basic works of reference, bibliographic guides, anthologies and reprints, critical and historical studies, and works of the major dramatists are included. Index of Subjects. Index of Authors.

ROBINSON, J. W. – Editor
British Writers and Their Work
University of Nebraska, 1966. 182pp. Paper $1.60. Essays on Christopher Marlowe, Ben Jonson, John Webster, and John Ford. Select Bibliographies on the authors and on English Renaissance drama are included.

RYE, WILLIAM BRENCHLEY
England as Seen by Foreigners in the Days of Elizabeth and James the First
Blom, 1967. 300pp. $12.50. Originally printed in 1865, this is a series of articles written by foreign travelers in England, reflecting the attitudes and life of the Elizabethan era. Illustrated. Index.

SCHELLING, FELIX E.
Elizabethan Drama: 1558 – 1642
Russell & Russell, 1959. Volume I: 606pp. Volume II: 685pp. Two volume set: $30.00. Originally published in 1908 and now reprinted, this is a history of the drama in England from the accession of Queen Elizabeth to the closing of the theatres. A resume of the early drama from its beginnings in England is included.

SCHELLING, FELIX E.
Elizabethan Playwrights
Blom, 1965. 349pp. $12.50. First published in 1925 and now reissued, this study traces the line of dramatic development and describes each playwright's contribution.

SCHOENBAUM, S.
Internal Evidence and Elizabethan Dramatic Authorship
Northwestern University, 1966. 281pp. $7.50. Professor Schoenbaum deals with the origins and history of inquiries into Elizabethan dramatic authorship. He surveys the hundreds of articles, monographs, and commentaries that have appeared on individual plays and playwrights, and comments on many disputed plays. Index.

SCHOENBAUM, S. – Editor
Renaissance Drama VII
Northwestern University, 1964. Volume One: 157pp. Volume Two: 49pp. Paper. Two volume set: $4.25.

With these volumes the annual report of the Modern Language Conference on Research Opportunities in Renaissance Drama becomes an independent annual. The journal has essays by T. W. Craik, David Bevington, Norman Rabkin, and others. The second volume is a checklist of works in progress and a record of the 1963 meeting.

SCHOENBAUM, S.—Editor
Renaissance Drama IX
Northwestern University, 1967. 317pp. $9.50. The ninth volume in the yearly series on Renaissance drama. Among the contributors to this volume of essays are: M. C. Bradbrook, R. W. Dent, Cyrus Hoy, and Alvin B. Kerman.

SCHUSTER, LOUIS A.
Henry VIII: A Neo-Latin Drama by Nicolaus Vernulaeus, Translated and Edited, with a History of the Louvain Academic Theatre
University of Texas, 1964. 331pp. $8.50. This study examines the life and work of the priest–playwright who died in 1649, studies his dramatic art and the purposes that motivated his theatre, presents a full historical and literary background for the play "Henry VIII," evaluates it as a literary achievement, and considers it as a document in the great political and religious struggle of the time. Bibliography. Index.

SELLERY, GEORGE CLARKE
The Renaissance: Its Nature and Origins
University of Wisconsin, 1964. 296pp. Paper $1.50. A reprint of the book first published in 1950, this study of the Renaissance considers its politics, economics, literature, fine arts, inventions, philosophy, criticism, and history. Index.

SISSON, C. J.
Lost Plays of Shakespeare's Age
Cass, 1970. 221pp. $10.00. Originally published in 1936 and now reissued. The author's aim was to add to the existing knowledge of the Elizabethan stage and to reveal something of the scores of plays of which nothing but the bare titles remain. Through his examination of contemporary records he is also able to throw new light on the various forms of popular drama such as the Jig, the May Game, and the Libel Proper. Illustrated. Appendix. Index.

STEVENS, JOHN
Music and Poetry in the Early Tudor Court
University of Nebraska, 1961. 483pp. $5.00. A study of the neglected field of early Tudor music, with the first full description of the three songbooks that contain virtually all the remains of English secular music between 1480 and 1530. The relation between poetry and music in the Reformation is considered. The literal texts of the songs are given, with commentaries.

STOUP, THOMAS B.
Microcosmos: The Shape of the Elizabethan Play
University of Kentucky, 1965. 235pp. $6.00. The author examines the relevance to Elizabethan drama of the widespread metaphor of the world as stage and of the view expressed in that metaphor that man and his world is a microcosm of a larger world. Index.

SYKES, H. DUGDALE
Sidelights on Elizabethan Drama
Cass, 1966. 231pp. $9.00. Originally published in 1924 and now reissued, this study deals with the authorship of sixteenth and seventeenth century plays. Mr. Sykes studies "Timon of Athens," "The Taming of the Shrew," "The Spanish Moor's Tragedy," "The Queen," "The Spanish Gypsy" and five others. There is an Appendix of notes on the authorship of various other Elizabethan and Jacobean plays. Index.

THOMPSON, ELBERT N. S.
The Controversy Between the Puritans and the Stage
Russell & Russell, 1966. 275pp. $9.50. First published in 1903, this reprinted edition is a study of morality and the Elizabethan stage. The major portion of the book is a history of English sentiment against the stage. The second portion is concerned with the reply of the actors and the dramatists to the Puritans. Index.

TILLYARD, E. M. W.
The Elizabethan World Picture
Random House, 1961. 116pp. Paper $1.45. A study of the basic Medieval idea of an ordered chain of being as it was transformed by the age of Shakespeare, Donne, and Milton.

TOMLINSON, T. B.
A Study of Elizabethan and Jacobean Tragedy
Cambridge, 1964. 232pp. $6.00. The author analyzes some of the main tragedies and shows that English tragedy in this period was able to treat evil, coarseness, and violence without the restrictions later, more polite periods would place on the theatre. Index.

WAITH, EUGENE M.
The Herculean Hero in Marlowe, Chapman, Shakespeare and Dryden
Columbia, 1962. 224pp. $6.00. A study of the anti-social behavior of the hero in classical and Renaissance drama. Among the plays studied are: Marlowe's "Tamburlaine," Chapman's "Bussy d'Ambois," Shakespeare's "Antony and Cleopatra" and "Coriolanus," Dryden's "The Conquest of Granada," "Aureng-Zebe," and "All for Love." Notes. Appendix. Index.

WALLACE, CHARLES WILLIAM
The First London Theatre
Blom, 1969. 296pp. $12.50. Originally published in 1913, this pioneer work helped to lay down the essential structure of the Elizabethan theatre and its production techniques. Wallace recorded all the pertinent historical documents and ranged them in chronological order for reference. Included is an introduction

on the history of the theatre from James Burbage in 1567 to the achievements of Shakespeare in 1599.

WATT, LAUCHLAN MACLEAN
Attic and Elizabethan Tragedy
See Page 37

WELLS, HENRY W.
Elizabethan and Jacobean Playwrights
Kennikat, 1964. 349pp. $11.00. This study, originally published in 1939, is concerned with the English drama from about 1576 to 1642. This edition includes a chronological list of extant plays produced in or about London 1581–1642. List of Biographies and Bibliographies. Index.

WELSFORD, ENID
The Court Masque: A Study of the Relationship Between Poetry and the Revels
Russell & Russell, 1962. 434pp. $12.00. A reprint of the first edition of 1927, this is a study of the English Court masque of the seventeenth century. The author considers the origin and history of the genre, the influence on pictorial art and poetry, and certain aspects that throw light on the nature of art and its social value.

WHANSLAW, H.W.
The Bankside Stage Book
Wells, Gardner, Darton, 256pp. $3.00. Full directions for making a model Elizabethan stage, enabling producers and directors to study, with figures, the most suitable groupings of the characters of a play. Details of Tudor costumes, furniture, music, and background are included with a short history of the stage. Illustrated.

WHITE, BEATRICE—Editor
An Index to "The Elizabethan Stage" and "William Shakespeare" by Sir Edmund Chambers
Blom, 1964. 161pp. $7.50. A reprint of the original 1934 edition, this index is based on the works themselves, although it makes use of the existing indices which it attempts to enlarge upon uniform lines. Players' names are included.

WICKHAM, GLYNNE
Early English Stages—1300 to 1660. Part II: 1576 to 1660
Columbia, 1963. 408pp. $15.00. The second volume in this history is divided into two main sections. The first half is an account of the imposition of state censorship during the Elizabethan era, shows its effects on the drama, and discusses the collapse of the theatres in the provinces. The second half examines the aesthetic principles which determined the structure of the playhouses and considers the stage conventions. Illustrated.

WILLIAMS, JOHN—Editor
English Renaissance Poetry: A Collection of Shorter Poems from Skelton to Jonson
Doubleday, 1963. 358pp. Paper $1.45. Included in this volume are poems by Skelton, More, Gascoigne, Ralegh, Spenser, Peele, Greene, Drayton, Shakespeare, Nashe, Donne, and Jonson, among others.

WILSON, F.P. and G.K. HUNTER
The English Drama: 1485—1585
Oxford, 1968. 244pp. $5.95. This is Volume IV—Part One of "The Oxford History of English Literature." It begins at the accession of Henry VII and discusses the new dramatic impulses produced by the combined pressures of Reformation and Renaissance. It ends in 1584 at the point where the drama of Lyly and Peele was about to begin its achievement. Chronological Table. Bibliography. Index.

WILSON, F.P.
The Plague in Shakespeare's London
Oxford, 1963. 228pp. Paper $1.50. A study of the plague in London and in the countryside with attention given to the rise of the Plague-Orders from the inception in 1518. Emphasis is placed on the great plague of 1603 and that of 1625 with their disrupting influence on social, commercial, and theatrical life. Index.

WITHERSPOON, ALEXANDER MACLAREN
The Influence of Robert Garnier on Elizabethan Drama
Archon, 1968. 192pp. $6.75. This work investigates the influences of the most eminent of French tragedians of the sixteenth century on Elizabethan drama. The basis of Garnier's appeal to English writers who accepted him as mentor and guide and the reasons for choosing him as a model are discussed in detail. Bibliography.

WRIGHT, LOUIS B.—Editor
The Elizabethan's America: A Collection of Early Reports by Englishmen on the New World
Edward Arnold, 1965. 295pp. $7.50. A collection of forty-two items, in modernized spelling, in which the Elizabethans put down their impressions of America. Mr. Wright's introduction deals with the economic, social, and diplomatic background of colonization.

WRIGHT, LOUIS B. and VIRGINIA A. LAMAR—Editors
Life and Letters in Tudor and Stuart England
Cornell University, 1962. 528pp. $7.50. A collection of essays on aspects of Elizabethan life. Several of the essays are concerned with the life, authorship, and theatre of Shakespeare.

WRIGHT, LOUIS B.
Middle-Class Culture in Elizabethan England
Cornell University, 1958. 733pp. $10.00. First published in 1935, this is a description of the intellectual background and interests of the literate common people who composed the rising middle class of

Elizabethan society. The literature that shaped their habits and tastes is discussed in detail. Index.

YATES, FRANCES A.
Theatre of the World
University of Chicago, 1969. 218pp. $10.00. The English public theatre is studied as an adaptation of the Vitruvian ancient theatre. Dr. Yates shows that it is from within a Renaissance world of thought that the English public theatres made their appearance. She suggests new approaches to the problem of the ground plan of the Globe Theatre and outlines its stage. Illustrated. Index.

STUDIES OF PLAYWRIGHTS

Beaumont and Fletcher

FLETCHER, IAN
Beaumont and Fletcher
Longman, 1967. 60pp. Paper $ .95. This short essay deals with the work of the seventeenth century English playwrights. It includes a Selected Bibliography of the joint and separate works and criticism.

GAYLEY, CHARLES MILLS
Beaumont the Dramatist
Russell & Russell, 1969. 442pp. $14.50. Originally published in 1914 and now reissued, this is an attempt to present the personality of playwright Francis Beaumont as conjoined with and distinguished from the personality of his co-author John Fletcher as seen from the background of the contemporary social, literary, and theatrical environment. Illustrated. Index.

LEECH, CLIFFORD
The John Fletcher Plays
Harvard, 1962. 108pp. $3.50. A general discussion of the trends taken by the late Elizabethan theatre with a close examination of Fletcher's plays and the reciprocal influences between him and Shakespeare.

McKEITHAN, DANIEL MORLEY
The Debt to Shakespeare in the Beaumont and Fletcher Plays
Gordian Press, 1970. 233pp. $10.00. The author's thesis is that Shakespeare's romantic dramas influenced Beaumont and Fletcher rather than that theirs influenced his. In this study, originally published in 1938 and now reprinted, the author discusses forty-five plays of joint or single authorship or authorship in association with other persons. Bibliography.

SPRAGUE, ARTHUR COLBY
Beaumont and Fletcher on the Restoration Stage
Blom, 1965. 335pp. $12.50. First published in 1926, this study of the theatrical history of the Beaumont and Fletcher plays from 1660 to 1710 details the productions of twenty adaptations of these plays in the period. The constrasting dramatic ideals of the Jacobean and the Restoration eras are described.

THORNDIKE, ASHLEY H.
The Influence of Beaumont and Fletcher on Shakespeare
See Page 84

WILSON, JOHN HAROLD
The Influence of Beaumont and Fletcher on Restoration Drama
See Page 175

Chapman, George

MacLURE, MILLAR
George Chapman: A Critical Study
University of Toronto, 1966. 241pp. $8.00. A critical study of the English Renaissance poet and playwright. All the works are considered in detail in relation to their genres and in terms of Chapman's intellectual and aesthetic development. Index.

REES, ENNIS
The Tragedies of George Chapman: Renaissance Ethics in Action
Harvard, 1954. 223pp. $5.50. Mr. Rees demonstrates, in this study of the Elizabethan dramatist's tragedies, that Chapman expounded the Christian—humanistic creed. Beginning with an analysis of Chapman's philosophy, then proceeding to a reinterpretation of the tragedies, Mr. Rees shows in detail how Chapman gave expression to his religious and ethical creed. Bibliography. Index.

Dekker, Thomas

CONOVER, JAMES H.
Thomas Dekker: An Analysis of Dramatic Structure
Mouton, 1969. 250pp. $12.50. A study of six plays by the English playwright which have been generally accepted as written by Dekker alone. Each of the plays is allotted an individual chapter and the author provides an analytical concluding chapter. Introduction. Appendix: Summaries of the Six Plays. List of Works Cited.

DEKKER, THOMAS
Thomas Dekker: Selected Prose Writings
Harvard, 1968. 374pp. $10.00. Edited by E. D. Pendry, this volume contains the texts of the major part of Dekker's prose writing. There is an introduction on the life and work of the seventeenth century author. Illustrated with facsimiles of the contemporary title pages, plates, and line drawings. Notes on Sources and Texts. Glossary.

HUNT, MARY LELAND
Thomas Dekker: A Study
Russell & Russell, 1964. 212pp. $8.50. Originally published in 1911 and now reprinted. The author has collected and arranged in chronological order the scattered material on the playwright's life and career. Among the items discussed are the early plays, the quarrel with Jonson, the influence of Middleton, the prose works, and Dekker's imprisonment. Bibliography. Index.

PRICE, GEORGE R.
Thomas Dekker
Twayne, 1969. 189pp. $4.50. A study of the seventeenth century playwright in which the author reappraises Dekker's accomplishment in the light of recent scholarship. The book includes an exhaustive list of all Dekker's writings. Chronology. Selected Bibliography. Index.

Fletcher, John

See: Beaumont and Fletcher

Ford, John

LEECH, CLIFFORD
John Ford and the Drama of His Time
Hillary House, 1957. 144pp. $3.75. A study of Ford's plays, poems, and collaborations, with special emphasis on the theme of "suffering, not action." List of Ford's writings and appearances of his plays on stages to 1955.

OLIVER, H.J.
The Problem of John Ford
Cambridge, 1955. 146pp. $5.50. A critical assessment of Ford's work, considering his relation to his age, his non-dramatic works, and with detailed expositions of eight of his plays. Appendix.

SENSABAUGH, G.F.
The Tragic Muse of John Ford
Blom, 1964. 196pp. $10.00. A reprint of the book first published in 1944, this study attempts to discover, through an examination of Ford's immediate milieu, what Ford attempted to say in his serious plays and why what he says sounds familiar to modern man. Index.

STAVIG, MARK
John Ford and the Traditional Moral Order
University of Wisconsin, 1968. 225pp. $6.95. A study of the seventeenth century playwright in which the author discusses the techniques, tone, and form of the plays as they might have been perceived by Ford's original audiences. Chapters deal individually with the works upon which Ford's reputation is based. Notes. Selected Bibliography. Index.

Greene, Robert

JORDAN, JOHN CLARK
Robert Greene
Octagon, 1965. 231pp. $9.00. Originally published in 1915 and now reissued, this biography of the sixteenth century playwright focuses on "the personality of Greene, and ... the nature of his activity." The author contends that Greene's place is secure to him for the historical reason that he was one of the Elizabethans and through the charm of his poems and romances. Bibliography. Index.

Heywood, John

JOHNSON, ROBERT CARL
John Heywood
Twayne, 1970. 159pp. $4.95. Professor Johnson evaluates the unique position of Heywood in the development of the English drama. He provides critical examinations of the "Epigrams," "The Dialogue of Proverbs," and the other poems. All six plays are also studied. Chronology. Selected Bibliography. Index.

MAXWELL, IAN
French Farce and John Heywood
Cambridge, 1946. 175pp. $3.75. A study of the influence of the French comic drama on the plays of Heywood.

Heywood, Thomas

CROMWELL, OTELIA
Thomas Heywood: A Study in the Elizabethan Drama of Everyday Life
Archon, 1969. 227pp. $8.25. Originally published in 1928 and now reissued, this is an effort to estimate Heywood's contribution to that phase of Elizabethan drama representing Elizabethan England in plot, character, or general atmosphere. Index.

HEYWOOD, THOMAS
A Woman Killed with Kindness
Barnes & Noble, 1961. 122pp. $6.50. Paper—Methuen, 1970. 122pp. $2.65. Edited by R.W. Van Fossen for the Revels Plays series, this is a critical edition of the play. The editor has provided an Introduction surveying previous scholarship on the sources, themes, and structure of the play. Appendix. Glossarial Index.

Jonson, Ben

BARISH, JONAS A. – Editor
Ben Jonson: A Collection of Critical Essays
Prentice–Hall, 1963. 180pp. $4.95. Paper $1.95. This volume views such masterpieces as "Volpone," "The Alchemist," and "Every Man in His Humour" through modern eyes. Among the contributors are: T.S. Eliot, Edmund Wilson, L.C. Knights, and Harry Levin. Chronology. Selected Bibliography.

BARISH, JONAS A.
Ben Jonson and the Language of Prose Comedy
Harvard, 1960. 335pp. $9.00. Paper – Norton, 1970. 335pp. $2.45. An analysis of Jonson's recurrent prose patterns. Their stylistic, theatrical, and philosophical import are investigated. Notes. Index.

BASKERVILL, CHARLES READ
English Elements in Jonson's Early Comedy
Gordian Press, 1967. 328pp. $11.50. This study, originally published in 1911 and now reissued, attempts to prove the author's theory that Jonson was indebted to certain specific trends in English literature rather than to specific works used as sources. Jonson's relation to the movements of English literature at the end of the sixteenth century is the primary problem of the study. Index.

BENTLEY, GERALD EADES
Shakespeare and Jonson
See Page 95

CHAMPION, LARRY S.
Ben Jonson's "Dotages": A Reconsideration of the Late Plays
University of Kentucky, 1967. 156pp. $6.50. Mr. Champion maintains that Ben Jonson's later plays were an attempt to create new dramatic modes that would broaden the appeal of realistic comedy for audiences captivated by the prevailing romantic dramas. Index.

CHUTE, MARCHETTE
Ben Jonson of Westminster
Dutton, 1953. 380pp. $6.50. Paper – 1960. $1.75. A biography of the playwright and a picture of his time based on contemporary documentary sources. Maps of London included.

DELUNA, B.N.
Jonson's Romish Plot
Oxford, 1967. 415pp. $12.50. A study of Jonson's classical drama, "Catiline," and the circumstances (personal, artistic, and political) surrounding the writing of it. Bibliography. Index.

DUNN, ESTHER CLOUDMAN
Ben Jonson's Art: Elizabethan Life and Literature as Reflected Therein
Russell & Russell, 1963. 159pp. $8.00. A reprint of the 1925 edition, the intention of this study is twofold: to determine Jonson's view of his time and to show how that view is reflected in his works.

ENCK, JOHN J.
Jonson and the Comic Truth
University of Wisconsin, 1966. 281pp. Paper $1.95. A reprint of the 1957 edition, this is a study of the plays, with special attention given to the language that Jonson contrived to fit each dramatic situation. Jonson's theory of the comic is analyzed in terms of stage diction.

EVANS, WILLA MCCLUNG
Ben Jonson and Elizabethan Music
Da Capo Press, 1965. 131pp. $5.95. A second edition with a new preface of the standard work in the field, first published in 1929. The new preface outlines the development of investigatory activity in the field. Jonson's rise and decline as a lyricist and playwright is shown to be allied with his degree of collaboration with musicians. Bibliography.

FISKIN, A.M.I.
The Alchemist: Notes
Cliff's Notes, 1967. 79pp. Paper $1.00. This is an introduction to Ben Jonson's life and work. Scene-by-scene analyses and summaries of "The Alchemist" are provided with critical comments and review questions. Selected Bibliography.

GILBERT, ALLAN H.
The Symbolic Persons in the Masques of Ben Jonson
AMS Press, 1969. 297pp. & plates. $13.75. Reprinted from the edition first published in 1948, the purpose of this volume is to show what the allegorical and mythological characters in Jonson's masques and entertainments looked like. Included are a Bibliography of works accessible to Jonson and works published after 1637. Illustrated. Appendix. Index.

GREG, W.W.
Jonson's Masque of Gipsies in the Burley, Belvoir, and Windsor Versions: An Attempt at Reconstruction
Oxford, 1952. 235pp. $6.95. Jonson's longest masque, which was performed in three different versions and preserved in five independent texts, is subjected to a detailed textual investigation in an effort to establish a definitive text.

HERFORD, C.H. and PERCY SIMPSON, EVELYN SIMPSON – Editors
The Oxford Jonson: Volumes One and Two – Ben Jonson: The Man and His Work
Oxford, 1965. 441pp. $10.75. The first two volumes in "The Oxford Jonson" are combined in this edition. Included are a life of Jonson, introductions to the plays, masques, poems, and prose works, and a series of Appendices in which the extant documents bearing upon Jonson are reproduced. Illustrated.

HERFORD, C.H. and PERCY SIMPSON, EVELYN SIMPSON – Editors
The Oxford Jonson: Volume Nine
Oxford, 1960. 732pp. $10.75. This volume of "The Oxford Jonson" contains a historical survey of the texts and the stage history of the plays, and a commentary on the plays. Illustrated.

HERFORD, C.H. and PERCY SIMPSON, EVELYN SIMPSON – Editors
The Oxford Jonson: Volume Ten
Oxford, 1961. 710pp. $11.50. This volume contains a continuation of the commentary on the plays and commentary on the early entertainments, masques, and the later entertainments.

HERFORD, C.H. and PERCY SIMPSON, EVELYN SIMPSON – Editors
The Oxford Jonson: Volume Eleven
Oxford, 1963. 668pp. $10.75. The final volume in the series. Included is a commentary on various works, Jonson's literary record, supplementary notes on the life of Jonson and on the masques, and a list of musical settings of Jonson's songs. Index.

JACKSON, GABRIELE BERNHARD
Vision and Judgment in Ben Jonson's Drama
Yale, 1968. 178pp. $8.00. Mrs. Jackson examines the meanings that "poet" and "poetry" had for Ben Jonson and analyzes his characteristic dramatic practices as logical corollaries of his beliefs. She investigates the principles upon which his plays are constructed in order to reveal his vision of the principles upon which the universe is constructed. Selected Bibliography. Index.

JONSON, BEN
Ben Jonson: The Complete Masques
Yale, 1969. 557pp. $16.00. A volume in the Yale edition of the plays of Ben Jonson. Edited by Stephen Orgel, these modernized versions of the masques are annotated and Jonson's own glosses and notes are included as well as explanatory notes which offer the most detailed critical commentary ever undertaken. Mr. Orgel's Introduction is in itself an essay on the Renaissance stage. Selected Bibliography.

JONSON, BEN
Ben Jonson: Selected Masques
Yale, 1970. 377pp. $13.50. Paper $3.45. Originally published in 1969 as "The Complete Masques" and now issued in an abridged edition, this collection includes the fifteen most important of the twenty-eight works and the Introduction by the editor, Stephen Orgel, which discusses Jonson's development of the masque in relation to Inigo Jones' development of the illusionistic stage. Notes. Appendix. Select Bibliography.

KERNAN, ALVIN B. – Editor
Ben Jonson's Volpone or The Fox
Yale, 1962. 231pp. $3.75. Paper – 1963. $1.45. A new critical edition of the play, the first in "The Yale Ben Jonson" series. A scholarly text, in modernized spelling, interpretative and critical essays are included. Notes. Glosses. Appendices.

KNOLL, ROBERT E.
Ben Jonson's Plays: An Introduction
University of Nebraska, 1964. 205pp. $5.50. In this chronological survey of the plays the overall theme is an attempt to define Jonson's dramatic ideas by an examination of the structure of the plays. Some of the major critical controversies concerning them are examined.

MEAGHER, JOHN C.
Methods and Meaning in Jonson's Masques
University of Notre Dame, 1966. 214pp. $6.50. Ben Jonson's masques are examined by Professor Meagher for both form and content. The study analyzes the actual methods employed to make the masques poetically sound as well as ethically effective. Costume sketches by Inigo Jones are included. Index.

ORGEL, STEPHEN
The Jonsonian Masque
Harvard, 1965. 216pp. $5.95. This study treats the masques as dramatic and poetic wholes, taking into account both the text and the methods of production. The development of the masque convention through mummings, Tudor disguisings, and Elizabethan entertainments is traced. Close readings of six masques are given.

PARTRIDGE, A.C.
Studies in the Syntax of Ben Jonson's Plays
Hillary House, 1953. 104pp. $3.75. A study of the grammatical function of the periphrastic auxiliary verb "do," of the nouns, pronouns (excluding "thou" and "you"), and the definite article in the plays.

PARTRIDGE, EDWARD B.
The Broken Compass: A Study of the Major Comedies of Ben Jonson
Columbia, 1958. 245pp. $6.25. The author approaches the plays through their imagery and metaphor, showing how Jonson's theories of metaphorical language reveal his sensitivity to decorum and how the satirical inversion of Christian values provides some of his most telling dramatic effects. Bibliography. Index.

REDWINE, JAMES D. – Editor
Ben Jonson's Literary Criticism
University of Nebraska, 1970. 203pp. $5.95. Paper $2.25. This volume collects the criticism of Ben Jonson from all his writings. Mr. Redwine, in his long critical introduction, looks at the body of this work in perspective. Selected Bibliography. Index.

SWINBURNE, ALGERNON CHARLES
A Study of Ben Jonson

University of Nebraska, 1969. 212pp. Paper $2.25. Originally published in 1889 and now edited and reissued with a new Introduction by Howard B. Norland, this is a general introduction to Ben Jonson. The editor's Introduction considers the major principles of Swinburne's criticism of Jonson and his critical technique. Textual and Explanatory Notes.

THAYER, C.G.
Ben Jonson: Studies in His Plays
University of Oklahoma, 1963. 280pp. $5.95. A chronological analysis of all the plays. The emphasis is on an explication of the ethical themes of the comic satires and on the manner in which Jonson weaves the figure of the poet into the dramatic fabric. The later plays are given special attention and their genuine value is stressed.

WOODBRIDGE, ELISABETH
Studies in Jonson's Comedy
Gordian Press, 1966. 103pp. $6.00. Originally published in 1898 and now reissued, this is a study of four of Jonson's plays with discussions of the playwright's theory of literary art, character treatment and structural features of his typical comedies. An Appendix offers brief discussions of the comedies not already treated in the body of the work. Bibliography. Index.

Kyd, Thomas

EDWARDS, PHILIP
Thomas Kyd and Early Elizabethan Tragedy
Longmans, 1966. 48pp. Paper $1.25. This study concentrates on "The Spanish Tragedy" by Kyd and places it in the perspective of the development of Elizabethan tragedy from the beginning of the Queen's reign to the time of Shakespeare's first essays in tragedy. Selected Bibliography.

FREEMAN, ARTHUR
Thomas Kyd: Facts and Problems
Oxford, 1967. 200pp. $8.50. This biographical and critical study of one of the most eminent pre-Shakespearean playwrights treats of Kyd's life, literary career, and the complicated events surrounding his imprisonment and death. The aim has been to estimate Kyd's achievement in our terms and our time as well as in his and Shakespeare's. Select List of Works Employed. Index.

MURRAY, PETER B.
Thomas Kyd
Twayne, 1969. 170pp. $4.50. Mr. Murray offers a study of the Elizabethan's one surviving play, "The Spanish Tragedy." He shows that Kyd combined elements from a number of sources and made these elements his own. Chronology. Notes and References. Selected Bibliography. Index.

Lodge, Thomas

RAE, WESLEY D.
Thomas Lodge
Twayne, 1967. 128pp. $4.95. A critical-analytical interpretation of the works of the Elizabethan playwright, essayist, and poet. The study traces Lodge's contribution to the development of English literature during the reigns of Elizabeth I and James I. Rae views Lodge as a Renaissance gentleman and a true representative of his age. Chronology. Notes and References. Selected Bibliography. Index.

Lyly, John

HUNTER, G.K.
John Lyly: The Humanist as Courtier
Harvard, 1962. 376pp. $8.50. A critical account of Lyly's work, including detailed studies of the eight plays. Their relation to the tradition of Court drama is stressed.

HUNTER, G.K.
Lyly and Peele
Longmans, 1968. 52pp. Paper $1.00. A short study of the sixteenth century dramatists. The two playwrights are usually catalogued as "university wits" and they are among the first English writers to bring the fruits of the new Humanist education to the service of popular commercial entertainment. Bibliography.

SACCIO, PETER
The Court Comedies of John Lyly: A Study in Allegorical Dramaturgy
Princeton, 1969. 233pp. $8.50. An investigation of allegory in the plays of the Elizabethan Court dramatists of the 1580's and 1590's, particularly in the comedies of John Lyly. The author examines Lyly's plots and their sources, his use of the techniques of Court staging, and his euphuistic dialogue, and discusses the means by which these elements cooperate in unique dramatic structures that present allegorical explorations of major Renaissance ideas. index.

Marlowe, Christopher

ARMSTRONG, WILLIAM A.
Marlowe's "Tamburlaine": The Image and the Stage
University of Hull, 1966. 18pp. Paper $1.25. Reprint of a lecture delivered in England in which Professor Armstrong discusses Marlowe's play, "Tamburlaine."

BAKELESS, JOHN
Christopher Marlowe: The Man in His Time
Washington Square Press, 1964. 335pp. Paper $ .90. First published in 1937 and now reprinted, this study

utilizes much material from manuscripts not available in the past, among them the last will of Marlowe's murderer and a series of documents on Marlowe's life at home.

BATES, PAUL A.
Faust: Sources, Works, Criticism
See Page 139

BATTENHOUSE, ROY W.
Marlowe's "Tamburlaine": A Study in Renaissance Moral Philosophy
Vanderbilt University, 1964. 266pp. $5.00. In this reprint of the study first printed in 1942, the author demonstrates the influence of the Reformation humanism on both parts of the play and shows how the play illustrates the standard Renaissance interpretations of fortune, providence, and the function of poetry. Index.

BOAS, FREDERICK S.
Christopher Marlowe: A Biographical and Critical Study
Oxford, 1940. 336pp. $7.50. A complete survey of Marlowe's life and work. The author suggests that the texts of "Doctor Faustus" and of "The Massacre of Paris" preserve more of the playwright's original work than hitherto suspected.

BOAS, FREDERICK S.
Marlowe and His Circle
Russell & Russell, 1968. 159pp. $7.50. Originally published in 1929 and now reissued, this is a biographical survey of the Elizabethan playwright in which the author attempts to take stock of the documentary materials available to historians in the 1920's. A second aim of the author has been to reconsider the case for and against the acceptance of the verdict in the killing of Marlowe. Index.

BROCKBANK, J. P.
Dr. Faustus: A Critical Study
Barron, 1962. 63pp. Paper $1.00. A brief survey of the Faust legend and Marlowe's use of it. Major themes of the play are analyzed.

CLARK, ELEANOR GRACE
Ralegh and Marlowe: A Study in Elizabethan Fustian
See Page 152

COLE, DOUGLAS
Suffering and Evil in the Plays of Christopher Marlowe
Princeton, 1962. 274pp. $6.75. Marlowe's handling of the themes of suffering and evil is examined in relation to the dramatic conventions of his day, his source materials, the intellectual trends, and his background as a theology student.

FANTA, CHRISTOPHER G.
Marlowe's "Agonists"
Harvard, 1970. 60pp. Paper $3.25. An approach to the ambiguity of Christopher Marlowe's plays plus a note on a theory of tragedy. Bibliography. Notes.

FARNHAM, WILLARD – Editor
Twentieth Century Interpretations of Doctor Faustus
Prentice–Hall, 1969. 120pp. $4.95. Paper $1.25. A collection of critical essays on Marlowe's drama by twenty-one authorities including M. C. Bradbrook, Helen Gardner, L. C. Knights, and George Santayana. An Introduction has been provided by the editor. Chronology. Selected Bibliography.

FIELER, FRANK B.
Tamburlaine, Part I and Its Audience
University of Florida, 1961. 80pp. Paper $2.00. A study of Marlowe's conscious manipulation of audience reaction to his main character in this play.

FITZWATER, EVA
Doctor Faustus: Notes
Cliff's Notes, 1967. 61pp. Paper $1.00. This volume serves as an introduction to Marlowe's work. Essays on the Faust legend, synopsis of the play, and summaries of each scene with critical commentaries. Review questions are also provided. Selected Bibliography.

INGRAM, JOHN H.
Christopher Marlowe and His Associates
Cooper Square, 1970. 305pp. $12.85. Originally published in 1904 and now reissued, this is a biography and study of Marlowe. Much of the volume is concerned with his contemporaries. Illustrated with twenty-seven plates. Appendices. Notes. Bibliograhy. Index.

JUMP, JOHN – Editor
Doctor Faustus: A Casebook
Aurora, 1970. 235pp. Paper $2.50. A selection of critical essays including extracts from earlier critics and recent studies by Helen Gardner, Nicholas Brooke, Harry Levin, and others. Select Bibliography. Index.

KLEINMAN, NEIL and RICHARD WASSON – Editors
Marlowe's "Jew of Malta" – The Grammar of Policy
Depot Press, 1967. 8pp. Paper $ .50. A monograph on Christopher Marlowe's play.

KNOLL, ROBERT E.
Christopher Marlowe
Twayne, 1969. 160pp. $4.50. A general introduction to the work of Marlowe. Each of the plays is considered to show its interrelationship of structure and theme. The author attempts to include relevant Marlovian criticism and scholarship. Notes. Selected Bibliography. Index.

KOCHER, PAUL H.
Christopher Marlowe: A Study of His Thought, Learning and Character
Russell & Russell, 1962. 345pp. $10.00. A reprint

of the 1946 edition, this is a study of the degree of Marlowe's subjectivity as a dramatist with special attention directed to the criticism of Christianity that emerged as Marlowe's most skillfully and passionately reiterated theme.

LEECH, CLIFFORD — Editor
Marlowe: A Collection of Critical Essays
Prentice—Hall, 1964. 184pp. $4.95. Paper $1.95. Essays by T. S. Eliot, Harry Levin, Ethel Seaton, Roy Battenhouse, Eugene M. Waith, W. W. Greg, Una Ellis-Fermor, J. P. Brockbank, and others. Chronology. Selected Bibliography.

LEVIN, HARRY
The Overreacher: A Study of Christopher Marlowe
Beacon, 1964. 204pp. Paper $1.75. A reassessment of Marlowe's work. Introductory chapters discuss the history of the theatre and the development of blank verse. The major plays are analyzed and a psychological portrait of Marlowe as a Faustian personality is developed.

MORRIS, BRIAN — Editor
Christopher Marlowe: Mermaid Critical Commentaries
Ernest Benn, 1968. 197pp. $4.50. Paper $3.00. An anthology of critical essays on the Jacobean playwright. Among the subjects are "The Jew of Malta" in the theatre, comic method in "Hero and Leander," Marlowe and comic distance, Marlowe and early Shakespeare, and Marlowe's naturalism. Index.

MULLANY, PETER F.
Christopher Marlowe's Doctor Faustus
Monarch, 1965. 122pp. Paper $1.00. A critical commentary on "Doctor Faustus" and four other plays. Discussion of the background of the plays and the plots, theme development, character analysis, critical commentary, and review questions and answers are provided. Bibliography.

NORMAN, CHARLES
The Muses' Darling: The Life of Christopher Marlowe
Macmillan, 1960. 272pp. Paper $1.85. A biography of the playwright which stresses the revolution he brought about in the theatre and his dominant influence on poets and playwrights.

O'NEILL, JUDITH — Editor
Critics on Marlowe
University of Miami, 1970. 127pp. $3.95. This is an anthology of criticism of Christopher Marlowe's work. Among the contributors are: Robert Greene, George Peele, William Hazlitt, T. S. Eliot, Una Ellis-Fermor, M. C. Bradbrook, Helen Gardner, John Russell Brown, Clifford Leech, and G. Wilson Knight. Selected Bibliography.

POIRIER, MICHEL
Christopher Marlowe
Archon, 1968. 216pp. $5.00. Originally published in 1951 and now reissued, this is a study of Marlowe's work which emphasizes the contrasts between his violent and tawdry life and the rhetoric of his poetry. The author provides a detailed critical analysis of the plays and poems and deals with the influences behind them, the form they take, and their reflection of Marlowe's nature. Selected Bibliography. Index.

RIBNER, IRVING — Editor
Christopher Marlowe's "Doctor Faustus"
Odyssey, 1966. 216pp. Paper $1.50. The text of the play with notes by Irving Ribner and a collection of essays by the major critics of the play. Selected Bibliography.

ROWSE, A. L.
Christopher Marlowe: A Biography
Harper, 1964. 220pp. $8.00. Based on the conclusion that Marlowe was Shakespeare's rival for Southampton's patronage and that the dating of the Sonnets could be determined by historical methods, this study re-examines the life of Marlowe and demonstrates that his early death was the greatest single loss to English literature.

ROWSE, A. L.
Christopher Marlowe: His Life and Work
Grosset & Dunlap, 1966. 220pp. Paper $2.65. This is a reprint of the study first published in 1964. Mr. Rowse provides a biography of the Elizabethan playwright and a critical study of his work including close readings of "Tamburlaine," "Edward the Second," and "Dr. Faustus." Illustrated. Notes. Index.

SIMS, JAMES H.
Dramatic Uses of Biblical Allusions in Marlowe and Shakespeare
See Page 83

STEANE, J. B.
Marlowe: A Critical Study
Cambridge, 1964. 381pp. $7.50. Paper — 1970. 383pp. $2.95. Detailed studies of all the works—plays, translations, and poems—prefaced by a biographical chapter. The author takes the poetry as his center of interest and offers a literary judgment of Marlowe's art rather than a study of background and sources. Appendices. Bibliography. Notes. Index.

TANNENBAUM, SAMUEL A.
The Assassination of Christopher Marlowe
Shoe String, 1962. 75pp. $4.50. This reprint of the 1928 work is a study of Thomas Kyd's accusation of treason by Christopher Marlowe and the circumstances surrounding the death of Marlowe. Included is a translation of the Coroner's report.

WILSON, F. P.
Marlowe and the Early Shakespeare
Oxford, 1953. 144pp. $3.00. Lectures on "Tamburlaine," "The Massacre at Paris," and "Edward II."

One lecture considers the relationship between Marlowe's and Shakespeare's history plays.

WRAIGHT, A.D. and VIRGINIA F. STERN
In Search of Christopher Marlowe
Vanguard, 1965. 376pp. $12.50. The authors attempt to reveal the multiplicity of concerns which engaged Marlowe's attention in his lifetime. A pictorial essay provides a comment on the text and recreates the world in which Marlowe moved. Historical documents of importance are presented in reproduction. Index.

Marston, John

FINKELPEARL, PHILIP J.
John Marston of the Middle Temple
Harvard, 1969. 275pp. $7.50. The author reconstructs the life at the Inns of Court during the late sixteenth and early seventeenth centuries, placing particular emphasis on the manners, morals, politics, and tastes of this restricted but influential world. He then proceeds to analyze Marston's works focusing on the influence of the social environment on the Elizabethan dramatist. Index.

Massinger, Philip

DUNN, T.A.
Philip Massinger: The Man and the Playwright
Thomas Nelson, 1957. 285pp. $7.50. A study of Massinger's stagecraft, dramatic structure, blank verse style, and world view, based on a critical examination with the tools of research developed since the 1920's for the study of Shakespeare and other major writers.

SPENCER, BENJAMIN T. – Editor
The Bondsman: An Antient Storie – Philip Massinger
Princeton, 1932. 266pp. $3.50. A definitive text of the play with a study of the sources, topical allusions, editorial problems, and influence. Notes give the stage history of Massinger's plays, critical estimation, and bibliographical information.

Middleton, Thomas

BARKER, RICHARD HINDRY
Thomas Middleton
Columbia, 1958. 216pp. $6.00. A comprehensive survey of the playwright which examines all the plays. Evidence on authorship is offered when necessary. Attention is given to Middleton's use of irony, and the relation between this use and his moral themes is demonstrated. Appendices discuss dating, lost works, and works attributed to him.

DUNKEL, WILBUR DWIGHT
The Dramatic Technique of Thomas Middleton in His Comedies of London Life
Russell & Russell, 1967. 126pp. $8.50. Originally published in 1925 and now reissued, this is an analysis of Middleton's plays with regard to his treatment of action, character, devices and conventions, emotional values and dialog. Appendix. Selective Bibliography.

SCHOENBAUM, SAMUEL
Middleton's Tragedies: A Critical Study
Columbia, 1955. 275pp. $6.00. Examinations of six tragedies by Middleton. Particular attention is paid to characterization and to the ironic method as well as to the psychological interpretation of sin and its self-destructive nature. Middleton's collaborations with Rowley are also discussed.

Milton, John

DIEKHOFF, JOHN S. – Editor
A Maske at Ludlowe
Case Western Reserve University, 1968. 280pp. $8.95. This is a collection of essays on "Comus," the seventeenth century masque by John Milton. Eleven essays by nine authors discuss the form of the masque, the stage by Henry Lawes (who also provided the music which is reproduced in the volume), and the argument and intent of the text. Also included is the text of the Bridgewater "Comus" which comes closest of all existing manuscripts to the acting version of the poem. Appendix. Bibliography.

Otway, Thomas

SCHUMACHER, EDGAR
Thomas Otway
Burt Franklin, 1970. 175pp. $13.50. Originally published in 1924 and now reissued, this is a study of the Elizabethan dramatist. The text is in the German language.

Peele, George

HORNE, DAVID H. – Editor
The Life and Minor Works of George Peele
Yale, 1952. 305pp. $10.00. The editor of this volume refutes the widely held opinion that Peele was a rake living a dissolute life among the university wits. The minor works include pageants, masques, and poetry. Index.

HUNTER, G.K.
Lyly and Peele

Longmans, 1968. 52pp. Paper $1.00. A short study of the sixteenth century dramatists. The two playwrights are usually catalogued as "university wits" and they are among the first English writers to bring the fruits of the new Humanist education to the service of popular commercial entertainment. Bibliography.

Shirley, James

NASON, ARTHUR HUNTINGTON
James Shirley, Dramatist
Blom, 1967. 471pp. $12.50. Originally published in 1915 and now reissued, this is a biographical and critical study of the English dramatist. Illustrated. Bibliography. Index.

Spenser, Edmund

McLANE, PAUL E.
Spenser's "Shepheardes Calender": A Study in Elizabethan Allegory
University of Notre Dame, 1961. 370pp. $5.00. An interpretation of Spenser's "Calender" as historical allegory. Mr. McLane pictures in full detail the religious situation in England in the late 1570's and deals with notable people, events, and institutions of Elizabethan biography, politics, and church history in interpreting the author's poem. Index.

WATKINS, W. B. C.
Shakespeare and Spenser
See Page 87

Webster, John

ANSARI, K. HABIBMOHAMED
John Webster: Image Patterns and Canon
Jalaluddin Rumi Publications, 1969. 296pp. $7.75. Published in India, this study of the image patterns of Webster demonstrates that Webster was not a decadent but that his ideal of life was the crown of fame. The imagery of disease, graveyard and death in his plays is didactic in function to underline the futility and ephemeral nature of the lower values. Dr. Ansari also restores the classic play "Appius and Virginia" to Webster after weighing arguments against the authorship. Appendices. Index.

BOGARD, TRAVIS
The Tragic Satire of John Webster
Russell & Russell, 1965. 158pp. $8.50. A reprint of the study first published in 1955, in this work the author approaches Webster's tragedies historically, seeing them in terms of the conventions of Jacobean tragedy, and critically, seeing them in terms of the scope and significance of Webster's vision of human suffering.

BOKLUND, GUNNAR
The Duchess of Malfi: Sources, Themes, Characters
Harvard, 1962. 189pp. $5.00. A discussion of the possible sources of John Webster's play with an analysis of the play itself. Notes. Index.

BROOKE, RUPERT
John Webster and the Elizabethan Drama
Russell & Russell, 1967. 276pp. $9.50. Originally published in 1916 and now reissued, this is a study of the Elizabethan playwright. Critical Appendices deal with the plays. Bibliography.

DENT, ROBERT WILLIAN
John Webster's Borrowing
University of California, 1960. 323pp. $6.75. The author establishes the probability that at least three-quarters of all Webster's works can be traced to specific sources. All the evidence is analyzed in detail.

HUNTER, G. K. and S. K. HUNTER – Editors
John Webster
Penguin, 1969. 328pp. Paper $2.25. This volume surveys and anthologizes Webster criticism. The account of stage and other adaptations draws on new material. Among the authorities who provide essays are: Charles Lamb, John Addington Symonds, William Archer, Rupert Brooke, T. S. Eliot, and Una Ellis-Fermor. Table of Dates. Select Bibliography. Index.

LEECH, CLIFFORD
The Duchess of Malfi: A Critical Study
Barron, 1963. 64pp. Paper $1.00. This study considers the general pattern of the play, examines the composition of the action, and analyzes themes and implications.

MOORE, DON D.
John Webster and His Critics: 1617 – 1964
Louisiana State University, 1966. 199pp. $4.00. Professor Moore examines in detail the critical responses to Webster's art over the past 350 years. Bibliography. Index.

MORRIS, BRIAN – Editor
John Webster
Ernest Benn, 1970. 237pp. $6.95. Paper $4.50. A volume in the Mermaid Critical Commentaries series. Papers dealing with staging and performance of Webster's plays and critical studies of the dramatist and his works are included. Eight pages of photographs. Index.

RABKIN, NORMAN – Editor
Twentieth Century Interpretations of "The Duchess of Malfi"
Prentice–Hall, 1968. 120pp. $3.95. Paper $1.25. This is a collection of twenty-five critical essays on

Webster's tragedy. The contributors explore the roles of fate and chance in the play, its moral vision, Webster's language, intentions and techniques, and the play's relationship to other Elizabethan dramas. Chronology of Important Dates.

STOLL, ELMER EDGAR
John Webster
Gordian Press, 1967. 216pp. $7.75. Originally published in 1905 and now reissued, this study is subtitled "The Periods of His Work as Determined by His Relations to the Drama of His Day." A chronology of the plays is attempted and the playwright's life is separated into periods: that of apprenticeship and partnership, the period of the revenge plays, and the Fletcherian and eclectic period. Appendices. Index.

Chronological Periods: Restoration and Eighteenth Century (1660-1880)

HISTORIES AND CRITIQUES

ADAMS, HENRY HITCH and BAXTER HATHAWAY – Editors
Dramatic Essays of the Neo-Classic Age
Blom, 1965. 412pp. $12.50. A reprint of the work first published in 1947, this collection assembles the most important and influential statements on dramatic theory of the period beginning in 1660. French and German critics who had strong influence in England are included. Index.

ANGELO, HENRY
The Reminiscences of Henry Angelo
Blom, 1970. 937pp. & plates. Two volume set: $28.50. Originally published in 1904 and now reissued in a facsimile edition, these memories and anecdotes of the eighteenth century were written by the foremost fencing master of the times. Introduction by Howard de Walden and Notes by H. Lavers Smith. Sixty-eight prints illustrate the volumes.

AVERY, EMMETT L. – Editor
The London Stage 1660 – 1800. Part Two: 1700 – 1729
Southern Illinois University, 1960. 1,300pp. Two volume set: $50.00. A calendar of plays, entertainments, and afterpieces, together with casts, box-receipts, and contemporary comment compiled from the playbills, newspapers, and theatrical diaries of the period. The two volumes that make up "Part Two" of this series contain critical introductions by William Van Lennep, Emmett L. Avery, Arthur H. Scouten, George Winchester Stone, Jr., and C. Beecher Hogan. (See other volumes listed by editor. William Van Lennep: Part One. Arthur H. Scouten: Part Three. George Winchester Stone, Jr.: Part Four. Charles Beecher Hogan: Part Five. See also entry directly below.)

AVERY, EMMETT L.
The London Stage 1700 – 1729: A Critical Introduction
Southern Illinois University, 1968. 192pp. Paper $2.25. The critical introduction to "The London Stage 1660—1800. Part Two: 1700—1729" in a separate volume. Illustrated. Index.

AVERY, EMMETT L. and ARTHUR H. SCOUTEN
The London Stage 1660 – 1700: A Critical Introduction
Southern Illinois University, 1968. 187pp. Paper $2.25. The critical introduction to "The London Stage 1660—1800. Part One: 1660—1700." Published for the first time separately, it deals with theatrical events recorded in the time period indicated. Illustrated. Index.

BATESON, F.W.
English Comic Drama 1700 – 1750
Russell & Russell, 1963. 158pp. $8.50. A reprint of the 1929 edition, this is a general introduction to the drama of the era with chapters on Colly Cibber, Steele, Mrs. Centilivre, John Gay, and Henry Fielding.

BOAS, FREDERICK S.
An Introduction to Eighteenth Century Drama 1700 – 1780
Oxford, 1953. 365pp. $6.50. A study of playwrights from Rowe, Farquhar, and Steele to Goldsmith, and Sheridan. Critical analyses of the plots of the plays are given and the sources of the drama and influences on it are studied. The predominance of Anglo-Irish playwrights during the era is examined. Index.

BOSWELL, ELEANORE
The Restoration Court Stage (1660 – 1702) with a Particular Account of the Production of "Calisto"
Barnes & Noble, 1966. 370pp. $10.50. A reprint of the 1932 study of the Restoration Court stage during the reign of Charles II. It includes information on the theatres, maintenance and production, the players and the plays, staging, lighting, music, and many other facets of the drama and theatre of the era. Illustrated. Index.

BROWN, JOHN RUSSELL and BERNARD HARRIS – Editors
Restoration Theatre
St. Martin, 1965. 240pp. $5.75. Paper – Putnam, 1967. 241pp. $1.65. A critical reappraisal of the Restoration theatre. Each of the ten essays is prefaced by explanatory notes by the editors that provide a background to the discussions and critiques that follow. Four illustrations. Index.

CHASE, LEWIS NATHANIEL
The English Heroic Play
Russell & Russell, 1965. 250pp. $9.00. First published in 1903, this critical study surveys the heroic type of drama with the object of determining the main

features. A history of the heroic play in England is given with the occasion of its introduction and the causes and stages of its decline. Included is a list of plays and representative references for the period 1656—1703.

CUNNINGHAM, JOHN E.
Restoration Drama
Evans, 1966. 160pp. $3.50. Paper $2.65. A study of the theatre and the playwrights of the Restoration. The author attempts to draw a general picture of the society and to introduce each of the major dramatists: Etherege, Dryden, Wycherley, Otway, and Congreve. Bibliography. Index.

DEANE, CECIL VICTOR
Dramatic Theory and the Rhymed Heroic Play
Cass, 1967. 235pp. $8.00. Originally published in 1931 and now reissued, Dr. Deane's examination of the Restoration theatre in England attempts to determine to what extent the heroic play observed the neo-Aristotelian rules of the drama as expounded by the French theorists, and to what degree the English genius contrived to impose its own individuality on forms borrowed from abroad. Bibliography. Index.

DOBREE, BONAMY
Restoration Comedy 1660—1720
Oxford, 1962. 182pp. $3.50. A reprint of the volume first published in 1924, this is a general view of comedy from Etherege to Farquhar with detailed examinations of the major plays. The question of French influence is studied. The author's contention is that Restoration comedy is a natural development of late Elizabethan drama.

DOBREE, BONAMY
Restoration Tragedy 1660—1720
Oxford, 1959. 189pp. $3.50. A reprinting of the 1929 edition, this study has a three-fold aim: to see why tragedy took the form known as heroic and to analyze what the term implies; to distinguish the characteristics of the major playwrights; to see what lessons can be learned for the tragic drama of the present times. The playwrights studied are: Dryden, Lee, Otway, and Rowe and there is a chapter on the tragedies of Congreve and Addison.

DONOHUE, JR., JOSEPH W.
Dramatic Character in the English Romantic Age
Princeton, 1970. 402pp. $14.50. Professor Donohue examines the change in concepts of dramatic character in the late eighteenth and early nineteenth centuries. He treats the essential nature of Romanticism in the drama and its development from origins in the Jacobean private theatre, and then analyzes three plays—Cumberland's "West Indian," Sheridan's "Pizzaro," and Shelley's "Cenci"—to provide evidence of the nature of the hero and his reflection of the social, political, and cultural opinions of audiences and readers. Illustrated. Bibliographical Note. Index.

DOWNES, JOHN
Roscius Anglicanus
Blom, 1968. 286pp. $12.50. Edited by the Reverend Montague Summers, this book was originally published in 1929 and is now reissued. It is a historical review of the English stage from 1660 to 1706. The author was bookkeeper and prompter at Sir William Davenant's theatre and attended all the rehearsals and performances there. Reverend Summers has provided explanatory notes to the text.

FUJIMURA, THOMAS
The Restoration Comedy of Wit
Barnes & Noble, 1968. 232pp. $8.00. A republication of the study first published in 1952. It is a study of the plays and playwrights of the English Restoration. Subjects covered include the nature of wit, the intellectual background of wit comedy, and the aesthetics of wit comedy. Etherege, Wycherley, and Congreve are discussed in separate chapters. Bibliography. Index.

GAGEN, JEAN
The New Woman: Her Emergence in English Drama (1600—1730)
Twayne, 1954. 193pp. $3.50. A study of the first appearance in drama of the type of emancipated woman with modern notions of independence and equality. The heroines of many seventeenth and early eighteenth century plays are examined. Bibliography.

GOLDSTEIN, MALCOLM
Pope and the Augustan Stage
Stanford University, 1958. 139pp. $4.00. The author's intention is twofold: to draw together the evidence—from his poetry and prose, in the prefaces to plays of his friends, and the eighteenth century letters and journals—that Pope considered the theatre a vital, influential, and meaningful experience; secondly, to demonstrate the appeal of early eighteenth century drama to a man of great taste and intelligence.

GRAY, CHARLES HAROLD
Theatrical Criticism in London to 1795
Blom, 1959. 333pp. $12.50. A reprint of the 1931 study of the available sources of opinion and information on eighteenth century English drama. The study indicates where discussions of the theatre may be found and suggests the quality of these discussions.

GREEN, CLARENCE C.
The Neo-Classic Theory of Tragedy in England During the Eighteenth Century
Blom, 1966. 245pp. $12.50. First published in 1934 and now reissued, this book attempts to supply a unified and complete history of the defeat of the neo-classic forces of the theory of tragedy at the hands of the eighteenth century critics. In his Introduction the author studies the development of the neo-classic theory of tragedy to 1699. Index of Authors and Critics.

HARBAGE, ALFRED
Cavalier Drama
See Page 154

HILL, AARON and WILLIAM POPPLE
The Prompter: A Theatrical Paper (1734 – 1736)
Blom, 1966. 208pp. $15.00. Selected and edited by William W. Appleton and Kalman A. Burnim, this is a series of papers originally published in the periodical which appeared from 1734 to 1736. Hill and Popple are regarded by the editors as the first professional theatre critics. Illustrated. Index.

HOGAN, CHARLES BEECHER – Editor
The London Stage 1660 – 1800. Part Five: 1776 – 1880
Southern Illinois University, 1968. 2,500pp. Three volume set: $75.00. The final volumes in the eleven volume set. Illustrated. Index. (See other volumes listed by editor. William Van Lennep: Part One. Emmett L. Avery: Part Two. Arthur H. Scouten: Part Three. George Winchester Stone, Jr.: Part Four. See also the entry directly below for the Introduction to Part Five in a separate volume.)

HOGAN, CHARLES BEECHER
The London Stage 1776 – 1800: A Critical Introduction
Southern Illinois University, 1968. 224pp. Paper $2.25. The critical introduction to "The London Stage 1660–1800. Part Five: 1776–1800" published separately. Illustrated. Index.

HOLCROFT, THOMAS
The Life of Thomas Holcroft
Blom, 1968. Volume One: 319pp. Volume Two: 346pp. Two volume set: $27.50. Originally published in 1925 and now reissued, this two volume set is an autobiography of the English actor and writer. William Hazlitt finished the work after Holcroft's death and Elbridge Colby edited it, wrote an Introduction, and provided notes. Chronology. Index.

HOLLAND, NORMAN
The First Modern Comedies: The Significance of Etherege, Wycherley, and Congreve
Harvard University, 1959. 274pp. $7.50. Paper – Indiana University, 1967. 274pp. $2.95. An evaluation of the eleven comedies of Etherege, Wycherley, and Congreve. To his close reading of each play in terms of plot, character, and language, the author adds discussions of the seventeenth century intellectual milieu. Notes. Index.

HOTSON, LESLIE
The Commonwealth and Restoration Stage
Russell & Russell, 1962. 424pp. $15.00. A reprint of the edition of 1928, this is a digest and evaluation of the most important records dealing with plays and entertainments of the period 1642–1660 and a study of the important playing companies from 1660 to 1704.

HUGHES, LEO
A Century of English Farce
Princeton, 1956. 307pp. $7.50. A study of farce and low comedy from the Restoration to the middle of the eighteenth century. The structure of the farce, its sources and influences, and the actors of the farce-plays are examined.

HUTCHINSON, ROBERT – Editor
Joe Miller's Jests, or The Wit's Vade-Mecum
Dover, 1963. 70pp. Paper $1.00. A facsimile edition of the original "Joe Miller," the most popular and most influential humor book in English. The book is an informal compendium of eighteenth century types and characters and reflects the favorite pastimes and hobbies of the age.

JUMP, JOHN D. – Editor
The Diary of Samuel Pepys
Washington Square Press, 1964. 336pp. Paper $ .60. Based on the Mynors Bright edition of 1875, this abridged edition contains selections from the period 1660 to 1669.

KRUTCH, JOSEPH WOOD
Comedy and Conscience After the Revolution
Columbia, 1961. 300pp. Paper $2.75. A reprint of the 1929 study of the development of Restoration comedy and its transformation into sentimental comedy. The study shows how the attacks on the excesses of the stage, the return of a conservative monarch, and the influences of the middle class brought about the end of the Restoration comedy.

LAWRENCE, W. J.
Old Theatre Days and Ways
Blom, 1968. 255pp. $12.50. Originally published in 1935 and now reissued, this is a collection of essays on little-known aspects of the English theatre in the Restoration and eighteenth century. Among the subjects covered are the variety of admission systems, famous theatrical cat-calls, and audience sing-alongs. Illustrated. Index.

LEECH, CLIFFORD
Shakespeare's Tragedies and Other Studies in Seventeenth Century Drama
See Page 56

LEFANU, WILLIAM – Editor
Betsy Sheridan's Journal: Letters from Sheridan's Sister 1784 – 1786, and 1788 – 1790
Rutgers University, 1960. 223pp. $4.50. The first complete edition of the journal kept by Richard Brinsley Sheridan's younger sister which she sent in the form of weekly letters from England to her elder sister Alice LeFanu in Dublin. The letters provide a picture of the eighteenth century world of respectable bohemians—actors, artists, and writers. Illustrated with plates including a portrait of Betsy Sheridan. Index.

LEONARD, STERLING A.
The Doctrine of Correctness in English Usage 1700–1800
Russell & Russell, 1962. 361pp. $11.50. A reprint of the 1929 edition, this book examines such topics as the eighteenth century interest in problems of language, the philosophical basis of language theories, the appeal to usage and its repudiation, the struggle of language elites, and the value of the eighteenth century critical dicta.

LICHTENBERG, GEORGE CHRISTOPH
Lichtenberg's Visits to England
Blom, 1969. 130pp. $12.50. Originally published in 1939 and reissued in a facsimile edition, this is a collection of letters and portions of the diary of the German author and critic, as translated and annotated by Margaret L. Mare and W. H. Quarrell. Among other subjects, the letters describe and give critiques of theatrical performances in the 1770's. Appendix. Bibliography. Index.

LOFTIS, JOHN
Comedy and Society from Congreve to Fielding
Stanford University, 1959. 154pp. $4.75. A study of how the social assumptions of dramatists conditioned the choice of subject and influenced the direction of dramatic satire.

LOFTIS, JOHN
The Politics of Drama in Augustan England
Oxford, 1963. 173pp. $6.00. The author contends that the hundreds of plays first produced in the late seventeenth and early eighteenth centuries constitute a particularized and voluminous record of the development of English political institutions. Sir Robert Walpole's Stage Licensing Act of 1737 is seen as the culmination of political and theatrical trends discernible since the Restoration. Index.

LOFTIS, JOHN—Editor
Restoration Drama: Modern Essays in Criticism
Oxford, 1966. 369pp. Paper $2.25. Essays by L. C. Knights, Guy Montgomery, Dale Underwood, Norman N. Holland, Bonamy Dobree, Clifford Leech, and others.

LOFTIS, JOHN
Steele at Drury Lane
University of California, 1952. 260pp. $5.00. A study of Steele's governorship of the Drury Lane Theatre from 1714 to 1729. Special attention is paid to his efforts to achieve a moral and artistic reform in the theatre and to his play, "The Conscious Lovers," as an example of what he felt an unoffending comedy should be like. Index.

McAFEE, HELEN—Editor
Pepys on the Restoration Stage
Blom, 1963. 353pp. $12.50. A reprint of the 1916 edition, this is a selection of the passages relating to the theatre and drama in Pepys' diary, annotated in the light of recent researches as well as the seventeenth century sources. The references are grouped according to topics. Bibliography. Index.

McCALL, JOHN
Eighteenth Century Restoration Plays
Monarch, 1965. 203pp. Paper $1.95. A critical study guide to the plays of Cibber, Congreve, Dryden, Etherege, Farquhar, and others. Plot summaries and commentary are provided with review questions.

MINER, EARL—Editor
Restoration Dramatists: A Collection of Critical Essays
Prentice–Hall, 1966. 479pp. $4.95. Paper $1.95. The essays collected here show how the tradition of English drama found expression in the plays of Dryden, Etherege, Wycherley, Otway, and Congreve. Chronology of Plays. Selected Bibliography.

NETTLETON, GEORGE HENRY
English Drama of the Restoration and Eighteenth Century (1642–1780)
Cooper Square, 1968. 366pp. $9.25. Originally published in 1932 and now reissued, this is an attempt to survey the continuous development of English drama from the closing of the theatres in 1642 to the culmination of eighteenth century drama in Sheridan. Among the playwrights discussed are Dryden, Otway, Congreve, Vanbrugh, Farquhar, Fielding, Goldsmith, and Sheridan. Bibliographical Notes. Index.

NICOLL, ALLARDYCE
A History of English Drama. Volume Two: Early Eighteenth Century Drama, 1700–1750
See Page 147

NICOLL, ALLARDYCE
A History of English Drama. Volume Three: Late Eighteenth Century Drama, 1750–1800
See Page 147

PALMER, JOHN
The Comedy of Manners
Russell & Russell, 1962. 308pp. $10.00. A reprint of the 1913 edition, this is a study of the rise and fall of the comic dramatists of the Restoration, presented from an historical point of view. The men are studied against the background of their era and their works are measured by the moral standards they accepted.

PASTON, GEORGE
Social Caricature in the 18th Century
Blom, 1968. 145pp. $32.50. In this study, originally published in 1905 and now reissued, the author attempts, with the aid of the Caricaturists, to give a view of the lighter side of social life in the eighteenth century. He offers information on the mores, habits, and costume of British life as well as a lengthy section on the popular entertainment of the time: operas,

pantomimes, and masquerades. The illustrations have been reproduced from prints and engravings in the British Museum. Index.

PEARCE, CHARLES E.
Polly Peachum: The Story of Lavinia Fenton and The Beggar's Opera
Blom, 1968. 382pp. $12.50. Originally published in 1931 and now reissued, this is a history of John Gay's ballad opera and the life of Lavinia Fenton, the girl who created the role of Polly Peachum. Illustrated. Index.

PERRY, HENRY TEN EYCK
The Comic Spirit in Restoration Drama: Studies in the Comedy of Etherege, Wycherley, Congreve, Vanbrugh, and Farquhar
Russell & Russell, 1962. 148pp. $7.50. A reprint of the original edition published in 1929, this is an analysis of the comic theory and practice of the leading playwrights of the era which pays close attention to the texts of the plays.

ROTHSTEIN, ERIC
Restoration Tragedy: Form and the Process of Change
University of Wisconsin, 1967. 194pp. $6.50. In tracing the development of English tragedy from the time of the Restoration in 1660 to the accession of Queen Anne in 1702, Mr. Rothstein provides a reassessment of a mode of drama that has been largely neglected. Its artistic merits, the importance of its techniques, and the significance of its pattern of change form the basis for a study of eighteenth century literature. Index.

SCOUTEN, ARTHUR H.—Editor
The London Stage 1660—1800. Part Three: 1729—1747
Southern Illinois University, 1961. 1,600pp. Two volume set: $50.00. The third part of the eleven volume set comprising a history of the Restoration and eighteenth century London stage. Critical Introduction by the editor. Illustrated. Index. (See also other volumes in the series listed by editor. William Van Lennep: Part One. Arthur H. Scouten: Part Two. George Winchester Stone, Jr.: Part Four. Charles Beecher Hogan: Part Five. See entry directly below for separate volume which contains the Introduction to Part Three.)

SCOUTEN, ARTHUR H.
The London Stage 1729—1747: A Critical Introduction
Southern Illinois University, 1968. 210pp. Paper $2.25. Published separately for the first time, this is the critical introduction to "The London Stage 1660—1800. Part Three: 1729–1747." Among the subjects of the volume are theatre plants, administration, acting, production, repertory, audience, and criticism. Illustrated. Index.

SHEPPARD, F.H.W.—Editor
The Theatre Royal, Drury Lane, and The Royal Opera House, Covent Garden
Oxford, 1970. 200pp. $22.50. Volume XXXV of a historical series, "The Survey of London," this is a study of the history of the two most famous theatres in London. The volume concentrates on three themes: the ownership of the two theatres, the buildings which successive proprietors erected, and the history of the patents granted to Thomas Killigrew and Sir William Davenant by Charles II. Sixty-eight pages of Illustrations. Index.

SHERBO, ARTHUR
English Sentimental Drama
Michigan State University, 1957. 181pp. $5.75. A study of the nature of the sentimental drama that was the dominant form of dramatic expression in the eighteenth century.

STONE, GEORGE WINCHESTER, JR.—Editor
The London Stage 1660—1800. Part Four: 1747—1776
Southern Illinois University, 1963. 2,400pp. Three volume set: $75.00. These three volumes bring the eleven volume set on the history of the Restoration and eighteenth century London stage up to date through 1776. Critical Introduction by the editor. Illustrated. Index. (See other volumes listed by editor. William Van Lennep: Part One. Emmett L. Avery: Part Two. Arthur H. Scouten: Part Three. Charles Beecher Hogan: Part Five. See also the entry directly below for a separate volume containing only the Introduction to Part Four.)

STONE, GEORGE WINCHESTER, JR.
The London Stage 1747—1776: A Critical Introduction
Southern Illinois University, 1968. 218pp. Paper $2.25. The critical introduction to "The London Stage 1660–1800. Part Four: 1747–1776" published separately for the first time. Illustrated. Index.

SUMMERS, MONTAGUE
The Playhouse of Pepys
Humanities, 1964. 485pp. $14.50. A reprint of the 1935 edition, this study contains chapters on Sir William Davenant, Thomas Killigrew, and other dramatists of the period from 1660 to 1682. Illustrated.

SUMMERS, MONTAGUE
The Restoration Theatre
Humanities, 1964. 352pp. $14.00. A reprint of the 1934 edition, this study examines seven aspects of the Restoration theatrical scene: the system of anannouncements and advertisements for plays; the system of admission; the composition of the audience, including the concessionaires; the use of the curtain, the prologue, and scene-change intervals; the epilogue; realism on the stage; and costume. Appendices. Illustrated. Index.

VAN LENNEP, WILLIAM—Editor
The London Stage 1660—1800. Part One: 1600—1700
Southern Illinois University, 1965. 752pp. $25.00. A calendar of plays, entertainments, and afterpieces together with casts, box-receipts, and contemporary comment compiled from the playbills, newspapers, and theatrical diaries of the period. This first volume in the series begins with Davenant and closes with Congreve and records all the known details of performances of the period. The critical introduction is by Emmett L. Avery and Arthur H. Scouten. Illustrated. Index. (See other volumes listed by editor. Emmett L. Avery: Part Two. Arthur H. Scouten: Part Three. George Winchester Stone, Jr.: Part Four. Charles Beecher Hogan: Part Five. See also the entry under Emmet L. Avery and Arthur H. Scouten for a separate volume containing only the Introduction to Part One.)

VICTOR, BENJAMIN
The History of the Theatres of London and Dublin
Blom, 1969. 722pp. $27.50. Originally published in 1761 and 1771 as a three volume set and now reissued in a one volume facsimile edition. The volume is a history of the theatres of London and Dublin from the year 1730 to 1771. The volumes were originally written as a sort of supplement to Colley Cibber's "Apology." They chronicle theatrical events, and comment on the noted actors of the period. The author was sub-manager and treasurer of the Drury Lane Theatre, London.

WILSON, JOHN HAROLD
The Influence of Beaumont and Fletcher on Restoration Drama
Blom, 1968. 156pp. $8.50. This study, originally published in 1928 and now reissued, seeks to show that the writers of the Restoration were acquainted with the works of Beaumont and Fletcher and that they altered and borrowed from the plays. Certain dramatists who continued on beyond the Restoration period—notably Farquhar and Vanbrugh—are also considered. An Appendix lists plays produced between 1660 and 1700. Also provided is a Selected Bibliography. Index.

WILSON, JOHN HAROLD
A Preface to Restoration Drama
Harvard, 1968. 208pp. $7.25. Paper—Houghton, Mifflin, 1965. 208pp. $2.50. This study is written primarily for the student and the general reader. It is a survey of the Restoration theatre, players, audience, and of the varieties of tragedies and comedies prevalent from 1660 to 1702. Professor Wilson tries "to define and describe the varieties of Restoration drama and to analyze outstanding examples of each kind objectively..." He offers fundamental critical appraisals, emphasizing that the plays discussed were intended to be produced on a stage, not read in the study. A Selected Bibliography is provided. Index.

STUDIES OF PLAYWRIGHTS

Behn, Aphra

LINK, FREDERICK M.
Aphra Behn
Twayne, 1968. 183pp. $3.95. A survey of the works of the writer of the Restoration period. The study encompasses the plays, poems, translations, and stories of the first woman to make a living by writing. Brief plot summaries of the plays are included. Notes and References. Selected Bibliography. Index.

Burney, Fanny

ADELSTEIN, MICHAEL E.
Fanny Burney
Twayne, 1968. 169pp. $3.95. This study describes and assesses Fanny Burney's achievement in literature as an eighteenth century novelist, playwright, and diarist. Selected Bibliography. Index.

Cibber, Colley

ASHLEY, L.R.N.
Colley Cibber
Twayne, 1965. 224pp. $3.95. A complete biography and critical study of this actor-playwright who occupied the stage for forty years, established the vogue for sentimental comedy, and wrote an autobiography that gives a brilliant theatrical gallery of the late seventeenth century. Bibliography. Index.

CIBBER, COLLEY
An Apology for the Life of Colley Cibber
University of Michigan, 1968. 372pp. $11.50. Edited by B. R. S. Fone, this is a history of English theatre, as the English playwright saw it, from the Restoration to 1733. Cibber tells how he wrote "Love's Last Shift" to provide a role for himself and how he eventually became actor-manager of Drury Lane. He gives us studies of the great actors of the era and provides a gossipy account of life backstage. Index.

CIBBER, COLLEY
An Apology for the Life of Mr. Colley Cibber
AMS Press, 1966. Volume One: 337pp. Volume Two: 416pp. Two volume set: $17.50. An edition, with notes and supplement by Robert W. Lowe, of Cibber's autobiography. It includes biographies of contemporary actors and actresses, a Bibliography of Cibber's works and an Index.

Congreve, William

AVERY, EMMETT L.
Congreve's Plays on the Eighteenth Century Stage
New York University, 1951. 226pp. $3.75. In this study of the stage history of Congreve's plays from 1693 to 1800, the author presents the plays in relation to other late seventeenth century plays and against the background of the principal events in the London theatre world of the eighteenth century. Appendices include a study of the revisions of the plays and a list of performances from 1700 to 1800 with cast lists where available. Index.

HODGES, JOHN C. – Editor
William Congreve: Letters and Documents
Harcourt, Brace, 1964. 295pp. $6.75. An edition of 157 letters and documents (by, to, or about the playwright) that reveal his personal and literary relations, his business and professional affairs, and his ideas on the art of drama. An Appendix deals with his death, his will, and his relation with Henrietta, the Duchess of Marlborough. Bibliography.

TAYLOR, D. CRANE
William Congreve
Russell & Russell, 1963. 252pp. $7.50. A reprint of the 1931 edition, this is a critical evaluation of Congreve's life and work, with chapters on the social and literary background, his ancestry, and early life, the plays and miscellaneous writings, his last days in the theatre, and his retirement. Included is a list of newspapers and magazines containing information on the playwright. Bibliography.

VAN VORIS, W. H.
The Cultivated Stance: The Designs of Congreve's Plays
Dufour, 1967. 186pp. $6.95. The approach of this study of Congreve's plays is to examine the author's main assumptions and show how they are revealed in the designs of his plays. Congreve's intricately plotted structures are studied fully and a concluding chapter examines the dramatic utility of his dialogue. Also included is a calendar of Congreve's life with a general background of the history of the time.

Davenant, William

COLLINS, HOWARD S.
The Comedy of Sir William Davenant
Humanities, 1967. 179pp. $8.95. In this examination of Davenant and his treatment of the comic spirit, Mr. Collins attempts to reveal Davenant as a playwright who employed his talent to portray the types of comedy in favor in his own time and who thus aided in transporting the traditions of one age of comedy across the gap of two decades. Bibliography.

Dryden, John

ALLEN, NED BLISS
The Sources of John Dryden's Comedies
Gordian Press, 1967. 298pp. $10.00. Originally published in 1935 and now reissued, this is a critical study of the comedies of Dryden. The author contends that there was no uniformity of development in Dryden's comic drama. She studies the plays separately and in groups and pays particular attention to the sources used by Dryden and to the conventions that influenced the playwright. Appendices quote sources of various of the plays. Select Bibliography. Index.

BARBEAU, ANNE T.
The Intellectual Design of John Dryden's Heroic Plays
Yale, 1970. 221pp. $11.50. Miss Barbeau investigates Dryden's heroic dramas in an attempt to prove they are informed by a clear and well-defined scheme of values. She contends that the plays have been underestimated because they have been judged by inappropriate aesthetic standards and she views them as tragedies of civilizations rather than individuals. List of Works Consulted. Index.

BREDVOLD, LOUIS I.
The Intellectual Milieu of John Dryden
University of Michigan, 1956. 185pp. Paper $1.75. This book accepts John Dryden's skeptical temperament as the basic explanation of the development of his ideas. The author examines skepticism in seventeenth century literature—its bearings on religious thought and on conservative political thought. Appendices. Index.

DRYDEN, JOHN
John Dryden: Selected Criticism
Oxford, 1970. 315pp. Paper $3.75. Edited by James Kinsley and George Parfitt, this volume contains not only well known essays such as "Of Dramatic Poesy," but also a wide selection of less accessible critical writings. Explanatory footnotes are supplemented by longer notes at the end of the book. Index.

DRYDEN, JOHN
Literary Criticism of John Dryden
University of Nebraska, 1966. 174pp. $5.95. Paper $2.25. Edited by Arthur C. Kirsch, this is a collection of essays and other works by the seventeenth century critic and playwright. Included are "Of Dramatic Poesy," a defense of that essay, and the Prefaces to several of the author's works. Selected Bibliography. Index.

DRYDEN, JOHN
Of Dramatic Poesy and Other Critical Essays
Dutton, 1962. Volume One: 322pp. Volume Two: 279pp. Price per volume: $3.95. A complete edition of Dryden's dramatic criticism. Collected are the

whole of the critical writings in whatever form they have survived: prefaces, essays, prologues, letters, and private notes. Glossary of Critical Terms.

HAMILTON, K.G.
John Dryden and the Poetry of Statement
Michigan State University, 1969. 193pp. $7.50. Professor Hamilton aims to provide a detailed analysis of the more important and characteristic elements of Dryden's poetry. He deals with the works written between 1682 and 1687. Bibliography. Index of Names.

HARTH, PHILIP
Contexts of Dryden's Thought
University of Chicago, 1968. 304pp. $10.00. Professor Harth presents an assessment of Dryden's attitudes toward reason and faith. He investigates the poet's intellectual formation at Trinity College and places particular emphasis on the elucidation of two of Dryden's longest poems: "Religio Laici" and "The Hind and the Panther." Index.

HOFFMAN, ARTHUR W.
John Dryden's Imagery
University of Florida, 1968. 172pp. $6.00. Originally published in 1962 and now reissued, this volume is a study of the kinds of imagery characteristically used by Dryden and of the range in his methods of employing this imagery. Representative examples of his non-dramatic poetry have been selected for examination. Index.

HUNTLEY, FRANK LIVINGSTONE
On Dryden's "Essay of Dramatic Poesy"
Shoe String, 1968. 71pp. $4.00. Originally published in 1951 and now reissued, this study seeks to discover what lies behind Dryden's essay, to find its organic unity, and to explain its final significance.

JENSEN, H. JAMES
A Glossary of John Dryden's Critical Terms
University of Minnesota, 1969. 135pp. $5.00. Professor Jensen has catalogued every important word that Dryden used in discussing critical matters about art, literature, or music. Under each word there is a general definition and, if needed, an essay on the word's origin, history, and general usage.

KING, BRUCE – Editor
All for Love: Twentieth Century Interpretations
Prentice–Hall, 1968. 120pp. $3.95. Paper $1.25. A collection of critical essays analyzing theme, style, genre, structural elements, artistic influence, and historical background of Dryden's play. Among the twenty essayists are Bonamy Dobree, T. S. Eliot, Kenneth Muir, and B. Ifor Evans. Chronology of Important Dates. Selected Bibliography.

KING, BRUCE – Editor
Dryden's Mind and Art
Oliver & Boyd, 1969. 213pp. $8.50. A collection of essays meant to serve as an introduction to Dryden's poetry, prose, and drama. The essays combine evaluation with close reading for a fuller understanding of Dryden's work. Selected Bibliography. Index.

KIRSCH, ARTHUR C.
Dryden's Heroic Drama
Princeton, 1965. 157pp. $5.95. The author contends that Dryden's heroic dramas should not be treated as a single unit but as a continuation of a particular kind of dramatic convention, with the early examples derived from Fletcherian and Cavalier tragicomedy and the later ones oriented towards sentimental drama of the 1670's.

MOORE, FRANK HARPER
The Nobler Pleasure: Dryden's Comedy in Theory and Practice
University of North Carolina, 1963. 264pp. $7.25. This is a detailed chronological examination of Dryden's critical statements and comic practice. The author traces Dryden's theory of comedy from 1663 to 1700. Bibliography. Index.

OSBORN, JAMES M.
John Dryden: Some Biographical Facts and Problems
University of Florida, 1965. 316pp. $8.50. Originally published in 1940 and now reissued in a revised second edition, this is a source work for students of the late seventeenth century. The first part is devoted to an examination of the biographies of Dryden that have been published since his death. The second half is made up of separate investigations of such subjects as the presentation of new documents, the re-examination of old ones, the synthesis of scattered evidence, and the analysis of specific problems. Illustrated. Appendices. Index.

PENDLEBURY, B.J.
Dryden's Heroic Plays
Russell & Russell, 1967. 138pp. $8.00. Originally published in 1923 and now reissued, this is a study of the origins of the plays of Dryden. Included is an essay on the heroic tradition before Dryden, comment on Dryden's dramatic theory, the development of the English heroic play, and the playwright's dramatic achievement. List of Books Consulted. Index.

RAMSEY, PAUL
The Art of John Dryden
University of Kentucky, 1969. 214pp. $6.50. Mr. Ramsey acknowledges Dryden's defects of style and occasional inconsistencies of thought but finds in Dryden's art a solid theory of poetics including the important principles of harmony and propriety. Although mainly concerned with Dryden's poetry there is a long chapter on "All for Love." Notes. Index of Names. Index of Subjects.

SCOTT, SIR WALTER
The Life of John Dryden

University of Nebraska, 1963. 471pp. $5.00. Paper $1.70. First published in 1808, this is the 1834 edition of the biography, edited and annotated by John Gibson Lockhart. The present editor, Bernard Kreisman, has provided a new Introduction and notes which are restricted to points of clarification and essential correction. The biography has been praised for its panoramic view of Restoration life and society as well as for its critical acuity. Index.

SHERWOOD, MARGARET
Dryden's Dramatic Theory and Practice
Russell & Russell, 1966. 110pp. $9.50. First published in 1898 and now reissued, this study of John Dryden takes into account the age in which he lived. His theory of the drama, his comedies, heroic plays, and tragedies are examined in separate chapters. The author contends that Dryden's dramatic work "is imitation, not organic creation. It lacks vital centre, and it has not endured." Bibliography. Index.

SMITH, DAVID NICHOL
John Dryden
Archon, 1966. 93pp. $3.50. An unaltered edition of the volume first published in 1950. These four lectures were originally delivered at Trinity College, Cambridge, on Dryden's early verse and criticism, his plays, his satires and religious poems, and his translations, odes, and fables. Index.

SWEDENBERG, H. T. – Editor
Essential Articles for the Study of John Dryden
Shoe String, 1966. 587pp. $10.00. A selection of articles and survey on the work of John Dryden. Among the contributors are Hugh MacDonald, George Williamson, Lillian Feder, and Ruth Wallerstein.

VAN DOREN, MARK
John Dryden: A Study of His Poetry
Indiana University, 1960. 298pp. Paper $1.75. An analysis of the achievements and the failures of the poet. This edition is a revised and enlarged reprint of the 1946 edition.

WARD, CHARLES E.
The Life of John Dryden
University of North Carolina, 1961. 380pp. $11.35. This biography of England's great man of letters provides a re-examination of Dryden's life and career as poet, dramatist, and man of letters. By closely examining the numerous autobiographical passages which Dryden inserted in dedications, prefaces, and critical essays and by interpreting these in the light of Dryden's relations to persons and contemporary situations, the author disproves some long-accepted explanations of Dryden's conduct in the political and religious aspects of his career. Appendices. Notes. Index.

WASSERMAN, GEORGE
John Dryden
Twayne, 1964. 174pp. $4.50. A critical survey of Dryden's total literary production in verse, drama, criticism, and translation. The works are seen as a consistent development of the implications of neo-Classical political and aesthetic principles. Bibliography. Index.

ZEBOUNI, SELMA ASSIR
Dryden: A Study in Heroic Characterization
Louisiana State University, 1965. 111pp. $3.00. Professor Zebouni offers a new concept of the hero as seen in Dryden's five heroic dramas. She considers the plays as drama and offers an interpretation of the archetype of heroic hero. This interpretation is concluded with a comparison of Corneille with Racine and of Dryden with both. Index.

Farquhar, George

FARMER, A. J.
George Farquhar
Longmans, 1966. 40pp. Paper $1.25. A study of the Restoration dramatist, his life, his novels, poems, letters, and plays. Selected Bibliography.

FARQUHAR, GEORGE
The Complete Works of George Farquhar
Gordian Press, 1967. Volume One: 401pp. Volume Two: 443pp. Two volume set: $42.50. Originally published in 1930 and now reissued, this two volume set of the works of Farquhar has been edited by Charles Stonehill. Besides the texts of the fifteen works, the editor has provided an Introduction, a chronological table, and textual and explanatory notes. The theatrical history of each play has also been included.

ROTHSTEIN, ERIC
George Farquhar
Twayne, 1967. 206pp. $3.95. This study extends scholarly and critical analysis to the seventeenth century dramatist. It reveals him as the originator of a new kind of comedy. Selected Bibliography. Chronology. Index.

Fielding, Henry

BANERJI, H. K.
Henry Fielding: His Life and Work
Russell & Russell, 1962. 342pp. $9.00. A reprint of the 1929 edition in which the author's intention is to rescue the plays, the pamphlets, the essays in periodicals, and other miscellaneous writings from the oblivion that has overtaken them. There are chapters on Fielding's art, the beginnings of his literary career, his early efforts in fiction, his political journalism, his major novels, and his plays. Bibliography.

Garrick, David (Also See Page 268)

BURNIM, KALMAN A.
David Garrick: Director
University of Pittsburgh, 1961. 234pp. $7.95. This study considers David Garrick's management and stage direction at the Drury Lane Theatre. The author treats his many activities as manager; his relations with authors; his selection and casting of plays; his rehearsal techniques; and his use of scenery, costumes, and lights. Provided is a detailed reconstruction of some of the most important productions. Illustrated. Bibliography. Index.

ENGLAND, MARTHA WINBURN
Garrick and Stratford
New York Public Library, 1962. 72pp. Paper $2.50. A study of the three day Shakespeare festival held in September, 1769, at Stratford-on-Avon on the occasion of the dedication of the Town Hall to Shakespeare. Illustrated.

HEDGCOCK, FRANK A.
David Garrick and His French Friends
Blom, 1969. 442pp. $12.50. This work, originally published in 1912 and now reissued, is a biography of the eighteenth century English actor and an appreciation of his qualities, an account of his visits to Paris and travels on the continent, and a collection of his French correspondence with actors, playwrights, men of letters and others. The text is fully annotated. List of Principal Works Quoted or Referred To. Illustrated. Index.

KNAPP, MARY E.
Checklist of Verse by David Garrick
University of Virginia, 1955. 69pp. $5.00. An alphabetical arrangement of the verse in four categories: occasional verse, prologues, epilogues, and theatrical skits and songs. The entries note time and place of publication.

LITTLE, DAVID M. and GEORGE M. KAHRL – Editors
The Letters of David Garrick
Harvard, 1963. 1,418pp. Three volume set: $35.00. The editors have assembled about 1,360 letters, of which over half are published for the first time. The letters are printed without corrections of the formal and stylistic characteristics of Garrick's hand. The introductions give the sources of the manuscripts, short titles, and a chronology. Illustrated. Appendices. Index. Boxed set.

OMAN, CAROLA
David Garrick
Hodder and Stoughton, 1958. 427pp. $8.50. A complete biography giving detailed information on Garrick's career as an actor, manager, and playwright. Illustrated.

PEDICORD, HARRY WILLIAM
The Theatrical Public in the Time of Garrick
Southern Illinois University, 1966. 267pp. $6.00. Paper $2.65. In this study, originally published in 1954 and now reissued, the author seeks to answer the questions of the size of the audiences, the economic aspects of eighteenth century playgoing, and the quality of the spectators, and the repertoire as measured in terms of popularity at the box-office. Included is a chronology of Garrick's writing for the theatre, attendance charts and box-office receipts for various theatres, a survey of the eighteenth century repertoire at the Drury Lane and Covent Garden theatres, a List of Works Cited, and an Index.

STEIN, ELIZABETH
David Garrick, Dramatist
Blom, 1967. 315pp. $12.50. Originally published in 1938, this is a reissue of a study of Garrick's playwriting career. The twenty-one plays written between 1740 and 1775 are examined by types and the author has drawn on "The MS Diaries of the Drury Lane Theatre" for the first hand account of play production from 1747 to 1776. Illustrated. Bibliography. Index.

Gay, John

IRVING, WILLIAM
John Gay, Favorite of the Wits
Russell & Russell, 1960. 334pp. $9.00. A reprint of the original 1940 edition, this study is based on letters, periodicals, theatrical records, and early biographies. Considered are the early years, the works on the "Scriblerus Papers," the success of "Three Hours After Marriage" and "The Beggar's Opera," and the last years of the playwright as well as his posthumous reputation.

SPACKS, PATRICIA
John Gay
Twayne, 1965. 176pp. $4.95. This study of John Gay's poetry and drama treats the work primarily in terms of its literary accomplishment. Gay is seen as not essentially a satirist, but as a poet led to satire by the literary climate of the eighteenth century. The author includes a chronology of events during Gay's lifetime. Selected Bibliography. Index.

Goldsmith, Oliver

GOODING, DAVID
Oliver Goldsmith's She Stoops to Conquer
Monarch, 1966. 126pp. $1.00. A critical guide to the play with background and plot discussion, character analysis, critical commentary, review questions and answers, and a Bibliography.

QUINTANA, RICARDO
Oliver Goldsmith: A Georgian Study
Macmillan, 1967. 213pp. $4.95. The author provides a portrait of the eighteenth century master of comedy and an appraisal of the entire body of his work. Quintana studies the works from the early essays through to the dramatic triumph in 1772 of "She Stoops to Conquer." Appendix on Goldsmith's miscellaneous work. Bibliographical Notes. Index.

SHERWIN, OSCAR
The Life and Times of Oliver Goldsmith
Collier, 1962. 351pp. Paper $ .95. A study of Goldsmith's career with examinations of his novels, plays, poems, and essays.

WARDLE, RALPH M.
Oliver Goldsmith
Archon, 1969. 330pp. $10.50. Originally published in 1957 and now reissued, this is a biography of the eighteenth century playwright which takes into account materials not available or utilized by earlier biographers. Illustrated. Notes. Index.

Killigrew, Thomas

HARBAGE, ALFRED
Thomas Killigrew, Cavalier Dramatist, 1612 – 1683
Blom, 1967. 247pp. $12.50. A study, originally published in 1930, of the Restoration period dramatist and manager of the Theatre Royal in Drury Lane. Illustrated. Bibliography. Index.

Sedley, Charles

PINTO, V. DE SOLA – Editor
The Poetical and Dramatic Works of Sir Charles Sedley
AMS Press, 1969. Volume One: 333pp. Volume Two: 264pp. Two volume set: $20.00. Reprinted from the edition of 1928, these two volumes contain the ninety-three poems and three plays of the seventeenth century dramatist. The editor has included a fourth play and other poetry ascribed to Sedley "on doubtful authority." Four illustrations. Editor's preface. Explanatory notes, textual notes, and a Bibliography are included. Index of First Lines.

PINTO, V. DE SOLA
Sir Charles Sedley: 1639 – 1701
AMS Press, 1969. 412pp. $20.00. Subtitled, "A Study in the Life and Literature of the Restoration," this volume was originally published in 1927 and is now reissued. The dramatic and non-dramatic works of this seventeenth century English dramatist and poet are studied. Two illustrations. Appendices. Index.

Shadwell, Thomas

BORGMAN, ALBERT S.
Thomas Shadwell: His Life and Comedies
Blom, 1969. 269pp. $12.50. Originally published in 1928 and now reissued, this is an attempt to bring together the facts of Shadwell's life and to review each of his thirteen plays. The literary and political controversies with which Shadwell was involved are detailed, and the author provides a stage history, a synopsis of the plot, and a critique of each of the plays. Borgman concludes that the playwright's place among the comic dramatists writing between 1660 and 1692 is next in importance to that occupied by Etherege and Wycherley. Index.

Sheridan, Richard Brinsley

FISKIN, A. M. I.
The Rivals and School for Scandal: Notes
Cliff's Notes, 1967. 79pp. Paper $1.00. These notes present a discussion of the action and thought of the two plays by Sheridan and provide a concise interpretation of their artistic merits and significance. Included are a life of Sheridan, essays on the comedy of manners, sentimental comedy, and Sheridan's comic art. Review questions and essay topics and a Selected Bibliography are provided.

PRICE, CECIL – Editor
The Letters of Richard Brinsley Sheridan
Oxford, 1966. 999pp. Three volume set: $30.00. A collection of the letters of the playwright. A number of the letters are printed here for the first time and they are drawn from libraries in Europe, Australia, and the United States.

SHERWIN, OSCAR
Uncorking Old Sherry: The Life and Times of Richard Brinsley Sheridan
Twayne, 1960. 352pp. $6.00. A study of Sheridan both as playwright and as orator. The disasters of his later life, beginning with his association with the Prince of Wales, are treated in detail. Illustrated.

Southerne, Thomas

DODDS, JOHN WENDELL
Thomas Southerne – Dramatist
Archon, 1970. 232pp. $8.75. Originally published in 1933 and now reissued, this is a consideration of Restoration drama and the tragedies of the eighteenth century playwright. Each of the ten plays is studied in a separate chapter and the author includes biographical information, a Chronology, a copy of Southerne's will and a Bibliography. Index.

Wycherley, William

ZIMBARDO, ROSE A.
Wycherley's Drama, A Link in the Development of English Satire
Yale, 1965. 175pp. $6.75. This study views the dramatist as a highly conscious craftsman, who enriched a tradition of English satire that originated in Anglo-Saxon magic and was fulfilled in the works of Marston, Shakespeare, and Jonson. Wycherley's work bridges the two great ages of English satire (the Renaissance and the Augustan) and is a substantial contribution to the development of an important literary tradition. Index.

Chronological Periods: Nineteenth Century

HISTORIES AND CRITIQUES

AGATE, JAMES
Buzz, Buzz! Essays of the Theatre
Blom, 1969. 235pp. $9.75. Originally published in 1918 and now reissued in a facsimile edition, these critical essays on the stage, plays, acting and actors are divided into three parts: lectures on the art of playgoing with some considerations for actors, essays on fourteen contemporary actors and actresses, and a long parable on the temperament of the artist.

AGATE, JAMES
These Were Actors
Blom, 1969. 150pp. $10.75. Originally published in 1943 and now reissued in a facsimile edition, this is a collection of extracts from newspaper articles dated 1811–1833, selected and annotated by Mr. Agate. The cuttings are reviews or appreciations of actors of the time including Sarah Siddons, Fanny Kemble, Talma, Edmund Kean, and the last appearance of the clown Grimaldi. Illustrated.

AMERONGEN, J.B. VAN
The Actor in Dickens
Blom, 1969. 301pp. $12.50. A study of the histrionic and dramatic elements in the novelist's life and works, originally published in 1926 and now reissued in a facsimile edition. The volume also includes a chapter on the stage in Dickens' play-going days, and an Appendix on the contemporary adaptation of Dickens' works for the stage. Illustrated. List of Books Studied or Consulted.

ARCHER, WILLIAM
The Theatrical World – 1893
Blom, 1969. 307pp. $12.50. Originally published in 1894 and now reissued in a facsimile edition, these are the theatrical criticisms of the English critic for the London season of 1893. Index.

ARCHER, WILLIAM
The Theatrical World – 1897
Blom, 1969. 452pp. $12.50. Originally published in 1898 and reissued in a facsimile edition, this volume contains criticisms of plays produced in London during the theatrical season of 1897. A synopsis of playbills of the year by Henry George Hibbert is included. Index.

AXTON, WILLIAM F.
Circle of Fire
University of Kentucky, 1966. 294pp. $7.25. Subtitled "Dickens' Vision and Style and the Popular Victorian Theatre," this is an exploration of the influence of the Victorian theatre upon Dickens' novels. Three distinctively Victorian dramatic modes–burlesquerie, grotesquerie, and the melodramatic–are applied to Dickens' works. Appendices. Index.

BANCROFT, MARIE and SQUIRE BRANCROFT
The Bancrofts: Recollections of Sixty Years
Blom, 1969. 462pp. $12.50. Originally published in 1909 and reissued in a facsimile edition, this is a biography and series of reminiscences of the successful nineteenth century English actor and his wife. They provide a picture of the life of the Victorian stage and its actors. Illustrated. Index.

BOOTH, MICHAEL
English Melodrama
Herbert Jenkins, 1965. 223pp. $6.50. Dr. Booth analyzes the nineteenth century golden age of melodrama; its rapid rise to prominence; its lengthy reign and its slow decline. He defines melodrama and traces its background and devotes several chapters to the various types. Bibliography. Index.

BOOTH, MICHAEL – Editor
Hiss the Villain: English and American Melodramas
Blom, 1964. 390pp. $8.75. The texts of the six plays are based on nineteenth century acting editions, and for each there are full production notes, original casts, dates of productions, etc. A long Introduction to the melodrama is included. Illustrated with old posters and woodcuts. The plays are Pocock's "The Miller and His Men," Haines' "My Poll and My Partner Joe," Pratt's "Ten Nights in a Bar-room," Phillips' "Lost in London," Daly's "Under the Gaslight," and Lewis' "The Bells.

BRANNAN, ROBERT LOUIS – Editor
Under the Management of Mr. Charles Dickens
Cornell, 1966. 173pp. $7.95. The editor has prepared an edition of the script of the production of "The Frozen Deep" which Charles Dickens wrote and in which he appeared in 1857. The play is based on the lost polar expedition of Sir John Franklin and was, in part, an answer to the charges of cannibalism leveled at its leader. In a long Introduction, Mr. Brannan describes the writing, staging, performance, and lasting influence of the play. Illustrated. Bibliography.

CLAPP, JOHN BOUVE and EDWIN FRANCIS EDGETT
Plays of the Present
Blom, 1969. 331pp. $12.50. Originally published in 1902 and now reissued in a facsimile volume, this is a catalogue of plays presented in England and the United States during the late nineteenth century. Production information, cast list, and a critical summary are provided. Illustrated with thirty-four photographs of actors of the period. Index.

CRUSE, AMY
The Englishman and His Books in the Early Nineteenth Century
Blom, 1968. 300pp. $12.50. Originally published in 1930 and now reissued, this volume describes the people who read the books and went to the plays, their tastes and attitudes, the popular literary fads, and the "new" writing and the old favorites. Illustrated. Index.

DARBYSHIRE, ALFRED
The Art of the Victorian Stage
Blom, 1969. 182pp. $12.50. Originally published in 1907 and reissued in a facsimile edition, this is a record of the experiences of stagecraft and art in nineteenth century England. The work of Charles Calvert and Sir Henry Irving is studied as well as other practicioners in the theatre during Queen Victoria's era.

FILON, PIERRE MARIE AUGUSTIN
The English Stage
Blom, 1970. 319pp. $12.50. Originally published in 1897 and reissued in a facsimile edition, this is an account of the development of English drama during the Victorian era. Translated by Frederic Whyte, the study shows continental attitudes and evaluations of English drama, playwrights, and actors.

FITZSIMONS, RAYMUND
Garish Lights: The Public Reading Tours of Charles Dickens
Lippincott, 1970. 192pp. $6.50. A study of the last three years of Charles Dickens' life, from 1858 to 1870, when he barnstormed across Britain and the United States reading from his own works. Illustrated with reproductions of drawings by Phiz for the Dickens' novels and with three photographs. Bibliography. Index.

FLETCHER, RICHARD M.
English Romantic Drama 1795—1843
Exposition, 1966. 226pp. $6.50. A critical history of verse plays including studies of works by Wordsworth, Browning, Coleridge, Shelley, Byron, and many others. Its purpose is to "bring poetic tragedy as a genre into sharper focus." Bibliography.

GRANT, JAMES
Penny Theatres
Society for Theatre Research, 1952. 35pp. Paper $1.75. An excerpt from "Sketches in London" originally published in 1838. Edited by Bertram Shuttleworth, it is an account of the nineteenth century theatres which were "cheap places of juvenile amusement." The author discusses the theatres, the performances, and the performers. Illustrated with two drawings by the contemporary cartoonist, "Phiz."

HACKETT, JAMES HENRY
Notes, Criticisms, and Correspondence Upon Shakespeare's Plays and Actors
See Page 93

HAZLITT, WILLIAM
Hazlitt on Theatre
Hill & Wang, 1957. 211pp. $3.00. Paper $1.25. Edited by William Archer and Robert Lowe, this is a collection of selections from "View of the English Stage" and "Criticisms and Dramatic Essays." Emphasis is placed on the quality of acting that distinguished the performances of such actors as Kean, Macready, Stephen Kemble, and Mrs. Siddons.

HOWARD, DIANA
London Theatres and Music Halls: 1850—1950
See Page 376

JACKSON, HOLBROOK
The Eighteen Nineties
Putnam, 1966. 304pp. Paper $1.95. A survey of the British literary and artistic movements that flourished in the last decade of the nineteenth century. It moves from a general survey of the period, its movements and leading figures, to specific discussions of the more notable examples. Illustrated. Index.

JONES, JOHN BUSH—Editor
W.S. Gilbert: A Century of Scholarship and Commentary
See Page 288

KNIGHT, G. WILSON
Byron and Shakespeare
Barnes & Noble, 1966. 381pp. $8.95. Professor Knight seeks to show how the life and thought of Byron reflect the main comedic and tragic experiences involved in the dramas of Shakespeare. The comparisons given seek to show that Shakespeare's dramas possess a relevance to the modern world. Index of Byronic Themes. Index of Names. Index of Titles.

LAVER, JAMES
Victoriana
Hawthorn, 1967. 256pp. $5.95. Every aspect of Victorian art, pastimes and trinkets is covered in this volume. The text is accompanied by 262 photographs with detailed captions. The theatre of the Victorian era is covered in a chapter on melodrama posters and one on "tinsel pictures" and toy theatres. Bibliography. Index.

MacINNES, COLIN
Sweet Saturday Night
See Page 281

MANDER, RAYMOND and JOE MITCHENSON
British Music Hall
See Page 281

MANDER, RAYMOND and JOE MITCHENSON
The Theatres of London
Rupert Hart—Davis, 1963. 292pp. Paper $3.00. A revised edition of the study first published in 1961, this volume contains descriptions not only of the public theatres of the West End and the suburbs, but also of the club theatres and buildings originally designed as theatres, but now used for other purposes.

MASON, A. E. W.
Sir George Alexander and the St. James' Theatre
Blom, 1969. 247pp. $12.50. Originally published in 1935 and reissued in facsimile edition, this is a history of the St. James' Theatre in London under the management of George Alexander from 1890 through 1918. A complete history of all the productions and actors appearing at the theatre is given. Illustrated. Appendices. Index.

MAYER, DAVID
Harlequin in His Element: The English Pantomine 1806—1836
See Page 348

MURRY, J. MIDDLETON
Keats and Shakespeare: A Study of Keats' Poetic Life from 1816 to 1820
See Page 51

NICHOLSON, WATSON
The Struggle for a Free Stage in London
Blom, 1966. 475pp. $12.50. A reprint of the 1906 study of the long nineteenth century struggle to free London of the theatrical monopoly which allowed only two theatres to play Shakespeare and other national drama. Bibliography. Index.

NICOLL, ALLARDYCE
A History of English Drama. Volume Four: Early 19th Century Drama, 1800—1850
See Page 147

RENDLE, ADRIAN
Everyman and His Theatre
Pitman, 1968. 114pp. $5.00. The object of this book is to review some of the major aspects of the English amateur theatre from the middle of the nineteenth century to the present. The author attempts to assess the acting and direction standards of the present day. Illustrated. Index.

REYNOLDS, ERNEST
Early Victorian Drama 1830—1970
Blom, 1965. 163pp. $7.50. A reprint of the volume first published in 1936, this study examines the cultural conditions of the period as they affected drama. The author considers comedy, farce, tragedy, and melodrama in the era. A discussion of the dramatization of fiction and a section on notable actors of the time are included. Bibliography. Index.

ROBINSON, HENRY CRABB
The London Theatre: 1811—1866
Society for Theatre Research, 1966. 227pp. Paper $10.50. This is a selection of writings from the diary of Henry Crabb Robinson, lawyer and theatre-afficiando. Edited by Eluned Brown, it is a record of Robinson's play-going and his friendships with the leading theatrical personalities of his time. Index to Plays. Index to Actors, Theatres, Subjects.

SHATTUCK, CHARLES H.—Editor
Bulwer and Macready: A Chronicle of the Early Victorian Theatre
University of Illinois, 1958. 278pp. $6.95. Letters, diary notes, and other memorabilia detailing the planning, writing, and staging of a body of Victorian plays. The collaboration between the playwright Bulwer and the actor-manager Macready is illustrated.

SHATTUCK, CHARLES—Editor
William Charles Macready's "King John"
University of Illinois, 1962. 75pp. $6.95. A facsimile reproduction of Macready's prompt-book for Shakespeare's "King John" with illustrations of the production. Mr. Shattuck examines six other relevant prompt-books and three "acting editions" and explains their relation to the production. Thirty-four plates provide illustrations of the Drury Lane Theatre, costume and set designs.

SHERSON, ERROLL
London's Lost Theatres of the Nineteenth Century
Blom, 1969. 392pp. $12.50. Originally published in 1925 and reissued in a facsimile edition, this is a study of nineteenth century theatres which are no longer in existence with notes on the actors and productions. Twenty-nine pages of illustrations of actors and productions. Indices.

SOUTHERN, RICHARD
The Victorian Theatre: A Pictorial Survey
Theatre Arts, 1970. 112pp. $8.95. The author describes in simple terms the achievements of theatre in England during the reign of Queen Victoria: 1837—1901. In text and more than 125 illustrations, the distinguishing features of nineteenth century theatre including theatre architecture, methods of scene-changing, actors, and productions are described. Bibliography. Index.

SPEAIGHT, ROBERT
William Poel and The Elizabethan Revival
See Page 94

TAYLOR, JOHN RUSSELL
The Rise and Fall of the Well Made Play
Hill & Wang, 1967. 175pp. $5.75. Paper—1969. 175pp. $1.95. This is a re-examination of the "well made" drama in Britain from the 1870's to the 1960's. Mr. Taylor argues that although plot is in disrepute today, it is one of the constants of drama. The work is a guide to the playwrights of the past one hundred years in Britain. Bibliographical Notes. Index.

TREWIN, J. C.—Editor
The Pomping Folk in the Nineteenth-Century Theatre
Dent, 1968. 230pp. $7.50. This anthology of the English stage in the nineteenth century concentrates on the pomping folk—the actors. Actors, actresses, dramatists and managers, critics, play-goers, historians and novelists, all tell about the stage people of the time and also of the taste and shifting opinions of the century.

VARDAC, A. NICHOLAS
Stage to Screen: Theatrical Method from Garrick to Griffith
See Page 442

WEINTRAUB, STANLEY—Editor
The Yellow Book: Quintessence of the Nineties
Doubleday, 1964. 373pp. Paper $1.45. A selection of works from the famous journal by such contributors as "Max," Henry James, Richard Le Gallienne, H. G. Wells, and W. B. Yeats. Illustrated.

STUDIES OF PLAYWRIGHTS

Baillie, Joanna

CARHART, MARGARET S.
The Life and Work of Joanna Baillie
Archon, 1970. 215pp. $7.50. Originally published in 1923 and now reissued, this is a biography of the Scots dramatist of the late eighteenth and early nineteenth centuries. Her biographer, in assessing her literary influence, concludes that she was "the greatest Scotch dramatist" and that her qualities as a writer—her aesthetic values, her moral tone, her vivid characterization—caused her contemporaries to place her above all women poets save Sappho. Bibliography of Works and References.

Boucicault, Dion (Also See Page 248)

WALSH, TOWNSEND
The Career of Dion Boucicault
Blom, 1967. 224pp. $12.50. A republication of the 1915 study of Dion Boucicault's life and career as an actor, manager, and playwright in the 1800's. Illustrated. Chronological List of Dramatic Works.

Jones, Henry Arthur

CORDELL, RICHARD A.
Henry Arthur Jones and the Modern Drama
Kennikat, 1968. 265pp. $11.00. Originally published in 1932, this is a study of the work of Henry Arthur Jones, nineteenth century playwright, and the state of the drama in England in the nineteenth century. Index.

Pinero, Arthur Wing

DUNKEL, WILBUR DWIGHT
Sir Arthur Pinero
Kennikat, 1967. 142pp. $7.50. Originally published in 1941, this volume is subtitled "A Critical Biography with Letters." Appendices include extracts from the first night reviews of the plays as well as a Bibliographical Note. Illustrated with reproductions of posters, playbills, letters, and a photograph of Pinero. Index.

Robertson, Thomas William

SAVIN, MAYNARD
Thomas William Robertson: His Plays and Stagecraft
Brown University, 1950. 168pp. $4.00. A study of the playwright with chapters on his translations and adaptations, his six successes produced at the Prince of Wales' Theatre, and his social philosophy.

Shelley, Percy Bysshe

CURRAN, STUART
Shelley's "Cenci": Scorpions Ringed with Fire
Princeton, 1970. 298pp. $11.00. A critical and historical exploration of Shelley's tragedy, "The Cenci." Professor Curran assesses its stylistic and structural dependence on the past, scrutinizes the thematic balancing of characters to the patterns of imagery and to the philosophical questions at the core of the tragedy. He analyzes the course of the play's professional stage history in an attempt to determime its indigenous dramatic values. Illustrated. Index.

Tennyson, Alfred Lord

JAPIKSE, CORNELIA G. H.
The Dramas of Alfred Lord Tennyson
Haskell House, 1966. 167pp. $13.25. A study of the dramatic work of the nineteenth century poet and playwright. A history and appreciation of the works, including their sources, other literary versions,

contemporary criticism, and their reflection of the times are provided. Illustrated. Appendices.

Wilde, Oscar

BECKSON, KARL – Editor
Oscar Wilde: The Critical Heritage
Routledge & Kegan Paul, 1970. 434pp. $16.50. A collection of critical reviews of Oscar Wilde's works from 1881 through 1928. The author has provided an Introduction. Bibliography. Index.

ELLMANN, RICHARD – Editor
Oscar Wilde: A Collection of Critical Essays
Prentice–Hall, 1969. 180pp. $5.95. Paper $1.95. Twenty-four critical essays on the life and work of Oscar Wilde. Among the contributors are: William Butler Yeats, Andre Gide, Alfred Douglas, James Joyce, Richard Ellmann, W. H. Auden, Thomas Mann, and Brendan Behan. Chronology of Important Dates. Selected Bibliography.

HARRIS, FRANK
Oscar Wilde
Michigan State University, 1959. 358pp. $7.00. A reprint of the 1916 edition of the biography of Oscar Wilde. Included is an Appendix: "My Memories of Oscar Wilde" by George Bernard Shaw. Index.

HOLLAND, VYVYAN
Oscar Wilde: A Pictorial Biography
Viking, 1960. 144pp. $6.50. The son of the playwright creates, through a unique collection of photographs and commentary, a portrait of his father.

JULLIAN, PHILIPPE
Oscar Wilde
Viking, 1969. 420pp. $7.95. Translated by Violet Wyndham, this is a full-scale biography of Oscar Wilde which won the Prix Femina Vacaresco in France. The author provides a revealing account of Wilde's upbringing and Irish background with portraits of his parents. Among his sources have been the 1962 edition of Wilde's collected letters. Illustrated with photographs and line drawings. Bibliography. Index.

REDMAN, ALVIN – Editor
The Wit and Humor of Oscar Wilde
Dover, 1962. 258pp. Paper $1.50. Originally published in England in 1952 as "The Epigrams of Oscar Wilde," this collection contains over 1,000 epigrams from Wilde's fiction and drama. They are divided into forty-nine categories: men, women, art, life, smoking, youth and age, etc. Bibliography.

SCHWARTZ, GRACE HOROWITZ
The Plays of Oscar Wilde
Monarch, 1965. 117pp. Paper $1.00. A critical guide to four plays with an Introduction on the playwright, critical commentary, essay questions and answers for review, and a Bibliography.

WEINTRAUB, STANLEY – Editor
The Literary Criticism of Oscar Wilde
University of Nebraska, 1968. 253pp. $5.95. Paper $2.25. A collection of Wilde's literary criticism ranging from his reviews from the early 1880's to a piece written in 1897. Professor Weintraub has contributed an introductory essay. Bibliography. Index.

WILDE, OSCAR
The Artist as Critic: Critical Writings of Oscar Wilde
Random House, 1969. 446pp. $10.00. Paper – Vintage, 1970. 446pp. $2.45. A selection of the best of Wilde's critical writings, edited by Richard Ellmann. The volume includes the revised version of "The Portrait of Mr. W. H.," the four essays of "Intentions," reviews, letters to editors, and some of Wilde's trial testimony. Index.

WILDE, OSCAR
The Letters of Oscar Wilde
Harcourt, Brace, 1962. 958pp. $7.95. This is a collection of 1,098 letters written to nearly 300 correspondents. The letters range in time from Wilde's youth in Oxford to the decline of his health and fortune in Paris. They are edited by Rupert Hart-Davis.

Chronological Periods: Twentieth Century

HISTORIES AND CRITIQUES

AGATE, JAMES
The Amazing Theatre
Blom, 1969. 304pp. $12.50. Originally published in 1939 and reissued in a facsimile edition, this is a collection of Mr. Agate's reviews and thoughts on the theatre in London from 1937 through 1939. Among the productions reviewed are the first performance of "Victoria Regina" with Helen Hayes in the leading role and the Old Vic production of "Macbeth" with Laurence Olivier in 1937. Index.

AGATE, JAMES
Immoment Toys
Blom, 1969. 264pp. $9.75. Originally published in 1945 and reissued in a facsimile edition, this is a survey of light entertainment on the London stage 1920–1943. Reviews of musical plays, pantomimes, and reviews are included. Index.

AGATE, JAMES
More First Nights
Blom, 1969. 359pp. $12.50. Originally published in 1937 and reissued in a facsimile edition, this is another collection of the theatre reviews of James Agate. Among the productions reviewed from 1934

through 1937 are John Gielgud's "Hamlet" of 1934, Komisarjevsky's revival of Chekhov's "The Sea Gull," and Rodgers' and Hart's "On Your Toes" in 1937. Index.

AGATE, JAMES
Playgoing : An Essay
Blom, 1969. 83pp. $5.75. Originally published in 1927 and reissued in a facsimile edition, this is an essay by the English dramatic critic on playgoing and play-acting. Mr. Agate compares the great actresses and provides anecdotes of actors and actresses of bygone days.

AGATE, JAMES
Red Letter Nights
Blom, 1969. 382pp. $12.50. Originally published in 1944 and reissued in a facsimile edition, this is a survey of post-Elizabethan drama in actual performance on the London stage, 1921—1943. All of the reviews first appeared in the London "Sunday Times." Among the plays reviewed are revivals of Restoration drama, plays by Ibsen, Shaw, Maugham, Coward, and O'Neill. Index.

AGATE, JAMES
A Short View of the English Stage: 1900—1926
Blom, 1969. 128pp. $6.75. Originally published in 1926 and reissued in a facsimile edition, this is a discussion of various aspects of the theatre in England during the early years of the twentieth century.

BABLET, DENIS
Edward Gordon Craig
Theatre Arts, 1966. 207pp. $7.75. The author has investigated the events of Craig's life, his writings, his designs, and his dealings with other theatre practicioners of his day. The book attempts to disentangle the facts from the legends and describes Craig's great creative period from the 1890's to World War I. Illustrated with photographs and reproductions of Craig's designs. Index.

BAKSHY, ALEXANDER
The Theatre Unbound
Blom, 1969. 124pp. $6.75. First published in 1923, this is, according to the author, "a plea on the behalf of the ill-used" theatre artists trapped by the demands of conventional theatre economics and stage realism. Chapters on the London theatre of the early twentieth century, George Bernard Shaw, and the problems of artistic cinema.

BEERBOHM, MAX
Around Theatres
Taplinger, 1969. 583pp. $6.50. This is a selection of the reviews and criticisms Max Beerbohm wrote for the "Saturday Review" in London from 1898 to 1910. Included among the playwrights reviewed are Shaw, Rostand, Ibsen, Barrie, Yeats, Synge, Wilde, and Henry James. Index of Plays and Books Criticized.

BEERBOHM, MAX
The Bodley Head Beerbohm
Bodley Head, 1970. 390pp. $8.95. Edited and introduced by David Cecil, this is a collection of essays, critiques, and other works by the twentieth century English essayist and caricaturist. Six essays written between 1901 and 1907 and originally collected in "Around Theatres" are included.

BEERBOHM, MAX
Last Theatres
Taplinger, 1970. 553pp. $15.00. Edited by Rupert Hart-Davis, this is a collection of Beerbohm's theatre criticism. The essays offer comments on the great plays, playwrights, and actors of the period from 1904—1910. Frontispiece. Index.

BEERBOHM, MAX
More Theatres
Taplinger, 1969. 624pp. $15.00. This is a collection of Max Beerbohm's drama criticism, edited and with an Introduction by Rupert Hart-Davis. The selections range from 1898 to 1903 and include essays on actors, the art of acting, the state of the theatre, Shakespeare, Shaw, and Ibsen. Index of Plays and Books Criticized.

BISHOP, G.W.
Barry Jackson and the London Theatre
Blom, 1969. 215pp. $12.50. Originally published in 1933 and reissued in a facsimile edition, this is a record of the London manager and producer's achievements in the theatre since the first World War. Among the productions discussed are a "Hamlet" in modern dress, several of Shaw's plays, and "The Barretts of Wimpole Street." An Appendix includes programs of plays presented by Jackson. Illustrated. Index.

BLAKELOCK, DENYS
Round the Next Corner
Gollancz, 1967. 190pp. $5.25. This is the autobiography of the English actor and teacher at London's Royal Academy of Dramatic Art. Mr. Blakelock appeared in some of the most renowned stage productions of the day and throws much light on London theatrical life in the 1920's and '30's. Illustrated with photographs.

BROWN, JOHN RUSSELL—Editor
Modern British Dramatists
Prentice—Hall, 1968. 176pp. $4.95. Paper $1.95. In this volume of critical essays twelve noted theatre critics and scholars, including John Russell Taylor, Martin Esslin, Laurence Kitchin, and Richard Gilman, offer studies of such playwrights as Osborne, Pinter, Wesker, and Arden. They provide insights into the plays and relate them to other plays and playwrights. Chronology. Selected Bibliography.

BROWN, JOHN RUSSELL
Shakespeare's Plays in Performance
See Page 93

BROWN, JOHN RUSSELL and BERNARD HARRIS—Editors
Stratford—Upon—Avon Studies IV: Contemporary Theatre
St. Martin's, 1962. 208pp. $5.75. Nine essays on the modern British theatre by Clifford Leech, G. W. Brandt, Allardyce Nicoll, R. D. Smith, and others. Among the playwrights and topics discussed are Arnold Wesker, Harold Pinter, George Bernard Shaw, verse and prose drama, the Irish theatre, and television drama.

BRYDEN, RONALD
The Unfinished Hero and Other Essays
Faber & Faber, 1969. 242pp. $6.75. This collection of essays covers the years from 1956 to 1966 during which Mr. Bryden has been a theatre and literary critic. The first half of the book is devoted to the theatre and includes reviews of the most important productions staged in England during the period the author was drama critic for "The New Statesman." Also included is a long essay on acting and his study of "Peter Pan." The second half of the volume contains the major book reviews written between 1958 and 1963.

CLINTON—BADDELEY, V. C.
Some Pantomime Pedigrees
Society for Theatre Research, 1963. 38pp. Paper $2.00. A short study of the beginnings, development, and history of some of the standard characters of English pantomime.

COUNSELL, JOHN
Counsell's Opinion
Barrie & Rockliff, 1963. 216pp. $5.00. The director of the Theatre Royal, Windsor, describes his twenty-five years of experience with the theatre.

DEMUTH, AVERIL—Editor
The Minack Open-Air Theatre
David and Charles, 1968. 128pp. $5.25. This is the story of the Minack Theatre which is built into the Cornish cliffs. The contributors to this symposium tell of the hazards and difficulties of producing in such an open air setting and describe many practical aspects, such as lighting and scenery, that will make the book useful for those staging plays in the open anywhere. Illustrated with photographs and a plan of the theatre. A list of productions from 1932 to 1968 is also included.

EPSTEIN, JOHN and LINDSAY DAVIDSON, ROBERT BURNE, REINER BURGER, and DAVID SAWYER
The Black Box: An Experiment in Visual Theatre
Latimer, 1970. 72pp. $7.50. Paper $3.95. The record of the evolution/invention of the Black Box medium which uses film, slides, ghost images, live actors and music. The experiment began with a series of paintings by John Epstein to illustrate a short story and the authors detail the birth-pangs of their group, their difficulties, their differing personal involvement in the medium, and the technical breakthroughs and set-backs they experienced. Illustrated with photographs and diagrams.

GARLAND, MADGE
The Indecisive Decade
MacDonald, 1968. 254pp. $12.00. This is a survey of the world of fashion and entertainment in the 1930's. Architecture and decoration, fashion, theatre and cinema, and painting and sculpture are all covered in separate sections to bring the era of the 1930's in England to life. Illustrated with contemporary photographs and paintings. Index.

GOODWIN, JOHN
Royal Shakespeare Theatre Company
See Page 93

GUTHRIE, TYRONE
A Life in the Theatre
McGraw—Hill, 1959. 357pp. $6.95. Paper $2.45. Sir Tyrone discusses his ideas about plays, players, and the director's art, and recalls famous productions and playwrights.

IRVING, HENRY
The Drama
See Page 412

ISAACS, J.—Editor
William Poel's Prompt-Book of "Fratricide Punished"
Society for Theatre Research, 1956. 35pp. Paper $3.00. This is an edition of William Poel's prompt-book of his English version of "Fratricide Punished" produced in London in 1924. The editor has provided an Introduction to the work of the producer, his achievements, his views on the play, and his treatment of the text. Illustrated with facsimiles of pages of the prompt-book and the stage plans.

KITCHIN, LAURENCE
Mid-Century Drama
Faber & Faber, 1969. 238pp. $8.50. Paper $2.95. Originally published in 1960 and revised in 1962, this is a survey of the English theatre today. The first part consists of a critical appraisal of the most outstanding work of living English playwrights, actors, and producers. The second part is a series of interviews with twenty-three theatrical personalities. Illustrated with photographs. Index.

MacCARTHY, DESMOND
The Court Theatre: 1904—1907
University of Miami, 1966. 182pp. $6.50. Originally published in 1907 and republished with a Foreword and additional material by Stanley Weintraub, this is an appraisal of the Royal Court Theatre under the management of John Vedrenne and Harley Granville-Barker during the era when the nineteenth century star system was abandoned and Shaw's plays were

beginning to win critical and public approval. An Appendix of reprinted first night programs is included.

MacINNES, COLIN
Sweet Saturday Night
See Page 281

MANDER, RAYMOND and JOE MITCHENSON
British Music Hall
See Page 281

MAROWITZ, CHARLES and SIMON TRUSSLER – Editors
Theatre at Work
Hill & Wang, 1968. 191pp. $5.00. This book contains interviews with leading British dramatists and directors of the past decade. They offer an insight into the processes of translating an idea into the script of a play and a script into a live performance. Among the contributors are John Whiting, John Arden, Harold Pinter, Joan Littlewood, Peter Hall, and Peter Brook. Illustrated with photographs. Index.

MARSHALL, AUDREY
Fishbones into Butterflies: A Kind of Remembering
Chatto and Windus, 1964. 221pp. $4.95. An account of the British provincial theatre before World War One, when the author's mother, Lydia Donavan, was one of the most popular heroines of the day. The author's father, Cyril Marshall Fulford, was also a leading performer. Introduction by Dame Sybil Thorndike. Illustrated.

MASON, A.E.W.
Sir George Alexander and the St. James' Theatre
See Page 183

MASTERS, SIMON
The National Youth Theatre
See Page 328

MELLY, GEORGE
Revolt Into Style: The Pop Arts in Britain
See Page 506

MERRYN, ANTHONY – Editor
The Stage Year Book
See Page 9

PHELPS, WILLIAM LYON
The Twentieth Century Theatre
See Page 26

PLAYFAIR, NIGEL
The Story of the Lyric Theatre, Hammersmith
Blom, 1969. 236pp. $12.50. Originally published in 1925 and reissued in a facsimile edition, this is the history of the Lyric Theatre and the plays produced there from 1918 to 1924. Eighteen plates illustrate costume and set designs and theatre posters. Appendix of Programs. Index.

REYNOLDS, ERNEST
Modern English Drama: A Survey of the Theatre from 1900
University of Oklahoma, 1949. 240pp. $3.50. A history of the important dramatic works, trends, and developments that have shaped the British stage. In addition, the playhouses and their equipment, technical experiments, and architecture are studied. Illustrated.

RUCK, S.K.
Municipal Entertainment and the Arts in Greater London
Allen & Unwin, 1965. 191pp. $9.50. After a brief account of how local government came to enter the sphere of entertainment, the author shows what each of the eighty-seven authorities in Greater London spent on entertainment in the year 1960–61. He describes the kind of provision made, and the part played by parks and baths, libraries and museums, arts festivals, evening classes, and Arts Councils. Finally, the author considers what sort of policy there should be behind the provision of public entertainment and what relative parts the new London Boroughs and the Greater London Council should play in this sphere. Illustrated. Bibliography. Index.

RUSSELL, BERTRAND
Portraits from Memory and Other Essays
Simon & Schuster, 1963. 246pp. Paper $1.45. A collection of essays in which the philosopher describes his relationships with some of the most famous men of the century, among them Bernard Shaw, Joseph Conrad, D.H. Lawrence, George Santayana, H.G. Wells, Alfred North Whitehead, and Lord John Russell. Included are six autobiographical sketches.

SHORT, ERNEST
Theatrical Cavalcade
Kennikat, 1970. 224pp. $11.75. Originally published in 1942 and reissued in a facsimile edition, this is a study of the theatre in Britain during the last years of the nineteenth century and the years of the twentieth-century up to 1939. Among the subjects are actors, playwrights such as Shaw, Galsworthy, Barrie, the art and craft of acting, and the plays of the war years from 1909 to 1939. Illustrated. Index.

SPANOS, WILLIAM V.
The Christian Tradition in Modern British Verse Drama
See Page 327

TAYLOR, JOHN RUSSELL
The Angry Theatre: New British Drama
Hill & Wang, 1969. 391pp. $7.50. Paper $3.95. A revised and expanded edition of the study published in 1962. It is a comprehensive look at the movement which has brought forward such dramatists as Osborne, Behan, Pinter, Simpson, Arden, Stoppard, Bond, and Wesker. Chapters on important writers have been

brought up to date and new writers have been added. Illustrated with photographs. Index. Paper bound edition is titled: "Anger and After."

TAYLOR, JOHN RUSSELL
The Rise and Fall of the Well Made Play
See Page 184

TREWIN, J.C.
The Birmingham Repertory Theatre 1913—1963
Barrie & Rockliff, 1963. 272pp. $7.50. A portrait of the founder of the Birmingham Repertory Theatre. The author reviews Sir Barry Jackson's significant productions of "Back to Methusalah," "Abraham Lincoln," "The Immortal Hour," and the trilogy of Shakespeare's "Henry VI" plays. Appendices. Bibliography. Index.

TREWIN, J.C.
Drama in Britain: 1951—1964
Longmans, 1965. 68pp. Paper $1.50. The author discusses the developments in dramatic writing, acting, staging, administration, and events in the West End of London and in the provinces during the period covered in the title. The rise of the National Theatre Company and the Royal Shakespeare Company are also detailed.

TREWIN, J.C.
Shakespeare on the English Stage: 1900—1964
See Page 94

VAN DAMM, SHEILA
We Never Closed
Hale, 1967. 191pp. $4.50. Miss Van Damm tells the story of London's Windmill Theatre. She reveals the behind-the scenes background of its nude tableaux and its variety shows and its stars, including Peter Sellers and Harry Secombe who won their first West End appearances at the Windmill. Illustrated with photographs. Index.

WEALES, GERALD
Religion in Modern English Drama
See Page 327

WILLIAMS, WILLIAM EMRYS—Chairman of the Committee
The Theatre Today in England and Wales
Arts Council of Great Britain, 1970. 79pp. $2.95. This is a report of the Arts Council Theatre Enquiry Committee which sat for two years to "investigate the theatre, both subsidized and non-subsidized, with particular reference to the extent and use of subsidy from all sources; and to recommend how the position should be improved." Among topics examined is the work of the Theatre Investment Fund.

WILSON, SHEILA
The Theatre in the Fifties
Library Association Publications, 1963. 63pp. Paper $2.75. A bibliography dealing with material published between 1950 and 1960 in the field of theatre and drama. The list covers material on theatre in Great Britain primarily, but there are sections on world theatre. Index.

STUDIES OF PLAYWRIGHTS

Arden, John

HAYMAN, RONALD
John Arden
Heinemann, 1968. 77pp. Paper $1.50. This study includes descriptions and critical assessments of all of John Arden's plays. Illustrations of important productions are provided. A Bibliography and a list of productions are also included.

Auden, W.H.

BLAIR, JOHN G.
The Poetic Art of W.H. Auden
Princeton, 1965. 210pp. Paper $1.95. A critical portrait of Auden as the anti-romantic, didactic, and impersonal artist. Professor Blair concentrates his attention on the style and tone of the poet. Bibliographical Note. Lists of Works Cited. Index.

DOBREE, BONAMY and J.W. ROBINSON—Editors
British Writers and Their Work
University of Nebraska, 1965. 158pp. Paper $2.00. A collection of three brief essays: "T.S. Eliot" by M.C. Bradbrook; "W.H. Auden" by Richard Hoggard;" "Dylan Thomas" by G.S. Fraser.

Bagnold, Enid

BAGNOLD, ENID
Enid Bagnold's Autobiography
Little, Brown, 1970. 382pp. $8.95. The autobiography of the English playwright, author of "The Chalk Garden" and seven other plays. Illustrated. Index.

Barrie, J.M.

DUNBAR, JANET
J.M. Barrie: The Man Behind the Image
Houghton Mifflin, 1970. 413pp. $8.95. This biography of the author of "Peter Pan" and other plays is an attempt by the author to understand the playwright in the light of his relationships with four women who influenced his life to a geat degree. Illustrated. Selected Bibliography. Index.

GREEN, ROGER LANCELYN
J.M. Barrie
Walck, 1961. 64pp. $2.75. A short critical account of the life and work of the playwright. Included is a list of Barrie's writings and of books about Barrie. Illustrated with a portrait of Barrie.

WALBROOK, H.M.
J.M. Barrie and the Theatre
Kennikat, 1969. 190pp. $9.00. Originally published in 1922 and now reissued, this is an appreciation of the work of playwright Barrie. Illustrated with drawings by W.W. Lendon. Index.

Bolt, Robert

HAYMAN, RONALD
Robert Bolt
Heinemann, 1969. 88pp. Paper $1.95. The author explores the work of the English playwright. He believes the plays are each stylistically distinct from the rest and this universal diversity is explored in two interviews with the playwright. Illustrated with photographs.

Bridie, James

LUYBEN, HELEN L.
James Bridie: Clown and Philosopher
University of Pennsylvania, 1965. 180pp. $8.00. This critical analysis of twelve plays demonstrates that Bridie was essentially a moralist and that he used religious myth to create a modern morality play. The study includes a defense of Bridie's craftmanship as a dramatist with special attention given to the structure of the plays and the metaphysical use of language. Chronology. Bibliography. Index.

Christie, Agatha

RAMSEY, G.C.
Agatha Christie: Mistress of Mystery
Dodd, Mead, 1967. 124pp. Paper $1.50. This is an appreciation of the novels and short stories of the English writer. Included are sixteen pages of illustrations. Appendices include a list of the books and stories made into films. Index.

Coward, Noel

COWARD, NOEL
The Lyrics of Noel Coward
See Page 294

LEVIN, MILTON
Noel Coward
Twayne, 1968. 158pp. $3.95. A critical study of Coward's writing with detailed analyses of individual titles. A biographical sketch and a brief description of the theatre during the first decades of the twentieth century provide an introduction and then the author devotes the bulk of the study to defining the chief genres Coward has essayed and to discussing major examples. Chronology. Selected Bibliography. Index.

MORLEY, SHERIDAN
A Talent to Amuse
Doubleday, 1969. 453pp. $8.95. This is a biography of Noel Coward: playwright, actor, author, composer, lyricist, and director. The author has interviewed more than 100 people and had access to Coward's own files of clippings, notes, and letters. Illustrated with photographs. Chronology. Bibliography. Index.

Delaney, Shelagh

DELANEY, SHELAGH
Sweetly Sings the Donkey
Putnam, 1963. 186pp. $4.00. A memoir by the author of "A Taste of Honey." In it Miss Delaney writes of growing up in England, of her exposure to success, and of the remarkable assortment of characters she has known.

Denholm, Reginald

DENHOLM, REGINALD
Stars in My Hair
See Page 266

Duncan, Ronald

DUNCAN, RONALD
All Men Are Islands: An Autobiography
Rupert Hart–Davis, 1964. 280pp. $6.95. The poet and playwright describes his life up to the middle of World War II. Ezra Pound has called Duncan "the lone wolf of English letters" and Duncan tells how he has remained true to that description.

HAUETER, MAX WALTER
Ronald Duncan: The Metaphysical Content of His Plays
Rebel Press, 1969. 160pp. Paper $2.95. Published in England, this is an analysis of the intentions of the poet/playwright. The author traces Duncan's thinking through its roots and development as it is reflected in his dramatic work. Bibliography.

Durrell, Lawrence

MOORE, HARRY T. — Editor
The World of Lawrence Durrell
Southern Illinois University, 1962. 239pp. $4.50. A group of seventeen critics and writers have been assembled by Professor Moore to discuss Durrell and his work. Among the essayists are Bonamy Dobree, Henry Miller, George Steiner, and Lionell Trilling. They discuss Durrell's fiction, poetry, plays, and miscellaneous writings. A feature of the book is a series of letters in which Durrell discusses many of the problems of the composition of the "Alexandria Quartet."

WEIGEL, JOHN A.
Lawrence Durrell
Twayne, 1965. 174pp. $3.95. Paper—Dutton, 1966. 174pp. $1.25. A critical study of the novelist, poet, and playwright. Bibliography. Index.

Eliot, T.S.

BRAYBROOKE, NEVILLE — Editor
T.S. Eliot: A Symposium for His Seventieth Birthday
Garnstone Press, 1970. 221pp. $8.75. Originally published in 1958 and now reprinted, this symposium is regarded as an important source book. Some errors of fact in the first edition are corrected in this reprint. Among the fifty contributors are E. Martin Browne, Vincent Cronin, Rose Macaulay, Iris Murdoch, Robert Speaight, and Vernon Watkins. Indices.

BROWNE, E. MARTIN
The Making of a Play: T.S. Eliot's "The Cocktail Party"
Cambridge, 1966. 46pp. Paper $ .95. A critical study of the play by Eliot's producer and friend.

BROWNE, E. MARTIN
The Making of T.S. Eliot's Plays
Cambridge, 1969. 349pp. $9.50. Mr. Browne worked closely with T. S. Eliot on all his plays and directed each of them in their first productions. He tells in detail how each play came to be written, the history of the first productions, and the evolution of the texts. Each play is dealt with separately and there are also chapters dealing with general features of Eliot's plays. Index.

CATTAUI, GEORGES
T.S. Eliot
Funk & Wagnalls, 1968. 128pp. $3.95. Paper $1.95. Translated from the French by Claire Pace and Jean Stewart, this is an analysis of the work of the poet and playwright from the early satirical verse to the late plays. A biographical chapter illuminates the influence of Eliot's background on his development. Bibliography.

DOBREE, BONAMY — Editor
British Writers and Their Work
See Page 189

DONOGHUE, DENIS
The Third Voice
See Page 24

ELIOT, T.S.
Selected Essays
Harcourt, Brace, 1950. 460pp. $7.50. Originally published in 1932 and now revised to include work up to 1950, this is the author's choice among all the prose he has written since 1917. It includes essays on poetic drama, dramatic poetry, and playwrights such as Euripides, Marlowe, Shakespeare, Ford, and Massinger among the thirty-seven selections.

ELIOT, T.S.
The Three Voices of Poetry
Cambridge, 1954. 39pp. Paper $ .75. A study of the mind and heart of the poet at the height of the creative process. Mr. Eliot makes special reference to his own work.

ELIOT, T.S.
To Criticize the Critic
Farrar, Straus, 1965. 189pp. $7.50. Edited by Valerie Eliot, this volume includes eight essays on literature and education. Among the subjects are Ezra Pound's poetry, the aims of education, American literature and the American language, Dante, and the literature of politics.

FRYE, NORTHROP
T.S. Eliot
Oliver & Boyd, 1963. 106pp. Paper $1.75. An introduction to Eliot which attempts to give the central facts about him in chapters which consider the man of letters, the critic, the satiric poet, and the devotional poet and dramatist. Bibliography.

GANNON, PAUL and STEPHEN LEVENSON
T.S. Eliot's "Murder in the Cathedral" and Selected Poems
Monarch, 1965. 108pp. Paper $1.00. A critical commentary on the play with a detailed analysis of the plot, character analyses, review questions and answers, critical commentary, and an Annotated Bibliography. Also included is a general introduction to the poetry and commentary on six major poems.

GEORGE, A.G.
T.S. Eliot: His Mind and Art
Asia Publishing House, 1969. 310pp. $8.50. Originally published in 1962 and revised and rewritten for this edition, this is an analytical study of Eliot as philosopher, religious thinker, critic of society and literature, poet, and playwright. Eliot's poetic technique, dramatic art, his major poems, and all his plays are considered. Bibliography. Index.

HEADINGS, PHILIP R.
T.S. Eliot
Twayne, 1964. 192pp. $3.95. Paper—College and University Press, 1964. 192pp. $2.45. This study views all of Eliot's work as a varied exploration of themes derived from a classical view of the world based on the theology and poetics of Dante.

JONES, D.E.
The Plays of T.S. Eliot
University of Toronto, 1960. 242pp. $4.75. Paper $1.95. The author explores the meaning of each of Eliot's plays in terms of a coherent theatrical production as well as through an exegesis of the text.

KENNER, HUGH
The Invisible Poet: T.S. Eliot
Citadel, 1964. 346pp. Paper $2.65. Mr. Kenner relates Eliot's verse and prose to the systematic anonymity of their creator. The sources of his criticism are revealed, the quality of his poetic procedures are uncovered, and the plays are located in his development. Index.

KENNER, HUGH—Editor
T.S. Eliot: A Collection of Critical Essays
Prentice–Hall, 1962. 210pp. $4.95. Paper $1.95. Essays on all aspects of Eliot's art by Wyndham Lewis, R.P. Blackmur, Allen Tate, Ezra Pound, and others. Chronology. Selected Bibliography.

LAIR, ROBERT L.
A Simplified Approach to T.S. Eliot
Barron, 1968. 117pp. Paper $ .95. Individual discussions, with critical commentary, of all the significant poems, essays, and plays. Also included are a short biography, chronology, and topics for review. Bibliography.

LEVY, WILLIAM TURNER and VICTOR SCHERLE
Affectionately, T.S. Eliot
Lippincott, 1968. 148pp. $4.95. The story of the friendship between an Episcopalian priest and the English poet-playwright from 1947 to 1965. The principle topics, both in correspondence and in their many conversations reported here, are literature and religion. Index.

MASON, W.H.
T.S. Eliot's Murder in the Cathedral
Barnes & Noble, 1962. 73pp. Paper $1.25. This brief study considers the nature of poetic drama, the historical background of the play, the triple theme, the various characters, the use of the chorus, and the verse.

MATTHIESSEN, F.O.
The Achievement of T.S. Eliot: An Essay on the Nature of Poetry, with a Chapter on Eliot's Later Work by C.L. Barber. Third Edition
Oxford, 1959. 248pp. $5.50. Paper $1.95. The first six chapters, published in 1935, deal with the nature of poetry as re-defined by the literary revolt of which Eliot was the prime mover. In the edition of 1947, Matthiessen added two chapters on the plays written up to the War and on "Four Quartets." C.L. Barber has written chapters on Eliot's work since then and on his criticism.

PEARCE, T.S.
T.S. Eliot
Arco, 1969. 160pp. Paper $1.95. A literary critique of Eliot's work. The author believes that Eliot developed new forms and styles while writing complex themes near the boundaries of thought. Illustrated. Bibliography. Index.

SMIDT, KRISTIAN
Poetry and Belief in the Work of T.S. Eliot
Humanities, 1961. 258pp. $7.50. A revised edition of the author's comprehensive examination of Eliot as poet and critic, first published in 1949. The various philosophical stands Eliot has taken are examined and the influence of the philosophy of F.H. Bardley and Henri Bergson is studied.

SMITH, CAROL H.
T.S. Eliot's Dramatic Theory and Practice: From Sweeney Agonistes to The Elder Statesman
Princeton, 1963. 250pp. $7.95. The first study to examine closely the relationship between the changes and development in Eliot's dramatic practice and his artistic and intellectual development. Eliot's conception of the need for order in religion and art is studied in the overtly religious works and in the symbolic plays.

SMITH, GROVER
T.S. Eliot's Poetry and Plays: A Study in Sources and Meanings
University of Chicago, 1956. 342pp. $8.50. Paper $2.45. A study of the creative ideas behind each work and of the literary echoes that enrich the meaning.

TAMBIMUTTU, M.J. and RICHARD MARCH—Editors
T.S. Eliot: A Symposium
Frank Cass, 1965. 259pp. $8.00. First published in 1948, this collection of essays and poems is of particular importance as a source book for the details of Eliot's life as a student and his early career. It is written chiefly by those who knew him, among them W.H. Auden, Edith Sitwell, Conrad Aiken, Mario Praz, and Wyndham Lewis.

TATE, ALLEN—Editor
T.S. Eliot: The Man and His Work
Dell, 1966. 400pp. $6.50. Paper $2.45. A critical evaluation by twenty-six distinguished writers including Bonamy Dobree, Ezra Pound, C. Day Lewis, G. Wilson Knight, Mario Praz, and Robert Speaight. The contributors offer essays in reminiscence and appreciation as well as criticism and illuminations of Eliot's works. Illustrated with photographs.

THOMPSON, ERIC
T.S. Eliot: The Metaphysical Perspective
Southern Illinois University, 1963. 186pp. $4.50. A study of the philosophical ideas behind Eliot's early criticism and of the idea of literature implicit in the criticism and poetry.

UNGER, LEONARD
T.S. Eliot
University of Minnesota, 1961. 48pp. Paper $ .95. A brief study of some of the major themes that appear throughout the poetry and plays. Special attention is given to the peculiarly "American" quality of much of his work.

UNGER, LEONARD
T.S. Eliot, Moments and Patterns
University of Minnesota, 1966. 190pp. Paper $1.95. Originally published in 1956, this volume includes seven essays which provide a cohesive view of the work of the English poet/playwright. Selected Bibliography. Index.

WILLIAMSON, GEORGE
A Reader's Guide to T.S. Eliot
Farrar, Straus, 1966. 270pp. $4.95. Paper $1.95. Originally published in 1953 and now issued in a revised edition. The author provides a poem-by-poem analysis, documenting his analyses with quotes from the poems. The work is arranged in chronological order. Bibliographical Notes. Index.

Fry, Christopher

ROY, EMIL
Christopher Fry
Southern Illinois University, 1968. 179pp. $4.95. Mr. Roy discusses Fry's sources, his imagery, and his relationship to theatrical traditions. With a chapter on each play, he shows how Fry has contributed to the modern theatre with his variety of dramatic techniques. Notes. Index.

Galsworthy, John

BARKER, DUDLEY
The Man of Principle
Stein & Day, 1970. 240pp. Paper $2.45. Originally published in 1969 and now reissued, this is a biography of John Galsworthy, English novelist and playwright. Bibliography. Index.

WILSON, ASHER B. – Editor
John Galsworthy's Letters to Leon Lion
Humanities, 1968. 223pp. $9.25. An annotated edition of letters written by Galsworthy to Lion over a period of eleven years from 1921 to 1932. The letters concern negotiations for revivals of Galsworthy's plays and give extensive listings of actors who were considered for parts in the plays, with text indicating the previous training of these actors, and suggestions for the production of the plays. Bibliography.

Golding, William

KINKEAD–WEEKES, MARK and IAN GREGOR
William Golding: A Critical Study
Faber & Faber, 1970. 257pp. Paper $2.75. Originally published in 1967 and now reissued, this is a study of the novels of William Golding, author of the play "The Brass Butterfly." Among the novels discussed is "Lord of the Flies."

Granville–Barker, Harley

MORGAN, MARGERY M.
A Drama of Political Man: A Study in the Plays of Harley Granville–Barker
Sidgwick & Jackson, 1961. 337pp. $6.50. This first comprehensive assessment of Granville-Barker's dramaturgy traces the development of his mind and art, using all the available published and unpublished materials, including five early plays and drafts of an unfinished play, composed between 1911 and 1914. Bibliography. Index.

Greene, Graham

ALLOT, KENNETH and MIRIAM FARRIS
The Art of Graham Greene
Russell & Russell, 1963. 253pp. $10.50. A reprint of the work first published in 1951, this is an analysis of the novels and entertainments from "The Man Within" to "The Heart of the Matter." The authors are concerned with refuting the charges that Greene's work is morbid and melodramatic.

DE VITIS, A.A.
Graham Greene
Twayne, 1964. 165pp. Paper $1.95. This study concentrates on Greene's use of religious belief and subject matter in his works and shows how his thought is developed out of his preoccupation with love, compassion, and belief.

EVANS, ROBERT O. – Editor
Graham Greene: Some Critical Considerations
University of Kentucky, 1963. 286pp. $5.50. Paper $2.75. A collection of fourteen essays on aspects of Greene's art. A comprehensive Bibliography of works by Greene and of criticism of them published up to 1963 is included.

LODGE, DAVID
Graham Greene
Columbia, 1966. 48pp. Paper $1.00. A critical study which also lists Greene's principal works and has a selected list of critical works and biographies.

Hardy, Thomas

ROBERTS, MARGUERITE
Hardy's Poetic Drama and the Theatre
Pageant, 1965. 110pp. $3.00. A study of Thomas Hardy's two works of poetic drama, "The Dynasts" and "The Famous Tragedy of the Queen of Cornwall." Dr. Roberts covers the background of the creation of the two plays and includes a critical analysis of their content and a history of their productions.

Lessing, Doris

BREWSTER, DOROTHY
Doris Lessing
Twayne, 1965. 173pp. $3.95. The first full-length study of the stories, personal narratives, and plays. The remote world of colonial Africa and the nearer world of British society are examined as controlling influences on Miss Lessing's work. Bibliography. Index.

Maugham, William Somerset

BARNES, RONALD E.
The Dramatic Comedy of William Somerset Maugham
Mouton, 1968. 190pp. $7.50. This study analyzes Maugham's strategy in his use of comedy. Eleven of the plays provide the nucleus for this analysis. Plot outlines are included as the author explores Maugham's attitude toward elements of society, his development of the comic aspect with that of the dramatic, and his concern with the inadequacy of society's moral structure. Bibliography.

BRANDER, LAURENCE
Somerset Maugham: A Guide
Oliver & Boyd, 1963. 220pp. Paper $3.25. A chronological survey of all of Maugham's works. The works are related to the personal and social background. Maugham's themes and the development of his techniques are examined. Bibliography. Index.

BROWN, IVOR
Somerset Maugham
A. S. Barnes, 1970. 85pp. $2.95. A profile and biography of the playwright. Included are a chronology and a list of publications. Illustrated with photographs. Selected Bibliography.

CORDELL, RICHARD A.
Somerset Maugham: A Biographical and Critical Study
Indiana University, 1961. 274pp. $5.95. A detailed study of Maugham's life from his medical school days to his last years at Villa Mauresque. Examinations of all the stories, novels, essays, plays, and autobiographical works are included. Illustrated.

CORDELL, RICHARD A.
Somerset Maugham: A Writer for All Seasons
Indiana University, 1969. 308pp. $6.95. Originally published in 1961 and now revised and brought up to date to include Maugham's last years and death, this is a detailed biographical and critical study of the English novelist and playwright. Detailed accounts of all the stories, novels, essays, plays, and autobiographical writings are included. Illustrated. Bibliography. Index.

KANIN, GARSON
Remembering Mr. Maugham
Atheneum, 1966. 314pp. $5.95. A portrait of Somerset Maugham by his friend, the famous playwright-director. The author made notes while his conversations were fresh and the book takes the form of a non-chronological journal and an informal series of impressions. Index.

MAUGHAM, ROBIN
Somerset and All the Maughams
New American Library, 1966. 270pp. $5.95. Paper $ .95. Not merely a biography, but an examination of the whole Maugham family and its heritage, particularly the gifted Frederic Herbert, a Lord Chancellor of England. The conflicting strains in Maugham's personality are studied. Twenty-four pages of illustrations are included in the volume. Notes. Appendices. Index.

MAUGHAM, W. SOMERSET
The Summing Up
Pocket Books, 1967. 230pp. Paper $ .95. Originally published in 1938 and now reissued, this is Maugham's personal testament and a distillation of his wisdom.

NAIK, M. K.
W. Somerset Maugham
University of Oklahoma, 1966. 222pp. $5.95. A critical study of all of Maugham's work from 1897 to the present. The author's conclusion is that Maugham left nothing of lasting creative achievement because of a deep-seated conflict between cynicism and humanitarianism. Mr. Naik traces this conflict throughout Maugham's writings in a complete critical analysis of the works. A Bibliography of works is included. Appendices. Index.

NICHOLS, BEVERLEY
A Case of Human Bondage
Secker & Warburg, 1966. 153pp. $4.25. The author purports to give the account of the break-up of the Maugham marriage.

Osborne, John

BANHAM, MARTIN
Osborne
Oliver & Boyd, 1969. 109pp. $3.95. Paper $1.95. This is an introduction to the plays of John Osborne. Six chapters of the volume are devoted to the thirteen plays presented in London between 1956 and 1968. A general introduction to the playwright's work and critical comments are also included. References. List of First Productions of the Plays. Select Bibliography.

CARTER, ALAN
John Osborne
Oliver & Boyd, 1969. 194pp. $10.95. A study of the English playwright. The volume is a detailed survey of all of Osborne's plays including the two latest: "Time Present" and "Hotel in Amsterdam." A biographical account of the playwright is also included. Appendices. Bibliography. Index.

HAYMAN, RONALD
John Osborne
Heinemann, 1968. 80pp. Paper $1.50. In this study, Mr. Hayman describes and critically assesses all of John Osborne's plays. There is a Bibliography and list of productions together with Illustrations of scenes from four of the plays.

TAYLOR, JOHN RUSSELL – Editor
Look Back in Anger: A Casebook
Macmillan, 1968. 206pp. $5.00. Paper $2.50. A selection of critical essays on John Osborne's plays. The volume includes a selection of early reviews, a selection of writings by Osborne, and a section on "Anger and Commitment." Contributors include Lindsay Anderson, Arthur Miller, Kenneth Tynan, and Arthur Wesker. Bibliography. Index.

TRUSSLER, SIMON
The Plays of John Osborne: An Assessment
Gollancz, 1969. 252pp. $6.95. Paper $3.95. A critical study of Osborne's twelve plays. Each plays is studied in a separate chapter and the author provides a full analysis of the characterization, language, themes, and theatrical techniques, as well as a personal interpretation of the work. Included is a Bibliography of works by the playwright and critical writings about the works. Cast lists of original productions are also provided.

Pinter, Harold

ESSLIN, MARTIN
The Peopled Wound: The Work of Harold Pinter
Doubleday, 1970. 270pp. $5.95. Paper $1.45. A study of the work of the English dramatist written with the assistance of the playwright himself. The author provides a Chronology, a chapter on Pinter's background and basic premises, a chapter on his use of language, an overall evaluation and an analysis of each of the works including the poetry and the screenplays. Bibliography. Index.

GORDON, LOIS G.
Strategems to Uncover Nakedness: The Dramas of Harold Pinter
University of Missouri, 1969. 63pp. Paper $1.50. This is a study of the plays from "The Room" in 1957 to "The Homecoming" in 1965.

HAYMAN, RONALD
Harold Pinter
Heinemann, 1968. 80pp. Paper $1.50. In this study of the English playwright, Ronald Hayman sees his plays as "one-man forays into the unarticulated and irrational no-man's-land inside the modern Everyman." All of Pinter's plays, including those written for television are discussed. Illustrated with photographs. Bibliography.

HOLLIS, JAMES R.
Harold Pinter: The Poetics of Silence
Southern Illinois University, 1970. 143pp. $4.95. The primary focus of this study is Pinter's relationship to and utilization of language. Hollis investigates the playwright's use of the metaphor of the room and the increasing intensity of Pinter's use of man's anxious search for himself and for the meaning back of the silence. Eleven major plays written between 1957 and 1969 are analyzed. Among these plays are: "The Room," "The Birthday Party," "A Slight Ache," "The Caretaker," "The Homecoming," and "Silence" and "Landscape." A Preface has been provided by Harry T. Moore, Professor at Southern Illinois University. Notes. Bibliography. Index.

KERR, WALTER
Harold Pinter
Columbia, 1967. 48pp. Paper $1.00. Mr. Kerr's thesis in this critical study is that Harold Pinter does not simply content himself with stating existentialist themes inside familiar forms of playmaking but he remakes the play altogether so that it will function according to existentialist principle. List of Published Plays. Bibliography.

KLEINMAN, NEIL and RICHARD WASSON – Editors
Pinter's Optics
Depot Press, 1967. 8pp. Paper $ .50. A short monograph on Harold Pinter's plays.

TAYLOR, JOHN RUSSELL
Harold Pinter
Longmans, 1969. 31pp. Paper $1.25. This introduction to the work of the playwright traces the development of the writing from the so-called comedy of menace to the later plays exploring the questions of personal identity. Select Bibliography.

Priestley, J. B.

EVANS, GARETH LLOYD
J. B. Priestley: The Dramatist
Heinemann, 1964. 230pp. $6.50. The author relates Priestley's time plays to his comedies and to his sociological plays. Bibliography. Index.

Shaw, George Bernard

Biographies and Studies

ABBOTT, ANTHONY S.
Shaw and Christianity
Seabury, 1965. 228pp. $4.95. A full-length study of Shaw's role as a critic of religion. The author seeks to present Shaw's attitudes through six of the plays. He considers the major religious themes in each plays, shows their relationship to one another, and comments on the significance of each in Shaw's development as an artist. Selected Bibliography. Index.

ADAM, RUTH
What Shaw Really Said
Schocken, 1966. 176pp. $4.00. An organized statement of Shaw's main ideas—the chapter headings include: Socialism, Sex and Marriage, War, Doctors, Bringing Up Children, and The Theatre. Mrs. Adam sketches in the background of his more outrageous pronouncements and summarizes his best known works. Index.

BENTLEY, ERIC
Bernard Shaw
New Directions, 1957. 256pp. Paper $1.95. A revised and amended edition of the book first published in 1947. This study treats of Shaw's politics, his religious opinions, his chief plays, and their themes as they are related to the whole pattern of the Shavian life.

BOXILL, ROGER
Shaw and the Doctors
Basic Books, 1969. 199pp. $5.95. Mr. Boxill examines Shaw's views on doctors and medicine. Notes. List of Works Consulted. Index.

BROWN, G. E.
George Bernard Shaw
Evans, 1970. 160pp. $3.50. Paper $1.95. Published in England, this study attempts to set Shaw against the theatrical background of his time. The author examines such topics as Shaw's reforming plays, Shaw and evolution, Shaw and religion, Shaw's humor, and his style. He assesses Shaw's stagecraft with the idea that the plays were written to be performed and not simply as exercises in literature. Illustrated. Reading List. Index.

BROWN, IVOR
Shaw in His Time
Nelson, 1965. 212pp. $6.00. Not a biography, but rather a study of the man as a product of the various periods in which he lived. The career of the playwright is traced from his early days of failure and poverty to his sucess as a journalist and spokesman for the new drama. Illustrated.

CHAPPELOW, ALLAN
Shaw – The Chucker Out
Allen & Unwin, 1969. 558pp. $10.95. This is a selection from Bernard Shaw's writings giving his own views on many controversial topics. Mr. Chappelow has selected, edited and arranged these views, with commentary where necessary, to present an appreciation and understanding of Shaw's personality. Illustrated. Index.

CHAPPELOW, ALLAN – Editor
Shaw the Villager and Human Being: A Biographical Symposium
Macmillan, 1962. 354pp. $10.00. A series of intimate, authentic and amusing impressions and reminiscences by those who knew Shaw in the moments when he was not living his "public figure" role.

CHESTERTON, G. K.
George Bernard Shaw
Hill & Wang, 1956. 190pp. Paper $ .95. A reprint of the work first published in 1910, this is a literary portrait that studies the three major influences on Shaw: his Irish background, his puritanism, and his progressive outlook.

COOLIDGE, OLIVIA
George Bernard Shaw
Houghton, Mifflin, 1968. 227pp. $3.95. Miss Coolidge describes the life of the Irish playwright and takes a fresh look at his wit and humor. Illustrated with photographs.

COSTELLO, DONALD P.
The Serpent's Eye: Shaw and the Cinema
University of Notre Dame, 1965. 209pp. $6.50. This study of Shaw's interest in the theory and practice of film shows the social-revolutionary theory that Shaw held and how that theory often led to disaster in the actual making of films from his plays. The relationship with Gabriel Pascal is examined in detail. Illustrated with forty stills from the films. Index.

CROMPTON, LOUIS
Shaw the Dramatist
University of Nebraska, 1969. 261pp. $7.95. The author's intention has been to write a general introduction to Shavian drama and to elucidate Shaw's major plays through a consideration of their social, philosophical, and historical backgrounds. Professor Crompton devotes a chapter to each of the eleven most popular plays.

DIETRICH, R. F.
Portrait of the Artist as a Young Superman: A Study of Shaw's Novels
University of Florida, 1969. 197pp. $7.50. The author contends in this study that Shaw worked out in the private art of his youthful novels the basic design of his public future. He reads the novels as an autobiography of the artist's mind showing how Shaw experimentally created the person he became. Illustrated with two photographs. Bibliography.

FROMM, HAROLD
Bernard Shaw and the Theatre in the Nineties
University of Kansas, 1967. 234pp. $5.00. In this study of Shaw's dramatic criticism, the author provides a picture of a major era in British theatre and throws light on Shaw's methods as a dramatist. Notes. Bibliography. Index.

GIBBS, A. M.
Shaw
Oliver & Boyd, 1969. 120pp. $3.95. Paper $1.95. This is a critical interpretation and assessment of the plays of George Bernard Shaw. Particular emphasis is placed upon the early and middle periods of Shaw's career. References. Bibliography.

HUGGETT, RICHARD
The Truth About "Pygmalion"
Random House, 1970. 195pp. $6.95. An account of the months before and after the premiere of Shaw's play, "Pygmalion." Mr. Huggett reconstructs the witticisms and temperaments of the principals involved, including Shaw, Mrs. Patrick Campbell and Sir Beerbohm Tree, from letters, diaries, contemporary press reports, and reminiscences of surviving members of the original company. Illustrated with drawings and photographs. Index.

KAUFMANN, R. J.—Editor
G. B. Shaw: A Collection of Critical Essays
Prentice—Hall, 1965. 182pp. $4.95. Paper $1.95. Essays by Brecht, Erik H. Erikson, Richard Ohmann, Bruce Park, G. Wilson Knight, Louis Crompton, T. R. Henn, Irving Fish, and others.

KAYE, JULIAN B.
Bernard Shaw and the Nineteenth-Century Tradition
University of Oklahoma, 1959. 222pp. $4.00. In an effort to explain the wrong headedness of Shaw's views of public events after the first World War, the author analyzes the influence of nineteenth century thought, especially romanticism, on the playwright.

KOZELKA, PAUL
A Glossary to the Plays of Bernard Shaw
Teachers College, 1959. 55pp. $1.75. A handbook for students to help them understand certain words and expressions which are uniquely Shavian or peculiarly British. Definitions of 862 words and phrases are included with play and scene noted.

MATTHEWS, JOHN F.
George Bernard Shaw
Columbia, 1969. 48pp. Paper $1.00. A short study of of the English playwright.

MAYNE, FRED
The Wit and Satire of Bernard Shaw
St. Martin's, 1967. 154pp. $6.95. Mr. Mayne provides a discussion of Shaw's political and sociological thoughts as they appear in his plays. These thoughts are treated only in so far as they are relevant to techniques of wit. Bibliography. Index.

MEISEL, MARTIN
Shaw and the Nineteenth Century Theater
Princeton, 1968. 477pp. Paper $3.45. A reprinting of the 1963 study in which Mr. Meisel presents Shaw as a dramatic resurrectionist, one who breathed life into nineteenth century drama and preserved the conventions and techniques of that day. He analyzes the relationship of Shaw's plays to the popular drama of his predecessors and recreates the stage of Boucicalut and the Adelphi. Illustrated. Bibliography. Index.

MILLS, JOHN A.
Language and Laughter: Comic Diction in the Plays of Bernard Shaw
University of Arizona, 1969. 176pp. $6.50. Mr. Mills examines and evaluates the devices Shaw used to exploit the comic possibilities of language. Notes. List of Works Cited. Index.

MINNEY, R. J.
Recollections of George Bernard Shaw
Prentice—Hall, 1969. 211pp. $7.95. Mr. Minney traces Shaw's career through the eyes of those who knew and loved him to gain new perspectives on his private thoughts and public pronouncements. Illustrated with a frontispiece. Index.

NETHERCOT, ARTHUR
Men and Supermen: The Shavian Portrait Gallery
Blom, 1966. 327pp. $12.50. A corrected second edition of the 1954 publication in which the author describes the entire gallery of Shavian characters. The literary sources and live models on which Shaw drew are also described. Appendix on Shaw's use of proper names. Index.

NICKSON, RICHARD
G. B. Shaw's Arms and the Man
Monarch, 1966. 72pp. Paper $1.00. A critical guide to the play with complete background, plot discussion, theme development, character analysis, critical commentary, typical essay questions and answers, and a Bibliography.

NICKSON, RICHARD
G. B. Shaw's Candida
Monarch, 1966. 78pp. Paper $1.00. A critical guide

to the play with complete background, plot discussion, theme development, character analysis, critical commentary, typical essay questions and answers, and a Bibliography.

NICKSON, RICHARD
G. B. Shaw's Man and Superman
Monarch, 1965. 112pp. Paper $1.00. A critical guide to the play providing complete background, plot discussion, theme development, character analysis, critcal commentary, typical essay questions and answers, and a Bibliography.

NOURSE, JOAN THELLUSSON
G. B. Shaw's Major Barbara
Monarch, 1965. 128pp. Paper $1.00. A critical guide to the play providing complete background, plot discussion, theme development, character analysis, critical commentary, typical essay questions and answers, and a Bibliography.

O'DONOVAN, JOHN
Shaw and the Charlatan Genius
Dolmen Press, 1965. 160pp. $4.50. The story of the "menage a trois" in which George Bernard Shaw was brought up in his native Dublin. This menage consisted of Shaw's parents and a singing teacher named George Vandeleur Lee. The author includes much hitherto unpublished material including eighteen photographs and reproductions of documents. Index.

OHMANN, RICHARD M.
Shaw: The Style and the Man
Wesleyan University, 1962. 200pp. $5.00. A study of Shaw's language and style which uses the methods of new linguistic studies to discover the relation between personality, thought, and expression.

PASCAL, VALERIE
The Disciple and His Devil
See Page 449

PEARSON, HESKETH
George Bernard Shaw: His Life and Personality
Atheneum, 1963. 480pp. Paper $1.95. A reprint of the 1942 edition, this is a biography of the playwright. Shaw, himself, collaborated with the author and supplied what he describes as "unique private history," correcting and checking facts. The concluding section of this edition was originally published separately.

PURDOM, C. B.
A Guide to the Plays of Bernard Shaw
Crowell, 1965. 344pp. $4.95. Paper $1.75. A brief account of the life of Shaw and a critical essay on the plays, followed by a complete survey of the plays from 1885 to 1947. Scene-by-scene descriptions of the action, a full list of characters, notes on the original and subsequent productions, and hints to future producers are provided.

ROCKMAN, ROBERT
The Plays of G. B. Shaw
Monarch, 1964. 94pp. Paper $1.00. A critical guide to the twelve plays of Shaw with an Introduction, plot discussion, theme development, character analysis, critical commentary, essay questions and answers for review, and a Bibliography.

SCHWARTZ, GRACE HOROWITZ
G. B. Shaw's Caesar and Cleopatra
Monarch, 1965. 86pp. Paper $1.00. A critical guide to the play with complete background, plot discussion, theme development, character analysis, critical commentary, typical essay questions and answers, and a Bibliography.

SCHWARTZ, GRACE HOROWITZ
George Bernard Shaw's Pygmalion
Monarch, 1965. 90pp. Paper $1.00. A critical guide to the play providing a short introduction to phonetics, a guide to the structure of the play with analysis and commentary, character analyses, critical commentary on the playwright, essay questions and answers for review, and a Bibliography.

SCHWARTZ, GRACE HOROWITZ
Shaw's Saint Joan
Monarch, 1965. 105pp. Paper $1.00. A critical guide to the play providing an Introduction, detailed scene-by-scene commentary, character analyses, critical commentary, essay questions and answers for review, and a Bibliography.

SHENFIELD, MARGARET
Bernard Shaw: A Pictorial Biography
Viking, 1962. 144pp. $5.95. A pictorial biography covering the people, places, events, manuscripts, and letters of the playwright's career. Included are 128 gravure Illustrations.

SMITH, J. PERCY
The Unrepentant Pilgrim: A Study of the Development of Bernard Shaw
Houghton, Mifflin, 1965. 274pp. $4.95. The author challenges the usual conceptions about Shaw's blustering personality and shows that the man was a shy and self-doubting individual with a serious religious conviction. Professor Smith details the varied careers that Shaw pursued before his success as a playwright. Shaw's Socialism is seen as a prelude to conversion to a religious attitude toward life and society. Index.

SMITH, WARREN S. – Editor
Bernard Shaw's Plays
Norton, 1970. 494pp. Paper $3.00. A critical edition of four plays by Shaw. The volume includes backgrounds and criticism on the playwright and the plays by such authorities as Harold Clurman, John Gassner, and Stanley Weintraub. The plays are: "Heartbreak House," "Saint Joan," "Too True to be Good," and "Major Barbara." Selected Bibliography.

STANTON, STEPHEN – Editor
A Casebook on Candida
Crowell, 1962. 292pp. Paper $3.50. The text of the play with samplings from Shaw's other writings that illuminate the themes, sources, and critical reaction to the work.

WARD, A. C.
Bernard Shaw
Longmans, 1966. 59pp. Paper $1.25. A revised edition of the 1950 study of Shaw's writing career and, in particular, his dramatic works. List of First Performances of the Plays. Selected Bibliography. Index of Miscellaneous Essays.

WATSON, BARBARA BELLOW
A Shavian Guide to the Intelligent Woman
Norton, 1964. 250pp. $6.00. Drawing on the plays, the comments on politics and economics, and on letters to women, this book examines Shaw's views on women in love, in marriage, in divorce, and in practical affairs.

WEATHERFORD, RICHARD M.
A Simplified Approach to Pygmalion
Barron, 1968. 77pp. Paper $ .95. A scene-by-scene summary with commentary, detailed analyses and interpretations. Included are sources, character sketches, essays on Shaw as playwright, comic writer, social critic, and language reformer. Selected critiques. Study questions. Bibliography.

WEINTRAUB, STANLEY
Private Shaw and Public Shaw: A Dual Portrait of Lawrence of Arabia and G. B. S.
Braziller, 1963. 302pp. $5.00. The first full account of the thirteen years of friendship between Shaw and T. E. Lawrence. During this time the author contends that Lawrence became a source of inspiration to the playwright and an object of paternal affection while Shaw became for Lawrence a trusted literary adviser and loyal friend.

WEINTRAUB, STANLEY – Editor
Shaw: An Autobiography 1856 – 1898
Reinhardt, 1970. 336pp. $10.00. Selected from Shaw's own writings (prefaces, reviews, speeches, and other sources) this is a biography of the first half of the playwright's life. Illustrated. Notes. List of Sources. Index.

WILLIAMSON, AUDREY
Bernard Shaw: Man and Writer
Collier, 1963. 224pp. $4.95. A biography of the playwright from his Dublin childhood to his death. The plays are evaluated and the influences of his personal relationships on his work are analyzed. Illustrated.

WILSON, COLIN
Bernard Shaw: A Reassessment
Atheneum, 1969. 306pp. $6.95. Part biography, part critical study, this is an appraisal of the legend and the reality of the Shaw persona. The author devotes much thought to Shaw's formative years between twenty and thirty and also attempts to show how Shaw's success at fifty affected his later career. Index.

WINSTEN, STEPHEN
Days with Bernard Shaw
Vanguard, 1949. 327pp. $3.75. Personal reminiscences by a neighbor of Shaw's at Ayot Saint Lawrence. Also included are Shaw's own comments on many subjects. Illustrated.

WOODBRIDGE, HOMER E.
G. B. Shaw: Creative Artist
Southern Illinois University, 1963. 181pp. $4.50. Paper $1.65. A study of the playwright which concentrates on his mastery of the arts of rhetoric and on the brilliance and clarity of his style. The effects of Shaw's involvement with political and social issues on his creative powers and on his playwriting are examined in detail. Included is a Preface by the authority on modern writers, Professor Harry T. Moore. Index.

ZIMBARDO, ROSE – Editor
Twentieth Century Interpretations of "Major Barbara"
Prentice–Hall, 1970. 124pp. $4.95. Paper $1.25. A collection of critical essays by eleven authorities. The essays range from Joseph Frank's comparison of the play with Dante's "Divine Comedy" to Donald Costello's account of the film version of the play. Chronology of Important Dates. Selected Bibliography.

Non–Dramatic Writings

GEDULD, HARRY M – Editor
The Rationalization of Russia
Indiana University, 1964. 134pp. $3.95. The unfinished and hitherto unpublished book based on Shaw's trip to the Soviet Union in 1931. There is a satirical exposition of the history of European capitalism and a critique of modern international banking and stock exchange transactions. Also included is an ideological continuity between the ideas found here and the plays: "Too True to Be Good" and "The Simpleton of the Unexpected Isles." Introduction by the editor.

LAURENCE, DAN H. – Editor
Bernard Shaw: Collected Letters 1874 – 1897
Dodd, Mead, 1965. 877pp. $12.50. The first in a planned series of four volumes. The present volume covers the period from Shaw's eighteenth year when he was a land agent's clerk in Dublin, through his Socialist and journalist apprenticeship in London, to the eve of his emergence as a playwright. Included are 700 letters to 170 correspondents. Illustrated. Index.

LAURENCE, DAN H. – Editor
How to Become a Musical Critic
Hill & Wang, 1961. 359pp. $5.00. Paper $2.45. A survey of Shaw's hitherto unreprinted opinions of music, covering the period 1876–1950. Shaw's earliest criticisms are included, as well as more than a dozen uncollected "Corno di Bassetto" contributions to "The Star." Introduction by the editor.

LAURENCE, DAN H. – Editor
Platform and Pulpit
Hill & Wang, 1961. 302pp. $5.00. The full text of more than thirty of Shaw's formal lectures, extemporary speeches, and debates, covering the period from 1885 to 1946, and including all the favorite Shavian subjects.

LAURENCE, DAN H. – Editor
Selected Non-Dramatic Writings of Bernard Shaw
Houghton, Mifflin, 1965. 455pp. $3.75. Paper $2.25. These writings include "An Unusual Socialist," "The Quintessence of Ibsenism," and various other essays.

MATTHEWS, JOHN – Editor
Shaw's Dramatic Criticism – 1895 – 1898
Hill & Wang, 1959. 306pp. Paper $1.45. A collection of approximately one-third of the 151 weekly theatre pieces Shaw wrote during his term as critic for "The Saturday Review" (January, 1895 through May,1898). Shaw's reaction to his predecessors, the work of his contemporaries, and the technical aspects of the theatre are covered.

ST. JOHN, CHRISTOPHER – Editor
Ellen Terry and Bernard Shaw: A Correspondence
Theatre Arts, 1949. 434pp. $6.45. This correspondence covers thirty years of letter writing between the actress and the playwright. Photographs. Index.

SHAW, BERNARD
Our Theatre in the Nineties
Constable, 1954. Volume One: 288pp. Volume Two: 292pp. Volume Three: 420pp. Three volume set: $17.95. An edition of the theatre critiques contributed to "The Saturday Review" from 1895 to 1898.

SHAW, BERNARD
The Quintessence of Ibsenism: Now Completed to the Death of Ibsen
Hill & Wang, 1957. 188pp. Paper $ .95. Originally written as a lecture for the Fabian Society on the theme of socialism in contemporary literature, this book developed into an analysis of the meaning of Ibsen's themes and their relevance to modern life.

SMITH, WARREN SYLVESTER – Editor
The Religious Speeches of Bernard Shaw
Penn State University, 1963. 104pp. $5.00. The first collection of the eleven speeches given by Shaw between 1906 and 1937 dealing with religious matters. Among the items discussed are Shaw's brand of "mysticism," religion and science, and religion and war. Foreword by Arthur H. Nethercot.

SMITH, WARREN SYLVESTER – Editor
Shaw on Religion
Dodd, Mead, 1967. 240pp. $5.00. Paper $1.95. The editor has chosen over two dozen extracts from Shaw's writings on religion, arranged them chronologically, identified each with introductory notes, and related them to the theological and philosophical discussions of our day. Included are three essays unpublished by Shaw.

TOMPKINS, PETER – Editor
To a Young Actress: The Letters of Bernard Shaw to Molly Tompkins
Potter, 1960. 192pp. $5.00. Letters written by Shaw to the young American actress between the years 1921–1949. Shaw's friendship with the actress and his constant stream of advice to her is documented in these photographic reproductions of the letters. An Introduction clarifies obscure references in the texts and deciphers difficult passages. Illustrated.

WARD, A. C. – Editor
Plays and Players: Essays on the Theatre
Oxford, 1952. 350pp. Paper $2.25. A selection from the three volumes of "Our Theatre in the Nineties," this volume contains forty essays chosen to provide a representative cross-section of English theatre history in the 1890's.

WEST. E. J. – Editor
Advice to a Young Critic and Other Letters
Putnam, 1960. 208pp. Paper $1.45. These letters were written to Reginald Golding Bright from 1884 to 1928. A great number include Shaw's observations on his own plays, their productions, and the theories behind their composition. The editor has provided notes on the letters and an Introduction.

WEST, E. J. – Editor
Shaw on Theatre
Hill & Wang, 1958. 306pp. $3.95. Paper $1.75. Letters and speeches and articles written over a period of sixty years. They constitute Shaw's only book on dramatic art and theory as such.

WILSON, EDWIN – Editor
Shaw on Shakespeare
Dutton, 1961. 284pp. $4.50. Paper $1.75. All the significant Shakespeare material, including over twenty reviews of productions, letters to Ellen Terry, Mrs. Patrick Campbell, and John Barrymore on playing Shakespeare, the essay "Better than Shakespeare," and other articles. Introduction by the editor.

WINSTEN, STEPHEN – Editor
The Wit and Wisdom of Bernard Shaw
Collier, 1962. 415pp. Paper $1.50. A collection of

essays and epigrams taken from the plays, prefaces, personal letters, and other sources. This edition was originally published as "The Quintessence of GBS" in 1949. Bibliography.

Sherriff, R. C.

SHERRIFF, R. C.
No Leading Lady: An Autobiography
Gollancz, 1968. 352pp. $7.50. Mr. Sheriff tells of the events that led to the writing of "Journey's End" and of what happened afterwards. He details his life in Hollywood as the movie industry's highest paid script writer and his work on such films as "The Invisible Man" and "Goodbye Mr. Chips."

Thomas, Dylan

ACKERMAN, JOHN
Dylan Thomas: His Life and Work
Oxford, 1964. 201pp. $5.75. This study examines the extent to which Thomas' poetry and prose were influenced by the Welsh environment and both the Anglo-Welsh and English literary traditions. Index.

BRINNIN, JOHN MALCOLM
A Casebook on Dylan Thomas
Crowell, 1960. 322pp. $4.95. Paper $3.25. This book presents ten major poems, and a collection of thirty-four essays which analyzes the poems in terms of their individual merit and their relation to the whole body of the poet's work. Bibliography. Index.

BRINNIN, JOHN MALCOLM
Dylan Thomas in America
Little, Brown, 1955. 302pp. $6.50. Paper—Avon, 1966. 302pp. $ .95. The author provides a candid account of Dylan Thomas' four trips to America and his personal involvement in the affairs of Thomas.

CLEVERDON, DOUGLAS
The Growth of Milk Wood
New Directions, 1969. 124pp. $8.50. This is a history of the text of Dylan Thomas' play through its eleven versions from its inception as an idea in 1939 through to the final publication of the acting edition in 1958. The second part of the volume contains an analysis of all the textual variants in the eleven versions.

COX, C. B.—Editor
Dylan Thomas: A Collection of Critical Essays
Prentice-Hall, 1966. 186pp. $4.95. Paper $1.95. The writers of these essays analyze the merits of Thomas' individual works and provide parallels and perspectives on the body of his poetry. Selected Bibliography. Index.

DAVIES, ANEIRIN TALFAN
Dylan: Druid of the Broken Body
Dent, 1964. 75pp. $3.25. In this assessment of Dylan Thomas as a religious poet, the author shows that the order of the "Collected Poems" was designed to reveal Thomas' progression of religious thought and belief and to demonstrate the ways he probed into the nature of man and his place in God's creation.

DOBREE, BONAMY—Editor
British Writers and Their Work
See Page 189

EMERY, CLARK
The World of Dylan Thomas
University of Miami, 1962. 319pp. $6.50. Studies of the hundred-odd poems included in the "Collected Poems." The poems are understood as taking their place within the tradition of English poetry, lyric and didactic, products of a craftsman who was an acute observer of the human scene and a teacher with a definite subject to teach. A Bibliographical Note lists books dealing with Dylan Thomas and his poetry.

FIRMAGE, GEORGE J.—Editor
A Garland for Dylan Thomas
October House, 1963. 171pp. $6.95. Paper $2.95. A gathering of eighty-four poems by seventy-eight poets written in tribute to Dylan Thomas. Illustrated with photographs of the poet and his country.

FITZGIBBON, CONSTANTINE
The Life of Dylan Thomas
Little, Brown, 1965. 370pp. $7.95. Paper $2.65. A fully documented biography that attempts to restore a perspective to the study of Thomas' achievements and limitations. Included is a definitive list of Thomas' broadcasts, film scripts, lectures, and readings. Index.

HOLBROOK, DAVID
Dylan Thomas and Poetic Dissociation
Southern Illinois University, 1964. 182pp. $4.50. Mr. Holbrook suggests that poetry's essential quality is metaphorical and must be governed by the impulse to extend morality and develop attitudes to life. He studies Dylan Thomas' work, especially "Under Milk Wood," to prove his thesis. Notes. Index.

KORG, JACOB
Dylan Thomas
Twayne, 1965. 204pp. $3.95. This study of Dylan Thomas undertakes a critical survey of his literary activity in fiction and drama as well as in poetry. His radio and film scripts and his stories are placed in relation to the major work as a poet. Selected Bibliography. Index.

MAUD, RALPH and ALBERT GLOVER
Dylan Thomas in Print: A Bibliographical History
See Page 549

MOYNIHAN, WILLIAM T.
The Craft and Art of Dylan Thomas
Cornell University, 1966. 304pp. $6.50. Paper $1.95. A study of the writings of Dylan Thomas in which the focus is on the poetry rather than on the man and his life although biographical material is introduced and his prose and dramatic writings are discussed. Index.

PRATT, ANNIS
Dylan Thomas' Early Prose: A Study in Creative Mythology
University of Pittsburgh, 1970. 226pp. $6.95. Paper $2.95. A full-scale treatment of the prose Dylan Thomas wrote before 1940. The author considers the work from both an internal textual viewpoint and from the external viewpoint of Thomas' affinities with Welsh mythology, Welsh religion, and occult traditions. Appendices. Index.

READ, BILL and ROLLIE McKENNA
The Days of Dylan Thomas: A Pictorial Biography
McGraw–Hill, 1964. 189pp. $5.95. Paper $1.95. Photographs show scenes of Thomas' family and friends, the places he knew and wrote about. The text is based on the poet's words and those of his friends.

STANFORD, DEREK
Dylan Thomas
Citadel, 1964. 212pp. Paper $1.95. This study recreates the life and personality of the poet, examines his themes and techniques in the poetry, studies the plays, and reviews his reputation.

THOMAS, DYLAN
Adventures in the Skin Trade and Other Stories
New American Library, 1960. 192pp. Paper $ .75. Stories by Dylan Thomas with an "Afterword" by Vernon Watkins. Bibliographical notes.

THOMAS, DYLAN
The Collected Poems of Dylan Thomas
New Directions, 1957. 203pp. $4.25. Paper—1971. $2.75. All the poems Thomas wished to preserve are included as well as the "Prologue in Verse" which he wrote for this edition.

THOMAS, DYLAN
The Notebooks of Dylan Thomas
New Directions, 1966. 364pp. $8.50. Edited and with an Introduction by Ralph Maud, this is a compilation of four manuscript notebooks dating from 1930–1934. They are concerned with 200 poems. Notes on related poems of the same period, revisions, later variants are given in the notes and in an Appendix. Index to Titles and/or First Lines.

THOMAS, DYLAN
Portrait of the Artist as a Young Dog
New Directions, 1955. 160pp. Paper $1.35. Autobiographical stories by the poet.

TINDALL, WILLIAM YORK
A Reader's Guide to Dylan Thomas
Farrar, Straus, 1962. 305pp. $4.95. Paper $1.95. Detailed explications of five volumes of poems: "Eighteen Poems," published in 1934; "Twenty-Five Poems," published in 1936; "The Map of Love," published in 1939; "Deaths and Entrances," published in 1946; and "In Country Sleep," published in 1952. Bibliography. Index.

Thomas, Gwyn

THOMAS, GWYN
A Few Selected Exits: An Autobiography of Sorts
Little, Brown, 1968. 239pp. $5.95. This is the autobiography of the Welsh playwright. The book spans the years from 1931 to the mid-sixties as Mr. Thomas describes his school days, his life at Oxford and in Spain, and his career as a schoolteacher, writer, and television personality. Illustrated with photographs.

Ustinov, Peter

RICHARDS, DICK—Compiler
The Wit of Peter Ustinov
Frewin, 1969. 146pp. $4.50. A compilation of the wit and wisdom of the British playwright collected from his writings, from conversations with Ustinov, and from the memories of his friends.

Wesker, Arnold

HAYMAN, RONALD
Arnold Wesker
Heinemann, 1970. 91pp. $3.95. Paper $1.50. An assessment of Wesker's plays from "The Kitchen" to "The Four Seasons." Two interviews with the playwright open and close the volume. Illustrated with four photographs. Biographical Outline. Bibliography.

RIBALOW, HAROLD U.
Arnold Wesker
Twayne, 1965. 154pp. $3.95. In this full-length study of the playwright, the plays are examined within the context of recent British social, cultural, and literary trends. Two as yet unproduced plays are discussed, along with the non-dramatic works. Bibliography.

WESKER, ARNOLD
Fears of Fragmentation
Cape, 1970. 128pp. $3.95. A collection of essays and lectures by the English playwright. They provide a picture of Wesker's attempts to compensate for the inadequacies he experienced as a result of being involved only with his art, and the fear of fragmentation

that separates work from art. Also included is a history of Centre Forty-two, Wesker's own experimental theatre in England.

Whiting, John

HAYMAN, RONALD
John Whiting
Heinemann, 1969. 98pp. Paper $1.95. The author describes and discusses all of Whiting's work for the theatre in this study. Illustrated with photographs. Bibliography.

WHITING, JOHN
The Art of the Dramatist
Calder & Boyars, 1970. 198pp. $6.95. Edited and with an Introduction by Ronald Hayman, this is a collection of work by the playwright ranging in date from 1947 to 1962. The collection includes three short stories, a fragment of a novel, a fragment of an unfinished play with the author's statement of his intentions for it, a narrative written for television, a film scenario in verse, and a selection of critical writings.

HOLLAND

KAISER, WALTER
Praisers of Folly: Erasmus, Shakespeare, Rabelais
See Page 85

INDIA

AMBROSE, KAY
Classical Dances and Costumes of India
See Page 320

ANAND, MULK RAJ
The Indian Theatre
Dobson, 1950. 60pp. $3.50. The author shows that the Indian theatre is complex because of the lack of communication between the provinces of the country. This lack encouraged the growth of regional myth and tradition, and it has been only on the wave of recent nationalism that the Indian intellectuals turned back to their own theatre and away from the West. Each chapter deals with the theatre of a particular province. Illustrated.

GARGI, BALWANT
Folk Theatre of India
University of Washington, 1966. 217pp. $8.95. Indian folk theatre is described by an Indian playwright and critic. He details staging, costumes, make-up, and performances. Illustrated with sixty-two photographs and fifty-four line drawings. Glossary. Index.

GARGI, BALWANT
Theatre in India
Theatre Arts, 1962. 245pp. $6.95. A study of the mimes, ancient myths, medieval pageants and dance dramas of India. The growth and trends of modern Indian theatre are considered. Illustrated.

HAAS, GEORGE C. O.
The Dasarupa: A Treatise on Hindu Dramaturgy by Dhanamjaya
AMS Press, 1965. 169pp. $12.00. A reprint of the 1912 edition translated from the Sanskrit. It is a treatise on the canons of dramatic composition in early India and also includes an introduction to this treatise, an Index of Sanskrit Technical Terms, and a General Index. Bibliography.

HORRWITZ, E. P.
The Indian Theatre
Blom, 1967. 215pp. $8.50. Originally published in 1912 and now reissued, this is a brief survey of the Sanskrit drama. The author provides chapters on the origin of Hindu drama, the influence of Greece, the Buddhist theatre, marionettes and pantomimes, politics on the stage, and includes a list of dates, a pronunciation and spelling guide and a Glossary of Words. Index.

KEITH, A. BERRIEDALE
The Sanskrit Drama in Its Origin, Development, Theory, and Practice
Oxford, 1924. 405pp. $5.25. This study deals with the origin of Sanskrit drama in Vedic and post-Vedic writings, the period of the great writers (Bhasa, Kalidasa, Harsha, Bhavabhuti, and Vishakhadatta), dramatic theory, and dramatic practice.

MATHUR, J. C.
Drama in Rural India
Taplinger, 1964. 122pp. $8.75. This study of the many forms that traditional drama takes in India demonstrates that the drama in Indian villages is more than a spontaneous expression of folk-life or a local folk-device to entertain the community. The continuous process of exchange between traditional-classic and traditional-folk drama is examined in detail.

SHEKHAR, I.
Sanskrit Drama: Its Origin and Decline
E. J. Brill, Netherlands, 1960. 214pp. $13.50. This study examines the origins of Sanskrit drama, traditional dramatic theory, plot and characters in the drama, dance elements, and the factors which contributed to the decline. Bibliography. Index.

WELLS, HENRY W.
The Classical Drama of India
Taplinger, 1963, 196pp. $8.50. The author's thesis is that the chief aim of Indian drama is the effort to achieve spiritual equilibrium. The relation between Indian religious and philosophical thought and the

practice of playwrights is examined, and the dramatic technique and language is studied. The author concludes with analyses of two forms of Indian drama: Prakarana and Nataka. Index.

INDONESIA

PEACOCK, JAMES L.
Rites of Modernization
University of Chicago, 1968. 306pp. $13.50. This is a study of the symbolic and social aspects of Indonesian proletarian drama. Mr Peacock analyzes Indonesian drama by interpreting symbolic forms as modes of expressing and creating crucial social realities. He shows how dances, songs, propaganda, and melodrama relate to the contemporary social situation. Illustrated with photographs and drawings. Glossary. Bibliography. Index.

IRELAND

Histories and Critiques

CLARK, WILLIAM SMITH
The Early Irish Stage: The Beginnings to 1720
Oxford, 1955. 227pp. $7.50. A study of the changes through which Irish drama passed from its beginnings in folk and Biblical plays up to the Dublin professional stage. Social conditions, methods of staging and playhouse customs are examined. Illustrated. Bibliography.

CLARK, WILLIAM SMITH
The Irish Stage in the Country Towns 1720–1800
Oxford, 1965. 405pp. $13.00. A continuation of the account of theatricals begun in the author's "Early Irish Stage." The period under study here saw professional theatre become a feature of town life throughout Ireland. Nine leading country seats are examined. Illustrations include rare portraits of founding acting families, early maps, and playbills of the period. Index.

DOOLEY, ROGER B.
Review Notes and Study Guide to Modern British and Irish Drama
See Page 145

ELLIS–FERMOR, UNA
The Irish Dramatic Movement
Barnes & Noble, 1954. 241pp. $4.00. Paper $3.50. This is a reprint of the study first published in 1939. It is largely a critical study of the dramatic work of Yeats, Lady Gregory, Synge, and their contemporaries and successors in the Irish dramatic movement which began approximately in 1899. Included are a chronological table, list of plays produced in London in the 1890's, a Subject Index of the main critical opinions of Yeats and Lady Gregory, and a note on editions and general works of reference for the period. Index.

GREGORY, LADY AUGUSTA
Our Irish Theatre
Putnam, 1965. 319pp. Paper $1.95. Lady Gregory's account of the history of the early years of the Irish theatre, its dramatists and actors, and the difficulties that made the Abbey Theatre a center of controversy. Introduction and supplements by Daniel Murphy.

HOGAN, ROBERT
After the Irish Renaissance
University of Minnesota, 1967. 282pp. $6.95. Professor Hogan has written a critical history of the Irish drama since "The Plough and the Stars." He provides critical introduction to some thirty or forty playwrights who have worked in Ireland since 1926. Illustrated with photographs. Bibliography of Plays and Criticism. Index.

HOLLOWAY, JOSEPH
Joseph Holloway's Abbey Theatre
Southern Illinois University, 1967. 296pp. $6.95. Edited by Robert Hogan and Michael J. O'Neill, this is a selection from the 221 volume journal "Impressions of a Dublin Play-goer." It is a detailed record of the plays and players of the Abbey Theatre from 1899 to 1926. Notes. Index.

HOLLOWAY, JOSEPH
Joseph Holloway's Irish Theatre
Proscenium Press. Volume One: 1968. 88pp. $2.00. Volume Two: 1969. 85pp. $2.00. Volume Three: 1970. 110pp. $2.50. Three Volume Set: $6.00. Edited by Robert Hogan and Michael J. O'Neill, this is a selection in three volumes from the theatrical diaries of one of Ireland's most passionate playgoers. The volumes cover the years 1926 through 1944 and the emphasis is on the history of the Abbey theatre and the then new playwrights and actors. Each volume has a section of notes and an Index. The first volume also includes an Introduction by the editors. All volumes are paper bound.

McCANN, SEAN
The Story of the Abbey Theatre
Four Square, 1967. 157pp. Paper $1.50. A history of the Abbey Theatre in Dublin—its productions, the playwrights, and the actors. Illustrated with drawings.

MacLIAMMOIR, MICHEAL
Theatre in Ireland
Mercier Press, 1964. 84pp. Paper $1.25. Originally published in 1949, and now reissued with additional material and new illustrations, this is a study of theatre in Ireland from the eighteenth century to the present day. Illustrated with photographs of the leading actors and productions.

MALONE, ANDREW E.
Irish Drama
Blom, 1965. 351pp. $12.50. First published in 1929, this reprinting of the history of the Irish theatre from 1880 describes the forces that created the Irish theatre and the playwrights who wrote for it. Mr. Malone has included production notes on all the plays from 1899 to 1928. Index.

MERCIER, VIVIAN
The Irish Comic Tradition
Oxford, 1962. 258pp. $8.00. Paper—1969. $1.95. This is an attempt to trace an unbroken comic tradition in Irish literature from approximately the ninth century to the present day. Irish humor, wit, satire, and parody each receive separate treatment in one or more chapters. Certain aspects of Swift, Joyce, Beckett, and many other Anglo-Irish writers are discussed. Index.

O'CONNOR, FRANK
A Short History of Irish Literature
Putnam, 1967. 264pp. $5.95. This is a survey of the past 1,000 years of Irish writing from its beginnings in the sixth century up to the work of Yeats, O'Casey, and Joyce. Many subjects are discussed: the metrical structure and distinctive rhythms of early Irish verse, the strong oral traditions, the fight against alien influences, and the effects of the Irish government and the Catholic church on Irish literature. Bibliography. Index.

SHELDON, ESTHER K.
Thomas Sheridan of Smock-Alley
Princeton, 1967. 530pp. $14.00. A study of the career of Thomas Sheridan as actor and as manager of Dublin's Smock-Alley Theatre. The author's account throws light on the problems and routines of Dublin theatres, the changing position of the eighteenth century actor and the tastes and attitudes of Dubliners. Included is a daily record of performances and casts at the theatre. Selected Bibliography. List of Sheridan's Works. Index.

SIMPSON, ALAN
Beckett and Behan and a Theatre in Dublin
Routledge & Kegan Paul, 1962. 193pp. $4.25. A joint biography of Brendan Behan and Samuel Beckett, written by a fellow-Dubliner who produced the first productions of both playwrights in their native city at his "The Pike" theatre. The author also tells the story of the modern Irish theatre.

STOCKWELL, LA TOURETTE
Dublin Theatres and Theatre Customs: 1687—1820
Blom, 1968. 426pp. $12.50. Originally published in 1938 and now reissued, this is a comprehensive history of the theatre in Dublin during the seventeenth and eighteenth centuries, with a list of performances given during the period and an extensive Bibliography. Illustrated. Index.

VICTOR, BENJAMIN
The History of the Theatres of London and Dublin
See Page 175

WEYGANDT, CORNELIUS
Irish Plays and Playwrights
Kennikat Press, 1966. 314pp. $12.00. Originally published in 1913 and now reissued, this is a study of the Irish theatre. Among the playwrights discussed in full chapters are Yeats, Lady Gregory, Synge, and William Sharp. An Appendix lists plays produced in Dublin by the Abbey Theatre Company. Illustrated. Index.

Studies of Playwrights

Behan, Brendan

BEHAN, BRENDAN
Borstal Boy
Knopf, 1958. 272pp. $4.50. Paper—Avon, 1970. 348pp. $1.25. An account of Behan's experiences from his arrest at the age of sixteen for agitating for the I. R. A. through his life in reform school.

BEHAN, BRENDAN
Confessions of an Irish Rebel
Bernard Geis, 1965. 245pp. $4.95. The sequel to "Borstal Boy" and the second part of Behan's autobiography. It details his I. R. A. activity, and his life in Dublin and Paris.

BEHAN, BRENDAN
The Wit of Brendan Behan
Leslie Frewin, 1968. 140pp. $3.50. Compiled by Sean McCann, this is a collection of the comic lines and anecdotes attributed to the irish playwright. There are pronouncements on himself, his family, drinking, court and prison, politics, Ireland, America, England, and Canada. Illustrated with photographs.

BEHAN, DOMINIC
My Brother Brendan
Four Square, 1966. 189pp. Paper $1.25. A reissue of the 1965 study of Brendan Behan by his brother. Illustrated with photographs.

BOYLE, TED E.
Brendan Behan
Twayne, 1969. 150pp. $4.50. Professor Boyle provides a comprehensive analysis of Behan's work. The author attempts to demonstrate those influences which shaped Behan's character and his talent as well as to indicate some of the reasons for the dissipation of those talents. Each of the three major works ("The Quare Fellow," "The Hostage," and "Borstal Boy") is analyzed in a separate chapter. The author has included a section of Notes and References as well as a Selected Bibliography. Index.

JEFFS, RAE
Brendan Behan, Man and Showman
Hutchinson, 1966. 256pp. $7.50. An account of the last years of Brendan Behan's life by the woman who served as his transcriber and, often, editor. Mrs. Jeffs depicts Behan's public personality and the private man which few were privileged to see. Illustrated with photographs. Chronology. Index.

McCANN, SEAN – Editor
The World of Brendan Behan
Twayne, 1966. 208pp. $4.00. Paper – Four Square, 1965. 208pp. $1.65. A collection of reminiscences of Brendan Behan by his friends: bar-room cronies and men who knew him in prison as well as those who knew him when he was a young house painter. Illustrated with drawings by Liam C. Martin.

Clarke, Austin

CLARKE, AUSTIN
A Penny in the Clouds
Routledge & Kegan Paul, 1968. 216pp. $6.00. The Irish poet and playwright writes about life in the earlier part of this century in this autobiography. He writes about his friends and enemies in Dublin, about Yeats, Lady Gregory, and others. Index.

Colum, Padraic

BOWEN, ZACK
Padraic Colum: A Biographical–Critical Introduction
Southern Illinois University, 1970. 162pp. $4.95. A first study of the Irish poet/playwright. The entire scope of his work is included: poems, plays, essays, novels, biographies, and books for children. The author's aim is to place in perspective the entire range of the work and to assess critically the literary and historical position of the work. Notes. Bibliography. Index.

Gregory, Lady Augusta

COXHEAD, ELIZABETH
J. M. Synge and Lady Gregory
See Page 209

Joyce, James

BURGESS, ANTHONY
Re Joyce
Ballantine, 1966. 349pp. Paper $ .95. Mr Burgess offers a guide through the whole body of James Joyce's work with particular emphasis on the aims and techniques of the two major novels.

CURRAN, CONSTANTINE
James Joyce Remembered
Oxford, 1968. 129pp. $5.95. Mr. Curran illuminates many of the particulars behind Joyce's assault upon Irish tradition and his repudiation of family and country. The author follows in some detail Joyce's reading as a university student. Illustrated with photographs. Index.

ELLMANN, RICHARD
James Joyce
Oxford, 1959. 842pp. Paper $3.95. The definitive biography of Joyce which won the National Book Award for non-fiction in 1959. Illustrated. Index.

GIVENS, SEON – Editor
James Joyce: Two Decades of Criticism
Vanguard, 1963. 486pp. $7.50. An augmented version of the 1948 work which includes an essay by T. S. Eliot, portraits of Jolas and Budgen, the first appearance of Hugh Kenner's study, and James T. Farrell's views. Bibliography.

GLASHEEN, ADALINE
A Second Census of Finnegans Wake
Northwestern University, 1963. 285pp. $8.95. A revised and expanded edition of the author's first index of characters and their roles in the novel first published in 1956. Included in this volume is a forty page synopsis of the narrative, a chart titled "Who is Who When Everybody is Someone Else" which identifies the transformation of major characters, and the alphabetically arranged census.

GROSS, JOHN
James Joyce
Viking, 1970. 102pp. Paper $1.65. An analysis of the life and work of the Irish novelist. The one surviving play, "Exiles," is mentioned briefly in the text. Bibliography. Index.

HART, CLIVE
Structure and Motif in Finnegans Wake
Northwestern University, 1962. 271pp. $6.95. This study is an attempt to re-examine and re-define some of the basic structural principles of the novel in light of recent knowledge. The architectonic patterns, the historical cycles, dream structures, and counterpoint rhythms are examined, and the hundreds of leitmotifs, by means of which Joyce makes his structure meaningful, are described in full. An Appendix notes more than 600 motifs. Bibliography.

JONES, WILLIAM POWELL
James Joyce and the Common Reader
University of Oklahoma, 1970. 170pp. $5.95. Paper $2.50. Originally published in 1955 and now reissued, this is an evaluation for the beginner of the work of

James Joyce. The evaluation is on the basis not only of the avant garde experimentalism but also of the mastery of the conventional literary forms. Advice for Further Reading. Index.

JOYCE, JAMES
The Letters of James Joyce
Viking, 1966. 1,496pp. Three volume set: $35.00. The collected correspondence of James Joyce, containing more than 1,500 letters. Edited by Richard Ellmann, this is a three volume boxed set. Illustrated. Index in each volume.

JOYCE, STANISLAUS
My Brother's Keeper: James Joyce's Early Years
McGraw–Hill, 1964. 266pp. Paper $2.85. Edited by Richard Ellmann, this biography is based on the journal kept by Stanislaus Joyce and used by him as a basis for a biographical study of his brother to the age of twenty-two.

KENNER, HUGH
Dublin's Joyce
Beacon Press, 1962. 372pp. Paper $2.25. A reprint of the 1956 work on the state of Joyce's native Dublin at the turn of the century and of how this milieu provided the fabric for Joyce's works. The author surveys Joyce's writings from "Chamber Music" to "Finnegans Wake."

LEVIN, HARRY
James Joyce
New Directions, 1960. 256pp. Paper $1.95. Revised and augmented edition of the 1941 study in which the author sums up the contributions of James Joyce. There is a new preface and a postscript entitled "Revisiting Joyce." Mr. Levin examines the works that have come to light in the last few years and some of the important later biographical and critical writings about Joyce. Index.

LEVIN, HARRY – Editor
The Portable James Joyce
Viking, 1963. 760pp. $2.45. Complete texts of "A Portrait of the Artist," "The Exiles," "Collected Poems," and "Dubliners." Also included are selected passages from "Ulysses" and "Finnegans Wake." Introduction and Notes by the editor. Bibliography.

LITZ, A. WALTON
James Joyce
Twayne, 1966. 141pp. $3.95. A general survey assessing Joyce's achievements and his place in modern literature. The author appraises the early poetry and discusses all of the later work. Bibliography. Index.

MAGALANER, MARVIN and RICHARD M. KAIN
Joyce: The Man, the Work, the Reputation
New York University, 1956. 377pp. $10.00. A study of the artist and his work with systematic examinations of each work and detailed explication of obscure passages. Bibliographies.

O'BRIEN, DARCY
The Conscience of James Joyce
Princeton, 1968. 258pp. $6.95. A study of the man as well as of the works, this book combines biographical perspective with textual analysis. Joyce's development is traced and particular reference is made to the letters from Joyce to his wife during 1909–1912 in which Joyce revealed his moral and emotional convictions with unusual frankness. Index.

TINDALL, WILLIAM YORK
A Reader's Guide to James Joyce
Farrar, Straus, 1959. 304pp. Paper $1.95. A study of all of Joyce's prose works. Bibliography. Index.

TYSDAHL, B. J.
Joyce and Ibsen: A Study in Literary Influence
Humanities, 1968. 255pp. $7.50. This book investigates Joyce's use of and dept to Ibsen, dealing with Joyce's total production, and examining the most important works one by one. The last chapter discusses the nature of literary influence and outlines a mutual interpretation of certain aspects of the works of Ibsen and Joyce. Bibliography. Index.

O'Casey, Sean

ARMSTRONG, WILLIAM A.
Sean O'Casey
Longmans, 1967. 39pp. Paper $ .95. A short study of the life and work of the Irish dramatist. Included are biographical and critical studies and a Selected Bibliography.

AYLING, RONALD – Editor
Sean O'Casey: Modern Judgements
Macmillan, 1969. 274pp. $7.95. Paper $3.50. A selection of critical essays by twenty-four authorities including: James Agate, Una Ellis-Fermor, John Gassner, G. Wilson Knight, G. B. Shaw, and W. B. Yeats. An Introduction is provided by the editor. Chronology. Selected Bibliography. Index.

COWASJEE, SAROS
Sean O'Casey: The Man Behind the Plays
Oliver & Boyd, 1963. 266pp. $7.50. Paper $3.75. The author concentrates on the first forty-six years of the playwright's life—his early years in Dublin, his involvement with the cause of Irish freedom, his work for the Abbey Theatre, and his self-imposed exile to London in 1926. Bibliography. Index.

FALLON, GABRIEL
Sean O'Casey: The Man I Knew
Little, Brown, 1965. 213pp. $5.00. The author, an

actor of O'Casey's plays at the Abbey Theatre between 1920 and 1927, became a close friend of the playwright until his critical views on the later plays caused a breech between them. Written just before O'Casey's death, this personal account of the playwright contains a chapter added after his death.

HOGAN, ROBERT
The Experiments of Sean O'Casey
St. Martin's, 1960. 215pp. $5.00. A study of the plays, with special attention paid to the so-called "failures" of O'Casey's later career. The bold dramaturgy of these late plays is analyzed. Documents relating to "The Silver Tassie" controversy and the break with the Abbey Theatre are given.

KOSLOW, JULES
Sean O'Casey: The Man and His Plays
Citadel, 1966. 117pp. Paper $1.75. Originally published in 1950 and now revised and expanded, this is a study of the dramatist and an analysis of all his major plays.

KRAUSE, DAVID
Sean O'Casey: The Man and His Works
Collier, 1962. 412pp. Paper $1.50. Originally published in 1960, this is a study of the complete works of O'Casey with individual analyses of each play. O'Casey's autobiographical works are studied as a revelation of the artist.

KRAUSE, DAVID
A Self-Portrait of the Artist as a Man
Dolmen Press, 1968. 37pp. Paper $2.25. The editor of O'Casey's letters presents a short essay in which he provides a new view of the writer. This view emerged from Krause's study of the extensive corresspondence.

O'CASEY, SEAN
Blasts and Benedictions
St. Martin's, 1967. 341pp. $6.50. A collection of articles, stories, and occasional writings from the years between 1926 and 1964. O'Casey discusses his own works and also criticizes Shakespeare, Chekhov, Synge, Shaw, and John Arden, among others. Index.

O'CASEY, SEAN
Drums Under The Windows
Macmillan, 1960. 431pp. Paper $1.65. The third volume of the autobiography is devoted to the playwright's activities in the Irish Rebellion.

O'CASEY, SEAN
Feathers from the Green Crow
University of Missouri, 1962. 256pp. $6.50. Edited by Robert Hogan, these are essays written between 1905 and 1925 for newspapers and periodicals. Two previously unpublished plays ("Kathleen Listens In" and "Nannie's Night Out"), a dozen songs, four short stories and notes and commentaries are included.

O'CASEY, SEAN
I Knock at the Door
Macmillan, 1956. 268pp. Paper $2.50. The first volume in the playwright's autobiography, written in the third person, describing his early years in the slums of North Dublin.

O'CASEY, SEAN
Inishfallen, Fare Thee Well
Macmillan, 1960. 396pp. Paper $1.65. A reprint of the 1949 edition, this is the fourth volume of the autobiography. It is devoted to the years in which the Abbey Theatre produced "Juno and the Paycock" and "The Plough and the Stars" and to O'Casey's departure from Ireland in self-imposed exile.

O'CASEY, SEAN
Pictures in the Hallway
Macmillan, 1960. 373pp. Paper $1.65. The second volume of the autobiography describes his life as a young man in Dublin, his first interest in politics and religion, and his introduction to the stage.

O'CASEY, SEAN
Sunset and Evening Star
Macmillan, 1961. 339pp. Paper $1.65. A reprint of the sixth volume in O'Casey's autobiography. Included are accounts of his visits to Cambridge, and of his friendship with George Bernard Shaw. A tribute to Ireland closes the volume.

O'CASEY, SEAN
Under a Colored Cap
St. Martin's, 1963. 277pp. $4.95. A collection of a variety of articles on a number of subjects. Among the longer papers are discussions of orthodox belief and the myth and mystery behind it, an analysis of contemporary culture, and several critical works.

Robinson, Lennox

O'NEILL, MICHAEL J.
Lennox Robinson
Twayne, 1964. 192pp. $4.95. Paper $1.95. This study concentrates on Robinson's contributions to the Irish theatre and particularly to his service to the Abbey Theatre as playwright, manager, producer, and director. The playwright's efforts to break away from the Abbey are also recounted. Chronology. Selected Bibliography. Index.

Shaw, George Bernard

SHAW, GEORGE BERNARD
See Page 196

Synge, J.M.

BICKLEY, FRANCIS
J.M. Synge and the Irish Dramatic Movement
Russell & Russell, 1968. 97pp. $7.95. Originally published in 1912 and now reissued, this is a study of Synge and his place in relation to his contemporaries and in the line of English-written drama. The author analyzes the qualities he feels make Synge's work so notable and provides information on the Irish dramatic movement as a background.

BOURGEOIS, MAURICE
John Millington Synge and the Irish Theatre
Blom, 1965. 353pp. $10.00. First published in 1913, this is a study of the complex personality of the great dramatist which examines his conflict with the age in which he lived. Synge's relation with the Abbey Theatre and the productions of his plays there are also among the items covered. There is a study of the Irish dialect of the plays.

CORKERY, DANIEL
Synge and the Anglo-Irish Literature
Russell & Russell, 1965. 247pp. $8.50. First published in 1931, this study attempts to explain the manner in which Synge stood apart from his contemporaries. Illustrated with a portrait of Synge. A Bibliography lists the published works of Synge and a selection of critical and biographical works.

COXHEAD, ELIZABETH
J.M. Synge and Lady Gregory
Longmans, 1962. 35pp. Paper $ .85. A brief essay on the contributions to the renaissance of Irish drama of each of these dramatists, and a study of their personal relationship. Bibliography.

GERSTENBERGER, DONNA
John Millington Synge
Twayne, 1964. 157pp. $3.95. A survey of the cannon of published works. The success and failure the playwright met in trying to find artistic statements for his belief and opinions are examined. A detailed exposition of "The Playboy of the Western World" is also provided.

GREENE, DAVID H. and EDWARD M. STEPHENS
J.M. Synge: 1871–1909
Collier, 1961. 319pp. Paper $ .95. A definitive and authorized biography of the playwright based on his personal papers. His turbulent and frustrated personal life and his friendships with the great figures of the Irish Renaissance are discussed. The writing and staging of his plays are treated in detail. Illustrated.

WHITAKER, THOMAS R.–Editor
Twentieth Century Interpretations of "The Playboy of the Western World"
Prentice–Hall, 1969. 122pp. $4.95. Paper $1.25. A collection of critical essays by twelve noted authorities including Cyril Cusack, Una Ellis-Fermor, Norman Podhoretz, and William Butler Yeats. Chronology. Selected Bibliography.

Yeats, William Butler

ALSPACH, RUSSELL K.–Editor
The Variorum Edition of the Plays of W.B. Yeats
Macmillan, 1966. 1,366pp. $40.00. This edition of all of Yeats' thirty-three plays brings together all of the work the playwright did including the revisions made in successive editions beginning with "The Island of Statues" in 1885 and ending with "The Death of Cuchulain" in 1939. The editor has provided an Introduction, Bibliography, Appendices and a Glossary.

BERRYMAN, CHARLES
W.B. Yeats: Design of Opposites
Exposition, 1967. 149pp. $6.00. A critical study of Yeats' art and philosophy beginning with the investigation of the origins and development of Yeats' philosophy of opposites. The author analyzes in detail selected plays, fiction and poems.

BLOOM, HAROLD
Yeats
Oxford, 1970. 500pp. $12.50. A critical study which sets forth in detail the relationships of all of Yeats' writings and places the author's achievements in historical and literary perspective. Notes. Index.

BRADFORD, CURTIS B.
Yeats at Work
Southern Illinois University, 1965. 407pp. $12.50. A study tracing the development of Yeats' work from the earliest surving manuscript. Plays treated are "Purgatory," "At the Hawk's Well," "The Words Upon the Window-Pane," "The Resurrection," and "A Full Moon in March."

BUSHRUI, S.B.
Yeats' Verse Plays: The Revisions 1900–1910
Oxford, 1965. 240pp. $7.95. Dr. Bushrui examines the five verse plays published between 1900 and 1910. He traces the effects of Yeats' growing practical experience of the theatre through these plays and their revisions. Selected Bibliography. Index.

CLARK, DAVID R.
W.B. Yeats and the Theatre of Desolate Reality
Dolmen Press, 1965. 125pp. $6.00. Mr. Clark studies a selected group of Yeats' plays which have a similarity in theme but which are representative of the early, middle, and late stages of Yeats' development. In his final chapter the author concludes that Yeats' drama provides the nearest thing to the Realist idea of a theatre that our age has achieved. Bibliography.

COWELL, RAYMOND
W. B. Yeats
Evans, 1969. 160pp. $3.50. Paper $1.95. This is a study of the work of W. B. Yeats. Mr. Cowell suggests that the work demands recognition both as modern poetry and as a record of a pursuit of self-knowledge. Reading List. Index.

ELLMANN, RICHARD
Eminent Domain
Oxford, 1967. 159pp. $4.95. William Butler Yeats attained pre-eminence early in life and was the focal center for both disciples and rebels. This is the first book to display the complicated interactions among Yeats, Wilde, Joyce, Pound, Eliot and Auden. Notes. Index.

ELLMANN, RICHARD
The Identity of Yeats
Oxford, 1964. 342pp. Paper $2.25. First published in 1954, this is a reprint of a study of Yeats' verse. The author examines the poet's choice among literary directions, his development of theme, symbol, style, and pattern. The edition has a new Introduction which re-examines the basic constancy underlying Yeats' flexible talent. Index.

ELLMANN, RICHARD
Yeats, the Man and the Masks
Dutton, 1948. 331pp. Paper $1.75. Based on some 50,000 pages of unpublished material left by Yeats on his death, this study attempts to reconstruct the poetic growth of the poet. Many poems and letters found in the material are published here for the first time.

ENGELBERG, EDWARD
The Vast Design: Patterns in W. B. Yeats' Aesthetic
University of Toronto, 1964. 224pp. $6.95. The first extensive study of Yeats' "critical prose," this book analyzes the aesthetic patterns Yeats developed and shows that early in his career the poet formulated an aesthetic which often preceded and always supported his poetic practice. Illustrations accompany a discussion of Yeats' criticism of art. Bibliography. Index.

FAULKNER, PETER
Yeats and the Irish Eighteenth Century
Dolmen Press, 1965. 16pp. Paper $1.25. The author traces Yeats' discovery of the Irish eighteenth century and its effect on his work in this short study.

HONE, JOSEPH
W. B. Yeats: 1865 – 1939
St. Martin's, 1962. 503pp. $9.50. Paper $5.25. A second edition of the biography first published in 1943. The author had the assistance of Mrs. Yeats in preparing the work as well as free access to the papers dealing with the poet's private life. Index.

JEFFARES, A. NORMAN and K. G. W. CROSS – Editors
In Excited Reverie: A Centenary Tribute to William Butler Yeats 1865 – 1939
Macmillan, 1965. 354pp. $10.00. This series of essays explores aspects of the thought and ideas, the background, the reading and the writing, of the poet, as well as the reactions of others to his life and work. Among the contributors are: Lennox Robinson, David Daiches, T. R. Henn, and Russell K. Alspach. Index.

MacMANUS, FRANCIS – Editor
The Yeats We Knew
Herder, 1965. 94pp. Paper $1.50. Five of Yeats' contemporaries recall him in portraits that differ in detail but add up to a picture of potent Irish personality.

NATHAN, LEONARD E.
The Tragic Drama of William Butler Yeats
Columbia, 1965. 307pp. $7.50. A chronological study of Yeats' tragedies that traces the development of his tragic art from his earliest experimentations to his late adaptations of Noh drama.

RONSLEY, JOSEPH
Yeats' Autobiography: Life as Symbolic Pattern
Harvard, 1968. 172pp. $5.00. This extended analysis treats Yeats' autobiography both on its own terms as an individual work and in terms of its special function among Yeats' other works. Mr. Ronsley attempts to discover the design underlying Yeats' presentation of events, people, and ideas. Index.

SKELTON, ROBIN and ANN SADDLEMYER – Editors
The World of W. B. Yeats
University of Washington, 1967. 231pp. $5.95. Paper $2.95. This is a revised edition of the collection of essays originally published in 1965. Divided into three parts: Beginnings; Creations; Contemporaries. In addition to essays by the editors, the volume contains contributions from David R. Clark, Joan Coldwell, Gwladys V. Downes, and Liam Miller, and twelve pages of Illustrations.

STOCK, A. G.
W. B. Yeats: His Poetry and Thought
Cambridge, 1964. 254pp. $5.50. Paper $1.95. This study considers three main elements of Yeats' thought: his pre-occupation with Irish tradition; his social and political outlook; and the influence of "The Vision." Stress is placed on Yeats' lifelong preoccupation with his Irish heritage.

TINDALL, WILLIAM YORK
W. B. Yeats
Columbia, 1966. 48pp. Paper $1.00. A short biographical and critical study of Yeats. Selected Bibliography.

UNTERECKER, JOHN
A Reader's Guide to William Butler Yeats
Farrar, Straus, 1959. 310pp. $5.00. Paper $2.25. An analytical commentary on the work of the Irish

playwright. The author provides a poem-by-poem analysis of Yeats' verse and explains the imagery and meanings of the individual lyrics. An examination of the poet's principal themes is included. Chronology. Bibliography. Index.

UNTERECKER, JOHN – Editor
Yeats: A Collection of Critical Essays
Prentice–Hall, 1963. 182pp. $4.95. Paper $1.95. Essays by T. S. Eliot, R. P. Blackmur, Allen Tate, Alec Zwerdling, and Richard Ellmann, with a Chronology and a Bibliography.

URE, PETER
W. B. Yeats
Peter Smith, 1965. 129pp. Paper $3.00. The author provides a biographical introduction to the poet, followed by a consideration of the poems and the plays. There is also a discussion of Yeats and the critics. Bibliography. Index.

URE, PETER
W. B. Yeats and the Shakespearian Moment
Queen's University, 1969. 25pp. Paper $1.25. This essay deals with W. B. Yeats' attitudes toward Shakespeare's work as those attitudes are revealed in his criticism and in his own work for the theatre. References.

URE, PETER
Yeats the Playwright
Barnes & Noble, 1963. 182pp. $6.75. Paper – Routledge & Kegan Paul, 1969. 182pp. $2.50. This is a study of aspects of Yeats' drama in which the stress is laid on the force and variety of Yeats' characterizations and construction. Notes. Chronology. Index.

VENDLER, HELEN HENNESSY
Yeats' Vision and the Later Plays
Harvard, 1963. 286pp. $7.50. The first part of this study analyzes "A Vision," describing its scheme and the material in it related to the creative process. The second part consists of a reading of twelve late plays. The plays are related to "A Vision" and similarities of symbolism are noted.

WILSON, F. A. C.
W. B. Yeats and Tradition
Methuen, 1968. 286pp. Paper $2.25. Originally published in 1958 and now reissued, this study examines the late plays and various related lyrics and places them in the context of Yeats' personal philosophy. Notes. Bibliography. Index.

WILSON, F. A. C.
Yeats' Iconography
Macmillan, 1960. 349pp. $5.00. This study is concerned with "Four Plays for Dancers" and "The Cat and the Moon," and with twelve related lyrics. In examining Yeats' verse plays written on the Noh formula the author is concerned with an explanation of the maximum symbolic meaning, using a broad system of reference. Bibliography. Index.

YEATS, WILLIAM BUTLER
Ah, Sweet Dancer
Macmillan, 1971. 144pp. $4.95. The correspondence of W. B. Yeats and Margot Ruddock, an actress and minor poet, as edited by Roger McHugh. Besides illuminating Yeats' views on poetry in general and on the problems of verse theatre in London and Dublin, the letters provide a demonstration of Yeats' technique of poetry in his revisions of Miss Ruddock's poems and his comments upon them. Illustrated. Appendices. Bibliography. Index.

YEATS, WILLIAM BUTLER
The Autobiography of W. B. Yeats
Collier, 1965. 404pp. Paper $1.95. This volume consists of three books: "Reveries Over Childhood and Youth;" "The Trembling of the Veil;" and "Dramatist Personae."

YEATS, WILLIAM BUTLER
Essays and Introductions
Collier, 1968. 530pp. Paper $2.45. Originally published in 1961, this is a collection of the poet-playwright's literary criticism. It contains over forty essays on subjects ranging from Shelley, Blake, Spenser, and Synge to summary statements on Shakespeare's history plays, Noh drama, poetry and tradition, and art and ideas.

YEATS, WILLIAM BUTLER
Letters to the New Island
Harvard, 1970. 222pp. $5.00. Originally published in 1934 and now reissued, this is a facsimile edition. Edited and with an Introduction by Horace Reynolds, this is a series of letters in which Yeats writes of his desire to bring a national theatre to Ireland and provides a glimpse behind the scenes of the Irish Renaissance. Illustrated with a portrait of Yeats.

YEATS, WILLIAM BUTLER
Uncollected Prose by W. B. Yeats: Volume One
Columbia, 1970. 437pp. $17.50. Collected and edited by John P. Frayne, this volume includes reviews and articles written by Yeats from 1886 to 1896. Mr. Frayne includes an introduction which traces the course of Yeats' literary career, gives a summary of the Irish literary scene of the time, and examines the taste and aesthetic principles which are central to Yeats' early criticism. Bibliography.

ZWERDLING, ALEX
Yeats and the Heroic Ideal
New York University, 1966. 196pp. $6.75. Paper $1.95. The author shows how Yeats' involvement in the Irish freedom movement, his interest in myth, religion, and the occult, and his praise of aristocratic values were all related expressions of his desire to re-establish the vision of heroism. Index.

ISRAEL

GERSHONY, G.K.
The Hebrew Theatre
Herzl Press, 1963. 28pp. Paper $ .25. This brief pamphlet describes the early development of the Hebrew theatre in the Diaspora, the first attempts to produce a play in Israel in 1894, and such modern groups as the Ohel Theatre, Hateatron Hakameri, and the Haifa Municipal Theatre. Illustrated with photographs.

KOHANSKY, MENDEL
The Hebrew Theatre: Its First Fifty Years
Ktav Publishing, 1969. 306pp. $13.50. A history of the Hebrew theatre from its beginnings in Moscow in 1918 to the current repertory theatres in Israel. Included among the subjects are the Habimah Theatre in Moscow, Stanislavsky and Vakhtangov, and the new Hebrew playwrights. A chronology of milestones is included as is a list of productions in the major theatres. Illustrated. Index.

MOREVSKI, ABRAHAM
There and Back: Memories and Thoughts of a Jewish Actor
See Page 274

SHAKOW, ZARA
The Theatre in Israel
Herzl Press, 1963. 143pp. Paper $1.25. The author discusses Israeli theatre groups including Ohel, Habima, Cameri, Haifa Municipal, and the Telem, or theatre for immigrants. Described are the foreign language theatres, the childrens' theatre, and theatre literature. Illustrated.

ITALY

Histories and Critiques

BEAUMONT, CYRIL W.
The History of Harlequin
Blom, 1967. 156pp. $13.50. A republication of the 1926 history of one of the most popular characters of Commedia dell'Arte. Sacheverell Sitwell has provided a long preface on Harlequin in art and there are many illustrations from contemporary sources. Two chapters are given to a study of English Harlequins and there is a complete text with production notes of a comic pantomime by Thomas Dibdin. Illustrated. Index.

COLLISON-MORLEY, LACY
Shakespeare in Italy
See Page 95

CORRIGAN, BEATRICE
Catalogue of Italian Plays, 1500–1700, in the Library of the University of Toronto
University of Toronto, 1961. 134pp. $4.25. A catalogue of one of the largest collections outside Europe of Italian Renaissance plays. The plays are identified, their dates given as accurately as possible, and their genres and forms indicated.

CROCE, BENEDETTO
Ariosto, Shakespeare and Corneille
See Page 48

DUCHARTE, PIERRE LOUIS
The Italian Comedy
Dover, 1966. 367pp. Paper $4.00. An unabridged republication of the 1929 edition, this study traces the history of the Commedia dell'Arte and describes the staging, masks, scenarios, acting troupes, and characters. More than 200 drawings and photographs are included. Bibliography. Index.

HERRICK, MARVIN T.
Italian Comedy in the Renaissance
University of Illinois, 1960. 238pp. $4.50. Paper $1.75. This study traces the significant development of the golden age of Italian comedy. Excerpts from the plays are given to illustrate the plots and dramatic structure of the works considered.

HERRICK, MARVIN T.
Italian Plays, 1500–1700, in the University of Illinois Library
University of Illinois, 1966. 92pp. $5.75. A bibliography of Italian plays published before 1701, mainly by sixteenth century authors. Index.

HERRICK, MARVIN T.
Italian Tragedy in the Renaissance
University of Illinois, 1965. 315pp. $6.75. This companion volume to the author's "Italian Comedy in the Renaissance," discloses the close relation between the French and English theatres of the Renaissance and those Italian playwrights who were experimenting with native tragedies. The plots, characters, and styles of the major plays of the period are studied in detail. Bibliography. Index of Italian and Latin Tragedies. Index of Names.

HEWITT, BARNARD
The Renaissance Stage: Documents of Serlio, Sabbattini and Furttenbach
University of Miami, 1958. 256pp. $5.50. Translations by Allardyce Nicoll, John H. McDowell, and George R. Kernodle of the three major sources of information about the stage scenery and scenic practices in the Italian Renaissance theatre. Illustrated with diagrams and engravings from the original edition of essays.

KENNARD, JOSEPH SPENCER
The Italian Theatre: From Its Beginning to the Close of the Seventeenth Century

Blom, 1964. Volume One: 243pp. Volume Two: 313pp. Two volume set: $18.50. This study attempts to "reflect the successive phases of the Italian social conscience and to depict the changing life of the Italian people." Volume One has chapters on the Classical and Christian origins of the theatre, Medieval theatre, the humanistic theatre, various types of theatre in the sixteenth century, the Renaissance, and the seventeenth century. Volume Two has chapters on many different playwrights. This is a reprint of the work first published in 1932. Bibliography. Index.

KENNARD, JOSEPH SPENCER
Masks and Marionettes
Kennikat, 1967. 129pp. $8.00. Originally published in 1935 and now reissued, this study is divided into two sections. The first deals with the Commedia dell'Arte: its history, players, companies, playwrights (including Goldoni, Gozzi, and Scala), and the scenarios. Nineteen plates accompany the text and show reproductions of period art work. The second section is concerned with the puppet theatre of Italy and is accompanied by three plates. Index.

LEA, K.M.
Italian Popular Comedy: A Study of the Commedia dell'Arte, 1560–1620, with Special Reference to the English Stage
Russell & Russell, 1962. Two volume set: 696pp. $20.00. In this reprint of the 1934 study, the nature and development of the professional improvised comedy of sixteenth and seventeenth century Italy is examined. The important relation of this comedy to English stage practice is analyzed.

MECCOLI, DOMENICO and GIOVANNI CALENDOLI, GUIDO CINCOTTI
Il Risorgimento Italiano nel Teatro e nel Cinema
Speedimpex, Undated. 236pp. $18.00. A pictorial and documentary account of the struggle for Italian unification and independence as it is represented in the plays and motion pictures of the nineteenth and twentieth centuries. Published in Italy, the text of the volume is in Italian, English, and French.

MOLINARI, CAESARE
Spettacoli Fiorentini del Quattrocento
Speedimpex, 1961. 122pp. & plates. $5.00. A study of the popular festivals and spectacles of the Renaissance in Florence and of their relation to the art of the drama. Forty-nine contemporary Illustrations. The text of the study is in Italian.

NICOLL, ALLARDYCE
The World of Harlequin
See Page 348

NIKLAUS, THELMA
Harlequin, or the Rise and Fall of a Bergamask Rogue
See Page 348

OREGLIA, GIACOMO
The Commedia dell'Arte
Hill & Wang, 1968. 158pp. $5.95. Paper $1.95. Translated by Lovett F. Edwards, and with an Introduction by Evert Sprinchorn, Oreglia's text describes the Commedia dell'Arte from the mid-sixteenth century through approximately two hundred years. The scenarios of a number of plays are given in full and chapters are devoted to the characters, their costumes, their roles, and the actors who specialized in the roles. Complementing the text are many illustrations from the work of contemporary artists. Bibliography. Index.

ORR, DAVID
Italian Renaissance Drama in England Before 1625
See Page 157

RADCLIFF–UMSTEAD, DOUGLAS
The Birth of Modern Comedy in Rennaissance Italy
University of Chicago, 1969. 285pp. $15.00. The author provides a detailed analytical and comparative study of Renaissance comedy in Italy and shows it to be an original drama which expressed Renaissance values and depicted contemporary customs. Appendices include the plots of Latin and Italian plays. Bibliography. Index of Names. Index of Plays.

REA, DOMENICO
Pulcinella e "La Canzone di Zeza"
See Page 348

SALERNO, HENRY F. – Editor
Scenarios of the Commedia dell'Arte
N.Y.U. Press, 1967. 411pp. $13.00. This is the first English translation of a comprehensive collection of working plots actually used by the Commedia dell'Arte companies. It is a reprint and translation of Flaminio Scala's "Il Teatro Delle Favole Rappresentative" first published in 1611. The fifty plays are in the form of plot summaries rather than in dialogue form. Illustrated.

SAND, MAURICE
The History of the Harlequinade
Blom, 1968. Two volume set: 622pp. $25.00. This two volume history, originally published in 1915, examines in detail each of the stock characters of the Commedia dell'Arte from the seventeenth century. The author describes the origin and meaning of each character and traces the history of famous interpretations and actors. Illustrated. Index.

SMITH, WINIFRED
The Commedia dell'Arte
Blom, 1964. 280pp. $13.75. A study of the origins of the Commedia dell'Arte which considers the influences of the Mountebanks and the Academies. The Commedia in Europe in the sixteenth and seventeenth centuries and in Elizabethan and Jocobean England is treated in detail. Typical scenarios are discussed. The volume has a portfolio of illustrations, many of which have never been reproduced before.

SMITH, WINIFRED
Italian Actors of the Renaissance
Blom, 1968. 204pp. $12.50. Originally published in 1930, this is a reissue of the author's study of individual acting companies, especially those of the Duke of Mantua and Giambattista Andreini. A final chapter traces the decline and fall of Lelia and Arlecchino in the early seventeenth century. Illustrated. Index.

SOLERTI, ANGELO
Musica, Ballo e Drammatica Alla Corte Medicea dal 1600 al 1637
Blom, 1968. 594pp. $28.50. Originally published in 1905 and now reissued, this is a collection of rare and previously unpublished texts of dramas and pageants performed at the court of the Medici, with commentaries on them drawn from a contemporary diary. Fully annotated by Professor Solerti. The text is in Italian. Illustrated. Index.

SPINGARN, JOEL E.
History of Literary Criticism in the Renaissance
See Page 541

THERAULT, SUZANNE
La Commedia dell'Arte
Centre National de la Recherche Scientifique, 1965. 311pp. $11.50. Six scenarios for Commedia dell'Arte productions by Placido Adriani. The text of the volume is in Italian and French. Illustrated.

TREVELYAN, RALEIGH – Editor
Italian Writing Today
Penguin, 1967. 285pp. Paper $1.45. Although it does not deal primarily with theatre, this volume includes an essay on "The Theatre of Today" by Nicola Chiaramonte.

Studies of Playwrights

Ariosto, Ludovico

CROCE, BENEDETTO
Ariosto, Shakespeare and Corneille
Russell & Russell, 1966. 440pp. $10.00. A reprint, translated by Douglas Ainslie, of the 1920 edition of three critical essays by the Italian philosopher/critic. Index.

Bertolazzi, Carlo

ALTHUSSER, LOUIS
Notes on a Materialist Theater
Depot Press, 1969. 19pp. Paper $ .75. This is a monograph on the play "El Nost Milan" written by the nineteenth century Italian playwright, Carlo Bertolazzi. The study is based on a production by the Piccolo Teatro of Milan in 1962.

Della Porta, Giambattista

CLUBB, LOUISE GEORGE
Giambattista Della Porta: Dramatist
Princeton, 1965. 359pp. $9.75. This study examines all the known facts on the life of one of Renaissance Italy's finest comic playwrights, closely analyzes his dramatic works as part of the literary scene in the late Renaissance, and evaluates the influence of his comedy on such dramatists as Jean Rotrou and Thomas Middleton. Bibliography and a list of possible new dates for the plays. Index.

Goldoni, Carlo

KENNARD, JOSEPH SPENCER
Goldoni and the Venice of His Times
Blom, 1967. 551pp. $12.50. This is a republication of the 1920 study of the eighteenth century playwright. Professor Kennard presents a study of Goldoni's life together with a detailed examination of the plays he wrote from 1734 to 1760. Emphasis is placed on Goldoni's Venetian inheritance and his respect for tradition. Illustrated. Chronological Summary of Goldoni's Life. Bibliography. Index.

Gozzi, Carlo

GOZZI, CARLO
Useless Memoires of Carlo Gozzi
Oxford, 1962. 285pp. $3.95. Originally published in three volumes in Venice in 1797–1798, this edition of the eighteenth century playwright's autobiography has been edited, revised, and abridged (from the John Addington Symonds translation) by Philip Horne. Gozzi's memoirs record his rivalry with Carlo Goldoni, the production of "The Love of Three Oranges," and his association with the company of Antonio Sacchi.

Machiavelli, Niccolo

MACHIAVELLI, NICCOLO
The Literary Works of Machiavelli
Oxford, 1961. 202pp. $3.75. Translations by J. R. Hale of two comedies, "Mandragola" and "Clizia," a short story, an essay on the Italian language as a medium of literary expression, and a selection from the correspondence.

Pirandello, Luigi

BISHOP, THOMAS
Pirandello and the French Theatre
See Page 124

CAMBON, GLAUCO – Editor
Pirandello: A Collection of Critical Essays
Prentice–Hall, 1967. 182pp. Paper $1.95. A collection of essays on the relationship between the fiction and the drama of Pirandello. The authors discuss Pirandello's influence on twentieth century literature. Selective Bibliography.

MacCLINTOCK, LANDER
The Age of Pirandello
Kraus, 1968. 341pp. $20.00. Originally published in 1951 and now reprinted, this is a study of the Italian theatre after World War I. Among the topics discussed are: the decline of the realistic tradition, the bourgeois tradition, the dialect theatre, cinema, and the theatre business. Notes. Bibliographical References.

STARKIE, WALTER
Luigi Pirandello, 1867 – 1936
University of California, 1965. 340pp. $5.00. Paper $2.25. A third revised edition of the study first published in 1926. Professor Starkie explains Pirandello's relationship to other writers of the modernistic dramatic movement known as the Teatro Grottesco and shows how, in the modern Italian theatre, Pirandello led the attack against the old-fashioned, bourgeois well-made play, and especially against the voluptuous drama of D'Annunzio. This edition has a new Introduction, a new chapter on the effect of Pirandello's work since his death, a revised epilogue, and an expanded Bibliography. Index.

JAPAN

For other books on this subject, see: Dance – Ethnic

ANDO, TSURUO
Bunraku: The Puppet Theatre
See Page 341

ARKI, JAMES T.
The Ballad-Drama of Medieval Japan
University of California, 1964. 289pp. $7.50. An historical account of the ballad-drama, or "Kowaka," a legacy of the heroic age which recounts the exploits of Samurai warriors. Synopses of fifty Kowaka, complete texts of two, and new translations. Illustrated.

ARNOTT, PETER
The Theatres of Japan
St. Martin's, 1969. 319pp. $12.50. This book traces the history of Japanese drama using as examples works which still may be seen. Topics include dances, the Noh drama, the Kabuki, imitators of the Japanese style, and the traditional influences on the modern Japanese film. Sixteen pages of plates. Glossary. Bibliography. Index.

BOWERS, FAUBION
Japanese Theatre
Hill & Wang, 1959. 194pp. Paper $2.25. A reprint of the 1952 edition, this is a history of the Kabuki and of other theatres in Japan. The Noh drama, early dance drama, and the doll theatres are studied. Three Kabuki plays are given in translation. Illustrated.

DE VERA, JOSE MARIA
Educational Television in Japan
See Page 487

DUNN, CHARLES J. and BUNZO TORIGOE
The Actors' Analects
See Page 411

DUNN, C.J.
The Early Japanese Puppet Theatre
See Page 342

ERNST, EARLE
The Kabuki Theatre
Oxford, 1956. 269pp. $7.50. Paper – Grove, 1969. 269pp. $3.95. An analysis of the Kabuki theatre as a manifestation of the philosophical, political, and aesthetic attitudes of the Japanese. The Kabuki techniques of expression are compared with those of Western theatre. Included are fifty-eight Illustrations of every phase of Kabuki.

GUNJI, MASAKATSU
Buyo: The Classical Dance
See Page 321

HALFORD, AUBREY S. and GIOVANNA M. HALFORD
The Kabuki Handbook: A Guide to Understanding and Appreciation
Tuttle, 1956. 487pp. $3.50. Synopses and explanations of the hundred-odd plays which form the main Kabuki repertoire, with notes on all aspects of the drama's history, its acting techniques, music, costuming, and production. Illustrated.

HIRONAGA, SHUZABURO
Bunraku: Japan's Unique Puppet Theatre
See Page 342

JAPANESE NATIONAL COMMISSION FOR UNESCO
Theatre of Japan
Japan Publications, 1963. 250pp. Paper $8.00. This work is intended to give an account of Japanese theatre in all its aspects. Chapters are included on the classic and the modern forms of drama. Illustrated.

KEENE, DONALD
Bunraku: The Art of the Japanese Puppet Theatre
See Page 342

KEENE, DONALD
No: The Classical Theatre of Japan
Kodansha, 1966. 311pp. $27.50. Mr. Keene presents the history, literary content, music and dance, and a critique of the aesthetic ideals of No drama. Kaneko Hiroshi has contributed hundreds of photographs of actual performances. Included is a recording of excerpts from the No play: "Funa Kenkei." Bibliography. Index.

KINCAID, ZOE
Kabuki: The Popular Stage of Japan
Blom, 1965. 385pp. $18.50. First published in 1925, this study is an account of the Kabuki drama. There are summaries of the most important plays and the text is supplemented by a series of fifty plates. Bibliography. Index.

KUSANO, EISABURO
Stories Behind Noh and Kabuki Plays
Japan Publications, 1962. 128pp. $2.75. The author has retold the classic plays of the Japanese theatre in story form, incorporating the folk-loric aspects in simple form for the Western reader. Illustrated with four photographs and with woodcuts. Appendices.

LOMBARD, FRANK ALANSON
An Outline History of the Japanese Drama
Haskell House, 1966. 358pp. $20.00. Originally published in 1928 and now reissued, this history of Japanese drama traces the evolution of the dramatic repertoire from song and symbolistic mimicry to the Noh dramas and the Kabuki plays. Many translations from the various forms are included. Illustrated. Index.

MALM, WILLIAM P.
Nagauta: The Heart of Kabuki Music
Tuttle, 1963. 344pp. $10.00. A study of one of the major elements in the music of the Kabuki theatre. The various forms found in Nagauta are studied, along with the techniques used for the various instruments. A separate insert volume contains the first transcription into Western notation of two complete Nagauta.

MILLER, ROY ANDREW
Masterpieces of Japanese Puppetry
See Page 342

MINER, EARL
The Japanese Tradition in British and American Literature
See Page 13

MINNICH, HELEN BENTON
Japanese Costume and the Makers of Its Elegant Tradition
See Page 400

MIYAKE, SHUTARO
Kabuki Drama
Tuttle, 1958. 157pp. $3.50. Information on the conventions and techniques of the Kabuki stage in its various forms and styles. Brief synopses of more than forty representative plays. Illustrated.

NISHIMOTO, MITOJI
Development of Educational Broadcasting in Japan
See Page 490

POUND, EZRA and ERNEST FENOLLOSA
The Classic Noh Theatre of Japan, with an Essay on the Noh by William Butler Yeats
New Directions, 1959. 163pp. Paper $1.50. Fifteen of the most famous Noh plays are given in their entirety and five in synopses. The Introduction provides a full history of the development of Noh drama and its techniques. Included is an essay, first published in 1916, by William Butler Yeats.

SCOTT, A. C.
The Kabuki Theatre of Japan
Barnes & Noble, 1964. 317pp. $8.95. Paper—Collier, 1966. 319pp. $2.95. This is a detailed study of the Kabuki theatre in which the author provides information on the plays, the music, and the actors' techniques. He relates the historical development of the drama against the social background of Japan. Scott also provides a comparison between Japanese and Chinese theatre. He includes a Select Bibliography, a List of Japanese Eras, a Glossary of Japanese terms, five illustrative plates and thirty-eight drawings. Index.

SCOTT, A. C.
The Puppet Theatre of Japan
See Page 342

TOITA, YASUJI
Kabuki: The Popular Theater
Lippincott, 1970. 245pp. $5.95. Translated by Don Kenny with an Introduction by Donald Keene, this is a largely visual approach to the world of Kabuki to show its history, techniques, repertoire, and actors. 181 Illustrations. Chronology.

TOKYO DOLL SCHOOL
The World of Japanese Dolls
See Page 342

WEBB, HERSCHEL
An Introduction to Japan
Columbia, 1960. 145pp. Paper $1.75. Originally published in 1955 and now reissued, this is a guide to Japan. The author introduces the reader to the land and its people and relates the history of its development from a primitive country to a world power. He considers the social and cultural life including the fine arts and literature, and the development of Japanese drama, poetry, and prose. Bibliographies are included for each topic.

NORWAY

BARRANGER, MILLY S.
Simplified Approach to Ibsen: Ghosts, The Wild Duck, Hedda Gabler
Barron, 1969. 108pp. Paper $ .95. Detailed analyses and interpretation of the three plays with discussion of each play, its theme and structure, characters and action, the author and the critics. Topics for discussion are included. Bibliography.

BARRANGER, MILLY S.
Simplified Approach to Ibsen: Peer Gynt, A Doll's House, An Enemy of the People
Barron, 1969. 124pp. Paper $ .95. Detailed analyses and interpretations of each of the three plays with discussions of the plays' themes and structures, the characters and action, the author and the critics. Topics for discussion are included. Bibliography.

BRADBROOK, M.C.
Ibsen, the Norwegian: A Revaluation
Shoestring, 1966. 173pp. $5.00. A new edition of the 1946 publication in which Dr. Bradbrook provides an analysis of the plays. She shows how the plays relate to the three chief phases of Ibsen's life and has written a new chapter for this edition about Ibsen's drama on the modern stage. Index.

BRANDES, GEORGE
Henrik Ibsen: A Critical Study
Blom, 1964. 172pp. $7.50. A reprinting of the authorized translation by Jessie Muir, first published in 1899, with an Introduction by William Archer. These three essays serve as summations of Ibsen's achievements in the years 1867, 1882, and 1898 and the author concentrates on presenting a defense of Ibsen's Naturalism. Also included in the volume is a forty-two page essay on Bjornstjerne Bjornson, one of Norway's greatest dramatists. Index.

BYRNES, EDWARD T.
The Plays of Ibsen
Monarch, 1965. 107pp. Paper $1.00. Edited by Stanley Brodwin, this is a critical commentary on eleven plays. Detailed act-by-act summaries are provided as are critical commentary, essay questions and answers for review. Bibliography.

FJELDE, ROLF – Editor
Ibsen: A Collection of Critical Essays
Prentice–Hall, 1965. 184pp. $5.95. Paper $1.95. A collection of critical essays on the Norwegian playwright. The editor has contributed an Introduction, a Chronology, and a Selected Bibliography. Among the essayists are Eric Bentley, Francis Fergusson, Richard Schechner, and E.M. Forster.

HAMSUN, KNUT
On Overgrown Paths
MacGibbon & Kee, 1968. 176pp. $6.75. Translated and with an Introduction by Carl I. Anderson, this memoir of the Norwegian novelist and playwright was written while he was interned from 1945 to 1948 on suspicion of treason. This book deals with the trial and internment of the Nobel prize winner rather than with his literary output.

HEIBERG, HANS
Ibsen: A Portrait of the Artist
University of Miami, 1971. 313pp. $10.00. Originally published in 1969 in England, this biography of the playwright has been translated by Joan Tate. It describes the early life of the writer in a small provincial town, his years of adversity and humiliation, and the withdrawal which occured at the same time his fame was growing. Chronology. Index.

HOLTAN, ORLEY I.
Mythic Patterns in Ibsen's Last Plays
University of Minnesota, 1970. 213pp. $7.95. Professor Holtan examines Ibsen's last eight plays. He identifies a mythic pattern and unity in these plays, based on elements of symbolism and mysticism. Notes. Bibliography. Index.

LAVRIN, JANKO
Ibsen: An Approach
Russell & Russell, 1969. 139pp. $9.00. Originally published in 1950 and now reissued, this is a study of the playwright. Bibliography. Index.

McFARLANE, JAMES WALTER – Editor
Discussions of Henrik Ibsen
D.C. Heath, 1962. 110pp. Paper $2.25. The essays in this collection discuss the meaning of Ibsenism and its influence, examine individual plays, consider the style, characterization, and evaluate the playwright's influence.

McFARLANE, JAMES WALTER – Editor
Henrik Ibsen: A Critical Anthology
Penguin, 1970. 476pp. Paper $3.25. A critical anthology of criticism on the playwright. Both contemporary and modern view-points are provided. A full selection from the writer on his own art is also included. The editor has contributed Introductions, a Table of Dates, a Bibliography, and a full Glossarial Index.

McFARLANE, JAMES WALTER and GRAHAM ORTON – Editors
The Oxford Ibsen – Volume One: Early Plays
Oxford, 1970. 715pp. $25.00. A scholarly edition, in a projected series of eight volumes, of all of Ibsen's plays. In his translations, Mr. McFarlane has worked from the original manuscripts and has included a selection of Ibsen's draft material where available. He has also provided a critical introduction to each volume and full bibliographical information. The plays in this volume include: "Catiline," "The Burial

Mound," "St. John's Night," "Lady Inger," "The Feast at Solhoug," and "Olaf Likjekrans."

McFARLANE, JAMES WALTER – Editor
The Oxford Ibsen – Volume Two: The Vikings at Helgeland, Love's Comedy, The Pretenders
Oxford, 1962. 378pp. $9.00. See Volume One for information.

McFARLANE, JAMES WALTER and GRAHAM ORTON – Editors
The Oxford Ibsen – Volume Four: League of Youth, Emperor and Galilean
Oxford, 1963. 616pp. $10.50. See Volume One for information.

McFARLANE, JAMES WALTER – Editor
The Oxford Ibsen – Volume Five: Pillars of Society, A Doll's House, Ghosts.
Oxford, 1961. 499pp. $9.50. See Volume One for information.

McFARLANE, JAMES WALTER – Editor
The Oxford Ibsen – Volume Six: An Enemy of the People, The Wild Duck, Rosmersholm
Oxford, 1960. 464pp. $8.00. See Volume One for information.

McFARLANE, JAMES WALTER – Editor
The Oxford Ibsen – Volume Seven: The Lady from the Sea, Hedda Gabler, The Master Builder
Oxford, 1966. 592pp. $14.75. See Volume One for information.

MEYER, MICHAEL
Henrik Ibsen: The Making of a Dramatist 1828 – 1864
Hart–Davis, 1967. 260pp. $10.00. Mr. Meyer reconsiders Ibsen's development as a man and as a writer and revalues his work, both individually and as a whole. He portrays the changing theatrical world of Ibsen's time and shows the impact of his life and work on his contemporaries. Selected Bibliography. Index.

MUIR, KENNETH
Last Periods of Shakespeare, Racine, Ibsen
See Page 123

SPRINCHORN, EVERT – Editor
Ibsen: Letters and Speeches
Hill & Wang, 1964. 360pp. $5.75. Paper $2.45. The first English edition of Ibsen's letters since 1905, this book contains, in chronological order, 276 letters, thirteen speeches, four prefaces and an autobiographical fragment. Chronology.

TENNANT, P.F.D.
Ibsen's Dramatic Technique
Humanities, 1965. 135pp. $6.00. Originally published in 1948, this study analyzes Ibsen's method of composition, his setting, stage directions, plot and action, exposition and endings. Appendices. Bibliography.

THOMPSON, REBECCA and ALICE BERNSTEIN
About "Hedda Gabler"
Definition Press, 1970. 14pp. Paper $1.00. An essay by the actress who appeared in the title role of the "Opposites Company" production of "Hedda Gabler" off-Broadway. This production was based on Eli Siegel's philosophy of Aesthetic Realism. Miss Bernstein has contributed "A Short History of Hedda Gabler Criticism 1890–1970."

TYSDAHL, B.J.
Joyce and Ibsen: A Study in Literary Influence
See Page 207

WEIGAND, HERMANN
The Modern Ibsen: A Reconsideration
Dutton, 1960. 416pp. Paper $1.95. An essay in creative interpretation which is devoted to a close analysis of the texts of the twelve social dramas. Most of the biographical data are omitted and there is no treatment of the first half of Ibsen's output.

POLAND

WELSH, DAVID
Adam Mickiewicz
Twayne, 1966. 168pp. $4.50. A biography of the nineteenth century Polish poet and playwright. Notes and References. Selected Bibliography. Index.

WELSH, DAVID
Ignacy Krasicki
Twayne, 1969. 150pp. $4.95. The first full-length study in English of the eighteenth century Polish writer. One chapter details the eight comedies written for the Polish National Theatre. Notes and References. Bibliography. Index.

WIENIEWSKA, CELINA – Editor
Polish Writing Today
Penguin, 1967. 206pp. Paper $1.45. An anthology of recent prose and poetry from Poland. The contributors include: Bochenski, Brandys, Herbert, and Szymborska. Jan Kott's essay, "A Short Treatise on Eroticism," is also included.

PORTUGAL

PARKER, JACK HORACE
Gil Vicente
Twayne, 1967. 169pp. $5.50. A study of the Court Dramatist of Portugal in the first third of the sixteenth century. The dramatist wrote in both Portuguese and Spanish and thus belongs to the literature of both countries. Parker attempts to assess Vicente's literary activity and his place in the history of theatre. Chronology. Selected Bibliography. Index.

RUSSIA

Histories and Critiques

BRAUN, EDWARD
Meyerhold on Theatre
Hill & Wang, 1969. 336pp. $8.50. This is a collection of Vsevolod Meyerhold's writings which cover his entire career as a director from 1902 to 1939. Mr. Braun has translated and edited the writings and provides critical commentary and descriptions of all the major productions. Included are fifty photographs of Meyerhold's designs and productions. Select Bibliography. Index.

CARTER, HUNTLY
The New Spirit in the Russian Theatre: 1917–1928
Blom, 1970. 348pp. $7.00. Originally published in 1929 and now reissued in a facsimile edition, this is a study of the Russian cinema and radio from 1919 to 1928. Illustrated. Appendices. Indices.

COURNOS, JOHN – Editor
A Treasury of Classic Russian Literature
Putnam, 1962. 584pp. Paper $2.45. This is an anthology of the best of Russian literature up to 1917. The editor has included such authors as Turgenev, Dostoevsky, Bakunin, Tolstoy, and Pushkin. Also provided are essays by Chekhov and Gorki on literary subjects and Gogol's play "The Inspector General."

FULOP–MILLER, RENE and JOSEF GREGOR
The Russian Theatre
Blom, 1968. 384pp. $32.50. This comprehensive study of the Russian theatre was first published in 1930. The four hundred illustrations give a pictorial history from the Court Theatre of the Tsars to the "Mass Theatre." Closely examined are the relationship between theatre and social conditions in Russia from the late nineteenth century through the early days of the Revolution. Index.

GORCHAKOV, NIKOLAI
The Theatre in Soviet Russia
Columbia, 1957. 480pp. $15.00. Translated by Edgar Lehman, this is a history of the growth and decline of Russian theatre in the twentieth century. Using original documents, the author traces the contributions of Stanislavsky and Danchenko and their early relationship with Chekhov. Meyerhold's contributions to staging and design are discussed. The manner in which the theatre was altered by the Soviet political repressions is analyzed in detail. Illustrated. Bibliography.

GRONICKA, ANDRE VON
The Russian Image of Goethe
See Page 140

HARRIS, LEON
The Moscow Circus School
Atheneum, 1970. 60pp. $4.50. A study for children of the school in Moscow where children learn to be circus performers. Illustrated with photographs.

KOHANSKY, MENDEL
The Hebrew Theatre: Its First Fifty Years
See Page 212

KOMISSARZHEVSKY, VICTOR
Moscow Theatre
Foreign Languages Publishing House, 1959. 219pp. $4.50. A survey of contemporary Moscow stage life, with descriptions of the best known playhouses, including the Bolshoi and the Maly. Illustrated with photographs of performances and portraits of actors and directors.

KOZINTSEV, GRIGORI
Shakespeare: Time and Conscience
See Page 94

LIPOVSKY, ALEXANDER – Compiler
Lenin Prize Winners: Soviet Stars, Master of Stage and Screen
Central Books, 1969. 368pp. $7.50. This is a collection of articles about actors, directors, cinematographers, and dance artists of the Soviet theatre, cinema and ballet who have been awarded the Lenin Prize for outstanding achievements in their field over the period 1957–1966. Published in Russia as translated by Katharine Villiers.

LIPOVSKY, ALEXANDER – Compiler
The Soviet Circus
See Page 347

MUCHNIC, HELEN
From Gorky to Pasternak: Six Writers in Soviet Russia
Random House, 1966. 438pp. Paper $2.45. A reprint of the 1961 study in which the author includes essays on Gorky, Pasternak, Mayakovsky, and Leonov. Index.

MUCHNIC, HELEN
An Introduction to Russian Literature
Dutton, 1964. 252pp. Paper $1.65. Originally published in 1947 and now reprinted, this is an analysis of the nature of Russian literature. Professor Muchnic's purpose is to uncover in the works of Russia's greatest writers certain traits that might be used toward an explanation of Russia's literary art. Individual chapters treat Gogol, Turgenev, Doestoevsky, Tolstoy, and Chekhov, among others. Bibliography. Index.

NEMIROVITCH–DANTCHENKO, VLADIMIR
My Life in the Russian Theatre
Theatre Arts, 1968. 365pp. $9.50. Paper $3.45. Translated by John Cournos, with an Introduction by Joshua Logan and a Chronology by Elizabeth Reynolds

Hapgood, this book by the co-founder of the Moscow Art Theatre was originally published in 1936. The volume details Dantchenko's relationship to the playwrights of the Moscow Art Theatre and gives an account of the first conversation between Stanislavsky and Dantchenko which lasted for eighteen hours. Illustrated with photographs. Index.

ROBERTS, SPENCER E.
Soviet Historical Drama: Its Role in the Development of a National Mythology
Martinus Nijhoff, 1965. 218pp. Paper $10.00. The author examines the literary and idealogical controversies which arose over the historical plays in the Soviet Union from 1917 and traces the evolution of the myths on which they are based. What historical materials were available to the playwrights and what uses they made of them are examined. The author tries to determine how much of the myths of a corrupt past, an encircling enemy, and a glorious defender are still officially sanctioned. Bibliography. Index.

SAMARIN, ROMAN and ALEXANDER NIKOLYUKIN – Editors
Shakespeare in the Soviet Union
Central Books, 1966. 275pp & plates. $3.95. Translated by A. Pyman, this is a selection of articles by distinguished Soviet writers, critics, scholars, and people of the theatre. Color plates of sets, costumes, posters, and illustrations of productions.

SIMMONS, ERNEST J.
Introduction to Russian Realism
Indiana University, 1965. 275pp. Paper $2.65. The author presents the development of realism in Russian fiction from its inception to the Soviet era. He takes into account the intellectual, social, and political movements in Russia and Western Europe, offers new insights into the achievements of six authors (Pushkin, Gogol, Dostoevsky, Tolstoy, Chekhov, and Sholokhov), and sheds new light on the meaning of realism. Index.

SIMONOV, RUBEN
Stanislavsky's Protege: Eugene Vakhtangov
Drama Book Specialists, 1969. 243pp. $6.95. Translated and adapted by Miriam Goldina, this is a book about the work of the Russian director. There is a detailed account of the rehearsals for Chekhov's "The Wedding," comparisons of Vakhtangov's and Stanislavsky's treatment of Chekhov works, and the Soviet theatre from 1919 to the present. Chronology.

SLONIM, MARC
From Chekhov to the Revolution: Russian Literature 1900 – 1917
Oxford, 1964. 253pp. Paper $1.50. This book,originally published in 1953, reproduces the first ten chapters of the author's "Modern Russian Literature." It offers a comprehensive view of Russian literature from the era of the great classics through Chekhov, Gorki, Bunin, Kuprin, and Andreyev, down to the modernist movement.

SLONIM, MARC
Russian Theatre from the Empire to the Soviets
Collier, 1962. 382pp. Paper $1.50. A study of the main trends in the development of the Russian stage. The emphasis is on the literary and aesthetic tendencies of each period. Special attention is given to the mood and manner of the post-Revolutionary stage.

Studies of Playwrights

Aleichem, Sholom

WAIFE–GOLDBERG, MARIE
My Father, Sholom Aleichem
Simon & Schuster, 1968. 333pp. $7.50. A biography of the author of the stories upon which the musical, "Fiddler on the Roof," is based. Included is a list of the works in translation from the Yiddish. Index.

Andreyev, Leonid

GORKY, MAXIM
Reminiscenses of Tolstoy, Chekhov, and Andreyev
See Page 223

KAUN, ALEXANDER
Leonid Andreyev: A Critical Study
Blom, 1969. 361pp. $12.50. Originally published in 1924 and now reissued, this is a study and biography of the Russian playwright of the early twentieth century. A comprehensive Bibliography is included. Index.

WOODWARD, JAMES B.
Leonid Andreyev: A Study
Oxford, 1969. 290pp. $11.00. This is the author's investigation of the unity and coherent body of ideas in the work of the Russian literary figure. Woodward is mainly concerned with Andreyev's fiction in this study. Index.

Chekhov, Anton

CHEKHOV, ANTON
Letters of Anton Tchehov to Olga Knipper
Blom, 1966. 401pp. $12.50. Translated and edited by Constance Garnett, these are the letters that Checkhov wrote to his wife from 1899 to 1904. The letters provide an intimate glimpse of Chekhov's life and thought and shed light on his ideas of the staging and acting of his plays. An Index has been especially compiled for this new edition.

CHEKHOV, ANTON
Letters on the Short Story, the Drama, and Other Literary Topics
Blom, 1964. 346pp. $8.50. Paper—Dover, 1966. 346pp. $2.00. A reprint of the 1924 edition, selected and edited by Louis S. Friedland, this is a collection of 470 letters which reveal Chekhov's attitudes toward his own work, his contemporaries, the theatre, and the critics. Index of Short Stories. Index to Persons and Subjects.

CHEKHOV, ANTON
Literary and Theatrical Reminiscences
Blom, 1965. 248pp. $8.50. Edited by S. S. Koteliansky, this reprint of the original 1927 edition contains Chekhov's diary, an autobiographical sketch, and two sections of literary and theatrical reminiscences. Eight hitherto unpublished works by Chekhov (short stories, sketches, fragments of stories, and a drama in one act titled "Tayana Riepin."). Index.

CHEKHOV, ANTON
The Notebooks of Anton Chekhov
Hogarth, 1967. 108pp. $2.50. This collection of "Themes, thoughts, notes and fragments" was found among Chekhov's papers and first published in 1921. Now reissued and combined with Maxim Gorky's "Reminiscences of Chekhov," first published in 1906. The works have been translated by S. S. Koteliansky and Leonard Woolf.

CHEKHOV, ANTON
The Selected Letters of Anton Chekhov
Farrar, Straus, 1955. 331pp. $4.95. New translations by Sidonie K. Ledered, edited by Lillian Hellman, of a number of letters by the playwright covering the period from 1885 to 1904. Some of the letters are previously unpublished and others contain passages which do not appear in earlier publications.

CHEKHOV, ANTON
Stories: 1895—1897
Oxford, 1965. 325pp. $6.75. Volume VII in the Oxford Chekhov series, this is a collection of all of Chekhov's fiction which was first published from 1895 through 1897. Included are four fragments never published during the playwright's lifetime. The volume has been translated and edited by Ronald Hingley. Bibliography. Notes. Appendices.

EHRENBURG, ILYA
Chekhov, Stendahl, and Other Essays
Knopf, 1963. 291pp. $5.95. Translated by Anna Bostock, Yvonne Kapp, and Tatiana Shebunina, with an Introduction by Harrison Salisbury, this is a collection of essays by the leading critic of current Soviet cultural standards.

GILLES, DANIEL
Chekhov: Observer Without Illusion
Funk & Wagnalls, 1968. 436pp. $10.00. Translated by Charles Lam Markmann, this a biography of the playwright and a study of his works. Bibliography. Index.

GORKY, MAXIM
Reminiscenses of Tolstoy, Chekhov, and Andreyev
See Page 223

HINGLEY, RONALD
Chekhov: A Biographical and Critical Study
Barnes & Noble, 1966. 256pp. $4.50. Paper $2.25. A revised edition of the study first published in 1950. The author provides a full account of the man and his work. Bibliography. Index.

JACKSON, ROBERT LOUIS—Editor
Chekhov: A Collection of Critical Essays
Prentice-Hall, 1967. 213pp. $5.95. Paper $1.95. This collection of essays ranges from studies of Chekhov's place in Russian literature through analyses of the plays and prose. Included are selections from Stanislavsky's prompt-book for "The Three Sisters." Bibliography.

MAGARSHACK, DAVID
Chekhov the Dramatist
Hill & Wang, 1960. 301pp. Paper $1.45. A study of the development of Chekhov's ideas on dramatic art. The author investigates the genesis and evolution of his plays and analyzes their structure.

MANN, THOMAS
Last Essays
See Page 13

SAUNDERS, BEATRICE
Chekhov: The Man
Dufur, 1960. 195pp. $6.00. Miss Saunders contends that Chekhov was aware from his early manhood of his exceptional literary talent and that he used this talent for the furtherance of the Russian cause and for the assistance of his family. Index.

SHESTOV, LEON
Chekhov and Other Essays
University of Michigan, 1966. 205pp. $4.50. Paper $1.95. First published in 1918 and now reissued with an Introduction by Sidney Monas, this is a collection of essays on Chekhov, Doestoevsky, Ibsen, Tolstoy, and Kant.

SIMMONS, ERNEST J.
Chekhov: A Biography
Little, Brown, 1962. 669pp. $10.00. Paper—University of Chicago, 1970. 669pp. $3.95. A comprehensive study of Chekhov's life and work, based on much evidence only recently made available in Russia. Bibliographic Survey. Index.

TOUMANOVA, NINA ANDRONIKOVA
Anton Chekhov, the Voice of Twilight Russia

Columbia, 1960. 238pp. $4.25. Paper $1.50. The life of Chekhov, told against the background of Russian social and intellectual life in the late nineteenth century. A reprint of the 1937 edition.

VALENCY, MAURICE
The Breaking String: The Plays of Anton Chekhov
Oxford, 1966. 324pp. $7.00. Paper—1969. $1.95. Professor Valency examines the Russian dramatic tradition and the work of other Russian writers in respect to their influence on Chekhov. He discusses the periods of Chekhov's life when he wrote his great plays and emphasizes the achievements of "The Sea Gull," "Uncle Vanya," "The Three Sisters," and "The Cherry Orchard." Index.

WEXFORD, JANE
The Plays of Anton Chekhov
Monarch, 1965. 127pp. Paper $1.00. A critical guide to five plays. Detailed act-by-act summaries are provided with critical commentary. Selected Bibliography.

WINNER, THOMAS
Chekhov and His Prose
Holt, Rinehart, 1966. 263pp. $5.00. The author traces the development of Chekhov's prose style from its start when Chekhov was writing for the "pulps" to the perfection of such stories as "The Peasants" and "The Duel." The technique of the modern short story is examined.

YACHNIN, RISSA
Chekhov in English: 1949–1960
New York Public Library, 1960. 47pp. Paper $1.00. A brief biographical sketch, followed by a list of works by and about Chekhov which were published from 1949 to 1960.

Gogol, Nikolai

ERLICH, VICTOR
Gogol
Yale, 1969. 230pp. $10.00. A survey of the works of the Russian writer. The author traces the gradual maturation of Gogol's art to show that his central theme was the intrusion of the demonic into the real world. Index.

GOGOL, NIKOLAI
Letters of Nikolai Gogol
University of Michigan, 1967. 247pp. $8.00. Carl R. Proffer has selected and edited about one-sixth of Gogol's letters as both representative of the total and particularly interesting to the specialist and the general reader. He has carefully annotated these letters and provided a detailed Bibliography. Index.

MAGARSHACK, DAVID
Gogol: A Life
Grove, 1969. 328pp. Paper $2.95. Originally published in 1957 and now reissued, this is a study of the Russian novelist and playwright. Mr. Magarshack attempts to define Gogol's place in Russian letters and the influence he had on the political life of his country. Bibliography. Index.

NABOKOV, VLADIMIR
Nikolai Gogol
New Directions, 1961. 172pp. Paper $1.75. A corrected edition of the 1944 study in which Nabokov examines the life and work of Gogol to bring to life the strange, unhappy, self-deluding man and his singular literary methods and achievements. Index.

SETCHKAREV, VSEVOLOD
Gogol: His Life and Works
New York University, 1965. 264pp. $8.00. Paper $2.25. A comprehensive account of Gogol's career, with an investigation of his realism, his political commitment, and his religious sentiments. Index.

Gorky, Maxim

BORRAS, F. M.
Maxim Gorky, the Writer: An Interpretation
Oxford, 1967. 195pp. $5.75. This book attempts to place Maxim Gorky as an artist in relation to his time and to evaluate his best work independently of propaganda and political factors. The events of his life are considered in relation to his writings. Bibliography. Index.

GORKY, MAXIM
The Autobiography of Maxim Gorky
Citadel, 1969. 616pp. Paper $3.45. Gorky's three autobiographical works—"My Childhood," "In the World," and "My Universities"—have been translated by Isidor Schneider and collected into one volume. Originally published in 1949 and now reissued.

GORKY, MAXIM
The Autobiography of Maxim Gorky
Collier, 1962. 638pp. Paper $1.50. The complete autobiography of the author with an illuminating account of life in Russia immediately preceding and following the Revolution.

GORKY, MAXIM
Childhood
Cambridge, 1965. 155pp. $2.25. Gertrude M. Foakes' translation, abridged and edited by David Holbrook.

GORKY, MAXIM
Literary Portraits
Foreign Languages Publishing House, Undated. 310pp. $2.50. Character sketches of Tolstoy, Chekhov, Korolenko, Kotsubinsky, Garin-Mikhailovsky, and Prishvin, based on the author's personal knowledge.

GORKY, MAXIM
My Childhood
Penguin, 1966. 234pp. Paper $1.25. The first part of Gorky's autobiography, translated by Ronald Wilks.

GORKY, MAXIM
Reminiscences of Tolstoy, Chekhov, and Andreyev
Viking, 1959. 182pp. Paper $1.25. Among these sketches, based on Gorky's diaries and notes, are Tolstoy's comments on "The Lower Depths;" Chekhov discussing "Uncle Vanya" and "The Cherry Orchard." Introduction by Mark Van Doren.

HARE, RICHARD
Maxim Gorky: Romantic Realist and Conservative Revolutionary
Oxford, 1962. 156pp. $4.25. This account of Gorky's life and achievement is based primarily on a close study of his works and of material published recently in Russia. Illustrated. Index.

KAUN, ALEXANDER
Maxim Gorky and His Russia
Blom, 1968. 620pp. $12.50. Originally published in 1931 and now reissued, this is a study of the author against the background of Russia in transition from the rule of the Tsars to the dictatorship of the Bolsheviks. Included is a list of important dates in Gorky's life and a list of his writings. Index.

LEVIN, DAN
Stormy Petrel: The Life and Work of Maxim Gorky
Appleton, 1965. 332pp. $7.95. A biography of Gorky which attempts to re-evaluate his life and achievements. Levin maintains the Gorky's creative works have been lost in the shadow of "the hero of the revolution" created by Soviet propaganda. He re-examines Gorky's place in the Russian revolutionary movement.

Mayakovsky, Vladimir Vladimirovich

WOROSZYLSKI, WIKTOR
The Life of Mayakovsky
Orion Press. 1970. 562pp. $15.00. Translated from the Polish by Boleslaw Taborski, this is a biography of the Russian writer. The events of the poet's life are described by the poet himself or by eye-witnesses in a collage of documentary sources. Illustrated. Notes. Index.

Nabokov, Vladimir

DEMBO, L. S. – Editor
Nabokov: The Man and His Work
University of Wisconsin Press, 1967. 282pp. $6.50. Paper $2.50. Featuring an exclusive interview with the Russian writer, this is a collection of essays which examine and study his major works of fiction, drama, and literary criticism. Selected Bibliography. Index.

FIELD, ANDREW
Nabokov: His Life in Art
Little, Brown, 1967. 397pp. Paper $2.95. A biography and criticism of the complete works of Vladimir Nabokov. A brief chronology is included as is a Bibliography of all the works and an Index.

NABOKOV, VLADIMIR
Speak, Memory: An Autobiography Revisited
Capricorn, 1970. 316pp. Paper $2.95. Originally published in 1966 and now reissued, this is the autobiography of the Russian author. The recollections cover the years from 1903 to 1940. Illustrated with photographs. Index.

Tolstoy, Leo

CHRISTIAN, R. F.
Tolstoy: A Critical Introduction
Oxford, 1969. 291pp. Paper $2.45. This is an introduction to the novels and short stories of the Russian author. "War and Peace" and "Anna Karenina" are discussed in detail and most of the other fiction is also discussed. There is one chapter on Tolstoy's drama and aesthetic theories. Chronology. Selected Bibliography. Index.

GIBIAN, G.
Tolstoy and Shakespeare
Humanities, 1957. 47pp. Paper $2.75. A study of Tolstoy's violent antagonism toward Shakespeare which shows that this attitude was not an expression of the author's old age but was a deeply felt sentiment of his youth and middle period.

GORKY MAXIM
Reminiscences of Tolstoy, Chekhov, and Andreyev
See preceding column

MATLAW, RALPH E. – Editor
Tolstoy: A Collection of Critical Essays
Prentice–Hall, 1967. 178pp. $4.95. Paper $1.95. A collection of essays evaluating the relationship between Tolstoy's artistic technique and his creative vision. Edmund Wilson, Isaiah Berlin, George Lukacs, and others study the individual works.

NOYES, GEORGE RAPALL
Tolstoy
Dover, 1968. 395pp. Paper $2.50. A republication of the 1918 edition, this is an exploration of the interrelations of Tolstoy's life and work, with examination of important writings. The work is based in part on interviews with Tolstoy. Bibliography. Index.

TOLSTOY, LEO
Childhood, Boyhood and Youth
Washington Square Press, 1968. 361pp. Paper $ .90. Translated, and with an Introduction, by Alexandra and Sverre Lyngstad, this is Tolstoy's autobiographical novel. Selected Bibliography.

Turgenev, Ivan S.

TURGENEV, IVAN S.
Literary Reminiscences and Autobiographical Fragments
Farrar, Straus, 1958. 309pp. $5.00. Written toward the end of his career, these pieces discuss the character of creative writing, the attitude of the artist toward his environment, the art of Pushkin, Gogol, Belinsky, Lermontov, and Krylov. An essay by Edmund Wilson explores the strange family background and upbringing of the author. Translated by David Magarshack. Introduction by Edmund Wilson.

TURGENEV, IVAN S.
Turgenev's Letters: A Selection
Knopf, 1961. 401pp. $5.00. Edited and translated from the Russian, French, and German originals by Edgar H. Lehrman. This is the first English translation of a selection from the vast correspondence, including letters to Tolstoy, Herzen, Dostoevsky, Flaubert, Henry James, Mme. Viardot, and Maupassant. A Bibliography is included.

YACHNIN, RISSA and DAVID H. STAM
Turgenev in English
New York Public Library, 1962. 55pp. $2.50. A checklist of works by and about Turgenev with an Introduction by Marc Slonim.

YARMOLINSKY, AVRAHM
Turgenev: The Man, His Art, and His Age
Collier, 1961. 384pp. Paper $1.50. A new, revised edition of the biography first published in 1929. Turgenev's early domination by his mother, his years as a student in Germany, his exile in Paris and Baden, his house arrest, and his bitter love affair with Mme. Viardot are considered. The literary output is analyzed and the influences on it are studied.

SOUTH AMERICA
(Including Latin American Countries)

CALLAN, RICHARD
Miguel Angel Asturias
Twayne, 1970. 182pp. $5.50. A study of the Guatemalan novelist, short story writer, and playwright. The main portion of the book is devoted to the fiction but one chapter studies the five dramas written by the author. Chronology. Notes and References. Selected Bibliography. Index.

COHEN, J. M. – Editor
Latin American Writing Today
Penguin, 1967. 267pp. Paper $1.25. This anthology includes translations of recent prose and poetry from Argentina, Brazil, Chile, Colombia, Cuba, Mexico, Peru, and Uruguay.

COHEN, J. M. – Editor
Writers in the New Cuba
Penguin, 1967. 191pp. Paper $1.25. An anthology of contemporary Cuban writing which includes stories, poems, and a play: "Cain's Mangoes" by Abelardo Estorino.

DAVISON, NED J.
Eduardo Barrios
Twayne, 1970. 152pp. $5.50. A general survey of the works of the Chilean novelist and playwright (1884–1963). Special attention is paid to the development of central themes and character-types, and the relationship of the author's life to his creations is also considered. Major emphasis is placed, however, on the personalities of the characters and their significance in relation to narrative structure, techniques, and literary style. Chronology. Notes and References. Selected Bibliography. Index.

JONES, WILLIS KNAPP
Behind Spanish American Footlights
University of Texas, 1966. 609pp. $9.50. A comprehensive study of the native drama, and the Spanish influences on it, in nineteen South American countries over a 500 year period. The study shows how the many cultural elements of both old and new worlds have been blended into the distinct national characteristics of each of the nations. With a Reading Guide, an extensive Bibliography, and an Index.

JONES, WILLIS KNAPP – Translator
Men and Angels: Three South American Comedies
Southern Illinois University, 1970. 191pp. $7.95. This volume includes translations of three South American comedies which look into human experience on both the conscious and unconscious levels. An Introduction by the translator traces the growth of Latin American theatre from the colonial days to the last few decades which have witnessed the flowering of a true national theatre. Included is a checklist of translations of Spanish-American plays. The texts of the plays included in the volume are by Darthes and Damel, Matto, and Frank.

WRIGHT, RICHARDSON
Revels in Jamaica
Blom, 1969. 378pp. $10.75. Originally published in 1937 and now reissued in a facsimile edition, this book by the newspaperman/historian details, in his own subtitle, "plays and players of a century,

tumblers and conjurors, musical refugees and solitary showmen, dinners, balls, and cockfights, darky mummers and other memories of high times and merry hearts'' during the period 1682–1838. The study covers Jamaican social life including the theatre of the time. Illustrated. Bibliography. Index.

SPAIN

Histories and Critiques

BLISTEIN, ELMER M. – Editor
The Drama of the Renaissance
See Page 98

COOK, JOHN A.
Neo–Classic Drama in Spain: Theory and Practice
Southern Methodist University, 1959. 576pp. $8.50. A general survey of Spanish drama, dramatic theory, and criticism in the eighteenth and early nineteenth centuries. The neo-classic drama of the period is studied in its relation to the golden age of Spanish drama.

CRAWFORD, J. P. WICKERSHAM
Spanish Drama Before Lope de Vega
University of Pennsylvania, 1967. 223pp. $6.50. Originally published in 1922, this is a reprint with corrections and a new Bibliographical Supplement by Warren T. McCready. Professor Crawford's study has been acknowledged as the best history of early Spanish drama ever published. Index.

GREEN, OTIS H.
Spain and the Western Tradition: The Castilian Mind in Literature from El Cid to Calderon
University of Wisconsin. Volume One: 1963. 329pp. $8.75. Paper $2.95. Volume Two: 1964. 365pp. $8.75. Paper $2.95. Volume Three: 1965. 507pp. $12.00. Paper $2.95. Volume Four: 1966. 345pp. $8.75. Paper $2.95. A four volume history and interpretation of Spanish culture. Volume One is concerned mainly with the two great themes of medieval secular literature: chivalry and love. Each chapter in Volume Two is a monograph on an important aspect of the thought patterns that determined the content of medieval and classical Spanish literature. Volume Three deals with the ways in which the intellectual life of Spain responded to the developments and changing pressures of the times. In Volume Four, the author outlines the display of originality and energy in Spanish literature during an era of decline in the greatness of Spain as a nation. Bibliographies and Indices in each volume with a Cumulative Index in Volume Four.

LEECH, CLIFFORD
Shakespeare's Tragedies and Other Studies in Seventeenth Century Drama
See Page 56

MCCLELLAND, I. L.
Spanish Drama of Pathos: 1750 – 1808
Liverpool Univeristy, 1970. 641pp. Two volume set: $32.00. A survey of the dramatic aspect of Spain's movement towards modern thinking. Volume One evaluates the better-known authors, the scholar-dramatists, with special reference to their European context and to the Spanish activity of the period in translation, opera, and parody. Volume Two deals with the little-known, popular playwrights who were of historical importance for their development of foreign social theses and their initiative in experimenting in new dramatic methods. Notes. Bibliography. Index.

McNEIR, WALDO F.
Studies in Comparative Literature
See Page 156

MOLINARO, J. A. and J. H. PARKER, EVELYN RUGG
A Bibliography of Comedias Sueltas in the University of Toronto Library
University of Toronto, 1959. 149pp. $4.25. This Bibliography gives information on the ''Comedias Sueltas'' published between 1703 and 1825.

POUND, EZRA
The Spirit of Romance
New Directions, Undated. 248pp. Paper $2.45. This is an attempt to define the literary traditions of Latin Europe. Pound gives the background of the transition from Latin to the Romance languages, studies the medieval narrative poetry of northern France, the Spanish epic of ''El Cid,'' and the Portuguese epic, ''The Lusiads.'' Also included is a chapter on the plays of Lope de Vega. Index.

RENNERT, HUGO ALBERT
The Spanish Stage in the Time of Lope de Vega
Dover, 1963. 403pp. Paper $2.75. A reprint of the 1909 edition, this study considers the early religious pageants, the ''corrales'' of Madrid and Seville, the staging of the comedies, costumes, women on the stage, actors, salaries, royal performances, relations between church and theatre, and the representations of ''autos sacramentales.''

SHERGOLD, N. D.
A History of the Spanish Stage from Medieval Times until the End of the Seventeenth Century
Oxford, 1967. 624pp. & plates. $20.00. This book aims to provide a complete account of the way in which the plays were staged in Spain from the Middle Ages until about 1700. it covers the early religious and secular drama, the public playhouse, the court theatre, morality plays. Texts of the plays of the period are studied and analyzed. Illustrated with contemporary theatrical drawings. Bibliography. Index.

THOMPSON, LAWRENCE S.
A Bibliography of Spanish Plays on Microcards
See Page 8

WILSON, MARGARET
Spanish Drama of the Golden Age
Pergamon, 1969. 221pp. $6.50. Paper $4.95. A study of theatre in Spain during the seventeenth century. The author analyzes the plays, the nature of the drama and the processes by which it evolved, the playwrights, and the merits and interest of the plays for the student of literature today. Among the playwrights studied are: Vega, Molina, Calderon, Alarcon, Castro, Guevara, and Amescua.

YOUNG, HOWARD T.
The Victorian Expression
University of Wisconsin, 1964. 223pp. Paper $1.95. A study of four contemporary Spanish playwrights: Unamuno, Machado, Jimenez, and Lorca. Accompanying the critical comment on each poet are excerpts from the works in Spanish, with English translations. In a general Introduction, Mr. Young provides a historical focus for the poetry and discusses the Spanish temperament.

Studies of Playwrights

Azorin (Martinez Ruiz)

FOX, EDWARD INMAN
Asorin as a Literary Critic
Las Americas, 1962. 176pp. Paper $5.25. An analysis of Azorin's criticism, based on the nine volumes of his collected works and his numerous newspaper articles, which demonstrates that a re-evaluation of Spanish literature had been one of his major concerns. The philosophy of his criticism is examined and special attention is given to his definition of the "generation of 1898" and his relation to Unamuno and Drauism. Bibliography. Index of Criticism Available.

LAJOHN, LAWRENCE ANTHONY
Azorin and the Spanish Stage
Hispanic Institute, 1961. 208pp. Paper $5.75. A study of the Spanish playwright and his own productions for the stage. Mr. Lajohn analyzes the plays and relates Azorin's dramatic theory to his practice. Bibliography.

Benavente, Jacinto

PENUELAS, MARCELINO C.
Jacinto Benavente
Twayne, 1969. 178pp. $4.95. The author attempts to place the most popular and important Spanish playwright of the first half of this century in his proper niche, considering him as a man and a writer of his time. The relationship of the dramatic works to the framework of the Spanish and European theatre is analyzed and the virtues and short-comings of the plays are considered in detail. Chronology. Selected Bibliography. Index.

Calderon de la Barca, Pedro

HESSE, EVERETT W.
Calderon de la Barca
Twayne, 1967. 192pp. $4.50. The craftsmanship of the dramatic legacy left by one of Spain's great playwrights is examined by Professor Hesse. He probes into Calderon's ideas and themes and closely analyzes representative dramas. Hesse also provides a consideration of Calderon's life and a background of seventeenth century Spain, the development of the national theatre, and the rise of the "commedia." Chronology. Selected Bibliography. Index.

HESSE, EVERETT W. – Editor
El Mayor Monstro Los Celos: A Critical and Annotated Edition from the Partly Holographic Manuscript of D. Pedro Calderon de la Barca
University of Wisconsin, 1955. 264pp. $4.75. An authoritative edition, based on the playwright's own manuscript, with a critical Introduction which establishes the holographic nature of the manuscript through a detailed and illustrated examination of Calderon's chirography.

PARKER, A.A.
The Allegorical Drama of Calderon
Oxford, 1968. 232pp. $7.50. Originally published in 1943 and now reissued, this is a fully annotated Introduction to the "Autos Sacramentales" in which Professor Parker studies the manner in which Calderon moulds the traditions of the liturgy, Christian dogma, and Christian ethics into the service of his own poetic ends. Index of Names.

WARDROPPER, BRUCE W.
Critical Essays on the Theatre of Calderon
New York University, 1965. 239pp. $8.00. Paper $2.25. These essays provide close readings of the major plays, studies of the persistent themes, and examinations of the historical background.

Cervantes, Miguel de

SCHEVILL, RUDOLPH
Cervantes
Ungar, 1966. 388pp. $6.50. A reprint of the 1919 edition of the biography of the Spanish author. Professor Schevill provides a reconstruction of Cervantes' life and a discussion of his "relation to the culture of the Renascence." He includes critical analyses of "Don Quixote" and of "The Exemplary Novels." The work was hailed as a "brilliant and particularly satisfying study" in the New York Times. Bibliography. Index.

Lorca, Federico Garcia

COBB, CARL W.
Garcia Lorca
Twayne, 1967. 160pp. $4.50. This is a critical-analytical study of the Spanish playwright in which the author contends that Lorca has too often been treated as a Spanish traditionalist when, in reality, his work is often an attack against his culture. Included is a Chronology of events during Lorca's lifetime and a Selected Bibliography.

DURAN, MANUEL – Editor
Lorca: A Collection of Critical Essays
Prentice–Hall, 1962. 181pp. $5.95. Paper $1.95. This collection of critical essays is introduced by a biographical sketch and commentary by the editor. The essays place Lorca as a master figure in twentieth century writing and emphasize his special Spanish qualities; they point to his sensitivity to Spanish folklore; and they provide an awareness of his sense of humor which balanced his preoccupation with death. Included in the volume are a Chronology of events during Lorca's lifetime and a Selected Bibliography.

HONIG, EDWIN
Garcia Lorca
New Directions, 1963. 239pp. Paper $1.80. A revision of the 1944 edition, this book is a critical survey of the life and all the presently available works of the poet, stressing the influence of Spanish folk and literary traditions as well as Gypsy and Arabic influences on his work. The principal plays are analyzed in detail. A new Introduction, new biographical information, and new Bibliography are added in this edition.

LIMA, ROBERT
The Theatre of Garcia Lorca
Las Americas, 1963. 338pp. $5.00. A comprehensive study of Lorca's theatre, with a biographical chapter that places each work within the scope of his growth, the influences on him, and his personal psychology. Puppet farces, folk tragedies, surrealistic plays, tragicomedies, and playlets are discussed. Bibliography.

LORCA, FEDERICO GARCIA
The Gypsy Ballads of Garcia Lorca
Indiana University, 1958. 64pp. $3.00. Paper $1.45. Eighteen ballads by Lorca, translated by Rolfe Humphries.

LORCA, FEDERICO GARCIA
The Selected Poems of Federico Garcia Lorca
New Directions, 1955. 180pp. Paper $1.35. Edited by Donald M. Allen, this volume includes selections from each of the published volumes of Lorca's poems, including posthumous works. Spanish texts and English translations are provided.

Moreto y Cabana, Agustin

CASA, FRANK P.
The Dramatic Craftsmanship of Moreto
Harvard, 1966. 187pp. $6.00. A study of the Spanish playwright, Agustin Moreto y Cabana (1618–1669). The author discusses five of the comedies and analyzes the source versions, then the Moreto versions, pointing out differences in characterization, dramatic elaborations, attitudes, and themes. Bibliography. Index.

Vega Carpio, Lope de

HAYES, FRANCIS C.
Lope de Vega
Twayne, 1967. 160pp. $4.50. Professor Hayes focuses his attention upon the life-like qualities of Lope's art, including his ability to portray real characters. A topical guide to the proverbs and sayings in Lope's works is provided as well as a chronology of his life. Selected Bibliography. Index.

MARIN, L. ASTRANA
Lope de Vega
Las Americas, 1963. 383pp. Paper $2.00. A study of the playwright with the text in the Spanish language. Bibliography.

PARKER, JACK H. and ARTHUR M. FOX – Editors
Lope de Vega Studies: 1937 – 1962
See Page 553

RENNERT, HUGO ALBERT
The Life of Lope De Vega
Blom, 1968. 587pp. $12.50. This life of the Spanish playwright was originally published in 1905 and is now reissued. Every known event in the life of Lope is recorded and commented upon by the author. He includes a 137 page annotated Bibliography of the works. Appendices include "A record of the action against Lope De Vega for libelling certain actors" and the 1627 version of Lope's will. Illustrated with a portrait and a page of manuscript. Index.

Zorilla, Francisco de Rojas

MacCURDY, RAYMOND R.
Francisco de Rojas Zorrilla
Twayne, 1969. 172pp. $4.95. This study has three principal aims: (1) to present essential factual information concerning the life and works of the Spanish dramatist; (2) to classify his authenticated works; (3) to present resumes of the plots of the plays and brief critical analyses of the principal ones. Chronology. Selected Bibliography. Index.

SWEDEN

COLLIS, JOHN STEWART

Marriage and Genius: Strindberg and Tolstoy: Studies in Tragi-Comedy

Cassell, 1963. 310pp. $8.25. A study of the problems of marriage as exemplified in the lives of two men of genius. Strindberg's marriage exemplifies the love-hate relationship that is often prevalent in the married state. Tolstoy and his wife illustrate what happens to a strong-willed couple whose respective ideals are antagonistic. Index.

DAHLSTROM, CARL E. W. L.

Strindberg's Dramatic Expressionism

Blom, 1965. 264pp. $7.50. First published in 1930 and now reissued, this is a study of the general characteristics of expressionism and the ideals of its founders: Marzynski, Pfister, Edschmid, Picard, and Bahr. Treated in detail are Strindberg's plays: "Miss Julie," "To Damascus," "A Dream Play," and the "Chamber Plays." A Bibliography includes listings of the published works and letters as well as a selection of critical literature. Index.

JOHANNESSON, ERIC O.

The Novels of August Strindberg

University of California, 1968. 317pp. $7.95. This study provides a general introduction to all of Strindberg's major novels. Chronology. Bibliography. Index of Proper Names.

JOHNSON, WALTER

Strindberg and the Historical Drama

University of Washington, 1963. 326pp. $6.50. A study of the more than twenty historical plays that are among Strindberg's greatest contributions to world drama. The six centuries of Swedish history that they cover are examined, as well as the playwright's developing ideas about the meaning of history, the nature of political power, and the search for order and harmony. Individual treatments of the major plays are provided.

KLAF, FRANKLIN S.

Strindberg: The Origin of Psychology in Modern Drama

Citadel, 1963. 192pp. Paper $1.75. Strindberg died leaving a series of autobiographical novels which represent the finest portrayal of mental illness in world literature. These writings are analyzed by Dr. Klaf who attempts to show how Strindberg's illness influenced all his later plays, and, through them, the entire course of Western drama. Bibliography. Index.

McGILL, V. J.

August Strindberg: The Bedeviled Viking

Russell & Russell, 1965. 459pp. $13.50. This comprehensive study examines such aspects of the playwright's life and work as his early years as protege of the King of Sweden, His work as a journalist, romantic influences on his work, his atheism, the rise of naturalism, his relation to Nietzsche, his marriages, and his psychological dilemmas. A reprint of the study first published in 1930. Bibliography. Index.

MORTENSEN, BRITA and BRIAN DOWNS

Strindberg: An Introduction to His Life and Work

Cambridge, 1959. 234pp. $3.75. Paper $1.75. In the biographical chapters of this volume, Professor Downs reveals the playwright's life of spiritual violence and tragedy and his search for himself. Miss Mortensen deals with the writings and the impact on Swedish audiences. She also estimates the place of the plays in European literature.

PALMBALD, HARRY V. B.

Strindberg's Conception of History

AMS Press, 1966. 196pp. $12.00. Originally published in 1927 and now reprinted, this study examines Strindberg's conception of history and the development of his historical thinking from about 1870 to the end of his life. Part I traces the development of the playwright's historical theories and includes a discussion of related ideas. Part II deals with the interpretation of history as shown in the historical or semi-historical works. Bibliography.

STRINDBERG, AUGUST

The Cloister

Hill & Wang, 1969. 160pp. $5.00. Edited by C. G. Bjurstrom, and translated with commentary and notes by Mary Sandbach, this is a fictionalized fragment of biography. It sheds light on the playwright's second marriage and introduces the reader to the circle of friends who played an important part in Strindberg's life in Berlin in 1892.

STRINDBERG, AUGUST

From an Occult Diary: Marriage with Harriet Bosse

Hill & Wang, 1965. 160pp. $4.00. Paper—Icon Books, 1966. 160pp. $1.50. This section of Strindberg's diary deals with his marriage to Harriet Bosse in 1901 and the obsession that she became for him after their divorce. Translated by Mary Sandbach and edited by Torsten Eklund.

STRINDBERG, AUGUST

Inferno, Abne and Other Writings

Doubleday, 1968. 429pp. Paper $1.75. Edited and introduced by Evert Sprinchorn, this is the last in the sequence of autobiographical works by the Swedish writer. These new translations by the editor are published for the first time.

STRINDBERG, AUGUST

Letters of Strindberg to Harriet Bosse

Grosset & Dunlop, 1959. 194pp. Paper $1.45. Edited and translated by Arvid Paulson, these letters of the playwright to his third wife contain many references to his plays and their characters, to his ideas on how the plays should be acted, and to his critical theories.

STRINDBERG, AUGUST
A Madman's Defense
Doubleday, 1967. 293pp. Paper $1.25. Newly translated and with an Introduction and notes by Evert Sprinchorn, this is one of the series of autobiographical novels by the Swedish playwright. It gives the author's version of his marriage to his first wife.

STRINDBERG, AUGUST
Open Letters to the Intimate Theatre
University of Washington, 1966. 323pp. $6.95. Paper–1967. $2.95. Translations by Walter Johnson of Strindberg's notes and letters to the members of the Intimate Theatre, a group founded in Sweden in 1907 for the purpose of presenting the works of Strindberg. These letters reveal his theories on acting, the role of the director, and the use of scenery. Strindberg analyzes "Hamlet" and other of Shakespeare's plays and also Goethe's "Faust." Index.

STRINDBERG, AUGUST
The Son of a Servant: The Story of the Evolution of a Human Being — 1849 – 1867
Doubleday, 1966. 243pp. Paper $1.25. A complete translation by Evert Sprinchorn of Strindberg's autobiographical work. Mr. Sprinchorn has also supplied an Introduction and Notes.

TURKEY

MARTINOVITCH, NICHOLAS M.
The Turkish Theatre
Blom, 1968. 125pp. $12.50. Originally published in 1933 and now reissued, in this volume the author discusses the three types of Turkish theatre and provides seven complete texts of plays. Fifteen full page illustrations complement the text. Vocabulary. Bibliography.

UNITED STATES

For other books on American theatre, see the sections on Musical Theatre and on Clowns and Circus.

General Histories and Critiques

ABRAMS, DOLORES M.
Theatre in the Junior College
American Educational Theatre Association, 1964. 58pp. Paper $2.50. A study of the theatre activity in junior colleges, examined by regions. Lists of courses offered, kinds and number of productions, range of theatre programs, and evaluations of the courses as a whole are given.

AYERS, RICHARD G. – Editor
Directory of American College Theatre: Second Edition
A. E. T. A., 1967. 195pp. Paper $6.00. This directory presents a comprehensive report on the educational theatre in the United States. More than 60,000 data are provided to describe this field as it is represented in 1,581 regionally accredited colleges and universities. Information is provided on undergraduate and graduate programs and there is a section of statistical summaries and reference materials.

BALIO, TINO and LEE NORVELLE
The History of the National Theatre Conference
National Theatre Conference, 1968. 119pp. Paper $2.95. This is the history of the banding together of the American non-professional theatre groups to foster the development of American theatre, particularly on the amateur, university and high school level. Bibliography. Index.

BAULAND, PETER
The Hooded Eagle: Modern German Drama on the New York Stage
Syracuse University, 1968. 299pp. $9.00. This is a history of the German drama that was presented in New York theatres from 1894 to 1965. The author examines each major movement of the German theatre, comparing the important plays produced in English in New York with their German texts. He devotes attention to the critical, scholarly, and commercial reception of these plays and discusses their relationship to native American drama. An Appendix lists pertinent available production information on all recorded plays of Germanic origin to appear in New York during the period covered. Bibliography. Index.

BLUM, DANIEL and JOHN WILLIS
A Pictorial History of the American Theatre 1860 – 1970
Crown, 1969. 416pp. $12.50. A third edition of the pictorial classic, revised and enlarged by John Willis. The presentation begins in 1860 and pictures all the legendary "greats." In this new edition, the seasons from 1960 to 1969–70 are included. Over 5,000 photographs illustrate the volume. Index.

BOND, FREDERICK W.
The Negro and the Drama
McGrath, 1969. 213pp. $13.00. This study was originally published in 1940. It details the contributions the American Negro has made to drama and the legitimate stage. The author considers the beginnings of the Negro participation in the early nineteenth century, minstrelsy, Negro authorship, white authorship

of Negro themes, the Federal theatre movement, and the period of the allied arts of dancing and music. Bibliography. Index.

BROWN, T. ALLSTON
History of the American Stage
See Page 261

CAHN, WILLIAM
A Pictorial History of the Great Comedians
See Page 261

DUSENBURY, WINIFRED L.
The Theme of Loneliness in Modern American Drama
University of Florida, 1967. 231pp. $6.50. The major approaches to the theme of loneliness in modern American drama are analyzed with examples from eighteen playwrights, including: Maxwell Anderson, Paul Green, Lillian Hellman, William Inge, Carson McCullers, Arthur Miller, Robert Sherwood, and Tennessee Williams. Notes. Bibliography. Index.

GILBERT, DOUGLAS
American Vaudeville: Its Life and Times
Dover, 1963. 427pp. $2.50. A history of the period between 1880 and 1930 when vaudeville was at the heights of its popularity. The author concentrates on the performers and the acts that made them famous. The activity of the impressarios, talent managers, theatre owners, and press agents is also examined. There is a discussion of the birth of the newspapers, Variety and Billboard. An unabridged republication of the original 1940 edition. Illustrated.

GOHDES, CLARENCE
Literature and Theatre of the States and Regions of the U. S. A.
See Page 554

GRAHAM, PHILIP
Showboats: The History of an American Institution
University of Texas, 1969. 224pp. $6.00. A reprint of the history first published in 1951, this is a record of America's floating theaters from 1831 to 1937. It is also a record of the men and women who built and performed on the stages and the audiences who enjoyed the performances. Illustrated. Bibliography. Index.

HATCH, JAMES V.
Black Image on the American Stage
See Page 558

HERRON, IMA HONAKER
The Small Town in American Drama
Southern Methodist University, 1969. 564pp. $12.50. Through more than three hundred plays, Miss Herron follows in detail the development of the drama of the village and small town. Beginning with the tragedies of religious persecution in the Puritan village, she proceeds to the frontier community, the trend toward realism after the Civil War, to the present century when plays with small town themes have offered evidence of "the chaos and decadence of modern life." Miss Herron offers information about American playwrights, plays, actors, staging, costuming, and every other aspect of American drama as it touches on the small town. Illustrated. Notes. Selected Bibliography. Index.

HERZBERG, MAX J. – Editor
The Reader's Encyclopedia of American Literature
Crowell, 1963. 1,280pp. $12.95. This reference work contains 6,500 articles on writers of drama, fiction, poetry, essays, important writers of non-literary fields, persons, places, and events alluded to in literature, literary groups, movements, and events. Included are 250 illustrations, eight geneological charts, and a Glossary of Literary Terms. Introduction by Van Wyck Brooks and articles by, among others: Paul Green, Max Lerner, John Gassner, and Philip Young.

HEWITT, BARNARD
Theatre U. S. A. 1668 to 1957
McGraw–Hill, 1959. 528pp. $11.50. A collection of eye-witness accounts of the development of the American theatre, placed in chronological order, with a narrative continuity by the author. Most of the selections are reviews of performances, both there are descriptions of such events as The Astor Place Riot, and the Iroquois Theatre fire. Illustrated. Bibliography.

HOBGOOD, BURNET – Editor
Directory of American College Theatre
A.E.T.A., 1960. 64pp. Paper $5.00. Data on 1,278 accredited and 159 non-accredited two year and four year institutions in the fifty states and three federally governed commonwealths.

HORNBLOW, ARTHUR
A History of Theatre in America
Blom, 1965. Volume One: 357pp. Volume Two: 374pp. Two volume set: $25.00. First published in 1919 and now reissued, these two volumes describe the entire field of American theatrical activity from colonial days, with particular attention paid to the lives of the great performers. Information is provided on non-literary aspects of theatre. Illustrated with 188 photographs and drawings showing actors and actresses, productions and theatres. Index.

HOYT, HARLOWE R.
Town Hall Tonight
Bramhall House, 1955. 292pp. $2.98. A study of the country theatres of the 1890's and 1900's, the "Town Halls" across the country that were hosts to such a wide variety of theatrical entertainment. The book has a selection of excerpts from typical melodramas of the day, as well as descriptions of lectures, readings, musical offerings, "freak shows," and circuses. Illustrated with contemporary prints and photographs. Index.

HUGHES, GLENN
A History of the American Theatre 1700 – 1950
Samuel French, 1951. 562pp. $5.00. A chronological survey, with chapters on theatre in Philadelphia, Boston, New York, and New Orleans in the eighteenth century. Information is provided on theatre on the frontier, famous actors and managers, theatre during the depression, and the state of the theatre up to 1950. Illustrated.

LAUFE, ABE
Broadway's Greatest Musicals
See Page 290

LIFSON, DAVID S.
The Yiddish Theatre in America
Thomas Yoseloff, 1965. 659pp. $12.00. A study of the Yiddish theatre from its birth in Rumania in 1876. The author describes how major European theatrical innovations were first brought to America via the Yiddish theatre companies. Notable directors, playwrights, and actors are examined. Illustrated with photographs.

LOVELL, JOHN – Editor
Digest of Great American Plays
Crowell, 1962. 452pp. $7.95. Paper – Apollo, 1965. 452pp. $2.25. An act-by-act retelling of more than one hundred famous plays, with casts of characters, historical notes on background, and ten separate indices listing authors, lyricists, composers, songs, outstanding roles, and literary sources and origins.

McLEAN, ALBERT, JR.
American Vaudeville as Ritual
University of Kentucky, 1965. 250pp. $6.50. A reexamination of vaudeville which shows it as a ritualistic enactment charged with symbols of the social beliefs and attitudes of the American industrial civilization arising during the period from 1885 to 1930.

McPHARLIN, PAUL
The Puppet Theatre in America
See Page 342

MESERVE, WALTER J.
An Outline History of American Drama
Littlefield, Adams, 1965. 378pp. Paper $2.75. This outline presents the developing trends in American drama—from the Colonial theatre to the theatre of the absurd—with supporting detail, play synopses, and critical observations. Index.

MOSES, MONTROSE J.
The American Dramatist
Blom, 1964. 474pp. $12.50. A reprint of the book first published in 1925, this study intends "to summarize the identifying qualities of those dramatists who have anything of an individual position, to enumerate those elements in the theatre that have served to check the original flow of native creativeness, thus limiting the dramatist's work." Bibliography. Index.

MOSES, MONTROSE J. and JOHN MASON BROWN – Editors
The American Theatre as Seen by Its Critics 1752 – 1934
Cooper Square, 1967. 391pp. $11.50. Originally published in 1934 and now reissued, this is a collection of American dramatic criticism. Its concern is with the native theatre in performance. Among the contributors are: Edgar Allan Poe, Walt Whitman, Henry James, Heywood Broun, George Jean Nathan, Alexander Woollcott, Stark Young, Brooks Atkinson, and Burns Mantle. Biographical sketches of actors and critics are included.

MOSES, MONTROSE J.
Famous Actor-Families in America
Blom, 1968. 341pp. $12.50. The story of the acting families who carried on a tradition of great performances (on and off stage). Professor Montrose examines the Booths, Jeffersons, Sotherns, Boucicaults, Hacketts, Drews and Barrymores, Wallacks, Davenports, Hollands, and Powers. Originally published in 1906 and now reissued. Illustrated.

NANNES, CASPAR
Politics in the American Drama
Catholic University, 1960. 256pp. $5.75. A study of theatrical depictions of politicians and political activity in stage presentations since the 1890's.

NOLAN, PAUL T. – Editor
Provincial Drama in America, 1870 – 1916: A Casebook of Primary Materials
Scarecrow, 1967. 234pp. $7.00. The author intends to direct the reader into a number of research projects dealing with the thousands of plays which have never been produced and/or published. Index.

PALMER, HELEN H. and JANE ANNE DYSON
American Drama Criticism
See Page 554

PHILLIPS, ELIZABETH C. and DAVID ROGERS
Modern American Drama
Monarch, 1966. 125pp. Paper $1.95. A critical guide to American drama from "The Prince of Parthia" in 1767 through the works of O'Neill, to the current writings of Albee. Critical analyses of the major playwrights' works, essay questions and answers for review, critical commentary, and Bibliographies are provided.

POGGI, JACK
Theater in America: The Impact of Economic Forces, 1870 – 1967
Cornell University, 1968. 328pp. $9.50. Mr. Poggi diagnoses the ailments of theater in America and argues that the sickness is of longer duration and

the causes are more deep-seated than most people realize. He traces two closely related economic trends that have affected the quality of American drama: centralization of production in New York City and the decline in theatrical activity since the 1920's. He assesses the impact on the theater of motion pictures, radio, television, rising costs, and subsidies from foundations and his conclusions often contradict the commonly held assumptions. A series of tables and graphs are included to illustrate the text. Bibliography. Index.

QUINN, ARTHUR HOBSON
A History of the American Drama: From the Beginning to the Civil War – Volume One
Appleton, 1943. 530pp. $9.00. First published in 1923 and now reissued in a second edition, this pioneer history deals with plays that were actually performed in the United States up to 1860. The works of the major playwrights are studied as units. Bibliography. Lists of Plays.

QUINN, ARTHUR HOBSON
A History of the American Drama: From the Civil War to the Present Day – Volume Two
Appleton, 1936. 432pp. $9.50. A second edition of the volume first published in 1927. This study has three aims: to study drama as a force in social history; to point out prevailing types and tendencies among playwrights; to indicate the relative merits of the dramatists. Playwrights from Daly to Clyde Fitch are treated historically and critically. For playwrights after the death of Moody, the treatment is more selective. Lists of Plays – 1860–1936. Illustrated. Bibliography.

RIGDON, WALTER – Editor
The Biographical Encyclopaedia and Who's Who of the American Theatre
J. H. Heinman, 1965. 1,101pp. $82.50. This reference book contains a list of New York theatre productions from January 1, 1900 through May 31, 1964; complete "Playbills" since 1959; lists of premieres of American plays abroad since 1946; complete biographies of important persons in every aspect of American theatre and of American theatre groups and their productions; records of theatre awards; biography and autobiography bibliography; discography of spoken records; and necrology.

SOBEL, BERNARD
A Pictorial History of Burlesque
Bonanza, 1956. 194pp. $10.00. A history of this art form from Aristophanes to Minsky with special emphasis on the American scene from 1860. Illustrated.

STRATMAN, CARL J.
Bibliography of the American Theatre: Excluding New York City
Loyola University, 1965. 397pp. $8.00. A systematic compilation, arranged by state and city, of books, periodical articles, theses and dissertations on all phases of American theatre. Included are such varied theatre activity as arena theatre, children's theatre, Chinese theatre in America, open air theatre, showboats, and theatre scenery.

TAUBMAN, HOWARD
The Making of the American Theatre
Putnam, 1967. 402pp. $10.00. A revised edition of the 1965 work which traces the rise of the American theatre from Colonial times to the twentieth century. Mr. Taubman brings the new volume up to date and adds the new developments to the critically acclaimed defintive work on the subject. Illustrated. Index.

WOOLLCOTT, ALEXANDER
Mrs. Fiske: Her Views on Actors, Acting, and the Problems of Production
Blom, 1968. 225pp. $12.50. Originally published in 1917 and now reissued, this is a volume of the noted drama critic's conversations with the actress/producer/director on such topics as Ibsen, the repertory system, Spanish theatre, and her own career, Illustrated.

Histories through the Nineteenth Century

ANONYMOUS
Early American Theatrical Posters
Cherokee, 1967. 519pp. $17.50. A collection of over 500 rare early American theatrical posters are reproduced in miniature form in this volume. The posters were originally published from 1869 to 1872 and depict scenes from the melodramas of the nineteenth century.

BERNARD, JOHN
Retrospections of America: 1797 – 1811
Blom, 1969. 380pp. $12.50. Originally published in 1887 and now reissued in a facsimile edition, these are selections from the autobiography of the eighteenth century English actor who toured America from 1797–1811. Introduction, Notes and Index by Laurence Hutton and Brander Matthews. Illustrated.

BIEBER, ALBERT A.
American Plays, Poetry, and Songsters
Cooper Square, 1963. 103pp. $8.95. This bibliography of 708 items consists of descriptive and critical entries on books published on early and modern American popular or folk literature and about such events as colonial life, the Revolution, the War of 1812, the Civil War, Lincoln, politics, Masonic songs, legal poetry, and various state and regional songs. There are many entries covering the works of obscure and forgotten minor playwrights, poets and song writers. Illustrated with reproductions of pages from original publications.

BOOTH, MICHAEL—Editor
Hiss the Villain
See Page 181

BOWEN, ELBERT R.
Theatrical Entertainments in Rural Missouri Before the Civil War
University of Missouri, 1959. 140pp. $3.50. A study of the wagon shows, circus boats, Negro minstrels and professional legitimate theatre in the period. Amateur and professional performers are discussed. Illustrated. Bibliography. Index.

BROWN, T. ALLSTON
A History of the New York Stage
Blom, 1964. Volume One: 523pp. Volume Two: 652pp. Volume Three: 671pp. Three volume set: $55.00. These volumes list each theatre operating in New York from 1732 to 1901, with description of physical plant, complete record of performances, casts, critical commentary, historical data, and subsequent history of the playhouse.

BUNN, ALFRED
Old England and New England
Blom, 1969. 315pp. $12.50. Originally published in 1853 and now reissued in a facsimile edition, these are observations on America and its history and people by a nineteenth century English writer. The volume includes a chapter on the origin of the American stage and some of the famous actors who appeared on it. Other comments on the stage and the stars of the period are distributed throughout the book.

BURTON, JACK
In Memoriam: Old Time Show Biz
Vantage Press, 1965. 102pp. $3.00. The author recalls the glamour and gaiety of the theatre that used to be: the minstrel show, grand op'ry house, road show, big top, vaudeville, and burlesque.

CARSON, WILLIAM G. B.
Managers in Distress: The St. Louis Stage, 1840–1844
Blom, 1949. 329pp. $10.00. The five theatrical seasons described in this book constitute a definite period in the history not only of the St. Louis stage but in that of the American theatre in general. The desperate efforts of the managers Noah Ludlow and Sol Smith to save their theate by staging anything from Shakespeare to the lowest farce with a double bill every night and a new bill every day are described in detail. Records of Performances. Index.

CARSON, WILLIAM G. B.
The Theatre on the Frontier: The Early Years of the St. Louis Stage
Blom, 1965. 361pp. $12.50. A study of the St. Louis stage from 1814 to 1839. The activities of Ludlow, Drake, Smith, and Caldwell are described. The performances at the Salt House and the New St. Louis Theatre are discussed. This second edition of the work originally published in 1932 has a new Introduction by the author. Bibliography. Index.

CLAPP, JOHN BOUVE and EDWIN FRANCIS EDGETT
Plays of the Present
See Page 182

CLAPP, WILLIAM WARLAND
Record of the Boston Stage
Blom, 1968. 492pp. $12.50. Originally published in 1853 and now reissued with a new Index especially prepared for this edition. These records cover the period from the earliest recorded performances to the middle of the nineteenth century, with biographical sketches of actors, commentary on acting styles, surveys of productions, and production techniques, and a great quantity of anecdotes and gossip.

COAD, ORAL SUMNER
William Dunlap: A Study of His Works and Life and of His Place in Contemporary Culture
Russell & Russell, 1962. 314pp. $11.00. A reprint of the 1917 edition, this is an account of Dunlap's life and work as playwright and manager, as biographer and historian, as journalist and novelist, and as painter. Detailed examination is made of his original plays and of the translations of French and German plays. Illustrated. List of Works and Paintings. Index.

DALY, CHARLES P.
First Theatre in America
Kennikat, 1968. 115pp. $8.00. Originally published in 1896, this is a study of the theatre in early America including "A consideration of the objections made to the stage."

DORMON, JAMES H.
Theatre in the Ante Bellum South: 1815–1861
University of North Carolina, 1967. 322pp. $9.50. Mr. Dormon traces in detail the development and nature of southern theatrical activity during the forty-five year period preceding the Civil War. There is also a study of the audiences of the region and time. Illustrated. Selected Bibliography. Index.

DUNLAP, WILLIAM
Diary of William Dunlap
Blom, 1969. 1,021pp. $28.50. A one volume edition of the 1930 three volume edition. The thousands of entries from 1797 to 1834 give an invaluable guide to the life, artistic climate, theatre activity, and historical scene of the era. Illustrated. Notes. Index.

DUNLAP, WILLIAM
History of the American Theatre, and Anecdotes of the Principal Actors
Burt Franklin, 1963. 799pp. $27.00. A reprint of the classic history of the eighteenth and early ninteenth

century American theatre, by the American playwright and stage-manager. Included are a list of early plays and "A Narrative of His Connection with the Old American Company 1792 — 1797" by John Hodgkinson.

DUNN, ESTHER CLOUDMAN
Shakespeare in America
See Page 93

FORD, PAUL LEICESTER
Washington and the Theatre
Blom, 1967. 86pp. $6.75. Originally published in 1899 and now reissued in a facsimile edition, this is a study of George Washington's involvement with the theatre as a patron and sponsor. Illustrated with contemporary material. The volume also includes a complete comic sketch: "Darby's Return" written by William Dunlap and performed in 1789.

FORD, PAUL LEICESTER
Washington and the Theatre
Burt Franklin, 1970. 84pp. $16.95. Originally published in 1899 and now reissued in a facsimile edition, this is a study of George Washington's involvement with the theatre as a patron and sponsor. Illustrated with contemporary material. The volume also includes a complete comic sketch, "Darby's Return," written by William Dunlap and performed in 1789.

GAER, JOSEPH — Editor
The Theatre of the Gold Rush Decade in San Francisco
Burt Franklin, 1970. 101pp. $11.75. Originally published in 1935 and now reissued, this volume lists plays, minstrel shows, operas, and other theatrical works produced in San Francisco from 1850 to 1859. Author, date, and theatre where performed are listed when possible. Lists of Authors and Composers.

GALLAGHER, KENT G.
The Foreigner in Early American Drama
Mouton, 1966. 206pp. $11.00. A critical study of early American attitudes towards the foreigner. Early American dramatic output containing material pertinent to the study has been broken down into five areas: the growth of American ideas of politico-economic separateness; the assertion of anti-foreign sentiments; attitudes evincing a sympathetic outlook towards foreigners; comic stereotypes; and romantic influences. An Appendix lists plays from pre-Revolutionary days to 1830. Bibliography. Index.

GALLEGLY, JOSEPH
Footlights on the Border: The Galveston and Houston Stage Before 1900
Humanities, 1962. 262pp. $8.50. A history of the development of the stage in Texas from the first recorded performance in 1838 to the end of the nineteenth century. The record shows that the supposedly uncivilized frontier shared fully in the development of theatre in America.

GARLAND, HAMLIN
Crumbling Idols
Harvard, 1960. 150pp. Paper $1.45. Twelve essays on art which deal chiefly with literature, painting, and the drama. This is a highly personalized account of various artistic developments in the 1890's, particularly in the United States. Bibliography.

GRIMSTED, DAVID
Melodrama Unveiled: American Theatre and Culture 1800 — 1850
University of Chicago, 1968. 285pp. $10.50. Mr. Grimsted seeks to answer the question of why the eighteenth century melodrama was so popular for so long. In this study of the early nineteenth century drama, he conveys the social and intellectual context of the times. Selected Bibliography. Index.

HILL, FRANK PIERCE
American Plays Printed 1714 — 1830
See Page 6

HODGE, FRANCIS
Yankee Theatre: The Image of America on the Stage, 1825 — 1850
University of Texas, 1964. 320pp. $6.00. This book examines the full range of the theatre activity of the "Stage Yankees" who, with their eccentric New England dialect comedy, entertained audiences at home and abroad. Lists of Yankee theatre plays and stories are included.

IRELAND, JOSEPH N.
Records of the New York Stage from 1750 to 1860
Blom, 1965. Volume One: 663pp. Volume Two: 740pp. Two volume set: $57.50. Originally published in 1866—1867 and now reissued in a facimile edition, this is a complete record of the New York stage written from theatrical memoranda kept by the author for forty years. Index.

IRELAND, JOSEPH N.
Records of the New York Stage from 1750 to 1860
Burt Franklin, 1968. Volume One: 663pp. Volume Two: 746pp. Two volume set: $45.00. Originally published in 1866—1867 and now reissued in a facsimile edition, this is a complete record of the New York stage written from theatrical memoranda kept by the author for forty years. Index.

JAMES, HENRY
The Scenic Art
See Page 25

McNAMARA, BROOKS
The American Playhouse in the Eighteenth Century
Harvard, 1969. 174pp. $9.95. This is an architectural history of the eighteenth century American playhouse from the theatre built at Williamsburg, Virginia about 1716 to the completion of the New York Park Theatre in 1798. Mr. McNamara traces the influence

of English stagecraft and theatre architecture, discusses the dominance of English acting companies, and recreates the settings of early American dramatic performances. Fifty-three illustrations include photographs and reproductions of period art showing the playhouses. Notes. Index.

MOORE, LESTER L.
Outside Broadway
Scarecrow Press, 1970. 182pp. $5.00. A history of the professional theatre in Newark, New Jersey from the beginning in 1799 to the last stock company before the demise of the stock system in 1867. The Appendices provide complete listings of plays performed in Newark, dates and places of performance, and players. Bibliography.

PATRICK, J. MAX
Savannah's Pioneer Theatre: From Its Origins to 1810
University of Georgia, 1953. 94pp. Paper $2.50. A study of the development of drama in Georgia from the plays produced by Royalist soldiers during the Revolution to the temporary decline in theatrics at the end of the first decade of the nineteenth century. Georgia's first native play, "The Mysterious Father" by William Bullock Maxwell, is examined. Handlist of Plays. Index of Performances: 1781–1810.

RANKIN, HUGH F.
The Theatre in Colonial America
University of North Carolina, 1965. 237pp. $7.50. This historical account moves from Levinston's first theatre, begun in Williamsburg in 1716, through the early years of struggle, to the height of the popularity of the playing groups in the years between 1770 and 1774. The touring groups, the native born actors, the building of playhouses, and various production practices are among the topics covered. Illustrated. Index.

SEILHAMER, GEORGE OVERCASH
History of the American Theatre
Blom, 1968. 1,210pp. Three volume set: $37.50. This three volume history was originally published in 1888–1891 and is now reissued. The volumes cover the period from 1749 to 1797 and give a chronological account of the theatre and its performers, managers, financial backing, and cultural impact, with exhaustive production notes and statistical tables. Professor Norman Philbrick has provided an Introduction.

SMITH, SOL
Theatrical Management in the West and South for Thirty Years
Blom, 1968. 294pp. $15.00. Originally published in 1868, this new edition has an Introduction and Index by Arthur Thomas Tees. It is the nineteenth century actor-manager's version of his life and career interspersed with anecodotal sketches. Illustrated with contemporary engravings. Index.

SMITHER, NELLE
A History of the English Theatre in New Orleans
Blom, 1967. 406pp. $12.50. A study of the theatre in New Orleans from 1806 to 1842. This second edition of the 1944 publication contains corrections of the original edition. The nature of the more than 900 plays performed and their critical and popular reception are studied in detail. Chronologically arranged records for each season are given and there are alphabetical lists of plays performed and actors and dancers who appeared in the period. Illustrated with a picture of the St. Charles Theatre, built in 1835.

TOMPKINS, EUGENE and QUINCEY KILBY
History of the Boston Theatre: 1854 – 1901
Blom, 1969. 551pp. $25.00. Originally published in 1908 and reissued in a facsimile edition, this volume is compiled from the records of the playhouse. The history ranges from grand opera stars to minstrels, from statesmen and clergymen to pugilists. Each season in the history of the playhouse is detailed in a separate chapter. The volume is lavishly illustrated with reproductions of photographs of actors and actresses and other figures of the theatre during the period covered. Index.

VARDAC, A. NICHOLAS
Stage to Screen: Theatrical Method from Garrick to Griffith
See Page 442

WALLACK, LESTER
Memories of Fifty Years
Blom, 1969. 232pp. $9.75. Originally published in 1889 and now reissued in facsimile edition, this volume is the autobiography of the prominent American actor of the late nineteenth century. It also deals with the history of Wallack's theatre in New York and the actors who appeared there. The editor of the work, Laurence Hutton, has provided an Introduction, a biographical sketch, and a list of the characters played by Wallack. Sixty-seven illustrations are provided. Index.

WEMYSS, FRANCIS C.
Chronology of the American Stage from 1752 to 1852
Blom, 1968. 191pp. $12.50. Originally published in 1852 and now reissued, this is a "List of Performers" alphabetically arranged, with short biographies. Also listed are the theatres of the period 1752 to 1852 with some data on them.

WILLIS, EOLA
The Charleston Stage in the XVIII Century
Blom, 1968. 483pp. $18.50. Originally published in 1924 and now reissued, this history of the Charleston, South Carolina stage is one aspect of theatrical activity in the early days of the Republic. Miss Willis' book is a detailed study of the social life of the city. Complete production lists for every major theatrical season are included.

Histories of the Twentieth Century

ADAMS, JOEY and HENRY TOBIAS
The Borscht Belt
Avon, 1969. 190pp. Paper $ .60. Originally published in 1966 and now reissued, this is the history of the resort hotels and the entertainers who appeared in the Pocono, Catskill, and Berkshire Mountains. Illustrated. Index.

AMORY, CLEVELAND and FREDERIC BRADLEE — Editors
Vanity Fair: A Cavalcade of the 1920s and 1930s
Viking, 1970. 327pp. $12.50. A selection of stories, articles, humor, photographs, and art from the magazine, "Vanity Fair," from 1914 to 1936. Among the contributions are works by Robert Benchley and Thomas Wolfe, Dorothy Parker, Gertrude Stein, Noel Coward, Cocteau, Somerset Maugham, Max Beerbohm, and Andre Gide. Photographers Steichen, Beaton, and others provide portraits of Broadway and Hollywood stars, literary and sports figures including Helen Hayes, Lillian Gish, Ethel Merman, Charles Chaplin, Fred Astaire.

ATKINSON, BROOKS
Broadway
Macmillan, 1970. 484pp. $12.50. An anecodotal history of theatre in New York from provincial pre-World War One to the current scene. The theatres, the companies, producers, directors, stars, playwrights, and composers from 1900 to 1950 are discussed with a postscript on the current American stage. Illustrated with photographs. Index.

BAUMOL, WILLIAM J. and WILLIAM G. BOWEN
Performing Arts: The Economic Dilemma
Twentieth Century Fund, 1966. 582pp. $7.50. Paper — M. I. T. Press, 1968. 582pp. $3.95. A study of problems common to theatre, opera, music, and dance. Commissioned by the Twentieth Century Fund, this volume provides the information and understanding necessary to gauge the economic requisites for a vital national life in the arts. Bibliography. Index.

BENTLEY, ERIC
The Dramatic Event: An American Chronicle
Beacon, 1956. 278pp. Paper $1.25. Originally published in 1954, this is a collection of criticisms of the American theatre including the plays, productions of plays, acting, and the economics of production. The essays deal mainly with Broadway productions of the years 1952 — 1954.

BENTLEY, ERIC
What Is Theatre? A Query in Chronicle Form
Atheneum, 1968. 273pp. $12.50. Paper $4.95. A companion volume to "The Dramatic Event," these essays cover the New York professional theatre seasons from 1954 to 1956. The concluding chapter is a long essay on the problems and future of theatre in America.

BENTLEY, ERIC
What Is Theatre? And The Dramatic Event
Atheneum, 1968. 491pp. $12.50. Paper $4.95. Originally published in 1956 as two separate volumes, this omnibus volume is a collection of essays and reviews from the period 1956 to 1967. Most of the essays were originally published in "The New Republic." Index.

BIGSBY, C. W. E.
Confrontation and Commitment: A Study of Contemporary American Drama 1959 — 1966
University of Missouri, 1967. 187pp. $4.95. Dr. Bigsby takes two meaningful concepts for the modern generation, confrontation and commitment, and finds in the frequently disparaging social plays of contemporary America a power and a hope for American drama. Among the playwrights studied are Arthur Miller, Edward Albee, James Baldwin, LeRoi Jones, and Lorraine Hansberry. Bibliography. Index.

BLAU, HERBERT
The Impossible Theatre: A Manifesto
Macmillan, 1964. 309pp. $10.00. Paper $1.95. The co-founder of the Actor's Workshop of San Francisco seeks new possibilities for the American theatre. He analyzes a major cause of the decline of theatre in America, "the timorousness and self-deceit of people in the theatre." The history of the Workshop is given in detail. The author also discourses on the art of the theatre. Illustrated with photographs.

BLUM, DANIEL — Editor
Theatre World
See Page 514

BROUSSARD, LOUIS
American Drama: Contemporary Allegory from Eugene O'Neill to Tennessee Williams
University of Oklahoma, 1962. 176pp. $4.95. A study of the allegorical theme of twentieth century man journeying through the confusion of his time, traced from its origins in Ibsen, Strindberg, Freud, and Bergson to its development in the plays of Elmer Rice, John Howard Lawson, Philip Barry, Thornton Wilder, Eugene O'Neill, and Tennessee Williams.

BROWN, JOHN MASON
Two on the Aisle
Kennikat, 1969. 321pp. $10.00. Originally published in 1938 and now reissued, this is a discussion of the American theatre in performance by the drama critic. It consists of reviews originally printed in the New York Evening Post in the 1930's. Among the performers reviewed are Katharine Cornell, Walter Huston, John Gielgud, the Lunts, Maurice Evans, Ruth Gordon, Eva Le Gallienne, Nazimova, and William Gilette. Index.

BROWN, JOHN MASON
Upstage: The American Theatre in Performance
See Page 24

BROWN, JOHN RUSSELL and BERNARD HARRIS — Editors
American Theatre
St. Martin's, 1967. 228pp. $5.75. Ten critics and scholars, including John Gassner, Gerald Weales, and Brian Way, have collaborated for this study. Each of the chapters forms part of a comprehensive, up-to-date, and varied account of American theatrical history. Among the topics discussed are: realism in the modern American theatre, the development of Eugene O'Neill, European influences, the Group Theatre, and Edward Albee and the theatre of the absurd. Notes to each chapter give bibliographical information. Index.

BRUSTEIN, ROBERT
Seasons of Discontent: Dramatic Opinions 1959 — 1965
Simon & Schuster, 1965. 322pp. $5.95. Paper — $1.95. This analytic record of a half-decade of professional theatre considers such topics as the history of The Living Theatre, the Broadway occultism of "Tiny Alice," the Brecht revival, and Robert Lowell. Index.

BUCH, ARTHUR T.
The Bible on Broadway
Archon, 1968. 175pp. $8.50. By examining a number of recent theatrical productions Dr. Buch guides the reader to an understanding and appreciation of today's culture as it is reflected in its plays and movies. He makes specific comparisons between Biblical concepts and the basic ideas and values contained in many of today's plays and movies. List of Plays and Movies Discussed. Books of the Bible and Verses Cited.

BUCHWALD, ART
Counting Sheep
Putnam, 1970. 219pp. $5.95. The full text of the Broadway political comedy, "Sheep on the Runway," by Mr. Buchwald with a "log" of the production which reveals the trials and tribulations of writing and producing a Broadway play. Illustrated with photographs.

CAPOTE, TRUMAN
The Muses Are Heard
Random House, 1956. 181pp. $3.00. Paper — Modern Library. $1.25. The author's account of the journey to Leningrad of ninety-four Americans and two dogs with the celebrated production of "Porgy and Bess." This tour was a milestone in the history of Soviet-American cultural relations.

CHAGY, GIDEON — Editor
Business in the Arts '70
Eriksson, 1970. 176pp. $6.95. A survey of corporate support of the visual and performing arts in the United States. Essays and reports examine the reason for the economic crisis in the arts and the various ways in which business is trying to help. Detailed case histories of business-arts projects and guidelines for involvement based on the experience of the country's leading corporate patrons are provided. Illustrated with photographs. Index.

CHAPMAN, JOHN
Best Plays Series
See Page 8

CHURCHILL, ALLEN
The Great White Way: A Re-creation of Broadway's Golden Age of Theatrical Entertainment
Dutton, 1962. 310pp. $4.95. A history of Broadway from the opening of "Floradora" in 1900 to the Actors Equity strike in 1919. Illustrated.

CLAPP, JOHN BOUVE and EDWIN FRANCIS EDGETT
Plays of the Present
See Page 182

CLARKE, NORMAN
The Mighty Hippodrome
Barnes, 1968. 144pp. $10.00. A history of the Hippodrome Theatre which flourished in New York City for thirty-four years in the early 1900's. Illustrated with photographs. Bibliography. Index.

CLURMAN, HAROLD
The Fervent Years: The Story of the Group Theatre and the Thirties
Hill & Wang, 1957. 302pp. Paper $1.75. The co-founder of the Group Theatre (1931 — 1941) writes about the plays he directed—among them "Golden Boy," "The Gentle People," "Awake and Sing," and "Night Music"—and the people who made up the theatre company, among them: Cheryl Crawford, Lee Strasberg, Elia Kazan, Clifford Odets, Irwin Shaw, Lee J. Cobb, and Franchot Tone.

CROWLEY, ALICE LEWISOHN
The Neighborhood Playhouse
Theatre Arts, 1959. 266pp. $5.00. The history of the Neighborhood Playhouse on New York's lower East Side, and of the years between 1915 and 1927 during which first performances of new and important works were given there. Joseph Wood Krutch writes an Introduction on the contributions of the Playhouse.

DEMOTT, BENJAMIN
Supergrow: Essays and Reports on Imagination in America
Dutton, 1969. 188pp. $5.95. Paper — Dell, 1970. 188pp. $2.25. This is a collection of recent essays in which the author assumes that our troubles stem

from failure of the imagination. Professor DeMott's essays examine almost every current or controversial phenomenon on the American scene: rock music, McLuhanism, student rebellion, camp, Vietnam, homosexual literature, education and violence in the South, Hollywood, and the "Tickle-Touch Theater."

DENNEY, REUEL
The Astonished Muse
University of Chicago, 1957. 264pp. $4.50. Paper — Grosset & Dunlap, 1964. 273pp. $2.50. A study of the leisure class mentality in America. The author suggests that vital art will develop only if Americans throw over the dictatorship of old-fashioned realism in the entertainment and art they appreciate.

DOWNER, ALAN S. — Editor
American Drama and Its Critics
University of Chicago, 1965. 258pp. $7.95. Paper — $2.45. A collection of critical essays originally written from 1897 to 1965. The essays are arranged to show the development of the American theatre from the first attempts to break with a stereotyped past to full awareness of the advances in dramatic writing and staging from the new theatre of Europe.

DOWNER, ALAN S. — Editor
The American Theatre Today
Basic Books, 1967. 212pp. $5.95. Sixteen authorities cover all aspects of the American theatre. The book is divided into four parts: Background, The Big Time, The Makers, Off-Broadway, and an epilogue on the future of the American theatre. Among the contributors are: John Gassner, Eric Bentley, Gerald Weales, Richard Barr, Edward Albee, Murray Schisgal, and Arthur Lithgow. Index.

DOWNER, ALAN S.
Recent American Drama
University of Minnesota, 1961. 46pp. Paper $ .95. Written by the co-founder and chairman of the American Society for Theatre Research, this essay discusses trends in modern American theatre.

FLANAGAN, HALLIE
Arena: The History of the Federal Theatre
Blom, 1965. 475pp. $12.50. First published in 1940, this is a history of the Federal Theatre from 1935 to 1939. The Theatre's work in bringing live performances to audiences that had never before experienced them; in producing classics and new playwrights; in experimental drama and foreign language drama—all at a top admission price of one dollar (with 65% of productions free)—are recorded by the director. Illustrated. Index.

FLORY, JULIA MCCUNE
The Cleveland Playhouse — How It Began
Western Reserve University, 1965. 136pp. $6.50. The history of the Cleveland Playhouse from 1915 to 1965. Illustrated.

FREE, WILLIAM and CHARLES LOWER
History Into Drama: A Source Book on Symphonic Drama
Odyssey, 1963. 243pp. Paper $3.00. The authors center their study around Paul Green's outdoor drama, "The Lost Colony." There is a full text of the play including revisions over a twenty-five year period, professional criticism of the play, and selected materials revealing the influences on and the purpose of this type of drama. Illustrated.

FRENZ, HORST — Editor
American Playwrights on Drama
Hill & Wang, 1965. 174pp. $3.95. Paper — $1.65. A collection of essays, casual articles, extracts from working notes, and reviews that reveal the views on theatre of such playwrights as Eugene O'Neill, Maxwell Anderson, John Howard Lawson, Thornton Wilder, Archibald MacLeish, Elmer Rice, Lorraine Hansberry, Edward Albee, and Paul Green.

GAGEY, EDMOND M.
Revolution in American Drama
Columbia, 1947. 315pp. $5.50. This history of the American theatre from 1912 to 1947 studies the changes in manners, morals, and tastes, the influences of European reformers, the "little theatre" movement, and the development of new techniques in stagecraft. Poetical and imaginative drama, realistic and social propaganda, high and low comedy, and musicals are examined.

GARD, ROBERT E. and MARSTON BALCH, PAULINE TEMKIN
Theatre in America, Appraisal and Challenge
Theatre Arts, 1968. 192pp. $6.50. Paper $4.95. This appraisal of the American contemporary theatre scene was undertaken by the National Theatre Conference. It is a view of what is being done in New York, on the Community Theatre scene, in the Educational Theatre, and on the Regional Repertory scene. Bibliography. Index.

GARDNER, R.H.
The Splintered Stage: The Decline of the American Theatre
Macmillan, 1965. 159pp. $4.50. With the thesis: "With the possible exception of Calvin and Cromwell, no two men have retarded the development of the drama more than Karl Marx and Sigmund Freud," this study indicts today's "misfit drama in which the sick and the obscure take the place of the normal and the significant."

GAVER, JACK
Season In, Season Out
Hawthorn, 1966. 221pp. $6.95. A diary of the 1965-1966 Broadway theatre: the stories behind each new play, various theatre awards, critical controversies, the background of the Actor's Studio, A. P. A., and A. N. T. A., etc.

GILDER, ROSAMOND and The Editorial Board of the International Theatre Institute of the U.S. — Editors
Theatre I
Drama Book Specialists, 1969. 128pp. Paper $4.95. A collection of essays on the American theatre 1967–68. Among the contributors are Arthur Miller, Roger Stevens, Clive Barnes, Brooks Atkinson, Richard Barr, Alan Schneider, Harold Clurman, Harold Prince, Tom O'Horgan, Ellen Stewart, and Paul Green. A thirty page insert has the articles translated into French. Illustrated with photographs and drawings. Slipcased.

GILDER, ROSAMOND et al — Editors
Theatre 2: 1968 — 1969
Theatre Arts, 1970. 176pp. Paper $4.95. A collection of essays on the American theatre 1968–1969. Among the contributors are Walter Kerr, Richard Schechner, Harold Clurman, John Lahr, Clive Barnes, Jean-Claude van Itallie, Ed Bullins, Peggy Clark, and Paul Baker. Illustrated with photographs and drawings.

GILDER, ROSAMOND et al — Editors
Theatre 3: The American Theatre 1969 — 1970
Scribner, 1970. 176pp. $9.95. Paper $4.95. The third annual volume of essays on the American theatre. Articles and essays on off-Broadway, off-off-Broadway, Broadway, and various American companies by such contributors as Walter Kerr, Peter Brook, Richard Schechner, John Lahr, Harold Clurman, Clive Barnes, Arthur Ballet, and Dan Sullivan. Illustrated with photographs and drawings. An extensive Bibliography of books published during the year is also provided.

GINGRICH, ARNOLD
Business and the Arts: An Answer to Tomorrow
See Page 25

GOLDEN, JOSEPH
The Death of Tinker Bell: The American Theatre in the 20th Century
Syracuse University, 1967. 181pp. $5.00. Mr. Golden claims that the freedom and magic of the American theatre have been destroyed because Americans have failed to provide a favorable environment for its growth. Economic pressure, suspicions of the artist, and a general moral upheaval have stifled the theatre's potential. The author analyzes representative selections from O'Neill, MacLeish, Wilder, Williams, and Miller. Suggested Reading List.

GOLDMAN, WILLIAM
The Season
Harcourt, Brace, 1969. 432pp. $6.95. Paper — Bantam, 1970. 434pp. $1.25. In this "candid look at Broadway," the author takes each production of the 1967–68 season and relates it to some aspect of the over-all Broadway scene. All aspects of the season and the people who made it are examined. The author supports his opinions with information from industry sources and a research survey initiated privately for this book. Illustrated with posters of productions. Index.

GOTTFRIED, MARTIN
A Theatre Divided: The Postwar American Stage
Little, Brown, 1967. 330pp. $7.50. Paper $2.65. Mr.Gottfried's thesis is that the Broadway stage is the victim of a disastrous schism which divides the American theatre. Borrowing his terms from politics, he places Broadway on the extreme right wing of the theatrical spectrum and the left wing is represented by the newer resident companies and off-and off-off-Broadway. These two wings should interact to evolve a growing and vital theatre, but in the postwar years, a chasm has developed which threatens the existence of both wings. Index.

GOULD, JEAN
Modern American Playwrights
Dodd, Mead, 1966. 302pp. $6.50. Paper $1.95. A popular survey of the modern American theatre and its playwrights. Among the fourteen playwrights studied at length are: Elmer Rice, Susan Glaspell, Philip Barry, Eugene O'Neill, Robert Sherwood, Maxwell Anderson, Lillian Hellman, Clifford Odets, Thornton Wilder, Edward Albee, and Tennessee Williams. Illustrated with photographs. Bibliography. Index.

GRAU, ROBERT
The Stage in the Twentieth Century
Blom, 1969. 360pp. $25.00. Originally published in 1912 and now reissued in a facsimile edition, this is a study of the American stage and its development and condition in the early part of the twentieth century. Illustrated with photographs.

GREEN, PAUL
Drama and the Weather
Samuel French, 1958. 220pp. $3.00. A collection of essays varied in range and treatment, all pointing toward the creation of a climate favorable to the development of the arts in America. An essay entitled "Symphonic Outdoor Drama" describes the author's experiments in writing and producing outdoor plays dealing with the American heritage, including "The Common Glory" and "The Lost Colony."

GREEN, PAUL
Plough and Furrow
Samuel French, 1963. 165pp. $3.00. A collection of essays on such topics as the National Theatre effort, the Group Theatre, the "Method" in acting, "Peer Gynt," Southern attitudes toward the theatre, and the Civil War celebration in the South. There are a number of dialogue playlets and sketches on such topics as over-confident Broadway critics and the plight of the Negro.

GUERNSEY, OTIS L. — Editor
Best Plays Series
See: General Reference Works — Annuals

GUTHRIE, TYRONE
A New Theatre
McGraw–Hill, 1964. 189pp. $5.00. An account of the Tyrone Guthrie Theatre in Minneapolis which opened in May, 1963, with Mr. Guthrie as Director, Peter Zeisler as Stage Director, and Oliver Rea as entrepreneur. In addition to discussing the work of organizing the theatre, Mr. Guthrie comments on the plight of the commercial theatre today; examines the advantages and disadvantages of open stage and proscenium stage; and analyzes the relation with the audience. Illustrated.

HEWES, HENRY – Editor
Best Plays Series
See Page 9

HIMELSTEIN, MORGAN Y.
Drama Was a Weapon: The Left-Wing Theatre in New York 1929 – 1941
Rutgers University, 1963. 300pp. $6.00. A history of the social theatre of the Depression as it was beset by the Communist Party. The author describes the Party's efforts to finance its own theatre groups, organize fronts, and infiltrate the theatre groups of other organizations. The early successes and final failure of the movement are examined.

HURRELL, JOHN D.
Two Modern American Tragedies
Scribner, 1961. 153pp. $3.50. A collection of reviews and criticisms of Miller's "Death of a Salesman" and Williams' "A Streetcar Named Desire" designed to serve as a guide to the methods of research paper writing and controlled research.

HYAMS, BARRY – Editor
Theatre: The Annual of the Repertory Theatre of Lincoln Center – Volume Two, 1965
Hill & Wang, 1965. 124pp. $3.95. Paper $1.95. A collection of essays on the function of Lincoln Center and the plays performed there since it opened. Among the contributors are: Henri Peyre, Lionel Abel, Nancy and Richard Meyer, and May Swenson. A record of a symposium on "The New Repertory" is also included. Among the contributors to that forum were: Sir Tyrone Guthrie, Herbert Blau, and Harold Clurman. Illustrated.

JONES, MARGO
Theatre-In-the-Round
McGraw–Hill, 1965. 244pp. Paper $2.45. Originally published in 1951 and now reissued, this is a log of the twenty-nine productions of Miss Jones' theatre in Dallas, Texas up to 1951. The producer/director analyzes the special problems of casting, costuming, directing, and lighting at the theatre. She provides hints on how to organize an arena theatre, lists contemporary arena theatres, and includes a Book List.

KELLNER, BRUCE
Carl Van Vechten and the Irreverent Decades
University of Oklahoma, 1968. 354pp. $7.95. Mr. Kellner traces the life of Carl Van Vechten through his varied careers as critic, essayist, novelist, photographer, and collector of the arts. The biography includes anecdotes of some of America's most celebrated men and women of letters: Theodore Dreiser, Eugene O'Neill, F. Scott Fitzgerald, George Gershwin, and Gertrude Stein. Illustrated with photographs including thirty-two of Van Vechten's own portrait studies. Bibliography. Index.

KERNAN, ALVIN B. – Editor
The Modern American Theatre
Prentice–Hall, 1967. 183pp. $4.95. Paper $1.95. A group of critics, directors, and playwrights (including Kenneth Tynan, Allan Kaprow, Robert Brustein, and Edward Albee) considers the range and variety of American theatre from the Broadway musical to the existential Theatre of Chance. Analyzed in detail are the work of five of our most successful playwrights: Albee, Inge, Miller, Wilder, and Williams. Bibliography.

KERR, JEAN
Please Don't Eat the Daisies
Doubleday, 1957. 198pp. $3.50. Paper – Fawcett. $ .50. Sketches of life with children, drama critics, and producers by a playwright and mother.

KERR, JEAN
The Snake Has All the Lines
Doubleday, 1960. 168pp. $3.95. Paper – Fawcett. $ .50. Another collection of parodies and commentaries on life and the theatre.

KERR, WALTER
Thirty Plays Hath November
See Page 29

KRONENBERGER, LOUIS – Editor
Best Plays Series
See Page 9

KRUTCH, JOSEPH WOOD
American Drama Since 1918
Braziller, 1967. 344pp. $6.00. Originally published in 1939, and now revised and expanded, this volume is a first hand account of the American theatre from the end of the first World War to the present day. The author stresses the effect in performance rather than the text to show the growth and development of a genuinely American drama. Index.

LAHR, JOHN
Up Against the Fourth Wall
See Page 30

LANGNER, LAWRENCE
The Play's the Thing
The Writer, 1967. 258pp. $5.95. This is a reissue of Mr. Langner's 1960 book. It is an informal record

of Mr. Langner's career over a forty year period and also provides insights into the working methods of some of the most memorable names of the theatre. The observations on play construction, rewriting, adaptation, and production will be of particular interest to playwrights.

LAUFE, ABE
Anatomy of a Hit: Long-Run Plays on Broadway from 1900 to the Present Day
Hawthorn, 1965. 350pp. $6.95. This study of plays that have had runs of more than 500 performances examines those qualities each possessed to make it a commercial success. The plays are studied from idea to opening night and critical reception. Index.

LEWIS, ALLAN
American Plays and Playwrights of the Contemporary Theatre: Revised Edition
Crown, 1970. 270pp. $5.95. Originally published in 1965 and now thoroughly revised and brought up to date. Dr. Lewis examines the topical revue, the musical theatre, new themes and forms, new trends and movements and analyzes the works of Miller, Hellman, Saroyan, Albee, Schisgal, Kopit, Horovitz, O'Horgan, and Grotowski as well as many of the other new voices on, off-and off-off-Broadway. Index.

LEWIS, ARTHUR H.
Carnival
Trident, 1970. 315pp. $5.95. A study of the American outdoor entertainment form as it exists today and as it was revealed to the author in his travels along the carnival trail for six months in thirty cities. In a humorous manner, the author describes the lives of the workers including snake charmers and tattooed ladies.

LEWIS, EMORY
Stages: The Fifty Year Childhood of the American Theatre
Prentice –Hall, 1969. 290pp. $7.95. Mr. Lewis discusses the development of the American theatre, decade by decade, from 1915 to the 1960's. He studies the plays and playwrights, actors and directors, producers, scenic designers, costumers, Broadway, off- and off-off-Broadway. He concludes that the promise of the American theatre lies in the aspirations of the nation's young to change America as reflected in the work of LeRoi Jones, Barbara Garson, Megan Terry, Cafe La Mama, the Living Theatre, and other revolutionary groups known and to be discovered. Index.

LEY–PISCATOR, MARIA
The Piscator Experiment: The Political Theatre
Heineman, 1967. 336pp. $8.50. Erwin Piscator's widow writes about her husband's friendship with Brecht, his productions of "total theatre," his politics, and his acquaintance with the playwrights and performers of the "Epic Theatre" stage. Bibliography. Index.

LIPSKY, LOUIS
Tales of the Yiddish Rialto
A. S. Barnes, 1962. 234pp. $3.75. A collection of reminiscences of playwrights and players in New York's Yiddish theatre during the early 1900's.

LITTLE, STUART W. and ARTHUR CANTOR
The Playmakers
Norton, 1970. 320pp. $7.95. An account of the contemporary Broadway theatre scene. The authors write about Broadway as a physical entity and the people who are responsible for the plays produced there. Illustrated. Index.

McCARTHY, MARY
Mary McCarthy's Theatre Chronicles: 1937–1962
Farrar, Straus, 1963. 248pp. $4.50. Paper $1.95. The pathology of the New York theatre is examined in articles originally written for "The Partisan Review," "The New York Times," and "The London Observer."

MANTLE, BURNS – Editor
Best Plays Series
See Page 9

MATHEWS, JANE DE HART
The Federal Theatre: 1935 – 1939
Princeton, 1967. 342pp. $8.50. A study of the WPA Theatre Project during the Roosevelt era. Mrs. Mathews explores the venture from its ambiguous origins through the Congressional hearings which occasioned its disbanding. Illustrated. Bibliography. Index.

MELNITZ, WILLIAM
Theatre Arts Publications in the United States: 1947 – 1952
See Page 4

MESERVE, WALTER – Editor
Discussions of Modern American Drama
D. C. Heath, 1966. 150pp. Paper $2.50. Essays on the American theatre by playwrights and critics. Among the contributors are: Lionel Trilling, Harold Clurman, Robert Brustein, Mary McCarthy, Eugene O'Neill, Tennessee Williams, and Edward Albee.

MOORE, THOMAS GALE
The Economics of the American Theater
Duke University, 1968. 192pp. $10.00. Professor Moore investigates the economic forces that have been shaping theatre in the U. S. He examines what has happened to costs, union's responsibilities for the theatre's financial difficulties, and the theatre patron. Other topics include subsidization and regional and touring theatre. Tables and Charts. Glossary. Appendices. Bibliography. Index.

MORISON, BRADLEY G. and KAY FLIEHR
In Search of an Audience

Pitman, 1968. 230pp. $5.95. This is a detailed history of a community action program on behalf of a theater. It tells how a group of experts drawn from advertising, public relations, and the community at large found an audience for the Tyrone Guthrie Theatre in Minneapolis. Preface by Sir Tyrone Guthrie. Bibliography.

MOSKOW, MICHAEL H.
Labor Relations in the Performing Arts: An Introductory Survey
Associated Councils of the Arts, 1970. 218pp. Paper $2.50. The basic purposes of this study are to survey the status of labor relations in some of the performing arts and to identify existing and possible future problem areas that will be of interest to scholars, managers, trustees, union leaders, performers, and community leaders. Illustrated with eighteen tables. Appendix. Footnotes.

NADEL, NORMAN
A Pictorial History of the Theatre Guild
Crown, 1969. 312pp. $10.00. A history of the Theatre Guild producing organization over the fifty years of its existence. Special material by Lawrence Langner and Armina Marshall is included as is an Introduction by Brooks Atkinson. Illustrated with more than 500 photographs. Lists of Theatre Guild Plays. Index.

NATHAN, GEORGE JEAN
Encyclopaedia of the Theatre
Fairleigh Dickinson University, 1970. 449pp. $10.00. Originally published in 1940 and now reissued with a new Introduction by Charles Angoff. Nathan expresses his knowledge and perceptions of the theaatre in alphabetized topics including, among many others, acting, Hollywood, the Lunts, musical shows, polite comedy, morality and burlesque, and producers versus critics.

NATHAN, GEORGE JEAN
Passing Judgments
Fairleigh Dickinson University, 1970. 271pp. $8.00. Originally published in 1935 and now reissued, this is a book on the theatre of the middle 1930's. In separate chapters, Nathan deals with such subjects as critics, the impact of the movies on the stage, critical presumptions, sex appeal, producers, summer theatre, and motion picture censorship. A new Introduction has been provided by Charles Angoff.

NATHAN, GEORGE JEAN
The Theatre of the Moment
Fairleigh Dickinson University, 1970. 310pp. $8.00. Originally published in 1936 and now reissued, the drama critic reflects on plays, playwrights, actors, and critics prominent in the 1930's. A new Introduction has been provided by Charles Angoff.

NEFF, RENFREU
The Living Theatre/USA
Bobbs—Merrill, 1970. 254pp. $7.50. A history of the six-month tour The Living Theatre company made in the United States beginning in September 1968. A history of the company and details of their productions are included. Illustrated with photographs. Bibliography. Index.

NEWQUIST, ROY
Showcase
Morrow, 1966. 412pp. $5.95. Interviews with twenty-five actors, directors, designers, and producers. These interviews follow certain major themes: how and why does one get into show business; what obligation the actor feels to the writer, director, and the audience; how the actor (or producer, or writer) prepares for the play; the difference between American and other audiences. Illustrations by Irma Selz.

NOVICK, JULIUS
Beyond Broadway: The Quest for Permanent Theatres
Hill & Wang, 1968. 393pp. $7.95. Paper $2.95. Mr. Novick records his visits to fifty professional theatres outside New York. He describes the companies, their backgrounds, history, budgets, buildings, productions, and personalities. Illustrated with photographs. Index.

PASOLLI, ROBERT
A Book on the Open Theatre
Bobbs—Merrill, 1970. 127pp. $7.50. A history and study of Joseph Chaikin's Open Theatre company from the beginning workshops in 1963. The author also provides a manual of the individual and ensemble acting exercises created by the group throughout its seven-year history. Illustrated with photographs.

PHELPS, WILLIAM LYON
The Twentieth Century Theatre
See Page 26

PORTER, THOMAS E.
Myth and Modern American Drama
Wayne State University, 1969. 286pp. $7.95. The author suggests an approach to drama criticism which relates drama to the cultural milieu in which it is produced. He analyzes nine American plays as they relate to the major components of the milieu. The plays are: "Mourning Becomes Electra," "The Cocktail Party," "J. B.," "Detective Story," "Death of a Salesman," "Streetcar Named Desire," "Our Town," "The Crucible," and "Who's Afraid of Virginia Woolf." Notes. Selected Bibliography. Index.

RABKIN, GERALD
Drama and Commitment: Politics in the American Theatre of the Thirties
Indiana University, 1964. 322pp. $6.00. An examination of the impact of politics upon the dramatic genre in the 1930's which traces the results of that impact on three developments in the Depression—theatre unions, the Group theatre, and the Federal Theatre.

The works of Odets, Behrman, Rice, Lawson, and Anderson are examined to determine the effects of political commitment on their dramatic achievements. A final chapter restates the problem in terms of present theatre and politics. Index.

REDFIELD, WILLIAM
Letters from an Actor
See Page 94

ROCKEFELLER PANEL
The Performing Arts: Problems and Prospects
McGraw–Hill, 1965. 258pp. Paper $1.95. The Rockefeller Panel Report on the future of theatre, dance, and music in America. This study examines such aspects as the financing of theatrical ventures, individual giving to the performing arts, corporate support, foundation support, the role of the federal government, the Universities and the professional theatre, and the building of greater appreciation of the performing arts. Lists of permanent theatres and orchestras. Index.

ROSTAGNO, ALDO with JULIAN BECK, JUDITH MALINA
We, The Living Theatre
Ballantine, 1970. 240pp. Paper $1.95. This is a pictorial documentation of the life and the pilgrimage of The Living Theatre in Europe and the U. S. and the productions recently mounted. Introduced by a panel discussion on "Theatre as Revolution" and including an Appendix of selected documents and reviews from the American press.

SANN, PAUL
Fads, Follies and Delusions of the American People
Crown, 1967. 370pp. $4.95. The subtitle of this volume is "A pictorial story of madnesses, crazes and crowd phenomena." Although not a theatre book, it gives an account of the way Americans amused themselves over a period of years and contains much material on entertainers and the entertainment industry. Illustrated. Index.

SCHAFFNER, NEIL E. and VANCE JOHNSON
The Fabulous Toby and Me
Prentice–Hall, 1968. 212pp. $5.95. This is the story of the Schaffner Players and the tent theatre of America. Mr. Schaffner's company toured the South and Mid-west for many years and he himself became identified with the "Toby" character. Illustrated with photographs. Index.

SCHECHNER, RICHARD
Public Domain
See Page 23

SIEVERS, W. DAVID
Freud on Broadway
Cooper Square, 1970. 479pp. $14.50. Originally published in 1955 and now reissued, this is a comprehensive survey of the impact of psychoanalysis upon the American theatre. Dr. Sievers provides concentrated summaries of hundreds of plays and critical evaluations of such American playwrights as Susan Glaspell, Eugene O'Neill, Elmer Rice, Thornton Wilder, Paul Green, Maxwell Anderson, Lillian Hellman, Clifford Odets, Arthur Laurents, Arthur Miller, Tennessee Williams, and others. Bibliography. Index.

SPEARMAN, WALTER and SAMUEL SELDEN
The Carolina Playmakers: The First Fifty Years
University of North Carolina, 1970. 178pp. $10.00. A history of the Carolina Playmakers from the inception of the group at The University of North Carolina in 1918 by Professor Frederick H. Koch. One chapter describes the popularization of the outdoor historical drama beginning with "The Lost Colony" in 1937. Illustrated with photographs. Index.

SPITZER, MARIAN
The Palace
Atheneum, 1969. 267pp. $8.95. A history of the Palace Theatre from its opening in 1913 through the great days of vaudeville and the many stars who played there: W. C. Fields, Nora Bayes, Smith and Dale, Ed Wynn, Fanny Brice, Sophie Tucker, and others, to its days as a movie house during the depression and then its resurgence as a legitimate theatre during the 1950's and 1960's. Illustrated with photographs. Index.

SPRATLING, WILLIAM and WILLIAM FAULKNER
Sherwood Anderson and Other Famous Creoles
University of Texas, 1966. 80pp. $5.00. Originally published in 1926 and now reissued in a facsimile edition with additional material. It includes caricatures of some of the famous and infamous people who were engaged in the arts in New Orleans in the 1920's, an article on Faulkner by Spratling entitled "Chronicle of a Friendship," and a reminiscence of Spratling by Robert David Duncan.

STAGG, JERRY
The Brothers Shubert
Random House, 1968. 431pp. $10.00. A biography of the three Shubert brothers, Samuel, J. J., and Lee, theatrical producers who became a living legend in the early 1900's and dominated the theatre scene, not only in New York but across America. The book not only details their lives but is a history of theatre in America during the 1900's. Illustrated with photographs. List of Shubert-Produced Plays in New York City. Index.

STEIGMAN, BENJAMIN
Accent on Talent: New York's High School of Music and Art
Wayne State University, 1964. 270pp. $7.95. A history of the High School of Music and Art, written by the man who was principal of the school for twenty-two years. The course of study at the school is described and a history of its alumni is given. Index.

STERNE, RICHARD L.
John Gielgud Directs Richard Burton in "Hamlet"
See Page 94

STEVENS, DAVID H. – Editor
Ten Talents in the American Theatre
University of Oklahoma, 1957. 299pp. $5.95. A collection of essays by ten professional men of the theatre which describes their efforts to communicate the American spirit through theatre. The contributors are: Robert Gard, Paul Baker, Alan Schneider, Margo Jones, Frederick McConnell, Barclay Leathem, Gilmor Brown, Leslie Cheek, Jr., George G. Izenour, and Paul Green.

STEWARD, DWIGHT
Stage Left
Tanager Press, 1970. 126pp. $4.95. Paper $2.95. The author analyzes recent movements in politically radical theatre and furnishes "rules of the game" instructions for prospective writers and producers. Scripts for improvisations, guerilla theatre, happenings, and agit-prop plays are provided.

SULLIVAN, FRANK
Frank Sullivan Through the Looking Glass
See Page 30

SYLVESTER, ROBERT
Notes of a Guilty Bystander
Prentice–Hall, 1970. 305pp. $7.95. Memories and chronicles of New York during the 1930's by the newspaper columnist. The essays deal with Broadway, the sports world, early television, and the hoods, saloon society, and jazz musicians of the decade. Illustrated with photographs. Index.

TAPER, BERNARD
The Arts in Boston
Harvard, 1970. 170pp. $6.00. Paper $2.95. An analysis of the social and economic characteristics of the arts in Boston, Massachusetts. The author seeks answers to the questions of what might be done to foster the arts and to make them more meaningful to a larger segment of the community. The author includes interviews with concerned artists in Boston and relates his analysis to the overall situation of the arts in America. Appendices. Notes. Index.

TOFFLER, ALVIN
The Culture Consumers: A Study of Art and Affluence in America
St. Martin's, 1964. 263pp. $5.00. Paper – Penguin, 1965. 288pp. $1.25. A portrait of the American as professional art lover, with comments on such topics as: culture as campus big business, art in executive suites, and the underpaid artist and the overpriced work of art.

TOOHEY, JOHN L.
A History of the Pulitzer Prize Plays
Citadel, 1967. 344pp. $14.95. Over 300 photographs illustrate the text of this history of the Pulitzer Prize plays from 1918 to 1967. Mr. Toohey presents and analyzes the forty-two award winning plays. The production history, credits, major reviews, and a full synopsis of each play are given. Index.

VAUGHAN, STUART
A Possible Theatre
McGraw–Hill, 1969. 255pp. $6.95. Mr. Vaughan provides not only an autobiography but also a documented study of the resident theatre movement in the U. S. His experiences as a pioneer director in the movement with the N. Y. Shakespeare Festival, the Phoenix Theatre, and the Seattle Repertory Theatre are detailed. Index.

WEALES, GERALD
American Drama Since World War II
Harcourt, Brace, 1962. 246pp. $5.95. A critical evaluation of Broadway (on and off-) with chapters on Miller, Williams, video playwrights, the "new Pineros," and musicals.

WEALES, GERALD
The Jumping Off Place: American Drama in the 1960's
Macmillan, 1969. 306pp. $6.95. Mr. Weales takes a critical look at the radical departures characteristic of the current dramatic scene on Broadway, off-Broadway, off-off-Broadway, Assemblage, Environments, and Happenings. Among the playwrights discussed are Tennessee Williams, Arthur Miller, Edward Albee, LeRoi Jones, James Baldwin, Robert Lowell, Lawrence Ferlinghetti, Bruce Jay Friedman, Joseph Heller, Jean-Claude van Itallie, Ellen Stewart, and Claes Oldenburg. Index.

WILLIS, JOHN – Editor
Theatre World
See Page 9

YOUNG, STARK
The Theatre
Hill & Wang, 1958. 124pp. Paper $ .95. A selection of Mr. Young's "New Republic" criticisms which reveal his philosophy of dramatic art. The essays cover the years 1921–1947.

The Negro in the American Theatre

See also listings for individual American playwrights.

ABRAMSON, DORIS E.
Negro Playwrights in the American Theatre: 1925 – 1959
Columbia, 1969. 335pp. $13.50. Paper $2.95. This is a study of the fifteen Negro playwrights and their eighteen plays which were produced in the professional

New York theatre between 1925 and 1959. The author studies the playwrights in a social and artistic context and examines their artistic development as writers. Each of the plays is studied in the perspective of the political, economic, and social scene of its time and of the prevailing attitudes in the professional theatre when each was produced. Notes. Bibliography. Index.

BAILEY, PEARL
The Raw Pearl
See Page 263

BOND, FREDERICK W.
The Negro and the Drama
See Page 229

BOWEN, ELBERT R.
Theatrical Entertainments in Rural Missouri Before the Civil War
See Page 233

BROWN, STERLING
Negro Poetry and Drama and the Negro in American Fiction
Atheneum, 1969. 351pp. Paper $3.45. This volume consists of two books originally published in 1937 and now reissued. Only forty pages deal with the Negro in American theatre but these chapters deal with the early drama of Negro life, Negro folk drama, and realistic and problem drama of the 1920's and 1930's. Lists of reference works are included.

CRUSE, HAROLD
The Crisis of the Negro Intellectual
Morrow, 1967. 594pp. $8.95. Paper $3.50. Mr. Cruse analyzes the American racial impasse and examines the Negro intellectual as a class that lacks continuity with its cultural, creative, and idealogical antecedents. The author traces the roots of the crisis back to the 1920's through the emergence of such figures as Paul Robeson, Martin Luther King, LeRoi Jones, and Lorraine Hansberry. Of particular interest is the section on the theatre of the 1960's and the Harlem Black Arts Theatre. Bibliography. Index.

DAVIS, SAMMY and BURT BOYAR, JANE BOYAR
Yes, I Can
See Page 266

DENT, THOMAS C. and RICHARD SCHECHNER – Editors
The Free Southern Theatre
Bobbs–Merrill, 1969. 233pp. $6.95. Paper $3.75. A study of the radical black theatre group, with journals, letters, essays, and a play written by those who built the group. Most of the writing dwells on the years 1965–67, on the concepts from which the theatre began and on the changes within the company as commitment deepened and experience strengthened their efforts. Illustrated with photographs.

GIBSON, DONALD B. – Editor
Five Black Writers
N. Y. U. Press, 1970. 310pp. $13.00. Paper $3.50. Essays by various critics on five black writers: Richard Wright, Ralph Ellison, James Baldwin, Langston Hughes, and LeRoi Jones. Introduction to the volume by the editor. Also included in the volume are a series of essays on "The Writer and Social Responsibility." Bibliography.

GREGORY, DICK with ROBERT LIPSYTE
Nigger
See Page 269

HATCH, JAMES V.
Black Image on the American Stage
See Page 558

HORNE, LENA and RICHARD SCHICKEL
Lena
See Page 270

HOYT, EDWIN P.
Paul Robeson: The American Othello
See Page 276

HUGHES, LANGSTON and MILTON MELTZER
Black Magic
Prentice–Hall, 1967. 375pp. $13.95. A pictorial history of the Negro in American entertainment, from the slave musicians up to such great modern Negro entertainers as Ella Fitzgerald, Sammy Davis, and Duke Ellington. It provides a comprehensive history of the whole scope of Negro entertainment in America and includes hundreds of photographs.

ISAACS, EDITH J. R.
The Negro in the American Theatre
McGrath, 1969. 143pp. $24.00. A reprint of the 1947 publication, this is a history of the contributions of the Negro in the American theatre from its earliest days to 1946. Illustrated with production photographs and portraits.

LITTLEJOHN, DAVID
Black on White
Viking, 1969. 180pp. Paper $1.45. Originally published in 1966 and now reissued, this is a critical survey of writing by American Negroes. One chapter concerns four Negro playwrights of the contemporary American theatre: Lorraine Hansberry, Ossie Davis, James Baldwin, and LeRoi Jones. Index.

MALONE, MARY
Actor in Exile: The Life of Ira Aldridge
See Page 263

MARGOLIES, EDWARD
Native Sons
Lippincott, 1969. 209pp. $5.95. Paper $1.95. This is a critical study of twentieth century American

Negro authors. Dr. Margolies reveals the significance of modern American Negro writing in terms of what it tells us about the quality of American life. The study expresses Negro thought from the point of view of the Negro writer and the work of a number of authors, including Richard Wright, Langston Hughes, James Baldwin, LeRoi Jones, and Malcolm X, is examined. Bibliography. Index.

MARSHALL, HERBERT and MILDRED STOCK
Ira Aldridge, the Negro Tragedian
See Page 263

MITCHELL, LOFTEN
Black Drama: The Story of the American Negro in the Theatre
Hawthorn, 1967. 248pp. $5.95. Paper $2.45. Mr. Mitchell examines every aspect of the Negro theatre with an awareness of the social, economic, and political atmosphere. He gives the reader a new perspective on plays written and produced by non-Negroes in which Negroes were important; he studies the Negro pioneers who opposed the minstrels, the Harlem theatre movements, the off-Broadway developments, and the plays of Baldwin, Jones, and Hansberry. Illustrated with photographs. Index.

NATHAN, HANS
Dan Emmett and the Rise of Early Negro Minstrelsy
See Page 290

NOBLE, PETER
The Negro in Films
See Page 440

OLIVER, PAUL
The Meaning of the Blues
See Page 292

RALPH, GEORGE
The American Theater, the Negro, and the Freedom Movement
See Page 558

REARDON, WILLIAM R. and THOMAS D. PAWLEY – Editors
The Black Teacher and the Dramatic Arts: A Dialogue, Bibliography, and Anthology
Negro Universities Press, 1970. 487pp. $17.50. Designed as a teaching aid for the training of black teachers in theatre education and the dramatic arts and as a working guide for theatre groups in predominantly black high schools and colleges. The Bibliography section embraces books, theses, articles, and plays from early twentieth century works to the present by Negroes and whites, dealing with all facets of Negro thinking and creative dramatic activity, listed by category and period of publication. The Anthology section provides five plays by C. B. Jackson, James Hatch, Ossie Davis, Loften Mitchell, and Ted Shine. Illustrated with photographs.

ROLLINS, CHARLEMAE
Famous Negro Entertainers of Stage, Screen and TV
See Page 262

SCHECHTER, WILLIAM
The History of Negro Humor in America
Fleet Press, 1970. 214pp. $8.95. A history, from early colonial times to the present day, of Negro humor in America. "Cakewalks," the minstrel period, ethnic jokes, and contemporary humorists such as Dick Gregory and Bill Cosby are all included to show the cultural contributions the Negro has made to American humor. Forty pages of Illustrations. Bibliography. Index.

SETON, MARIE
Paul Robeson
See Page 276

WATERS, ETHEL with CHARLES SAMUELS
His Eye Is on the Sparrow
See Page 278

Studies of Playwrights

Albee, Edward

AMACHER, RICHARD E.
Edward Albee
Twayne, 1969. 190pp. $4.50. A study of the playwright in which Dr. Amacher presents analyses of the plays and assesses the achievements of the American leader of "the theatre of the absurd." Chronology. Notes and References. Selected Bibliography. Index.

BIGSBY, C. W. E.
Albee
Oliver & Boyd, 1969. 120pp. $4.50. Paper $2.45. An evaluation of Edward Albee's plays. The author analyzes all of the plays but concentrates on "Who's Afraid of Virginia Woolf." Dr. Bigsby believes that Albee's work challenges comparison with the plays of Arthur Miller and Eugene O'Neill. Bibliography.

COHN, RUBY
Edward Albee
University of Minnesota, 1969. 48pp. Paper $ .95. A short study of the playwright. A Selected Bibliography includes lists of plays and essays and critical studies.

DEBUSSCHER, GILBERT
Edward Albee: Tradition and Renewal
Center for American Studies, 1969. 94pp. Paper $3.50. Originally published in 1967 and now reprinted, this study was published in Brussels and has been translated from the French by Mrs. Anne D. Williams. The author analyzes the dominant themes, the recurrent images and symbols, and the structural development

of each work from the first one-act plays through "Tiny Alice." An opening chapter examines the American tradition since O'Neill and a concluding chapter examines the scope of Albee's accomplishments to date. Bibliography.

RUTENBERG, MICHAEL E.
Edward Albee: Playwright in Protest
Drama Book Specialists, 1969. 280pp. $6.95. Paper—Avon, 1970. 255pp. $1.65. Professor Rutenberg begins his analysis of Albee's plays, from "Zoo Story" through "Box-Mao-Box," by discussing the playwright's early position as a defender of society's outcasts. He clarifies Albee's attack on hypocrisy and corruption and explores the playwright's understanding of modern man's sense of futility and isolation. Included are transcripts of two interviews with the playwright, footnotes, chronology of openings, and a Selected Bibliography.

Anderson, Maxwell

AVERY, LAURENCE G.—Compiler
A Catalogue of the Maxwell Anderson Collection at the University of Texas
University of Texas, 1968. 175pp. $10.00. This is an inventory of Maxwell Anderson's papers which are being preserved at the University of Texas. Plays, poems, essays, letters and diaries, published and unpublished, are covered. For each published play the chronology of the various drafts is established and every manuscript is described. The remaining literary manuscripts are described in chronological order and a summary of the draft is provided. Illustrated. Index.

Anderson, Sherwood

ANDERSON, DAVID D.
Sherwood Anderson: An Introduction and Interpretation
Barnes & Noble, 1967. 182pp. $5.50. A critical biography of Sherwood Anderson's life and work. The works are approached as a chronological unit and the close relationship between Anderson's life and work is studied. Illustrated with photographs. Chronology. Selected Bibliography. Index.

ANDERSON, ELIZABETH and GERALD R. KELLY
Miss Elizabeth: A Memoir
Little, Brown, 1969. 315pp. $6.75. A memoir of the second wife of playwright Sherwood Anderson. It tells of Mrs. Anderson's early life, contact with literary figures in New York during the early 1900's, her meeting and life with Anderson in New Orleans, Paris, and Virginia, and her later life in Mexico and the notables she encountered there.

BURBANK, REX
Sherwood Anderson
Twayne, 1961. 156pp. $4.50. Paper—1962. 159pp. $2.45. An examination of those facts of the writer's life that shaped the tales and romances he wrote. There is detailed criticism of "Winesburg, Ohio."

HOWE, IRVING
Sherwood Anderson: A Biographical and Critical Study
Stanford University, 1951. 271pp. $6.00. Paper—1966. $2.95. A critical biography of Anderson and his work. The author traces Anderson's career through the tales of "Winesburg, Ohio" and ties together the characters and the central theme of their lostness. Also analyzed is the narrative method of the short stories. Bibliographical Notes. Index.

WEBER, BROM
Sherwood Anderson
University of Minnesota, 1964. 48pp. Paper $ .95. A short study of the novelist/playwright. Selected Bibliography.

WHITE, RAY LEWIS—Editor
Sherwood Anderson's Memoirs: A Critical Edition
University of North Carolina, 1969. 579pp. $15.00. Newly edited from the original manuscripts, this is a scholarly edition of Mr. Anderson's memoirs. Mr. White has completely retranscribed over 2,200 pages of Anderson's manuscripts, explained the composition and textual state of the work, and annotated the biographical and bibliographical facts of Anderson's career. Illustrated with photographs. Bibliography. Index.

Baldwin, James

ECKMAN, FERN MARJA
The Furious Passage of James Baldwin
Lippincott, 1966. 254pp. $4.50. Miss Eckman has based this book on hours of taped interviews with Baldwin and with the people involved in his life. Bibliographic Notes.

Barry, Philip

ROPPOLO, JOSEPH PATRICK
Philip Barry
Twayne, 1965. 159pp. $4.50. Paper $2.45. This chronological survey of Barry's life and work begins with his first appearance in print, as a child, and follows him through his college publications, his apprenticeship under George Pierce Baker in the Harvard Workshop, and through three decades of Broadway productions. A Bibliography provides lists of critical discussions and biographical materials.

Bellow, Saul

TANNER, TONY
Saul Bellow
Oliver & Boyd, 1965. 119pp. Paper $1.75. Published in England, this is a brief study of the principal themes in the fiction of Saul Bellow. The author has included a list of critiques as well as a list of Bellow's works in the Bibliography.

Benet, Stephen Vincent

STROUD, PARRY E.
Stephen Vincent Benet
Twayne, 1962. 173pp. Paper $2.45. A critical study of Benet's writings which argues that their significance arises from the importance of the author's national themes, from the craftsmanship of his work, and from the liberal philosophy which underlies it. A chapter is devoted to ''John Brown's Body'' and one to his radio drama which was written during World War II. Selected Bibliography. Index.

Bird, Robert Montgomery

DAHL, CURTIS
Robert Montgomery Bird
Twayne, 1963. 144pp. Paper $2.45. A study of the career and writings of the dramatist of the early nineteenth century. Professor Dahl describes how the author was cheated of the monetary gains of his dramas by Edwin Forrest and how he was forced to turn to the teaching of medicine for a livelihood. Selected Bibliography. Index.

Boucicault, Dion (Also See Page 184)

HOGAN, ROBERT
Dion Boucicault
Twayne, 1969. 146pp. $4.50. A modern account of the nineteenth century actor and playwright. The author singles out from among Boucicault's dozens of plays those few which he considers to have literary merit and discusses the theatrical validity of the potboilers. Notes and References. Bibliography. Index.

Chapman, John Jay

BERNSTEIN, MELVIN H.
John Jay Chapman
Twayne, 1964. 144pp. $3.95. Paper $2.45. Chapman was a turn-of-the-century essayist, poet, and dramatist who has recently been neglected. Professor Bernstein examines the causes of this neglect and attempts to catch Chapman's censure of our intellectual and moral timidity. Chronology. Selected Bibliography. Index.

Chase, Mary Ellen

WESTBROOK, PERRY D.
Mary Ellen Chase
Twayne, 1965. 176pp. Paper $2.45. This is an assessment of the American writer's fictional and autobiographical writings. Selected Bibliography. Index.

Connelly, Marc

CONNELLY, MARC
Voices Offstage: A Book of Memoirs
Hott, Rinehart, 1968. 258pp. $5.95. This volume of memoirs details the theatrical and personal life of the author of ''The Green Pastures.'' Intimate portraits of the great actors, writers, publishers and wits of the era emerge.

MONTGOMERY, MARILYN M.
Connelly's The Green Pastures
Monarch, 1966. 64pp. Paper $1.00. A critical guide to the play with discussions on the background, thematic analysis, character analysis, critical commentary, essay questions and answers for review, and a Bibliography.

NOLAN, PAUL T.
Marc Connelly
Twayne, 1969. 175pp. $4.50. Dr. Nolan describes over thirty plays, dozens of short stories and essays, and a novel. Much of the book is based on a series of interviews with the playwright. Chronology. Selected Bibliography. Index.

Crawford, Francis Marion

PILKINGTON, JOHN, JR.
Francis Marion Crawford
Twayne, 1964. 223pp. Paper $1.95. This is the first study of Crawford's life and work to be published. Although emphasis is placed upon the novels, his dramas of the 1890's are also studied and discussed. Chronology. Selected Bibliography. Index.

Cummings, E. E.

MARKS, BARRY A.
E. E. Cummings
Twayne, 1964. 156pp. $3.95. Paper $2.45. A study

of Mr. Cummings' poetry. The author analyzes a relatively small number of poems to show how Cummings handled a single selected subject, its effect on his poetic technique, and its relation to his ideas and attitudes. Bibliography. Index.

NORMAN, CHARLES
e. e. cummings
Dutton, 1967. 246pp. Paper $1.45. A biography of the American poet, first published in 1958 and now considerably revised and brought up-to-date. Interpolated are many quotations from Cummings' letters, poetry, and other writings. Index of Persons and Places.

TRIEM, EVE
E. E. Cummings
University of Minnesota, 1969. 48pp. Paper $ .95. This short critical study of the American poet and playwright is concerned principally with the poetry. A Selected Bibliography is provided.

Dunlap, William

CANARY, ROBERT H.
William Dunlap
Twayne, 1970. 162pp. $4.50. A study of the playwright/manager-director/historian and printer of the eighteenth century. The author takes account of the wide range of Dunlap's activities but concentrates on his dramas and histories. Chronology. Notes. Selected Bibliography. Index.

Faulkner, William

BACKMAN, MELVIN
Faulkner: The Major Years
Indiana University, 1966. 212pp. $5.75. Paper $1.95. A critical study of Faulkner's major contributions from 1929 to 1942. Mr. Backman has selected the major novels and stories to study as parts of a larger design. He considers in chronological detail the relationships among the symbols, themes, images, characters, and situations among the stories. Bibliography. Index.

IZARD, BARBARA and CLARA HIERONYMUS
Requiem for a Nun: On Stage and Off
Aurora, 1970. 331pp. Paper $3.95. The authors study William Faulkner's drama, particularly it's offstage life. They deal with the genesis of the drama, the questions of the author's intent, and the mysteries that surrounded it from the time of its writing in 1950 to its performance on Broadway in 1959. More than fifty photographs and illustrations of the manuscript. Bibliography. Index.

RUNYAN, HARRY
A Faulkner Glossary
Citadel, 1966. 310pp. Paper $2.25. A guide to the titles, fictional characters, and places in the published writings of William Faulkner. The author includes a biographical sketch, bibliographies and histories of the principal families of Yoknapatawpha County.

Frost, Robert

SQUIRES, RADCLIFFE
The Major Themes of Robert Frost
University of Michigan, 1969. 119pp. $3.95. Paper $1.95. Originally published in 1963 and now reissued, this is a synoptic discussion of Frost's works. Included here is an analysis of "A Way Out," a relatively unknown drama by the poet. Chronology. Selected Bibliography. Index.

Gale, Zona

SIMONSON, HAROLD P.
Zona Gale
Twayne, 1962. 157pp. Paper $2.45. A study of the life and work of the 1921 Pulitzer Prize winner for drama. The volume reviews Miss Gale's achievements in fiction, drama, poetry, and criticism. Chronology. Selected Bibliography. Index.

Gibson, William

GIBSON, WILLIAM
A Mass for the Dead
Atheneum, 1968. 431pp. $7.95. Paper—Bantam, 1969. 393pp. $1.25. The author of "The Miracle Worker" tells the story of his childhood years in New York City.

GIBSON, WILLIAM
The Seesaw Log
Knopf, 1959. 273pp. $4.95. This is a complete record of the day-to-day making of a hit play. It is the playwright's own account of what happened to his play from option to opening and is a portrait of the contemporary theatre at work. Complete text of the play is included.

Glaspell, Susan

WATERMAN, ARTHUR E.
Susan Glaspell
Twayne, 1966. 144pp. $3.95. Paper $2.45. A study

of the life and work of the novelist/playwright who won a Pulitzer Prize in 1931 for her play ''Alison's House.'' The crucial role she played in the growth of the Provincetown Players and the plays she wrote for that theatre is included as is a study of her fiction. A concluding chapter evaluates Miss Glaspell's place in America's literary history. The author has included a Chronology of events during Miss Glaspell's lifetime, a section of notes and references, and a Selected Bibliography of works and criticism. Index.

Green, Paul

GREEN, PAUL
Home to My Valley
University of North Carolina, 1970. 140pp. $5.95. Originally published in 1928 and now reissued, this is a collection of autobiographical pieces and folk tales of North Carolina where the author, Paul Green, grew up. The author is the playwright of ''In Abraham's Bosom,'' ''The Lost Colony,'' and ''The Common Glory.'' Illustrated.

LAZENBY, WALTER S.
Paul Green
Steck—Vaughn, 1970. 44pp. Paper $1.00. A study of the playwright. Material from an interview with Green is included. Selected Bibliography.

Hart, Moss

HART, MOSS
Act One
Modern Library, 1959. 444pp. $2.95. Paper — New American Library, 1960. 383pp. $ .95. Critically acclaimed on its original publication, this autobiography of Moss Hart is an account of his early years. Hart recalls his childhood in the Bronx, his life as a social director on the ''Borscht Circuit,'' and his successful collaboration with George S. Kaufman on the script of ''Once in a Lifetime.''

Hecht, Ben

HECHT, BEN
A Child of the Century
Ballantine, 1970. 608pp. Paper $1.25. Originally published in 1954 and now reissued, this is an autobiography of the playwright, film writer, and reporter. Anecdotes about Hollywood, the New York theatre, and his work as a journalist are included as are anecdotes about the famous people who were his friends, enemies, and/or co-workers. Illustrated with sixteen pages of photographs. Index.

Hellman, Lillian

ADLER, JACOB H.
Lillian Hellman
Steck—Vaughn, 1969. 44pp. Paper $1.00. A short study of the work of the American playwright. Selected Bibliography.

HELLMAN, LILLIAN
An Unfinished Woman
Little, Brown, 1969. 280pp. $7.50. Paper — Bantam, 1970. 244pp. $1.50. Miss Hellman offers a memoir of her life in the world outside the theatre. It details her experiences in New York, New Orleans, and Hollywood, in Spain during the Civil War, in Moscow and Leningrad during the Second World War, and through the great events of our times. Illustrated with photographs.

TRIESCH, MANFRED — Compiler
The Lillian Hellman Collection at the University of Texas
University of Texas, 1967. 167pp. $7.50. This is a descriptive catalogue of the collection of Miss Hellman's manuscripts at the University of Texas. The entries for each play are preceded by a short comment on the play. Reviews of opening night performances are included and an Appendix includes scenes from various of the works with the additions or deletions Miss Hellman made. Illustrated with photographs. Index.

Hughes, Langston

DICKINSON, DONALD C.
A Bio-bibliography of Langston Hughes: 1902 – 1967
Archon, 1967. 267pp. $12.00. Dr. Dickinson has written an introduction to the life and work of the poet/playwright. The biographical section gives a summary of Hughes' career and the bibliographical listing of his publications provides a guide to the work. References. Index.

EMANUEL, JAMES A.
Langston Hughes
Twayne, 1967. 192pp. $4.95. Paper $2.45. This study of the works of Langston Hughes examines the best and most representative of his literary productions, predominantly his short stories and poems. The author has included a Chronology of events during the lifetime of Hughes as well as a Selected Bibliography. Index.

HUGHES, LANGSTON
The Big Sea
Hill & Wang, 1968. 335pp. $4.95. Paper $1.95. This is a reissue of Mr. Hughes' autobiography, originally published in 1963. It tells the story of his early years,

particularly the years in Paris in the 1920's and the years of the "Black Renaissance" when he was a rising young poet.

HUGHES, LANGSTON
I Wonder as I Wander: An Autobiographical Journey
Hill & Wang, 1964. 405pp. $5.95. Paper $2.45. Mr. Hughes recreates his life in the 1930's when he traveled through Cuba, Russia, Central Asia, Spain, and Japan, and met the famous and the humble. A reissue of the second volume of the autobiography.

MELTZER, MILTON
Langston Hughes: A Biography
Crowell, 1968. 281pp. $4.50. This biography of the American poet and playwright was written for young people. Bibliography. Index.

Inge, William

SHUMAN, R. BAIRD
William Inge
Twayne, 1965. 190pp. $3.95. Paper—College and University Press, 1966. 190pp. $2.45. This study examines Inge's probing of the themes of loneliness, isolation, insecurity, and anxiety in the plays. Bibliography. Index.

James, Henry

EDGAR, PELHAM
Henry James: Man and Author
Russell & Russell, 1964. 350pp. $10.00. A reprint of the study first published in 1927. Chapters are devoted to such topics as the American short stories, the literary and artistic stories, the stories of the supernatural, the dramas, the letters, prefaces, and literary criticism, and the major novels. Index.

McELDERRY, BRUCE R., JR.
Henry James
Twayne, 1965. 192pp. Paper $2.45. This critical biography treats all aspects of Henry James' career. All of his fiction, travel essays, criticism, and plays are considered. A list of all of James' novels and stories in the order of their first publication is given. Selected Bibliography. Index.

TANNER, TONY—Editor
Henry James: Modern Judgments
Aurora, 1970. 351pp. Paper $2.50. This volume includes a selection of the best recent criticism of the work of Henry James. The editor has contributed an extensive Introduction as well as a Chronology of events during the author's career and a Selected Bibliography of additional criticism. Index.

Jeffers, Robinson

CARPENTER, FREDERICK I.
Robinson Jeffers
Twayne, 1962. 159pp. $3.95. Paper $2.45. This study examines the rise and fall of Jeffers' standing with critics and interprets the poet and playwright as a figure in the creation of our "American myth." The long poems are seen as myth and not classic tragedy.

RIDGEWAY, ANN N.—Editor
The Selected Letters of Robinson Jeffers: 1897—1962
Johns Hopkins, 1968. 407pp. $10.95. With a Foreword by Mark van Doren and photographs by Leigh Wiener, this is a collection of nearly 400 letters, arranged chronologically, that present an image of Jeffers from the age of ten until the day before his death. Index.

Lowell, Robert

MARTIN, JAY
Robert Lowell
University of Minnesota, 1970. 48pp. Paper $ .95. A short analysis of the American poet/playwright's work. This pamphlet discusses "Prometheus Bound," "The Old Glory," and "Phaedra." Selected Bibliography.

PARKINSON, THOMAS—Editor
Robert Lowell: A Collection of Critical Essays
Prentice-Hall, 1968. 176pp. $4.95. Paper $1.95. The essays in this volume probe the complexities of Lowell's life and work. The contributors concentrate on the poetry but an essay on "Benito Cereno" is also included. Chronology of Important Dates. Selected Bibliography.

McCarthy, Mary

STOCK, IRVIN
Mary McCarthy
University of Minnesota, 1968. 47pp. Paper $ .95. A short critical study of the work of the American novelist and critic. The study is concerned only with Miss McCarthy's fictional writings. A Selected Bibliography includes listings of the works and of critical and biographical studies.

McCullers, Carson

EDMONDS, DALE
Carson McCullers
Steck-Vaughn, 1969. 43pp. Paper $1.00. In this short study of the novelist/short story writer, the

author concentrates on Miss McCullers' fiction but also provides notes on her two plays. Selected Bibliography.

EVANS, OLIVER
The Ballad of Carson McCullers: An Intimate Biography
Putnam, 1965. 220pp. $5.00. Drawing on his long friendship with Carson McCullers and on hitherto unpublished biographical material made available to him, the author presents an in depth study of the personal factors that have created the world of her literature. Illustrated with eight pages of photographs. The author has also included Mrs. McCullers' original version of "The Heart is a Lonely Hunter." Index.

GRAVER, LAWRENCE
Carson McCullers
University of Minnesota, 1969. 48pp. Paper $ .95. A short critical study of the work of the American novelist and playwright. Selected Bibliography.

MacLeish, Archibald

FALK, SIGNI
Archibald MacLeish
Twayne, 1965. 189pp. $3.95. Paper $2.45. A chronological interpretation of MacLeish's development in poetry, drama, and prose, with attention given to his literary techniques and to those patterns of thought that have conditioned his point of view on self-government. Index.

MacNeice, Louis

MacNEICE, LOUIS
The Strings are False
Oxford, 1966. 288pp. $6.00. An unfinished biography of the late poet and playwright. Also included is a description of John Hilton, and of Mr. MacNeice's school and university days. Index.

Mailer, Norman

LEEDS, BARRY H.
The Structured Vision of Norman Mailer
New York University, 1969. 270pp. $6.95. Paper $2.45. In his examination of Mailer's fiction, Dr. Leeds contends that the artist's thematic concern with the plight of the individual in contemporary society is a legacy of the thirties, modified by Mailer's own perspective. Leeds appraises the non-fiction, tracing the development of the writer's narrative voice. Bibliography. Index.

Millay, Edna St. Vincent

BRITTIN, NORMAN A.
Edna St. Vincent Millay
Twayne, 1967. 192pp. $4.95. Paper $2.45. A study of the work of the poet/playwright including the libretto of an opera. Chronology. Selected Bibliography. Index.

GOULD, JEAN
The Poet and Her Book
Dodd, Mead, 1969. 308pp. $6.50. This is a biography of Edna St. Vincent Millay. Illustrated with photographs. Selected Bibliography. Index.

Miller, Arthur

CALANDRA, DENIS M. and JAMES L. ROBERTS
The Crucible: Notes
Cliff's Notes, 1968. 73pp. Paper $1.00. Included in this volume are scene-by-scene analyses and summaries of Miller's play. Also provided are essays and comments on the play. Selected Bibliography.

CORRIGAN, ROBERT W. – Editor
Arthur Miller: A Collection of Critical Essays
Prentice–Hall, 1969. 176pp. $5.95. Paper $1.95. An analysis of Miller's evolution as man and artist. Among the essayists are Harold Clurman and Herbert Blau. Chronology. Selected Bibliography.

EVANS, RICHARD I.
Psychology and Arthur Miller
Dutton, 1969. 136pp. $4.50. Paper $1.75. This is a dialogue between the playwright and the psychologist in which they discuss how a writer creates, character motivation, play structure, and critics and audiences. The final section of the dialogue deals with Miller's ideas of the writer's function in society. List of Recommended Readings. Index.

HAYASHI, TETSUMARO
Arthur Miller Criticism (1930 – 1967)
See Page 559

HAYMAN, RONALD
Arthur Miller
Heinemann, 1970. 82pp. $3.75. Paper $1.50. A study of the plays of Arthur Miller from "All My Sons" in 1947 to "The Prize" in 1968. The book opens with an interview with the playwright. Scenes from several of the plays are shown in photographs. Biographical Outline. Bibliography.

HOGAN, ROBERT
Arthur Miller
University of Minnesota, 1964. 48pp. Paper $ .95. This study maintains that Miller's plays embody the

austere tradition of Western tragedy derived from classical models.

HUFTEL, SHEILA
Arthur Miller: The Burning Glass
Citadel, 1965. 257pp. $4.50. This study examines the plays of Miller as a fusion of social and psychological drama in a form not seen since Ibsen. Miller's private life, including a survey of his political evolution and a discussion of his marriage with Marilyn Monroe, is also studied. Introduction by J. C. Trewin. Illustrated. Index.

MOSS, LEONARD
Arthur Miller
Twayne, 1967. 160pp. $3.50. Paper $2.45. A study of the playwright centering attention on Miller's technical resources—dialogue style, symbolic devices, and structural principles. Chronology. Selected Bibliography. Index.

MURRAY, EDWARD
Arthur Miller, Dramatist
Ungar, 1967. 186pp. $5.00. Paper $1.95. A study in depth of the important plays of Arthur Miller. Mr. Murray discusses Miller's plays for both form and content. Each of the seven plays studied is approached as a dramatic whole and all the elements—structure, character, language, and theme—are studied. Bibliography.

NELSON, BENJAMIN
Arthur Miller: Portrait of a Playwright
McKay, 1970. 336pp. $5.95. A comprehensive study of the work and thought of the playwright, set against the context of his life and times. The author delineates plot, characterization, mood, and motivation for each work, and ends with an assessment of Miller's place in the history of the American theatre. Selected Bibliography. Index.

NOURSE, JOAN THELLUSSON
Arthur Miller's Death of A Salesman and All My Sons
Monarch, 1965. 121pp. Paper $1.00. A critical guide to the two plays with detailed summary and analysis, analyses of major characters, critical commentary, review questions and answers, and a Bibliography.

NOURSE, JOAN THELLUSSON
Arthur Miller's The Crucible
Monarch, 1965. 96pp. Paper $1.00. A critical guide to "The Crucible" and four other of Miller's plays. The author provides background and plot discussion, thematic analysis, critical commentary, essay questions and answers for review, and a Bibliography.

WEALES, GERALD
Arthur Miller's "Death of a Salesman."
Text and Criticism
Viking, 1967. 426pp. Paper $2.50. The text of Miller's play and a collection of essays about the play including several writings by Mr. Miller on the play. Bibliography.

WELLAND, DENNIS
Arthur Miller
Oliver & Boyd, 1961. 124pp. Paper $1.75. A brief biography of the playwright, followed by a detailed examination of his fiction and drama and a Bibliography.

WHITE, SIDNEY HOWARD
Guide to Arthur Miller
Merrill, 1970. 47pp. Paper $1.00. This essay is aimed at the beginning student and is designed to give him perspective and background on the American playwright and his plays.

Moody, William Vaughn

HALPERN, MARTIN
William Vaughn Moody
Twayne, 1964. 208pp. Paper $2.45. The aim of this volume is to provide a thorough, objective appraisal of Moody's published work—both poetry and drama. This dramatist of the late 1890's and early 1900's is shown to have left behind a body of dramatic writing which establishes him as a pioneer in modern drama. The author has included a Chronology of events during Moody's lifetime as well as a Selected Bibliography. Index.

Munford, Robert

BAINE, RODNEY M.
Robert Munford, America's First Comic Dramatist
University of Georgia, 1967. 132pp. $5.00. This is a biography of America's first dramatic farce and legitimate comedy writer. Dr. Baine supplies previously unavailable information on the eighteenth century writer's early life and devotes the last part of the book to a critical study of the two plays: "The Candidates" and "The Patriots." Notes. Bibliography. Index.

Nemerov, Howard

MEINKE, PETER
Howard Nemerov
University of Minnesota, 1968. 48pp. Paper $ .95. This is a short study of the American poet. The work concentrates on the poetry rather than on the fiction or the verse plays. The author has provided a selected Bibliography which includes lists of works by Nemerov and lists of critical articles and reviews of the works.

Odets, Clifford

MURRAY, EDWARD
Clifford Odets: The Thirties and After
Ungar, 1968. 229pp. $5.50. An analytical study of Clifford Odets' major plays. The author argues that the playwright expanded his themes from the "proletarian" school of the thirties to suit the temper of the forties and fifties. He attempts to show that the later plays possess qualities of craftsmanship and insight into the dilemmas of man that constitute significant and lasting drama. A List of References is included.

SHUMAN, R. BAIRD
Clifford Odets
Twayne, 1962. 160pp. $4.50. Paper $2.45. A critical study in which the author seeks to bring some order out of the critical chaos surrounding the late plays by demonstrating the allegorical overtones in them and by showing the continued presence of the social concern and proletariat sympathy that marked the earlier works. Shuman includes a Chronology of events during the playwright's lifetime as well as a Selected Bibliography of the works and of studies.

O'Neill, Eugene

ALEXANDER, DORIS
The Tempering of Eugene O'Neill
Harcourt, Brace, 1962. 301pp. $5.95. An account of the intense family drama, the powerful individuals, and the forces of rebellion, despair, and self-discovery that shaped the life of the playwright and are seen in his plays.

CALLAHAN, JOHN M.
A Simplified Approach to Mourning Becomes Electra
Barron, 1970. 91pp. Paper $ .95. Detailed analyses and interpretations of O'Neill's plays with background essays on Greek tragedy and the Oresteia, discussion of O'Neill's style, analytical comparison of the Greek and modern versions of the play, an essay on the man and the playwright, Bibliography, and questions for study and review.

CARGILL, OSCAR and BRYLLION N. FAGIN, WILLIAM J. FISHER – Editors
O'Neill and His Plays: Four Decades of Criticism
New York University, 1962. 528pp. $8.50. Paper $3.95. A collection of reviews of plays, essays, and critiques on the playwright. A selection of O'Neill's letters and articles, in which he reveals his views on the theatre and his work, is included.

CARPENTER, FREDERIC I.
Eugene O'Neill
Twayne, 1964. 191pp. $3.95. Paper $2.45. A study of the evolution of the playwright's creative process, and a study of the individual plays, based on the playwright's own suggestions to the author. There is a discussion of O'Neill's theory of tragedy.

CLARK, BARRETT H.
Eugene O'Neill, The Man and His Plays
Dover, 1947. 182pp. Paper $1.50. A revision of the 1926 study, this is an analysis of O'Neill's plays from "The Web" to "The Iceman Cometh" with detailed descriptions of the environment in which each was first produced. A checklist of first editions and performances is included.

CLARK, PETER
The Emperor Jones and The Hairy Ape: Notes
Cliff's Notes, 1966. 58pp. Paper $1.00. Notes on the life and background of the playwright, scene-by-scene summaries and commentaries on the two plays, character analyses, critical notes, questions for review, and a Selected Bibliography.

COOLIDGE, OLIVIA
Eugene O'Neill
Scribner, 1966. 223pp. $3.95. Mrs. Coolidge records the life of the dramatist and the theatrical era on which he left his mark. Index.

FALK, DORIS V.
Eugene O'Neill and the Tragic Tension
Rutgers University, 1958. 211pp. $9.00. An interpretation of the plays in which the psychological techniques of Carl Jung, the neo-Freudians, Karen Horney and Eric Fromm among them, are used to explain the pull of opposites found in them. Notes. Index.

FRAZER, WINIFRED DUSENBURY
Love as Death in The Iceman Cometh
University of Florida, 1967. 63pp. Paper $2.00. A monograph on O'Neill's play in which the author proposes that the theme of the play, that love is death, is ironical in that man supposedly lives by the illusion that love is life.

GANNON, PAUL W.
Eugene O'Neill's Desire Under the Elms
Monarch, 1965. 39pp. Paper $1.00. A critical guide to the play with background and plot discussion, theme development, character analysis, critical commentary, review questions and answers, and a Bibliography.

GANNON, PAUL W.
Eugene O'Neill's Long Day's Journey Into Night: A Critical Commentary
Monarch, 1965. 80pp. Paper $1.00. A guide to the play providing complete background and plot discussion, theme development, character analysis, critical commentary, review questions and answers, and a Bibliography.

GASSNER, JOHN
Eugene O'Neill
University of Minnesota, 1965. 48pp. Paper $ .95. This brief introduction to the playwright examines the two careers in the theatre that he experienced—the period up to 1934, then the revival after 1946—and the two different styles, realism and expressionism, that he developed.

GASSNER, JOHN
O'Neill: A Collection of Critical Essays
Prentice–Hall, 1964. 180pp. $5.95. Paper $1.95. Essays by Stark Young, Eric Bentley, Robert F. Whitman, and others.

GELB, ARTHUR and BARBARA GELB
O'Neill
Harper, 1962. 970pp. $15.00. A comprehensive biography based upon exhaustive research and extensive interviews. Brooks Atkinson has provided an Introduction. Illustrated.

GREENE, JAMES J.
Eugene O'Neill's Strange Interlude: A Critical Commentary
Monarch, 1965. 120pp. Paper $1.00. A critical guide to the play with an Introduction, discussions of the structural analysis of the play, analyses of characters, a review of criticism, examination questions and answers for review, and a Selected Bibliography.

LONG, CHESTER CLAYTON
The Role of Nemesis in the Structure of Selected Plays by Eugene O'Neill
Humanities, 1968. 231pp. $10.25. The author studies "nemesis," the personification of an idea or the idea of justice-in-action, in eight of the American playwright's plays. O'Neill's characters are presented as creatures having the power to choose and their choices are shown to be important in shaping the nemesis that overtakes them. Bibliography.

MILLER, JORDAN Y.
Eugene O'Neill and the American Critic: A Summary and Bibliographical Checklist
Shoestring, 1962. 313pp. $17.00. A collection of all important published items on O'Neill from his earliest successes to 1959 in an annotated Bibliography. There is also a brief summary of the major factors that led up to O'Neill's long absence from the theatre and his subsequent posthumous revival.

MILLER, JORDAN Y.
Playwright's Progress: O'Neill and the Critics
Scott, Foresman, 1965. 184pp. Paper $3.50. This collection of essays by various critics covers the six periods of O'Neill's career: apprenticeship, 1913–1919; the period of search for theme and form, 1920–1925; triumph and decline, 1926–1934; the decade of silence, 1935–1945; steps toward revival, 1946–1956; revival and re-evaluation, post–1956.

NUGENT, ELIZABETH
Eugene O'Neill's Mourning Becomes Electra: A Critical Commentary
Monarch, 1965. 58pp. Paper $1.00. A guide to play with complete background discussion, and notes on plot, theme development, character analysis, critical commentary, review questions and answers, and a Bibliography.

NUGENT, ELIZABETH M.
Eugene O'Neill's The Iceman Cometh: A Critical Commentary
Monarch, 1965. 44pp. Paper $1.00. A study guide to the play with a biography of the playwright, general introduction, critical comment, essay questions and answers for review, and a Bibliography.

RAGHAVACHARYULU, D.V.K.
Eugene O'Neill: A Study
Heinman, 1965. 232pp. $8.50. The author of this book attempts to view O'Neill's work as a single act of creation reflecting an unique and characteristic sensibility that shaped and controlled his imagination. He relates the story of the playwright's inner growth, change, and conflict through four distinct phases. Bibliography. Index.

RALEIGH, JOHN HENRY – Editor
The Iceman Cometh: Twentieth Century Interpretations
Prentice–Hall, 1968. 117pp. $3.95. Paper $1.25. A collection of critical essays by twenty-one distinguished critics who examine O'Neill's play and offer evaluations of the work's comic and tragic elements. Among the essayists are Eric Bentley, Robert Brustein, and Mary McCarthy. Chronology of Important Dates. Bibliography.

RALEIGH, JOHN HENRY
The Plays of Eugene O'Neill
Southern Illinois University, 1965. 304pp. $4.50. In analyzing the plays of O'Neill, the author considers the autobiographical elements in each and considers the plays' relationship to American culture as a whole. The plays are not analyzed in chronological order but are considered as one organic whole, made up of a Strindbergian variety of themes, characters, and preoccupations. Each play is seen as psychological, moral, historical, and philosophical document. The author asserts that O'Neill's late plays showed an immense range of impulses, influences, and cross-purposes. Notes. Index.

ROBERTS, JAMES L.
Mourning Becomes Electra: Notes
Cliff's Notes, 1966. 57pp. Paper $1.00. This volume includes scene-by-scene summaries of O'Neill's play, an introduction to the playwright's work, character analyses, critical evaluation of the play, essays on naturalism, the Greek myth and O'Neill's use of it, questions for review, and a Selected Bibliography.

ROGERS, DAVID
The Plays of Eugene O'Neill: A Critical Commentary
Monarch, 1964. 83pp. Paper $1.00. A critical guide to ten of the plays of O'Neill. The author analyzes O'Neill's action and character development, scene-by-scene, recounts O'Neill's difficulties with the establishment, traces his situations and themes, and provides a Bibliography.

SANBORN, RALPH and BARRETT H. CLARK
A Bibliography of the Works of Eugene O'Neill. The Collected Poems of Eugene O'Neill
Blom, 1965. 203pp. $12.50. Originally published in 1931 and now reprinted, this Bibliography is the most complete record of O'Neill's writings up to 1930. O'Neill gave the editors permission to publish his early poems in the volume in order that the record would be complete.

SHEAFFER, LOUIS
O'Neill: Son and Playwright
Little, Brown, 1968. 543pp. $10.00. This is a biography based on many sources hitherto unknown or inaccessible. Among the subjects covered are O'Neill's equivocal relations with his parents, a comprehensive account of his life as a seaman, and his preoccupation with the subject of insanity. The volume closes in 1920 when O'Neill's play, "Beyond the Horizon" was produced on Broadway.

SKINNER, RICHARD DANA
Eugene O'Neill: A Poet's Quest
Russell & Russell, 1964. 242pp. $11.00. In this reprint of the 1935 study the author maintains that there is an inner continuity in the plays, a quality of continuous poetic progression, that links them all together by a bond of inner relation. There is a corrected chronology of plays as furnished by the playwright.

TIUSANEN, TIMO
O'Neill's Scenic Images
Princeton, 1968. 388pp. $10.00. The director of the Finnish National Theatre traces Eugene O'Neill's artistic development in terms of his increasing control over various scenic means of expression: setting, lighting, sound effects, props, gestures, and dialogue. All of O'Neill's forty-six published plays and three unpublished ones are discussed from the scenic point of view. Illustrated with photographs of various productions of the plays.

TORNQVIST, EGIL
A Drama of Souls
Yale, 1969. 284pp. $10.00. Subtitled, "Studies in O'Neill's Super-Naturalistic Technique," the primary aim of this study is to demonstrate how Eugene O'Neill sought to create what he called a drama of souls. The author analyzes most of the playwright's forty-six published plays and discusses at length several of these plays in an attempt to shed new light not only on O'Neill's dramatic technique but also on the meaning of the dramas. Chronology of Plays. Bibliography. Indices.

WINTHER, SOPHUS KEITH
Eugene O'Neill: A Critical Study
Russell & Russell, 1961. 319pp. $11.00. A reprint of the study first published in 1934. The work analyzes the major themes found in O'Neill. A final chapter in this edition considers the four plays published since 1934.

Payne, John Howard

HARRISON, GABRIEL
John Howard Payne: His Life and Writings
See Page 275

Rice, Elmer

DURHAM, FRANK
Elmer Rice
Twayne, 1970. 161pp. $4.50. A study of the American playwright. About thirty of his fifty plays are treated. Chronology. Notes. Selected Bibliography. Index.

HOGAN, ROBERT
The Independence of Elmer Rice
Southern Illinois University, 1965. 164pp. $4.50. A study of Rice's works from his first play, "A Defection from Grace," written when he was a young law clerk, to "Love Among the Ruins" first produced in 1963. Analyses of two unpublished and unproduced recent scripts, "Slaves of the Lamp" and "Court of Last Resort," are included. Index.

Riggs, Lynn

ERHARD, THOMAS A.
Lynn Riggs: Southwest Playwright
Steck–Vaughn, 1970. 44pp. Paper $1.00. A study of the playwright who is perhaps best-known for his play "Green Grow the Lilacs" upon which "Oklahoma" was based. A Selected Bibliography of plays, books containing material on Riggs, and articles about Riggs are included.

Saroyan, William

FLOAN, HOWARD R.
William Saroyan
Twayne, 1966. 176pp. $3.95. Paper $2.45. A study of the American author which surveys the entire body of his work and gives especially close attention to the young Saroyan's search for a subject and a suitable technique and to his contribution to the American theatre. Chronology. Selected Bibliography. Index.

SAROYAN, WILLIAM
Not Dying
Harcourt, Brace, 1963, 244pp. $4.95. This autobiography is a record of a year Mr. Saroyan spent in Paris, during which he worked on three books simultaneously, and in his spare time helped his teen-age son and daughter discover Paris, one another, and themselves. Saroyan reflects on life and love, parents and children, and success and failure. Illustrated with abstract line drawings.

Sheldon, Edward

BARNES, ERIC WOLLENCOTT
The Man Who Lived Twice: The Biography of Edward Sheldon
Scribner, 1956. 367pp. $5.95. The story of the author of such international hits of the early part of the century as ''Salvation Nell,'' ''The High Road,'' ''Romance,'' and other plays, and of his influence on the theatre from 1910 to 1946, during which time he was bedridden, paralyzed, and blind. The volume is illustrated with photographs.

Sherwood, Robert E.

BROWN, JOHN MASON
The Ordeal of a Playwright
Harper & Row, 1970. 320pp. $10.00. Edited and with an Introduction by Norman Cousins, this volume traces Robert E. Sherwood's struggle against World War II, his war work with President Roosevelt, and the record of his writing of the play, ''There Shall Be No Night,'' a play testifying to his strong feelings about the Russian invasion of Finland. The text of the play is included. Index.

BROWN, JOHN MASON
The Worlds of Robert Sherwood
Harper & Row, 1965. 409pp. $7.95. A biography of the Pulitzer Prize winning dramatist who also served as speech writer and intimate adviser to Franklin Delano Roosevelt. It is not merely a biography of Sherwood but also a record of the times in which he lived.

LINDROTH, COLETTE and JAMES R. LINDROTH
Sherwood's Abe Lincoln in Illinois: A Critical Commentary
Monarch, 1966. 48pp. Paper $1.00. A critical guide to the play with discussions of background, thematic and character analysis, critical commentary, essay questions and answers for review, and a Bibliography.

SHUMAN, R. BAIRD
Robert E. Sherwood
Twayne, 1964. 160pp. $4.50. Paper $2.45. A critical study of Sherwood with emphasis on the period from 1932 to 1941 during which his major plays were produced.

Stein, Gertrude

BRIDGMAN, RICHARD
Gertrude Stein in Pieces
Oxford, 1970. 411pp. $12.50. Professor Bridgman offers a descriptive reading of Miss Stein's work, relating it to the events of her life and the stages of her development. Selected Bibliography. Appendices. Index.

HOFFMAN, FREDERICK J.
Gertrude Stein
University of Minnesota, 1961. 48pp. Paper $ .95. A short study of the author with a Bibliography.

Taylor, Charles

TAYLOR, DWIGHT
Blood-and-Thunder
See Page 277

Thurber, James

MORSBERGER, ROBERT E.
James Thurber
Twayne, 1964. 224pp. Paper $2.45. This is a study of the work of one of America's greatest humorists. Chronology. Selected Bibliography. Index.

Tyler, Royall

TANSELLE, G. THOMAS
Royall Tyler
Harvard, 1967. 281pp. $7.50. The first book-length study of Royall Tyler (1757–1826). Tyler is best known for his play, ''The Contrast,'' the first American comedy produced professionally. The author provides a fascinating sketch of Tyler's life and studies in turn his plays, poems, novels, and essays. Selected Bibliography. Notes. Index.

Vidal, Gore

WHITE, RAY LEWIS
Gore Vidal
Twayne, 1968. 157pp. $3.95. Using the author's private papers and his public statements, Mr. White provides the biographical and the bibliographical data that are essential to appreciation of Vidal's ten novels and four plays, all of which Mr. White critically examines and evaluates. Notes and References. Selected Bibliography. Index.

Warren Robert Penn

LONGLEY, JOHN L.
Robert Penn Warren
Steck–Vaughn, 1969. 43pp. Paper $1.00. A study of the American novelist/poet. The author concentrates on Warren's non-dramatic work. A Selected Bibliography includes listings of Warren's principal works and of books and articles pertaining to his life and works.

West, Nathanael

MARTIN, JAY
Nathanael West: The Art of His Life
Farrar, Straus, 1970. 435pp. $10.00. Mr. Martin had access to West's letters, notebooks, scrapbooks, and unpublished works for his biography of the American novelist. He interviewed and consulted several hundred people who knew West and traced his life from the early days in New York to the final days in Hollywood where West worked on screenplays. Twenty pages of photographs. Notes on Sources. Index.

Wilder, Thornton

BURBANK, REX
Thornton Wilder
Twayne, 1961. 156pp. $3.50. Paper $2.45. A critical examination of the novels and four full-length plays. Wilder's achievement is measured against his total artistic intent and he is evaluated in terms of his rightful place in the American literary tradition.

GEMME, FRANCIS R.
Thornton Wilder's Our Town and Other Works
Monarch, 1965. 96pp. Paper $1.00. A critical guide to "Our Town," "The Skin of Our Teeth," and three novels. Analyses of the form, meaning, and style are provided through plot discussions, theme development, character analysis, critical commentary, review questions and answers, and a Bibliography.

GOLDSTEIN, MALCOLM
The Art of Thornton Wilder
University of Nebraska, 1965. 179pp. $6.50. In this chronological survey of the novels and plays, the author comments on specific literary sources, investigates each work's relation to the ideas underlying all of Wilder's works, and analyzes the coordination of form and meaning in each. The basic continuity of Wilder's thought and the broadening of his range of ideas is demonstrated. Bibliography. Index.

GREBANIER, BERNARD
Thornton Wilder
University of Minnesota, 1964. 48pp. Paper $ .95. This brief pamphlet concentrates on the paradoxical nature of Wilder's personality and his work.

HABERMAN, DONALD
The Plays of Thornton Wilder: A Critical Study
Wesleyan University, 1967. 162pp. $7.00. Paper $1.45. This is a treatment of Wilder's work as literary artist in the drama. Mr. Haberman organizes his study in terms of Wilder's intellectual concerns and the techniques by which they are made manifest. There is a full treatment of the virtually unknown "Alcestiad" with extensive quotations from the text. Bibliography. Index.

Williams, Tennessee

DONAHUE, FRANCIS
The Dramatic World of Tennessee Williams
Ungar, 1964. 243pp. $5.50. The major themes of the plays are examined: the destruction of the sensitive by the insensitive; the conflict between flesh and spirit; the consequences of non-conformity; the destructiveness of time.

FALK, SIGNI L.
Tennessee Williams
Twayne, 1962. 224pp. $4.50. Paper $2.45. A critical analysis of the playwright's work which evaluates his materials and attitudes, appraising his technical skills and shortcomings. His contribution to contemporary theatre is estimated.

JACKSON, ESTHER MERLE
The Broken World of Tennessee Williams
University of Wisconsin, 1965. 179pp. $5.95. Paper $1.75. Williams' role in the history of Western drama is examined and a comprehensive review of his output is given. Williams is placed in relation to the technical developments of Elia Kazan, Jo Mielziner, and Lee Strasberg. Illustrated. Bibliography. Index.

NELSON, BENJAMIN
The Plays of Tennessee Williams
Monarch, 1965. 96pp. Paper $1.00. The author summarizes and comments on eleven of Williams' plays.

He examines the structure, symbolism, and themes of each play and provides a Bibliography and sample essay questions and answers in this study guide.

NELSON, BENJAMIN
Tennessee Williams: His Life and Work
Astor–Honor, 1961. 262pp. $6.50. The author draws upon biographical material supplied by the playwright to arrive at an understanding of the plays.

RATHBUN, GILBERT L.
Tennessee Williams' A Streetcar Named Desire
Monarch, 1965. 72pp. Paper $1.00. A study guide providing complete background, plot discussion, theme development, character analysis, critical commentary, essay type questions and answers, and a Bibliography.

RATHBUN, GILBERT L.
Tennessee Williams' The Glass Menagerie: A Critical Commentary
Monarch, 1965. 75pp. Paper $1.00. A critical guide providing analysis of the form, meaning and style in the play by means of complete background, theme development, plot discussion, character analysis, critical commentary, review questions and answers, and a Bibliography.

STEEN, MIKE
A Look at Tennessee Williams
Hawthorn, 1969. 318pp. $6.95. A series of interviews with artistic collaborators and personal friends of the playwright. Among the contributors are Hermione Baddeley, Hume Cronyn, George Cukor, Mildred Dunnock, William Inge, Deborah Kerr, Margaret Leighton, Geraldine Page, Maureen Stapleton, Eli Wallach, Hal Wallis, and Shelley Winters. Mr. Steen has included a brief introduction to each of the twenty interviews. Illustrated with photographs. Index.

TISCHLER, NANCY M.
Tennessee Williams
Steck–Vaughn, 1969. 44pp. Paper $1.00. A study of the work of the American playwright. The author provides notes on Williams' fictional works as well as the plays. Selected Bibliography.

TISCHLER, NANCY M.
Tennessee Williams: Rebellious Puritan
Citadel, 1965. 319pp. Paper $1.95. This study, originally published in 1961, examines the works and the milieu that produced them. Included are summaries of the major plays and evaluations of the critical and popular response to them.

WEALES, GERALD
Tennessee Williams
University of Minnesota, 1965. 46pp. Paper $ .95. A critical essay on the life and work of the playwright. Included is a Bibliography of Williams' works, essays about the the playwright, and interviews, biographical and critical works.

Williams, William Carlos

BRINNIN, JOHN MALCOLM
William Carlos Williams
University of Minnesota, 1963. 48pp. Paper $ .95. A short study of the poet and playwright. Brinnin is concerned with the poetry in this monograph. He includes a Selected Bibliography of the principal poetic works and of critical studies.

GUIMOND, JAMES
The Art of William Carlos Williams
University of Illinois, 1968. 257pp $6.95. Paper $2.45. This study of the poetry and prose of William Carlos Williams analyzes the major changes and stages in his techniques and themes from 1909 through the works of the late '50's. Although primarily concerned with his non-dramatic work, there are many references to "Many Moons" and other plays. Bibliography. Index.

WHITAKER, THOMAS R.
William Carlos Williams
Twayne, 1968. 183pp. $3.95. This is a critical assessment of the poetry and prose of William Carlos Williams. Biography is subordinated to comment on the works and the author shows how Williams sought in his writing to abandon habits and conventions to renew contact with "that eternal moment in which we alone live." Chronology. Notes and References. Selected Bibliography. Index.

WILLIAMS, WILLIAM CARLOS
The Autobiography of William Carlos Williams
New Directions, 1967. 402pp. $6.50. Paper $2.25. Mr. Williams' autobiography in which he tells of his two roles as doctor and author. He relates how each of the roles stimulated and supported the other. He also writes of the literary and artistic personalities of the period: Ezra Pound, Marianne Moore, Joyce, Hemingway, Gertrude Stein, and Ford Madox Ford. Index.

Willis, Nathaniel P.

AUSER, CORTLAND P.
Nathaniel P. Willis
Twayne, 1969. 175pp. $4.95. Paper $2.45. An assessment of the late nineteenth century journalist, travel essayist, short story writer, and playwright. Although the author is mainly concerned with the fiction of the writer, Willis' two plays are described in the study. Auser concludes that these two plays, "Bianca Visconti" and "Tortesa," were the equal in dramatic merit of the romantic dramas of the time. The author includes a Chronology of events during the lifetime of Willis, a section of Notes and References, and a Selected Bibliography. Index.

Wilson, Edmund

FRANK, CHARLES P.
Edmund Wilson
Twayne, 1970. 213pp. $4.50. An analysis and evaluation of Edmund Wilson's major and minor work—his criticism, fiction, poetry, journalism, and drama. Chronology. Notes and References. Selected Bibliography. Index.

Wolfe, Thomas

PAYNE, LADELL
Thomas Wolfe
Steck–Vaughn, 1969. 43pp. Paper $1.00. This study concentrates on the prose works of the author. Selected Bibliography.

Woollcott, Alexander

HOYT, EDWIN P.
Alexander Woollcott: The Man Who Came to Dinner
Abelard–Schuman, 1968. 357pp. $6.50. A biography of the playwright, drama critic, and columnist. Illustrated with photographs. Index.

Wright, Richard

BONE, ROBERT
Richard Wright
University of Minnesota, 1969. 48pp. Paper $ .95. A short study of the American author with a Selected Bibliography of his books and essays and a list of critical works about the author.

BRIGNANO, RUSSELL CARL
Richard Wright: An Introduction to the Man and His Works
University of Pittsburgh, 1970. 201pp. $6.95. Paper $2.95. This analysis of Richard Wright gives a critical, historical, and biographical perspective on the Afro-American writer. Brignano discusses Wright's artistry and his major public concerns as revealed in his novels, short stories, essays, and poetry. Notes. Selected Bibliography. Index.

McCALL, DAN
The Example of Richard Wright
Harcourt, Brace, 1969. 202pp. $5.95. A critical study of the first major black writer in American literature. Of particular interest is the section comparing Wright's "Native Son" with Genet's "The Blacks." Index.

MARGOLIES, EDWARD
The Art of Richard Wright
Southern Illinois University, 1969. 180pp. $4.95. The author traces the development of Richard Wright's major themes: freedom, existential horror, and black nationalism. Notes. Selected Bibliography. Index.

WEBB, CONSTANCE
Richard Wright
Putnam, 1968. 443pp. $8.95. This is a biography of the Negro author and playwright. It is a combination of personal reminiscence, scholarship, and literary analysis. It is based in part on Mr. Wright's diaries, letters, unpublished novels, and tape-recorded conversations. Illustrated. Bibliography. Index.

YIDDISH THEATRE

FRIEDMAN, MAURICE – Editor
Martin Buber and the Theatre
See Page 325

KOHANSKY, MENDEL
The Hebrew Theatre: Its First Fifty Years
See Page 212

LIFSON, DAVID S.
The Yiddish Theatre in America
See Page 231

LIPSKY, LOUIS
Tales of the Yiddish Rialto
See Page 241

MOREVSKI, ABRAHAM
There and Back: Memories and Thoughts of a Jewish Actor
See Page 274

PICON, MOLLY
So Laugh A Little
See Page 275

BIOGRAPHIES OF STAGE PERSONALITES

COLLECTED (By Author)

ALPERT, HOLLIS
The Barrymores
Dial, 1964. 397pp. $7.95. A chronicle of the theatrical and private fortunes of Ethel, John, and Lionel, based on much previously unavailable material. Written by the film critic for the "Saturday Review." Illustrated.

AMORY, CLEVELAND and EARL BLACKWELL – Editors
Celebrity Register
Harper & Row, 1963. 677pp. $9.95. Irreverent biographies of over 1,800 people—famous and infamous. Illustrated with photographs of the personalities.

BANCROFT, MARIE
The Bancrofts: Recollections of Sixty Years
See Page 181

BENNETT, JOAN and LOIS KIBBEE
The Bennett Playbill
Holt, Rinehart, 1970. 332pp. $6.95. A record of five generations of the famous theater family, from the eighteenth century to Miss Bennett's own career in the theatre and in films. Illustrated with photographs.

BROWN, T. ALLSTON
History of the American Stage
Burt Franklin, 1969. 421pp. $20.50. Originally published in 1870 and now reissued in a facsimile edition, this is a collection of biographical sketches of nearly every member of the profession who has appeared on the American stage from 1733 to 1870. Illustrated with portraits of eighty of the actors and actresses.

CAHN, WILLIAM
A Pictorial History of the Great Comedians
Grosset & Dunlap, 1970. 224pp. $7.95. A revised edition of "The Laugh Makers – A Pictorial History of American Comedians," originally published in 1957. In pictures and text, the author surveys the traditions of American comedy, the comedians themselves, and the forms and media that have shaped American humor from Thomas Wignell of Revolutionary days to Rowan and Martin today. Included are over 200 illustrations and photographs. Index.

CLARK, BARRETT H.
Intimate Portraits
Kennikat, 1970. 232pp. $10.50. Originally published in 1951 and now reissued, this is a series of portraits and reminiscences of six men with whom the author worked or maintained a friendship. Among the six are playwrights Maxim Gorky, John Galsworthy, Edward Sheldon, George Moore, and Sidney Howard. Index.

FREEMAN, LUCY – Editor
Celebrities on the Couch
Price/Stern/Sloan, 1970. 234pp. $5.95. A collection of accounts by famous people of the problems that sent them into analysis and of the progress and results of their treatment. Among the fourteen celebrities are: Sid Caesar, Patty Duke, William Inge, Josh Logan, Claudia McNeil, Jayne Meadows, Vivian Vance, and Tennessee Williams.

GAYE, FREDA – Editor
Who's Who in the Theatre: 14th Edition
See Page 5

GRUEN, JOHN
Close-Up
Viking, 1968. 206pp. $7.50. A collection of interviews with nearly forty figures in the arts. Among the subjects of Mr. Gruen's scrutiny are Federico Fellini, Joseph Losey, Ruby Keeler, Vivien Leigh, Mario Montez, Samuel Beckett, Arthur Miller, George S. Kaufman, Tennessee Williams, Stella Adler, Ned Rorem, and Leonard Bernstein. Each interviewee is pictured in a photograph.

KIMMEL, STANLEY
The Mad Booths of Maryland
Dover, 1969. 418pp. Paper $3.75. A revised and enlarged edition of the biography of the Booth family originally published in 1940. A complete biography of Edwin and a full account of John Wilkes as actor, conspirator and fugitive. Included are a new Foreword, six supplementary articles and eighty-three illustrations including photographs taken by the author as he traced the route used by John Wilkes Booth during his escape after the assassination of President Lincoln. Revised Index.

KNEPLER, HENRY
The Gilded Stage: The Years of the Great International Actresses
Morrow, 1968. 347pp. $7.50. A book about the lives of four great actresses: Rachel Felix, Adelaide Ristori, Sarah Bernhardt, and Eleanora Duse. From the 1840's to the 1920's, these actresses dominated the stage and transcended the limitation of language and national culture to perform to international acclaim. Twenty-four pages of illustrations of the actresses and their era. Selected Book List. Index.

MOSES, MONTROSE J.
Famous Actor-Families in America
Blom, 1968. 341pp. $12.50. Originally published in 1906 and now reissued, this is a study of the families who carried on a tradition of great performances. The author examines the Booths, Jeffersons, Sotherns, Boucicaults, Hacketts, Drews, Barrymores, Wallacks, Davenports, Hollands, and Powers. Illustrated.

MURDOCH, JAMES
The Stage
Blom, 1969. 510pp. $12.50. Originally published in 1880 and now reissued in a facsimile edition, this is a series of sketches of prominent nineteenth century actors and actresses and essays on acting techniques of the author's time. Illustrated. Index.

PEARSON, HESKETH
Extraordinary People
Heinemann, 1965. 267pp. $5.95. Mr. Pearson's volume is made up of short accounts written at various times in his career, together with his latest work—studies of Henry Fielding and Frank Harris, and an essay, "Beyond the Pale," which brings together several men of note whose natures were sufficiently heterodox to make them distinctive. The short biographies are of Wilkie Collins, Erasmus Darwin, Thomas Day, Johnston Forbes-Robertson, Sir Francis Galton, Samuel Ogden, Thomas Paine, Anna Seward, and Bernard Shaw.

PHELPS, ROBERT and PETER DEANE
The Literary Life
Farrar, Straus, 1968. 244pp. $4.95. Subtitled, "A scrapbook almanac of the Anglo-American literary scene from 1900 to 1950," this is a collection of pictures, gossip, homage, letters, and lists of facts about poets, novelists, and dramatists who were working during the years covered. Illustrated.

PORTER, HAL
Stars of the Australian Stage and Screen
Angus & Robertson, 1965. 304pp. $5.95. This is the history of the Australian theatre told through studies of the stars of the productions from 1796 to the present time. Illustrated with photographs. List of Australian Films. Index.

RIGDON, WALTER – Editor
The Biographical Encyclopaedia and Who's Who of the American Theatre
See Page 5

ROLLINS, CHARLEMAE
Famous Negro Entertainers of Stage, Screen and TV
Dodd, Mead, 1967. 123pp. $3.50. Following a short introduction about the origin of Negro entertainment on the Southern plantations, the author presents sixteen outstanding Negro entertainers from various fields. An account of the entertainer's life and an appraisal of the professional career are included for Marian Anderson, Josephine Baker, Harry Belafonte, Sidney Poitier, Paul Robeson, Louis Armstrong, and others. Illustrated. Index.

STONE, HENRY DICKINSON
Theatrical Reminiscences
Blom, 1969. 316pp. $17.50. Originally published in 1873 and now reissued in a facsimile edition, this is a collection of sketches of prominent nineteenth century actors and actresses, "their chief characteristics, original anecdotes of them, and incidents connected therewith." Illustrated.

WAGENKNECHT, EDWARD
Merely Players
University of Oklahoma, 1966. 270pp. $5.95. A recounting of the lives, private and public, of eight great actors. Starting with David Garrick, Mr. Wagenknecht follows the course of acting through Edmund Kean, William Charles Macready, Edwin Forrest, Edwin Booth, Henry Irving, Joseph Jefferson, and Richard Mansfield. Illustrated. Bibliography. Index.

WAGENKNECHT, EDWARD
Seven Daughters of the Theatre
University of Oklahoma, 1964. 234pp. $5.95. Studies of Jenny Lind, Sarah Bernhardt, Ellen Terry, Julia Marlowe, Isadora Duncan, Mary Garden, and Marilyn Monroe. The study of Miss Monroe is a memorial tribute to the actess the author believes could have been one of the great performers of our time. Illustrated. Bibliography.

WILLIAMS, P.C.
English Shakespearian Actors
Regency, 1966. 61pp. Paper $2.95. The author reviews the acting of some of the chief portrayors of Shakespeare's characters from Alleyn, Burbage and Betterton, to Wolfit, Gielgud and Olivier.

WINTER, WILLIAM
The Jeffersons
Blom, 1969. 252pp. $9.75. Originally published in 1881 and now reissued in a facsimile edition, this is a biography of the Jefferson family of actors. The family appeared on the English and American stages from the early eighteenth to the late nineteenth centuries. The fourth Jefferson, Joseph, is most famous for his production of "Rip Van Winkle." Illustrated. Index.

INDIVIDUAL (By Subject)

Adams, Maude

ROBBINS, PHYLLIS
The Young Maude Adams
Marshall Jones, 1959. Unpaged. $4.00. This biography, based on the author's own friendship with the actress, studies the background and early career of Maude Adams, up to her creation of "Peter Pan." Illustrated.

Aldridge, Ira

MALONE, MARY
Actor in Exile: The Life of Ira Aldridge
Crowell, 1969. 88pp. $3.95. A biography, written for young people, of the great Negro actor of the 1800's. Denied an acting career in America and England because of racial discrimination, Aldridge achieved success in Europe and Russia. The volume includes ten pages of illustrations by Eros Keith. Index.

MARSHALL, HERBERT and MILDRED STOCK
Ira Aldridge, The Negro Tragedian
Southern Illinois University, 1968. 355pp. Paper $2.85. Originally published in 1958, this is a reprint of the biography of the Negro actor who played all the great tragic roles during the middle 1800's. Illustrated. List of References. Index.

Angelou, Maya

ANGELOU, MAYA
I Know Why the Caged Bird Sings
Random House, 1970. 281pp. $5.95. The autobiography of a black girl from Arkansas who became a dancer, teacher, actress, and producer of a ten part television series on African issues in American life. The work is concerned with the formulative phase of her life in Arkansas.

Bailey, Pearl

BAILEY, PEARL
The Raw Pearl
Harcourt, Brace, 1968. 206pp. $5.75. Paper—Pocket Books, 1969. 189pp. $ .95. The autobiography of the entertainer. It details her struggles and triumphs, the story of her love and marriage and there is a meaningful chapter on racial conflict. Illustrated with photographs.

Barnum, P. T.

BARNUM, P. T.
Struggles and Triumphs of P. T. Barnum Told by Himself
Macgibbon, 1967. 188pp. $7.50. P. T. Barnum published his own autobiography in 1882 and it is now reissued. Here, in his own words, is the story of his beginnings as a grocer and hardware merchant and his rise to the "greatest showman of all time."

FITZSIMONS, RAYMUND
Barnum in London
St. Martin's, 1970. 180pp. $6.95. Mr. Fitzsimons recounts the adventures of the American showman, P. T. Barnum and his star attraction Tom Thumb, in London during the nineteenth century. Barnum set out to prove that the British could be just as vulgar and as gullible as they believed Americans to be. The volume is illustrated with sixteen pages of photographs and contemporary cartoons. Bibliography. Index.

Barrymore, Diana

BARRYMORE, DIANA and GEROLD FRANK
Too Much, Too Soon
New American Library, 1957. 380pp. Paper $ .50. Miss Barrymore's account of her troubled life, from her early conflict with her father and mother, to her failures on Broadway, in international society, and in her personal life. Illustrated.

Barrymore, Ethel

NEWMAN, SHIRLEE P.
Ethel Barrymore, Girl Actress
Bobbs Merrill, 1966. 200pp. $2.50. This is not only the story of Ethel Barrymore's career, but it also depicts the nature of the theatrical world in which Miss Barrymore lived.

Beaton, Cecil

BEATON, CECIL
The Years Between: Diaries 1939–1944
Holt, Rinehart, 1965. 352pp. $5.95. As official photographer to the wartime Ministry of Information, Beaton led photographic safaris to the far ends of the world and saw the war from many different viewpoints. These diaries record his experiences.

Beerbohm, Max

RIEWALD, J. G.
Sir Max Beerbohm: Man and Writer
Nijhoff, 1953. 369pp. $12.00. A critical analysis of the work of the English essayist-caricaturist. A brief biography and a comprehensive Bibliography complete the volume. Illustrated with four plates. Index.

Bell, Mary Hayley

BELL, MARY HAYLEY
What Shall We Do Tomorrow?
Lippincott, 1969. 235pp. $5.95. The autobiography of the actress/playwright, wife of John Mills, and mother of Juliet, Jonathan, and Hayley. She tells of her early childhood in China, her years as an actress in England, her marriage to Mr. Mills, and the later years as a playwright and film writer. Illustrated with photographs.

Benchley, Robert

ROSMOND, BABETTE
Robert Benchley: His Life and Good Times
Doubleday, 1970. 239pp. $6.95. A biography of the author/actor/humorist. Illustrated with photographs from the Benchley family album, stills from his short films, and cartoons by Gluyas Williams. List of books and short films.

Bernhardt, Sarah

AGATE, MAY
Madame Sarah
Blom, 1969. 223pp. $8.75. Originally published in 1945 and now reissued, this is a volume of reminiscences about Sarah Bernhardt and her acting classes. The author, a former pupil of Bernhardt, gives her impressions of Madame Sarah as a teacher of the naturalistic method of acting, and describes the actress's famous roles. Frontispiece. Index of Plays.

BERNHARDT, SARAH
Memories of My Life
Blom, 1968. 456pp. $12.50. Originally published in 1908 and now reissued, these personal recollections are filled with anecdotes of Bernhardt's life on and off stage. Illustrated with thirty-one plates.

BERTON, MME. PIERRE
The Real Sarah Bernhardt
Award Books, 1967. 238pp. Paper $ .75. A reprint of the 1924 biography of "The Divine Sarah" as told to her friend and confidante and edited by Basil Woon. It details the life, and the legends, of the famous French actress of the nineteenth century.

HOPE, CHARLOTTE
The Young Sarah Bernhardt
Roy, 1965. 143pp. $3.25. Written primarily for young readers, this is the biography of Sarah Bernhardt to her fifteenth year and includes an epilogue which tells of her later life. Illustrated.

NOBLE, IRIS
Great Lady of the Theatre: Sarah Bernhardt
Messner, 1960. 192pp. $3.50. An intimate portrait of the actress, concentrating on her personal life, her struggles to perfect her art, and her romantic involvements.

SKINNER, CORNELIA OTIS
Madame Sarah
Houghton, Mifflin, 1966. 356pp. $6.95. Paper—Dell, 1968. 352pp. $ .95. A biography of Sarah Bernhardt. Miss Skinner chronicles many other aspects of Bernhardt's life as well as her career. Partial list of plays and roles is included. Bibliography. Illustrated. Index.

Booth, Edwin

GOODALE, KATHERINE
Behind the Scenes with Edwin Booth
Blom, 1969. 328pp. $7.50. Originally published in 1931 and now reissued in a facsimile edition, these are reminiscences by the actress, Kitty Molony, who shared Booth's private railroad car with two other young actresses during a forty week tour of the United States in 1886. The volume provides one of the few close-ups of Booth and is based on the actress' diary. Included is a Foreword by Mrs. Minnie Maddern Fiske. Illustrated. Index.

GROSSMAN, EDWINA BOOTH
Edwin Booth: Recollections by His Daughter
Blom, 1969. 292pp. $12.50. Originally published in 1894 and now reissued in a facsimile edition, this is a short reminiscence of the American actor and a collection of his letters to his daughter and his friends. Illustrated. Index.

RUGGLES, ELEANOR
Prince of Players
Norton, 1953. 401pp. $6.95. The story of Edwin Booth, of his famous father, Junius Brutus Booth, and of his fellow actors: Henry Irving, Joseph Jefferson and Barrett. Illustrated.

SHATTUCK, CHARLES H.
The Hamlet of Edwin Booth
University of Illinois, 1969. 321pp. $10.95. The author presents the complete life of the Hamlet role as Edwin Booth played it from 1852 to his farewell appearance in 1891. He relates Booth's attempts to find his acting style and establish himself as a star and observes the personal and intellectual forces which shaped his conception of Hamlet. Shattuck presents Charles Clarke's factual and interpretive record of Booth's 1870 performance scene by scene, word by word, in a 166 page section of the volume. Illustrated. Index.

Bruce, Lenny

BRUCE, LENNY
The Essential Lenny Bruce
Douglas Books, 1970. 243pp. $5.95. Paper—Ballantine, 1967. 319pp. $ .95. This is a collection of the material used by Bruce in his night club performances, transcribed from tapes and edited by John Cohen. Index.

BRUCE, LENNY
How to Talk Dirty and Influence People
Simon & Schuster, 1963. 188pp. $5.00. Paper—Pocket Books, 1966. 240pp. $ .75. Lenny Bruce brings his own unique brand of comic relief to his story of a depression childhood, his Navy service, his marriage, and his emergence as the top-billed performer on the nightclub circuit. The continual difficulties with narcotics and obscenity arrests are detailed. Illustrated.

Bull, Peter

BULL, PETER
I Say, Look Here!
Peter Davies, 1965. 200pp. $5.00. This is the autobiography of the English actor. Illustrated with a portrait.

Burton, Philip

BURTON, PHILIP
Early Doors: My Life and the Theatre
Dial, 1969. 238pp. $5.95. The theatrical memoirs of Philip Burton from his childhood in a South Wales mining town to his present eminence in today's theatre as Director of the American Musical and Dramatic Academy. Mr. Burton recalls his friendships with some of the foremost literary and theatrical figures of our times and presents his personal analysis of particular plays in sometimes surprising interpretations. Illustrated with photographs.

Byng, Douglas

BYNG, DOUGLAS
As You Were
Duckworth, 1970. 176pp. $6.75. The biography of one of London's most famous cabaret artistes. Highlighted are his career in musical comedy and in the Cochran reviews, and his night club appearances. Illustrated with photographs. Index.

Campbell, Mrs. Patrick

CAMPBELL, MRS. PATRICK
My Life and Some Letters
Blom, 1969. 451pp. $12.50. Originally published in 1922 and now reissued in a facsimile edition, this is the autobiography of the nineteenth century actress. Mrs. Campbell's sketches of her stage career, American tours, and popular roles are interspersed with a collection of letters from her family and friends, and notes of criticism and appreciation of her acting. A chapter is devoted to Sir James Barrie, and another to George Bernard Shaw. Illustrated with photographs. Index.

Chevalier, Maurice

CHEVALIER, MAURICE
I Remember It Well
Macmillan, 1970. 221pp. $5.95. Chevalier's journal of two years during which he embarked on his "Eightieth Birthday Tour" through the United States, South America, Japan, Canada, and Europe. Illustrated with sixteen pages of photographs.

Cochran, C. B.

HEPPNER, SAM
Cockie
Frewin, 1969. 288pp. $6.50. A biography of C. B. Cochran, the British showman and impresario, whose career spanned menageries, wild west shows, boxing, wrestling, circus, nightclubs, cabaret, revue, and the serious theatre. Noel Coward has provided a Foreword. Illustrated with photographs.

Coppin, George Selth

BAGOT, ALEC
Coppin the Great: The Father of the Australian Theatre
Cambridge, 1965. 356pp. $12.50. This biography of George Selth Coppin (1819—1906) describes his career as a "low" comedian, impresario, adventurer, politician, and philanthropist. The biography is based on material (including journals, biographical notes, press cuttings, playbills, and letters) made available by Coppin's daughter. Coppin's early life in England, his emigration to Australia, and his success as an actor/manager, as well as his other activities, are described. Thirteen pages of illustrations are included. Index.

Cornell, Katherine

MALVERN, GLADYS
Curtain Going Up! The Story of Katherine Cornell
Messner, 1966. 243pp. $3.50. Originally published in 1943 and now reissued, this is a biography of Miss Cornell, written for young people. There is a Foreword by Miss Cornell. Index.

Crabtree, Lotta

DEMPSEY, DAVID with RAYMOND P. BALDWIN
The Triumphs and Trials of Lotta Crabtree
Morrow, 1968. 341pp. $6.95. Lotta Crabtree was one of the most popular actresses of the late nineteenth century. This book details the later years of her life and the courtroom drama that followed her death. Illustrated with photographs. Index.

Crosby, Caresse

CROSBY, CARESSE
The Passionate Years
Southern Illinois University, 1968. 370pp. $7.00. Paper $2.85. Originally published in 1953 and now reissued, this autobiography includes anecdotes of some of the most famous people of the 1920's. Among the visitors to the Paris home of Mrs. Crosby were Hemingway, Fitzgerald, Joyce, Picasso, Pound, Eliot, and Douglas Fairbanks, Sr. Illustrated. Index.

Cushman, Charlotte

BARRETT, LAWRENCE
Charlotte Cushman: A Lecture
Burt Franklin, 1970. 44pp. $16.95. Originally published in 1899 and now reissued in a facsimile edition, this is a tribute to the nineteenth century actress. Included is a chronological list of performances. Illustrated with a portrait.

LEACH, JOSEPH
Bright Particular Star: The Life and Times of Charlotte Cushman
Yale, 1970. 453pp. $12.50. Making use of diaries, letters, memoirs, and contemporary newspaper clippings, the author provides a biography of the nineteenth century American actress. He offers a portrayal of the pains and pleasures of a theatrical career as well as a commentary on the country that produced and admired her talent. Notes. Bibliographical Notes. Index. Illustrated.

Dale, James

DALE, JAMES
Pulling Faces for a Living
Gollancz, 1970. 158pp. $5.95. The British actor reminisces about his fifty years in the theatre including his work in a popular English radio series. Index.

Davenport, Edward Loomis

EDGETT, EDWIN FRANCIS – Editor
Edward Loomis Davenport: A Biography
Burt Franklin, 1970. 145pp. $16.95. Originally published in 1901 and now reissued in a facsimile edition, this is a biography of the prominent nineteenth century American actor. Illustrated with photographs. Index.

Davis, Jr., Sammy

DAVIS, SAMMY and JANE BOYAR, BURT BOYAR
Yes, I Can
Farrar, Straus, 1965. 612pp. $6.95. Paper – Pocket Books, 1966. 626pp. $ .95. A self-portrait of the entertainer. He describes his struggle to reach the peak of fame. Illustrated.

Dean, Basil

DEAN, BASIL
Seven Ages: An Autobiography 1888 – 1927
Hutchinson, 1970. 340pp. $11.75. The autobiography of the English theatrical producer. His early years as an actor in the early part of the century and his later productions of plays by Galsworthy, Maugham, and Barrie are all covered. Illustrated with photographs. Index.

Denholm, Reginald

DENHOLM, REGINALD
Stars in My Hair
Max Reinhardt, 1958. 256pp. $4.00. The author's account of his forty years in the theatre during which time he has worked with such men as Beerbohm Tree and Benson. Denholm considers his career since 1922 as a producer, playwright, and/or director of such hit plays as "Ladies in Retirement," "Dial M for Murder," and "The Bad Seed." Illustrated with photographs.

Durang, John

DOWNER, ALAN S.
The Memoir of John Durang, American Actor, 1785–1816
University of Pittsburgh, 1966. 176pp. $7.00. An account of the life of the American actor during his years as a circus clown, puppeteer, dancer, actor, and producer in the Eastern U. S. and Canada. It is a source of much information about the early American theatre. Illustrated with watercolors by Mr. Durang. Index.

Duse, Eleonora

LE GALLIENNE, EVA
The Mystic in the Theatre: Eleonora Duse
Bodley Head, 1965. 185pp. $4.50. This is Miss Le Gallienne's examination of the Duse art of acting. The volume records the effect of Duse's art on an audience, the means she took to create that effect, and the personal memoirs of the meeting of the author and the actress.

MAPES, VICTOR
Duse and the French
Blom, 1969. 56pp. $6.75. Originally published in 1898 and now reissued in a facsimile edition, this is a short study of Madame Eleonora Duse's appearances in France and her apparent initial failure and ultimate triumph in that country. Illustrated with a frontispiece of Madame Duse.

RHEINHARDT, E. A.
The Life of Eleonora Duse
Blom, 1969. 292pp. $12.50. Originally published in 1930 and now reissued in a facsimile edition, this is a biography of the Italian actress. Using personal information received from Duse's trusted friend, Olga Resnevic Signorelli, as well as other sources, the author attempts to reconstruct an image of the celebrated actress by recounting the events of her life, her achievement as the greatest tragedienne of her day, and her tragic affair with D'Annunzio. Illustrated. Bibliography.

SIGNORELLI, OLGA
Eleonora Duse
European Publishers Representatives, 1955. 411pp. $8.50. This biography of the great actress was published in Italy. It includes forty-five photographs. The text is in the Italian language.

STUBBS, JEAN
Eleonora Duse
Stein and Day, 1970. 320pp. $6.95. A "documentary novel" about the life of the nineteenth century Italian actress.

SYMONS, ARTHUR
Eleonora Duse
Blom, 1969. 164pp. $12.50. Originally published in 1927 and reissued in a facsimile edition, this is a study and appreciation of the nineteenth century actress. Illustrated with a portrait.

VERGANI, LEONARDO
Eleonora Duse
Martello, 1958. 321pp. $11.95. A biography of the Italian actress. The volume is lavishly illustrated with photographs. Please note that the text is in the Italian language.

Dybwad, Johanne

WAAL, CARLA RAE
Johanne Dybwad, Norwegian Actress
Humanities, 1967. 354pp. Paper $8.00. An account of the career of the Norwegian actress based upon works by Scandinavian theatre historians, contemporary newspaper articles, private letters, an unpublished biography, and interviews. The work includes a review of the repertory and major events in the history of the theatres in Norway from 1867 to 1950. A survey of the dramatic works of Norwegian playwrights and a study of Miss Dybwad's portrayals of characters in plays by Ibsen is included. Illustrated with photographs. Bibliography. Index.

Elliott, Maxine

FORBES–ROBERTSON, DIANA
My Aunt Maxine: The Story of Maxine Elliott
Viking, 1964. 306pp. $7.50. The daughter of Maxine Elliott's sister describes the theatrical and social career of her celebrated aunt. Miss Forbes–Robertson takes the legendary figure back to her youth in Maine, through her first years in the theatre, and her triumphs in America and England. Illustrated. Chronology. Index.

Elliston, Robert William

RAYMOND, GEORGE
Memoirs of Robert William Elliston
Blom, 1969. 992pp. $27.50. Originally published in 1846 and reissued in a facsimile edition, this is a biography and appreciation of the nineteenth century actor and theatrical manager. An account of the actor's funeral and a list of the characters he played are included. Illustrated.

Fechter, Charles Albert

FIELD, KATE
Charles Albert Fechter
Blom, 1969. 205pp. $9.75. Originally published in 1882 and now reissued in a facsimile edition, this is a biography of the English nineteenth century actor. Included are a series of press notices on Fechter's acting. Illustrated. Index.

Fennell, James

FENNELL, JAMES
An Apology for the Life of James Fennell
Blom, 1969. 510pp. $25.00. Originally published in 1814 and now reissued in a facsimile edition, this is the biography of an eighteenth century actor.

Fogerty, Elsie

COLE, MARION
Fogie: The Life of Elsie Fogerty
Peter Davies, 1967. 229pp. $10.00. This is a biography of the English pioneer of speech training for the theatre. Many of the great actors of the present day studied with Miss Fogerty who established a new tradition of simple and effective speech. Her methods influenced the attitude toward speech studies in the universities and in the use of speech therapy. Foreword by Sir Laurence Olivier. Illustrated with photographs. Index.

Forrest, Edwin

BARRETT, LAWRENCE
Edwin Forrest
Blom, 1969. 171pp. $7.50. First published in 1881 and now reissued in a facsimile edition, this is a brief account of the domestic life and stage success of the nineteenth century actor. Mr. Barrett, a fellow actor, describes Forrest's bitter defeat in the contest over the separation from his wife and his unfortunate quarrel with Macready which resulted in the "Astor Place Riot." Illustrated. Index.

MOSES, MONTROSE J.
The Fabulous Forrest
Blom, 1969. 369pp. $12.50. Originally published in 1929 and now reissued in a facsimile edition, this biography of the American actor views his life in relation to the background of national surroundings. Illustrated. Bibliography. Index.

Fraser, Grace Lovat

FRASER, GRACE LOVAT
In the Days of My Youth
Cassell, 1970. 285pp. $8.95. The memoirs of the widowof Claud Lovat Fraser, the artist and designer who had a revolutionary effect on English stage design, up to her husband's death in 1921. The author details the Nighel Playfair London productions of "As You Like It" and "The Beggar's Opera" for which Lovat designed the costumes and sets. Illustrated with twelve pages of photographs. Index.

French, Harold

FRENCH, HAROLD
I Swore I Never Would
Secker & Warburg, 1970. 206pp. $7.95. The English actor, director and film producer, writes of his boyhood in the days before World War I and his early career as a child actor, including the time he shared living space with Noel Coward. Illustrated with two photographs of the author. Introduction by Terence Rattigan.

Furse, Jill

WHISTLER, LAURENCE
The Initials in the Heart
Houghton Mifflin, 1964. 248pp. $4.95. Mr. Whistler, a British poet, tells the story of his life with Jill Furse, the promising young English actress, and of their five-year marriage cut short by death. Illustrated with photographs.

Garrick, David (Also See Page 179)

DAVIES, THOMAS
Memoirs of the Life of David Garrick
Blom, 1969. 883pp. Two volume set: $18.75. Published originally in 1808 and reissued in a facsimile edition with notes by Stephen Jones. This is a contemporary account of the life and theatre of the English actor. Appendices include a list of Garrick's dramatic works, a list of characters acted by Garrick, and the text of his will, plus a section of testimonies to Garrick's "genius and merits." Illustrated with a portrait of the actor.

GARRICK, DAVID
The Poetical Works of David Garrick
Blom, 1968. 540pp. Two volume set: $27.50.

Originally published in 1785 by publisher George Kearsley and now reissued, this is the only collected edition of the verse written by David Garrick. A biography of Garrick and a list of the roles he played is included.

HEDGCOCK, FRANK A.
David Garrick and His French Friends
See Page 179

KNIGHT, JOSEPH
David Garrick
Blom, 1969. 346pp. $12.50. Originally published in 1894 and now reissued in a facsimile edition, this is a biography of the eighteenth century actor. Illustrated with an etched portrait. Index

MURPHY, ARTHUR
The Life of David Garrick
Blom, 1969. 776pp. $22.50. First published in London in 1801 and reissued in a facsimile edition, this is a biography of the eighteenth century actor. Appendices include Garrick's will.

OMAN, CAROLA
David Garrick
Hodder and Stoughton, 1958. 427pp. $8.50. A complete biography giving detailed information on Garrick's career. Illustrated. Index.

PARSONS, MRS. CLEMENT
Garrick and His Circle
Blom, 1969. 417pp. $12.50. Originally published in 1906 and reissued in a facsimile edition, this is a series of vignettes illustrating the character and career of David Garrick, the eighteenth century actor. The work is chiefly devoted to Garrick's theatre, his acting, and his associations. Illustrated with thirty-six plates. Lists of Works Consulted. Almanac of Contemporary Events. Appendices. Index.

WEIR, ROSEMARY
The Young David Garrick
Roy, 1963. 136pp. $3.25. An account, written especially for young people, of David Garrick's youth up to the time he left Litchfield, his schoolday home, with Samuel Johnson. Illustrated with drawings by Anne Linton.

Goodman, Cardell

WILSON, JOHN HAROLD
Mr. Goodman, The Player
University of Pittsburgh, 1964. 153pp. $4.95. In recreating the life of this Restoration actor, the author describes the violence, hazards, and delights of theatrical life when England was shaking off the inhibitions of the Puritan Commonwealth.

Gregory, Dick

GREGORY, DICK with ROBERT LIPSYTE
Nigger
Dutton, 1964. 224pp. $4.95. Paper—Pocket Books, 1965. 209pp. $ .75. The story of the Negro comedian from his youth as a welfare case in St. Louis, through his school days as star athlete, to his front-page participation in the Civil Rights movement. Illustrated.

Grimaldi, Joseph

DICKENS, CHARLES
Memoirs of Joseph Grimaldi
See Page 347

Gwynn, Nell

BAX, CLIFFORD
Pretty Witty Nell
Blom, 1969. 262pp. $12.50. Originally published in 1932 and republished in a facsimile edition, this is an account of the seventeenth century actress, Nell Gwynn, and her environment. Illustrated. Bibliography. Appendices. Index.

BEVAN, BRYAN
Nell Gwyn
Roy, 1969. 190pp. $5.95. A biography of the English actress of the Restoration period. Her youth, her career as an actress, her life as the mistress of Charles II, and her last years after the death of Charles are detailed. Illustrated with eight pages of plates. Notes. Bibliography. Index.

DASENT, ARTHUR IRWIN
Nell Gwynne 1650–1687
Blom, 1969. 322pp. $12.50. Originally published in 1924 and now reissued in a facsimile edition, this is a biography of the seventeenth century actress. It is an attempt "to give a more detailed account of Nell's stage career than has hitherto been attempted ... (and) to present the atmosphere of the Court of Charles the Second throughout." Illustrated. Appendices include a chronological list of plays in which the actress appeared at Drury Lane. Index.

Hamilton, Edith

REID, DORIS FIELDING
Edith Hamilton: An Intimate Portrait
Norton, 1967. 175pp. $5.00. A biography of the

literary figure whose translations of the classical tragedies, renderings of the Greek myths, and introductions to the world of the Greeks and Romans have become classics. Illustrated with photographs.

Hancock, Freddie

HANCOCK, FREDDIE and DAVID NATHAN
Hancock
Kimber, 1969. 191pp. $8.50. This is a biography of the comedian who appeared on British radio and television and on the English stage before his death in 1969. Illustrated with photographs.

Hayes, Helen

HAYES, HELEN
A Gift of Joy
Lippincott, 1965. 254pp. $4.95. Paper—Fawcett, 1966. 224pp. $ .75. This is a collection of Miss Hayes' thoughts, reminiscences, and personal anecdotes. Also included is a selection of passages from her favorite authors. Illustrated.

HAYES, HELEN
On Reflection: An Autobiography
Lippincott, 1968. 253pp. $5.95. Paper—Fawcett, 1969. 224pp. $ .95. This autobiography sets down all the family stories, the backstage anecdotes, and the recollections of spiritual struggles as a legacy for Miss Hayes' grand-children. The details of the private world of the famous actress are enhanced by sixteen pages of photographs.

Hill, George Handel

HILL, GEORGE HANDEL
Scenes from the Life of an Actor
Blom, 1969. 247pp. $12.50. Originally published in 1853 and now reissued in a facsimile edition, this is the autobiography of "Yankee Hill," a comedian of the nineteenth century. Illustrated.

Holloway, Stanley

HOLLOWAY, STANLEY
Wiv a Little Bit O'Luck
Stein & Day, 1967. 223pp. $5.95. Best known for his portrayal of Alfred Doolittle in "My Fair Lady," Mr. Holloway tells his story from the beginnings as a choirboy soprano to his hits on stage, in the movies, and in television. Among the personalities he recalls are Gracie Fields, Vivien Leigh, Moss Hart and the cast of characters of "My Fair Lady." Illustrated.

Horne, Lena

HORNE, LENA and RICHARD SCHICKEL
Lena
Doubleday, 1965. 300pp. $4.95. Paper—New American Library, 1966. 300pp. $ .75. Miss Horne's autobiography includes a candid discussion of her own response to the civil rights issue as it has affected her. She includes a number of anecdotes about the celebrities she has known and worked with in her career.

Hull, Josephine

CARSON, WILLIAM G. B.
Dear Josephine: The Theatrical Career of Josephine Hull
University of Oklahoma, 1963. 313pp. $6.50. Miss Hull was associated with the American theatre for more than half a century. This biography is told against the background of changes in styles of acting, directing, and playwriting. Illustrated.

Hunter, Ruth

HUNTER, RUTH
Barefoot Girl on Broadway
Exposition Press, 1965. 115pp. $4.00. The story of the creator of the harelipped girl in "Tobacco Road." Miss Hunter played the role 1,013 times and saw theatre history made as the play turned from total failure to smash hit. Carl Sandburg has contributed a Preface.

Irving, Henry

CRAIG, EDWARD GORDON
Henry Irving
Blom, 1969. 252pp. $9.75. Originally published in 1930 and now reissued in a facsimile edition, this biography of the nineteenth century actor also includes Craig's own reminiscences of eight years of work with Irving. The author also provides extracts from three of Irving's most famous roles. Illustrated. Index.

JONES, HENRY ARTHUR
The Shadow of Henry Irving
Blom, 1969. 111pp. $8.75. Originally published in 1931 and now reissued in a facsimile edition, this is a study of nineteenth century actor Henry Irving.

SAINTSBURY, HENRY ARTHUR and CECIL PALMER – Editors
We Saw Him Act
Blom, 1970. 424pp. $12.50. Originally published in 1939 and now reissued in a facsimile edition, this is a symposium on the art of Sir Henry Irving, nineteenth century English actor. Essays, articles and anecdotes, personal reminiscences and dramatic criticisms written by forty-nine of Irving's contemporaricc. Illustrated with sketches, drawings, and photographs. Index.

Jefferson, Joseph

DOWNER, ALAN S. – Editor
The Autobiography of Joseph Jefferson
Harvard, 1964. 363pp. $5.95. Jefferson's autobiography, which covers his debut in 1833 at the age of four to his retirement one year before his death in 1904, is an account not only of a man of the theatre but of the art of the drama in America in the nineteenth century. In this annotated edition, Mr. Downer supplies data not included in the edition of 1890, including notes on Jefferson's later career. Thirty-six engravings. Index.

Jordan, Dorothy

JERROLD, CLARE
The Story of Dorothy Jordan
Blom, 1969. 439pp. $12.50. Originally published in 1914 and reissued in a facsimile edition, this biography of the eighteenth century actress attempts to clear up disputed points in earlier accounts by giving authorized statements concerning Mrs. Jordan's parentage and other facts. Illustrated. Index.

Jorgensen, Christine

JORGENSEN, CHRISTINE
Christine Jorgensen: A Personal Autobiography
Eriksson, 1967. 332pp. $6.95. The autobiography of the world-famous transsexual in which she reveals the details of her early life, the motivations that led to the Danish operation, and her adjustments to her new role. Illustrated.

Kean, Edmund

HILLEBRAND, HAROLD NEWCOMB
Edmund Kean
A.M.S. Press, 1966. 387pp. $18.00. Originally published in 1933, this is a reissue of the biography of the eighteenth century English actor. Included are many contemporary illustrations of Kean in his most famous performances. Index.

MacQUEEN–POPE, W.
Edmund Kean
Nelson, 1960. 84pp. $2.50. This biography of the nineteenth century actor was written for young people and published in England. Illustrated with drawings and water color paintings reproduced in color.

Kelly, Al

ROSE, ALEXANDER
Al Kelly's Double Life
Frederick Fell, 1966. 220pp. $4.95. A biography of the master of double-talk and gibberish, with emphasis on the many celebrities who have listened and made sense out of his nonsense. Illustrated.

Kemble, Charles

WILLIAMSON, JANE
Charles Kemble: Man of the Theatre
University of Nebraska, 1970. 267pp. $7.95. A biography of the nineteenth century actor/manager/dramatist. Miss Williamson's study attempts to illumine nineteenth century English theatrical history by bringing together information about the multiple roles which Kemble played in it. Frontispiece. Bibliography. Index.

Kemble, Fanny

KEMBLE, FAMNY
The Journal of Frances Anne Butler
Blom, 1970. 600pp. $12.50. Originally published in 1835 and reissued in a facsimile edition this is the diary of the nineteenth century English actress.

KERR, LAURA
Footlights to Fame: The Life of Fanny Kemble
Funk & Wagnalls, 1962. 217pp. $3.50. A biography, written for the teen-age reader, of the daughter of the famous theatrical family who was at first prevented from going on the stage.

Kronenberger, Louis

KRONENBERGER, LOUIS
No Whippings, No Gold Watches
Little, Brown, 1970. 309pp. $6.95. Subtitled "The Saga of a Writer and His Jobs," this is a personal account of Mr. Kronenberger's career on magazines, in the publishing houses, as a drama and literary critic, and as a writer and teacher. The biography covers forty-five years beginning in the 1920's. One chapter details his twenty-three years as a drama critic in New York and includes his own criteria for drama criticism. Index.

Lahr, Bert

LAHR, JOHN
Notes on a Cowardly Lion
Knopf, 1969. 394pp. $8.95. Paper—Ballantine, 1970. 459pp. $1.25. The biography of Bert Lahr, written by his son. Drawing on his father's recollections and the memories of those who worked with him, Lahr's life is recreated from the days of the two-a-day in vaudeville, the years on Broadway, and his disappointments in Hollywood. Brooks Atkinson has said of this volume, "one of the finest theatre biographies." A series of the sketches Lahr did in vaudeville is included. Illustrated with photographs. Index.

Lawrence, Gertrude

ALDRICH, RICHARD STODDARD
Gertrude Lawrence as Mrs. A.
Bantam, 1968. 377pp. Paper $ .95. A reissue of the 1954 biography by Miss Lawrence's husband. It tells the story of their romance and marriage and the death of the Broadway musical star.

THOMAS, BOB
Star!
Bantam, 1968. 150pp. Paper $ .75. Adapted from the screenplay by William Fairchild, this is a novelized version of the film about Gertrude Lawrence. Sixteen pages of sketches by Al Hirschfeld of Julie Andrews on the set are included.

Leigh, Vivien

DENT, ALAN
Vivien Leigh: A Bouquet
Hamish Hamilton, 1969. 219pp. $6.95. This is a collection of memories and anecdotes about the motion picture and stage actress. Listing, with credits, of the nineteen films and thirty plays in which she appeared between 1934 and 1966. Illustrated.

ROBYNS, GWEN
Light of a Star: Vivien Leigh
See Page 477

Lemaitre, Frederick

BALDICK, ROBERT
The Life and Times of Frederick Lemaitre
Hamish Hamilton, 1959. 283pp. $4.00. A biography of the great French actor of the nineteenth century. His contemporaries called him the "French Kean" and he was the idol of the French theatre for whom some of the most famous Romantic dramas were specially written. Illustrated. Bibliography. Index.

Leman, Walter M.

LEMAN, WALTER M.
Memories of an Old Actor
Blom, 1969. 406pp. $12.50. Originally published in 1886 and now reissued in a facsimile edition, this is the biography of a nineteenth century American actor. His reminiscences include observations on the theatre and actors of his time. Illustrated with a portrait.

Levant, Oscar (Also See Page 565)

LEVANT, OSCAR
The Unimportance of Being Oscar
Putnam, 1968. 255pp. $5.95. A collection of reminiscences, anecdotes, witticisms, and commentaries about show biz, TV, Hollywood, writers, politicians, musicians, and the whole bizarre world of Oscar Levant. Illustrated with photographs.

Lister, Moira

LISTER, MOIRA
The Very Merry Moira
Hodder & Stoughton, 1969. 189pp. $6.95. A biography of the English actress and television comedy star. Miss Lister tells of her early life and stage debut in Africa, and the stage successes in London, the films she has made, and her television appearances. Illustrated with photographs.

Lunt, Alfred and Lynn Fontanne

ZOLOTOW, MAURICE
Stagestruck: The Romance of Alfred Lunt and Lynn Fontanne
Harcourt, Brace, 1965. 278pp. $5.95. Paper—Fawcett, 1968. 320pp. $ .95. A dual biography of the acting couple from their first success as an acting team in "The Guardsman" in 1924. Their off-stage life is also described. Illustrated.

Mac Kaye, Steele

MacKAYE, PERCY
Epoch: The Life of Steele Mac Kaye
Scholarly Press, 1968. Volume I—536pp. Volume II—579pp. Two volume set—$39.00. Originally published in 1927 and now reissued in a facsimile edition, this is a biography of and tribute to one of the leading American actors of the eighteenth and nineteenth centuries. The volumes touch upon records of over a hundred years and focus on about three decades. In Volume I, devoted to the life record, are chapters on acting, lecturing, and play producing. Volume II continues the narrative with comments on the lives of MacKaye's contemporaries, and also contains a play chart, an acting chart of MacKaye's roles, etc. Illustrated. Appendices. Bibliography. Index.

Macklin, Charles

APPLETON, WILLIAM W.
Charles Macklin: An Actor's Life
Harvard, 1960. 280pp. $6.00. This biography of the eighteenth century actor draws on unpublished materials to illustrate stage conditions during the eighteenth century in England and Ireland.

Mac Liammoir, Micheal

MacLIAMMOIR, MICHEAL
All For Hecuba: A Theatrical Autobiography
Branden, 1966. 440pp. $6.95. A revised edition of the 1961 autobiography of Mr. MacLiammoir, the Irish actor, whose one man show based on the writings of Oscar Wilde has been a world wide success. Illustrated. Index.

MacLIAMMOIR, MICHEAL
An Oscar of No Importance
Heinemann, 1968. 234pp. $6.50. This is an account of the actor/author's adventures with his one man show about Oscar Wilde, "The Importance of Being Oscar." Photographic frontispiece. Index.

McMaster, Anew

PINTER, HAROLD
Mac
Pendragon Press, 1968. 21pp. $4.50. A short reminiscence of the actor, Anew McMaster, upon the occasion of his death. It is by the English playwright, author of "The Homecoming" and "The Birthday Party."

Macready, William Charles

DOWNER, ALAN S.
The Eminent Tragedian: William Charles Macready
Harvard, 1966. 392pp. $10.00. Making use of family papers and other materials not previously available, Mr. Downer combines in this biography an account of the theatre in the first half of the nineteenth century with a detailed study of the actor's theories of acting and staging. Illustrated. Index.

MACREADY, WILLIAM CHARLES
The Diaries of William Charles Macready 1833—1851
Blom, 1969. Volume I—512pp. Volume II—543pp. Two volume set: $28.50. Originally published in 1912 and reissued in a facsimile edition, edited by William Toynbee, these are the journals of the nineteenth century actor. Illustrated with forty-nine portraits. Index.

TREWIN, J.C.—Editor
The Journal of William Charles Macready 1832—1851
Southern Illinois University, 1970. 315pp. Paper $2.85. An abridged edition of the 1967 publication of the journal of the nineteenth century actor. Mr. Trewin's interpolations provide a background to the diarist's entries. Illustrated. Index.

Master Betty

PLAYFAIR, GILES
The Prodigy: The Strange Life of Master Betty
Secker & Warburg, 1967. 190pp. $7.25. From 1804 to 1806, Master Betty, a teen-aged actor, played all the great parts of the English stage: Macbeth, Hamlet, and Romeo. In this documented account Mr. Playfair tells Master Betty's story and also examines the reasons for the "Bettymania" that swept England. Illustrated. Bibliography. Index.

Menken, Adah Isaacs

EDWARDS, SAMUEL
Queen of the Plaza
Alvin Redman, 1964. 307pp. $4.95. Paper—Mayflower, 1969. 252pp. $1.75. This is a biography of Adah Isaacs Menken, the nineteenth century actress who became a symbol of glamour and wickedness before she died at the age of 33. This book was published in the United States in 1964 under the same title but the author was listed as Paul Lewis.

Modjeska, Helena

MODJESKA, HELENA
Memories and Impressions of Helena Modjeska
Blom, 1969. 571pp. $12.50. Originally published in 1910 and reissued in a facsimile edition, this is the autobiography of the nineteenth century actress. She describes her youth in Poland, her stage experiences in Europe and America, and comments on her co-stars, including Edwin Booth, Otis Skinner, and Maurice Barrymore. Illustrated. Index.

Montez, La

WYNDHAM, HORACE
The Magnificent Montez
Blom, 1969. 288pp. $6.75. Originally published in 1935 and reissued in a facsimile edition, this is a biography of La Montez, the nineteenth century courtesan and theatrical personality. Illustrated with photographs. Appendices. Index.

More, Kenneth

MORE, KENNETH
Kindly Leave the Stage
Michael Joseph, 1965. 128pp. $3.75. The British stage and screen star describes some of the pitfalls of a life as a celebrity. Illustrated with drawings by John Jensen.

Morevski, Abraham

MOREVSKI, ABRAHAM
There and Back: Memories and Thoughts of a Jewish Actor
Warren H. Green, 1967. 256pp. $7.50. This biography of an actor with the Yiddish theatre details his life from his days on the Russian stage to his career in Poland, and with Maurice Schwartz's Yiddish Art Theatre in New York. Illustrated with photographs and drawings. Index.

Morley, Robert

MORLEY, ROBERT and SEWELL STOKES
Robert Morley: A Reluctant Autobiography
Simon & Schuster, 1967. 285pp. $6.95. The autobiography of the English stage and screen actor. Illustrated with photographs. Index.

O'Conner, Lois

O'CONNER, LOIS
The Bare Facts. Candid Confessions of a Stripper
MacFadden, 1964. 126pp. Paper $ .50. The story of a strip-teaser's career.

Olivier, Laurence

FAIRWEATHER, VIRGINIA
Olivier: An Informal Portrait
Coward—McCann, 1969. 183pp. $4.95. A memoir of the English actor/director/producer. It records Sir Laurence's participation in some of the most decisive developments of the English theatre over the last two decades including the establishment of the National Theatre Company. Illustrated with photographs. Index.

WHITEHEAD, PETER and ROBIN BEAN
Olivier—Shakespeare
See Page 478

WILLIAMS, P.C.
English Shakespearean Actors
See Page 262

Oppenheimer, George

OPPENHEIMER, GEORGE
The View from the Sixties: Memories of a Spent Life
McKay, 1965. 273pp. $5.00. The author, drama critic of "Newsday" and author of stage, screen, and television plays, describes a celebrity-crowded life in a number of creative fields.

Orr, Mary

ORR, MARY and REGINALD DENHAM
Footlights and Feathers
Pageant, 1967. 278pp. $4.95. This is the story of the Australian and New Zealand tour of the comedy, "Never Too Late," in which Miss Orr played the lead. It is also a personal account of the authors' journey back home through Aisa and a description of the wildlife they encountered. Illustrated with photographs.

Otero

LEWIS, ARTHUR H.
La Belle Otero
Trident, 1967. 257pp. $5.95. Paper—Pocket Books, 1968. 243pp. $ .95. This is the story of the singer-dancer who first appeared in America in 1890 and who became mistress to at least five members of royalty and to some of the wealthiest men in the world. The era in which Otero operated is captured by the author and he illustrates the text with twenty-seven photographs of the courtesan.

Parker, Dorothy

KEATS, JOHN
You Might As Well Live
Simon and Schuster, 1970. 319pp. $7.50. A biography of the American poet/short-story writer/drama critic, Dorothy Parker. Her life at the center of the cultural and intellectual excitement of the day, in New York, Paris, Spain, and Hollywood, is described. Illustrated with sixteen pages of photographs.

Payne, John Howard

HARRISON, GABRIEL
John Howard Payne: His Life and Writings
Blom, 1969. 404pp. $12.50. Originally published in 1875 and now reissued in a facsimile edition, this is a biography of the nineteenth century actor/dramatist. The author traces the manifold activities of Payne, and includes selections from Payne's journals, letters, and manuscript plays. The book contains much that relates to the stage of the period. List of Payne's dramatic works. Illustrated. Index.

OVERMYER, GRACE
America's First Hamlet
New York University, 1957. 439pp. $7.50. A biography of the man who wrote "Home, Sweet Home" and who was the first American to play the title role in "Hamlet." Miss Overmeyer deals fully with John Howard Payne's career as a successful playwright and as a famous actor on the London stage. Frontispiece. Notes. Bibliography. Index.

Petomane, Le

NOHAIN, JEAN and F. CARADEC
Le Petomane
Sherbourne Press, 1967. 96pp. $2.50. An account of the career of the artist who was the main attraction at the Moulin Rouge from 1892 to 1914. His anal emissions shocked and amused Europeans and out-drew even Sarah Bernhardt. Illustrated with photographs.

Picon, Molly

PICON, MOLLY and ETH CLIFFORD ROSENBERG
So Laugh A Little
Simon and Schuster, 1962. 175pp. $3.00. Paper—Paperback Library, 1966. 160pp. $ .60. The autobiography of Molly Picon, covering her activity in the Yiddish theatre for fifty years with anecdotes about the one hundred plays in which she appeared.

Rachel

AGATE, JAMES
Rachel
Blom, 1969. 94pp. $6.75. Originally published in 1924 and now reissued, this is a biography of the nineteenth century French actress who started out as a street singer and became France's unrivaled tragedienne. A short Bibliography is included as is a frontispiece portrait.

BEAUVALLET, LEON
Rachel and the New World
Abelard, 1967. 224pp. $5.00. Edited by Colin Clair, this is the account of the tours the French actress made with her acting troupe in the United States in the 1850's. Written by a member of the troupe, it is a portrait of the actress and of America in that time. Illustrated.

COST, MARCH
I, Rachel
Vanguard, 1957. 480pp. $4.95. A biographical novel about the nineteenth century French actress.

Richman, Harry

RICHMAN, HARRY and RICHARD GEHMAN
A Hell of a Life
Meredith, 1966. 242pp. $4.95. A biography of the entertainer of the 1920's, 1930's, and 1940's. Illustrated.

Ristori, Adelaide

RISTORI, ADELAIDE
Memoirs and Artistic Studies
Blom, 1969. 263pp. $12.50. Originally published in 1907 and reissued in a facsimile edition as translated by G. Mantellini. Part I relates the principal events of her stage career, her numerous travels and tours. Part II includes a record of her prominent roles and closely follows the text of an earilier autobiography. An Appendix contains biographical reminiscences by L. D. Ventura. Illustrated with thirty-two pages of photographs and engravings of Ristori and other contemporary personalities including Duse, Rachel, Bernhardt, Salvini, and Racine. Index.

Robeson, Paul

HOYT, EDWIN P.
Paul Robeson: The American Othello
World, 1967. 228pp. $5.95. A biography of the singer/actor, his rise to the pinnacle of international prominence, and the tragedy of his fall from popularity due to his outspoken support of the Communist cause in the 1930's.

SETON, MARIE
Paul Robeson
Dennis Robson, 1958. 254pp. $5.95. Paper $2.50. This is a biographical study of the Negro singer/actor which details his early life, his success as an athlete, his rise to international fame, and his controversial political stand. Illustrated with photographs. Index.

Rogers, Paul

WILLIAMSON, AUDREY
Paul Rogers
Barrie & Rockliff, 1956. 125pp. $3.00. Published in England, this is an illustrated study of the work of the English stage and screen actor. A chronology of his career on the stage, in films, and on television through 1956 is included.

Rogers, Will

DAY, DONALD
Will Rogers
McKay, 1962. 370pp. $6.95. The first full-scale biography of the man Damon Runyon called "America's most complete human document."

Rose, Billy

CONRAD, EARL
Billy Rose, Manhattan Primitive
World, 1968. 272pp. $6.95. This is the candid biography of "a Broadway scoundrel," Billy Rose. It details Rose's sensational rise to infamy and fortune from the ghetto slums of the lower East side of New York. Illustrated with photographs.

GOTTLIEB, POLLY ROSE
The Nine Lives of Billy Rose
Crown, 1968. 290pp. $5.95. Paper—Signet, 1969. 240pp. $ .95. Billy Rose's sister tells his story from his days as a stenography champion to his last years as an art collector, philanthropist, and millionaire. His nine careers and five marriages are all detailed and there are seventy-five photographs included. Index.

Rose, Clarkson

ROSE, CLARKSON
Red Plush and Greasepaint
Museum Press, 1964. 152pp. $4.50. Britain's most famous music hall performer describes the life of the Halls from his first appearance at the age of six through the next fifty years of his active career. Illustrated. Index.

Shubert Family

STAGG, JERRY
The Brothers Shubert
Ballantine, 1969. 466pp. Paper $1.25. Originally published in 1968 and now reissued, this is a biography of the three Shubert Brothers: Samuel, Jacob J., and Lee. Beginning with a chain of theatres in New York State, the Shuberts eventually created a nation-wide network of their own theatres to become the most powerful producing and booking corporation in the country. Illustrated with photographs of theatrical personalities and productions. List of Shubert productions. Index.

Siddons, Sarah

MACKENZIE, KATHLEEN
The Great Sarah: The Life of Mrs. Siddons
Evans, 1968. 144pp. $4.50. A biography of the eighteenth and early nineteenth century English actress who was universally acclaimed as the greatest actress on the English stage during her own lifetime. Miss Mackenzie gives a picture of the theatre of the day, the people who worked in it, and the plays they performed as well as telling the story of the actress. Illustrated with contemporary prints. Bibliography. Index.

PARSONS, MRS. CLEMENT
The Incomparable Siddons
Blom, 1969. 298pp. $12.50. Originally published in 1909 and reissued in a facsimile edition, this is a biography of the eighteenth century actress. The author includes comments on her acting style, ideals, and methods, as well as on the theatre of the period and the prominent theatrical personalities. Illustrated with portraits of the actress and her family. Chronology. List of Works Consulted. Appendices. Index.

Skinner, Cornelia Otis

SKINNER, CORNELIA OTIS
Family Circle
Houghton Mifflin, 1948. 310pp. $4.95. A history of the family life of Maud, Otis, and Cornelia Otis Skinner. The account is completed up to the debut of Miss Skinner in "Blood and Sand," in which she appeared with her father. Illustrated.

Sobol, Louis

SOBOL, LOUIS
The Longest Street
Crown, 1968. 448pp. $7.50. Reminiscences by the popular columnist. It is a record of the past forty years and the glamorous people Mr. Sobol encountered in the world of the speakeasys, burlesque and vaudeville, and Broadway and Hollywood. Illustrated with photographs. Index.

Speaight, Robert

SPEAIGHT, ROBERT
The Property Basket: Recollections of a Divided Life
Collins & Harvill, 1970. 416pp. $11.50. Memoirs of the English actor/author/teacher. He records the original productions of "Journey's End" and "Murder in the Cathedral," his love of Shakespeare and of France, and his friendships with French and English writers and thinkers. Illustrated with photographs. Index.

Talma, Francois—Joseph

COLLINS, HERBERT F.
Talma: A Biography of an Actor
Hill & Wang, 1964. 407pp. $7.95. A study of Francois-Joseph Talma and of his efforts, as a lifelong member of The Comedie Francaise, to reform costume, decorum, and declamation on the stage. Talma's relation with Napoleon and his affair with the Princess Borghese, Napoleon's sister, are examined in detail. The author has included a list of the roles created by Talma from 1788 to 1826. Illustrated. Selected Bibliography. Index.

Taylor, Charles

TAYLOR, DWIGHT
Blood-and-Thunder
Atheneum, 1962. 232pp. $4.50. A biography of Charles A. Taylor, the author of numerous melodramas, and of Laurette Taylor, the much put-upon heroine of these extravaganzas.

Taylor, Laurette

COURTNEY, MARGUERITE
Laurette
Atheneum, 1968. 445pp. $7.95. Originally published in 1955 and now reissued, this is the life story of Laurette Taylor by her daughter. This work is considered one of the classic theater biographies and the new edition contains eleven photographs of the actress, some never before published. Index.

Terry, Ellen

MANVELL, ROGER
Ellen Terry
Putnam, 1968. 390pp. $6.95. This biography contains much hitherto unpublished material, including letters, extracts from the actress' diaries, and her notes for her performances with Henry Irving. Illustrated with photographs. Bibliography. Index.

TERRY, ELLEN
Ellen Terry's Memoirs
Blom, 1969. 367pp. $12.50. A facsimile edition of the American actress' autobiography as published in 1932, with a Preface, notes, and additional biographical chapters by Edith Craig and Christopher St. John. More than seventy pages of illustrations and photographs. Index.

Vestris, Madame

PEARCE, CHARLES E.
Madame Vestris and Her Times
Blom, 1969. 314pp. $12.50. Originally published in 1923 and reissued in a facsimile edition, this is a biography of the nineteenth century actress, Lucia Elizabetta Bartolozzi—Madame Vestris. Illustrated with eighteen plates. Index.

Viertel, Salka

VIERTEL, SALKA
The Kindness of Strangers
Holt, Rinehart, 1969. 338pp. $6.95. A biography of the actress and writer who worked on all the major films in which Greta Garbo starred. Her early life as an actress in Vienna and her work in post-World War I Germany is detailed as is the career in Hollywood.

Wallack, Lester

WALLACK, LESTER
Memories of Fifty Years
See Page 235

Waters, Ethel

WATERS, ETHEL with CHARLES SAMUELS
His Eye Is on the Sparrow
Pyramid, 1967. 278pp. Paper $ .75. Originally published in 1950 and now reissued, this autobiography depicts Miss Waters' life from her under-privileged youth to her success in the theatre. She recreates the era of the great blues singers and gives a picture of the discrimination in the paths of Negro entertainers.

Webster, Margaret

WEBSTER, MARGARET
The Same Only Different
Knopf, 1969. 410pp. $7.95. Miss Webster relates the theatrical history of her family. The first part of the book is dominated by the first Ben Webster, who in the 1790's founded a fashionable dancing school and fathered eleven acting and dancing children. Miss Webster's parents' life is then detailed during the time when they were the leading actors of the turn of the century touring both England and America. The author brings her history to a close with the details of her early life and debut as director of Maurice Evans' "Richard II." Illustrated. Geneology. Index.

Woffington, Peg

DUNBAR, JANET
Peg Woffington and Her World
Houghton Mifflin, 1968. 245pp. $7.95. A biography of the eighteenth century English actress. It details her life with David Garrick and the theatrical world of the times. Illustrated with sixteen pages of photographs. Bibliography. Index.

Yurka, Blanche

YURKA, BLANCHE
Bohemian Girl
Ohio University, 1970. 306pp. $8.95. The autobiography of the actress which covers over sixty years of the theatre in this century. Illustrated with photographs. Index.

MUSICAL THEATRE

REFERENCE WORKS, HISTORIES, AND CRITIQUES

APEL, WILLI
Harvard Dictionary of Music
Harvard, 1969. 935pp. $17.50. This is the second edition, revised and enlarged, of the dictionary originally published in 1944. It has been established as the standard reference work for anyone concerned with music. In addition to definitions of words, there are articles on individual countries, discussions of both theory and history, bibliographies, drawings, music examples, diagrams, charts, and a full-page outline of the history of music. Lists of music libraries and collections with summaries of their holdings.

BAMBERGER, CARL – Editor
The Conductor's Art
McGraw–Hill, 1965. 322pp. $6.50. Paper $2.95. A collection of essays on conducting by such musicians as Von Weber, Berlioz, Robert Schumann, Liszt, Wagner, Felix Weingartner, Richard Strauss, Pablo Casals, Bruno Walter, Stokowski, Furtwangler, Sir Adrian Boult, Hermann Scherchen, Sir John Barbirolli, Leonard Bernstein, and Gunther Schuller. Index.

BERANEK, LEO L.
Music, Acoustics and Architecture
John Wiley, 1962. 586pp. $18.50. A detailed exploration in non-technical language of the essential meaning of acoustics to the performance and appreciation of music. The author shows how size, shape, building materials, and construction affect the sound in music. He outlines a new terminology to be used in describing the acoustics of a hall. Photographs, drawings, and critical evaluations of fifty-five of the world's most important halls. Philharmonic Hall in New York is described in detail.

BERNSTEIN, LEONARD
The Infinite Variety of Music
Simon & Schuster, 1966. 286pp. $6.50. Mr. Bernstein discourses on music: from Mozart to the canned music we hear in planes and elevators; from the classic tradition to the serious avant-grade of today. He provides insights into his own way of writing music and discusses what is "American" in American music. Illustrated.

BERNSTEIN, LEONARD
The Joy of Music
Simon and Schuster, 1954. 303pp. $6.50. Paper $2.45. Also: Paper – New American Library, 1967. 299pp. $ .95. This is a collection of seven expanded "Omnibus" television scripts plus essays and imaginary conversations that range in subject from an explanation of how music is dubbed onto a motion picture sound-track to an analysis of a Beethoven symphony. Illustrated with photographs and musical diagrams.

BORNOFF, JACK – Editor
Music Theatre in a Changing Society
UNESCO, 1968. 144pp. Paper $3.00. This is a survey of the application of modern techniques in the creation of works written for the stage; the transmission through the media of radio, television, and film of works written for the stage; and the creation of works especially for these media. Bibliography.

BRIFFAULT, ROBERT
The Troubadors
Indiana University, 1965. 296pp. Paper $2.45. Edited by Lawrence Koons, this volume provides the first comprehensive work on the poetic heritage of the Medieval troubadors and their impact on the tradition of Italian and English verse. Illustrated. Bibliography. Index.

BRITTEN, BENJAMIN and IMOGEN HOLST
The Wonderful World of Music
Doubleday, 1968. 96pp. $3.95. The authors study the history of music through the ages. First they define their terms: music is organized sound and rhythm. Then they show how sounds and music have been organized; how a language of music was evolved; how instruments were developed; and how styles of expressing ideas and emotion in sound have arisen and changed. Illustrated with contemporary drawings, prints, paintings, and photographs. Glossary of Musical Terms. Chronological List of Composers. Index.

BULL, STORM
Index to Biographies of Contemporary Composers
Scarecrow, 1964. 405pp. $10.75. Vital statistics on each composer, with lists of the sources in which biographical material can be found. Composers are listed if their works are found in reference sources, and if the composer is still alive or was born in 1900 or later.

CAGE, JOHN
Notations
Something Else Press, 1969. Unpaged. $15.00. Paper $4.50. This book illustrates a collection of music manuscripts which shows the many directions in which music notation is now going. The manuscripts are arranged alphabetically according to the composer's name. The text for the book is the result of a process employing I-Ching chance operations.

CAGE, JOHN
Silence
Wesleyan University, 1961. 276pp. $10.00. Paper – M.I.T. Press, 1967. 276pp. $3.95. Lectures and writings by the avant-garde composer.

CAGE, JOHN
A Year From Monday
Wesleyan University, 1969. 167pp. $7.95. Paper $1.95. Originally published in 1967 and now reissued, this is a collection of the lectures and writings of one of America's foremost modern composers.

CLENDENIN, WILLIAM R.
Music: History and Theory
Doubleday, 1965. 464pp. Paper $2.45. A college course guide to the historical development of music. The growth of major, as well as less significant, forms are traced from primitive times through the modern era. Illustrated with musical examples.

CRON, THEODORE O. and BURT GOLDBLATT
Portrait of Carnegie Hall
Macmillan, 1966. 217pp. $9.95. A pictorial history of the more than seven decades of activity at Carnegie Hall, showing the famous performers, musical and otherwise, and the many different kinds of performances. Discography. Index.

CROSS, MILTON and DAVID EWEN
The Milton Cross New Encyclopedia of the Great Composers and Their Music
Doubleday, 1969. 1,284pp. Two volume set $12.95. A revised and enlarged two volume edition of the encyclopedia originally published in 1953. Sixty-seven chapters, on the composers who have contributed most to the history of music, each present a comprehensive essay on the composer's life, his musical style, and his contributions. A brief history of music before and since Bach, a revised section on the home record library, an analysis of the symphony orchestra, and explanation of musical form, as well as an expanded Glossary of Musical Terms are all included. Slipcased.

DAMASE, JACQUES
Les Folies du Music-Hall
Spring Books, 1970. 190pp. $6.00. Originally printed in Paris in 1960 and now reissued, this is a history of the music-hall in Paris from 1914 to 1959. Two hundred photographs of the acts and spectacles that appeared in the music-halls are included.

DOLAN, ROBERT EMMETT
Music in Modern Media
See Page 468

DUKE, VERNON
Listen Here! A Critical Essay on Music Depreciation
Obolensky, 1963. 406pp. $5.95. Paper $1.95. A caustic view of music, popular and serious, as it is practiced and listened to today. The author questions the assumption that greater opportunity to hear music indicates a more musical age. Mr. Duke polled conductors of repute throughout the world with a series of questions, the answers to which he interprets. General Index. Index of Musical Compositions.

EDITORS OF HIGH FIDELITY MAGAZINE
Records In Review: 1968
Scribner, 1969. 517pp. $10.00. The thirteenth annual collection of record reviews from "High Fidelity." Reviews are organized alphabetically by composer with discussions on composition, performance, fidelity, and comparisons with earlier releases. Index.

EDITORS OF HIGH FIDELITY MAGAZINE
Records In Review: 1969
Scribner, 1969. 521pp. $10.00. The fourteenth annual edition of reviews of classical and semi-classical records. Index of Performers.

EWEN, DAVID
The World of Twentieth Century Music
Prentice–Hall, 1968. 989pp. $14.95. In this volume the author explores the development of music from 1900 to the present day. An individual section on each composer gives a critical consensus, a brief biography, and a listing of his works in order of composition and illuminated with programmatic and analytical notes. Alphabetical list of schools, styles, techniques, idioms, trends, movements, tendencies in twentieth-century music. List of Sources. Index.

FINKELSTEIN, SIDNEY
Composer and Nation: The Folk Heritage of Music
International, 1960. 333pp. $4.50. Paper $1.85. A study of the ideas expressed in music and of the popular and folk sources of the melodies of the great composers from the Renaissance to the twentieth century. The influence of social change on music is also studied.

FOOTE, HENRY WILDER
Three Centuries of American Hymnody
Archon, 1968. 441pp. $8.50. Originally published in 1940 and now reprinted with a new Appendix, "Recent American Hymnody," this volume traces the story of hymns and hymn writers from the early colonial days to the present. Index of Names and Subjects. Index of Psalm Books and Hymn Books. Index of First Lines.

FULD, JAMES J.
The Book of World Famous Music: Classical, Popular, and Folk
Crown, 1966. 564pp. $12.50. This reference book traces almost 1,000 of the best known melodies, of over 500 years, back to their sources. There is a complete Index of songs, composers, operas, ballets, and lyricists.

HOWARD, JOHN TASKER
Our American Music. Fourth Edition
Crowell, 1965. 944pp. $12.95. A comprehensive history of American music from 1620 to the present. Information on nearly 100 composers who have come into prominence since the 1950's is included and scores of new titles have been added to the extensive Bibliography. Index.

HUGHES, RUPERT
Music Lovers' Encyclopedia
Doubleday, 1954. 900pp. Paper $4.95. First published in 1903 and now completely revised and edited by Deems Taylor and Russell Kerr, this is the standard reference book on music. It contains a pronouncing biographical dictionary, a dictionary of more than 7,000 terms, stories of ninety operas with factual information, the lives of famous composers, brief biographical sketches of the great musicians, a series of essays on such subjects as acoustics, harmony, counterpoint, jazz, etc. "Introduction to Music," an essay by Rupert Hughes, is also included.

INTERNATIONAL SOCIETY FOR MUSIC EDUCATION – Compilers
International Directory of Music Education Institutions
UNESCO, 1968. 115pp. Paper $2.00. A trilingual directory of music education institutions, workshops, courses, competitions, festivals, libraries and archives, collections of musical instruments, national and international organizations and music periodicals. Seventy-two countries are included.

JENKINS, ELLA
This Is Rhythm
Oak, 1962. 96pp. Paper $2.95. A musically-therapeutic record book, aimed at the lower grades of elementary school, with sections on the broader meaning of rhythm, descriptions of ten rhythm instruments, and a discussion of bell-tones. The print and illustrations are designed for the convenience of the sight-saving classes.

KOSTELANETZ, RICHARD – Editor
John Cage
Praeger, 1970. 237pp. $12.50. Paper $4.95. Selected readings by and about the pioneer avant-garde composer. The Cagean contribution to sound is analyzed by such composers and critics as Virgil Thomson, Henry Cowell, Edward Downes, and Michael Zwerin. Cage's comments about his works as well as an essay on the future of music, and his remarks about composers who influenced his development are included. Illustrated with scores, music diagrams and photographs. Chronology. Bibliography. Catalogue of Compositions. Discography. Index.

KRAGEN, KENNETH and KENNETH FRITZ
Successful College Concerts
Watson–Guptill, 1967. 87pp. $4.95. A step-by-step guide to the planning, development, production and supervision of the college concert. It includes a list of major booking agencies, illustrations of sample tickets, manifest, statement of receipts and disbursements, schedule of advertising, and box office statements. Index.

LEVY, LESTER S.
Grace Notes in American History
University of Oklahoma, 1967. 410pp. $12.50. A view of America in the nineteenth century is revealed through Mr. Levy's examination of the popular sheet music from 1820 to 1900. The book is divided into two parts: "Mores" and "History." Material included within each section is treated topically. Illustrated with reproductions of sheet music covers. Bibliographical Notes. Index.

MacINNES, COLIN
Sweet Saturday Night
MacGibbon & Kee, 1967. 160pp. $5.25. This is a study of the English Music Hall and the performers and songs from Charles Chaplin to Wee Georgia Wood and "Act on the Square, Boys" to "You Could Almost Shut Your Eyes." It is a nostalgic look at the pop song era from 1840 to 1920. Index of Names. Index of Titles.

McPHEE, COLIN
Music in Bali: A Study in Form and Instrumental Organization in Balinese Orchestral Music
Yale, 1966. 430pp. $30.00. A study of music in Bali as it was practiced in the decade preceding World War II, with emphasis on musical form, rhythm, technical devices, and orchestration. The place of music in Balinese culture and the relation of music to drama and dance are also studied. Illustrated with photographs. Index.

MANDER, RAYMOND and JOE MITCHENSON
British Music Hall: A Story in Pictures
Studio Vista, 1965. 207pp. $10.00. The story of more than a century of popular entertainment, told through 300 pictures of artists and performers. Many of the photographs are from the private collection of the authors and many have never been published before.

NEWCOMB, WILBURN W.
Lute Music of Shakespeare's Time
Penn State University, 1966. 115pp. $9.50. The author includes a biography of William Barley, the sixteenth century musician, notes on the instruments used and described by Barley, and a discussion of the musical forms employed. "The New Book of Tabliture" is included in its entirety with critical notes and a keyboard transcription of the music for the lute. Illustrated.

REED, LANGFORD
The Writer's Rhyming Dictionary
The Writer, 1961. 244pp. $2.95. More than 25,000 rhymes for the most common sounds. Divided into two sections: one containing rhyme sounds of one syllable; the other, the more difficult two-syllable rhymes.

RICH, ALAN
Careers and Opportunities in Music
Dutton, 1964. 224pp. $4.95. The five parts of this book are: the musical world, a consideration of

musical talent and training; the performer's world, in which the activities of each type of performer are described; the world of the composer, which considers special problems in each aspect of music; the world of the teacher and the writer; and the rewards—financial expectations in the field. Illustrated.

ROREM, NED
Music and People
Braziller, 1968. 250pp. $5.95. From an opening essay on the Beatles to a final chapter on "Where is Our Music Going?" Mr. Rorem writes about contemporary music and musicians and provides a running commentary on his life, his friendships, the national differences between musicians, and the making of an opera and a ballet. Bibliography of Published Musical Compositions by Ned Rorem. Index of People.

ROREM, NED
Music from Inside Out
Braziller, 1967. 144pp. $4.00. Mr. Rorem attempts to answer questions about composers and music, to show "from inside out" the how and why of music. He considers how songs are written, the relationship of the song and the singer, the composer and the performance, and the difference between listening and hearing.

ROTH, ERNST
The Business of Music
Oxford, 1969. 269pp. $7.50. This book details the vast changes that have occurred in the music industry with the arrival of the mechanical and electronic age. Dr. Roth discusses the commercial implications of these changes in the matter of copyright and performing rights. He also writes about the art of music and reminisces about the great composers he has known.

SCHOLES, PERCY A.
The Concise Oxford Dictionary of Music
Oxford, 1964. 636pp. $7.00. A second revised edition, edited by John Owen Ward, with new entires relating to performers and composers. Some 3,500 items are included with diagrams and explanatory pictures.

SCHONBERG, HAROLD C.
The Great Pianists from Mozart to the Present
Simon and Schuster, 1966. 448pp. Paper $2.45. The author traverses the development of piano performance since its inception 200 years ago. The book forms not only a survey of the field but also honors the great development of performance as an art. Illustrated. Index.

SESSIONS, ROGER
Questions About Music
Harvard, 1970. 166pp. $5.95. The contemporary composer writes about music from the point of view of the practicing artist. He discusses such matters as the difficulty of talking about the non-verbal arts, composing, the gap between the composer and the public, and what the composer expects of his listeners.

SETTLE, RONALD
Music in the Theatre
See Page 359

SHARP, HAROLD and MARJORIE Z. SHARP – Compilers
Index to Characters in the Performing Arts: Part II – Operas and Musical Productions
Scarecrow, 1969. 1,253pp. Two volume set: $32.50. The purpose of this compilation is to identify characters in opera, operetta, musical comedy, and plays in which music is introduced. The compilers tell something about the character, indicate the author of the material, and provide information on composer and first production. Coverage runs from thirteenth century folk plays to the 1965/66 Broadway season. 2,542 productions and 20,000 characters are identified.

SHAW, BERNARD
How to Become A Musical Critic
Hill & Wang, 1967. 359pp. Paper $2.45. This edition of the 1961 publication is edited by Dan H. Laurence. It is a collection of Shaw's music criticisms and other writings on music. Biographical Index. General Index.

SHEMEL, SIDNEY and M. WILLIAM KRASILOVSKY
More About This Business of Music
Watson—Guptill, 1967. 160pp. $6.95. A guide book dealing with the legal complexities of four major segments of the music business: serious music, tape cartridge, background music and transcriptions, and production and sale of printed music. Index.

SIMPSON, CLAUDE M.
The British Broadside Ballad and Its Music
Rutgers University, 1966. 922pp. $20.00. The Broadside Ballad was a medium of mass communication, influential primarily from the middle of the sixteenth century to the beginnings of the eighteenth. Much of the music for these songs has become dissociated from the texts and Mr. Simpson has based his work on contemporary evidence. 540 tunes are reproduced and the text traces the history of their use for broadsides. List of Sources. Indices.

STECHESON, ANTHONY and ANNE STECHESON
Stecheson Classified Song Directory
Wehman, 1961. 503pp. $25.00. A compilation of over 100,000 song titles, classified by category. The publisher of each song is listed with the writer and the year of composition.

STRAVINSKY, IGOR and ROBERT CRAFT
Retrospectives and Conclusions
Knopf, 1969. 361pp. $7.95. This is a collaboration between the composer and the conductor/author. The volume includes a collection of Stravinsky's essays, reviews and interviews, and a selection of the writings from Craft's diary from 1948 to 1968. Appendices include the hitherto unpublished notes on Henry Berg's "Lulu." Indices.

TAUBMAN, HOWARD – Editor
The New York Times Guide to Listening Pleasure
Macmillan, 1968. 328pp. $6.95. Following Mr. Taubman's introductory survey of music, this guide provides twelve chapters on all the various forms of music from opera and classical music to jazz, folk, and the music of the theatre. Such experts as Martin Bookspan, Igor Kipnis, John S. Wilson, and Pru Devon have written these chapters. Discography. Index.

WECHSBERG, JOSEPH
Vienna, My Vienna
Macmillan, 1968. 300pp. $14.95. The author presents a portrait of Vienna, past and present. He discusses the city's contributions to the world of the arts, especially in music and the theater. He examines the Viennese "character" and analyzes the factors that have made the city one of myth, charm, and beauty. Werner Forman, the Czech photographer, has provided over 100 photographs of the city. Index.

OPERA AND OPERETTA

BERGES, RUTH
The Backgrounds and Traditions of Opera
A. S. Barnes, 1970. 269pp. $7.95. Originally published in 1961 as "Opera: Origins and Sidelights" and now revised and expanded, this is an in-depth study of opera including the major composers and librettists and with a special long section on Wagner. Illustrated. Selected Bibliography. Index.

BERGES, RUTH
Opera: Origins and Side Lights
Yoseloff, 1961. 192pp. $5.95. This book is not a standard introduction to opera; rather it selects, from a wide range of operas and composers, a mass of little known facts to give insight into the whole range of operatic art. Illustrated. Bibliography. Index.

BRIGGS, JOHN
Requiem for a Yellow Brick Brewery
Little, Brown, 1969. 359pp. $8.95. A history of the Metropolitan Opera. The author takes the reader behind the scenes and offers a collection of hitherto unpublished humorous and candid anecdotes gathered from thirty years of personal experience. Illustrated with photographs. Chronology. Index.

BRIGGS, THOMAS H.
Opera and Its Enjoyment
Teachers College, 1960. 243pp. $5.25. An introduction to opera. The author provides chapters on the creation of an opera, conventions of opera, how to prepare for an opera experience, and other subjects. The elements of opera including the libretto, vocal music, the orchestra, stage settings and costumes, dance and ballet in opera are studied in separate chapters. Appendix.

BROCKWAY, WALLACE and HERBERT WEINSTOCK
The World of Opera
Random House, 1962. 723pp. $10.00. Also Modern Library, 1966. 723pp. $4.95. A history of opera, with a two-hundred page alphabetically arranged "Annals of Performance." A revision of the authors' "The Opera: A History of Its Creation and Performance: 1600–1941."

BROPHY, BRIGID
Mozart the Dramatist
Faber & Faber, 1964. 328pp. $6.50. This study examines opera in relation to eighteenth century society, with special attention given to the influence of eighteenth century thought on Mozart's operas. The operas are examined in detail as dramas, and specific details are treated at length. Bibliography. Index.

CONE, JOHN F.
Oscar Hammerstein's Manhattan Opera Company
University of Oklahoma, 1966. 399pp. $7.95. A history of the Metropolitan Opera's chief competition during the years 1906 to 1910. Illustrated. Index.

CROSS, MILTON
The New Complete Stories of the Great Operas
Doubleday, 1955. 688pp. $4.95. This is the revised and enlarged edition, edited by Karl Kohrs, of Mr. Cross's book about opera. It includes synopses of seventy-six operas, a section on how to enjoy opera, a short history of the development of opera as an art form, and a discussion of ballet as a traditional part of opera. Selected Reading Guide. Index.

CULSHAW, JOHN
Ring Resounding
Viking, 1967. 276pp. $7.50. This is the account of how Wagner's "Der Ring des Nibelungen" was recorded in its entirety for the first time and how it took seven years to produce the fifteen recorded hours with the Vienna Philharmonic Orchestra and some of the world's finest Wagnerian singers such as Dietrich Fischer-Dieskau and Kirsten Flagstad. Illustrated. Index.

DAVIS, RONALD
Opera in Chicago
Appleton, 1966. 393pp. $12.95. A social and cultural history of opera in Chicago from 1850 to 1955. List of leading singers and the operas in which they sang. Illustrated. Index.

DEMUTH, NORMAN
French Opera: Its Development to the Revolution
Artemis Press, 1963. 337pp. $12.50. A study of the evolution of opera in France from liturgical drama to Gluck and Rameau, seen against a background of social and historical change. All aspects of opera are discussed—music, libretto, performers, design and montage, patrons and audience. The works of Lully are examined in detail and the rivalry between Italian

and French taste is considered. 100 musical examples. Discography. Bibliography. Index.

DENT, EDWARD J.
Foundations of English Opera: A Study of Musical Drama in England During the Seventeenth Century
Da Capo Press, 1965. 242pp. $8.95. A republication of the study first issued in 1928, with a new Introduction by Dr. Michael Winesanker. The study considers the English masques, plays with music, French influences, and chamber opera. Index.

DENT, EDWARD J.
Mozart's Operas. Second Edition
Oxford, 1962. 276pp. Paper $2.50. First published in 1913 and completely revised for this edition, this pioneer study has chapters on all the major operas of Mozart.

DENT, EDWARD J.
Opera
Penguin, 1965. 206pp. Paper $1.45. First published twenty-five years ago, this book traces the development of opera from the start of the seventeenth century to the modern British composers. Illustrated.

EATON, QUAINTANCE
The Boston Opera 1909–1915
Appleton, 1965. 338pp. $8.95. A history of the Boston Opera under the direction of Henry Russell, with a discussion of the performances of great singers and a retelling of famous anecdotes. Complete list of operas and full production notes for the period and a list of boxholders. Index. Illustrated.

EATON, QUAINTANCE
The Miracle of the Met
Meredith, 1968. 490pp. $10.95. Miss Eaton has written an informal history of the Metropolitan Opera from 1883 to 1967. Dozens of hitherto unpublished anecdotes are included and Miss Eaton dwells at length on the triumphs and tribulations of the hundreds of singers who have created one Golden Age after another. Illustrated with photographs. Index.

EATON, QUAINTANCE
Opera Production: A Handbook
University of Minnesota, 1961. 266pp. Designed as a reference book for producers, students, singers, and writers, this work contains information on 150 full length operas and 109 shorter ones. With descriptions of settings, size of orchestra, chorus, ballet, number of singers, their relative importance and individual requirements, sources for obtaining materials, previous American performances, and the entire story of the opera. Supplementary information on 260 more operas.

EBERS, JOHN
Seven Years of the King's Theatre
Blom, 1969. 395pp. $17.50. First published in 1828 and reissued in a facsimile edition, this is a history of the King's Theatre Opera House in London by the manager of that theatre from 1821 to 1827. The productions and performers of those years are detailed. Illustrated with portraits of some of the singers who appeared at the theatre. Appendices.

EWEN, DAVID
The Book of European Light Opera
Holt, Rinehart, 1962. 297pp. $7.50. A list of plots, composers, production histories, musical highlights, and critical evaluations of 167 European light operas.

EWEN, DAVID
Encyclopedia of the Opera
Hill & Wang, 1963. 594pp. $7.50. A new enlarged edition of this reference work first published in 1955. Included are stories of 505 operas, 105 complete act-by-act synopses and analyses, a complete "who's who" of opera personalities, and 1,000 biographies of composers.

FELLNER, RUDOLPH
Opera Themes and Plots
Simon & Schuster, 1958. 354pp. $4.95. Paper $1.75. A presentation of the essential materials for an understanding of thirty-two operas from the standard repertoire. The musical excerpts are printed on the left-hand page, the dramatic material on the right. Each musical excerpt is numbered to correspond to a numbered commentary for ready reference.

GAGEY, EDMOND MCADOO
Ballad Opera
Bloom, 1965. 272pp. $12.50. A detailed history of the ballad operas produced in England between 1728 and 1750, including all the many types that were developed after the successful "The Beggar's Opera." The extensive Bibliography lists all published and unpublished examples and survivals of the type between 1750–1835.

GOLDMAN, ALBERT and EVERT SPRINCHORN
Wagner on Music and Drama
Dutton, 1964. 447pp. $5.95. Paper $2.75. The eight parts of this collection of Wagner's writings are: criticisms of art and culture; a study of the Greek theatre; a critical history of opera, drama and music; specifications for the art-work of the future; his artistic development; practical problems of conducting, orchestration, acting, and singing; accounts of the founding of the Festspielhaus at Bayreuth; late political writings.

GOLDOVSKY, BORIS
Bringing Opera to Life
Appleton, 1968. 424pp. $10.00. Dr. Goldovsky's book is designed primarily for those planning operatic careers either as singers or as directors. He discusses opera from the viewpoints of the singer, the stage director, and the intelligent listener. Included in the work are detailed discussions of scenes from many of

the major operas, reflecting the responsibilities of the stage director in working with opera and the singer's role in presenting a convincingly dramatic as well as musical production. Over 100 diagrams illustrate the placement and movement of singers in specific scenes, and over 150 musical examples further clarify the problems of bringing opera to life. Index of Operas.

GOLLANCZ, VICTOR
The Ring at Bayreuth and Some Thoughts on Operatic Production
Dutton, 1966. 121pp. $3.50. Wieland Wagner's revolutionary productions at Bayreuth are discussed. Also included are two essays on opera production in general. Index.

HOLDE, ARTHUR
The Treasury of Great Operas
Bantam, 1965. 218pp. Paper $ .95. Stories of the great operas in the standard repertory with over 100 photographs taken at actual performances.

HOWARD, PATRICIA
Gluck and the Birth of Modern Opera
St. Martin's, 1964. 118pp. $7.50. This study discusses Gluck's role as a reformer and considers his innovations in the development of the operatic aria, the recitative, the chorus, and the overture. His abilities as a dramatist are also examined. Bibliography. Index.

HURD, MICHAEL
Young Person's Guide to Opera
Roy, 1966. 119pp. $3.25. This brief introduction to opera is designed to answer the young person's questions on how an opera is prepared for production, how the composer works, what the singer's life is like, and what the opera house is like. A history of opera from the seventeenth century to the present is given. Index.

INTERNATIONAL MUSIC CENTRE, VIENNA – Compilers
Films for Music Education and Opera Films
UNESCO, 1962. 114pp. Paper $1.25. Compiled by the International Music Centre, Vienna, for UNESCO, with a general introduction by Egon Kraus and an introduction to opera films by Jack Bornoff, this is an international catalogue of music films. The films are categorized and all salient information is included. Index of Titles. Index by Countries. Index by Composers.

JACOBS, ARTHUR and STANLEY SADIE
The Pan Book of Opera
Pan, 1969. 492pp. Paper $1.95. A revised edition of the 1964 publication, this reference work describes in detail the composer, story, and musical content of sixty-six operas by thirty-one composers. The authors have included a chapter on early opera and another on the modern scene. Bibliography.

JOHNSON, H. EARLE
Operas on American Subjects
Coleman–Ross, 1964. 125pp. $5.95. A bibliography of operas on American subjects, arranged alphabetically by composer. A short synopsis of the work is given, the name of the librettist and the date of first performance are provided. List of Titles by Topics and Locales. Selective Bibliography. Index of Titles. General Index.

KERMAN, JOSEPH
Opera as Drama
Knopf, 1956. 269pp. $5.00. Paper – Vintage, 1956. 275pp. $1.45. Musical-dramatic analyses of the central works of the operatic repertoire. The author's thesis is that opera is a valid form of dramatic expression.

KOLODIN, IRVING
The Metropolitan Opera: 1883 – 1966
Random House, 1966. 809pp. $15.00. A complete history of the Metropolitan Opera Company from its opening in 1883 to its last performance on April 16, 1966 in the building at Broadway and 39th Street. Illustrated with 183 photographs. Index.

KRALIK, HEINRICH
The Vienna Opera
James Heinman, 1963. 188pp. $15.00. This book describes the unique role of the Vienna Opera in Viennese social life from the days of the Opera's beginnings through the era of patronage by the Hapsburg emperors, its progress under Herbeck and Jauner, the era of prosperity under Jahn, and the great days of Gustav Mahler. The destruction and rebirth of the opera in 1955 are also described. Illustrated with drawings and paintings in color and black-and-white. Index.

LUBBOCK, MARK and DAVID EWEN
The Complete Book of Light Opera
Appleton, 1962. 953pp. $12.95. A comprehensive reference work covering all the leading schools of operetta, opera buffa, and musical comedy, European and American, from 1850 to the present. Plot synopses, casts of characters, information on first performances, and musical excerpts are given. The American section is by Mr. Ewen. Twenty pages of photographs of productions.

McSPADDEN, J. WALKER
Grand Opera in Digest Form
Apollo, 1961. 397pp. Paper $1.95. Act-by-act synopses of 172 operas with lists of characters, information on libretto, biographies of composers, and facts on premieres and first American productions. Index of Characters.

MARETZEK, MAX
Crochets and Quavers
Da Capo Press, 1966. 345pp. $6.95. This autobiography

of the manager and conductor of the Italian Opera Company was originally published in 1855 and is now reissued. It reveals in detail many aspects of operatic, concert, and popular music during America's pre-Civil War era. Also available in paper. See entry directly below.

MARETZEK, MAX
Revelations of an Opera Manager in 19th Century America
Dover, 1968. 440pp. Paper $2.75. This volume combines Mr. Maretzek's two volume autobiography: "Chrotchets and Quavers" and "Sharps and Flats." It reveals in detail many aspects of operatic and concert life during America's pre-Civil War era. Originally published in 1855 and 1890, an Introduction by Charles Haywood has been provided for this new edition. Illustrated. Index.

MARTIN, GEORGE
The Opera Companion: A Guide for the Casual Operagoer
Dodd, Mead, 1961. 751pp. $12.50. The operatic experience explained to the opera-goer who cannot read music. Included are synopses of forty-seven popular operas.

MATZ, MARY JANE
Opera: Grand and Not So Grand
Morrow, 1966. 222pp. $5.95. A behind-the-scenes view of opera today. Miss Matz explores the changes that are taking place with emphasis on the problems of size, rapid transportation, shortage of stars, and dominance of the stage over the music. Index.

MAYNARD, OLGA
Enjoying Opera
Scribner, 1966. 308pp. $6.95. A book for the general reader and average theatre-goer which reveals the romantic evolution of opera from the Renaissance to the start of the twentieth century. Forms and styles of opera are identified, personalities of the great composers and singers are discussed, and the language and instruments are explained. Illustrated. Index.

MERKLING, FRANK – Editor
The Opera News Book of "Figaro"
Dodd, Mead, 1967. 146pp. $5.00. Selected background articles on music, plot, character, history, and the composer of "The Marriage of Figaro" from the official publication of the Metropolitan Opera Guild. Sixteen pages of illustrations plus musical examples in the text. Index.

MOORE, FRANK LEDLIE – Editor
Crowell's Handbook of World Opera
Crowell, 1961. 683pp. $7.50. This encyclopedic guide contains information on more than 500 operas, entries on more than 1,500 singers and composers. Glossary. Dictionary. List of Recordings of Complete Operas. Introduction by Darius Milhaud.

MORGENSTERN, SAM and HAROLD BARLOW
A Dictionary of Opera and Song Themes
Crown, 1950. 547pp. $5.95. Originally published as "A Dictionary of Vocal Themes," this volume shows the music of more then 8,000 themes, together with words, arranged for easy reference to enable the reader to find the exact music of any important vocal composition. Line Index. Title Index. Notation Index.

MORLEY, ALEXANDER
The Harrap Opera Guide
Harrap, 1970. 320pp. $7.95. Sir Alexander describes in alphabetical order eighty-eight of today's most frequently performed operas. After a general introductory note to each work, in which the author assesses it and places it in its musical and historical context, he provides a summary of the action and most significant dialogue. Index.

NEWMAN, ERNEST
Great Operas
Vintage, 1958. Volume One: 441pp. Volume Two: 439pp. Paper. Each volume: $1.95. These two volumes contain essays on thirty masterpieces of the operatic repertoire with 652 musical examples.

OSBORNE, CHARLES
The Complete Operas of Verdi
Knopf, 1970. 485pp. $10.00. An interpretive study of the librettos and music and their relation to the Italian composer's life. The author sets the twenty-six operas against the human background of their creation, relates the events in Verdi's life, retells the libretto of each opera, and analyzes each of the scores, complete with musical examples and extracts from the librettos. Bibliography. Index.

PAULY, REINHARD G.
Music and the Theatre
Prentice–Hall, 1970. 462pp. $13.95. An introduction to opera for novices. The author explores the essence of opera through an investigation of basic operatic conventions. He traces the significant development in opera from its roots in ancient Greece through the works of Mozart, Wagner, Puccini, Stravinsky, and others. Illustrated with photographs and musical examples. Glossary. Index.

PELTZ, MARY ELLIS and ROBERT LAWRENCE
The Metropolitan Opera Guide
Modern Library, 1939. 497pp. $3.95. Detailed synopses of the operas in the standard repertory at the Metropolitan Opera, with biographies of composers, motives and musical themes of principal arias, and commentaries on major roles. Bibliography. Index.

PLEASANTS, HENRY
The Great Singers
Simon & Schuster, 1966. 382pp. $7.50. Mr. Pleasants recreates the personalities and performances, the lives and art of the great singers. Beginning with the

age of bel canto in the seventeenth century, he extends his history to the singers of own own time. Illustrated. Index.

PRAWY, MARCEL
The Vienna Opera
Praeger, 1970. 224pp. $25.00. A history of the Vienna State Opera House and Company from 1810 to the present. A chapter is devoted to each of the directors as the author discusses the conductors and singers who performed in the House as well as the operas in which they appeared. The volume is lavishly illustrated with hundreds of photographs, sketches, and reproductions of programs, cartoons and caricatures. Appendix on the Opera Ballet. Index.

RAPHAEL, ROBERT
Richard Wagner
Twayne, 1969. 153pp. $4.95. A study of the music dramas (operas) of the German composer. The author analyzes the dramas as prime documents of European culture in the ninteenth century. He examines each drama in chronological order with the aim of revealing the corpus of Wagner's ten major works for the stage as a single drama of immense proportions in ten acts. Notes and References. Bibliography. Index.

REYNOLDS, ERNEST
The Plain Man's Guide to Opera
Michael Joseph, 1964. 160pp. $4.50. A guide for the casual opera-goer. Each school is examined and individual works of importance are discussed in detail.

ROSENTHAL, HAROLD and JOHN WARRACK—Editors
The Concise Oxford Dictionary of Opera
Oxford, 1964. 446pp. $6.50. Over 3,000 entries covering composers, singers, conductors, librettists, synopses, details of first performances, characters in operas, and the first lines of famous arias. Technical terms and jargon are explained.

ROSENTHAL, HAROLD
Opera at Covent Garden: A Short History
Gollancz, 1967. 192pp. $4.75. A recounting of the history of the Covent Garden Opera House. Mr. Rosenthal shows how changes in public taste have been reflected in the policies of the Opera House managements. Illustrated with forty-eight photographs. Appended is a complete List of Operas Produced at Covent Garden from 1847 to 1965.

ROSENTHAL, HAROLD—Editor
The Opera Bedside Book
Gollancz, 1965. 317pp. $5.50. The essays in this book include discussions of opera critics by Benjamin Britten and Winston Dean, artists on the art by Sylvia Fisher and Helga Pilarczyk, studies of Ponselle, Martinelli, and Callas, and various productions, recordings, and opera houses.

SHAW, GEORGE BERNARD
The Perfect Wagnerite: A Commentary on the Niblung's Ring
Dover, 1968. 136pp. Paper $1.50. A republication of the 1923 edition of Shaw's commentary on the cycle of four Wagner operas known as "The Ring." Shaw discusses Wagner's life, the character of music drama as opposed to grand opera, the role of the Leitmotif in unifying the cycle and delineating character, and other related questions. Prefaces to all four editions of the commentary are included.

SIMON, HENRY W.
The Victor Book of the Opera: Thirteenth Edition
Simon & Schuster, 1968. 475pp. $8.50. Originally published in 1929 and now completely revised by Mr. Simon, this volume contains the historical background and act-by-act summaries of 120 operas and complete listings of the best available recordings, an outline history of opera, and over 400 illustrations of the great composers, the great singers and the great scenes of Grand opera. Index of Names.

SKELTON, GEOFFREY
Wagner at Bayreuth
Braziller, 1965. 239pp. $6.50. A complete history of the staging of Wagner's opera at Bayreuth. It traces the background of the Festpielhaus, describes Wagner's own productions and includes sidelights on Wagner productions in Germany, Britain, and America. Illustrated. Index.

SMITH, PATRICK J.
The Tenth Muse
Knopf, 1970. 436pp. $12.95. A historical study of the opera libretto beginning in the early seventeenth century and continuing on to the twentieth century librettists: von Hofmannsthal, Brecht, and Gertrude Stein. The author analyzes the lives, works and collaboration with their composers of the librettists and studies the relationships within opera of drama, dance, words, and music. Illustrated. Selective Bibliography. Index.

SMITH, WILLIAM C.—Compiler
The Italian Opera and Contemporary Ballet in London: 1789–1820
Society for Theatre Research, 1955. 191pp. Paper $11.00. This is a record of opera and ballet performances in London with reports from the journals of the time: 1789–1820. Several Indices are included as is a List of Works Consulted. The compiler has included an Introduction to the subject. Illustrated.

SONNECK, OSCAR G.
Early Opera in America
Blom, 1964. 230pp. $15.00. First published in 1915, this volume in the series, "Roots and Sources of the American Theatre," under the general editorship of Richard Moody, consists of a brief survey of pre-Revolutionary opera, and gives a detailed study

of opera from 1793 to 1800 in New York, Philadelphia, Boston, Baltimore and the South. There is a chapter on French opera in America. Lists of Performances. Illustrated. Index.

SPENDER, STEPHEN
The Magic Flute
Putnam, 1966. Unpaged. $3.95. A retelling for children of Mozart's opera with illustrations by Beni Montresor.

VOLBACH, WALTHER R.
Problems of Opera Production
Shoe String, 1967. 218pp. $11.50. Originally published in 1953 and now reissued in a revised edition, this is a guidebook for workers in the lyric theatre, professional, civic, or educational, on stage or backstage, in the pit or in the office, outlining for them the best means of achieving productions of high standard. Sections are devoted to the historical background of opera, basic concepts and general production problems, the organization behind the production, the roles of the singer, conductor, stage director, and designer. Illustrated with scene designs and plans and photographs. Glossary. Bibliography. Index.

WEAVER, WILLIAM
Puccini Librettos
Doubleday, 1966. 471pp. Paper $1.95. Mr. Weaver here translates Puccini's librettos for "La Boheme," "Tosca," "Madame Butterfly," "Gianni Schicchi," and "Turandot." This is a bilingual version with the original Italian on facing pages. Mr. Weaver includes stage directions and changes in the Italian texts made after the first performances.

WEISSTEIN, ULRICH – Editor
The Essence of Opera
Macmillan, 1964. 372pp. $7.95. An anthology of writings about opera which includes as wide a range as possible of disparate views broached by composers, librettists, and aestheticians during the past 350 years. Every period and every national style of opera is covered.

WESTERMAN, GERHART VON
Opera Guide
Dutton, 1968. 584pp. Paper $2.95. Originally published in 1964 and now reissued, this guide has been edited by Harold Rosenthal who also provides an Introduction. The guide presents synopses and casts of almost 200 operas together with a detailed account of developments and trends from the first emergence of opera to the present day. Illustrated with sixty-two photographs of historical productions. Indices.

WHITE, ERIC WALTER
Benjamin Britten: His Life and Operas
University of California, 1970. 256pp. $10.00. Originally published in 1948 and now completely revised and substantially expanded to bring the study up to date. Included are detailed scrutinies of all Britten's major operas and the recent musical-dramatic works. Chronological list of original works with a list of first productions of the operas with cast lists. Illustrated with musical examples and twenty-four photographs. Bibliography. Index.

GILBERT AND SULLIVAN

BLASHFIELD, JEAN
The Gondoliers
Nelson, 1966. Unpaged. $1.90. The Gilbert and Sullivan operetta retold for children by Miss Blashfield with color illustrations by Anne and Janet Grahame Johnstone.

CELLIER, FRANCOIS and CUNNINGHAM BRIDGEMAN
Gilbert and Sullivan and Their Operas
Blom, 1970. 443pp. $12.50. A study of the composers and their works first published in 1914 and now reissued in a facsimile edition. Recollections and anecdotes of D'Oyly Carte and other famous Savoyards are included. Illustrated with photographs and facsimiles of letters. Appendix. Index.

GREEN, MARTYN
Martyn Green's Treasure of Gilbert and Sullivan
Simon & Schuster, 1962. 715pp. $15.00. The complete librettos of eleven operettas accompanied by Mr. Green's comments on their history, on their staging, and on performing them. Included are the words and music to more than 100 songs. Illustrated.

HARRIS, PAULA
The Young Gilbert and Sullivan
Roy, 1965. 128pp. $3.25. This biography of the composers concentrates on their youth. It was written especially for children. Illustrated.

HEWITT, TONY
The School Gilbert and Sullivan
Albyn Press, 1949. 48pp. Paper $ .65. A guide to producing Gilbert and Sullivan operettas for and with youngsters. All aspects of production are briefly covered, from selecting the work and casting it, to scenery, props, costumes and lighting, to actual performance.

JONES, JOHN BUSH – Editor
W.S. Gilbert: A Century of Scholarship and Commentary
New York University, 1970. 321pp. $10.00. A collection of critical and scholarly essays on Gilbert and the Victorian drama. A chronological arrangement is followed ranging from the reviews of "The Bab Ballads" through articles of research in the 1960's. The articles range in scope from general

appreciations and criticisms, studies of sources and parallels, to analysis of individual works, and bibliographical and editorial investigations. Foreword written by Bridget D'Oyly Carte. Selected Bibliography.

MANDER, RAYMOND and JOE MITCHENSON
A Picture History of Gilbert and Sullivan
Studio Vista, 1962. 158pp. $7.50. Through more than 380 pictures and descriptive text the authors tell the story of the great partnership and the separate work. Bridget D'Oyly Carte has contributed a Foreword and allowed her vast archives to be explored and used by the authors. A section is included dealing with the unofficial, burlesque, ballet, and film versions of the operas.

MEARNS, MARTHA
H.M.S. Pinafore
Nelson, 1966. Unpaged. $1.90. A retelling for children of the Gilbert and Sullivan opera. Color drawings by Anne and Janet Grahame Johnstone.

MEARNS, MARTHA
The Yeomen of the Guard
Nelson, 1966. Unpaged. $1.90. Gilbert and Sullivan's operetta is retold by Miss Mearns with drawings by Anne and Janet Grahame Johnstone in color.

MOORE, FRANK LEDLIE – Editor
Crowell's Handbook of Gilbert and Sullivan
Crowell, 1962. 264pp. $4.95. An encyclopedic guide to the operettas, with detailed synopses of each work, casts of characters, settings, songs, choruses, biographies of the authors and of Richard D'Oyly Carte, and musical themes of famous songs.

MUSICAL COMEDY

BARAL, ROBERT
Revue: The Great Broadway Period
Fleet Press, 1970. 296pp. $10.00. Originally published in 1962 and now revised, this is a reprise of the period of the 1920's and 1930's when the revue form of musical comedy was at its high point in New York and London. The productions, the stars and the writers and producers are all discussed. Illustrated. Appendix of Casts and Credits. Index.

BURTON, JACK
The Blue Book of Broadway Musicals
Century House, 1952. 320pp. $10.00. An anthology covering all the musical productions that have had a Broadway opening the last fifty years. The half-century is divided into five major periods, each of which is provided with a general introduction followed by a listing of the musicals and their songs arranged according to the composers of scores. The casts of the Broadway productions are given. Illustrated. List of Long Running Shows. Discography. Index of Shows.

CORIO, ANN and JOSEPH DIMONA
This Was Burlesque
Grosset & Dunlap, 1968. 206pp. $9.95. A history of burlesque: the famous comics, the comedy acts, the singers, the candy butchers, the chorus lines, the producers, the censors and the audiences as seen through the eyes of one of its leading ladies. A feature of the book is its inclusion of several of the leading comedy scenes. Illustrated with photographs.

ENGEL, LEHMAN
The American Musical Theatre: A Consideration
Macmillan, 1967. 236pp. $12.50. A study of the American musical theater by one of the best known musical conductors of Broadway musicals. It is a penetrating and comprehensive book about this theatre genre and includes chapters on the beginnings, the revue, the contemporary musical, and Broadway opera. Lavishly illustrated. Included are a Discography, a List of Published Librettos and Vocal Scores, Bibliography, and Index.

ENGEL, LEHMAN
Planning and Producing the Musical Show
Crown, 1966. 148pp. $3.95. A handbook of practical advice for producers of amateur musicals. All aspects of production are covered including budgeting. A checklist of seventy-six popular musicals is included. Illustrated.

EWEN, DAVID
Composers for the American Musical Theatre
Dodd, Mead, 1968. 270pp. $5.00. Mr. Ewen describes the roots of the modern musical theatre in foreign importations, the minstrel show, farce, and burlesque. He recalls the operettas and discusses the productions of Cohan, Kern, Berlin, Gershwin, Porter, Rodgers, and others. Fourteen composers and the works they have created for the American musical theatre are discussed in a chapter apiece. Illustrated with photographs of the composers. Index.

EWEN, DAVID
New Complete Book of the American Musical Theatre
Holt, Rinehart, 1970. 800pp. $15.00. A completely revised guide, originally published in 1958, to more than 500 musical shows from "The Black Crook" in 1866 to "Applause." Included are some 160 composers, librettists, and lyricists, with plot summaries, production history, stars, and songs. Over sixty photographic illustrations. Appendices. Indices.

EWEN, DAVID
The Story of America's Musical Theatre
Chilton, 1968. 278pp. $5.50. This is a revised edition of the history of musical entertainment in America from the first performance in 1735 to the current Broadway hits. Originally published in 1961, it has been brought up-to-date and includes the stories behind the productions of "Cabaret" and "The Apple Tree" among many others. Index.

GREEN, STANLEY
The World of Musical Comedy
A. S. Barnes, 1968. 541pp. $12.00. A revised and enlarged edition of the work first published in 1960. This is a history of the American musical stage as told through the careers of its foremost composers and lyricists. The revisions and enlargements bring the book up to date through current composers such as Jerry Herman and Fred Ebb and John Kander. An Appendix lists production information for every Broadway and off-Broadway musical with scores written by the composers and lyricists discussed in the book. Illustrated with photographs. Index.

LAUFE, ABE
Broadway's Greatest Musicals
Funk & Wagnalls, 1970. 480pp. $10.00. Originally published in 1969 and now enlarged and illustrated, this volume gives facts, figures, and background details on all the people who contributed to the greatest musical hits of the Broadway stage from 1884 to the present. Precise summaries of plot, behind-the-scenes anecdotes, descriptions of costumes and sets and excerpts from reviews are included. Illustrated with photographs. Bibliography. Appendix. Indices.

MANDER, RAYMOND and JOE MITCHENSON
Musical Comedy: A Story in Pictures
Taplinger, 1969. 64pp. & plates. $10.00. Over 230 pictures and a long introduction detail the history of musical comedy in England. Indices of Musicals Illustrated, Sources, Authors and Lyricists, Authors of Sources, Composers, and Actors. Foreword by Noel Coward.

MATES, JULIAN
The American Musical Stage Before 1800
Rutgers University, 1962. 331pp. $6.00. A study of the first American musicals, from the early adaptations of European material and conventions to the first production in 1796 of "The Archers," the first musical written entirely by Americans.

MATTFELD, JULIUS
Variety Music Cavalcade: Musical–Historical Review 1620–1961
Prentice–Hall, 1962. 713pp. $15.00. A complete chronological survey of music published in the U. S. from 1620. Included are titles, composers, lyricists, publishers and copyright data.

NATHAN, HANS
Dan Emmett and the Rise of Early Negro Minstrelsy
University of Oklahoma, 1962. 496pp. $12.50. A historical, biographical, and musicological study of the early songs, lyrics, dances, and performers of the American minstrel show. Treated in detail is the life and work of Dan Emmett, singer/comedian and composer of "Dixie." Illustrated with 119 musical examples and sixty reproductions of contemporary art work.

O'HARA, MARY
A Musical in the Making
Taplinger, 1966. 260pp. $3.95. The history of how Miss O'Hara's musical, "The Catch Colt," reached the stage in Cheyenne, Wyoming.

SMITH, CECIL
Musical Comedy in America
Theatre Arts, 1950. 374pp. Paper $2.60. A history of musicals from 1864 to 1950, with sixty-four illustrations from important shows and a twenty page Index of titles, actors, composers, and critics.

SPENCER, PETER A.
Let's Do A Musical
See Page 360

STAMBLER, IRWIN
Encylopedia of Popular Music
See Page 293

TUMBUSCH, TOM
The Theatre Student: Complete Production Guide to Modern Musical Theatre
Richards Rosen, 1969. 187pp. $5.97. Written for students and teachers of theatre involved in the production of musicals, this text gives all the information necessary for producing a musical from how to choose the script to the duties of all members of the production staff. A list of major musicals produced on and off-Broadway since 1866 is included. illustrated with photographs. Bibliography.

POPULAR MUSIC

BART, TEDDY
Inside Music City, U. S. A.
Aurora, 1970. 164pp. $4.95. Paper $1.95. Mr. Bart explores the role of several key contributors to the "Nashville Sound" in music. The role of the music publisher and the functions of the performing rights societies as well as such songwriters as Jack Clement, Harlan Howard, Hank Cochran, and John D. Laudermilk are discussed. Illustrated with photographs. List of Publishers.

BELZ, CARL
The Story of Rock
Oxford, 1969. 256pp. $5.95. A survey of rock music describing its history in terms of major artists and groups. The author seeks to define rock's origins, its essential nature, and its musical significance. Illustrated with photographs. Selected Discography: 1953–1963. Index.

BURTON, JACK
The Blue Book of Hollywood Musicals
Century House, 1953. 296pp. $10.00. A complete listing of performers, songs, composers, and avail-

able recordings covering Hollywood musicals from 1927 to 1952. Illustrated.

BURTON, JACK
The Blue Book of Tin Pan Alley
Century House, 1962. 528pp. Two volume set: $21.00. Originally published in 1951 and now reissued in a revised edition this is a reference book listing biographies and compositions of America's songwriters from Stephen Foster to Irving Berlin and Richard Rodgers. Song titles and available recordings are listed.

CHARTERS, SAMUEL
Jazz New Orleans 1885–1963: An Index to the Negro Musicians of New Orleans
Oak, 1963. 173pp. Paper $2.95. A revised second edition of the book first published in 1958, this Index brings up to date the research into the lives and musical activities of the musicians of the period.

CHARTERS, SAMUEL
The Poetry of the Blues
Oak, 1963. 112pp. Paper $1.95. A study of the Negro folk blues as literature. Illustrated with photographs.

COHN, NIK
Rock from the Beginning
Stein & Day, 1969. 256pp. $5.95. A history and study of rock music from its beginnings in the mid-fifties to the groups current today. Among the subjects covered are: Bill Haley, Elvis Presley, the Beatles, the Rolling Stones, Bob Dylan, and The Who. Illustrated with photographs. Index.

EISEN, JONATHAN – Editor
The Age of Rock–2
Random House, 1970. 339pp. $8.95. Paper $2.95. A collection of articles and essays on "sights and sounds of the American Cultural Revolution." Rock groups, Bob Dylan, the Altamont concert, and the Woodstock Nation are among the many subjects and personalities discussed. Illustrated with photographs.

EWEN, DAVID
Great Men of American Popular Song
Prentice–Hall, 1970. 387pp. $12.95. The history of the American popular song through the lives, careers, achievements, and personalities of its foremost composers and lyricists—from William Billings of the Revolutionary War to the "folk-rock" of Bob Dylan. Index.

EWEN, DAVID
The Life and Death of Tin Pan Alley
Funk & Wagnalls, 1964. 380pp. $5.95. A study of the musical scene in the era of Paul Dresser, Harry von Tilzer, the young Irving Berlin, Kern, Herbert, and Gershwin. A review of popular music in America is given. The influences of the Alley in the period before 1930 and the changes since then with the rise of ASCAP, radio, motion pictures, and phonographs are traced. Index.

FEATHER, LEONARD
The Encyclopedia of Jazz in the Sixties
Horizon, 1966. 312pp. $15.00. A complete new survey of the entire field of jazz. Included are 1,100 biographies of musicians. Illustrated with 200 photographs. List of Recordings. Bibliography.

FERNETT, GENE
A Thousand Golden Horns
Citadel, 1966. 175pp. $7.50. The story of the great dance bands of 1935–1945 and the men in them. Among the bands mentioned are those of Miller, Dorsey, Goodman.

GILLETT, CHARLIE
The Sound of the City: The Rise of Rock and Roll
Dutton, 1970. 375pp. Paper $2.95. A history and sociological investigation of rock and roll music. The author studies the music, the lyrics, the audience, and the sources of the music. List of Recordings. Notes. Bibliography. Index.

GITLER, IRA
Jazz Masters of the '40's
Macmillan, 1966. 290pp. $5.95. This is the story of the emergence in the 1940's of bebop, the modern jazz statement of that era. The author evokes the personalities and achievements, the places and the movements of the music. Discography. Illustrated. Index.

GOLDBERG, ISAAC
Tin Pan Alley
Ungar, 1961. 371pp. Paper $1.95. Originally published in 1930 and now reissued, this is a history of American popular music and musicians. A supplement: "From Swing and Sweet to Rock 'N Roll" by Edward Jablonski recounts the rise of the Hollywood musical, the beginning of Swing, and the flowering of the American musical theatre in the 1940's, through the rock 'n roll craze of the 1950's. Illustrated. Index.

GOLDSTEIN, RICHARD
Goldstein's Greatest Hits
Prentice–Hall, 1970. 228pp. $7.95. Essays on rock and roll music by the editor of "New York Magazine." The reviews, essays, and interviews are collected from the various publications in which they originally appeared from 1966 through 1969. Index.

HALL, DOUGLAS KENT and SUE C. CLARK
Rock: A World Bold As Love
Cowles, 1970. 192pp. $7.95. A collection of comments on the music, the performers, and the world of "Rock." Hundreds of personalities from the music industry were interviewed for their comments. Lavishly illustrated with photographs of the performers. Index.

HEMPHILL, PAUL
The Nashville Sound: Bright Lights and Country Music
Simon & Schuster, 1970. 289pp. $5.95. A description of what country and western music is, where it came from, where it's going, and what it means to the listeners and the people who write, play, and make their livings from it. Index.

HOPKINS, JERRY
The Rock Story
Signet, 1970. 222pp. Paper $ .95. A history of rock and roll music with a selection of essays on how a hit is made, the fans, the rock star, and the rise and fall of a group. Illustrated with photographs. Discography.

JONES, LE ROI
Black Music
Morrow, 1968. 221pp. Paper $1.95. Originally published in 1967 and now reissued, this is a collection of essays, reviews, interviews, musical analyses, and personal impressions of jazz musicians. All of the pieces were written between 1959 and 1967. Four photographs.

JONES, LE ROI
Blues People
Morrow, 1970. 244pp. Paper $1.95. Originally published in 1963 and now reissued, this is an interpretation of Negro music in America. Mr. Jones attempts to place jazz and the blues within the context of American social history. Index.

LIEBER, LESLIE
How to Form a Rock Group
Grosset & Dunlap, 1968. 128pp. $3.95. A step-by-step guide for young musicians on forming their own rock music group. The history of a group named the Forum Quorum is detailed. Information on buying instruments, rehearsing, auditioning, making recordings and commercials, costumes, and production of the total act is provided. Illustrated with photographs.

LINDSAY, MARTIN
Teach Yourself Songwriting
Dover, 1968. 160pp. $2.50. Originally published in 1955 and now reissued in a revised edition. The author sets forth "the tricks of the trade" of writing songs. The popular song market, the lyric and the melody, and the selling of the completed song are all covered. Appendices. Glossary. Index.

MABEY, RICHARD
The Pop Process
Hutchinson, 1969. 190pp. $7.50. A critical account of the world of "pop" music in the 1960's. The social and musical importance of the music is analyzed with special emphasis on the achievements of the Beatles and Bob Dylan. List of Books for Further Reading.

MALONE, BILL C.
Country Music, U.S.A.
University of Texas, 1968. 422pp. $7.50. A history of country music and its performers from its beginnings in the Southern rural culture before the 1920's through the Nashville sound of the 1960's. Illustrated. Bibliography. Index.

MARCUSE, MAXWELL F.
Tin Pan Alley in Gaslight: A Saga of the Songs that Made the Gay Nineties "Gay"
Century House, 1959. 448pp. $12.00. A history of the most important and most successful songs of the period, 1870–1910, with biographical sketches of important composers. Illustrated with reproductions of sheet music and posters of the period.

MELLY, GEORGE
Revolt Into Style: The Pop Arts in Britain
See Page 506

MELTZER, RICHARD
The Aesthetics of Rock
Something Else Press, 1970. 346pp. $6.95. A kaleidoscopic philosophical inquiry of rock and roll music by one of its practicioners. Illustrated with photographs. Index.

MYRUS, DONALD
Ballads, Blues and the Big Beat
Macmillan, 1966. 136pp. $3.95. Highlights of American folk singing from Leadbelly to Bob Dylan. Illustrated. Index.

NETTI, BRUNO
An Introduction to Folk Music in the United States
Wayne State University, 1962. 69pp. Paper $2.50. A study of the variety of forms and cultures represented in the folk music in this country. The emphasis is on the music itself rather than the words. The author goes beyond what is usually included in folk music to discuss and show the use of folk music in the modern city, in the professional singer's repertory, and in art music. Illustrated with thirty-two musical examples. Bibliography.

OLIVER, PAUL
The Meaning of the Blues
Collier, 1963. 383pp. Paper $ .95. A study of the historical development of the blues. The book is also a social history of the Negro in America. Foreword by Richard Wright. A Discography of quoted blues songs is given.

OLIVER, PAUL
The Story of the Blues
Chilton, 1969. 176pp. $12.50. Illustrated with more than 500 photographs and drawings, numerous musical examples, blues lyrics, and a Selective Discography, this is the complete story of the blues from the African slaves in post-Civil War America, the

blues in New Orleans, and the influence of blues in modern rock. Among the great musicians reviewed are: Leadbelly, Ma Rainey, Bessie Smith, Jelly Roll Morton, Fats Domino, and hundreds of others. Index.

RAMSEY, JR., FREDERIC
Been Here and Gone
Rutgers University, 1969. 177pp. Paper $2.95. A reprint of the 1960 publication, this is a record of the life and musical activity of black Americans in the deep South. The volume helps to reveal the development of Afro-American music in the United States. The text is illustrated with photographs.

RIVELLI, PAULINE and ROBERT LEVIN – Editors
The Rock Giants
World, 1970. 125pp. $5.95. A collection of articles, interviews, and profiles from "Jazz and Pop Magzine" on the music and attitudes of today's young musicians in the "pop revolution." Among the musicians interviewed are Eric Clapton, Frank Zappa, Donovan, Canned Heat, Jefferson Airplane, and John and Yoko Lennon. Illustrated with photographs.

ROHDE, H. KANDY
The Gold of Rock & Roll: 1955 – 1967
World, 1970. 352pp. $8.95. Paper $4.95. A week-by-week, year-by-year recall of the most popular recordings and artists in the popular music field. Special appreciations of the music, people, and events are included. Illustrated with photographs. Indices.

ROXON, LILLIAN
Rock Encyclopedia
Grosset & Dunlap, 1969. 613pp. $9.95. A reference book on rock music. Biographies, discographies, commentary, analysis, and miscellany on over 1,200 personalities and 22,000 songs. Illustrated with photographs. Appendices.

SHAPIRO, NAT and NAT HENTOFF – Editors
Hear Me Talkin' to Ya
Dover, 1966. 429pp. Paper $2.50. Originally published in 1955 and now reissued, this is the story of jazz as told by the men who made it, among them: Louis Armstrong, King Oliver, Duke Ellington, Jelly Roll Morton, Billie Holiday, and many others. Index.

SHAW, ARNOLD
The World of Soul
Cowles, 1970. 306pp. $6.95. The author traces the evolution of American black music from the itinerant country blues through the classic singers and black pop artists of today. Mr. Shaw analyzes each stage in the growth of the music, how style changes have occurred, and gives insights into the lives and personalities of the artists involved. Among the musicians studied are Blind Lemon Jefferson, Bessie Smith, Louis Armstrong, and Aretha Franklin. Illustrated with photographs. Selected Discography. Index.

SHELTON, ROBERT and BURT GOLDBLATT
The Country Music Story
Bobbs-Merrill, 1966. 256pp. $7.50. A picture history of country and western music over the past forty years. Illustrated. Index.

SIMON, GEORGE T.
The Big Bands
Macmillan, 1967. 537pp. $9.95. Mr. Simon recreates the era of the mid-thirties to the mid-forties when the big bands held forth. The full story of each of 400 bands including Duke Ellington, Tommy Dorsey, Benny Goodman, Guy Lombardo, and many others. The role of the leaders, the arrangers, the soloists, the vocalists, the managers, the publishers, and the public are all discussed. More than 250 photographs are included and Frank Sinatra has written a Foreword. Index.

STAMBLER, IRWIN and GRELUN LANDON
Encyclopedia of Folk, Country, and Western Music
St. Martin's, 1969. 396pp. $12.50. This reference work includes approximately 500 entries ranging from biographies of folk and country music personalities, definition of terms, and discussions of major classes of the various types of music. Entries cover special events and instruments. Bibliography. Discography. Illustrated with nearly a hundred photographs.

STAMBLER, IRWIN
Encyclopedia of Popular Music
St. Martin's, 1965. 359pp. $10.00. More than 300 entries, plus articles, provide a comprehensive survey of the entire field of popular music, concentrating on the period from 1925. Synopses of over seventy major musicals, biographies of leading composers and performers, and information on unions and organizations are included. Illustrated. Discography. Index.

STEARNS, MARSHALL W.
The Story of Jazz
Oxford, 1970. 379pp. Paper $2.95. Originally published in 1956 and now reissued with an expanded Bibliography and syllabus, this is a history of jazz from the African Negro's musical heritage to the birth of American jazz in New Orleans and its dissemination to St. Louis, Chicago, Kansas City, and New York to the evolution of rock in the 1950's. Illustrated with photographs. Index.

WILLIAMS, MARTIN
Jazz Masters in Transition 1957 – 69
Macmillan, 1970. 288pp. $6.95. This collection of reviews, interviews, profiles, and narratives provides an encyclopedic record of the contemporary jazz music scene of the last decade. Illustrated with eight pages of photographs.

WILLIAMS, MARTIN – Editor
Jazz Panorama
Macmillan, 1964. 318pp. $4.95. Paper $1.50. An

anthology of selections from "The Jazz Review," with interviews, reminiscences, and reviews that cover the jazz scene from the birth of Dixieland to the latest "third stream" innovations.

WILLIAMS, MARTIN
The Jazz Tradition
Oxford, 1970. 232pp. $6.50. Essays on sixteen major figures describing their music in detail, evaluating their contributions, and showing how they have influenced one another. Some of the musicians studied are Jelly Roll Morton, Louis Armstrong, Billie Holiday, Duke Ellington, Miles Davis, and Ornette Coleman. Discographical Notes.

SONG BOOKS

ALDRIDGE, ALAN – Editor
The Beatles Illustrated Lyrics
Delacorte, 1969. 156pp. $5.95. A collection of the lyrics of the English music group. Autobiographical comments and quotes and interpretation of the lyrics by the Beatles themselves are included. Photographs of the group and full-color illustrations by internationally known artists complete the book.

ASCH, MOSES and ALAN LOMAX – Editors
The Leadbelly Songbook
Oak, 1963. 97pp. Paper $1.95. A collection of the ballads, blues, and folk songs of Huddie Ledbetter. Musical transcriptions have been made by Jerry Silver. The editors have provided essays and biographical sketches. Illustrated. Discography. Index.

AUDEN, W.H. and CHESTER KALLMANN, NOAH GREENBERG
An Anthology of Elizabethan Lute Songs, Madrigals, and Rounds
Norton, 1970. 242pp. Paper $1.95. Originally published in 1955 as "An Elizabethan Song Book" and now reissued, this is a collection of songs from the Elizabethan period. An introduction on the poetry by Auden and Kallman and an introduction to the music by Greenberg are provided. Indices.

BACHARACH, BURT and HAL DAVID
The Bacharach and David Song Book
Simon & Schuster, 1970. 127pp. $7.50. The words and music for thirty-seven of the songs of the popular composer and lyricist. Introduction by Dionne Warwick. Music arranged for piano and guitar by Norman Monath.

BONI, MARGARET BRADFORD
Fireside Book of Folk Songs
Simon & Schuster, 1947. 323pp. $6.95. 147 favorite folk songs arranged for piano and guitar by Norman Lloyd and illustrated in color by Alice and Martin Provensen. Index of First Lines.

BRECHT, BERTOLT and HANNS EISLER
The Brecht-Eisler Song Book
Oak, 1967. 192pp. $10.00. A book of songs and poems by Brecht and Eisler in German and English. Forty-two songs are included with piano arrangements and guitar chords. The music has been edited by Earl Robinson, well-known composer, and Eric Bentley has written notes on the songs. A Bibliography and a Discography are included.

CHAPPELL, WILLIAM
The Ballad Literature and Popular Music of the Olden Time
Dover, 1965. 822pp. Paper. Two volume set $5.50. A comprehensive anthology of English secular ballads, songs, and dance tunes. More than 400 airs are given with music, words and variants. The collection ranges from the beginning of the Middle Ages to the end of the eighteenth century. Index of First Lines. Subject Index.

COWARD, NOEL
The Lyrics of Noel Coward
Heinemann, 1965. 418pp. $13.50. A complete collection of the lyrics of Mr. Coward's songs from the 1920's through the production of "The Girl Who Came to Supper" in the 1960's. Coward includes a General Introduction and a note on each era.

DEUTSCH, LEONHARD
A Treasury of the World's Finest Folk Song
Crown, 1967. 400pp. $12.50. A revised edition of the 1942 publication, this collection contains 171 folk songs from thirty languages, all with piano and guitar accompaniments. Songs are grouped by country or region, and Claude Simpson has provided a text that is an informal history of folk song, giving the background of each national group and commenting on each song.

EWEN, DAVID
American Popular Songs: From the Revolutionary War to the Present
Random House, 1966. 507pp. $10.00. An encyclopedia of over 4,000 American songs with more than 1,000 cross-references to the composers, lyricists, musical comedies and motion pictures.

FLEMING–WILLIAMS, NAN and PAT SHULDHAM–SHAW
A Popular Selection of English Dance Airs. Book One
English Folk Dance and Song Society, 1965. 16pp. Paper $1.00. The music for country dance tunes from the seventeenth and eighteenth centuries.

FRIEDMAN, ALBERT B.
The Viking Book of Folk Ballads of the English-Speaking World
Viking, 1956. 469pp. $4.95. Paper $2.25. Drawing upon the entire folk literature of England, Scotland, Ireland, Canada, the United States, the West Indies,

and Australia, this collection presents authentic texts of complete ballads with many variant readings. Ballads are grouped according to subject or locale and there is an introductory note for each group. Bibliography. Glossary. Index.

GERSHWIN, GEORGE and IRA GERSHWIN
The George and Ira Gershwin Song Book
Simon & Schuster, 1960. 178pp. $10.00. All the extra verses and choruses and patter from the songs as they were originally sung with introductions and marginalia on the songs by Ira Gershwin and Gershwin's piano arrangements. Edited by Dr. Albert Sirmay. An Appendix gives information on all the shows and films.

GERSHWIN, IRA
Lyrics on Several Occasions
Knopf, 1959. 362pp. $5.00. A collection of lyrics written over the last thirty-five years by Ira Gershwin in collaboration with such musicians as George Gershwin, Jerome Kern, Kurt Weill, Harold Arlen, Arthur Schwartz, and others.

GLAZER, TOM
A New Treasury of Folk Songs
Bantam, 1961. 182pp. Paper $ .60. An anthology of 152 songs of all types with words and easy guitar accompaniments. Self-instruction lessons for playing the guitar are included.

HATTORI, RYUTARO
Japanese Folk Songs with Piano Accompaniment
Japan Times, 1964. 100pp. Paper $3.75. A collection of thirty-eight songs from all sections of the Japanese Islands. Texts are in Japanese and English.

HAYWOOD, CHARLES
Folk Songs of the World
Putnam, 1966. 320pp. $10.95. This collection presents 180 songs from 119 countries. The volume also contains a General Introduction, commentary on the musical culture of each area, notes on each song, chord suggestions, and a Bibliography.

HEALEY, JAMES N.
Ballads from the Pubs of Ireland
Herder, 1965. 142pp. Paper $2.00. Lyrics of old Irish ballads. Index of First Lines.

HILLE, WALDEMAR – Editor
The People's Song Book
Oak, 1959. 128pp. Paper $1.95. The four parts of this collection are: Songs that Helped Build America; World Freedom Songs; Union Songs; Topical-Political Songs. Foreword by Alan Lomax.

JACKSON, GEORGE PULLEN
Spiritual Folk-Songs in Early America
Dover, 1964. 244pp. Paper $2.00. A collection of 250 tunes, with texts, dating from the 1800's, which illustrate how religious lyrics were adapted to secular melodies. Notes on the history of each song. Twelve half-tone illustrations.

LEHRER, TOM
Tom Lehrer's Second Song Book
Crown, 1968. 64pp. $2.95. A collection of fifteen songs with words and music by the noted singer and composer. Piano transcriptions have been provided by Frank Metis.

LERNER, ALAN JAY and FREDERICK LOEWE
The Lerner and Loewe Song Book
Simon & Schuster, 1962. 255pp. $10.00. The words and music for forty-six songs arranged for voice and piano, with guitar chords. The songs are from such shows as "My Fair Lady," Paint Your Wagon," "Brigadoon," "The Day Before Spring," "Gigi," and "Camelot." Stories of the shows, production histories and pictures are included.

LOMAX, ALAN
The Folk Songs of North America
Doubleday, 1960. 623pp. $8.50. A collection of words and music of over 300 songs. In each case the origin and development of each is explained by detailed quotations from folk tales, biographies, and from other American documents. The whole work is a folk history of the United States. Illustrated with drawings and end maps. Index.

LOMAX, ALAN – Editor
The Penguin Book of American Folk Songs
Penguin, 1964. 159pp. Paper $1.95. Music and lyrics for 111 ballads, love songs, lullabies, work and cowboy songs, and spirituals popular in America from Colonial days to the present. Guitar chords and an illustrated method for learning to play the guitar accompaniments are provided. Piano arrangements are by Elizabeth Poston.

LOMAX, JOHN A. and ALAN LOMAX
American Ballads and Folk Songs
Macmillan, 1966. 625pp. $8.95. Originally published in 1934, this collection of ballads and folk songs includes short notes about the origins of the tunes, a Bibliography and an Index.

LOMAX, JOHN A. and ALAN LOMAX
Folk Song U.S.A.
New American Library, 1966. 512pp. Paper $ .95. This is a reprint of the 1947 work. It includes 111 American ballads with words and music for piano and guitar, plus folk tales and anecdotes about collecting. Music arrangements are by Charles and Ruth Seeger. Index.

MacCOLL, EWAN and PEGGY SEEGER
Ewan MacColl-Peggy Seeger Songbook
Oak, 1963. 94pp. Paper $2.45. The collection of songs in this volume includes songs of labor, songs of social protest, and propaganda songs, mainly those

that have grown out of the "Ban the Bomb" movement. Glossary of archaic words, a Discography, and an Index to Titles and First Lines.

McKUEN, ROD
The World of Rod McKuen
Random House, 1968. 113pp. $4.95. Twenty-two songs with music by Rod McKuen. Piano arrangements for these never-before-published songs have been provided by Ben Kendall. Helen Miljakovich provided the photographic illustrations of the songwriter.

OKUN, MILTON – Arranger
Something to Sing About!
Macmillan, 1968. 241pp. $8.95. Paper $3.95. More than seventy folk songs chosen by America's most distinguished folk artists as their own favorites. Each song has been arranged by Mr. Okun for piano and guitar. Also provided is a brief analysis and critique of each artist. Illustrated with photographs.

PORTER, COLE
The Cole Porter Song Book
Simon & Schuster, 1959. 215pp. $12.50. The complete music and lyrics to forty songs by Porter with a Foreword by Moss Hart. Data on productions with songs by Porter is provided.

ROBINSON, EARL – Editor
Young Folk Song Book
Simon & Schuster, 1963. 112pp. $5.95. Paper $2.95. The most popular songs of Joan Baez, Bob Dylan, Jack Elliott, the Greenbriar Boys, the New Lost City Ramblers, and Peggy Seeger, published for the first time as they sing them, with arrangements for voice, piano, guitar, banjo, and mandolin by Earl Robinson. Introduction by Pete Seeger.

SANDBURG, CARL
The American Songbag
Harcourt, Brace, 1927. 495pp. $5.95. The words and music to 280 songs, ballads, and ditties which have been sung throughout American history. Each song is introduced by Mr. Sandburg, and there is a summary of its theme and historical background.

SCOTT, JOHN ANTHONY
The Ballad of America
Grosset & Dunlap, 1967. 404pp. $5.95. This book attempts to show the history of America through its songs. Songs for each period of American history are included. There are words and music to more than 125 songs with guitar chords for many of them. Index of Titles and First Lines. General Index.

SEEGER, PETE
American Favorite Ballads: Songs and Tunes As Sung by Pete Seeger
Oak, 1961. 96pp. Paper $1.95. A collection of more than eighty ballads in the versions sung by Mr. Seeger. Each song has chord notations for the guitar. Mr. Seeger introduces each song, and there are illustrations from period prints and a Discography.

SHELTON, ROBERT and WALTER RAIM
The Josh White Song Book
Quadrangle, 1963. 191pp. $6.95. Paper $2.95. The biographical section by Mr. Shelton traces White's life from his boyhood in South Carolina through the decades of the '30's and '40's, to his present position as the foremost ballad singer. The music section, fifty-seven songs arranged for piano and guitar by Mr. Raim, embraces the best of Josh White. Discography and Index of First Lines.

SHELTON, ROBERT and WALTER RAIM
The Mitchell Trio Song Book
Quadrangle, 1964. 144pp. $6.95. Paper $2.95. A collection of thirty-five of the Trio's most famous songs with a Discography.

SIEGMEISTER, ELIE – Editor
The Joan Baez Songbook
Crown, 1964. 189pp. $5.95. Paper $3.95. Sixty-six songs from the repertory of one of America's best known folk singers. The songs are arranged for voice and piano with chord progressions for guitar.

SILBER, IRWIN – Editor
Lift Every Voice!: The Second People's Songbook
Oak, 1953. 96pp. Paper $1.95. The sections of this collection are entitled: "Study War No More," "Commonwealth of Toil," "Wasn't That A Time," and "A Man's A Man for All That." Introduction by Paul Robeson.

VOCAL TRAINING

ADLER, KURT
Phonetics and Diction in Singing
University of Minnesota, 1967. 161pp. Paper $1.95. Originally published in 1965 and now reissued, this book provides rules and illustrative examples for the study of songs and opera in the leading foreign languages of musical literature. Following a general discourse on phonetics and diction in singing, there are separate chapters on Italian, French, Spanish, and German phonetics and diction. The text is illustrated with musical examples and drawings and diagrams of vocal techniques. Index.

BERKOWITZ, SOL and GABRIEL FRONTRIER, LEO KRAFT
A New Approach to Sight Singing
Norton, 1960. 330pp. $6.50. In five chapters with supplementary exercises in musical drill, this book presents a coordinated body of musical material specifically composed for sight reading. Glossary of Foreign Language Terms.

FUCHS, VICTOR
The Art of Singing and Voice Technique
Calder & Boyars, 1967. 219pp. Paper $2.95. A handbook for voice teachers, professional and amateur singers. This is a new and revised edition of the work first published in 1963. Illustrated with drawings, diagrams, and photographs.

GRIFFITH, GEORGE
Artistry in Singing
Belle-Maria, 1965. 246pp. Paper $3.95. This is an approach to the study of lieder for the American singer. This book presents a background in lieder and traces the changing emphasis in the settings of German lieder. Illustrated with musical examples. Bibliography. Index.

HERBERT–CAESARI, E.
Vocal Truth
Robert Hale, 1969. 110pp. $4.50. Published in England, this is a discussion of the author's own approach and modus operandi in teaching vocal technique and singing to his students. Special emphasis is laid on the question of establishing the particular category of voice the student possesses and on the question of breathing.

KLEIN, JOSEPH J. and OLE A. SCHJEIDE
Singing Technique: How to Avoid Vocal Trouble
Van Nostrand, 1967. 145pp. $6.95. This is an explanation for singers and speakers on the basic fundamentals of voice production. The authors explain support and how to get it to work, explain the falsetto, and provide practical exercises to control muscles for vowel and resonance formation. Illustrated. Index.

LIEBERMAN, MAURICE
Ear Training and Sight Singing
Norton, 1959. 326pp. Paper and spiral bound. $7.50. This text aims to help the student in development of his ear training skills. It offers almost a thousand carefully selected melodies and rhythm exercises. There are also exercises in tonal and rhythmic drill, intervals, memorization, modulation, etc. Illustrated with musical passages. Glossary.

METZGER, ZERLINE MUHLMAN
Individual Voice Patterns
Carlton Press, 1966. 93pp. $3.00. This is a guide to the author's method for uncovering inborn correct vibrato patterns for the individual singer. Mrs. Metzger discusses such varied subjects as the origin of the Individual Voice Pattern Concept, the influences that affect the singer, the procedure for discovering and applying individual voice patterns, and she includes many of her own devices for vocal improvement. Illustrated with musical examples. Index.

PUNT, NORMAN A.
The Singer's and Actor's Throat
Heinemann, 1967. 99pp. Paper $3.95. Originally published in 1952, this second edition studies the vocal mechanism of the professional voice user and its care in health and disease. The author is adviser to The National Theatre Company, The Royal Shakespeare Company, and other companies in England. Bibliography. Index.

REID, CORNELIUS L.
The Free Voice: A Guide to Natural Singing
Coleman–Ross, 1965. 225pp. $6.95. Mr. Reid derives his system of vocal training from the nature of the vocal function itself. His practical program for achieving volitional control over involuntary muscular responses within the laryngeal complex is set forth. Index.

SUNDERMAN, LLOYD F.
Artistic Singing: Its Tone Production and Basic Understandings
Scarecrow, 1970. 159pp. $5.25. A guidebook to help vocal students and teachers, professional singers, and choral directors attain the desirable tone quality essential to artistic singing. Discussion and a series of exercises aid in understanding and overcoming problems associated with resonance, register development, and diction. Twenty-two detailed lessons on vowel, consonant, and dipthongal actions are included. Illustrated with drawings and musical examples. Bibliography.

THORPE, C. R.
A Short Course in Singing
Funk & Wagnalls, 1968. 124pp. Paper $ .95. Originally published in 1954 and now reissued, this is a course in singing for the amateur. Six weeks of progressive daily lessons are systematically arranged in two sections. Part I is devoted to the cultivation of the singing voice and Part II trains in sight reading.

WINSEL, REGNIER
The Anatomy of Voice: An Illustrated Manual of Vocal Training
Exposition, 1966. 96pp. $4.00. Mr. Winsel, a coach and teacher, has developed a method based on physical, psychological and acoustical laws, combined with special exercises to balance and strengthen the vocal mechanism and coordinate the action with the proper mental impulses.

BIOGRAPHIES

Collected (By Author)

CHILTON, JOHN
Who's Who of Jazz: Storyville to Swing Street
Bloomsbury, 1970. 447pp. $18.50. Biographies of over 1,000 musicians born before 1920 in the United States. Illustrated with photographs.

KUTSCH, K. J. and LEO RIEMENS
A Concise Biographical Dictionary of Singers
Chilton, 1969. 487pp. $14.95. Originally published in Europe and now translated by Harry Earl Jones, this is an international reference book with full biographies on almost 1,500 artists and performers from forty countries. Almost every artist who has recorded from the 1880's to the present is included. Roles, recordings, personal and professional data, description of voice and repertory, and publications are all included. Glossary. List of Operas, Operettas, and Composers.

WAGENKNECHT, EDWARD
Seven Daughters of the Theatre
See Page 262

Individual (By Subject)

Anderson, Marian

ANDERSON, MARIAN
My Lord, What a Morning
Avon, 1956. 222pp. Paper $ .60. An autobiography by the famous singer.

Armstrong, Louis

ARMSTRONG, LOUIS
Satchmo
Signet, 1970. 191pp. Paper $ .95. The biography of the great jazz musician told in his own words. Originally published in 1954 and now reissued.

Arnold, Eddy

ARNOLD, EDDY
It's A Long Way From Chester County
Hewitt House, 1969. 154pp. $4.95. The autobiography of the country music singer. It details all the aspects of his successful climb to fame from sharecropping in Tennessee to hosting "Grand Ole Opry" to his present status as concert, recording, and television star. Illustrated with photographs.

Baez, Joan

BAEZ, JOAN
Daybreak
Dial, 1968. 159pp. $3.95. Paper—Avon, 1969. 191pp. $.95. This is an informal self-portrait by the folk singer. In the anecdotes and retelling of her dreams, she acknowledges her commitments to music, love, and peace.

Bailey, Pearl

BAILEY, PEARL
The Raw Pearl
See Page 263

Beatles, The

ANONYMOUS
The Beatle Book
Lancer, 1964. Unpaged. Paper $ .50. A biography and appreciation of the musical quartet from their early days to the 1960's. Illustrated with almost 100 photographs.

DAVIES, HUNTER
The Beatles: The Authorized Biography
McGraw—Hill, 1968. 357pp. $6.95. Paper—Dell, 1969. 405pp. $ .95. The author has pieced together the complete story of the Beatles from their school days to the present. The four musicians and their friends and families give candid information on their personalities, their lives and their music. Illustrated with photographs. Discography.

DAVIS, EDWARD E.—Editor
The Beatles Book
Cowles, 1968. 213pp. $5.95. Fourteen essays on the popular entertainers by critics and writers. The quartet's movies, poetry, religion, and their social thought are all discussed by contributors Timothy Leary, William F. Buckley, Jr., Ned Rorem, Ralph J. Gleason, and others. A Discography is included.

EPSTEIN, BRIAN
A Cellarful of Noise
See Page 300

FAST, JULIUS
The Beatles: The Real Story
Putnam, 1968. 252pp. $5.95. This biography of the Beatles is an in-depth profile of their achievements in their lives, past and present, and in their music. The music is analyzed with a view to understanding what the composers are doing and what their sounds mean. Illustrated with photographs.

SCADUTO, ANTHONY
The Beatles

Signet, 1968. 157pp. Paper $ .75. A biography of the English musical group which concentrates on their lives since the popular success. Illustrated with photographs.

Belafonte, Harry

SHAW, ARNOLD
Belafonte
Pyramid, 1967. 287pp. Paper $ .50. Reprint of the biography of Harry Belafonte, the popular singer. Eight pages of photographs.

Bernstein, Leonard

EWEN, DAVID
Leonard Bernstein
Chilton, 1960. 153pp. $4.25. An account of the composer-conductor's career from the night he substituted as conductor for the New York Philharmonic and created a sensation to his success on Broadway with "West Side Story." A list of works and recordings is included.

GRUEN, JOHN
The Private World of Leonard Bernstein
Viking, 1968. 191pp. $12.50. In text, and in pictures by Ken Heyman, the private life of composer-conductor, Leonard Bernstein, is revealed. Included are reports on an evening with Charlie Chaplin and a complete description by Mr. Bernstein of his debut as a conductor in 1943.

Boulton, Laura

BOULTON, LAURA
The Music Hunter
Doubleday, 1969. 513pp. $8.95. This is the autobiography of the noted musicologist. it details her search to discover and record the traditional and liturgical music of the people living in little known parts of the world. Illustrated. Index.

Bradford, Perry

BRADFORD, PERRY
Born with the Blues
Oak, 1965. 175pp. $5.95. Paper $2.95. The autobiography of Perry Bradford, song writer and publisher, this book is also a history of the early days of jazz. Illustrated. Index.

Campbell, Glen

KRAMER, FREDA
The Glen Campbell Story
Pyramid, 1970. 125pp. Paper $ .75. A biography of the popular singer from his youth in Arkansas to his success as a singer with hit records, and television and movie stardom. Illustrated with sixteen pages of photographs.

Carmichael, Hoagy

CARMICHAEL, HOAGY with STEPHEN LONGSTREET
Sometimes I Wonder
Redman, 1966. 312pp. $5.50. Hoagy Carmichael's story of his life and his careers as a lawyer, piano player, singer, composer, and star of motion pictures, radio, and television.

Chaliapin, Feodor

GORKY, MAXIM
Chaliapin: An Autobiography
Stein & Day, 1967. 320pp. $10.00. Paper $3.95. The first publication in the West of the opera star's life as he told it to his contemporary, Maxim Gorky. The work has been translated, compiled, and edited from the original Russian by Nina Froud and James Hanley. Included is a large selection of Chaliapin's correspondence, a listing of the singer's repertoire, notes on persons mentioned, and a Bibliography. Illustrated with eighty-nine photographs and reproductions of art work. Index.

Christie, John

BLUNT, WILFRID
John Christie of Glyndebourne
Theatre Arts, 1968. 303pp. $7.45. This is the biography of the founder of the Glyndebourne Festival Opera House in England. It tells of his childhood, the manor house which was deeded to him, his marriage to opera star, Audrey Mildmay, and his creation of the Opera Festival. Illustrated with photographs. Index.

Cotton, Billy

COTTON, BILLY
I Did It My Way
Harrap, 1970. 192pp. $6.50. The autobiography of the late English entertainer and musical personality. Dubbed ''Mr. Show Business'' in England, the author details the spirited dance crazes of the 1920's, the nightlife of the '30's, his appearances on radio and television, and his repeated Royal Command performances. Illustrated with photographs. Index.

Davis, Jr., Sammy

DAVIS, SAMMY and BURT BOYAR, JANE BOYAR
Yes, I Can
See Page 266

Dylan, Bob

KRAMER, DANIEL
Bob Dylan
Citadel, 1967. 159pp. $2.95. Paper—Pocket Books, 1968. 214pp. $ .95. The photographer attempts to capture a segment of folk singer-composer Bob Dylan's life in words and pictures during the period of two years in which he became the most popular musician in the folk music world.

Epstein, Brian

EPSTEIN, BRIAN
A Cellarful of Noise
Pyramid, 1965. 127pp. Paper $ .50. An autobiography by the man who discovered and managed the Beatles. Epstein details their world-wide success from the day he first heard the singers in Liverpool, England. Illustrated with four pages of photographs.

Flagstad, Kirsten

McARTHUR, EDWIN
Flagstad: A Personal Memoir
Knopf, 1965. 343pp. $7.95. An intimate portrait of Kirsten Flagstad from her first appearance at the Metropolitan Opera House in 1935 to her death on December 2, 1962. An Appendix lists her roles with date of first performance and number of performances. Illustrated.

Gallo, Fortune T.

GALLO, FORTUNE T.
Lucky Rooster
Exposition, 1967. 304pp. $6.00. This is the autobiography of the impresario and founder of the San Carlo Opera Company. Included are anecdotes about most of the theatrical greats of the twentieth century including Anna Pavlova, Caruso, Lillian Russell, Helen Traubel, John McCormack, and George M. Cohan.

Gershwin, George

BRYANT, BERNICE
George Gershwin: Young Composer
Bobbs Merrill, 1965. 200pp. $2.75. Written for young people, this is the story of the childhood of Gershwin through the first public performance of the ''Rhapsody in Blue'' in 1924. Illustrated.

EWEN, DAVID
George Gershwin: His Journey to Greatness
Prentice–Hall, 1970. 354pp. $7.95. Originally published as ''A Journey to Greatness,'' this biography has now been rewritten, expanded and up-dated. The author has traced Gershwin's development from first hand information obtained from the Gershwin family, personal letters, scrapbooks, diaries, and interviews with famous contemporaries. Illustrated with photographs. Appendices include lists of works. Index.

GOLDBERG, ISAAC and EDITH GARSON
George Gershwin: A Study in American Music
Ungar, 1958. 387pp. $6.50. Paper $1.95. Originally published in 1931 and now supplemented by Edith Garson, this is a biography of the American composer. Selected Discography. Illustrated. Index.

RUSHMORE, ROBERT
The Life of George Gershwin
Macmillan, 1966. 177pp. $3.50. A biography of the composer. Illustrated. Discography. Index.

Guthrie, Woody

GUTHRIE, WOODY
Bound for Glory
Dutton, 1968. 430pp. $6.95. Paper $2.45. Also—New American Library, 1970. 320pp. Paper $1.25. Originally published in 1943, this new edition of the biography of the American folk song composer and performer covers the period from his birth to 1942 when he was on the theshold of fame. Pete Seeger has contributed a Foreword. Illustrated with drawings by Guthrie.

Horne, Lena

HORNE, LENA and RICHARD SCHICKEL
Lena
See Page 270

Jackson, Mahalia

JACKSON, MAHALIA with EVAN MCLEOD WYLIE
Movin' On Up
Hawthorn, 1966. 212pp. $5.95. Paper—Avon, 1969. 224pp. $ .75. The autobiography of the American Negro gospel singer. Illustrated with photographs. A Discography is included.

Jones, Tom

JONES, PETER
Tom Jones
Regnery, 1970. 161pp. $4.95. The biography of the popular singer from Wales. The author details his life from his youth as a miner's son to his international success as a recording and television star and the highest paid entertainer in the history of British show business. Illustrated with twenty-four pages of photographs. The author has also included a complete Discography.

Kelly, Michael

KELLY, MICHAEL
The Reminiscences of Michael Kelly
Blom, 1969. 424pp. $18.50. Originally published in 1826 and now reissued in a facsimile edition, compiled by Theodore Edward Hook, this is the biography of the eighteenth century opera tenor and composer. The volume includes many anecdotes of his travels in Europe and meetings with famous opera and theatre personalities.

Kern, Jerome

EWEN, DAVID
The Story of Jerome Kern
Holt, Rinehart, 1962. 140pp. $3.59. A study of the man and his music, written for children in grades 7—9. Lists of songs, stage shows, and motion pictures for which he composed music are provided. Discography.

EWEN, DAVID
The World of Jerome Kern: A Biography
Holt, Rinehart, 1960. 178pp. $3.95. A comprehensive biographical study with a history of all Kern's major works and complete listing of his output. Illustrated.

Lauder, Harry

IRVING, GORDON
Great Scot!
Frewin, 1968. 184pp. $5.95. The biography of Sir Harry Lauder, Scots entertainer. The early years and struggles before he won world reknown, his American tours, and his success in the English and Scots music halls are all detailed. Illustrated with photographs. A list of the songs he composed is also included. Index.

Lawrence, Marjorie

LAWRENCE, MARJORIE
Interrupted Melody: The Story of My Life
Southern Illinois University, 1968. 307pp. $7.00. Paper $2.85. Originally published in 1949, and now reissued, this is the autobiography of the renowned opera singer who suffered infantile paralysis at the height of her career. The overcoming of that disability is detailed in the singer's book. Illustrated with sixteen pages of photographs. Index.

Merrill, Robert

MERRILL, ROBERT and SANFORD DODY
Once More from the Beginning
Macmillan, 1965. 286pp. $5.95. The story of Moishe Miller, the boy from the Brooklyn tenement who became Robert Merrill, one of the great baritones. The singer records his years at the Metropolitan Opera, his flop in Hollywood, and his fight with Rudolph Bing. Illustrated with sixteen pages of photographs. Index.

Morrison, Jim

JAHN, MIKE
Jim Morrison and the Doors
Grosset & Dunlap, 1969. 96pp. Paper $1.00. "An unauthorized book" about the rock musicians. Illustrated with photographs.

Peters, Roberta

PETERS, ROBERTA and LOUIS BIANCOLLI
A Debut at the Met
Meredith, 1967. 86pp. $3.50. This is the story of Miss Peters' preparation for her career as a singer and her debut at the Metropolitan Opera in 1950.

Piaf, Edith

PIAF, EDITH
The Wheel of Fortune
Chilton, 1965. 192pp. $4.50. The autobiography of the celebrated French singer. Illustrated.

Porter, Cole

EELLS, GEORGE
The Life that Late He Led
Putnam, 1967. 383pp. $6.95. A definitive biography of Cole Porter. The author had access to Porter's private papers and journals and conducted extensive interviews with Porter's friends and colleagues. Also included is a complete Bibliography of the works and the first publication of Porter's Hollywood diary. Illustrated. Index.

EWEN, DAVID
The Cole Porter Story
Holt, Rinehart, 1965. 192pp. $3.50. Porter's days at Harvard as an undergraduate, his service in the French Foreign Legion, his marriage to a Kentucky socialite, and their life with the international set—all the aspects of the lighter side of the Porter story are treated in this book.

Richard, Cliff

FERRIER, BOB
The Wonderful World of Cliff Richard
Peter Davies, 1964. 247pp. $5.00. Published in England, this is a biography of the popular entertainer. Illustrated with five pages of photographs.

WINTER, DAVID
New Singer, New Song
Hodder & Stoughton, 1967. 192pp. Paper $1.50. A biography of English popular singing star, Cliff Richard. Published in England, this "rags-to-riches" success story includes a list of recordings, films, and stage appearances. Illustrated with eight pages of photographs.

Richman, Harry

RICHMAN, HARRY and RICHARD GEHMAN
A Hell of A Life
See Page 276

Ritchie, Jean

RITCHIE, JEAN
Singing Family of the Cumberlands
Oak, 1963. 258pp. Paper $2.95. An autobiography by the folk-singer in which she recreates her early life with her family in terms of the songs they sang and taught her. Included are words and music for forty-two songs. Illustrated with sketches by Maurice Sendak.

Rodgers, Richard

EWEN, DAVID
With a Song in His Heart
Holt, Rinehart, 1963. 216pp. $3.95. This is the biography of composer Richard Rodgers. Written for young people, it details his long career and association with Oscar Hammerstein. List of Recommended Recordings. List of Productions. Bibliography. Index.

Rorem, Ned

ROREM, NED
The New York Diary
Braziller, 1967. 218pp. $5.95. The composer continues his biography from the point where his Paris diary left off. This is the story of the years from 1955 to 1960. Rorem describes his diaries as "The cinema of myself." He provides a record of an artist whose concerns are not only aesthetic, but social, sexual, and philosophic. Illustrated with sixteen pages of photographs and art work.

ROREM, NED
The Paris Diary of Ned Rorem
Braziller, 1966. 240pp. $5.95. A selection from the diaries of the reknowned composer of art songs and the opera, "Miss Julie." This is the story of a young American composer in the Paris of the early 1950's and includes word portraits of some of the people he knew. Illustrated.

ROREM, NED
The Paris and New York Diaries
Avon, 1970. 431pp. Paper $2.45. Originally published

in 1966 and 1967 as two separate volumes and now reissued in a single volume edition, this is the biography of the American composer from 1951 through 1961. Illustrated with photographs.

Rose, Clarkson

ROSE, CLARKSON
Red Plush and Greasepaint
See Page 276

Roth, Lillian

ROTH, LILLIAN
I'll Cry Tomorrow
Frederick Fell, 1954. 347pp. $5.95. Paper—Popular Library, 1960. 347pp. $ .60. A biography of Miss Roth's life from her days as a child star, to her triumphs on Broadway and in Hollywood before she was twenty, through her fight with alcoholism and her ultimate triumphs.

Sargeant, Winthrop

SARGEANT, WINTHROP
In Spite of Myself: A Personal Memoir
Doubleday, 1970. 264pp. $6.95. The music critic for "The New Yorker" tells the story of his own journey of self-discovery through psychiatry. The crucial events of his life from his days as a child prodigy to his troubled adulthood are all detailed.

Shaw, Artie

SHAW, ARTIE
The Trouble with Cinderella
Collier, 1963. 352pp. Paper $ .95. This fragment of an autobiography is an attempt by the musician to put in proper perspective the two lives he has been forced to lead—that of highly-publicized musician and that of the private man.

Sutherland, Joan

BRADDON, RUSSELL
Joan Sutherland
Collins, 1969. 254pp. Paper $1.65. Originally published in 1962 and now reissued, this is a biography of the Australian opera singer. Particular attention is paid to her romance with and marriage to Richard Bonynge. Illustrated with photographs.

Swann, Donald

SWANN, DONALD
Space Between the Bars
Simon & Schuster, 1969. 160pp. $4.95. Subtitled, "A Book of Reflections," this semi-autobiography of the English entertainer/composer is a sharing of experiences, ideas, jokes, music, and friends the author has encountered during his career.

Thomson, Virgil

THOMSON, VIRGIL
Virgil Thomson
Knopf, 1966. 424pp. $7.95. The autobiography of the American classic composer. Illustrated.

Vallee, Rudy

VALLEE, RUDY and GIL McKEAN
My Time Is Your Time
Astor–Honor, 1962. 244pp. $5.95. The life of the singing star of the 1920's. Illustrated.

Waters, Ethel

WATERS, ETHEL with CHARLES SAMUELS
His Eye Is on the Sparrow
See Page 278

Williams, Bert

CHARTERS, ANN
Nobody: The Story of Bert Williams
Macmillan, 1970. 157pp. $6.95. A biography of the Negro entertainer whose career flourished from 1892 to 1922. It is also the record of one man's struggle against racial prejudice. His career in vaudeville, musical comedy, and the Ziegfeld Follies are recorded as is the introduction and success of his

own trademark song, ''Nobody.'' Illustrated with photographs and reproductions of the words and music of his famous songs. Discography. Index.

Williams, Hank

WILLIAMS, ROGER
Sing a Sad Song

Doubleday, 1970. 275pp. $5.95. A biography of composer/singer Hank Williams. The author considers Williams to be the archetype of the American success pattern and he records the life of the man behind the legend—the tortured man who destroyed himself with drugs and alcohol. During his brief stardom, Williams wrote such song hits as ''Your Cheatin' Heart,'' ''Jambalaya,'' and ''Hey, Good Lookin'.'' Illustrated with eight pages of photographs.

DANCE

GENERAL HISTORIES, CRITIQUES, AND APPRECIATIONS

ANDREWS, GLADYS
Creative Rhythmic Movement for Children
Prentice–Hall, 1954. 198pp. $11.35. An analysis of movement as a form of expression, with chapters on the psychology of childhood, children and creative experiences, creative movement experiences, movement exploration, development of movement, effects of space, rhythm, percussion, and the ideas behind movement education. Illustrated.

BEAUMONT, CYRIL W.
Bibliography of Dancing
Blom, 1965. 228pp. $12.50. A guide to hundreds of books pertaining to the dance and ballet, ancient and modern. It is the only bibliography which gives full collation (especially valuable for rare and early books). Descriptive notes and commentary are provided.

BELKNAP, S. YANCEY
Guide to Dance Periodicals
University of Florida. A subject and author index to articles, reviews, essays, and photographic essays about dance with occasional descriptive commentary. The following volumes are available.

Volume 1.	1931 – 1935.	$ 7.50
Volume 5.	1951 – 1952.	7.50
Volume 6.	1953 – 1954.	7.50
Volume 7.	1955 – 1956.	7.50

BRUCE, V.
Dance and Dance Drama in Education
Pergamon, 1965. 118pp. Paper $2.95. Published in England, this book is based on the work of Rudolf Laban. The author provides an exposition of the language of movement and the way it can be utilized educationally in the primary and secondary school. There are sections devoted to the childrens' own contributions. Illustrated with photographs. Bibliography.

CARROLL, JEAN and PETER LOFTHOUSE
Creative Dance for Boys
Dufour, 1970. 71pp. $4.95. Originally published in England in 1969 and now issued in the United States, this is an introduction for men teachers on the subject of how to teach dance to boys. Each of the five chapters takes an aspect of movement and relates it educationally to boys between the ages of ten and sixteen. The various aspects are placed within the educational setting and the author gives specific examples of their applications. Illustrated with twenty-eight plates. Index.

CHUJOY, ANATOLE and P. W. MANCHESTER – Editors
The Dance Encyclopedia
Simon & Schuster, 1967. 993pp. $20.00. A completely revised and enlarged edition of the one-volume international reference work on the art and science of dance. Close to 5,000 entries are included and illustrated with 274 photographs. Subjects covered include history, biography, criticism, choreography, terminology, technique, instruction, and education; in addition classical and modern dance works are covered with plot summaries, names of choreographers, composers, designers, original casts, musical detail, and dates of original performance.

COHEN, SELMA JEANNE – Editor
The Ballad of Nancy Dawson
Dance Perspectives, 1966. 45pp. Paper $2.95. A biography and study of the eighteenth century dancer. Illustrated with contemporary material.

COLE, ARTHUR C.
The Puritan and Fair Terpsichore
Dance Horizons, 1966. 36pp. Paper $1.25. A treatise on the opposition of Puritanism in the nineteenth century to dance. Originally published in 1942 and now reprinted.

CUNNINGHAM, JAMES P.
Dancing in the Inns of Court
Jordan, 1965. 44pp. Paper $1.50. A study of the terpsichoreal activities at the Inns of Court during the sixteenth and seventeenth centuries.

DAVIES, JOHN
Orchestra, or, A Poem of Dancing
Dance Horizons, 1970. 55pp. Paper $1.95. Originally published in 1945 and now reissued, this is an Elizabethan poem celebrating the dance. Introduction. Notes.

DEAN, BETH
The Many Worlds of Dance
Tri-Ocean, 1967. 175pp. $5.95. A survey of ethnic and folk dance, ballet and modern theatre, their origins and their developments in many parts of the world. Illustrated with photographs and drawings. Also included are a Glossary, a list of dance schools, and a Critical Bibliography. Index.

DELZA, SOPHIA
Body and Mind in Harmony
McKay, 1961. 184pp. $3.95. The first popular explanation in English of T'ai Chi Ch'Uan (Wu style), the ancient Chinese system of activating the body for the development of physical, emotional, and mental well-being. Each movement is illustrated by drawings.

DENBY, EDWIN
Dancers, Buildings, and People in the Streets
Horizon, 1965. 287pp. $5.95. The noted dance critic

discusses some of the major dance achievements of the modern era, especially the work of the New York City Ballet, the Bolshoi, the Royal Ballet, and the Kabuki. Balanchine's work in America is given special treatment. Index.

DE ZOETE, BERYL
The Thunder and the Freshness
Theatre Arts, 1963. 160pp. $4.25. A collection of essays by the ballet teacher and critic. Among the essays are a tribute to Jacques Dalcroze, a study of Frederick Ashton, a discussion of English ballet in wartime, three B. B. C. talks on ballet directed to the Far East, and a previously unpublished essay on the Oasus of Siwa.

DOLMETSCH, MABEL
Dances of England and France: 1450 – 1600
Routledge & Kegan Paul, 1949. 163pp. $12.50. Reconstructions of the dances of England and France from the late fifteenth and the sixteenth-centuries. The author describes the steps and provides musical examples as well as the origins and history of the steps. Reproductions of contemporary illustrations. Bibliography. Index.

DOLMETSCH, MABEL
Dances of Spain and Italy: From 1400 to 1600
Routledge & Kegan Paul, 1954. 174pp. $12.50. Reconstructions of the dances of four and five hundred years ago in Spain and Italy. The author describes the steps and their music, their origins and history. Musical examples and illustrations. Bibliography. Index.

EAMES, MARIAN
When All the World Was Dancing: Rare and Curious Books from the Cla Farnaroli Collection
New York Public Library, 1957. 16pp. Paper $1.00. An extensively notated descriptive catalogue of unique books from the collection donated to the N. Y. Public Library by Walter Toscanini.

FLETCHER, IFAN KYRLE, et. al.
Famed for Dance: Essays in the Theory and Practice of Theatrical Dancing in England 1660 – 1740
New York Public Library, 1960. 64pp. Paper $1.50. The three essays in this volume are: "Ballet in England, 1660–1740," by Mr. Fletcher; "The Theory and Practice of Theatrical Dancing," by S. J. Cohen; and "Dr. Burney, John Weaver, and the Spectator," by Roger Lonsdale.

GRAY, VERA and RACHEL PERCIVAL
Music, Movement & Mime for Children
Oxford, 1969. 110pp. $3.50. Originally published in 1962 and now reprinted, the aim of this book by a musician and dancer is to provide teachers with material for the teaching of music and dance to children. Based on a popular BBC television series. Illustrated with photographs and musical examples. Appendices.

HABERMAN, MARTIN and TOBIE MEISEL – Editors
Dance – An Art in Academe
Teachers College Press, 1970. 172pp. $10.50. Essays on the nature of dance and its place in education. Specific problems are analyzed, possible solutions examined, guiding principles and model programs proposed. The volume is divided into eight parts: Dance as Art, Dance and Communication, Developing Curricula in the Arts, Dance in Higher Education, Dance in Public Education, The Teaching of Dance, Evaluation in the Arts, and The Child: Artist and Audience.

HASKELL, ARNOLD L.
The Wonderful World of Dance
Doubleday, 1969. 96pp. $3.95. Originally published in England in 1960 and now issued in the United States, this volume traces the evolution of dance. Mr. Haskell explains how dance began, the reasons why people dance, and explores ritual dancing. Illustrated with color and black-and-white photographs. Glossary. Index.

HAWKINS, ALMA M.
Creating Through Dance
Prentice–Hall, 1964. 164pp. Paper $6.50. A study of the relationship between the creative aspects of dance and the development of the dance instrument. Illustrated. Index.

HAYES, ELIZABETH R.
Dance Competition and Production for High Schools and Colleges
Ronald Press, 1955. 210pp. $5.00. This text examines the basic principles of the dance as an art form, and presents a program of dance studies based on movement techniques, the use of space, elements of rhythm, sensory and ideational stimuli, and structural motifs. Included is a section on music for dance composition. Index.

HAYES, ELIZABETH R.
An Introduction to the Teaching of Dance
Ronald Press, 1964. 340pp. $6.00. This comprehensive text examines such factors as movement fundamentals, preparation for the dance, creative modern dance teaching techniques, ballroom dance techniques, folk dancing, dance performances, and music accompaniment. Illustrated. Index.

H'DOUBLER, MARGARET N.
Dance: A Creative Art Experience
University of Wisconsin, 1962. 168pp. Paper $1.45. A reprint of the work first published in 1940. The author relates dance to the personal experience of the teacher and student and applies the dance form to the changing cultural pattern. Illustrated with drawings.

HOOPER, KATRINE AMORY
Dance Pageantry in History and Legend
Vantage, 1964. 210pp. $4.95. Directions and

suggestions for costuming, choreographing, and scoring in the staging of pageants. Dances of ancient Egypt, Greece, the era of Charlemagne, and early America. Illustrated with drawings by the author.

HORST, LOUIS
Pre-Classic Dance Forms
Dance Horizons, 1970. 140pp. Paper $2.95. An unabridged republication of the edition first published in 1937. Mr. Horst studies the classic court dances of the early sixteenth century—each in a separate chapter. Illustrated with photographs, drawings and musical examples.

KINKELDEY, OTTO
A Jewish Dancing Master of the Renaissance: Guglielmo Ebreo
Dance Horizons, 1966. 44pp. Paper $1.45. A treatise on the art of the dance in the fifteenth century. Originally published in 1929 and now reissued. Illustrated. Bibliography.

LABAN, RUDOLF
Choreutics
MacDonald, 1966. 214pp. $20.00. This book gives a cogent account of the basis of Laban's Space Harmony which is based on the unity of space and movement. There is an explicit presentation of the grammatical and syntactical aspects of the language of movement together with consideration of its notation. The text is annotated and edited by Lisa Ullmann. Illustrated with diagrams. Index.

LABAN, RUDOLF
The Mastery of Movement
Drama Book Specialists, 1960. 186pp. $8.00. Originally published in England and now distributed in the United States in an expanded and revised edition edited by Lisa Ullmann, this is an examination of movement in relation to the stages of human life and the "artistic enhancement of human movement" in theatrical activity. The basic principles are clarified, the roots of mime are examined, and movement expression in group scenes is studied. This edition also includes three mime plays. Also provided are exercises, study scenes, examples of movement sequences, and movement scenes. Index.

LAMBRANZI, GREGORIO
New and Curious School of Theatrical Dancing
Dance Horizons, 1966. 169pp. Paper $3.95. A reprint of the 1928 edition of the 1716 publication of the collection of seventeenth and eighteen century engravings of the Venetian choreographer. Translated by Derra De Moroda and edited by Cyril W. Beaumont.

LATCHAW, MARJORIE and JEAN PYATT
A Pocket Guide of Dance Activities
Prentice–Hall, 1958. 234pp. Spiral bound $6.00. Materials in this book have been prepared for the elementary classroom teacher as practical aids in bridging the gap between the theoretical aspects of dance and the actual teaching situation. Exploratory movement experiences, including illustrations of how dance may be stimulated from a variety of sources, are included. Illustrated with drawings and musical examples. Index.

LAWLER, LILLIAN B.
The Dance in Ancient Greece
Wesleyan, 1964. 160pp. $5.75. Paper – University of Washington, 1967. 160pp. $2.95. A full examination of dance from ancient Knossos to the year 527 when dancer-courtesan Theodora became Empress of Byzantium. The roots of dance in religious rites, the dances of Crete and Mycenea, animal dances, temple dances, and dance in the ancient theatre are among the topics covered.

LESTER, SUSAN
Dancers and Their World: A Young Person's Guide
Gollancz, 1965. 144pp. $2.75. Miss Lester opens her book with a discussion of dance in general, then treats classical ballet, modern dance, the teaching of dance, and dance-therapy. Conditions of every branch of the profession in England are covered. List of Books for Further Reading.

LOFTHOUSE, PETER
Dance
Heinemann, 1970. 56pp. Paper $1.50. Published in England, this is a brief guide to the latest theory and methods of teaching children the fundamentals of dance in the primary school grades. Index.

LOHSE–CLAUSE, ELLI
Dance
Abbey Library, 1964. 17pp. and 46 plates. $4.50. A collection of forty-six color plates representing all forms of dance in the arts of sculpture, painting, stained glass, etc. A text on the history of dance in art, from prehistoric times to the present, also describes the plates.

MAGRIEL, PAUL DAVID
A Bibliography of Dancing
Blom, 1966. 230pp. $17.50. Originally published in 1936 and now reissued, this is a list of books and articles on the dance and related subjects. It includes general works and works on various aspects of the dance including history, criticism, folk dance, the art of dancing, ballet, mime and pantomine, masques, decor, costume, and music.

MARTIN, JOHN
Introduction to the Dance
Dance Horizons, 1965. 363pp. Paper $4.95. A reprint of the 1939 edition, this history examines the nature of movement, form and composition in the dance, the basis of style, the nature of recreational, spectacular, and expressional dance, and the position of dance in education.

MARTIN, JOHN
John Martin's Book of the Dance
Tudor, 1963. 192pp. $8.95. The former Dance Editor of the "New York Times" traces the development of dance from primitive times to the modern era. The four parts of the study discuss the basic elemental nature of all dance; folk and ballroom dancing; the rise of ballet from its courtly beginnings through the era of Fokine and Diaghilev to Balanchine, Tudor, DeMille, and others; and the contributions of choreographers and interpretative dancers from Isadora Duncan to Martha Graham. Negro dance and the "integrated" companies are discussed in a final chapter. Illustrated.

MELCER, FANNIE HELEN
Staging the Dance
Wm. C. Brown, 1955. 85pp. $2.00. A manual of information pertaining to the theatrical part of staging a dance program in high schools. The technical suggestions are made with considerations of budget and student ability in mind. In addition to the technical stage matters covered there are suggestions on programs, and advice on public relations and general administration. Bibliography. Illustrated.

MITCHELL, JACK
American Dance Portfolio
Dodd, Mead, 1964. 128pp. $10.00. A gallery of 159 portraits of leading personalities in the field of modern ballet, ethnic, and theatrical dance by the master photographer of the ballet. Foreword by Walter Terry. Index.

MITCHELL, JACK and CLIVE BARNES
Dance Scene, U.S.A.
World, 1967. 144pp. $12.50. Clive Barnes has contributed a commentary on the American dance scene to accompany more than 200 photographs by Jack Mitchell, America's foremost dance photographer. Represented are the companies and stars of American Ballet Theatre, Martha Graham, New York City Ballet, Robert Joffrey Ballet, the Harkness Ballet, the Paul Taylor Dance Company, and many other important groups. Index.

MOORE, LILLIAN
Artists of the Dance
Blom, 1969. 320pp. $17.50. Paper—Dance Horizons, 1969. 320pp. $4.95. A reprint of the edition first published in 1938, this is a collection of short biographies of great dancers from the early classical ballet, the romantic ballet, the Russian ballet, the Spanish dance, and modern dance. Illustrated. Glossary. Index.

MOORE, LILLIAN
Images of the Dance: Historical Treasures of the Dance Collection, 1581–1861
New York Public Library, 1965. 80pp. $6.75. An essay in the form of a running commentary on pictorial materials from sixteenth century Versailles and Venice, through eighteenth century London and Paris, to the romantic ballet of early nineteenth century Europe and America. A frontispiece in color and eighty-four of the unique prints and engravings in the Library's collection are included.

MURRAY, RUTH LOVELL
Dance in Elementary Education: A Program for Boys and Girls
Harper & Row, 1963. 451pp. $13.25. The second edition of the teaching manual originally published in 1953. For secondary schools and colleges, with sections on dance for younger children, there are discussions on creating dance and teaching dance movements, rhythm, and coordination. A list of aids to teaching dance is included. Illustrated.

NADEL, MYRON HOWARD and CONSTANCE GWEN NADEL—Editors
The Dance Experience: Readings in Dance Appreciation
Praeger, 1970. 388pp. $13.95. The editors bring together past and contemporary thought on a wide variety of dance subjects and problems to provide a broad-based view of the critical literature of dance. The editors provide extensive sectional introductions, brief comment on each selection, questions for discussion, and original articles on the spiritual nature of dance, the ballet, and the role of dance in a liberal arts education. Among the contributors are: Selma Jeanne Cohen, Doris Humphrey, Faubion Bowers, Alwin Nikolais, Antony Tudor, Walter Sorell, and Martha Graham. Index.

NASH, BARBARA
Tap Dance
Wm. C. Brown, 1969. 54pp. Paper $1.25. This is a guidebook for the beginner tap dancer. After a summary of the history of tap dancing, the author analyzes movement, content and style, time and space, and the structure of a dance. Illustrated with diagrams. Appendices include sources of taps and shoes, records, and information. Index.

PERCIVAL, RACHEL
Discovering Dance
Dufour, 1966. 136pp. $2.95. Miss Percival traces the history of dance from the primitive war-dances of prehistoric man to ballroom dancing of today. Ballet, the dance of Greece and Rome, the Court balls of Tudor times, stage and film dancing are all discussed. A chapter on dance music is also included. Illustrated with drawings, diagrams, and photographs.

PRESTON, VALERIE
A Handbook for Modern Educational Dance
MacDonald & Evans, 1968. 187pp. $4.50. Originally published in 1963 and now reissued, this book, by a pupil of the late Rudolf Laban, gives sixteen basic themes, based on principles formulated by Laban. Each theme is concerned with a particular aspect of

bodily movement and forms a logical progression. These themes cover work appropriate for students of all ages, from primary classes to adults. Symbols and diagrams illustrate the text. Index.

RAFFE, W. G. and M. E. PURDON
Dictionary of the Dance
A. S. Barnes, 1964. 583pp. $20.00. The 5,000 entries in this dictionary cover all periods of history and every area of the world. Included is a Bibliography of books from the fifteenth century to the present. Illustrated.

SACHS, CURT
World History of the Dance
Norton, 1963. 469pp. Paper $2.45. A reprint of the 1937 edition, this history of the dance is divided into two parts. Part One, "Dance Through the World," deals with the physiological and aesthetic basis of dance movements, the themes and types of dance, and the forms and choreography of dance. Part Two, "Dance Throughout the Ages," treats of dance in the stone age, the evolution of dance in Europe, and other subjects. Illustrated. Index.

SELLARS, DOROTHY RAINER
The Dance Teacher Today
Dance Magazine, 1969. 71pp. $5.75. This is a collection of articles originally printed in "Dance Magazine" from 1967 to 1969. Illustrated with drawings by Doug Anderson.

SHEETS, MAXINE
The Phenomenology of Dance
University of Wisconsin, 1966. 158pp. $4.75. This book examines the philosophy and aesthetics of dance, the gap between the goals of dancer and dance educator, and the place of dance in education. Among the items covered are the illusion of force in dance, the plastic components of force, dynamic line, a phenomenological concept of rhythm, and dance as a composition of form and art. Index.

SORELL, WALTER — Editor
The Dance Has Many Faces
Columbia, 1966. 267pp. $9.00. This collection of twenty-nine essays discusses important phases of ballet, modern, and ethnic dance. American and European backgrounds of the dance are dealt with by various experts including Frederick Ashton, George Balanchine, Birgit Cullberg, Doris Humphrey, Rudolf Laban, John Martin, Walter Terry, and Charles Weidman. Illustrated. Index.

SORELL, WALTER
The Dance Through the Ages
Grosset, 1967. 304pp. $14.95. This is a chronicle of ancient, Oriental, folk, ballet, modern, and experimental dance which traces the history of the dance from primitive rites to the dancers currently exploring the frontiers of the art. Over 250 illustrations, eighteen of which are in color. Selected Reading List. Chronology of Dance. Index.

STEARNS, MARSHALL and JEAN STEARNS
Jazz Dance: The Story of American Vernacular Dance
Macmillan, 1968. 464pp. $9.95. A history of jazz dancing, from its African origins to the present. The material is taken from more than two hundred interviews with dancers, musicians, choreographers, and observers of jazz. A list of films (documentaries, television productions, and full-length motion pictures) has been compiled by Ernest Smith. Also offered is an analysis (in Labanotation) of basic jazz dance movements by Nadia Chilkovsky Nahumck, noted dancer and teacher. Illustrated with photographs. Selected Bibliography. Index.

SZYPULA, GEORGE
Tumbling and Balancing for All
Wm. C. Brown, 1968. 209pp. $5.50. A second edition of the book first printed in 1957, this is a text on gymnastics — tumbling, balancing, and related activities. After an initial chapter on the responsibilities of instructors and students, there are chapters on individual tumbling, pyramid building, advanced individual routines, lesson plans, and competitive tumbling. All chapters include detailed instructions for the exercises and routines. Illustrated with photographs and line drawings. Spiral bound.

TAYLOR, MARGARET FISK
A Time to Dance
See Page 327

TERRY, WALTER
The Dance in America
Harper & Row, 1956. 248pp. $5.95. A history of all types of dance in America from colonial times to the fifties. The influence of traditional and romantic ballet on current dance is described. Biographies of leading dance figures are included.

TODD, MABEL ELSWORTH
The Thinking Body
Dance Horizons, 1968. 314pp. Paper $4.95. Originally published in 1937, this republication of the "study of the balancing forces of dynamic man" is an approach to teaching body balance and motion to produce more efficient mechanics of movement. The basic principles of action and control of the body activity and the influence of unconscious sensations on body control and action are stressed. Illustrated. Bibliography. Index.

WEBSTER, T. B. L.
The Greek Chorus
See Page 37

WIENER, JACK and JOHN LIDSTONE
Creative Movement for Children
Reinhold, 1969. 112pp. $7.50. In text and more than

300 photographs, the authors provide a dance program for the classroom. They explore the teaching situation and the relationship of the teacher to the students.

WILLIS, JOHN
Dance World
This is an annual pictorial and statistical record of the activities and personnel of professional ballet, modern, and ethnic dance groups that performed in the United States in the various dance seasons covered in the individual volumes. A special section is devoted to the biographies and portraits of choreographers and dancers. Each volume is illustrated with more than 450 photographs. Index. Volumes available are listed below.
Volume One: 1966. Crown, 1966. 244pp. $10.00.
Volume Two: 1967. Crown, 1967. 224pp. $10.00.
Volume Three: 1968. Crown, 1968. 224pp. $10.00.
Volume Four: 1969. Crown, 1970. 224pp. $10.00.
Volume Five: 1970. Crown, 1970. 224pp. $10.00.

WOOD, MELUSINE
Advanced Historical Dances
Imperial Society of Teachers of Dancing, 1960. 189pp. $8.95. This collection of dances from the eighteenth and nineteenth centuries is intended for the advanced dance student. Full directions for the performance of the dances are given with musical examples. List of Works Consulted. Index.

WOOD, MELUSINE
Historical Dances: 12th to 19th Century
Imperial Society of Teachers of Dancing, 1964. 154pp. Paper $5.95. Originally published in 1952 and now reissued, this is a collection of dances covering a period of 600 years. Short notes are provided to relate the dances to their period. The origin and evolution of each dance is explained and then followed by practical instructions for the performance of the dance. Bibliography. Index.

WOOD, MELUSINE
More Historical Dances
Imperial Society of Teachers of Dancing, 1956. 159pp. $8.95. This is a companion book to "Historical Dances 12th to 19th Century." Dances are studied in relation to a definite syllabus. Detailed instructions for the execution of the steps and special exercises for the development of technical ability are given. Musical examples. Table of Dates. Index.

WOODY, REGINA J.
Young Dancer's Career Book
Dutton, 1966. 185pp. $4.50. Originally published in 1958 and now reprinted, this is a guide for the beginning young dancer. It offers advice on subjects from how to evaluate your own talent to how to get a Ph. D. in modern dance. How to train for the classic ballet, choreography for modern dance, how to get a job, and other pertinent questions are answered. Illustrated with photographs and drawings. Bibliography. Index.

TYPES OF DANCE

Ballet

AMBROSE, KAY
Ballet Lover's Companion
Knopf, 1949. 80pp. $3.50. A study of the aesthetics of dance for the ballet student. The book emphasizes the means whereby the techniques of dance can be developed to produce artistically pleasing movement. Chapters are included on basic training, practical science, on music and the dancer, and on partnering. Illustrated with drawings. Index.

AMBROSE, KAY
Ballet Lover's Pocket–Book
Knopf, 1945. 64pp. $3.50. Instructions in basic technique for the beginner. Supplementary notes on costume, lighting, make-up, curtain call procedures, etc., are included.

AMBROSE, KAY
Ballet Student's Primer
Knopf, 1954. 80pp. $3.50. A concentrated guide for beginners of all ages. All the basic ballet exercises and steps are described in drawings.

ATKINSON, MARGARET and MAY HILLMAN
Dancers of the Ballet: Biographies
Knopf, 1955. 174pp. $4.49. Biographical sketches of the leading ballerinas and premier danseurs of the United States, England, and France are included in this volume. Photographs of the artists are provided.

BALANCHINE, GEORGE
Balanchine's New Complete Stories of the Great Ballets
Doubleday, 1968. 626pp. $8.95. Originally published in 1954 and now completely revised, this volume describes 231 ballets. Included are descriptions of each ballet, sections on how to enjoy the ballet, a chronology of outstanding events in dance from 1469 to today, a chapter on ballet for children and on careers in ballet. Also provided is a guide to selected reading, an annotated section on recorded ballet music, an illustrated glossary, and notes and comments on dancing, dancers, and choreography. The volume has been edited by Francis Mason. Marta Becket has provided drawings and the volume is also illustrated with photographs. Index.

BEAUMONT, CYRIL W.
The Ballet Called Giselle
Dance Horizons, 1969. 143pp. Paper $2.95. First published in 1945, this is a study of the evolution of the ballet, "Giselle," from conception to realization. Forty-seven pages of photographs. Index.

BIRDWHISTELL, RAY I. – Introducer
The Male Image

Dance Perspectives, 1969. 48pp. Paper $2.95. This latest publication by Dance Perspectives Foundation is introduced by Mr. Birdwhistell and includes statements by five leading contemporary male dancers on the masculine image in ballet. The contributors are: Igor Youskevitch, Bruce Marks, Helgi Tomasson, Luis Fuente, and Edward Villella. Illustrated with photographs.

BLASIS, CARLO
An Elementary Treatise Upon the Theory and Practice of the Art of Dancing
Dover, 1968. 64pp. Paper $1.35. Originally published in 1820 and now reissued, as translated by Mary Stewart Evans, this work is the direct ancestor of the many subsequent ballet teaching guides. The author, director of the Imperial Academy at Milan in the nineteenth century, singles out common errors of technique and taste and suggests how they should be remedied. Biographical sketch and Foreword by the translator. Illustrated with sketches by the author.

BRINSON, PETER
Background to European Ballet
Humanities, 1966. 196pp. Paper $5.25. A guide to ballet material available in libraries, museums, archives and collections in European centers. Illustrated. Index.

BRINSON, PETER and CLEMENT CRISP
Ballet For All
Pan, 1970. 281pp. Paper $1.75. A guide, published in England, to the current international repertoire of the world's ballet companies. The authors describe in detail over 100 ballets by thirty-eight choreographers, with production credits, synopses and commentary. Chapters on the historical background of ballet and a short survey of modern Soviet ballet. Illustrated with photographs.

BRUHN, ERIK
Beyond Technique
Dance Perspectives, 1968. 76pp. Paper $2.50. The Danish dancer discusses his life and technique of dancing. Twenty-six pages of photographs by Fred Fehl show Mr. Bruhn in performance.

BRUHN, ERIK and LILLIAN MOORE
Bournonville and Ballet Technique
A. & C. Black, 1961. 71pp. $5.00. A volume of studies and comments on the technique of dancing the choreography of August Bournonville. The authors discuss and describe some of the techniques as they are taught at the Royal Danish Ballet School. Included are some of Bournonville's own remarks regarding the exercises. Illustrated with photographs.

CLARKE, MARY
Dancers of Mercury: The Story of Ballet Rambert
A. & C. Black, 1962. 240pp. $4.50. This is a detailed history of the Ballet Rambert which has been called the cradle of British ballet. The author includes an appraisal of the achievements of the company, its choreographers, dancers, and repertoire, and discusses the place the company will occupy in the future development of British ballet. Illustrated with photographs and drawings. List of Ballets Produced. Index.

COHEN, SELMA JEANNE
Stravinsky and the Dance
New York Public Library, 1962. 60pp. Paper $3.00. Prepared in honor of Stravinsky's eightieth birthday, this is a survey of ballets choreographed to Stravinsky's music from 1910 to 1962. An essay by Herbert Read, "Stravinsky and the Muses," is included.

COOPER, DOUGLAS
Picasso Theatre
See Page 368

CULBERG, BIRGIT
Ballet: Flight and Reality
Dance Perspectives, 1967. 52pp. Paper $2.95. Translated from the Swedish by Laura de la Torre Bueno with an Introduction by Anna Greta Stahle, this is an essay on ballet by the choreographer. List of ballets choreographed. Illustrated with photographs.

de MILLE, AGNES
And Promenade Home
Little, Brown, 1956. 301pp. $6.50. A sequel to "Dance to the Piper," this book recounts the artistic success that followed Miss DeMille's years of struggle. The choreographer's work in "Oklahoma," "One Touch of Venus," "Carousel," and "Bloomer Girl" is analyzed. Illustrated.

de MILLE, AGNES
Dance to the Piper
Little, Brown, 1951. 342pp. $7.50. The first part of Miss DeMille's autobiography which describes her early life in Hollywood with such stars as Chaplin, Geraldine Farrar, and her Uncle Cecil. Her long struggle to be a dancer and her six years of work in England with Anthony Tudor and Hugh Laing are treated in detail. Illustrated. Index.

de MILLE, AGNES
Lizzie Borden: A Dance of Death
Little, Brown, 1968. 302pp. $6.95. Miss DeMille tells the story of the genesis and artistic realization of the ballet, "Fall River Legend." She describes historical facts, the liberties she had to take with them, the encouragement she received from the composer (Morton Gould), and the anguish of the rehearsals. Illustrated with photographs. Index.

de MILLE, AGNES
Russian Journals
Dance Perspectives, 1970. 57pp. Paper $2.95. Miss De Mille visited the Soviet Union in 1966 and 1969

and this is the record of her observations and impressions. Illustrated with photographs.

de MILLE, AGNES
To a Young Dancer
Little, Brown, 1960. 175pp. $4.95. Paper $2.25. A handbook for dance students, parents, and teachers, illustrated by Milton Johnson. Miss DeMille describes the discipline and training and problems the young dancer faces, and the joys of her art. A list of colleges offering dance courses, repertories of dance companies, and films dealing with dance are included.

DENBY, EDWIN
Looking at the Dance
Horizon, 1968. 432pp. $7.95. Originally published in 1949, this is a new edition of the classic work on dance. Mr. Denby has divided the volume into ten major parts which encompass all phases of classical dance: meaning in ballet, ballets in recent repertory, dancers in performance, ballet music and decoration, ballet in books, prints, photographs and films, modern dancers, and dancing in shows. Index.

DOLIN, ANTON
Pas De Deux: The Art of Partnering
Dover, 1969. 61pp. Paper $1.50. Originally published in 1949 and now reissued with a new Preface by the author. Mr. Dolin gives practical advice on all aspects of partnering and includes step-by-step presentations of three adagios from the classical repertory. Illustrated with drawings and photographs.

DOLIN, ANTON
The Sleeping Ballerina
Muller, 1966. 130pp. $7.00. This is the biography of Olga Spessivtzeva, the legendary ballerina whose perfection of technique and sensitive understanding of her roles has never been surpassed. Illustrated with photographs. Index.

DRAPER, NANCY and MARGARET F. ATKINSON
Ballet for Beginners
Knopf, 1951. 115pp. $3.95. The basic ballet positions are shown in more than 100 photographs and drawings, with diagramatic charts indicating procedure for home practice.

ELLFELDT, LOIS
A Primer for Choreographers
National Press, 1967. 121pp. $6.60. Dr. Ellfeldt attempts to explain choreography to beginning students. From an introductory chapter on what dance is, to the role of the choreographer, and the process of making dances, she provides a series of movement exercises which answer questions of would-be choreographers. Illustrated with drawings by Sue Powell. Glossary. Selected Bibliography.

FEATHERSTONE, DONALD F.
Dancing Without Danger
A. S. Barnes, 1970. 258pp. $5.95. A guide to the prevention and treatment of injuries liable to occur in ballet dancing. Illustrated with photographs and diagrams. Index.

FISHER, HUGH
Margot Fonteyn
A. & C. Black, 1964. 40pp. $2.95. A brief biography of Dame Margot, followed by a complete record of all her important roles, illustrated with photographs. This third edition of the book first published in 1952 has been revised by Mary Clarke.

FORRESTER, F.S.
The Ballet in England
Library Association, 1968. 224pp. $13.50. A bibliography and survey of ballet in England, 1700—June 1966. The volume provides a guide to books, periodicals, and articles. Each chapter is preceded by an introductory survey. Aspects dealt with include publishing and bibliography, reference and general works, history, technique and notation, choreography, design and costume, music film, and television. Illustrated with five photographs. Appendices. Index.

GEESLIN, MARTHA
Ballet Time
Dance Publications, 1957. 44pp. Paper $1.00. Written for parents of beginning ballet students, this primer explains and illustrates basic terms and techniques.

GELABERT, RAUL
Anatomy for the Dancer
Dance Magazine, 1964. 115pp. Two volume set $11.00. This is an approach to avoiding and correcting physical ailments in ballet training. Photographic representations of exercises are provided as well as textual explanations. Anatomical drawings are also included.

GERAGHTY, ANNE—Editor
Ballet
William Collins, 1970. 380pp. $6.95. An anthology of fictional works, essays, appreciations, and biographies based on ballet and its artists. Provided are articles concerned with visiting the ballet, works on ballet as a professional career, the mechanics of creating a ballet, the background and history of ballet through the personalities who influenced its development. A reprint of "The Blue Train" by Joan Selby-Lowndes is included. This is the long out-of-print, highly praised biography of Anton Dolin. Photographs, line drawings, by Robert Geary, and cartoons illustrate the volume.

GLENNON, JAMES
Making Friends with Ballet
Crescendo, 1970. 80pp. Paper $1.50. The author gives, in non-technical language, the history of the dance and the stories of thirty ballets with

analytical notes on the music. Short biographies of important dance personalities are included as is a Glossary of ballet terms.

GRANT, GAIL
Technical Manual and Dictionary of Classical Ballet
Peter Smith, 1967. 127pp. $3.50. Originally published in 1950, this second revised edition is augmented with 100 additional terms and an improved phonetic translation of each. Miss Grant fully describes and defines over 800 ballet steps, movements, and poses, and other expressions and concepts. There is also a fifteen page pictorial supplement of diagrams showing the exact positions for the proper execution of the more common ballet steps and movements. Bibliography.

GREGORY, JOHN
Understanding the Ballet
Oldbourne, 1965. 124pp. $8.50. An introduction to the world of the ballet, with a brief historical account and a study of the dancer's world from classroom to stage. A section of photographs by Mike Davis illustrates the ballet positions and shows the great ballet artists in their most famous roles. Glossary. Bibliography. Index.

GREY, JENNIFER
So They Want to Learn Ballet
Dufour, 1966. 60pp. $2.95. A practical guide for parents whose children want to learn ballet. The many questions parents should consider before sending their child to ballet class are explored and the basic and primary ballet steps are illustrated in drawings and photographs.

GUEST, IVOR
Dandies and Dancers
Dance Perspectives, 1969. 49pp. Paper $2.95. A study of dance audiences during the Victorian era in London. Illustrated.

GUEST, IVOR
The Empire Ballet
Society for Theatre Research, 1962. 111pp. Paper $3.95. The story of the Empire Theatre, London, from 1884 to 1915 and of the ballet company which appeared there during those years. A complete list of ballets produced, principal dancers, and selected scenarios are included. Illustrated with photographs. Index.

GUEST, IVOR
The Romantic Ballet in Paris
Wesleyan University, 1966. 314pp. $15.00. A history of the romantic ballet in the nineteenth century. Such figures as Marie Taglioni, Fanny Essler, Carlotta Grisi, and the first performances of "Giselle" and "La Sylphide" are treated in detail. Illustrated with forty-one pages of plates. Appendices. Bibliography. Notes. Index.

HAGGIN, B. H.
Ballet Chronicle
Horizon Press, 1970. 223pp. $17.50. A collection of writings from "The Nation" and "The Hudson Review" from 1940 to 1970. The period includes the entire lifetime of the New York City Ballet, of which Mr. Haggin, in effect, provides a history. He also reports on the seasons of other American and some foreign companies, describes the long series of ballets created by Balanchine for the New York City Ballet, and describes the performances of a succession of great dancers. Illustrated with 250 action photographs including sequences from films.

HALL, FERNAU
The World of Ballet and Dance
Hamlyn, 1970. 140pp. $3.95. A history of the renaissance of ballet and modern dance throughout the world from the time of Diaghilev in the part of this century until the present day. Special sections on the Royal Ballet, North American ballet, modern dance, Soviet ballet, classical dances of the East, and Rudolf Nureyev. Illustrated with 141 photographs in black-and-white and in color by Mike Davis. Index.

HARRIS, LEON
The Russian Ballet School
Atheneum, 1970. 60pp. $4.75. A study in text and photographs of what it is like to attend ballet school in Leningrad and Moscow.

HASKELL, ARNOLD
Balletomania: The Story of An Obsession
AMS Press, 1968. 350pp. $14.50. Originally published in 1934, this is the story of one man's concern with and love for the art form of the classical ballet. The reknowned critic and balletomane tells of his lifelong obsession with the ballet, the companies and the dancers. Illustrated with photographs and drawings. Index.

HASKELL, ARNOLD
The Russian Genius in Ballet
Pergamon, 1963. 50pp. $2.25. Paper $2.00. This is a short study of Russian ballet: its birth, the Russian school, Diaghilev and the Russian ballet in Western Europe, and Soviet ballet today. Illustrated with photographs.

HASKELL, ARNOLD
What Is A Ballet?
MacDonald, 1965. 160pp. $3.75. A study of the development of the English ballet form from its French and Russian sources, with an analysis of the roles played by dancers, choreographers, impresarios, painters, and composers. List of Important Dates and Works. Bibliography. Index.

HILL, LORNA
La Sylphide: The Life of Marie Taglioni
Evans, 1967. 142pp. $3.95. A biography of the

nineteenth century ballerina. It is also the story of the founding of romantic ballet and its innovations as well as the woman and the dancer. Illustrated with photographs. Glossary. Index.

INTERNATIONAL MUSIC CENTRE, VIENNA – Compilers
Ten Years of Films on Ballet and Classical Dance: 1956 – 1965
UNESCO, 1968. 105pp. Paper $3.00. This is a catalogue of films on dance, listed by country of origin. Information is included on title, producer, choreographer, composer, dancers, and other technical credits; also a short synopsis, and the distributor of each film is given. Index by Country. Index of Choreographers. Index of Composers.

KARSAVINA, TAMARA
Ballet Technique
Theatre Arts, 1968. 48pp. $3.45. A republication of the series of essays first issued in 1956. It is a textbook on Madame Karsavina's method of teaching ballet technique. Illustrated with photographs.

KERENSKY, OLEG
The World of Ballet
Coward–McCann, 1970. 302pp. $7.95. A guide to the aesthetics of ballet, its history, recent developments, traditions, and predictions for the future. The volume includes a description of the creation of a new ballet from the choreographer's original conception to its final realization. The final section of the book covers the contributions of the great ballet and modern dance companies of the world. Illustrated with thirty-four photographs. Index.

KERSLEY, LEO and JANET SINCLAIR
A Dictionary of Ballet Terms
A. & C. Black, 1969. 112pp. $3.95. Originally published in 1952, enlarged in 1964, and now reprinted with corrections, this dictionary explains, and illustrates with drawings by Peter Revitt, all the terms and expressions of basic ballet technique. Index.

KIRSTEIN, LINCOLN, et al
The Classic Ballet: Basic Techniques and Terminology
Knopf, 1952. 243pp. $10.00. A condensed history of the evolution of ballet. Carlus Dyer has contributed 156 pages of line drawings to illustrate preparation, practice, direction, significance, and motion of basic ballet steps. Explanatory Introductions and Notes by Muriel Stuart. George Balanchine has provided a Preface. Index.

KIRSTEIN, LINCOLN
Movement and Metaphor: Four Centuries of Ballet
Praeger, 1970. 290pp. $17.50. Mr. Kirstein discusses ballet as movement, as art, as theatrical spectacle, and as history. He surveys five basic elements of theatrical dance-choreography, gesture and mime, music, costume, and decor—as they have developed over 400 years of performance in the West. Centerpiece of the work is the author's interpretation of fifty seminal ballets, beginning with the French court spectacles of the sixteenth century and including major productions of Balanchine, Ashton, and Robbins. More than 400 rare illustrations are included from European and American archives. Among the illustrations are many photographs of productions and dancers. Bibliography. Index.

KIRSTEIN, LINCOLN
Three Pamphlets Collected
Dance Horizons, 1967. 267pp. Paper $4.95. A collection of three articles on dance originally published in 1937, 1939 and 1959. The titles are "Blast at Ballet," "Ballet Alphabet," and "What Is Ballet All About." Illustrated.

KNIGHT, DENNIS
Ballet: An Instant Picture Book
Patterson–Blick, 1968. 12pp. Paper $1.00. A book for young children. In the short text Mr. Knight discusses the history of ballet, the great dancers, ballet exercises, and also provides drawings of sets and dancers in action.

KOCHNO, BORIS
Diaghilev and the Ballets Russes
Harper & Row, 1970. 293pp. $35.00. A history of Diaghilev's ballet company, the Ballets Russes, from 1909 until his death twenty years later. The author presents his recollections of Diaghilev at work and relates them to the sixty great ballets he choreographed. 312 black-and-white illustrations, and seventy in color, show the creations of the great artists who created set designs and costumes for the company, as well as the dancers in their greatest roles. Autobiographical notes by Diaghilev. Index.

KROKOVER, ROSALYN
The New Borzoi Book of Ballets
Knopf, 1956. 320pp. $8.95. Notes on the stories, music, choreography, sets, costumes, and performances of fifty-seven ballets in the repertory of Ballet Theatre and the New York City Ballet companies. Illustrated.

LASSAIGNE, JACQUES
Marc Chagall Drawings and Watercolors for the Ballet
Tudor, 1969. 155pp. $37.50. The first volume to reproduce in full color the original designs for "Aleko," "The Firebird," and "Daphnis and Chloe." Sixty-eight reproductions in full color of the decors and the costumes with an original color lithograph by Chagall created especially for this edition. The text describes the preparation of the designs, their reception, and evaluates Chagall's work for the ballet.

LAWSON, JOAN
Classical Ballet: Its Style and Technique

A. & C. Black, 1960. 167pp. $6.50. This book attempts to record the principles common to the French, Russian, Italian, and other schools of dance, particularly as they have been discussed and understood at the Royal Ballet School under Dame Ninette de Valois. The author discusses the physical and musical qualities of the steps and poses, describing how famous choreographers have used them in their ballets. The drawings by Peter Revitt form an integral part of the volume. Bibliography. Index of Technical Terms. Index of Ballets.

LAWSON, JOAN and PETER REVITT
Dressing for the Ballet
A. & C. Black, 1958. 96pp. $3.95. A practical how-to-do it book for dancers giving instructions on the making of suitable costumes. Drawings of many types and styles of patterns together with full instructions for cutting out and sewing.

MALVERN, GLADYS
Dancing Star: The Story of Anna Pavlova
Messner, 1942. 280pp. $3.95. Miss Malvern has written a biography of Anna Pavlova for young people. It details the childhood days in St. Petersburg through the triumphs of the dancing years. Illustrated by Susanne Suba. Bibliography. Index.

MARA, THALIA
The Language of Ballet
Dance Horizons, Undated. 120pp. Paper $2.95. This reprint of the 1966 publication provides more than 600 entries of the unique words and terms constituting the vocabulary of ballet. Illustrated.

MARCELIAIRE, PHILIPPE
Ballet and the Dance
Harrap, 1970. 24pp. $1.75. A simple definition of dance, for young people, showing how ballet has developed as an art form. Illustrated with full color illustrations on every page by Edith Dasnoy.

MASSINE, LEONIDE
My Life in Ballet
St. Martin's, 1969. 318pp. $8.95. The autobiography of the celebrated dancer-choreographer. He describes his early training at the Moscow Theatre School, his first engagements at the Maly and Bolshoi Theatres, his work with Ballets Russes, and the choreographing of his great ballets. Illustrated with photographs. Catalogue of Ballets. Index.

MONEY, KEITH
The Art of the Royal Ballet
World, 1968. 272pp. $12.50. Originally published in 1965 and now revised, this is a record of the Royal Ballet during the time Sir Frederick Ashton was beginning to guide the company as its Director. The many photographs show all of the Company's artists in a variety of roles and a record of Christopher Gable's career with the Company. Photographs show rehearsals as well as performances and there are also many shots of Fonteyn, Nureyev, and Gable in action.

MONEY, KEITH
The Royal Ballet Today
World, 1969. 272pp. $15.00. Over 250 illustrations include eight pages of full color showing Britain's Royal Ballet in performance and in rehearsal. The leading dancers and the ballets featured in the repertoire are all illustrated.

MOORE, LILLIAN
New York's First Ballet Season: 1792
New York Public Library, 1961. 18pp. Paper $1.00. This monograph describes in detail the first visit by a professional ballet company to New York. The company featured M. and Mme. Placide, "first rope dancers to the King of France." Illustrated.

MYERS, ELISABETH P.
Maria Tallchief: America's Prima Ballerina
Grosset & Dunlap, 1966. 175pp. $2.95. A biography of the ballerina written for children. It relates the struggles to reach the top from Miss Tallchief's early days as the daughter of an Indian chief in Oklahoma to her success with the New York City Ballet Company. Illustrated with drawings.

NIJINSKY, VASLAV
The Diary of Vaslav Nijinsky
Cape, 1963. 160pp. $4.95. Paper—University of California, 1968. 187pp. $2.25. First published in England in 1937, "The Diary" is a record of the year 1918–1919 when Nijinsly had retired to St. Moritz, suffering extreme mental agony from his efforts to break the hold of Diaghilev over his personal life. Edited, with a Preface, by Romola Nijinsky.

NOVERRE, JEAN GEORGES
Letters on Dancing and Ballet
Dance Horizons, 1966. 169pp. Paper $3.95. The letters of the noted eighteenth century choreographer are considered to be an exposition of the theories and laws governing ballet and dance representation and a contemporary history of dancing. Translated by Cyril W. Beaumont. Illustrated.

NUREYEV, RUDOLPH
Nureyev: An Autobiography
Dutton, 1963. 160pp. $5.95. This autobiography begins with an account of Russian ballet dancer Rudolph Nureyev's defection from the Leningrad Kirov Ballet Company in Paris in 1961, then returns to his early years of poverty in a remote Baskir village, his first dancing experiences, and his rise to prominence despite great opposition and prejudice against his "insubordination, non-assimilation, and dangerous individualism." The volume is illustrated with photographs by Richard Avedon, Michael Peto, and others. Preface by Alexander Bland.

PERCIVAL, JOHN
Modern Ballet
Dutton, 1970. 159pp. Paper $1.95. Mr. Percival charts and explains the changes that have taken place in ballet over the last few years. He also suggests some developments that may be still to to come. The work of fifty companies in Europe, Russia and the United States is discussed, as are world-renowned choreographers and dancers. Illustrated with over 100 photographs. Index.

READE, BRIAN
Ballet Designs and Illustrations: 1581 – 1940
British Information Service, 1967. 58pp. & 173 plates. $20.00. This catalogue of the balletic material in the Victoria and Albert Museum, London, provides a pictorial survey of ballet history. There is a considerable range of contemporary prints showing costumes and performances from sixteenth century Italy to the work of Diaghilev in the present century.

REYNA, FERDINANDO
A Concise History of Ballet
Grosset & Dunlap, 1964. 255pp. $5.95. The evolution of ballet from its beginnings in fifteenth century Italy, as seen in the gradual transformation of the art from dancing mixed with singing and recitation to the formal ballet of modern times. The influences, traditions, techniques, and personalities that have shaped ballet's history are examined. Over 200 illustrations from all periods are included. Index.

RYAN, JUNE
Ballet History
Roy, 1960. 72pp. $3.95. A brief history of the development of the European ballet from the seventeenth century to the present with descriptions of the more important ballets and brief biographies of leading dancers and choreographers. Drawings by the author.

SALTAN, PIERRE – Editor
A Day with Galina Ulanova
Cassell, 1960. 32pp. $2.75. A pictorial survey of the art of Ulanova with detailed photographs of the ballerina at practice.

SALTAN, PIERRE – Editor
A Day with Marjorie Tallchief and Georges Skibine
Cassell, 1960. 32pp. $2.75. A pictorial study of the husband and wife ballet team showing them in practice, rehearsal, and performance.

SALTAN, PIERRE – Editor
A Day with Yvette Chauvire
Cassell, 1960. 24pp. $2.75. A pictorial essay on the art of the ballerina with photographs of the dancer in performance.

SELBY–LOWNDES, JOAN
How A Ballet Is Produced
Routledge & Kegan Paul, 1958. 145pp. $3.50. In this book, written for young people, the author illustrates the development of a ballet production, giving an account of every stage of the work and the responsibilities of every member of the production group. Illustrated with drawings and photographs.

SHERBON, ELIZABETH
On The Count of One
National Press, 1968. 168pp. Paper $6.65. A guide to movement and progression for the teacher in ballet class. After initial chapters on approach and the vocabulary of dance, basic technique exercises are provided and a special chapter on dance for men is included. Suggested lesson plans are provided and there are lists of records, films, books, and periodicals on dance. Illustrated with sketches of exercises.

SKEAPING, MARY
Ballet Under the Three Crowns
Dance Perspectives, 1967. 62pp. Paper $2.95. A study of Swedish ballet history. Illustrated in color and black-and-white.

SLONIMSKY, YURI
The Bolshoi Ballet
Central Books, 1960. 176pp. $4.95. Published in Russia, this is a history of the Bolshoi Ballet Company. The author provides a chapter which poses the aesthetic precepts of Soviet ballet. Illustrated with photographs of the dancers and the productions.

SMITH, WILLIAM C. – Compiler
The Italian Opera and Contemporary Ballet in London: 1789 – 1820
See Page 287

SOKOLOVA, LYDIA
Dancing for Diaghilev
John Murray, 1960. 287pp. $5.95. Edited by Richard Buckle, these are the memoirs of Diaghilev's principal character dancer. Miss Sokolova danced with the Diaghilev Ballet company in the early days of Nijinsky, Karasavina, and Fokine, and was still with the company when Diaghilev's death in 1929 ended the enterprise. Illustrated with photographs. Index.

STILLER, SONIA
Dancing in Action
Borden, 1953. 46pp. Paper $1.50. This ballet book recreates the illusion of movement in twelve color pictures designed to be viewed through three-dimensional glasses provided. There are 350 dance illustrations and 250 dance terms are explained.

STREATFIELD, NOEL
The First Book of the Ballet
Watts, 1953. 69pp. $3.75. Basic exercises and steps presented in simple text for the young reader.

SWIFT, MARY GRACE
The Art of the Dance in the U.S.S.R.

University of Notre Dame, 1968. 405pp. $15.00. Through close scrutiny of the librettos of many ballets performed in Russia, and documentation of government criticism, approval, or ostracism of the most famous and talented directors and writers and dancers, the use of the ballet by the Soviet government for political purposes is studied. Illustrated with photographs. Selected Bibliography. Notes. Index.

SWINSON, CYRIL – Editor
Dancers and Critics
A. & C. Black, 1950. 80pp. $1.95. Thirteen of the leading ballet critics tell how they assess a ballet, a dancer, or a choreographer. Among these critics are: Cyril Beaumont, Anatole Chujoy, Arnold Haskell, and Walter Terry. Illustrated with photographs.

TAPER, BERNARD
Balanchine
Collins, 1964. 288pp. $4.50. A biography of the founder of the New York City Ballet. The author discusses his youth in Russia, his association with Diaghilev during the 1920's, his early work in America, Broadway and Hollywood activity, and the establishment of the City Center Company. Illustrated. Appendices. Index.

TER–ARUTUNIAN, ROUBEN
In Search of Design
Dance Perspectives, 1966. 49pp. Paper $2.95. An essay by the reknowned scenic designer on his work for the ballet. Illustrated with photographs and reproductions of the designs. List of Designs: 1950–1966.

TERRY, WALTER
Ballet: A Pictorial History
Van Nostrand, 1970. 64pp. $5.95. Written especially for young people, this is an introduction to ballet history from its beginning in approximately 1581 to the dancers currently practicing the art today. Illustrated with contemporary art work and photographs. Index.

TERRY, WALTER
The Ballet Companion: A Popular Guide for the Ballet–Goer
Dodd–Mead, 1968. 236pp. $5.95. The eminent critic presents information about every aspect of ballet. He discusses the history, technique, the companies, and the productions, costumes, and the interpretations of roles. Sixteen pages of photographs are included as well as line drawings by Mel Juan. Also provided is a glossary of dance terms. List of ballets with production details. Index.

UNTERMEYER, LOUIS
Tales from the Ballet
Golden Press, 1969. 92pp. $5.95. Stories of the great ballets as adapted by Mr. Untermeyer with illustrations in color by A. and M. Provensen. The stories are especially adapted for children and the adapter provides production notes on each of the twenty ballets.

VAGANOVA, AGRIPPINA
Basic Principles of Classical Ballet: Russian Ballet Techniques
Dover, 1969. 171pp. Paper $2.00. A reprint of the 1946 publication, translated from the Russian by Anatole Chujoy. All basic principles of ballet movement, grouped by fundamental types, are covered. Diagrams show exact positions. The volume includes a sample lesson with musical accompaniment. Index.

VERDY, VIOLETTE
Giselle
McGraw–Hill, 1970. 56pp. $4.95. This is an adaptation and retelling of the libretto of the ballet by Theophile Gautier. It is intended for young people and is illustrated by Marcia Brown.

WALKER, KATHRINE SORLEY
Eyes on the Ballet
Putnam, 1963. 192pp. $4.50. Written especially for the young reader, this book examines ballet from the standpoint of the audience and shows the many interests a love of dance can help to cultivate in the young. Illustrated. Index.

WHITTAKER, HERBERT
Canada's National Ballet
McClelland & Stewart, 1967. 112pp. $12.00. The story of the development of Canada's National Ballet from the early nineteen-forties to its maturity as a company of international stature. The author provides an intimate glimpse of some of the people who have built the ballet in Canada and the current repertoire of the company. An Appendix includes the artists of the company and the repertoire from 1951 through 1967. Illustrated with over 160 photographs.

WINTER, GINNY LINVILLE
The Ballet Book
Astor–Honor, 1962. 47pp. $2.95. Designed for little girls about to take their first steps in ballet. Each movement is illustrated and described in simple verse.

WOODWARD, IAN
Ballet
Wills & Hepworth, 1969. 52pp. $ .95. The author tells the story of the development of ballet from the early days of dancing in the Royal Courts. He explains the language of ballet and classical mime and deals with such subjects as styles of dancing, training, clothes, and backstage preparation. Twenty-three pages of illustrations are provided.

WOODWARD, IAN
Balletgoing
Museum Press, 1967. 144pp. $5.95. This book aims at providing a sound basis for appreciation of ballet. The author lays stress on the technical aspects. Ballet as a career is considered and information on English contracts, salaries, and working conditions is given. Illustrated with drawings and photographs. Indices.

ZAIDENBERG, ARTHUR
How to Draw Ballet and Other Dancers
Abelard–Schuman, 1968. 64pp. $3.75. Mr. Zaidenberg demonstrates how to capture in drawings the spirit of the dance. His illustrations show ballet, ethnic, and social dancers.

Modern

ARMITAGE, MERLE
Martha Graham
Dance Horizons, 1966. 132pp. Paper $2.95. A reprint of the 1937 appreciation of Miss Graham and her work by such renowned dance figures as John Martin, Lincoln Kirstein, and many others. Included are lists of New York concerts, repertoire, and concert tours. Illustrated.

CHENEY, GAY and JANET STRADER
Modern Dance
Allyn & Bacon, 1969. 85pp. Paper $1.65. A guidebook to modern dance in which the authors map out a pattern of experiences the student dancer might have. Illustrated. Bibliography.

COHEN, SELMA JEANNE – Editor
The Modern Dance: Seven Statements of Belief
Wesleyan, 1966. 106pp. $6.50. Paper – 1969. 106pp. $1.95. Articles by Jose Limon, Anna Sokolow, Erick Hawkins, Donald McKayle, Alwin Nikolais, Pauline Koner, and Paul Taylor on the aesthetics and methods of their choreography. Illustrated with photographs of the artists.

CUNNINGHAM, MERCE
Changes: Notes on Choreography
Something Else Press, 1968. Unpaged. $8.95. These are the choreographer/dancer's in-progress notes for his dances. Cunningham approaches the dance in terms of its primary elements—movement in space and time—and the source from which they spring—stillness. He examines the theatre in terms of the presence or absence of movement, light, sound, decor, and costume. Profusely illustrated.

DUNCAN, IRMA
Duncan Dancer: An Autobiography
Wesleyan, 1965. 352pp. $6.95. The adopted daughter of Isadora Duncan describes her relation with the great dancer and her own career as teacher and dancer, from her youth through her triumphs in Europe and America. Illustrated. Index.

DUNCAN, IRMA
Isadora Duncan: Pioneer in the Art of Dance
New York Public Library, 1959. 15pp. Paper $1.00. The author, one of the original pupils in Isadora Duncan's first school, describes the Duncan ideas and ideals that revolutionized the dance. Illustrated.

DUNCAN, ISADORA
The Art of the Dance
Theatre Arts, 1969. 147pp. $12.50. Originally published in 1928, these are the dancer's notes and essays, speeches, and program notes in which Miss Duncan sets down her ideas on dance. Edited and with an Introduction by Sheldon Cheney, the book includes thirty-three drawings, paintings, and photographs of the dancer.

DUNCAN, ISADORA
My Life
Liveright, 1942. 359pp. $5.95. Paper – Universal, 1969. 319pp. $ .95. A biography of the internationally celebrated creator of modern dance. Originally published in 1927 and now reissued.

HALL, FERNAU
The World of Ballet and Dance
See Page 313

HORST, LOUIS and CARROLL RUSSELL
Modern Dance Forms in Relation to the Other Modern Arts
Dance Horizons, 1967. 149pp. Paper $2.95. A republication of the 1961 edition of the study of dance as an art form. The elements of dance: space design, rhythm, and texture, the backgrounds or souces of dance, and the immediacies of modern life that inspire modern dance are studied. Suggested musical accompaniments are included. Illustrated.

HUMPHREY, DORIS
The Art of Making Dances
Grove, 1962. 189pp. Paper $1.95. Written just before her death in 1958, this is Miss Humphrey's autobiography in art, and a practical source book on choreography. It contains a short history on the dance and various chapters on design, dynamics, and rhythm. A check list of composers of dances and a list of all Miss Humphrey's dances are added.

HUMPHREY, DORIS
New Dance: An Unfinished Autobiography
Dance Perspectives, 1966. 81pp. Paper $2.50. A brief sketch by Miss Humphrey of the beginning of her career, through the foundation and achievements of the Denishawn Company. Introduction by John Martin. Illustrated.

LLOYD, MARGARET
The Borzoi Book of Modern Dance
Dance Horizons, 1970. 382pp. Paper $5.95. An unabridged republication of the 1949 edition, this is a history of the development of modern dance in the United States. Thirty-two pages of photographs. Bibliography. Indices.

LOCKHART, AILEENE and ESTHER E. PEASE
Modern Dance: Building and Teaching Lessons
Wm. C. Brown, 1966. 189pp. & Plates. Spiral bound

$5.00. A guide to modern dance for the beginning dance teacher and for the student studying dance. Suggestions for structuring lessons, development of technique and style, accompaniment for dance, and terminology are all included. Illustrated with photographs. Piano accompaniments for lessons are provided. Selected Dance Bibliography.

McDONAGH, DON
The Rise and Fall and Rise of Modern Dance
Dutton, 1970. 344pp. $6.95. The author seeks to explain what modern dance is all about. Through a series of individual profiles, he gives a panoramic view of the aims and achievements of the new dancers including Paul Taylor, Merce Cunningham, Meredith Monk, Twyla Tharp, Alwin Nikolais, James Waring and others. An introductory chapter traces the development of modern dance from Isadora Duncan to Martha Graham to Merce Cunningham. Illustrated with photographs. Chronologies of each of the major artists. Index.

MARTIN, JOHN
America Dancing
Dance Horizons, 1968. 320pp. Paper $4.95. Originally published in 1936, this book details the background and personalities of the modern dance. The companies and the dancers as well as the theories and development of the field are covered. Illustrated with photographs. Index.

MARTIN, JOHN
The Modern Dance
Dance Horizons, 1965. 123pp. Paper $2.95. First printed in 1933 and now reissued, this is a discussion of the characteristics, form, and techniques of modern dance and its relation to other art forms.

MAYNARD, OLGA
American Modern Dancers: The Pioneers
Little, Brown, 1965. 218pp. $4.50. An introduction to modern dance through the biographies of the first creative workers in the field. Arranged for teacher-student use in classes. Illustrated.

NORRIS, DOROTHY E. KOCH and REVA P. SHINER
Keynotes to Modern Dance
Burgess, 1969. 229pp. Paper $7.00. Originally published in 1964 and now revised, this is a practical guide for teaching modern dance. Illustrated. Lists of recordings and films. Glossary. Selected Bibliography. Index.

PENROD, JAMES and JANICE GUDDE PLASTINO
The Dancer Prepares: Modern Dance for Beginners
National Press, 1970. 58pp. $3.95. Paper $1.65. The author introduces the student to modern dance. Such rudiments of the dancer's craft as basic techniques, care of the body, choreographic fundamentals, and evaluation procedures are discussed. Illustrated with photographs and drawings. List of References.

ST. DENIS, RUTH
An Unfinished Life
Dance Horizons, 1970. 391pp. Paper $5.95. Originally published in 1939 and now reissued, this is the autobiography of one of the founders of the modern dance movement. Index.

SCHEYER, ERNST
The Shapes of Space: The Art of Mary Wigman and Oskar Schlemmer
Dance Perspectives, 1970. 48pp. Paper $2.50. An appreciation of the dance art of Mary Wigman and Oskar Schlemmer. Illustrated with photographs.

SCHLUNDT, CHRISTENA L.
The Professional Appearances of Ruth St. Denis and Ted Shawn: A Chronology and an Index of Dances, 1906 – 1932
New York Public Library, 1962. 85pp. $3.00. The complete dance programs for the "Denishawn" performances here and abroad. Illustrated with eighteen photographs of the dancers. Index of Dances.

SCHNEIDER, ILYA ILYICH
Isadora Duncan: The Russian Years
Harcourt, Brace, 1968. 221pp. $6.95. Translated from the Russian by David Magershack, this is a record of Isadora's performances, her school, her methods of teaching, and her personal life during the five years she lived in Russia. Illustrated with thirty-two pages of photographs and reproductions of drawings and paintings of the dancer. Index.

SHAWN, TED
Every Little Movement
Dance Horizons, 1968. 127pp. Paper $2.95. A republication of the 1954 book about Francois Delsarte and his science of "Applied Aesthetics," the science of the effects of emotion upon the human body as seen in gesture and in speech. Mr. Shawn applies the science to the art of the dance.

SHURR, GERTRUDE and RAPHAEL DUNAVEN YOCOM
Modern Dance: Techniques and Teaching
Ronald Press, 1949. 191pp. $6.25. The authors analyze, illustrate and organize for teaching purposes some of the techniques of modern dance to provide a reference and a guide for teachers and students. The left hand page provides visual analysis and the right hand page provides descriptive analysis for more than seventy-five warm-ups, exercises, and techniques. Illustrated with photographs. Glossary.

SIEGEL, MARCIA B. — Editor
Dancer's Notes
Dance Perspectives, 1969. 49pp. Paper $2.95. Essays by eight modern dancers and choreographers on their art. Among the contributors: Lucas Hoving, Daniel Nagrin, Murray Louis, Remy Charlip, and Judith Dunn. Illustrated.

SORELL, WALTER
Hanya Holm: The Biography of an Artist
Wesleyan, 1969. 226pp. $7.95. A biography of the dancer, teacher, and choreographer. It is the story of her career, a statement of her aesthetic principles and an analysis of her performances. Miss Holm's own view of her life and work (A significant part of the text is in her own words.) provides the basis of the book. A chronology including choreographed works is provided. Illustrated with photographs. Index.

STEWART, VIRGINIA and MERLE ARMITAGE
The Modern Dance
Dance Horizons, 1970. 107pp. Paper $3.95. Originally published in 1935 and now reprinted, this is a symposium of statements on the modern dance in Germany and in America by such practicioners as Mary Wigman, Harold Kreutzberg, Martha Graham, Doris Humphrey, Charles Weidman, and Hanya Holm. Illustrated with twenty-four photographs.

TERRY, WALTER
Miss Ruth
Dodd, Mead, 1969. 206pp. $6.95. A biography of Ruth St. Denis, the dancer and dance innovator. Mr. Terry provides an authoritative account of "Miss Ruth's" romance, marriage, her partnership and relationship with Ted Shawn, and the creation of the Denishawn schools and companies. Illustrated with thirty-two pages of photographs. Index.

VAN TUYL, MARIAN
Anthology of "Impulse": Annual of Contemporary Dance 1951 – 1966
Dance Horizons, 1969. 150pp. Paper $2.95. This is a collection of essays on dance reprinted from the magazine, "Impulse." Among the contributors are: Martha Graham, Louis Horst, Ann Hutchinson, and Ann Halprin. The volume includes excerpts from the script of "A Dancer's World," a conversation with Anna Sokolow, and articles on notation, dance movies, and the performing arts workshop. illustrated.

WAGENKNECHT, EDWARD
Seven Daughters of the Theatre
University of Oklahoma, 1964. 234pp. $5.95. Studies of six actresses and one modern dancer. The portraits include: Jenny Lind, Sarah Bernhardt, Ellen Terry, Julia Marlowe, Mary Garden, Marilyn Monroe, and Isadora Duncan. Illustrated. Bibliography. Index.

WIGMAN, MARY
The Language of Dance
Wesleyan, 1966. 118pp. $12.50. Translated by Walter Sorell, this is the great German dancer-choreographer's considerations on the art of the dance: Its aesthetics, its nature as expression and as interpretation, and its relation to the spiritual needs of man. She also considers some of her own more notable dance creations. Illustrated with photographs.

Ethnic

ALFORD, VIOLET
Sword Dance and Drama
Merlin Press, 1962. 222pp. $6.00. A study of the sword dance in Great Britain and Europe and of its origins in ancient miming. The connection between the dance and English Mummers' plays is traced and analogies are seen in the folk drama of Piedmont, Rumania, Greece and, ultimately, in the Dionysiac threshing floor rites. Illustrated. Bibliography.

AMBROSE, KAY
Classical Dances and Costumes of India
Hillary House, 1965. 96pp. $7.00. Originally published in 1950 and now reissued, this is a study of Indian dancing which explains the development, construction, design, and significance of the dances: their choreography, rhythm, and costume. Introduction by Ram Gopal. Fifty-three photographs and many drawings illustrate the volume. Bibliography. Index.

BACKMAN, E. LOUIS
Religious Dances
Allen & Unwin, 1952. 364pp. $4.95. This is an account of the origins and history of religious dances and their significance in the Christian church. The author attempts to assess the role which religious dancing has played in the history of medicine and pays particular attention to the dancing epidemics of the Middle Ages. Illustrated. Bibliography. Index.

BIEMILLER, RUTH
Dance: The Story of Katherine Dunham
Doubleday, 1969. 144pp. $3.50. Written for young people, this is the story of Katherine Dunham's career as a dancer, choreographer, and anthropologist. Illustrated with photographs of Miss Dunham and her company.

BOURGUIGNON, ERIKA
Trance Dance
Dance Perspectives, 1968. 61pp. Paper $2.95. This is a study of ecstatic dance, the dance connected in some way with the phenomena of trance. Its various forms and rituals throughout history and the world are studied. Illustrated.

BOWERS, FAUBION
The Dance in India
AMS Press, 1967. 175pp. $12.00. Originally published in 1953 and now reissued, this is a study of the Indian dance as it is in the present day. The book is divided into five sections, each of which details a different type of dance: Bharata Natya, Kathakali, Kathak, Manipuri, and Folk Dances. The volume is illustrated with seventeen pages of photographs of the dances and dancers described in the text. Index.

BOWERS, FAUBION
Theatre in the East: A Survey of Asian Dance and Drama
See Page 116

BRANDON, JAMES R.
Theatre in Southeast Asia
See Page 116

BROWNING, MARY
Micronesian Heritage
Dance Perspectives, 1970. 49pp. Paper $2.95. The Autumn 1970 issue of Dance Perspectives covers dancing in the Marshall, Mariana, Caroline and Gilbert Islands in the South Pacific. Illustrated with photographs.

CHIZHOVA, ALEXANDRA
Beryozka Dance Company
Central Books, 1969. Unpaged. $3.95. Published in Russia, this is the history of the Russian folk dance company which is under the direction of Nadezhda Nadezhdina. Translated by R. Flaxman and profusely illustrated with color and black-and-white photographs.

CZARNOWSKI, LUCILE K.
Folk Dance Teaching Cues
National Press, 1963. 93pp. Spiral bound $3.35. The intention of this volume is to assist the new teacher of folk dance in solving some of the basic problems he may encounter and to stimulate the experienced teacher to find new ideas and methods. Musical illustrations and diagrams for forty-eight folk dances.

DE ZOETE, BERYL
Dance and Magic Drama in Ceylon
See Page 118

DUGGAN, ANNE SCHLEY and JEANETTE SCHLOTTMANN, ABBIE RUTLEDGE
The Teaching of Folk Dance
Ronald Press, 1948. 116pp. $6.00. Topics discussed include definitions and sources of folk dance, specific methods of teaching, evolution of teaching, and production of folk festivals and folk dance parties.

DUNHAM, KATHERINE
Island Possessed
Doubleday, 1969. 280pp. $6.95. Miss Dunham explains her approach to Haiti and its culture during her thirty-year fascination with the island and its people and customs. She explains how the rites and rhythms of Haiti came to dominate her art and how she became an initiate of voodoo. Glossary.

DUNHAM, KATHERINE
A Touch of Innocence
Harcourt, Brace, 1969. 312pp. Paper $1.45. Published in 1959, and now reissued, these memoirs recount the early years of Miss Dunham's life. The dancer/choreographer provides a portrait of a racially mixed family rooted in the American Middle West and also an objective reminiscence of her youth.

FLETT, J.F. and T.M. FLETT
Traditional Dancing in Scotland
Vanderbilt University, 1966. 313pp. $8.95. A factual picture of many little-known aspects of Scottish dancing. The period covered extends up to about 1914 and the book gives the social background, descriptions of dances and steps, and the histories of the dances. Illustrated. Index.

GARFIAS, ROBERT
Gagaku: The Music and Dances of the Japanese Imperial Household
Theatre Arts, 1959. 40pp. Paper $1.50. A brief essay on the origins and development of Gagaku, with a study of its techniques, music, and costume. Introduction by Lincoln Kirstein. Photographs illustrate performances. Bibliography. Discography.

GILBERT, CECILE
International Folk Dance at a Glance
Burgess, 1969. 171pp. Paper $5.25. A manual of sixty-seven folk dances with step-by-step instructions. Basic movements are described, and teaching suggestions and record sources are provided. Illustrated with drawings. Bibliography.

GUNJI, MASAKATSU
Buyo: The Classical Dance
Lippincott, 1970. 207pp. $5.95. Translated by Don Kenny with an Introduction by James R. Brandon, this is an introduction to one of Japan's oldest performing arts. The author shows that Buyo has been the chief feature of celebratory occasions from ancient times and its role as the ancestor of the drama is still apparent in the Japanese theater today. 153 photographs in black-and-white and color show dance types and roles, scenes from famous dance pieces, notable performers, and paintings and prints from dance history. Chronology.

HALL, J. TILLMAN
Folk Dance
Goodyear, 1969. 106pp. Paper $2.35. The author provides chapters on the history, value, fundamentals of folk dancing as well as hints for teaching. Explicit instructions for execution of dances from all over the world are included. Suggested Readings. Illustrated with photographs.

HARRIS, JANE A. and ANNE PITTMAN, MARLYS S. WALLER
Dance A While
Burgess, 1969. 386pp. Spiral bound $8.65. Originally published in 1950 and now revised and updated, this is a handbook of folk, square and social dance. The purpose is to provide the teacher and recreation

leader with practical suggestions for dance teaching. Each dance is described in a step-by-step procedure with record sources. Illustrated with drawings. Glossary. Bibliography. Index.

ILUPINA, ANNA and YELENA LUTSKAYA
Moiseyev's Dance Company
Central Books, 1966. Unpaged. Paper $3.50. Published in Russia, this is the story of the Russian folk dance company, told mainly in photographs by Yevgeny Umnov.

IVANOVA, ANNA
The Dance in Spain: A History
Praeger, 1970. 202pp. $10.00. A comprehensive account of the development of Spanish dance over four hundred years. Such indigenous forms as the gypsy flamenco dance are also reported on. Included are seventy-one illustrations. Appendices. Bibliography. Index.

JENSEN, CLAYNE R. and MARY BEE JENSEN
Beginning Folk Dancing
Wadsworth, 1966. 60pp. Paper $1.65. A handbook on the values, history, and basic skills of folk dancing. Step-by-step instructions are provided for twenty-four selected dances. Illustrated with photographs. Glossary. Bibliography. Index.

JENSEN, CLAYNE R. and MARY BEE JENSEN
Beginning Folk Dancing
Wadsworth, 1966. 62pp. Paper $1.65. This handbook provides information on the values, history, and basic skills of square dancing. Information on square dance calling is included. Step-by-step directions are given for selected dances. Illustrated with photographs. Glossary. Bibliography.

JERSTAD, LUTHER G.
Mani–Rimdu: Sherpa Dance–Drama
University of Washington, 1969. 192pp. $8.50. The author describes the Nepalese form of Cham, a traditional Tibetan Buddhist dance-drama, as he observed it among the Sherpas of northeastern Nepal. Mr. Jerstad focuses on the religious and historical message which the dances convey and describes in detail the physical setting of the drama, the musical instruments, the costumes, masks, and the training of the actors who participate. Illustrated with photographs and line drawings. Glossary. Bibliography. Index.

JONES, CLIFFORD R. and BETTY TRUE JONES
Kathakali
Theatre Arts, 1970. 116pp. Paper $3.95. An introduction to the dance drama of Kerala, India, with chapters on tradition and preparation, costume and makeup, the various forms of the dance, choreographic structure, musical accompaniment, and acting techniques. Lavishly illustrated with photographs. Notes. Glossary.

MARTI, SAMUEL and GERTRUDE PROKOSCH KURATH
Dances of Anahuac: The Choreography and Music of Precortesian Dances
Aldine, 1964. 251pp. $12.50. This study of Mayan and Aztec dances describes them and relates them to religious rites, social structure, and daily life. Source materials on the chronology and evaluation of artifacts and pictorial evidence are given. An analysis of dance movements and studies of comparative choreographies from other regions are included.

MASON, BERNARD S.
Dances and Stories of the American Indian
Ronald Press, 1944. 269pp. $8.00. A study of American Indian dances with explicit instructions for each of the dances. Make-up, costume, and dance accessories are also studied. Illustrated with line drawings, and photographs. Index.

MATTEO
Woods that Dance
Dance Perspectives, 1968. 49pp. Paper $2.50. This is a history of castanets from their development in prehistoric times through their use by performers today. Illustrated with reproductions of drawings and paintings and with photographs.

MYNATT, CONSTANCE V. and BERNARD D. KAIMAN
Folk Dancing for Students and Teachers
Wm. C. Brown, 1968. 113pp. Spiral bound $3.95. This is a guidebook to presenting folk dances. After an introductory chapter on the history of folk dance, the authors present instruction on the teaching of this type of dance including facilities and equipment, and suggestions for planning the material, and preparation for the lesson. Complete instructions for sixty-five dances are provided. Illustrated with drawings.

NETTLEFORD, REX
Roots and Rhythms: Jamaica's National Dance Theatre
Hill & Wang, 1970. 128pp. $6.50. The author records the history of the Jamaica National Dance Theatre Company which was founded in 1962. A complete synopsis of the repertoire is included. Maria La Yacona has provided more than 130 photographs of the company and its dancers.

OESTERLEY, W. O. E.
The Sacred Dance
Dance Horizons, 1968. 234pp. Paper $3.95. A republication of the 1923 study which attempted to estimate the part played by the sacred dance among the peoples of antiquity as well as among the uncultured races in modern times. Index.

PETRIDES, THEODORE and ELFLEIDA PETRIDES
Folk Dances of the Greeks
Exposition Press, 1961. 78pp. $4.00. Twenty-five

folk dances are presented in step-by-step illustrations, with drawings of foot patterns, notes on style, historical background, and characteristics.

RIDGEWAY, WILLIAM
The Dramas and Dramatic Dances of the Non-European Races
Blom, 1964. 448pp. $17.50. A reprint of the 1915 edition, this is an examination of the religious ritual, ceremonials, and dance theatrics of the major Asian peoples. The author maintains that dance and dance drama originated in the indigenous worship of dead leaders and he shows how the traditional and the contemporary dances of these peoples still reflect this origin. Appendix on the origin of comedy.

SARABHAI, MRINALINI
The Eight Nayikas: Heroines of the Classical Dance of India
Dance Perspectives, 1966. 49pp. Paper $2.95. A study of the dance and dancers of India. Illustrated with photographs.

SASPORTES, JOSE
Feasts and Folias: The Dance in Portugal
Dance Perspectives, 1970. 50pp. Paper $2.95. A study of the dance in Portugal with contemporary illustrations. Notes. List of Foreign Artists Dancing in Portugal from 1752 to 1807.

SCHNEIDER, GRETCHEN ADEL
Pigeon Wings and Polkas
Dance Perspectives, 1969. 57pp. Paper $2.95. A study of the dance of the California miners during the gold rush. Illustrated with contemporary material. Bibliography.

SINCLAIR, OLGA
Dancing in Britain
Blackwell, 1970. 62pp. $1.95. Written especially for children, with illustrations in color and black-and-white, this is a survey of the folk dance in the British Isles. Index.

SINGHA, RINA and REGINALD MASSEY
Indian Dances: Their History and Growth
Braziller, 1967. 264pp. $12.50. The authors provide a comprehensive survey of classical Indian dancing, include technical information for the specialist in the field, and offer a guide to the audience of this art. Illustrated. Glossary of Terms. Bibliography. Index.

SOCIETY FOR INTERNATIONAL FOLK DANCING
A Selection of European Folk Dances: Volumes 1, 2, and 3
Pergamon, 1964. Three volumes—each volume: 39pp. Paper $1.75. Instructions and music for folk dances from various European countries.

SQUIRES, JOHN L. and ROBERT E. McLEAN
American Indian Dances
Ronald Press, 1963. 132pp. $5.50. The steps, rhythms, costumes, and interpretation of American Indian dances. Illustrated.

Social

ARBEAU, THOINOT
Orchesography
Dover, 1967. 266pp. Paper $2.50. Translated by Mary Stewart Evans, with a new Introduction and notes by Julia Sutton and a new Labanotation section by Mireille Backer and Julia Sutton, this is a republication of the 1948 English edition of the 1589 treatise on sixteenth century dance and dance music. It is written as a dialogue in which Arbeau instructs a young man in the art of "ballroom" dancing. Fourteen of the dances described in the text have been translated into Labonatation. Illustrated. Bibliography. Index.

ARBEAU, THOINOT
Orchesography
Dance Horizons, 1965. 174pp. Paper $3.95. Written in 1589 and translated in 1925 by Cyril W. Beaumont, and now reissued, this is a detailed thesis on sixteenth century dance and dance music. Practical instructions for dancing several of the dances are provided.

CRATHORN, CHARLES
Old Time Dancing
Arco, 1963. 158pp. $3.25. A manual of pre-World War I dances.

FEUILLET, RAOUL AUGER
For the Further Improvement of Dancing
Dance Horizons, 1970. 88pp. Paper $2.95. Originally published in London in 1710 and now reissued in a facsimile edition, this is a "treatise of choreography or y Art of Dancing Country Dances." Complete diagrams of "foot movements."

SPENCER, FRANK and PEGGY SPENCER
Come Dancing
A. S. Barnes, 1969. 190pp. $5.95. A guide to English-style ballroom dancing which includes a history of competitive ballroom dancing. Information about the various dances, including photographic presentations, and advice about competitions is included. Illustrated with photographs. Discography. List of Champions.

WHITMAN, WALTER and VICTOR SILVESTER
The Complete Old Time Dancer
Jenkins, 1967. 256pp. $3.25. Step-by-step, the authors provide the basic principles of social dances of pre-World War I vintage. From the two-step to the tango, the barn dance to the Brittania Saunter, the basic steps are enumerated. Index.

YOUMANS, JOHN G.
Social Dance
Goodyear, 1969. 86pp. Paper $2.00. This volume includes instruction in nine different social dances. Illustrated with photographs.

DANCE NOTATION

BENESH, RUDOLF and JOAN BENESH
An Introduction to Benesh Movement–Notation: Dance
Dance Horizons, 1970. 56pp. Paper $1.95. Originally published in 1956 and now reissued, this is an introduction to a method of dance notation. Illustrated.

HUTCHINSON, ANN
Labanotation
Theatre Arts, 1970. 528pp. Paper $4.95. A revised and expanded second edition of the study first published in 1954. Miss Hutchinson attempts to answer all questions from teachers of Labanotation and those attempting to master this system of analyzing and recording movement. Preface by George Balanchine. Illustrated. Glossaries. Appendices. Index.

LABAN, RUDOLF
Principles of Dance and Movement Notation
Dance Horizons, 1970. 56pp. Paper $1.95. Originally published in 1956 and now reissued, this is an introduction to a method of dance notation. Illustrated. Indices.

PRESTON–DUNLOP, VALERIE
An Introduction to Kinetography Laban
Macdonald and Evans, 1966. 32pp. Paper $1.25. Kinetography is a system of recording movement by means of written symbols. This system was originally propounded by Rudolf Laban some forty years ago and is herewith explained. Examples of how to use these symbols to describe the broad outline and the detail of a variety of movements are given. Illustrated.

PRESTON–DUNLOP, VALERIE
Practical Kinetography Laban
Dance Horizons, 1969. 216pp. Paper $3.95. This book is designed as a practical introduction to Laban's system of movement notation. It has been prepared as a step-by-step guide for student-teachers of movement, and contains examples of notation of creative movement, dance, athletics, and gymnastics. Illustrated.

STEPANOV, V. I.
Alphabet of Movements of the Human Body
Dance Horizons, 1969. 47pp. Paper $1.95. A republication of the study in recording the movements of the human body by means of musical signs. Translated by Raymond Lister from the French edition of 1892. Illustrated.

OTHER CATEGORIES OF THEATRE

RELIGIOUS THEATRE

Histories and Critiques

ANDERSON, MARY D.
Drama and Imagery in English Medieval Churches
See Page 148

BATES, KATHARINE LEE
The English Religious Drama
Kennikat, 1966. 254pp. $10.00. Originally published in 1893, this is a history of religious drama in England. Passion plays, saint plays, miracle plays, and moralities are all described. An Appendix lists extant plays and general references.

BATTENHOUSE, ROY W.
Shakespearean Tragedy: Its Art and Its Christian Premises
See Page 54

BAXTER, K.M.
Contemporary Theatre and the Christian Faith
Abingdon Press, 1964. 112pp. $2.75. A study of contemporary drama from "Waiting for Godot" to "West Side Story." The author maintains that the secular playwright and the Christian theologian have insights of critical importance to each other and for the public. Index.

BLUEM, A. WILLIAM
Religious Television Programs
See Page 487

BRYANT, JOSEPH A.
Hippolyta's View: Some Christian Aspects of Shakespeare's Plays
See Page 85

BUCH, ARTHUR T.
The Bible on Broadway
See Page 237

BUTLER, IVAN
Religion in the Cinema
See Page 433

CARLSON, JAMES R. and WARREN KLIEWER – Editors
Religious Theatre: Number 7 – Biblical Drama
Religious Theatre Publs., 1969. 90pp. Paper $1.50. This latest issue of the periodical contains a symposium on biblical drama, a section of news and comment, and a complete play: "The Brief and Violent Reign of Absalom" by James D. Pendleton, with notes on the production.

CAWLEY, A.C. – Editor
The Wakefield Pageants in the Towneley Cycle
See Page 148

COX, ROGER L.
Between Earth and Heaven: Shakespeare, Dostoevsky and the Meaning of Christian Tragedy
See Page 81

CRAIG, HARDIN
English Religious Drama of the Middle Ages
See Page 148

DRIVER, TOM F.
The Sense of History in Greek and Shakespearean Drama
See Page 33

EDYVEAN, ALFRED R.
Religious Drama Project Play List
See Page 6

EVERSOLE, FINLEY – Editor
Christian Faith and the Contemporary Arts
Abingdon Press, 1962. 255pp. $5.00. Mr. Eversole has brought together twenty-eight essays by writers, artists, and authorities to establish a point of contact between faith and culture, church and world. This symposium discusses the communication between Christian faith and contemporary culture. Illustrated. Index.

FRIEDMAN, MAURICE – Editor
Martin Buber and the Theater
Funk & Wagnalls, 1969. 170pp. $7.95. The theatre as a central aspect of the Austrian theologian/philosopher's life and thought is the theme of this work. Dr. Friedman includes three essays concerning Buber's relationship with the theatre and the first English translation of Buber's religious mystery play, "Elijah," written in 1955 but not made public until 1963. Index.

FRYE, ROLAND MUSHAT
Shakespeare and Christian Doctrine
See Page 81

GARDINER, HAROLD C.
Mysteries' End: An Investigation of the Last Days of the Medieval Religious Stage
See Page 149

HARDISON, JR., O.B.
Christian Rite and Christian Drama in the Middle Ages
See Page 149

HARRISON, JANE
Prolegomena to the Study of Greek Religion
See Page 34

HARRISON, JANE
Themis
See Page 34

HATFIELD, LOUIS DUANE
As the Twig Is Bent: Therapeutic Values in the Use of Drama and the Dramatic in the Church
Vantage, 1965. 166pp. $2.95. Mr. Hatfield traces the history of therapeutic drama from the earliest examples in the rituals of primitive peoples through to the psychodrama of the present day. He considers the elements of drama, religion, and therapy in his explanation of the therapeutics of religious drama and concludes with specific present-day examples of religious plays and programs using a consciously therapeutic approach. Bibliography.

HEATON, VERNON
The Oberammergau Passion Play
Robert Hale, 1970. 160pp. $5.95. A history of the Passion Play as produced in Oberammergau for almost 350 years. The actors who devoted so much of their lives to the play, the building that today holds an audience of 5,000, the company of more than 700 actors and musicians required for the play, and the attitude of the villagers during Passion Year are all discussed. Photographs of the village, scenes from the play, and portraits of some of the actors are included. Index.

HUNNINGHER, BENJAMIN
The Origin of the Theatre
See Page 12

HURLEY, NEIL P.
Theology Through Film
See Page 436

JONES, G. WILLIAMS
Sunday Night at the Movies
See Page 437

KAUFMANN, WALTER
From Shakespeare to Existentialism
See Page 137

KNIGHT, G. WILSON
Shakespeare and Religion
See Page 86

KOLVE, V.A.
The Play Called Corpus Christi
Stanford University, 1966. 337pp. $8.50. A critical study of the Corpus Christi drama which held the stage for more than 200 years. It investigates the medieval idea of theatre as play and game. Each of the four extant Corpus Christi plays is examined. Bibliography. Notes. Index.

LONGSWORTH, ROBERT
The Cornish Ordinalia: Religion and Dramturgy
Harvard, 1967. 173pp. $6.50. The Cornish "Ordinalia" consists of three plays written at the start of the fourteenth century which depict man's fall and regeneration through Biblical episodes. Mr. Longsworth's discussion of the dramatic, liturgical, and the theological elements of these plays indicates their complexity and their importance in medieval drama. Bibliography. Index.

MENDL, R.W.S.
Revelation in Shakespeare
See Page 86

MERCHANT, W. MOELWYN
Creed and Drama: An Essay in Religious Drama
SPCK, 1965. 119pp. $3.50. Paper—Fortress Press, 1966. 119pp. $1.95. The author "tries to trace one argument only, the relation between certain beliefs concerning human destiny and the dramatic form in which they were successively cast." Especial attention is given to Shakespeare, whom the author describes as the artist who "supremely bridged the imaginative gap between the sacred and the secular." Bibliography.

MOSELEY, J. EDWARD
Using Drama in the Church
Bethany Press, 1963. 96pp. Paper $1.00. Originally published in 1939 and revised in 1962, this book may be used by drama groups in local churches. Among the subjects discussed are the relationship of drama to the church, how to use drama and the technique of informal dramatization, an introduction to the field of religious drama with source materials and suggestions for practical projects. Appendices.

PROSSER, ELEANOR
Drama and Religion in the English Mystery Plays
See Page 149

ROSTON, MURRAY
Biblical Drama in England from the Middle Ages to the Present Day
Northwestern University, 1968. 335pp. $12.50. The twofold aims of this history of biblical drama are to provide a critical evaluation of the plays themselves in the context of their own times, and at the same time to suggest the insights they afford into the religious history of the English people. Dr. Roston surveys each period from the middle ages to the present day on its own terms, bringing out the varying relation over the years between regard for the sanctity of the scriptural text and the demands of art. Among the works studied are the mystery cycles as well as the works of Milton, Byron, Yeats, Fry, and MacLeish. The author includes a Select List of Plays and an Index.

SALTER, F.M.
Mediaeval Drama in Chester
See Page 149

SPANOS. WILLIAM V.
The Christian Tradition in Modern British Verse Drama
Rutgers University, 1967. 400pp. $12.50. In this critical examination of the religious verse drama in England, the author deals with the problem of the disintegration of the Judeo-Christian system of beliefs and symbols and the artists' search for fresh means of reconciling reality and value. The Christian verse drama movement is explored and extended analyses are given of representative plays by Eliot, Masefield, Fry, and others. Bibliography. Index.

SPEAIGHT, ROBERT
Christian Theatre
Hawthorn, 1960. 140pp. $3.95. A study of Christian influence on drama from the Middle Ages to the present, with chapters on liturgical drama, Miracle, Mystery and Morality plays, Christian theatre in the Reformation and the Renaissance, Shakespeare, the Jesuit drama, Calderon, Corneille, Racine, and Christianity in the modern theatre.

STEIN, WALTER
Criticism as Dialogue
See Page 14

STICCA, SANDRO
The Latin Passion Play: Its Origins and Development
State University of New York, 1970. 220pp. $10.00. A study of the Latin Passion play in which Professor Sticca examines the medieval liturgical ceremonies commemorating the events in Christ's Passion and traces their gradual change in character from the contemplative to the dramatic. Illustrated with four facsimile page plates. Bibliography. Index.

TUNISON, JOSEPH S.
Dramatic Traditions of the Dark Ages
See Page 14

VAN ABBE, DEREK
Drama in Renaissance Germany and Switzerland
See Page 137

VOS, NELVIN
The Drama of Comedy: Victim and Victor
John Knox, 1966. 125pp. Paper $1.95. A study of the works of Thornton Wilder, Eugene Ionesco, and Christopher Fry from a theological point of view. Bibliography.

WEALES, GERALD
Religion in Modern English Drama
University of Pennsylvania, 1961. 317pp. $9.00. An examination into the ways in which religion has been used on the commercial stage in England since World War II. The history of the church drama movement is studied and the post-war developments by Eliot, Fry, and their followers are analyzed. List of dramas: 1879–1955. Bibliography. Index.

WICKHAM, GLYNNE
Shakespeare's Dramatic Heritage
See Page 85

WILLIAMS, ARNOLD
The Characterization of Pilate in the Towneley Plays
See Page 150

WILLIAMS, ARNOLD
The Drama of Medieval England
See Page 150

YOUNG, KARL
The Drama of the Medieval Church
See Page 150

Production

ALLEN, ARTHUR B.
Religious Drama for Amateur Players
Faber & Faber, 1958. 204pp. $3.95. This book of practical advice contains complete examples, of varying degrees of complexity, of mimes and plays suitable for production. Two mimes of the Nativity, a cycle for Holy Week, and a play based on "The Pilgrim's Progress" have been especially written for this volume by the author. An Appendix lists suitable plays for amateur groups.

COLLINS, FREDA
Let's Prepare a Nativity Play
Garnet Miller, 1954. 30pp. $1.95. The author describes her own experiences in producing Nativity plays in a children's settlement. Movement, grouping, costume, and the conduct of rehearsals are all discussed. A short Nativity play, "The Angels at Bethlehem," with notes on production, is included. Illustrated. Bibliography.

EASTMAN, FRED and LOUIS WILSON
Drama in the Church
Samuel French, 1960. 187pp. $2.00. This manual sums up the most important things drama groups should know before they begin to produce plays in church. The plays are considered as means of ministering to the souls of men rather than as mere entertainment. Lists of Plays.

JOHNSON, ALBERT
Best Church Plays
See Page 6

TAYLOR, MARGARET FISK
A Time to Dance: Symbolic Movement in Worship
United Church Press, 1967. 180pp. Paper $2.95. Mrs. Taylor tells, step-by-step, how to be a leader of a dance-choir. She explains how many members there should be, what kind of robes to wear, how to get men and boys to join the group, and she describes

dance dramas, processions, narrative outlines, and special programs for religious holidays. She also includes a history of religious dance and details the renaissance of dance movement in twentieth century worship. Illustrated. Bibliography.

CHILDREN AND THE THEATRE

General Reference Works

See also sections on:
Speech, Puppets, Model Theatres, Circus, and Magic.

CHORPENNING, CHARLOTTE
Twenty-One Years with Children's Theatre
Anchorage, 1954. 112pp. $3.50. Information on writing and producing plays for children, based on the author's experiences at the Goodman Theatre, Chicago. Illustrated.

CROSSCUP, RICHARD
Children and Dramatics
Scribner's, 1966. 271pp. $5.95. Mr. Crosscup introduces the reader to the need of children for the broadening emotional commitment of dramatics and the ways in which an adult can use dramatics to contribute to a child's development. He deals thoroughly with the practical matters of speech, movement, scenery, lighting, properties, costume, and make-up. Index.

DAVIS, JED H. – Editor
A Directory of Children's Theatres in the United States
A.E.T.A., 1968. 205pp. Paper $3.55. A compilation of children's theatre organizations that stage or sponsor productions for children. Each entry includes name and address of organization and contact, category of group, year program began, paid staff, type, number, and cast and crew member information, and source of income. A list of other national organizations concerned with children's theatre, and a list of publishers of children's theatre plays are included.

LEACH, ROBERT
Theatre for Youth
Pergamon, 1970. 133pp. $6.50. Published in England, this is a summary of the work currently being done to involve young people in the theatre—especially by the growing number of professional theatres in England. The author also gives a detailed account of the work in one theatre workshop where he explores the potentialities of young people in drama. The production of a play from choice of script to direction is also analyzed. Illustrated. Suggestions for Reading. Index.

MASTERS, SIMON
The National Youth Theatre
Longmans, 1969. 86pp. $4.95. A comprehensive account of the English National Youth Theatre which was founded in 1956 from a group of schoolboy actors. It has grown into a national organization staging up to seven productions a year in London's West End, the Provinces, and on the Continent during school holidays. The history, its way of working, and its members are all detailed. Illustrated with photographs.

MEARNS, HUGHES
Creative Power: The Education of Youth in the Creative Arts
Dover, 1958. 320pp. Paper $2.50. A second revised edition, with an Introduction by Winifred Ward, of the book first published in 1929. The Mearns Method of encouraging the child to express himself in drama, music, and creative writing is analyzed.

SIKS, GERALDINE BRAIN and HAZEL BRAIN DUNNINGTON
Children's Theatre and Creative Dramatics
University of Washington, 1961. 277pp. $6.95. Paper—$3.95. A collection of articles on children's theatre. Nellie McCaslin presents a concise history of children's theatre in the United States; Kenneth Graham brings out the value for children of good theatre; Albert Mitchell discusses productions by adult groups: Winifred Ward contributes an outline of creative dramatics in elementary schools. Also included are nineteen other articles. Illustrated. Bibliography. Index.

SIKS, GERALDINE BRAIN
Directory of American Colleges and Universities Offering Training in Children's Theatre and Creative Dramatics
A.E.T.A., 1963. 28pp. Paper $1.00. This is a list, compiled by state, of training opportunities in children's theatre. Two addendums dated 1965 and 1966 are included.

SLADE, PETER
Child Drama
Verry, 1954. 379pp. $10.00. A textbook on the development of the dramatic play instinct in children. Instructions on children's theatre production techniques, films, puppets, masks, and marionette shows. Illustrated with photographs and diagrams. Foreword by Dame Sybil Thorndike.

SLADE, PETER
Children's Theatre and Theatre for Young People
Stacey, 1968. 25pp. Paper $ .75. Based on a talk given to the British Children's Theatre Association, this short pamphlet conveys Mr. Slade's ideas on theatre for children.

TAYLOR, ALISON
Off Stage and On: An Introduction to Youth Drama
Pergamon, 1969. 72pp. Paper $2.25. The author discusses the possible value to young people of drama as a means of expression. Stress is laid on the value

for young people of creating drama in their own way. Lists of relevant books and information about the work and facilities offered by professional theatre companies in England are included.

WAGNER, JEARNINE and KITTY BAKER
A Place For Ideas: Our Theatre
Principia Press of Trinity University, 1965. 208pp. $8.00. This book is a collage of ideas-in-action presented as they occur in the children's theatre work of Jearnine Wagner. In this work the children and their teachers are closely associated in the exploration of many different media. Art, writing, acting, movement, and music are presented as experiences in learning. Illustrated.

WARD, WINIFRED
Theatre for Children
Anchorage Press, 1950. 378pp. $4.00. Written primarily for the young inexperienced person who is to direct plays for children, either with children or adult performers. A history of children's theatre is given, both in the United States and abroad. Extensive information and instruction on organizing and presenting productions. Illustrated.

Drama in the Classroom

ADLAND, D. E.
The Group Approach to Drama
Longmans, 1964. Five volume set. Paper $7.95. Published in England, this set of five volumes consists of a teacher's guide and four pupils' books. The author offers a four year course in creative dramatic experience. The teacher's book explores the nature and function of dramatic activity as the author examines dramatic experience and experiment within groups. Each of the pupils' books offers short plays and synopses of plays with suggestions for the pupils' own creative outlets. Illustrated. Bibliography.

ALINGTON, A. F.
Drama and Education
Dufour, 1966. 105pp. $3.25. This book outlines a progressive course in creative and interpretative dramatic work from beginning to end of school life. Movement, mime, improvisation, speech, and pupils' own productions are studied. Also referred to is the training of potential teachers for dramatic work.

ALLSTROM, ELIZABETH
Let's Play A Story
Friendship Press, 1957. 165pp. Paper $2.95. This handbook for teachers gives detailed and practical advice on how to use informal dramatics as an educational tool. The values of playing out a story are outlined and the most effective ways to introduce stories to children are discussed. Suggestions for settings and props. Illustrated.

BARNFIELD, GABRIEL
Creative Drama in Schools
Hart, 1969. 268pp. $10.00. Paper 292pp. $2.95. This book details how to teach creative drama. It explores a full range of techniques and methods and gives detailed guidance on the problems of producing drama. How the dramatic possibilities latent in all children can be inspired, encouraged, and developed by teachers lacking special training is set out in notes made by the author after his own teaching sessions. Illustrated with sketches and photographs. Bibliography. Index.

BOGARD, TRAVIS – Editor
International Conference on Theatre Education and Development
A.E.T.A., 1968. 126pp. Paper $2.00. This special issue of the "Educational Theatre Journal" is a report on the conference sponsored by A.E.T.A. in 1967. Educators and theatre professionals from twenty-four countries discussed matters concerning "Education and Theatre:" the education of students for the theatre, the education of audiences by the theatre, and the development through education of the theatre itself.

BROWN, JOHN RUSSELL
A University and the Theatre
University of Birmingham, 1968. 16pp. Paper $ .85. This lecture by Professor Brown was delivered at the University of Birmingham in England in 1967 and deals with the study of drama in the university.

BURNISTON, CHRISTABEL
Creative Oral Assessment: Its Scope and Stimulus
Pergamon, 1968. 124pp. $4.50. The author sets out the philosophic principles and practical techniques for the teaching and examining of spoken English. in scope it covers all aspects: the imaginative interpretation of drama and poetry, the art of reading aloud, the functional presentation of personal projects, the art of guiding questions and discussions. The book adheres to the examining forms and precepts held by the English Speaking Board, London. References and background reading lists are included.

BYERS, RUTH
Creating Theatre
Trinity University, 1968. 225pp. $8.00. Based upon actual experiences with students in creative playwriting, this book describes specific steps in the process of originating and developing ideas for play creation, writing, and production. Among the methods the author suggests for channeling creativity into productive work are guidelines for before-class preparation, advice to teachers on providing an atmosphere conductive to creative activity, and suggestions for study plans. The book contains nine original scripts which represent the efforts of students from six to eighteen. The plays are complete with suggestions for staging, costuming, and design. Illustrated.

CASCIANI, J.W. and IDA WATT
Drama in the Primary School
Thomas Nelson, 1966. 44pp. Paper $1.60. The purpose of this book is to provide the teacher with matter and method for dramatic activity in primary schools. Each section contains procedural steps and a sample lesson. Illustrated.

CHAMBERS, DEWEY W.
Storytelling and Creative Drama
Wm. C. Brown, 1970. 92pp. Paper $2.25. A guidebook for teachers in the art of storytelling and the teaching of creative drama to children. Illustrated. Selected References. Index.

CHILVER, PETER
Improvised Drama
Dufour, 1967. 159pp. $4.50. Mr. Chilver's book suggests how improvisation can develop a greater command of language, an interest in drama, theatre and literature. He discusses improvisation based on situations drawn from current events, based on excerpts from novels, short stories, and plays, based on detailed instructions for each character, and as a way of producing and rehearsing the school play.

CITRON, SAMUEL J.
Dramatics for Creative Teaching
United Synagogues of America, 1961. 405pp. $8.50. A book of techniques for teaching drama in the school curriculum. The subject matter is related to teaching in schools for Jewish students.

COLE, NATALIE ROBINSON
Arts in the Classroom
John Day, 1940. 137pp. $5.25. The author tells how she guides her elementary school pupils in creative art activities, setting them free to work things out according to their own inner feelings. Illustrations of the pupils' work in painting, clay work, block-printing, dancing, and writing.

CORNWELL, PAUL
Creative Playmaking in the Primary School
Chatto & Windus, 1970. 137pp. Paper $4.75. Published in England, this is an account of some experiments in the use of creative playmaking in the primary school as a stimulus for spoken and written language. The students were ten to eleven year olds who, at the end of the school year, produced Homer's "Odyssey" as rewritten and organized entirely by the children. Illustrated with drawings and photographs.

COSTELLO, LAWRENCE and GEORGE N. GORDON
Teach with Television: A Guide to Instructional TV
See Page 492

COURTNEY, RICHARD
Play, Drama and Thought
Cassell, 1968. 288pp. $7.95. This text examines the intellectual background of drama in education. Starting with the concept that the creative imagination is dramatic in character, the author relates this to the philosophic traditions of Western thought. Part I is philosophic, ranging from Plato to modern thought. Part II considers the contributions made by psychoanalysis to the understanding of the child's dramatic play. Part III examines sociological thought and the origins of drama. Part IV is concerned with cognition and how thought itself is based upon the dramatic imagination. Bibliography. References. Index.

COURTNEY, RICHARD
Teaching Drama
Cassell, 1965. 118pp. $4.25. Published in England, this is a handbook for the teaching of drama in schools. Mr. Courtney's subjects include: The Value of Drama, Improvisation, Playmaking, Movement and Mime, Speech, The Printed Play, The Theatre Arts, and Drama for Older Pupils. Bibliography. Index.

CULLUM, ALBERT
Push Back the Desks
Citation Press, 1967. 223pp. Paper $2.85. Mr. Cullum's method of teaching includes student involvement and participation. This book presents descriptions of some of the projects and techniques he has evolved, including panel discussions, exhibitions, total environments, trips, and demonstrations. Illustrated with photographs.

CURRY, LOUISE H. and CHESTER M. WETZEL
Teaching with Puppets
See Page 341

DOHERTY, G.D. and J.A. BLEAKLEY
Moving into Drama
Schofield & Sims, 1968. Four volume set: 302pp. Spiral bound $12.00. Published in England, this four volume set provides an introduction to "child drama." The work is based on principles used by the authors in English schools. The set consists of two teacher's books and two pupil's books. The teacher's volumes contain the complete children's book with inter-leaved pages of commentary on how to use the material and how to develop it. Illustrated.

DURLAND, FRANCES CALDWELL
Creative Dramatics for Children: A Practical Manual for Teachers and Leaders
Antioch Press, 1952. 181pp. $2.75. Paper $1.60. A handbook of techniques for developing the dramatic instinct in children, with selections from actual scripts written by children's groups, notes on their productions, and studies of what they meant to the children in them.

FRAZIER, CLIFFORD and ANTHONY MEYER
Discovery in Drama
Paulist Press, 1969. 208pp. Paper $3.95. This is a guide for the use of "spontaneous drama" in teenage educational situations. The authors probe basic

human needs, as expressed in contemporary social situations, through dramatic improvisation. Illustrated with drawings and photographs.

GAHAGAN, WINIFRED and THE AMERICAN EDUCATIONAL THEATRE ASSOCIATION'S COMMITTEE ON THE SECONDARY SCHOOL LEVEL
A Course Guide in the Theatre Arts at the Secondary School Level
A.E.T.A., 1968. 118pp. Paper $3.00. This guide suggests materials to be used in school situations to bring theatre study to students. The course concentrates on the individual, using acting as the fundamental teaching method of learning the entire theatre art. On each left hand page are suggestions for the teacher to adapt and direct to the student. On each right hand page are suggestions for the teacher in conducting the activities and evaluating the students. Bibliography.

GOODRIDGE, JANET
Drama in the Primary School
Heinemann, 1970. 158pp. Paper $2.50. Published in England, this handbook aims to provide some ideas for teachers of drama who are working with young children. Each chapter contains suggestions for scenes and a book list.

HAGGERTY, JOAN
Please Can I Play God?
Bobbs–Merrill, 1966. 152pp. $4.00. Miss Haggerty taught seven to ten year olds in England in 1965 and this is a record of her experiences with these children. She is convinced that there is value in using psychodrama as an educational device to develop children's imaginative resources and to create a commitment brought by a total involvement in the learning process.

LIGHTWOOD, DONALD
Creative Drama for Primary Schools
Blackie, 1970. 53pp. Paper $1.75. A handbook of activities, movement, mime, and improvised plays, for children in primary schools. It provides the teacher with exercises and plans for starting improvised work in the classroom.

LOVE, MARGARET
Let's Dramatise
See Page 580

McCASLIN, NELLIE
Creative Dramatics in the Classroom
McKay, 1968. 165pp. $4.50. Paper $3.25. A guide for classroom teachers who wish to initiate dramatic activities. The author maintains that the principles of dramatic creativity and response provide a positive approach to learning for all age levels through the appeal of play and imagination. The contents include a rationale for creative dramatics with specific objectives, exercises in pantomime, improvisations, and play structure, and the basic procedures involved in preparing a play for an audience. Selected Bibliography. Index.

McINTYRE, BARBARA M.
Informal Dramatics: A Language Arts Activity for the Special Pupil
Stanwix House, 1963. 97pp. Paper $3.25. A practical handbook based on sound educational principles in the use of drama with children. The manual builds a background in informal drama in general for the untrained teacher. A special section on informal dramatics for the mentally retarded child develops a program consistent with the child's reading program. Included are six original stories for dramatization. A seventh story is analyzed to show what constitutes a good story on which a creative play can be based. Illustrated with photographs. List of Books for Further Reading.

MERSAND, JOSEPH
Index to Plays with Suggestions for Teaching
See Page 7

MIZENER, ARTHUR – Editor
Teaching Shakespeare
See Page 102

MOFFETT, JAMES
Teaching the Universe of Discourse
Houghton–Mifflin, 1968. 215pp. Paper $3.95. These essays represent one teacher's efforts to theorize about discourse, expressly for teaching purposes. There is a long chapter on drama, which the author defines as the recording of "what is happening" as opposed to fiction which is the reporting of "what happened."

MORGAN, ELIZABETH
A Practical Guide to Drama in the Primary School
Ward Lock, 1968. 125pp. $3.95. This book deals with the practical problems which face teachers whose task is to teach drama in the primary school. All aspects of drama are covered from basic introductory exercise, through exercises designed to give children an awareness of their hands, feet, or heads, to dance-drama, mime, and spoken improvisation. Line drawings and photographs illustrate points made in the text. Index.

MOTTER, CHARLOTTE KAY
Theatre in High School: Planning, Teaching, Directing
See Page 359

MUNKRES, ALBERTA
Helping Children in Oral Communication
Teachers College, 1959. 102pp. Paper $1.95. An aid to teachers to help children learn effective and correct oral language expression. Material is organized around five aspects of oral communication: conversing and discussing, storytelling, reporting, and making speeches, dramatizing, and using words well.

PEMBERTON–BILLING, R. N. and J. D. CLEGG
Teaching Drama
University of London, 1965. 156pp. $3.50. The theory and practice of teaching drama are linked throughout this practical British handbook for everyone interested in the teaching of drama. The authors emphasize the value of drama in awakening the child's awareness of life. Illustrated with photographs. Index.

PRITNER, CALVIN LEE – General Editor
A Selected and Annotated Bibliography for the Secondary School Theatre Teacher and Student
See Page 4

SANDERS, SANDRA
Creating Plays with Children
Citation Press, 1970. 95pp. Paper $1.25. The author describes her tested system of having children write their own plays based on a familiar story. Included in the volume are six plays created by her students, with production notes for each.

SCHATTNER, REGINA
Creative Dramatics for Handicapped Children
Putnam, 1967. 160pp. $6.00. Miss Schattner believes that the arts can act as a force of liberation, a vehicle for growth, and a molder of personality for the handicapped child. All aspects of play production are reviewed and there are thirteen short plays presented as examples. There is also a section of "Suggested Resources."

SIKS, GERALDINE BRAIN
Creative Dramatics: An Art for Children
Harper & Row, 1958. 472pp. $12.00. A guide for the teacher on the methodology, techniques, and philosophy of children's dramatics, as developed at the University of Washington. Eighteen creative dramatics classroom experiences are correlated with social studies, language arts, music, and related arts. A list of works for dramatization is included. Illustrated. Bibliography.

SLADE, PETER
Child Drama and Its Value in Education
Stacey, 1965. 22pp. Paper $ .75. This is a reprint of a talk Mr. Slade originally gave in 1965 at the first Conference on Drama at Bangor University, Wales. It details some of his thoughts and experiences from working with children.

SLATER, DEREK
Plays in Action
Pergamon, 1964. 175pp. $4.95. Paper $2.45. Intended for use by teachers in English grammar schools, the author's approach to his subject is based on the idea that plays should be considered as literature and as material for further enjoyment of the drama. The first section of the work is a broad discussion of the nature and meaning of drama. Plays studied include: "Noah," "The Devil's Disciple."

STEIGMAN, BENJAMIN
Accent on Talent: New York's High School of Music and Art
See Page 243

WALKER, BRENDA
Teaching Creative Drama
Batsford, 1970. 144pp. $4.50. Designed for the teacher of children in the nine to fifteen years age group, this is a guide to teaching creative drama with a sense of progression. After a comprehensive introduction, the author provides chapters on beginning work in the classroom, progression of the drama lesson, and correlation of drama with other school subjects. Published in England, the volume is illustrated with extracts from the works of Dylan Thomas, William Shakespeare, and Charles Dickens, and a documentary drama on "War," devised by fifteen year olds.

WARD, WINIFRED
Playmaking with Children
Appleton, 1957. 341pp. $7.95. A revised edition of the 1947 text for the teacher of children from kindergarten through junior high school. Basic techniques for all manner of creative dramatic activity are provided with step-by-step instructions. Lists of stories for dramatization and a list of recordings are included. Illustrated. Bibliography. Index.

WAY, BRIAN
Development Through Drama
Longmans, 1967. 308pp. Paper $3.50. The author presents his ideas on the development of children through the use of drama in education. Using his years of practical experience in England, he considers facets of personality, participation in the classroom, use of imagination, use of movement and sound, speech, improvisation, playmaking and playbuilding, and the use of the classroom. Book List. Record List. Index.

WELKER, DAVID
Educational Theatre Journal: A Ten Year Index
See Page 4

WILES, JOHN and ALAN GARRARD
Leap to Life!: An Experiment in Youth Drama
Chatto & Windus, 1968. 154pp. $5.00. Originally published in 1957 and now revised and brought up to date, this book describes the work of the County Drama Adviser for Buckinghamshire, England, which is designed mainly for the benefit of the child and which Mr. Garrard calls Dance Drama, a method of movement and mime to music. This work has proved a success with all types of adolescents and pre-adolescents and impressed teachers from many countries. Illustrated with photographs.

WILT, MIRIAM E.
Creativity in the Elementary School
Appleton, 1959. 72pp. Paper $1.75. The author's

viewpoint is that creative expression in the elementary school is another means of communication rather than an artist-training course. She points out the common denominators of all creative endeavor in the elementary age group: readiness, activities, media, self-evaluation, and adult acceptance. Illustrated with photographs. Lists for Further Reading. Index.

WOOD, D. NEVILLE
On Tape: The Creative Use of the Tape Recorder
Ward Lock, 1969. 120pp. $6.95. Published in England, this is an explanation in non-technical terms of how to operate a tape recorder. The author discusses the advantages and disadvantages of various types when used in schools and offers practical hints on calculating playing time and getting good value when buying spools and tapes. The main part of the book is devoted to providing suggestions for use of the tape recorder in all normal school subjects. Illustrated with photographs. Bibliography. Index.

Music and Movement

For other books on this subject, see: Dance—Ballet

BRUCE, V.
Dance and Dance Drama in Education
Pergamon, 1965. 118pp. $5.00. Paper $2.95. Published in England, this work is based on the techniques of Rudolf Laban. The author provides an exposition of the language of movement and the way it can be utilized in the primary and secondary schools. There are sections devoted to the students' own contributions. Illustrated with photographs. Bibliography. Index.

COLLINS, CLAUDETTE
Practical Modern Educational Dance
Macdonald & Evans, 1969. 83pp. $2.95. Published in England, this book deals with the teaching of dance to children. The author provides a number of suggestions which will be of help to teachers. Illustrated with diagrams. Music Suggestions. Index.

DRIVER, ANN
Music and Movement
Oxford, 1966. 122pp. Paper $3.20. Originally published in 1936 and now reissued, this book sets out the author's principles of education through rhythm. she shows teachers how the child's own natural rhythm can be released and then used to build up his knowledge and appreciation of music. Illustrated with drawings.

GRAY, VERA and RACHEL PERCIVAL
Music, Movement and Mime for Children
See Page 306

HABERMAN, MARTIN and TOBIE MEISEL—Editors
Dance—An Art in Academe
See Page 306

HEWITT, TONY
The School Gilbert and Sullivan
See Page 288

LABAN, RUDOLF and F.C. LAWRENCE
Effort
Macdonald & Evans, 1967. 88pp. $3.50. Originally published in 1947 and now reissued in England, this work is a collaboration between an artist and an industrialist. It is their common conviction that the study of human effort is necessary for individuals in every field of activity. They reveal a method of instruction and training which should lead to increased enjoyment of work through the awareness and practice of the rhythmic character of that work. Index.

LABAN, RUDOLF and LISA ULLMANN
Modern Educational Dance
Macdonald & Evans, 1966. 114pp. $5.00. Originally published in 1948 and now revised by Miss Ullmann, this book is devised as a guide for teachers and parents. It provides an introduction to the study of modern educational dance and provides information on the rudiments of a free dance technique and the principles of movement. Sixteen themes, suitable for different age groups, correspond to the progressive movement experience of the growing child. Miss Ullmann has amplified and revised Laban's text and diagrams. Index.

LOFTHOUSE, PETER
Dance
See Page 307

MAYNARD, OLGA
Children and Dance and Music
Scribner, 1968. 311pp. $6.95. Miss Maynard offers practical ideas for integrating the arts and the values of the arts in ordinary life and in elementary education. She insists that the human intimate approach must be sustained in this machine dominated age. Illustrated with photographs. Index.

MONSOUR, SALLY and MARILY CHAMBERS COHEN and PATRICIA ECKERT LINDELL
Rhythm in Music and Dance for Children
Wadsworth, 1966. 99pp. Spiral bound $7.35. This book contains a variety of approaches, teaching media, materials, and activities to enable teachers of various backgrounds to conduct lessons in rhythm using music and dance for children in the first eight grades. Each of the three sections of the volume is designed to promote an increased understanding of rhythm including all aspects of duration in music and movement. Illustrated with diagrams. Appendices include a list of recordings suitable for movement exercises. Annotated Bibliography. Index.

NYE, ROBERT EVANS and VERNICE TROUSDALE NYE
Music in the Elementary School
Prentice–Hall, 1963. 405pp. $8.95. Originally published in 1957 and now reissued in revised edition, this is a textbook for music teachers in the elementary grades. The authors provide a background for the teacher's concept of musical activities in a classroom situation. The sections include classroom management and planning, rhythm introduction, playing of instruments, singing, performing for audiences, and an evaluation of the teacher's role in the profession and community. Illustrated. Index of Songs. General Index.

PRESTON, VALERIE
A Handbook for Modern Educational Dance
See Page 308

REDFERN, BETTY
Introducing Laban Art of Movement
Macdonald & Evans, 1965. 32pp. Paper $1.00. Published in England, this guide explains the general principles of the art of movement as formulated by Rudolf Laban. Taken into consideration are movement in industry, in the theatre, in recreation, and the therapeutic value of movement.

ROWEN, BETTY
Learning Through Movement
Teachers College, 1963. 77pp. Paper $1.50. Mrs. Rowen offers advice to teachers wishing to insert move and better movement experiences in their curriculum. Movement is discussed as a part of classroom activity as the author describes her teaching methods. Lists of books recommended for teachers and summaries of published stories and poems are included. Illustrated. Selected List of Recordings.

RUSSELL, JOAN
Creative Dance in the Primary School
Praeger, 1968. 68pp. $7.00. Practical suggestions and examples of work found suitable for the various age groups of students in primary schools are found in this volume, originally published in London in 1965 and now reissued in the United States. A feature of the book is the series of photographs which analyze the reactions of children to the various stages of movement experience. Index.

RUSSELL, JOAN
Creative Dance in the Secondary School
Macdonald & Evans, 1969. 120pp. $4.95. This study presents the case for including the art of movement in the secondary school curriculum. It stresses the need for creative activity to balance the academic work. The core of the book is a suggested syllabus, given year by year. The author also considers the content of the lesson, the type of accompaniment, suitable music and combined work in the arts. Illustrated. Index.

RUSSELL, JOAN
Modern Dance in Education
Macdonald & Evans, 1966. 99pp. $5.00. Originally published in 1958 and now reissued, this book is devoted to the theory underlying the art of movement and the application of that theory within the infant, junior and secondary schools, as well as in the adult field. Included is an Appendix which is a collection of definitions, together with a list of suitable British recordings and music. Illustrated with photographs. Index.

SHEEHY, EMMA D.
Children Discover Music and Dance
Teachers College, 1970. 207pp. Paper $5.25. Originally published in 1959 and now reissued, this is a guide book for teachers. The author explores the fundamentals of music and dance for children and offers suggestions based on her own experiences in the classroom enjoyment of singing, instrumental music, dance, records, radio, television, and concerts. Lists of Reference Works. Index.

WIENER, JACK and JOHN LIDSTONE
Creative Movement for Children
See Page 309

Films, Television, and Radio

AMELIO RALPH J. and ANITA OWEN, SUSAN SCHAEFER
Willowbrook Cinema Study Project
See Page 433

ANDERSON, YVONNE
Make Your Own Animated Movies
See Page 467

ANDERSON, YVONNE
Teaching Film Animation to Children
See Page 467

BATEMAN, ROGER
Instructions in Filming
See Page 460

BEAL, J.D.
How to Make Films at School
See Page 460

CASSIRER, HENRY H.
Television Teaching Today
See Page 487

COSTELLO, LAWRENCE and GEORGE N. GORDON
Teach With Television: A Guide to Instructional TV
See Page 492

DE VERA, JOSE MARIA
Educational Television in Japan
See Page 487

GORDON, GEORGE N.
Classroom Television: New Frontiers in ITV
Hastings House, 1970. 248pp. $8.95. Paper $7.50. Dr. Gordon analyzes the poor start of television in the educational world and discusses the uses of instructional television in the future. It is related to recent discoveries in learning theory, research in educational technology, and the problems of teachers and administrators. Problems of cost, installing and staffing television installations, training teachers, and preparation of special materials for students' needs are covered in detail. Diagrammatic illustrations by Lawrence Garfinkel accompany the text. Notes. Bibliography. Glossary. Index.

GORDON, GEORGE N.
Educational Television
See Page 622

GRIFFITH, BARTON L. and DONALD W. MacLENNAN – Editors
Improvement of Teaching by Television
See Page 488

HARCOURT, PETER and PETER THEOBALD – Editors
Film Making in Schools and Colleges
See Page 461

HERMAN, LEWIS
Educational Films: Writing, Directing, and Producing
See Page 493

HEYER, ROBERT and ANTHONY MEYER
Discovery in Film
See Page 436

HIGGINS, A. P.
Talking About Television
See Page 489

INTERNATIONAL MUSIC CENTRE, VIENNA – Compilers
Films for Music Education and Opera Films
See Page 285

KITSES, JIM and ANN MERCER
Talking About the Cinema
See Page 437

KOENIG, ALLEN E. and RUANE B. HILL
The Farther Vision: Educational Television Today
See Page 489

KUHNS, WILLIAM and ROBERT STANLEY
Exploring the Film
See Page 461

KUHNS, WILLIAM
Themes – Short Films for Discussion
See Page 438

LARSON, RODGER and ELLEN MEADE
Young Filmmakers
See Page 462

LIDSTONE, JOHN and DON McINTOSH
Children As Film Makers
Reinhold, 1970. 111pp. $7.95. This book is designed for classroom teachers and other enthusiasts who would like to work with children in film making. A detailed text explains the basics of camera operation, editing, splicing, animation, titling, and projection. Ways to guide children toward successful structuring of their films, methods for practical classroom organization of supplies and equipment, and ideas for the exhibition of films are all discussed. Illustrated with drawings and photographs. Bibliography. Index.

LOWNDES, DOUGLAS
Film Making in Schools
See Page 462

MacLEAN, RODERICK
Television in Education
See Page 489

MANCHEL, FRANK
Movies and How They Are Made
See Page 462

NISHIMOTO, MITOJI
Development of Educational Broadcasting in Japan
See Page 490

ROBERTS, FREDERICK
Radio and Television
See Page 494

ROBINSON, JOHN – Editor
Educational Television and Radio in Britian
See Page 623

SCHILLACI, ANTHONY and JOHN M. CULKIN – Editors
Films Deliver
Citation, 1970. 348pp. Paper $5.25. A guide for film use in schools; these are the published results of the efforts of the staff and participants of Fordham University's National Film Study Project to develop materials and methods to help teachers teach with films. The volume moves from the rationale for film study to case histories of successful projects and how-to-do-it practices, and examples of student filmmaking. Extensive Appendices of annotated filmographes and bibliographies are included as are lists of sources and sample teachers' guides. A Title Index to all film titles mentioned or discussed is also provided. Illustrated with photographs.

SCHRAMM, WILBUR
The Impact of Educational Television
See Page 623

SCHRAMM, WILBUR and JACK LYLE, ITHIEL DE SOLA POOL
The People Look at Educational Television
See Page 490

SCHRAMM, WILBUR and JACK LYLE, EDWIN B. PARKER
Television in the Lives of Our Children
See Page 491

TAYLOR, LOREN E.
Radio Drama
See Page 500

WRIGHT, ANDREW
Designing for Visual Aids
Van Nostrand, 1970. 96pp. $5.50. Paper $2.75. Written for designers and teachers, this is a guide to the various visual media that play an increasing part in modern visual education. The author covers in detail the various media such as overhead projectors, slides and filmstrips, television, programmed learning and teaching machines, and wallposters and books. Illustrated. Bibliography.

Acting for Children

BOAS, GUY
Shakespeare and the Young Actor
See Page 409

BURGER, ISABEL B.
Creative Play Acting
Ronald Press, 1966. 233pp. $6.00. The author sets forth practical procedures for organizing creative dramatics projects. These procedures are based on successful experiences in directing the Baltimore Children's Theatre Association for twenty-three years. Illustrated. Bibliography. Index.

CARLSON, BERNICE WELLS
Act It Out
Abingdon, 1956. 160pp. $2.50. Paper $1.60. Instructions for acting for children are provided in this volume. Among the exercises are acting games, pantomines, and puppet manipulation. Instructions for making several kinds of puppets are included. Illustrated.

CHILVER, PETER
Stories for Improvisation in Primary and Secondary Schools
Batsford, 1969. 188pp. $3.50. To provide the teacher with an imaginative anthology of stories for use in improvisation, the author has adapted and retold some thirty stories: most of them folk stories or legends. The author stresses that pupils should be encouraged to use, build on, and extend the stories so that each one is a stimulus to develop the children's ideas in their own speech and dialogue.

DOHERTY, G.D. and J.A. BLEAKLEY
Moving Into Drama
Schofield & Sims, 1968. Four volume set. Spiral bound $12.00. Published in England, this four volume set provides an introduction to "child drama." The work is based on principles used in English schools by the authors. The set consists of two graduated teacher's books and two pupil's books. The teacher's book contains the complete children's book with interleaved pages of comments on how to use this material and how to develop it. The emphasis in Book One is on individual work especially in space and body awareness. In Book Two the authors suggest more work in pairs and small groups. Illustrated.

GRAYSON, MARION F.
Let's Do Fingerplays
Robert B. Luce, 1962. 109pp. $5.25. A one-volume collection of the best-loved traditional "fingerplays," with songs and poems. Many new rhymes are given and each verse has instructions on the appropriate movements. Illustrated.

JOHNSON, ALBERT and BERTHA JOHNSON
Drama for Classroom and Stage
See Page 358

JONES, ERIC
Make-Up for School Plays
See Page 421

KASE, ROBERT C.
Stories for Creative Acting
Samuel French, 1961. 269pp. $5.00. A collection of seventy-two stories recommended and used successfully by leading creative dramatics teachers. The selections are arranged in groups according to age and selected for the ability to stimulate the imagination of the child. Each story is evaluated and its particular characteristics noted. Illustrated by Gilbert Boyd Davenport.

KERMAN, GERTRUDE
Plays and Creative Ways with Children
Harvey House, 1961. 289pp. $6.95. The author provides information on each facet of informal dramatics from preliminary exercises through the making and the directing of a complete play. Twelve non-royalty plays are included with production notes; however, the flexibility of possible presentation is stressed. Illustrated with drawings by Margaret Zimmerman. Glossary. Bibliography. Index.

LEADLEY, TOM and TERENCE DIXON
The Stage: A Picture Career Book
See Page 422

LEWIS, MARY KANE
Acting for Children: A Primer
John Day, 1969. 176pp. $5.95. The author provides a complete course on teaching children the fundamentals of acting. From the introduction of the subject by the teacher to the presentation of an actual scene or play, the thirty-two lessons provide instruction, homework, and class participation in improvisation, speech, miming and music, using a script, and preparation for play. The author's method may be used with children aged approximately eight to twelve. Five short playlets are included. Illustrated with photographs and diagrams.

LOVE, MARGARET
Let's Dramatise
See Page 580

NUTTALL, KENNETH
Your Book of Acting
Faber & Faber, 1957. 68pp. $2.50. A book of simplified instructions on the technique of dramatic expression for young actors. Included are chapters on production techniques, stage management, and playwriting. Illustrated.

OAKDEN, DAVID
The Make-A-Play Series
Blond, 1968. Four volume set: 252pp. Paper $7.00. Each of the four volumes in this set contains simple stories for children to dramatize with suggestions for costumes, scenery, and props that the children can make themselves. Illustrated. Titles of the individual volumes are: "Let's Pretend," "Let's Make a Play," "Let's Act," and "Stories for Acting."

SCHUON, KARL
The First Book of Acting
See Page 415

SEVERN, BILL
Magic Comedy: Tricks, Skits and Clowning
David McKay, 1968. 144pp. $3.95. Written for children, this volume includes skits, stunts, magical jokes, gags, and full outlines for magicians. Illustrated with drawings.

SIKS, GERALDINE BRAIN
Children's Literature for Dramatization
Harper & Row, 1964. 331pp. $10.00. A collection of fifty-six stories and eighty-three poems which are strong in dramatic content and which are designed to appeal to children from four to fourteen. Selections are divided according to degree of difficulty of presentation and notes on production are included.

TAYLOR, LOREN E.
Choral Drama
Burgess, 1965. 81pp. Paper $2.50. The values and techniques of choral speaking for children are discussed and three plays are included. Illustrated.

TAYLOR, LOREN E.
Formal Drama and Children's Theatre
Burgess, 1965. 118pp. Paper $2.50. An introduction to formal dramatics for children. Chapters on all phases of theatre for children, from selecting the play to preparing the actor. Illustrated.

TAYLOR, LOREN E.
Informal Dramatics for Young Children
Burgess, 1965. 68pp. Paper $2.50. The term, informal dramatics, is used to distinguish extemporaneous dramatic expression from the formal study of ready-made scripts. Mr. Taylor suggests that informal dramatics may take many forms ranging from children's games to improvisations, skits, and stunts for older children. Illustrated.

TAYLOR, LOREN E
Pantomime and Pantomime Games
Burgess, 1965. 79pp. Paper $2.50. An introduction to pantomime for children, including individual, dual and group pantomimes. A selection of plays is included. Illustrated.

TAYLOR, LOREN E.
Stunts and Skits
Burgess, 1965. 112pp. Paper $2.50. A collection of stunts and skits for children from the sixth grade up. Lists of sources for skits is included. Illustrated.

VERNON, HOWARD
Acts for Comedy Shows
Sterling, 1964. 28pp. $2.95. Designed for the ten to fourteen year old audience, this volume includes acts for one or two players and skits for several players. Plays, pantomimes, and examples of jokes are provided with complete instructions for staging of the show. Illustrated.

WARD, WINIFRED – Editor
Stories to Dramatize
Anchorage Press, 1952. 339pp. $6.00. This is a collection of stories which will be useful in improvising drama with children. The stories are grouped in four sections to provide material for children from five to fourteen years of age. Material is provided on the philosophy and techniques of creative dramatics, on the basis of choosing stories to dramatize, and on the correlation of various subjects with a creative play at the center. A list of other recommended stories and books is provided. Index.

WHITE, TESSA
Visual Poetry for Creative Interpretation
Macdonald & Evans, 1969. 32pp. Paper $1.75. Published in England, the aim of this volume is to encourage children in primary schools to express themselves with fluency and freedom. Twenty-eight poems are presented as a basis for other activities such as dance, drama, mime, writing, art, and musical rhythm and composition.

Speech for Children

RUMSEY, H. ST. JOHN
Speech Training for Children
J. Garnet Miller, 1957. 68pp. $1.95. Originally published in 1939, expanded in 1950, and now revised and reissued, this is a handbook dealing with the problems of teaching children to properly produce their voices. The author explains the methods teachers should use and analyzes the vowel sounds which are such an important part of voice production. Index.

SWANN, MONA
Trippingly on the Tongue
Walter Baker, 1938. 32pp. Paper $ .70. A collection of speech games and practice rhymes for children.

Production of Plays

ALLEN, JOHN
Play Production with Children and Young People
Dennis Dobson, 1950. 55pp. $1.00. A brief discussion of theatre as a creative experience for young people. Creative values in each element of production are explained.

BERK, BARBARA
The First Book of Stage Costume and Make-Up
Edmund Ward, 1966. 45pp. $3.50. Written in simple language, this volume provides suggestions for costumes and make-up that children can improvise for themselves. Illustrated with drawings by Jeanne Bendick.

CHILVER, PETER and ERIC JONES
Designing a School Play
Batsford, 1968. 96pp. $5.00. A guide book for those concerned with the staging of a school play—directors, or actors. It places the work of the designer into perspective with the work of all those involved in the production. Sections include: a basic approach to stage design, lighting, building, painting, and a Glossary of terms used in staging and scenic design. Illustrated. Index.

CHILVER, PETER
Staging a School Play
Harper & Row, 1967. 150pp. $4.95. Mr. Chilver has written a guide book for school and amateur play production. He covers every aspect of the subject from choosing the right play to taking bows. The book is designed primarily for the director and is arranged into chapters on each of the crafts involved such as directing, acting, lighting, scenery, and make-up. General chapters on the problems of rehearsals and flexible staging are included. Also included are suggestions of plays for production and a list of play publishers. Illustrated with drawings. Index.

CITRON, SAMUEL J.
Dramatics the Year Round
United Synagogues of America, 1956. 543pp. $8.50. Plays, operettas, and dramatic ceremonial services of Jewish content for schools, community centers, and summer camps, with production notes.

COCHRANE, JENNIFER—Editor
National Costume
See Page 389

COLLINS, FREDA
Let's Prepare A Nativity Play
See Page 327

COURTNEY, RICHARD
Drama For Youth
See Page 586

DAVIS, JED H. and MARY JANE WATKINS, ROGER M. BUSFIELD
Children's Theatre: Play Production for the Child Audience
Harper & Row, 1950. 416pp. $13.00. A comprehensive instruction book dealing with the direction, lighting, costuming, rehearsing, and performance of plays for and with children.

FITZGERALD, BURDETTE S.
World Tales for Creative Dramatics and Storytelling
Prentice—Hall, 1962. 332pp. $10.50. An anthology of tales designed to introduce children to the world's cultures. The author shows the storyteller how to choose, prepare and enact each story. Instructions on developing the educational value of dramatic art are given.

FORKERT, OTTO MAURICE
Children's Theatre That Captures Its Audience
Coach House, 1962. 158pp. $12.50. A pictorial and documentary account of producing the play, "Tom Sawyer," at the Goodman Memorial Theatre, Chicago. An album of 182 photographs of seventy-six productions staged by Charlotte B. Chorpenning and Louise Dale Spoor is included.

FOX, LILLA M.
Folk Costume of Western Europe
See Page 398

GREY, ELIZABETH
Behind the Scenes in the Theatre
See Page 358

JOHNSON, ALBERT and BERTHA JOHNSON
Drama for Classroom and Stage
See Page 358

JONES, ERIC
Stage Construction for School Plays
See Page 373

KASE, ROBERT C.
Children's Theatre Comes of Age
Samuel French, 1956. 32pp. Paper $ .60. A brief survey of the children's theatre movement in the United States. Advice on creating a company, touring, publicity, and production is given.

MILLER, HELEN LOUISE
Pointers on Producing the School Play
See Page 359

MURPHY, DONN B.
A Director's Guide to Good Theatre
See Page 7

NUTTALL, KENNETH
Play Production for Young People
See Page 359

OWENS, JOAN LLEWELYN
Working in the Theatre
See Page 359

PARISH, PEGGY
Costumes to Make
See Page 406

PETERS, JOAN and ANNA SUTCLIFFE
Making Costumes for School Plays
See Page 406

PLAY LIST REVISION COMMITTEE OF THE SECONDARY SCHOOL THEATRE CONFERENCE
Plays Recommended for High Schools
See Page 7

SMITH, MOYNE RICE
Plays and How to Put Them On
Walck, 1961. 169pp. $4.50. Advice to the amateur producer of children's plays on script selection, rehearsal techniques, lighting, costuming, make-up, and publicity. Included are seven scripts, with production notes, for children.

SNOOK, BARBARA
Fancy Dress for Children
See Page 392

TAYLOR, LOREN E.
Pageants and Festivals
Burgess, 1965. 84pp. Paper $2.50. How to plan, write, produce and stage pageants and festivals. Two scripts are included. Illustrated.

TAYLOR, LOREN E.
Radio Drama
See Page 500

WALKER, PAMELA PRINCE
Seven Steps to Creative Children's Dramatics
Hill & Wang, 1957. 150pp. $3.00. Basic information on how to cast and produce a play with children. Included are three full-length original plays: "Rumplestiltskin," "Land of Jesters," and "Around the World in Eighty Days."

Books for Children

Histories of Theatre

CLARKE, R. F.
The Growth and Nature of Drama
See Page 20

COCHRANE, JENNIFER – Editor
The Theatre
See Page 20

COOMBS, CHARLES I.
Window on the World: The Story of Television Production
See Page 492

FLOHERTY, JOHN J.
Television Story
See Page 488

GOULD, JACK
All About Radio and Television
See Page 496

GREY, ELIZABETH
Behind the Scenes in the Theatre
See Page 358

HODGES, C. WALTER
Shakespeare and The Players
See Page 90

HODGES, C. WALTER
Shakespeare's Theatre
See Page 90

JOSEPH, STEPHEN
The Story of The Playhouse in England
See Page 146

MALE, DAVID
The Story of the Theatre
See Page 22

MARCELIAIRE, PHILIPPE
Ballet and the Dance
See Page 315

PRIESTLEY, J. B.
The Wonderful World of the Theatre
See Page 22

ROBERTS, FREDERICK
Radio and Television
See Page 494

TAYLOR, ALISON
The Story of the English Stage
See Page 147

TERRY, WALTER
Ballet: A Pictorial History
See Page 317

Biographies

BRYANT, BERNICE
George Gershwin: Young Composer
See Page 300

GREEN, ROGER LANCELYN
J. M. Barrie
See Page 190

HAMMONTREE, MARIE
Walt Disney: Young Movie Maker
See Page 473

HOPE, CHARLOTTE
The Young Sarah Bernhardt
See Page 264

KATZ, MARJORIE
Grace Kelly
Coward–McCann, 1970. 96pp. $3.95. Written for younger readers, this is a biography of Grace Kelly, movie star and Princess of Monaco.

KERR, LAURA
Footlights to Fame: The Life of Fanny Kemble
See Page 271

MacQUEEN–POPE, W.
Edmund Kean
See Page 271

MALONE, MARY
Actor in Exile: The Life of Ira Aldridge
See Page 263

MALVERN, GLADYS
Curtain Going Up! The Story of Katherine Cornell
See Page 266

MYERS, HORTENSE and RUTH BURNETT
Cecil B. DeMille, Young Dramatist
See Page 457

MYERS, HORTENSE and RUTH BURNETT
Edward R. Murrow: Young Newscaster
See Page 497

NEWMAN, SHIRLEE P.
Ethel Barrymore, Girl Actress
See Page 263

NOBLE, IRIS
William Shakespeare
See Page 51

NORMAN, CHARLES
The Playmaker of Avon
See Page 51

REESE, M. M.
William Shakespeare
See Page 51

SISSON, ROSEMARY ANNE
The Young Shakespeare
See Page 52

THOMAS, BOB
Walt Disney: Magician of the Movies
See Page 473

WEIR, ROSEMARY
The Young David Garrick
See Page 269

Shakespeare and His Plays

BUCKMAN, IRENE
Twenty Tales from Shakespeare
See Page 97

CULLUM, ALBERT
Shake Hands with Shakespeare
See Page 97

GRACZYK, ED
The Rude Mechanicals
See Page 97

HODGES, C. WALTER
Shakespeare and the Players
See Page 90

JOHNSON, ALBERT
Shakespeare Vignettes: Adaptations for Acting
See Page 97

KERMAN, GERTRUDE LERNER
Shakespeare for Young Players
See Page 97

LAMB, CHARLES and MARY LAMB
Tales from Shakespeare
See Page 97

NESBIT, E.
The Children's Shakespeare
See Page 98

SERRAILLIER, IAN
The Enchanted Island
See Page 98

PUPPETS AND MARIONETTES

General Histories

ARNOTT, PETER D.
Plays Without People: Puppetry and Serious Drama
Indiana University, 1964. 157pp. $4.50. After a brief historical introduction which evaluates the condescending attitudes toward puppet plays found in America and England, the author demonstrates that, for certain types of serious drama, productions with marionettes are often more effective than with live actors. The author's productions of "Medea" and "Dr. Faustus" are illustrated.

BAIRD, BIL
The Art of the Puppet
Macmillan, 1965. 251pp. $19.95. Mr. Baird recounts the history of the art of the puppet as he explains the nature of puppetry and how it operates from the point of view of a member of the craft. The book is lavishly illustrated in color and black-and-white by Arie de Zanger. Bibliography. Index.

CURRY, LOUISE H. and CHESTER M. WETZEL
Teaching with Puppets
Fortress, 1966. 119pp. $3.50. The authors have experimented through the years in the use of puppets for teaching purposes. Among the topics covered as they impart their experiences are: creating the puppet, creating puppet plays, staging and production techniques. Illustrated. Glossary of Terms. Bibliography. Index.

FRASER, PETER
Punch and Judy
Van Nostrand, 1970. 120pp. $3.95. An introduction to the history of the Punch and Judy show with instructions for making traditional puppets, and the libretto for the rare classical play taken down by John Payne Collier in 1828. Illustrated with drawings. List of Suppliers. Bibliography.

NICULESCU, MARGARETA and THE EDITORIAL BOARD OF UNION INTERNATIONALE DES MARIONETTES
The Puppet Theatre of the Modern World
Harrap, 1967. 228pp. $14.95. Published in England, this profusely illustrated book has been compiled by an international team of experts in the field of puppetry. A total of thirty-six countries are represented and more than 200 illustrations provide a comprehensive coverage of the modern marionette art. Index of Illustrations.

PHILPOTT, A.R.
Dictionary of Puppetry
Macdonald, 1969. 291pp. $7.95. Published in England, this is a guide, in dictionary format, to the many different aspects of puppetry—technical, historical, and biographical. Articles on the techniques of puppet making and presentation, the history of the subject, the origins of Punch and Judy, and biographical studies are included. Illustrated.

PHILPOTT, A.R.
Let's Look at Puppets
Muller, 1966. 64pp. $2.50. Intended for children, this is a short history of puppets in the various countries of the world. Illustrated with drawings by Norma Burgin.

RANSOME, GRACE GREENLEAF
Puppets and Shadows: A Bibliography
See Page 583

SPEAIGHT, GEORGE
Punch and Judy: A History
Studio Vista, 1970. 160pp. $15.00. Originally published in 1955 as "History of the English Puppet Theatre" and now completely revised, this is a study of the history of puppets throughout the world with an emphasis on the Punch and Judy tradition. Included is a Punch and Judy play dating from 1854. Illustrated in color and black-and-white. Selected Bibliography. Index.

VON BOEHN, MAX
Dolls and Puppets
Cooper Square, 1966. 522pp. $19.50. A complete history of dolls and puppets from prehistoric idols to the puppets of today. Included is "The Puppet Play of Doctor Faust" as originally presented in 1850. 494 Illustrations are provided. Bibliography. Index.

Puppets of Various Nations

ABBE, DOROTHY
The Dwiggins Marionettes: A Complete Experimental Theatre in Miniature
Abrams, 1970. 232pp. $45.00. A history of the experimental theatre of William Addison Dwiggins and of the puppets he created for it. In text and more than 368 illustrations, the puppets, the productions, and the theatres are described and detailed. Among the illustrations are sixty-six plates in color and sixty line drawings.

ANDO, TSURUO
Bunraku: The Puppet Theatre

Lippincott, 1970. 222pp. $4.95. A behind-the-scenes look at the history, techniques, and repertoire of the puppet theatre of Bunraku. The book is lavishly illustrated with black-and-white photographs. A chronology of events in the history of the puppet theatre from 1100 to 1967 is included.

BRANDON, JAMES R.
On Thrones of Gold: Three Javanese Shadow Plays
Harvard, 1970. 407pp. $15.00. Three traditional Javanese shadow plays complete with 143 photographs and with descriptions of the music, the puppet movements, and the stylized performance techniques. The author's detailed introduction provides historical background and a discussion of the theatrical tradition within which these plays evolved. Appendices. Bibliography. Glossary. Index.

DUNN, C. J.
The Early Japanese Puppet Drama
Luzac, 1966. 153pp. $18.50. This book investigates the puppets, stage, and plays of the puppet drama in Japan. The author shows how the puppet drama began and how it developed into an art form. Illustrated with photographs and drawings. Bibliography of works in Japanese and English. Index.

HIRONAGA, SHUZABURO
Bunraku: Japan's Unique Puppet Theatre
Japan Publications, 1964. 386pp. $7.00. The first part of this study describes the three elements of Bunraku: puppet manipulation, "joruri" recitation and samisen accompaniment. There are descriptions of the construction of the dolls, stage mechanisms, and the manufacture of the doll's heads. The second part of the volume is a history of the art. Part three gives synopses of 100 important plays. Illustrated. Index.

KEENE, DONALD
Bunraku: The Art of the Japanese Puppet Theatre
Kodansha, 1965. 287pp. $27.50. The highly refined art of the puppet theatre is described in text and pictures in this folio size book. The text analyzes the history of the theatre, the plays, the chanters, the puppets and the operators, and the elaborate system of gestures. Over 400 photographs by Kaneko Hiroshi, ten in full color, are included. Also provided is a list of plays, a chronology, and a phonograph record of a monologue from one of the plays. Bibliography.

KENNARD, JOSEPH SPENCER
Masks and Marionettes
See Page 213

McPHARLIN, PAUL
The Puppet Theatre in America: A History 1524 – 1948
Plays, Inc., 1969. 734pp. $12.95. Originally published in 1949 and now reissued with a supplement, "Puppets in America Since 1948" by Marjorie Bathelder McPharlin, this is a definitive history of puppets and puppetry in America. The author describes the origins of puppetry, traces the history of puppetry in Europe and England, describes the development and production of puppet shows in America, and includes anecdotes of the many pioneers and devotees of the art. Illustrated. List of Puppeteers: 1524—1948. Bibliography. Index.

MILLER, ROY ANDREW
Masterpieces of Japanese Puppetry
Tuttle, 1958. 91pp. $27.50. This collection of thirty-two full-color plates shows examples of the sculptured heads of the puppets of the Bunraku puppet theatre. The author also provides an essay on the art of Bunraku and its development.

PURSCHKE, HANS R.
Liebenswerte Puppenwelt
George Efron, 1962. 211pp. $7.50. Published in Germany, this collection of photographs of puppets and marionettes shows over 250 examples of the art as practiced in Germany. The text is in German.

SCOTT, A. C.
The Puppet Theatre of Japan
Tuttle, 1963. 174pp. $3.50. A history of the development of puppet drama with a study of the techniques of the puppeteers, musicians, and narrators. Ten popular plays are summarized. Illustrated with maps and photographs. Glossary of Terms. Index.

SPEAIGHT, GEORGE
The History of the English Puppet Theatre
Harrap, 1955. 350pp. $7.95. Mr. Speaight traces in detail the development of the puppet show and the popular theatre of mimes and masks from its origins in ancient Greece to its flowering in Renaissance Europe. Extensive notes, lists of all English puppet showmen who flourished between 1600 and 1914 and the plays performed on the English puppet stage between 1500 and 1914 are given. Illustrated. Index.

TOKYO DOLL SCHOOL
The World of Japanese Dolls
Tuttle, 1962. 115pp. $4.75. A history of the Japanese doll with color reproductions of the most famous. Instructions are provided for creating various dolls and puppets.

Instruction Books

ACKLEY, EDITH FLACK
Marionettes: Easy to Make! Fun to Use!
Lippincott, 1939. 115pp. $5.95. Written for children in grades five through nine, this volume provides directions for making marionettes out of cloth, stuffed with cotton, with instructions on costuming, manipulation, and staging. Four original plays are given. A series of full-size pattern sheets for making

bodies, faces and costumes is included. Illustrated with drawings.

ADAIR, MARGARET WEEKS
Do–It–In–A–Day Puppets for Beginners
John Day, 1964. 86pp. $3.98. By following the simple techniques described here, children, from kindergarten through third grade, can put on a puppet production—from the construction of the puppets through the creation of the script to the actual performance—within the space of a single school day. Scripts of three familiar tales are included to illustrate how the spontaneous method is applied. Illustrated.

BAINBRIDGE, CECIL
Hand Puppets
Museum Press, 1968. 46pp. $3.50. This book deals in detail with the construction of hand puppets from the paper bag type to more sophisticated models. Subjects covered include modeling heads of various types, painting, dressing, manipulation, and building the stage. Illustrated with drawings and photographs.

BATCHELDER, MARJORIE
Puppet Theatre Handbook
Harper & Row, 1947. 293pp. $7.50. A complete guide to all phases of puppet making and play presentation.

BATCHELDER, MARJORIE and VIRGINIA LEE COMER
Puppets and Plays: A Creative Approach
Harper & Row, 1956. 241pp. $5.50. Instructions for creating, rehearsing, and presenting puppet plays. The basic principles of playwriting are discussed and improvised stages that allow freedom of movement are illustrated. Illustrated with drawings and photographs.

BENBOW, MARY and EDITH DUNLOP, JOYCE LUCKIN
Dolls and Doll-Making
Plays Inc., 1968. 95pp. $6.95. A volume in the art and craft of making and dressing dolls. The authors show how the basic figure can be constructed, include a series of graded exercises for costume making, and conclude with the more sophisticated aspects of finishing and decorating. The instructions are illustrated with practical diagrams and photographs of the finished dolls.

BENBOW, MARY and EDITH DUNLOP, JOYCE LUCKIN
Dolls: Traditional and Topical and How to Make Them
Plays, Inc., 1970. 93pp. $6.95. A selection of historically accurate and colorful costume dolls with easy-to-follow instructions for making and dressing. Illustrated with photographs and patterns.

BODOR, JOHN
Creating and Presenting Hand Puppets
Reinhold, 1967. 144pp. $7.95. The author demonstrates, through text and photographs, techniques for making puppets simple enough for children but versatile enough to hold the interest of adults. There is complete information on obtaining materials, manipulating puppets, making a stage, costumes, and props, and setting up lighting and sound effects.

BRAMALL, ERIC and CHRISTOPHER C. SOMERVILLE
Expert Puppet Techniques
Faber & Faber, 1963. 104pp. $5.00. This handbook for production contains chapters on the "philosophy" of puppets, writing the play, recording the play script, designing and manipulating the puppets, setting the stage, and performing. Illustrated with diagrams.

BRAMALL, ERIC
Making a Start with Marionettes
G. Bell, 1960. 111pp. $3.00. A practical introduction for adults and older children to the art of making, manipulating, and presenting marionettes. Included is a script for a production of "Hansel and Gretel." Illustrated with diagrams and photographs.

BRAMALL, ERIC
Puppet Plays and Playwriting
G. Bell, 1960. 154pp. $3.75. The principles of the art of writing plays for puppets, with seven plays by the author. Each play has a commentary describing how it originated and how it was constructed to fit the puppet stage.

BURSILL, HENRY
Hand Shadows
See Page 349

CRAVEN, WINIFRED M.
Costume Dolls and How to Make Them
Pitman, 1962. 109pp. $6.50. An introduction to the making and dressing of costume dolls. Chapters discuss the materials needed, the anatomy of the doll, stands, and props. Detailed instructions and step-by-step diagrams for sixteen dolls are included. List of English sources of craft material.

CUMMINGS, RICHARD
101 Hand Puppets: A Guide for Puppeteers of All Ages
David McKay, 1962. 147pp. $3.95. Step-by-step instructions for making every kind of hand puppet, from the simplest handkerchief type to a modern version of the elaborate Osaka puppet. Included are scripts for three plays. Illustrated with diagrams.

FAIRHURST, RONALD
How–To–Do Puppetry
Nelson, 1969. 29pp. $2.50. A simplified explanation for children on how to make and use various types of puppets including instructions on how to make a puppet theatre. Illustrated with drawings.

FRASER, PETER
Introducing Puppetry
Watson—Guptill, 1968. 120pp. $7.95. This practical text provides guidance in the art of puppetry. There are sections on various kinds of puppets and marionettes, costumes, theatres, and the actual methods of play production. Emphasis is on simple methods of making a range of puppets and the technique of the performance. Illustrated with drawings.

FRENCH, SUSAN
Presenting Marionettes
Reinhold, 1964. 96pp. $6.95. The author illustrates, in text and over 150 photographs and drawings, the making of marionettes. Among the subjects covered are casting the heads, cutting and assembling the bodies, creating unusual forms, stringing and controlling, designing costumes, and building a stage. A history of puppets is included as is a puppet play based on the myth of Persephone. All the puppets and accessories needed for the play are described. Index.

GOAMAN, MURIEL
Judy's and Andrew's Puppet Book
Plays, Inc., 1963. 48pp. $3.95. Miss Goaman explains, for children in grades four through nine, an easy way to make both glove and string puppets, how to paint and dress them and how the strings work. There are simple instruction for making theatres and suggestions for plays, including versions of "Punch and Judy" and "Hansel and Gretel." Illustrated.

GREEN, M.C. and B.R.H. TARGETT
Space Age Puppets and Masks
Plays, Inc., 1969. 84pp. $5.95. Two craft teachers give instructions for making a collection of puppets, marionettes, and masks from readily available materials. The simple projects are intended to capture the interest of children and help stimulate their creative ability. Illustrated with drawings and photographs.

HAWKESWORTH, ERIC
Making a Shadowgraph Show: Apparatus and Routines for a Complete Programme
Faber & Faber, 1969. 59pp. $2.95. Instructions and diagrams for making and operating a shadowgraph screen, basic hand formations and how to adapt them, making and using cardboard cut-out accessories, and the patter that accompanies the action.

HOWARD, VERNON
Puppet and Pantomime Plays
Sterling, 1962. 108pp. $2.95. Simple directions for creating hand and stick puppets, with scripts and instructions on producing puppet plays.

JAGENDORF, MORITZ
Penny Puppets, Penny Theatre, and Penny Plays
Plays, Inc., 1966. 190pp. $6.95. The author provides easy to follow directions for making puppets and producing puppet plays. The step-by-step directions are illustrated with drawings and diagrams to help a child use simple materials to create his own puppets and marionettes. A selection of easy to produce plays is included.

JAGENDORF, MORITZ
Puppets for Beginners
Plays, Inc. 1962. 68pp. $3.95. An introduction to puppets with easy directions for making and working with various kinds of puppets. Three very short plays are included. Illustrated.

JOHNSON, LILLIAN
Papier—Mache
David McKay, 1958. 88pp. $4.95. Complete, step-by-step instructions for working in papier-mache, with suggestions for making holiday decorations, stage props, window displays, puppets, and dolls. Illustrated with photographs.

JONES, JOSEPHINE M.
Glove Puppetry
Brockhampton, 1965. 93pp. $2.00. Instructions on how to make glove puppets and how to manipulate them. The author provides details on how to write a glove puppet play, how to build a theatre, paint scenery for it, and collect properties, and choose music for the performance. Illustrated with diagrams and drawings.

LAURY, JEAN RAY
Doll Making: A Creative Approach
Van Nostrand, 1970. 136pp. $9.95. A complete guide to doll making showing the techniques needed to make a number of different types of dolls. The text explains the materials and methods and application of various crafts used by the author. Illustrated with photographs and drawings.

LEWIS, SHARI and LILLIAN OPPENHEIMER
Folding Paper Puppets
Stein & Day, 1962. 78pp. $3.95. Illustrated instructions on how to make animated toys, simple puppets, and inexpensive party decorations by Origami, the Japanese art of paper folding.

LEWIS, SHARI and LILLIAN OPPENHEIMER
Folding Paper Toys
Stein & Day, 1963. 93pp. $3.95. This illustrated book of carefully prepared instructions for the beginner in Origami shows how to make playthings that actually move.

LEWIS, SHARI
Making Easy Puppets
Dutton, 1967. 86pp. $4.50. Written for children, this book describes over thirty simple puppets with suggestions on dramatic activities. Illustrated with drawings and photographs. A Bibliography of books about puppets is included.

MULHOLLAND, JOHN
Practical Puppetry
Arco, 1962. 191pp. $4.95. Starting with a history of puppets, this book examines the educational and entertainment value of the art in various countries with special emphasis on the Russian experiments. The major portion of the book is devoted to a complete course in puppet construction and play production.

PELS, GERTRUDE
Easy Puppets
Crowell, 1951. 104pp. $3.95. Written for children in grades two to five, this book provides more than 100 diagrammatic illustrations showing how to make a wide variety of puppets from inexpensive household materials.

PHILPOTT, A. R.
Modern Puppetry
Michael Joseph, 1966. 128pp. $3.95. This introduction to the art of puppetry describes the making and operating of many kinds of puppets. Instructions on the construction of puppet stages and on the art of acting with puppets is also provided. Illustrated.

PRATT, LOIS H.
The Puppet Do–It–Yourself Book: A Handbook for Beginners and Teachers
Exposition Press, 1957. 76pp. $4.00. Instructions for making puppets with simple and fully moulded heads. Three plays are included with lists of props and stage directions.

RASMUSSEN, CARRIE and CAROLINE STORCK
Fun Time Puppets
Children's Press, 1952. 41pp. $2.75. A simplified construction manual for the young puppet maker in grades two through six. Illustrated.

REINIGER, LOTTE
Shadow Theatres and Shadow Films
Watson–Guptill, 1970. 128pp. $10.00. The author provides a guide to the shadow theatre and the shadow film as a creative medium. Mrs. Reiniger deals with the history of the shadow theatre in Asia and Europe, describes shadow puppets and theatres, provides instructions on the cutting out and assembling of the figures, and details for production of plays. Among the many details discussed in relation to shadow films are animation, photography, story boards, settings, synchronization of sound, and other aspects. More than 100 illustrations—color plates, photographs, drawings, and diagrams. Glossary. List of Suppliers.

RENFRO, NANCY
Puppets for Play Production
Funk & Wagnalls, 1969. 128pp. $6.95. Explicit directions for making puppets of various materials and details for further use of the puppets. Information includes how to plan and choose a play or write one, how to make scenery and a stage, how to use sound effects and properties, and how to stage an actual production. A section on how to teach puppetry, how to use puppetry as a teaching aid, and how to direct and put on shows. Illustrated. Bibliography.

RUTTER, VICKI
ABC Puppetry
Plays, Inc., 1969. 78pp. $3.95. In this introduction to puppetry, the author describes the main types of puppets and gives detailed instructions for making glove puppets and marionettes. The volume also includes sections on staging, scenery, properties, lighting, production, scripts and the choice of programs. Illustrated with diagrams and photographs.

SCHONEWOLF, HERTA
Play with Light and Shadow
Reinhold, 1968. 95pp. $6.95. This handbook on the art and techniques of shadow theatre is divided into three parts. The first section deals with theory: light and images, flatness and depth, time and movement, words and sound. Part Two describes techniques: figure construction, masks and costumes, lighting and stage construction. Part Three is a section on the actual practice of the art: how to play with light and shadow, stage directions, and the performance. Illustrated with diagrams and photographs.

SLADE, RICHARD
You Can Make A String Puppet
Plays, Inc., 1957. 47pp. $3.95. A collection of photographs, with descriptive captions, illustrating each step in the process of making the string puppet.

SNOOK, BARBARA
Puppets
Batsford, 1965. 95pp. $3.95. Both glove and string puppets are studied with drawings and instructions for construction, stage manipulation, and drama-writing. Index.

STOCKWELL, A.
Puppetry
Collins, 1966. 127pp. $1.75. A book on puppetry for the amateur. Mr. Stockwell summarizes the history of puppetry, gives advice on construction, costume, manipulation, and transportation of puppets. There is also a chapter on stages. Illustrated with line drawings. Index.

STROBL–WOHLSCHLAGER, ILSE
Make Your Own Dolls
Watson–Guptill, 1968. 56pp. $2.50. The author shows how to construct fifty animals, dolls and jumping jacks from scraps of cloth and stuffing, yarn, cardboard and papier-mache, pipe cleaners, and wooden balls. Sixty-three Illustrations, seven in full color, are included.

WALL, L. V. and G. A. WHITE, A. R. PHILPOTT
The Puppet Book
Plays, Inc., 1965. 301pp. $7.95. Originally published in 1950 and now revised, this is a practical guide to puppetry in schools, training colleges, and clubs. Chapters are included on the uses of puppetry, the making and manipulation of puppets, stages and scenery for puppet plays, play production, and the possible future development of the art. Illustrated.

WITZIG, H. and G. E. KUHN
Making Dolls
Sterling, 1969. 96pp. $3.95. A book of instructions for making dolls from everything from twigs to foam rubber. Illustrated with diagrams and photographs.

WORRELL, ESTELLE ANSLEY
Be a Puppeteer!
McGraw–Hill, 1969. 96pp. $4.95. This is a step-by-step instruction book on how to make and dress puppets, choose and write plays for them, and design a stage and scenery. The volume is written for children from grade three and and includes full size patterns for the puppets. Index.

Plays for Puppets

For other books of puppet plays, see:
Puppets – Instruction Books.

BAUMANN, HANS
Caspar and His Friends
Phoenix House, 1967. 95pp. $3.00. Ten puppet plays, based on the german puppet character Caspar or Kasperl, are included in this volume. The book includes some general hints on the presentation of puppet plays. Illustrated with drawings by Wanda Zacharias.

ESTES, ELEANOR
The Lollipop Princess
Harcourt, Brace, 1967. 30pp. $2.50. A play for paper dolls in one act. Illustrated by the author, this play was written especially for young people.

PHILPOTT, A. R. – Editor
Eight Plays for Hand Puppets
Plays, Inc. 1968. 74pp. $4.00. After a short introduction on puppet plays and puppet play production, the editor provides eight short plays written expressly for puppets.

STAHL, LEROY and EFFA A. PRESTON
The Master Puppet Book
Denison, 1965. 400pp. $3.95. A collection of plays, with complete production notes and instructions on making and manipulating puppets.

TICHENOR, TOM
Folk Plays for Puppets You Can Make
Abingdon, 1959. 96pp. $2.50. Written for children in grades two through five, this volume presents directions for making puppets and puppet stages with five plays. Production notes are provided for the plays. Illustrated with diagrams.

VON BOEHN, MAX
Dolls and Puppets
See Page 341

MINIATURE THEATRES

BUSSELL, JAN
The Model Theatre
Dennis Dobson, 1948. 31pp. Paper $1.00. The author provides instructions for building a miniature theatre from cardboard or wood. He also includes suggestions for scenery and lighting.

SCAPING, MARY
Toy Theatre
Premier, 1967. 24pp. Spiral bound $2.00. Published in England, this volume provides instructions for building a toy theatre. This craft is illustrated in drawings and photographs and a complete toy theatre play is included.

SPEAIGHT, GEORGE
The History of the English Toy Theatre
Studio Vista, 1969. 224pp. $16.95. A revised version of "Juvenile Drama: The History of the English Toy Theatre" originally published in 1946. It is a study of the toy theatre that had its origin in the days of the Regency. This version is completely revised and expanded with new illustrations including twelve plates in color and more than forty black-and-white illustrations. Lists of Plays Published. Bibliography. Index.

WHANSLAW, H. W.
The Bankside Stage Book
Wells Gardner, Undated. 256pp. $3.00. Directions are provided for making a model Elizabethan stage. Details of Tudor costumes, furniture, music, and background are included. A short history of the stage is included. Illustrated.

WILLIAMS, GUY R.
Making a Miniature Theatre
Plays, Inc. 1967. 79pp. $4.95. In simple language, Mr. Williams gives instructions for making a miniature theatre. He explains what equipment is needed and how to use it, and gives a detailed account of the construction. He also tells how to make the curtains and draperies, scenery, lights, and special effects. Illustrated with diagrams and photographs.

WILSON, A. E.
Penny Plain – Two Pence Coloured

Blom, 1969. 118pp. $18.75. Originally published in 1932 and now reissued in a facsimile edition, this is a stage history of English toy theatres with chapters on famous scenic designers, sellers of plays, and kinds of drama. Illustrated. Appendices. Bibliography. Index.

CLOWNS, CIRCUS, PANTOMIME, COMMEDIA DELL'ARTE

For other books on this subject, see: Italian Theatre.

CLINTON–BRADDELEY, V. C.
Some Pantomime Pedigrees
See Page 187

DE REGNIERS, BEATRICE SCHENK and AL GIESE
Circus
Viking, 1966. Unpaged. $3.95. Color photographs of the circus are provided in this volume. The performers, both animals and human, are shown in actual performance.

DICKENS, CHARLES
Memoirs of Joseph Grimaldi
Stein & Day, 1968. 311pp. $6.95. This is a revised edition, edited by Richard Findlater with new notes and Introduction, of the work first published in 1838. It is a biography of England's great clown who won fame in the early nineteenth century for his pantomimes. Illustrated by George Cruikshank. Index of People Mentioned.

DISHER, M. WILLSON
Clowns and Pantomimes
Blom, 1968. 362pp. $17.50. Originally published in 1925 and now reissued, this is one of the few books to treat in detail the Commedia dell'Arte throughout the history of the English theatre. Illustrated with fifty-seven plates. Index.

FENNER, MILDRED SANDISON and WOLCOTT FENNER – Editors
The Circus: Lure and Legend
Prentice–Hall, 1970. 208pp. $9.95. A collection of pictures, prose, and poetry by circus people and circus lovers. Essays on the history of the circus, animals and their trainers, clowns and other performers, the side show, life behind the scenes and on the road. Sixteen pages of circus posters and paintings in color. Among the contributors are Jack London, James Thurber, Charles Dickens, Charles Chaplin, and many others.

GOLLMAR, ROBERT H.
My Father Owned a Circus
Caxton, 1965. 205pp. $5.00. This is the story of how the Gollmar Brothers Circus grew from its beginnings as a small wagon show in 1891 to become the fourth largest railroad circus in America in 1916. There is material on the advertising methods, the street parades, the specialty acts, the spectacles and the animal acts. Illustrated with photographs.

GROCK
Life's A Lark
Blom, 1969. 276pp. $9.75. Originally published in 1931 and now reissued in a facsimile edition, this is the biography of the German clown. Illustrated with caricatures and photographs.

HARRIS, LEON
The Moscow Circus School
See Page 219

HUBBARD, FREEMAN
Great Days of the Circus
Harper & Row, 1962. 153pp. $5.95. Compiled by the editors of "American Heritage" Magazine, with a text by Mr. Hubbard in consultation with Leonard V. Farley, this is a history of the circus from the eighteenth century tent shows to the present day. Illustrated with contemporary paintings, drawings, prints, posters, and photographs. Selected Bibliography. Index.

LANO, DAVID
A Wandering Showman, I
Michigan State University, 1957. 290pp. $5.75. An autobiography of the entertainer who for 75 years was a showman with circuses and road shows. Eyewitness accounts are provided of famous circuses of the past including the Holland and McMahon Circus, the Hurd and Berry show, and others. Illustrated.

LENO, DAN
Dan Leno – Hys Booke
Hugh Evelyn, 1968. 60pp. $1.75. This book of anecdotes was written by the leading English music-hall comic of the nineteenth century. Factual notes and an Introduction have been provided by Roy Hudd. Illustrated with contemporary drawings of the comic.

LIPOVSKY, ALEXANDER – Compiler
The Soviet Circus
Progress Publishers, 1967. 234pp. $3.95. Published in Russia, but printed in the English language, this is a collection of articles about the Soviet circus and its artists. Illustrated with photographs.

MAY, EARL CHAPIN
The Circus from Rome to Ringling
Dover, 1968. 332pp. Paper $2.75. Originally published in 1932 and now reissued, this history of the circus traces its development from the Roman Circus Maximus to the modern extravaganzas of the Ringling Brothers. A new Introduction by L. V. Farley brings the history up-to-date from 1932 to 1963. Illustrated with photographs and contemporary prints.

MAYER, DAVID
Harlequin in His Element: The English Pantomime 1806–1836
Harvard, 1969. 400pp. $18.00. The author examines the structures, conventions, and characters of pantomime, outlining their development and showing how they were defined and stabilized during the period of Grimaldi: 1806–1836. Mr. Mayer discusses in detail how pantomime reflected and recorded the social, economic, political, and aesthetic issues of the time. An Appendix presents the only extant contemporary document discussing the construction and operation of pantomime trick-work. Also included are five pieces of pantomime music. Illustrated with eighty-one contemporary illustrations. Bibliography. Index of Pantomimes. General Index.

MILLS, CYRIL BERTRAM
Bertram Mills Circus
Hutchinson, 1967. 272pp. $8.50. Written by Bertram Mill's son, this is the story of the famous London circus from 1920 to its last Olympia Theatre season in 1965/66. Illustrated with photographs. Glossary of Circus Terms. Index.

NICOLL, ALLARDYCE
The World of Harlequin
Cambridge, 1963. 243pp. $18.50. A full length investigation of the Commedia dell'Arte. The growth of the Commedia in Italy during the sixteenth and seventeenth centuries and its relation to English theatre of the period are among the topics pursued. The technique of staging and acting and the scenarios used are also examined. Illustrated with a rare collection of contemporary paintings and engravings in black-and-white and with a color frontispiece.

NIKLAUS, THELMA
Harlequin, or the Rise and Fall of a Bergamask Rogue
Braziller, 1956. 259pp. $7.50. A history of the harlequin figure, tracing his ancestry in Italy and his development in France and England. Celebrated players of the role are discussed and the scenarios and early pantomime books are examined. Illustrated.

PLOWDEN, GENE
Those Amazing Ringlings and Their Circus
Caxton, 1967. 303pp. $6.50. A history of the Ringling Brothers Circus from the 1880's, to the 1930's when the circus moved aboard railroad cars, to the story of how it moved from the ashes of the tragic fire in Hartford to be presented in the auditoriums and sports arenas as it is today. Illustrated with photographs. Bibliography.

POPOV, OLEG
Russian Clown
Macdonald, 1970. 164pp. $6.50. The autobiography of Russia's great clown. Popov describes his career from the days when he trained at the Moscow Circus School to the world-wide trips he took with his company. He also gives an insight into the traditional art of circus clowning. Seventeen pages of illustrations.

REA, DOMENICO
Pulcinella e "La Canzone di Zeza"
Edizione Scientifiche Italiane, 1968. 54pp. $30.00. This folder contains folio sized loose pages. These pages provide the scenario for "The Love Song of Zeza" —a Harlequin play—and a long Introduction to the play and the characters. This text is, however, in the Italian language. Illustrated with black-and-white drawings and reproductions, in color, of paintings by Mario Cortiello.

SANGER, "LORD" GEORGE
Seventy Years a Showman
Macgibbon, 1966. 176pp. $7.50. "Lord" George Sanger was the founder of the Sanger circus. This is his autobiography, originally published in 1910 and now reissued. He recalls the life of the last century and describes the showman's tricks, the fun of the fair, and the lives of the itinerant show people of the era.

SAXON, A. H.
Enter Foot and Horse
Yale, 1968. 249pp. $7.50. This history traces the development of the presentation of plays in which animals, especially horses, were given leading actions, especially in England and France in the nineteenth century. Mr. Saxon focuses on the unique facilities for such productions at Astley's Theatre in London and at the Cirque Olympique in Paris. Detailed descriptions of many of the productions are supplemented by illustrations. Selected Bibliography. Indices.

SUTTON, FELIX
The Book of Clowns
Grosset & Dunlap, 1953. 26pp. $1.00. Written for children, this volume includes elementary information on the history of clowns, clown make-up, and various clown acts. The text is illustrated with color illustrations by James Schuker on every page.

WILLEFORD, WILLIAM
The Fool and His Scepter
Northwestern University, 1969. 265pp. $8.50. Subtitled "A Study in Clowns and Jesters and Their Audience," this is an examination of the materials of folly, the nature of the fool spectacle, and the interactions between the fool actor and his audience. The fool is considered in his relations to mimetic motives in various religions. The author draws upon records of folk festivals and court jesters, the fool literature of the Middle Ages and the Renaissance, plays by Shakespeare and others, vaudeville and circus clown skits, and slapstick films. Twenty-seven plates include reproductions of period drawings and paintings and other art and contemporary photographs. Notes. Index.

MAGIC

ABRAHAM, R. M.
Easy-To-Do Entertainments and Diversions with Coins, Cards, String, Paper and Matches
Dover, 1961. 186pp. Paper $1.25. Originally published in 1932 as "Winter Night's Entertainment," this volume contains instructions for over 300 tricks, games, puzzles, and pastimes for youngsters. Illustrated.

ADAIR, IAN
Conjuring as a Craft
Barnes, 1970. 160pp. $5.95. The presentation of tricks and illusions is described stage-by-stage so that the reader can build up a skill. Action photographs of the conjuror's hands at work help explain the secret moves. Also illustrated with drawings and sketches. Bibliography. Index.

BURSILL, HENRY
Hand Shadows
Dover, 1968. Unpaged. Paper $1.00. Originally published in 1859 and now reissued, this volume contains eighteen full page illustrations which show the exact positioning for fingers and hands which create hand shadows. The author's original Preface is included.

CHRISTOPHER, MILBOURNE
Houdini: The Untold Story
Crowell, 1969. 281pp. $6.95. Paper—Pocket Books, 1970. 298pp. $ .95. A biography of the magician and escape artist, Harry Houdini. The author follows Houdini's life, career, his crusade against fraudulent mediums and psychics, and the accident that led to his death. Bibliography. Index.

CHRISTOPHER, MILBOURNE
Panorama of Magic
Dover, 1962. 216pp. Paper $3.00. A history of the development and the changes in the art of conjuring from the time of the Pharaohs. Illustrated with a rare collection of prints and bills.

DICK, WILLIAM BRISBANE
Dick's 100 Amusements
Something Else Press, 1967. 182pp. $4.50. Paper $2.25. Originally published in 1873 and now reissued in a facsimile edition with the original illustrations, this is a collection of do-it-yourself games, magic tricks, and songs.

DUNNINGER, JOSEPH
Dunninger's Complete Encyclopedia of Magic
Lyle Stuart, 1967. 288pp. $4.95. This is a complete course of training for the amateur magician. Most of the material in the volume was originally published in three volumes under the title: "Dunninger's Popular Magic." The illusions described include sleight-of-hand, telepathy, and spirit writing. Illustrated.

GIBSON, WALTER B.
The Complete Illustrated Book of Card Magic
Doubleday, 1969. 470pp. $12.95. Principles and professional techniques revealed in text and photographs of basic secrets, master methods, and magic tricks done with cards. Illustrated. Glossary. Index.

GIBSON, WALTER B. and MORRIS N. YOUNG
Houdini's Fabulous Magic
Chilton, 1961. 214pp. $4.50. Written for teenagers, the spectacular stunts of Houdini are described and explained.

GIBSON, WALTER, B.
The Master Magicians: Their Lives and Most Famous Tricks
Doubleday, 1966. 221pp. $4.50. Written for teenagers, this is a history of magic told through the lives of the great magicians. Illustrated with forty-eight pages of photographs, period drawings, posters, and showbills. Index.

GIBSON, WALTER B.
Secrets of Magic: Ancient and Modern
Grosset & Dunlap, 1967. 147pp. $3.95. Written for teenagers, this volume includes seventy famous feats of magic. Using more than 100 illustrations and diagrams, Mr. Gibson reveals how the effects are achieved.

GRESHAM, WILLIAM LINDSAY
Houdini: The Man Who Walked Through Walls
Macfadden, 1961. 263pp. Paper $ .95. A biography of Harry Houdini with special attention paid to his great illusion tricks and escapes. Originally published in 1959 and now reprinted, the volume is illustrated. Annotated Bibliography.

HAY, HENRY—Editor
Cyclopedia of Magic
Tudor, 1949. 498pp. $4.95. In addition to explaining every standard principle, trick, and stage illusion, this encyclopedia offers a wide variety of historical and bibliographical information. There are special contributions on pantomime, music, stage settings, children's shows, and literature of magic. Illustrated with over 400 drawings, photographs and portraits.

HOPKINS, ALBERT A.
Magic: Stage Illusions and Scientific Diversions
Blom, 1968. 556pp. $25.00. First printed in 1897 and now reissued, this is a study of stage magic. It contains four hundred illustrations from contemporary sources. Bibliography. Index.

HOUDINI, HARRY
Houdini on Magic
Dover, 1953. 280pp. Paper $2.00. Edited by Walter B. Gibson and Morris N. Young, this is Harry Houdini's own account of his exploits, supplemented with photographs and posters, first hand material

from periodicals and pamphlets, and instructions for performing forty-four of his famous stage tricks. Illustrated. Bibliography.

HOULDEN, DOUGLAS
Ventriloquism for Beginners
A. S. Barnes, 1967. 63pp. $3.50. Mr. Houlden teaches how to train the voice for ventriloquism and how to manipulate a figure. Several sample dialogues and acts are given. Written primarily for young people and illustrated with drawings and photographs.

HUGARD, JEAN
Modern Magic Manual
Faber & Faber, 1969. 372pp. Paper $4.95. Originally published in 1957 and now reissued, this is a textbook on magic for beginners. No intricate or expensive equipment is required for the effects. Illustrated with drawings. Index.

HUNT, DOUGLAS and KARI HUNT
The Art of Magic
Atheneum, 1967. 216pp. $4.95. Written for children in grades five and up, this is a history of the art of magic. The authors include descriptions of many famous magicians' tricks and conclude the volume with a series of tricks for those who wish to perform themselves. Illustrated. Bibliography.

HUNTER, NORMAN
The Puffin Book of Magic
Penguin, 1968. 128pp. Paper $ .95. A book of magic tricks for children. The tricks are explained and easy directions for props are included. Illustrated with diagrams.

JONSON, WILFRID
Magic Tricks and Card Tricks
Dover, 1954. 196pp. Paper $1.50. Originally published in 1950 as two separate books and now republished in a single volume. The two books provide instruction in the art of conjuring and impromptu deceptions. A special feature of the book is the portrait gallery of fifty-one famous magicians. Bibliography. Index.

MULHOLLAND, JOHN
John Mulholland's Book of Magic
Scribner, 1963. 329pp. $6.50. A complete course in magic, designed to teach a great number of tricks in a short time. None of the tricks require use of sleight of hand.

NELMS, HENNING
Magic and Showmanship: A Handbook for Conjurers
Dover, 1969. 322pp. Paper $2.50. Mr. Nelms deals with the showmanship on which the real art of conjuring depends. He shows how techniques developed by playwrights, directors, and actors can dramatize the conjuring art. Sixty original routines are included from simple card effects to the sudden disappearance of the performer. The author has provided nearly 200 drawings. Index.

PERMIN, IB
Hokus Pokus
Sterling, 1969. 120pp. $3.95. Written especially for teenagers, the tricks in this book of magic range from very simple to professional. Only two things are required: an ability to read and follow directions and a determination to practice. Most of the equipment can be found around the home. Illustrated with photographs and diagrams. Glossary. Index.

SCHONEWOLF, HERTA
Play with Light and Shadow
See Page 345

SEVERN, BILL
Magic Comedy: Tricks, Skits and Clowning
McKay, 1968. 144pp. $3.95. Written for children, this volume includes skits, stunts, magical jokes, gags, and full outlines for magicians. Illustrated with drawings.

VERMES, HAL G.
The Quick and Easy Guide to Magic
Collier, 1963. 94pp. Paper $1.50. The author includes instructions on such popular forms of magic as tricks with money, matches, paper, handkerchiefs, string, rope, and cards as well as mental tricks. Instructions on performance technique are provided. Illustrated with drawings.

WIT AND HUMOR

DOLBIER, MAURICE
All Wrong on the Night
Walker, 1966. 86pp. $3.50. This is a book about the things that have gone wrong on opening nights in the theatre. A humorous retelling of the stories theatrical people tell each other. Illustrated with drawings by Michael Ffolkes.

KRONENBERGER, LOUIS
The Cutting Edge
Doubleday, 1970. 178pp. $5.95. A collection of quips, comments, retorts and witticisms ranging through the entire history of the written and spoken word. Index.

MAY, ROBIN – Compiler
The Wit of the Theatre
Leslie Frewin, 1969. 126pp. $4.50. Published in England, this is a compilation of the wit of actors and actresses, managers and playwrights, and critics and audiences. Illustrated with drawings.

MENDOZA, GEORGE
The Marcel Marceau Alphabet Book

Doubleday, 1970. Unpaged. $5.95. Twenty-six full-page photographs by Milton H. Green in which Marcel Marceau illustrates the alphabet.

RICHARDS, DICK – Compiler
The Wit of Noel Coward
Sphere, 1970. 112pp. Paper $1.35. Originally published in England in 1968 and now reissued, this is a compilation of the wit of the English playwright. The quips and quotes are categorized under such topics as "The World of the Theatre," "Films and Television," "Personalities," and "The Coward Image." Illustrated with eight pages of photographs.

RUSSELL, RAY
The Little Lexicon of Love
Sherbourne Press, 1966. 244pp. $5.95. A humorous and satirical book with chapters on Hollywood and Broadway, TV Soap operas, Shirley MacLaine, and Tennessee Williams.

PART TWO

BOOKS ON TECHNICAL ARTS

PART TWO: BOOKS ON TECHNICAL ARTS

PRODUCTION

GENERAL REFERENCE WORKS

Note: For other books on this subject, see:
Children and the Theatre

ABRAHALL, CLARE
Amateur Dramatics
Collins, 1967. 160pp. $2.00. A reprint of the guide first published in 1963 for amateur theatrical groups. Beginning with advice on founding an amateur society and joining one, the author pases to the question of choosing a play. Subsequent chapters deal with the work of the producer, stage manager, those responsible for decor, lighting, sound, prompting, wardrobe, and make-up. Illustrated with drawings and eight photographs illustrating make-up technique. Index.

ALBRIGHT, H.D. and WILLIAM P. HALSTEAD, LEE MITCHELL
Principles of Theatre Art
Houghton Mifflin, 1968. 547pp. $11.75. A second edition of the text originally published in 1955. New material has been added and other material has been revised and updated. Chapters on drama as art, the dramatic composition, characterization, language, acting, the theatre structure, set, lighting and costume design, the function of the director, directing for the open stage, and conduct of rehearsals are all provided. A series of Appendices detail projects and exercises for the student, the art of costuming and make-up. Illustrated with photographs and drawings. Selected Bibliography. Index.

ALLEN, ARTHUR B.
Religious Drama for Amateur Players
See Page 327

AUSTELL, JAN
What's In A Play?
Harcourt, Brace, 1968. 160pp. $3.50. The author has chosen three plays—"Our Town," "Macbeth," and "The Glass Menagerie"—to show how to read, enjoy, and fully understand a play. The author analyzes the plots, portrayal of characters, and the appropriate staging and direction of each play to help clarify the playwright's message and the importance of drama as a form of literary expression. There are Appendices on direction, lighting, and floor plans with sample plans for each of the three plays.

BAKER, HENDRIK
Stage Management and Theatrecraft
Theatre Arts, 1968. 304pp. $8.75. Written by an English stage manager, this book deals with the development of a stage production and with present day practice in England: marking scripts, conducting rehearsals, stage staff, the stage itself, first night, and running the play. Illustrated with photographs and line drawings. Glossary. Suggestions for Further Reading. Index.

BRADBURY, A.J. and W.R.B. HOWARD
Stagecraft
Herbert Jenkins, 1957. 94pp. $1.75. A guide book for the amateur production team, with chapters on planning all aspects of the show. Index.

BRANDT, ALVIN G.
Drama Handbook for Churches
See Page 580

BROWN, ANDREW
Drama
Arc Books, 1962. 160pp. $2.50. Paper $ .95. A comprehensive guide and instruction book dealing with all aspects of theatre from its history, through the theories and methods of famous producers and directors. Instructions on play production, and suggestions to the actor on voice, diction, costume, make-up, and props. Illustrated.

BRUDER, KARL C.
The Theatre Student: Properties and Dressing the Stage
Richards Rosen Press, 1969. 126pp. $5.97. A practical guide for those who are beginning their work with stage properties. A study of props as a design problem is included. Illustrated with production photographs from Kansas State Teachers College and with drawings.

BURTON, PETER and JOHN LANE
New Directions: Ways of Advance for the Amateur Theatre
MacGibbon & Kee, 1970. 373pp. $12.50. Introduced by John Arden, this volume is about some of the ways people concerned with the amateur theatre can develop their work. The authors examime the possibilities of work with puppetry, film-making and playwriting, as well as documentaries, street theatre, and sound ballads. They discuss the role of the director, choosing the play, staging and setting, costumes, props and furniture, music and sound, make-up, lighting, stage management, and organizing the performance. Also provided is an exhaustive list of sources of help for the amateur group in England. Illustrated with drawings and photographs. Index.

CANOVA, SIRENA M. – Editor
Contact Book: 1970
Celebrity Service, 1969. 152pp. Paper $4.00. A trade directory for the entertainment industry. Listings of advertising agencies, agents, air lines, professional associations, theatres, scenic and property materials, television producers, recording studios, and other services. The major cities are all covered.

CAPBERN, A. MARTIAL
The Drama Publicist
Pageant Press, 1968. 119pp. $5.00. The author has compiled a how-to-do-it book on the technique of publicizing amateur theater productions. From the proper use of news media to a publicity-program timetable, every aspect of drama publicity is explored. Illustrations of mailing pieces, spot TV and radio announcement formats, newspaper stories and editorials are included.

CAREY, GRACE
Stagecraft for Small Drama Groups
Albyn Press, 1948. 62pp. Paper $ .85. A handbook for amateur groups by an English producer and actor. All aspects of production are covered briefly from forming the group and choosing the play to rehearsals, production, costume and make-up, lighting, and instituting a drama festival. Illustrated with sketches.

CARTER, CONRAD and A. J. BRADBURY, W. R. B. HOWARD
The Production and Staging of Plays
Arc Books, 1963. 186pp. $2.50. Paper $ .95. A concise handbook, intended mainly as a guide for amateur productions, which describes every aspect of the producer's, the stage manager's, and the designer's art. Chapters on script preparation, staff organization, casting, interpretation of roles, set designing, publicity, etc. Introduction by Sir Donald Wolfit. Illustrated.

CARTMELL, VAN H.
Amateur Theatre: A Guide for Actor and Director
Funk & Wagnalls, 1968. 218pp. Paper $1.50. A handbook for the beginning director and actor. It covers play selection, casting, and rehearsals. Mr. Cartmell anticipates every problem the novice might encounter and he gives advice about prompters and property men, rehearsal discipline, costumes, and make-up. A working script of the one-act play, "George," illustrates the principles discussed throughout the book. A glossary of stage terms and an Appendix on "The Duties of a Production Manager" are included.

CHALLENER, ROBERT B.
Play Production, Arena Style
Dramatic Publishing, 1967. 151pp. Paper $2.25. This is a manual for producing plays in arena theatres. It traces the history of the arena theatre and guides the director on his own arena productions. Illustrated with photographs and diagrams. Included is the full text of "The Importance of Being Earnest," by Oscar Wilde, as directed for arena by Mr. Challener with floor plans, property list, and suggestions for costuming.

CLAY, JAMES H. and DANIEL KREMPEL
The Theatrical Image
McGraw-Hill, 1967. 300pp. $8.95. The authors attempt to define how theatre creates its effect. They explore the working methods that create these effects from interpretation to evaluation of the production. Discussed are examples of productions and interpretations. Illustrated with photographs. Notes. Index.

CLAY, ROBERTA
Promotion in Print
A. S. Barnes, 1970. 94pp. $4.95. A guide for publicity chairmen. The author discusses newspaper publicity at length and the general material concerns club publicity. Two chapters are devoted, however, to specific suggestions about public information for schools, churches, civic projects, businesses, health organizations, and the arts.

COGER, LESLIE IRENE and MELVIN R. WHITE
Readers Theatre Handbook
Scott Foresman, 1967. 259pp. Paper $4.25. Subtitled, "A Dramatic Approach to Literature," this is an introduction to the type of theatre in which the actors or readers carry copies of the script they are reading. The origins and history of the medium, the forms it has taken on both the professional and educational stage, and some of the dynamics and procedures involved in its presentation are considered. Sample scripts are provided. Illustrated. Bibliography. Index.

COLLINS, FREDA
Children in the Marketplace
See Page 580

COLLINS, FREDA
Let's Prepare a Nativity Play
See Page 327

CORRY, PERCY
Amateur Theatrecraft
Museum Press, 1961. 159pp. $3.95. A practical handbook designed for the amateur working with limited resources. Chapters on types of theatres, play selection, the actor, scenery, dress rehearsal procedure, and performance. Illustrated.

DAUBENY, PETER
Stage by Stage
John Murray, 1952. 162pp. $3.50. Published in London, this volume discusses the ideas on the techniques of stage production of the producer/manager of such hits as "The Late Edwina Black," "Fallen Angels," and "The Gay Invalid." There is a section on the American theatre and an account of an interview with the Lunts. Illustrated. Index.

DEMUTH, AVERIL – Editor
The Minack Open-Air Theatre
David & Charles, 1968. 128pp. $5.25. This is the story of the Minack Theatre which is built into the Cornish cliffs. The contributors to this symposium tell of the hazards and difficulties of producing in such an open air setting and describe many practical

aspects such as lighting and scenery that will make the book useful for those staging plays in the open anywhere. Illustrated with photographs and a plan of the theatre. A list of productions from 1932 to 1968 is also included.

DODRILL, CHARLES W.
Theatre Management Selected Bibliography
See Page 586

DOLMAN, JOHN
The Art of Play Production
Harper & Row, 1946. 421pp. $12.50. Addressed primarily to the student and the amateur interested in building a permanent theatre group, this text covers the whole range of theatre production from preparation of the script, through styles of acting, to the organization of back-stage and box-office. Appendices include sample working scripts, and excerpts from Vitruvius. A revision of the 1928 edition.

EASTMAN, FRED
Drama in the Church
See Page 327

EATON, QUAINTANCE
Opera Production: A Handbook
See Page 284

EDE, CHRISTOPHER
Drama Festivals and Adjudications
Herbert Jenkins, 1955. 96pp. $1.50. A book on the amateur staging of festival plays, with Appendices on British Drama League rules for festivals, rules for local festivals, and a sample balance-sheet for a festival.

EEK, NAT
A Touring Manual
A.E.T.A., 1965. 27pp. Paper $1.00. A mimeographed manual for those organizations which would like to tour outside their immediate environment. It covers facets from play selection to contracts, fees, royalties, the company, budget, union relations, scenery, lighting, sound, props and costumes. The preparation of this manual was supervised by The American Educational Theatre Association.

EHRENSPERGER, HAROLD
Religious Drama: Means and Ends
See Page 580

ENGEL, LEHMAN
Planning and Producing the Musical Show
See Page 289

FARBER, DONALD C.
From Option to Opening
Drama Book Specialists, 1970. 134pp. $7.50. Originally published in 1968 and now revised and reissued, this is a guide for the off-Broadway producer. It explains all the facets of professional production and is applicable to professional theatre anywhere. Mr. Farber discusses finding the property, taking an option, forming the production company, raising money, signing a theatre lease, hiring qualified personnel, dealing with unions, contracts, and all legal responsibilities. Included are examples of an option agreement, production and operating budgets, and a theatrical financial offering.

FARBER, DONALD C.
Producing on Broadway: A Comprehensive Guide
Drama Book Specialists, 1969. 399pp. $15.00. A practical guide to every phase of producing on Broadway. Analyzed and explained in detail are the twelve union contracts, the Securities and Exchange Commission offering circular, out-of-town and Broadway theatre licensing agreements, co-production and limited partnership agreements. Every phase of producing on Broadway is discussed and examples of budgets and legal forms are included.

FISHMAN, MORRIS
Play Production: Methods and Practice
Herbert Jenkins, 1965. 174pp. $4.95. An introductory chapter discusses the rise of the modern producer, after which the author examines the requirements and functions of play producers in general. Play production from first reading of the script to long-run hit is treated in detail. Bibliography. Index.

GASSNER, JOHN
Producing the Play: with The New Scene Technician's Handbook by Philip Barber
Holt, Rinehart, 1953. 915pp. $14.50. A revision of the 1941 edition, this is a complete guide to production. Contributors include Harold Clurman, Margaret Webster, Worthington Miner, Lee Strasberg, M. Gorelik, Guthrie McClintic, Robert Lewis, Alfred DeLiagre, Jr., and others. Illustrated with charts, diagrams, and photographs.

GOFFIN, PETER
The Art and Science of Stage Management
J. Garnet Miller, 1953. 120pp. $3.95. A critical study of the aesthetic and technical aspects of play production written by a producer/designer. Bibliography.

GOODMAN, RANDOLPH
Drama on Stage
Holt, Rinehart, 1961. 475pp. Paper $8.50. A collection of six plays with essays on the first productions, modern production techniques, costuming, designing, directing, and acting. Illustrated. The plays included are: "Medea," "Everyman," "Macbeth," "The Misanthrope," "A Streetcar Named Desire," and "The Visit."

GRAHAM–CAMPBELL, A. and FRANK LAMBE
Drama for Women

G. Bell, 1960. 160pp. $3.50. A book devoted to the problems involved in producing plays with all women casts for the amateur groups.

GREY, ELIZABETH
Behind the Scenes in the Theatre
Roy, 1969. 112pp. $3.95. Written for young people, this is an account of the work of each person in the theatre: on-, or back-stage, or in the front of the house. Miss Grey writes about the whole range of theatre from English Club and provincial repertory to the commercial West End in London. Illustrated with sixteen pages of photographs plus drawings. Index.

GROTOWSKI, JERZY
Towards a Poor Theatre
Simon & Schuster, 1969. 262pp. $6.50. Paper $2.45. This volume contains texts by Grotowski, interviews with this revolutionary Polish theatre director/producer, and other supplementary material presenting his method and training. Peter Brook has contributed a Preface to the volume. Illustrated with drawings and diagrams and forty-four pages of photographs showing productions and exercises.

GRUVER, BERT
The Stage Manager's Handbook
Drama Book Specialists, 1961. 202pp. $4.50. An authoritative handbook for all members of the production staff of the amateur or professional theatre, with chapters on pre-rehearsal period, rehearsals, managing the performance, and touring. Appendices on the manuscript as received from the playwright, the stage manager's working prompt script, the finished prompt script, union rules, and off-Broadway stage managing.

HEFFNER, HURBERT C. and SAMUEL SELDEN, HUNTON D. SELLMAN
Modern Theatre Practice: A Handbook of Play Production
Appleton, 1959. 662pp. $13.25. This revised fourth edition of the 1935 publication is a comprehensive analysis of three essential aspects of production: directing, scenery, and lighting. An introductory section covers the arts of the theatre and drama in general terms. Included is a section on the technique of play analysis. An Appendix by Fairfax Proudfit Walkup is included on costume and make-up. Glossary. Illustrated. Bibliography.

HEWITT, TONY
The School Gilbert and Sullivan
See Page 288

ISAACS, J. – Editor
William Poel's Prompt-Book of "Fratricide Punished"
See Page 187

JOHNSON, ALBERT
Church Plays and How to Stage Them
See Page 580

JOHNSON, ALBERT and BERTHA JOHNSON
Drama for Classroom and Stage
A. S. Barnes, 1969. 569pp. $9.50. The authors have written a textbook and guide for aspiring young actors. They trace the history and development of the theatre with a special chapter on the institutional theatre in the first section of the volume. "Actors on Stage" is the focal point of the book: it is a complete guide to all phases of acting with chapters on the role of the director, musical theatre, television production, make-up, and analysis of acting methods. The third section is concerned with the behind-the-scenes work of production, stage design, scenery, props and costumes, sound, and publicity with a final chapter on evaluation of the total performance. Index.

LITTO, FREDRIC M.
Directory of Useful Addresses
A.E.T.A., 1966. 20pp. $ .75. This is a mimeographed list of names and addresses useful for the academic theatre. It includes theatrical and general organizations, theate collections, research libraries, magazines, publishers, booksellers, authors' agents, and technical theatre organizations and supply houses.

LOUNSBURY, WARREN C.
Theatre Backstage from A to Z
University of Washington, 1967. 172pp. $9.00. Spiral bound $5.95. A revised and expanded version of "Backstage from A to Z" originally published in 1959, this is a manual of all the technical aspects of theatrical production. The two topics covered in greatest detail are lighting and set construction. The most up-to-date equipment available commercially is described, illustrated, and evaluated and an Appendix supplies a directory of sources of supply. Bibliography. Illustrated.

LOVE, MARGARET
Let's Dramatise
See Page 580

LOWENTHAL, JEFF
Stage and Theatre Photography
Chilton, 1965. 128pp. $4.95. A guide book on photographing events in the theatre, night clubs, or concert hall. The difficult techniques of photographing in dimly lit or spot-lighted theatres are examined in detail. Illustrated.

McCALMON, GEORGE and CHRISTIAN MOE
Creating Historical Drama: A Guide for the Community and the Interested Individual
Southern Illinois University, 1965. 393pp. $12.50. Written for the non-specialist, the teacher of university courses in theatre, and the director of the little theatre group, this book shows charts of organization and production structure, drawings of stage arrangements for productions in churches, stadiums and outdoors. Advice for playwrights, four plays, and production information are included. Index.

MacKENZIE, FRANCES
Plays and Pleasure
J. Garnet Miller, 1964. 81pp. $3.25. A handbook on producing a play and organizing a dramatic group. Included is a chapter on the "Pleasure of Presentation" by Donald Fitzjohn, and Mr. Fitzjohn's one-act play, "Exercise Conflict."

MELVILL, HARALD
Stage Management in the Amateur Theatre
Barrie & Rockliff, 1963. 194pp. $6.25. This book is a handbook of stage practices, with chapters on all aspects of the technical end of production. In addition, there is a long discussion of the work of the stage manager during rehearsal and performance. Illustrated. Index.

MELVILL, HARALD
Theatrecraft: The A to Z of Show Business
Barrie & Rockliff, 1954. 228pp. $4.75. A detailed survey of back-stage activity illustrating the work of the management, the producer, stage manager, property head, wardrobe staff, actors, and understudies. Glossary of British Stage Terms. Illustrated.

MILLER, HELEN LOUISE
Pointers on Producing the School Play
Plays, Inc., 1960. 112pp. $3.50. Designed to help teachers and drama directors produce a school play or drama program, with a guide to rehearsals, coaching techniques, various kinds of school entertainments, full-length plays, and musicals. Glossary.

MOORE, MAVOR – Editor
The Awkward Stage
See Page 118

MOTTER, CHARLOTTE KAY
Theatre in High School: Planning, Teaching, Directing
Prentice–Hall, 1970. 187pp. $9.00. Primarily concerned with the problems inherent in high school drama teaching and directing, this volume also covers a philosophy of educational theatre and relationships between the high school program and the community. Extensive practical guides are offered including course planning, play directing, and producing. Illustrated with photographs. Appendices include suggested reading for drama students, publicity summary, plays recommended for high schools, and recommended reference material.

NELMS, HENNING
Play Production
Barnes & Noble, 1958. 301pp. Paper $1.95. Originally published in 1950 and now revised, this is a survey of the entire field of play production, from organization of the company, financing, and choice of script, to the taking of curtain calls. Included are chapters on the technical aspects of production. Illustrated. Bibliography. Index.

NUTTALL, KENNETH
Play Production for Young People
Faber & Faber, 1963. 199pp. $4.50. Published in England, the three parts of this book consider organization of the company, setting the stage, and the art of acting. A list of suitable plays, and some useful addresses for obtaining materials in Great Britain are included. Illustrated. Glossary. Index.

OWENS, JOAN LLEWELYN
Working in the Theatre
Bodley Head, 1964. 187pp. $3.95. The careers investigated include theatre administration, play direction, acting, stage management, design, lighting, electronics, costume, and properties.

PLUMMER, GAIL
The Business of Show Business
Harper & Row, 1961. 238pp. $6.75. A handbook for managers that offers a systematic analysis of the techniques necessary to make amateur and professional theatrics profitable.

RAE, KENNETH and RICHARD SOUTHERN
International Vocabulary of Technical Theatre Terms in Eight Languages
Theatre Arts, 1960. 139pp. $5.25. The technical vocabulary of the theatre in American English, Dutch, English, French, German, Italian, Spanish, and Swedish. Complete Indices and marginal space for notations are included.

REISS, ALVIN H.
The Arts Management Handbook
Law–Arts Publishers, 1970. 655pp. $12.50. A guide for those involved with the administration of cultural institutions. The material on the problems of support of the visual and performing arts has been collected from articles originally published since 1962 in the "Arts Management" periodical. Information included ranges from how to raise funds, how to promote programs, how to attract audiences, to how to organize a board of directors. Illustrative case histories follow theoretical articles.

SETTLE, RONALD
Music in the Theatre
Herbert Jenkins, 1957. 96pp. $1.75. A complete guide to the use of music in the theatre, with chapters on the development of background music, use of the tape recorder, "ghosting," music in children's plays, period plays, and Shakespearean songs. An Index of music suitable for various moods is included.

SIMON, BERNARD – Editor
Simon's Directory of Theatrical Materials, Services, and Information
Package Publicity Service, 1970. 320pp. Paper $5.00. A classified guide, listing where to buy, rent, lease, or find out about everything needed for the production of stage attractions and the management of

theatres. This fourth edition covers the entire United States and Canada. A special feature is the listings of books, booksellers, research sources, organizations, conventions and conferences, training schools, New York theatres and hotels, long-running plays, and a four year record of the New York stage.

SMITH, MILTON
Play Production for Little Theatres, Schools, and Colleges
Appleton, 1948. 482pp. $8.50. A detailed examination of the many individual elements which combine in making a successful production. The emphasis in this book is not only on the technique of production but on the rationale behind each element of production technique. Illustrated.

SPENCER, PETER A.
Let's Do a Musical
Studio Vista, 1968. 128pp. $6.50. Mr. Spencer, a producer for two London, England, amateur stage companies, offers practical suggestions for the production of amateur musicals. He covers in detail a production from its initial conception through to the first performance taking in such aspects as the producer's script and prompt book, music rehearsals, principal and ensemble coaching, dancing, setting and lighting the show, properties and costumes, legal aspects, publicity, and first nights. Illustrated with photographs, line drawings, and diagrams. Bibliography. Index.

STACEY, ROY
Choosing a Play
Herbert Jenkins, 1961. 95pp. $2.00. A complete guide to play selection, with chapters on how to read a play, methods of selection, casting, purposes of the play, type of stage, amateur versus professional play selection, names and addresses of publishers and agents and the kinds of plays they specialize in. A list of other sources of guidance for the amateur producer is provided.

STACEY, ROY – Editor
Theatre Directory: Suppliers and Organizations
Stacey, 1968. 32pp. Paper $ .75. This pamphlet lists English suppliers and organizations of theatre materials: publishers and agents, costumes, scenery and scenic materials, furniture and properties, make-up and wigs, lighting and general equipment, publicity, magazines, drama festivals, and training schools.

SWEETING, ELIZABETH
Theatre Administration
Pitman, 1969. 229pp. $10.50. Published in England, this is a guide to the organization and financing of theatres of all types. Included are theatres in London, provincial and touring theatres, and repertory, university, and civic theatres. The author covers all aspects of theatre administration such as financing, mounting a production, legal responsibilities, and personnel. Illustrated. Appendices show typical forms used in British theatres. Index.

TANNER, FRAN AVERETT
Basic Drama Projects
Clark, 1966. 284pp. Paper $4.75. A text book for drama instructors. Each chapter consists of a complete activity project worked out in detail and aimed at giving students practical experience in drama. The book is divided into sections dealing with "Inner Resources," movement, oral interpretation, characterization, playing the part, make-up, costuming, directing, set and lights, and production. There is also a section dealing with dramatic criticism and several Appendices. Index.

TAUBMAN, JOSEPH – Editor
Financing a Theatrical Production
Federal Legal Publications, 1964. 499pp. $15.00. This book is a record of the Symposium of the Committee on the Law of the Theatre of the Federal Bar Association of N. Y., N. J., and Conn. It is the only book which deals with all the laws governing the financing of stage, motion picture, and television productions. Complete copies of all laws discussed are included, in addition to a supplement which contains the newly enacted Article 26-A of the General Business Law, as proposed by Attorney General Louis Lefkowitz. Copies of all legal forms required in forming a production unit are given.

THEATRICAL VARIETY GUIDE – 1966
Theatrical Variety Publications, 1966. 100pp. Paper $5.00. A directory listing union offices, agents, performers, advertising agencies, broadcasting stations, recording companies, theatres, producers, etc. for the entertainment industry.

THOMPKINS, DOROTHY LEE
Handbook for Theatrical Apprentices: A Practical Guide in All Phases of Theatre
Samuel French, 1962. 181pp. Paper $1.75. A guide to theatre practice for workers in summer stock, students in drama schools, and members of community theatre groups.

TUMBUSCH, TOM
The Theatre Student: Complete Production Guide To Modern Musical Theatre
Richards Rosen Press, 1969. 187pp. $5.97. Written for students and teachers of theatre involved in the production of musicals, this text gives all the information necessary in producing a musical from how to choose the script to the duties of all members of the production staff, to tickets, program, and promotion. Illustrated with photographs. A list of major musicals produced since 1866 is included. Bibliography.

VOLBACH, WALTHER R.
Problems of Opera Production
See Page 288

WHITE, EDWIN C.
Problems of Acting and Play Production
Pitman, 1955. 170pp. $4.50. A discussion of movement, gesture, and voice on the stage, with an analysis of techniques of staging, grouping the actors, rehearsals, and production management. Published in England, the volume includes a list of plays suitable for various age groups.

WHITING, FRANK M.
An Introduction to the Theatre
See Page 22

WILLIAMS, WILLIAM EMRYS – Chairman of the Committee
The Theatre Today in England and Wales
See Page 189

WYKES, ALAN
The Handbook of Amateur Dramatics
Arthur Barker, 1966. 154pp. $5.25. Published in England, this volume covers every aspect of amateur theatrics from the forming of the company to the raising of the curtain. This handbook is designed for all those in the amateur theatre—from the beginner to the experienced. Illustrated.

YOUNG, JOHN WRAY and MARGARET MARY YOUNG
How to Produce the Play: The Complete Production Handbook
Dramatic Publishing, 1960. 96pp. Spiral bound $3.75. Instructions on organizing the production, designing and building sets, building properties and costumes, and designing the lighting for amateur productions. Illustrated.

INDIVIDUAL ASPECTS OF PRODUCTION

PLAYWRITING

ARCHER, WILLIAM
Play-Making: A Manual of Craftsmanship
Dover, 1960. 277pp. Paper $2.50. Instructions on such topics as theme choice, exposition, foreshadowing, tension, obligatory scene, dialogue, characterization, and psychology. An Introduction by John Gassner gives a critical evaluation of Archer's theories and shows how they were modified by later playwrights.

AUBIGNAC, FRANCOIS HEDELIN
The Whole Art of the Stage
Blom, 1968. 320pp. $25.00. Originally published in 1684 and now reissued, this was the first book on playwriting to be published in English. Written "by command of Cardinal Richelieu," who intended to make the author "Overseer of the Theatres of France."

BADER, A. L. – Editor
To the Young Writer
University of Michigan, 1964. 196pp. Paper $1.95. A collection of essays by Saul Bellow, John Ciardi, Malcolm Cowley, John Gassner, Alfred Kazin, Archibald MacLeish, Arthur Miller, Howard Nemerov, and others.

BARRY, JACKSON G.
Dramatic Structure: The Shaping of Experience
See Page 10

BENTLEY, ERIC
The Life of the Drama
See Page 10

BOULTON, MARJORIE
The Anatomy of Drama
Routledge & Kegan Paul, 1960. 212pp. $3.50. An introduction to drama for those who do not have easy access to the live theatre and must study plays chiefly as printed books. The author's emphasis is on Shakespeare but most forms of drama receive some share of attention. A study of the techniques of plot, dialogue, and characterization help the reader to a deeper appreciation of the problems and success of the dramatist. Index.

BURACK, A.S. – Editor
The Writer's Handbook
The Writer, 1970. 774pp. $10.00. A complete guide to all phases of the craft of writing. One hundred authorities have each written a chapter containing practical instruction in the writing of novels and short stories, articles, verse, humor, television scripts, juvenile books, and plays. Information on the business side of writing (manuscript preparation, agents, copyright, etc.) is also given. A list of markets for the sale of manuscripts is provided.

CLARK, BARRETT H.
European Theories of the Drama
Crown, 1965. 628pp. $7.50. A revised edition by Henry Popkin. This fully annotated collection of writing about drama from Aristotle to the present contains commentaries, biographies, and bibliographies on all entries. The new edition includes Ibsen, Strindberg, and Chekhov, and representatives of important modern movements in drama and such new "schools" as realism, problem drama, poetic drama, folk drama, epic theatre, theatre of the absurd. Index.

COLE, TOBY – Editor
Playwrights on Playwriting: The Meaning and Making of Modern Drama from Ibsen to Ionesco
Hill & Wang, 1960. 299pp. $3.95. Paper $1.95. The beliefs, theories and practices of playwrights in their own words. The playwrights include Ibsen, Strindberg, Chekhov, Maeterlink, Yeats, Galsworthy, Shaw, Synge, Cocteau, Pirandello, Lorca, Giraudoux,

O'Neill, Brecht, Wilder, Sartre, Eliot, Williams, Fry, Duerennmatt, O'Casey, Ionesco, Miller, and Osborne.

EGRI, LAJOS
The Art of Creative Writing
Citadel, 1965. 224pp. $2.50. Paper $1.95. The author presents the fundamentals of good writing. He offers a step-by-step guide for the development of fiction, plays, television and radio scripts.

EGRI, LAJOS
The Art of Dramatic Writing
Simon & Schuster, 1960. 305pp. Paper $1.95. A revised and enlarged edition of the author's "How to Write a Play," originally published in 1942. This study emphasizes character as the center of a play. Included are analyses of five plays, hints on marketing manuscripts, and lists of plays that have been financial successes and those sold to the films.

ENGLE, PAUL – Editor
On Creative Writing
Dutton, 1966. 244pp. Paper $1.35. A collection of articles by specialists in the creative writing disciplines. Lionel Abel, playwright and teacher, contributes the essay, "On Writing A Play."

FOLLETT, WILSON
Modern American Usage: A Guide
Hill & Wang, 1966. 436pp. $7.50. This is a guide to educated usage and good taste in language. Edited and completed, after Mr. Follett's death, by Jacques Barzun, it is intended to be read with pleasure and used by those who are interested in good English.

FOSTER, HARRIS
The Basic Patterns of Plot
University of Oklahoma, 1959. 119pp. $3.50. Although mainly a basic book on the patterns and principles of plotting in fiction, the author provides an analysis of the physiology and the anatomy of story, directions concerning the development of viewpoint, character and dimensions, and the techniques of revision and selling. The book may be helpful to students of playwriting.

FREYTAG, GUSTAV
Technique of the Drama
Blom, 1968. 395pp. $12.50. Originally published in 1904, as translated by Elias J. MacEwan, and now reissued, this is an exposition of dramatic composition and art. Freytag's method of diagramming the structure of complex plays is one of the most useful aids to understanding the playwrights' craft. His experience as the foremost nineteenth century German exponent of the "well-made" play and his knowledge of classic drama made this book an important contribution to the technical literature of the drama. Index.

GREBANIER, BERNARD
Playwriting
Apollo, 1965. 386pp. Paper $1.95. A reprint of the 1961 edition, this is a complete course in playwriting, with special emphasis on form and structure. A number of plays, ranging from "Hamlet" to "The Zoo Story," are examined in detail. A list of suggested exercises is included.

GREENWOOD, ORMEROD
The Playwright: A Study of Form, Method and Tradition in the Theatre
Pitman, 1950. 214pp. $4.00. Published in England, this volume examines plays from "The Oresteia" to "The Family Reunion" as the author considers such topics as the playwright's choices and limitations, the literary and popular theatre, the structure of a play, writing comic plays, cutting and revision techniques, and the mastery of stagecraft. Plays with similar themes, from different periods, are studied.

HEATH, ERIC
Story Plotting Simplified
The Writer, 1954. 243pp. $3.95. An interpretation, in terms of contemporary literary standards, of George Polti's "The Thirty-Six Dramatic Situations." A chapter is devoted to each "situation" and each is analyzed in terms of modern usage.

HULL, RAYMOND
Profitable Playwriting
Funk & Wagnalls, 1968. 257pp. $5.95. This handbook takes the apprentice playwright step-by-step through all the stages of conceiving the plot, establishing character, and blocking the action within the theatre of his own mind. The author demonstrates by actual examples the technique of devising dialogue, situation, and dramatic climaxes. Appendix.

KAZIN, ALFRED – Editor
Writers at Work: The Paris Review Interviews – Third Series
Viking, 1967. 368pp. $7.95. In this third volume of interviews with writers, the authors discuss their natural concern with the craft of writing and the peculiar demands that our contemporary world imposes on the imaginative writer. Among the fourteen authors interviewed are: Edward Albee, Saul Bellow, Jean Cocteau, Lillian Hellman, Norman Mailer, Arthur Miller, and Harold Pinter.

KERR, WALTER
How Not to Write A Play
The Writer, 1955. 244pp. $5.95. The drama critic discusses weaknesses of theme, plot, language, and characterization as illustrated by recent Broadway entries.

KLINE, PETER
The Theatre Student: Playwriting
Richards Rosen, 1970. 186pp. $6.96. A guide to playwriting for students. Among the subjects covered are the elements of drama, building a plot, creating

characters, designing dialogue, revisions, working with a play in production. Appendices include scenes from student-written plays. Bibliography.

LAWSON, JOHN HOWARD
Theory and Technique of Playwriting
Hill & Wang, 1960. 313pp. Paper $1.95. A history of dramatic technique, with an analysis of representative plays, that stresses the relation between the play and the audience. This reprint of the 1936 edition contains a long introduction on the theatre since World War II.

LEAVITT, HART DAY
An Eye for People: A Writer's Guide to Character
Bantam, 1970. 224pp. Paper $ .95. In text and more than 150 illustrative photographs the author attempts to teach the art of creative observation and character study to student writers. The book may also be of some value to students of acting.

MacGOWAN, KENNETH
A Primer of Playwriting
Random House, 1951. 210pp. $4.50. A discussion of the essential skills of the playwright and an analysis of the elements by which dramatic form is distinguished from the narrative forms. Glossary of Terms. Appendix.

MAROWITZ, CHARLES and SIMON TRUSSLER – Editors
Theatre at Work
See Page 188

MATTHEWS, BRANDER – Editor
Papers on Playmaking
Hill & Wang, 1957. 312pp. Paper $1.35. A collection of essays on playwriting by Pinero, Dumas fils, de Vega, Labiche, Bronson Howard, Goethe, Sardou, W. S. Gilbert, Sarcey, Coquelin, Legouve, and Augier. Preface by Henry W. Wells and notes on the essayists by Mr. Matthews are included.

MILLER, J. WILLIAM
Modern Playwrights at Work: Volume I
Samuel French, 1968. 576pp. $10.00. This study centers on eight playwrights: Ibsen, Strindberg, Chekhov, Shaw, Galsworthy, Pirandello, O'Neill and Williams. The playwrights' letters, speeches, notebooks, work, and the testimony of representative critics and biographers, as well as friends, relatives, and employees, were consulted. The author has attempted to compile the most authoritative information on modern playwriting in one volume. The Appendix includes many suggestions for further study as well as lists of plays. Illustrated with portraits of the playwrights studied. Index.

NEAL, HARRY EDWARD
Nonfiction From Idea to Published Book
Funk & Wagnalls, 1964. 236pp. $3.95. Paper $1.50. Among the items covered in this book are how to get a salable idea, how to do research, conducting an interview to your advantage, obtaining free illustrations and photographs, agents and their ways, copyright regulations, and contracts. Index.

NICHOLSON, MARGARET
A Manual of Copyright Practice
Oxford, 1970. 273pp. $7.50. Originally published in 1945 and reissued in 1956, this manual is now reprinted with a new Preface detailing the changes in copyright practice since the 1956 edition. Miss Nicholson covers all aspects of copyright practice and includes a section of sample copyright forms, the U. S. copyright law, and a Selected Bibliography. Index.

NIGGLI, JOSEFINA
New Pointers on Playwriting
The Writer, 1967. 166pp. $5.00. Miss Niggli has written a practical guide to the techniques of playwriting. Carefully selected examples from classical and modern plays are used to illustrate how a play "works" on stage and to analyze the behind-the-scene dramatic devices and techniques of various dramatists. The three fundamental types of plays are discussed and the structure and foundation of scene are explained along with chapters on all the problems playwrights must solve.

PILPEL, HARRIET and THEODORA ZAVIN
Rights and Writers: A Handbook of Literary and Entertainment Law
Dutton, 1960. 384pp. $7.50. An up-to-date treatment of libel, privacy rights, copyright law and regulations, the protection of ideas, unfair competition, contracts, taxes, and censorship in the U. S. today. Included is a discussion of the Supreme Court's decision in the Roth case, the Court's last word on the law of obscenity.

PLIMPTON, GEORGE – Editor
Writers at Work: The Paris Review Interviews – Third Series
Viking, 1968. 368pp. Paper $1.95. A collection of interviews with writers from the Paris Review. Among the authors interviewed are: Louis-Ferdinand Celine, Norman Mailer, Harold Pinter, Jean Cocteau, Arthur Miller, Edward Albee, and Lillian Hellman.

POLTI, GEORGES
The Thirty-Six Dramatic Situations
The Writer, 1954. 181pp. $4.00. An outline of the basic plots in dramatic literature. The author traces them to their first appearance in print, and illustrates their use in ancient drama and contemporary drama. A reprint of the 1916 edition.

ROWE, KENNETH THORPE
A Theatre in Your Head: Analyzing the Play and Visualizing Its Production

Funk & Wagnalls, 1960. 438pp. $6.95. Paper $2.95. A complete dramaturgy for the reading of plays, from the visualization of an ideal production to the detailed critical evaluation of dramatic structure. Scenes from John Gielgud's prompt book for "The Lady's Not for Burning" and excerpts from Elia Kazan's notebooks for "Death of a Salesman" are included. For study of dramatic construction, the author has included the complete text of the full length play "Our Lan'" by Theodore Ward.

ROWE, KENNETH THORPE
Write That Play
Funk & Wagnalls, 1968. 418pp. Paper $2.95. Originally published in 1939 and now reissued, this is an introduction to playwriting. The author has organized his work to lead the writer from the simpler to the more advanced technical problems. He gives detailed examinations and parallel analyses of "A Night at the Inn," "Riders to the Sea," and "A Doll's House."

SANDERS, THOMAS E.
The Discovery of Drama
Scott, Foresman, 1968. 632pp. Paper $5.75. Beginning with an analysis of dramatic structure, this book attempts to help the student explore the nature of dramatic reality. Nine plays are studied with critical analyses and suggested assignments for the student reader. In the final chapter, guidelines for writing a one-act play are given as well as aids for writing about the play. Index.

STRUNK, WILLIAM, JR. and E. B. WHITE
The Elements of Style
Macmillan, 1959. 71pp. Paper $ .95. Professor Strunk's original 1935 essay has been expanded and rewritten by E. B. White. It deals with usage and style in the writing of good English.

WAGER, WALTER – Editor
The Playwrights Speak
Dial Press, 1967. 290pp. $6.00. Paper – Dell, 1968. 290pp. $2.25. In these eleven interviews with playwrights who have shaped today's theatre, the dramatists disclose the fears, thoughts, questions, and theories which assist them, plague them, and motivate them to write. Harold Clurman's Introduction is a summation of each playwright's work, providing the necessary context in which the interviews may be fully understood and interpreted. The editor has provided brief biographies of each dramatist, among whom are included: Edward Albee, John Arden, Eugene Ionesco, Friedrich Durrenmmatt, Arthur Miller, John Osborne, Harold Pinter, Peter Weiss, Arnold Wesker, and Tennessee Williams.

WINCOR, RICHARD
Literary Property
Crown, 1967. 154pp. $5.00. This is a textbook and guide to the business practices of the communications industry, including television, the legitmate theatre, motion pictures, and book publishing. The author is a lawyer and he details what to expect when you enter negotiations for a piece of property, either as an owner or a user. An Appendix provides reproductions of actual contract forms. Glossary of Industry Terms. Index.

YOUNG, JAMES N.
101 Plots Used and Abused
The Writer, 1961. 71pp. $2.95. Mr. Young summarizes 101 plots which constantly turn up on editors' desks. This summary of what plots not to use will help beginning writers. The author's positive advice and twenty-eight requisites for successful authorship supplement the main body of the book.

DIRECTING

BRAUN, EDWARD
Meyerhold on Theatre
Hill & Wang, 1969. 336pp. $8.50. This is a collection of Vsevolod Meyerhold's writings. The Soviet director is considered a forerunner of such directors as Brecht and Piscator. These writings cover his entire career as a director from 1902 to 1939. Mr. Braun has translated and edited the writings and provides critical commentary which relates Meyerhold to his period and provides descriptions of all his major productions. Included are fifty photographs of Meyerhold's designs and productions. Select Bibliography. Index.

BROOK, PETER
The Empty Space
Atheneum, 1968. 141pp. $5.00. Paper – Avon, 1969. 128pp. $1.65. The English director explains and discusses the theories and techniques by which he made triumphs of such plays as "King Lear," "The Visit," and "Marat/Sade" and which helped to guide the Royal Shakespeare Company into international acclaim as an experimental theatre. He categorizes theatre into four parts and analyzes what makes each one different.

BROWN, BEN W.
Upstage—Downstage: Directing the Play
Walter Baker, 1946. 94pp. Paper $1.75. A guide for the director of the small amateur or college drama group.

BROWN, GILMOR and ALICE GARWOOD
General Principles of Play Direction
Samuel French, 1936. 190pp. $2.75. Mr. Brown, director of the Pasadena Community Playhouse, describes in detail his method of making a script come alive on the stage. Illustrated.

CANFIELD, CURTIS
The Craft of Play Directing
Holt, Rinehart, 1963. 349pp. $11.50. A study in two

parts: Part One, "The Director's Material," discusses the qualifications the director must possess and develop in order to analyze a script. The author illustrates methods of interpreting dramatic meaning from an analysis of the play's subject, theme, characterization, and atmosphere. Part Two, "The Director's Medium," deals with the craft involved in translating the play into theatre. Studies of blocking, rehearsal, stage design, etc., are given. Illustrated.

CARTMELL, VAN H.
Amateur Theatre
Van Nostrand, 1961. 220pp. $3.95. A handbook for the beginning director, covering play selection, casting, and rehearsals. Included is the working script of a one-act play.

COLE, TOBY and HELEN KRICH CHINOY
Directors on Directing
Bobbs–Merrill, 1963. 464pp. Paper $4.25. Originally titled, "Directing the Play," this revised edition includes a new chapter on staging Shakespeare, with statements by Laurence Olivier, Tyrone Guthrie, Margaret Webster, and others. Also available for the first time in English is Stanislavsky's production plan for a scene from Gorky's "The Lower Depths." Brecht's notes for the "Courage-Modell" are given. Other sections of the book provide a history of the rise of the modern director and his place in the modern theatre. There is a section of twenty essays on the theory and practice of modern directors, and a section of excerpts from prompt-books and notes to illustrate the directors' work. Illustrated.

DAWLEY, HERBERT M.
Directing is Fun: A Blue-Print of Play Production
Samuel French, 1952. 32pp. Paper $ .60. A brief summary of the various aspects of production that come under the director's control, with suggestions for dealing with each.

DEAN, ALEXANDER
The Fundamentals of Play Directing
Holt, Rinehart, 1965. 368pp. $12.50. A revision of the book first published in 1944. Professor Lawrence Carra applies Dean's basic principles to the contemporary stage, includes a chapter on central staging, and describes latest technical developments. There are twenty-one new production photographs and thirty-eight drawings illustrating the principles of stage composition. Index.

DIETRICH, JOHN E.
Play Direction
Prentice–Hall, 1953. 484pp. $10.50. This study applies psychological and aesthetic principles to the technique of stage direction. Illustrated. Glossary of Directorial Terms.

FEATHERMAN, KAREN
The Director's Dilemma
Walter Baker, 1966. 39pp. Paper $1.35. A primer for directors of amateur theatre groups.

FERNALD, JOHN
Sense of Direction: The Director and His Actors
Stein & Day, 1968. 189pp. $6.95. Paper $1.95. Mr. Fernald describes the director's relation to the actors, designers, lighting experts, and architects. He stresses the need for a director to dominate the actors yet allow them to express themselves fully. He gives his own insights into directing, a schedule of the procedures to follow before production, during rehearsal, and during the run of a show. Illustrated with diagrams and a photo of the author.

GIELGUD, JOHN
Stage Directions
Random House, 1963. 146pp. $5.95. Paper—Putnam, 1966. 146pp. $1.45. Sir John discusses the arts of acting and directing, beginning with a general study of the means the actor uses to master the technical art of presenting character, mood, and emotion. The problems involved in directing the classics are examined, with illustrations from famous productions. Among specific plays treated are "Richard II," "Hamlet," "The Importance of Being Earnest," the plays of Chekhov, and Granville-Barker's "King Lear." Illustrated with photographs. Index.

GREGORY, W. A.
The Director: A Guide to Modern Theatre Practice
Funk & Wagnalls, 1968. 369pp. $6.95. The author sets out the considerations that present themselves to the working director in his roles as artist, craftsman, and pilot of the theatrical enterprise. Analyzing specific cases that arise in theatrical practice, he gives suggestions for inducing actors to function at their highest level as artists. The technical questions of stagecraft and the larger questions of artistic interpretation are both covered. Bibliography. Index.

GROTOWSKI, JERZY
Towards a Poor Theatre
Simon & Schuster, 1969. 262pp. $6.50. Paper $2.45. This volume contains texts by Grotowski, interviews with the revolutionary Polish theatre director/producer, and other supplementary material presenting his method and training. Peter Brook has contributed a preface to the volume. Illustrated with drawings and diagrams and forty-four pages of photographs showing productions and exercises.

HOPKINS, ARTHUR
Reference Point
Samuel French, 1948. 135pp. $2.50. Based on a series of papers on the theatre read by the author at the 1947 Summer Theatre Seminar sponsored by Fordham University, this book includes essays on community theatre, directing classics, the director and the actor, and the director and modern plays.

JOHNSON, ALBERT and BERTHA JOHNSON
Directing Methods
A. S. Barnes, 1970. 443pp. $9.50. The authors cover the evolution of the director, the directing theories of the Meininger, Antoine, Otto Brahm, Stanislavski, Meyerhold, Reinhardt and many others, including many contemporary directors. A treatment of dramatic analysis, theatrical styles, the dynamics of movement, theatre technology, and management and promotion are also provided. Appendices include a list of professional schools and institutions offering graduate degrees in theatre arts and a directory of theatre companies in the United States, England, and Canada. Bibliography. Index.

KOZELKA, PAUL
The Theater Student: Directing
Richards Rosen, 1968. 184pp. $5.97. This book for students and teachers of the theatre presents detailed information on the subject of directing. Actual examples of the handling of specific material, techniques, and methods of working are provided. Among the subjects covered are: choosing a play, inventory of sources and resources, preparing schedules, analyzing the play, preparing for the first rehearsal, tryouts, rehearsals, and dress rehearsals, and performances. A one act play by Betty Smith and Chase Webb, "Lawyer Lincoln," is included with notes on producing and words and music for two songs. An Appendix also contains lists of plays, musicals, and plays for a child audience, and a Bibliography of other books on theatre. Illustrated with photographs.

LATHAM, JEAN LEE
Do's and Don'ts of Drama: 555 Pointers for Beginning Actors and Directors
Dramatic Publishing, 1935. 172pp. Paper $1.50. A collection of more than 500 practical suggestions on a variety of problems. Illustrated with charts, the volume covers its field from collecting stage properties to planning stage movements.

McMULLAN, FRANK
The Directorial Image: The Play and the Director
Shoe String Press, 1962. 249pp. Paper $5.50. A study of the director's technique in classic and modern drama. The author examines the problem of the director's creative latitude and his obligation to serve the play and the playwright's intention faithfully.

McMULLAN, FRANK
The Director's Handbook: An Outline for the Teacher and Student of Play Interpretation and Direction
Shoe String Press, 1964. 181pp. Paper $5.00. This book presents, in outline form, the main points to be considered in the study of who the director is, his general position and function in the theatre, his psychological work with the actors, pre-rehearsal procedures and problems, pictorial dramatizations, pantomime, movement, rhythm, and creative interpretation. Bibliography.

MILLER, LEON C.
How to Direct the High School Play
Dramatic Publishing, 1968. 70pp. Spiral bound $3.50. The author's aims are to help those with or without educational training who wish to stage and direct plays. The suggestions given are directed primarily to high school teachers. The topics include selecting and casting the play, rehearsal, technical organization, and the performance itself. Illustrated with charts and diagrams. A list of references and suggested further reading is included.

ROOSE–EVANS, JAMES
Directing a Play
Theatre Arts, 1968. 96pp. $6.95. Mr. Roose-Evans sets down his theories on how to mount a play successfully. Each detail from the first reading to the opening night and after is discussed. The author describes the training which a director should have and the ways to develop the necessary understanding of literature, dramatic values, human nature, reality, and life. The points are illustrated with examples from his own productions. Photographs show how the director achieved the effect he was seeking.

SHARP, WILLIAM L.
Language in Drama: Meanings for the Director and the Actor
Chandler, 1970. 162pp. $7.50. Paper $3.50. The author's purpose is to examine the way in which language helps actors and directors to discover how a play moves on stage. Professor Sharp examines a number of plays, from Greek tragedy to Harold Pinter, with the purpose of suggesting the kinds of information that the playwrights' words can give to the prospective director or actor. Bibliographical Essay. Index.

SIEVERS, W. DAVID
Directing for the Theatre
Wm. C. Brown, 1965. 390pp. $7.50. A text for a basic college level course in play directing with chapters on the values and purpose of educational theatre, on play selection, interpretive movement, tempo and climax, production procedures, rehearsing, and backstage techniques. Included are lists of plays for high schools, lists of recordings of dialects, and lists of scenes and exercises. Illustrated. Bibliography. Index.

SIMONOV, RUBEN
Stanislavsky's Protege: Eugene Vakhtangov
Drama Book Specialists, 1969. 243pp. $6.95. Translated and adapted by Miriam Goldina, this is a book about the work of the great Russian director who contributed so much to the growth of the Russian theatre and the art of theatre in general. There is a detailed account of the rehearsals of Chekhov's "A Wedding," comparison of Vakhtangov and Stanislavsky's treatment of Chekhov, and the Soviet theatre from 1919 to the present. Also dealt with are the production

of "The Miracle of St. Anthony," the attempts of Maeterlink, Meyerhold and Vakhtangov to work together, and Meyerhold's search for new theatre forms. Chronology.

SPOLIN, VIOLA
Improvisation for the Theatre: A Handbook of Teaching and Directing Techniques
Northwestern University, 1963. 399pp. $8.50. This study is divided into three parts: the first is concerned with the theory and foundations for teaching and directing theatre, with a discussion of the seven aspects of spontaneity the director must cultivate, and pointers on the physical set-up of the workshop. Part Two gives an outline of over 200 exercises. Part Three contains discussions of children in the theatre and on techniques for directing the formal play for community workshops.

TAIROV, ALEXANDER
Notes of a Director
University of Miami, 1969. 153pp. $6.50. This is the record of the first six years of the Moscow Kamerny Theatre and an exposition of the theories which stimulated its foundation and animated its work. Originally published in Moscow in 1921, this is its first publication in English. Tairov was one of the great theatrical innovators of the twentieth century and his book is a major document in the history of a theatre. It is also of practical pertinence as a significant treatment of the current problem of freeing the theatre from the demands of realism. Illustrated. Notes. Index.

STAGE AND THEATRE DESIGN

Reference Works and General Histories

APPIA, ADOLPHE
Music and the Art of the Theatre
University of Miami, 1962. 221pp. $6.50. Edited by Barnard Hewitt, this is the first authoritative translation of the work of the artist whose theories elucidated the basic aesthetic principles of modern scenic design, analyzed the fundamental technical problems of the art, and formed a charter of freedom for designers. Illustrated with examples of Appia's work.

ARNHEIM, RUDOLF
Visual Thinking
University of California, 1969. 345pp. $11.50. Professor Arnheim contends that all thinking is basically perceptual in nature. He shows that the fundamental processes of vision involve mechanisms typical of reasoning and he describes problem solving in the arts as well as imagery in the thought-models of science. The volume is of interest to the educator for the function of art in education and for visual training in all fields of learning. Students of scenic design will find it interesting. Illustrated. Bibliography. Index.

ARNOTT, PETER
Greek Scenic Conventions of the Fifth Century B.C.
See Page 32

BABLET, DENIS
Le Decor de Theatre
Editions du Centre National de la Recherche Scientifique, 1965. 443pp. $22.00. Published in France, this is a study of stage settings and scenery in the French theatre from 1870 to 1914. 179 illustrations are included. Note that the text is in the French language. Index.

BAGNARA, FRANCESCO and GIUSEPPE BERTOJA, PIETRO BERTOJA
Scenografi Veneziani dell'Ottocento
Speedimpex, 1962. Unpaged. $3.00. A study of Venetian stage design in the nineteenth century. 139 illustrations are included. The text is in the Italian language.

BASOLI, ANTONIO
Collezione Di Varie Scene Teatrali
Blom, 1969. Unpaged. $47.50. Originally published in 1821 and now reissued, this is a collection of 100 plates created in the eighteenth and nineteenth centuries by the Italian stage designer. Basoli represents the concluding phase of the neo-classicism style of stage design and the beginning of the new approach of romanticism.

BERVE, HELMUT and GOTTFRIED GRUBEN
Greek Temples, Theatres and Shrines
See Page 32

BJURSTROM, PER
Giacomo Torelli and Baroque Stage Design
Almqvist & Wiksell, 1962. 271pp. $13.75. Published in Sweden, this is a study of Torelli as a stage designer, with a catalogue of his works, reproductions of his designs, contemporary accounts of his settings, and a history of seventeenth century stage designs and conditions.

BURNACINI, LUDOVICO
Il Fuoco Eterno – Das Vestalische Ewige Feur
Blom, 1970. 158pp. $27.50. First published in Vienna in 1674 and now reissued, this is a facsimile reproduction of the libretto for the festive opera with Burnacini's engraved plates for the settings. The thirteen plates show the seventeenth century designer's settings, the painted act drop, the ornamented proscenium arch of the Hoftheater, many scenes from the festival drama, and the stage machinery. The Introduction is in English but the libretto of the opera is in the German language.

CAMPBELL, LILLY B.
Scenes and Machines on the English Stage During the Renaissance: A Classical Revival
Barnes & Noble, 1960. 302pp. $10.00. A reprint of

the study first published in 1923, this volume begins with an analysis of the classical revival in stage decoration in Italy, considering the influence of Vitruvius and Serlio. Stage decoration in England during the sixteenth and seventeenth centuries is also studied. Illustrated with diagrams and engravings.

CHENEY, SHELDON
Stage Decoration
Blom, 1966. 138pp. & plates. $12.50. Originally published in 1928, this study tries to put into proper perspective the revolution in stage design which took place in the twentieth century. Mr. Cheney examines stage decor and production techniques from the ancient Greeks to the present day. A series of 156 illustrations, fully annotated, describes each style of design and each type of play produced.

COOPER, DOUGLAS
Picasso Theatre
Abrams, 1968. 360pp. $25.00. The author has tried to give an accurate account not only of the circumstances in which Picasso was led to design decors for various theatrical productions, but also of when and where they were executed and how they looked on stage. Over 400 plates plus eighty-four illustrations in the text are included. Also provided are a list of theatrical productions on which Picasso has collaborated, some unpublished letters and documents, a list of plates, a list of illustrations, and a Bibliography.

COREY, IRENE
The Mask of Reality: An Approach to Design for Theatre
Anchorage, 1968. 124pp. $20.00. The author uses her sixteen years of experience in educational theatre to form a plan of action for theatrical design. Her book is for the working theatre artist who wishes to enhance and expand his own knowledge and capabilities for imaginative productions, particularly in the field of costume design and make-up. Illustrated with 174 color and black-and-white photographs. Index.

CRAIG, EDWARD
Gordon Craig
Knopf, 1968. 398pp. $10.00. Written by his son, this is the first full-scale biography of one of the major innovators in modern stagecraft. Illustrated with line drawings and photographs. General Bibliography. Index.

CRAIG, EDWARD GORDON
On the Art of the Theatre
Theatre Arts, 1958. 298pp. $6.50. A reprint of the book of essays first published in 1911 in which the author discusses the function of the director-scenic designer in the theatre. Among the essays are "The Actor and the Uber-Marionette," "The Theatre in Russia, Germany, and England," "The Ghosts in the Tragedies of Shakespeare," "Realism and the Actor," "Open Air Theatres," "Symbolism." Seven illustrations of designs for scenes and costumes are included.

CRAIG, EDWARD GORDON
Scene
Blom, 1968. 27pp. & 19 plates. $12.50. Originally published in 1923, this is a reissue of Craig's essay on scene design illustrated with nineteen plates. John Masefield has contributed a Foreword and an introductory poem.

CRAIG, EDWARD GORDON
Towards a New Theatre
Blom, 1969. 90pp. $27.50. Originally published in 1913 and reissued in a facsimile edition, this volume includes forty designs for stage scenes with critical notes by Craig.

CROFT–MURRAY, E.
John Devoto: A Baroque Scene Painter
Society for Theatre Research, 1963. 16pp. Paper $3.00. A short study devoted to the work of the eighteenth century artist of stage scenery. Included are twelve illustrations of the work.

DIDEROT, DENIS and JEAN LE ROND D'ALEMBERT – Editors
Theatre Architecture and Stage Machines
Blom, 1969. 89pp. $37.50. This edition of eighty-nine plates illustrating theatre architecture and stage machines consists of engravings from "Encyclopedie, ou Dictionnaire raisonne des sciences, des arts, et des metiers" first published in 1762–1772. The text is reproduced in the original French language.

DINE, JIM
Jim Dine Designs for "A Midsummer Night's Dream"
Museum of Modern Art, 1968. 31pp. Paper $1.50. Reproductions in color and black-and-white of painter Jim Dine's avant-garde costume designs for a San Francisco Actor's Workshop production of Shakespeare's comedy. Introduction is an essay by Virginia Allen on the designs.

FERRERO, M. VIALE
Filippo Juvarra: Scenografo e Architetto Teatrale
Blom, 1970. 391pp. $37.50. A study of the eighteenth century Italian stage designer and architect with a collection of his designs in color and black-and-white. 160 illustrations are included plus thirty tipped-in color plates, and 300 illustrations in the text. Note that the text of the volume is in the Italian language.

FINIGUERRA, MASO and SIDNEY COLVIN
A Florentine Picture-Chronicle
See Page 399

FUERST, WALTER RENE and SAMUEL J. HUME
Twentieth Century Stage Decoration

Dover, 1967. Two volume set: 191pp. & plates. Paper $6.00. First published in 1929, this is an unabridged, corrected, two volume edition of the study of the theory and practice of stage setting. The authors cover both Europe and America from the end of the nineteenth century to the late 1920's. Volume One includes the text and Volume Two has 393 photographs and drawings ranging from Stanislavsky's work to Appia's settings for "Tristan und Isolde."

GALLIARI, GASPARE
Numbero XXIV Invenzioni Teatrali
Blom, 1970. 10pp. & plates. $27.50. This volume, originally published in Italy in 1803, includes twenty-four plates dating from 1000 which show the essential scenic concepts developed by the Italian sconographer. Introduction by Denise Addis.

GOTCH, J. ALFRED
Inigo Jones
Blom, 1968. 271pp. $12.50. Originally published in 1928 and now reissued, this is a biography of the seventeenth century English architect, artist, and scenic designer. The volume includes thirty-one plates showing costume designs, theatre designs, sketches of buildings, and photographs of completed buildings. Chronology. Index.

GRUBE, MAX
The Story of the Meininger
University of Miami, 1963. 117pp. $6.50. Edited by Wendell Cole, this is the first English translation, by Ann Marie Koller, of the 1926 study of George II, Duke of Saxe-Meiningen. The Meininger productions made European directors aware of the technique of the Regisseur—the director who unifies the production through his control of the actor's interpretation and movements, and the details of setting, lighting, costuming, and make-up. The volume is illustrated with sixteen plates.

HAINAUX, RENE and YVES-BONNAT – Editors
Stage Design Throughout the World Since 1935
Theatre Arts, 1965. 224pp. $29.95. Out of print for a number of years, and now reissued in its original format, this is a pictorial survey of recent international experiments in scenic design (1935–1950) in opera, ballet, and drama. The 176 illustrations, thirty-five in full color, are fully documented and indexed separately under designers, or by the work of composers, authors, or choreographers. Introduction by Kenneth Rae.

HAINAUX, RENE – Editor
Stage Design Throughout the World Since 1950
Theatre Arts, 1964. 276pp. $32.50. The second book on stage design published for the International Theatre Institute under the auspices of UNESCO. There are 190 pages of black-and-white illustrations, 16 pages in full color, showing stage designs from countries all over the world. In the 56 pages of text special attention is given to new materials and new techniques, with selections from comments by noted designers on their use of new materials. With a Who's Who of designers.

HEWITT, BARNARD
The Renaissance Stage: Documents of Serlio, Sabbattini, and Furttenbach
University of Miami, 1958. 256pp. $6.50. Translations by Allardyce Nicoll, John H. McDowell, and George R. Kernodle of the three major sources of information about stage scenery and scenic practice in the Italian Renaissance theatre. Illustrated with diagrams and engravings from the original editions of the essays.

JACQUOT, JEAN and ANDRE VEINSTEIN
La Mise en Scene des Oeuvres du Passe
Editions du Centre National de la Recherche Scientifique, 1957. 307pp. $6.00. A collection of essays on scene design. Among the essays are one on scene design for Shakespearean productions, settings for productions of "Peer Gynt," and the Stanislavsky production of "Marriage of Figaro." Index. The essays are in the French language.

JEUDWINE, WYNNE
Stage Designs
Country Life Books, 1968. 64pp. Paper $2.50. Published in England, this volume includes an essay and illustrations of the stage designs of the "Theatre of Illusion" from the sixteenth to the nineteenth centuries. The volume is illustrated with contemporary drawings and engravings. Reading List.

JONES, ROBERT EDMOND
The Dramatic Imagination: Reflections and Speculations on the Art of the Theatre
Theatre Arts, 1941. 157pp. $3.95. A collection of essays by the designer on the theory and practice of the art. The essays are: "A New Kind of Drama," "Art in the Theatre," "The Theatre as It Was and as It Is," "To a Young Designer," "Some Thoughts on Stage Costume," "Light and Shadow in Theatre," "Toward a New Stage," "Behind the Scenes."

JONES, ROBERT EDMUND
Drawings for the Theatre
Theatre Arts, 1970. 24pp. & plates. $13.50. Originally published in 1925 and now reissued in a second edition with a biographical introduction by Donald Oenslager. The thirty-five plates show Jones' designs for productions from 1916 to 1946.

KOMISARJEVSKY, THEODORE and LEE SIMONSON
Settings and Costumes of the Modern Stage
Blom, 1966. 132pp. $15.00. First published in 1933 and now reissued, this book covers the period between 1925 and 1933 when new styles, theories and methods were revolutionizing the theatre. There are 197 illustrations—complete with full production data and notes.

LAMBOURNE, LIONEL
Diaghilev
See Page 397

LARSON, ORVILLE K.—Editor
Scene Design for Stage and Screen
Michigan State University, 1961. 334pp. $6.00. A collection of essays on the aesthetics and methodology of scene design for theatre, opera, musical comedy, ballet, motion pictures, television, and arena theatre. Among the contributors are Robert Edmond Jones, Lee Simonson, Norris Houghton, Howard Bay, and Oliver Smith.

MacGOWAN, KENNETH and ROBERT EDMOND JONES
Continental Stagecraft
Blom, 1964. 223pp. $12.50. Originally published in 1922, this is a description of the production methods and theories of the founders of modern theatre: Appia, Reinhardt, Craig, Stanislavsky, Jessner, and Copeau. Details on technique, styles of acting, architecture, and stage design are included. Forty full page plates reproduce the designs of Robert Edmond Jones.

MANCINI, FRANCO
Scenografia Napoletana Dell'Eta Barocca
Speedimpex, 1964. 259pp. $12.00. Published in Italy, this is a historical survey of the styles and tastes in theatre buildings and stage designs from the seventeenth through the nineteenth centuries in Naples, Italy. Full descriptive notes are supplied for all the illustrations which reproduce paintings, drawings, and engravings of the period. The text is in the Italian language.

MIELZINER, JO
Designing for the Theatre: A Memoir and a Portfolio
Atheneum, 1965. 241pp. $5.95. Mr. Mielziner recounts the history of his career with particular attention given to the creation and special problems involved in producing "Death of a Salesman." A portfolio of designs is accompanied by explanatory texts which focus on the particular nature of each production and the challenge it presented. Ninety-six pages of drawings—sixteen of which are in color. Index.

MOSCHINI, VITTORIO
Canaletto
Dover, 1969. 72pp. Paper $1.75. A collection of seventy-two drawings by the Venetian eighteenth century master who was trained as a painter of theatrical scenery and who worked on opera sets until 1720. Each plate is fully documented.

MOUSSINAC, LEON
The New Movement in the Theatre
Blom, 1967. 152pp. $35.00. Originally published in 1932 and now reissued with the original Foreword by Gordon Craig, this is a survey of developments in European and American stage design in the 1920's and 1930's. Included are 128 pages of plates from eleven countries. Bibliography. Index to Text and Plates.

MYERSCOUGH-WALKER, R.
Stage and Film Decor
Pitman, 1948. 192pp. & plates. $8.50. A reprint of the volume first published in 1939, this work provides a full study of decor from the simplicity of the Greek drama to the complicated structures in use in the modern theatre and cinema. Full details are given of the techniques involved in conception and construction of sets from the designer's first impression of the script to the final execution. Short studies of the careers and work of six leading designers are included. Eleven tipped-in color illustrations of set, stage and costume designs are included as are ninety-one monochrome illustrations of designs for all types of productions.

NASH, GEORGE
Edward Gordon Craig
Her Majesty's Stationary Office, 1967. 66pp. Paper $2.50. An introduction to the work of the scenic designer. After a short introduction, the volume concludes with sixty-three plates with descriptions.

NEUMANN, ECKHARD—Editor
Bauhaus and Bauhaus People
Reinhold, 1970. 256pp. $13.50. Translated from the German by Eva Richter and Alba Lorman, this is a collection of personal opinions and recollections of former Bauhaus members and their contemporaries. Forty-eight of these members discuss their experiences in the 1920's and 1930's, and the postwar years at the Bauhaus in Germany. Illustrated with photographs. Index.

NICOLL, ALLARDYCE
The Development of the Theatre: A Study of Theatrical Art from the Beginnings to the Present Day
Harcourt, Brace, 1967. 292pp. $15.00. This revised edition of the comprehensive survey of theatre buildings, theatrical decorations and arrangements makes special reference to the English stage. The theatres of the Greeks and Romans, the Middle Ages, the Renaissance, the Commedia dell'Arte, Elizabethan England, eighteenth century France, Restoration and eighteenth and nineteenth century England are studied. There is a section on the Oriental theatre and the theatre of the twentieth century. Included are 288 illustrations. Bibliography. Index.

OENSLAGER, DONALD
Scenery Then and Now
Russell & Russell, 1966. 265pp. $18.00. A reissue of the 1936 edition. Mr. Oenslager explains his theories of scenic design and views the theatre of the past to reveal the original purposes of the conventions and traditions and to devise ways and means of putting them to work in the theatre of today. Illustrated.

PARKER, W. OREN and HARVEY K. SMITH
Scene Design and Stage Lighting: Second Edition
Holt, Rinehart, 1968. 496pp. $12.00. Originally published in 1963, this expanded and updated edition reflects the many new theatre forms and technical advancements in recent years. It covers the changing emphasis in design resulting from the popularity of thrust and arena stages and the latest production innovations and technical devices. Illustrated with complete lighting layouts for seven different types and styles of productions. Bibliography. Index.

PAROLA, RENE
Optical Art: Theory and Practice
Reinhold, 1969. 144pp. $14.95. A study and definition of optical art and some of the elements to which we respond in our perception of it. The various facets of the art form are clarified including the composition of the image, progressions and pattern, and color. Although not essentially a theatre book, the study may be of some value to scenic designers and painters. Bibliography. Index.

RISCHBIETER, HENNING – Editor
Art and the Stage in the Twentieth Century
New York Graphic Society, 1969. 306pp. $35.00. This is a comprehensive survey and critical evaluation of the contributions made to the theatre by major painters and sculptors of the twentieth century. The survey has been documented by Wolfgang Storch. Mr. Rischbieter provides an Introduction which traces stage design from the Baroque period to the theatre of today. Among the more than seventy painters and sculptors discussed are Munch, Picasso, Calder, Dali, Cocteau, Kandinsky, Leger, Chagall, and Dine. Their sets and costume designs are evaluated in terms of the interrelationship of the plastic and performing arts. Each artist's work is recorded with details of original production, extant designs, ownership, and bibliography. Illustrated with photographs, diagrams, and drawings. Index.

ROWELL, KENNETH
Stage Design
Reinhold, 1968. 96pp. $5.50. Paper $2.75. A brief historical outline of stage design in this century and a survey of the contemporary scene. Illustrated with photographs of designs and productions. Glossary of Technical Terms. Bibliography.

SCHLEMMER, OSKAR and LASZLO MOHOLY–NAGY, FARKAS MOLNAR
The Theatre of the Bauhaus
Wesleyan University, 1961. 109pp. $7.50. The first English edition of the trail-blazing work "Die Buhne im Bauhaus" (1924) in which the theatrical aesthetic of the Bauhaus experimental theatre found its most complete verbal expression. The essays in the book are: "Man and Art Figure," and "Theatre (Buhne)" by Schlemmer; "Theatre, Circus, Variety," by Moholy-Nagy; and "U-Theatre," by Molnar with an Introduction by Walter Gropius. Illustrated with photographs, drawings and fold-out tables.

SIMONSON, LEE
The Stage Is Set
Theatre Arts, 1963. 581pp. Paper $3.95. A new edition of the theatre classic, first published in 1932. A new Introduction brings the economics of the theatre up-to-date. The book is a critical history of stagecraft and a philosophical discussion of its importance. 103 illustrations are included as is an amended Bibliography. Notes. Index.

SIMONSON, LEE – Editor
Theatre Art
Cooper Square, 1969. 68pp. & plates. $8.75. Originally published in 1934, this is a volume of essays by Lee Simonson and others on design for the theatre. Over seventy plates are also collected showing set designs and costume designs from the pioneers of modern theatre art in Austria, Czechoslovakia, Denmark, and England, France, Germany, Italy, the United States, and Soviet Russia.

SIMPSON, PERCY and C.F. BELL
Designs by Inigo Jones for Masques and Plays at Court
Russell & Russell, 1966. 158pp. $42.50. A descriptive catalog of drawings for scenery and costumes designed by Inigo Jones from 1605 to 1640. There are fifty-one plates included.

STRONG, ROY
Festival Designs by Inigo Jones
Los Angeles County Museum of Art, 1967. Unpaged. Paper $6.00. This is the catalogue for an exhibition of drawings for scenery and costumes designed for the Court masques of James I and Charles I, designed and drawn by Inigo Jones. The Introduction by Mr. Strong deals with Jones' life and work. Profusely illustrated in color and black-and-white.

STUART, DONALD CLIVE
Stage Decoration in France in the Middle Ages
A.M.S., 1966. 230pp. $14.00. The author of this study, originally published in 1910, shows that no single kind of stage can be said to be typical of the Middle Ages. There were many different kinds of stages for many different kinds of plays. Mr. Stuart studies the thirteenth century setting of the "Adam" play, the tableaux and pantomimes, the Miracles of Notre Dame, the Passions and pantomimes of the fifteenth century and the indoor stage of Paris.

SUMMERSON, JOHN
Inigo Jones
Penguin, 1966. 149pp. Paper $2.25. A study of the sixteenth century English classical architect. Included are over sixty illustrations of Jones' designs. The seven surviving architectural works are show in photographs. Bibliography. Index.

TER–ARUTUNIAN, ROUBEN
In Search of Design
See Page 317

THOMAS, RICHARD K.
Three-Dimensional Design: A Cellular Approach
Reinhold, 1969. 96pp. $6.95. This is not a theatre book; however, set designers may be interested in the author's approach to forms and structures in the form of "cells." Divided into two parts, Theory and Application, Mr. Thomas describes cellular theory and how to construct polygonal and polyhedral cellular systems and how to apply the theories in display, lighting, housing design, and urban planning. Illustrated with nearly 100 line drawings and photographs. Bibliography. Index.

VARDY, JOHN
Some Designs of Inigo Jones and William Kent
Gregg, 1967. 53pp. $50.00. Originally published in England in 1733 and now reissued, this is a collection of plates which illustrate the work of Inigo Jones, the English architect whose set, costume, and stage machinery designs had such a considerable influence on later theatrical design.

VOLBACH, WALTHER R.
Adolphe Appia: Prophet of the Modern Theatre
Wesleyan University, 1968. 242pp. $12.50. This study of the details of the work and the extent of the influence of the early twentieth century stage designer concentrates on Appia's aesthetic ideas, writings, and professional accomplishments. The steps in Appia's career are shown in relation to the cultural milieu, especially the theatre, of his place and time. Illustrated. List of Writings. Bibliography. Index.

YARWOOD, DOREEN
Robert Adam
Dent, 1970. 221pp. $10.00. A biography and summary of the work of the eighteenth century architect and interior designer. Although, not a theatre book, the work in environmental planning and architectural design may be of interest to stage designers. Illustrated with photographs and line drawings. Glossary. List of Surviving Works. Bibliography. Index.

Manuals and Instruction Books

ADIX, VERN
Theatre Scenecraft: For the Backstage Technician and Artist
Anchorage Press, 1956. 309pp. $7.00. A manual for the inexperienced designer-technician on the construction, painting, riggin, and shifting of scenery and props. Illustrated with drawings and photographs of productions. List of sources of materials is included.

BUERKI, FREDERICK A.
Stagecraft for Nonprofessionals
University of Wisconsin, 1955. 131pp. Paper $2.50. Originally published in 1945 and now reissued, this is a concise discussion of the building, painting, and lighting of scenery, for school and little theatre productions. Illustrated.

CHILVER, PETER and ERIC JONES
Designing a School Play
See Page 338

CONWAY, HEATHER
Stage Properties
Barrie & Jenkins, 1960. 96pp. $1.75. A manual, published in England, on the making of inexpensive properties for historical plays of all eras. Illustrated.

CORNBERG, SOL and EMANUEL L. GEBAUER
A Stage Crew Hand-Book
Harper & Row, 1957. 291pp. $5.95. A textbook in stagecraft for the stage carpenter, painter, property manager, technical director, and scenic designer. Originally published in 1941 and now revised, the volume is illustrated with detailed charts, diagrams, and drawings.

FLETCHER, IFAN KYRLE and ARNOLD ROOD
Edward Gordon Craig: A Bibliography
Society for Theatre Research, 1967. 117pp. $4.50. An annotated listing of over 650 items relating to the career and work of Edward Gordon Craig. Entries are listed by date with place of publication, record of editions, and illustrations. The volume contains books, introductions or contributions to books, books illustrated, texts of plays produced, periodicals edited, periodicals with contributions, and several other categories.

GILLETTE, A.S.
An Introduction to Scene Design
Harper & Row, 1967. 210pp. $15.35. This text is intended as an introduction to the field of scene design. It should prove helpful to those directors of little theatres and to those teachers who have not had any special training in the subject who find themselves with the problem of designing and painting scenery for their own productions. Illustrated. Bibliography. Index.

GILLETTE, A.S.
Stage Scenery: Its Construction and Rigging
Harper & Row, 1959. 315pp. $15.35. A complete manual of instruction, with information on staff-organization, the relation between designer and technical staff, building two and three dimensional scenery, and special rigging problems. Illustrated.

GRAHAM, FRANK D.
Carpenters and Builders Guide
Audel, 1965. Volume One: 472pp. Volume Two:

358pp. Volume Three: 342pp. Volume Four: 406pp. Set of four volumes: $18.00. An all-inclusive reference set covering the use and care of carpenter's tools, plus the construction and application of wood joints. This is a reference for anyone desiring a knowledge of woodworking tools and techniques. Illustrated. Index.

HAKE, HERBERT V.
Here's How: A Basic Stagecraft Book
Samuel French, 1958. 128pp. Spiral bound $3.95. A guide to the building, decorating, and lighting of stage sets, with step-by-step, illustrated instructions. The economic use of materials is stressed throughout, and sample budgets are included.

JONES, ERIC
Stage Construction for School Plays
Batsford, 1969. 88pp. $5.75. The author examines and illustrates some basic ideas about staging. He suggests ways to get the most out of many different staging facilities available. Improvising space, flats, individual units, screen backgrounds, traverse curtains, open staging, and lighting are all discussed. A short glossary of terms is provided. Illustrated with drawings. Index.

JONES, LESLIE ALLEN
Painting Scenery: A Handbook for Amateur Productions
Walter Baker, 1935. 107pp. $2.25. A simplified manual for the non-professional, illustrated with diagrams.

JOSEPH, STEPHEN
Scene Painting and Design
Pitman, 1964. 132pp. $6.95. Published in England, in this volume the art of scene design is analyzed against a background which includes an account of the function of scenery and its original connection with stage architecture. The problems of the open stage and of proscenium stage are discussed. Building and painting flats and lighting them are also described.

KENTON, WARREN
Stage Properties and How to Use Them
Pitman, 1964. 119pp. $5.00. This book, published in England, presents the basic techniques of constructing properties in paper and paste, wood and wire, etc. Methods of construction are illustrated in detail and there are step-by-step labeled drawings of representative properties.

MELVILL, HARALD
Designing and Painting Scenery for the Theatre
Barrie & Jenkins, 1963. 99pp. $5.00. Published in England, this is a manual on the designing and painting of scenery for large or small theatres. Illustrated with thirty diagrams and ground plans and seventy-six photographs of settings. Glossary of British Terms.

NAPIER, FRANK
Curtains for Stage Settings
J. Garnet Miller, 1949. 146pp. $2.95. Originally published in 1937 and now reissued, this is an illustrated guide to the making and arranging of stage curtains, built pieces, exterior and interior scenes. Mr. Napier tells how to provide the most suitable scenery with the minimum of trouble and expense. Illustrated. List of English Suppliers. Index.

NELMS, HENNING
A Primer of Stagecraft
Dramatists, 1941. 162pp. $1.75. A manual detailing methods and materials for building scenery and properties from stock units that can be used over again. A list of approximate prices is included. Illustrated.

NELMS, HENNING
Scene Design: A Guide to the Stage
Sterling Publishing, 1970. 96pp. $6.95. The principles of scene design and practical ways to "do it" are provided by the author. Among the subjects discussed are types of sets, the nature of scenery, model scenery, designing with a model, and arena design. Illustrated by the author with drawings and diagrams of sets and set pieces. Index.

NORTON, DORA MIRIAM
Freehand Perspective
Bell, 1970. 91pp. $1.98. Originally published in 1957 and now reissued in a revised edition, this study of perspective includes 184 drawings to illustrate the text.

PARKER, W. OREN and HARVEY K. SMITH
Scene Design and Stage Lighting: Second Edition
Holt, Rinehart, 1968. 496pp. $12.00. Originally published in 1963, this expanded and updated edition reflects the many new theatre forms and technical advancements in recent years. Illustrated with complete lighting layouts for seven different types and styles of productions. Bibliography. Index.

PARKER, W. OREN
Sceno-Graphic Techniques
Carnegie Institute of Technology, 1964. 85pp. $5.75. This book is designed to assist the stage designer in the planning portion of his craft, and includes details on the basic drafting and presentation of the set, pattern development, perspective foreshortening, projection distortion and other technical problems pertaining to construction. Detailed stage design planning diagrams are included.

PHILIPPI, HERBERT
Stagecraft and Scene Design
Houghton Mifflin, 1953. 448pp. $11.00. Instructions on every aspect of stage setting with chapters on back-stage equipment, types of scenery, painting, supporting, and shifting of scenery, properties,

lighting, sound, and special effects. An Appendix on the designer's and technician's vocabulary is included. Illustrated. Glossary of Terms. Bibliography. List of Sources of Supply. Index.

SANTOS, LOUISA
Projected Scenery for the School Stage
Walter Baker, 1949. 28pp. Paper $ .75. A brief manual on the use of lantern slide scenes to provide inexpensive and artistically effective scenes for amateur productions. Illustrated.

SELDEN, SAMUEL and HUNTON D. SELLMAN
Stage Scenery and Lighting
Appleton, 1959. 394pp. $8.95. A guide for little theatre and non-professional groups. Among the topics covered are forms of scenery, building, painting, and assembling sets, means of lighting, elementary electricity, lighting control, and color. Illustrated with charts and diagrams.

SOUTHERN, RICHARD
Proscenium and Sight-Lines
Theatre Arts, 1964. 235pp. $7.45. A complete system of scenery planning, and a guide to the laying out of stages for scene designers, producers, stage-managers, theatre architects and engineers, theatrical history research workers, and those concerned with the planning of stages for small halls. A second, revised edition of the book first published in 1933, with a new Introduction. Illustrated with drawings. Index.

SOUTHERN, RICHARD
Stage-Setting for Amateurs and Professionals
Theatre Arts, 1964. 272pp. $5.95. A guide for the amateur stage-manager and set designer and a record of professional procedure in a particular type of theatrical setting. The usual professional methods of today are here collected and described. Revised from the out-of-print 1937 edition. Bibliography. Index.

STELL, W. JOSEPH
The Theatre Student: Scenery
Richards Rosen, 1969. 256pp. $7.97. Written for students and teachers of the theatre involved in producing drama and musicals, this is an introduction to set design and scenery. An introduction to the design process leads to the problems of the one-set and the multisetting show, musicals and children's plays, and special design problems and techniques. Appendices include a Glossary of Stage Terminology. Lists of Tools, Hardware, and Materials, and A List of Suppliers of Stage Materials. Illustrated with drawings, diagrams, and photographs. Bibliography.

WARRE, MICHAEL
Designing and Making Stage Scenery
Reinhold, 1966. 104pp. $8.95. A practical handbook on scenic design describing developments from early forms to current practice. There are sixty designs which cover five centuries of scenic art and a short history of world theatre practice. The second part of the volume includes many line drawings and diagrams which help to explain the craft of planning, building, painting, and setting up stage scenery today. Illustrated. Index.

WELKER, DAVID
Theatrical Set Design: The Basic Techniques
Allyn & Bacon, 1969. 349pp. $12.00. This is a complete guide to the functions and practices of the scenic designer. Beginning with an interpretation of the role of the designer and the functions of scenery, the author continues with an analysis of the steps in designing, the preliminary analysis, designing for mood and locale, and designing for aesthetics. The third section of the volume is a study of the actual recording of the designs with techniques examined and materials explained. Complete information on materials and methods, and types of stage and set machinery is given. Illustrated with drawings and photographs. Index.

WYATT, JENIFER
Stage Scenery
Barrie & Jenkins, 1957. 93pp. $1.75. Instructions on the construction and painting of scenery, in two parts. Part One describes traditional types of scenery, offers hints on carpentry, and discusses the use of alternative materials to wood. Part Two describes the basic techniques of scenery painting. Illustrated.

Auditoriums and Stages

ALOI, ROBERTO
Architetture per lo Spettacolo
Speedimpex, 1958. 504pp. $25.00. Published in Italy, this is an exhaustive survey of contemporary theatre architecture covering a wide range of types and locales. The Preface is in Italian but the illustrative descriptions are in English, German, French, and Italian. Included are 345 illustrations in black-and white, twenty-one color plates, and 454 sketches, blueprints, and diagrams of theatres. Index.

AMERICAN THEATRE PLANNING BOARD
Theatre Check List: A Guide to the Planning and Construction of Proscenium and Open Stage Theatres
Wesleyan University, 1969. 71pp. Paper $3.95. This guide has been prepared under the chairmanship of Jo Mielziner by a committee of theatre specialists organized to bring to the attention of the new theatre builder or renovator information and recommendations which will result in better planned theatres. It includes a study of the proscenium stage theatre vs. the open stage theatre, a check list of facilities for both types of theatres, a section of considerations applicable to all types of theatres,

and a recommendation for permanently installed lighting equipment. The volume is illustrated with drawings and diagrams by Ming Cho Lee as well as photographs and diagrams of the Theatre Royal, in Bristol, England, the Vivian Beaumont Theatre in Lincoln Center, New York, and the Stratford, Ontario, Shakespeare Festival Theatre. Index.

ANONYMOUS
Theatre and Concert Halls Seating Plans
Stubs, 1967. 100pp. Paper $2.00. A guide to the theatres and concert halls of London. It includes seating plans, short histories of the theatres, how to get to them, and a short section on restaurants near each of the theatres.

BERANEK, LEO L.
Music, Acoustics and Architecture
See Page 279

BIBIENA, GIUSEPPE GALLI
Architectural and Perspective Designs
Dover, 1964. 103pp. Paper $2.50. An unabridged reprint of the 1740 edition of fifty designs by Bibiena. These full page plates show illustrations of the Viennese Court Riding School, Baroque funeral monuments, settings for religious dramas, and sets and costumes for court pageants. A. Hyatt Major has contributed an Introduction.

BOCHIUS, JOHANNES
The Ceremonial Entry of Ernst, Archduke of Austria, into Antwerp, June 14, 1594
Blom, 1970. 227pp. $37.50. Originally published in 1595 and now reissued in a folio sized facsimile, this is an illustrated account of Archduke Ernst's ceremonial entry into Antwerp. The actual account is in the original language; however, an Introduction by Hans Mielke on ceremonial entries and the theatre in the sixteenth century is in the English language. Among the plates are views of the ampitheatres on a turntable and illustrations of the stage settings provided for the ceremony.

BURRIS–MEYER, HAROLD and EDWARD COLE
Theatres and Auditoriums
Reinhold, 1964. 376pp. $27.50. This new enlarged edition attempts to amplify the basic principles of production techniques set forth in the first edition, particularly in regard to the use of new materials, new construction and operational techniques for the purpose of economy and efficiency, and in the relative value of varying types of theatres. This book makes it possible for persons concerned in the planning of theatres, though unfamiliar with theatrical practices, to understand what constitutes a good theatre and to govern their plans accordingly. The technical reasons for the size, shape, arrangements and equipment of the spaces which comprise the theatre building are given. Selected pictures give examples of good practice in theatre planning.

CORRY, PERCY
Planning the Stage
Pitman, 1961. 148pp. $7.95. A practical guide to the planning and equipping of stages. The special problems of the civic theatre, the little theatre, arena theatre, and the multi-purpose hall are given special attention.

COURTNEY, RICHARD
The Drama Studio
Pitman, 1967. 146pp. $9.25. The first major work on architectural design and equipment for dramatic education. It should serve as a basis for planning studios and for making the best of existing facilities. Part I discusses drama in school, college and university and the basic physical requirements. Part II provides a design procedure for studios. Part III gives specimen studio layouts. Illustrated with drawings, diagrams, and photographs. List of English Manufacturers and Suppliers. Bibliography of books on theatre architecture, acoustics, lighting, and sound. Index.

DE FILIPPI, JOSEPH and CLEMENT CONSTANT
Parallele des Principaux Theatres Modernes de l'Europe et Des Machines Theatrales
Blom, 1968. 163pp. & plates $75.00. First published in 1860 and now reissued, this is a study of theatre architecture and descriptions of theatres that existed in the nineteenth century. The second part of the book consists of 133 plates showing the various component parts of the theatre in general and some theatres in particular. The text is in the French language.

DUMONT, GABRIEL PIERRE MARTIN
Parallelle de Plans des Plus Belles Salles de Spectacles d'Italie et de France
Blom, 1968. Unpaged. $37.50. Architectural plans and drawings of theatre buildings, stages, and stage machinery by a master French architect of the eighteenth century. Many cross-sections, elevations, and full views are given, frequently of theatres not depicted in any other source. The eighty plates have been assembled from all editions of the book published in the eighteenth century and this is the first publication in a single volume of all of Dumont's theatre architecture drawings.

DUNCAN, C. J.
Modern Lecture Theatres
Oriel Press, 1968. 340pp. $15.00. The editor has provided a comprehensive reference book for all concerned with the planning, design, and use of lecture theatres and teaching rooms. Contributions by experts over the whole field were first presented in Manchester, England, in 1961 during a course on "Designing and Equipping Modern Lecture Theatres." Other material collected by the editor since that conference has been included. Illustrated with photographs, drawings, and diagrams. A forty page section of equipment currently available is included.

HOWARD, DIANA
London Theatres and Music Halls: 1850–1950
Library Association, 1970. 291pp. $18.50. An annotated directory of theatres in use in London during the century covered. Details of architecture and management are provided from official records and contemporary accounts. Illustrated. Bibliography of General Works. Index to Names of Buildings.

JOSEPH, STEPHEN – Editor
Actor and Architect
University of Toronto Press, 1964. 118pp. $4.50. Paper $1.95. This is a collection of lectures by a group of British experts on the theatre. They explore the architecture of the theatre as a public building, showing how and why the shape and form of the traditional theatre is changing, that change is possible and often very desirable. The essayists include Tyrone Guthrie, Hugh Hunt, Sean Kenny, Richard Southern, Christopher Stevens, and John English. Illustrated. Index.

JOSEPH, STEPHEN
New Theatre Forms
Theatre Arts, 1968. 144pp. $6.25. This book provides a guide to the new forms of the stage—arena, apron, and their various related forms— which are to some extent taking the place of the traditional picture frame stage. The various factors involved are considered in detail from the point of view of designers, producers, playwrights, and actors. Illustrated with plans and illustrations. Book List.

MIELZINER, JO
The Shapes of Our Theatre
Clarkson N. Potter, 1970. 160pp. $6.95. Edited by C. Ray Smith, with an Introduction by Brooks Atkinson, this book is about planning and designing the interior shapes of theatre buildings, primarily those for spoken drama and comedy and musical theatre. Mielziner points out basic faults and omissions in much of current theatre planning. Illustrated with drawings. Appendices. Index.

MULLIN, DONALD C.
The Development of the Playhouse
University of California, 1970. 197pp. $15.00. A survey of theatre architecture from the Renaissance to the present. The author explains the principal elements of each architectural concept, defining and comparing the diverse styles of theatre construction through the centuries. Illustrations are integrated with the text and drawn, whenever possible, from sources contemporary with the structures. Illustrated with photographs, drawings, and plans. Appendices. Bibliography. Index.

PUPPI, LIONELLO
Il Teatro Olimpica
Speedimpex, 1963. 63pp. Paper $2.25. Published in Italy, this is a study of the first theatrical building in the city of Vicenza, inaugurated in 1585. The classical Roman sources of the building are discussed and the author shows that the building is the epitome of the work of Palladio. Fifty-two plates from contemporary sources and photographs are included. The text is in the Italian language.

ROBINSON, HORACE W.
Architecture for the Educational Theatre
University of Oregon, 1970. 147pp. $7.50. Based on a conference which examined the physical requirements for theatre activity in secondary schools, this study considers the physical plant: auditorium and stage, public service areas, backstage work areas, equipment, teaching areas, alternate forms to the proscenium stage, and other related considerations. Illustrated with drawings of proposed facilities. Bibliography. Index.

SACHS, EDWIN O. and ERNEST A. E. WOODROW
Modern Opera Houses and Theatres
Blom, 1968. Three volumes. $110.00. Originally published in 1896, 1897, and 1898, and now reissued, this is a collection of articles, photographs, drawings, and diagrams of some of the most famous theatres all over the world. Volume One contains 100 plates and ninety-three illustrations in the text. Volume Two includes 100 plates and ninety-five illustrations. Volume Three provides twenty plates and 860 illustrations as well as the major text: "A Treatise on Theatre Planning." Sections are included on service arrangement, construction, equipment, and safety of life.

SAUNDERS, GEORGE
A Treatise on Theatres
Blom, 1968. 94pp. & plates, $25.00. Originally published in London in 1790 and now reissued in a facsimile edition, this is an "inquiry into the essentials of a good theatre." It includes twenty plates illustrating various theatres.

SCHATTNER, MEYER
Stubs: The Seating Plan Guide
Citadel Press, 1969. 128pp. Paper $1.00. Seating plans of all New York theatres, sports stadia, and music halls including many off-Broadway theatres and some nearby out-of-state theatres.

SHEPPARD, F. H. W. – Editor
The Theatre Royal, Drury Lane, and The Royal Opera House, Covent Garden
See Page 174

SILVERMAN, MAXWELL
Contemporary Theatre Architecture: An Illustrated Survey
New York Public Library, 1965. 100pp. $10.00. With a Foreword by George Freedley, this volume includes floor plans, cross sections, and photographs of more than forty recently built theatres, concert halls, and

performing arts centers in Europe and America. Ned Bowman's "A Checklist of Publications: 1946–1964" is included in the volume. It lists 1,700 references to world literature, arranged geographically and indexed by subject and theatre location.

Acoustics

BERANEK, LEO L.
Acoustics
McGraw–Hill, 1954. 481pp. $18.95. This is a text book on acoustics published in 1954. The basic wave equation and its solutions are discussed in detail. Radiation of sound, components of acoustical systems, microphones, loudspeakers, and horns are treated. Extensive treatment of such problems as sound in enclosures, methods for noise reduction, speech intelligibility, and psychoacoustic criteria for comfort. Illustrated with diagrams and charts. Appendices. Index.

BERANEK, LEO L.
Music, Acoustics and Architecture
See Page 279

BURRIS–MEYER, HAROLD and VINCENT MALLORY
Sound in the Theatre
Theatre Arts, 1959. 95pp. $6.95. A detailed exposition of what can be done with sound by electronic control. The requirements for control are developed from the necessities of the performance, the characteristics of the audience, and the way sound is modified by environment, hall, and scenery. Techniques for control are illustrated by means of thirty-two specific problems. Illustrated.

PARKIN, P.H. and H.R. HUMPHREYS
Acoustics, Noise and Buildings
Faber & Faber, 1963. 331pp. Paper $4.95. Originally published in 1958, this is a reissue of the study on acoustics. Subjects covered include the nature of sound, the behavior of sound in rooms, the design of rooms for speech and for music, the design of studios, the design of high quality speech reinforcement systems, sound insulation and noise control, sound measurement, and criteria for sound insulation and noise control. Appendices. Illustrated. Index.

SABINE, WALLACE CLEMENT
Collected Papers on Acoustics
Dover, 1964. 279pp. Paper $3.00. First presented in 1922 and republished with a new Introduction by F.V. Hunt of Harvard University, this volume includes eleven essays written by the father of architectural acoustics. Sabine was the first to bring quantitative measurements to bear upon the problems of acoustics in architecture. Optimal reverberation time, total absorption, duration of residual sound, and building materials are among the topics covered.

WOOD, ALEXANDER
Acoustics
Dover, 1966. 594pp. Paper $3.50. This is an unabridged republication of the 1960 edition of the study of the theory of sound. Some of the subjects covered include: wave motion, forced vibrations, resonators, filters, dissipation of energy of sound waves, reflection and refraction of sound waves, pitch and frequency, recording and reproduction of sound, and acoustics of buildings. Illustrated with tables and figures. Bibliography. Indices.

Stage Decoration

Architecture

ACKERMAN, JAMES S.
Palladio
Penguin, 1966. 195pp. Paper $2.25. A study of the sixteenth century architect, this is the first full account of his career to be published in English. Included are photographs and architectural drawings of his great buildings. Bibliographical Notes. Index.

CHAMBERS, WILLIAM
A Treatise on the Decorative Part of Civil Architecture
Blom, 1968. 137pp. & plates. $37.50. This is a facsimile reproduction of the study first published in London in 1791. The aim of the treatise is to provide a course of instruction on architecture. Chambers examines, compares, and abstracts a series of precepts and designs. Direct observations of French, Italian, and English architecture are made. The fifty-three plates show primitive buildings, mouldings, pilasters, capitals, arches, arcades, columns, pediments, doors, windows, and ornaments for ceilings, etc.

FOCILLON, HENRI
Giovanni Battista Piranesi
Speedimpex, 1963. 390pp. $50.00. Published in Italy, the text of this volume is in Italian. It is a study of the style and work of the eighteenth century architect and engraver. The volume includes over 250 illustrations of Piranesi's work.

GIBBS, JAMES
A Book of Architecture
Bloom, 1968. 28pp. & plates. $47.50. Originally published in 1728, and now reissued in a facsimile edition, this book includes 150 plates showing buildings, designs, and ornaments used in architecture in the eighteenth century.

HIND, ARTHUR M.
Giovanni Battista Piranesi: A Critical Study
Da Capo, 1967. 95pp. & plates. $25.00. Originally published in 1922 and now reprinted, this is a catalogue of Piranesi's two major series of etchings: the

prisons and the views of Rome. Introductory notes on the origins, dates, and contents of Piranesi's work in relation to existing documents and an estimate of his place in the history of art, a short biography, and some descriptions of his drawings are included along with a list of the published works. The plates comprise 146 illustrations of Piranesi's work.

HOWELLS, JOHN MEAD
The Architectural Heritage of the Piscataqua
Architectural Book Publishers, 1965. Unpaged. $4.95. Included in this volume are 300 photographs and drawings of the architecture and gardens of Portsmouth, New Hampshire, and its vicinity. The volume gives a picture of an American town in the Colonial and early Federal periods. William Lawrence Bottomley has provided an Introduction.

ISON, LEONORA and WALTER ISON
English Architecture Through the Ages: Secular Building
Coward–McCann, 1967. 124pp. $5.00. A history of English secular architecture ranging from the earliest buildings to the most recent. Every important type of public and private building is represented with captioned illustrations. Over 400 drawings are provided. Indices.

JORDAN, ROBERT FURNEAUX
Victorian Architecture
Penguin, 1966. 278pp. Paper $2.95. Mr. Jordan attempts to answer the questions: why are we interested in Victorian architecture and why did it exist. His study includes over 130 illustrations of surviving churches, palaces, buildings and furniture. Bibliography. Index.

KIESLER, FREDERICK
Inside the Endless House: Art, People and Architecture – A Journal
Simon & Schuster, 1965. 576pp. $15.00. This is the journal of the architect, sculptor, painter, poet, and stage designer, covering the years from 1956 to 1964. From accounts of his travels (in Italy, to the South American city of Brasilia, and to Israel) to reminiscences of dinner parties and other social events, from vignettes of people to penetrating insights into the economic and aesthetic problems that face every artist, it is a document by a man who was a major force in the world of art during his lifetime. Thirty of the author's drawings are scattered throughout the text.

LICKLIDER, HEATH
Architectural Scale
Braziller, 1965. 232pp. $5.00. This book is designed to give the student a description of scale that will help him discover the complex relationship between the lines he draws on paper, the three-dimensional results, and the experience those buildings may afford the viewer.

LOCKARD, WILLIAM KIRBY
Drawing as a Means to Architecture
Reinhold, 1968. 96pp. Spiral bound. $10.95. The author views drawing as an inseparable part of the design process. He describes and demonstrates the various ways architectural projects can be conceived, refined, and communicated graphically. Full size drawings and tissue overlays are used to illustrate the use of drawing in the design process.

LOS ANGELES COUNTY MUSEUM OF ART
Agostino Mitelli
Los Angeles County Museum of Art, 1965. 79pp. Paper $4.95. This museum catalogue of drawings by the seventeenth century artist includes fifty-three plates illustrating his concept of ceiling design—a major expression of Baroque art. Also included is a critique on the artist and his work by Ebria Feinblatt. Selected Bibliography.

NASH, JOSEPH
The Mansions of England in the Olden Time
Crown, 1970. Unpaged. $9.95. Originally published in 1906 and now reissued, this volume contains 100 lithographic plates of the nineteenth century artist. These plates were originally published between 1839 and 1849 and show architectural details of the Tudor and Elizabethan periods. Preface by George B. Tatum and Introduction by C. Harrison Townsend.

NYBERG, DOROTHEA
Oeuvre De Juste Aurele Meissonnier
Blom, 1969. 43pp. & 74 plates. $42.50. A reissue of the 1750 edition of Meissonnier's designs. Professor Nyberg's commentary underlines the fact that Meissonnier was not only one of the most original designers of the age but one of the most influential. The plates illustrate both the architectural designs plus the decorative details of his work.

SERLIO, SEBASTIAN
The Book of Architecture
Blom, 1969. 412pp. $27.50. Originally published in London in 1611 and reissued in a facsimile edition, this is one of the seminal documents in the history of art. The fifteenth century architect has provided a comprehensive illustrated guide to the theory and practice of architecture. Introduction by A. E. Santaniello. Bibliography. Illustrated.

STOTZ, CHARLES MORSE
The Architectural Heritage of Early Western Pennsylvania
University of Pittsburgh, 1966. 293pp. $17.50. A record of building before 1860 from the first log houses to the pre-Civil War Gothic revival in Western Pennsylvania. Illustrated with 416 photographs and eighty-one measured drawings of the buildings.

STUART, JAMES and NICHOLAS REVETT
The Antiquities of Athens

Blom, 1968. Volume One: 53pp. & plates. Volume Two: 46pp. & plates. Volume Three: 64pp. & plates. Three volume set: $112.50. The 226 full-page engravings in these three volumes are of unique importance in the history of architecture. Originally published in three volumes from 1762 to 1795, the volumes fostered the taste for classic design that culminated in the Greek revival.

WATKINSON, RAY
William Morris as Designer
Reinhold, 1967. 84pp. & plates. $16.50. The ideas and lectures of William Morris have influenced architecture, town planning, and printing ever since the late 1800's. Mr. Watkinson presents every aspect of Morris' output and includes ninety-one illustrations of his work. Bibliography Index.

Furniture

ARONSON, JOSEPH
The Encyclopedia of Furniture
Crown, 1965. 484pp. $7.95. This third, revised edition of the standard reference work has descriptions of new materials, styles, and trends. The nineteenth century is given full treatment. The 2,000 photographs range in scope from pictures of earliest museum pieces to noteworthy items of today's designers. Glossary of Terms.

BAKER, HOLLIS S.
Furniture in the Ancient World
Macmillan, 1966. 351pp. $17.95. The first book to consider ancient furniture as a whole and to compare the types that evolved in the different civilizations of the world. Correlated with the text are more than 500 black-and-white pictures and sixteen color plates. The text covers furniture from 3100 to 475 B.C. Index.

BOGER, LOUISE ADE
Complete Guide to Furniture Styles
Scribners, 1969. 500pp. $17.50. An enlarged edition of the 1959 comprehensive guide to the stylistic development of domestic furniture from classical times to the present in Europe, America, and China. Outstanding examples of furniture from every period are illustrated in over 600 photographs. Bibliography. Index of Artists and Craftsmen. General Index.

BOGER, LOUISE ADE
Furniture, Past and Present
Doubleday, 1966. 520pp. $12.95. A history of furniture styles from ancient to modern in the Western world. 582 photographs of furniture have been chosen as epitomes of the historical period from which they came. Index.

BRETT, GERARD
English Furniture and Its Setting
University of Toronto, 1965. 117pp. $6.50. A collection of illustrations of later sixteenth to early nineteenth century furniture in the Royal Ontario Museum. It provides insights into English social history as well as information on furniture. Illustrated. Index.

BUTLER, DAVID F.
Simplified Furniture Design and Construction
A. S. Barnes, 1970. 118pp. $5.95. A handbook for the amateur builder showing simplified construction methods for furniture to be built with a minimum of tools. Among the projects described and illustrated with diagrams and photographs are: bedside table, bookcase, lamps, cabinets, and cocktail table. Index.

CESCINSKY, HERBERT
English Furniture from Gothic to Sheraton
Dover, 1968. 406pp. Paper $4.95. This is an unabridged republication of the 1938 edition which is considered the finest single volume coverage of British furniture in the classical period. A full text covers each period or major style and there are more than 900 illustrations. Bibliography. Index of illustrations.

CESCINSKY, HERBERT
The Gentle Art of Faking Furniture
Dover, 1967. 168pp. Paper $4.00. This unabridged, unaltered edition of a book first published in 1931 is a comprehensive study of how to tell fakes from genuine antique furniture. For each period of English furniture, the author tells what to look for and the hallmarks of the original pieces. Illustrated with 563 photographs of interesting fakes and also genuine pieces. Index.

CHIPPENDALE, THOMAS
The Gentleman and Cabinet-Maker's Director
Dover, 1966. Unpaged. Paper $3.50. An unaltered and unabridged republication of the 1762 edition of Thomas Chippendale's catalog of his designs. The plates contain drawings of the furniture plus construction diagrams, elevations, moldings, and other details. This volume also includes a supplement of photographs of eighteenth century Chippendale-style pieces and a short biographical sketch of Chippendale. 200 plates plus photos.

COLLISCHON, DAVID
Furniture Making
Watson—Guptill, 1968. 104pp. $2.50. Simple methods of construction and veneering are detailed in this instruction book. The author details every stage in the construction and veneering in non-technical terms and illustrates the steps with diagrams and photographs. Index.

COMSTOCK, HELEN
American Furniture: A Complete Guide to Seventeenth, Eighteenth, and Early Nineteenth Century Styles
Viking, 1962. 336pp. $17.50. Chapters on Jacobean, William and Mary, Queen Anne, Chippendale,

classical, and early Victorian styles of furniture are included in this guidebook. Historical background is furnished for each period and style, descriptions of known craftsmen are provided, and also included are over 700 illustrations of individual pieces of furniture as well as full room settings.

COMSTOCK, HELEN – Editor
The Concise Encyclopedia of American Antiques
Hawthorn, 1966. 848pp. $12.95. Written by experts in their field, this volume contains sections on paintings, wall-paper, folk sculpture, furniture, pewter and glass, hooked rugs, and many more. Each subject has its own Glossary and Bibliography. 160 pages of photographs are included. Index.

CORNELIUS, CHARLES OVER
Furniture Masterpieces of Duncan Phyfe
Dover, 1970. 86pp. $2.50. Originally published in 1922 and now reissued, this is an appreciation and survey of Phyfe's furniture in text and photographs. The volume includes fifty-six full-page plates of actual examples of the furniture plus a set of measured drawings which supply precise technical details.

COWIE, DONALD and KEITH HENSHAW
Antique Collector's Dictionary
Arc Books, 1969. 208pp. Paper $1.45. Originally published in 1962 and now reissued, this is a dictionary of 1,600 terms dealing with antiques. The terms are alphabetically arranged and many are illustrated with photographs and drawings.

DECRISTOFORO, R. J.
How to Build Your Own Furniture
Harper & Row, 1965. 176pp. $3.95. The author's "Component System" enables you to build any piece of furniture in any style with a few basic components —broad surfaces or slabs, rails, and legs. Included are construction details, design elements, assembly procedures, and techniques. Illustrated with drawings and photographs. Glossary of Terms. Index.

DELDERFIELD, ERIC R.
Church Furniture
Taplinger, 1967. 157pp. $5.00. A guide to the things to be found in and around almost any church. Alphabetically arranged, each piece is described and set in its place in history. Bibliography. Index of Churches.

DURDICK, JAN et al
The Pictorial Encyclopedia of Antiques
Hamlyn, 1970. 496pp. $5.95. Seven authors, all experts in their fields, have combined to describe the major historical styles throughout Europe. This encyclopedia is divided into sections dealing with furniture, tapestries, carpets, etc. At the end of each chapter there is a text offering advice to the collector. Illustrated with over 650 monochrome photographs and sixty-seven color plates. Bibliography. Glossary. Index of Museums. Subject Index.

EDWARDS, RALPH and L. G. G. RAMSEY – Editors
The Connoisseur's Complete Period Guides
Bonanza, 1968. 1,536pp. $12.50. Originally published in the 1950's in three volumes and now reissued in one volume, this is a complete guide to the houses, decoration, furnishings, and chattels of the classic periods of Tudor, Stuart, Georgian, Regency, and early Victorian style. Every article has been contributed by an acknowledged expert in his particular field. Included are 576 pages of black-and-white photographs plus numerous line drawings, diagrams, and contemporary prints. Index.

EDWARDS, RALPH
English Chairs
British Information Service, 1965. 26pp. & plates. Paper $2.95. A selection of the chairs to be found in the Victoria and Albert Museum in London. Included are 120 photographs of chairs from the sixteenth to the nineteenth century. Each example is described in the text and a history of the English chair is included.

EDWARDS, RALPH
A Short History of English Furniture
British Information Service, 1966. 32pp. & plates. $4.50. Paper $3.50. This short review provides a quick survey of the main styles of English furniture over the centuries. The volume includes 100 plates of some of the items in the Victoria and Albert Museum in London. Each example is described in the text.

FASTNEDGE, RALPH
English Furniture Styles: 1500 – 1830
Penguin, 1967. 321pp. Paper $2.45. This is a reprint of the 1955 edition of the historical survey of the evolution of English furniture. The book contains quotations from old memoirs, diaries, and letters which help to recreate the social conditions under which the designers and makers worked. Several Appendices are included: Glossaries of makers, woods, and specialized terms. Illustrated with over 100 line drawings and sixty-four pages of plates.

FRY, PLANTAGENET SOMERSET
The World of Antiques
Paul Hamlyn, 1970. 141pp. $7.95. An introduction to antiques for the collector. The author explains the workings of the salesrooms, describes some of the more spectacular bids at auctions, and reveals some of the hazards of the antique trade. Included are over 140 illustrations, of which twenty-six are in color. Bibliography. Index.

GLOAG, JOHN
A Short Dictionary of Furniture
Allen & Unwin, 1969. 813pp. $23.95. Originally published in 1952 and now revised, this dictionary is divided into five sections. The first and second concern the description and design of furniture; the

third is occupied with the 2,612 entries in alphabetical order; section four gives a list of the principal furniture makers in Britain and North America; and section five records books and periodicals on furniture and design. The concluding section sets out in tabular form the periods with the materials used and types of craftsmen employed from 1100 to 1950. Illustrated with over 1,000 reproductions from contemporary sources.

GLOAG, JOHN
A Social History of Furniture Design from BC 1300 to AD 1960
Crown, 1966. 202pp. $12.50. The changing character of furniture is described and illustrated, from the work of ancient Egyptian and Greek craftsmen to the age of the great French and English craftsmen in the eighteenth century and the contemporary style of today. 344 illustrations. Index.

GRANDJEAN, SERGE
Empire Furniture 1800 to 1825
Faber & Faber, 1966. 120pp. $17.50. The author calls attention to the quality of French furniture and its influence on the furniture produced throughout Europe and in the Americas. Illustrated with ninety-six plates.

HAYWARD, CHARLES H.
English Period Furniture Designs
Arco, 1969. 111pp. $4.95. Scale drawings and explanatory details of English period furniture. Basic furniture pieces through the ages and mouldings are also illustrated.

HAYWARD, HELENA – Editor
World Furniture
McGraw –Hill, 1965. 320pp. $17.95. This volume includes 130,000 words of text, over 1,00 black-and-white illustrations, and fifty-two color plates. It provides a survey and illustrated history of furniture throughout the world. Glossary. Reading List. Index.

HAYWARD, JOHN F.
Tables in the Victoria and Albert Museum
British Information Service, 1961. 18pp. & plates. Paper $1.50. A catalogue of some of the tables found in the British museum. A complete description is included along with the fifty-three illustrated examples.

HEPPLEWHITE, GEORGE
The Cabinet-Maker and Upholsterer's Guide
Dover, 1969. 176pp. Paper $3.00. An unabridged, unaltered republication of the third (1794) edition of the catalogue of Hepplewhite's furniture designs with a new Introduction by Joseph Aronson. 128 plates illustrate the volume.

KOVEL, RALPH and TERRY KOVEL
American Country Furniture: 1780 – 1875
Crown, 1965. 248pp. $7.50. The more than 700 close-up photographs with detailed captions provide a means of identifying styles, construction, wood, finish, hardware and other characteristic features. All classifications of furniture are included with special sections on Pennsylvania Shaker, and spool furniture. An illustrated glossary of accessories and terms is included. Index.

MacDONALD – TAYLOR, MARGARET
English Furniture from the Middle Ages to Modern Times
Putnam, 1965. 299pp. $8.95. An overall survey of the evolution of English furniture with discussions of the major craftsmen. Each type of furniture is treated in a separate chapter and the volume is illustrated with eighty photographs of important pieces. Chronological Chart. Glossary. Bibliography. Index.

MARGON, LESTER
Masterpieces of American Furniture, 1620 – 1840
Architectural Book Pub., 1965. 256pp. $12.50. This book contains 150 photographs of fine pieces and settings, with fifty measured drawings of furniture masterpieces from leading museums. The drawings are accompanied by photographic views and by the author's commentary. One hundred additional photographs show other pieces that are related to those presented in the drawings. Index.

MARGON, LESTER
Masterpieces of European Furniture
Architectural Book Pub., 1968. 288pp. $14.00. A compendium with photographs, measured drawings, and descriptive commentary of European furniture from 1300 to 1840. There are 137 photographs and fifty-nine drawings. The book is a companion piece to the author's "Masterpieces of American Furniture." Index.

MICHAEL, GEORGE
The Treasury of New England Antiques
Hawthorn, 1969. 210pp. $7.95. A guide to New England antiques. Mr. Michael discusses the best values to look for, clues for distinguishing authentic items from imitations, characteristics of different periods, and methods of restoring antiques. He also explores the many factors that have contributed to the recent rise in the popularity of antiques. Illustrated with photographs. Index.

MILLER, EDGAR G.
American Antique Furniture
Dover, 1966. 1,106pp. Two volume set. Paper $7.50. A two volume reprint of the 1937 edition, these volumes are organized around a collection of 2,115 illustrations, arranged in chronological order in chapters on the various kinds of furniture. Index.

MONTGOMERY, CHARLES F.
American Furniture: The Federal Period
Viking, 1966. 497pp. $25.00. In five chapters and

twenty essays, the author introduces Federal furniture with emphasis on the way it was made and used. 491 pieces are illustrated and complete descriptions are given. Illustrated. Bibliography. Index.

MOODY, ELLA
Modern Furniture
Dutton, 1966. 160pp. Paper $1.95. Miss Moody traces the development of furniture design from the time of William Morris to the present day. More than 150 photographs provide a pictorial anthology of some of the best of the world's furniture. Bibliography.

NUTTING, WALLACE
Furniture of the Pilgrim Century (Of American Origin) 1620–1720
Dover, 1965. 776pp. Two volume set. Paper $5.50. An extensive coverage of American furniture in an unabridged two volume reprint of the revised enlarged edition of the 1924 study. More than 1,500 photographs and drawings are keyed to descriptive captions in the text that give details about the owner, design, dimensions, history, and other data about the furniture.

NUTTING, WALLACE
Furniture Treasury: Volumes I and II
Macmillan, 1971. Unpaged. $17.50. Originally published in two volumes in 1928 and now reissued in a one volume unabridged edition. The volume includes 5,000 examples, illustrated by photographs and brief descriptive comments, of furniture and utensils, mostly of American origin, dating approximately from 1650 to the end of the Empire period. The contents include ninety generic and specific furniture or accessory types. Index.

NUTTING, WALLACE
Furniture Treasury: Volume III
Macmillan, 1969. 548pp. $12.95. Originally published in 1933 and now reissued, this is a record of designers, details of design and structure, with lists of clock makers in America. The designs are mostly of American origin and there are 1,000 illustrations. The author describes in the text how to collect antique furniture, how to recognize various styles, how to appreciate the special qualities of antiques, how to detect the genuine, and how to repair and restore antiques. Glossary of Furniture Terms. Index.

ORMSBEE, THOMAS H.
Field Guide to Early American Furniture
Little, Brown, 1951. 352pp. $5.95. Paper—Bantam, 1961. 352pp. $1.95. An illustrated dictionary of early American furniture containing information on upholstery, hardware, and woods, as well as style and construction.

ORMSBEE, THOMAS HAMILTON
The Story of American Furniture
Pyramid, 1966. 271pp. Paper $ .95. The classic guide to antique American furniture first published in 1934 and now reissued. It includes over 100 illustrations. Glossary. Index.

RANDALL, RICHARD H.
American Furniture in the Museum of Fine Arts – Boston
October House, 1965. 276pp. Boxed: $25.00. A catalogue of the collection of American furniture in the Boston Museum of Fine Arts. Included are 218 plates showing important pieces and descriptive text. Index.

SCHUTZE, ROLF
Making Modern Furniture
Reinhold, 1967. 95pp. $4.50. The well-known Danish sculptor and woodworking teacher tells how to construct and assemble chairs, desks, shelves and bookcases of modern design. Precise drawings and instructions for making, veneering, and finishing the pieces are included. In addition there are helpful hints for variations on the designs and creations of new ones. Illustrated.

STAFFORD, MAUREEN and ROBERT KEITH MIDDLEMAS
British Furniture Through the Ages
Putnam, 1966. 112pp. $5.00. In 570 drawings, this book displays the entire course of development of British furniture. The drawings express the growth and change of man and society through the different styles. A short caption relates every illustration to its type and context. Index.

WILLIAMS, HENRY LIONEL
Country Furniture of Early America
A. S. Barnes, 1964. 138pp. $3.95. A reference work of furniture put together by the skilled craftsmen of early America for everyday use. It contains photos, drawings, and precise information on the types of wood, construction of joints, and finishes that the craftsman must have to reproduce the pieces described. Illustrated. Index.

WILSON, JOSE and ARTHUR LEAMAN
Decorating Defined: A Dictionary of Decoration and Design
Simon & Schuster, 1970. 191pp. $9.95. A wide range of furniture and furnishings, from antique to contemporary designs, is included in 1,400 definitions and 450 illustrations. Bibliography.

Decorative Arts and Design

ALEXANDER, MARY JEAN
Handbook of Decorative Design and Ornament
Tudor, 1965. 128pp. $4.95. Paper $1.95. A book of over 1,000 representative motifs and patterns of all periods.

ANDERSON, DONALD M.
Elements of Design
Holt, Rinehart, 1966. 218pp. Paper $9.00. The material in this book is arranged to help an instructor prepare a foundation college-level course in two-dimensional graphic representation and to help a student understand it. Among the topics discussed are: motivation in design, perception and space illusion, sources of design, the natural environment, the function of texture, fundamentals of color, motion, and color in action. Illustrated. Glossary. Index.

AUDSLEY, W. and G. AUDSLEY
Designs and Patterns from Historic Ornament
Dover, 1968. 14pp. & 60 plates. Paper $2.50. This is an unabridged republication of the 1882 edition of a rendering of ornaments and designs. The sixty plates contain over 250 line drawings derived from architectural motifs, textile designs, patterns from ceramics, etc. A brief text specifies sources for many of the designs and captions identify national origin.

BIRREN, FABER
Color: A Survey in Words and Pictures
University Books, 1966. 223pp. $8.50. The story and mysteries of color through many fields of learning: history, anthropology, archaeology, religion, mythology, art, painting, sculpture, architecture, science, and natural history. Illustrated. Index.

BOGER, LOUISE ADE and H. BATTERSON BOGER
The Dictionary of Antiques and the Decorative Arts
Scribner, 1967. 662pp. $17.50. This is an enlarged edition of the 1957 publication. It is a complete reference book of all the decorative arts and contains over 5,500 entries. Also included are 750 drawings and 182 photographs of all styles, periods, terms, methods, processes, and craftsmen in American, European, and Oriental decorative art.

BUTSCH, ALBERT FIDELIS
Handbook of Renaissance Ornament: 1290 Designs From Decorated Books
Dover, 1969. 231pp. Paper $4.50. Originally published in 1878 and 1880 and reissued with a new Introduction and captions by Alfred Werner. The 226 plates reproduce material including ornamental initials, title pages, and other decorations. Indices of Printers, Artists, and Cities of Origin.

CHAMBERS, WILLIAM
Designs of Chinese Buildings, Furniture, Dresses, Machines and Utensils
Blom, 1968. 19pp. & plates. $29.50. Originally published in London in 1757, and now reissued in a facsimile edition, the major portion of this book is given to twenty-one plates engraved by William Chambers from "the originals drawn in China." Descriptions of the temples, buildings, gardens, and houses of China are included.

CHEVREUL, M.E.
The Principles of Harmony and Contrast of Colors
Reinhold, 1967. 256pp. $27.50. Originally published in France in 1839, this book of the principles of color is reprinted with an Introduction and explanatory notes by Faber Birren, a leading color authority. Chevreul's principles dominated the schools of Impressionistic art and exerted influence on the later schools, including today's Op artists, and they are basic in color training throughout the world. The volume contains twenty-eight color plates and numerous black-and-white illustrations depicting Chevreul's life and work. Index.

CHIEFFO, CLIFFORD T.
Silk-Screen as a Fine Art
Reinhold, 1967. 120pp. $10.95. Step-by-step, this book shows the reader the complete process of silk-screen printing for use in the fine arts. All forms of stencil making techniques are explored. More than 120 photographs as well as detailed diagrams illustrate the equipment and techniques. Glossary. Bibliography. Index.

CIRKER, HAYWARD and BLANCHE CIRKER
Monograms and Alphabetic Devices
Dover, 1970. 227pp. Paper $4.00. An unabridged republication of four volumes of monograms and allied devices published between 1830 and 1881. Over 2,500 monogrammatic and alphabetic designs are displayed in the plates. Index of Monograms and Ciphers. Index of Names and Devices.

CONNELL, PATRICK – Editor
Greek Ornament
Dover, 1968. 127pp. $4.95. A visual survey of the styles and forms of Greek ornament. Drawings illustrate the motifs; photographs show their application; outline diagrams make clear the traditional shapes; and an Introduction surveys the origins and development of Greek ornament over some 5,000 years. Select Bibliography.

COOK AND COMPANY
Illustrated Catalogue of Carriages
Dover, 1970. 226pp. Paper $4.00. An unabridged, unaltered republication of the original 1860 edition of an advertising catalogue showing 104 basic carriage types manufactured by a New Haven, Connecticut, carriage maker. All carriages are illustrated and described. Also included in the volume are 101 other early advertisements for such wares as fruit baskets, hardware, and clothing.

CROY, PETER
Graphic Design and Reproduction Techniques
Hastings, 1968. 282pp. $14.00. A reference source on all stages of the transformation of design to the printed page. Various printing processes are detailed from letterpress through offset-lithography and photogravure. Sections on craft printing and silk screen,

the techniques of reproducing illustrations, information on the raw materials of the printing process, and the tools of the printer are presented. Typography, layout, graphic design, photography are all included. Illustrated. Index.

DE VRIES, JAN VREDEMAN
Perspective
Dover, 1968. 86pp. Paper $2.25. An unabridged republication of the work first published in 1604 and 1605. A new Introduction hs been written by Adolf K. Placzek for this collection of engravings by the sixteenth century architect-painter-engraver which demonstrate his theories of perspective and include exteriors of architectural structures, Gothic interiors, gardens, townscapes and views into domes or vaults and down many-tiered stairwells.

DREYFUSS, HENRY
Designing for People
Grossman, 1967. 230pp. Paper $3.95. The author has designed for the theatre as well as for Bell Telephone, RCA Radio, and Lockheed. His theories of engineering, human anatomy, the psychological effect of color and aesthetics, and how he has used these theories "to make people comfortable" are herewith elucidated. Illustrated.

ENCISO, JORGE
Design Motifs of Ancient Mexico
Dover, 1953. 153pp. Paper $2.50. Originally published in 1947, this is a collection of pictorial material for artists, designers, and handicraft workers. 766 illustrations of primitive designs derived from early Mexican cultures.

FINCH, CHRISTOPHER
Pop Art: Object and Image
Dutton, 1968. 168pp. Paper $2.45. An account of the way in which modern artists have drawn increasingly on their everyday environments. The author discusses the context in which this phenomenon has occurred and the work of such precursors as Marcel Duchamp. Illustrated with reproductions of the work of Jim Dine, Robert Rauschenberg, Andy Warhol, and other modern artists. Index.

GARRAHER, RONALD G. and JACQUELINE B. THURSTON
Optical Illusions and the Visual Arts
Reinhold, 1966. 127pp. $7.50. A creative guide for artists, designers, photographers, teachers and students. This book analyzes the nature of perceptual effects and optical illusions and illustrates their role in photography, fine and graphic art.

HALE, WILLIAM HARLAN and ROBERT PAYNE and THE EDITORS of HORIZON MAGAZINE
The Horizon Book of Ancient Rome
Doubleday, 1966. 415pp. $18.95. This book presents the history and heritage of the Roman epoch in 350 illustrations and text. The book includes a chronology of Roman history, many maps, illustrations of the lands, architecture, weapons, dress, furnishings, jewelry. Excerpts from contemporary philosophers, poets, historians, and playwrights. Index.

HAYETT, WILLIAM
Display and Exhibit Handbook
Reinhold, 1967. Unpaged. $7.50. This is a handbook of practical ideas and specific ways to plan an exhibit within a realistic budget and timetable. Over 100 illustrations give a clear idea for the use of posters, signs, display panels, table-top exhibits, island arrangements and storage plus methods of construction and directions for finishing exhibits and displays. Also included are a Glossary of Display, Graphics, and Exhibit Terminology.

HENRION, F. H. K. and ALAN PARKIN
Design Coordination and Corporate Image
Reinhold, 1967. 208pp. $25.00. Design coordination is the concerted and related planning of all activities of a corporation's top management which can be seen in buildings, products, packaging, transport, stationery, publications, signs, uniforms, and all kinds of promotion. The authors show twenty-seven examples of successful design coordination drawn from nine countries ranging from designs for international corporations to designs for British road signs and the Tokyo Olympics. Illustrated.

HILLIER, BEVIS
Art Deco
Dutton, 1968. 168pp. Paper $2.45. An exploration of the origins and scope of the 1920's and 1930's art style of Odeon architecture of liner and hotel interiors, of suburbia and the mass-produced arts. The way in which the moods of two decades affected the arts is illustrated in both text and in the 120 illustrations. The author covers silver, jewelry, ceramics, glass, textiles, metalwork, architecture, and the revival of Art Deco today. Index.

HOLLIS, H. F.
Teach Yourself Perspective Drawing
Dover, 1955. 198pp. Paper $2.50. An introduction to the art of perspective drawing. There are chapters on theory and geometrical constructions, practical advice to the professional designer and draughtsman who must use quick and efficient methods, and information for the artist who must have an understanding of perspective. Illustrated with diagrams.

ITTEN, JOHANNES
Design and Form: The Basic Course at the Bauhaus
Reinhold, 1963. 190pp. $13.95. The first complete description of one of the landmarks of modern art education, written by the man who organized the course at the invitation of Walter Gropius, in 1919, at Weimar, Germany. Itten describes his methods of encouraging the students to creative use of light

and dark, material and texture, rhythm, expressive and subjective forms, and color. Nearly 200 illustrations with detailed descriptions. Translation by John Maass. Index.

JACOBS, FLORA GILL
A History of Doll's Houses
Scribner, 1965. 342pp. $15.00. A revised edition of the 1963 history, this volume includes chapters on doll's houses and furnishings of all countries over the last four hundred years. Among the noted doll's houses shown are those in the collections of Colleen Moore, Helena Rubenstein, and Queen Mary of England. The volume is illustrated in color and black-and-white and may be of value to the set designer.

JOHNSON, PAULINE
Creating with Paper: Basic Forms and Variations
University of Washington, 1958. 206pp. $7.95. A complete guide to the creation of imaginative objects with paper. Chapters on tools, cutting techniques, curling, bending, folding, scoring, screen models, geometrics, moving forms, planes, and fastening. Illustrated.

JOHNSTON, RANDOLPH WARDELL
The Book of Country Crafts
A. S. Barnes, 1964. 211pp. $3.95. A reference guide to projects made with wood, clay, metals and stone. The author provides formulae and processes based on research and experiment. A chapter on color details the making of dyes and paints with simple materials. Illustrated. Index.

KETTELL, RUSSELL HAWKES – Editor
Early American Rooms: 1650–1858
Dover, 1967. 200pp. Paper $4.50. This is a republication of the 1937 edition. Twelve rooms, each representative of a significant period in America's past, are illustrated and described in articles written by a team of twenty authorities. Illustrated with plans and elevations, line drawings, and colored drawings. Index.

KORNFIELD, ALBERT
Doubleday Book of Interior Decorating
Doubleday, 1965. 360pp. $14.95. A comprehensive volume of decorating knowledge. The book contains a 100 page encyclopedia of furniture identification and a forty-four page do-it-yourself guide for results with minimal cost and labor. Illustrated. Index.

LEHNER, ERNST
Alphabets and Ornaments
Dover, 1968. 256pp. Paper $3.50. Originally published in 1952 and now reissued, this book is divided into eight sections which show examples of alphabets and ornaments from many periods of history. Each section is introduced with notes on uses, history and other backgrounds. Over 750 illustrations are included. Bibliography.

LUCKIESH, M.
Visual Illusions: Their Causes, Characteristics and Applications
Dover, 1968. 252pp. Paper $2.00. Originally published in 1922 and now reissued with a new Introduction by W. H. Ittelson, this is an introduction to visual illusions. The author arranges virtually all types known in categories with one or two examples to illustrate each. Chapters suggest practical applications for illusions in the fields of painting, architecture, interior decoration, and lighting. Illustrated with drawings and photographs. Index.

McCLINTON, KATHARINE MORRISON
Collecting American Victorian Antiques
Scribners, 1900. 288pp. $8.95. A guide for the collector of American Victorian furniture, decorative accessories, glass, pottery and porcelain, silver and silver plate. Illustrated with over 200 photographs. Index.

MEYER, FRANZ SALES
Handbook of Ornament
Dover, 1957. 548pp. Paper $2.75. Reproducing art motifs from classic times through the nineteenth century, this book gives artists, designers, set builders, and costumers more than 3,300 royalty-free designs, in 300 full-page plates.

NAYLOR, GILLIAN
The Bauhaus
Dutton, 1968. 159pp. Paper $1.95. A history of the Bauhaus movement in design education. Illustrated. List of Sources. Index.

NELMS, HENNING
Thinking with a Pencil
Barnes & Noble, 1966. 347pp. Paper $1.95. This reprint of the 1964 edition is a self-instruction book in drawing for those who wish to use drawing as a tool for thought and communication but lack knowledge of how to draw. There are 692 illustrations of easy ways to make and use drawings. Bibliography. Index.

NESBITT, ALEXANDER – Editor
Decorative Initials and Alphabets
Dover, 1959. Unpaged. Paper $2.75. Included in this volume are 123 full page plates. Ninety-one alphabets in varying styles are illustrated as the author show manuscript initials from the eighth to the fifteenth centuries and initials from printed books from the fifteenth to the eighteenth centuries. Victorian letters and types and twentieth century alphabets are also illustrated. Each section has an historical introduction and each plate has a descriptive caption. Bibliography.

NESBITT, ALEXANDER
The History and Technique of Lettering
Dover, 1957. 300pp. Paper $2.50. A republication

of the 1950 study, this is a history of the development of letter forms from the point of view of the artist or typographer. A practical course in lettering is a special feature of the book. The author provides illustrations of eighty-nine complete alphabets and more than 165 additional specimens of letters. Bibliography. Index.

NOGUCHI, ISAMU
A Sculptor's World
Harper & Row, 1968. 259pp. $20.00. This autobiography of the sculptor takes him from his youth as Brancusi's stonecutter in Paris to his position of influence in today's art world. The book includes photographs of his theatre designs as well as his sculpture, architecture, and designs for gardens and playgrounds. Illustrated. Index.

PEGLER, MARTIN
The Dictionary of Interior Design
Crown, 1966. 500pp. $7.50. In over 3,500 entries and 2,500 illustrations every element of design for all periods is covered in this reference work on decoration. Furniture, tapestries, architecture, tools, foreign language terms in current use in America, and room layouts are all included in alphabetical order.

PERGOLESI, MICHELANGELO
Classical Ornament of the Eighteenth Century
Dover, 1970. 99pp. Paper $4.00. A collection of sixty-seven plates containing 435 designs by the eighteenth century engraving artist. The designs are authentic examples of neo-classicism. An Introduction has been provided by Edward A. Maser.

SARGENT, WALTER
The Enjoyment and Use of Color
Dover, 1964. 274pp. Paper $2.50. The author explains the relation between colors in nature and in art. He points out facts about color values, intensities, effects of high and low illumination, complimentary colors, and color harmonies. This republication of the 1923 guide includes seven full page color plates among its thirty-six illustrations. Index.

SAVAGE, GEORGE
A Concise History of Interior Decoration
Grosset & Dunlap, 1966. 285pp. Paper $3.95. This is a history of interior decoration in Europe and America. Mr. Savage discusses the origins and proper settings of the decorative arts from the first century A. D. to the present day. He explains how styles of furniture and accessories changed and developed in the light of technical innovations, economic pressures, or social and religious opinions. Illustrated with over 200 gravure photographs. Bibliography. Index.

SCHAEFER, HERWIN
Nineteenth Century Modern: The Functional Tradition in Victorian Design
Praeger, 1970. 211pp. $17.50. This is a study of design in the nineteenth century. Among the objects studied are instruments and machines, consumer goods, metalware, ceramics and glass, means of transportation, and furniture. Illustrated with 289 photographs and drawings. Bibliography. List of Sources of Objects. Index.

SCHEIDIG, WALTHER
Weimar Crafts of the Bauhaus
Reinhold, 1967. 150pp. $16.50. An account of the organization of the Bauhaus during 1919–1923 and of the Bauhaus theory of design which emphasized utility and beauty of form. The author has included ninety illustrations, forty-seven of them in color. Bibliography. Index of Names.

SCHWARZ, HANS
Colour for the Artist
Watson–Guptill, 1968. 104pp. $2.50. The author discusses the problems of color in painting for the amateur artist and the student. Its main aim is to help the beginner with the problems both of color and technique. There are chapters on optics, and the appearance of color, the theory of primary and secondary colors, how color can be used, and the permanence of different pigment. Illustrated in color and black-and-white with diagrams, photographs and reproductions of art work. Index.

SCOTT, ROBERT GILLAM
Design Fundamentals
McGraw–Hill, 1951, 199pp. $13.25. The author treats design as a fundamental discipline. Among the subjects discussed in this study are contrast, figure organization, movement and balance, proportion and rhythm, color, depth and plastic illusion, three-dimensional organization, light and movement, and design in action. Illustrated with diagrams, drawings, and photographs. Index.

SNEUM, GUNNAR
Teaching Design and Form
Reinhold, 1965. 125pp. $8.95. This book concentrates on the instructional materials that come into question when pupils have progressed beyond the early stages and have reached the point where the emphasis is on experimentation with materials and spontaneous expression. The exercises include experiments in narrative drawing, decoration, design and form, and lettering and studies in the design principles of symmetry, rhythm, harmony, texture, color and tone. Subject and Illustration Indices.

SPELTZ, ALEXANDER
The Styles of Ornament
Dover, 1959. 647pp. Paper $3.75. A collection of 3,765 illustrations representing the entire range of ornament from pre-historic times to the middle of the nineteenth century. The different uses of ornaments are shown.

STOUDT, JOHN JOSEPH
Early Pennsylvania Arts and Crafts
A. S. Barnes, 1964. 364pp. $12.00. A definitive history of all the arts and crafts of early Pennsylvania. The author includes sections on architecture, furniture, fine arts, painting on glass, crafts, and the art of illumination. Illustrated. Index.

TOLLER, JANE
Papier–Mache in Great Britain and America
Branford, 1962. 126pp. $8.25. A general history of papier-mache in the eighteenth and nineteenth centuries. The author considers the work of the foremost manufacturers in Birmingham, Oxford, London, and Wolverhampton, considers the various styles of decoration, and illustrates the major types of articles made in papier-mache. Advice to collectors is provided. Illustrated. Index.

VERONESI, GIULIA
Style and Design: 1909 – 1929
Braziller, 1968. 372pp. $15.00. Originally published in Italy in 1925, and now reissued, this is a study of the decorative arts during a period which saw the flowering of decoration for its own sake. The author traces the history of the conflicting trends and illustrates her survey with 256 plates. Glossary and Who's Who. Index.

WHITE, GWEN
Perspective. A Guide for Artists, Architects, and Designers
Watson–Guptill, 1968. 80pp. $8.50. This book demonstrates how an effect of perspective is achieved and the geometrical or optical causes which bring it about. Individual sections of the book are on: Parallel and Angular Perspective, Oblique Perspective, Shadows, and Reflections. These are illustrated by such examples as a stage set, a spiral staircase, and a film set. A particular feature of the book is the use of semi-opaque paper, whereby Miss White shows simultaneously a succession of perspective drawings and the skeleton of lines of which the perspective itself is composed. 300 drawings and diagrams are included.

WILSON, EVERETT B.
America's Vanishing Folkways
A. S. Barnes, 1965. 224pp. $4.95. This book describes and pictures a wide range of customs and manners of our forebears. Touched upon are such diversified topics as dress, homes, religion, foods, laws, and forms of punishment. Illustrated with photographs and engravings from contemporary publications of the 1870's, 1880's, and 1890's.

WITZLEBEN, ELISABETH VON
Stained Glass in French Cathedrals
Reynal, 1968. 264pp. $45.00. This is a historical survey of the art of glass painting in the great cathedrals of France. The volume includes forty-six Color plates and ninety-six black-and-white plates. Bibliography. Index.

Lighting

BELLMAN, WILLARD F.
Lighting the Stage: Art and Practice
Chandler, 1967. 348pp. $15.00. This text is intended for the serious student of theatre lighting who wishes to gain a complete understanding of the tools, technology, and artistic considerations of that art. The author covers not only the latest technical developments in stage lighting but also the practical design. Bibliography. Index.

BENTHAM, FREDERICK
The Art of Stage Lighting
Taplinger, 1969. 447pp. $14.95. The author's object is to make stage lighting not only a technical engineering feat but also an art. The book is divided into three major sections: an introduction which covers the general background including theatre architecture and a short history of stage lighting; chapters discussing the technical material used; and five chapters dealing with the actual processes of painting the stage with light. Illustrated with photographs and diagrams. Glossary. Index.

BONGAR, EMMET W.
The Theatre Student: Practical Stage Lighting
Richards Rosen, 1971. 124pp. $5.97. The author explains the reasons for use of a proper system of lighting for the stage and provides basic lighting concepts. Among the subjects are: what equipment to use, where to get it, how to use it, and how to make it. Illustrated with drawings and photographs. Appendices. Bibliography.

FUCHS, THEODORE
Home-Built Lighting Equipment for the Small Stage
Samuel French, 1939. 39pp. Paper and Spiral bound $3.50. A guide for the amateur lighting technician in the construction of all the necessary equipment for lighting the stage. Detailed fold-out charts, in accurate scale, illustrate each lighting unit. Included are a list of lighting construction materials and a list of sources of supply.

FUCHS, THEODORE
Stage Lighting
Blom, 1963. 495pp. $15.00. First published in 1929 and now reprinted, this book has become a classic in its field and remains an invaluable aid to the lighting designer despite the changes in the instrumentation and techniques of lighting that have evolved since it first appeared. The book studies the history of stage lighting, electricity, light, color, equipment, home-built equipment, stage-lighting control, color media, and special effects. Illustrated. Index.

GOFFIN, PETER
Stage Lighting for Amateurs
Coach House Press, 1955. 158pp. $3.50. A comprehensive treatment of the problems of stage lighting. Consideration is given to elementary theory, electrical apparatus, and the practical necessities of the small stage. General procedures for lighting a play and the dramatic qualities of light are studied. Illustrated.

HARTMANN, LOUIS
Theatre Lighting
Drama Book Specialists, 1970. 138pp. $7.50. A reprint of the 1930 manual of the stage switchboard by David Belasco's lighting designer. The book is still considered vital and provoking by many professional lighting designers. Unchanging concepts of form and color are explored. Foreword by David Belasco. Illustrated. Bibliography. Index.

KNAPP, JACK STUART
Lighting the Stage with Homemade Equipment
Walter Baker, 1933. 86pp. $2.25. A book of simplified instructions for the amateur group. Illustrated.

McCANDLESS, STANLEY
A Method of Lighting the Stage
Theatre Arts, 1958. 144pp. $3.25. A revision of the 1932 edition, in this volume the author provides a fixed layout plan which presents a simple formula for lighting an entire production without the necessity of individual scene set-ups and changes. An Appendix provides a schedule of spread and intensity for spotlights.

McCANDLESS, STANLEY
A Syllabus of Stage Lighting
Drama Book Specialists, 1964. 135pp. $8.50. This eleventh edition contains revisions that take cognizance of recent developments. The third chapter on "Controls" has been rewritten and the outline form of the earlier editions has been filled out for easier reading and teaching.

OST, GEOFFREY
Stage Lighting
Barrie & Jenkins, 1957. 96pp. $1.75. Designed for amateur productions with limited budgets, this guide book describes each stage from the lighting plan to the performance. Illustrated. Index.

PARKER, W. OREN and HARVEY K. SMITH
Scene Design and Stage Lighting
See Page 371

PILBROW, RICHARD
Stage Lighting
Reinhold, 1970. 152pp. $10.00. The author divides his text into two sections: "Design" and "Mechanics." He introduces the basic principles of lighting design and discusses in detail the procedures involved in lighting a production. The second part is in the form of a designer's notebook. Line drawings and half-tone illustrations are included. Glossary of Lighting Terms in English, French, and German. List of Suppliers. Bibliography. Index.

RUBIN, JOEL and LELAND H. WATSON
Theatrical Lighting Practice
Theatre Arts, 1954. 142pp. $5.95. A handbook for students and specialists covering indoor productions, proscenium and arena staging, puppet shows, and television. A survey of job opportunities and a directory of manufacturers are included. Illustrated.

COSTUME

General Histories

ALLEN, AGNES
The Story of Clothes
Roy, 1958. 260pp. $4.95. A history of the development of clothing from the era of the caveman to the present day. Illustrated with drawings by Agnes and Jack Allen.

ANTHONY, PEGARET and JANET ARNOLD
Costume: A General Bibliography
Costume Society of the Victoria & Albert Museum, 1966. 49pp. Paper $1.00. A listing of over 400 books and journals dealing with Western costume in its historic aspect. Author, title, publisher, year of publication, and a short resume of the books are given.

BARTON, LUCY
Appreciating Costume
Walter Baker, 1969. 124pp. Paper $2.95. A book that explains the "why" of theatre costumes: what a costume should mean to designer, director, actor and audience. Reference Notes and Bibliographies.

BARTON, LUCY
Historic Costume for the Stage
Walter Baker, 1935. 609pp. $9.95. This is a comprehensive survey of the historic background of costume with precise descriptions of the garments and the manner in which they were made and worn. Approximately 600 separate sketches of costumes from ancient Egypt to the early twentieth century are included. Patterns and instructions on cutting garments are also provided.

BARTON, LUCY and DORIS EDSON
Period Patterns: A Supplement to Historic Costume for the Stage
Walter Baker, 1942. 106pp. Spiral bound $3.25. A book of charts made from surviving costumes, from diagrams in tailor's books, and from paper patterns. The charts illustrate costumes from 1500 A. D. to

the present. Photographs of the construction of costumes are provided. References are given to pages in "Historic Costumes for the Stage" where details of the costumes are to be found.

BENNETT–ENGLAND, RODNEY
Dress Optional: The Revolution in Menswear
Peter Owen, 1967. 240pp. $9.50. An analysis of the developments in menswear through the ages and an examination of the influences at work on modern men's fashions in England. There are chapters on design, manufacture and materials. Top designers such as Hardy Amies, Pierre Cardin, and John Weitz give predictions of fashion's future. Illustrated with photographs and sketches. Index.

BRADLEY, CAROLYN G.
Western World Costume: An Outline History
Appleton, 1954. 451pp. $8.95. Each historical period in this outline is treated as a separate entity, but chapters are arranged under uniform topics so that the reader can trace the evolution of a particular item of dress from period to period. Short historical sketches and chronologies are given, with lists of the significant motifs of each period, major influences, and names of artists whose works influenced and reflected the fashions of the times. Drawings and maps illustrate the volume. Index.

BROBY–JOHANSEN, R.
Body and Clothes
Reinhold, 1968. 236pp. $12.50. The author traces the history of clothing with all it's religious, political, psychological and sexual overtones. He discusses the social and geographical conditions that spawned various styles. Illustrated with contemporary materials throughout.

BROOKE, IRIS
Medieval Theatre Costume
Theatre Arts, 1967. 112pp. $6.95. This is a practical guide to the construction of garments worn in the Middle Ages by various classes and includes the delineation of the actual costumes of the Mystery and Morality plays of the period. Miss Brooke provides scale drawings and diagrams to enable costumers to make garments without patterns and with a maximum of simplicity. Illustrated with a color frontispiece, a sixteen page section of diagrams for measurement, and drawings throughout the volume. Index.

BRUHN, WOLFGANG, and MAX TILKE
A Pictorial History of Costume
Zwemmer, 1955. 274pp. $30.00. A survey of costume of all periods from antiquity to modern times including national costumes in Europe and non-European countries. Illustrated with over 120 plates in color and eighty plates in gravure which represent more than 40,000 figures and details of costumes. Detailed explanations of all illustrations are provided in the text.

COCHRANE, JENNIFER – Editor
National Costume
Macdonald, 1970. 61pp. $1.75. This volume, written for children and published in England, describes the costumes worn by people of the world. It touches on the reasons for wearing a national costume with relation to natural resources and climate. Illustrated with photographs in color. Glossary. Index.

CONTINI, MILA
Fashion from Ancient Egypt to the Present Day
Golden, 1965. 321pp. $8.95. Edited by James Laver, with a Foreword by Emilio Pucci, and an Introduction by Jane Ironside, this volume contains nearly 550 illustrations, almost all in full color, describing the changing story of fashion through the ages. Index.

COOPER, EDMUND J.
Let's Look at Costume
F. Muller, 1965. 64pp. $3.00. Written for children and illustrated by Norma Ost, this book studies costume to see how and why costume began. The author traces the development of garments and fashion through all the major periods of history. Index.

CORSON, RICHARD
Fashions in Eyeglasses
Dufour, 1967. 288pp. $27.50. Mr. Corson traces the history of eyeglasses from the fourteenth through the twentieth century. His account shows how the variations in use and appearance were dictated by fashion and desire for social status as well as by optical considerations. Over 120 period prints and drawings show the manufacture, selling, and wearing of spectacles. Also included are 500 annotated drawings illustrating a representative range of eyeglasses. Index.

CRAIG, HAZEL T.
Clothing: A Comprehensive Study
Lippincott, 1968. 468pp. $7.50. This is a textbook for the high school girl on clothing and fashion. It details the origin and evolution of clothing, fashion and the garment industry, the social and psychological aspects of clothing, selection and care, careers in clothing and textiles, and the construction of clothing. Illustrated. Glossary. Index.

CUNNINGTON, PHILLIS
Costume
A. & C. Black, 1966. 64pp. $3.00. This book tells the story of changing fashions in clothes from the time of Alfred the Great to the present day. There are over 180 illustrations all taken or copied from pictures of the period. Costume collections in British museums are listed. Illustrated. Index.

D'ASSAILLY, GISELE
Ages of Elegance: Five Thousand Years of Fashions and Frivolity
New York Graphic Society, 1968. 251pp. $29.95. This folio sized book follows the historical evolution

of fashion elegance. The text recounts the "inside" story of fashion's foibles and how they reflected the changing attitudes of the day. Five hundred illustrations in color and black-and-white are drawn from period documents and works of art to show how men and women dressed and the mannerisms and attitudes of the day.

DAVENPORT, MILLIA
The Book of Costume
Crown, 1948. 958pp. $14.95. A chronological survey of costume from the ancient Orient to the end of the American Civil War, with a historical summary of each period and an outline of changes in dress. Costume, jewelry, ornament, and coiffure are covered. 3,000 illustrations from contemporary documents are included. A Costume Index lists names and locations of biographies of designers and artists.

EVANS, MARY
Costume Throughout the Ages
Lippincott, 1950. 359pp. $8.95. A third revised edition of the study first published in 1930. The author provides a history of the development of styles in dress, with chapters on the costume of the ancients, on French, English, and American dress throughout history, and on the national costumes of Europe, North Africa, Asia, and the Americas. Illustrated.

FABRE, MAURICE
History of Fashion
Leisure Arts, 1966. 112pp. $6.50. Translated by Joan White, this study details the trends of fashion from ancient times to the present day. Illustrated with drawings and photographs in black-and-white and color.

FAIRCHILD, JOHN
The Fashionable Savages
Doubleday, 1965. 200pp. $4.95. Personal interviews, acute observations and uninhibited opinions covering fashion designers and fashion wearers are all combined in Mr. Fairchild's book. Illustrated. Index.

GARLAND, MADGE
Fashion
Penguin, 1962. 160pp. Paper $1.25. Written for the young reader, this is a study of the growth of the fashion industry from the small Paris shop of Charles Frederick Worth to the vast international industry of today. The work of the designer, buyer, merchandiser, reporter, and illustrator is examined.

GERNSHEIM, ALISON
Fashion and Reality, 1840–1914
Faber & Faber, 1963. 104pp. $13.00. The first costume book illustrated entirely with contemporary photographs, thus enabling the reader to see what well-dressed persons actually wore, as opposed to the ideal images of the fashion-plates. Practically all of the 235 photographs show full-length figures in a wide variety of costumes. The photographers include David Octavius Hill, Lewis Carroll, Rejlander, Silvy, Alice Hughes, and others. Bibliography. Index.

GORSLINE, DOUGLAS
What People Wore: A Visual History of Dress from Ancient Times to Twentieth Century America
Viking, 1952. 266pp. $12.95. An illustrated survey of dress, with 1,800 line drawings and twelve pages in full color. Of special interest is the long section on American dress from mid-nineteenth century—the time when it began to acquire specific national characteristics—to 1925. A historical survey and calendars of events are provided.

GREEN, RUTH M.
The Wearing of Costume
Pitman, 1966. 171pp. $6.50. The changing techniques of wearing clothes are studied in this volume. The author describes the technique of moving in costumes from all periods of history. Illustrated. Index.

HANSEN, HENNY HERALD
Costumes and Styles
Dutton, 1956. 160pp. $8.95. A study of the evolution of fashions from early Egypt to 1954, with 685 examples of historic costumes in color. The similarities within a period and the differences between stylistic periods are analyzed. The illustrations are not exact reproductions, but composites designed to emphasize drape, detail, and style.

HEAD, EDITH and JANE KESNER ARDMORE
The Dress Doctor
See Page 615

HEAD, EDITH
How to Dress for Success
Random House, 1967. 212pp. $4.95. How to look younger, prettier, slimmer, and how to attract men. Miss Head shows how to analyze a woman's figure, cope with its defects and guides the reader in how to shop for and build a personal wardrobe. Illustrated.

HEAL, EDITH
Fashion as a Career
Messner, 1967. 191pp. $3.95. For those interested in a fashion career this book will serve as a guide. The author covers the philosophy, history, and the work of the fashion makers: designers, manufacturers, buyers, editors, copy-writers, columnists, and models. Miss Heal discusses outstanding textbooks and teachers of fashion, and lists established schools. Illustrated. Bibliography. Index.

HILER, HILAIRE and MEYER HILER
Bibliography of Costume
Blom, 1967. 911pp. $18.50. This is a reprint of the 1939 edition, edited by Helen Grant Cushing. About 8,000 books and periodicals dealing with costume and adornment in all languages are cataloged. Full

bibliographic information is given for each book. Each phase of costume is brought out under subject headings.

HILL, MARGOT HAMILTON and PETER A. BUCKNELL
The Evolution of Fashion: Pattern and Cut from 1066 to 1930
Reinhold, 1967. 225pp. $18.50. This is a source book for male and female fashions from 1066 to 1930. Miss Hill has provided fifty-six drawings illustrating the changing trends of dress and Mr. Bucknell has provided a dressmaker's pattern drawn to scale. In addition there is an accompanying text by Mr. Bucknell for each period. Most useful for the theatrical designer are the technical notes on completing the costumes from the scale patterns.

HOLMES, M. R.
Stage Costume and Accessories
Her Majesty's Stationery Office, 1968. 94pp. Paper $2.50. A catalog of the collection in the London Museum. This volume also includes an article on the assembling of the collection and one on the development of theatrical costume. Illustrated with photographs of many of the costumes and accessories.

HUENEFELD, IRENE PENNINGTON
International Directory of Historical Clothing
Scarecrow, 1967. 175pp. $5.50. This volume lists authentic clothing of various periods and countries found in museums, art galleries, historical societies, libraries and churches, located in Canada, the U. S., and Europe. Clothing is categorized by both century and sex. Part I indicates collections in North America and Part II collections in Europe.

IRONSIDE, JANEY
A Fashion Alphabet
Michael Joseph, 1968. 263pp. $9.00. A dictionary of the expressions and terms of reference which are relevant today. Clothes and their outlines are divided into a number of sections with separate treatment of furs, jewelry, dressmaking terms, and other items. Each section is introduced and discussed by Mrs. Ironside. Illustrated with drawings.

KELLY, FRANCIS M. and RUDOLPH SCHWABE
Historic Costume: A Chronicle of Fashion in Western Europe
Blom, 1968. 305pp. $13.75. Originally published in 1929, this study of costume details the cut and proportion of attire and accessories that differentiate one decade from another. It is illustrated with contemporary art work. Bibliography. Glossary. Index.

KNIGHT, DENNIS
Fashion Through the Ages: An Instant Picture Book
Patterson Blick, 1967. 13pp. Paper $1.00. A concise history of costume, written for children, with text and drawings in color by Mr. Knight.

KOHLER, CARL
A History of Costume
Dover, 1963. 594pp. Paper $3.50. This is an unabridged reprint of the 1928 examination of costumes of the world. The author studies costume from the ancient peoples of the Mediterranean lands and of Asia Minor to the eighteenth and nineteenth centuries. Clear, measured patterns are given for costumes from all walks of life.

KOMISARJEVSKY, THEODORE
The Costume of the Theatre
Blom, 1968. 178pp. $12.50. This study of clothing for the stage was first published in 1931 and is now reissued. The author details how costume actually "works" in terms of the total stage spectacle and the creation of character. Illustrated. Index.

KOMISARJEVSKY, THEODORE and LEE SIMONSON
Settings and Costumes of the Modern Stage
See Page 369

KYBALOVA, LUDMILA and OLGA HERBENOVA, MILENA LAMAROVA
The Pictorial Encyclopedia of Fashion
Hamlyn, 1968. 608pp. $10.00. Divided into two parts, the first half of the volume comprises a concise history of fashion from the fourth millennium B. C. to the present day. The second half consists of a detailed glossary of the various garments and accessories which make up fashion. Each of the sections is arranged chronologically. Illustrated with over 1,000 photographs. Foreword by James Laver.

LANGNER, LAWRENCE
The Importance of Wearing Clothes
Hastings, 1959. 349pp. $7.95. An analysis of the relationship between clothes and the life of the human race. Over 300 illustrations show the variety of dress affected by man in all eras.

LAVER, JAMES
The Concise History of Costume and Fashion
Abrams, 1969. 288pp. Paper $3.95. A survey of the history of costume and its relationship to shifting cultural patterns. The illustrations, drawings, paintings, and photographs in color and black-and-white represent the major changes that have occurred from prehistoric times to the 1960's. Bibliography. Index.

LAVER, JAMES
Costume in the Theatre
Hill & Wang, 1964. 223pp. $6.50. Paper $1.95. This volume describes costumes in primitive dance rituals, in Greek and Roman theatre, in Medieval drama, in early ballet and opera, in the Commedia dell'Arte, in Shakespeare's plays, and in ballet from Noverre to Diaghilev. The author was former Keeper of the Victoria and Albert Museum and created the most important theatre collection in existence. Illustrated. Select Bibliography. Index.

LAVER, JAMES
Costume Through the Ages
Simon & Schuster, 1963. 144pp. $5.95. Paper $2.45. This history of costume from the first century A. D. to 1930 includes 120 pages of black-and-white drawings which the author has based on sources contemporary with the styles shown.

LAVER, JAMES
Dress
Murray, 1966. 48pp. $3.95. Mr. Laver's purpose is to elucidate what fashion is by studying that particular department of design in which its influence is most clearly manifest—in clothes. He explains how and why fashions in men's and women's clothes have changed during the past few hundred years. Illustrated.

LAVER, JAMES
Modesty in Dress
Heinemann, 1969. 186pp. $12.50. Mr. Laver offers an answer to the question of why we wear clothes. He maintains that clothes are to affirm one's status or to emphasize one's allure and his study ranges from the loin cloth to the dress suit. Separate chapters are included on military uniforms, dress fetishism, children's dress, and sport clothes. Illustrated from contemporary sources. Bibliography.

LISTER, MARGOT
Costume: An Illustrated Survey from Ancient Times to the 20th Century
Barrie & Jenkins, 1967. 347pp. $12.95. This is a reference work for anyone who has an interest in the changing style of dress. 355 line drawings were made specially for this book and each is accompanied by a description of the costume and its appropriate accessories, hair styles, fabrics and colors. The author is chiefly concerned with costume in England and France and there are examples of ecclesiastical, military, trades people's, laborer's and leisured class dress.

LISTER, MARGOT
Stage Costume
Barrie & Jenkins, 1954. 96pp. $1.75. A survey of costumes and accessories and how they are worn, from Ancient Egypt to the present day, written for the amateur costumer.

PAYNE, BLANCHE
History of Costume: From the Ancient Egyptians to the Twentieth Century
Harper & Row, 1965. 607pp. $20.00. A study of costume in each major period of civilization. Emphasis is on the study and presentation of actual garments as the authentic source of information. The 375 photographs are of contemporary works of art. Also included are 241 line drawings and pattern drafts for thirty costumes. The patterns are reproduced in precise 1/8 scale on graph paper with notes on linings and reinforcements. Bibliography. Index.

PRINGLE, PATRICK
Fashion
Thomas Nelson, 1970. 44pp. Paper $1.25. A study of fashion in women's clothes and why fashions change. Illustrated.

SAINT-LAURENT, CECIL
The History of Ladies Underwear
Michael Joseph, 1968. 222pp. $12.50. This study traces the development and change of fashion in underclothes in relation to morals, sensibility, sex, and practical considerations from Sumerian and Egyptian costumes to the present day. Over 200 black-and-white illustrations and thirty-two pages of color plates show examples from all periods. Bibliography.

SNOOK, BARBARA
Fancy Dress for Children
Batsford, 1969. 96pp. $3.95. Pictures and descriptions of more than 100 costume designs for children. The range is from the traditional (Alice in Wonderland, Pirate, Cowboy, Pierrot) to the unexpected and exotic (Parcel, Seaweed, Rain, Night, Skeleton).

SPENCER, CHARLES
Erte
Crown, 1970. 198pp. $15.95. An assessment of the work of the costume designer, Erte, from 1913 to the present day. His contributions to the French music hall, Broadway, Hollywood, and the great opera houses of the world are described and illustrated in color and black-and-white in over 180 reproductions. Selected Bibliography. Index.

STAVRIDI, MARGARET
The History of Costume: Volume One – The Nineteenth Century
Plays, Inc., 1968. Unpaged. $15.00. The first volume of a four part history. Miss Stavridi covers the fashions of the nineteenth century in the western world in this volume. Faith Jaques has contributed a series of colored illustrations of men's, women's, children's, servant's, and colonial dress.

STAVRIDI, MARGARET
The History of Costume: Volume Two – 1660 – 1800
Plays, Inc., 1968. Unpaged. $15.00. The costumes of the seventeenth and eighteenth centuries are described by Miss Stavridi and illustrated in color by Faith Jaques. The plates and text provide a comprehensive picture of the dress of the working people, the fashionable world, and of children.

STAVRIDI, MARGARET
The History of Costume: Volume Three – 1500 – 1660
Plays, Inc., 1968. Unpaged. $15.00. This volume covers the period in European history when the city states emerged as nations and when the effects of the Renaissance and the Reformation spread across Europe. Twenty color plates by Faith Jaques illustrate national costumes and style changes.

STAVRIDI, MARGARET
The History of Costume: Volume Four – 4 B.C. – 1500 A.D.
Plays, Inc., 1970. Unpaged. $15.00. The last volume in this series shows the origins of European costume and reveals how the barbaric dress of the invaders of Greece became a distinctive Western style through the centuries of the Dark and Middle Ages. Faith Jaques has contributed twenty color plates to illustrate the study.

TAYLOR, BOSWELL – Editor
Picture Reference Book of Costume
Brockhampton Press, 1967. 32pp. Paper $1.50. This is a brief introduction to costume and it provides general background information and material on the subject. There are 335 illustrations which span the time from prehistoric cultures to the modern dress of the astronaut.

TILKE, MAX
Costume Patterns and Designs
Zwemmer, 1967. 120pp. $28.50. A survey of costume patterns and designs of all periods and nations from antiquity to modern times, this is a supplement to "A Pictorial History of Costume" edited by Wolfgang Bruhn and Max Tilke. Illustrations, the majority in a scale of one to ten, show the garments spread out to emphasize their materials and decorations.

TRUMAN, NEVIL
Historic Costuming
Pitman, 1956. 152pp. $6.00. A reference book covering each period from the ancient Greek to 1910. There is a chapter on fashions in armour and an Appendix of drawings showing the evolution of a number of styles in dress.

VOLLAND, VIRGINIA
Designing Woman
Doubleday, 1966. 197pp. $4.95. The designer of costumes for "Two for the Seesaw," "Raisin in the Sun," and "Sunrise at Campobello" discusses such topics as how to enter the field of costuming, how to find a job, unions, techniques of design, and how to handle rehearsals, out of town tryouts, and long runs.

VON BOEHN, MAX
Miniatures and Silhouettes
Blom, 1970. 214pp. $18.50. A supplemental volume to the "Modes and Manners" series. First published in 1928 and now reissued, the volume records the history and technique of miniatures and the application to jewelery, fans, personal belongings, furniture and interior decoration. Illustrated. Index of Artists and Sitters.

VON BOEHN, MAX
Modes and Manners
Blom. 1970. 1,143pp. Two volume set: $47.50. Originally published in 1932 in a four volume edition and now reissued in a two volume set, this is a history of European clothing. The subject treatment is chronological, encompassing the entire range of Continental and English cultures from the decline of the ancient world through the eighteenth century. The text includes social anecdotes with an account of usage and economic and mechanical details. Illustrations reproduce contemporary works of art such as paintings and graphics as well as artifacts.

VON BOEHN, MAX
Modes and Manners of the Nineteenth Century
Blom, 1970. 747pp. Two volume set: $47.50. First published in 1909 in a four volume edition and now reissued in a two volume set, this is a continuation of von Boehn's history and study of modes and manners. Illustrated.

VON BOEHN, MAX
Ornaments
Blom, 1970. 293pp. $18.50. Originally published in 1929 and now reissued, this is a supplemental volume to the "Modes and Manners" series. The volume illustrates and comments on lace, fans, gloves, walking-sticks, parasols and umbrellas, jewelry and trinkets. There are 257 illustrations included.

WALKUP, FAIRFAX PROUDFIT
Dressing the Part: A History of Costume for the Theatre
Appleton, 1966. 423pp. $15.75. Originally published in 1950 and revised for this edition, this is a comprehensive history of costume drom the earliest recorded time in Egypt, Mesopotamia, and Asia Minor, Greece, and Rome through to the twentieth century. Historical data are included and costumes are described and illustrated with diagrams and drawings. Appendices include lists of materials for costumes and lists of plays for each period covered in the text. Bibliography. Index.

WAUGH, NORA
Corsets and Crinolines
Theatre Arts, 1970. 176pp. $11.95. Paper $4.95. Originally published in 1954 and now reissued, this volume shows how the silhouette of women's dress has been in a state of continuous change. Miss Waugh itemizes cycles in the last 400 years and provides structural drawings and patterns. Included are 115 illustrations. Appendices on the repair and manufacture of corsets are included. Glossary of Terms and Materials. Index.

WAUGH, NORA
The Cut of Men's Clothes: 1600 – 1900
Theatre Arts, 1964. 160pp. $11.50. This study traces the evolution in style of men's dress through a sequence of diagrams accurately drawn and scaled down from patterns, many of them rare museum specimens. Quotations from period sources give descriptions of

costumes, comment on fashions, and details of bills. Included in the volume are twenty-nine plates, forty-two cutting diagrams, and twenty-seven tailor's patterns. Index of Artists and Engravers.

WAUGH, NORA
The Cut of Women's Clothes: 1600–1930
Theatre Arts, 1968. 336pp. $21.00. This study of women's clothes is written from the viewpoint that each period in the history of costume has produced its own characteristic line and silhouette, derived from a cut and construction which varies from age to age. Patterns have been selected from actual dresses to show the typical cut of each period. Notes on the production of women's dress with references to early technical books and quotations from period sources are included with numerous illustrations which show the dresses as worn complete with hair styles, jewelry, and decorative accessories. Glossary of Materials. Bibliography. Index.

WILCOX, R. TURNER
The Dictionary of Costume
Scribner, 1969. 406pp. $15.00. More than 3,200 entries pertaining to costume and covering articles of clothing from all over the world and from all periods of history, Accessories, materials, folk costume, high fashion, and specialized dress, tailoring and dressmaking tools and terms, brief biographies of famous figures in the fashion world are all included. Hundreds of drawings accompany the text and illustrate every aspect of the subject. Bibliography.

WILCOX, R. TURNER
The Mode in Costume
Scribner, 1969. 463pp. $10.00. Paper $4.95. This history of clothing and accessories from 3000 BC to the present has been revised and expanded from the original 1942 edition. Descriptive notes and 1,300 drawings of full length figures, accessories, and design motifs are included. Bibliography.

WILCOX, R. TURNER
The Mode in Hats and Headdress
Scribner, 1959. 348pp. $10.00. A revision of the 1945 edition, this is a survey of the changing styles in headwear from ancient Egypt to the present. 198 full page illustrations and detailed line drawings supplement the chapters on hair styles, jewelry, and cosmetics.

WILSON, EUNICE
A History of Shoe Fashions
Pitman, 1969. 334pp. $19.50. This is a study of shoe design in relation to costume. The volume constitutes a history of shoe fashions from pre-Roman Britain to the 1950's in England, with a separate chapter for various types of American shoes. Ten pages of plates plus 220 drawings by the author and by Jay Lloyd clarify the text and illustrate shoe design throughout the ages. Bibliography. Index.

YOUNG, AGATHA BROOKS
Recurring Cycles of Fashion: 1760–1937
Cooper Square, 1966. 216pp. $8.00. Originally published in 1937 and now reprinted, this is a discussion which shows that, when typical annual fashions are arranged chronologically over a long term of years, their changes appear to follow laws of modification and development within an almost unchanging pattern of evolution. The central feature of the volume is a continuous annual series of illustrations of typical costumes worn from 1760 to 1937. Practically all the text is a discussion of these pictures. Index.

ZAIDENBERG, ARTHUR
How to Draw Period Costumes
Abelard, 1966. 64pp. $3.50. Mr. Zaidenberg begins with the basic human figure and in simple steps shows how to draw a proportionate figure alive enough to wear any of the costumes which the young artist may wish to draw. Illustrated.

British Costume

ANONYMOUS
English Historic Costume Painting Book
Winsor & Newton, 1963. 28pp. Paper. Each volume: $1.00. Each volume in this series consists of twelve simple line drawings of costume styles for the major periods in English history. Each volume also includes an explanatory introduction and a chronology of the period. An inserted guide shows the costumes in colors.

No. 1. Saxon Period: 450–1066
No. 2. Norman Period: 1066–1154
No. 3. Henry II–Edward I: 1154–1307
No. 4. Edward II–Henry IV: 1307–1461
No. 5. Edward IV–Mary: 1461–1558
No. 6. Elizabeth and James I: 1558–1625
No. 7. Charles I and the Commonwealth: 1625–1660
No. 8. Charles II–William and Mary: 1660–1702
No. 9. Anne–George II: 1702–1760
No. 10. George III, Part 1: 1760–1789
No. 11. George III, Part 2: 1789–1820
No. 12. George IV–William IV: 1820–1837
No. 13. Victoria, Part 1: 1837–1870
No. 14: Victoria, Part 2: 1870–1901
No. 15. Edward VII–George V: 1901–1914
No. 16. George V–Edward VIII: 1914–1936

BARFOOT, AUDREY I.
Discovering Costume
University of London, 1967. 128pp. $3.25. This is a reprint of the 1959 study of the development of English men's and women's clothing since early Saxon times. There are nearly 300 black-and-white illustrations and four color plates which reveal the pattern of continuity. There is a Glossary of technical terms, a list of books for further reference and a full Index.

BRADFIELD, NANCY
Costume in Detail: Women's Dress 1730 – 1930
Plays, Inc., 1968. 391pp. $16.95. This study of women's dress provides documented drawings and photographs of garments in private collections. The drawings reveal not only the outside of the garment from various views but the inside construction as well. Over 360 full page drawings plus twelve color photographs are included. List of books for further reading. Index.

BROOKE, IRIS
English Children's Costume Since 1775
Barnes & Noble, 1958. 87pp. $3.75. A reprint of the 1930 publication, this is a study of the development of children's dress as a fashion distinct from that of adults from 1775 to 1920. Included are illustrations by the author and an Introduction by James Laver.

BROOKE, IRIS
English Costume in the Age of Elizabeth: The Sixteenth Century
Barnes & Noble, 1963. 89pp. $3.75. A second edition of the 1930 publication which shows drawings of costumes based on manuscript illustrations, ivory effigies, and other sources. Descriptive notes are included.

BROOKE, IRIS
English Costume of the Early Middle Ages: The Tenth to the Thirteenth Centuries
Barnes & Noble, 1964. 86pp. $3.75. A reprint of the 1930 collection of drawings of costumes. The drawings are based on manuscript illustrations and other sources and the volume includes descriptive text and notes on social customs.

BROOKE, IRIS
English Costume of the Eighteenth Century
Barnes & Noble, 1964. 87pp. $3.75. A reprint of the 1931 edition, this volume includes drawings in color and black-and-white by Miss Brooke with text by James Laver.

BROOKE, IRIS
English Costume of the Later Middle Ages: The Fourteenth and Fifteenth Centuries
Barnes & Noble, 1963. 87pp. $3.75. A reprint of the 1930 publication showing costume drawings by Miss Brooke with descriptive text.

BROOKE, IRIS
English Costume of the Nineteenth Century
Barnes & Noble, 1964. 89pp. $3.75. A reprint of the 1930 publication, in this volume Miss Brooke shows the effect of the political and economic revolutions of the nineteenth century. The text is by James Laver.

BROOKE, IRIS
English Costume of the Seventeenth Century
Barnes & Noble, 1964. 89pp. $3.75. A reprint of the 1930 collection of drawings of the Stuart, Commonwealth, and Restoration periods with descriptive text.

BROOKE, IRIS
A History of English Costume
Methuen, 1968. 224pp. $4.50. A reprint of the study first published in 1937, this volume covers the history of dress in England from the earliest times through 1900. The author/illustrator has included a text, four color plates, and nearly 300 line drawings.

BUCK, ANNE M.
Victorian Costume and Costume Accessories
Barrie & Jenkins, 1961. 215pp. $8.95. A study of the changes in fashion during the Victorian period. Men's, women's, and children's dress are considered with period illustrations.

CALTHORP, DION CLAYTON
English Costume: 1066 – 1830
Barnes & Noble, 1963. 463pp. $8.00. A history of the development of English dress from the period of William the Conqueror to the time of George IV. Included are line drawings and sixty-one plates in color.

CLARKE, JOAN
English Costume Through the Ages
English Universities Press, 1966. 178pp. $2.50. A compact summary of the development of English costume from the Anglo-Saxon period to the end of the nineteenth century. Included is a series of test questions for students. Illustrated. Selected Bibliography. Index.

COOKE, PATRICIA GERRARD
English Costume: Its History and Its Design
Gallery Press, 1968. 127pp. $3.50. Miss Cooke describes and illustrates the development of English fashions from Anglo-Saxon times to the 1960's. She shows how the styles of each period have been affected by historical events and by the influence of famous people. The book concludes with a section of practical advice on how to recreate period costumes from easily obtainable materials.

CUNNINGTON, CECIL WILLETT and PHILLIS E. CUNNINGTON
A Dictionary of English Costume: 900 – 1900
A. & C. Black, 1960. 281pp. $8.95. Concise descriptions of all items of costume and the manner of wearing them. The authors have included an extensive glossary of materials and a list of obsolete color names and their modern equivalents. Illustrated.

CUNNINGTON, CECIL WILLETT and PHILLIS E. CUNNINGTON
Handbook of English Costume in the Eighteenth Century
Faber & Faber, 1960. 443pp. $12.95. A long

introductory chapter considers the social background and indicates the direction taken by fashion during the period covered. Illustrations from period sources are provided. Glossary of Materials. List of Illustrative Prices.

CUNNINGTON, CECIL WILLETT and PHILLIS E. CUNNINGTON
Handbook of English Costume in the Nineteenth Century
Plays, Inc., 1970. 617pp. $14.95. Originally published in 1959 and now revised and reissued in a third edition, this volume provides detailed information about all the main garments and accessories worn by men, women, and children in the nineteenth century. Illustrations by Phillis Cunnington, Cecil Everitt, and Catherine Lucas. Glossary of Materials. List of Sources. Index.

CUNNINGTON, CECIL WILLETT and PHILLIS E. CUNNINGTON
Handbook of English Costume in the Seventeenth Century
Faber & Faber, 1966. 222pp. $10.00. Originally published in 1955 and now revised throughout, this volume illustrates the changes in fasions for both sexes throughout the seventeenth century. Illustrated with drawings. Glossary. List of Sources. Index.

CUNNINGTON, CECIL WILLETT and PHILLIS E. CUNNINGTON
Handbook of English Costume in the Sixteenth Century
Faber & Faber, 1970. 244pp. $10.95. Originally published in 1954 and now revised, this is a study of fashion in the period. Detailed commentary on each item of dress and all accessories is provided by the authors. Illustrated with seventy-six line drawings. Index.

CUNNINGTON, CECIL WILLETT and PHILLIS E. CUNNINGTON
Handbook of English Medieval Costume
Plays, Inc., 1969. 210pp. $7.95. Originally published in England in 1952 and now revised and brought up to date, this is an account of English costumes from 800 A. D. to 1500 A. D. Clothes of men and women are illustrated and described in the text. Two new sections on children's costume and working peoples' costume are included. Glossary. Bibliography. Index.

CUNNINGTON, PHILLIS E.
Costumes of the Nineteenth Century
Plays, Inc., 1970. 80pp. $3.95. The author describes the clothes worn by English men, women, and children in the nineteenth century in England. Line drawings and text illustrate and describe not only the main garments but also accessories including hats, shoes, and hairstyles and the make-up worn by the women. An Index is provided.

CUNNINGTON, PHILLIS E.
Costumes of the Seventeenth and Eighteenth Centuries
Plays, Inc., 1970. 120pp. $3.95. The author describes the apparel of English men, women and children. She includes details such as hats and shoes as well as the main garments. Illustrated with line drawings. Index.

CUNNINGTON, PHILLIS E.
Medieval & Tudor Costume
Plays, Inc., 1968. 77pp. $3.95. An account of the clothes worn by the English people from the Norman conquest to the end of the reign of Elizabeth I. It deals with the clothes of working people as well as fashionable clothes, Written for children, the book is fully illustrated with line drawings based on period sources. Index.

CUNNINGTON, PHILLIS E. and ANNE BUCK
Children's Costume in England: 1300–1900
A. & C. Black, 1965. 236pp. $8.95. This account of the dress of children from infancy to the age of sixteen is based on the evidence of period writings and illustrations and on surviving examples of childeren's dress. The authors deal particularly with garments and styles which show how the dress of children has had its own fashionable changes. Index.

CUNNINGTON, PHILLIS E. and CATHERINE LUCAS
Occupational Costume in England from the Eleventh Century to 1914
Barnes & Noble, 1967. 427pp. $12.95. In describing the clothes of working men, the authors show how the garments gradually evolved from a comparative uniformity in Medieval times to the later rich variety related to particular occupations. Illustrated from original English sources. Bibliography. Index.

CUNNINGTON, PHILLIS E. and ALAN MANSFIELD
English Costume for Sports and Outdoor Recreation from the Sixteenth to the Nineteenth Centuries
A. & C. Black, 1969. 388pp. $13.50. This is a source for historically accurate information on costumes for popular sports during almost 400 years in England. The sports include hunting, archery, hawking, cricket, and bathing and they are fully described with references to period writings and illustrations. Included are sixty-four plates and 254 drawings. General Bibliography. Index.

GIBBS–SMITH, CHARLES H.
The Fashionable Lady in the Nineteenth Century
British Information Service, 1960. 184pp. $6.50. Paper $4.50. The author presents a group of fashion plates for each fifth year throughout the century, from 1800 to 1900, and includes both day and evening dresses, corsets, and a small number of artists' impressions for each section. Preceding the 200 illustrations is an Introduction which details the main fashion changes. List of Sources.

HALLS, ZILLAH
Men's Costume: 1580 – 1750
Her Majesty's Stationery Office, 1970. 52pp. Paper $1.50. Illustrated with period portraits, this is an historical introduction to men's dress in England. The illustrations show a series of costume specimens, selected from the London Museum collection, which detail the continous development of style. Bibliography.

HOUSTON, MARY G.
Medieval Costume in England and France
Barnes & Noble, 1950. 228pp. $8.50. An account of the style and construction of dress in the thirteenth, fourteenth, and fifteenth centuries. Included are accounts of royal, ecclesiastical, academic, legal, and civilian fashions with details of embroidery, jewelry, ornaments, and hair dressing. The author has provided eight plates in color and 350 drawings.

KELLY, FRANCIS M.
Shakespearian Costume for Stage and Screen
Theatre Arts, 1970. 123pp. $8.75. Revised by Alan Mansfield from the original 1938 edition, this study supplies information on Shakespearian costume from period documents, both literary and pictorial. Illustrations include eight plates and fifty drawings from the costume collections of the Royal Shakespeare Theatre and the London Museum. Bibliography. Index.

KELLY, F. M. and R. SCHWABE
A Short History of Costume and Armour: Chiefly in England 1066 – 1515
Blom, 1968. 168pp. & plates. $13.75. Originally published in 1931 and now reissued, this is a history of costume and armour, illustrated with contemporary art. Glossary. Bibliography. Index.

LAMBOURNE, LIONEL
Diaghilev
British Arts Council, 1967. 19pp. Paper $ .75. Introduced by Richard Buckle, this catalogue for an exhibition of costume and set designs (chiefly for Diaghilev's ballets) includes six reproductions of the costume designs.

LAVER, JAMES
Dandies
Weidenfeld & Nicolson, 1968. 123pp. $4.50. Mr. Laver offers a study of dandyism as a social phenomenon in the Regency period and since. Illustrated with contemporary photographs and drawings. List of books for further reading. Index.

LINTHICUM, M. CHANNING
Costume in the Drama of Shakespeare and His Contemporaries
See Page 90

MORSE, H. K.
Elizabethan Pageantry
Blom, 1969. 128pp. $15.00. Originally published in 1934 and reissued in a facsimile edition, this is a pictorial survey of costume actually worn by the upper classes from 1560 to 1620. Quotations from contemporary sources complement the illustrations. Glossary. List of Authors and Works Cited. Index to the Illustrations.

OAKES, ALMA and MARGOT HAMILTON HILL
Rural Costume: Its Origin and Development in Western Europe and the British Isles
Reinhold, 1970. 248pp. $12.95. This study illustrates and details the history of the folk costumes, head-dresses, and footwear of all the countries of Western Europe including Switzerland, Holland, and South Germany, as well as England. Illustrated with line drawings. Glossary. Appendices. Bibliography. Index.

SIMPSON, PERCY and C. F. BELL
Designs by Inigo Jones for Masques and Plays at Court
Russell & Russell, 1966. 158pp. $42.50. A descriptive catalog of drawings for scenery and costumes designed by Jones from 1605 to 1640. Fifty-one plates reproduce the designs.

TAYLOR, BOSWELL – Editor
Picture Reference Book of the Elizabethans
Brockhampton, 1965. 32pp. Paper $1.00. This is one of a series of books about the different periods in British history. Several illustrations are shown on each page. Illustrations and text describe and show how people lived, worked, and played during the time of Elizabeth I.

TAYLOR, BOSWELL – Editor
Picture Reference Book of the Early Stuarts: 1603 – 1660
Brockhampton, 1969. 32pp. Paper $1.00. Illustrations and text show and describe how the people lived, worked, and played during the early seventeenth century in Great Britain.

TAYLOR, BOSWELL – Editor
Picture Reference Book of the Later Stuarts: 1661 – 1714
Brockhampton, 1970. 32pp. Paper $1.00. Another in the series of books about the different periods of British history. Illustrations and text show and describe how the people lived, worked and played during the late seventeenth and early eighteenth centuries.

TAYLOR, BOSWELL – Editor
Picture Reference Book of the Middle Ages
Brockhampton, 1967. 32pp. Paper $1.00. Another in the series of volumes describing various periods in the history of England. The 227 illustrations include line drawings by Valerie Bell and reproductions of period material to show the period between 1066 and 1485.

TAYLOR, BOSWELL – Editor
Picture Reference Book of the Saxons, Vikings and Normans
Brockhampton, 1968. 32pp. Paper $1.00. Another in the series of books showing different ages and periods and achievements in British history. The illustrations show how people lived, worked, and amused themselves during the centuries throughout which the Saxons, Vikings, and Normans in turn dominated Great Britain.

TAYLOR, BOSWELL – Editor
Picture Reference Book of the Tudors
Brockhampton, 1967. 32pp. Paper $1.00. This volume in the series shows how people lived, worked, played, and fought in Tudor times. The illustrations are taken from period sources.

TAYLOR, BOSWELL – Editor
Picture Reference Book of the Victorians
Brockhampton, 1965. 32pp. Paper $1.00. The detailed line drawings in this volume have been provided by Leslie Marshall. The volume also includes photographs and reproductions of period material to show how people lived and amused themselves during the period when Queen Victoria was ruler of England.

YARWOOD, DOREEN
English Costume from the Second Century BC to 1967
Batsford, 1967. 302pp. $9.50. This is the third edition of the historical survey of costume. Prefaced by introductory chapters on costume in ancient Egypt, Greece, Rome, and Byzantine, it describes the major stylistic features of each period and presents each article of dress in outline. Illustrated with drawings and photographs of contemporary material. Index.

YARWOOD, DOREEN
Outline of English Costume
Batsford, 1967. 48pp. $3.75. The changing styles in dress and decoration from Norman times to the present day are presented with clarity in the author's almost 300 drawings. Miss Yarwood's text summarizes the distinguishing features of fashions in each age and there are half page plates for each period which illustrate a typical group of figures in an authentic historical setting. Selected Bibliography. Sources of Information on Costume. Index.

ZAIDENBERG, ARTHUR
How to Draw Shakespeare's People
Abelard, 1967. 64pp. $3.50. Taking a representative selection of Shakespeare's plays, Mr. Zaidenberg shows how the main characters can be depicted in various poses and scenes in costumes typical of their era. He demonstrates how the student of Shakespeare can draw his own interpretation of the characters. Among the plays for which Mr. Zaidenberg has drawn sketches are: "Julius Caesar," "Othello," "Romeo and Juliet," and "Macbeth."

European Costume

General

BROOKE, IRIS
Western European Costume and Its Relation to the Theatre. Volume One: Thirteenth to Seventeenth Centuries
Theatre Arts, 1963. 151pp. Paper $2.85. This second edition of the book first published in 1939 describes and illustrates the principal costumes of the period in European countries other than Britain. The author attempts to aid the designer to reconstruct the dress required for plays of the period. Sixteen plates and ninety-five illustrations in the text emphasize the construction of the costume.

BROOKE, IRIS
Western European Costume and Its Relation to the Theatre. Volume Two: Seventeenth to Early Nineteenth Centuries
Theatre Arts, 1966. 144pp. Paper $2.85. A second edition of the book first published in 1940 describes the principal dress of the period in European countries and delineates the costumes used on the contemporary stage. The author presents a brief survey of the staging of the plays of the period and in detail discusses the clothing worn by various classes in the principal countries. Twenty-eight plates and eighty-one drawings are provided. Index to Volumes One and Two.

FOX, LILLA M.
Folk Costume of Western Europe
Plays, Inc., 1969. 64pp. $3.95. A guide to regional costumes of Western Europe with a detailed examination of such features as headdresses and embroidery. Written for children from eight to twelve years old, the volume is illustrated with drawings by the author. Index.

MANN, KATHLEEN
Peasant Costume in Europe
A. & C. Black, 1961. 191pp. $8.50. Examples of typical peasant costumes and accessories from all European countries, with sixteen plates in color and 125 pages of drawings.

WILCOX, R. TURNER
Folk and Festival Costume of the World
Scribners, 1965. 111 plates and text. $7.95. A survey of traditional dress all over the world, ranging in alphabetical order, from Afghanistan to Yugoslavia, from the Amish of Pennsylvania to Zulu of South Africa. The plates illustrate clothes from more than 150 countries and races in detail. Bibliography. Index.

French

BECHTEL, EDWIN DE T.
Jacques Callot
Braziller, 1955. Unpaged $15.00. A collection of 237 reproductions in 100 plates depicting the work of the "father of French etching." The forty-eight pages of descriptive text plus the plates illustrate the characters and costumes, the entertainments and occupations, of seventeenth century France.

HOUSTON, MARY G.
Medieval Costume in England and France
See Page 397

Spanish

ANDERSON, RUTH MATILDA
Costume of Candelario, Salamanca
Hispanic Society of America, 1932. Six plates. $1.50. This is a series of color plates of costumes of the village of Candelario in Spain. The plates are included in a folder with a short introduction and descriptions of the costumes.

ANDERSON, RUTH MATILDA
Costumes Painted by Sorolla in His Provinces of Spain
Hispanic Society of America, 1957. 208pp. $4.00. In 1919 the Spanish artist Joaquin Sorolla y Bastida completed fourteen paintings for the Hispanic Society of America. These paintings presented the peoples of eleven Spanish regions, and a single group of Portuguese. These paintings are shown in black-and-white reproductions in this volume along with preliminary sketches and other material. The author has provided exhaustive descriptions of the costumes and of the regional characteristics of the people depicted. Index.

ANDERSON, RUTH MATILDA
Spanish Costume: Extremadura
Hispanic Society of America, 1951. 334pp. $11.00. The author provides descriptions and illustrations of the costumes of a particular region of Spain: Extremadura on the Portugese/Spanish border.

HISPANIC SOCIETY OF AMERICA
Spain: Costume Details
Hispanic Society of America, 1932. 30 plates. $ .75. This is a set of thirty photographs of Spanish costume and accessories. All of the photographs are from the collection of the Hispanic Society of America. They are enclosed in a set of three envelopes and include ten photographs of women's festival dress of Montehermoso, ten photographs of women's coiffures from various areas, and ten examples of jewelry. All of the photographs are 5''x7''.

Other European Countries

FINIGUERRA, MASO and SIDNEY COLVIN
A Florentine Picture-Chronicle
Blom, 1970. 131pp. & plates. $57.50. First published in 1898 and now reissued, this volume includes ninety-nine drawings by the artist Finiguerra with a critical and descriptive text by Sidney Colvin. The fifteenth century master engraver's drawings show figures from the Bible, from pagan legends, and from secular history and they may be of value to costume or stage designers seeking Renaissance material. The ninety-nine plates are supplemented by 117 illustrations in the text.

GRANGE, R. M. D.
A Short History of the Scottish Dress
Macmillan, 1966. 120pp. $17.00. A short history of Scottish dress from the earliest times. There are eight plates in full color and nearly fifty in monochrome, many of which depict the tartan as worn prior to 1746. Bibliography. Index of Sources.

PETTIGREW, DORA W.
Peasant Costume of the Black Forest
A. & C. Black, 1937. 89pp. $3.75. The author provides illustrations and descriptive commentary on the peasant costumes of the remote valleys and farmsteads of the German Black Forest. Hats and headgear, shoes, and other accesories are described in addition to the main garments. Included are eight color plates and thirty-two pages of drawings.

Other National Costumes

AMBROSE, KAY
Classical Dances and Costumes of India
See Page 320

CORDRY, DONALD and DOROTHY CORDRY
Mexican Indian Costumes
University of Texas, 1968. 373pp. $15.00. This volume approaches the study of Mexican Indian costumes by examining the general history of the costume, the tools and techniques used in the making of the costume, and the nature and variation of the particular garments and accessories and how they are worn. Analyzed in detail are the costumes of some twenty-seven villages and linguistic groups. Illustrating the volume are 276 plates (sixteen in color) and several detailed maps, as well as a number of drawings and diagrams. List of Works Consulted. Index.

EARLE, ALICE MORSE
Two Centuries of Costume in America
Blom, 1968. Two volumes: 864pp. $27.50. Originally published in 1903 and now reissued in a facsimile edi-

tion, Volume One of this two volume set describes the apparel of men, women, and children in the colonies including costume details and accessories. Volume Two covers the period from the middle of the eighteenth century to 1820. Illustrated with ninety-seven full page plates from contemporary sources.

EARLE, ALICE MORSE
Two Centuries of Costume in America
Dover, 1970. Volume One: 338pp. Volume Two: 459pp. Paper. Each volume: $3.75. Originally published in 1903 and now reissued in an unabridged slightly corrected edition. Mrs. Earle has assembled a wealth of precise evidence on clothing and its importance in society in early America from 1620 to 1820. Illustrated with over 350 drawings and reproductions of contemporary paintings. Index.

HOFSINDE, ROBERT
Indian Costumes
Morrow, 1968. 96pp. $2.95. The author describes selected examples of dress from ten representative American Indian tribes. He shows what typical Indian costumes looked like and explains, where possible, how they were made. Illustrated. Index.

McCLELLAN, ELISABETH
Historic Dress in America 1607 – 1870
Blom, 1969. 863pp. $22.50. Originally published as two separate volumes in 1904 and 1910 and now reissued in one volume, this was one of the first books to be published on costume in America. It shows the everyday clothes of the period in over 700 black-and-white illustrations. Glossary. Index.

MINNICH, HELEN BENTON
Japanese Costume and the Makers of Its Elegant Tradition
Tuttle, 1963. 374pp. $19.50. A history of Japanese achievement in the textile and costume arts from legendary times to the present. The study is primarily a history of the kimono and its evolution. There are fifty-three plates in color, 119 in black-and-white, and twelve line drawings. These illustrations include pictures from contemporary sources—scrolls, and woodblock prints—and photographs of kimono masterpieces and representative textiles.

RUBENS, ALFRED
A History of Jewish Costume
Valentine, 1967. 220pp. $10.00. By means of contemporary sources, the author shows how Jewish costume remained distinctive im most parts of the world throughout the ages. He also adopts a new approach to the study of costume in the Bible by reconciling traditional beliefs with modern archaeological discoveries. More than 300 illustrations are included. Bibliography. Glossarial Index.

SCOTT, A.C.
Chinese Costume in Transition
Theatre Arts, 1960. 110pp. Paper $3.25. An illustrated study of costume developments from the old style of the middle of the nineteenth century to the present day. Sketches by the author.

SHAVER, RUTH M.
Kabuki Costume
Tuttle, 1966. 396pp. $22.50. Over 250 illustrations show the attire of the characters of the Kabuki theatre of Japan. 110 of the illustrations are in color. Glossary. Bibliography. Index.

TOKYO DOLL SCHOOL
The World of Japanese Dolls
See Page 342

WARWICK, EDWARD and HENRY C. PITZ, ALEXANDER WYCOFF
Early American Dress: The Colonial and Revolutionary Periods
Blom, 1965. 428pp. $17.50. An examination of dress and the social, economic, and political factors that influenced the changes in styles in the period. Of special importance is the collection of ninety-six full page plates of rarely seen early American art. The value of contemporary art as a guide to the dress of the period is analyzed in full.

WILCOX, R. TURNER
Five Centuries of American Costume
Scribners, 1963. 207pp. $10.00. A comprehensive survey of American dress including a study of the costume of the aboriginal dweller on both American continents. Also provided are discussions of the dress of early explorers and settlers, military dress, children's costume, and everyday wear of all periods. Illustrated with 107 pages of line drawings.

Ancient Dress

HOPE, THOMAS
Costumes of the Greeks and Romans
Dover, 1962. 300pp. Paper $2.50. A reprinting of the book first published in 1812 under the title "Costume of the Ancients." Over 700 illustrations of the costumes and decorations of people from all walks of life have been taken from contemporary sources.

HOUSTON, MARY
Ancient Egyptian, Mesopotamian, and Persian Costume and Decoration
A. & C. Black, 1954. 190pp. $8.50. Originally published in 1920, this second edition of the study of ancient costume includes flat patterns which show the cut of the garments. Bibliography.

HOUSTON, MARY
Ancient Greek, Roman, and Byzantine Costume and Decoration

A. & C. Black, 1947. 182pp. $8.50. Second edition of the book first published in 1931 in which the author illustrates and provides comment on details of costume, textiles, accessories, and hair arrangement of the various ancient eras. Over 200 illustrations are provided. Bibliography.

SAUNDERS, CATHARINE
Costume in Roman Comedy
A. M. S. Press, 1966. 145pp. $9.00. Originally published in 1909 and now reissued, this study gathers all the information that the extant comedies have to offer on costume. Dr. Saunders compares or contrasts this evidence with that afforded by the frescoes and reliefs at Pompeii and elsewhere to describe the costumes of the period. Bibliography.

TAYLOR, BOSWELL – Editor
Picture Reference Book of the Ancient Egyptians
Brockhampton, 1970. 32pp. Paper $1.00. A brief introduction and background material to the lives of the Ancient Egyptians. The volume is almost completely composed of illustrations which show how the people lived, worked, and played.

TAYLOR, BOSWELL – Editor
Picture Reference Book of the Ancient Romans
Brockhampton, 1970. 32pp. Paper $1.00. This volume shows how the Ancient Romans lived and entertained themselves. Profusely illustrated with line drawings and photographs.

Military Dress, Arms and Armour

ASHDOWN, CHARLES HENRY
British and Continental Arms and Armour
Dover, 1970. 348pp. Paper $3.50. An unabridged republication of the 1909 edition, this is a study of arms and armour from the prehistoric period to the beginning of studded and splintered armour about 1355 AD. Included are 455 illustrations in the text and forty-two plates. Index.

ASHDOWN, CHARLES HENRY
European Arms and Armour
Brussel & Brussel, 1967. 384pp. $10.00. This is a study of arms and armour from prehistoric man through the introduction of gunpowder. It includes 450 engravings in the text and forty-two plates from actual examples. Index.

BLACKMORE, HOWARD L.
Arms and Armour
Dutton, 1965. 160pp. Paper $1.95. A brief survey, with illustrations based on contemporary sources, of all types of armour.

BRITISH WAR OFFICE
Dress Regulations for the Army – 1900
Tuttle, 1970. 118pp. & 79 plates. $10.00. Originally published in 1900 and now reissued, this volume illustrates the uniforms, badges, swords, and devices used by all officers of the British Army as published by the British War Office. Illustrated with seventy-nine pages of plates.

BROOKE-LITTLE, JOHN
Knights of the Middle Ages
Walker, 1966. Unpaged. $15.00. Mr. Brooke-Little has provided a commentary on the life, heraldry, and armour of each of twelve notable feudal lords from the reigns of English kings from Richard I to Richard III. John Rollo has provided illustrations in color of each of the twelve knights.

D'AMI, RINALDO D. – Editor
World Uniforms in Colour: Volume I – The European Nations
Patrick Stephens, 1968. 93pp. $5.95. Ceremonial uniforms of the European nations today, illustrated in color with explanatory texts. This volume includes the twenty European nations. Index.

D'AMI, RINALDO D. – Editor
World Uniforms in Color: Volume 2 – The Nations of America, Africa, Asia and Oceania
Patrick Stephens, 1969. 93pp. $5.95. This volume includes the ceremonial uniforms of forty-four nations illustrated in color with explanatory notes. Index.

DEL GIUDICE, ELIO and VITTORIO DEL GIUDICE
Uniformi Militari Italiane: Volume One
Bramante Editions, 1968. Unpaged. $52.50. A survey of Italian military uniforms from 1861 to 1933. Each uniform is described and illustrated in color. The text is in the Italian language. General Index.

DEL GIUDICE, ELIO and VITTORIO DEL GIUDICE
Uniformi Militari Italiane: Volume Two
Bramante Editions, 1968. Unpaged. $40.00. This volume in the survey of Italian military uniforms covers the period from 1934 to the present time. Each uniform is described and illustrated. The text is in the Italian language. General Index.

FFOULKES, CHARLES
The Armourer and His Craft
Blom, 1967. 199pp. $18.50. A reprint of the 1912 publication, this is a study of the actual processes by which armour and accessories were manufactured and worn from the eleventh to the sixteenth century. Each phase of the manufacturing process is described, the question of decoration is discussed, and there is a chapter on the cleaning and maintenance of metal armour. Illustrated. Glossary. List of European Armourers. Index.

FFOULKES, CHARLES and E. C. HOPKINSON
Sword Lance and Bayonet
Arco, 1967. 145pp. $7.50. Originally published in

1938, this second edition is reproduced in facsimile. It is an attempt at a consecutive account of the arms that have come into general and official use since the discarding of armor. Illustrated. Index.

HAKUSEKI, ARAI
The Armour Book in Honcho-Gunkiko
Tuttle, 1964. 132pp. $20.00. Originally published in 1913 and now revised and edited by H. Russell Robinson, the text of this volume is made up of the nine volumes of Hakuseki's large work which dealt with armour and military clothing worn in Japan up to about 1550. Illustrations are taken from the two volumes of woodcuts in the original work with many photographs of the armours preserved today. Additional diagrams and line drawings show detail of armours and their construction. Glossary of technical terms. Bibliography. Index.

HAYWARD, J.F.
European Armour
British Information Services, 1965. Unpaged. Paper $1.95. This is a catalogue of a portion of the armour collection, which dates from the late fifteenth to the early seventeenth century, at the Victoria and Albert Museum, London. Forty plates picture all the elements of armour which are identified and described in the accompanying text.

JISL, LUMIR
Swords of the Samurai: The Spendours of Japanese Sword Furniture
Artia Press, 1967. 62pp. & plates. $5.95. Published in Czechoslovakia, this study of the Japanese sword details the materials, the techniques of manufacture, famous sword masters and schools, the cult of the sword, and the status of the swordsmith. Sixty plates in sepia tone and color show the details of the sword. Glossary of Terms. Bibliography.

KANNIK, PREBEN
Military Uniforms of the World in Color
Macmillan, 1968. 278pp. $4.95. This is an encyclopedia of military uniforms. It contains 128 pages of color illustrations showing more than 500 dress and combat uniforms dating from the sixteenth century to the present. The accompanying text fully describes each uniform and gives the details of origin, development, and variations. Also included are a general history of uniforms and a guide to military terminology. Index.

LATHAM, JOHN WILKINSON
British Military Swords from 1800 to the Present Day
Crown, 1967. 91pp. $5.95. This is a survey and identification of British swords since 1800. Over 100 different sword patterns are described and illustrated in photographs and drawings. Index.

LATHAM, R.J. WILKINSON
British Military Bayonets from 1700 to 1945
Arco, 1969. 94pp. $8.50. This volume is a source of information for the accurate identification of British bayonets over a period of almost 250 years. The author has identified and catalogued 119 bayonet types all of which are illustrated in the photographic plates. Appendices. Glossary. Index.

LAWSON, CECIL C.P.
A History of the Uniforms of the British Army
Kaye & Ward, Volume One: 1962. 213pp. $10.00. Volume Two: 1963. 276pp. $10.00. Volume Three: 1961. 264pp. $10.00. Volume Four: 1966. 202pp. $15.00. Volume Five: 1967. 184pp. $15.00. All branches of the British army are dealt with in text and illustrations from the beginnings through the early nineteenth century. The five volumes each include drawings by the author, Bibliographies, and Indices.

LORD, FRANCIS A. and ARTHUR WISE
Uniforms of the Civil War
A. S. Barnes, 1970. 174pp. $10.00. With text by Dr. Lord and illustrations selected by Mr. Wise, this is a history of the varied uniforms worn by the soldiers of the American Civil War. An Appendix includes the names of suppliers and patents issued to both sides. Illustrated with photographs and drawings. Bibliography. Index.

MANN, JAMES
An Outline of Arms and Armour in England from the Middle Ages to the Civil War
British Information Services, 1966. 44pp. Paper $1.00. This is a reprint of a chapter from "Medieval England" which consists of a brief outline of arms and armour in England illustrated with contemporary art work and photographs of examples. It includes a list of books for reference.

MARTIN, PAUL
Arms and Armour from the Ninth to the Seventeenth Century
Tuttle, 1968. 298pp. $15.00. An illustrated guide to the history of arms and armour. The author describes the history of armour and its accessories from the days of Charlemagne up until the general use of firearms. Illustrated with contemporary drawings, paintings, and photographs of pieces described. Bibliography. Index.

MARTIN, PAUL
European Military Uniforms: A Short History
Spring Books, 1967. 144pp. $7.95. The author studies the development of military costume in Europe to show how each nation in turn introduced a distinctive dress for its fighting men, stemming from such simple motives as the need to distinguish one's own forces from those of the enemy. The illustrations include forty-four pages of color plates—prints, lithographs, and watercolors by contemporary artists. The volume also includes numerous drawings in the text.

MOLLO, JOHN
Uniforms of the Royal Navy During the Napoleonic Wars
Hugh Evelyn, 1965. 43pp. $15.00. This volume provides a series of twenty color plates showing the uniforms worn by officers of the Royal Navy during the years 1793–1815. The illustrations are in the form of silhouettes and textual matter describing the uniforms and their history accompanies the plates.

NORTH, RENE
Military Uniforms: 1686 – 1918
Grosset & Dunlap, 1970. 159pp. $3.95. A condensed history of military dress. Accompanying the text are 240 color illustrations depicting the campaign and dress uniforms of European and American men-at-arms. Glossary. Bibliography. Index.

PETERSON, HAROLD L.
Daggers and Fighting Knives of the Western World from the Stone Age Till 1900
Walker, 1968. 90pp. $7.50. The author introduces his subject by setting it in its historico-geographical context and continues with a full account of Middle Eastern, Asian, and European weapons from prehistory to the end of the nineteenth century. Illustrated with photographs. Selected Bibliography. Index.

PETERSON, HAROLD L.
History of Body Armor
Scribners, 1968. 64pp. $3.50. This guide demonstrates how man has succeeded in making a protective body cover through the centuries. Illustrated by Daniel D. Feaser. Index.

POPE, DUDLEY
Guns from the Invention of Gunpowder to the Twentieth Century
Delacorte, 1965. 256pp. $12.95. The author tells the story of the gun in all its forms. Illustrated in color and black-and-white photographs and with reproductions of contemporary paintings and engravings. Cross section drawings by Max Millar are also included.

RAWSON, P.S.
The Indian Sword
Arco, 1969. 108pp. $8.50. This study attempts to account for the different forms of the Indian sword by a historical survey of their development. Swords of all periods and locales are discussed and illustrated in photographs and sketches. Notes. Bibliography. Index.

ROBINSON, H. RUSSELL
Japanese Arms and Armor
Crown, 1969. 54pp. & plates. $14.95. This is a profusely illustrated volume of Japanese arms and armor with an historical introduction. The arms and armor are illustrated in thirty-nine color and 112 black-and-white plates plus line drawings.

ROBINSON, H. RUSSELL
Oriental Armour
Walker, 1967. 257pp. $12.50. This book presents a general picture of the development of military equipment in the principal countries of the Orient. Emphasis is placed on the origins and their influence over the armour of other cultures. Included are 112 line drawings and thirty-two pages of photographs which show the armour, its decoration, and its defensive qualities. Bibliography. Glossary. Index.

ROBINSON, H. RUSSELL
A Short History of Japanese Armour
British Information Services, 1965. 47pp. Paper $1.00. This history of Japanese armour starts with the protohistoric and Asuka periods of the fourth and fifth centuries AD and describes armour through the Edo period of 1603–1867. Photographs of examples are included. Glossary of Japanese Technical Terms. Select Bibliography.

SMITHERMAN, P.H.
Cavalry Uniforms of the British Army
Plays, Inc. 1970. Unpaged. $15.00. A new edition of the 1963 publication of twenty detailed engravings in color. The drawings and descriptive notes illustrate almost every cavalry regiment in the British Army from 1705 to 1960.

SMITHERMAN, P.H.
Infantry Uniforms of the British Army: 1660 – 1790
Hugh Evelyn, 1965. Unpaged. $15.00. In twenty full color plates, Colonel Smitherman illustrates and describes the development of infantry dress from the Restoration up to the period immediately preceding the Napoleonic Wars.

SMITHERMAN, P.H.
Infantry Uniforms of the British Army: 1790 – 1880
Hugh Evelyn, 1966. Unpaged. $15.00. The twenty full color plates in this volume illustrate the development of British Infantry uniforms from 1790 up to the years immediately preceding the Crimean War.

SMITHERMAN, P.H.
Uniforms of the Royal Artillery: 1716 – 1966
Hugh Evelyn, 1966. Unpaged. $15.00. This volume provides twenty plates in full color of the uniforms of the Royal Artillery during its 250 year history. Accompanying text describes the uniforms and their histories.

SMITHERMAN, P.H.
Uniforms of the Scottish Regiments
Hugh Evelyn, 1963. Unpaged. $15.00. This volume includes twenty color prints of Scottish regiment uniforms from 1730 to 1959. Accompanying text describes the uniforms and their histories.

SMITHERMAN, P.H.
Uniforms of the Yeomanry Regiments: 1783 – 1911

Hugh Evelyn, 1967. Unpaged. $15.00. In this volume, Colonel Smitherman has illustrated the uniforms of twenty of the yeomanry regiments with plates in full color. The plates and descriptive text provide a history of this colorful arm of the British service.

SNODGRASS, A.M.
Arms and Armour of the Greeks
Cornell University, 1967. 151pp. & plates. $6.50. Dr. Snodgrass contends that the superiority of Greek weapons was an important factor in their many military victories. He traces the development of armaments in Greece and discusses the role that military events played in the history of Greece. Sixty black-and-white plates show examples of the armour and military equipment. Index.

STIBBERT, FREDERICK
Civil and Military Clothing in Europe
Blom, 1968. 224pp. $25.00. This book contains 217 engraved plates, based on carefully documented sources, of arms, armour, and costumes. It is an illustration of the development of styles in armour and dress from the first to the eighteenth century.

TILY, JAMES C.
The Uniforms of the United States Navy
Yoseloff, 1964. 338pp. $15.00. This documented study is a history of Naval uniforms from the establishment of the Federal government in 1789 to the present. Major emphasis is placed on the Civil War period when the essential features of the modern uniform emerged. Included are over 400 illustrations in black-and-white. Appendices include Uniform Regulations: 1852 and 1958 and Insignia and Devices of the Civil War. Index.

WAGNER, EDUARD
Cut and Thrust Weapons
Spring Books, 1967. 491pp. $17.50. This comprehensive work records the development of steel weapons of every kind against a background of the times. The use of swords, sabres, and broadswords is documented from artistic and literary sources. An important accompaniment to the text is the author's illustrated supplement depicting the weapons in drawings. Also included are more than 200 plates illustrating the weapons.

WILKINSON, FREDERICK
Battle Dress
Doubleday, 1970. 272pp. $12.95. Subtitled, "A Gallery of Military Style and Ornament," this volume presents some of the most significant and attractive milestones in the evolution of military dress. Illustrated with monochrome and color photographs from England's most important collections. Bibliography. Index.

WILKINSON, FREDERICK
Edged Weapons
Doubleday, 1970. 270pp. $12.95. Mr. Wilkinson traces the story of all the main categories of hand weapons, from neolithic times up to the twentieth century. Illustrated with color and black-and-white photographs. Bibliography. Index.

WILKINSON, FREDERICK
Militaria
Hawthorn, 1969. 256pp. $5.95. This work covers all aspects of militaria: medals and decorations, helmets and headdresses, uniforms, badges, military prints, weapons, and police items. Illustrated profusely with photographs. List of Military Museums. Bibliography. Index.

WILKINSON, FREDERICK
Swords and Daggers
Hawthorn, 1968. 256pp. $5.95. Examples of swords and daggers from all over the world are discussed and illustrated. There are sections on the history, manufacture and care of weapons and, following the text, 150 pages of photographs of weapons. Index.

WILKINSON–LATHAM, ROBERT and CHRISTOPHER WILKINSON–LATHAM
Cavalry Uniforms
Macmillan, 1969. 215pp. $4.95. Illustrations in color by Jack Cassin-Scott with descriptions of the uniforms by the authors. The ninety-six illustrations cover the mounted troops of Britain and the Commonwealth.

WILKINSON–LATHAM, ROBERT and CHRISTOPHER WILKINSON–LATHAM
Infantry Uniforms: Book One
Macmillan, 1970. 199pp. $4.95. Illustrations in color by Jack Cassin-Scott with descriptions of the uniforms by the authors. The uniforms were worn in the period from 1742 to 1855 and include artillery and other supporting troops of Britain and the Commonwealth. Appendices. Select Bibliography. Index.

WILKINSON–LATHAM, ROBERT and CHRISTOPHER WILKINSON–LATHAM
Infantry Uniforms: Book Two
Macmillan, 1970. 227pp. $4.95. Illustrations in color by Jack Cassin-Scott with descriptions of the uniforms by the authors. The authors describe the main features of each uniform and the important historical data on the regiments from 1855 to 1939. Appendices. Select Bibliography. Index.

WISE, ARTHUR
Weapons in the Theatre
See Page 418

ZAIDENBERG, ARTHUR
How to Draw Military and Civilian Uniforms
Abelard–Schuman, 1965. 64pp. $3.50. A collection of sketches of uniforms which illustrate the techniques involved in drawing every type of uniform from ancient Mongolian fighters to the livery of the modern doorman.

Instruction and Pattern Books

ASH, BERYL and ANTHONY DYSON
Introducing Dyeing and Printing
Watson—Guptill, 1970. 119pp. $6.95. In text and more than 200 illustrations, the mechanics of dyeing and printing of cloth are explained. Four principal methods are included and a selection of recipes for dyes is provided. Also included is a list of suppliers. Bibliography. Index.

BARTON, LUCY
Costumes by You: Eight Essays from Experience
Walter Baker, 1940. 92pp. Paper $1.00. A guide for the amateur costume designer with easy to follow diagrams.

BERK, BARBARA
The First Book of Stage Costume and Make-Up
See Page 338

BISHOP, EDNA BRYTE and MARJORIE STOTLER ARCH
The Bishop Method of Clothing Construction
Lippincott, 1966. 284pp. Paper $3.95. This revised edition of the 1959 publication details the Bishop method. It is based on accuracy in preparing, cutting, and marking fabric, cutting to fit, perfection in stitching, pressing, and detail work. Photographs and diagrams illustrate the volume.

BORRETT, EVE
How to Make Hats
Pitman, 1967. 92pp. $3.75. Printed in England, this is a guide to the subject of home millinery. The contents include discussions of equipment, shapes, styles, useful stitches, fabrics, linings, and trimmings. Illustrated. Index.

DOTEN, HAZEL R. and CONSTANCE BOULARD
Costume Drawing
Pitman, 1956. 64pp. Paper $1.25. The authors provide instructions in the technique of drawing costumes with illustrations of every major stylistic period from Ancient Egypt to the fashions of the 1950's.

DOTEN, HAZEL R. and CONSTANCE BOULARD
Fashion Drawing: How to Do It
Harper & Row, 1953. 224pp. $8.50. A revised edition of the manual on drawing the fashion figure. The authors discuss synthetic materials, the changes in styles and techniques, and the history of fashion in the period from 1930 to 1950.

FERNALD, MARY and EILEEN SHENTON
Costume Design and Making: A Practical Handbook
Theatre Arts, 1967. 159pp. $4.75. The second edition of the volume originally printed in 1937, this is an introduction to and diagrams of English costume from Anglo-Saxon times to the end of the nineteenth century. The diagrams have been drawn to scale from working patterns. The authors provide information on materials, coloring, costume plotting, and lighting.

GEEN, MICHAEL
Theatrical Costume and the Amateur Stage
Arco, 1968. 150pp. $6.50. The author provides a simple approach to the making, altering, and storing of theatrical costumes, both period and modern. There are details on measuring, cutting and adjusting, as well as a glossary of materials and their uses. A survey of period costumes from the Greeks to the present day is also included. Drawings by William Langstaffe. Index.

HOLLEN, NORMA R.
Flat Pattern Methods
Burgess, 1965. 167pp. Spiral bound $5.00. Originally published in 1961, this second edition has been revised and expanded. It is a guidebook for making patterns based on the use of a simple pattern which is changed or modified by specific directions to create a pattern for a chosen design. The volume is illustrated with line drawings and photographs. A series of ¼ and ½ scale paterns are included.

JACKSON, SHEILA
Simple Stage Costumes and How to Make Them
Watson—Guptill, 1968. 96pp. $5.95. This is a guide to the designing and making of stage costumes using readily available and adaptable materials. Full practical instructions for achieving effects in the simplest way, with each step covered in text and illustrations. The author describes and illustrates patterns and decorations for all types of drama from Greek to modern. A section is devoted to actual patterns drawn to scale. Illustrated with diagrams, drawings, and photographs. Lists of Suppliers. Index.

JOHNSTON, MEDA PARKER and GLEN KAUFMAN
Design on Fabrics
Reinhold, 1967. 156pp. $12.50. This is a comprehensive guide to the principles and techniques of fabric decoration. A discussion of the basic elements as well as a section of exercises offers the craftsman an opportunity to experiment. Detailed information about dyes and pigments, block printing, batik, and tie-dyeing is given. Complete lists of equipment and the procedures are outlined for each technique. Illustrated.

MARGOLIS, ADELE P.
How to Make Clothes That Fit and Flatter
Doubleday, 1969. 296pp. $6.95. Easy to follow step-by-step instructions, how-to drawings, and styling tips for proper fit in women's dressmaking. Some of the instructions include how to make a flat pattern, how to alter the pattern, how to use the pattern, how to use a dress form, and instructions on fitting procedures. Illustrated with drawings and diagrams. Index.

MILLER, EDWARD
Textiles: Properties and Behavior
Theatre Arts, 1969. 192pp. $6.95. A book for those who are in any way concerned with fabrics. Technical explanation of the processes of manufacture is provided to enable the student to understand why fabrics differ in appearance, texture, and properties. Relationship between yarns and fabrics, techniques by which they are manufactured, and ultimate behavior when finally woven into fabrics, are shown and illustrated in the line illustrations. Bibliography.

MORI, MARIA
Basic Pattern Cutting
Taplinger, 1970. 160pp. $6.95. Precise patterns, drawings, and instructions for sewing an entire wardrobe—skirts, suits, coats, capes, rain apparel, and dresses. Instructions for measuring, drawings of the basic pattern blocks, lists of suppliers, and Appendices on pressing, cutting, machine sewing, etc. are included.

MOTLEY
Designing and Making Stage Costumes
Studio Vista, 1964. 144pp. $7.95. With the aid of sketches, illustrations, and diagrams, Motley (in reality three different stage designers) shows the amateur how to create authentic period and modern costumes with a minimum of money and material. The authors treat the practical problems of working with directors and producers, and the use of color on stage, as well as the importance of stage properties and fabrics. Bibliography. Index.

MOULTON, BERTHA
Garment-cutting and Tailoring for Students
Theatre Arts, 1968. 223pp. $16.50. First published in 1949 and now revised, this is a fully illustrated and practical manual of tailoring for the stage. Individual sections of the book cover all necessary detail: measurements, garment-cutting, sports garments, adaptations, tailoring stitches, fittings, and alterations. More than 250 patterns and line illustrations are provided. Index.

MOULTON, BERTHA
Simplified Tailoring
Theatre Arts, 1969. 111pp. $4.95. Miss Moulton makes clear the techniques of tailoring through drawings and diagrams as well as text. Dealing with suit making for boys as well as for women, individual sections of the book are concerned with choosing the pattern and material, cutting the material, tailoring stitches, pockets, lining, fitting, and pressing.

NAYLOR, BRENDA
The Technique of Dress Design
Batsford, 1967. 154pp. $11.95. Miss Naylor has provided a series of drawings and photographs illustrating the principle of good design in England. These principles are based on the relation of cut and style to the human figure. Illustrations show basic garments, details, and ideas on how to change them.

PARISH, PEGGY
Costumes to Make
Macmillan, 1970. 111pp. $3.95. Illustrated by Lynn Sweat, this is a guidebook of simple, step-by-step instructions for making fifty costumes, ranging from historical dress and storybook characters to special holiday and animal outfits, for young children's costume parties, plays, and Halloween.

PETERS, JOAN and ANNA SUTCLIFFE
Making Costumes for School Plays
Batsford, 1970. 112pp. $6.95. All the necessary basic information to help young people make costumes for school drama productions. Under various headings the authors give practical suggestions for making costumes of all periods. illustrated witn 140 photographs. List of Books for Further Reading. List of Suppliers.

PRISK, BERNICE
Stage Costume Handbook
Harper & Row, 1966. 198pp. Paper $10.00. Pattern making instructions for a set of basic patterns, as well as a list of standards for constructing average stage costumes. The author provides sections on historical, national, and traditional dress. Bibliography.

ROBINSON, RENEE and JULIAN ROBINSON
Streamlined Dressmaking
Crown, 1967. 128pp. $3.95. A make-it-yourself instruction book which provides simple explanations, drawings, and diagrams for the woman who has never sewn before. Illustrated. Index.

SCRASE, PAT
Let's Start Designing
Reinhold, 1966. 60pp. $6.50. Miss Scrase attempts to stimulate the imaginative processes with simple ideas based on geometric shapes and the shapes, textures, and colors of animals, fish, moths, and fruit. These designs can be applied to embroidery, printmaking, fabric printing, stenciling, or any craft incorporating two-dimensioned patterns and images. Illustrated.

SNOOK, BARBARA
Costumes for School Plays
Branford, 1965. 96pp. $3.75. Prepared for school productions, this book contains chapters on color, dyeing, painting and stenciling on fabric, costumes and armor of all periods, properties, masks, make-up, storage of costumes, and Green Room organization. Bibliography. Index.

TOMPKINS, JULIA
Stage Costumes and How to Make Them
Pitman, 1969. 166pp. $6.75. The author, an English costumer and wardrobe mistress, explains how to

dress any production from the Saxon times to the 1930's. Simple basic patterns and clear diagrams with average measurements show how to make costumes simply and cheaply. Illustrated. List of Useful Books. List of English Suppliers. Index.

WHITE, ALICE V.
Making Stage Costumes for Amateurs
Routledge & Kegan Paul, 1957. 73pp. $2.75. A guide for building a basic theatre wardrobe by creating garments adaptable to various historical periods. Diagrams show easy methods of converting the costumes with suggestions on making jewelry, armour, and weapons of various periods.

ZAIDENBERG, ARTHUR
How to Draw Costumes and Clothes
Abelard—Schuman, 1964. 64pp. $4.75. In this volume written for students in grades five to ten, the author illustrates national costumes and shows simple methods of drawing the people and clothes of other lands.

ZIRNER, LAURA
Costuming for the Modern Stage
University of Illinois, 1957. 49pp. Paper $3.95. The author illustrates steps in the creation of convertible costumes for period plays. The costumes are made up of basic units which can be elaborated on or changed.

Jewelry

BATES, KENNETH F.
The Enamelist
World, 1967. 246pp. $3.95. A complete course of study in enameling. The author begins with a history of the art and then deals with the major aspects of teaching enameling from preparation to tests. The buying of materials, planning class projects, encouraging student creativity, and arranging exhibits are all covered. Illustrated with photographs. Bibliography. Glossary of Terms. Index.

FLOWER, MARGARET
Jewelry: 1837 – 1901
Walker, 1969. 64pp. $2.95. This is a study of jewelry as made and worn during the Victorian period. Illustrated with photographs. Glossary.

GREGORIETTI, GUIDO
Jewelry Through the Ages
McGraw—Hill, 1970. 319pp. $14.95. Translated from the Italian by Helen Lawrence, this is an exploration of the recorded history of jewelry from the cave and rock paintings of 40,000 years ago to the personal adornment of the present day. Illustrated with 400 photographs and reproductions of contemporary paintings, drawings, etc., more than half in full color. Table of Precious Stones. Bibliography. Index.

LAMMER, JUTTA
Make Your Own Enamels
Watson—Guptill, 1968. 57pp. $2.50. This detailed handbook introduces the art of enameling. Step-by-step instructions detail materials and tools, how to prepare and apply enamel to the material and how to finish and mount each piece. Illustrated.

ROSE, AUGUSTUS F. and ANTONIO CIRINO
Jewelry Making and Design
Dover, 1967. 306pp. Paper $2.75. This is a revised and enlarged fourth edition of the 1949 publication in which the authors detail the making of jewelry, give helpful methods for developing original designs, and illustrate thoroughly all the processes. Illustrated. Bibliography. Index.

SOCHER, MILLI V.
Jewelry to Make Yoyrself
Taplinger, 1967. 95pp. $2.95. This book contains more than 100 suggestions and ideas for jewelry which can be made from beads, wood, metal wire, ceramic, enamel, etc. Fully illustrated with diagrams and photographs.

Masks

CUMMINGS, RICHARD
101 Masks
McKay, 1968. 173pp. $4.25. An introduction to the art of mask making, including instructions on the use of different materials, three complete plays, and suggestions for several other mask entertainments. Written for young people, it includes sections on simple masks, more advanced work, and instructions for making masks for decorative use. Illustrated with drawings. Index.

GREGOR, JOSEPH
Masks of the World: An Historical and Pictorial Survey of Many Types and Times
Blom, 1968. 31pp. & plates. $32.50. Originally published in 1937 and now reissued, this is a study of the mask and its uses. Ninety-one plates show 225 examples of the mask from all periods of history.

HUNT, KARI and BERNICE WELLS CARLSON
Masks and Mask Makers
Abingdon, 1961. 67pp. $3.50. A brief history of the mask with illustrations showing masks from noted collections. Written for children from grade four, the volume includes instructions for making a variety of masks.

LEWIS, SHARI and LILLIAN OPPENHEIMER
Folding Paper Masks
Dutton, 1965. 92pp. $3.95. Simple instructions for folding twenty-one masks with large photographs of each mask in its completed stage. Bibliography.

MONTI, FRANCO
African Masks
Hamlyn, 1969. 158pp. $2.95. Originally published in Italy in 1966 and issued in England in translation by Andrew Hale, this study reveals the background of the African tribal artist and his place and function in the tribe. It shows how the mask, part of a dance costume, is linked via the public ceremonial life of the tribe to the most secret religious customs. Full notes allow the reader to follow without difficulty the background to an art which has had much influence on Western painting and sculpture. Included are sixty-nine plates in color.

SLADE, RICHARD
Masks and How to Make Them
Transatlantic, 1964. 48pp. $4.50. Written for children, this book gives an outline of the history of masks plus instructions for making masks of various types and materials. Illustrated with diagrams and photographs.

Heraldry

ALLCOCK, HUBERT
Heraldic Design: Its Origin, Ancient Forms, and Modern Usage
Tudor, 1962. 96pp. $4.95. Paper $1.95. Over 500 illustrations trace the history and meaning of symbols used in heraldry. The evolution of symbols and devices from medieval armour and shields to present-day trademarks is examined.

FOX–DAVIES, ARTHUR CHARLES
The Art of Heraldry: An Encyclopedia of Armory
Blom, 1968. 504pp. & plates. $37.50. Originally published in 1904 and now reissued, this is a comprehensive study of the entire field of coats of arms and armour. Thousands of examples, precise technical descriptions, and a historical survey of the development of all branches of armory are included. More than 1,000 drawings in the text and 153 plates illustrate the volume.

FRANKLYN, JULIAN
Heraldry
A. S. Barnes, 1968. 154pp. $8.50. A detailed examination of every aspect of this Gothic art which, in the author's opinion, represents the epitome of pure design. Illustrated in color and black-and-white. Index.

LOUDA, JIRI
European Civic Coats of Arms
Hamlyn, 1966. 265pp. $2.95. Civic heraldry, the coats of arms of towns and cities, is studied by the author. The book is devoted to the towns and cities of the European continent and includes 320 illustrations in color. Glossary. Index.

WOODWARD, JOHN and GEORGE BURNETT
A Treatise on Heraldry – British and Foreign
Tuttle, 1969. 858pp. $17.50. Originally published in 1891 and now reissued, this study of heraldry traces the history and meaning of symbols and devices used in Great Britain and Europe. Illustrated with fifty-six full page plates, most in color, and 106 illustrations in the text. English and French Glossaries. Index.

THE ACTOR AND HIS CRAFT

THEORIES AND HISTORIES OF ACTING

Note: For further books on this subject, see: Children and the Theatre – Acting for Children

ABENEDETTI, ROBERT L.
The Actor at Work
Prentice–Hall, 1970. 177pp. $8.75. Using techniques similar to those of Gestalt psychology, the author offers the acting student a program of self-discovery and development of his expressive behavior. This is related to the aesthetics of stage performance. The first part of the book deals with expressive technique. The second part treats in detail the techniques of textual analysis – language, play structure, action and characterization. Exercises included are intended as training devices rather than rehearsal techniques. Illustrated with drawings and photographs.

AGGERTT, OTIS J. and ELBERT R. BOWEN
Communicative Reading
Macmillan, 1967. 482pp. $8.95. The second edition of the 1963 publication. It is an approach for the teaching of the beginning course in interpretative reading. The authors explore the idea of interpretative reading, discuss how to find the meaning and how to express and intensify this meaning, and give generous selections for reading and interpretation. Index of Authors and Titles. Index of Topics.

ALBERTI, EVA
A Handbook of Acting: Based on The New Pantomime by Madame Eva Alberti
Samuel French, 1932. 205pp. $2.50. Edited by R. Hyndman, this is a course in acting designed to give the student the physical, mental, and emotional foundation necessary for creative acting. A history of pantomime is included, with two pantomime plays written by Mme. Alberti.

ALBRIGHT, HARDIE
Acting: The Creative Process
Dickenson, 1967. 287pp. Spiral bound $8.95. A handbook on acting by a professional actor and teacher. The textbook is the revised edition of Mr. Albright's notes for a university extension course.

Acting theories and methods are discussed and applied to exercise scenes. Illustrated. Index.

ALBRIGHT, H.D.
Working Up a Part: A Manual for the Beginning Actor
Houghton Mifflin, 1959. 246pp. Paper $4.50. A second edition of the book first published in 1947, the author includes chapters on analyzing a role, on movement, speech, characterization, and playing the role. Each chapter has a check list of essential points and a series of exercises. A selected group of poetry and prose readings and scenes for rehearsal is included. Illustrated. Glossary. Bibliography.

ARCHER, WILLIAM
Masks or Faces? with The Paradox of Acting by Denis Diderot
Hill & Wang, 1957. 240pp. Paper $1.65. Diderot's essay, first published in 1830, presents a theory of acting that rejects the emotionalist point of view. William Archer's essay is the classic rejoinder to Diderot, first published in 1888. Archer questioned the leading actors of his day on the basis of their art and this questionnaire formed the background for his reply. Introduction by Lee Strasberg.

AVRAM, RACHMAEL BEN
The Act and The Image
Odyssey Press, 1969. 292pp. Paper $3.95. This book is addressed to the beginning actor who wants to learn the discipline of acting. Each chapter takes up a single aspect of acting and provides exercises to give the student actor an opportunity to test the principle in action. All of the exercises relate either directly or by analogy with the acting problems to be found in "Romeo and Juliet" and "Our Town," both of which plays are included in the volume.

BAKER, ROGER
Drag: A History of Female Impersonation on the Stage
Triton, 1968. 256pp. $7.95. A study of female impersonation on the stage from the playhouses of ancient China, Japan, Greece, and medieval England to the pantomime "dame" and professional impersonators of modern times. Illustrated with sixty-five pages of photographs. Bibliography. Index.

BARRAULT, JEAN–LOUIS
The Theatre of Jean-Louis Barrault
Hill & Wang, 1959. 244pp. $5.00. France's great man of the theatre reviews the accumulated experience of his career, especially that of his own company and theatre. Part One discusses the foundation and development of the Madelaine Renaud, Jean-Louis Barrault theatre company; Part Two contains four essays on the craft of acting.

BARTHOLOMEUSZ, DENNIS
Macbeth and the Players
See Page 69

BERNHARDT, SARAH
The Art of the Theatre
Blom, 1969. 224pp. $12.50. Originally published in 1924 and now reissued in a facsimile edition, this is a volume of reminiscences by the actress, dictated during the last months of her life. A few instructions on make-up, voice, and the qualities necessary in an actor are given. Translated by H. J. Stenning, the volume includes a Preface by James Agate.

BLAKELOCK, DENYS
Advice to a Player: Letters to a Young Actor
Heinemann, 1958. 84pp. $2.25. Written in the form of letters to an imaginary young actor, this is not a book of technical instruction but a series of helpful hints to the actor who has already acquired a technique.

BLUNT, JERRY
The Composite Art of Acting
Macmillan, 1966. 450pp. $10.00. This book presents a wide selection of theories and techniques on all aspects of dramatic art. Various practice scenes are incorporated throughout the book. The format is designed to provide ample space for making notes in the margins. Plays studied in depth include: "Hamlet," "The Imaginary Invalid," and "She Stoops to Conquer." Index.

BOAS, GUY
Shakespeare and the Young Actor
Dufour, 1955. 126pp. $4.50. A simplified method of training and rehearsal for school productions. Twelve productions are described and illustrated in detail.

BOLESLAVSKY, RICHARD
Acting: The First Six Lessons
Theatre Arts, 1933. 122pp. $3.25. Essays in dialogue form on concentration, memory of emotion, dramatic action, characterization, observation and rhythm. The author was a member of the Moscow Art Theatre and Director of its first Studio.

BOURNE, JOHN
Teach Yourself Amateur Acting
Dover, 1949. 208pp. $2.00. A revised edition of the 1939 publication, this is an examination of the techniques of acting for the non-professional. The author's intention is to stimulate creative work without laying down hard and fast rules. Included are discussions of acting techniques, play analysis, and rehearsal procedures.

BROWN, JOHN RUSSELL
Shakespeare's Dramatic Style
See Page 57

BROWN, JOHN RUSSELL
Shakespeare's Plays in Performance
See Page 93

BUELL, WILLIAM ACKERMAN
The Hamlets of the Theatre
See Page 64

BURNISTON, CHRISTABEL
Creative Oral Assessment: Its Scope and Stimulus
Pergamon, 1968. 124pp. $4.50. The author sets out the philosophic principles and practical techniques for the teaching and examining of spoken English. In scope he covers all aspects: the imaginative interpretation of drama and poetry, the art of reading aloud, the functional presentation of personal projects, the art of guiding questions and discussions. The book adheres to the examining forms and precepts held by the English Speaking Board, London. References and background reading lists are included.

BURTON, HAL – Editor
Acting in the Sixties
British Broadcasting Corp., 1970. 256pp. $14.95. This book is based on a series of programs originally shown on BBC television. It is devoted to the current young generation of actors and actresses who talk about acting in films, in television, and on the stage. Each of the interviews in fully illustrated with photographs to show the wide range of parts played by the actors. The interviewees are: Richard Burton, Harry H. Corbett, Albert Finney, John Neville, Eric Porter, Vanessa Redgrave, Maggie Smith, Robert Stephens, and Dorothy Tutin.

BURTON, HAL – Editor
Great Acting
Hill & Wang, 1967. 192pp. $8.95. Eight actors reveal why they became actors, how they learnt their craft, and discuss in depth some of the major parts with which they have become identified. The actors are: Laurence Olivier, Sybil Thorndike, Ralph Richardson, Peggy Ashcroft, Michael Redgrave, Edith Evans, John Gielgud, and Noel Coward. There are sixty-four pages of photographs showing the range of parts each actor has played and there is also a chart which gives all the parts each played in the theatre and lists the important events in the theatre at the time.

BURTON, PHILIP
The Sole Voice: Character Portraits from Shakespeare
See Page 57

CARLISLE, CAROL JONES
Shakespeare from the Greenroom
See Page 99

CHEKHOV, MICHAEL
To the Actor: On the Technique of Acting
Harper & Row, 1953. 201pp. $6.00. Yul Brynner has provided a Preface to this text on acting. Chapters on the actor's body and psychology, imagination, improvisation, the psychological gesture, characterization, and composition of the performance are included. Exercises on each aspect of technique are also provided. Illustrated with drawings by Nicolai Remisoff.

CHING, JAMES
Performer and Audience
Neil A. Kjos, 1947. 96pp. Paper $2.50. A psychological study of nervousness and stage fright. The author offers a practical approach for the overcoming by performers of nervousness and stage fright.

CHISMAN, ISABEL and HESTER E. RAVEN–HART
Manners and Movement in Costume Plays
Walter Baker, 1934. 122pp. Paper $1.75. A guide to the proper use of garments and accessories in period plays. Instructions on ceremonial usage, handling of weapons, and dancing are included.

COGER, LESLIE IRENE and MELVIN R. WHITE
Readers Theatre Handbook
See Page 356

COLE, TOBY and HELEN KRICH CHINOY – Editors
Actors on Acting
Crown, 1970. 715pp. $8.95. Originally published in 1949 and now revised and enlarged, this is a comprehensive collection of actors' thoughts and writings on the theories, techniques, and practices of acting. More than 100 selections extend from Thespis in the sixth century B. C. to the leading actors of the international stage today. Introductory essays to the fourteen separate national sections form a concise history of the actor and there are more than 100 biographies of the great performers. Bibliography of over 1,000 titles. Index.

COLLIER, GAYLAN JANE
Assignments in Acting
Harper & Row, 1966. 330pp. Paper $10.00. A workbook of thirty-two assignments in realistic acting techniques designed to explore the psychology of character, the inner motivation of the actor, and the technique of portrayal. Each assignment requires the creating of a character analysis chart to guide the young actor.

COLLINS, FREDA
Let's Prepare a Nativity Play
See Page 327

COQUELIN, CONSTANT
The Art of the Actor
Allen & Unwin, 1932. 77pp. $2.50. A translation, by Elsie Fogerty, of Coquelin's 1894 treatise. The essay illustrates the existing traditions of the Comedie Francaise and the Conservatoire de Musique et de Declamation in France.

CRAUFORD, LANE
Acting: Its Theory and Practice
Blom, 1969. 248pp. $12.50. Originally published in

1930, this is a study of the technique of acting "with illustrative examples of players past and present." Index.

D'ANGELO, ARISTIDE
The Actor Creates
Samuel French, 1939. 96pp. $2.00. Instructions in play analysis, the preparation of a role, and in acting technique written by an instructor at the American Academy of Dramatic Arts.

DIDEROT, DENIS
The Paradox of Acting
See listing under: **ARCHER, WILLIAM: Masks or Faces?**

DOW, MARGUERITE R.
The Magic Mask: A Basic Textbook of Theatre Arts
St. Martin, 1968. 367pp. $6.50. Originally published in Canada in 1966 and released in the United States for the first time, this textbook was designed to offer training in the fundamental principles of theatre arts to students of all aspects of the theatre. Each passage of explanation is followed by exercises in both theory and practice. There are a selection of scenes for student practice, two one act plays, and a suggested list of plays for student production. Illustrated. Bibliography. Index.

DOWNER, ALAN S. – Editor
Oxberry's 1822 Edition of "King Richard III"
See Page 114

DUERR, EDWIN
The Length and Depth of Acting
Holt, Rinehart, 1962. 590pp. $13.25. A history of acting that covers all theories from Aristotle to Brecht, with a record of changing styles in plays and playhouses and the conflict between different aims and methods of acting.

DUNN, CHARLES J. and BUNZO TORIGOE
The Actors' Analects
Columbia, 1969. 308pp. $11.00. A collection of advice and notes left by great actors of the popular theatre of Japan at the end of the seventeenth century. The notes have been translated and edited with full annotation to provide an insight into the lives, principles, mentality, and aesthetics of Kabuki actors of the time. Material about the organization of the theatre of the period in Kyoto and Osaka is also included. Appendices include a Glossary, List of Actors, Subject List, and a Bibliography. Illustrated.

EUSTIS, MORTON
Players at Work
Blom, 1969. 127pp. $6.75. Originally published in 1937 and reissued in a facsimile edition, this is a study of various actor's ideas and opinions on acting as translated by the author. The actors represented are: Helen Hayes, Lunt and Fontanne, Nazimova, Katherine Cornell, Ina Claire, Burgess Meredith, and Fred Astaire. Lotte Lehmann has contributed an essay on "The Singing Actor." Illustrated with photographs.

FAST, JULIUS
Body Language
Lippincott, 1970. 192pp. $4.95. Although this is not a theatre book, the new science of kinesics may be of value to actors. The author discusses the movements of the body that may amplify or contradict verbal expression. Selected References.

FRANKLIN, MIRIAM A.
Rehearsal: The Principles and Practice of Acting for the Stage
Prentice–Hall, 1963. 282pp. Spiral bound $11.25. Originally published in 1938, this is the fourth edition of a text for the beginning actor in college classes. It contains chapters on the physical, mental, and emotional aspects of acting. Lengthy excerpts for exercise are included with marginal reminders and pointers. Illustrated with photographs, drawings, and diagrams. Index of Authors. Index of Titles. Index of Topics.

FUNKE, LEWIS and JOHN E. BOOTH
Actors Talk About Acting
Avon, 1963. 442pp. Paper $1.25. Originally published in 1961, this is a series of interviews conducted via tape recorder. The questions were designed to discover the actors' approaches to their own theory and practice of acting. Actors interviewed are: John Gielgud, Alfred Lunt, Lynn Fontanne, Helen Hayes, Jose Ferrer, Maureen Stapleton, Katherine Cornell, Vivien Leigh, Morris Carnovsky, Shelley Winters, Bert Lahr, Sidney Poitier, Paul Muni, and Anne Bancroft.

GEIGER, DON
The Dramatic Impulse in Modern Poetics
Louisiana State University, 1967. 165pp. $6.00. This study treats the theory of poetry as dramatized discourse: the utterance of the poem's implied speaker. The perspective of the dramatic speaker and its implications for modern poetics are explored. The author examines the differences, interrelations, and points of influence and connection among the dramatic, contexualist, impersonal, and Romantic theories, and traces the lines of descent in theoretical criticism.

GILDER, ROSAMOND
Enter the Actress: The First Women in the Theatre
Theatre Arts, 1931. 312pp. Paper $1.95. A history of the pioneers who broke down the prejudice against women in the theatre. The first women playwrights, directors, and actresses from the tenth century nun, Hrotsvitha, to Mme. Vestris are discussed. Examined are the theories of acting held by some of the actresses. Illustrated.

GORCHAKOV, NIKOLAI
The Vakhtangov School of Stage Art
Foreign Languages Publishing House, Undated. 206pp. $4.50. Written by a pupil of Yevgeny Vakhtangov and published in Russia, this volume contains a number of personal impressions of the director and notes on his productions and on his methods of rehearsal. The text is in English.

GOULD, ELEANOR CODY
Charles Jehlinger in Rehearsal
American Academy of Dramatic Art, 1958. 30pp. Paper $1.25. Verbatim notes transcribed by Eleanor Cody Gould during a number of rehearsal classes conducted by Jehlinger at the American Academy from 1918 to 1952.

GRAHAM, KENNETH L.
Relationships Between Educational Theatre and Professional Theatre: Actor Training in the United States
A.E.T.A., 1966. 76pp. Paper $2.00. This report by the American Educational Theatre Association is concerned with the mutual problems and relationships between educators and practicing theatre professionals. The development of professional training, the present standards, and several developmental projects are considered.

GREEN, MICHAEL
Downwind of Upstage
Hawthorn, 1966. 175pp. $4.95. Subtitled, "The Art of Coarse Acting," this is a humorous study of amateur acting. Drawings by Arthur Wallower.

GREEN, RUTH M.
The Wearing of Costume
See Page 390

GROTOWSKI, JERZY
Towards a Poor Theatre
See Page 365

HAMMERTON, J. A.—Editor
The Actor's Art
Blom, 1969. 267pp. $10.50. Originally published in 1897 and now reissued in a facsimile edition, this is a volume of theatrical reminiscences, methods of study, and advice to actors by the leading actors of the nineteenth century. Among the actors contributing are: Sir Henry Irving, H. Beerbohm Tree, Mrs. Kendal, Ellen Terry, Sarah Bernhardt, and Arthur Playfair.

HARRAL, STEWART
When It's Laughter You're After
University of Oklahoma, 1962. 414pp. $6.50. A guide for the after-dinner speaker. The author provides information on how to build a file of gags, jokes, and anecdotes, how to break down audience resistence, tips on developing a style of humor,and ways of blending a joke with a speech theme. The main portion of the book includes more than 4,000 jokes alphabetized under topics. Index.

HAYMAN, RONALD
Techniques of Acting
Methuen, 1969. 188pp. $7.50. The author attempts to describe the different approaches that the actor needs to make to different media—theatre, film, and television—and to show how the art of acting has entered into a new phase of growth. Mr. Hayman looks both at the lessons to be drawn from the theories of directors such as Stanislavski and Brecht and those to be drawn from some of the great performances of individual actors in our time. Performances by modern actors are viewed in perspective against such actors of the past as Bernhardt and Salvini. Index.

HODGSON, JOHN and ERNEST RICHARDS
Improvisation: Discovery and Creativity in Drama
Barnes & Noble, 1966. 209pp. $7.50. Paper $3.00. The authors illustrate the way improvisation helps actors to draw upon their imaginative resources and to extend their awareness of themselves and others. They first outline ways of improvising without a script and then show how improvisation can illuminate the text of a play both for study and for practical rehearsal purposes. Index.

IRVING, HENRY
The Drama
Blom, 1969. 164pp. $6.75. Originally published in 1893 and reissued in a facsimile edition, this volume contains a series of four lectures by the nineteenth century English actor. Two of the lectures concern "The Art of Acting;" one is about Burbage, Betterton, Garrick, and Kean; and the fourth concerns the stage in Irving's time.

JAMES, HENRY
The Scenic Art
See Page 25

JOHNSON, ALBERT
Church Plays and How to Stage Them
See Page 580

JOHNSON, ALBERT
Drama: Technique and Philosophy
See Page 13

JOSEPH, BERTRAM
Acting Shakespeare
Theatre Arts, 1969. 199pp. Paper $2.25. Originally published in 1960 and reissued in a revised edition, this is a consideration of the fundamental principles of acting Shakespeare's plays. Mr. Joseph attacks the dual problem of creating character and making the Elizabethan playwright's poetry compelling for the audience. He provides examples and simple exercises for the training of body and voice. Illustrated with seven photographs. Glossary. Index.

JOSEPH BERTRAM
Elizabethan Acting
Oxford, 1964. 115pp. $5.50. This revised edition of the study first published in 1951 uses sixteenth and seventeenth century sources to ascertain the nature of the Elizabethan stage play. The author asserts that methods which the modern theatre employs to ensure intense and truthful representation of emotion were used on the Elizabethan stage. Index of Persons, Places, and Works.

JOSEPH, BERTRAM
The Tragic Actor
Theatre Arts, 1959. 415pp. $9.75. A survey of tragic acting in England from Burbage and Alleyn to Forbes-Robertson and Irving. Contemporary notices, eyewitness accounts, and biographical studies supply information on the theories and practices of the major tragic actors. Illustrated. Bibliography.

KAHAN, STANLEY
An Actor's Workbook
Harcourt, Brace, 1967. 320pp. $8.75. This spiral-bound workbook is intended as a working source for the actor or director who wants a large collection of materials to use with his particular approach to acting. The scenes have been chosen for variety and style and for opportunities for different combinations of actors from two character dialogues to ensemble scenes. The fifty scenes range from Shakespeare to modern verse drama to comedy and serious scenes.

KAHAN, STANLEY
Introduction to Acting
Harcourt, Brace, 1962. 312pp. $9.25. A text for college acting and drama classes. Chapters on radio and television acting are included, along with many exercises and plays designed to illustrate theory. Illustrated with photographs and diagrams.

KESTER, KATHARINE
Problem-Projects in Acting
Samuel French, 1937. 217pp. $2.00. A collection of scenes varying in length from two to fifteen minutes. Each scene is treated as a complete unit and floor plans are included for each. The projects are designed to give the beginning acting student insight into the various related factors in acting.

KIERKEGAARD, SOREN
Crisis in the Life of an Actress and Other Essays on Drama
Harper & Row, 1967. 154pp. Paper $1.45. Translated with an Introduction and Notes by Stephen D. Crites, this is a series of three essays, by the Danish philosopher, on three actors and their craft. The title essay concerns an actress and the crisis in her professional life as she grows older. Other essays include one on the portrayal of a role in "Don Giovanni" and one on how the actor Phister played a role in the comic opera "Ludovic." Index.

KLINE, PETER
The Theatre Student: Scenes to Perform
Richards Rosen, 1969. 190pp. $5.97. The author attempts to give to the student some idea of the background information and interpretation techniques that an experienced actor utilizes when preparing a role. Each of the nine scenes for single men and eight scenes for single women includes commentary on the play, the character, the scene, and vocal and physical characterization notes. Illustrated. Bibliography.

KRANZ, SHELDON – Editor
Aesthetic Realism: We Have Been There
Definition Press, 1969. 119pp. $4.95. Paper $1.95. Six essays on the theory of Aesthetic Reality as propounded by Eli Siegel, founder and teacher of the philosophy. Also included are two essays by Siegel on his theories. Illustrated.

LAING, R. D.
The Politics of Experience
Ballantine, 1968. 190pp. Paper $ .95. Originally published in 1967 and now reissued, this book by a young British psychiatrist attacks the Establishment assumptions about "normality" with a radical view of the mental sickness built into our society. The volume may be of value to students of acting in the "new" theatre.

LEAVITT, HART DAY
An Eye for People: A Writer's Guide to Character
See Page 363

LIGGETT, CLAYTON E.
The Theatre Student: Concert Theatre
Richards Rosen, 1970. 185pp. $6.96. Mr. Liggett clarifies "Concert Theatre" for the student and explains how such performances can be put on by students. The three basic types—in all of which the material is read from the printed page and the reader does not attempt to "become the character physically"—are Readers' Theatre, Chamber Theatre, and Choric Theatre. Illustrated. List of Material. Bibliography.

MACKAY, EDWARD and ALICE B. MACKAY
Elementary Principles of Acting
Samuel French, 1934. 253pp. $2.50. A textbok aid for teachers and students, this is an adaptation of F. F. Mackay's 1913 manual, "The Art of Acting." The authors have retained the technical scheme of the original publication and apply the basic principles to plays from the modern repertoire. They include drills and exercises as well as examples of drama chosen to give actual practice on all teaching points.

MacKENZIE, FRANCES
The Amateur Actor
Theatre Arts, 1966. 122pp. $3.00. This is the third revised edition of a practical book for the amateur.

The author deals with all the most important problems including: speech, movement, gesture, creation of atmosphere, working to a climax, entrances and exits, and falls. She includes a useful series of exercises to help the actor master the elementary techniques and there is also a chapter on stage management.

MAISEL, EDWARD — Editor
The Resurrection of the Body
University Books, 1969. 204pp. $5.95. This is a selection of the writings of F. Matthias Alexander, an Australian, who developed a practical technique for restoring the body as a means towards better health, greater awareness, and freedom from habit. He was the forerunner of the Esalen movement and his body-mind technique has come into wide use for training actors in the contemporary theatre. Mr. Maisel has provided a long critical introduction to the writings. Illustrated with a portrait of Alexander.

MATTHEWS, BRANDER — Editor
Papers on Acting
Hill & Wang, 1958. 303pp. $3.75. Paper $1.65. A collection of essays on acting. The essays range from the eighteenth century to the present and among the authors included are: Coquelin, Talma, Boucicault, Edwin Booth, Henry Jenkins, and Robert Lloyd.

MURDOCH, JAMES
The Stage
See Page 262

NEWTON, ROBERT G.
A Creative Approach to Amateur Theatre
Coach House, 1967. 211pp. $5.00. This volume contains three books bound together: "Together in Theatre," "Exercise Improvisation," and "Improvisation Steps Out."

NEWTON, ROBERT G.
Exercise Improvisation: A Manual for the Use of Improvisation
J. Garnet Miller, 1960. 47pp. $1.75. A brief introdution to the technique of improvisation with exercises in feeling, characterization, and telling a story.

NEWTON, ROBERT G.
Improvisation Steps Out
J. Garnet Miller, 1967. 46pp. Paper $1.75. This is an extension of some of the ideas in "Exercise Improvisation." The author suggests approaches to working out dramatic comment on contemporary and other subjects and shows how improvisation may help overcome some difficulties that often arise during the rehearsal period. Practical exercises are included.

NEWTON, ROBERT G.
Together in Theatre
J. Garnet Miller, 1954. 119pp. $2.50. A study of the relationship between the actor and the other members of a theatre group with special reference to amateur and community groups.

ORMSBEE, HELEN
Backstage with Actors
Blom, 1969. 343pp. $9.50. Originally published in 1938 and now reissued in a facsimile edition, this is a study of the progress of acting in the English speaking theatre from the time of Shakespeare to the late 1930's. After a prologue on the author's idea of what constitutes good acting, players are discussed, including Thomas Betterton, Garrick, Siddons, Edmund Kean, the Booths, Ellen Terry, Maude Adams, Katharine Cornell. Leslie Howard, George M. Cohan, and Lunt and Fontanne. Illustrated with photographs. Notes. Index.

OXENFORD, LYN
Design for Movement: A Textbook on Stage Movement
Theatre Arts, 1951. 96pp. $2.95. A study of individual and group movement on stage. Realistic, stylized and period acting requirements are considered. Emphasis is placed on dance training for both actors and directors. The author has included a chapter on religious drama and pageants.

OXENFORD, LYN
Playing Period Plays
J. Garnet Miller, 1958. 318pp. $6.50. Simple stage directions for producing and acting period plays of various eras. The periods covered in the four parts of the volume are: Medieval and Early Tudor, Elizabethan and Jacobean, Restoration and Georgian, Victorian and Edwardian. Illustrated.

PASOLLI, ROBERT
A Book on the Open Theatre
See Page 242

PEGRAM, MARJORIE
Overture and Beginners
Samuel French, 1958. 28pp. Paper $1.00. A guide to stage movement and the wearing of costumes. Foreword by Sir John Gielgud.

PERLS, FREDERICK with RALPH F. HEFFERLINE and PAUL GOODMAN
Gestalt Therapy
Dell, 1970. 470pp. Paper $2.65. Originally published in 1951 and now reissued, this is a presentation of the method and theory of a challenging approach to the study of man's personality. In a series of eighteen experiments, the reader is an active participant in the growth of self-discovery. This is not a book on acting, but actors may find it of some value. Index.

REDGRAVE, MICHAEL
The Actor's Ways and Means
Theatre Arts, 1966. 90pp. Paper $2.65. Originally published in 1953, this volume presents a survey of the literature of acting and includes Sir Michael's

own theories and practices. Illustrated with photographs.

REDGRAVE, MICHAEL
Mask or Face: Reflections in an Actor's Mirror
Theatre Arts, 1958. 188pp. $4.15. A survey of the acting profession with discussions of Stanislavsky, Brecht, the approach to acting Shakespeare, the relation between acting and audience, the art of the film, and the actor and the director. Illustrated.

ROCKWOOD, JEROME
The Craftsmen of Dionysus
Scott, Foresman, 1966. 230pp. Paper $3.95. An approach to the "representational" school of acting—the methods and procedures for attaining truth on stage. The author discusses all of the elements of the actor's style and art from marking the script to actual performance. Illustrated. Index.

ROSENSTEIN, SOPHIE and LARRAE A. HAYDON, WILBUR SPARROW
Modern Acting: A Manual
Samuel French, 1936. 129pp. $2.00. A textbook in acting fundaments as taught at the University of Washington. The approach and method are described and illustrated for adoption by other teachers and students.

ROSS, LILLIAN and HELEN ROSS
The Player: A Profile of an Art
Simon & Schuster, 1968. 459pp. Paper $2.95. Originally published in 1962, this is a reprint of interviews with 55 outstanding actors and actresses of our time, in which they portray themselves and their craft and recreate the whole world of the contemporary drama and theatre. Among the actors are Ingrid Bergman, Melvyn Douglas, John Gielgud, Margaret Leighton, Frederic March, Geraldine Page, Francoise Rosay, Paul Scofield, and Maureen Stapleton. Illustrated with photographs. Index.

SCHRECK, EVERETT M.
Principles and Styles of Acting
Addison–Wesley, 1970. 354pp. $11.95. A text for the study of acting. "Part One: Principles of Acting" is planned to meet the needs of the beginning actor, while "Part Two: Styles of Acting" may serve as an advanced course. Exercises and practice excerpts from plays are provided. Illustrated with photographs. Index.

SCHUON, KARL
The First Book of Acting
Franklin Watts, 1965. 64pp. $2.65. A book of instructions on acting for young people. Illustrated with drawings.

SCHUTZ, WILLIAM C.
Joy: Expanding Human Awareness
Grove, 1967. 223pp. $5.50. Paper $1.25. A leading group psychologist describes new techniques for preserving one's identity amid the pressures of mass society. He demonstrates how, through group thinking, touching, and acting out life-situations, one can develop a more integrated personality, deeper consciousness, and greater physical and psychic powers. Dr. Schutz's methods are based on methods used at the Esalen Institute at Big Sur, California and they may be of some help to actors endeavoring to acquire a deeper sense of characterization.

SCOTT, BERTIE
The Life of Acting
Bertie Scott Foundation, 1967. 123pp. Paper $3.75. Mr. Scott was a speech and acting teacher who was highly praised for his work. This book elucidates his principles of good speech and acting.

SCOTT, CLEMENT
Some Notable Hamlets
Blom, 1969. 193pp. $9.75. Originally published in 1900 and now reissued in a facsimile edition, this is an appreciation of some Hamlets of the nineteenth century including: Sarah Bernhardt, Henry Irving, Wilson Barrett, Beerbohm Tree, and Forbes Robertson. Illustrated with portraits by W. G. Mein.

SELDEN, SAMUEL
First Steps in Acting
Appleton, 1964. 382pp. $10.75. A revised edition of the 1947 text in acting. The author emphasizes the two lines of training: The recognition, planning and communication of evocative stage imagery; and the development of pantomimic and vocal instruments for the communication of this image. Included are twenty-five scenes for various group and individual performance. Glossary of Acting Terms.

SELDEN, SAMUEL
The Stage in Action
Southern Illinois University, 1967. 324pp. Paper $2.85. A reprint of the 1941 publication, this is a text on acting techniques with special attention paid to the relation between the actor and the director. Examples are drawn in particular from the plays of Paul Green. Illustrated with drawings and photographs. A list of books useful to the actor and the director is included. Index.

SEYLER, ATHENE and STEPHEN HAGGARD
The Craft of Comedy
Theatre Arts, 1957. 114pp. $2.75. In the form of letters, this book deals with the problems of specific characterizations and scenes in plays that range from Schnitzler's "Anatol" to Restoration and Elizabethan plays.

SHARP, WILLIAM L.
Language in Drama: Meanings for the Director and the Actor
See Page 366

SIDDONS, HENRY
Practical Illustrations of Rhetorical Gesture and Action
Blom, 1968. 408pp. $17.50. Originally published in 1822 and now reissued, this is a study of gesture and action as it applied to the early nineteenth century stage. Illustrated with sixty-nine engravings "expressive of the various passions and representing the modern costume of the London theatres." Index.

SPOLIN, VIOLA
Improvisation for the Theatre: A Handbook of Teaching and Directing Techniques
See Page 367

STRICKLAND, F. COWLES
The Technique of Acting
McGraw–Hill, 1956. 306pp. $10.50. The core of this book is a series of exercises designed to develop in the young actor a technique of expression. The exercises are arranged to develop each aspect of the complete technique. Chapters on the entrance, phrasing, progressions, building a climax, timing, pointing, invention of action, rhythm, tempo, pace, style, and the design of a role. Illustrated.

TURNER, CLIFFORD
The Stage as a Career
Museum Press, 1963. 122pp. $3.50. The author maintains that the stage is not a career in the accepted sense of the word and therefore the stage aspirant needs qualities of a different nature. Among topics covered are the development of inherent qualities in the actor, the nature of technique, the function of each member of the production, and the development of various professional areas in the theatre. Illustrated. Index.

WHITE, EDWIN C.
Problems of Acting and Play Production
See Page 361

WHITE, EDWIN and MARGUERITE BATTYE
Acting and Stage Movement
Arc Books, 1963. 182pp. Paper $ .95. A concise course of instruction in all phases of acting and movement. Illustrated.

WHITE, G. PATERSON
Acting for Amateurs
Albyn Press, 1948. 56pp. Paper $ .85. A guide to acting for beginning actors. Speech characterization, movement, and gesture are covered in this short book by an English actor–producer.

WILLIAMS, P.C.
English Shakespearian Actors
Regency, 1966. 61pp. Paper $2.95. The author reviews the acting of some of the chief portrayors of Shakespeare's characters from Alleyn, Burbage, and Betterton to Wolfit, Gielgud, and Olivier.

WILSON, GARFF B.
A History of American Acting
Indiana University, 1966. 310pp. $6.95. A detailed analysis of the careers and styles of outstanding performers from the Colonial period to the twentieth century, using contemporary comment to show how these actors appeared to the critics of their time. The author also discusses style as applied to the art of the actor, the technique of acting for motion pictures, and the phenomenon of the growing campus and regional repertory theatres. Illustrated. Index.

WITKER, KRISTI
How to Be an Absolutely Smashing Public Speaker Without Saying Anything
American Heritage, 1970. 60pp. $2.95. Originally published in 1892 as "Gestures and Attitudes" and now condensed and reissued, these are Professor Edward B. Warman's methods of gesture as taught by Delsarte. The original illustrations are commented upon in a humorous manner.

ZORN, JOHN W. – Editor
The Essential Delsarte
Scarecrow, 1968. 205pp. $5.50. A previously out-of-print selection of material on the Delsarte System of speech and acting. The nineteenth century system of oratory was based on a "trinitarian philosophy of Life, Mind, and Soul." Illustrated with diagrams and drawings.

THE STANISLAVSKY METHOD

COLE, TOBY – Editor
Acting: A Handbook of the Stanislavsky Method
Crown, 1955. 223pp. $3.95. Paper $1.45. Essays by Stanislavsky and his associates on such topics as the actor's responsibility, directing and acting, the creative process, preparing for the role, production plans for "Othello," and the principles of directing. Included is a collection of photographs of Stanislavsky's roles at the Moscow Art Theatre.

EASTY, EDWARD DWIGHT
On Method Acting
Allograph Books, 1966. 191pp. Paper $2.25. A book on "method acting" for young actors and layman. Mr. Easty relates the reality of the actor's art to the reality with which the actor lives his daily life.

EDWARDS CHRISTINE
The Stanislavsky Heritage
New York University, 1965. 345pp. $13.50. Paper $3.50. This study examines the origin and development of the Russian theatre in the nineteenth century, the life and work of Stanislavsky, the sources of early American acting techniques, and the reception of Stanislavsky's techniques in the United States. Illustrated. Bibliography. Index.

GORCHAKOV, NICOLAI
Stanislavsky Directs
Funk & Wagnall, 1954. 402pp. $4.95. Paper $2.95. Translated by Miriam Golding from notes and diaries kept by Gorchakov when he attended Stanislavsky's lectures and rehearsals from 1924 to 1936, this volume studies production plans for five plays: "The Battle of Life," "Much Woe from Wit," "Lev Gurytch Sinitchkin," "Merchants of Glory," and "The Sisters Gerard." Foreword by Norris Houghton. Glossary.

HETHMON, ROBERT H. – Editor
Strasberg at The Actors Studio
Viking, 1968. 428pp. $10.00. Paper $1.95. Tape recorded sessions from Lee Strasberg's classes at The Actors Studio, edited and arranged by topic to reveal the systematic approach to training actors that Strasberg has developed. Index of Technical Terms and Topics. Index of Names and Titles.

LEWIS, ROBERT
Method or Madness?
Samuel French, 1958. 165pp. $3.50. Eight lectures on the method of acting developed by Stanislavsky. Some popular variations on it and some misconceptions about it are examined.

McGAW, CHARLES
Acting is Believing: A Basic Method for Beginners
Holt, Rinehart, 1966. 219pp. $8.50. Not a complete exposition of Stanislavsky's method of acting, but a handbook giving those aspects of the system which have proved to be practical in helping beginning actors to develop an effective technique. A revised edition of the 1962 edition with the texts of "The Typists" and "The Proposal."

MOORE, SONIA
The Stanislavsky System
Viking, 1965. 112pp. Paper $1.25. Also Paper – Pocket Books, 1967. 126pp. $ .75. A revised and enlarged edition of "The Stanislavsky Method," originally published in 1962. Miss Moore makes use of the latest research in Russia including physiologists' confirmation of the scientific importance of "the method of physical actions." A new chapter on directing and one on Stanislavsky's disciple, Eugene Vakhtangov, are included. Preface by John Gielgud. Foreword by Joshua Logan.

MOORE, SONIA
Training an Actor: The Stanislavsky System in Class
Viking, 1968. 260pp. $5.75. Paper $2.45. Miss Moore demonstrates the process of mastering Stanislavsky's techniques. In dialogues with her students, and in comments on the exercises and scenes they perform, she emphasizes her conviction that our theatre will not come of age until all the actors are properly trained in "the method." Appendices include scenes from Chekhov's "The Three Sisters" and notes on some scenes used in the classes. Index.

MUNK, ERICA – Editor
Stanislavski and America
Fawcett, 1967. 270pp. Paper $ .95. A reprint of the 1966 anthology of writings on "the method" and its influence on the American theatre. Among the contributors are: Stella Adler, Eric Bentley, Bertolt Brecht, Robert Lewis, Sanford Meisner, Lee Strasberg, and Geraldine Page.

STANISLAVSKY, CONSTANTIN S.
An Actor Prepares
Theatre Arts, 1936. 295pp. $4.45. The basic acting method evolved by the director, presented in the first book of a series illustrating his life work with actors and productions.

STANISLAVSKY, CONSTANTIN S.
An Actor's Handbook
Theatre Arts, 1963. 160pp. Paper $1.95. An alphabetical arrangement of comments by the director on acting, on his system, and on other theatre matters. Edited and translated by Elizabeth Reynolds Hapgood.

STANISLAVSKY, CONSTANTIN S.
Building a Character
Theatre Arts, 1949. 293pp. $4.95. A sequel to "An Actor Prepares," this is the second half of the director's technique for the realization of character. It covers characterization in physical terms—speech and voice, movement, gesture, tempo, rhythm— and the training necessary to make these components convincing.

STANISLAVSKY, CONSTANTIN S.
Creating a Role
Theatre Arts, 1961. 271pp. $4.45. The third volume, completing the series on Stanislavsky's life work, this book is made up of three drafts of the unfinished volume long thought lost. Three plays are discussed in detail: "Much Woe from Wit," "Othello," and "The Inspector General." Translated by Elizabeth Reynolds Hapgood.

STANISLAVSKY, CONSTANTIN S.
My Life in Art
Theatre Arts, 1924. 586pp. $6.75. The director's story, from his early childhood in Moscow, his failure as an amateur actor, through the establishment of the group that was to become the most celebrated acting company of modern times. Translated by J. J. Robins. Index.

STANISLAVSKI, CONSTANTIN S.
Stanislavsky's Legacy
Theatre Arts, 1968. 209pp. $5.50. Paper $2.45. Originally published in 1958 and now revised and expanded by Elizabeth Reynolds Hapgood, this collection of comments on a variety of aspects of an actor's art and life now includes a series of letters about the interpretation of "Othello." Index.

STANISLAVSKY, CONSTANTIN S.
Stanislavsky on the Art of the Stage
Hill & Wang, 1961. 311pp. Paper $1.95. This volume includes a collection of lectures given in Moscow between 1918 and 1922, transcripts of five rehearsals of Massenet's opera "Werther," and an analysis of Stanislavsky's system of acting by David Magarshack. Illustrated.

STANISLAVSKY, CONSTANTIN S.
Stanislavsky Produces Othello
Theatre Arts, 1948. 244pp. $5.95. Compiled from the instructions the director sent to the Moscow Art Theatre from Nice in 1929. Illustrated with diagrams of blocking for the production. Translated by Dr. Helen Nowak.

WEAPONS ON STAGE

BEAUMONT, C–L. DE
Teach Yourself Fencing
English Universities Press, 1968. 127pp. $1.95. This book aims to guide beginners step-by-step through the intricacies of every aspect of the foil, the epee, and the sabre. All terms used in fencing are explained and the book contains a large number of illustrations. Glossary. Index.

BEAUMONT, C–L. DE
Your Book of Fencing
Faber & Faber, 1970. 91pp. $3.95. Published in England, this is a guide for the beginning fencer. The author concentrates on the foil but also deals with the epee and the sabre. Equipment, handling of the weapon, stance, and defensive and offensive tactics are described. Illustrated with line drawings. Glossary.

BEHMBER, R. H.
Fencing
Arco, 1965. 97pp. $5.00. This book examines such questions as how to join a fencing club, the cost of equipment, and the use of electric foil, epee, sabre, and ordinary foil. Illustrated.

CASTELLO, HUGO and JAMES CASTELLO
Fencing
Ronald Press, 1962. 116pp. $7.25. A guide to fencing in text and pictures. The authors discuss theory and give instruction in fundamental moves, practice, drills, and the competitive bout. Glossary. Bibliography. Index.

CROSNIER, ROGER
Fencing with the Electric Foil: Instruction and Tactics
A. S. Barnes, 1961. 93pp. $5.00. Chapters on the influence of the electric foil and apparatus on traditional forms of fencing, with detailed discussions of equipment, basic movements, and tactics. Final chapters give suggestions on presiding at matches, and on special problems associated with this kind of foil. Illustrations.

CROSNIER, ROGER
Fencing with the Foil: Instruction and Technique
Faber & Faber, 1967. 277pp. $8.25. This is a new edition of the 1951 publication. Professor Crosnier has added a Revised Syllabus for Class Instruction for Leaders' Examination. Each fencing movement is clearly defined, its execution is analyzed, its technical use is described and the appropriate method for class instruction is laid down. Illustrated with drawings and photographs.

CURRY, NANCY, L.
Fencing
Goodyear, 1969. 79pp. Paper $2.00. Designed to aid the student in the understanding and mastery of the sport, the author covers the fundamentals of fencing—the beginning techniques, rules and customs, equipment and terms. Evaluation Questions. Suggested Readings. Illustrated with photographs and drawings.

HOBBS, WILLIAM
Stage Fight
Theatre Arts, 1967. 96pp. $6.95. From swords to firearms, from fisticuffs to slapstick, the stage fight is analyzed and explained. The author stresses the need to shape a fight so that it holds interest and furthers the characterization and he explains the role of movement patterns, rhythm, the element of surprise, and the need for safety precautions. There are thirty-two pages of plates showing a variety of fight scenes from eighteenth century productions to the present day.

THIMM, CARL A.
A Complete Bibliography of Fencing and Duelling
Blom, 1968. 538pp. $28.50. Originally published in 1896 and now reissued in a facsimile edition, this bibliography enumerates books and manuscripts, newspaper and magazine notices and articles, and accounts of duels. It contains thirty-four portraits, title-pages, frontispieces, and illustrations. An Index in Chronological Order, according to language, is also included as are Notes on Duelling and Fencing.

WISE, ARTHUR
Weapons in the Theatre
Barnes & Noble, 1968. 139pp. $10.00. Mr. Wise considers the factors that have prompted dramatists to make such wide use of the theatrical possibilities of physical violence and the relevance of violence in classical dramas to the present theatrical scene. He studies in detail the problems of mounting fights in the theatre: their plotting and rehearsal, and their integration into the total theatrical intention. Weapons in films and in television are also considered. Illustrated with drawings, diagrams, and photographs. Bibliography. Index.

PANTOMIME

ALBERTI, EVA
A Handbook of Acting
See Page 408

AUBERT, CHARLES
The Art of Pantomime
Blom, 1970. 210pp. $12.50. Originally published in 1927 and now reissued in the Edith Sears translation, this is a study of body, face and hand expression in pantomime for the theatre. Illustrated with drawings.

BROADBENT, R. J.
A History of Pantomime
Blom, 1965. 226pp. $5.75. A reprint of the study first published in 1901, this history traces the origins and development of pantomime from the ancient civilizations to the English theatre of the late eighteenth and nineteenth centuries. The techniques of such great English mimes as Grimaldi, Rich, and Weaver are discussed.

BRUFORD, ROSE
Teaching Mime
Barnes & Noble, 1969. 235pp. $5.95. First published in 1958 and now reprinted with corrections, this is a text providing a graduated program in mime with notes on the relation of mime to other subjects in the school curriculum. Included are a number of mime plays designed for large groups. Index.

CLINTON–BADDELEY, V. C.
Some Pantomime Pedigrees
See Page 187

DORCY, JEAN
The Mime
Robert Speller, 1961. 116pp. $4.95. A study of the art of the modern French mime, with chapters on the Ecole du Vieux-Colombier, the Comediens-Routiers, the Compagnie des Quinze, and the Compagnie Theatrale Proscenium. There are essays by Etienne Decroux, Jean-Louis Barrault, and Marcel Marceau. Illustrated.

ENTERS, ANGNA
On Mime
Wesleyan University, 1965. 132pp. $5.00. Developed from a log Miss Enters kept in which she recorded the adventure of trying to communicate her process of work to a group of young dancers, this book describes her complete theatre technique and theory. Illustrated with drawings by Miss Enters.

HUNT, DOUGLAS and KARI HUNT
Pantomime: The Silent Theatre
Atheneum, 1964. 115pp. $3.95. A history of pantomime from the earliest times with chapters on the modern day pure pantomimists and what they have contributed to the ancient art. Instructions are included on the basic skills. Illustrated. Bibliography.

LANDER, BARBARA
Music for Mime
Methuen, 1965. 118pp. Paper $5.00. A reprint of the 1958 edition, this book contains forty-eight musical selections for mime exercises plus the complete music for five mime plays by Rose Bruford. The music is intended to used in conjunction with Miss Bruford's book: "Teaching Mime."

SIDDONS, HENRY
Practical Illustrations of Rhetorical Gesture and Action
See Page 416

WALKER, KATHRINE SORLEY
Eyes on Mime: Language Without Speech
John Day, 1969. 190pp. $4.95. The author traces mime's development through history, the technique of different gesture languages belonging to different cultures, and the varying ways in which mime is used today. Illustrated with over thirty photographs of mimes and mime productions. Selected Bibliography. Selected Filmography. Index.

MAKE-UP

ANGELOGLOU, MAGGIE
A History of Make-Up
Macmillan, 1970. 144pp. $8.95. Originally published in England and now released in the United States, this is a study of make-up from the primitive ages to the present day. Illustrated with over eighty photographs and reproductions of period drawings and advertisements, ten of them in color. Bibliography. Index.

ASSER, JOYCE
Historic Hairdressing
Pitman, 1966. 134pp. $6.00. This book describes and illustrates hair styles from Assyrian times to the present day. Miss Asser is a leading authority on hairdressing. Illustrated. Glossary. Index.

BAIRD, JOHN F.
Make-Up: A Manual for the Use of Actors, Amateur and Professional
Samuel French, 1957. 132pp. $2.00. A revision of the 1930 edition, this is a simplified guidebook on the technique of make-up. Illustrated.

BAMFORD, T. W.
Practical Make-Up for the Stage
Pitman, 1965. 146pp. $5.95. The author analyzes the technique and practice of make-up. He discusses various racial types, character make-up, individual features, and the hair. Illustrated with drawings and photographs. Index.

BELL, SUSAN
250 Hair Styles
Pyramid, 1967. 127pp. Paper $ .60. Hairstyles for modern women are described and illustrated.

BENOLIEL, M. H.
Stage Make-Up Made Easy
Deane, 1967. 108pp. $2.25. Step-by-step instructions on make-up for amateurs. Illustrated.

BERK, BARBARA
The First Book of Stage Costume and Make-Up
See Page 338

BLORE, RICHARD
Stage Make-Up
Stacey, 1969. 24pp. Paper $1.75. A revised edition of the 1965 discussion of the general principles of make-up. List of Supplies.

BOTHAM, MARY and L. SHARRAD
Manual of Wigmaking
Heinemann, 1964. 112pp. $4.50. A manual for the trainee-wigmaker and hairdressing student, offering a detailed explanation of the processes involved in all aspects of hairdressing. Diagrams accompany each chapter. Among the items covered are boardwork, preparation of hair, weaving, uses of hair weft, preparing the pattern, foundation making, knotting, maintenance of Postiche. Glossary. Index.

BOUBLIK, VLASTIMIL
The Art of Make-Up for Stage, Television & Film
Pergamon, 1968. 187pp. $7.00. Translated from the Czech language, this is a detailed handbook on the use of make-up. The largest part of the book is devoted to the actual art of make-up: corrective make-up, changing the actor's personality and age, with and without the use of special accessories, the correct technique, new types of make-up and the technique of handling them. The book contains a large number of photographs and line drawings. Index.

CHARLES, ANN and ROGER DEANFRASIO
The History of Hair
Bonanza, 1970. 287pp. $4.95. An illustrated review of hair fashions for men throughout the ages from primitive times to the twentieth century. Also included in the volume is a guide to hair care for men. Subjects include styles, beards and moustaches, hair coloring, and hair care. Illustrated with photographs and drawings. Bibliography.

CORDWELL, MIRIAM and MARION RUDOY
Hair Design and Fashion
Crown, 1970. 288pp. $7.95. The fifth revised edition of the work originally published in 1956. Information about hairstyling and care, hair coloring, wigs and wiglets, make-up tricks, and grooming hints for the modern woman. Illustrated with drawings and photographs.

CORSON, RICHARD
Fashions in Hair
Humanities, 1969. 701pp. $24.00. Originally published in 1965 and now reissued, this is a comprehensive historical survey of the diversity of men's and women's hair styles through the ages. It ranges from Ancient Egyptian, Greek, Roman, and Anglo-Saxon times to recent trends in fashion. Over 3,000 drawings by the author illustrate the text. List of Sources. Index.

CORSON, RICHARD
Stage Make-Up
Appleton, 1967. 456pp. $11.00. A complete guide to every type of stage make-up. In this revised and enlarged fourth edition of the book first published in 1949, there is included a make-up color chart that offers a coordinating system of designating shades and tints of make-up sold by various manufacturers. Technical and historical information on hair is included as are 228 photographs and drawings and twenty-one plates illustrating various hair styles. Appendices. Index.

COX, J. STEVENS
An Illustrated Dictionary of Hairdressing and Wigmaking
Hairdressers' Technical Council, 1966. 359pp. Paper $10.50. Published in England, this is the first and only dictionary to provide the names and details of the different kinds of wigs, beards, moustaches, and hair styles of all periods of the past, and the processes of hairdressing, with their history, descriptions and meanings. An Appendix provides proverbs and popular sayings connected with human hair. Illustrated. Bibliography.

EMERALD, JACK
Make-Up in Amateur Movies, Drama, and Photography
Fountain, 1966. 93pp. $6.95. The author takes the reader through every aspect of make-up technique from basics for men and women to character, youth, old age, corrective techniques, and reconstruction of facial structure. Illustrated with sixty-nine halftone illustrations. Index.

HARRISON, MOLLY
Hairstyles and Hairdressing
Ward Lock, 1968. 71pp. $3.75. Published in England, this volume traces the history and development of hairstyles from the seventeenth century to the present. The styles are illustrated in drawings and photographs. Index.

HYMAN, REBECCA
The Complete Guide to Wigs and Hairpieces
Grosset & Dunlap, 1968. 96pp. Spiral bound $1.95. A guide to the purchase, fitting, setting, cleaning, and styling of wigs and hairpieces. The volume is illustrated with photographs showing Miss Hyman's techniques and a gallery of the latest styles.

HYMAN, REBECCA
Hairpieces and Wigs
Bantam, 1968. 96pp. Paper $ .50. What to buy, how to spot good quality, professional secrets for fitting, setting, cutting, tinting, conditioning, cleaning, and storing—professional tips on wigs from a professional. Illustrated with photographs and drawings.

JONES, ERIC
Make-Up for School Plays
Batsford, 1969. 94pp. $5.00. Published in England, this book concentrates on the make-up needs of the school production and the young performer. All aspects of make-up are covered in straightforward instruction and in drawings by the author. Index.

KEHOE, VINCENT J–R.
The Technique of Film and Television Make-Up
Hastings House, 1969. 280pp. $16.50. Originally published in 1957 and now fully revised, this is essentially a new book. Reflected herein are all the advances made in compatible systems which require make-up to be photographed in both color and black-and-white simultaneously. Information on facial anatomy, the make-up kit and tools, the make-up department, straight and corrective make-up, character, age, racial and national types, period and historical types, special effect techniques, and hair goods are all included. Illustrated with drawings and photographs. Index.

KEYES, JEAN
A History of Women's Hairstyles: 1500 to 1965
Methuen, 1967. 86pp. $4.50. This is a series of drawings and commentary on women's hairstyles. Printed in England, it also includes a selection of accessories and jewelry illustrated in black-and-white. Index.

LISZT, RUDOLPH G.
The Last Word in Make-Up
Dramatists Play Service, 1970. 138pp. $3.50. A completely rewritten version of the 1942 course in make-up for the stage, with sections on street make-up,methods for photography, and make-up for television. The book is arranged in a series of courses, ranging from the basic to the advanced. Illustrated with drawings, photographs and make-up charts. Index.

MELVILL, HARALD
Magic of Make-Up for the Stage
Theatre Arts, 1967. 89pp. $3.50. This is an illustrated guide to modern methods of make-up for the stage. Originally published in 1958, this revised edition is a practical manual giving the most modern methods. Illustrated with photographs and drawings. List of Make-up Materials. Index.

PERROTTET, PHILLIPPE
Practical Stage Make-Up
Reinhold, 1967. 96pp. $8.50. This book deals comprehensively and in an up-to-date and profesfessional manner with make-up. It sets out to describe the purpose of make-up, the basic equipment and materials needed, and exactly how to set about achieving a sucessful result. Basic make-ups, character make-ups, how to make the face look older or younger, and racial, stylised and fantastic make-ups are described and the use of putty, wigs, and false hair are included. How to apply a complete body make-up is also included. The text is illustrated with line drawings by Motley and with photographs. List of Suppliers. Index.

SEQUEIRA, HORACE
Stage Make-Up
Barrie & Jenkins, 1953. 94pp. $1.75. Basic instructions for amateur actors, with chapters on implements, greasepaints, character and straight make-up, open air performances, and character make-up in fiction and history. Illustrated with drawings. Index.

THOMAS, CHARLES
Make-Up: The Dramatic Student's Approach
Theatre Arts, 1968. 48pp. $2.25. Originally published in 1951 and revised for this edition, the emphasis in this volume is on the reasons for using make-up. It is the author's aim to send the player to his mirror knowing exactly what he wants to do to his face and why. Bibliography.

VOEGE, RAY
Beauty Secrets for the Black Woman
Simon & Schuster, 1970. 96pp. Paper $1.00. A book on make-up for the black woman by a television make-up artist. Illustrated with photographs and drawings.

VOEGE, RAY
Look Like a Star
Simon & Schuster, 1969. 96pp. Paper $1.00. NBC—TV make-up artist, Ray Voege, presents a guide to make-up for the modern woman. Basic and corrective make-up, make-up for the teenage girl and the black woman are covered in drawings and photographs.

CAREER OPPORTUNITIES

BLAKELOCK, DENYS
Making the Stage Your Career
W. & G. Foyle, 1965. 82pp. $1.25. A guide for those considering the stage as a career. Mr. Blakelock, an English actor, teacher and coach, provides information and advice on careers in acting, design, lighting, stage management, and production. Illustrated with photographs. List of Drama Schools in England. List of Books for Suggested Reading. Index.

CAPON, ERIC
Drama as a Career

Batsford, 1963. 127pp. $3.25. The Director of Drama Studies at Britain's Guildhall School of Music and Drama discusses the vicissitudes and rewards of a career in the theatre. He considers opportunities available in theatre, television, and radio, and discusses the role of agents and the function of British Actors' Equity. Also included are lists of useful names, addresses, books. Illustrated. Index.

DALRYMPLE, JEAN
Careers and Opportunities in the Theatre
Dutton, 1969. 256pp. $5.95. A guide for those who wish to have a career in the theatre. Miss Dalrymple deals with all aspects of the theatre today: what it is like to be an actor, how to survive in New York, how auditions, tryouts and rehearsals are conducted, what are the special qualifications of the musical actor, and the specifics of training for each type of theatre. There are sections on the theatre from the actor's point of view, musical theatre, the playwright, and careers backstage. Appendices provide a sample resume, lists of schools, teachers, agents, and repertory and summer stock theatres. Illustrated. Index.

GRAY, DULCIE and MICHAEL DENISON
The Actor and His World
Gollancz, 1964. 160pp. $3.50. A guide for the young person on careers in the theatre. The English authors provide chapters on training, the different fields for the actor, careers backstage, and advice on subjects from professional behavior to the best way to cope with success—or failure.

HIRSCHFELD, BURT
Stagestruck: Your Career in Theatre
Messner, 1963. 191pp. $3.95. This guide to opportunities for the beginner considers the work of actors, business managers, choreographers, dancers, designers, directors, playwrights, press agents, and stagehands. Bibliography. Glossary. Index.

HOOKS, ED – Compiler
Agents by Building
Ed Hooks, 1970. 27pp. Paper $1.35. All Manhattan SAG, AFTRA and Equity agents are arranged geographically by street and building with an alphabetical cross reference.

JOELS, MERRILL E.
How to Get Into Show Business
Hastings House, 1969. 157pp. $5.95. A revised and expanded edition of the 1955 publication, "Acting Is a Business." Mr. Joels provides a practical approach to obtaining experience, breaking in, and getting work in theatre and films, television and radio. Appendix of Sources and Services. Illustrated.

LAGOS, POPPY
Geographic Casting Guide
Lagos Enterprises, 1970. 15pp. Paper $1.75. A listing of over 350 New York City casting contacts for performers. The contacts are arranged geographically with an alphabetical cross-reference guide.

LEADLEY, TOM and TERENCE DIXON
The Stage: A Picture Career Book
Lutterworth Press, 1970. 80pp. $4.50. Published in England, this is a book for young people about to embark on a career in the theatre. Details on how to make a start, with a section on British drama schools and a special Appendix on opportunities and training. There is also a feature on teaching drama. Illustrated with photographs.

LERCH, JOHN H. – Editor
Careers in Broadcasting
See Page 496

MOORE, DICK
Opportunities in Acting: Stage, Motion Pictures, and Television
Universal, 1963. 128pp. Paper $1.95. A realistic discussion of the business of acting, stressing the practical aspects of the professsion. Information on unions, agents, contracts, auditions, interviews, making rounds, and landing a job.

NICHOLSON, DIANNE
Turn On to Stardom
Simon & Schuster, 1968. 192pp. Paper $1.45. This is a guidebook for individuals who would like to break into show business. It discusses how to prepare at home or in professional schools, the opportunities in various major cities, photographs and resumes, where to look for jobs, what talent agents and managers do, and how to audition.

ROWLEY, LILLIAN
So You Want to Go on the Stage
Kenneth Mason, 1970. 69pp. $3.95. A guide to the training available in England in the various entertainment fields: drama, music, ballet, singing, musical instruments. Facts on the training necessary, financial rewards available, how to find an agent, plus a directory of schools in England.

SOLOTAIRE, ROBERT SPENCER
How to Get Into Television
See Page 496

MODELING

JONES, CANDY
Modeling and Other Glamour Careers
Harper & Row, 1969. 227pp. $5.95. Paper – Pocket Books, 1970. 248pp. $ .95. Miss Jones analyzes the modeling and glamour industries and guides would-be models on how to get started and modeling opportunities. Illustrated. Index.

JONES, CANDY
More Than Beauty
Harper & Row, 1970. 175pp. $5.95. Miss Jones tells the story of her years as one of America's top models and provides advice on modeling careers.

KENMORE, CAROLYN
Mannequin: My Life as a Model
Bantam, 1970. 341pp. Paper $ .95. Originally published in 1969 and now reissued, this is a behind-the-scenes look at the world of the model.

SHULL, LEO – Editor
Models Guide
Leo Shull, 1969. 128pp. Paper $2.75. A guide for models and would-be models. Provided are listings of model agencies and firms that employ models.

SCENES AND MONOLOGUES

BOLTON, BARBARA and JOHN RICHMOND
The New Drama: A Selection of Fifty Speeches for Actors
Samuel French, 1966. 57pp. $2.25. The three to five minute speeches in this collection are for actors of various age ranges from twenties to elderly. Among the extracts are scenes from "Entertaining Mr. Sloane" and "The Caretaker."

BOLTON, BARBARA and JOHN RICHMOND
The New Drama: A Selection of Fifty Speeches for Actresses
Samuel French, 1966. 57pp. $2.25. The speeches in this anthology are for actresses ranging in age from fifteen to elderly. The speeches range in length from three to five minutes and include cuttings from such plays as "Anne Frank," "Gigi," and "Mother Courage."

CARROLL, ROBERT F.
All For the Ladies
Samuel French, 1949. 103pp. Paper $1.50. A collection of twenty-five monologues for women. The characters range from the social climber to the saleslady.

COSGROVE, FRANCES – Editor
Scenes for Student Actors: Volume One
Samuel French, 1934. 129pp. $2.00. Monologues for one man or one woman, scenes for one man and one woman, for two men or two women, and group scenes for men, boys, or women. Forty-five cuttings from plays including "Ah, Wilderness!" "Berkeley Square," "Springtime for Henry," "Girls in Uniform," "Holiday," "Cavalcade," "The Barretts of Wimpole Street," and "Elizabeth the Queen."

COSGROVE, FRANCES – Editor
Scenes for Student Actors: Volume Two
Samuel French, 1935. 142pp. $2.00. Identical in format with Volume One, this collection contains forty-six cuttings from plays by Maxwell Anderson, S. N. Behrman, Noel Coward, Emlyn Williams, Lynn Riggs, Sommerset Maugham, J. B. Priestley, Paul Green and others.

COSGROVE, FRANCES – Editor
Scenes for Student Actors: Volume Three
Samuel French, 1937. 127pp. $2.00. The same format as Volumes One and Two. The scenes have been chosen to illustrate a problem in acting such as sustaining a theme, utilizing props, speaking in dialect, building a scene to a climax, or portraying a character in an unusual situation. Among the playwrights are: Lynn Riggs, Harold Brighouse, the Spewacks, Sidney Howard, Robert Sherwood, and Maxwell Anderson.

COSGROVE, FRANCES – Editor
Scenes for Student Actors: Volume Four
Samuel French, 1939. 132pp. $2.00. Fifty scenes for one actor, one actress, two men or two women, one man and one woman, or groups. The selection includes both comedy and dramatic scenes from plays including: "Idiot's Delight," "French Without Tears," "Golden Boy," "Night Must Fall," "Stage Door," "Tovarich," and "Of Mice and Men."

COSGROVE, FRANCES – Editor
Scenes for Student Actors: Volume Five
Samuel French, 1942. 114pp. $2.00. Forty-five scenes for one man, one woman, two men, two women, one man and one woman, or three women. Playwrights include William Saroyan, James Thurber, J. B. Priestley, Robert Sherwood, Philip Barry, S. N. Behrman, Lynn Riggs, Patrick Hamilton, and John Van Druten.

COSGROVE, FRANCES – Editor
Scenes for Student Actors: Volume Six
Samuel French, 1958. 102pp. $2.00. Forty-three scenes in a format identical to the volumes above. Selections from plays: "The Rainmaker," "Caine Mutiny Court-Martial," "A Hatful of Rain," "Time Limit," "Witness for the Prosecution," "Ondine," "The Reluctant Debutante," "Medea," "The Innocents," "Anastasia," and "Come Back Little Sheba," among others.

DOWNS, HAROLD – Editor
Anthology of Play Scenes, Verse and Prose
Pitman, 1949. 258pp. $4.50. Two hundred and two short play scenes or cuttings from poetry or prose works. Among the playwrights represented are: Shakespeare, Sheridan, Barrie, Priestley, Rattigan, O'Neill, and Steinbeck.

DOWNS, HAROLD – Editor
A Second Anthology of Play Scenes, Verse, and Prose
Pitman, 1951. 278pp. $3.75. Identical in format to the above. Among the playwrights included are:

Shakespeare, Sheridan, Van Druten, Saroyan, Wilde, Chekhov, and Christopher Fry.

GREENSLADE, MARY and ANNE HARVEY
Scenes for Two: Book One – Dialogues for Young Players
Samuel French, Undated. 117pp. Paper $2.00. A selection of forty-five scenes for young people up to the age of about fifteen; however, many of the scenes do require older actors and actresses. Cuttings include extracts from "Tom Sawyer," "Beauty and the Beast," "The Blue Bird," "Hansel and Gretel," "Heidi," "Junior Miss," "The Member of the Wedding," "Pinocchio," and "The Wizard of Oz."

GREENSLADE, MARY and ANNE HARVEY
Scenes for Two: Book Two – Duologues for Girls and Women
Samuel French, Undated. 140pp. Paper $2.00. A selection of forty-five scenes for two women. Among the extracts are scenes from: "Antigone," "The Chalk Garden," "Five Finger Exercise," "The Glass Menagerie," "Hedda Gabler," "Look Back in Anger," "Pygmalion," "Rebecca," and "A Taste of Honey."

HALL, WILLIS and KEITH WATERHOUSE – Editors
Writers' Theatre
Heinemann, 1967. 113pp. $3.50. Selections from ten plays by English playwrights with introductions to the plays by the editors. The cuttings require various numbers of actors of various ages and both sexes. Among the represented authors are John Arden, Henry Livings, John Mortimer, John Osborne, Harold Pinter, N. F. Simpson, and Waterhouse and Hall.

HODAPP, WILLIAM
Face Your Audience
Hasting House, 1956. 130pp. $2.95. Twenty-eight audition readings for actors. Four complete sketches for various combinations of actors and actresses, six monologues, an anecdote, a commercial, a complete television script, and thirteen cuttings from long plays are included. Appendix. Bibliography.

HOLGATE, JOHN and RONA LAURIE
Eleventh Anthology of Poetry, Prose and Play Scenes
Guildhall School, 1969. 269pp. $4.50. More than 200 selections for a single actor or actress. Among the playwrights represented are: Shakespeare, Beaumont and Fletcher, Wilde, Shaw, Anouilh, Osborne, Brecht, O'Neill, and Moliere.

KLINE, PETER
The Theatre Student: Scenes to Perform
Richards Rosen, 1969. 190pp. $6.96. The author has chosen a selection of scenes for the theatre student. Each scene is prefaced with commentary on the playwright, the scene, the character, and the characterization. Nine scenes for men and eight scenes for women include cuttings from, among other plays, "The Taming of the Shrew," "Macbeth," "Peer Gynt," "An Ideal Husband," "Hamlet," "Richard III," "The Miser," and "Cyrano de Bergerac."

MASTERS, EDGAR LEE
The New Spoon River
Collier, 1968. 325pp. Paper $1.25. Originally published in 1924 and now reissued, this is the continuation of Master's "Spoon River Anthology." Included are 322 microbiographies describing the lives and relationships of the citizens of a small American town in the 1920's.

MASTERS, EDGAR LEE
Spoon River Anthology
Collier, 1962. 318pp. Paper $1.25. Originally published in 1915, this is a series of poetic monologues by 244 former inhabitants (both real and imagined) of Spoon River, Illinois. The monologues are in free verse form.

OLFSON, LEWY – Editor
Fifty Great Scenes for Student Actors
Bantam, 1970. 318pp. Paper $ .95. Scenes for various combinations of actors and actresses are included in this anthology. Among the playwrights represented are: Shakespeare, Chekhov, O'Neill, Ibsen, Arthur Miller, Terence Rattigan, and Tennessee Williams.

PERTWEE, E. GUY
For the Actress
Samuel French, Undated. 81pp. $2.25. Fifty speeches from well-known plays for actresses. Among the playwrights represented are Chekhov, Wilde, Maugham, Priestley, Fry, Milne, Congreve, and Rattigan.

RUBINSTEIN, H. F. and J. C. TREWIN – Editors
The Drama Bedside Book
Atheneum, 1966. 542pp. $7.50. A collection of scenes from the plays of the past 2,400 years. Each scene is prefaced by brief notes to orient the reader and bring the plot into focus. Among the playwrights represented: Sophocles, Marlowe, Shakespeare, Jonson, Ford, Moliere, Goldoni, Sheridan, Goethe, Ibsen, Strindberg, Wilde, Chekhov, Pinero, Shaw, Synge, O'Casey, Yeats, Fry, Bagnold, and Wesker.

RYERSON, FLORENCE and COLIN CLEMENTS
Isn't Nature Wonderful?
Dramatists Play Service, 1938. 78pp. Paper $1.50. A book of twenty-one monologues for men and women.

SELIGMAN, MARJORIE and SONYA FOGLE
More Solo Readings for Radio and Class Work
Dramatists Play Service, 1944. 50pp. Paper $1.50. Twenty-six cuttings for women and twenty-three cuttings for men are included in this anthology of solo readings. Among the authors represented are: Lillian Hellman, Moss Hart, John Steinbeck, Robert Sherwood, Elmer Rice, F. Hugh Herbert, and Mary Orr and Reginald Denham.

SELIGMAN, MARJORIE and SONYA FOGLE
Solo Readings for Radio and Class Work
Dramatists Play Service, 1941. 55pp. Paper $1.50. Among the forty-nine selections in this anthology are extracts from the works of leading playwrights. Scenes are included for ingenues, juveniles, leading men and women, and character men and women. Among the playwrights included are: Ben Hecht, Irwin Shaw, Edna Ferber and George S. Kaufman, Elmer Rice, Clare Booth, Sidney Kingsley, and Arthur Kober.

SELIGMAN, MARJORIE and SONYA FOGLE
Still More Solo Readings for Radio and Class Work
Dramatist, 1947. 57pp. Paper $1.50. Thirty cuttings for women, and twenty-seven cuttings for men, both serious and comic. Among the plays from which selections are included: "Dear Ruth," "Snafu," "Laura," "The Corn Is Green," "State of the Union," "Deep Are the Roots," "The Searching Wind," The Hasty Heart," and "The Late George Apley."

STEFFENSEN, JAMES L. – Editor
Great Scenes from The World Theatre
Avon, 1965. 573pp. Paper $1.65. Eighty-six scenes from more than fifty plays, selected for the professional use of actors, teachers, and students. Arranged in chapters which parallel the approaches of basic acting courses, the selections include monologues and scenes for two or more characters. Among the playwrights included: Mary Chase, Eugene O'Neill, Elmer Rice, Tennessee Williams, Arthur Kopit, William Inge, Arthur Miller, Arthur Laurents, Phillip Barry, Jean Kerr, and many others. Index.

THOMPSON, ARNOLD – Editor
Listen: Dramatic Monologues and Dialogues
English Universities Press, 1968. 86pp. $2.25. A collection of thirty-eight selections in English verse. Among the poets included are: John Betjeman, D. H. Lawrence, Robert Browning, T. S. Eliot, John Donne, W. H. Auden, and Theodore Roethke. Index to Further Readings. Appendix of Notes, Questions, and Suggestions for Written Work.

WALKER, MAVIS – Editor
Audition Pieces for Actresses
Samuel French, Undated. 75pp. $2.25. Fifty speeches from contemporary drama for actresses. Among the playwrights represented are: Anouilh, Brecht, Coward, Eliot, Priestley, Rattigan, Sartre, Chekhov and Williams.

YAEGER, MARSHALL
Micro Plays: Volume One
Embassy, 1968. 92pp. Paper $1.50. A collection of original scenes written for students to use in scene study classes and for auditions. The twelve scenes include five scenes for women, three scenes for men, and four scenes for couples.

YAEGER, MARSHALL
Micro Plays: Volume Two
Embassy, 1968. 183pp. Paper $1.50. Thirteen original scenes for students including four scenes for couples, six for actors over twenty-five, and three scenes for "senior citizens."

YOUNG, JOHN WRAY
Audition Scenes for Students
Dramatic Publishing Company, 1967. 176pp. Paper $1.75. Twenty-four monologues or scenes for various combinations of actors. The editor has provided notes on each scene. Among the selections are cuttings from works by Aeschylus, Shakespeare, John Osborne, William Golding, and Guy Bolton.

SPEECH

Training

For other books on this subject, see the "Vocal Training" section of Musical Theatre.

ANDERSON, VIRGIL A.
Training the Speaking Voice
Oxford, 1961. 453pp. $8.50. A second edition, revised, of the book first published in 1942, this text is designed for use in courses that study voice, diction, speech, and other subjects that stress the use of the voice as a basic approach to the problems of self-expression and communication. A long section deals with diction with practice exercises in the use of the phonetic alphabet. Illustrated. Bibliography.

AVERY, ELIZABETH and JANE DORSEY, VERA A. SICKELS
First Principles of Speech Training
Appleton, 1956. 518pp. $5.50. A presentation of the scientific principles of speech training and their application to the improvement of everyday speech. The authors discuss speech in its relation to the general education of the student, study voice and its articulation, and survey the elementary principles of group discussion, debate, public speaking, and oral reading. Exercises are provided for practice in posture, breathing, voice production articulation, and public speaking. Illustrated. Bibliography.

BENEDICT, STEWART H.
Famous American Speeches
Dell, 1967. 224pp. Paper $ .50. A collection of twenty-two American speeches—most of them political but also including humorous and inspirational speeches as well.

BLACK, JOHN W. and RUTH B. IRWIN
Voice and Diction: Applied Phonation and Phonology
Charles E. Merrill, 1969. 296pp. $9.50. A text book on speech in which the authors explain the processes

which underlie the production of speech, discuss diction and pronunciation, and develop a motor theory of speech perception. Exercise selections are provided. Appendices. Index.

BRAUDE, JACOB M.
The Complete Art of Public Speaking
Bantam, 1970. 217pp. Paper $ .95. A guide for public speakers with general rules on speech-making. More than 1,000 ideas, quotations and anecdotes are arranged in categories. Subject Index.

BROCKETT, OSCAR and SAMUEL L. BECKER, DONALD C. BRYANT
A Bibliographical Guide to Research in Speech and Dramatic Art
See Page 3

COFFIN, L. CHARTERIS
Stage Speech
Barrie & Jenkins, 1963. 96pp. $1.75. Basic lessons in speaking for the stage, with chapters on the communication of emotion, characterization, conventions of stage speech, speech for the verse play, and style. Bibliography. Index.

COLSON, GRETA
Speech Practice
Museum Press, 1970. 80pp. $2.50. A series of passages in verse and prose, originally published in 1967 and now reissued. The material is intended to exercise the speech organs and increase awareness of sounds and words.

COLSON, GRETA
Voice Production and Speech
Museum Press, 1963. 80pp. $2.95. An attempt to define the terms used in speech training in view of technical advances and to place the theory on a thoroughly practical basis. Sections on breath, note, and tone, and exercises for practice. Illustrated with diagrams. Bibliography.

COPELAND, LEWIS and LAWRENCE LAMM – Editors
The World's Great Speeches
Dover, 1958. 745pp. Paper $4.00. A collection of 255 speeches by 216 speakers from antiquity to the present.

DESFOSSES, BEATRICE
Your Voice and Your Speech: Self-Training for Better Speaking
Hill & Wang, 1959. 293pp. $4.95. A revised edition of the book first published in 1946, this text aims at developing confidence in the beginning speaker. The author provides examples that clarify the techniques of relaxation, posture, breath-control, and articulation.

DRAGONETTE, JESSICA
Your Voice and You
Rodale Books, 1966. 243pp. $4.95. Miss Dragonette sets down her own rules for developing skill in speaking. Written for the layman, the volume describes the techniques of improving and using the vocal instrument. Index.

ECROYD, DONALD H. and MURRAY M. HALFOND, CAROL C. TOWNE
Voice and Articulation: A Handbook
Scott, Foresman, 1966. 144pp. Paper $3.00. A text designed to help students understand language formation and delivery, to provide them with the tools to analyze their own speech, and to help them determine what changes are desirable. Illustrated. Index.

EISENSON, JON
The Improvement of Voice and Diction
Macmillan, 1965. 370pp. $6.95. This is the second edition, revised, of the text originally published in 1958. Consideration is given to the mechanism for speech, to breathing, tone production, resonance, pitch, vocal variety, speech patterns, and study of American-English sounds. Appendices include a Glossary of Terms, Voice Improvement Check List, and Pronunciation and Articulation Check List. Illustrated with drawings and diagrams. Index.

FAIRBANKS, GRANT
Voice and Articulation Drillbook
Harper & Row, 1960. 196pp. $7.35. Originally published in 1937, this is a completely rewritten edition. It is a book of practice materials for the improvement of voice and articulation. It stresses auditory discrimination and takes its organization from the phonetic and acoustic figures of speech. Illustrated. List of References. Index.

GRASHAM, JOHN A. and GLENN G. GOODER
Improving Your Speech
Harcourt, Brace, 1960. 326pp. Paper $6.25. This text for voice and diction improvemet begins with an evaluation of the individual student's speech, and progresses to an introduction to the speech process and the procedures to be followed for speech improvement. The authors discuss control of breathing, vocal power, and improvement of articulation. Exercises are provided and the authors include an instructor's test sheet at the end of every chapter. Illustrated with drawings, diagrams, and charts. Index.

HEDDE, WILHELMINA G. and WILLIAM NORWOOD BRIGANCE, VICTOR M. POWELL
The New American Speech
Lippincott, 1968. 535pp. $7.50. Originally published in 1942 as "American Speech," this is the third edition of this textbook. The authors' purposes are to teach students how to listen efficiently and how to speak effectively All phases of theatre speech are covered and practical exercises for students are included. Suggested classroom activities are also provided as are comprehensive lists of references. Illustrated with photographs. Index.

HEFFNER, ROE-MERRILL S.
General Phonetics
University of Wisconsin, 1964. 253pp. Paper $4.50. A detailed explanation of the physiology of speech and the physics of speech sounds. The principle types of speech sound are described with their variations and their occurrence both as individual phenomena and as speech sounds in context. Index.

HELLIER, MARJORIE
How to Develop a Better Speaking Voice
Wilshire Book Co., 1959. 124pp. Paper $1.00. A brief manual of basic instructions in voice improvement, illustrated with drawings.

HORNER, A. MUSGRAVE
Movement, Voice and Speech
Methuen, 1970. 142pp. $4.50. Paper $2.50. The author, an experienced teacher/broadcaster/producer, provides four main features in this volume: a statement of the basis of effective speech, guidance towards expressive extemporaneous speech, a creative approach to interpretational speech, and an approach to "theory" and "technique" of speech. Glossary. Reading List. Index.

HORNER, A. MUSGRAVE
Speech Training: A Handbook for Students
A. & C. Black, 1969. 176pp. $3.50. Originally published in 1951 and reprinted in 1959 with corrections, this is a collection of information on speech. There are chapters and exercises on vocal expression, breathing, voice production, and movement allied to speech as well as a section of selections for study and practice. List of Books for Further Study.

JONES, DANIEL
English Pronouncing Dictionary
Dutton, 1967. 544pp. $7.00. Edited by A. C. Gimson, this is a completely revised and enlarged thirteenth edition of the text first published in 1917. It contains over 58,000 words in the International Phonetic transcription and a Glossary of Phonetic Terms.

JONES, DANIEL
The Pronunciation of English
Cambridge, 1966. 223pp. $3.75. Paper $1.95. This manual of phonetics deals particularly with English pronunciation. It is written from the viewpoint of the English student and is the standard work on the subject. First published in 1909, it has been regularly revised to bring it up-to-date. This is a reprint of the fourth edition of 1956 with minor corrections. Illustrated with diagrams, charts, and photographs.

KARR, HARRISON M.
Developing Your Speaking Voice
Harper & Row, 1953. 506pp. $12.50. A text for beginning college classes in which the author presents a developmental program for voice improvement. Corrective exercises and drill exercises are provided. The text is divided into two sections: producing the voice and using the voice. Illustrated with drawings and diagrams. Index.

LESSAC, ARTHUR
The Use and Training of the Human Voice
Drama Book Specialists, 1967. 297pp. $8.00. First published in 1961, this second edition has been completely revised, rewritten and re-illustrated. In his text the author demonstrates that vocal skills cannot be separated from speech skills, and training cannot be separated from use. In three sections, the book takes the student from a new look at the fundamentals of voice and speech training, through Lessac's specific principles and practice, into the creative and exploratory use of the trained skills. Illustrated.

LEVY, LOUIS and EDWARD W. MAMMEN, ROBERT SANKIN
Voice and Speech Handbook
Prentice–Hall, 1960. 138pp. Paper $4.95. This is a revised edition of the authors' "Voice and Diction Handbook." It is intended as a brief, practical text for beginning courses in speech on the college level.

McBURNEY, JAMES H. and ERNEST J. WRAGE
Guide to Good Speech
Prentice–Hall, 1965. 339pp. $8.95. This new edition of the text originally published in 1955 is designed to present a concise statement of the principles of good speech as a basis for speech improvement. Each chapter contains exercises for the student and there is a selection of sample speeches. Illustrated. Index.

MACHLIN, EVANGELINE
Speech for the Stage
Theatre Arts, 1966. 246pp. $6.75. Dr. Machlin sets down the essence of her experience in teaching speech. After showing how to re-educate the actor's voice projection, she describes acoustics and the way the body functions to produce speech. With the help of exercises, she deals with such elements as relaxation, phonetics, articulation, resonance, pitch, rate of speech, and stress. There are chapters on speech in Shakespeare, the use of dialects, sight reading, auditioning, and actual performance. Illustrated. Index.

McLEAN, MARGARET PRENDERGAST
Good American Speech
Dutton, 1968. 381pp. $7.95. Originally published in 1928, this speech text has been acclaimed as one of the most scientific and most explicit by professionals and laymen. It offers a self-teaching tool to everyone concerned with good speech. This edition offers a special new Introduction and a revised chapter on current speech conditions in America. Bibliography. Index.

MANSER, RUTH B.
Speech Improvement on the Contract Plan
Chilton, 1961. 408pp. $6.00. Originally published

in 1935, this is a revised third edition of the manual of speech improvement for adults. The author breaks the corrective program into small work-units for individualized action.

MILES–BROWN, J.
Speech Training and Dramatic Art
Pitman, 1963. 184pp. $6.50. Published in England, this guide discusses the technicalities of voice and speech, prosody, acting, stage management, and improvised drama. Included are exercises for speech and voice training, with suggestions for those taking examinations and those judging voice and acting competitions. Illustrated with diagrams and plates.

O'CONNOR, J.D.
Better English Pronunciation
Cambridge, 1967. 179pp. Paper $1.95. This is a systematic introduction to the pronunciation of English, especially written for the foreign learner, and it starts from the analysis of English speech sounds provided by phonetic research. After an introduction to the general problems of pronunciation, a survey of the basic sounds, and an introduction to phonetic notation, the author takes the categories of sounds one by one. Practice material is given and remedial exercises provided.

PRICE, AUDREY and DAVID PRICE
Speak for Yourself
Mills & Boon, 1965. 96pp. $1.95. This book is intended to point the way to efficient speech. Among the topics discussed are audibility, vocabulary, preparation and delivery of a talk, impromptu speaking, reading aloud, and verse speaking. The authors include practical exercises.

PUNT, NORMAN A.
The Singer's and Actor's Throat
Heinemann, 1967. 99pp. Paper $3.95. Originally published in 1952, this is a second edition of the work by the adviser to the National Theatre Company, the Royal Shakespeare Company, and other companies in England. The author studies the vocal mechanism of the professional voice user and its care in health and disease. Bibliography. Index.

ROBINSON, DARL F. and CHARLOTTE LEE
Speech in Action
Scott, Foresman, 1965. 506pp. $6.75. A text on speech for high school students. The essentials of speech are covered in six sections. Each section includes a selection of activities and exercises for the student. Illustrated. Bibliography. Index.

SARNOFF, DOROTHY
Speech Can Change Your Life
Doubleday, 1970. 346pp. $6.95. Miss Sarnoff draws on her experience as a singer and an actress to develop a method of freeing speech from distracting vocal blemishes. Exercises in breathing, pronunciation, and speech delivery are provided. Appendices include a selection of speeches to read aloud and a group of short punchlines to use in speeches. Index.

SHERIDAN, THOMAS
A Course of Lectures on Elocution
Blom, 1968. 262pp. $13.75. Originally published in London in 1762 and now reissued, this is a facsimile edition of a series of lectures on elocution. The volume also contains "Two Dissertations on Language."

SKINNER, EDITH WARMAN
Speak With Distinction
Edwards, 1965. 274pp. Spiral bound $5.50. This volume provides speech exercises for the actor. Among the subjects studied are: voice production, vowels, consonants, dipthongs, syllibication, pronunciation, and phrasing.

THURBURN, GWYNNETH L.
Voice and Speech
Nisbit & Co., 1965. 156pp. $3.95. Originally published in England in 1939 and now reprinted, this book on speech was written primarily for teachers of general subjects who must include speech training among their activities. It is an introduction to the subject and Miss Thurburn provides explanations and exercises for rhythm, breathing, pitch, development of muscular activity, verse speaking and choral speaking.

WISE, CLAUDE MERTON
Applied Phonetics
Prentice–Hall, 1957. 546pp. $15.50. The aim of this book is to apply phonetic symbols and nomenclature to the description of the principle varieties of the English language in America and the British Isles. The student is introduced to the use of the International Phonetic Alphabet as a tool applied to English and certain foreign languages. Standard and sub-standard speech are examined.

WOOLBERT, CHARLES HENRY and SEVERINA E. NELSON
The Art of Interpretative Speech
Appleton, 1968. 586pp. $8.95. This fifth and revised edition of the text first published in 1956 studies the techniques of interpretative speech through controlled use of vocal and bodily skills. New material includes chapters on structure, meaning, and point of view in literature, and a fuller anthology of literature. Index of Names. Index of Selections.

Dialects

BLUNT, JERRY
Speech Dialects
Chandler, 1967. 156pp. $8.00. The author provides a single source for the study of the most used stage

dialects. Provided are key sounds, word drill, sounds in sentence context, and practice exercises. Among the dialects studied are: Standard English, American Southern, Brooklynese, Japanese, Irish, French, Italian, German, and Russian. Index.

BRONSTEIN, ARTHUR J.
The Pronunciation of American English
Appleton, 1960. 320pp. $9.65. An introduction to phonetics. The text is written for use in classes and deals with the sounds of American English. The author deals with the basic concept of phonetics and the subject of dialects. He details the sounds and discusses special aspects of the sound system. Included are a question and review section and a selection of exercises. Illustrated. Bibliography. Index.

HERMAN, LEWIS and MARGUERITE SHALETT HERMAN
Foreign Dialects: A Manual for Actors, Directors, and Writers
Theatre Arts, 1943. 415pp. $8.50. Thirty of the principal foreign dialects of various national groups are given with character studies, speech peculiarities, and examples of the dialects in phonetic monologues. Musical inflection graphs show the pace and pitch of delivery. A simplified visual phonetic system is used. The authors provide a slip-out card showing symbols.

PART THREE

BOOKS ON MOTION PICTURES, TELEVISION, AND RADIO

PART THREE: BOOKS ON MOTION PICTURES, TELEVISION, AND RADIO

MOTION PICTURES

WORLD CINEMA

Histories, Appreciations and Critiques

ALTSHULER, THELMA and RICHARD PAUL JANARO
Responses to Drama
See Page 10

AMELIO, RALPH J. with ANITA OWEN, SUSAN SCHAEFER
Willowbrook Cinema Study Project
Pflaum, 1969. 84pp. Paper $4.00. A guidebook to a program offered at a high school in Illinois. This two-semester course on film as a medium for intellectual and aesthetic experience is described with suggested activities correlated. A suggested calendar is provided. Annotated Bibliography. List of Periodicals.

ARNHEIM, RUDOLF
Film As Art
University of California, 1960. 230pp. Paper $1.95. A collection of reviews, originally written in the 1930's, in which the major thesis is that the silent film makers were using the limitations of the medium to create a new art form until mechanical advances led to greater realism and a loss of artistry. The talking picture is evaluated as a medium of expression.

BALL, ROBERT HAMILTON
Shakespeare on Silent Film
See Page 93

BALSHOFER, FRED J. and ARTHUR C. MILLER
One Reel a Week
University of California, 1967. 218pp. $6.95. Two veteran film-makers write of their experiences and observations during the years when the patterns of the movie industry were being formed. The history covers the years 1905 to the 1950's and is Illustrated with working scenes from the early studios and with stills from films. Index.

BAXTER, JOHN
Science Fiction in the Cinema
A. S. Barnes, 1970. 240pp. Paper $2.45. A study of science fiction films from 1902 to 1968. Illustrated with photographs. Bibliography. Selected Filmography.

BAZIN, ANDRE
What Is Cinema?
University of California, 1967. 183pp. $5.75. Paper $2.25. A series of essays by the editor of "Cahiers du Cinema." The ten essays cover such subjects as "The Myth of Total Cinema," "The Evolution of the Language of the Cinema," "Charlie Chaplin," and "Theatre and Cinema," Index.

BLUM, DANIEL and JOHN KOBAL
A New Pictorial History of the Talkies
Grosset & Dunlap, 1970. 352pp. $9.95. A history of the talking moving-picture. Originally published in 1958 as compiled by Daniel Blum and now updated through 1968 by John Kobal. Over 4,000 stills from the films are included. Index.

BOBKER, LEE R.
Elements of Film
Harcourt, Brace, 1969. 303pp. Paper $6.00. A study of the technical and aesthetic elements of film-making. The emphasis is on the relationship between the techniques and their creative application. Chapters on script, image, sound, editing, the work of the major contemporary directors, and the function of film criticisim are included. Lists of films for study and books for supplementary reading follow each chapter. Illustrated. Index.

BRITISH UNIVERSITIES' FILM COUNCIL
Film and the Historian
British Universities Film Councils, 1968. 50pp. Paper $1.25. This pamphlet is a record of the proceedings of the conference held in London In April, 1968. The intention of the conference was to record what has been done in making film an effective medium for historians and how to enlarge on that function. An Appendix lists some of the films which document history.

BROWNLOW, KEVIN
The Parade's Gone By
Knopf, 1968. 593pp. $13.95. Paper—Ballantine, 1969. 691pp. $3.95. The author recreates the earliest days of the movies, tells how the first moving pictures were actually shot, and how the first film-makers responded to the new medium. Using interviews and his own accounts of the roles of such men as Griffith and Chaplin, Mr. Brownlow provides a history of silent film. Illustrated with almost 300 photographs of the films and the artists at work. Index.

BUTLER, IVAN
Horror in the Cinema
A. S. Barnes, 1970. 208pp. Paper $2.95. A revised edition of the study of horror film which was first published in 1967. The macabre in the silent cinema through to the use of horror in Polanski's film, "Repulsion," are studied. Illustrated. Selected Bibliography. Index.

BUTLER, IVAN
Religion in the Cinema
A. S. Barnes, 1969. 208pp. Paper $2.45. A survey of the treatment of Biblical history and Christian

practice in the commercial film. The author has selected those films in which religious function has some definite bearing on the story. There is a section on anti-religious films. Illustrated with stills from the films assessed. Selected Bibliography. Index.

CAMERON, IAN – Editor
Second Wave
Praeger, 1970. 144pp. $4.95. Paper $2.50. Considerations of eight important directors whose work is post-New Wave in approach as well as date. The directors are: Dusan Makavejev, Jerzy Skolimowski, Nagisa Oshima, Ruy Guerra, Glauber Rocha, Gilles Groulx, Jean-Pierre Lefebvre, and Jean-Marie Straub. Illustrated with photographs. Filmographies.

CLARENS, CARLOS
An Illustrated History of the Horror Film
Putnam, 1967. 256pp. $6.95. Paper – Capricorn, 1968. 256pp. $2.75. An introduction to the horror film by a widely known critic. Starting with the fantasies of George Melies and ending with "Alphaville" and "Fahrenheit 451," the author traces the evolution of the horror film through its various stages. Included are the complete credits for 300 movies and 135 stills that span the time range from Melies to Truffaut. Index.

DE BARTOLO, DICK
A Mad Look at Old Movies
New American Library, 1966. 192pp. Paper $ .50. Satires on the movies in comic strip form.

DIMMITT, RICHARD BERTRAND
An Actor Guide to the Talkies
Scarecrow, 1967. Two volume set: 1,555pp. $38.50. This is a comprehensive listing of 8,000 feature length films made from January 1949 to December 1964. Both foreign and domestic films are listed alphabetically with year of release, producing company, and players with character names. The second volume lists some 30,000 actors with page numbers of entries in Volume One which detail the films the actors made during the period covered.

DIMMITT, RICHARD BERTRAND
A Title Guide to the Talkies
Scarecrow, 1965. Two volume set: 2,133pp. $50.00. A comprehensive listing of 16,000 feature films produced from October 1927 to December 1963, listed alphabetically with the title of the original source, the author's name, place of publication, publisher, and date.

DOUGLAS, DRAKE
Horror
Macmillan, 1966. 309pp. $6.95. Paper – Collier, 1969. 277pp. $1.50. A light-hearted approach to horror films from the first true example, "The Cabinet of Dr. Caligari," in 1919, to the present day. Illustrated. Film List. Index.

DURGNAT, RAYMOND
Eros in the Cinema
Calder & Boyars, 1966. 207pp. $7.50. Paper $5.00. The author deals with the subject of eroticism in the cinema on an historical basis and includes a detailed examination of the techniques employed to present it. Beginning with the great silent classics, the development is traced through the heyday of Hollywood, the emergence of the sex symbol, and the development of the subject in Europe. Profusely illustrated with stills from the films considered.

DURGNAT, RAYMOND
Films and Feelings
M. I. T. Press, 1967. 288pp. $6.95. Mr. Durgnat examines hundreds of films from "Birth of a Nation" to the films of the '60's in his endeavor to prove that an aesthetic of the film is possible. He discusses the union of film style and content, the connection between film as entertainment and as a comment on the facts of social life, the gap between popular responses and those of "high culture," and produces evidence of the existence of cinematic poetry in the commercial film. Illustrated. Index of Films.

ENSER, A. G. S.
Filmed Books and Plays 1928 – 1967
Andre Deutsch, 1968. 448pp. $15.00. This volume consists of a complete list of books and plays from which English language films have been made from 1928 to 1967. There are three Indices: A film title index, an author index, and a change of original title index. Information includes the name of the maker or distributing company, the year the film was registered, the author of the original book, and name of the publisher.

EVERSON, WILLIAM K.
The Bad Guys: A Pictorial History of the Movie Villain
Citadel, 1968. 241pp. Paper $3.45. Originally published in 1964, this is a survey of film villainy which divides sixty years of movie history into twenty categories and examines the types of villains in each. Illustrated.

FENSCH, THOMAS
Films on the Campus
A. S. Barnes, 1970. 534pp. $15.00. A study of film production on college and university campuses. The author provides an accurate picture of the extent of the growth of film courses and programs—their philosophies, requirements, faculty interest, and students. Several examples of student shooting scripts that can be used for study are included as is a lexicon that defines new and old words in the film-making industry. Illustrated with over 200 photographs. Index.

FEYEN, SHARON and DONALD WIGAL – Editors
Screen Experience: An Approach to Film

Pflaum, 1969. 273pp. Paper $5.95. The editors hope to "stimulate, encourage and expand the awareness which is brought to and from the film experience." An outline history of film styles is followed by a chapter on the present scene and the probable future of movies. Succeeding chapters cover specific aspects of film such as literary adaptations, the short film, the western, the documentary, the role of the director, etc. Suggestions for film series are provided. Illustrated with photographs. Annotated Film List. List of Film Distributors. Bibliography. Index of Film Titles.

FIELDING, RAYMOND – Editor
A Technological History of Motion Pictures and Television
See Page 461

FULTON, A.R.
Motion Pictures
University of Oklahoma, 1960. 320pp. $6.95. A history of the development of the motion picture as an art form, with particular attention paid to the role of technical developments and the achievements of important directors. Illustrated. Glossary of Terms.

GESSNER, ROBERT
The Moving Image
Dutton, 1968. 444pp. $8.95. Paper $3.95. Professor Gessner analyzes the nature of movies as a storytelling medium and explores the relationship between the narrative, dramatic, and cinematic processes to discover the unique patterns and structures that make cinema an art. The range of screenplays excerpted or explored runs from "Nanook of the North" to "Bonnie and Clyde." Illustrated. Bibliography. Glossary. Index.

GIFFORD, DENIS
Movie Monsters
Dutton, 1969. 159pp. $4.95. Paper $1.95. Classified into twelve different species, movie monsters from a vampire, vintage 1896, to the creations of Karloff, Lugosi, and Chaney are resurrected by a leading authority on film. Complete filmographies list every known monster movie giving year, title, director and stars. Lavishly illustrated with photographs.

GORDON, GEORGE N. and IRVING FALK, WILLIAM HODAPP
The Idea Invaders
See Page 505

GOW, GORDON
Suspense in the Cinema
A. S. Barnes, 1968. 167pp. Paper $2.25. Through a study of ninety-two films from all over the world, Mr. Gow contends that suspense has a place in the cinema and gives historical examples. Illustrated with photographs. Filmography.

GRAHAM, PETER
A Dictionary of the Cinema
A. S. Barnes, 1968. 175pp. $4.95. Paper $2.45. A revised edition of the 1964 publication. This dictionary has over 600 entries covering all aspects of films and film personalities, directors, writers, actors, etc. Efforts have been made to provide information on all major films begun up to January, 1968. Illustrated with photographs of major personalities prominent in international cinema. Guide to Technical Terms. Index of Film Titles.

GRAU, ROBERT
The Theatre of Science
Blom, 1969. 378pp. $25.00. Originally published in 1914 and now reissued in a facsimile edition, this volume is subtitled, "A Volume of Progress and Achievement in the Motion Picture Industry." It is a history of the film industry from the 1870's to 1914. All phases of the industry are detailed. Illustrated with eighty-seven pages of photographs.

GROVES, PETER D.
Film in Higher Education and Research
Pergamon, 1966. 332pp. $9.25. Paper $6.75. This study is concerned with film in universities and other institutes of higher education. The author emphasizes recent developments in the field. The contents are grouped into five sections: the place of film within the university setting; the problems of supply, catalogue, distribution and use; the place of film as a teaching medium; aspects of the film as a research tool; and the production of films by amateurs and professional film units. Illustrated with charts, diagrams, and photographs. Index.

GUBACK, THOMAS H.
The International Film Industry: Western Europe and America Since 1945
Indiana University, 1969. 244pp. $12.00. Mr. Guback studies international cooperation in film making. He discusses the increase of American investment in European film companies, the search for wider markets, postwar quota and tariff restrictions, the use of boycott to force a foreign market for U. S. films, the increasing acceptance of European films in the U. S., and the American government's backing of the industry and use of film for propaganda purposes. Illustrated with tables. Selected Bibliography. Index.

HALLIWELL, LESLIE
The Filmgoer's Companion
Hill & Wang, 1970. 1,072pp. $15.00. The third edition of the international encyclopedia of film information. Newly revised and expanded, the volume contains over 6,000 entries on films, film-makers—directors, actors, composers, writers, and cameramen—themes, and technical terms. Each entry contains biographical or historical notes and a selected list of principal credits for each of the personalities involved.

HARDY, FORSYTH – Editor
Grierson on Documentary
University of California, 1966. 411pp. $8.50. A history of the documentary film movement, first published in 1947 and now reissued with revisions and additions. John Grierson comments on a wide range of cinematic subjects. A new section bears on the international role of documentary film and there is additional material on television documentaries. Illustrated. Index.

HENDRICKS, GORDON
Beginnings of the Biograph
Beginnings of the American Film, 1964. 78pp. $6.00. The story of the technical, commercial, and theatrical beginnings of the company which gave shape and direction to the art of the American film. The author presents the facts surrounding the invention of the Biograph camera and projector and describes the making of the Biograph's first movies and their screen debut. Illustrated with photographs. Index.

HENDRICKS, GORDON
The Kinetoscope
Beginnings of the American Film, 1966. 182pp. $10.00. A history of America's first contribution to commercial motion picture exhibition. The author describes the invention and first exhibitions of the kinetoscope and its movies in 1894. Illustrated with photographs. Index.

HEYER, ROBERT and ANTHONY MEYER
Discovery in Film
Paulist Press, 1969. 219pp. Paper $4.50. The authors explore the use of short non-feature films for educational purposes. They discuss seventy-eight films, catalogued according to five themes: communication, freedom, love, peace, and happiness. The authors comment on each film as to content and style, provide discussion questions, resource materials, and background data. Appendices on three major propaganda films and an essay on "Teaching the Film." Illustrated with photographs. Index.

HIBBIN, NINA
Screen Guide: Eastern Europe
A. S. Barnes, 1969. 239pp. Paper $3.50. An illustrated guide to the postwar work of film directors, players, and technicians in Albania, Bulgaria, Czechoslovakia, East Germany, Hungary, Poland, Romania, the Soviet Union, and Yugoslavia. Illustrated with photographs. Index to 2,500 Films.

HOUSTON, PENELOPE
The Contemporary Cinema
Penguin, 1963. 222pp. Paper $1.45. A detailed examination of the cinema from the neo-realism of the postwar period to the "new wave." The author shows how the cinema industry has adjusted to the more critical audiences of the present, has encouraged new talent in directors and actors, and has met the challenge of television. Illustrated.

HUACO, GEORGE A.
The Sociology of Film Art
Basic Books, 1965. 229pp. $6.50. This book examines the rise and fall of three great schools of moviemaking and the social, economic and political worlds that gave each its inspiration and shape. German expressionism from 1920 to 1931, Soviet expressive realism from 1925 to 1930, and Italian neo-realism from 1945 to 1955 are examined in detail. Bibliography. Index.

HUGHES, ROBERT – Editor
Film: Book Two – Films of Peace and War
Grove, 1962. 256pp. Paper $2.45. A study based on articles, interviews, and responses to questionnaires on the difficulties film-makers have encountered in making films about peace and war. Included are the complete scenarios of two banned films: John Huston's "Let There Be Light" and Alain Resnais' "Night and Fog." Illustrated.

HUNNINGS, NEVILLE MARCH
Film Censors and the Law
Hillary House, 1968. 474pp. $10.00. Originally published in England in 1967 and now released in the United States, this is a survey of the reasons for censorship and the ways in which it has been enforced. A detailed history of film censorship in England is followed by an examination of the complex developments in the United States. Censorship in India, Canada, Australia, Denmark, France, and Soviet Russia are also discussed. Illustrated. Bibliography. Index.

HUNTLEY, JOHN
Railways in the Cinema
Ian Allen, 1969. 168pp. $7.50. A detailed survey of the many hundreds of films which are about, or have contained scenes of, railways throughout the world. Feature films, documentaries, newsreels, television programs, and official records are all covered. The book combines information on the films as well as an analysis of the locomotives and rolling stock involved. The Index of Films includes credits and a short synopsis of the film where possible. Illustrated with photographs.

HURLEY, NEIL P.
Theology Through Film
Harper & Row, 1970. 212pp. $5.95. The author sees films as a powerful means of mass communication and believes that films have the potential to create the basis of community through shared experiences. He centers his study of motion pictures on several elements of cinematic theology. One or two films are chosen which best illustrate the capacities or inabilities of man to cope with a particular issue, and other films are discussed briefly to complement and support the point being made. A chapter is provided on "A Cinematic Theology of the Future." Illustrated with photographs. Notes. Index of Directors and Films.

HUSS, ROY and NORMAN SILVERSTEIN
The Film Experience: Elements of Motion Picture Art
Harper, 1968. 172pp. $6.95. Paper—Dell, 1969. 172pp. $1.95. The authors provide a description of principles and techniques of the motion picture art, written to sharpen the moviegoer's understanding and enjoyment. They draw upon films of all eras and most filmmaking countries to show how motion pictures can be more than just another way to tell a story. Illustrated with photographs. Index.

INTERNATIONAL MUSIC CENTRE, VIENNA—Compilers
Films for Music Education and Opera Films
See Page 285

JACOBS, LEWIS
The Emergence of Film Art
Hopkinson & Blake, 1969. $8.50. Paper $3.95. This is a study of the evolution and development of the motion picture as an art from 1900 to the present. The book is divided into three sections: The Silent Film, The Sound and Color Film, and The Creative Present. Each section is introduced by Mr. Jacobs' own observations. A selection of the writings of film-makers, critics and fellow historians illuminates the advances that transformed the motion picture from a commercial novelty into a dominant force in our culture. Illustrated with photographs. Index.

JACOBS, LEWIS—Editor
The Movies as Medium
Farrar, Straus, 1970. 335pp. $8.95. Paper $3.65. Selected, arranged, and introduced by Lewis Jacobs, this is an anthology of essays written by experts in every area of film-making. These essays undertake to investigate the nature of film as a medium and scrutinize the basic resources of film expression. The opening section includes comments by thirty-six directors who express their divergent personal views about moviemaking. Movement, time and space, color, and sound are also scrutinized. Illustrated with photographs. Bibliography. Index.

JENNINGS, GARY
The Movie Book
Dial, 1963. 211pp. $3.95. A history of the motion picture from the cave-artist's attempts to illustrate movement to the current stereoscopic, stereophonic productions. A section is devoted to each of the special types of films: comedies, epics, westerns, serials, jungle movies, cartoons, science-fiction, sex melodrama, television films, and newsreels. Illustrated. Bibliography. Index.

JOBES, GERTRUDE
Motion Picture Empire
Shoestring, 1966. 398pp. $11.50. This study of the motion picture industry describes the innovations in techniques in making films, the financial struggles of the companies, and the influence on the industry of powerful bankers and industrialists. Emphasis is placed on the "czars" of the industry and the ambitions that drove them to create their empires.

JONES, G. WILLIAMS
Sunday Night at the Movies
John Knox Press, 1967. 127pp. Paper $1.95. The author contends that the church should involve itself in film interpretation and criticism and use contemporary films as parables to communicate Christian faith. He shows how groups can plan, execute, and follow up a film discussion program. An Appendix lists movie rental sources, discussion guide sources, and a listing by topics of 248 feature length and short films. Illustrated. Bibliography.

KENNEDY, DONALD
So You Think You Know Movies
Ace, 1970. 160pp. Paper $ .60. A quiz book on the movies.

KEPES, GYORGY—Editor
The Visual Arts Today
See Page 505

KITSES, JIM and ANN MERCER
Talking About the Cinema
British Film Institute, 1966. 98pp. Paper $2.50. Published in England, this volume is subtitled, "Film Studies for Young People," and is an account of the authors' work with young people in England and their methods of teaching. Illustrated with photographs from the films under study.

KNIGHT, ARTHUR
The Liveliest Art: A Panoramic History of the Movies
New American Library, 1959. 352pp. Paper $1.25. A history of the films from 1895 to the present, with a consideration of such items as the technique of D. W. Griffith, the art of Chaplin, the rise of the star system, European films in the 1920's and 1930's, the first talking pictures, and television's effect on the movies. Illustrated. A Bibliography contains lists of sources of 16mm films.

KNIGHT, DERRICK and VINCENT PORTER
A Long Look at Short Films
Pergamon, 1967. 185pp. Paper $3.00. The authors provide a study of the short film industry in Great Britain. The contents are grouped under four main headings: Introductory Facts; the Entertainment Film; the Factual Film; and Conclusion. Within this framework many specialized aspects are covered. Bibliography. Index.

KOBAL, JOHN
Gotta Sing. Gotta Dance. A Pictorial History of Film Musicals
Hamlyn, 1970. 320pp. $6.75. Published in England, this is a lavishly illustrated history of film musicals

from the film short in 1926 which featured the New York Philharmonic Orchestra and opera stars to "Funny Girl" and "Sweet Charity." Among the special features is a section on foreign language film musicals. Many stills from Busby Berkeley production numbers are included among the 670 photographs. Index.

KOENIGIL, MARK
Movies in Society: Sex, Crime and Censorship
Robert Speller, 1962. 214pp. $5.95. An examination of the social influence of the movies. The effects of the exploitation of sex and violence are studied. Individual case histories are cited to prove the author's contention that movies play a role in crime and delinquency.

KOSTELANETZ, RICHARD – Editor
Moholy–Nagy
Praeger, 1970. 238pp. $12.50. Paper $4.95. Writings by Laszlo Moholy-Nagy form the core of this collection. Reprinted are interviews with the artist, essays and articles on Moholy's theories of art, his social vision, his principles of education, and the potentialities of motion pictures, still photography, technology of art, and art and industry. More than eighty photographs, including nine in color, illustrate the volume. Chronology. Bibliography. Index.

KRACAUER, SIEGFRIED
Theory of Film: The Redemption of Physical Reality
Oxford, 1960. 364pp. $12.50. Paper $2.75. A comprehensive examination of all the technical and artistic aspects of the film arts. Among the topics covered are the background of films in still photography, the problems inherent in historical and fantasy films, the novel as a cinematic form, experimental films, documentaries, the role of the actor, the use of dialogue, sound techniques, and the use of music. Illustrated.

KUHNS, WILLIAM and ROBERT STANLEY
Exploring the Film
See Page 461

KUHNS, WILLIAM
Themes: Short Films for Discussion
Pflaum, 1968. 296pp. $11.00. A guidebook to the showing of films in the classroom. Seventy-six films are described and their use in classroom instruction is discussed. The author includes suggested questions for student review. Illustrated with photographs. Bibliography. List of Addresses of Distributors. Thematic Index. Curriculum Index. The volume is bound in a loose-leaf binder.

LAHUE, KALTON C.
Collecting Classic Films
Hastings House, 1970. 159pp. $6.95. A guide book on the art of film collecting: the problems of beginning a collection through the care of equipment to the collecting of movie memorabilia. The author details where to buy films, a discussion of copyright, film reproduction and size, and how to add color or sound to films. Lists of distributors, sources for musical scores and selected sources of film history are included. Illustrated with photographs.

LAWSON, JOHN HOWARD
Film: The Creative Process
Hill & Wang, 1964. 384pp. $7.95. Paper $2.95. This study begins with a general history of the development of the film from the kinetoscope through the work of Griffith, von Stroheim, and Chaplin, to the work of the contemporary directors. The difference between film and theatre is treated in detail with special reference to Pudovkin's production of Gorki's "Mother" and John Ford's film, "The Grapes of Wrath." Illustrated. Bibliography. Index.

LEE, RAYMOND
Not So Dumb: Animals in the Movies
A. S. Barnes, 1970. 380pp. $8.50. A survey of animal actors in the seventy years of cinema history. The animals, their trainers, and the producers, directors, and stars who worked with them are all detailed. Illustrated with photographs.

LEONARD, HAROLD – Editor
The Film Index: A Bibliography. Volume I: The Film as Art
Arno Press, 1966. 723pp. $22.50. This index, prepared by the staff of the New York City WPA Writers' Project, makes available for the first time the information about films housed in libraries and museums all over the United States. There are works on history and technique and various types of films. Illustrated. Index.

LEWIS, LEON and WILLIAM DAVID SHERMAN
Landscape of Contemporary Cinema
Buffalo Spectrum Press, 1967. 95pp. Paper $2.00. The authors provide a series of brief essays with which they hope to give the reader some sense of current cinematic landscape and their own love of the movies. The volume is divided into three sections: Hollywood in the Sixties; Directors; and Films Around the World.

LEYDA, JAY
Films Beget Films
Hill & Wang, 1964. 176pp. $4.95. Paper $1.95. A critical study of the "compilation" film—the form that makes use of earlier films for effects ranging from drama to propaganda. Edwin S. Porter's "Life of an American Fireman," the first compilation film made in 1902, is studied in detail. Also examined are the work of Esther Schub in Russia in the 1920's, the techniques of Balasz in the 1930's, Nazi propaganda films, and the current use of film stock on television. Appendices include a list of significant films using the compilation form. Index.

LIDSTONE, JOHN and DON McINTOSH
Children as Film Makers
Reinhold, 1970. 111pp. $7.95. This book is designed for classroom teachers and other enthusiasts who would like to work with children in film-making. It demonstrates how films can be created by children. A detailed text explains the basics of camera operation, editing, splicing, animation, titling, and projection. Ways to guide children toward successful structuring of their films, methods for practical classroom organization of supplies and equipment, and ideas for the exhibition of films are all discussed. Illustrated with drawings and photographs. Bibliography. Index.

LINDEN, GEORGE W.
Reflections on the Screen
Wadsworth, 1970. 297pp. $10.00. Dr. Linden examines the form, function, material, and philosophical-psychological background of film. He develops analogues of film and drama, film and fiction, film and photography, and film and social message. The author analyzes film theories and evaluates contemporary film-makers. Illustrated with photographs. Bibliography. Index.

LINDSAY, VACHEL
The Art of the Moving Picture
Liveright, 1970. 324pp. $6.50. Paper $2.95. Originally published in 1915 and revised in 1922, this book is now reissued with a new Introduction by Stanley Kauffmann. The author provides an analysis and interpretation of film and its art. The volume is considered a classic in film aesthetics. Index.

McANANY, G. and ROBERT WILLIAMS
The Filmviewer's Handbook
Paulist Press, 1965. 198pp. Paper $ .95. A handbook for those who wish to start a film study society. The authors include a compendium of motion picture history, an essay on the language (or techniques) of film, and a sample series of films of twenty-nine international directors with a background of the director, a critique of his films, and suggestions on how to present the films to a study group. Appendices. Bibliography.

MacGOWAN, KENNETH
Behind the Screen
Dell, 1967. 528pp. Paper $2.95. Originally published in 1965, this is a study of the history and techniques of the motion picture which begins with a survey of the historical background of film and the film pioneers. Mr. Macgowan also discusses the era of the silent screen, the films of the 1920's, the coming of sound and color, the wide screen, and the age of television. Techniques of movie making are reviewed in great detail and the functions of the various technicians are fully explained and analyzed. Illustrated with photographs, drawings, diagrams, and tables. Index.

McVAY, DOUGLAS
The Musical Film
A. S. Barnes, 1967. 175pp. Paper $2.25. A study of film musicals, comic or dramatic films with isolated sequences of song or dance, and cartoons which include musical numbers. The author studies the musical films of each year from 1927 through 1966. Illustrated. Selected Bibliography. Index to Titles.

MANCHEL, FRANK
Terrors of the Screen
Prentice–Hall, 1970. 122pp. $4.25. The history of horror on film from the fantasy films of Melies to the modern thrillers of Hitchcock, Clouzot, and Polanski. Illustrated with photographs. Bibliography. Index.

MANCHEL, FRANK
When Movies Began To Speak
Prentice–Hall, 1969. 76pp. $3.95. Written for young people, this is a history of the "talkies." Starting with "The Jazz Singer," the author tells the story of sound films right up to "This Is Cinerama" and the new techniques demonstrated at Expo '67. Illustrated with stills from films. Bibliography. Index.

MANCHEL, FRANK
When Pictures Began To Move
Prentice–Hall, 1969. 76pp. $3.95 Written for young people, this is the story of the beginnings of motion pictures. From the legend of Father Athanasius Kircher who reputedly developed a magic lantern in 1604, through Edison's camera, and the Lumiere brothers, to the early directors and stars such as Mack Sennett, D. W. Griffith, Charlie Chaplin, and Greta Garbo, all the pioneers are discussed. Illustrated. Bibliography. Index.

MANVELL, ROGER
New Cinema in Europe
Dutton, 1966. 160pp. Paper $1.95. A concise, pictorial survey of the new cinema and its leading directors. Illustrated with over 140 stills, the book surveys the whole period from the second World War to the present.

MANVELL, ROGER
What Is a Film?
Macdonald, 1965. 184pp. $3.75. The early history of the film is explored and the part played by the director, producer, actor, writer, and technician is analyzed. Sections on television and films, documentaries, and animated films. Index.

MAYER, MICHAEL F.
Foreign Films on American Screens
Arco, 1965. 119pp. $4.50. Paper $2.00. The themes, techniques, and methods of foreign films and the differences between them and their Hollywood counterparts are discussed. The book includes over 150 photographs, lists of films, and National Legion of Decency classifications.

MECCOLI, DOMENICO
Il Risorgimento Italiano nel Teatro e nel Cinema
See Page 213

MILNER, MICHAEL
Sex on Celluloid
Macfadden, 1964. 224pp. Paper $ .95. A detailed study of sex as it has appeared in films and of the reactions to it. There are Appendices which list the Production Code and the Standards of Public Regulation in the U.S. Illustrated.

MINNEY, R.J.
The Film Maker and His World
Gollancz, 1964. 160pp. $2.75. Published in England, this is a young person's guide to the many branches of the film industry, the opportunities for entry, the influence of the unions, the necessary qualifications, the course of training and the eventual prospects. Mr. Minney also deals with the financial aspect of the industry. Included is a complete account of the making of a picture.

MONTAGU, IVOR
Film World
Penguin, 1964. 327pp. Paper $1.75. The four parts of this book—Film as Science, Film as Art, Film as Commodity, and Film as Vehicle—cover such aspects of the film as its history, its resemblance to and difference from other art forms, its aesthetic laws, the compound effects of sound and vision, and the inherent tendency towards production monopoly. Illustrated. Index.

MONTGOMERY, JOHN
Comedy Films 1894–1954
Allen & Unwin, 1968. 286pp. $9.00. Published in England, this is a revised edition of the 1954 history of comedy films and the men and women who made them. The beginnings of comic motion pictures and the pioneer work of the early artists in England and Europe are traced; the rise of the American comic film is studied; and the development of sound and its effect on the comedians is explained. The careers of Chaplin, Lloyd, Keaton, the Marx Brothers, Bob Hope, Fernandel, and Alec Guiness, among others, are traced. Illustrated with photographs. Index.

MUNSTERBERG, HUGO
The Film: A Psychological Study
Dover, 1970. 100pp. Paper $2.00. An unabridged republication of the work originally published in 1916 under the title "The Photoplay: A Psychological Study." A new Foreword has been written by Richard Griffith for this study of the film in 1916. General techniques and aesthetics are discussed in this study of the psychology of the viewer.

NEWHALL, BEAUMONT
Latent Image: The Discovery of Photography
Doubleday, 1967. 148pp. Paper $1.25. This is a scientific and technological history of photography, showing how the early pioneers learned from each other and produced a universal technique. Illustrated. Bibliography. Index.

NOBLE, PETER
The Negro in Films
Kennikat, 1969. 288pp. $13.50. Originally published in 1948 and now reissued, this is a critical study of the history of the Negro in films. A short introduction on the Negro on the stage leads to the portrayals in American silent and sound films and in European films. Short biographies of some of the most prominent actors and actresses are included. Illustrated with photographs. Bibliography. List of films 1902–1948. Index.

O'LEARY, LIAM
The Silent Cinema
Dutton, 1965. 160pp. Paper $1.95. A concise record of the outstanding achievements of the silent screen with 140 photographs showing the work of the great directors who made movies in the period. Index.

PUDOVKIN, V.I.
Film Technique and Film Acting
Vision Press, 1968. 388pp. $7.95. Paper—Grove, 1970. 388pp. $1.95. Translated and edited by Ivor Montagu, this is a revised and enlarged edition of the 1949 publication. These two works have become basic landmarks of cinema theory and practice. The ideas set out by Pudovkin remain fundamental to any philosophy of the film and the author is able to create an understanding in the reader of what the director is doing when he creates an effect on the screen. Also included is a personal memoir by Mr. Montagu and a revised and complete record of the author's film work. Illustrated with photographs.

RAMSAYE, TERRY
A Million and One Nights: A History of the Motion Picture
Simon & Schuster, 1964. 868pp. $10.00. Paper $3.95. Originally published in a two volume limited edition in 1926, this classic study is an investigation of the movies from the beginnings to 1926. The movie art is examined and evaluated from its origins in the ancient pantomime, drawing, and sculpture, through the great age of the silent films. Index.

RANDALL, RICHARD S.
Censorship of the Movies
University of Wisconsin, 1968. 280pp. $7.95. The author provides a history of the social and political control of the motion picture industry. He summarizes and analyzes such legal approaches as prior censorship and traces changes in the definition of obscenity. He describes the operation of censorship boards and includes reports on negotiations between censors and film owners. He contrasts legal censorship with extra

legal social and political control. Illustrated with tables. Notes. Index.

RICHARDSON, ROBERT
Literature and Film
Indiana University, 1969. 149pp. $4.95. Mr. Richardson argues that film and literature are not antithetical disciplines. He shows the relationship of film to literature, outlining differences and similarities, and common goals as well as divergent aims, demonstrating how each form is able to illuminate the other. He presents some of the literary influences that have significantly affected films since the era of D. W. Griffith, and he discusses film's major influences on modern literature including an extended exploration of the relationship of film to poetry.

ROBINSON, DAVID
The Great Funnies
Dutton, 1969. 160pp. Paper $1.95. A history of film comedy from the anonymous actors in the one minute animated jokes of the 1890's to the current comics. The author traces the origins of screen comedy in the music hall and popular theatres of the nineteenth century and shows the recent influences of television. Brief evaluations of some of the great comics are given and the comedy films made in Europe during the early years of the century are discussed. Illustrated with photographs. Index.

ROBINSON, W. R. – Editor
Man and the Movies
Louisiana State University, 1967. 371pp. $7.95. Paper – Penguin, 1969. 371pp. $1.95. An exploration of the impact of the movies on American culture. Realism and the Western, horror movies, the aesthetic of the movies, the relationship between movies and television, essays on Hitchcock, Griffith, Bergman, and Fellini, and the impact of motion pictures on viewers are some of the topics discussed. Illustrated. Indices.

ROEBURT, JOHN
The Wicked and the Banned
See Page 23

ROSS, T. J. – Editor
Film and the Liberal Arts
Holt, Rinehart, 1970. 419pp. Paper $6.50. A collection of essays keyed to the multiple nature of the cinema and designed to introduce the student to the multiple concerns and possibilities of communications and culture in general. Each set of essays revolves around film and one of the liberal arts to highlight the language of film and its mode of communication. Each essay is followed by exercises and questions on the content of the essay. List of Recommended Films. Selected Bibliography. Index.

ROTHA, PAUL and SINCLAIR ROAD, RICHARD GRIFFITH
Documentary Film
Hastings House, 1963. 412pp. $10.00. This study examines the use of the film medium to interpret creatively and in social terms the life of the people as it exists in reality. There are chapters on the social, economic, and propagandistic value of the film, and discussions of the evolution of the documentary film and its techniques. Illustrated. List of 100 important documentary films. Appendix.

ROTHA, PAUL and RICHARD GRIFFITH
The Film Til Now: A Survey of World Cinema
Twayne, 1958. 820pp. $15.00. The theoretical and technical basis of movie making is examined and actual productions are analyzed. Trends in world-wide motion picture activity from the beginnings to 1958 are reviewed. This third enlarged edition has a new section written by Richard Griffith. Illustrated. Appendices list production units of some outstanding films. Glossary. Bibliography.

SAMUELS, CHARLES THOMAS
A Casebook on Film
Reinhold, 1970. 250pp. Paper $4.75. A selection of essays defining the art of film, discussing its principal techniques, and considering the methods by which we can judge its results. Included are essays on "The Graduate," "Blow-Up," and "Bonnie and Clyde." A projects section provides opportunities for analytical writing and research. Questions accompanying each essay are designed to suggest ways in which the topic might be pursued. Selective Bibliography. Glossary.

SCHICKEL, RICHARD
Movies: The History of an Art and an Institution
Basic Books, 1964. 208pp. $7.50. After a summary of the early attempts to capture movement in pictures, this history examines the innovations of Georges Melies, D. W. Griffith, Mack Sennett, and Eisenstein, and the new directors. Illustrated.

SCHILLACI, ANTHONY and JOHN M. CULKIN – Editors
Films Deliver
See Page 335

SHARP, DENNIS
The Picture Palace and Other Buildings for the Movies
Praeger, 1969. 224pp. $12.50. Mr. Sharp offers a history of the movie house—from nickelodeons and Kinetoscope parlors to drive-ins, from the picture palace to the art theatre—in America, England, and Continental Europe. The author treats problems of sight lines, ventilation, acoustics, projection and decoration, and concludes with an assessment of the latest developments in the design of movie houses. Illustrated with photographs, sketches, and plans. Selected List of Cinemas. Bibliography. Index.

STEELE, ROBERT
The Cataloging and Classification of Cinema Literature

Scarecrow, 1967. 133pp. $5.00. Mr. Steele states the problems of cataloging and classifying cinema literature. He explains the major systems of classification at various institutions and the possibilities for expansion. Bibliography. Index.

STEPHENSON, RALPH and J.R. DEBRIX
The Cinema as Art
Penguin, 1965. 270pp. Paper $1.45. An examination of the cinema which describes the stages whereby the director isolates what is mentally and emotionally significant in a situation and creates his film by exploiting all the cinematic techniques. Illustrated with photographs from major films. Index.

STEWART, DAVID C.
Film Study in Higher Education
American Council on Education, 1966. 174pp. Paper $3.95. This report is designed to provide assistance to college teachers who plan to initiate courses in the history, criticism, and appreciation of motion pictures. There are five essays on courses and three essays by reknowned critics and educators. Appendices provide lists of film distributors, professional associations, archives, libraries, film societies, and tables of courses in 100 colleges. Bibliography.

THOMAS, D.B.
The Origins of the Motion Picture
Her Majesty's Stationery Office, 1964. 32pp. Paper $ .60. An introduction to the pre-history of the cinema. Illustrated with photographs and drawings. List of Books for Further Reading.

THOMPSON, DENYS – Editor
Discrimination and Popular Culture
See Page 507

THOMSON, DAVID
Movie Man
Stein & Day, 1967. 234pp. $6.95. Paper $2.95. Mr. Thomson traces the progress of commercial motion pictures to show how society shapes the uses of a discovery such as moving pictures. He discusses many directors and their films. Illustrated. Filmography. Index.

TOPFFER, RODOLPHE
Enter: The Comics
University of Nebraska, 1965. 80pp. $5.95. Translated and edited with an Introduction by E. Wiese, this volume includes Topffer's "Essay on Physiognomy" and "The True Story of Monsieur Crepin." Topffer was the nineteenth century author and teacher who discovered the art of the comic strip and thus laid a foundation for the cinema and for the development of the vast potential of education through pictures. "Essay" is the record of Topffer's search for a language of facial expressions and "Monsier Crepin" demonstrates his technique. Illustrated. List of Works Cited.

TYLER, PARKER
Classics of the Foreign Film: A Pictorial Treasury
Citadel, 1967. 252pp. Paper $3.45. A reprint of the 1962 selection by Mr. Tyler of his choice of the seventy-five greatest foreign films made from 1919 through 1961. Commentary and hundreds of photographs are included.

TYLER, PARKER
Sex Psyche Etcetera in the Film
Horizon Press, 1969. 239pp. $7.50. Mr. Tyler presents his film criticism to delineate the modern psyche in film, sex ritual in film, the film artist in crisis, and the pros and cons of film aesthetics. The author discusses "I Am Curious (Yellow)," "La Dolce Vita," Chaplin, Antonioni, Bergman, Orson Welles, and film as a force in visual education. Index.

TYLER, PARKER
The Three Faces of the Film
A. S. Barnes, 1967. 141pp. $6.95. A revised edition of the 1960 publication, this study is a development of Mr. Tyler's unorthodox approach to film criticism. This criticism combines the sociological and the psychological with the aesthetic. The image of the artist as portrayed by the movies, the basic structure of the experimental film, the film form as ritual and myth, are all discussed. Illustrated.

TYLER, PARKER
Underground Film: A Critical History
Grove, 1969. 249pp. $7.50. Paper $1.75. A history of the experimental film movement. The author discusses such underground film-makers as Stan Brakhage, Gregory Markopoulos, Maya Deren, Kenneth Anger, Ed Emshwiller, Ron Rice, Andy Warhol, and Willard Maas to show the variety of current aims and techniques. Tyler traces the origin of experimental films to the art movements known as Dada and Surrealism. Illustrated with photographs. Filmography.

VARDAC, A. NICHOLAS
Stage to Screen: Theatrical Method from Garrick to Griffith
Blom, 1968. 283pp. $12.50. Originally published in 1949, this is a study in which the author describes how the early cinema evolved out of the spectacles, melodramas, and panoramas of the nineteenth century stage. Illustrated.

VIZZARD, JACK
See No Evil
Simon & Schuster, 1970. 381pp. $6.95. Mr. Vizzard reveals the inside story of movie self-censorship from the days of the Will Hays office to the modern controversies over such films as "I am Curious (Yellow)." Appendices include a copy of the 1930 Motion Picture Code.

WAGENKNECHT, EDWARD
The Movies in the Age of Innocence

University of Oklahoma, 1962. 288pp. $7.95. A personal account of the silent films which records how the generation for whom they were created responded to the first motion pictures and stars.

WEINBERG, HERMAN G.
Saint Cinema – Selected Writings (1929 – 1970)
Drama Book Specialists, 1970. 354pp. $8.95. A collection of the writings of the film critic and historian. Fritz Lang has provided a Preface. An Introduction relates the past to the present. The aesthetics of cinema are discussed by Weinberg.

WHITAKER, ROD
The Language of Film
Prentice Hall, 1970. 178pp. $10.00. Paper $6.50
The author has designed his book to explore the elements of filmic expression from the creative and perceptual points of view. Each element is described first in terms of the film-maker and then in terms of content and effect. Illustrated. Indices.

WISEMAN, THOMAS
Cinema
A. S. Barnes, 1965. 181pp. $12.00. This book studies the cinema as an international industry and as a creative art within which men and women of genius struggled for recognition and freedom of expression. There are chapters on Chaplin and the star-system, early developments in Germany, Russia and France, the growth of Hollywood, the money-making formula, the non-conformists, the decline of Hollywood, and the new personalities in the international market. Illustrated.

WLASCHIN, KEN
Bluff Your Way in the Cinema
Wolfe, 1969. 64pp. Paper $ .95. An amusing series of facts about movies and their makers for people who would like to appear knowledgeable about films.

WOLFENSTEIN, MARTHA and NATHAN LEITES
Movies: A Psychological Study
Atheneum, 1970. 316pp. Paper $4.75. Originally published in 1950 and now reissued, this is a study of contemporary American films which attempts to discover the recurrent patterns and how they are arrived at. Comparisons with French and British films are made to show common themes and contrasting effects. Illustrated with photographs. Index.

WOLLEN, PETER
Signs and Meaning in the Cinema
Indiana University, 1969. 168pp. $5.95. Paper $1.95. The author explores the way in which a new approach to cinema can be combined with a new approach to aesthetics. The first section of the book deals with the work of Eisenstein. The "auteur" theory is investigated in the second part of the volume wherein the author studies the recurrence of themes and images throughout a director's career, with special reference to the films of John Ford and Howard Hawks. Part Three shows how the study of cinema can be considered as a province of the general study of the arts. Illustrated with photographs.

WOLLEN, PETER – Editor
Working Papers on the Cinema: Sociology and Semiology
British Film Institute, 1969. 36pp. Paper $1.50. A series of annotated papers on the sociology of the cinema by five leading educators and/or critics.

YOUNGBLOOD, GENE
Expanded Cinema
Dutton, 1970. 432pp. $9.95. Paper $4.95. In this study the author traces the evolution of cinematic language to the end of fiction, drama, and realism. New technological extensions of the medium such as computer films, laser movies, and multiple-projection environments are analyzed in detail. Methods of production are described and interviews with artists and technologists are included. R. Buckminster Fuller has written an Introduction for the volume. Illustrated with 284 photographs including sixty photographs in color. Selected Bibliography. Index.

ZWERDLING, SHIRLEY – Editor
Film and TV Festival Directory
Drama Book Specialists, 1970. 174pp. $10.00. A world-wide directory of film and television festivals with names of directors, locations, dates, participants, awards, and purposes. Festivals are located by country and, in a separate listing, by month. Cross Index of Categories. Index.

Collected Reviews and Essays

ADLER, RENATA
A Year in the Dark
Random House, 1969. 354pp. $7.95. A collection of approximately 130 reviews from the daily "New York Times" and 50 essays that appeared in the Sunday drama section during 1968–69. Miss Adler is intent on conveying the experience of being a movie reviewer for a daily newspaper and of what can be learned about our society and the art form of motion pictures.

AGEE, JAMES
Agee on Film: Volume One
Grosset & Dunlap, 1967. 432pp. $7.50. Paper $2.95. A new edition of the collection of reviews and essays originally published in 1958. Included are the complete series of reviews written for "The Nation" from 1942 to 1948 and a selection of the reviews for "Time" from 1948. Two long essays originally printed in "Life Magazine" are also included.

ALPERT, HOLLIS and ANDREW SARRIS – Editors
Film 68/69

Simon & Schuster, 1969. 281pp. $6.95. Paper $1.95. A collection of reviews and essays on the most noteworthy films of 1968 by the members of the National Society of Film Critics. More than sixty films are discussed by such critics as Hollis Alpert, Harold Clurman, Penelope Gilliatt, Stanley Kauffmann, Pauline Kael, Andrew Sarris, and John Simon. Index.

BATTCOCK, GREGORY – Editor
The New American Cinema: A Critical Anthology
Dutton, 1967. 256pp. Paper $1.75. A collection of twenty-nine essays by both critics and film-makers of underground films. Among the contributors are Susan Sontag, Stan Brakhage, Andrew Sarris, and Gregory Markopolous. Illustrated. Index.

COWIE, PETER
Seventy Years of Cinema
A. S. Barnes, 1969. 287pp. $15.00. A selection of the films which the author considers to be the high points in the development of cinema from 1895. Reviewed are 235 films with a checklist for each year of hundreds of other films of significance. A listing of facts of interest for each year is included. Illustrated with over 250 photographs. Index.

CRIST, JUDITH
The Private Eye, the Cowboy and the Very Naked Girl
Holt, Rinehart, 1968. 292pp. $6.95. One of America's best known movie critics has here collected some of her articles and reviews. In the Introduction she tells how she became interested in movies and details some of her experiences as a theatre and film critic. Her reviews span the 1960's. Index.

CROWTHER, BOSLEY
The Great Films: Fifty Golden Years of Motion Pictures
Putnam, 1967. 258pp. $10.00. The well-known film critic presents a history of motion pictures through his choice of the fifty greatest films from all over the world. Analytical studies of the fifty films are provided with cast and credit lists and illustrations of scenes from the films. There is also a supplementary list of 100 other outstanding films. Bibliography. Index.

KAEL, PAULINE
Going Steady
Little Brown, 1970. 304pp. $6.95. A collection of the writings of the film critic for "The New Yorker" magazine from 1968 and 1969. The writings are in sequence so the reader can, as the author says, "follow not only what was evolving in films during a crucial period of .... change ... but follow the reviewer's developing responses."

KAEL, PAULINE
I Lost It at the Movies
Bantam, 1966. 323pp. Paper $1.25. A reprint of the 1965 selection of Miss Kael's writings on films. Included are articles and reviews originally written for, among other periodicals, "Sight and Sound," "The Atlantic," "The New York Times," and "Film Quarterly." Index.

KAEL, PAULINE
Kiss Kiss Bang Bang
Little Brown, 1968. 404pp. $7.95. Paper – Bantam, 1969. 498pp. $1.25. A collection of Miss Kael's writings on the past, present, and future of movies. She reviews over 300 films in either short paragraphs or long essays. A previously unpublished day-by-day account of the filming of "The Group" is included. Index.

KAUFFMANN, STANLEY
A World on Film
Harper & Row, 1966. 437pp. $7.95. A collection of reviews from "The New Republic." The author, one of America's leading film critics, includes a new essay explaining the rise of film to its present eminence among the arts. Mr. Kauffmann also tries to gauge the cinema in the future. Index.

LENNING, ARTHUR – Editor
Classics of the Film
Wisconsin Film Society Press, 1965. 238pp. Paper $2.25. A discussion of some of the great masterpieces of the motion picture art. Articles are included on American, French, German, and Scandinavian films as well as one on the horror film. Illustrated.

MACDONALD, DWIGHT
Dwight Macdonald on Movies
Prentice–Hall, 1969. 492pp. $9.95. Mr. Macdonald takes a look at what's been happening, and failing to happen, in world cinema for the past forty years. He offers an original view of the message behind the medium of the motion picture screen. He discusses actors, directors, critics, and films in this collection of essays and reviews. Index.

MALTIN, LEONARD – Editor
TV Movies
Signet, 1969. 536pp. Paper $1.25. A guide to more than 8,000 movies now being shown on television. Information includes directors, stars, plots, dates, and original length plus a concise capsule summary and review of each film. Thirty-two pages of photographs.

ROTHA, PAUL
Rotha on the Film
Faber & Faber, 1958. 338pp. $6.00. Mr. Rotha has chosen the best of his criticisms of important films, his appreciations of screen personalities, and general articles about the film industry for this collection. A Foreword has been written by Mr. Rotha to introduce the collection. Twenty-seven pages of illustrations are included. Indices.

SARRIS, ANDREW
Confessions of a Cultist
Simon & Schuster, 1970. 480pp. $8.95. A collection of film reviews and articles which have appeared, mainly in "The Village Voice," from 1955 to 1969. Index.

SARRIS, ANDREW – Editor
The Film
Bobbs–Merrill, 1968. 64pp. Paper $1.25. A collection of film criticism by major critics. The work of three American directors, two French directors, two Italian directors, and the "new wave" are criticized or studied by such critics as Pauline Kael, Hollis Alpert, Richard Roud, John Simon, and Dwight Macdonald. Suggestions for discussion and writing by film students are included.

SCHEUER, STEVEN H. – Editor
Movies on TV
Bantam, 1969. 404pp. Paper $1.25. The 1969–70 edition of the guide to films now being shown on television. Stars, stories, and ratings for over 7,000 films are included.

SCHICKEL, RICHARD and JOHN SIMON – Editors
Film 67/68
Simon & Schuster, 1968. 320pp. $6.95. Paper $1.95. This anthology brings together reviews and essays on the films of 1967 by the members of the National Society of Film Critics. The recipients of the annual awards for film achievement are discussed in detail. Among the contributors are Hollis Alpert, Brendan Gill, Pauline Kael, Stanley Kauffmann, Arthur Knight, Andrew Sarris, and John Simon. Index.

SIMON, JOHN
Private Screenings: Views of the Cinema of the Sixties
Macmillan, 1967. 316pp. $6.95. A collection of reviews originally printed in "The New Leader" from 1963 to 1966. Added to these reviews are essays specifically written for the book including Mr. Simon's "Critical Credo" in which he sets forth his views of film criticism. Index.

SITNEY, P. ADAMS – Editor
Film Culture Reader
Praeger, 1970. 438pp. $12.50. Paper $4.95. A collection of film writings from the periodical "Film Culture," edited and introduced by the current editor of the magazine. The writings trace the evolution of the magazine from its beginnings, and in the process, define the evolution of the American non-commercial cinema. Illustrated with photographs. Appendix. Index.

TALBOT, DANIEL – Editor
Film: An Anthology
University of California, 1966. 404pp. Paper $2.25. A collection of outstanding writings on the film. The essays range from personal reminiscence to aesthetic analysis. Among the contributors are James Agee, Jean Cocteau, Pauline Kael, Siegfried Kracauer, Paul Rotha, and Gilbert Seldes. Bibliography. Index.

Annuals

AARONSON, CHARLES S. – Editor
International Motion Picture Almanac
Quigley Publications.
The annual volume of the facts, figures, and personalities of the motion picture industry. Included are statistics and information on productions, corporations, awards and polls, theatre circuits, buying and booking organizations, equipment suppliers, talent and literary agencies, the world market, and many other subjects. Illustrated. Indices. See also entry under: **RICHARD GERTNER**.
1969. 840pp. $15.00.
1970. 848pp. $15.00.

BLUM, DANIEL – Editor
Screen World
Biblo and Tannen.
The annual volume of pictorial and statistical analysis of the film season. Each volume includes cast lists and production credits for each film released in the United States during the year covered, a section illustrating promising personalities, an obituary section, and a section of biographical data on actors and actresses. Index. Each of these volumes is a reissue of volumes originally published under another imprint. See also entry under: **JOHN WILLIS**.
1949. Volume 1. 256pp. $15.00.
1951. Volume 2. 255pp. $15.00.
1952. Volume 3. 192pp. $15.00.
1953. Volume 4. 192pp. $15.00.
1954. Volume 5. 224pp. $15.00.
1955. Volume 6. 240pp. $15.00.
1956. Volume 7. 239pp. $15.00.
1957. Volume 8. 240pp. $15.00.
1958. Volume 9. 240pp. $15.00.
1959. Volume 10. 240pp. $15.00.

COWIE, PETER – Editor
International Film Guide
A. S. Barnes.
The annual guide to film production around the world. Sections are included on festivals, awards, film shorts, animation, archives, film books and magazines, with essays on directors, interviews, and critical reviews of films. Illustrated. Index.
1966. 304pp. Paper $3.95.
1967. 328pp. Paper $3.95.
1968. 336pp. $5.95. Paper $3.95.
1969. 336pp. Paper $3.95.
1970. 448pp. $5.95. Paper $3.95.
1971. 480pp. $5.95. Paper $3.95.

GERTNER, RICHARD – Editor
International Motion Picture Almanac – 1971

Quigley, 1970. 776pp. $15.00. The latest edition of the reference book dealing with the business of the screen. Statistics, who's who, productions, corporations, circuits, drive-ins, equipment, services, world market, organizations, and films in Great Britain are all covered. Alphabetical Index of Subjects. See also entry under: **CHARLES S. AARONSON.**

NOBLE, PETER – Editor
The British Film and Television Year Book
British and American Film Press.
This annual reference book lists film and television companies, distributors, film studios, laboratories, recording studios, trade organizations, agents, press representatives, and biographical information on film and television personalities. Illustrated with photographs.
1969. 494pp. $12.50.
1970. 500pp. $12.50.

SPEED, F. MAURICE – Editor
Film Review
A. S. Barnes.
An annual survey of world cinema. Plots, casts, and production credits are provided for films released in England during the period covered. Also included are lists of annual awards, essays on various facets of the film industry and its artists, obituary section, and interviews. Illustrated with photographs. Index.
1969–1970. 228pp. $6.95.
1970–1071. 240pp. $6.95.

WILLIS, JOHN – Editor
Screen World
Crown.
The comprehensive pictorial and statistical record of the movie season. Each volume lists cast and production credits, Academy Award winners, a section of obituaries, a section of photographs of promising personalities, biographical data on actors and actresses. Illustrated with photographs. Index. See also entry under: **DANIEL BLUM.**
1966. Volume 17. 256pp. $15.00.
1967. Volume 18. 256pp. $15.00.
1968. Volume 19. 256pp. $15.00.
1969. Volume 20. 256pp. $ 8.95.
1970. Volume 21. 256pp. $ 8.95.

FILMS OF PARTICULAR COUNTRIES

Egypt

KAHN, M.
An Introduction to the Egyptian Cinema
Informatics, 1969. 93pp. Paper $3.50. This is a history of the Egyptian film industry from 1853 to 1969. Illustrated with photographs.

France

ARMES, ROY
The Cinema of Alain Resnais
A. S. Barnes, 1968. 175pp. Paper $2.25. This is a study of the French film-maker from his first film at the age of thirteen to the later acclaimed work. All of Resnais' completed films are studied, including the short subjects, and illustrated with photographs. Filmography. Bibliography

ARMES, ROY
French Cinema Since 1946. Volume One: The Great Tradition
A. S. Barnes, 1966. 175pp. Paper $2.25. A survey of the French film since 1946, including summaries of the work of the great directors and critical analyses of their films. Illustrated.

ARMES, ROY
French Cinema Since 1946. Volume Two: The Personal Style
A. S. Barnes, 1966. 175pp. Paper $2.25. This volume includes critical analyses of the newer directors in France. Franju, Chabrol, Truffaut, Godard, Varda, Resnais, Vadim, Malle, and Etaix are some of the ones included. Illustrated.

ARMES, ROY
French Film
Dutton, 1970. 159pp. Paper $2.25. A study of the characteristic styles and personalities of over three dozen principal directors of the French cinema. The author demonstrates the range and variety of French film-making over the last seventy-five years. He concentrates on the contributions of the directors, from Melies to Godard, but does not neglect the efforts of the actors, writers, and technicians. Over 120 photographs illustrate the text.

CAMERON, IAN – Editor
The Films of Jean-Luc Godard
Studio Vista, 1967. 144pp. $4.95. Paper $1.95. A collection of articles on the films directed by the French film-maker. Among the contributors are Barry Boys, Ian Cameron, Daymond Durgnat, Paul Mayersberg, and Robin Wood. A Filmography and a Bibliography are included. Stills from the films illustrate the text.

CAMERON, IAN – Editor
The Films of Robert Bresson
Praeger, 1970. 144pp. $4.95. Paper $2.50. A group of critics with widely divergent attitudes to his work discuss the films of Bresson, director of "Diary of a Country Priest" and "Mouchette." Illustrated with photographs. Filmography. Bibliography.

COCTEAU, JEAN
Beauty and the Beast

New York University, 1970. 441pp. $14.95. Edited and annotated by Robert M. Hammond, this is a bilingual edition of the scenario of the classic film. An extensive Introduction indicates what cuts were made between preparation of the script and the appearance of the film, what additions and other discrepancies appear, and discusses the various versions and prints of the film which have come to light. Also included are excerpts from Cocteau's diary which apply to specific shots in the film. Illustrated with photographs.

COCTEAU, JEAN
My Contemporaries
See Page 131

COLLET, JEAN
Jean-Luc Godard: An Investigation into His Films and Philosophy
Crown, 1970. 218pp. Paper $2.95. Originally published in France in 1963 and now translated into English by Ciba Vaughan. In this study the author contends that Godard expresses the anger, confusion, and the existential despair of our contemporary world. The study is supplemented by selections from Godard's own thoughts on film-making and society, excerpts from screenplays, and a selection of critical and personal opinion. Illustrated with photographs. Bio-filmography. Bibliography. Index.

DURGNAT, RAYMOND
Franju
University of California, 1967. 144pp. $4.95. Paper $1.95. A study of the film director, Georges Franju, who directed a remarkable series of shorts and features. Durgnat analyzes Franju's savagely beautiful images and traces their artistic antecedents. Illustrated with photographs. Bibliography. Filmography.

GILSON, RENE
Jean Cocteau: An Investigation into His Films and Philosophy
Crown, 1969. 192pp. Paper $2.95. A study of the cinematic work of Cocteau, supplemented by selections from Cocteau's own thoughts, by excerpts from screenplays and from a broad spectrum of critical opinion. Illustrated. Filmography. Bibliography. Discography. Phonography. Chronology of References.

GRAHAM, PETER
The New Wave
Doubleday, 1968. 184pp. $4.95. Paper $2.95. A study of the French film scene during the late 1950's—its directors, films, and criticisms. Included are an interview with Francois Truffaut and several articles by leading film critics. Illustrated with photographs. Bibliography.

MORRISSETTE, BRUCE
Alain Robbe–Grillet
Columbia, 1965. 48pp. Paper $1.00. A brief essay on the work of the experimentalist novelist and film writer.

MUSSMAN, TOBY – Editor
Jean-Luc Godard
Dutton, 1968. 319pp. Paper $2.45. A critical anthology of essays and articles which discuss the French film-maker's fifteen feature films. Also included are three interviews with Godard, two scenarios, and five pieces by Godard himself. Illustrated with photographs. Chronology. Filmography.

PETRIE, GRAHAM
The Cinema of Francois Trauffaut
A. S. Barnes, 1970. 240pp. Paper $2.95. This is an in-depth study of the French film director and his work. All the films are studied from "The Mischief Makers" in 1958 to "The Wild Child" in 1970. Illustrated with photographs. Filmography. Bibliography.

ROUD, RICHARD
Jean-Luc Godard
Indiana University, 1970. 192pp. $5.95. Paper $2.25. Originally published in 1967 and now revised and reissued, this study of the French director is brought up to date to take account of the latest phase in Godard's oeuvre, the "political" cinema. Illustrated with photographs. Complete Filmography.

WARD, JOHN
Alain Resnais or The Theme of Time
Doubleday, 1968. 167pp. $4.95. Paper $2.95. Mr. Ward looks at the films of Alain Resnais, French director. Each of the four major films is concerned in some way with the concept of time and Ward traces the philosophical and social attitude throughout the films. Illustrated with scenes from the films. A complete Filmography of the features and the short subjects is included.

WOOD, ROBIN and MICHAEL WALKER
Claude Chabrol
Praeger, 1970. 144pp. $4.95. Paper $2.50. This book covers all of the features of the major French director who has assimilated into his personal style the influence of Alfred Hitchcock. The author concentrates on the major works from "Les Cousins" and "Les Bonnes Femmes" to "Les Biches" and "Le Boucher." Illustrated with photographs. Filmography.

Germany

BUCHER, FELIX
Germany – An Illustrated Guide
A. S. Barnes, 1970. 298pp. Paper $3.50. A guide to the work of over 400 directors, players, technicians, and other leading figures of the German cinema. Preference has been given to the artists responsible for the creation of German films between 1919 and 1933.

Illustrated with photographs. The Index lists over 6,000 films.

BYRNE, RICHARD B.
Films of Tyranny
College Printing & Typing, 1966. 152pp. Paper $4.50. The author studies the style, structure, composition, action, lighting, decor, and editing of three films of German expressionism: "The Cabinet of Dr. Caligari,""The Golem," and "Nosferatu." Illustrated.

EISNER, LOTTE H.
The Haunted Screen
University of California, 1969. 360pp. $10.95. Originally published in 1952 in France and now issued with new material in English, this is an analysis of expressionism in the German cinema and the influence of Max Reinhardt. Miss Eisner traces the stylistic and thematic developments from the beginnings of the expressionist film, "The Cabinet of Dr. Caligari," to the coming of sound. She links the work of Lang, Murnau, Pabst, Mayer, and many others to larger developments in the Germany of the twenties. More than 250 photographs. Selective Filmography 1913–33. Index.

HULL, DAVID STEWART
Film in the Third Reich
University of California, 1969. 291pp. $8.95. This is the first detailed comprehensive study of the German cinema of the Nazi period. The films of the period from 1933 to 1945 have all been studied by the author and he has interviewed more than a hundred members of the industry to write this history of film in a totalitarian state. One chapter on the anti-Semitic film traces the production of "Jud Suss," and the documentary," "Der ewige Jude." Illustrated with photographs. Notes. Bibliography. Index.

JENSEN, PAUL M.
The Cinema of Fritz Lang
See Page 456

KRACAUER, SIEGFRIED
From Caligari to Hitler
Princeton, 1966. 361pp. Paper $2.95. A psychological history of the German film from 1920 to the time of Hitler. Sixty-four stills from major films of the period are included. Bibliography. Index.

WEINBERG, HERMAN G.
The Lubitsch Touch
See Page 459

Great Britain

BALCON, MICHAEL
Michael Balcon Presents ....
See Page 471

BROWNLOW, KEVIN
How It Happened Here
Doubleday, 1968. 184pp. $4.95. Paper $2.95. This volume details how the film "It Happened Here" was made in England. The scenario deals with the imagined occupation of England by German forces during World War II. Illustrated with scenes from the film.

CURRY, GEORGE
Copperfield '70
Ballantine, 1970. 210pp. Paper $ .95. The story of the making of the film version of "David Copperfield," which was released in England and Europe as a motion picture and in the United States as a television spectacular. Included in the volume is the complete screenplay. Illustrated with sixteen pages of photographs.

GIFFORD, DENIS
British Cinema: An Illustrated Guide
A. S. Barnes, 1968. 176pp. Paper $2.45. A guide to 546 of the leading players and directors of the British cinema. Personal as well as professional data is included and a chronological Filmography for each entry is provided. Illustrated with photographs. Index to Film Titles.

LEAHY, JAMES
The Cinema of Joseph Losey
A. S. Barnes, 1967. 175pp. Paper $2.25. A study of the films of Joseph Losey, director of "The Servant," "Modesty Blaise," and "Accident." It consists partly of interviews with the director and partly of the author's opinions and point of view. Filmography. Selected Bibliography. Illustrated.

LOW, RACHAEL
The History of the British Film: 1906–1914
Allen & Unwin, 1949. 309pp. $6.00. This volume tells of the social, commercial, and artistic developments which took place in the British cinema industry from 1906 to 1914. The size and composition of the audience, the growth of the movie houses, the early labor struggles, and other matters of sociological interest are covered in Part One. Part Two gives an account of the content and treatment of factual, comic, and dramatic films with detailed studies of three major films: "East Lynne," "Richard III," and "David Copperfield." Illustrated. Bibliography. Index.

LOW, RACHAEL
The History of the British Film: 1914–1918
Allen & Unwin, 1950. 332pp. $8.00. This is the third volume in the history of the film industry in England. The author treats the growth of the audience, finances, trade organizations, the subject matter of the films, directorial techniques, and examines in detail two films: "Jane Shore" and "The Vicar of Wakefield." Miss Low surveys the standard

of film technique and provides complete production information on 500 films made between 1900 and 1920. Illustrated. Index.

MANVELL, ROGER
New Cinema in Britain
Dutton, 1969. 169pp. Paper $1.95. An assessment of British film over the last twenty years. The author discusses the changes which have taken place in the arts and shows how they form part of the general pattern of British cinema in the 1950's and 1960's. He studies the close relationship that exists between contemporary cinema and television drama and the recession of film censorship. The work of many feature directors is described and the work is illustrated with more than 100 stills. Index of Directors.

MILNE, TOM – Editor
Losey on Losey
Doubleday, 1968. 192pp. $4.95. Paper $2.95. Film director Joseph Losey talks about his work for the cinema and the theatre, examines his intentions and his failures, and explains why he did things as he did. Illustrated with stills from the films. Filmography.

MOSLEY, LEONARD
Battle of Britain: The Making of a Film
Stein & Day, 1969. 249pp. $10.00. Paper – Ballantine, 1969. 249pp. $ .95. The author tells about the making of the film, "Battle of Britain," from its inception as a story idea in 1965 to the conclusion of filming in 1968. Illustrated with color photographs.

PASCAL, VALERIE
The Disciple and His Devil
McGraw–Hill, 1970. 357pp. $8.95. A biography of Gabriel Pascal, the director who produced the film versions of G. B. Shaw's plays and whose idea it was to transform "Pygmalion" into a musical. The work is highlighted by quotations from the correspondence between Shaw and Pascal. Illustrated with photographs.

SPRAOS, JOHN
The Decline of the Cinema
Allen & Unwin, 1962. 168pp. $5.50. This book studies the causes of the drastic decline in theatre attendance and operating movie houses in Great Britain in the last decade. The influence of television and the shortage of films in this decline are examined in detail. The author also studies the patterns of cinema closures and evaluates their effect, discusses the rise in cost of productions as a factor, and considers proposals for revitalizing the industry. Illustrated with statistical tables.

SUSSEX, ELIZABETH
Lindsay Anderson
Praeger, 1970. 96pp. $4.95. Paper $1.95. The author discusses the film work of the highly acclaimed director. Illustrated with photographs. Filmography.

WHITEHEAD, PETER and ROBIN BEAN
Olivier – Shakespeare
See Page 478

WILCOX, HERBERT
Twenty-Five Thousand Sunsets
Bodley Head, 1967. 233pp. $6.50. This is the autobiography of Herbert Wilcox, the English director and producer. Mr. Wilcox gives vivid impressions of the stars, writers, and directors with whom he has worked and also details the films he made with his wife, the actress Anna Neagle. Illustrated. Index.

Hungary

NEMESKURTY, ISTVAN
Word and Image: History of the Hungarian Cinema
Clematis Press, 1968. 246pp. $7.50. Translated by Zsuzsanna Horn, this study of the cinema in Hungary is complete from its beginnings (1896–1911) through the work of the directors of the 1960's. A list of feature films made between 1945 and 1966 is included with names of directors and leading actors. Illustrated with forty-eight pages of photographs. Index.

India

BARNOUW, ERIK and S. KRISHNASWAMY
Indian Film
Columbia, 1963. 301pp. $10.00. The fifty year history of Indian film, viewed against a background of social change. The early films on mythological subjects, the musicals of the 1930's and 1940's, the post-war films, and the current international reputation are considered. The relation of the government of India to the industry is also considered.

Italy

CAMERON, IAN and ROBIN WOOD
Antonioni
Praeger, 1969. 144pp. $4.95. Paper $2.50. In this film-by-film analysis of Antonioni's career, Ian Cameron deals with the films up to "The Eclipse" while Robin Wood assesses the color films, "Red Desert" and "Blow Up." Illustrated with stills from the films. Filmography. Bibliography.

GUARNER, JOSE LUIS
Roberto Rossellini
Studio Vista, 1970. 144pp. $4.95. Paper $2.50. Translated from the original French by Elisabeth Cameron, this is a study of the work of the Italian director from 1941 to 1970. Illustrated with photographs. Filmography. Bibliography.

NOWELL–SMITH, GEOFFREY
Visconti
Doubleday, 1968. 192pp. $4.95. Paper $2.95. Mr. Nowell-Smith traces the links and connections in the work of the Italian film director of "The Leopard," "Rocco and His Brothers," and other films. Illustrated with scenes from the films. Filmography.

RONDI, BRUNELLO
Il Cinema de Fellini
Maestro, 1965. 418pp. $10.00. An Italian language discussion of Federico Fellini's major motion pictures. Illustrated.

SALACHAS, GILBERT
Federico Fellini: An Investigation into His Films and Philosophy
Crown, 1969. 224pp. Paper $2.95. A study of Italian director Federico Fellini. The study is supplemented by selections from Fellini's own thoughts on film-making, by excerpts from screenplays, and by a spectrum of critical and personal opinion. Illustrated. Selected Bibliography. Filmography. Index.

SOLMI, ANGELO
Fellini
Merlin, 1967. 183pp. $8.50. Mr. Solmi has written an autobiographical examination of the Italian film director. He delineates the constantly recurring themes in Fellini's films and shows how they are part of the director's own experience and philosophy. He also gives an account of the plots of the films and the intricacies of their actual making and their reception by the public. Illustrated with photographs. Bibliography. List of Films.

STACK, OSWALD
Pasolini on Pasolini
Indian University, 1970. 176pp. $5.95. Paper $2.25. In an extended series of interviews the author has drawn from Pier Paolo Pasolini, the Italian film-maker, a wealth of comment on his career to date. Stack discerns two opposing tendencies in Pasolini's work: a realism allied to his professed Marxism and a desire linked to his Catholicism to reach deeper levels of reality. "The Gospel According to Saint Matthew" is one of the films commented upon. Illustrated with photographs. Filmography. Bibliography.

ZAVATTINI, CESARE
Sequences from a Cinematic Life
Prentice–Hall, 1970. 297pp. $10.50. Translated and with an Introduction by William Weaver, this is the journal of the Italian cinema writer. Divided into four parts, it chronicles Zavattini's experiences with Vittoria De Sica in the founding of the neo-realist school of cinema, gives a behind-the-scenes view of movie making in Europe, reveals the man's personal and public hatreds, the sources of his radical politics, and his identification with the working classes. Illustrated with photographs.

Japan

ANDERSON, JOSEPH L. and DONALD RICHIE
The Japanese Film
Grove, 1960. 456pp. Paper $3.95. A reprint of the 1959 edition, this is a history of the Japanese film since 1898. Included are synopses of every major film and a list of the directors and leading players. Also included is a collection of 144 stills from the films. Index.

RICHIE, DONALD
The Films of Akira Kurosawa
University of California, 1965. 218pp. $11.00. Paper—1970. 223pp. $5.95. This is a critical study of the Japanese film director. All of Kurosawa's films are examined in detail with excerpts from the scripts, notes on camera usage and sound. Passages from the author's conversations with the director are included and biographical sections of the book are given in Kurosawa's own words. Illustrated with photographs.

RICHIE, DONALD
The Japanese Movie: An Illustrated History
Japan Publications, 1965. 200pp. $10.00. This collection of photographs, many reproduced for the first time, provides a history of the Japanese film industry. Supplementing the stills is an extensive commentary that provides comparison between the films of Japan and other countries. Richie analyzes the reasons Japan's movies have reflected the social and philosophical issues of the nation. The photographs and text reflect a span of seventy years. Index.

Poland

BUTLER, IVAN
The Cinema of Roman Polanski
A. S. Barnes, 1970. 192pp. Paper $2.95. A study of the man and his films. Each of the five full-length films as well as the shorts are studied in a separate chapter. Complete cast and production credits are provided as are synopses and critiques. Illustrated with photographs.

Russia

BRITISH FILM INSTITUTE
Fifty Years of Soviet Cinema: 1917—1967
British Film Institute, 1968. Unpaged. Paper $1.25. This folio of twenty-seven 8" x 10" plates is printed on heavy glossy paper and includes scenes from the major Soviet films produced during the fifty years since 1917.

CARTER, HUNTLY
The New Spirit in the Russian Theatre 1917—1928
See Page 219

EISENSTEIN, SERGEI
Film Essays with a Lecture
Praeger, 1970. 220pp. $6.95. Paper $2.95. A series of essays by the great Russian film director. Starting with his earliest theories and ending with his analyses of montage and composition, these essays provide an insight into Eisenstein's philosophy of cinema. Edited by Jay Leyda with a Foreword by Grigori Kozintsev. Illustrated with photographs. List of the Published Writings (1922–1964). Index.

EISENSTEIN, SERGEI
Film Form
Harcourt, Brace, 1969. 279pp. Paper $2.45. Together with "The Film Sense," this is one of the classic statements on the aesthetics of film-making. Translated and edited by Jay Leyda, the volume draws together twelve essays written between 1928 and 1945 that demonstrate key points in the development of Eisenstein's film theory and his analysis of the sound film medium. Illustrated with drawings and photographs.

EISENSTEIN, SERGEI
The Film Sense
Harcourt, Brace, 1969. 288pp. Paper $2.45. Translated and edited by Jay Leyda, this volume is considered to be one of the classic statements on the aesthetics of film-making. Eisenstein discusses films as a more expressive and profound medium that would appeal to all the senses as well as the emotions and the intellect. An analysis of audio-visual correspondences in a sequence from "Alexander Nevsky" is included. A complete listing of Eisenstein's pre-film and film work, sequences from his scenarios, and a Bibliography are also provided. Illustrated with drawings and diagrams. Index.

EISENSTEIN, SERGEI
Notes of a Film Director
Dover, 1970. 240pp. Paper $3.00. A corrected republication of the first English translation, by X. Danko, of Eisenstein's collection of twenty essays, articles, and letters written between the early 1930's and 1948. This collection provides an insight into Eisenstein's theories of film-making. Provided are seventy-eight illustrations including twenty-eight pages of the author's drawings and sketches.

GEDULD, HARRY M. and RONALD GOTTESMAN – Editors
Sergei Eisenstein and Upton Sinclair: The Making and Unmaking of "Qui Viva Mexico!"
See Page 454

KOZINTSEV, GRIGORI
Shakespeare: Time and Conscience
See Page 94

LEYDA, JAY
Kino: A History of the Russian and Soviet Film
Hillary, 1970. 494pp. $11.25. A comprehensive history of film in Russia that begins with the filming of the Czar's coronation in 1896, discusses the importance of the Pre-Revolutionary film industry, and shows the links between that and the achievements of the early Soviet films. The social and political backgrounds are also examined.

MONTAGU, IVOR
With Eisenstein in Hollywood
See Page 457

MOUSSINAC, LEON
Sergei Eisenstein
Crown, 1970. 226pp. Paper $2.95. An investigation into the films and philosophy of the film director. Supplemented by selections from Eisenstein's own thoughts of film-making, by excerpts from screenplays, and by a spectrum of critical and personal opinion. The volume was originally published in France in 1964 and has been translated by D. Sandy Petrey. Illustrated with photographs. Bio-Filmography. Bibliography. Index.

NIZHNY, VLADIMIR
Lessons with Eisenstein
Hill & Wang, 1962. 182pp. $5.75. Paper $1.95. This account of Eisenstein's classes at the State Institute of Cinematography in Moscow was translated and edited by Ivor Montagu and Jay Leyda. The essentials of Eisenstein's own rules for film direction are illustrated by scenes from "Pere Goriot," "Black Majesty," and "Crime and Punishment." Illustrated. Notes. Index.

PUDOVKIN, V. I.
Film Technique and Film Acting
See Page 440

Spain

DURGNAT, RAYMOND
Luis Bunuel
University of California, 1968. 152pp. Paper $1.95. This study interprets all of Luis Bunuel's films from "Un Chien Andalou" in 1928 to "Belle de Jour" in 1966. The study is illustrated with stills from the films. Also included are a Filmography and a Bibliography.

Sweden

COWIE, PETER
Sweden I
A. S. Barnes, 1970. 224pp. Paper $3.50. An Illustrated guide to the work of the leading directors, players, technicians, and other figures in the Swedish cinema. Credits and plot outlines for more than seventy important films are included. Illustrated with photographs. Index to 1,000 Titles.

COWIE, PETER
Sweden 2
A. S. Barnes, 1970. 256pp. Paper $3.50. A comprehensive assessment of the themes, trends, and directors in Swedish cinema. Among the directors studied are Victor Sjostrom, Mauritz Stiller, Alf Sjoberg, Arne Sucksdorff, Ingmar Bergman, and Bo Widerberg. Illustrated with photographs. Bibliography.

GIBSON, ARTHUR
The Silence of God: Creative Response to the Films of Ingmar Bergman
Harper & Row, 1969. 171pp. $5.95. Paper $2.25. Professor Gibson offers an intensive analysis of each of seven films, prefaced in every case by a brief synopsis of plot, to examine the theme of modern man's experience of the silence, presence, or absence of God. Illustrated with nine stills from the films.

PENSEL, HANS
Seastrom and Stiller in Hollywood
See Page 457

SJOMAN, VILGOT
I Was Curious: Diary of the Making of a Film
Grove, 1968. 217pp. $5.95. Paper $2.45. This is an account of the making of the controversial film: "I Was Curious—Yellow." The diary presents the preparations for the film, the filming itself, and reflections on the result. Illustrated with photographs.

WOOD, ROBIN
Ingmar Bergman
Praeger, 1969. 192pp. $5.95. Paper $2.50. A study of the work of the Swedish director. Particular attention is paid to the important films of Bergman's mature period: the trilogy, "Persona," "Hour of the Wolf," and "Shame." Illustrated. Filmography.

United States

AGEL, JEROME — Editor
The Making of Kubrick's "2001"
Signet, 1970. 368pp. Paper $1.50. This volume includes Arthur C. Clarke's original story, "The Sentinel." Essays on the special effects of the film, letters to Kubrick, interviews with scientists and theologians, samples of reviews and criticism are also included. Illustrated with more than ninety-six pages of photographs of the film.

AUSTIN, JOHN
Hollywood's Unsolved Mysteries
Ace, 1970. 190pp. Paper $ .75. A collection of essays on the deaths or scandals of Hollywood personalities.

BARBOUR, ALAN G.
Days of Thrills and Adventure
Collier, 1970. 168pp. $6.95. Paper $3.95. A pictorial history of the movie serial from the 1930's and 1940's to the final productions in the mid 1950's. The author chronicles the great movie names that emerged from the serials: Lon Chaney, Jr., Tom Mix, George Brent, and Jennifer Jones among them. There are also stories of the celebrities from other fields who worked in the medium. Particular attention is paid to Pearl White and Buster Crabbe. A complete list of sound serials is included. Illustrated with photographs.

BARRY, IRIS
D. W. Griffith: American Film Master
New York Graphic Society, 1965. 88pp. $6.95. Paper $2.95. A biography of the film director whose achievements justified the new medium to the world and became a source of motion picture development. Eileen Bowser has contributed an annotated list of films. Illustrated.

BAXTER, JOHN
The Gangster Film
A. S. Barnes, 1970. 160pp. Paper $3.50. An illustrated guide to over 200 key figures in the gangster and crime film. Actors, directors, producers, and screenwriters, as well as some terms frequently used in the films, are listed alphabetically with biographical and professional information. Illustrated. Index of over 900 films in the genre.

BAXTER, JOHN
Hollywood in the Thirties
A. S. Barnes, 1968. 160pp. Paper $2.25. A critique of the motion picture industry in the 1930's. The films and the artists who made them are reviewed and discussed. Illustrated with photographs. Index.

BLUM, DANIEL
Pictorial History of the Silent Screen
Grosset & Dunlap, 1953. 334pp. $7.95. A picture record of the silent film from 1889 to 1930 with descriptive text. Over 3,000 photographs, many of them rare or unique, of the great personalities of the silent screen are included. Index.

BOGDANOVICH, PETER
Fritz Lang in America
Studio Vista, 1967. 144pp. $4.95. Paper $1.95. In this interview book, Fritz Lang describes his experiences and looks back at his American films. Among these films, an average of one per year from 1936 to 1956, were "Fury," "Scarlet Street," and "Rancho Notorious." A complete Filmography with production and cast credits is included. Illustrated.

BOGDANOVICH, PETER
John Ford
University of California, 1967. 144pp. $4.95. Paper $1.95. A study of the American film director. In a series of interviews Ford sums up his career in the cinema. Mr. Bogdanovich also provides an Introduction

on the style and methods of the director. Illustrated with photographs. Filmography.

BRUNO, MICHAEL
Venus in Hollywood
Lyle Stuart, 1970. 257pp. $6.95. A history of the "sex-goddesses" who made Hollywood prosper. In his analysis of the evolution of the movies, the author charts the fashions, revolutions, and the mythology of Hollywood's dream girls from Mary Pickford and Vilma Banky to Jane Fonda and Jeanne Moreau. The public images and the private lives of the stars are discussed. Illustrated with photographs. Bibliography. Index.

BULL, CLARENCE and RAYMOND LEE
The Faces of Hollywood
A. S. Barnes, 1968. 256pp. $10.00. Clarence Bull was the chief portrait photographer for MGM studios for over thirty years. He has included hundreds of his photographs of the great stars and his own personal observations and anecdotes about them in this book. A Technical Appendix is included.

BURROWS, MICHAEL
John Ford and Andrew V. McLaglen
Primestyle, 1970. 32pp. Paper $1.35. A short study of the films of the two American directors. Illustrated with photographs. Bibliography. Filmography.

BURROWS, MICHAEL
John Steinbeck and His Films
Primestyle, 1970. 33pp. Paper $1.35. The author provides a commentary on films made from Steinbeck's fiction. Illustrated with photographs.

BURTON, JACK
Blue Book of Hollywood Musicals
See Page 290

BUTLER, IVAN
The Cinema of Roman Polanski
See Page 450

CALDER–MARSHALL, ARTHUR
The Innocent Eye: The Life of Robert J. Flaherty
Harcourt, Brace, 1963. 302pp. $6.95. Paper—Penguin, 1970. 303pp. $2.25. Using a wealth of research material gathered by Paul Rotha and Basil Wright, the author analyzes Flaherty's movie-making techniques as seen in such films as "Moana," "Man of Aran," "Louisiana Story," and "Nanook of the North." Flaherty's pioneering methods and his personality are studied. Appendices by Rotha and Wright. Illustrated with seventy photographs. index.

CAREY, GARY
Lost Films
Museum of Modern Art, 1970. 91pp. Paper $4.95. The author documents thirty American motion pictures from the 1920's that have been destroyed. in addition to discussing the films and providing a synopsis and credits for each, the author touches on the problems of film preservation. More than 150 photographs from the films illustrate the volume. Index.

CARMEN, IRA H.
Movies, Censorship and the Law
University of Michigan, 1966. 339pp. $7.95. This story of motion-picture censorship begins in 1915 when the Supreme Court denied freedom of the press to movies and follows the history of movie censorship to the present day. This book includes a series of interviews with film censors in major U.S. cities and reveals how such censors think, what kinds of films they suppress and for what reasons. Recent court decisions on censorship are also included. Bibliography. Index.

CASTY, ALAN
The Films of Robert Rossen
Museum of Modern Art, 1969. 94pp. Paper $2.50. A critical introduction to the films of producer/director/writer Robert Rossen. A Filmography with complete cast and production credits plus a photograph from each film is included. Bibliography.

COPLANS, JOHN
Andy Warhol
New York Graphic Society, 1970. 160pp. $10.00. With contributions by Calvin Tompkins and Jonas Mekas, this book sets out to provide a viewing of a broad spectrum of Warhol's painting and sculpture, from 1960 to 1964, and his recent films. The essays cover the man, the art, and the films. Also included are a Selective Bibliography of Published Writings on Warhol's art and a Filmography. Illustrated with eighteen color plates and 100 black-and-white reproductions and photographs.

CRONE, RAINER
Andy Warhol
Praeger, 1970. 332pp. $22.95. A major assessment of Warhol's position in the current art scene. The author's comments are supplemented by a comprehensive catalog of Warhol's works. Documented are 650 paintings, prints and objects. More than 325 illustrations in color and black-and-white provide an exhaustive visual record of the Warhol output. A Filmography and an extensive Bibliography of over 600 entries include a record of Warhol's interviews and his major exhibitions.

DEMING, BARBARA
Running Away From Myself
Grossman, 1969. 210pp. $6.95. The author subtitles this volume "a dream portrait of America drawn from the films of the 1940's." It is an examination of America based on the films of that era. Miss Deming's work has appeared in various national magazines. Illustrated with photographs from the films discussed. Index.

DUNNE, JOHN GREGORY
The Studio
Farrar, Straus, 1969. 255pp. $5.95. Paper – Bantam, 1970. 207pp. $ .95. The author provides a study of Hollywood at work. Mr. Dunne was allowed to be present in the board rooms of Twentieth Century Fox as well as on the sound stages and he provides information and anecdotes on the filming of "Star!," "The Boston Strangler," "Hello, Dolly!," and "Dr. Doolittle," as well as other films.

DURGNAT, RAYMOND
The Crazy Mirror: Hollywood Comedy and the American Image
Horizon, 1970. 280pp. $7.50. The author provides an analysis of comedy films and attempts to explain some of the "crazy images" of Hollywood comedy. The book explores the great comic films and the great comedians from Chaplin, Lloyd, Conklin, and Keaton to the Marx Brothers, Carole Lombard, and Katherine Hepburn. Illustrated with photographs. Index of Films. Index of Names.

EPHRON, NORA
Wallflower at the Orgy
Viking, 1970. 179pp. $5.95. A collection of articles originally printed in various periodicals between 1967 and 1970. In interviews and essays, Miss Ephron discusses or talks with some of the figures in popular culture. Among the entertainers included are Mike Nichols, Helen Gurley Brown, Jacqueline Susann, Julia Child, Ayn Rand, and there is also an article on the location shooting of the film "Catch 22."

ESSOE, GABE and RAYMOND LEE
DeMille: The Man and His Pictures
A. S. Barnes, 1970. 319pp. $8.50. A study of the life and work of the film director. Reminiscences by Charlton Heston, Henry Wilcoxon, and Charles Bickford, among others, are included. Lavishly illustrated with photographs. Complete Filmography: 1913–1956.

ESSOE, GABE
Tarzan of the Movies
Citadel, 1968. 208pp. $8.95. A pictorial history of more than fifty years of the Edgar Rice Burroughs' hero. The text reveals the back-stage machinations in the production of the films, the rivalry between film-makers for film rights, the events that took place during production. There are profiles of all the actors who have appeared in the title role and comparisons of their approaches to the role. More than 400 pictures appear throughout the text.

EVERSON, WILLIAM K.
A Pictorial History of the Western Film
Citadel, 1969. 246pp. $10.00. Using nearly five hundred stills as illustrations, Mr. Everson examines the whole range of the Western film as one aspect of film culture. Beginning with the first version of "The Great Train Robbery," the book traces Westerns through the two-and three-reelers on to the epics of the 1950's and 1960's. Index.

EYLES, ALLEN
The Western: An Illustrated Guide
A. S. Barnes, 1967. 183pp. Paper $2.25. A guide to the stars, supporting players, directors, screenwriters, composers, cameramen, authors, and others who have contributed to the Western film genre. A record of screen portrayals of the most famous real-life Westerners is included. Illustrated. Index to 2,200 films.

FENTON, ROBERT W.
The Big Swingers
Prentice–Hall, 1967. 258pp. $6.95. A full-scale biography of Edgar Rice Burroughs, creator of "Tarzan." It also includes the history of the Tarzan films and includes photographs of all the movie Tarzans. Index.

FINLER, JOEL W.
Stroheim
University of California, 1968. 144pp. $4.95. Paper $1.95. This monograph considers Stroheim's career as an actor and director. The author recreates the full version of "Greed" and links it to Stroheim's other films. Filmography. Illustrated.

FRANKLIN, JOE
Classics of the Silent Screen: A Pictorial Treasury
Citadel, 1967. 255pp. Paper $3.95. Originally published in 1959 and now reissued, this volume is a nostalgic look at the films of the silent screen. The author provides an analysis of fifty films and the careers of seventy-five stars and has illustrated the book with over 400 photographs.

FREDRIK, NATHALIE
Hollywood and the Academy Awards
Ace, 1970. 203pp. Paper $1.50. A listing of the Oscar winners from 1927 through 1969 with biographies of all acting-award winners and resumes of the winning films. Also listed are technical awards. Illustrated with over 200 photographs.

FRENCH, PHILIP
The Movie Moguls
Weidenfeld & Nicolson, 1969. 170pp. $7.95: An informal history of the Hollywood tycoons. The author considers the background, characters and careers of such men as Louis B. Mayer, Samuel Goldwyn, Adolph Zukor, William Fox, the Warner Brothers, Walt Disney, and others. Illustrated with photographs. Biographical notes. Bibliography. Index.

GEDULD, HARRY M. and RONALD GOTTESMAN – Editors
Sergei Eisenstein and Upton Sinclair: The Making and Unmaking of "Qui Viva Mexico!"
Indiana University, 1970. 449pp. $15.00. A study

of the conception, development, and abortive end of the film Eisenstein attempted to make in Mexico in the early 1930's. Actual correspondence of the main participants is included in the commentary by the editors. Illustrated with photographs. Chronology and Itinerary. Glossary of Principal Persons and Places. Annotated Bibliography. Index.

GISH, LILLIAN and ANN PINCHOT
Lillian Gish: The Movies, Mr. Griffith and Me
See Page 475

GRAHAM, SHEILAH
The Garden of Allah
Crown, 1970. 258pp. $5.95. A history of the Hollywood hotel during the thirty-two years of its life as the playground of such film personalities as Robert Benchley, Greta Garbo, John Barrymore, Errol Flynn, and Humphrey Bogart. Illustrated with photographs. Index.

GRIFFITH, MRS. D.W. (LINDA ARVIDSON)
When the Movies Were Young
Blom, 1968. 495pp. $12.50. Paper—Dover, 1969. 266pp. $2.50. A history of the early days of the movies by the wife of the celebrated film director. Originally published in 1925 and now reissued, the volume is illustrated with photographs.

GRIFFITH, RICHARD and ARTHUR MAYER
The Movies
Simon & Schuster, 1970. 495pp. $19.95. Originally published in 1957 and now completely revised and updated, this is the classic history of American motion pictures. All of the original material from the first edition is here and new pages of text show what happened during the 1960's, including the advent of the television era and the growth of the Underground Film and the new generation of young film-makers. Lavishly illustrated with over 1,300 photographs. Index.

HAMBLETT, CHARLES
The Hollywood Cage
Hart, 1969. 447pp. $6.95. A British magazine writer observes Hollywood. Closeups of Marilyn Monroe, Humphrey Bogart, Elizabeth Taylor, Marlon Brando, and many of the other great stars are included. Illustrated with photographs. Index.

HAMBLETT, CHARLES
Who Killed Marilyn Monroe?
Leslie Frewin, 1966. 175pp. $6.50. This book is Mr. Hamblett's assessment of Hollywood as a system and as a "set-up." He uses quotes from well-known Hollywood figures to inquire into that system. He contends that the system kills as it creates and destroys as it builds. Illustrated with photographs.

HAMPTON, BENJAMIN B.
History of the American Film Industry from Its Beginnings to 1931
Dover, 1970. 456pp. Paper $4.00. Originally published in 1931 and now reissued with a new Introduction by Richard Griffith. The author documents the early experiments with motion pictures, the rise of the stars, the battle for control of the movie theatres, and his own experiences with the great figures of the early industry. Illustrated with 191 photographs. Index.

HARDY, PHIL
Samuel Fuller
Praeger, 1970. 144pp. $4.95. Paper $2.50. The author examines the thematic and stylistic continuity of Fuller's film work, assessing its defects as well as its virtues. All eighteen of the films are studied. Illustrated with photographs. Filmography.

HENDERSON, ROBERT M.
D.W. Griffith: The Years at Biograph
Farrar, Straus, 1970. 250pp. $7.50. An exploration in depth of the years between 1908 and 1913 when silent film director D. W. Griffith began his directing career at the Biograph studio in New York. Illustrated with photographs. Bibliography. Appendices. Index.

HIGHAM, CHARLES
The Films of Orson Welles
University of California, 1970. 210pp. $10.95. Paper $5.95. In this study of the American film director, the author discusses all of Welles' films. A chapter is devoted to each film giving the circumstances of its production and analyzing its dramatic structure and stylistic strategies. Illustrated with more than 230 stills. Filmography. Bibliography.

HIGHAM, CHARLES
Hollywood Cameramen
Indiana University, 1970. 176pp. $5.95. Paper $2.25. A collection of interviews with cameramen who have worked during various periods of motion picture history. The work of seven men is elucidated by the cameramen themselves and the author provides an Introduction as well as checklists of the films mentioned. Illustrated with photographs. Index.

HIGHAM, CHARLES and JOEL GREENBERG
Hollywood in the Forties
A. S. Barnes, 1968. 192pp. Paper $2.25. This is an assessment of the creative achievements of the motion picture industry in the 1940's. Illustrated with twenty pages of photographs. Index.

HITCHENS, GORDON—Editor
Hollywood Blacklisting
Film Culture, 1970. 84pp. Paper $2.00. This is a special double issue of the periodical, "Film Culture," devoted to Hollywood Blacklisting during the 1940's and 1950's. Among the contributors are Nedrick Young, Alvah Bessie, Dick Powell, John Howard Lawson, Dalton Trumbo, Abraham Polonsky, Joseph Losey, and Joseph Strick. Actual transcripts

of some of the testimony before the Committee on Un-American Activities is provided. Illustrated with photographs.

HOFFMAN, CHARLES
Sounds for Silents
Drama Book Specialists, 1970. Unpaged. $10.00. The author traces the history of music in the film from before 1900 to 1930. The volume is profusely illustrated with production stills, comparative musical scores, cue sheets, and many important film scores never before reproduced. Foreword by Lillian Gish. A recording of musical backgrounds for four films is included.

JACOBS, LEWIS
The Rise of the American Film: A Critical History
Teachers College Press, 1968. 631pp. $8.50. Paper $3.95. Originally published in 1939 and now reissued with additional material, this book relates the artistic, technical, and industrial aspects of film-making to the forces at work in American society. The author traces the development of the movies from their introduction to 1939. He offers critical interpretations of hundreds of films, analyzing the contributions of inventors, artists, technicians, and financiers. Included in this new edition is an essay on "Experimental Cinema in America: 1921–1947." Illustrated with photographs. Bibliography. Film Index. Name Index.

JENSEN, PAUL M.
The Cinema of Fritz Lang
A. S. Barnes, 1969. 223pp. Paper $2.45. An appreciation and critique of the work of the German film director. His early work in the silent films and his later work in Hollywood are both covered. Illustrated. Filmography. References to Books and Periodicals.

KITSES, JIM
Horizons West: Studies of Authorship within the Western
Indiana University, 1970. 176pp. $5.95. Paper $2.25. An examination of Western films by three directors: Budd Boetticher, Sam Peckinpah, and Anthony Mann. The personal visions of the directors are related to the Western films they have made. Illustrated with photographs. Selected Filmographies.

LAHUE, KALTON C.
Continued Next Week: A History of the Moving Picture Serial
University of Oklahoma, 1964. 293pp. $6.95. The silent serial, a financial mainstay of production for at least two major companies in the 1920's and an important part of the entire industry's life between 1914 and 1930, is examined in detail. An Appendix lists credits for serials between 1912 and 1930. Illustrated.

LAHUE, KALTON C. and TERRY BREWER
Kops and Custards
University of Oklahama, 1968. 177pp. $5.95. Utilizing the memories of individuals who took part in the films and the data found in various private collections, the authors present an appraisal of the Keystone comedies and their creator. A complete listing of the comedies is appended together with production information. illustrated with scenes from the films. Bibliography. Index of Titles. General Index.

LAHUE, KALTON C.
World of Laughter
University of Oklahoma, 1966. 240pp. $5.95. Subtitled "The Motion Picture Comedy Short, 1910–1930," this book deals with the men and the companies who made laughter standard fare in the motion picture theatres of yesterday. It is a history of the silent comedy short rather than a treatment of the nature of comedy. Bibliography. Appendix of films of famous comedians. Index. Illustrated.

LEE, RAYMOND
Fit for the Chase: Cars and the Movies
A. S. Barnes, 1969. 237pp. $8.50. A photographic essay on the history of the automobile in motion pictures. In text and more than two hundred photographs, the use of the automobile as a comic prop, a chase vehicle, a lover's rendezvous, or a dramatic object is detailed.

LEVIN, MARTIN – Editor
Hollywood and the Great Fan Magazines
Arbor House, 1970. 224pp. Paper $3.95. In the format of a giant fan magazine, the editor collects articles from the literature of Hollywood in the 1930's. Articles about the stars, photographs, and features from the popular fan magazines of the era are included.

MADSEN, AXEL
Billy Wilder
Indiana University, 1969. 168pp. $5.95. Paper $1.95. A study of the film director in which the author assesses all twenty of the films on which Wilder collaborated as writer and director from 1942 to 1966. Filmography with complete production and cast credits. Illustrated with stills from the films and candid photographs.

MANVELL, ROGER
New Cinema in the U.S.A.
Dutton, 1968. 160pp. Paper $1.95. A companion volume to "New Cinema in Europe," this is a discussion of the development of the American film since 1946. The author shows how each generation of film-makers has contributed a new and sometimes highly individual slant to the accepted forms of entertainment. Illustrated. Index.

MARLOWE, DON
The Hollywood That Was
Branch-Smith, 1969. 192pp. $5.95. Recollections

of the 1930's and 1940's by a former member of the "Our Gang" comedy series. Reminiscences of Bela Lugosi, Humphrey Bogart, Tom Mix, Oliver and Hardy, and others are included. Almost one hundred pages of photographs are provided.

MAYERSBERG, PAUL
Hollywood the Haunted House
Penguin, 1967. 188pp. $6.25. Paper—1969. 172pp. $1.50. Also Paper—Ballantine, 1969. 211pp. $ .95. This is an account of how Hollywood movies are planned, financed, written, directed, shot, cut, and publicized. The British film critic relates anecdotes and experiences of many film-makers including Hitchcock, Stanley Kramer, Delmar Daves, and George Cukor. Bibliography.

MICHAEL, PAUL
The Academy Awards: A Pictorial History
Crown, 1968. 374pp. $3.95. A revised edition of the volume originally published in 1964. Nearly 300 photographs of the stars and the films which have won the "Oscar" from 1928 through 1967 are included. David O. Selznick has contributed a Foreword to the volume. Index.

MICHAEL, PAUL—Editor
The American Movies Reference Book: The Sound Era
Prentice—Hall, 1969. 629pp. $29.95. A comprehensive reference book covering the history, players, films, directors, producers, and awards of the film industry from the beginning of the sound era through the present day. Over six hundred actors and actresses are shown in a scene from one of their films with biographical material and a complete filmography. Each of over 1,000 films is illustrated with a still and complete cast and production credits. More than one hundred Filmographies of directors and producers are included. Illustrated. Bibliography. Index.

MILNE, TOM
Mamoulian
Indiana University, 1970. 176pp. $5.95. Paper $2.25. A critical study of film director Rouben Mamoulian in which the author examines each of the director's sixteen films from "Applause" in 1929 to "Silk Stockings" in 1957. Illustrated with photographs. Filmography.

MONTAGU, IVOR
With Eisenstein in Hollywood
International Publishers, 1969. 356pp. Paper $1.95. This volume is the author's memoirs of the days in the 1930's when he collaborated with Sergei Eisenstein and Grigory Alexandrov on two original film scenarios which were never produced. The volume includes the publication of the two film scripts: "An American Tragedy" and "Sutter's Gold." Illustrated with photographs and drawings. Bibliography. Index.

MUNSTERBERG, HUGO
The Film: A Psychological Study
Dover, 1970. 100pp. Paper $2.00. An unabridged republication of the original 1916 edition formerly titled "The Photoplay: A Psychological Study." Munsterberg treats an area of film experience—the psychology of the viewer—which is usually glossed over or omitted. A new Foreword has been provided for this edition by Richard Griffith.

MYERS, HORTENSE and RUTH BURNETT
Cecil B. DeMille, Young Dramatist
Bobbs-Merrill, 1963. 200pp. $2.75. The story of Cecil B. DeMille's childhood and his early years in Hollywood. The book is written for young people and is illustrated by Nathan Goldstein.

O'DELL. PAUL
Griffith and the Rise of Hollywood
A. S. Barnes, 1970. 163pp. Paper $2.95. A study of the work of D. W. Griffith and other pioneers of the film industry from the beginnings of cinema's adulthood in 1915 with the premiere of "The Birth of a Nation" to the development of the star system in 1919. Illustrated with photographs. Bibliography. Index.

PENSEL, HANS
Seastrom and Stiller in Hollywood
Vantage, 1969. 106pp. $3.50. This is a study of Victor Seastrom and Mauritz Stiller, two Swedish film directors, and their work in Sweden and Hollywood silent films from 1923 to 1930. Illustrated with photographs. Filmographies. Bibliography.

PRATLEY, GERALD
The Cinema of John Frankenheimer
A. S. Barnes, 1969. 240pp. Paper $2.45. A study of the work of director John Frankenheimer. Each of the twelve films is covered in a separate chapter and there are chapters on his television work, his methods, and his opinions on film, and the artist in politics. Illustrated.

QUIGLEY, MARTIN and RICHARD GERTNER
Films in America: 1929—1969
Golden Press, 1970. 379pp. $12.95. The authors discuss every aspect of the motion picture world in this volume, from the stars and the movies that made them to the economic ups and downs of the film business. Their aim has been to furnish concise, comprehensive information and analysis of a representative number of films significant in the United States from the first sound film to the present. Nearly 400 notable screen works are discussed and each is accompanied by at least one photograph that highlights its particular flavor. Index.

RENAN, SHELDON
An Introduction to the American Underground Film
Dutton, 1967. 318pp. Paper $2.25. A fully illustrated

handbook to the art of the underground film and its makers. The author discusses subject matter, elements of style and technique, and the ways that underground films are made. He gives a general history of the avant-garde film in America and provides detailed accounts of the careers and films of twenty-six of the most prominent film-makers. Index of Distributors. Bibliography. Illustrated. Index.

RINGGOLD, GENE and DE WITT BODEEN
The Films of Cecil B. DeMille
Citadel, 1969. 377pp. $10.00. Paper $3.95. A history of the motion-picture director's career and his silent and sound films. Each of the films has production and cast credits, a resume of the plot, and extracts from the contemporary reviews as well as many scenes from the film. In addition there is a section on "The Lux Radio Theatre" productions with a complete chronology. The Introduction to the volume includes a biographical sketch and notes on the films and players.

ROBINSON, DAVID
Hollywood in the Twenties
A.S. Barnes, 1968. 176pp. Paper $2.25. A critical assessment of the films and film-makers of the 1920's. Illustrated with twenty pages of photographs. Index.

ROSENBERG, BERNARD and HARRY SILVERSTEIN
The Real Tinsel
Macmillan, 1970. 436pp. $9.95. The authors have assembled an insider's chronicle of Hollywood, from beginnings to the present, as told by twenty-four of the pioneer contributors: producers, directors, stars, publicist, stuntman, voice animator, music director, cameraman, sound director, writer, and critic. Among these contributors: Hal Roach, Dore Schary, Mae Marsh, Fritz Lang, Max Steiner, and Arthur Knight. Illustrated. Index.

ROSS, LILLIAN
Picture
Avon, 1969. 220pp. Paper $1.25. Originally published in 1952 and now reissued, this is the story of the making of John Huston's film, "The Red Badge of Courage." It is factual reporting written in the form of a novel and details the ideals and ordeals of film-making.

SARRIS, ANDREW
The Films of Josef von Sternberg
New York Graphic Society, 1966. 56pp. $5.95. Paper $2.95. Josef von Sternberg's career and reputation are critically estimated in this survey of the director's eighteen films. Illustrated with stills from the films.

SLIDE, ANTHONY
Early American Cinema
A.S. Barnes, 1970. 192pp. Paper $2.95. A history of the early motion picture in the United States from the beginnings of Edison and Lubin in the late 1890's to the sensational serial queens before and during World War I. Illustrated with photographs. Selected Bibliography. Index.

SNYDER, ROBERT L.
Pare Lorentz and the Documentary Film
University of Oklahoma, 1968. 232pp. $6.95. Professor Snyder has written an account of the production of the 1930's documentary films that developed new techniques in filming and set new standards and which are regarded now as classics. A critical examination of each of three major films is provided: "The Plow that Broke the Plains," "The River," and "The Fight for Life." Illustrated with photographs. Appendices. Selected Bibliography. Index.

SPRINGER, JOHN
All Talking! All Singing! All Dancing!
Citadel, 1966. 256pp. $10.00. Paper $3.45. A history of the movie musical from silent films to the present day. The emphasis is on the American film but the foreign classics are also included. Illustrated with stills from all the great films from "The Jazz Singer" to "My Fair Lady." Introduction by Gene Kelly. Index.

STERNBERG, JOSEF VON
Fun in a Chinese Laundry
Secker & Warburg, 1967. 348pp. $7.95. Originally published in 1965, this is the autobiography of the director of such films as "The Blue Angel" and "Morocco," and the discoverer of Marlene Dietrich. Illustrated. Index.

THORPE, EDWARD
The Other Hollywood
Michael Joseph, 1970. 174pp. $6.25. The subjective impressions of the author attempt to capture the atmosphere of Hollywood today, the Hollywood that exists outside the fantasy of the film world. Illustrated with photographs.

TRUFFAUT, FRANCOIS
Hitchcock
Simon & Schuster, 1967. 256pp. $10.00. Paper $3.75. With the collaboration of Helen G. Scott, Francois Truffaut has provided a definitive study of Alfred Hitchcock and his films from the beginning of his career to the present. Composed in a question and answer format, the dialogues show how an idea is transformed into a cinematic image and the way a director imposes a story with the imprint of his own personality. Illustrated with 472 photographs taken directly from Hitchcock's films. Production and cast credits from all the films are included. Selected Bibliography. Index.

TYLER, PARKER
The Hollywood Hallucination
Simon & Schuster, 1970. 246pp. $5.95. Paper $1.95.

First published in 1944 and long out-of-print, this is a reissue of the pioneering study of the expressive style which developed out of the convergence of the beliefs and values of the American people and the peculiar technical properties of the medium of the film. Tyler shows how the qualities Hollywood flaunts constitute an art and how the screen image reflects the aspirations, frustrations, fears, and beliefs of the audience.

TYLER, PARKER
Magic and Myth of the Movies
Simon & Schuster, 1970. 283pp. $5.95. Paper $1.95. Originally published in 1947 and long out-of-print, this republished volume shows why the movie is the folk art of the American people. The author explores the ways in which the screen reflects the values and beliefs of the American culture.

VALLANCE, TOM
The American Musical
A. S. Barnes, 1970. 192pp. Paper $3.50. A guide to the artists who have worked on-and off-camera in the making of Hollywood's musical films. Musical film credits with basic biographical material and comment are included. Illustrated with photographs. Index.

WALKER, ALEXANDER
The Celluloid Sacrifice
Hawthorn, 1967. 241pp. $5.95. Paper—"Sex in the Movies" Penguin, 1968. 284pp. $1.65. This is an attempt to apply psychology, biography, film history, and film criticism to the problem of the personalities of some significant stars (Dietrich, Garbo, Mae West, and Elizabeth Taylor among them) and to see why each achieved her success. The author especially examines the sexual appeal of the star personality. Illustrated. Index.

WALKER, ALEXANDER
Stardom: The Hollywood Phenomenon
Stein & Day, 1970. 392pp. $10.00. A study of the Hollywood phenomenon of stardom. The author inquires into the processes by which some stars are made and the reasons why the products turn out as they do. He examines the emergence of stars in the silent films, the birth of the star system, the coming of the talkies, and the regime of studio rulers. The relationship between acting and the star personality is also studied. Illustrated with photographs. Appendices. Index.

WEINBERG, HERMAN G.
Josef von Sternberg
Dutton, 1967. 254pp. Paper $1.95. A critical study of the film director. The author includes detailed analyses of all Sternberg's films, how he selected the subjects, how he adapted them, and how he controlled all aspects of them. Also included are a Filmography, Bibliography, and more than fifty illustrations.

WEINBERG, HERMAN G.
The Lubitsch Touch
Dutton, 1968. 344pp. Paper $2.95. A critical study of the film director. Included are interviews, reminiscences, anecdotes, and tributes from those who knew and worked with Lubitsch. A special feature of the volume is the publication of almost the whole of the screenplay for "Ninotchka" and excerpts from "Trouble in Paradise." The book is illustrated with almost eighty photographs, most of which have never before been published.

WEST, JESSAMYN
To See the Dream
Harcourt, Brace, 1956. 314pp. $3.95. A journal kept while Miss West was working as script writer and technical advisor to William Wyler on the film production of her novel, "Friendly Persuasion." The personalities of the film colony are discussed.

WHITE, DAVID MANNING and RICHARD AVERSON
Sight, Sound, and Society: Motion Pictures and Television in America
See Page 507

WOOD, ROBIN
Arthur Penn
Praeger, 1970. 144pp. $4.95. Paper $2.50. Originally published in 1969 and now reissued in a revised version to include the film director's two latest films. Each of Penn's seven films is studied in a separate chapter and there is a chapter on the problems of editing. Filmography. Illustrated with photographs.

WOOD, ROBIN
Hitchcock's Films
A. S. Barnes, 1969. 204pp. Paper $2.45. Originally published in 1965 and now reissued in an enlarged edition, this is a lengthy analysis of Hitchcock's style, themes, techniques, with detailed studies of eight of the films. Filmography. Bibliography. Illustrated with photographs.

WOOD, ROBIN
Howard Hawks
Doubleday, 1968. 200pp. $4.95. Paper $2.95. Mr. Wood discusses the themes and attitudes of film director Howard Hawks' films. He emphasizes the films' stress on the human qualities of courage, endurance, responsibility, and a stoic attitude towards death. Among the films analyzed are "Scarface," "Red River," "The Big Sleep," "To Have and Have Not," and "Gentlemen Prefer Blondes." A complete Filmography is included. Illustrated with photographs.

WOOD, TOM
The Bright Side of Billy Wilder, Primarily
Doubleday 1970. 257pp. $6.95. A candid profile of the writer/producer/director, maker of such films as "Sunset Boulevard," "The Lost Weekend," "Some Like It Hot," and "Seven Year Itch." The volume

is a close-up of the techniques, methods, and philosophy of the film maker and includes anecdotes of some of the stars with whom Wilder worked: Marilyn Monroe, Jack Lemmon, Walter Matthau, Kim Novak, and Shirley MacLaine. Illustrated with photographs. Filmography. Index.

ZIEROLD, NORMAN
The Moguls
Coward—McCann, 1969. 354pp. $6.95. This is the story of the motion picture pioneers, of their ascent to power, of the struggles to keep themselves on top, their personalities, achievements, and blunders. The author conducted more than 200 interviews to obtain information about the heads of the motion picture studios in the 1920's, '30's, and '40's. Among the men examined are: DeMille, Selznick, Mayer, and the brothers Warner. Illustrated with photographs. Index.

ZINMAN, DAVID
Fifty Classic Motion Pictures
Crown, 1970. 311pp. $9.95. A collection of critical commentary, cast listings, notes on production details, and stills of fifty of Mr. Zinman's favorite motion pictures from the 1930's and 1940's. Among the films selected are: "Ninotchka," "The Letter," "Top Hat," "The Bank Dick," and "Gone with the Wind." Selected Bibliography. Index.

TECHNIQUES OF PRODUCTION

General Reference Works

BADDELEY, W. HUGH
The Technique of Documentary Film Production
Hastings House, 1969. 268pp. $10.00. Originally published in 1963 and now revised, this volume deals with all aspects of the production of the factual film. The means and methods of producing such films are treated step-by-step from the initial idea to the making of release prints and their distribution. Illustrated with drawings and diagrams. Glossary. Index.

BATEMAN, ROGER
Instructions in Filming
Museum Press, 1967. 124pp. $5.00. The author's emphasis is on filming within a limited budget by school and youth club film units. Illustrated with photographs. Index.

BEAL, J.D.
How to Make Films at School
Focal Press, 1968. 147pp. $5.00. This is practical advice on film-making, choice and use of equipment, and an analysis of the making of the film, "The Miraculous Mandarin," by school children. Illustrated with drawings. Glossary. Index.

BENDICK, JEANNE and ROBERT BENDICK
Filming Works Like This
McGraw—Hill, 1970. 95pp. $4.95. Written for young people, this is a step-by-step guide to the filming of motion pictures. Information on how to choose a movie camera, how to set up a film budget, how to write a script, how to organize a film making team and other pertinent topics are included. Illustrated with black-and-white drawings. Index.

BOBKER, LEE R.
Elements of Film
See Page 433

BOWLER, STANLEY W. and TONY WIGENS, PHILIP GROSSET
Making Home Movies
B.B.C. Publications, 1967. $1.25. This is a series of sixteen pocket-sized cards with basic instructions for use by the amateur movie-maker. The first eight are reference cards for use during filming and editing. Cards nine through sixteen provide story-boards to help the amateur create his own scenarios for such occasions as a wedding, on the beach, or bathing the children. Enclosed in a plastic case.

BRODBECK, EMIL E.
Handbook of Basic Motion-Picture Techniques
Chilton, 1966. 224pp. $6.95. This volume provides a complete course in the cinema. Mr. Brodbeck provides a general discussion of the basic techniques and a specific discussion of mechanics and equipment, including the latest advancements. Illustrated with over 200 motion picture stills, drawings, and diagrams. Index.

BRYNE—DANIEL, J.
Grafilm
Van Nostrand, 1970. 96pp. $5.50. Paper $2.75. The art of grafilm combines a wide variety of graphic and illustrative techniques on film stock. The emphasis in this book is on a graphic/poetic approach to film-making and it is based around a series of projects, progressively planned to widen the film-maker's vocabulary and to encourage a balance between technique, aesthetics, and education. Illustrated. Glossary.

CATLING, GORDON and RICHARD SERJEANT
Movie Making for the Young Cameraman
Leisure Time, 1965. 128pp. $4.00. This book contains information on kinds of equipment to buy, subjects for films, judging exposures, lighting, editing and titling, tricks and special effects, projection, and care of equipment. Illustrated. Index.

DE WITT, JACK
Producing Industrial Films
A.S. Barnes, 1968. 148pp. $7.50. The author relates, in a non-technical manner, the methods and problems involved in making films for industry, science, the military, and home movies. The producer,

the audience to whom the film is aimed, the script, lighting techniques, the cutting room, and sound techniques are all discussed in detail. A hypothetical film is discussed and as the reader follows the making of this film he is exposed to many valuable hints and suggestions. Illustrated. Glossary. Index.

FERGUSON, ROBERT
How to Make Movies
Viking, 1969. 88pp. $5.95. A practical introduction to the art of making films. Mr. Ferguson encourages groups to explore and discover their own talents and limitations through experiments with film-exercises. He covers all aspects of script writing, shooting, directing, acting, and editing. Advice is given on lighting, sound synchronization, effects, how to choose a subject, and semi-professional techniques. Illustrated with stills from both amateur and commercial films. Bibliography. Index.

FIELDING, RAYMOND – Editor
A Technological History of Motion Pictures and Television
University of California, 1967. 255pp. $14.00. This anthology has been compiled from the pages of "The Journal of the Society of Motion Picture and Television Engineers." The development of the technology is traced to provide a historical perspective and a point of departure for further study. Illustrated with photographs, sketches, charts and diagrams. Bibliography.

GORDON, JAY E.
Motion Picture Production for Industry
Macmillan, 1961. 352pp. $11.50. A complete guide to the successful operation of a film department. Procedures are provided for preparing, producing, and distributing small-budget motion pictures to be used for training, sales promotion, engineering progress reports, historical documentation, college public relations, and school science work.

GREY, ELIZABETH
Behind the Scenes in a Film Studio
Phoenix, 1967. 102pp. $3.75. Published in England, this is a description of how each member of the team plays his part in the making of a film. Included are twenty-nine pages of photographs and line drawings. Glossary. Index.

GROSSET, PHILIP
The Complete Book of Amateur Film Making
Evans, 1967. 220pp. $8.00. A book of practical advice to the amateur on making films. Mr. Grosset deals with the choice of equipment, its use, and the various aspects of compiling a film, from using the camera to scripting and titling. Several professional films are analyzed in an instructive way and specialized techniques are introduced by one of England's leading amateur film-makers. Illustrated with charts, diagrams, and photographs. Index.

GROSSET, PHILIP
Planning and Scripting Amateur Movies
Fountain Press, 1963. 127pp. $3.95. Published in England, this study is divided into three sections to show how to make a successful film through planning before, during, and after filming. Suggestions on how to find and develop ideas and how to build them into full shooting scripts are given. Illustrated with drawings and photographs.

HALAS, JOHN and WALTER HERDEG
Film and TV Graphics
Hastings House, 1967. 199pp. $16.50. An international survey of film and television graphics covering advertising films, entertainment films, sponsored and experimental films, titles and captions, and preproduction designs (storyboards, etc.). There is a detailed review of each sector of animated film activity by John Halas and more than 1,000 illustrations.

HARCOURT, PETER and PETER THEOBALD – Editors
Film Making in Schools and Colleges
British Film Institute, 1966. 80pp. Paper $2.00. A series of articles on film-making in education. The editors offer descriptions of work being done in England and Mr. Theobald contributes an Introduction on method. Illustrated.

HERMAN, LEWIS
Educational Films: Writing, Directing, and Producing
See Page 493

HILL, ROGER
Teach Yourself Film-Making
English Universities Press, 1970. 149pp. $2.50. The author discusses general principles of film-making, combining the technical with the aesthetic side of film-making. Separate chapters on the camera, film, the projector, care of equipment, shooting, editing, etc. are provided. Illustrated with photographs and drawings. An Appendix lists English film distributors. List of Books for Further Reading.

KNIGHT, BOB
Quick and Easy Guide to Making Home Movies
Collier, 1965. 98pp. Paper $1.95. Basic movie-making techniques, special effects, and story-line analysis for the amateur. A study of super 8mm film equipment is included.

KUHNS, WILLIAM and ROBERT STANLEY
Exploring the Film
Pflaum, 1968. 284pp. Two volume set: $8.95. The first of the two volumes studies the making of films. The second volume is a teacher's manual for the use of the volumes in a film study course in schools. Illustrated with photographs, drawings, and a comic-strip. Lists of recommended short films and distributors, feature films and distributors, sources for films, organizations, and periodicals. Bibliography.

LARSON, RODGER and ELLEN MEADE
Young Filmmakers
Dutton, 1969. 190pp. $5.95. Paper $3.95. Pioneers in film teaching for teenagers, the authors detail the basic essentials of the film-making experience and help young film-makers understand how to use the technical means at their command. The opening sections of this volume describe some of the films teenagers are making today. Other sections deal with such matters as the nature of film language, and the actual shooting of the picture beginning with the formulation of an idea and script, including the responsibilities of the film-maker as his own director and cameraman. Illustrated. Glossary. Index.

LEVITAN, ELI L.
An Alphabetical Guide to Motion Picture, Television, and Videotape Production
McGraw–Hill, 1970. 797pp. $24.50. Arranged alphabetically, the entries in this guide describe the materials and equipment and the many processes and methods that produce special effects. Photographs, diagrams, and charts complement the text. Subject Guide to Entries.

LINDGREN, ERNEST
The Art of the Film
Macmillan, 1963. 258pp. $7.50. Paper—1970. 340pp. $2.95. Originally published in 1948 and revised in 1963, this is one of the standard works on the development of film technique. Chapters are included on the mechanics and techniques of film production, including editing, sound, camera, story, music, acting, and other production facets as well as evaluations of the early innovators and some of the modern practitioners. Illustrated with forty stills. Glossary. Selected Bibliography. Index.

LOWNDES, DOUGLAS
Film Making in Schools
Watson–Guptill, 1968. 128pp. $6.95. A manual for teachers and students engaged in film-making. The author provided a comprehensive manual day-to-day work in the classroom. He analyzes the role of film in school curricula, surveys the basic equipment, provides a series of projects, and concludes with a technical section which defines film terminology, lists and describes equipment, explains operation of equipment, and provides lists of suppliers. Illustrated with line drawings and photographs.

MANCHEL, FRANK
Movies and How They Are Made
Prentice–Hall, 1968. 71pp. $3.95. Written for grades three to seven, this book follows the making of a film from the first idea for a plot through the opening of the film in a theatre. The author provides information on the producing, writing, directing, staging, casting, financing, shooting, editing, and promotion of a film. Illustrated with drawings. Glossary.

MANOOGIAN, HAIG
The Film-Maker's Art
Basic Books, 1966. 340pp. $9.95. After examining the film as an art form and studying the various types of films and their historical development, the author explores the transition from scenario to shooting script, the techniques of film craft, and the process of film composition—master shot, matched shot, cutaway, and establishing shots. Chapters on the use of optics and montage are included. Index.

PETZOLD, PAUL
All-In-One Movie Book
Amphoto, 1969. 222pp. $5.95. The author has written a basic book on the use of the amateur movie camera. Planning, scripting, timing, cutting, editing, and all equipment are dealt with in simple terms. Illustrated with drawings. Index.

PINCUS, EDWARD
Guide to Filmmaking
New American Library, 1969. 256pp. Paper $1.50. The aim of this guide is to provide complete technical knowledge needed to make a professional film. Every aspect is covered from the operation of the camera to the final printing and projection of the film. Illustrated with diagrams and photographs. Bibliography. Charts on Comprehensive Depth of Field. Index.

PITTARO, ERNEST M.
TV and Film Production Data Book
Morgan & Morgan, 1959. 448pp. $2.95. This quick-reference data book is designed to cut down on costly research in production planning. Categories of information include material on world television stations, television cameras and equipment, video tape, kinescope recording, television commercial standards, sound recording data, lighting and lighting equipment, general studio equipment, motion picture cameras and equipment. 132 photographs and drawings and 128 tables are included. Directory of Manufacturers. Index.

PROVISOR, HENRY
8mm/16mm Movie-Making
Chilton, 1970. 272pp. $8.95. All the materials, techniques, and attitudes needed to make professional quality movies using 8mm and 16mm amateur equipment are covered in this in-depth guide to movie-making. More than 100 photographs illustrate the techniques and equipment discussed. Index.

PUDOVKIN, V. I.
Film Technique and Film Acting
See Page 440

REGNIER, GEORGE
Movie Techniques of the Advanced Amateur: 8 & 16mm from Script to Screen
Amphoto, 1959. 160pp. $7.95. Published in England as translated from the original French language

edition, this is a text on the procedures and methods of professional film-making, adapted and restated in terms for the amateur. Detailed discussions are provided on scripting, shooting, directing of actors, lighting, documentary techniques, editing and sound. Additional material, by Myron A. Matzkin, has been provided specifically for the American film-maker. Illustrated with photographs and drawings.

RILLA, WOLF
A – Z of Movie Making
Viking, 1970. 128pp. $6.95. A handbook analyzing the whole process of film-making. Information on basic film grammar, pre-production procedures, lighting, set-ups, sound, handling of actors, editing and dubbing. Illustrated. Reading List. Index.

SMALLMAN, KIRK
Creative Film-Making
Collier–Macmillan, 1969. 245pp. $7.95. Paper $3.95. A concise introduction to the fundamentals of film-making. The author includes discussions of film, cameras, lighting and exposure, lenses, editing, recording and mixing sound, special effects, and using non-actors. A complete sample script is also included indicating how various techniques can produce desired effects on a small budget. Illustrated with drawings, diagrams, and photographs.

SPOTTISWOODE, RAYMOND
Film and Its Techniques
University of California, 1958. 516pp. $9.50. The essential techniques of documentary film-making, beginning with the preparation of scenario, forming of the production unit, and organization of the technical staff. The mechanism of the camera, editing procedures, optical printing, and negative cutting are considered. A chapter studies the physics of sound methods of recording and aesthetics of sound, as well as current color processes and 16mm techniques. Glossary. Bibliography.

SPOTTISWOODE, RAYMOND
The Focal Encyclopedia of Film and Television Techniques
Hastings House, 1969. 1,100pp. $37.50. The work of over 100 contributors, this volume contains 1,600 entries in alphabetical order covering both British and American photographic and electronic practices in the field of film and television. All entries are cross-referenced and most offer guides for further reading. Nearly 1,000 illustrations are included. An Index of 10,000 references concludes the book. A special feature is a survey of some 40,000 words which sums up the overall structure of both film and television technologies.

SPOTTISWOODE, RAYMOND
A Grammar of the Film: An Analysis of Film Technique
University of California, 1950. 328pp. Paper $1.75. The aim of this study is to isolate the fundamental principles of film art and to teach in concrete detail how these principles are well or badly applied in film production. The history of films is considered, and the aesthetic factors governing the use of camera angle, movement, cuts, dissolves, and sound are examined in detail.

TAYLOR, THEODORE
People Who Make Movies
Doubleday, 1967. 158pp. $3.95. Paper – Avon, 1968. 191pp. $ .75. Mr. Taylor describes how movies are made. All the various people and departments that contribute to the finished product are covered: Producer, director, actors, make-up men, stunt men, dubbing studio personnel, the art department, cutting room, and publicity and distribution experts. Illustrated with photographs. Glossary. Index.

WALLACE, CARLTON
Making Movies
Evans, 1965. 143pp. $3.50. Advice for the amateur film-maker is included in this volume. Provided are chapters on all aspects of film making. Samples of scripts are included. Illustrated. Glossary.

Lists of Sources

COWIE, PETER – Editor
International Film Guide – 1968
A. S. Barnes, 1967. 336pp. Paper $2.95. The fifth annual edition of the guide to film activities and production in twenty-three countries, with sections on festivals, short films, animation, art cinemas, archives, film books and magazines, film designers, and the five directors of the year. Illustrated.

COWIE, PETER – Editor
International Film Guide – 1969
A. S. Barnes, 1968. 336pp. $4.95. Paper $2.95. The sixth annual issue of the handbook. Information is provided on film-makers and suppliers of equipment in twenty-nine countries with articles and information on many aspects of film-making. Essays on five directors and an interview with director John Frankenheimer are included. Indices.

GOLD, MAGGE – Editor
Madison Avenue – Europe
Peter Glenn, 1970. Unpaged. Paper $6.95. The 1970 edition of the handbook for commercial European travellers, geared especially to the advertising, film, fashion, and photography world. Information and addresses for transportation services, hotels, restaurants, stores, advertising agencies, publications, public relations firms, television and film producers, illustrators, photographic studios, and model agencies in England, France, Germany, and other European countries.

GOLD, MAGGE – Editor
Madison Avenue – London
See Page 493

GOLD, MAGGE – Editor
Madison Avenue – Paris
See Page 493

GOLD, MAGGE – Editor
Madison Avenue – West Germany
See Page 493

TARCHER, JEREMY – Editor
West Coast Theatrical Directory – 1970
Tarcher/Gousha Guides, 1969. 296pp. Paper $6.95. This is a guide for the entire entertainment industry and related fields on the West Coast, including Los Angeles, San Francisco, Las Vegas, and Hawaii. Provided are listings of artists representatives, broadcasting/radio-television and associated services, live show production, motion picture and television production and distribution, music and photography services, public relations, theatrical instruction, unions and trade associations, and local facilities including airlines, hotels, restautants, etc. Indices.

TRIANDOS, PAT and CHUCK RUTHERFORD – Editors
Madison Avenue West
Peter Glenn, 1970. Unpaged. Paper $5.95. A directory covering visual communication services in Los Angeles. Listings include advertising agencies, television and film producers and their suppliers, photographers, models, actors, and talent agencies.

Cinematography

CAMPBELL, RUSSELL – Editor
Photographic Theory for the Motion Picture Cameraman
A. S. Barnes, 1970. 160pp. Paper $2.95. An introduction to the photographic process. Film stock, processing, image formation, grain structure, printing, color photography, and color balance are all covered in this guidebook. Illustrated with charts, drawings, and photographs. Bibliography. Index.

CAMPBELL, RUSSELL – Editor
Practical Motion Picture Photography
A. S. Barnes, 1970. 192pp. Paper $2.95. A study of the work of the film cameraman with emphasis on the technical side of the art. Film stock, light meters, exposure control, filters, special techniques, and style are covered in separate chapters. Eighteen professional cameramen were interviewed and their comments are the basis for the volume. Illustrated with photographs and diagrams. Bibliography. Index.

CLARKE, CHARLES G.
Professional Cinematography
American Society of Cinematographers, 1968. 192pp. $10.00. This is a second edition, revised, of the 1964 guide for the cinematographer. Among the items covered are the camera, lenses, film, filters, exposure, exterior equipment, lighting, special effects, composition, and trick effects. Illustrated. Bibliography. Index.

KRASZNA-KRAUSZ, A. – Chairman of Editorial Board
The Focal Encyclopedia of Photography
McGraw–Hill, 1969. 1,699pp. $14.00. Originally published in 1956 and revised and enlarged for this desk edition, this reference work includes 2,400 articles by 276 authors from twenty-eight countries. The technology of photography is covered in all its aspects in text and over 1,700 illustrations.

MASCELLI, JOSEPH V.
The Five C's of Cinematography: Motion Picture Filming Techniques Simplified
Cine/Grafic Publications, 1965. 250pp. $15.00. A study of camera angles, continuity, cutting, close-ups, and composition, designed so that low-budget production units can employ professional techniques. Illustrated with photographs and diagrams. Index.

MILLER, ARTHUR C. and WALTER STRENGE
American Cinematographer Manual
Amphoto, 1969. 650pp. $15.00. This is the third edition of the manual, originally compiled by J. V. Mascelli in 1960. The manual is designed to provide the technical data necessary for solving production problems confronting cinematographers. The authors consider the camera, lenses, films, exposure, filters, color, lighting, background process, sound, and special techniques. Illustrated with formulae, conversion tables, and electrical data.

SOUTO, H. MARIO RAIMONDO
The Technique of the Motion Picture Camera
Hastings House, 1969. 322pp. $16.00. Originally published in 1967, this is a revised and enlarged second edition of the comprehensive study of the modern film camera. The author provides the professional cameraman with complete information and comparative material on the latest equipment and techniques. Tables of camera characterisitics and lists of manufacturers and equipment suppliers are included. Illustrated with drawings and diagrams. Glossary. Index.

WALLACE, CARLTON
Cine-Photography All the Year Round
Evans, 1965. 128pp. $3.50. The author guides the beginner in the techniques of making films in various kinds of weather as well as indoors. Among other subjects, he discusses exposure settings and the processing of the film. Illustrated. Index.

WHEELER, LESLIE J.
Principles of Cinematography: A Handbook of Motion Picture Technology
Fountain Press, 1969. 440pp. $15.95. Originally published in 1953 and now reissued in a fourth completely revised and rewritten edition. The author explains in detail the processes and apparatus used in the production and exhibition of motion pictures. A short history of each main subject is included. Considerable portions of the work are devoted to the work of film laboratories, camera and projector mechanisms, film in television, and sound recording. Illustrated with line drawings and photographs. The Bibliography includes 1,024 references. Index.

Directing

General Reference

LIVINGSTON, DON
Film and the Director
Putnam, 1969. 209pp. Paper $1.95. A reprint of the 1953 guide to film-making. Among the topics covered are basic composition, continuity, the possibilities and limitations of photographic and sound equipment, all types of staging, movement, and acting. Special attention is given to problems of editing. Illustrated. Bibliography. Index.

REYNERTSON, A. J.
The Work of the Film Director
Hastings House, 1970. 259pp. $13.50. Paper $9.50. The author is concerned with the aesthetics of the film from the central position of the director as well as practical directing techniques. Dr. Reynertson discusses the design concept, the realization of the design, composition, sound, film ideas, the actor, and the director's work in terms of the audience. Illustrated with photographs and drawings. Notes. Film and Directorial References. Select Bibliography. Glossary. Index.

Interviews with Directors

GEDULD, HARRY M. — Editor
Film Makers on Film Making
Indiana University, 1967. 302pp. $6.75. Paper—1969. $1.95. This is a view of the art and craft of the film as conceived by thirty of the leading film directors. The articles offer insights into the personalities and purposes of these directors and range from an analysis of the techniques of slapstick comedy to the aesthetics of the "nouvelle vague" film. Among the contributors are: Sennett, Griffith, Flaherty, Chaplin, Eisenstein, Dreyer, Hitchcock, Bergman, Fellini, Cocteau, Antonioni, and Wajda. The Index to Contributors lists biographical data and films.

GELMIS, JOSEPH
The Film Director as Superstar
Doubleday, 1970. 316pp. $6.95. Paper $3.50. Interviews with sixteen film-makers who represent the importance of film as "a director's medium." Each expresses his personal view of film-making, from aesthetics to finances. Among the directors interviewed are Kubrick, Lester, Mailer, Nichols, Penn, and Polanski. Illustrated with photographs.

KANTOR, BERNARD R. and IRWIN R. BLACKER, ANNE KRAMER
Directors at Work: Interviews with American Film-Makers
Funk & Wagnalls, 1970. 442pp. $10.00. In-depth interviews with ten of the top movie directors in the U. S. The directors explain how they work and how they feel about film-making. The directors interviewed are: Richard Brooks, George Cukor, Norman Jewison, Elia Kazan, Stanley Kramer, Richard Lester, Jerry Lewis, Elliot Silverstein, Robert Wise, and William Wyler. A filmography for each director is included.

RHODE, ERIC
Tower of Babel
Chilton, 1967. 214pp. $5.95. In a series of essays on eleven directors, including Eisenstein, Jennings, Lang, Fellini, Resnais, Wajda, and Ray, Mr. Rhode seeks to cast some light on the question of how the cinema became an art. He show how, in terms of style, the director relates his particular insights to some general view of the world. Index.

SARRIS, ANDREW
The American Cinema: Directors and Directions — 1929 – 1968
Dutton, 1968. 383pp. $7.95. Paper $2.95. Mr. Sarris presents a comprehensive look at the American sound film from its beginnings to the present. He discusses the work of 200 directors, their strengths and weaknesses, their best pictures and their worst, from Griffith, Chaplin, Lubitsch, and Sternberg to Nichols, Kubrick, Antonioni, and Truffaut. Two special features are a chronology of the most important films of each year from 1929 to 1967 and an alphabetical list of over 6,000 films with the year of release and director included.

SARRIS, ANDREW
Interviews with Film Directors
Bobbs—Merrill, 1967. 478pp. $10.00. Paper—Avon, 1969. 557pp. $1.65. This is an anthology of conversations and interviews with forty of the world's great film-makers who discuss their own work and the art of the film. An Introduction on the relation of the director to cinema art is provided, and each interview is prefaced with a brief essay evaluating the director's career with a filmography. Among the directors included are: Antonioni, Bergman, Bunuel, Brook, Cukor, Eisenstein, Fellini, Godard, Hitchcock, Kurosawa, Riefenstahl, and Welles.

SHERMAN, ERIC and MARTIN RUBIN
The Director's Event
Atheneum, 1970. 200pp. $6.95. Interviews with five American film directors: Budd Boetticher, Peter Bogdanovich, Samuel Fuller, Arthur Penn, and Abraham Polonsky. The approach of the authors is that a director's films express his own unique and consistent view of the world. Complete filmographies of each director. Illustrated with scenes from the director's films.

TAYLOR, JOHN RUSSELL
Cinema Eye, Cinema Ear: Some Key Film-Makers of the Sixties
Hill & Wang, 1964. 294pp. $5.95. Paper $2.25. A study of the revolution in modern film-making, seen in terms of the major directors who have created the new film. Antonioni, Fellini, Bunuel, Robert Bresson, Bergman, and Hitchcock are studied in detail. Illustrated with sixteen pages of photographs. A Bibliography lists material vitally relevant to the film-makers discussed in the book. Filmographies are also provided. Index.

Sound

HOLE, R.A.
How to Do Sound Films
Focal Press, 1969. 155pp. $4.50. Originally published in 1954 under the authorship of D.M. Neale and now revised by Mr. Hole. The many forms of sound recording and synchronization are described for the amateur cine enthusiast. Indexed Glossary.

NISBETT, ALEC
The Technique of the Sound Studio
Hastings House, 1970. 559pp. $13.50. Originally published in 1962 and now completely revised and enlarged, this is the standard work in the field of radio, record production, television, and film recording. The author is concerned with general principles rather than engineering principles but information is provided on the characteristics of studios and microphones, the control of sound levels, mixing, editing of sound recordings, and radiophonics and its parent techniques in electronic music. Illustrated with drawings and diagrams. Glossary. Bibliography. Index.

Writing

BLUESTONE, GEORGE
Novels Into Film
University of California, 1961. 237pp. Paper $2.45. Originally published in 1957 and now reissued, this is a discussion of the aesthetic limitations of the novel and the film form, with close analyses of six films made from major novels. The films are: "The Informer," "Wuthering Heights," "The Grapes of Wrath," "Pride and Prejudice," "The Ox-Bow Incident," and "Madame Bovary." Illustrated.

HERMAN, LEWIS
A Practical Manual of Screen Playwriting: For Theatre and Television Films
World, 1963. 294pp. Paper $3.95. Originally published in 1952, this is a complete handbook on screen playwriting. The author covers the basic principles of dramaturgy and the technical requirements of the film media.

PARKER, NORTON S.
Audiovisual Script Writing
Rutgers University, 1968. 330pp. $12.50. Mr. Parker presents the fundamentals of writing scripts for audiovisual media such as films and television. Complete scrips for six half-hour films are provided with commentary. The reader can follow the genesis of a script from the original idea to the finished product. The author also includes advice on fees, job opportunities, budgeting of time for research and writing, and the "care and feeding" of producers and sponsors. Selected Glossary of Film Terms.

Special Effects

BRODBECK, EMIL
Movie and Videotape Special Effects
Chilton, 1968. 192pp. $8.95. Mr. Brodbeck explores the range of special effects that can be accomplished on motion picture film and videotape. He examines the motion-picture camera, shows how it is constructed, and details what effects are or are not possible with cameras of certain specification. Tricks with camera speed, reversing the action, stop-motion and time-lapse photography, creating ghost images, superimposition, distortion, and other matters are illustrated and described. He also suggests special effects that can be obtained with videotape. Illustrated. Index.

CLARK, FRANK P.
Special Effects in Motion Pictures
Society of Motion Picture and TV Engineers, 1966. 238pp. $9.50. This book describes those effects, both mechanical and optical, which are used during principal motion picture photography and which can be created by average production units with modest capabilities. An Appendix lists sources of materials. Bibliography. Index.

FIELDING, RAYMOND
The Techniques of Special-Effects Cinematography
Hastings House, 1965. 396pp. $15.00. Emphasizing low-budget techniques for film-makers in the educational, industrial, and television fields, this book aims to acquaint producers and directors with the variety of special effects that exist and that can be used to enhance the quality of films.

Set Design

LARSON, ORVILLE K. – Editor
Scene Design for Stage and Screen
See Page 370

MYERSCOUGH–WALKER, R.
Stage and Film Decor
See Page 370

Editing

BURDER, JOHN
The Technique of Editing 16MM Films
Hastings House, 1968. 152pp. $9.50. Starting with basic matters of film gauge, equipment and editing facilities, the author goes on to discuss the pure mechanics of editing. Particular attention is given to sound editing. The various forms of soundtrack, commentary, effects, and arrangements for dubbing are examined with their respective operations on the visual side. Illustrated with diagrams and drawings. Glossary of Technical Terms. Index.

REISZ, KAREL and GAVIN MILLAR
The Technique of Film Editing
Hastings House, 1968. 410pp. $13.50. Paper $9.50. This is the second enlarged edition of the text first published in 1953. A new section has been contributed by Gavin Millar in consultation with Karel Reisz. It surveys and records the contemporary approach to film editing by new schools of film-makers all over the world. Professor Thorold Dickinson has contributed a new Preface followed by a series of notes on passages in the original text which, in his opinion, are no longer valid. Illustrated. Selected Bibliography. Glossary of Terms. Index.

WALTER, ERNEST
The Technique of the Film Cutting Room
Hastings House, 1969. 282pp. $11.50. The author describes the functions of the editor on each stage of the production of a film. Illustrated with diagrams and drawings. Glossary. Index.

Animation

ANDERSON, YVONNE
Make Your Own Animated Movies
Little, Brown, 1970. 102pp. $5.95. The author explains the techniques used by young people, from ages five to nineteen, in making their own cartoon films at the Yellow Ball Workshop in Lexington, Massachusetts. Information is included on equipment and supplies, how to set up and use cameras and lights, details of positioning, shooting, and editing, instructions for making cut-outs, clay figures, and information on special and sound effects, and other techniques. Illustrated with photographs and drawings. Index.

ANDERSON, YVONNE
Teaching Film Animation to Children
Van Nostrand, 1970. 112pp. $8.95. Miss Anderson explains for teachers, parents, and group leaders the methods of guiding children in exploring film animation. All essential phases of camera work and of the sound track are covered in addition to chapters on editing, splicing, and adapting of cameras. The special techniques used by children in creating their own films can be a mode of self-expression and communication, according to the author's thesis. Illustrated. Index.

HALAS, JOHN and ROGER MANVELL
Art in Movement: New Directions in Animation
Hastings House, 1970. 191pp. $17.50. The authors describe the various fields open to the graphic artist and the opportunities open to him involving design in time and space. They suggest ways in which the technical facilities available through the contemporary motion picture camera can be applied to the development of both graphic art and the art of film. Illustrated in color and black-and-white. Index.

HALAS, JOHN and ROGER MANVELL
The Technique of Film Animation
Hastings House, 1968. 360pp. $10.95. The second edition of the 1959 publication has been revised and updated to include new developments and experiments in animation. Examples of every type are included in the hundreds of stills reproduced from animated films originating all over the world. Diagrammatic illustrations are also included, derived from every area of the creative process. Glossary of Animation Terms. Selected Book List. Index.

KINSEY, ANTHONY
How to Make Animated Movies
Viking, 1970. 95pp. $6.95. An introduction, designed for the interested layman, to the techniques and usage of animated film. Illustrated with diagrams, sequence drawings, and photographs. Bibliography. Index.

MADSEN, ROY P.
Animated Film: Concepts, Methods, Uses
Pitman, 1969. 234pp. $14.75. An introduction to the art of animation. Every known technique and its uses in education, entertainment, television, industrial and scientific film production are included. Introduced at the level of the novice, the reader is then led progressively to the most sophisticated concepts with diagrams, charts, and artwork. The historical background of animation since its inception to modern day usage throughout the world is included. Illustrated. Glossary. Bibliography. Filmography. Index.

REINIGER, LOTTE
Shadow Theatres and Shadow Films
See Page 345

STEPHENSON, RALPH
Animation in the Cinema
A. S. Barnes, 1967. 176pp. Paper $2.25. A history of animated films and animation all over the world. Filmographies of major directors. Illustrated. Bibliography.

Music

DOLAN, ROBERT EMMETT
Music in Modern Media
Schirmer, 1967. 181pp. $5.50. Mr. Dolan examines and explains the processes that produce the sounds and music in tape, disc, and film recording, motion picture and television recording, and electronic music. The book is illustrated with film mathematics, charts, diagrams, designs of materials, and music examples from the scores of such prominent composers as Aaron Copland, Alfred Newman, and Alex North. Glossary of Terms.

EISLER, HANNS
Composing for the Films
Dennis Dobson, 1951. 165pp. $5.95. An analysis of the art and technique of film music, with chapters on the dramaturgical requirements of films, on the function of film music, on the composer's role in relation to the whole film-making process. An Appendix gives musical analyses of scores of a number of films, and there is a sequence from Mr. Eisler's score for the film "Rain."

MANVELL, ROGER and JOHN HUNTLEY
The Technique of Film Music
Hastings House, 1957. 299pp. $12.50. Written by Manvell and Huntley in collaboration with a Committee set up by the British Film Academy, this is a comprehensive survey of the technique of composing music for films. Detailed analyses are provided of the scores for "Odd Man Out," "Henry V," "Louisiana Story," and "Julius Caesar," Illustrated with photographs, diagrams, and musical examples. Also included is an Index of British and American recordings of film music. Select Bibliography. Index.

SKINNER, FRANK
Underscore
Criterion, 1960. 239pp. $6.00. A study of the technique of scoring music for motion pictures or television. The author discuss the use of the "moviola," cue lines, dubbing, writing the score, dance routines, click track, scoring of themes, and the use of instrumentation. A slip-out folder gives the mechanics of scoring music for 35mm film, with a film footage table. Glossary of Terms.

Acting

PATE, MICHAEL
The Film Actor
A. S. Barnes, 1970. 245pp. $9.50. A manual of motion picture and television acting for the young professional. The author discusses all the stages of getting a part and playing it, discussing acting in general, relating personal experiences, and describing what the beginning actor may encounter in the field. Practical exercises and short scenes with diagrams of actor and camera movement are included. Glossary. Illustrated with diagrams. Index.

PUDOVKIN, V. I.
Film Technique and Film Acting
See Page 440

BIOGRAPHIES AND APPRECIATIONS OF SCREEN PERSONALITIES

Collected (By Author)

AMMANNATI, FLORIS LUIGI and LEONARDO FIORAVANTI, MICHELE LACALAMITA — Editors
Filmlexicon Degli Autori e Delle Opere
Speedimpex. 1958—1967. Seven Volumes. Price per volume: $28.50. Seven volume set: $200.00. The entries in this seven volume directory consist of biographical data, complete list of films, and bibliographical notes on figures in the motion picture field. The biographical notes give the name of the picture, the role played, in the case of actors, and the year in which the film was made. Bibliographical entries cover articles and magazine references in addition to books. All persons of importance in all branches of the film industry are covered. The seven volumes list names from A to Z. Illustrated. The text is in the Italian language.

BURROWS, MICHAEL
Charles Laughton and Frederic March
Primestyle, 1969. 41pp. Paper $1.95. Published in England, this is an appreciation of the careers of the two film actors. Filmographies are included. Illustrated with photographs.

CAHN, WILLIAM
A Pictorial History of the Great Comedians
See Page 261

CAMERON, IAN and ELISABETH CAMERON
Broads
Praeger, 1969. 144pp. $4.95. Paper $2.50. Articles are included on a selection of Hollywood actresses of the last twenty-five years who have specialized in not being ladies. A short assessment of the career, biographical information, and a list of films

(from 1939) is included for each of the seventy-two "broads." Illustrated with photographs

CAMERON, IAN and ELISABETH CAMERON
The Heavies
Praeger, 1969. 144pp. $4.95. Paper $2.50. This volume introduces the actors who in the past twenty-five years have been the "bad men" in American movies. There are photographs of each of the eighty-four actors, notes on the characteristics of each, biographies, and a film list. Illustrated with portraits of the actors and stills from the films.

CARR, LARRY
Four Fabulous Faces
Arlington House, 1970. 492pp. Slipcased: $40.00. Illustrated with over one thousand rare photographs—many never before in print—and a sixteen page color section of old movie magazine covers, this is a testimonial to the beauty of Gloria Swanson, Greta Garbo, Joan Crawford, and Marlene Dietrich. Biographical material, film critiques, and anecdotes probe the lives, careers, and influence of the four stars.

CORNEAU, ERNEST N.
The Hall of Fame of Western Film Stars
Christopher Publishing, 1969. 307pp. $9.75. A history of all the important cowboy stars in motion pictures over a span of more than fifty years from Bronco Billy Anderson to the current television cowboy heroes. Biographies and illustrations of all the stars with chapters about the serials, the horses, the sidekicks, and the villains. Index.

FALLACI, ORIANA
The Egotists
Regnery, 1968. 256pp. $5.95. A collection of sixteen interviews with some of the trend-setters of our time in politics, the arts, and the entertainment field. Among the interviewees are Norman Mailer, Sean Connery, Ingrid Bergman, H. Rap Brown, Nguyen Cao Ky, Federico Fellini, Sammy Davis, Jr., Jeanne Moreau, and Alfred Hitchcock. Illustrated with photographs.

GRIFFITH, RICHARD
The Movie Stars
Doubleday, 1970. 498pp. $25.00. An examination of the phenomenon of the movie star. The rise of the star system, its decline, the careers of the most popular stars, the producers and directors of the films, and the special qualities that made these men and women so successful are all discussed. Profusely illustrated with hundreds of photographs. Index.

GRUEN, JOHN
Close-Up
See Page 261

LAHUE, KALTON C. and SAM GILL
Clown Princes and Court Jesters
A. S. Barnes, 1970. 406pp. $8.50. A pictorial history of fifty comedians of the silent screen. The authors outline their screen careers in brief, mentioning some of their best films, and supplying a great many photographs. Among the comedians are: Fatty Arbuckle, Andy Clyde, Chester Conklin, Louise Fazenda, Harry Langdon, Mabel Normand, and Ben Turpin.

LAHUE, KALTON C.
Winners of the West
A. S. Barnes, 1970. 353pp. $10.00. A collection of biographies and appreciations of the heroes and heroines of the silent screen Western film. Thirty-eight of the leading Western players are included in separate chapters. Illustrated with photographs.

LAMPARSKI, RICHARD
Whatever Became of ....?: First Series
Crown, 1967. 208pp. $4.95. Paper—Ace, 1970. 208pp. $1.25. The story of what has happened to famous personalities of the immediate past. The author provides the background for each of 100 celebrities, from childhood to the time he or she became a public figure, then he tells what has happened since and what each is doing now. Illustrated with then-and-now photographs for each of the personalities. Among the subjects are: Annabella, Adele Astaire, Freddie Bartholomew, Bobby Breen, Judy Canova, Irene Dunne, Sonja Henie, Lum'n Abner, Miss America of 1919, Ramon Novarro, Jack Pearl, Irene Rich, Arthur Tracy, and Bert Wheeler.

LAMPARSKI, RICHARD
Whatever Became of....?: Second Series
Crown, 1968. 207pp. $4.95. Paper—Ace, 1970. 207pp. $1.25. The author tells what has happened to another 100 celebrities. Again, he provides background information on the personalities, and tells what each is doing now. Illustrated with then-and-now photographs. Subjects include: Axis Sally, William Boyd, Ina Claire, Dizzy Dean, Branda Frazier, Billy Gilbert, Horace Heidt, Arthur Lake, Colleen Moore, Margaret O'Brien, and Fay Wray.

LAMPARSKI, RICHARD
Whatever Became of ....?: Third Series
Crown, 1970. 207pp. $4.95. Based on his national network radio interview show, Mr. Lamparski details the backgrounds and histories of one hundred celebrities and recounts their present whereabouts and activities. Among the subjects are: the Andrews Sisters, Betty Bronson, Jerry Colonna, Jimmy Fidler, Jon Hall, Ezra Stone, Tokyo Rose, Tonto, and Vera Zorina. Illustrated with then-and-now photographs.

McCAFFREY, DONALD W.
Four Great Comedians
A. S. Barnes, 1968. 175pp. Paper $2.25. A study of four comedians of the silent screen: Chaplin, Lloyd, Keaton, and Langdon. The text sets the comedians in their milieu and examines their major films. Illustrated with photographs. Bibliography.

MALTIN, LEONARD
Movie Comedy Teams
New American Library, 1970. 352pp. Paper $1.50. Studies of the great comedy teams of the films. Twelve teams are studied in detail and eight others are examined briefly. Complete Filmographies are included. Illustrated with photographs. Index.

MARTIN, PETE
Pete Martin Calls On ...
Simon & Schuster, 1962. 510pp. $5.95. Forty of Pete Martin's interviews with celebrities of Hollywood and Broadway. They range from the young Shirley Temple in 1946 to the young Anna Marie Alberghetti in 1961.

MEYERS, WARREN B.
Who Is That?
Personality Posters, 1967. Unpaged. Paper $1.50. A guide to movie stars and lesser-known actors now appearing on television in revivals of Hollywood films. Illustrated with photographs. Index of Names.

MILLER, EDWIN
Seventeen Interviews Film Stars and Superstars
Macmillan, 1970. 384pp. $6.95. This collection of fifty-eight interviews was originally printed in "Seventeen" magazine. Each interview is illustrated with a photograph of its subject. Among the interviewed are: Julie Andrews, Warren Beatty, the Beatles, Julie Christie, Mia Farrow, Jane Fonda, Arlo Guthrie, Sophia Loren, Laurence Olivier, and Leonard Whiting and Olivia Hussey.

NEWQUIST, ROY
A Special Kind of Magic
Rand McNally, 1967. 156pp. $4.95. Mr. Newquist interviews Spencer Tracy, Katherine Hepburn, Sidney Poitier, Katherine Houghton, and Stanley Kramer. The actors and director of "Guess Who's Coming to Dinner" discuss their careers, Hollywood in general and the film in particular. Illustrated with photographs.

REED, REX
Conversations in the Raw
World, 1969. 312pp. $5.95. Paper—New American Library, 1970. 256pp. $1.25. A collection of the interviews and other writings of the candid journalist whose portraits have appeared in The New York Times, Esquire, and in his earlier "Do You Sleep in the Nude?" Among the subjects are Bette Davis, Ruth Gordon, Uta Hagen, Simone Signoret, Patricia Neal, Colleen Dewhurst, Jean Seberg, Oskar Werner, Paul Newman and Joanne Woodward, Joseph Losey, Omar Sharif, Albert Finney, Mart Crowley, Burt Bacharach, and Jon Voight.

REED, REX
Do You Sleep in the Nude?
New American Library, 1968. 276pp. $5.95. Paper—Signet, 1969. 255pp. $ .95. A series of thirty-four essays based on interviews with celebrities. Candid observations and off-guard statements are included from: Michelangelo Antonioni, Warren Beatty, Franco Corelli, Marlene Dietrich, Ava Gardner, the actors of the Living Theatre, Angela Lansbury, Mike Nichols, Otto Preminger, Barbra Streisand, and Lester Maddox.

ROLLINS, CHARLEMAE
Famous Negro Entertainers of Stage, Screen and TV
See Page 262

SHIPMAN, DAVID
The Great Movie Stars: The Golden Years
Crown, 1970. 576pp. $10.00. Biographies of 181 movie stars who achieved stardom before or during World War II. For each star there is a detailed career survey and an analysis of their critical and financial success. The stars range from Abbot and Costello to Roland Young. Illustrated with photographs. List of Sources.

TWOMEY, ALFRED E. and ARTHUR F. McCLURE
The Versatiles
A. S. Barnes, 1969. 304pp. $10.00. A study of supporting character actors and actresses in the American motion picture, 1930—1955. Photographs and biographical information containing personal and career backgrounds, and anecdotal material for 400 supporting players, and photos and brief career facts for 200 other actors and actresses are included. A Foreword by Irene Dunne, and an introductory essay devoted to the historical significance of supporting players are included.

WILDE, LARRY
The Great Comedians Talk About Comedy
Citadel, 1968. 382pp. $6.95. Each of the sixteen interviews included in this volume was taped by the author. He introduces the comedians with brief biographical sketches and provides samples of the humor which have made the comedians internationally acclaimed personalities. Among those interviewed are: Woody Allen, Milton Berle, Jack Benny, George Burns, Phyllis Diller, Jimmy Durante, Bob Hope, Danny Thomas, and Ed Wynn.

Individual (By Subject)

Agee, James

AGEE, JAMES
The Collected Short Prose of James Agee
Houghton—Mifflin, 1968. 243pp. $5.95. Edited and with a "Memoir" by Robert Fitzgerald, this is a volume of Agee's previously uncollected prose. In addition to short stories, there are notes for motion pictures, scenarios, and plans for projected works.

OHLIN, PETER
Agee

Astor–Honor, 1966. 247pp. $7.95. Paper $2.95. A critical study of James Agee's work in which the author seeks to place and relate the work. Ohlin deals primarily with the aesthetic problems which Agee confronted in his commitment to the holiness of human reality and his refusal to become part of a literary fashion. Notes. Bibliography.

SEIB, KENNETH
James Agee: Promise and Fulfillment
University of Pittsburgh, 1968. 175pp. $5.95. Paper $2.50. This critical survey of James Agee treats the entire range of his work—the poetry, scenarios, fiction, and criticism—in terms of an aesthetic ideal. Mr. Seib contends that Agee's progress through the various media was a natural fulfillment of his creative vision, culminating in his work in films. List of Published Works. Bibliography. Index.

Aherne, Brian

AHERNE, BRIAN
A Proper Job
Houghton–Mifflin, 1969. 355pp. $7.95. Mr. Aherne tells of his work in silent films in London, his tours with Dion Boucicault's company, and his work on Broadway, on the London stage, and in Hollywood. Thirty-two pages of photographs are included.

Andrews, Julie

COTTRELL, JOHN
The Unauthorized Life Story of a Super–Star: Julie Andrews
Dell, 1968. 212pp. Paper $ .75. This biography of the singer-actress tells of her beginnings as a child singer, her rise to world fame as a motion picture star, her success and her heartbreaks.

WINDELER, ROBERT
Julie Andrews: A Biography
Putnam, 1970. 253pp. $6.95. A biography of the film and stage actress. Her early life in England, her sensational career on Broadway, and her success in Hollywood are all detailed as is her private life. Illustrated with photographs. Index.

Astaire, Fred

THOMPSON, HOWARD
Fred Astaire: A Pictorial Treasury of His Films
Falcon Enterprises Inc., 1970. 158pp. $3.95. A catalogue of the films of the actor/dancer. In text and pictures the author explores the life and screen work of Mr. Astaire. A complete catalogue of the films from 1933 to 1968 is included with dates of New York openings. Illustrated with more than 100 photographs from the films.

Balcon, Michael

BALCON, MICHAEL
Michael Balcon Presents ... A Lifetime of Films
Hutchinson, 1969. 239pp. $9.50. The autobiography of the English film producer. From his first film in 1922 through the beginnings of the sound film to the days of the ''Ealing'' comedies with Alec Guinness, the author reveals the eccentricities and artistry of many of the greats of the film world. Illustrated with thirty-two pages of photographs. Index.

Barrymore, Diana

BARRYMORE, DIANA with GEROLD FRANK
Too Much, Too Soon
See Page 263

Barrymore, Ethel

NEWMAN, SHIRLEE P.
Ethel Barrymore, Girl Actress
See Page 263

Beaton, Cecil

BEATON, CECIL
The Years Between
See Page 263

Bell, Mary Hayley

BELL, MARY HAYLEY
What Shall We Do Tomorrow?
See Page 264

Bergman, Ingrid

QUIRK, LAWRENCE J.
The Films of Ingrid Bergman
Citadel, 1970. 224pp. $9.95. The author provides a complete recapitulation of Ingrid Bergman's film and stage career. Every film is chronicled with a cast and credit list, a synopsis, and extracts from the reviews. Appearances in stage productions are also documented. The author includes a biographical study of the actress' public and private life as well. More than four hundred photographs illustrate the volume, including many candid shots from the star's private collection.

Bogart, Humphrey

GOLDSCHIMIDT, ANTHONY – Editor
Bogart's Face

Stanyan Books, 1970. Unpaged. $3.00. This is a collection of fifty-four photographs of Humphrey Bogart. There is no text.

HYMANS, JOE
Bogie
New American Library, 1966. 210pp. $4.95. Paper $ .75. A biography of Humphrey Bogart. His widow, Lauren Bacall, has provided an Introduction. Illustrated with photographs.

McCARTY, CLIFFORD
Bogey: The Films of Humphrey Bogart
Citadel, 1970. 191pp. Paper $3.45. Originally published in 1965 and now reissued, this is a recapitulation of the film career of the late star. The volume includes synopses, credits, and stills from all the films. A biographical sketch is also included.

Carroll, Nancy

NEMCEK, PAUL
The Films of Nancy Carroll
Lyle Stuart, 1969. 223pp. $7.95. This is a recapitulation of the film career of the star of the 1920's and 1930's. A short biography and a portrait gallery are included as are credits, synopses, reviews, and stills from all the films.

Chaplin, Charles

CHAPLIN, CHARLES
My Autobiography
Pocket Books, 1966. 560pp. Paper $ .95. This is a reprint of the 1964 autobiography in which the great actor/director discusses his early, poverty-stricken years, his first experiences in the films, the evolution of his style of acting, his rise to fame, and his association with the great stars and films of the golden age of the movies. Detailed are the post-war years, including the humiliation of the paternity suit and the political controversy that drove him from the United States to his present home in Switzerland. Illustrated with photographs.

QUIGLY, ISABEL
Charlie Chaplin: Early Comedies
Dutton, 1968. 159pp. Paper $1.95. Miss Quigly recalls the early days of Chaplin's career when he developed his tramp creation. She shows how different was this character from that of his creator and she examines the moods and feelings of the early comedies. Illustrated with photographs.

Chaplin, Michael

CHAPLIN, MICHAEL
I Couldn't Smoke the Grass on My Father's Lawn
Ballantine, 1967. 171pp. Paper $ .75. Originally published in 1966 and now reissued, this is the biography of Charles Chaplin's son. He tells of his life with his father, why he ran away to London at the age of sixteen, and of his experience with drugs. Illustrated with photographs.

Cohn, Harry

THOMAS BOB
King Cohn
Putnam, 1967. 381pp. $6.95. Paper $ .95. A biography of the president of Columbia Pictures. Starting out in the 1920's, Harry Cohn raised the studio to major status and in the course of his career was responsible for many movie classics and the creation of two of America's greatest sex symbols—Rita Hayworth and Kim Novak. Illustrated with photographs. Note: the paper edition has no illustrations.

Cooper, Gary

CARPOZI, GEORGE
The Gary Cooper Story
Arlington House, 1970. 263pp. $6.95. A biography of the late film star from his beginnings as a cowhand to his place as the highest wage earner in the country. A Filmography of ninety-five films with cast and production credits is included as is a gallery of fifty-seven photographs. Index.

DICKENS, HOMER
The Films of Gary Cooper
Citadel, 1970. 281pp. $10.00. A documented pictorial life of the screen star. Included are a biographical study of Cooper, as well as a record of all the films in which he appeared. Synopses, cast listings, other credits, and reviews are provided. More than 400 photographs from the films are presented as well as many candid shots and studio portraits.

Coward, Noel (Also See Page 294)

MORLEY, SHERIDAN
A Talent to Amuse
See Page 190

Crawford, Joan

QUIRK, LAWRENCE J.
The Films of Joan Crawford
Citadel, 1968. 222pp. $7.95. Paper $3.95. A complete recapitulation of the Crawford career, this book includes stills from all her films, as well as cast lists, synopses, production credits, and reviews. There is also a biographical sketch of the star. Many photographs of her private life are included.

Dandridge, Dorothy

DANDRIDGE, DOROTHY and EARL CONRAD
Everything and Nothing: The Dorothy Dandridge Tragedy
Abelard—Schuman, 1970. 215pp. $6.95. Prepared by Mr. Conrad from tape-recordings made by Miss Dandridge before her death in 1965, this is the autobiography of one of the first black movie stars. It describes the effects of segregation and the social prejudice she suffered. Illustrated with photographs.

Davis, Bette

RINGGOLD, GENE
The Films of Bette Davis
Citadel, 1970. 191pp. Paper $3.45. Originally published in 1966 and now reissued, this is a recapitulation of the film career of the star. The volume includes a biographical sketch, synopses, reviews, credits and stills from all the films through 1966.

Davis, Jr., Sammy

DAVIS, JR., SAMMY with JANE BOYAR, BURT BOYAR
Yes, I Can
See Page 266

Dietrich, Marlene

DICKENS, HOMER
The Films of Marlene Dietrich
Citadel, 1968. 223pp. $7.95. Paper $3.95. All of Miss Dietrich's films from 1923 through 1964 are documented and illustrated, including five early German films never before listed. Credits and synopses of each film are provided. Photographs of the theatre work in Berlin, the tours during World War II, and the current stage and night club appearances are also included as is a biographical sketch of the star.

FREWIN, LESLIE
Dietrich
Stein & Day, 1967. 192pp. $5.95. The intimate story of Marlene Dietrich from her start as a Hamburg chorus girl to her appearances at the Cafe de Paris in London. An up-to-date and fully documented record of all the Dietrich films is included. Illustrated.

KOBAL, JOHN
Marlene Dietrich
Dutton, 1968. 160pp. Paper $1.95. Marlene Dietrich's life, films, relationship with von Sternberg, her work with other directors, and her impression on Hollywood are all related here by the author. Illustrated. Filmography. Bibliography.

Disney, Walt

HAMMONTREE, MARIE
Walt Disney: Young Movie Maker
Bobbs—Merrill, 1969. 200pp. $2.75. A biography of Walt Disney from his early boyhood on a farm in Missouri through the opening of Disneyland in 1955. The book is written for children and has been illustrated by Fred Irvin. A Glossary of words that may be unfamiliar to the reader is included as is a Chronology of the events during Disney's lifetime.

SCHICKEL, RICHARD
The Disney Version
Simon & Schuster, 1968. 384pp. $6.50. Paper—Avon, 1969. 330pp. $1.25. The author recounts the legends and the facts of Walt Disney's life, times, art, and commerce. He studies "the flaws in the Disney version of the American vision" as well as his individualism, his pragmatism, and his appreciation of the possibilities in technological progress. Bibliography. Index.

THOMAS, BOB
Walt Disney: Magician of the Movies
Grosset & Dunlap, 1966. 176pp. $2.95. A biography of Walt Disney for young readers. It details his childhood on his father's farm in Kansas, his early struggles, his pioneering of the cartoon film form and the opening of Disneyland. Illustrated with drawings.

Fields, W. C.

ANOBILE, RICHARD J.—Editor
Drat!
World, 1968. 128pp. $4.95. Paper—New American Library, 1969. 149pp. $ .95. A series of photographs of W. C. Fields with captions taken from his own words. An essay on the comedian by Richard F. Shepard is included.

DESCHNER, DONALD
The Films of W. C. Fields
Citadel, 1969. 192pp. Paper $2.95. A reprint of the 1967 record of Field's films, complete with cast lists, credits, synopses, reviews, and photographs. There are also two articles on comedy by Fields and studies of the comedian and his methods by Otis Ferguson and Heywood Broun. Index.

MASON, PAUL—Editor
W. C. Fields: I Never Met a Kid I Liked
Random House, 1970. 57pp. $3.00. A collection of some of the thoughts and gag lines of the great film comedian. Illustrated with portraits and scenes from his films.

TAYLOR, ROBERT LEWIS
W. C. Fields: His Follies and Fortunes
New American Library, 1967. 286pp. Paper $1.25.

A reprint of the 1949 edition, this is a portrait of the golden age of comedy in America and an analysis of Field's eccentric personality. The relationship between the public awareness of Field's unconventional life and its acceptance of him is considered in detail. Illustrated.

Flynn, Errol

THOMAS, TONY and RUDY BEHLMER, CLIFFORD McCARTY
The Films of Errol Flynn
Citadel, 1969. 223pp. $8.95. A complete record of the film career of Errol Flynn. All fifty-eight films are detailed with synopses, casts and credits, reviews, and hundreds of stills. A biographical study of Flynn is included in the text. Foreword by Greer Garson. Illustrated.

Fonda, Henry

SPRINGER, JOHN
The Fondas
Citadel, 1970. 279pp. $10.00. A study of the film careers of Henry Fonda and his children, Jane and Peter. Credits, synopses, and critical summaries are provided for all the films of each of the actors. Articles by Joshua Logan, Robert Ryan, and John Steinbeck are included. Illustrated with scenes from the films, candid and studio photographs.

Fox, William

ALLVINE, GLENDON
The Greatest Fox of Them All
Lyle Stuart, 1969. 244pp. $5.95. A biography of William Fox, creator of 20th Century Fox Film Studios. Illustrated with photographs. Index.

Gable, Clark

ESSOE, GABE
The Films of Clark Gable
Citadel, 1970. 255pp. $10.00. A record of Gable's career beginning with the early days on the stage to the final film, "The Misfits." Each film is documented with cast and credit listings, synopses, and reviews. The volume also includes appreciations by performers, directors, and technicians. Illustrated with more than 400 photographs.

WILLIAMS, CHESTER
Gable
Fleet, 1968. 154pp. $5.95. A biography of Clark Gable from the early rise from poverty to the final overwhelming success. A chronology of the films and a series of photographs are included.

Garbo, Greta

CONWAY, MICHAEL and DION MCGREGOR, MARK RICCI
The Films of Greta Garbo
Citadel, 1968. 155pp. Paper $2.95. Originally published in 1963 and now reissued, this is a pictorial survey of all of Greta Garbo's films from the first in Sweden in 1922 to the last one produced in Hollywood in 1941. A synopsis of each film, cast and production credits, and reviews are provided. A long contribution, "The Garbo Image," by Parker Tyler is also included.

ZIEROLD, NORMAN
Garbo
Stein & Day, 1969. 196pp. $5.95. A biography of Greta Garbo which examines the mystique and explores the effects the legend had on the woman and the degree to which the woman manipulated the legend. An extensive Appendix lists Garbo's films, the co-stars and directors, plot summaries, and the comment of critics at the time. Included is a sixteen page photographic section. Bibliography. Index.

Gargan, William

GARGAN, WILLIAM
Why Me? An Autobiography
Doubleday, 1969. 311pp. $5.95. This is the biography of the film star which includes the story of his struggle with throat cancer, his determination to speak again, and his success in helping not only himself but thousands of other cancer victims. Illustrated with photographs.

Garland, Judy

MORELLA, JOE and EDWARD EPSTEIN
Judy: The Films and Career of Judy Garland
Citadel, 1969. 217pp. $8.95. Paper $3.95. A history of Judy Garland's career in films, on the concert stage, in night clubs, and on television. Her life is also covered in text, photographs, and news clippings. The authors comment on the films, provide production and cast credits, and excerpts from the reviews. Judith Crist evaluates the Garland career in an Introduction and comments on Judy's life and personality are included by Arthur Freed, E. Y. Harburg, Gene Kelly, George Murphy, and Joe Pasternak. The volume is illustrated with more than 300 photographs and reproductions of advertisements.

STEIGER, BRAD
Judy Garland
Ace, 1969. 190pp. Paper $ .95. A biography of the motion picture singer. A feature of the volume is a horoscope and handwriting analysis. Also included are synopses of all of the films with cast lists and excerpts from critical reviews. Illustrated.

TORME, MEL
The Other Side of the Rainbow: with Judy Garland on the Dawn Patrol
Morrow, 1970. 241pp. $6.95. A record of the nine month period when Judy Garland was the star of her own television series. Torme was the "music consultant" for the series and he provides an in-depth portrait of the star and a look at the inner workings of a network television program. Illustrated with photographs.

Gish, Lillian

GISH, LILLIAN and ANN PINCHOT
Lillian Gish: The Movies, Mr. Griffith, and Me
Prentice–Hall, 1969. 388pp. $7.95. Paper–Avon, 1970. 388pp. $1.25. Miss Gish relates her own experiences and memories of the growth and development of motion pictures. Of particular interest is the account of the years Miss Gish worked with D. W. Griffith and the inside story of the making of his classic films. Illustrated. Index.

Glyn, Elinor

GLYN, ANTHONY
Elinor Glyn
Hutchinson, 1968. 356pp. $9.95. A reprint of the edition first published in 1955 and now revised. It is the biography of the English novelist, screenplay writer, and creator of "It." It is also a portrait of the Edwardian era in England and the great silent days of Hollywood. Illustrated with a color portrait of the subject. Index.

Graham, Sheilah

GRAHAM, SHEILAH
Confessions of a Hollywood Columnist
Morrow, 1969. 309pp. $5.95. Paper–Bantam, 1970. 310pp. $1.25. Reminiscenses and anecdotes about the stars of the motion pictures. Miss Graham offers examinations and explanations of the reasons for the success, the unhappiness, the restlessness, and the moments of strength and weakness of such celebrities as Barbra Streisand, Marilyn Monroe, Frank Sinatra, Cary Grant, Richard Burton, and Elizabeth Taylor, among many others.

GRAHAM, SHEILAH
The Rest of the Story
Coward McCann, 1964. 320pp. $4.95. Paper–Bantam, 1968. 215pp. $ .75. A sequel to "Beloved Infidel," this autobiography covers the years from 1940 to the present. The work contains new material on F. Scott Fitzgerald. There is a survey of life in Hollywood in the 1940's. Illustrated. Paper edition has no illustrations.

Harlow, Jean

CONWAY, MICHAEL and MARK RICCI – Editors
The Films of Jean Harlow
Citadel, 1969. 159pp. $2.95. Originally published in 1965 and now reissued, this is a recapitulation of the career of the actress. Each of the twenty-three films is documented with a synopsis, cast and production credits, and extracts from critical reviews. Conway has provided a biographical essay and a commentary on the star. Illustrated with more than 200 photographs including scenes from the films and studio and candid shots. Paper edition.

Hart, William S.

HART, WILLIAM S.
My Life East and West
Blom, 1968. 363pp. $12.50. Originally published in 1929 and now reissued, this is the biography of one of the great Western stars. Illustrated with photographs. Index.

Hayden, Sterling

HAYDEN, STERLING
Wanderer: An Autobiography
Knopf, 1963. 434pp. $7.95. This is an account of the famous trip to the South Seas which was undertaken with the actor's four children in defiance of a Federal Court order. It is also an appraisal of the "successful" life in Hollywood and what it does to a man of independent spirit.

Holloway, Stanley

HOLLOWAY, STANLEY
Wiv A Little Bit O'Luck
See Page 270

Horne, Lena

HORNE, LENA with RICHARD SCHICKEL
Lena
See Page 270

Hughes, Howard

GARRISON, OMAR
Howard Hughes in Las Vegas
Lyle Stuart, 1970. 293pp. $5.95. The author traces the development of the business deals which have made Howard Hughes the most powerful man in the state of Nevada. He examines in detail episodes from Hughes' early life to sift fact from rumor. Illustrated with photographs.

GERBER, ALBERT B.
Bashful Billionaire
Dell, 1968. 352pp. Paper $ .95. This is an unauthorized biography of Howard Hughes. It details his founding and/or association with RKO Pictures, Northeast Airlines, TWA, the Hughes Tool Company and his involvement with the careers of Jean Harlow and Jane Russell.

KEATS, JOHN
Howard Hughes
Random House, 1966. 304pp. $5.95. A biography of the controversial Hughes. Included are chapters on the making, and censorship troubles, of "Scarface" and "The Outlaw." Illustrated.

Karloff, Boris

ACKERMAN, FORREST J.
The Frankenscience Monster
Ace, 1969. 191pp. Paper $ .95. An appreciation of and tribute to Boris Karloff. Articles, interviews and biographies by many contributors as well as essays by the editor are included. A complete listing of all the Karloff films, alphabetical and chronological, completes the volume. Illustrated.

Keaton, Buster

BRITISH FILM INSTITUTE
Buster Keaton
British Film Institute, 1968. Unpaged. Paper $ .75. This folio of eleven 8" by 10" plates is printed on heavy glossy paper. They cover the milestones in Buster Keaton's career from 1917 to 1931.

KEATON, BUSTER and CHARLES SAMUELS
My Wonderful World of Slapstick
Allen & Unwin, 1967. 282pp. $5.95. Originally published in 1960 and now reprinted, this is the autobiography of the great film comedian. He tells of his early days in vaudeville and the "Golden Age of Comedy" in Hollywood during the 1920's. Illustrated.

LEBEL, J. P.
Buster Keaton
A. S. Barnes, 1967. 179pp. Paper $2.95. A review of the career and analysis of the work of the great screen comedian. There is a listing of all the films and many illustrations from them.

ROBINSON, DAVID
Buster Keaton
Indiana University, 1969. 199pp. $5.95. Paper $1.95. An account of the silent films of the great comedian. Each of the major films is analyzed to show the development of the skills as a performer, stunt-man, and director. Illustrated with photographs. Filmography of Silent Films.

Kelly, Grace

KATZ, MARJORIE
Grace Kelly
Coward—McCann, 1970. 96pp. $3.95. Written for younger readers, this is a biography of Grace Kelly, movie star and Princess of Monaco.

Lahr, Bert

LAHR, JOHN
Notes on a Cowardly Lion
See Page 272

Lake, Veronica

LAKE, VERONICA and DONALD BAIN
Veronica
Citadel, 1971. 281pp. $6.95. The autobiography of film star Veronica Lake. Miss Lake tells not only of how she succeeded but also how she failed. Her story of a woman on the way out is not the typical Hollywood biography. Illustrated with thirty-two photographs. Index.

Lamarr, Hedy

LAMARR, HEDY
Ecstacy and Me
Fawcett, 1967. 256pp. Paper $ .75. A reprint of the 1966 autobiography of Miss Lamarr. The film star has since disowned the work as the writings of someone else. Illustrated with photographs.

Laughton, Charles

BROWN, WILLIAM
Charles Laughton: A Pictorial Treasury of His Films
Falcon Enterprises, 1970. 161pp. $3.95. In text and photographs, the author explores the life and screen work of the actor. Mr. Brown details the struggles, defeats and triumphs that contributed to Laughton's ultimate success. A Filmography lists all of the films from 1929 to 1962 with cast and directorial credits and a brief summary of the plot. The volume is illustrated with more than 130 photographs including scenes from the films.

Laurel and Hardy

BARR, CHARLES
Laurel and Hardy
University of California, 1967. 144pp. $4.95. Paper $1.95. A critical appreciation of the screen's great comedy team. Illustrated with photographs. Filmography. Bibliography. Index.

McCABE, JOHN
Mr. Laurel and Mr. Hardy
Grosset & Dunlap, 1966. 262pp. $3.95. Paper—New American Library, 1968. 175pp. $ .95. A biography of the screen's great comedy team and a portrait of their era. Originally published in 1961 and now reprinted, the volume is illustrated with scenes from the films and also includes a listing of the films. Index.

Leigh, Vivien

DENT, ALAN
Vivien Leigh: A Bouquet
See Page 272

ROBYNS, GWEN
Light of a Star
A. S. Barnes, 1970. 256pp. $5.95. This biography of Vivien Leigh details her life from her birth in India to her death in 1967. The marriage to Laurence Olivier and their successful partnership on stage and in the films is recorded. Illustrated with photographs. Index.

Levant, Oscar

LEVANT, OSCAR
The Memoirs of an Amnesiac
See Page 565

LEVANT, OSCAR
The Unimportance of Being Oscar
See Page 272

Lister, Moira

LISTER, MOIRA
The Very Merry Moira
See Page 272

McKenna, Virginia

McKENNA, VIRGINIA and BILL TRAVERS
On Playing with Lions
Harcourt, 1966. 124pp. $3.95. The story of the filming of the motion picture, "Born Free," with many photos taken by actor Bill Travers.

MacLaine, Shirley

MacLAINE, SHIRLEY
Don't Fall Off the Mountain
Norton, 1970. 270pp. $5.95. The memoirs of the film actress cover not only her public career but also her adventures in Africa, India, Japan, and the Himalaya mountain kingdom of Bhutan. Her active role in politics and the problems of race are also discussed.

Marx Brothers

EYLES, ALLEN
The Marx Brothers: Their World of Comedy
A. S. Barnes, 1966. 175pp. Paper $2.45. A history of the Marx Brothers' work in films. Each of the films from 1929 to 1949 is covered in a separate chapter. Illustrated with photographs. Appendices include a Filmography and a Bibliography.

MARX, GROUCHO
The Groucho Letters
Simon & Schuster, 1967. 319pp. $4.95. Paper—New American Library, 1968. 238pp. $ .75. Letters to and from Groucho Marx are included in this volume. The screen star writes to comics, corporation presidents, and Presidents of the United States, as well as some of the great wits of our day.

ZIMMERMAN, PAUL D. and BURT GOLDBLATT
The Marx Brothers at the Movies
Putnam, 1968. 224pp. $7.95. Paper—New American Library, 1970. 262pp. $1.25. This book recreates the gags and sight gags to show how the Marx Brothers built their laughs. Casts and credits, plots and dialogue, background information and more than 200 illustrations are included.

Monroe, Marilyn

CONWAY, MICHAEL and MARK RICCI
The Films of Marilyn Monroe
Citadel, 1968. 160pp. Paper $2.45. A reprint of the 1964 survey of Miss Monroe's twenty-eight films. Included are synopses, cast and production credits, contemporary reviews, and scenes from the films. Also provided is an essay by Mark Harris tracing the career of the actress and a tribute by Lee Strasberg.

GUILES, FRED LAWRENCE
Norma Jean
McGraw—Hill, 1969. 341pp. $8.95. Paper—Bantam, 1970. 406pp. $1.25. The author studies the life and career of Marilyn Monroe. He probes in detail the complex elements of her identity as a person and as a star and traces her final withdrawal from public exposure during the last months of her life. Most of the material for this biography came from lengthy interviews over a period of five years with those closest to the late star. Illustrated. Index.

WAGENKNECHT, EDWARD—Editor
Marilyn Monroe: A Composite View
Chilton, 1969. 200pp. $5.95. A collection of essays, interviews, recollections, and memories of people who knew or were associated with the film star. Among the contributors are Hollis Alpert, Edith Sitwell, Norman Rosten, Cecil Beaton, Lee Strasberg, and Mr. Wagenknecht. Illustrated with eight pages of photographs.

WAGENKNECHT, EDWARD
Seven Daughters of the Theatre
See Page 262

Moore, Colleen

MOORE, COLLEEN
Silent Star
Doubleday, 1968. 262pp. $5.95. Miss Moore, a star of the silent screen and the talkies, tells her own story and describes the golden age of Hollywood. Anecdotes of the adventures and misadventures of the great stars are detailed. Illustrated with photographs.

More, Kenneth

MORE, KENNETH
Kindly Leave the Stage
See Page 274

Morley, Robert

MORLEY, ROBERT and SEWELL STOKES
Robert Morley: A Reluctant Autobiography
See Page 274

Murphy, George

MURPHY, GEORGE and VICTOR LASKY
Say, Didn't You Used to Be George Murphy?
Bartholomew House, 1970. 438pp. $6.95. The autobiography of the former stage and film star and ex-United States Senator. Illustrated with photographs.

Neal, Patricia

FARRELL, BARRY
Pat and Roald
Random House, 1969. 241pp. $6.95. This is the story of Patricia Neal's extraordinary recovery from a series of massive strokes and of her triumphant return to her acting career in "The Subject Was Roses." It is also the story of the faith and love of her husband, Roald Dahl, and his part in her recovery. Illustrated with photographs.

Negri, Pola

NEGRI, POLA
Memoirs of a Star
Doubleday, 1970. 453pp. $7.95. The autobiography of the film star. Miss Negri describes her childhood in Poland, her start in Germany's film industry, the height of her career in Hollywood in the 1920's and '30's, and her romances with Charles Chaplin and Rudolph Valentino. Illustrated with photographs. Index.

Olivier, Laurence

FAIRWEATHER, VIRGINIA
Sir Laurence Olivier: An Informal Portrait
See Page 274

WHITEHEAD, PETER and ROBIN BEAN
Olivier – Shakespeare
Lorimer, 1966. 40pp. & plates. Paper $1.95. Published in England, this is a short biography of Laurence Olivier complete with a Filmography and stills from all his Shakespearean films. Illustrated.

WILLIAMS, P. C.
English Shakespearian Actors
See Page 416

Oppenheimer, George

OPPENHEIMER, GEORGE
The View from the Sixties
See Page 274

Pickford, Mary

LEE, RAYMOND
The Films of Mary Pickford
A. S. Barnes, 1970. 175pp. $8.95. A record of the film career of the silent screen star. The 125 short features and fifty-two full-length films are all included with production and cast credits where available. Illustrated with over 200 stills from the films and a fifty-eight page section of portraits and candid photographs.

Poitier, Sidney

EWERS, CAROLYN H.
Sidney Poitier: The Long Journey
New American Library, 1969. 126pp. Paper $ .60. A biography of the motion picture star with twenty-four pages of photographs.

Reagan, Ronald

BOYARSKY, BILL
The Rise of Ronald Reagan
Random House, 1968. 269pp. $5.95. A biography which features California Governor Ronald Reagan's political career from his involvement as a union leader in the Screen Actors Guild to his current position. Illustrated with photographs. Index.

Rogers, Dale Evans

ROGERS, DALE EVANS
Angel Unaware
Pyramid, 1963. 64pp. Paper $ .50. Originally published in 1953 and now reprinted, this is the story of the life and death of the infant daughter of Dale Evans and Roy Rogers.

Rogers, Ginger

RICHARDS, DICK
Ginger – A Salute to a Star
Clifton, 1969. 192pp. $5.95. A biography of film star Ginger Rogers, from her beginnings to her current work on the Broadway and London stages. Illustrated. Filmography. Index.

Rogers, Will

DAY, DONALD
Will Rogers
See Page 276

Scott, Audrey

SCOTT, AUDREY
I Was a Hollywood Stunt Girl
Dorrance, 1969. 119pp. $3.95. Miss Scott describes the feats of skill she performed as a double for many film stars from the silent screen era to the late 1950's.

Sellers, Peter

EVANS, PETER
Peter Sellers: The Mask Behind the Mask
Prentice–Hall, 1968. 249pp. $6.95. A biography of the film star from his days as a "Goon Show" personality to his present superstar status. Candid interviews with Sellers' late mother, his wife, his friends, enemies, and co-workers are included. Illustrated with photographs.

Sinatra, Frank

SHAW, ARNOLD
Sinatra: Twentieth-Century Romantic
Holt, Rinehart, 1968. 371pp. $5.95. Paper – Pocket Books, 1969. 370pp. $ .95. This biography of Frank Sinatra places him in the pop-culture world from which he emerged. From the beginning days with Harry James and Tommy Dorsey to the days of "the Clan" and the great films and records, the singer's life is detailed and analyzed. Illustrated with sixteen pages of photographs. Appendices include a recapitulation of Sinatra's career as a recording artist and a list of films.

Stewart, James

McCLURE, ARTHUR F. and KEN D. JONES, ALFRED E. TWOMEY
The Films of James Stewart
A. S. Barnes, 1970. 256pp. $8.50. A review of the high-lights of the career of James Stewart. Detailed summaries, complete credits, and excerpts from contemporary reviews are included for each film. Illustrated with nearly 250 photographs. Selected Bibliography.

Swanson, Gloria

HUDSON, RICHARD and RAYMOND LEE
Gloria Swanson
A. S. Barnes, 1970. 269pp. $8.50. The career of the film star is detailed in more than 300 photographs including stills from the films, candid shots, and portraits. A complete Filmography lists each of the films and includes credits where possible.

Thalberg, Irving

THOMAS, BOB
Thalberg: Life and Legend
Doubleday, 1969. 416pp. $7.95. A biography of Irving Thalberg which details the growth of M. G. M. into the greatest film factory in movie history. Summaries of the most famous productions are included as are 144 photographs. List of major Academy Award winning Thalberg films. Bibliography. Index.

Tracy, Spencer

DESCHNER, DONALD
The Films of Spencer Tracy
Citadel, 1968. 255pp. $8.95. A survey of the actor's films. Each film is documented with a synopsis, cast and credit lists, extracts from reviews, and stills from the films. The authors have included a biographical essay on the actor. There are also appreciations and tributes to Tracy by various of his co-workers, including an essay by Stanley Kramer, "Film-Making with Spencer Tracy." Illustrated with scenes from the films and other photographs.

SWINDELL, LARRY
Spencer Tracy
World, 1969. 319pp. $6.95. A biography of the motion picture star from his childhood in Milwaukee to his great films in the 1940's, 1950's, and 1960's. Illustrated with thirty-two pages of movie stills and other photographs. Filmography. Index.

Travers, Bill
See Page 477 under **McKENNA, VIRGINIA**

Trumbo, Dalton

TRUMBO, DALTON
Additional Dialogue
Lippincott, 1970. 576pp. $12.50. Edited by Helen Manfull, this is a collection of the letters of Dalton Trumbo from 1942 to 1962. The letters detail the screenwriter's struggles through the period of the blacklist in Hollywood. Mr. Trumbo is the author of the screenplays of "Exodus," "Spartacus," "Lonely Are the Brave," "Kitty Foyle," and other films. Index.

Valentino, Rudolph

SHULMAN, IRVING
Valentino
Pocket Books, 1968. 404pp. $ .95. A reprint of the 1967 biography of "The Great Lover." Shulman details the legend of Rudolph Valentino and how that legend continued long after his death as motion picture companies struggled to recoup their investments in unreleased films and the cultists founded what approximated a religion honoring the silent film star. Illustrated.

Waters, Ethel

WATERS, ETHEL with CHARLES SAMUELS
His Eye Is on the Sparrow
See Page 278

Wayne, John

RICCI, MARK and BORIS ZMIJEWSKY, STEVE ZMIJEWSKY
The Films of John Wayne
Citadel, 1970. 288pp. $9.95. A complete record of John Wayne's career in Hollywood. Information on the 144 films includes synopses and cast and credit lists. The authors have also provided a biographical study of the actor in an attempt to cast new light on Wayne as a performer, a person, and a legend. More than 400 photographs, including studio and candid shots and scenes from the films, illustrate the volume.

West, Mae

WEINTRAUB, JOSEPH – Editor
The Wit and Wisdom of Mae West
Putnam, 1967. 94pp. $2.95. Paper – Avon, 1970. 143pp. $ .95. A collection of the witticisms of Mae West combined with a series of photographs of the actress. The paper edition does not contain as many photographs as the original edition but it does include a biographical memoir of the actress by Mr. Weintraub. This memoir is not included in the cloth edition.

White, Pearl

WELTMAN, MANUEL and RAYMOND LEE
Pearl White, The Peerless Fearless Girl
A. S. Barnes, 1969. 266pp. $8.50. A biography of the silent film actress which presents the essential facts of her life as if the book were a scenario for one of her serials. Much of the story is told in the form of dialogue between Miss White and her friends, directors, family, and servants. Illustrated with nearly 300 photographs. Filmography.

SCREENPLAYS

AGEE, JAMES
Agee on Film: Volume Two
Grosset & Dunlap, 1969. 488pp. Paper $2.95. A new edition of the collection of film scripts originally published in 1960. The complete scripts included are: "Noa Noa," "The African Queen," "The Night of the Hunter," "The Bride Comes to Yellow Sky," and "The Blue Hotel." John Huston has provided a Foreword.

ANDERSON, LINDSAY and DAVID SHERWIN
If . . .
Simon & Schuster, 1970. 167pp. Paper $1.95. The screenplay of the film with an essay by Lindsay Anderson and complete cast and production credits. Illustrated with photographs from the film.

ANDERSON, ROBERT
I Never Sang for My Father
New American Library, 1970. 159pp. Paper $ .95. The screenplay for the film starring Melvyn Douglas, directed by Gilbert Cates from Mr. Anderson's own adaptation of his Broadway play. The volume includes an Introduction by Mr. Anderson and notes on the making of the film by Mr. Cates. Illustrated with stills from the film.

ANTONIONI, MICHELANGELO and ELIO BARTOLINI, TONINO GUERRA
L'Avventura
Grove, 1969. 288pp. Paper $1.95. The scenario of Antonioni's film reconstructed from the finished film. Completing the volume are a number of interviews and critical pieces. Illustrated with over eighty photographs.

ANTONIONI, MICHELANGELO
Four Screenplays
Grossman, 1971. 361pp. Paper $3.95. This volume includes four screenplays by the Italian film-maker. An Introduction to the volume has been written by Antonioni, and cast and production credits for each of the films are included. The volume is illustrated with scenes from the films and photographs of the director at work. The screenplays have been translated by Louis Brigante and Roger J. Moore.

L'Avventura

La Notte
Il Grido
L'Eclisse

BAKER, FRED
Events
Grove, 1970. 128pp. Paper $1.75. Complete scenario of the film in which a young film-maker makes "stag" films in order to raise money to make a legitimate film. Illustrated with over 100 stills from the film.

BECKETT, SAMUEL
Film
Grove, 1969. 95pp. Paper $1.95. The complete scenario of Beckett's only film script. Notes on the script are included. Alan Schneider has provided an essay on directing the film. Stills from the film, which starred Buster Keaton, and production shots are also included.

BELLOCCHIO, MARCO
China Is Near
Orion Press, 1969. 160pp. $5.95. Paper $1.95. The complete script of the Italian director's screenplay, as translated by Judith Green. An Introduction by Tommaso Chiaretti, an interview with the director, and complete cast and production credits are also included. Illustrated with scenes from the film.

BERGMAN, INGMAR
A Film Trilogy
Orion, 1967. 143pp. $5.95. The scripts for three films by Bergman illustrated with scenes from the films.
Through a Glass Darkly
Winter Light
The Silence

BERGMAN, INGMAR
Four Screenplays
Simon & Schuster, 1960. 384pp. Paper $2.95. The screenplays of four of the Swedish director's films. Included are a Preface by Bergman's producer, Carl Anders Dymling, and an Introduction in which Bergman discusses film-making. Also provided are a chronology of films directed by Bergman and a list of major prizes won by Bergman films. Illustrated with stills from the films.
Smiles of a Summer Night
The Seventh Seal
Wild Strawberries
The Magician

BERGMAN, INGMAR
Three Films
Grove, 1970. 143pp. Paper $2.45. The screenplays for three of the Swedish director's films. Illustrated with stills from the films.
Through a Glass Darkly
Winter Light
The Silence

BERGMAN, INGMAR
Wild Strawberries
Simon & Schuster, 1970. 124pp. Paper $1.95. Included in this volume are the complete text of the filmscript, an essay on film-making by Bergman, a "Cutting Continuity" section, and a list of cast and production credits for the film. Illustrated.

BROOK, PETER et al
Tell Me Lies
Bobbs–Merrill, 1968. 214pp $6.00. Paper $3.25. The script of the Royal Shakespeare film production of their stage play "U. S." which created enormous controversy when it ran at the Aldwych Theatre in London. This is a record of the production, its sources, and the processes of working which led to the completed production. Reactions from press and audience are also included and the book is illustrated with production stills, news photographs, and original documents.

BUNUEL, LUIS
L'Age D'Or and Un Chien Andalou
Simon & Schuster, 1968. 124pp. Paper $1.95. The scripts of the two films with an introduction to each, cast and production credits, and notes by Bunuel. Illustrated with photographs.

BUNUEL, LUIS
Three Screenplays
Orion, 1969. 245pp. $6.95. Paper $3.50. The screenplays for three of the writer/director's films. Illustrated with stills from the films.
Viridiana
The Exterminating Angel
Simon of the Desert

BURROUGHS, WILLIAM
The Last Words of Dutch Schultz
Cape Goliard Press, 1970. 81pp. $6.00. Paper $2.50. A screenplay by the author of "Naked Lunch." The script is based on the transcript of the dying words of the 1930's American gangster.

CARNE, MARCEL and JACQUES PREVERT
Children of Paradise
Simon & Schuster, 1968. 218pp. Paper $2.95. The scenario of the classic French film which starred Arletty, Barrault, and Pierre Brasseur. The volume also includes an interview with Carne and one with Prevert and complete production and cast credits. Illustrated with photographs.

CARSON, L.M. KIT
David Holzman's Diary
Farrar, Straus, 1970. 126pp. $4.95. Paper $2.25. The screenplay of the film by Jim McBride which has won awards at the Mannheim and Brussels film festivals. The leading character films and records the people and events of his life in order to find a form for his existence. Illustrated with frames from the film.

CASSAVETES, JOHN
Faces
New American Library, 1970. 319pp. Paper $1.50. The screenplay for the award-winning film by Cassavetes. The making of the film is described in detail and parallel page comparisons of the original treatment and the final script are provided. Sixteen pages of photographs from the film.

CLAIR, RENE
A Nous la Liberte and Entr'Acte
Simon & Schuster, 1970. 140pp. Paper $2.45. The scripts for the French film-maker's two classic films, "A Nous la Liberte" and "Entr'Acte," in English translations and with descriptions of the action by Richard Jacques and Nicola Hayden. Included in the volume are cast and production credits and essays on the films. Illustrated with twenty-four pages of frames from the films.

CLAIR, RENE
Four Screenplays
Orion Press, 1970. 439pp. Paper $4.95. This anthology contains texts of the French director's films as translated by Piergiuseppe Bozzetti. Commentaries on each of the films are provided by Clair. Illustrated with scenes from the films. Cast and production credits are provided.

Le Silence Est d'Or
Less Belles-de-Nuit
La Beaute du Diable
Les Grandes Manoeuvres

COCTEAU, JEAN
Beauty and the Beast
New York University, 1970. 441pp. $14.95. Edited and annotated by Robert M. Hammond, this is the first publication of the scenario for Cocteau's classic film. This is a bilingual edition with both the French and English texts printed on facing pages. An extensive Introduction indicates the cuts that were made between preparation of the script and release of the film, and the discrepancies between the various versions and prints of the film. An Appendix provides excerpts from Cocteau's diary which apply to specific shots in the film. Illustrated with sixty photographs.

COCTEAU, JEAN
The Holy Terrors
New Directions, 1966. 183pp. Paper $1.95. The novel version of Cocteau's film, "Les Enfants Terribles," translated by Rosamond Lehmann, and published in paper for the first time. Includes twenty of Cocteau's drawings.

COCTEAU, JEAN
Two Screenplays
Orion, 1968. 147pp. $5.95. Paper—Penguin, 1969. 147pp. $1.25. The scripts of two of Cocteau's films translated from the French by Carol Martin-Sperry. Also included are some of Cocteau's writings on the cinema. Illustrated with sixty photographs.

Blood of a Poet
Testimony of Orpheus

CURRY, GEORGE
Copperfield '70
Ballantine, 1970. 211pp. Paper $ .95. The story of the making of the film version of "David Copperfield." Included in the volume is the complete screenplay. The film was released on television in the U. S. Sixteen pages of photographs. Index.

DE SICA, VITTORIO
The Bicycle Thief
Simon & Schuster, 1970. 100pp. Paper $1.95. Complete script of the neo-realist film, with an Introduction by the translator, Simon Hartog, and credits. Illustrated with twenty-two pages of stills.

DE SICA, VITTORIO
Miracle in Milan
Orion, 1968. 121pp. $5.00. Paper—Penguin, 1969. 121pp. $1.25. The text of the screenplay with a long Introduction by de Sica which tells why and how he made this and several of his other films. Illustrated with photographs from the film and of the director at work.

DREYER, CARL THEODOR
Four Screen Plays
Indiana University, 1970. 312pp. $12.00. Paper $3.95. The scripts of four films by Dreyer as translated by Oliver Stallybrass. Introduction by Ole Storm with a biographical note and Filmography. Thirty-two pages of photographs from the films are included.

The Passion of Joan of Arc
Day of Wrath
Vampire
The Word

DURAS, MARGUERITE
Hiroshima Mon Amour
Grove, 1961. 112pp. Paper $1.95. The complete text of the film by Alain Resnais with the author's original synopsis and notes. The volume has been edited by Robert Hughes and it includes over seventy stills from the film.

DURAS, MARGUERITE
Hiroshima Mon Amour and Une Aussi Longue Absence
Calder & Boyars, 1966. 191pp. $6.00. Paper $3.50. Two screenplays by the French writer. The volume is illustrated with scenes from the films.

EASTMAN, CHARLES
Little Faus and Big Halsy
Farrar, Straus, 1970. 164pp. $4.95. Paper $2.25. Paper—Pocket Books, 1970. 160pp. $1.25. The screenplay of the new film about motorcycle racing. Robert Redford and Michael J. Pollard play the

leading roles. Cast and production credits are provided and the volume is illustrated with stills from the film.

EISENSTEIN, SERGEI
Ivan the Terrible
Simon & Schuster, 1970. 264pp. Paper $3.25. The film script of all three parts of Eisenstein's classic film. Essays on the film are included with complete production and cast credits. Illustrated with photographs from the film.

EISENSTEIN, SERGEI
Potemkin
Simon & Schuster, 1968. 104pp. Paper $1.95. Translated by Gillon R. Aitken, this is the scenario for the classic Russian film with an Introduction by the director. Illustrated with stills from the film.

FELLINI, FEDERICO
Federico Fellini's Juliet of the Spirits
Orion, 1965. 183pp. $5.95. Edited by Tullio Kerich, this volume includes the complete screenplay for Fellini's film together with the only long interview Fellini has ever given. Translated from the Italian by Howard Greenfield. Illustrated.

FELLINI, FEDERICO
Fellini's Satyricon
Ballantine, 1970. 280pp. Paper $3.95. Edited by Dario Zonelli and translated by Eugene Walter and John Matthews, this is the complete screenplay for Fellini's film. Essays on the film are included as are many photographs of scenes from the film.

FELLINI, FEDERICO
Three Screenplays
Orion, 1970. 288pp. $7.95. Paper $3.50. Three of the Italian director's film scripts as translated by Judith Green. Cast and production credits are included and the volume is illustrated with scenes from the films.

I Vitelloni
Il Bidone
The Temptations of Dr. Antonio

FONDA, PETER and DENNIS HOPPER, TERRY SOUTHERN
Easy Rider
New American Library, 1969. 191pp. Paper $1.25. The complete script of the film plus interviews and articles dealing with the film and its stars. Illustrated with stills from the film.

FOOTE, HORTON
To Kill a Mockingbird
Harcourt, Brace, 1962. 117pp. Paper $1.85. The screenplay of Harper Lee's novel.

GINSBERG, MILTON MOSES
Coming Apart
Lancer, 1969. 208pp. Paper $1.25. The script of the film written and directed by Mr. Ginsberg. Cast and production credits are included as are many stills from the film.

GODARD, JEAN–LUC
Le Petit Soldat
Lorimer, 1967. 95pp. Paper $1.95. The screenplay for the film together with a Godard Filmography. Illustrated with scenes from the film.

GODARD, JEAN–LUC
Masculine Feminine
Grove, 1969. 288pp. Paper $1.95. The script of the film which introduced Godard's personal and artistic involvement with the new generation of young Parisians. Also included are two stories by de Maupassant upon which the film is based, a number of interviews and critical pieces, and a selection of over 100 illustrations.

GODARD, JEAN–LUC
Pierrot Le Fou
Lorimer, 1969. 104pp. Paper $1.95. An English translation, by Peter Whitehead, of Godard's film. The volume also includes an interview with the director and complete credits for the film. Illustrated with photographs from the film in color and black-and-white.

GOLDMAN, WILLIAM
Butch Cassidy and the Sundance Kid
Bantam, 1969. 185pp. Paper $ .75. The screenplay of the film which won an Academy Award in 1969. The volume also includes a portfolio of on-location photographs.

GREENE, GRAHAM and CAROL REED
The Third Man
Simon & Schuster, 1968. 134pp. Paper $1.95. This volume includes the complete script of the film, an Introduction by Andrew Sinclair, cast and production credits, and a characterization of all the major roles in the film. Illustrated with photographs.

HERNDON, VENABLE and ARTHUR PENN
Alice's Restaurant
Doubleday, 1970. 141pp. Paper $1.95. The complete screenplay of the film based on Arlo Guthrie's song. Introductory pieces by the scriptwriter and the director. Illustrated with stills from the film.

HUGHES, ROBERT – Editor
Film: Book 2 – Films of Peace and War
Grove, 1962. 256pp. Paper $2.45. A study based on articles, interviews, and responses to questionnaires on the difficulties film-makers have encountered in making films about peace and war. Included are two complete scenarios of banned films: John Huston's "Let There Be Light" and Alain Resnais' "Night and Fog." Illustrated.

JOHN, ERROL
Force Majeure. The Dispossessed. Hasta Luego
Faber & Faber, 1967. 194pp. $5.00. The screenplays for three film scripts by the author of "Moon on a Rainbow Shawl."

KAZAN, ELIA
America America
Stein & Day, 1962. 190pp. $4.95. The director's first novel, written in a form that approximates that of a screenplay.

KRONHAUSEN, PHYLLIS and EBERHARD KRONHAUSEN
Freedom to Love
Grove, 1970. 171pp. Paper $1.75. The screenplay of the film about current trends in sexuality and the freedom to publish, perform, and view what has here-to-fore been considered "pornography." Illustrated with more than 100 photographs from the film. Appendices include full texts of interviews by the Doctors Kronhausen with various sexual freedom leaders.

KUROSAWA, AKIRA
Ikiru
Simon & Schuster, 1968. 88pp. Paper $1.95. A complete scenario of the classic Japanese film. The volume has been edited and Introduced by Donald Richie. Cast and production credits are included as are photographs from the film.

KUROSAWA, AKIRA
Rashomon
Grove, 1969. 256pp. Paper $1.95. The complete script of the Japanese film. Also included are the two Akutagawa stories upon which the film was based. Essays on interpretation by Parker Tyler, James F. Davidson, and Donald Richie, and the first sequence from the screenplay titled "The Outrage" by Michael Kanin are also included. Illustrated with over 200 photographs from the film.

LANG, FRITZ and THEA VON HARBOU
M
Simon & Schuster, 1968. 112pp. Paper $1.95. The scenario of the great film which starred Peter Lorre. The volume also includes an Introduction by Nicholas Garnham and complete cast and production credits. Illustrated with photographs.

MAYSLES, ALBERT and DAVID MAYSLES
Salesman
New American Library, 1969. 128pp. Paper $ .75. The script of the film with an Introduction by Harold Clurman. Also included are production notes by Howard Junker and a Filmography of the Maysles Brothers. Illustrated with photographs.

OSBORNE, JOHN
Tom Jones
Grove, 1964. 192pp. Paper $1.95. The script of the Academy Award winning film adapted from the novel by Henry Fielding. Included are over 200 stills from the film plus cast and production credits.

PREVERT, JACQUES and MARCEL CARNE
Le Jour se Leve
Simon & Schuster, 1970. 128pp. Paper $2.25. The script of the classic French film. An essay on the film and credit and cast lists are provided as are photographs from the film.

RENOIR, JEAN
Grand Illusion
Simon & Schuster, 1968. 108pp. Paper $1.95. The scenario for the classic French film which starred Erich von Stroheim, Jean Gabin, and Pierre Fresnay. Translated from the French by Marianne Alexandre and Andrew Sinclair and illustrated with stills from the film.

RENOIR, JEAN
Rules of the Game
Simon & Schuster, 1970. 172pp. Paper $2.25. The script of the French film originally produced in 1939. Translated by John McGrath and Maureen Teitelbaum with several interviews with Jean Renoir and other essays on the film, production and cast credits. Profusely illustrated with stills from the film.

ROBBE–GRILLET, ALAIN
Last Year at Marienbad
Grove, 1962. 168pp. Paper $1.95. Translated by Richard Howard, this is the text of the film by Alain Resnais which won the grand prize at the Venice Film Festival. The volume includes an Introduction by Robbe-Grillet and is illustrated with over 140 photographs.

SEMPRUN, JORGE
La Guerre Est Finie
Grove, 1967. 192pp. Paper $2.45. The scenario for the film by Alain Resnais which deals with the effects of the Spanish Civil War on the lives of a group of exiles living in France. It includes 114 frame-enlargements from the film and production credits.

SHAW, BERNARD
Saint Joan
University of Washington, 1968. 162pp. $6.95. Paper $2.45. A screenplay adapted from his own drama by Shaw. Professor Bernard Dukore has edited and provided an Introduction. Twenty-two photographs of various productions of the play are included.

SJOMAN, VILGOT
I Am Curious (Blue)
Grove, 1970. 219pp. Paper $1.75. The complete scenario of the second part of the "I Am Curious" films. Translated from the Swedish by Martin Minow and Jenny Bohman, the volume includes over 270 illustrations from the film.

SJOMAN, VILGOT
I Am Curious (Yellow)
Grove, 1968. 254pp. Paper $1.75. The complete scenario of the Swedish film which has been acclaimed by critics around the world for its portrayal of the social, political, and sexual problems of today's youth. 266 stills from the film illustrate the volume and an Appendix of pertinent testimony about the film by key witnesses in the U.S. District Court pornography case is included.

SONTAG, SUSAN
Duet for Cannibals
Farrar, Straus, 1970. 129pp. $4.95. Paper $2.25. The screenplay directed in Stockholm from her own screenplay by Miss Sontag. Illustrated with stills from the film.

STERNBERG, JOSEF VON
The Blue Angel
Simon & Schuster, 1968. 111pp. Paper $1.95. The screenplay of the German film which introduced Marlene Dietrich. Sternberg has provided an Introduction to the volume. Illustrated with stills from the film.

THOMAS, DYLAN
The Doctors and the Devils and Other Scripts
New Directions, 1966. 229pp. $5.00. Collected in this volume are Thomas' principal works for films and radio. Also included is a series of captions for some photographs published in a British magazine and an essay by Ralph Maud on the writing of "Under Milk Wood."

The Doctor and the Devils—film script
Twenty Years A-Growing—film script
The Londoner—radio script

THOMAS, DYLAN
Rebecca's Daughters
Little, Brown, 1965. 144pp. $4.50. Written in the form of a novel, this book was originally commissioned as a screenplay.

THOMAS, DYLAN
Twenty Years A-Growing
J.M. Dent, 1964. 91pp. $3.50. This unfinished film script by Thomas was based on an autobiography by the Irish writer, Maurice O'Sullivan.

THOMPSON, ROBERT E.
They Shoot Horses, Don't They?
Avon, 1969. 319pp. Paper $ .95. This edition of Horace McCoy's novel about the dance marathons of the 1930's also includes the complete screenplay of the film by Mr. Thompson.

TRUFFAUT, FRANCOIS
The 400 Blows
Grove, 1969. 256pp. Paper $1.95. The script of the French director's first film, complete with scenes omitted from the finished film, complete credits, two interviews with the director, a selection of critical reviews, and essays on the film. Over 100 frame enlargements from the film are included.

TRUFFAUT, FRANCOIS
Jules and Jim
Simon & Schuster, 1968. 104pp. Paper $1.95. Translated from the French by Nicholas Fry, this is the screenplay of the internationally successful film written and directed by Truffaut and starring Jeanne Moreau, Oskar Werner, and Henri Serre. Complete cast and production credits are included as are many stills from the film.

VISCONTI, LUCHINO
Three Screenplays
Orion Press, 1970. 313pp. $7.95. Paper $3.50. Three scripts of highly regarded films translated from the Italian by Judith Green. Cast and production credits are provided. Illustrated with scenes from the films.

White Nights
Rocco and His Brothers
The Job

VISCONTI, LUCHINO
Two Screenplays
Orion Press, 1970. 186pp. $6.95. Paper $2.50. Two of Visconti's best known screenplays translated from the Italian by Judith Green. Cast and production credits are provided. Illustrated with scenes from the films.

La Terra Trema
Senso

WARHOL, ANDY
Blue Movie
Grove, 1970. 128pp. Paper $1.75. The scenario for the film which has been banned in most communities in the United States for its detailed photography of sexual intercourse and its explicit language. Over 100 photographs from the film are included.

WEXLER, NORMAN
Joe
Avon, 1970. 128pp. Paper $ .95. The screenplay of the film dealing with the unrest of contemporary middle America. It is a commentary on the consequences of racial violence. Introductory review by Judith Crist and sixteen pages of photographs are included.

TELEVISION

HISTORIES AND CRITIQUES

AARONSON, CHARLES S. — Editor
International Television Almanac: 1968
Quigley, 1967. 774pp. $9.50. The thirteenth annual edition of the almanac which includes several thousand biographies, statistical data, and inumerable facts on companies, organizations, producers, station operators, and other information on television.

AARONSON, CHARLES S. — Editor
International Television Almanac: 1969
Quigley, 1968. 784pp. $15.00. The fourteenth annual volume of information on the television industry. Statistical information, biographies, listings of television stations, producers, service companies, and the industry outside of the United States are all covered. Indices.

ARLEN, MICHAEL J.
Living-Room War
Viking, 1969. 242pp. $5.95. The thirty-six essays in this volume assess the place, role and presence of television in our lives today. The essays include several on television and the war in Vietnam, the most recent political conventions, educational television, and television on Sunday.

BACH, ROBERT O. — Editor
Communication: The Art of Understanding and Being Understood
Hastings House, 1963. 140pp. $6.95. This collection of essays examines verbal, written, and pictorial communication from a variety of angles. Contributors include: S. I. Hayakawa, Saul Bass, Oleg Cassini, Charles Coiner, and others. This is the complete report of the seventh annual Visual Communications Conference sponsored by the Art Directors Club of New York. Illustrated.

BARNOUW, ERIK
The Image Empire
Oxford, 1970. 396pp. $10.75. Volume three in the author's "History of Broadcasting in the United States." Mr. Barnouw traces the history from 1953, analyzing the programs, personalities, and other aspects of the entire television and radio industry. He emphasizes the medium's effect on public issues and its role in furthering American policies. Illustrated. Appendices. Bibliography. Index. Also see "The Golden Web" and "The Tower of Babel" in the section on Histories of Radio.

BARNOUW, ERIK
Mass Communication
See Page 505

BARBER, RED
The Broadcasters
Dial, 1970. 271pp. $6.95. Mr. Barber recounts the landmarks of his profession of radio sports broadcasting and the highlights of his own career at the microphone. The author recalls and evaluates dozens of his radio and television colleagues and tells of the ethics and personal how-to of his craft.

BARRETT, MARVIN — Editor
Survey of Broadcast Journalism: 1968 – 1969
Grosset & Dunlap, 1969. 132pp. Paper $1.95. This is a study of how television and radio report the news, serve the public, and how they are governed by the Federal Communications Commission. Included is a study of media coverage of the 1968 political campaign. Appendices. Index.

BARRETT, MARVIN — Editor
Survey of Broadcast Journalism: 1969 – 1970
Grosset & Dunlap, 1970. 156pp. Paper $1.95. Subtitled, "Year of Challenge, Year of Crisis," this is a report on how radio and television covered the news events of the year and the controversy surrounding the attacks on broadcasting by Vice President Agnew. Index.

BELSON, WILLIAM A.
The Impact of Television: Methods and Findings in Program Research
Crosby Lockwood, 1967. 400pp. $12.00. Dr. Belson urges the use of research to measure the effects of television on society and as an aid to program planning. He describes techniques for conducting research and illustrates these with actual inquiries he has conducted in England. Bibliography. Index.

BERTON, PIERRE — Editor
Voices from the Sixties
Doubleday, 1967. 242pp. $4.95. Mr. Berton has collected, arranged, annotated, and edited twenty-two interviews with men and women who have made the 1960's unique. From his Canadian television program, these interviews with Mrs. Ian Fleming, Malcolm X, Paul Anka, Lenny Bruce, Ray Bradbury, Mort Sahl, and others are concerned with people who are involved with this decade and with each other through the mass medium of television.

BLUEM, A. WILLIAM
Documentary in American Television: Form, Function, Method
Hastings House, 1965. 311pp. $8.95. An analysis of the heritage of the television documentary as it is found in other media. The major achievements in documentary production, the people who have shaped the form, and the problems and the potentials of its use in a free society are analyzed. News and theme documentary materials are examined in detail as well as significant new developments. Full production notes are provided on 100 important films. Illustrated.

BLUEM, A. WILLIAM
Religious Television Programs
Hastings House, 1969. 220pp. $4.95. The author provides a study of the achievements and problems of religious broadcasting and its relevance to American life today. It is based on one of the most extensive surveys of religious television programming ever undertaken. Professor Bluem examines, discusses and describes the programs presented on the air nationally and locally. A series of Appendices includes a list of stations, selected references, and a short history of religious broadcasting. Index.

BLUEM, A. WILLIAM and JOHN F. COX, GENE McPHERSON
Television in the Public Interest
Hastings House, 1961. 192pp. $6.95. Practical information for the layman on how he can make better use of the television medium for public service causes. Illustrated.

BLUEM, A. WILLIAM and ROGER MANVELL – Editors
Television: The Creative Experience
Hastings House, 1967. 328pp. $7.95. An anthology of thirty-seven essays and dialogues by sixty-three leading writers, producers, directors, educators, and performers. The articles were originally published in "Television Quarterly" and "English Journal of the Society of Film and Television Arts." Indices.

BLUMLER, JAY G. and DENIS McQUAIL
Television in Politics: Its Uses and Influences
University of Chicago, 1969. 379pp. $13.25. Originally published in England and now issued in the United States, this study is approached from two perspectives. The first is that of the viewer's feelings and opinions about political television. In addition, the book charts the impact of television, in conjunction with other communication sources, upon the political outlook of electors. In conclusion, the authors propose a radical reform of the structure of political broadcasting. Included are several Appendices on the authors' methods of sampling and compiling the results of their survey. Bibliography. Index of Sources Cited. Index of Subjects.

BRODHEAD, JAMES E.
Inside Laugh–In
New American Library, 1970. 159pp. Paper $ .75. A behind-the-scenes look at the popular television program. Illustrated with photographs.

CARNEGIE COMMISSION ON EDUCATIONAL TELEVISION
Public Television: A Program for Action
Bantam, 1967. 254pp. Paper $1.00. Non-commercial television is the subject of this report of the Carnegie Commission. Fifteen distinguished Americans, after a year of intensive study, recommend changes to bring into being a system of Public Television.

CARTER, HUNTLY
The New Spirit in the Russian Theatre: 1917 – 1928
See Page 219

CASSIRER, HENRY H.
Television Teaching Today
UNESCO, 1960. 267pp. $4.00. A volume in the UNESCO series on "Press, Film, and Radio in the World Today." The volume is designed to assist in improving the use of mass communications media. Aspects of production and the present state of the media in the United States and other countries are covered.

CHESTER, EDWARD W.
Radio, Television, and American Politics
Sheed & Ward, 1969. 342pp. $7.50. A complete history of the role of radio and television in American politics. Notes on sources follow each chapter and a Selected Bibliography of some 500 items is included. Index.

COLEMAN, HOWARD W. – Editor
Color Television: The Business of Colorcasting
Hastings House, 1968. 287pp. $8.95. This is a survey of color television and an exploration of the components that make color-casting a vital communications force. Appendices of industry data are included. Glossary of U. S. and British terminology. Illustrated with charts and diagrams. Index.

COONS, JOHN E.
Freedom and Responsibility in Broadcasting
Northwestern University, 1963. 252pp. $5.00. Representatives of the industry, of the Federal Communications Commission, and of the legal profession give their views on the place of broadcasting in American society. The major contributors are LeRoy Collins, Newton N. Minow, Louis L. Jaffe, and Roscoe L. Barrow. Included is an Appendix dealing with the extent of the authority of the F. C. C.

DE VERA, JOSE MARIA
Educational Television in Japan
Tuttle, 1967. 140pp. $6.00. This is the first attempt to offer in a Western language, a study, both descriptive and analytical, of the subject of educational television in Japan. The author discusses the concept of educational television as shaped by history and the Japanese broadcasting laws. His study embraces the content of educational television, the audience for it, and the effects and effectiveness of television on the learning process. The text is illustrated with forty-nine tables. A Bibliography lists books and articles on the subject in both the English and Japanese languages.

DONNER, STANLEY T. – Editor
The Meaning of Commercial Television
University of Texas, 1967. 157pp. Paper $2.50. A collection of speeches presented at a seminar on

commercial television in 1966. Among the contributors are George Schaefer, Paul Goodman, and Marshall McLuhan. Also in the book are summaries of the discussions which followed each of the speeches, and an examination of the overall impact of the meeting and the conclusions that might be drawn from it.

ELLISON, HARLAN
The Glass Teat
Ace, 1970. 318pp. Paper $1.25. A collection of columns that originally appeared in "The Los Angles Free Press." The essays and critiques on television contain assaults on situation comedies, talk shows, and the racism, corrupt politics, bad taste, and the blindness of the Establishment which the author contends are rampant on television.

FANG, IRVING E.
Television News
Hastings House, 1968. 285pp. $8.95. Paper $7.50. All the skills required by the television journalist—writing, editing, filming, broadcasting—are fully described and analyzed in this detailed guidebook. The book is an examination of the who, what, when, where, and especially, the how of television newscasts. Sample newscasts are included in the Appendix. Illustrated. Index.

FAULK, JOHN HENRY
Fear on Trial
Simon & Schuster, 1964. 398pp. $6.50. The radio and television personality describes his fight against the slander with which the vigilante group called AWARE, INC. undermined his career. The book gives much of the court transcript of the eleven week libel trial, conducted for Mr. Faulk by Louis Nizer, which resulted in an unprecedented $3,500 judgment against AWARE. The entertainment industry's weakness before such blacklisting attempts is also a subject of Mr. Faulk's book.

FLOHERTY, JOHN J.
Television Story
Lippincott, 1957. 160pp. $4.95. A survey of television from its origins to the present day, for the young reader.

GALANOY, TERRY
Down the Tube, or Making Television Commercials Is Such a Dog-Eat-Dog Business It's No Wonder They're Called Spots
Regenery, 1970. 257pp. $5.95. A light-hearted and informative look at the world of television commercials. The author looks at the advertisers, the agents, and the creative talents of the commercial industry and reports on what the agencies hope to accomplish and whether or not they succeed.

GLICK, IRA O. and SIDNEY J. LEVY
Living with Television
Aldine, 1962. 262pp. $6.75. Based on extensive field research conducted by Social Research, Inc., this study interprets the results of over 13,000 interviews with viewers to give a scientific basis to speculations about the composition of the television audience, its tastes, and its reactions to programs.

GORDON, GEORGE N.
Classroom Television: New Frontiers in ITV
See Page 335

GREEN, MAURY
Television News: Anatomy and Process
Wadsworth, 1969. 352pp. $10.00. The author, a newsman who has won the Emmy for documentary news/drama and the Golden Mike award, provides a study of the various aspects of television news. All the technical processes of television as a news medium are treated: writing, reporting in the field and on the air, film and video tape editing, production, and news department management. The author relates these techniques to television news ethics, to social values, and to the impact of television on politics. Illustrated. Suggestions for Further Reading. Glossary. Index.

GRIFFITH, BARTON L. and DONALD W. MacLENNAN – Editors
Improvement of Teaching by Television
University of Missouri, 1964. 238pp. $4.00. The proceedings of the National Conference of the National Association of Educational Broadcasters at the University of Missouri in 1964 are included in this volume. The papers are an assessment of the status of instructional television. They include discussion topics that range from the mechanics of presenting course material to relationships between faculty members and institutions.

GROSS, BEN
I Looked and I Listened
Arlington House, 1970. 373pp. $8.95. Originally published in 1954 and now reissued in a revised edition, this is a volume of informal recollections of radio and television by the critic and editor. New material brings the volume up-to-date. Illustrated with forty-eight pages of photographs. Index.

HAMM, VICTOR M.
Taste and the Audio-Visual Arts
Marquette University, 1960. 8pp. Paper $ .50. A brief essay on the standards of artistic judgement that should be brought to bear on current television productions.

HAZARD, PATRICK D. – Editor
TV As Art
National Council of Teachers of English, 1966. 221pp. Paper $1.65. These essays on and criticisms of television include such subjects as politics and mass communications in America, Shakespeare on the television screen, and television for children.

HEATH, R. B.
Radio and Television
Hamish Hamilton, 1969. 184pp. Paper $2.75. Published in England, this volume documents the media of radio and television. The author surveys the impact and influence of these media, the early history, the programs, and some technical aspects. Specific assignments and questions are included at the end of each chapter. The volume includes a short Glossary and a list of books for further reading. Illustrated.

HIGGINS, ANTHONY P.
Talking About Television
British Film Institute, 1966. 108pp. Paper $2.50. A personal account of the methods of teaching and some of the examples of the work which has been done with secondary school pupils in England by the author. Illustrated with photographs from the tele-plays under discussion.

HILDICK, E.W.
A Close Look at Television and Sound Broadcasting
Faber & Faber, 1967. 132pp. $2.50. After a survey of the importance of broadcasting as reflected in the practical concern of politicians, advertisers, and sociologists, the author goes on to embrace such aspects of broadcasting as general organization, measure of government control, and sources of revenue. There are also sections concerning the pursuit of mass audiences, the comparable advantages and limitations of newspapers and magazines, and the possible abuses of these powerful media in the social and political fields. Illustrated. Notes for Teachers.

HILLIARD, ROBERT L. — Editor
Understanding Television: An Introduction to Broadcasting
Hastings House, 1964. 254pp. $6.95. Paper $4.95. A collection of essays on television. Among the subjects are producing for television, writing, directing, staging, and the mechanics of the equipment. Bibliography. Index.

HOOD, STUART
A Survey of Television
Heinemann, 1967. 186pp. $6.00. Mr. Hood discusses the structure of the British television industry today, how this affects professionals, and compares conditions in other countries. He assesses some of the landmarks and recent developments in television journalism, education, and drama. Index.

HOPKINSON, PETER
Split Focus
Hart–Davis, 1969. 224pp. $16.00. This is Mr. Hopkinson's report of two decades as a cameraman/reporter. He describes the development of television documentary from its origins as cinema newsreel and tells of his involvement with the first uncensored film ever to be made in Soviet Russia, the filming of the first eighteen months of the independence of India, and other world-wide journeys to document contemporary history. Illustrated with photographs. Index.

JOHNSON, NICHOLAS
How to Talk Back to Your Television Set
Little Brown, 1970. 228pp. $5.75. Paper — Bantam, 1970. 246pp. $ .95. Mr. Johnson is a member of the Federal Communications Commission. He inquires into television's performance and criticizes its inadequacies as well as proposing some reforms. Examination of the values that television promotes, citation of the amount of violence that appears, and discussion of industry censorship are all included. Mr. Johnson also advises on how to reach those in responsible positions to improve the quality of television broadcasting.

KAHN, FRANK J. — Editor
Documents of American Broadcasting
Appleton, 1968. 598pp. $6.50. A collection of primary sources of laws, decisions, reports, and other documents on broadcasting. The five sections under which the documents are grouped are: Development of Broadcast Regulation, Broadcast Journalism, Regulation of Broadcasting, Regulation of Competition, and Educational Broadcasting. Each section contains a Bibliography of related reading materials.

KLAPPER, JOSEPH T.
The Effects of Mass Communication
See Page 505

KOENIG, ALLEN E. and RUANE B. HILL
The Farther Vision: Educational Television Today
University of Wisconsin, 1967. 371pp. $7.50. Paper $2.95. A series of articles on educational television. The emphasis is on operations that concentrate soley on ETV and the articles offer a perspective of the field, discuss major types of ETV stations and networks, examine the development and uses of instructional television, and deal with the current financial and research problems. Appendices. Index.

MACLEAN, RODERICK
Television in Education
Methuen, 1968. 151pp. $5.00. Paper $2.95. Mr. MacLean surveys the developments of educational television in the British school system and the implications for the future. He discusses current techniques and equipment and analyzes the roles and purposes of the educator and the television professional. Illustrated with photographs. List of References. Bibliography. Index.

MacNEIL, ROBERT
The People Machine
Eyre & Spottiswoode, 1970. 364pp. $10.00. A study of the influence of television on American politics. The author is concerned with how politics are sold to the electorate and subordinated to mass

entertainment values. In an Introduction and Postscript, Mr. MacNeil discusses the same developments in Britain. Notes. Index.

MANNES, MARYA
Who Owns the Air?
Marquette University, 1960. 20pp. Paper $ .50. A brief essay and negative report on the artistic status of television.

MICHAEL, PAUL and JAMES ROBERT PARISH
The Emmy Awards: A Pictorial History
Crown, 1970. 384pp. $9.95. A comprehensive pictorial history of the "Emmy" awards for excellence in television. Lists of all winners since 1948 with interesting highlights of each year's awards, plus complete details on losers, new award categories, and area awards for every year. Preface by Loring Mandel and Foreword by Newton N. Minow. Illustrated. Index.

MOIR, GUTHRIE
Into Television
Pergamon, 1969. 94pp. Paper $2.75. An introduction to television in England, designed to provide all the basic knowledge required for prospective workers in the field. Included are brief surveys of the BBC and ITV, the production of a program, the various types of programs, the audience and the advertisers, and the prospects for the future. Illustrated with photographs. Book List. Index.

MURROW, EDWARD R.
In Search of Light: The Broadcasts of Edward R. Murrow 1938 – 1961
Knopf, 1967. 376pp. $6.95. A selection of Mr. Murrow's broadcasts including those from wartime London, the wedding of Queen Elizabeth, and the "See It Now" telecasts on Senator Joseph McCarthy. Illustrated. Index.

NISHIMOTO, MITOJI
The Development of Educational Broadcasting in Japan
Tuttle, 1969. 287pp. $12.50. A history of the thirty-five years of experience in school broadcasting and fifteen years of school telecasting in Japan. The author provides guidelines and warnings for educational systems in other countries where there are current problems. Illustrated with charts and graphs. Index.

PAULU, BURTON
British Broadcasting in Transition
University of Minnesota, 1961. 250pp. $5.00. This sequel to an earlier study gives an account of developments in broadcasting in England between 1955 and 1961, when commercial television began to complete with the BBC. The legal and financial structures of the BBC and the ITA are examined and their program policies and operations are detailed.

PAULU, BURTON
British Broadcasting: Radio and Television in the United Kingdom
University of Minnesota, 1956. 457pp. $6.00. A study of the development of broadcasting in the British Isles from its inception to 1955. The development of the BBC is described and the factors that led to the emergence of the commercial Independent Television Authority are noted. Emphasis is placed on program description, audience reaction, staff and technical facilities, and finances.

PENNYBACKER, JOHN H. and WALDO W. BRADEN – Editors
Broadcasting and the Public Interest
Random House, 1970. 176pp. Paper $3.25. A selection of speeches and writings by important spokesmen on the mass media, particularly television. Essays on the Federal Communications Commission, programming, the fairness doctrine, and the implications of the communications revolution. Bibliographies.

ROE, YALE
The Television Dilemma: Search for a Solution
Hastings House, 1962. 184pp. $4.50. An analysis of the influence of television on the public's moral values, judgments, and attitudes. The dilemma created by the many forces seeking to motivate and control the medium is examined in detail.

ROE, YALE – Editor
Television Station Management: The Business of Broadcasting
Hastings House, 1964. 251pp. $6.95. Paper $4.95. The five parts of this book cover the finances of broadcasting, managing the station, programming, production, and publicity, sales management, and technical services. The essays are by Lawrence H. Rogers, Edward Wetter, D. Friedland, Richard B. Rawls, George A. Baker, Joseph K. Mitita, Vernon F. Cook, Colby Lewis, Jay Crouse, Howard W. Coleman, and John B. Sias.

RUBIN, BERNARD
Political Television
Wadsworth, 1967. 200pp. Paper $6.50. An account of the dramatic reshaping of elections and the Presidency by television. The book fixes on the five years preceding the general election of 1964, in the context of two presidential campaigns, in an attempt to show why and how television has become able to exert profound political influence. Index.

SCHRAMM, WILBUR – Editor
Mass Communications
See Page 506

SCHRAMM, WILBUR and JACK LYLE, ITHIEL DE SOLA POOL
The People Look at Educational Television
Stanford University, 1963. 209pp. $6.50. Based on

more than 30,000 interviews, this book answers such questions as: how large is the educational television audience, what is its make-up, what is its reaction to programs, and what is the impact of educational television on children, adults, and the entire community. Index.

SCHRAMM, WILBUR and JACK LYLE, EDWIN B. PARKER
Television in the Lives of Our Children
Stanford University, 1961. 324pp. $8.50. Paper $2.95. This study analyzes the chief effects which have been ascribed to television, such as juvenile delinquency and debasement of taste, and tests the validity of these claims. It sums up everything so far discovered by research concerning the effect of television on children.

SETTEL, IRVING and WILLIAM LAAS
A Pictorial History of Television
Grosset & Dunlap, 1969. 210pp. $7.95. This profusely illustrated volume traces the complete history of television from the pre-DuMont days to the McLuhan era. Beginning with the origins of electronic picture communications, it is a study of how television was developed and how it works. The great television personalities, the playwrights, the newscasters, and the programs are all included in text and hundreds of pictures. Index.

SHAYON, ROBERT
Television: The Dream and the Reality
Marquette University, 1960. 16pp. Paper $ .50. A brief essay on the morality of the television industry as revealed in the scandals over the "fixing" of quiz shows.

SKORNIA, HARRY J. and JACK WILLIAM KITSON — Editors
Problems and Controversies in Television and Radio
Pacific Books, 1968. 503pp. $10.00. A collection of articles, statements, and speeches by leaders in broadcasting, advertising, government, education, and other fields on the various issues, policies, practices, problems, and effects of television and radio. The result is a source book for anyone concerned with any aspect of television and radio broadcasting. Most of the fifty-four articles are either out-of-print or published here for the first time.

SKORNIA, HARRY J.
Television and Society: An Inquest and Agenda for Improvement
McGraw–Hill, 1965. 268pp. $7.50. Paper $2.95. Basing his reports on corporation records, Congressional hearings and an analysis of the control of mass media, the author concludes that business corporations cannot be expected to put public interest above profit. Items covered are leadership in the industry, economics, and ratings and mass values. Proposals for reform are included.

SKORNIA, HARRY J.
Television and the News: A Critical Appraisal
Pacific Books, 1968. 232pp. $5.75. A documented analysis of the state of broadcast journalism in the United States. Mr. Skornia points out the conditions that prevent news broadcasting from being a profession and suggests steps needed to achieve professionalism and to provide the type of news service the nation needs but is not getting. He examines the various problems in detail and presents cases and incidents. Index.

SMALL, WILLIAM
To Kill a Messenger
Hastings House, 1970. 302pp. $8.95. The director of CBS News in Washington examines the role of television news in our society. He tells of the problems of selecting and presenting news and how men of power examine, measure, and sometimes control the influence of television news. In depth discussions of past and recent events are provided and there is an analysis of television news in its relations with government and the pressures which are brought to bear on it. Index.

SOPKIN, CHARLES
Seven Glorious Days, Seven Fun-Filled Nights
Ace, 1970. 255pp. Paper $ .75. Originally published in 1968 and now reissued, this is one man's report of one week of television programs from sign-on to sign-off on all six New York City stations.

STEINER, GARY A.
The People Look at Television: A Study of Audience Attitudes
Knopf, 1963. 422pp. $7.95. A comprehensive study of popular opinions on television and how these opinions are related to viewing habits. The report is based on a study made at the Bureau of Applied Social Research at Columbia University.

STROUD, JEAN
Special Correspondent
Ward Lock, 1969. 160pp. $5.95. This is a history of news reporting on English television. Miss Stroud details the behind-the-scenes stories of the historic missions undertaken by broadcasters and commentators. Illustrated with photographs. Index.

SUMMERS, ROBERT E. and HARRISON B. SUMMERS
Broadcasting and the Public
Wadsworth, 1966. 402pp. $8.95. An introduction to radio and television that offers a detailed description of our system of broadcasting, American audiences, and the government. There is a brief history of American broadcasting, comparisons of the American and European broadcasting systems, and an evaluation of criticisms leveled at the industry. Illustrated. Index.

SWALLOW, NORMAN
Factual Television

Hastings House, 1966. 228pp. An examination of the role of television in politics, public affairs, education, and the arts. The social and political policies that modify or temper the presentation of news and controversy in a democracy, and the advantages and defects of news reported by television are also studied. Index.

THOMPSON, DENYS – Editor
Discrimination and Popular Culture
See Page 507

TORME, MEL
The Other Side of the Rainbow
See Page 475

WHALE, JOHN
The Half-Shut Eye: Television and Politics in Britain and America
St. Martin, 1969. 219pp. $6.95. Mr. Whale offers a theory and history of the relationship between television and politics. The author draws freely on his experiences as political correspondent of British Independent Television News, in the elections of 1966 and 1968. Notes. Index.

WHITE, DAVID MANNING and RICHARD AVERSON
Sight, Sound, and Society: Motion Pictures and Television in America
See Page 507

WHITEFIELD, STEPHEN E. and GENE RODDENBERRY
The Making of "Star Trek"
Ballantine, 1968. 414pp. Paper $ .95. This is a "biography" of the adult science-fiction television program with the story of how its rocket ships, weaponry, and equipment were designed, the original concept behind the show, background of the characters, and biographies of the stars. Illustrated.

WHITEHOUSE, MARY
Cleaning Up TV: From Protest to Participation
Blandford, 1967. 240pp. Paper $1.45. Mrs. Whitehouse is the co-founder of the "Clean Up TV" campaign in England. This campaign was a protest of the flagrant disregard of good taste and decency alleged to have been shown by the BBC in some of its programming. The author outlines some of the ways she believes television could be used constructively. Index.

WORSLEY, T.C.
Television: The Ephemeral Art
Alan Ross, 1970. 255pp. $9.00. A collection of articles on television which were originally printed in England in "The Financial Review." Full-length reviews of plays by Harold Pinter, David Mercer, John Hopkins, and other television playwrights are included as are essays on documentary television, adaptations of classical plays and other literature, and policy problems of television. Index.

ZWERDLING, SHIRLEY – Editor
Film and TV Festival Directory
See Page 443

TECHNIQUES OF PRODUCTION

General Reference Works

AARONSON, CHARLES S. – Editor
International Television Almanac – 1970
Quigley, 1970. 792pp. $15.00. This is the fifteenth annual edition of the almanac, appearing for the first time as a separate volume after years as part of the "International Motion Picture and Television Almanac." Contents include biographies of television personalities, statistics on stations, services, agencies, representatives, and programs. The industry in Great Britain, Ireland, and Canada is also surveyed. Indexes.

BADDELEY, W. HUGH
The Technique of Documentary Film Production
See Page 460

BRETZ, RUDY
Techniques of Television Production
McGraw–Hill, 1962. 474pp. $14.95. Designed to bridge the gap between the creative production man and the technically minded engineer, this book concentrates on the principles underlying television equipment and techniques. This is the second edition of the volume first published in 1953. Illustrated.

COLEMAN, HOWARD W.
Case Studies in Broadcast Management
Hastings House, 1970. 95pp. $4.95. Paper $4.50. The author offers detailed exploration of broadcast areas in which problems are serious and the solutions require long-range planning. Among the problems covered are finding and enlarging the audience, station revenue, programming, sales and promotion policies, and station management. List of Suggested Readings.

COOMBS, CHARLES I.
Window on the World: The Story of Television Production
World, 1965. 125pp. $4.50. A behind-the-scenes look at the technical end of a television production from commercials to live drama. Written for children in grades four to nine, the author discusses the latest developments. Illustrated. Index.

COSTELLO, LAWRENCE and GEORGE N. GORDON
Teach with Television: A Guide to Instructional TV
Hastings House, 1965. 192pp. $5.95. Paper $4.45. This is the second edition of the manual which shows how to produce and use instructional television most effectively on all educational levels.

DAVIS, DESMOND
The Grammar of Television Production
Barrie & Jenkins, 1966. 80pp. $3.50. John Elliot has revised this textbook on television production and this edition reflects the changes that have taken place in approach and technique since the book's first publication in 1960. New material has been added and the whole text brought up-to-date. A set of rules and suggestions for editing, lenses, composition, camera work, use of studio equipment, recording and filming are given. Drawings by Michael Knight, Vic Symonds, and Frank White.

DIAMANT, LINCOLN – Editor
The Anatomy of a Television Commercial
Hastings House, 1970. 191pp. $12.50. An account of the process of constructing a television commercial. Eastman Kodak's two minute film, "Yesterdays," is examined and the making is recounted by major participants. They explain each phase of the development from market planning through distribution. Included are the copywriter's original draft idea and the as-aired final script. Photographs from each of the commercial's forty-two scenes are provided. Glossary. Index.

GERTNER, RICHARD – Editor
International Television Almanac: 1971
Quigley, 1970. 746pp. $15.00. The latest edition of the reference book dealing with the business of television. Statistics, who's who, producers, corporations, services, and program notes are provided. Indices.

GIBSON, TONY
The Practice of ETV
Hutchinson, 1970. 189pp. Paper $6.50. Published in England, this is a book for all those who are becoming involved in the administration, production, use, and evaluation of education television, particularly in its closed circuit application. Illustrated with photographs, drawings, and diagrams. Appendices. Glossary. Index.

GOLD, MAGGE – Editor
Madison Avenue – Europe
See Page 463

GOLD, MAGGE – Editor
Madison Avenue – London
Peter Glenn, 1970. 64 + pp. Spiral bound $2.00. A listing of information and addresses for London firms in the advertising, film, fashion, and photography services.

GOLD, MAGGE – Editor
Madison Avenue – Paris
Peter Glenn, 1970. 64 + pp. Spiral bound $2.00. Information on service firms in Paris in the fields of advertising, film, fashion, and photographs as excerpted from the "Madison Avenue – Europe" guide.

GOLD, MAGGE – Editor
Madison Avenue – West Germany
Peter Glenn, 1970. 64 + pp. Spiral bound $2.00. Information on service firms in West Germany in the fields of advertising, film, fashion, and photography as excerpted from the "Madison Avenue – Europe" guide.

GOULD, JACK
All About Radio and Television
Random House, 1958. 144pp. $2.95. Written for children in grades four to six, this is a simplified illustrated account of how the radio and television media work.

HALAS, JOHN and WALTER HERDEG
Film and TV Graphics
See Page 461

HERMAN, LEWIS
Educational Films: Writing, Directing, and Producing for Classroom, Television and Industry
Crown, 1965. 338pp. $5.95. Written for grades nine and up, this manual covers all technical aspects of film-making. The author analyzes the separate responsibilities of each member of the creative team, discusses types of film organization and development, and examines such special problems as audience participation, narrative writing, recreation of history, and the use of suspense. Index.

INDEPENDENT TELEVISION AUTHORITY
ITV 1969: A Guide to Independent Television
I.T.A., 1969. 236pp. Paper $2.25. A guide to the Independent Television System in England. It describes the system, its program policy and control, its audience, its programs, method of advertising control, staff and organization, technical operations, and code of advertising standards and practice. Illustrated with photographs. Bibliography. Index.

JONES, PETER
The Technique of the Television Cameraman
Hastings House, 1965. 243pp. $10.00. This first comprehensive study in the field deals in non-technical terms with studio equipment and camera, with composition and movement, the essentials of good camera technique, lighting, and special problems of outside or remote broadcasts. Illustrated. Index.

KINGSON, WALTER K. and ROME COWGILL
Television Acting and Directing: A Handbook
Holt, Rinehart, 1965. 298pp. Paper $11.50. This book provides instructions in the fundamentals of production, acting and directing, in addition to a series of scripts designed to lead from basic skills to advanced techniques of acting and directing. The last section consists of specific production aids: forms, marked scripts, title cards, set designs, and studio hand signals. Glossary. Index.

LEVITAN, ELI L.
An Alphabetical Guide to Motion Picture, Television, and Videotape Production
See Page 462

LEWIS, COLBY
The TV Director/Interpreter
Hastings House, 1968. 255pp. $8.95. Paper $7.25. A guide to help television directors translate the meaning of their programs through the media of cameras and microphones. Step-by-step diagrammatic illustrations clarify the text. The author covers: planning picture statements, visual clarity, preserving form, keeping up with the action, concealing mechanics, spatial relationships, visual transitions, director as interpreter, from script to camera plan, making floor plans, calling the shots, selecting lenses. Index.

MILLERSON, GERALD
The Technique of Television Production
Hastings House, 1968. 440pp. $13.50. Paper $9.50. Originally published in 1961 and now revised and updated throughout, this is an encyclopedic textbook on the basics of television production. Illustrated with diagrams and drawings. Bibliography. Index.

NISBETT, ALEC
The Technique of the Sound Studio
See Page 466

NOBLE, PETER – Editor
The British Film and Television Year Book
See Page 446

PITTARO, ERNEST M.
TV and Film Production Data Book
See Page 462

QUAAL, WARD L. and LEO A. MARTIN
Broadcast Management: Radio and Television
Hastings House, 1968. 251pp. $8.95. Paper $7.50. This is an exploration of all the management aspects of American radio and television broadcasting. Set in historical perspective, some of the problems analyzed are: audience, programming, engineering and technical factors, sales and profit management, governmental regulations, and professional involvements. Index.

ROBERTS, FREDERICK
Radio and Television
Studio Vista, 1965. 80pp. $2.50. Written for children, and published in England, this book explains how a radio studio is organized, tells how to set up a simple one, gives suggestions for script writing and production, and helps readers to understand the techniques of television production. Illustrated with line drawings by the author.

ROSS, RODGER J.
Color Film for Color Television
Hastings House, 1970. 165pp. $10.00. The author describes a unified film-television system for producing high quality color television with film. After a concise introduction to the principles of color television, the author describes the currently available color films and processes in detail. Illustrated with diagrams. Index.

STASHEFF, EDWARD and RUDY BRETZ
The Television Program: Its Direction and Production
Hill & Wang, 1968. 336pp. Paper $2.95. Originally published in 1951 and now completely revised, this is a complete guide to television production. The author includes discussions of program format, types of shots and lenses, technical terms, composition, lighting, and special effects. Appendices cover camera set-ups for a variety of shows with excerpts from actual scripts. Illustrated. Index.

SPOTTISWOODE, RAYMOND – General Editor
The Focal Encyclopedia of Film and Television Techniques
See Page 463

TAYLOR, CECIL P.
Making a TV Play
Oriel Press, 1970. 95pp. $8.50. A complete guide from conception to production of the play "Charles and Cromwell" seen on BBC Television in England. Apart from the technical and creative problems involved in writing a television play, the author records the processes involved in selling a play from the submission of the first outline to the acceptance of the final script. Excerpts from a sample "camera script" are included. Illustrated with photographs and drawings.

TRIANDOS, PAT and CHUCK RUTHERFORD – Editors
Madison Avenue West
Peter Glenn, 1970. Unpaged. Paper $5.95. A directory covering the visual communications services in Los Angeles. Listings include advertising agencies, television and film producers and their suppliers, photographers, models and actors, talent agencies, prop sources, and listings of hotels, restaurants, and transportation services.

ZETTL, HERBERT
Television Production Handbook
Wadsworth, 1969. 541pp. $12.65. Originally published in 1961 and now reissued in a second revised edition, this is a handbook with a comprehensive discussion of the many elements of television production – lighting, scene design, graphics, special effects, video tape, film, and creative camera work. The latest equipment is described and illustrated and there are separate chapters on cameras and lenses. Contains over 300 illustrations. Glossary. List of books for further reading. Index.

ZETTL, HERBERT
Television Production Workbook
Wadsworth, 1968. 208pp. Paper $6.00. Originally published in 1965, this handbook sets out to test systematically the student's factual knowledge of production details, such as his familiarity with television equipment and terminology. The author suggests ways in which this material can be applied in a creative way. Most of the exercises can be completed without the use of television equipment. Illustrated with drawings.

Script Writing

ASHLEY, PAUL P.
Say It Safely: Legal Limits in Publishing, Radio, and Television
University of Washington, 1969. 181pp. $5.00. This is the fourth and revised edition of the study first published in 1956. This is a manual on the libel laws, the copyright laws, and the American right of privacy. The development of the rule of the New York Times case of 1964 is brought up-to-date, and a new chapter on "Copyrights and Literary Property" is included. This chapter discusses the background of the copyright law, the kinds of material that can be copyrighted, and the various kinds of infringements. Index.

BARNOUW, ERIK
The Television Writer
Hill & Wang, 1962. 180pp. $3.95. A detailed examination of the technical problems of the writer in this field, with suggestions on how the writer can play a role in shaping and reforming the industry.

BURACK, A.S. – Editor
The Writer's Handbook
See Page 361

BURACK, A.S. – Editor
Writing and Selling Fillers and Short Humor
The Writer, 1959. 144pp. $3.95. Eight articles on how to write and sell a variety of short and humorous pieces. The professional writers contributing to the volume include: Richard Armour, Parke Cummings, and Mart T. Steyn. A list of 300 available markets is provided.

DUNBAR, JANET
Script-Writing for Television
Museum Press, 1965. 125pp. $3.75. Published in London, this book is intended as a guide for people who desire to write for television and for those already experienced in other media but who are not knowledgeable about requirements for television. Index.

HARRAL, STEWART
The Feature Writer's Handbook
See Page 505

HERMAN, LEWIS
A Practical Manual of Screen Playwriting for Theatre and Television Films
See Page 466

HILLIARD, ROBERT L.
Writing for Television and Radio
Hastings House, 1967. 320pp. $7.95. This new edition of the 1962 text on writing for the mass media has been updated. The author concentrates on the practical elements of preparation for a writing job in television and radio. The various types of programs are analyzed in separate chapters, and an extensive chapter is devoted to the television and radio play. Excerpts from sample scripts are included. Index.

PARKER, NORTON S.
Audiovisual Script Writing
See Page 466

ROBERTS, EDWARD BARRY
Television Writing and Selling
The Writer, 1967. 504pp. $8.95. Originally published in 1954 and now revised, this is a complete guide to the process of writing for television from writer's conception through actual production. Sample scripts, with scene-by-scene analysis, are given. Television terms are defined and explained and the Television Code is quoted. Sixteen pages of illustrations are included.

ROSS, WALLACE A. – Editor
Best TV and Radio Commercials
Hastings House, 1968. 191pp. $16.50. This is a collection of analyses of the 1967 CLIO award winners of television and radio commercials. Television and cinema winners include storyboards and analyses. Radio winners include scripts and analyses and there is a recording of these winners. Illustrated with color and black-and-white photographs.

SWINSON, ARTHUR
Writing for Television Today
A. & C. Black, 1963. 262pp. $6.50. An exposition of the basic requirements of every type of television writing, with chapters on television's affinities to radio, film, and stage writing, the studio and its equipment, lay-out of scripts, background and documentary scripts, the drama on television, children's programs, and light entertainment. Glossary of British television terms. Illustrated. Index.

TRAPNELL, COLES
Teleplay: An Introduction to Television Writing
Chandler, 1966. 245pp. Paper $5.00. The theory and practice of writing for television from the mechanics of creation to the final script are included in this volume. The author includes a complete script by James E. Moser, "Question: What Is Truth," which was the pilot teleplay for the television series, "Slattery's People."

WAINWRIGHT, CHARLES ANTHONY
Television Commercials: How to Create Successful TV Advertising
Hastings House, 1970. 318pp. $8.95. Paper $7.50. Originally published in 1965 as "The Television Copywriter" and now reissued under the new title, this is an examination of the television commercial from idea to finished film. Information on casting, use of sets, studio procedures, costs, background music, video-tape, and use of jingles is included. Lists of production studios and agencies. Appendices. Index.

WILLIS, EDGAR E.
Writing Television and Radio Programs
Holt, Rinehart, 1967. 372pp. $8.95. Professor Willis provides practical step-by-step instruction for the aspiring writer on all major forms of dramatic and non-dramatic television and radio scripts. He explains the theory and technique of successful scripts and offers detailed guidance in building effective plots, developing and revealing character, constructing dialogue, capturing and maintaining interest, and arousing suspense. Excerpts from finished scripts are analyzed. Two chapters deal with commercials and with comedy. Bibliography. Index.

WYLIE, MAX
Writing for Television
Cowles, 1970. 456pp. $9.95. A complete guide to the techniques of writing for television. Examples and analyses of representative scripts from successful shows—soaps, serials, and packages—are included. Among these scripts are samples from "The Flying Nun," "Get Smart," "Twilight Zone," "Love of Life," and "Gomer Pyle." A series of Appendices include articles by various critics. Index.

Acting and Career Opportunities

BENDER, JAMES F. – Editor
NBC Handbook of Pronunciation
T. Y. Crowell, 1964. 418pp. $6.95. This handbook, originally published in 1943, has been revised and updated by Thomas Lee Crowell, Jr. The work has been expanded to more than 20,000 entries with a special supplement of "Names in the News," and a separate listing of hundreds of contemporary public figures whose names are not easy to pronounce. Each entry is given three ways: first the correct spelling, then respelled phonetically, then in the International Phonetic Alphabet symbols.

BRANDENBERGER, BARBARA
Working in Television
Bodley Head, 1965. 176pp. $4.50. Published in England, this is a study of the scope and nature of the various positions available in television media in England and the methods of entering the field.

GORDON, GEORGE N. and IRVING A. FALK
Your Career in TV and Radio
Messner, 1966. 221pp. $3.95. Written by experts in the field, this book explores the entire broadcast industry. It stresses the qualifications, education, background, skills, and personality needed for a successful career in TV or radio. For every occupation: director, playwright, researcher, announcer, engineer, and others, the authors take the reader backstage and reveal both the duties performed and the working atmosphere of each job. Illustrated with photographs. Index.

HENNEKE, BEN GRAF and EDWARD S. DUMIT
The Announcer's Handbook
Holt, Rinehart, 1959. 293pp. Paper $7.95. An analysis of the announcer's work with drill material in all kinds of announcing. The drills are taken from actual commercial continuity. The authors have included special sections on the pronunciation of foreign words and phrases and the phonetic alphabet is included. Bibliography.

KINGSON, WALTER K. and ROME COWGILL
Television Acting and Directing: A Handbook
See Page 493

LERCH, JOHN H. – Editor
Careers in Broadcasting
Appleton, 1962. 113pp. $3.95. Essays on how to make a career in the television and radio media. Contributions are included by Robert Sarnoff, Curt Gowdy, Steve Allen, Hugh Downs, Pat Boone, and others. The volume has been written for grades nine through twelve and is illustrated.

LEWIS, BRUCE
The Technique of Television Announcing
Hastings House, 1966. 264pp. $10.00. A complete manual for all who appear or aspire to appear "on camera." Illustrated. Index.

SOLOTAIRE, ROBERT SPENCER
How to Get Into Television
Sheridan House, 1957. 189pp. $5.00. A guide to careers in television: advertising, management, writing, and acting. Detailed information is provided on what the various jobs require in the way of training.

BIOGRAPHIES OF TELEVISION PERSONALITIES

ALLEN, STEVE
The Funny Men
Simon & Schuster, 1956. 280pp. $3.95. The comedian analyzes sixteen television comedians and discusses their styles.

BANNISTER, HARRY
The Education of a Broadcaster
Simon & Schuster, 1965. 352pp. $5.95. A nostalgic

recreation of the beginnings of commercial broadcasting, both radio and television, written by a pioneer broadcaster.

BRAUN, BOB
Here's Bob
Doubleday, 1969. 191pp. $5.95. The host of a popular television show in the Midwest, The Fifty-Fifty Club, describes the high points of his twenty year career in radio and television. Illustrated with photographs.

CAHN, WILLIAM
A Pictorial History of the Great Comedians
See Page 261

DIXON, PAUL
Paul Baby
World, 1968. 250pp. $4.95. Mr. Dixon is the star of a morning television show which is seen throughout the Midwest. He writes of the early days of radio and of the hectic days in early television, as well as of his present television show. Introduction by Bob Hope. Illustrated with photographs.

EPHRON, NORA
And Now ... Here's Johnny!
Avon, 1968. 220pp. Paper $ .75. A biography of television personality, Johnny Carson, master-of-ceremonies of the "Tonight" show. Illustrated with photographs.

FRIENDLY, FRED W.
Due to Circumstances Beyond Our Control ...
Random House, 1967. 325pp. $8.95. Paper—Vintage, 1968. 339pp. $1.95. A memoir of Mr. Friendly's sixteen years at C. B. S. He evaluates current programming, analyzes network profits, and condemns the failure of the F. C. C. to police the industry.

FULTON, EILEEN and BRETT BOLTON
How My World Turns
Taplinger, 1970. 208pp. $5.95. The autobiography of the heroine of "As the World Turns," the popular television daytime program. A forty-eight page album of photographs is included.

GRAHAM, VIRGINIA and JEAN LIBMAN BLOCK
There Goes What's Her Name
Prentice—Hall, 1965. 246pp. $4.95. Paper—Avon, 1966. 224pp. $ .75. The television mistress-of-ceremonies talks about her life. There is special attention given to her "Girl Talk" television show. Illustrated.

GREGORY, DICK with ROBERT LIPSYTE
Nigger
See Page 269

HARRIS, MICHAEL DAVID
Always on Sunday — Ed Sullivan: An Inside View
Meredith, 1968. 215pp. $4.95. Paper—Signet, 1969. 280pp. $ .95. Mr. Harris follows the career of Ed Sullivan from his boyhood through his long years as a television showman. Illustrated with photographs.

HUNTLEY, CHET
The Generous Years
Fawcett, 1970. 160pp. Paper $ .75. Originally published in 1968 and now reissued, these are the reminiscences of the television commentator's boyhood on a Montana ranch.

KENDRICK, ALEXANDER
Prime Time
Little, Brown, 1969. 548pp. $8.95. Paper—Avon, 1970. 608pp. $1.65. A biography of Edward R. Murrow. The author tells of Murrow's profound belief in the educative function of the television medium, his controversial programs about Senator Joe McCarthy, his struggles with sponsors, networks, and the Establishment. The wartime radio broadcasts from Europe, England, Africa, and Korea are all detailed. Illustrated. Bibliography. Index.

LISTER, MOIRA
The Very Merry Moira
See Page 272

LYONS, EUGENE
David Sarnoff
Pyramid, 1967. 431pp. Paper $ .95. Originally published in 1966 and now reissued, this is the story of the president of R. C. A. and his pioneering work in electronics and communications. Illustrated. Index.

MYERS, HORTENSE and RUTH BURNETT
Edward R. Murrow: Young Newscaster
Bobbs—Merrill, 1969. 200pp. $2.50. Written for children, this is a biography of the newscaster and commentator. The authors concentrate on his boyhood and early life but the later years are also covered. Illustrated with drawings.

ROLLINS, CHARLEMAE
Famous Negro Entertainers of Stage, Screen and TV
See Page 262

TELEVISION SCRIPTS

CAPOTE, TRUMAN and ELEANOR PERRY, FRANK PERRY
Trilogy
Macmillan, 1969. 276pp. $6.95. This volume includes the original Capote stories and the television adaptations of those stories. Film credits, notes on adaptations, and reminiscenes by Perry and Capote are also included. Illustrated with photographs.

A Christmas Memory
Miriam
Among the Paths to Eden

GRAY, SIMON
Sleeping Dog
Faber & Faber, 1968. 73pp. $3.50. This story of the bizarre delusions of a retired colonial administrator and their hideous consequences was seen on B. B. C. television in 1967. Mr. Gray is the author of the controversial stage play, "Wise Child."

JUPP, KENNETH
A Chelsea Trilogy
Calder & Boyars, 1969. 176pp. $5.95. Paper $2.95. Three television plays by the English playwright. All of the plays have been produced on English television and some of the actors who have appeared in them include Susannah York, Honor Blackman, Robert Stephens, Ian Hendry, Derek Jacobi, and Michael Bryant. Illustrated with photographs from the productions.

Photographer
Explorer
Tycoon

KAUFMAN, WILLIAM I.
Great Television Plays
Dell, 1969. 301pp. Paper $ .75. Six television plays selected by Mr. Kaufman with an Introduction by Ned E. Hoopes.

Twelve Angry Men: Reginald Rose
The Big Deal: Paddy Chayefsky
The Final War of Olly Winter: Ronald Ribman
Requiem for a Heavyweight: Rod Serling
Lee at Gettysburg: Alvin Sapinsley
The Lottery: Ellen Violett

MERCER, DAVID
On the Eve of Publication and Other Plays
Methuen, 1970. 131pp. Paper $1.95. Three television plays originally presented on English television. The plays all relate to different aspects of the same character, a left-wing novelist and Nobel prize-winner.

On the Eve of Publication
The Cellar and the Almond Tree
Emma's Time

MERCER, DAVID
The Parachute with Two More TV Plays
Calder & Boyars, 1967. 156pp. $5.95. Paper $2.95. Three television plays by the English playwright, author of "Morgan—A Suitable Case for Treatment."

The Parachute
Let's Murder Vivaldi
In Two Minds

MERCER, DAVID
Three Television Comedies
Calder & Boyars, 1966. 140pp. $5.00. Paper $2.95. Published in England, this is a collection of three plays by the popular English playwright. "A Suitable Case for Treatment" was a prize-winning film under the title of "Morgan."

A Suitable Case for Treatment
For Tea on Sunday
And Did Those Feet

MORTIMER, JOHN
Five Plays
Methuen, 1970. 201pp. $5.50. Paper $2.50. All five of these plays have been presented on the stage or on television in England.

The Dock Brief
Collect Your Hand Baggage
What Shall We Tell Caroline?
I Spy
Lunch Hour

ORTON, JOE
Funeral Games and The Good and Faithful Servant
Methuen, 1970. 90pp. $4.50. Paper $1.95. Two television plays, originally shown in England in 1967 and 1968, by the author of "Entertaining Mr. Sloane." "Funeral Games" deals with bogus religion, a severed hand, and a corpse in the cellar. "The Good and Faithful Servant" is a study of the disintegration of an old man when he retires after fifty sterile years in the sevice of a factory.

VIDAL, GORE—Editor
Best Television Plays
Ballantine, 1956. 250pp. Paper $ .95. A collection of eight plays presented on television over the years.

The Mother: Paddy Chayefsky
My Lost Saints: Tad Mosel
Man on a Mountain: R. A. Aurthur
The Rabbit Trap: J. P. Miller
The Strike: Rod Serling
Thunder on Sycamore Street: Reginald Rose
Visit to a Small Planet: Gore Vidal
A Young Lady of Property: Horton Foote

RADIO

HISTORIES AND CRITIQUES

BARNOUW, ERIK
The Golden Web
Oxford, 1968. 391pp. $10.75. The second volume in Mr. Barnouw's "History of Broadcasting in the United States." The author evokes the era, from 1933 to 1953, during which radio touched almost every American's life; he describes the growth of news broadcasting and the behind-the-scenes struggles for power between the giants of the radio world, the stranglehold of the advertising agencies on radio programming, and the purges of the early 1950's. Illustrated. Chronology. Bibliography. Index.

BARNOUW, ERIK
The Image Empire
See Page 486

BARNOUW, ERIK
Mass Communication
See Page 505

BARNOUW, ERIK
A Tower in Babel
Oxford, 1966. 344pp. $10.75. Volume One in Mr. Barnouw's "History of Broadcasting in the United States." This first of three volumes begins with Marconi's work in wireless telegraphy and carries the story through 1933 and the rise of the media both as a business and an entertainment industry. Illustrated. Bibliography. Index.

BARRETT, MARVIN – Editor
Survey of Broadcast Journalism: 1968 – 1969
See Page 486

BARRETT, MARVIN – Editor
Survey of Broadcast Journalism: 1969 – 1970
Grosset & Dunlap, 1970. 156pp. Paper $1.95. Subtitled "Year of Challenge, Year of Crisis," this is a report on how radio and television covered the news events of the year. The controversy surrounding the attacks on broadcasting by Vice President Agnew is also discussed. Index.

BRIGGS, ASA
The History of Broadcasting in the United Kingdom
Volume I: The Birth of Broadcasting
Oxford, 1961. 425pp. $10.50. This first volume in a projected three or four volume history covers early amateur experiments in America and the United Kingdom, the pioneer days at Writtle in Essex and elsewhere, the coming of organized broadcasting, the first four years of the B. B. C., and the conversion of the private company into a public corporation in 1927. Emphasis is placed on the forging of the instruments of public control in the early period. Illustrated. Bibliographical Note. Appendices. Index.

BRIGGS, ASA
The History of Broadcasting in the United Kingdom
Volume 2: The Golden Age of Wireless
Oxford, 1965. 688pp. $16.00. This volume covers the period from the beginning of 1927 when the B. B. C. ceased to be a private company and became a public corporation, up to the outbreak of war in 1939. Chapters deal with the programs and program-makers, the listeners and the way their needs were met or not met, public attitudes to the B. B. C., the coming of television, and the preparations for war. Illustrated. Index.

CARROLL, CARROLL
None of Your Business
Cowles, 1970. 288pp. $6.95. Recollections of an advertising agency writer who tells how radio programs were conceived, promoted, and produced at the J. Walter Thompson Agency. Illustrated with photographs. Index.

CHESTER, EDWARD W.
Radio, Television, and American Politics
See Page 487

COONS, JOHN E.
Freedom and Responsibility in Broadcasting
See Page 487

FAULK, JOHN HENRY
Fear on Trial
See Page 488

HARMON, JIM
The Great Radio Comedians
Doubleday, 1970. 195pp. $6.95. Memories and reminiscences of the comedians who appeared on radio. Material is taken from hundreds of actual scripts from the broadcasts of Amos and Andy, Fred Allen, Edgar Bergen, Burns and Allen, Eddie Cantor, and many others. Some of the unconscious humor of the more serious programs is also related. A short recording of W. C. Fields and Burns and Allen is included. Illustrated with photographs. Index.

HARMON, JIM
The Great Radio Heroes
Doubleday, 1967. 263pp. $4.95. Paper – Ace, 1970. 253pp. $ .75. A nostalgic re-creation, including actual scripts, of the radio programs and characters in those programs from the 1930's, 1940's, and 1950's. The authors, actors, and sponsors are discussed in the anecdotes and included in the data.

HEATH, R. B.
Radio and Television
See Page 489

HILDICK, E.W.
A Close Look at Television and Sound Broadcasting
See Page 489

KAHN, FRANK J. – Editor
Documents of American Broadcasting
See Page 489

KLAPPER, JOSEPH T.
The Effects of Mass Communication
See Page 505

KOCH, HOWARD
The Panic Broadcast
Little, Brown, 1970. 163pp. $4.95. The author re-creates the events of the evening when Orson Welles broadcast his radio program, "The War of the Worlds." Thirty-three pages of contemporary photographs, cartoons, and newspaper articles depict the event and its aftermath. Also included is a full script of the program.

LACKMANN, RON
Remember Radio
Putnam, 1970. 128pp. $6.95. A collection of photographs, reminiscences, and short excerpts from the actual scripts of the radio programs of the 1930's, 1940's, and the early 1950's. The author covers the full range of heroes, heroines, and shows from The A & P Gypsies to Young Dr. Malone. Index.

MURROW, EDWARD R.
In Search of Light: The Broadcasts of Edward R. Murrow
See Page 490

PAULU, BURTON
British Broadcasting in Transition
See Page 490

PAULU, BURTON
British Broadcasting: Radio and Television in the United Kingdom
See Page 490

SCHRAMM, WILBUR – Editor
Mass Communications
See Page 506

SETTEL, IRVING
A Pictorial History of Radio
Grosset & Dunlap, 1967. 192pp. $6.95. The hundreds of personalities and programs that make up the history of radio's glamourous fifty years are all pictured in this book. There are hundreds of photographs to illustrate the volume. Index.

SKORNIA, HARRY J. and JACK WILLIAM KITSON – Editors
Problems and Controversies in Television and Radio
See Page 491

SUMMERS, ROBERT E. and HARRISON B. SUMMERS
Broadcasting and the Public
See Page 491

TECHNIQUES OF PRODUCTION

General Reference Works

GOULD, JACK
All About Radio and Television
See Page 496

HILLIARD, ROBERT L.
Radio Broadcasting
Hastings House, 1967. 190pp. $6.95. Paper $5.50. This is an introduction to the principles and techniques of modern radio broadcasting. Experts in their fields discuss management and programming, operating and studio facilities, producing and directing, writing, and performing. Illustrated. Bibliography. Index.

MILTON, RALPH
Radio Programming: A Basic Training Manual
Geoffrey Bles, 1968. 384pp. $6.50. This manual of the basic principles of responsible radio programming has been designed for students in Asia, Africa, the Middle East, and Latin America who cannot take part in the programs the World Association of Christian Broadcasting sponsors in Britain to teach these students. All phases of programming are covered. Appendices include a Glossary, a Selected Bibliography, and a section on sound effects. Illustrated.

QUAAL, WARD L. and LEO A. MARTIN
Broadcast Management: Radio and Television
See Page 494

ROBERTS, FREDERICK
Radio and Television
See Page 494

TAYLOR, LOREN E.
Radio Drama
Burgess, 1965. 100pp. Paper $2.50. The author explains all phases of radio and includes two sample scripts.

Script Writing

ASHLEY, PAUL P.
Say It Safely: Legal Limits in Publishing, Radio, and Television
See Page 495

HARRAL, STEWART
The Feature Writer's Handbook
See Page 505

HILLIARD, ROBERT L.
Writing for Television and Radio
See Page 495

ROSS, WALLACE A. – Editor
Best TV and Radio Commercials
See Page 495

WILLIS, EDGAR E.
Writing Television and Radio Programs
See Page 496

Sound Recording and Audio Techniques

CROWHURST, NORMAN H.
ABC's of Tape Recording
Bobbs–Merrill, 1971. 94pp. Paper $2.95. A revised edition of the 1961 guidebook which explains how tape recorders work, which type to buy, and gives suggestions for using the machine. Glossary.

DOLAN, ROBERT EMMET
Music in Modern Media
See Page 468

HELLYER, H.W.
How to Choose and Use Tape Recorders
Fountain Press, 1970. 239pp. $8.95. The author tells a prospective purchaser what to look for in the way of functions, facilities, types, variations and specifications of tape recorders. Separate chapters deal with heads, the tape deck, tracks and speeds, microphones, special applications, cleaning, splicing, frequency correction, how to service the deck, and tests and measurements. Illustrated with diagrams and photographs. Index.

NISBETT, ALEC
The Technique of the Sound Studio
See Page 466

ORINGEL, ROBERT S.
Audio Control Handbook for Radio and TV Broadcasting
Hastings House, 1968. 154pp. $7.95. Originally published in 1956 and now revised and enlarged in this third edition, this text gives complete step-by-step directions and full explanations of every phase of audio control—covering problems encountered in all types of broadcasting. The book's many diagrams and photographs supplement the text and clarify points that might be obscure. Review Questions accompany each chapter. Glossary of Broadcasting Terminology. Index.

VILLCHUR, EDGAR
Reproduction of Sound
Dover, 1965. 92pp. Paper $1.25. The author attempts to give the reader an understanding of the nature of sound and of how the different parts of a reproduction system work. After discussions of sound in general, he devotes individual chapters to the component parts of a sound system. Illustrated with drawings and diagrams. Index.

WOOD, D. NEVILLE
On Tape: The Creative Use of the Tape Recorder
See Page 333

Acting

BENDER, JAMES F. – Editor
NBC Handbook of Pronunciation
Page

GORDON, GEORGE N. and IRVING A. FALK
Your Career in TV and Radio
See Page 496

HENNEKE, BEN GRAF and EDWARD S. DUMIT
The Announcer's Handbook
See Page 496

LERCH, JOHN H. – Editor
Careers in Broadcasting
See Page 496

PATE, MICHAEL
The Film Actor
See Page 468

BIOGRAPHIES OF RADIO PERSONALITIES

BANNISTER, HARRY
The Education of a Broadcaster
See Page 496

FRIENDLY, FRED W.
Due to Circumstances Beyond Our Control ...
See Page 497

HIGBY, MARY JANE
Tune In Tomorrow
Ace, 1970. 226pp. Paper $ .95. Originally published in 1968, this is the autobiography of Miss Higby who has appeared on most of the popular "soap-operas" from the mid-1930's to today. It is also the behind-the-scenes story of the era of the soap-opera and all facets of the radio industry. Illustrated with photographs. Bibliography.

KENDRICK, ALEXANDER
Prime Time
See Page 497

LYONS, EUGENE
David Sarnoff
See Page 497

McCARTHY, JOE – Editor
Fred Allen's Letters
Pocket Books, 1966. 259pp. Paper $ .75. Originally published in 1965 and now reissued, this is a collection of letters by the radio comedian. The letters are grouped under subject headings such as The Early Days, Old Friends, Show Biz People, Youngsters, and The Last Years. The editor has provided an Introduction.

MYERS, HORTENSE and RUTH BURNETT
Edward R. Murrow: Young Newscaster
See Page 497

ROLLINS, CHARLEMAE
Famous Negro Entertainers of Stage, Screen and TV
See Page 262

WARREN, TONY
I Was Ena Sharples Father
Duckworth, 1969. 128pp. $5.95. This is a record of the longest-lasting television serial in the history of English television. The author of ''Coronation Street'' details the history of the program from his own diaries, from viewers' letters, and from photographs. Illustrated with photographs.

RADIO SCRIPTS

ACE, GOODMAN
Ladies and Gentlemen – Easy Aces
Doubleday, 1970. 211pp. $5.95. Eight scripts of the classic radio dialogues of Jane and Goodman Ace: radio's ''Easy Aces'' from 1931 to 1949. The book also contains a recording of one of the radio programs.

CANTRIL, HADLEY
The Invasion from Mars
Harper & Row, 1966. 224pp. Paper $2.75. Subtitled ''A study in the psychology of panic,'' this is an account of the aftermath of the broadcast of Orson Welles' ''The War of the Worlds'' in 1938. It is a study of collective behavior and mass communications. The complete script of the radio broadcast is included.

EICH, GUNTER
Journeys
J. Cape, 1968. 111pp. Paper $1.50. This volume contains two radio plays by the contemporary German poet. They have been translated by Michael Hamburger.

- The Rolling Sea at Setubal
- The Year Lacertis

KOCH, HOWARD
The Panic Broadcast
See Page 500

LANG, HAROLD and KENNETH TYNAN
The Quest for Corbett
Gaberbocchus Press, 1960. 111pp. Paper $3.95. Originally broadcast on B.B.C. radio in 1956, this is a parody of British and American advertising, theatre, literature, and cinema of the last thirty years. Illustrated.

LIND, JAKOV
''The Silver Foxes Are Dead'' and Other Plays
Hill & Wang, 1968. 95pp. $3.95. Paper $1.75. These four short plays were originally written for radio. Mr. Lind writes about obsessive insanity to make the madness in modern society clear.

- The Silver Foxes Are Dead
- Anna Laub
- Hunger
- Fear

MacNEICE, LOUIS
Persons from Porlock
B. B. C. Corp., 1969. 144pp. $7.50. Four plays written for radio by the renowned poet. W. H. Auden has made the selection and provided an Introduction.

- Persons from Porlock
- East of the Sun and West of the Moon
- They Met on Good Friday
- Enter Caesar

STOPPARD, TOM
Albert's Bridge
Samuel French, 1969. 38pp. Paper $1.00. This is a radio play by the author of ''Rosencrantz and Guildenstern Are Dead. The play requires a cast of fourteen males and two females. Acting edition.

STOPPARD, TOM
Albert's Bridge and If You're Glad I'll Be Frank
Faber & Faber, 1969. 64pp. $3.95. Paper $1.95. These two plays were originally produced on radio in London. The critic for ''The London Times'' described ''Albert's Bridge'' as ''almost a textbook example of what a radio play ought to be.''

THOMAS, DYLAN
The Doctors and the Devils and Other Scripts
See Page 485

PART FOUR

THE MASS MEDIA AND THE POPULAR ARTS

PART FOUR: THE MASS MEDIA AND THE POPULAR ARTS

GENERAL HISTORIES AND CRITIQUES

AGEE, WARREN K.
Mass Media in a Free Society
University Press of Kansas, 1969. 96pp. $5.00. Paper $1.95. Six spokesmen from mass media discuss the challenges and the problems to be met today and in the future by newspapers, television, motion pictures, and magazines. Contributors are: Ben H. Bagdikian, Bill Moyers, Carl T. Rowan, Theodore F. Koop, Stan Freberg, and Bosley Crowther.

BARNOUW, ERIK
Mass Communication: Television, Radio, Film, Press
Holt, Rinehart, 1956. 280pp. $7.95. A discussion of the rise of the popular media and the psychological problems associated with each of them. Subtitled "The Media and Their Practice in the United States of America," the volume includes case histories of the successful communication between business, government, and non-profit organizations. Bibliographies. Index.

BLUM, ELEANOR
Reference Books in the Mass Media
University of Illinois, 1963. 103pp. Paper $1.50. An annotated, selected booklist covering books published, broadcasting, films, newspapers and magazines, and advertising. The author provides sources for facts, figures, names, addresses, and other bibliographic information and suggests starting points for research on the background, structure, function, content, and effects of mass media.

CASSOU, JEAN
Art and Confrontation: The Arts in an Age of Change
N. Y. Graphic Society, 1970. 203pp. $7.50. Paper $2.95. Nine essays on questions currently being raised about the place and stature of art in our society as a result of the Paris uprisings of May and June, 1968. Translated from the French by Nigel Foxell, the essays are by Jean Cassou, Gilbert Lascault, Raymonde Moulin, Pierre Gaudibert, Alain Jouffroy, and others.

DONOHUE, JODY
Your Career in Public Relations
Messner, 1967. 192pp. $3.95. This book explores and defines the varying nature of public relations work in such media as newspapers, magazines, radio and television. It surveys the opportunities, offers specific advice on how to obtain the proper education, and how to break into the field. Illustrated with photographs. List of schools offering degrees or courses is included. Bibliography. Index.

GORDON, GEORGE N. and IRVING FALK, WILLIAM HODAPP
The Idea Invaders
Hastings House, 1963. 256pp. $4.95. A study of mass communications and propaganda on the international and national scenes. The authors contend that the United States has lost the international war for men's minds and suggest remedies for this situation. Index.

HALL, JAMES B. and BARRY ULANOV
Modern Culture and the Arts
McGraw–Hill, 1967. 560pp. $5.95. This collection of fifty-six essays explores the condition of the arts and humanities in our time and the problems central to them. Areas under consideration include music, painting, sculpture, theatre, dance, television, motion pictures, photography, and the design arts of architecture and city planning. Illustrated with photographs.

HARRAL, STEWART
The Feature Writer's Handbook
University of Oklahoma, 1958. 342pp. $6.95. A complete reference book for free-lance writers, newspaper reporters, publicists, magazine editors, and all professional writers. A feature of the book is the "treasury" of 2,000 tested ideas for feature stories. Illustrated.

JACOBS, NORMAN – Editor
Culture for the Millions?
Beacon Press, 1964. 200pp. Paper $2.45. This is a far-reaching inquiry into the possible effects of contemporary television, radio magazines, and newspapers on the arts in modern America. Among those concerned with the production and distribution of culture who offer essays are: James Baldwin, Oscar Handlin, and Arthur Schlesinger, Jr.

KEPES, GYORGY – Editor
The Visual Arts Today
Wesleyan University, 1960. 272pp. $10.00. More than fifty contributors discuss the bases and meanings of today's art and its relation to modern living. Seven essays deal with the background of the visual arts today; six essays discuss advertising, motion pictures, and pictorial arts; four essays consider the relation between arts and sciences; and a last four essays deal with the interpretation of values. Illustrated.

KLAPPER, JOSEPH T.
The Effects of Mass Communication
Free Press of Glencoe, 1960. 320pp. $6.95. An analysis of research on the effectiveness and limitations of mass media in influencing the opinions, values, and behavior of their audience. These studies suggest that many commonly expressed fears are without basis, and that the media seldom operate directly and alone on the viewer.

KOSTELANETZ, RICHARD – Editor
The New American Arts
Collier, 1967. 270pp. Paper $1.95. A reprint of the 1965 edition, this is a collection of essays on theatre, fiction, painting, dance, film, music and poetry. The collection is intended to provide a basis for understanding the new currents in these arts.

LEVY, ALAN
The Culture Vultures
Putnam, 1968. 380pp. $6.95. The author explores the cultural explosion and the corrupting influences behind commercialized culture—including the theater, art, music, literature, the lecture world, and book clubs. The book ranges from the art dealers who manipulate prices and reputations, to the would-be-writer industry, to the theater party industry, to the world of the book clubs. Index.

LEWIS, JOHN
Typography: Basic Principles
Reinhold, 1964. 96pp. Paper $2.45. The author sets out to demonstrate what typography is, and particularly what it is to the modern graphic designer. The first chapter describes the influences that have shaped modern typography and this is followed by a presentation of present trends and methods of preparing layout for books and periodicals. Illustrated.

MELLY, GEORGE
Revolt Into Style: The Pop Arts in Britain
Allen Lane, 1970. 245pp. $8.95. An analytic history of popular culture in Britain during the 1960's. The television critic deals not only with the music but also with the pop-art movement and its impact on advertising and the mass media, with pop fashion, with pop theatre, and television, as well as with the underground press and the permissive society. Index.

PENNYBACKER, JOHN H. and WALDO W. BRADEN – Editors
Broadcasting and the Public Interest
See Page 490

ROSENBERG, BERNARD and DAVID MANNING WHITE – Editors
Mass Culture: The Popular Arts in America
Free Press, 1964. 561pp. $5.50. Paper $3.50. Essays on the movies, literature, television, advertising, and popular music by forty-nine literary critics, philosophers, political journalists, and sociologists.

RUCKER, BRYCE W.
The First Freedom
Southern Illinois University, 1968. 322pp. $12.50. This is an account of the dangers threatening the mass media through monopoly, chain, and cross-media ownership trends. The author focuses particularly on the appalling lack of diversity of voices in the marketplace of ideas. He provides a brief historical base for each medium discussed and includes thirty-five tables to illustrate the trends in mass communication ownership. Index.

SCHAEFFER, FRANCIS A.
Escape from Reason
Tyndale Press, 1968. 96pp. Paper $ .95. Dr. Schaeffer traces the way in which art and philosophy have reflected the dualism in Western thinking. This dualism is expressed today in a despair of rationality and an escape into a non-rational world which alone offers hope. Various chapters deal with literature, art and music, theatre and cinema, television and popular culture. Index.

SCHRAMM, WILBUR – Editor
Mass Communications
University of Illinois, 1969. 695pp. Paper $4.50. Originally published in 1960 and now reissued in a revised second edition, this is a comprehensive basic reader for the study of the subject. Outstanding authorities in the field of the social sciences contribute articles on the development, structure and function, control and support, process, content, audiences, effects, and responsibility of mass communications. Suggestions for Further Reading. Index.

SCHRAMM, WILBUR
Mass Media and National Development
Stanford University, 1964. 333pp. $8.50. Paper $3.25. This book analyzes the role of information in economic and social development and describes what the mass media can do directly to serve underdeveloped countries and to help these countries move from traditional society to social and economic modernity. The costs and requirements of mass media systems are examined. Fernand Terrou has contributed a chapter on international and legal problems of mass media.

STEINBERG, CHARLES S.
The Communicative Arts: An Introduction to Mass Media
Hastings House, 1970. 371pp. $7.50. A historical and critical survey of every area of mass communication from newspapers and magazines to comics to movies. After a chapter on man's earliest efforts as a communicator, what is known about the development of speech and writing is explored and the author reviews various theories which attempt to explain the process of personal and mass communication. Separate chapters then focus on the various mediums of communication. Each section closes with a List of Suggestions for Further Reading. Appendices. Index.

STEINBERG, CHARLES S. – Editor
Mass Media and Communication
Hastings House, 1966. 530pp. $11.50. Paper $7.50 A collection of essays which seeks to determine the impact of the mass media on society. The structure

and development of mass communication, public opinion, international communication, and propaganda are studied. Appendices give the various codes of ethics in the industry. Bibliography. Index.

THOMPSON, DENYS – Editor
Discrimination and Popular Culture
Penguin, 1964. 199pp. Paper $1.25. The essays in this collection deal with the modern mass-produced media: newspapers, films, radio, television, magazines, commercial design, and pop songs. Among the essayists are Frank Whitehead, Philip Abrams, Graham Martin, David Holbrook, and Michael Farr. The editor has provided an Introduction.

WHITE, DAVID MANNING and RICHARD AVERSON
Sight, Sound, and Society: Motion Pictures and Television in America
Beacon Press, 1968. 466pp. $7.50. This is an evaluation of the interplay between the sight and sound mass media and American social institutions. Thirty-two contributors range over the influence of motion pictures and television on politics, the Negro revolution, children, education, and the business of communication. A final essay urges specific research in modern communication practice and theory. Index.

WORKS ON THE ADVERTISING INDUSTRY

BOGART, LEO
Strategy in Advertising
Harcourt, Brace, 1967. 336pp. Paper $2.85. Concentrating on the qualities of mass communication that lend themselves to marketing purposes, Dr. Bogart focuses on media strategy in this commentary on and study of advertising. Bibliography. Index.

CONE, FAIRFAX M.
With All Its Faults
Little, Brown, 1969. 335pp. $6.95. The autobiography of Mr. Cone which details his forty years in the advertising industry. The author investigates the advertising mystique, the television commercial, and the function and future of advertising in American life. Illustrated with some of the "classic" advertisements. Index.

DELLA FEMINA, JERRY
From Those Wonderful Folks Who Gave You Pearl Harbor
Simon & Schuster, 1970. 253pp. $6.50. Edited by Charles Sopkin, this is a behind-the-scenes look at the world of the advertising agencies. It is an irreverent and frank account of the infighting between agencies and the "classic" ads.

GLATZER, ROBERT
The New Advertising
Citadel, 1970. 191pp. $10.00. A behind-the-scenes look at twenty of the most successful advertising campaigns of the recent years. Illustrated with original advertisement and television and radio commercials reproduced in each chapter, and discussed in the text, along with comments by the participants about the ads.

KIRKPATRICK, C. A.
Advertising: Mass Communication in Marketing
Houghton, Mifflin, 1964. 514pp. $11.50. This is a second edition of the 1959 study of advertising. Dr. Kirkpatrick examines his subject in general terms and in detail, from brand names and trade-marks through the various media and the implementation of campaigns. This edition has been revised and two new chapters summarize the field of marketing. Illustrated. Index.

LYON, DAVID G.
Off Madison Avenue
Putnam, 1966. 246pp. $5.95. A collection of observations on the business of advertising.

SCHWAB, VICTOR O.
How to Write a Good Advertisement
Harper & Row, 1962. 227pp. $5.95. A concise and specific book of information on every phase of copywriting. Index.

WORKS ON MARSHALL McLUHAN

McLUHAN, MARSHALL with WILFRED WATSON
From Cliche to Archetype
Viking, 1970. 213pp. $7.50. Mr. McLuhan's latest statement on today's culture and technology. It is also a study of the process of inter-media action. Illustrated.

McLUHAN, MARSHALL
The Gutenberg Galaxy
New American Library, 1969. 294pp. Paper $1.25. Originally published in 1962, this is McLuhan's contribution to the problems of advanced communication theory. His hypothesis is that the basic experience of Western man has been shaped mainly by the invention of type. Bibliographic Index.

McLUHAN, MARSHALL
The Mechanical Bride: Folklore of Industrial Man
Beacon Press, 1967. 157pp. Paper $2.95. Originally published in 1951, this is the book which first established McLuhan's reputation as the foremost critic of modern mass communications. Examples from ads, comic strips, columnists, etc. show how mass entertainment and suggestion make information irrelevant.

McLUHAN, MARSHALL and QUENTIN FIORE
The Medium is the Massage
Bantam, 1970. 160pp. Paper $1.65. The authors attempt to reveal how electronic technology is reshaping and restructuring the patterns of social

interdependence. They look at our world to see what is happening and why. Illustrated.

McLUHAN, MARSHALL
Understanding Media: The Extensions of Man
New American Library, 1966. 318pp. Paper $1.25. A reprint of the 1965 edition, this is a study of communications and how they affect mankind. The author interprets the entire process of communication from the invention of movable type through the electronic age. Bibliography.

McLUHAN, MARSHALL
Verbi-Voco-Visual Explorations
Something Else Press, 1967. 62+pp. $6.95. Paper $2.95. This is McLuhan's first essay on the arts that relates them to their impacts in a way relevant to the later writings. He documents, analyzes and details the implications of the arts through their sensual impact on the intellect and, especially, through their cumulative effect. Also included are contributions by six other essayists.

McLUHAN, MARSHALL and QUENTIN FIORE
War and Peace in the Global Village
Bantam, 1968. 192pp. Paper $1.45. This is a study into the dynamics of change. It highlights causes and processes rather than viewpoints. The authors contend that, with the advent of an electric information environment, all the territorial aims and objectives of business and politics tended to become illusory. Illustrated.

McNAMARA, EUGENE – Editor
The Interior Landscape: The Literary Criticism of Marshall McLuhan 1943 – 1962
McGraw–Hill, 1969. 239pp. $6.95. Selected, compiled, and edited by Mr. McNamara, these fourteen essays reflect three centers of interest: the attempts by various modern artists to cope with their universe; a consideration of several Romantic and Victorian poets; and the American landscape (The Southern tradition; Poe in the light of that tradition; and the arguments between rhetoricians and dialecticians).

ROSENTHAL, RAYMOND – Editor
McLuhan: Pro and Con
Funk & Wagnalls, 1968. 308pp. $5.95. Paper—Penguin, 1969. 308pp. $1.45. A collection of commentary on Marshall McLuhan and his theories. The editor introduces the volume by putting the McLuhan phenomenon into perspective. Among the contributors are Hugh Kenner, Dwight Macdonald, John Simon, Richard Kostelanetz, and Anthony Burgess.

STEARN, GERALD EMANUEL – Editor
McLuhan Hot and Cool: A Critical Symposium
Dial, 1967. 312pp. $6.95. Paper – New American Library, 1969. 304pp. $ .95. The material in this symposium covers not only McLuhan's best known book, "Understanding Media," but follows the formulation of his ideas from his first published work in 1951 up to the present. Among the contributors are Tom Wolfe, Dwight Macdonald, Susan Sontag, and George Steiner, as well as McLuhan himself. The transcript of a conversation between McLuhan and Stearn gives the reader a chance to see McLuhan at work as he replies to his critics. A Selected Bibliography of books and articles by McLuhan is included.

SUPPLEMENT

PART ONE: BOOKS ON THEATRE AND DRAMA

GENERAL REFERENCE WORKS

BIBLIOGRAPHIES

COLEMAN, ARTHUR and GARY TYLER
Drama Criticism: Volume II
Swallow, 1971. 446pp. $16.75. A checklist of interpretation since 1940 of classical and continental plays. Entries are arranged alphabetically by author and then by play. The bibliographical section following the checklist includes books in which drama criticism was found, books researched but yielding no entries, and a partial list of those works still in print but which were not researched due to original publication prior to 1940. A Periodicals Bibliography lists all journals researched.

GREG, W. W.
A Bibliography of the English Printed Drama to the Restoration – Volume IV
See Page 542

LIEVSAY, JOHN L.
The Sixteenth Century: Skelton Through Hooker
Appleton, 1968. 132pp. Paper $2.50. A selective bibliography of Renaissance English literature and culture with the emphasis on work published in the twentieth century. Only token recognition is given to dramatic works. Index.

PENCE, JAMES HARRY – Compiler
The Magazine and the Drama: An Index
Burt Franklin, 1970. 190pp. $16.95. Originally published in 1896 and now reissued in a facsimile edition, this is a guide to the literature "concerning the acted drama and the men and women directly connected with it" as published in magazines up to 1896. The material is indexed according to writers and subjects.

PRITNER, CALVIN LEE and STEPHEN M. ARCHER – Editors
A Selected and Annotated Bibliography for the Secondary School Theatre Teacher and Student
A. E. T. A., 1970. 38pp. Paper $1.95. Originally published in 1968 and now revised, this is a selective bibliography of readily available books on the theatre. Among the types of works listed are bibliographies and reference works, and books on: drama theory and criticism, theatre history, creative drama and children's theatre, acting, directing, costuming, radio, television, and film.

STRATMAN, CARL J.
British Dramatic Periodicals: 1720 – 1960
New York Public Library, 1962. Unpaged. Paper $2.50. A bibliography listing all important periodicals devoted to the theatre.

DICTIONARIES

BAND–KUZMANY, KARIN – Compiler
Glossary of the Theatre
Elsevier, 1969. 130pp. $12.95. A compilation of words and phrases covering the fields of drama, the history of the theatre, stagecraft, acting, scene design, and allied subjects including stage slang. Entries in the Basic Table are given in English with their French, Italian, and German equivalents. Alphabetical indices are provided for the foreign words.

ENCYCLOPEDIAS

ANDERSON, MICHAEL and JACQUES GUICHARNAUD et al
Crowell's Handbook of Contemporary Drama
Crowell, 1971. 505pp. $10.00. A comprehensive, alphabetically arranged guide to the drama of Europe and the Americas since the Second World War. Entries include surveys of the drama in England, France, Germany, the United States, Russia, Poland, the Scandinavian countries; biographical sketches of hundreds of playwrights with critical appraisals of their careers; descriptions and evaluations of significant or representative plays; and brief discussions of important movements, theorists, directors and companies that have influenced dramatic form. The fourteen specialists in American and European drama who have combined their knowledge include authorities from the United States, Great Britain, France, the Soviet Union, and many other countries.

KRONENBERGER, LOUIS and EMILY MORISON BECK – Editors
Atlantic Brief Lives: A Biographical Companion to the Arts
Little, Brown, 1971. 900pp. $15.00. A one-volume biographical companion to the literature and arts of the West. Major figures in our culture are included in over 200 essays and 1,000 short factual biographies. No living figures are included although the volume provides entries for the world of the theatre over the centuries.

PLAY GUIDES AND INDICES

CHICOREL, MARIETTA – Editor
Chicorel Theatre Index to Plays in Anthologies, Periodicals, Discs & Tapes: Volume One
Chicorel Library Publishing, 1970. 572pp. $38.25. This index lists plays in over fifty-five collections in print, and in current periodicals. Plays on discs and tapes will be listed in a forthcoming volume. This volume includes approximately 10,000 entries.

CHICOREL, MARIETTA – Editor
Chicorel Theatre Index to Plays in Anthologies, Periodicals, Discs & Tapes: Volume Two
Chicorel Library Publishing, 1971. 502pp. $42.50. This index locates additional plays in 500 more collections and periodicals. The volume includes approximately 10,000 entries. Plays on discs and tapes are not included in this volume.

KELLER, DEAN H.
Index to Plays in Periodicals
Scarecrow Press, 1971. 558pp. $15.00. An index to more than 5,000 plays published in 103 selected periodicals. The Author Index provides the main entry with all information necessary to locate the play: author, date, title, number of acts, description, citation of journal, names of translators, and language in which play appears. A Title Index, keyed by author and citation number, follows.

ANNUALS

BLUM, DANIEL – Editor
Theatre World: Volume 14
Drama Book Specialists, 1971. 256pp. $15.00. Originally published in 1958, allowed to go out-of-print, and now distributed by Drama Book Specialists, this is a pictorial and statistical record of all off-Broadway and Broadway productions for the 1957/58 season, plus records of other professional companies, and national touring company productions. Biographies of actors and an obituary section are included. Illustrated with hundreds of photographs. Index.

GUERNSEY, JR., OTIS L. – Editor
The Best Plays of 1970 – 1971
Dodd, Mead, 1971. 450pp. $12.50. The latest edition of "The Burns Mantle Theater Yearbook." Features include the listings of all plays produced in New York, detailed information on the London and European seasons, annual awards, vital statistics of productions, and lists of prizes and publications. The editor has chosen ten plays to represent the season's best, and summarizes nine with excerpts from the script with the tenth summarized in excerpts and photographs from the production. An additional thirty-two pages of photographs record the season's highlights. Sixteen pages of Al Hirschfeld's drawings are also included. The editor's ten best play choices are: "Home," "The Trial of the Catonsville Nine," "Boesman and Lena," "Steambath," "Sleuth," "Conduct Unbecoming," "The Gingerbread Lady," "Follies," "The Philanthropist," and "The House of Blue Leaves." Index.

GUERNSEY, JR., OTIS L. – Editor
Directory of the American Theater 1894 – 1971
Dodd, Mead, 1971. 343pp. $25.00. Compiled and edited as a cumulative index to the "Best Plays" series, as begun by Burns Mantle in 1920, this volume contains the names of all playwrights, librettists, composers, and lyricists, as well as all the titles of Broadway off-Broadway, and off-off-Broadway productions, listed in the fifty-two "Best Plays" volumes and the three retrospective volumes. The Directory contains an entry for each time a name is mentioned in the "Best Plays," volumes.

WILLIS, JOHN
Theatre World: 1970 – 1971
Crown, 1971. 288pp. $8.95. Volume 27 in the annual pictorial and statistical record of the Broadway and off-Broadway seasons. This volume covers the 1970–71 season and includes more than 750 photographs of the plays and players. Leading regional companies are included as are national touring companies. Biographies of actors and an obituary section are included. Illustrated. Index.

PHILOSOPHY OF THEATRE

THEORIES OF DRAMATIC ART

BAIRD, MARTHA
Two Aesthetic Realism Papers
Definition Press, 1971. 59pp. Paper $1.45. Two essays on the philosophy of Aesthetic Realism: "Opposites in the Drama" and "Opposites in Myself." Miss Baird provides examples of "the making one of opposites" in drama from Aeschylus to the present day.

BOYNTON, ROBERT W. and MAYNARD MACK
Introduction to the Play
Hayden, 1969. 386pp. $7.25. Paper $5.25. In this text, the authors emphasize that the reading of plays has demands and rewards as part of the study of literature. The first part of the volume is organized for analysis and discussion of the nature of drama with reference to specific lines and scenes from the plays anthologized. Discussed are the theatrical conventions of the several different periods of the plays. Included are the texts of: Shaw's "The Devil's Disciple," Ibsen's "Ghosts," Sophocles' "Oedipus the King," Shakespeare's "Henry IV, Part I," and Cocteau's "The Infernal Machine."

BROWN, JOHN RUSSELL – Editor
Drama and the Theatre: An Outline for the Student
Routledge & Kegan Paul, 1971. 192pp. $6.95. Paper $3.50. Written for those contemplating a career in the theatre and for students interested in the theatre arts, this volume includes a wide range of topics, including acting; production; design and equipment; and work in film, radio, and television. Separate chapters, each by a specialist in the field, look at drama and society, and drama and education. Published in England, the volume includes contributions by J. F. Arnott, John Fernald, Kenneth Muir, and other authorities. Illustrations. Book List. Index.

CLARK, BRIAN
Group Theatre
See Page 586

CULP, RALPH BORDEN
The Theatre and Its Drama: Principles and Practice
See Page 586

DAWSON, S. W.
The Critical Idiom: Drama and the Dramatic
Methuen, 1970. 100pp. $3.75. Paper $1.95. The author begins by studying the meaning of drama and the dramatic as related to the action upon a stage and proceeds to argue that a real understanding of the dramatic convention is a recognition that the action is evoked by the language and that the language creates the dramatic world of the play. Mr. Dawson considers the various requirements for a dramatic situation and shows how modern criticism lays emphasis upon these dramatic qualities. Bibliography. Index.

ESTRIN, MARC
ReCreation
See Page 556

EVREINOV, NIKOLAS
The Theatre in Life
Blom, 1971. 296pp. $10.50. Originally published in 1927 and now reissued, this is a discussion of the modern tendency in the theatre: the revolt against dramatic realism. The author was a prominent figure in the symbolist movement of the Russian theatre during the early 1900's. Illustrated by B. Aronson.

FERLITA, ERNEST
The Theatre of Pilgrimage
Sheed & Ward, 1971. 172pp. $6.00. Paper $2.95. The author explores eight plays that make explicit use of the metaphor of journey or pilgrimage, plays in which that metaphor is employed to reveal something about man's search for meaning. The plays range from "King Lear" to Ionesco's "Hunger and Thirst." Appendix of Related Readings. Bibliography.

HATLEN, THEODORE W. – Editor
Drama: Principles and Plays
Appleton, 1971. 522pp. Paper $7.25. Originally published in 1967 and now reissued, this is an anthology of twelve plays with an Introduction by the editor on "Theatre and Drama," "Tragedy," and "Comedy." Each play has a separate introduction on the play and the playwright, review questions, and a series of photographs illustrating a major production of the play. The plays are: "Antigone," "Hamlet," "The Miser," "The School for Scandal," "An Enemy of the People," "Miss Julie," "Major Barbara," "Desire Under the Elms," "The Caucasian Chalk Circle," "The Glass Menagerie," "The Leader," and "Act Without Words." Bibliography. Glossary.

HILL, PHILIP G.
The Living Art: An Introduction to Theatre and Drama
Rinehart Press, 1971. 578pp. $13.25. This anthology of world drama seeks to provide a foundation in theatre for the beginning student, to give him a broad understanding of the way diverse literary and theatrical elements function together to create a unified work of art. There are essays on the various crafts and arts of the theatre including acting, directing, set design, costume design, lighting, properties, make-up, and sound. The plays anthologized are listed below. The author has also provided a discussion of each script. Illustrated with photographs. Glossary. Index.

The Little Foxes   Footdeath

JB	Cyrano de Bergerac
Twelfth Night	The Importance of Being Earnest
Tartuffe	Oedipus the King
Galileo	A View from the Bridge

JOHNSON, STANLEY and JUDAH BIERMAN, JAMES HART
The Play and the Reader
Prentice–Hall, 1971. 583pp. Paper $6.50. Written as a text for students in introductory courses on the drama, the author provides an Introduction on the nature of the drama, and sections on tragedy, comedy, and new departures. Essays by Aristotle, Elder Olson, Lionel Abel, Robert Corrigan, Martin Esslin, and others. Plays by Sophocles, Shakespeare, Ibsen, Anouilh, Pirandello, Moliere, Brecht, Frisch, and Thornton Wilder complete the volume. Appendix of Further Readings.

KERNODLE, GEORGE and PORTIA KERNODLE
Invitation to the Theatre: Brief Edition
Harcourt Brace, 1971. 331pp. Paper $6.50. Originally published in a 677 page edition in 1967 and now reissued in a revised, updated and condensed edition. The authors present first, in historical perspective, the kinds of plays—realism and romance, tragedy and comedy, etc.—and then describe how the director, actor, and designer work together to create the play. A final chapter details some recent experiments in new forms of theatre. Illustrated with photographs, some of which are in color. Bibliography. Index.

MACLAY, JOANNA HAWKINS
Readers Theatre: Toward a Grammar of Practice
See Page 587

MITCHELL, ROY
Creative Theatre
Drama Book Specialists, 1969. 256pp. $7.50. Paper $4.95. Originally published in 1929 and now reissued, this work deals with theatre aesthetics in relation to modern dramatic art. Considered a visionary book when first published, Mr. Mitchell predicted much that has happened in the modern theatre to date, and is credited with helping regional and community theatres to become so important a force in the American theatre. Illustrated with seventeen wood-block projections by Jocelyn Taylor.

REASKE, CHRISTOPHER RUSSELL
How to Analyze Drama
Monarch Press, 1966. 112pp. Paper $1.50. A study guide for analysis of drama. After a brief history of the genre, the author analyzes dramatic structure, characterization, language and rhetoric, various dramatic techniques, interpretation of the author's theme, how to evaluate and criticize, and how to present a full analysis. A Bibliography is included. Index.

RILOVA, AUGUSTO CENTENO Y and DONALD SUTHERLAND
The Blue Clown: Dialogues
University of Nebraska, 1971. 204pp. $5.00. In eight dialogues a master and his disciple argue about the theatre—ancient, renaissance, and modern—attempting to situate it within an ontology and a scheme of aesthetic values. The content is chiefly concerned with present movements, particularly the theatre after Antonin Artaud.

ROBERTS, VERA MOWRY
The Nature of Theatre
Harper & Row, 1971. 500pp. $12.50. Paper $9.75. The author analyzes the total experience within the playhouse. "The Experience of Theatre" covers seeing a play, the nature of art, and the art of theatre. "Ways of Seeing" discusses the play itself, the development of dramatic forms, and the modes and conventions of drama. This is followed by a section devoted to genres and then by a discussion of the artists of the theatre. The final section treats films and television as separate but uniquely constituted forms. Information on vocational opportunities is provided. Illustrated with more than 250 photographs from recent Broadway, off-Broadway, and regional theatre productions. Selected List of Books for Additional Reading. Index.

SCHOLES, ROBERT and CARL H. KLAUS
Elements of Drama
Oxford, 1971. 78pp. Paper $1.25. The authors explain drama in relation to both literary and theatrical contexts and the way these contexts interact to produce the experience of drama. They discuss the modes and elements of drama, illustrating their points by references to "Oedipus Rex," "A Midsummer Night's Dream," "The Misanthrope," and "Endgame."

STATES, BERT O.
Irony and Drama: A Poetics
Cornell University, 1971. 243pp. $7.50. This new theory of the drama is based upon the principles of irony and dialectic. Mr. States treats irony as a means of confronting reality. He views drama as a vehicle for perceiving and ordering the possibilities of human experience. After setting forth his thesis, the author explores other modes such as the epic and the lyric and shows how they interact with the dramatic principle. Index.

WALKLEY, A.B.
Dramatic Criticism
Kennikat, 1970. 125pp. $7.50. Originally published in 1903 and now reissued, this volume includes three essays on "The Ideal Spectator," "The Dramatic Critic," and "Old and New Criticism."

WELLS, STANLEY
Literature and Drama

Routledge & Kegan Paul, 1970. 117pp. $5.00. Paper $2.50. The author attempts to explore and illustrate the implications of the statement: "Most drama has some literary quality, and most dramatic scripts can give literary pleasure when read, but the reading of a play is a necessarily incomplete experience." Most of the illustrations are taken from the English drama of the sixteenth and seventeenth centuries. Some of the problems created by the instability of dramatic art are considered in relation to recent productions of plays by Marlowe, Tourneur, and Shakespeare. Bibliography.

THEORIES OF COMEDY AND TRAGEDY

KROOK, DOROTHEA
Elements of Tragedy
Yale, 1969. 279pp. $6.95. Paper $2.95. Using examples from a range of dramas, Mrs. Krook isolates the elements fundamental to the universal tragic pattern: an act or situation of shame or horror which precipitates a spectacle of intense human suffering followed by a deeper knowledge of man's condition issuing in a final reaffirmation of the value of human life. She tests the validity of her scheme by examining plays by Sophocles, Shakespeare, Ibsen, Chekhov, and Thomas Middleton. Notes. Index.

McCOLLOM, WILLIAM G.
The Divine Average: A View of Comedy
Case Western Reserve Univ., 1971. 231pp. $7.50. A critical study of comedy in which the author analyzes form and attitude in comedy, the area of comedy, types of comic structure, and character and speech in comedy. He includes analyses of eight well-known comic plays, including three by Marivaux, and "The Birds," "Much Ado About Nothing," "Bartholomew Fair," "Tartuffe," and "Major Barbara." Bibliography. Index.

NATHAN, DAVID
The Laughtermakers: A Quest for Comedy
See Page 546

SZELISKI, JOHN VON
Tragedy and Fear: Why Modern Tragic Drama Fails
University of North Carolina, 1971. 257pp. $14.65. This is a study of the relationship between the worldview in modern serious playwriting and the effectiveness of modern attempts at tragic drama. It is also an examination of the problem of tragic spirit: is tragedy optimistic or pessimistic? The author discusses a number of tragic drama, among them plays by Eugene O'Neill, Maxwell Anderson, Theodore Dreiser, Elmer Rice, Tennessee Williams, Arthur Miller, and others. The volume also includes a number of Appendices and a Bibliography. Index.

WORLD THEATRE

COMPREHENSIVE REFERENCE WORKS

Histories and Critiques

GEISINGER, MARION
Plays, Players, & Playwrights
Hart Publishing, 1971. 767pp. $20.00. An illustrated history of the theatre. The profusely illustrated volume offers a complete survey of the English-speaking theatre from the early Greek drama through the Broadway season of 1971. The chapters include: The Greek and Roman Theatre, The Medieval Theatre, The Elizabethan Theatre, The Commedia dell'Arte, The Restoration Theatre, The English 18th Century Theatre, The English 19th Century Theatre, The English 20th Century Theatre, The Russian Theatre, The Early American Theatre, The 20th Century American Theatre, and The American Musical Comedy. Over 400 drawings and photographs and reproductions of memorabilia and playbills of every era illustrate the text. Index.

MODERN THEATRE (Dating from Henrik Ibsen)

Histories and Critiques

ANDERSON, MICHAEL and JACQUES GUICHARNAUD et al
Crowell's Handbook of Contemporary Drama
See Page 513

BROCKETT, OSCAR G.
Perspectives on Contemporary Theatre
Louisiana State University, 1971. 158pp. $6.50. A perceptive look at the radical trends in modern drama. Professor Brockett demonstrates that many of the aspects of contemporary theatre are rooted in the traditions of Western stage and society. He traces the shifts in values over the past century and shows how these changes have affected modern drama. He examines a wide range of playwrights and discusses plays from "Waiting for Godot" to "Hair" and "Che!"

CHENEY, SHELDON
The New Movement in the Theatre
Blom, 1971. 309pp. $12.50. Originally published in 1914 and now reissued in a facsimile edition, this is a collection of critical essays on the new ideals of stage scenery and the new dramatists that recreated the theatre in the early twentieth century. Cheney discusses Craig and Reinhardt, the new English dramatist, the American playwright and the drama of sincerity, the new stagecraft, and other aspects of the theatre. Sixteen illustrations. Index.

DRIVER, TOM F.
Romantic Quest and Modern Query: A History of the Modern Theatre
Dell, 1971. 496pp. Paper $2.95. Originally published in 1970 and now reissued, this study traces the history of the modern theatre across the nineteenth and twentieth centuries. Dr. Driver highlights the work of the great dramatists—Goethe, Kleist, Ibsen, Strindberg, Chekhov, Shaw, Pirandello, Brecht, and Genet among them—in his contention that man's search for self-understanding has culminated in a spirit of self-alienation. Selected Bibliography. Indices.

GOODMAN, RANDOLPH
From Script to Stage: Eight Modern Plays
Rinehart Press, 1971. 623pp. $15.95. An anthology designed for the student of drama. The eight plays chosen for the volume are representative of the dramatic styles that have been dominant in the twentieth century theatre. The author provides an introductory essay on the theatre since the Restoration, critical essays and comments on the plays and playwrights, and interviews with directors, designers, and actors involved in various productions of the plays. The plays are by Ibsen, Strindberg, Chekhov, Shaw, O'Neill, Brecht, Pinget, and Aspenstrom. List of Works for Further Study. Index.

GROSSMAN, MANUEL L.
Dada: Paradox, Mystification, and Ambiguity in European Literature
Bobbs–Merrill, 1971. 192pp. $6.95. Paper $2.25. A history of the Dada movement in European literature and an attempt to assess the importance of Dada as a phenomenon. The author discusses the artistic and intellectual climate that led to the founding of Dada and its most important precursors, the movement's life span, the literary experiments, and its overall importance. In the course of the study, Dada in the theatre is commented upon. Selected Bibliography. Notes. Index.

HANSON, GILLIAN
Original Skin
See Page 600

HINCHLIFFE, ARNOLD P.
The Absurd
Barnes & Noble, 1970. 105pp. $4.00. Paper $1.65. Originally published in England in 1969 and now issued in the United States, this is an introductory study of the literary form of "the absurd," a term which has been used to describe a body of plays. Among the playwrights studied are Sartre, Camus, Ionesco, Artaud, Brecht, Beckett, and Genet. Select Bibliography. Index.

HOUGHTON, NORRIS
The Exploding Stage: An Introduction to Twentieth Century Drama
Weybright and Talley, 1971. 269pp. $6.95. This is, as the author states in his subtitle, "An Introduction to Twentieth Century Drama." Mr. Houghton begins with a chapter on the nature of drama, a brief history of the theater's evolution, and a critique of the contributions of playwrights from the time of the Greek civilization to the late nineteenth century. He demonstrates how these men have directly influenced the great modern dramatists and brings out the ideas and philosophies behind the playwrights who now represent the classic avant-garde. Finally he provides a chapter on the situation of the theatre today. Index.

KIENZLE, SIEGFRIED
Modern World Theater
Ungar, 1971. 509pp. $14.50. Translated from the German by Alexander and Elizabeth Henderson, this is a guide to productions in Europe and the United States since 1945. The author surveys a cross-section of the productions. His entries include plot analysis and concise interpretation for plays arranged alphabetically by author and by titles under each author. First production, original language, place and year of first publication, translator and/or adaptor's name are all provided for the 578 plays included. Index of Play Titles.

KILLINGER, JOHN
World in Collapse: The Vision of Absurd Drama
Dell, 1971. 184pp. Paper $2.45. A survey and evaluation of the Theater of the Absurd. Professor Killinger traces the development through its leading exponents: Beckett, Ionesco, Arrabal, Genet, Pinter, Albee, Gelber, Kopit, and others. Their particular approach and treatment is analyzed in depth. Bibliography. Index.

KIRBY, MICHAEL
Futurist Performance
Dutton, 1971. 335pp. $8.95. Paper $3.95. The author attempts to survey the developments of the art movement known as "Futurism." Kirby covers Futurist work in the fields of drama, scenography, acting, dance, music, cinema, and radio. He concerns himself both with actual performance and with performance theory. An Appendix contains translations from the Italian of thirteen manifestos and forty-eight playscripts. Included is a selected chronology of Futurist performances from 1909 to 1933. Illustrated. Selected Bibliography. Index.

KRASSNER, PAUL
How a Satirical Editor Became a Yippie Conspirator in Ten Easy Years
Putnam, 1971. 319pp. $6.95. A collection of the writings of the editor of "The Realist." The writings range in time from 1958 to 1970 and satirize politics and politicians, sex, war, protest, television, films, civil rights, and other matters. Among his subjects are Mort Sahl, Ken Kesey, Richard Nixon, Woody Allen, Norman Mailer, Dick Gregory, Terry Southern, and many others who have helped to make our cultural and social climates what they are today.

LEWIS, ALLEN
The Contemporary Theatre
Crown, 1971. 374pp. $5.95. Originally published in 1962 and now revised and updated, this is a general introduction to the modern European and American theatres. The author provides an in-depth analysis of theatre, providing a background for every contemporary development. Among the playwrights and groups discussed are Ibsen, Strindberg, Chekhov, Pirandello, Shaw, Brecht, Albee, Kopit, Shepard, Hansberry, and Jones; and The Living Theatre, The Performance Group, The Polish Laboratory Theatre, and The La Mama Company. Foreword by John Gassner. References. Index.

ROOSE-EVANS, JAMES
Experimental Theatre
Avon, 1971. 159pp. Paper $1.65. Originally published in 1970 and now reissued, this is a record of the major experiments that, over the past hundred years, have extended the range of theatre as art. The author gives an account of the work of such key figures as Stanislavsky, Meyerhold, Craig, Appia, Artaud, Piscator, and Brecht, as well as discussing current experiments in America by Allen Kaprow, Ann Halprin's Dancers' Workshop Company, Yayoi Kusama, and Peter Schumann's Bread and Puppet Theatre. The volume includes sixty-four pages of illustrations, mostly photographs. Bibliography. Index.

SYKES, GERALD
The Perennial Avantgarde
Prentice–Hall, 1971. 239pp. $6.95. A dissection of the current situation in the fine arts and the calibre of our thinking about them. This essay on contemporary aesthetics covers painting and sculpture, music, theatre, architecture, science and art, and politics. Appendix.

WELLWARTH, GEORGE E.
The Theatre of Protest and Paradox: Developments in the Avant-Garde Drama. Revised Edition
New York University, 1971. 409pp. $10.00. Paper $3.95. A revision of the 1964 study of the avant-garde drama in which the author traces the sources of the new movement and suggests that although individual plays may differ radically, they share a common theme—protest—and a common technique—paradox. Wellwarth explores the theatre of France, Germany, England, Spain, and America. The original chapters have been expanded and updated, and a new section on Spanish theatre is included. Bibliography. Index.

Collections of Essays

ESSLIN, MARTIN

Reflections: Essays on Modern Theatre

Doubleday, 1971. 226pp. Paper $1.95. Originally published in 1969 and now reissued, this is a collection of essays covering the entire range of modern theatre from Ibsen and Pirandello to Brecht, Ionesco, Beckett, and Weiss. Index.

GILMAN, RICHARD

Common and Uncommon Masks: Writings on Theatre 1961 – 1970

Random House, 1971. 321pp. $8.95. In this collection of his theatre criticism, Mr. Gilman discusses contemporary playwrights and productions. A concluding essay is on the Polish Laboratory Theatre of Jerzy Grotowski. Index.

JOHNSTON, JILL

Marmalade Me

Dutton, 1971. 316pp. $8.95. Paper $2.45. A selection of the writings which originally appeared in the "Village Voice" in the period 1960–1970. Miss Johnston started as a critic of dance, painting, sculpture, happenings, and forms of intermedia, but her later writing represents a radical departure from existing notions concerning the role and function of criticism. It has evolved into her present style of autobiographical writing. Illustrated with photographs

GREEK AND ROMAN THEATRE

REFERENCE WORKS AND GENERAL HISTORIES

ARNOTT, PETER D.
The Ancient Greek and Roman Theatre
Random House, 1971. 167pp. Paper $3.95. A study of the Greek and Roman theatre from its beginnings to the late Empire. The author deals with the ways in which the plays were performed and surveys the changing modes of stage settings, acting, costuming, and production. Illustrated with photographs. Selected Bibliography. Index.

BALDRY, H.C.
The Greek Tragic Theatre
Chatto & Windus, 1971. 143pp. $6.00. Paper $2.95. In this introduction to Greek tragedy, Professor Baldry sees the plays of Aeschylus, Sophocles, and Euripides in their original settings, the festivals of Dionysus at Athens in the fifth century. He considers the organization and financing of the festivals, the theatre and its audience, the appearance and function of actors and chorus. Against this background, he discusses the plays: their form, dramatization of legend, and treatment of character, illustrating the differences between the three great tragic playwrights by their versions of the Orestes' theme. Five pages of illustrations. Bibliography. Index.

DUCKWORTH, GEORGE E.
The Nature of Roman Comedy: A Study in Popular Entertainment
Princeton, 1971. 501pp. Paper $3.95. Originally published in 1952 and now reissued, this is a study of the background and history of Roman comedy: the staging and presentation of the plays, the nature of the comedies (with attention to stage conventions, the structure of the plots, the delineation of character, the moral tone of the plays), the problem of the originality of Plautus and Terence and their relation to the Greek originals, and some consideration of their extensive influence on later comedy. Brief plot summaries of twenty-six comedies are included. Appendix. Bibliography. Index.

LLOYD–JONES, HUGH
The Justice of Zeus
University of California, 1971. 230pp. $8.50. The author examines early Greek legend and morality to create a sympathetic understanding of the early Greek view of the world. Among his subjects, he includes the Homeric epic, Herodotus, Aeschylus, Sophocles, and Euripides. The study also contains a new hypothesis about the missing plays of Aeschylus' Promethean trilogy. Notes. Glossary. Index of Modern Authors. General Index.

SIFAKIS, G.M.
Parabasis and Animal Choruses
Athlone Press, 1971. 150pp. $17.35. Professor Sifakis offers a critical analysis of the evidence on two topics concerning the origins and development of Greek comedy. This examination into the function, form, and origins of those parts in which the chorus addressed the audience in the poet's name is based upon the author's conviction that all earlier analyses of the subject have been based on the false premise that the parabasis interrupted the dramatic illusion. Illustrated. Notes. Bibliography. Indices.

TRENDALL, A.D. and T.B.L. WEBSTER
Illustrations of Greek Drama
Phaidon, 1971. 159pp. $28.50. The aim of the authors is to present a series of illustrations representative of the history of Greek dramatic performances from the earliest times down to the third century B.C. Most of the 200 illustrations are taken from Greek and South Italian vase-paintings. The authors have confined the illustrations to those specifically dealing with dramatic performances. These have been divided into five sections: Predramatic, Satyr-plays, Tragedy, Old and Middle Comedy, and New Comedy. Each of the sections provides descriptions of the art work illustrated, a commentary on the play, and a Select Bibliography. The authors' Introduction deals with the theatre, scenery, and costumes in Attica and South Italy in successive periods. List of Illustrations. Indices.

STUDIES OF PLAYWRIGHTS

Aeschylus

AHRENS, ROBERT H.
The Plays of Aeschylus
Monarch Press, 1966. 138pp. Paper $1.00. A critical guide providing an in-depth analysis of the form, meaning, and style of the playwright's works. A complete background of Aeschylus, plot discussion, theme development, character analysis, critical commentary, and study questions and answers are provided. Bibliography.

LEBECK, ANNE
The Oresteia: A Study in Language and Structure
Harvard University, 1971. 222pp. $11.25. A study of Aeschylus' "Oresteia" in which the author presents an analysis of the meaning of the images in their immediate context, their meaning as part of cumulative repetition within the individual play, and their meaning within the context of the trilogy as a whole. Notes. Index.

Aristophanes

MacDOWELL, DOUGLAS M. – Editor
Aristophanes: Wasps
Oxford, 1971. 346pp. $10.50. An annotated edition of Aristophanes' play, edited with an Introduction and commentary by Mr. MacDowell. An "apparatus criticus" based on a fresh examination of the manuscripts is included. The text of the play is in the Greek language, but the notes and commentary are all in English. Indices.

NEUVILLE, H. RICHMOND
The Plays of Aristophanes
Monarch Press, 1966. 85pp. Paper $1.00. A critical guide to the plays of the Greek playwright. A complete background to each of the plays is provided, with thematic and character analysis, critical commentary, essay questions and answers for review, and a Bibliography.

WALTER, WILLIAM
The Plays of Euripides, Aeschylus, and Aristophanes
See entry in EURIPIDES section

Euripides

BARLOW, SHIRLEY
The Imagery of Euripides
Barnes & Noble, 1971. 169pp. $12.50. A study which demonstrates that Euripides' use of poetic language, and imagery in particular, is worthy of close analysis and can be favorably compared with the poetic talents of Aeschylus and Sophocles. Notes. Bibliography. Index to Poetic Texts Cited. General Index.

STEVENS, P. T. – Editor
Andromache
Oxford, 1971. 255pp. $8.00. Euripides' play, in the text and apparatus criticus of G. Murray, with commentary on this text by the editor. An Introduction deals with problems of date and place of production, with the legendary material and Euripides' treatment of it, with the structure of the play and its main theme. The notes are intended to deal briefly with linguistic, textual, and metrical questions and also to interpret the play in its dramatic and literary aspects. The text of the play is in the Greek language but all other material is in English. Indices.

WALTER, WILLIAM
The Plays of Euripides
Monarch Press, 1966. 111pp. Paper $1.00. Revised and edited by Eugenie Harris, this is a critical guide to the work of Euripides. The author provides a complete background on the playwright, plot discussion, character analysis, theme development, critical commentary, study questions and answers, and a Bibliography.

WALTER, WILLIAM
The Plays of Euripides, Aeschylus, and Aristophanes
Monarch Press, 1963. 105pp. Paper $1.00. A critical guide to the plays of the Greek playwrights. A general Introduction is provided, then each of the playwright's work is studied individually. The author provides review questions and answers and a Bibliography.

Plautus

SEGAL, ERICH
Roman Laughter: The Comedy of Plautus
Harper & Row, 1971. 229pp. Paper $3.00. Originally published in 1968 and now reissued, this is a study of Plautus and his theatrical art. Mr. Segal pursues the question of the contemporary appeal of the comedies. Notes. Index of Passages. General Index.

Seneca

TOBIN, RONALD W.
Racine and Seneca
See Page 534

Sophocles

KNOX, BERNARD
Oedipus at Thebes
Norton, 1971. 279pp. Paper $1.95. Originally published in 1957 and now reissued, this is a study of Sophocles' tragic hero. Mr. Knox distinguishes between Oedipus as a universal figure who transcends the play and as a character "in time," shaped by the ideas and circumstances of fifth century Greece. Notes. Selected Bibliography. Index.

VELLACOTT, PHILIP
Sophocles and Oedipus
University of Michigan, 1971. 256pp. $9.50. A study of "Oedipus Tyrannus" with a new translation in verse. Seven chapters contain a systematic exposition of the play based on a close study of the Greek text. The author presents an original and controversial interpretation of Sophocles' play: that it explores the world of knowing and not-knowing and shows not only the central character of Oedipus, but other characters also, as exhibiting a wide and complex range

of awareness—providing material for the theme of knowledge as a matter of choice and will. Index of Lines Discussed. Index of Subjects Discussed.

WALTER, WILLIAM
The Plays of Sophocles
Monarch Press, 1963. 119pp. Paper $1.00. A critical guide to the plays of the Greek playwright. The author includes an in-depth analysis of the form, meaning, and style of the works of Sophocles by means of a discussion of the complete background of the plots of the plays. He also provides analyses of the themes and characters of the plays. A selection of questions and answers for student study is also included, as is a guide for research.

SHAKESPEARE

REFERENCE WORKS

Bibliographies

HOWARD–HILL, T.H.
Shakespearian Bibliography and Textual Criticism: A Bibliography
Oxford, 1971. 322pp. $17.25. Nearly 1,900 entries are listed under three main headings: "General Bibliographies and Guides," "Works," and "Textual Studies." The volume covers Shakespeare bibliographies and checklists and material published between 1890 and 1969 on the bibliography and text of Shakespeare's works. The author has also included a Supplement to "The Bibliography of British Literary Bibliographies" which lists some 1,000 additions to the end of 1969 and includes a note of corrections. Index.

Concordances, Dictionaries, Glossaries

HOWARD–HILL, T.H.—Editor
The Oxford Shakespeare Concordance Series
Oxford, 1971.
New volumes in the series are listed below. Each concordance is based on the text of the first folio. The editor takes into account every word of the text and represents their occurrence by frequency counts, line numbers, and reference lines, or a selection of these according to the interest of the particular word.
Henry IV. Part I. 388pp. $10.50.
Henry IV. Part II. 366pp. $10.50.
Henry V. 357pp. $16.00.
Henry VI. Part III. 314pp. $10.50.
Henry VIII. 336pp. $16.00.
Richard II. 284pp. $16.00.
Richard III. 365pp. $16.00.

SCHMIDT, ALEXANDER and GREGOR SARRAZIN
Shakespeare Lexicon and Quotation Dictionary
Dover, 1971. Volume One: 755pp. Volume Two: 730pp. Paper Two volume set: $12.50. An unabridged republication of the 1902 edition, revised and enlarged by Gregor Sarrazin. The volumes contain every word Shakespeare used in the plays and the poems. The author distinguishes between shades of meaning for each word, and provides exact definitions, plus governing phrases and locations, including the numbered line of the Cambridge edition of Shakespeare. More than 50,000 quotations are included, arranged under the words of the quotation itself, and precisely located. Appendices on basic grammatical observations, a Glossary of provincialisms, a list of words taken from foreign languages, and a list of words which form the latter part of word-combinations are also provided.

Quotation and Quiz Books

HUGHES, TED—Selector
A Choice of Shakespeare's Verse
Faber & Faber, 1971. $7.95. Paper $2.95. Selected and with an Introduction by Hughes, this is an anthology of passages from Shakespeare's works. Following the text, the editor has included a Note in which he describes a view of Shakespeare which emerged from his work on the selection. Index of First Lines.

McGOVERN, ANN—Collector
Shakespearean Sallies, Sullies, and Slanders
Crowell, 1969. 116pp. $3.95. Subtitled "Insults for All Occasions," this collection of quotations from Shakespeare's plays provides "a devastating retort, a thundering threat, a broadly funny squelch for every boor or bore or villain in life." Illustrated with drawings by James and Ruth McCrea.

QUENNELL, PETER
Quotations from Shakespeare
Plays, Inc., 1971. 279pp. $5.95. Originally published in Sweden and now issued in the United States with an Introduction and prefatory notes by Peter Quennell, this is a collection of short quotations from the plays of Shakespeare with drawings in color by Ake Gustavsson. The Introduction details Shakespeare's life and works.

SCHMIDT, ALEXANDER and GREGOR SARRAZIN
Shakespeare Lexicon and Quotation Dictionary
See entry in previous column

Annuals

MUIR, KENNETH
Shakespeare Survey 24
Cambridge, 1971. 184pp. $11.75. This is the annual survey of Shakespearean study and production. The central theme of the volume is "Shakespeare: Theatre Poet." Contributors include Anne Barton, J. P. Brockbank, John Russell Brown, Robert Hapgood, Terence Hawkes, Kenneth Muir, Richard Proudfoot, and Norman Sanders. Also provided is a review of critical studies recently published; a review of books on Shakespeare's life, times, and stage; and a review of recent textual studies. Eight photographs of recent productions in England are included. Index.

BIOGRAPHIES AND GENERAL SURVEYS

BROWN, IVOR
Shakespeare and the Actors
Coward–McCann, 1971. 208pp. $5.95. This volume completes the trilogy that began with "How Shakespeare Spent the Day" and continued with "The Women in Shakespeare's Life." Mr. Brown uses his knowledge of the theatre of today to draw a picture of playhouse conditions when Shakespeare was an actor. Illustrated. List of Books Consulted. Index.

CHARNEY, MAURICE
How to Read Shakespeare
McGraw–Hill, 1971. 149pp. $6.95. Paper $1.95. The author addresses himself to the problem of reading Shakespeare's plays with an awareness of their status as plays to be presented in a theatre. He suggests ways of approaching character, structure, staging, and poetic meaning that take into account the playwright's mastery of dramatic form and style. Mr. Charney calls attention to various aspects of staging—gesture, costume, music, use of the physical theatre, etc.—as essential to understanding the plays. Eight pages of illustrations are found in the cloth edition of this volume but are not included in the paper bound edition. List of Books for Further Reading.

EDITORS OF ARNOLDO MONDADORI EDITORE
Shakespeare: His Life, His Times, His Works
McGraw–Hill, 1971. 167pp. $4.95. Translated from the Italian by Catherine Jandine Hill, this is an introduction to Shakespeare's life and works. What is known of Shakespeare's life is set forth, many of the plays are analyzed in detail, and there is a review of criticism from the playwright's own time until the present. A sixty-four page anthology of passages from the works has been prepared for the volume by Louis Untermeyer. Illustrated with forty pages of color plates plus many illustrations in black-and-white.

HALLIDAY, F. E.
Shakespeare in His Age
Duckworth, 1971. 362pp. $3.95. Originally published in 1956 and now reissued, this is a study of the political, social, religious, and economical background of the age in which Shakespeare lived. A year-by-year presentation of the important events in his lifetime is given to show the influence of the times on the poet. Illustrated. Index.

HUSSEY, MAURICE
The World of Shakespeare and His Contemporaries
See Page 540

JOSEPH, B. L.
Shakespeare's Eden: The Commonwealth of England 1558 – 1629
Blandford, 1971. 368pp. $13.25. Paper $5.00. A study of Shakespeare's England which explains those aspects of life, art, and thought necessary for an understanding of the culture of the period. The author treats many aspects of the social, political, economic, and cultural life and includes chapters on literature in the age of Shakespeare, drama in the age of Shakespeare, and Shakespeare in his age. Eight pages of illustrations. Bibliography. Index.

MARTIN, MICHAEL RHETA and RICHARD C. HARRIER
The Concise Encyclopedic Guide to Shakespeare
Horizon, 1971. 450pp. $14.95. A guide to the world of Shakespeare—past and present. The main encyclopedic section is alphabetically arranged and covers the plays, the characters, meanings of words, quotations, critics, and scholars. Synopses of all the plots, details of the setting and the characters, original sources of the plays, summarizing comments by major critics, the background and significance of each character, the lines characterizing him, and separate entries for lesser known as well as significant quotations, with summaries of the contributions of important figures in Shakespearean scholarship from the seventeenth century to the present. Also included in separate sections are a biographical account of the playwright, lists of members of the Shakepearean contemporary theatre with concise biographical information, entries covering significant stage productions and major films, and information on composers of music for Shakespearean productions and recordings of works. Illustrated with fifty reproductions of art work or photographs. Introductory Reading List. Genealogical Charts.

MOMEYER, ARLINE BRYANT and WALTER M. BACH
All The World's a Stage
Christopher Publishing, 1969. 176pp. $2.95. An interpretation of the life of Shakespeare, written in the blank verse of the Elizabethan period.

MUIR, KENNETH and S. SCHOENBAUM – Editors
A New Companion to Shakespeare Studies
Cambridge, 1971. 298pp. $12.50. Paper $3.95. A new edition of "Companion to Shakespeare Studies" edited in 1934 by Harley Granville-Barker and G. B. Harrison. The editors of this edition have followed in general the lines laid down by the original editors and present an up-to-date and authoritative introduction to the whole field of Shakespeare studies. Topics include: Shakespeare's life, the theatre of his day and the ways in which he used it, the intellectual and social climate of his age, discussions of the plays and their performances, and a review of Shakespeare criticism. Illustrated. Notes and Reading Lists. Chronological Table. Index.

PARKER, MICHAEL ST. JOHN
Shakespeare and Stratford-upon-Avon

Pitkin Pictorials, 1971. 24pp. Paper $ .85. A description of Stratford-upon-Avon at the time Shakespeare lived. Illustrated with photographs in color and black-and-white.

RALLI, AUGUSTUS
A History of Shakespearian Criticism
Humanities, 1965. Volume One: 566pp. Volume Two: 582pp. Two volume set: $26.25. Originally published in 1932 and now reissued, this work aims to follow the course of aesthetic opinion on Shakespeare from his own time to the end of 1925 in England, Germany, and France. A selection of work on the subject has been made, and the author provides an exposition of each followed by a commentary. Alphabetical List of Critics. Index.

SALAMAN, MALCOLM C.
Shakespeare in Pictorial Art
Blom, 1971. 183pp. $18.50. Originally published in 1916 and now reissued, this is a collection of black-and-white plates which illustrate Shakespeare's plays. The text has been edited by Charles Holme. Among the artists whose works are included are: William Blake, Ford Madox Brown, E. Delacroix, Martin Droeshout, George Romney, and sixty-eight others. List of Artists.

SHAKESPEARE'S WORKS

General Studies of Shakespearean Comedy

McCUTCHAN, J. WILSON
Plot Outlines of Shakespeare's Comedies
Barnes & Noble, 1965. 174pp. Paper $1.50. This volume provides a scene-by-scene analysis of Shakespeare's comedies.

MARTZ, WILLIAM J.
Shakespeare's Universe of Comedy
David Lewis, 1971. 146pp. $6.00. This study employs comparative analysis to describe and define the dynamics of Shakespearean comedy. Five plays are examined: "The Taming of the Shrew," "A Midsummer Night's Dream," "As You Like It," "Much Ado About Nothing," and "Twelfth Night." Bibliographical Note.

PALMER, D. J. – Editor
Shakespeare's Later Comedies
Penguin, 1971. 460pp. Paper $3.75. An anthology of modern criticism of Shakespeare's comedies: "All's Well That Ends Well," "Measure for Measure," "Pericles," "Cymbeline," "The Winter's Tale," and "The Tempest." Critics include Northrop Frye, A. P. Rossiter, M. C. Bradbrook, G. E. Bentley, Allardyce Nicoll, and Stanley Wells.

RANALD, MARGARET
Notes on Selected Comedies
Monarch Press, 1964. 141pp. Paper $1.00. A study guide to "The Comedy of Errors," "The Taming of the Shrew," "The Two Gentlemen of Verona," "Love's Labour's Lost," "The Merry Wives of Windsor," "All's Well That Ends Well," and "The Winter's Tale." Act-by-act discussion of each of the plays is provided as well as critical commentary, essay questions and answers for review, and a Bibliography.

General Studies of Shakespearean Tragedy

CHARLTON, H. B.
Shakespearian Tragedy
Cambridge, 1971. 246pp. $6.00. A reprint of the study first published in 1948. The author is concerned with the humane rather than the technical aspects of Shakespearean drama. After a general discussion of the nature of tragedy, Professor Charlton studies the development of Shakespeare's technical skill from his first experiments in the tragic form ("Titus Andronicus," "Richard III," and "Richard II") through the four great tragedies ("Hamlet," "Othello," "Macbeth," and "King Lear"). Index.

McCUTCHAN, J. WILSON
Plot Outlines of Shakespeare's Tragedies
Barnes & Noble, 1965. 165pp. Paper $1.50. A detailed synopsis of each of Shakespeare's tragedies is included in this volume.

Studies of Plays in Groups

BROWER, REUBEN A.
Hero and Saint: Shakespeare and the Graeco-Roman Heroic Tradition
Oxford, 1971. 424pp. $7.50. Professor Brower approaches the idea of the heroic in Shakespeare's plays along two paths. One is the "sources" of the tragedies, in the context of Elizabethan translations of those sources; and the other is the dramatist's own resources, or what he brings to the work. Among the plays studied are: "Othello," "Titus Andronicus," "Julius Caesar," "Troilus and Cressida," "Hamlet," "Antony and Cleopatra," "King Lear," and "Coriolanus." Index.

CALDERWOOD, JAMES L.
Shakespearean Metadrama
University of Minnesota, 1971. 192pp. $7.50. Professor Calderwood attempts to demonstrate that in the five plays under study Shakespeare writes about his dramatic art—its nature, its media of

language and theatre, its generic forms and conventions, its relationship to truth and social order. The plays studied are: "Titus Andronicus," "Love's Labour's Lost," "Romeo and Juliet," "A Midsummer Night's Dream," and "Richard II." Index.

DAVIES, THOMAS
Dramatic Miscellanies
Blom, 1971. 859pp. $37.50. Originally published in 1784 and now reissued in a facsimile edition, this is a volume "consisting of critical observations on several plays of Shakespeare with a review of his principal characters, and those of various eminent writers, as represented by Mr. Garrick and other celebrated comedians, with anecdotes of dramatic poets, actors, etc." The plays studied include: "King John," "Richard II," "Henry IV – Part One and Part Two," "Henry VIII," "All's Well That Ends Well," "Macbeth," "Julius Caesar," "King Lear," "Antony and Cleopatra," and "Hamlet." Other playwrights studied include: Ben Jonson, Beaumont and Fletcher, Dryden, Otway, Congreve, Betterton, and Cibber. Indices.

EAGLETON, TERENCE
Shakespeare and Society: Critical Studies in Shakespearean Drama
Schocken, 1971. 208pp. Paper $2.75. Originally published in 1967 and now reissued, this is a critical study of some of Shakespeare's tragedies, problem plays, and late comedies, which sets out to examine the relationship between man and society as Shakespeare conceived it. Separate chapters deal with "Troilus and Cressida," "Hamlet," "Measure for Measure," "Coriolanus," "Antony and Cleopatra," "Macbeth," "The Winter's Tale," and "The Tempest," and the author includes a note on "Timon of Athens."

FARNHAM, WILLARD
The Shakespearean Grotesque
Oxford, 1971. 175pp. $8.50. The author presents Shakespeare's contribution to the realm of the "grotesque." He follows the stages of transformation in grotesque conception before and during the Renaissance and then turns critical attention to the shaping and placing within context of the characters of Falstaff, Hamlet, Iago, Caliban, and the Shakespearean fools. Three illustrations. Index.

FOAKES, R.A.
Shakespeare: The Dark Comedies to the Last Plays
University Press of Virginia, 1971. 186pp. $7.75. Professor Foakes seeks to understand Shakespeare's plays as dramatic structures. Starting with the dark comedies, the author examines the ways in which Shakespeare was affected by the new techniques and possibilities for drama opened up by the innovations of the years after 1600, notably by the rise in childrens, companies. A major part of the book is devoted to analyses of "Cymbeline," "The Winter's Tale," "The Tempest," and "King Henry VIII." Index.

JAMESON, MRS.
Characteristics of Women – Moral, Poetical, and Historical
A. M. S. Press, 1971. 391pp. $18.00. Originally published in 1889 and reprinted first in 1967, this is a facsimile edition of the study of the characteristics of Shakespeare's heroines. Twenty-three of the femal characters are analyzed as characters of intellect, passion, imagination, and affection, and as historical characters.

McCUTCHAN, J. WILSON
Plot Outlines of Shakespeare's Histories
Barnes & Noble, 1965. 184pp. Paper $1.50. A detailed synopsis of each of Shakespeare's ten history plays is included in this volume. Also provided is a biographical index to characters in the plays.

NUGENT, ELIZABETH M.
Notes on Troilus and Cressida and Titus Andronicus, Timon of Athens, Pericles, Cymbeline
Monarch Press, 1965. 154pp. Paper $1.00. A study guide to five of Shakespeare's plays with act-by-act discussion of the plots, character analyses, critical commentary, essay questions and answers for review, and Bibliographies.

PIERCE, ROBERT B.
Shakespeare's History Plays: The Family and the State
Ohio State University, 1971. 261pp. $8.75. Mr. Pierce examines the nine history plays in the approximate sequences of their composition to discover in them the elaboration and development of the correspondence between the family and the state which Shakespeare made into an effective dramatic technique. Index.

SISSON, C. J.
Shakespeare's Tragic Justice
Drama Book Specialists, Undated. 106pp. Paper $3.95. This volume includes an Introduction and four studies of justice in action. The four plays studied are: "Macbeth," "Othello," "Hamlet," and "King Lear." The author also provides an Appendix on "Hamlet."

Studies of Individual Plays

Antony and Cleopatra

MARKELS, JULIAN
The Pillar of the World
Ohio State University, 1968. 191pp. $6.00. Subtitled

"Antony and Cleopatra in Shakespeare's Development," this study traces the development of Shakespeare's concern with the conflict between public and private values. Mr. Markels suggests that Cleopatra's decision to join Antony in death can be said to exemplify the transition from a political to an ethical concern that distinguishes Shakespeare's most mature creations. Bibliographic Note. Index.

Hamlet

ALEXANDER, NIGEL
Poison, Play, and Duel: A Study in Hamlet
University of Nebraska, 1971. 212pp. $6.50. The author attempts to provide new insights into the thought and technique behind "Hamlet." He contends that the violence in the play, and the response to that violence, create the moral and psychological problems of the play. Four illustrations. Bibliography. Index.

FISCH, HAROLD
Hamlet and the Word: The Covenant Pattern in Shakespeare
Ungar, 1971. 248pp. $8.75. A new study of "Hamlet" in which the author introduces into the canons of Shakespearean criticism a new category, that of the biblical covenant. Professor Fisch shows how the idea of a covenant is inherent in the imagery and design of the play and how the leading character becomes the divine instrument of a moral purging. The insights gained from this analysis are applied to Shakespeare's other plays. Appendix. Notes. Index.

PROSSER, ELEANOR
Hamlet and Revenge
Stanford University, 1971. 304pp. $8.95. Paper $2.95. A second edition, revised, of the work first published in 1967. Miss Prosser re-examines the Elizabethan attitudes toward revenge and then analyzes the convention of revenge in the plays of Shakespeare and his contemporaries. A detailed explication of Shakespeare's play provides the core of the book, and the author supports her interpretation with a survey of "Hamlet" criticism and productions. Appendices. Index.

Henry VI

RIGGS, DAVID
Shakespeare's Heroical Histories: Henry VI and Its Literary Tradition
Harvard, 1971. 194pp. $8.75. Focusing on the trilogy of "Henry VI," this is an account of the rise of the Elizabethan history play as well as an examination of much of the serious English drama produced between 1587 and 1592. The author looks backward to the humanistic tradition on which Shakespeare drew and argues that the trilogy embodies an extended treatment of ethical topics that originated in classical rhetoric and historiography. Notes. List of Works Cited. Index.

Macbeth

JORGENSEN, PAUL A.
Our Naked Frailties: Sensational Art and Meaning in Macbeth
University of California, 1971. 234pp. $10.00. Mr. Jorgensen's study is intended as a tribute to both the art and moral vision of Shakespeare. It is his contention that "Macbeth" is a "sensational" work of art: it is a drama of sensation, of intense feeling. The author analyzes the literary techniques whereby sensation is achieved and attempts to suggest an underlying explanation for the sensationalism which he deems peculiarly organic to the play. Index.

Othello

ROSENBERG, MARVIN
The Masks of Othello
University of California, 1971. 313pp. $12.00. From the evidence of the play's stage history, the author searches for the identity of the three leading characters as portrayed by three centuries of leading actors and as reported on by critics. Illustrated with a frontispiece. Appendix. Notes. Index.

Richard II

CUBETA, PAUL M.—Editor
Twentieth Century Interpretations of Richard II
Prentice—Hall, 1971. 121pp. $4.95. Paper $1.45. Essays by nine of the world's foremost Shakespearean scholars and critics, including Jan Kott, E. M. W. Tillyard, Irving Ribner, Derek Traversi, and Peter Ure, which examine "Richard II" as a historical record and social document as well as a work of dramatic art. Discussing such wide-ranging aspects of the play as Richard's psychological motivation, the comparison of Richard and Bolingbroke, and the sophistication of the poetry, the contributors testify to the play's reputation as a masterpiece of Elizabethan drama. Chronology of Important Dates. Selected Bibliography.

Studies of Songs, Sonnets, and Poems

BOOTH, STEPHEN
An Essay on Shakespeare's Sonnets
Yale, 1971. 218pp. Paper $2.45. Originally published in 1969 and now reissued. Mr. Booth suggests that the source of pleasure in Shakespeare's "Sonnets" is in the line-to-line experience of reading them. He describes and illustrates the various patterning systems that coexist in the individual sonnets and then analyzes representative sonnets in terms of the reading experiences they evoke. Notes. Index of Sonnets.

MONCURE-SIME, A.H.
Shakespeare: His Music and Song
Blom, 1971. 196pp. $12.00. Originally published in 1915 and now reissued in a facsimile edition, this is a study of the use of music and song and musical allusions in the plays of Shakespeare. The author describes the place of music in Elizabethan life, then devotes a chapter to each of the plays, analyzing all the musical allusions in the verse. There are notes on references to musical instruments in the plays, to the use of song-birds in imagery, and to traditional melodies for new songs. Illustrated with a frontispiece and two reproductions of contemporary musical instruments. Appendices include seven musical examples of traditional melodies and a list of musical settings for twenty-two of the plays.

Editorial Problems

CAPELL, EDWARD
Notes and Various Readings to Shakespeare
Burt Franklin, 1970. Volume One: 533pp. Volume Two: 556pp. Volume Three: 669pp. Three volume set: $70.80. Originally published in 1779, 1780, and 1783 and now reissued in facsimile editions. The first two volumes contain notes and variant readings to eighteen of Shakespeare's plays based on an eighteenth century publication of the plays. The third volume includes extracts from books that were in print during Shakespeare's lifetime. Index of Books Extracted. Index of Words and Phrases.

HINMAN, CHARLTON and FREDSON BOWERS
Two Lectures on Editing: Shakespeare and Hawthorne
Ohio State University, 1969. 70pp. Paper $1.75. These two lectures were originally delivered at Ohio State University in 1968. Charlton Hinman has provided "Basic Shakespeare: Steps Toward an Ideal Text of the First Folio." He describes the search toward a definitive version of the First Folio of Shakespeare's works. Mr. Bowers' lecture is concerned with "Practical Texts and Definitive Editions" particularly of Nathaniel Hawthorne's works.

SHAKESPEARE'S CRAFTSMANSHIP

Shakespearean Techniques

JONES, EMRYS
Scenic Form in Shakespeare
Oxford, 1971. 269pp. $12.95. This study focuses attention on Shakespeare's invention and shaping of scenes in his plays. The author describes Shakespeare's mastery of scenic organization, and goes on to some related topics concerning scene and sequence. The book finally examines in detail four of the mature tragedies: "Othello," "King Lear," "Macbeth," and "Antony and Cleopatra." Index.

LEVIN, RICHARD
The Multiple Plot in English Renaissance Drama
See Page 541

LONG, JOHN H.
Shakespeare's Use of Music: The Histories and the Tragedies
University of Florida, 1971. 306pp. $11.00. This volume presents the results of a study of Shakespeare's use of performed music in his history plays and tragedies. Professor Long attempts to determine the functions of the performed music, the manner of performance, the original music scores or notation where possible, and the significance of these data to peripheral problems of interpretation, text, staging, and stage history. Appendices include musical examples. Also illustrated with musical examples in the text. Bibliography. Index.

THOMPSON, KARL F.
Modesty and Cunning: Shakespeare's Use of Literary Tradition
University of Michigan, 1971. 176pp. $6.95. An examination of Shakespeare's use of Renaissance literary tradition—a tradition which the Globe Theatre's audience recognized and appreciated. The author details Shakespeare's use of conventional materials such as standard elements of plot and characterization to fashion character, structure, and meaning. Notes. Index.

Shakespearean Themes

BARTON, DUNBAR PLUNKET
Shakespeare and the Law
Blom, 1971. 167pp. $11.50. Originally published in 1929 and now reissued in a facsimile edition, this book collects the various links which are discoverable between Shakespeare and the law. Shakespeare's relation to the Inns of Court and Chancery; his references to judges, advocates, and trials; and his allusions to law are all studied. Illustrated. Index.

FERGUSSON, FRANCIS
Shakespeare: The Pattern in His Carpet
Dell, 1971. 331pp. Paper $2.95. Originally published in 1970 and now reprinted, in this volume Dr. Fergusson seeks the poetic intention of each of Shakespeare's thirty-seven plays in order to bring out the recurrent themes. The plays are grouped chronologically according to the main parts of Shakespeare's career. Bibliographical Notes. Index.

KNIGHT, G. WILSON
The Shakespearian Tempest
Barnes & Noble, 1971. 332pp. Paper $4.50. Originally published in this revised edition in 1953, this is a volume of Shakespearean studies, tracing through the plays and poems the central symbols of tempest and music. A "Chart of Shakespeare's Dramatic Universe" gives Shakespeare's various values and symbolic powers, and, in effect, sums up Mr. Knight's whole work on the poet.

RICHMOND, HUGH M.
Shakespeare's Sexual Comedy: A Mirror for Lovers
Bobbs–Merrill, 1971. 210pp. $7.50. A study of the sexual relationships in Shakespeare's works. The author asserts that Shakespeare has much to teach the present generation about love. Moving from play to play, Mr. Richmond demonstrates his thesis: far from being something to fall into, love is far too dangerous to be left to the inexperienced or the doctrinaire. Sexual disaster can be averted only through resilience, realism, and a sense of humor. List of References.

TURNER, FREDERICK
Shakespeare and the Nature of Time
Oxford, 1971. 193pp. $7.75. A critical study of some of the moral and philosophical themes in the works of Shakespeare, particularly in "The Sonnets," "Romeo and Juliet," "As You Like It," "Twelfth Night," "Hamlet," "Troilus and Cressida," "Othello," "Macbeth," and "The Winter's Tale." The author's intention is to make possible new readings of specific passages, to suggest relationships within plays and groups of plays, and to examine "the core of Shakespeare's art." Appendix. List of Works Consulted. Index.

Shakespearean Sources

BOAS, FREDERICK S.
Shakespeare and His Predecessors
Gordian Press, 1968. 555pp. $11.50. Originally published in 1896 and now reissued, this is a discussion of Shakespeare's works in relation to their sources, emphasizing their points of contact with the playwright's predecessors and with contemporary literature. The author also discusses the Mediaeval drama, the early Renaissance drama, Marlowe, Kyd, Lyly, Peele, and Greene. Appendices. Index.

Playhouses and Productions in Shakespeare's Time

BOAS, FREDERICK S.
Shakespeare and the Universities
Blom, 1971. 272pp. $12.75. Originally published in 1923 and now reissued in a facsimile edition, this is a book of studies in Elizabethan drama. A portion of the volume is concerned with the university stage and its productions, particularly of Shakespeare's plays. Other subjects include stage censorship under Charles I and Charles II, a seventeenth century theatrical repertoire, and a non-Shakespearean "Richard II." Illustrated with reproductions of three contemporary documents. Appendices. Index.

KING, T. J.
Shakespearean Staging: 1599 – 1642
Harvard, 1971. 163pp. $9.00. A survey of pre-Restoration staging techniques. The author examines all the extant plays first performed by English professional actors between 1599 and 1642. Material from 276 texts has been assembled to show how Shakespeare's plays and those of his contemporaries were staged during the period. Illustrated. Appendices. Notes. Index.

EIGHTEENTH CENTURY TO THE PRESENT

Productions

AGATE, JAMES
Brief Chronicles
Blom, 1971. 311pp. $12.50. Originally published in 1943 and now reissued, this is a collection of the English theatre critic's reviews of London productions of Shakespeare's works in the 1930's and early 1940's. Index.

ENGLAND, MARTHA WINBURN
Garrick's Jubilee
See Page 542

MANVELL, ROGER
Shakespeare and the Film
See Page 601

RICHARDS, KENNETH and PETER THOMSON – Editors
Nineteenth Century British Theatre
See Page 545

SPRAGUE, ARTHUR COLBY and J.C. TREWIN
Shakespeare's Plays Today
University of South Carolina, 1971. 147pp. $4.95. Originally published in England in 1970 and now issued in the United States, this study traces the development of Shakespearean production in the United States and England throughout this century. The authors discuss the differing attitudes of the theatre towards the plays themselves, and they describe the changing fashions and conventions of visual presentation and interpretation of characters. Illustrated with nine plates. Notes. Index of Persons. Index of Plays.

Shakespeare's Reputation

ROBINSON, HERBERT SPENCER
English Shakespearian Criticism in the Eighteenth Century
Gordian Press, 1968. 300pp. $11.50. The purpose of this study, originally published in 1932, is to present a survey of English Shakespearean criticism from Nicholas Rowe's "Account" to Richard Cumberland's essays on the characters of Macbeth, Richard III, and Falstaff. The author offers the contention that there is no basis for the view that the eighteenth century was deficient in the appreciation of Shakespeare and that such appreciation anticipated nineteenth century thought and feeling. Appendices. Chronological Table. Topical Analysis. Index.

Adaptations of Plays

BAKER, PAUL
Hamlet ESP
Dramatist Play Service, 1971. 256pp. Paper $3.25. An adaptation of Shakespeare's "Hamlet" as presented at the Dallas Theatre Center, Texas, in 1970. The volume includes the director's notes on the production, a ground plan for the scene design, and a property list. Acting edition.

ESSAYS ON VARIOUS SUBJECTS

BERRY, FRANCIS
The Shakespeare Inset: Word and Picture
Southern Illinois University, 1971. 173pp. Paper $1.95. Originally published in 1965 and now reissued, this is a study of Shakespearean drama in performance. The author pursues the question of the relationship between the language being heard from the stage and the picture being exhibited. The divergence between what the audience hears and sees is examined. Index.

FOAKES, R.A. – Editor
Coleridge on Shakespeare
Routledge & Kegan Paul, 1971. 171pp. $7.75. A new edition of the lectures delivered by S.T. Coleridge in 1811–1812. It is based on hitherto unpublished transcripts of the lectures. Professor Foakes' Introduction and Appendices demonstrate the extent to which the transcriber, J.P. Collier, revised and altered Coleridge's words for the edition he published in 1856. The editor believes this edition provides a better and more authoritative text of Coleridge's lectures than has hitherto been available. Illustrated with five plates. Index.

HARBAGE, ALFRED
Shakespeare Without Words
Oxford, 1969. 18pp. Paper $1.50. The annual Shakespeare Lecture of the British Academy. The author suggests that Shakespeare's plays were written to be enjoyed and that criticism of the plays is unneccessary to their enjoyment.

HARBAGE, ALFRED
Shakespeare Without Words and Other Essays
Harvard, 1972. 229pp. $12.65. A collection of essays and lectures previously uncollected. The first eight essays are devoted to the debate of critical issues involving Shakespeare and his fellow dramatists. The last four essays relate to the history of the Elizabethan drama and raise questions of chronology and authorship. Index.

JACKSON, B.W. – Editor
Stratford Papers on Shakespeare – 1960
Drama Book Specialists, 1961. 112pp. Paper $3.95. Seven essays originally delivered at the Shakespeare Seminar at Stratford, Canada, in 1960. Among the contributors are: C.J. Sisson, John Cook, R.A. Huber, and Robertson Davies. The essays range in subject from a study of "King John" to Shakespeare and music to Shakespeare's development as a writer.

JACKSON, B.W. – Editor
Stratford Papers on Shakespeare – 1961
Drama Book Specialists, 1962. 231pp. Paper $3.95. The annual volume of Shakespeare lectures from Stratford, Canada. Twelve essays by such authorities as: Northrop Frye, Michael Langham, Peter Dwyer, R.B. Parker, Alfred Harbage, A.W. Trueman, Herbert Howarth, J. Mavor Moore, and J.W. Crow. The essays range in subject from Shakespeare's works to Shakespeare and witchcraft.

JACKSON, B.W. – Editor
Stratford Papers on Shakespeare – 1962
Drama Book Specialists, 1963. 238pp. Paper $3.95. These papers were delivered at Strarford, Canada, in 1961. The eight essays are by: Nevill Coghill, G.B. Harrison, R.A. Foakes, and Frank Jessup. The subjects range from Shakespearean comedy to G.B. Shaw's criticism on Shakespearean works.

JACKSON, B. W. – Editor
Stratford Papers on Shakespeare – 1963
Drama Book Specialists, 1964. 177pp. Paper $3.95. A collection of nine essays by Clifford Leech, Harry Levin, John Bayley, Joseph Papp. G. Wilson Knight, W. Moelwyn Merchant, Richard Morton, and Peter Smith. Most of the essays are concerned with the Greek plays.

JACKSON, B. W. – Editor
Stratford Papers on Shakespeare – 1964
Drama Book Specialists, 1965. 200pp. Paper $3.95. A collection of ten essays from the seminars held at Stratford, Canada. The essays were written to avow our debt to the playwright or to celebrate his fame on the four hundredth anniversary of his birth. The contributors are: Northrop Frye, Derek Traversi, Arthur Humphreys, Herbert Whittaker, F. E. Halliday, Robert Speaight, Roy W. Battenhouse, and Gordon Vichert.

KERMODE, FRANK
Shakespeare, Spenser, Donne: Renaissance Essays
Viking, 1971. 308pp. $7.95. A collection of essays and studies on the works of Shakespeare, Spenser, Donne, and Milton. Five of the eleven works are based on Shakespeare and his plays. The titles of these five essays are: "The Patience of Shakespeare," "Survival of the Classic," "The Mature Comedies," "The Final Plays," and "Shakespeare's Learning." Index.

McKEITHAN, DANIEL MORLEY
The Debt to Shakespeare in the Beaumont and Fletcher Plays
See Page 161

MORGANN, MAURICE
Shakespearean Criticism
Oxford, 1972. 444pp. $27.35. Edited with introductions and notes by Daniel A. Fineman, this volume publishes for the first time Morgann's revisions on his "Essay on Falstaff" together with the eighteenth century essay itself and also the author's commentaries on "The Tempest." Introductory materials include an account of Morgann's life and subsequent reputation.

PERRIN, NOEL
Dr. Bowdler's Legacy
Doubleday, 1971. 226pp. Paper $1.45. Originally published in 1969 and now reissued, this is a history of expurgated books in England and America. The author includes a chapter on the censoring of Shakespeare's works over the years. Notes. Index.

SCHOLARLY EDITIONS OF PLAYS

Plays in Series

OLIVER, H. J. – Editor
The Merry Wives of Windsor
Methuen, 1971. 149pp. $10.65. A volume in the "Arden Shakespeare" series. It contains not only the text, collations, and explanatory notes but also a full Introduction. This includes an extended critical analysis, discussions of the sources, probable date of composition, and the relation of the comedy to the other Falstaff plays; and a special study of the difficult textual problems created by the fact that the Quarto edition of 1602 is corrupt and inferior in some respects to the Folio version of 1623.

One Volume Editions

CRAIG, W. J. – Editor
Oxford Complete Works of Shakespeare
Oxford, $9.00 per volume.
Originally published from 1911 to 1912, these three volumes contain the texts of the plays and the poems of Shakespeare, as prepared by W. J. Craig. Introductory studies by Edward Dowden preface each of the plays and the poems. A General Introduction by Algernon Charles Swinburne is included in the volume of comedies. Each volume also includes a Glossary. "The Comedies" provides texts of fourteen plays. "The Histories and Poems" includes ten plays, five poems, and the Sonnets. "The Tragedies" includes thirteen plays.
The Comedies of Shakespeare. 1967. 1,128pp.
The Histories and Poems of Shakespeare. 1966. 1,214pp.
The Tragedies of Shakespeare. 1966. 1,315pp.

Single Editions of Works

BALLOU, ROBERT O. – Introducer
The Sonnets of William Shakespeare
Crown, 1961. 88pp. $1.00. This volume includes the 154 Sonnets, complete with the Temple Notes, and an Introduction by Robert O. Ballou. Also provided are eight illustrations of Shakespeare and of places associated with the playwright.

NATIONAL THEATRES

AFRICA

EAST, N. B. – Editor
African Theatre: A Checklist of Critical Materials
African Publishing, 1970. 47pp. Paper $3.75. This bibliography attempts to draw together wide-ranging references to secondary materials related to African drama. The work is divided into seven areas: Bibliographies, General, North, South, East, West, and Films. The entries include author, title, publisher or periodical, and date of appearance.

OKPAKU, JOSEPH – Editor
New African Literature and the Arts: Volume One
Crowell, 1971. 359pp. $8.95. An anthology of writing from Africa. Included in the volume are poetry, short stories, a segment from a film script by Oyekan Owomoyela, and essays on music, dance, art, and African literature and writers. Also included is a play by Joseph Okpaku: ''Born Astride the Grave.'' Hezbon Owiti has illustrated the volume with a selection of linocuts.

OKPAKU, JOSEPH – Editor
New African Literature and the Arts: Volume Two
Crowell, 1971. 251pp. $8.95. A second volume of writing from contemporary Africa. This volume contains essays, poetry, short stories, plays by Cosmo Pieterse and Leonard Kibera, and article on Les Ballets Africains, profiles of African artists, and a Bibliography. Ten photographs are included.

AUSTRALIA

HANGER, EUNICE – Editor
Drama for High Schools
University of Queensland, 1971. 281pp. Paper $5.65. Published in Australia, this is an anthology of short complete plays, sketches, and extracts from long plays. The primary purpose of the editor is to provide the twelve-to-sixteen-year-old high school student with selections which will be useful in his study of drama. Short introductions and conclusions provide information for the student and suggest approaches to the plays. It includes several selections from Australia as well as cuttings from contemporary English and American plays and from plays by Shakespeare, Marlowe, Sheridan, and Sophocles. A list of other plays is included. Illustrated with five drawings.

IRVIN, ERIC
Theatre Comes to Australia
University of Queensland, 1971. 260pp. $11.95. This is a history of Australia's first permanent theatre—Sydney's Theatre Royal. The author deals with the architecture of the Theatre Royal, its stage, equipment, actors, audiences, critics, and the plays presented. An Appendix lists every play presented at the theatre in the period 1832–1838. Illustrated. Bibliography. Index.

CHINA

ANSLEY, CLIVE
The Heresy of Wu Han
University of Toronto, 1971. 125pp. $9.25. The author provides a translation of a key document in the Chinese cultural revolution, ''Hai Jui's Dismissal,'' produced by the Peking Opera in 1961 and subsequently produced all over China. The play about a virtuous Ming Dynasty offical was used to lampoon Chairman Mao Tse-Tung and the core policies of the Chinese Communist Party and the name began to have a double meaning for many who had become disenchanted with Mao's rule. Mr. Ansley provides analytical and historical text which charts the reaction to the play and examines the charges made against the playwright by Chairman Mao and the Party. Notes. Bibliography.

HUNG, JOSEPHINE HUANG – Translator
Classical Chinese Plays
Drama Book Specialists, 1971. 275pp. $8.50. This volume contains translations of five of the most popular plays of the Chinese opera, with an Introduction and notes. They are among the four hundred written for the Chinese opera and belong to the ''wen-hsi,'' plays about social and domestic life. The plays are of unknown authorship and date. The translator has included six color plates, plus black-and-white illustrations, showing standard stage props, and musical instruments. Bibliography.

LEVENSON, JOSEPH
Revolution and Cosmopolitanism: The Western Stage and the Chinese Stages
University of California, 1971. 64pp. $6.75. Based on an analysis of a wide selection of Western plays translated into Chinese during the twentieth century, this is an attempt to set the Communist Cultural Revolution into historical perspective. Notes. Bibliography.

LU, STEVE
Face Painting in Chinese Opera
See Page 596

PE–CHIN, CHANG
Chinese Opera and Painted Face
See Page 596

FRANCE

Pre-Classical Period

Histories and Critiques

LEWIS, W.H.
The Splendid Century: Life in the France of Louis XIV
Morrow, 1971. 306pp. Paper $2.50. A reprint of the 1953 account of France under Louis XIV. The author explores the political, economic, social, and artistic forces which developed under the reign of the "Sun King." A summary of the work of the playwrights of the seventeenth century in France is included in a chapter on "The World of Letters." Notes for Further Reading. Index.

Classical Period: Histories and Critiques

MOORE, WILL G.
The Classical Drama of France
Oxford, 1971. 138pp. $4.35. Paper $2.15. The author's purpose is to discuss what we mean by "classical" French drama, to describe the theatrical and social conditions in which it flourished, to examine its origins, and to consider the theories of drama to be found in the writings of dramatic critics and of the dramatists themselves. A Note on Further Reading. Index.

NURSE, PETER
Classical Voices
Harrap, 1971. 230pp. $10.50. Studies of Corneille, Racine, Moliere, and Madame de Lafayette which attempt to capture the characteristic "voice" of each author by analyzing one or two of their more celebrated writings. Treated are such perennial aesthetic problems as the nature of the tragic and the comic, and the ethical function of art, with paritcular reference to the distinction between comedy and satire. Five pages of illustrations. Notes. Select Bibliography.

REISS, T.J.
Toward Dramatic Illusion: Theatrical Technique and Meaning from Hardy to "Horace"
Yale, 1971. 212pp. $10.00. This is an analysis of the changes which occurred in the French theatre of 1600–1650. The author approaches the dramatic text as one element in an artistic whole which also encompasses physical and verbal acting, scenic decoration, and the emotional and intellectual predispositions of the spectators. Mr. Reiss discusses and examines the plays of Alexandre Hardy, Francois Tristan l'Hermite, Georges de Scudery, de Monleon, Jean Mairet, Jean Rotrou, and Pierre Corneille. Appendices provide notes on the dating of the "Comedies des comediens" of Gougenot and Scudery, and on "The Ballets de Cour." A Bibliography lists primary and secondary sources which have been used in the formulation of the study. Index.

Studies of Playwrights

Corneille, Pierre

BROOME, J.H.
A Student's Guide to Corneille
Heinemann, 1971. 101pp. Paper $1.95. A study of Corneille's four greatest plays: "Le Cid," "Horace," "Cinna," and "Polyeucte." The author also provides an outline of Corneille's life and a survey of the development of French tragedy. Bibliography.

Racine, Jean

TOBIN, RONALD W.
Racine and Seneca
University of North Carolina, 1971. 173pp. Paper $7.50. A study of the debt owed by Racine to Seneca. The first of three parts treats Senecan dramaturgy; the Senecan tradition in the French tragedies of the sixteenth and seventeenth centuries is discussed in part two; the final section of the work deals with the affinity between Racine and Seneca as seen in the structure, characterization, thematic content, and style of Racinian tragedy. In the book's conclusion, some theories are advanced for Racine's well-known silence about his debt to Seneca. Select Bibliography. Index of Authors.

Rotrou, Jean de

NELSON, ROBERT J.
Immanence and Transcendence: The Theater of Jean Rotrou (1609 – 1650)
Ohio State University, 1969. 245pp. $8.00. A study of the dramatic works of the seventeenth century French dramatist. The author suggests that Rotrou was preoccupied with the relation between the human and the divine and his works demonstrate the continuity of, as well as the disparity between, Christianity and the classical heritage. Appendices. Notes. Bibliography. Index.

Eighteenth and Nineteenth Centuries

AFFRON, CHARLES

A Stage for Poets: Studies in the Theatre of Hugo & Musset

Princeton, 1971. 254pp. $11.00. Ten plays by Victor Hugo and Alfred deMusset are analyzed by the author. He considers those characteristics of lyric poetry which bring us closest to the attitudes of the playwrights, then examines the texts of the ten plays, including such topics as poetic time, the scope of analogy, theatrical and poetic rhetoric, the guises of the poet-hero, and the manner of sounding the poet's voice upon the stage. Eight pages of illustrations. Appendix. Selected Bibliography. Index.

BALDICK, ROBERT

Dinner at Magny's

Coward, McCann, 1971. 253pp. $5.95. A reconstruction of six evenings at the famed Parisian restaurant Magny where, from 1862 to 1872, the reigning geniuses of literature gathered to eat and talk. Among those attending these dinners were Flaubert, Turgenev, the Goncourts, and George Sand. Included among topics of conversation were politics, religion, literature, and sex. The author provides a picture of life in Paris during the last years of the Second Empire. Eight pages of photographs. Glossary. Bibliography. Index.

DU BOSE, ESTELLE and LA ROCQUE DU BOSE

Cyrano de Bergerac Notes

Cliff's Notes, 1971. 63pp. Paper $1.00. A scene-by-scene summary of and commentary on Rostand's play. An introduction to the life and works of the playwright, a note on scene divisions, listing of characters, and brief synopsis are included as are review questions and essay topics, and a Bibliography.

HENDERSON, JOHN A.

The First Avant-Garde: 1887 – 1894

Harrap, 1971. 175pp. $10.00. Published in England, this volume is subtitled "Sources of the Modern French Theatre." The author suggests that the avant-garde movement in France during the period from 1887 to 1894 transformed the French theatre, which took on a form recognizably similar to that we know today. Index.

HOUSSAYE, ARSENE

Behind the Scenes of the Comedie Francaise

Blom, 1971. 543pp. $15.75. Originally published in 1889 and now reissued, this is a translation by Albert D. Vandam of the author's reminiscences of the performances at the Comedie Francaise, and the actors who played there from about 1848 to 1856 while Houssaye was director of the theatre. One chapter discusses the French stage in the nineteenth century, and there are comments on the actress Rachel, on Victor Hugo, Alfred deMusset, and other prominent figures of the period. The translator has also edited the volume and provided notes. Illustrated with twelve plates.

JOSEPHS, HERBERT

Diderot's Dialogue of Gesture and Language: Le Neveu de Rameau

Ohio State University, 1969. 288pp. $8.00. Mr. Josephs studies Diderot's concern with the language of physical gesture. He devotes the first part of his book to a study of theories of language and gesture as they are suggested in the writings of Diderot and his contemporaries. He then offers an interpretation of "Le Neveu de Rameau" that focuses attention on the dialogue form of the work. Notes. Selected Bibliography. Index.

RAITT, A.W.

Prosper Merimee

Eyre & Spottiswoode, 1970. 453pp. $15.00. A biography of the French novelist, dramatist, and man of letters. Dr. Raitt presents Merimee's life against a background of the Romantic movement of the 1820's and 1830's, the revolutions of 1830 and 1848, and the rise to power of Napoleon and the Second Empire. All Merimee major writings are analyzed. Appendices include the texts of some unpublished Merimee letters. Illustrated with twenty-seven plates. Bibliography. Index.

SCHWARZ, H. STANLEY

Alexandre Dumas, fils: Dramatist

Blom, 1971. 216pp. $13.25. Originally published in 1927 and now reissued in a facsimile edition, this is a biography and study of the dramatic works of the nineteenth century dramatist. Bibliography. Index.

Twentieth Century: Histories and Critiques

SWERLING, ANTHONY

Strindberg's Impact in France: 1920 – 1960

See Page 554

Twentieth Century: Studies of Playwrights

Anouilh, Jean

ARCHER, MARGUERITE

Jean Anouilh

Columbia, 1971. 48pp. Paper $1.00. A critical study of the playwright. Included is a Selected Bibliography.

Artaud, Antonin

ARTAUD, ANTONIN
Collected Works: Volume Two
Calder & Boyars, 1971. 240pp. $10.00. Translated by Victor Corti, this volume includes the famous manifestos of the revolutionary Alfred Jarry Theatre, production plans, notes, and critical articles. Also included is a series of articles on literature and the plastic arts. Illustrated with eight photographs.

GREENE, NAOMI
Antonin Artaud: Poet Without Words
Simon & Schuster, 1971. 256pp. $7.95. Paper $2.95. The author traces the development of the major themes in the work of Artaud. Introduction by Janet Flanner. Notes. Bibliography. Index.

KNAPP, BETTINA L.
Antonin Artaud: Man of Vision
Avon, 1971. 255pp. Paper $1.65. Originally published in 1969 and now reissued, this is a study of Artaud's intellectual, philosophical, and psychological development through his own works. Dr. Knapp studies Artaud's theories and practice in the theatre and literature. Preface by Anais Nin. Notes. Bibliography. Index.

Beckett, Samuel

BARNARD, G. C.
Samuel Beckett: A New Approach
Dodd, Mead, 1971. 144pp. Paper $1.75. Originally published in 1970 and now reissued, this is a study of the novels and plays for the general reader. The author attempts to shed light on the condition of the main characters and the identity of all the heroes of the novels. Bibliography. Index of Names. Index of Subjects.

HASSAN, IHAB
The Literature of Silence: Henry Miller and Samuel Beckett
Knopf, 1967. 234pp. Paper $3.95. The author proposes that literature has adopted a new attitude toward itself and that silence is its metaphor, and the result is anti-literature. Two figures, Miller and Beckett, are proposed as masters of anti-literature. Selected Bibliography. Index.

HESLA, DAVID H.
The Shape of Chaos: An Interpretation of the Art of Samuel Beckett
University of Minnesota, 1971. 252pp. $9.75. A new interpretation of Beckett's art, focusing particularly on the sources and analogues of his ideas in pre-Socratic philosophy, the rationalists of the seventeenth century, and the phenomenologists and existentialists of the nineteenth and twentieth centuries. Among the works studied are five novels, two prose pieces, the plays "Waiting for Godot" and "Endgame," and, more briefly, the poetry and the shorter plays. Notes. Bibliography. Index.

MILLER, WALTER JAMES and BONNIE E. NELSON
Beckett's Waiting for Godot and Other Works
Monarch, 1971. 120pp. Paper $1.00. A critical guide to the themes, structure, and style of four of Samuel Beckett's plays: "Waiting for Godot," "Krapp's Last Tape," "All That Fall," and "Endgame." Also provided are guides to three of Beckett's novels. Included are model test questions and essay answers. Bibliography of Beckett's Works and Important Critical Writings About His Works.

Camus, Albert

FREEMAN, E.
The Theatre of Albert Camus
Barnes & Noble, 1971. 178pp. $8.75. A critical study of Camus as a dramatist. The author relates Camus' plays to his other writings and assesses them in their own right and in the context of the French theatre of 1930–1960. Notes. Bibliography. Index.

KING, ADELE
Camus
Capricorn, 1971. 120pp. Paper $1.25. Originally published in England in 1964 and now published in the United States, this is an introduction to the life and work of Albert Camus. A report on published criticism is included. Selected Bibliography.

LEBESQUE, MORVAN
Portrait of Camus
Herder & Herder, 1971. 174pp. Paper $2.95. Originally published in France in 1963 and now translated by T. C. Sharman and released in the United States, this is an illustrated biography of the French author. Chronology. Bibliography.

POLLMANN, LEO
Sartre & Camus: Literature of Existence
See Page 537

Duras, Marguerite

CISMARU, ALFRED
Marguerite Duras
Twayne, 1971. 171pp. $5.50. A study of the novelist/playwright. The plays and the film scripts are dealt with in separate chapters from the novels.

Notes and References. Chronology. Selected Bibliography. Index.

Genet, Jean

SARTRE, JEAN-PAUL
Saint Genet: Actor and Martyr
New American Library, 1971. 625pp. Paper $3.95. A new edition of the 1952 study of Jean Genet's life and work.

Gide, Andre

ROSSI, VINIO
Andre Gide: The Evolution of an Aesthetic
Rutgers University, 1967. 198pp. $7.50. Dr. Rossi analyzes Gide's early literary efforts to trace his "imaginative processes and fictional techniques in their evolution towards the formal perfection attained..." Notes. Selected Bibliography. Index.

Giraudoux, Jean

LEMAITRE, GEORGES
Jean Giraudoux: The Writer and His Work
Ungar, 1971. 220pp. $8.75. A study of the French playwright and novelist which examines how the substance of Giraudoux's writings reflects his perception of the world. Notes. Selected Bibliography. Index.

Ionesco, Eugene

BONNEFOY, CLAUDE
Conversations with Eugene Ionesco
Holt, Rinehart, 1971. 187pp. $4.95. In a series of exchanges with the French critic, Bonnefoy, Ionesco speaks candidly about the formative influences of his childhood, the challenges of the dramatist, his relationship with society, the theatre of the absurd, and the potential of the modern theatre. Translated from the French by Jan Dawson.

COE, RICHARD N.
Ionesco: A Study of His Plays
Methuen, 1971. 206pp. $6.95. Paper $2.95. Originally published in 1961 and now revised and enlarged, this study covers twenty years of Ionesco's work in the theatre and follows the development of his later plays. Included is a previously unpublished text, "The Neice-Wife." Illustrated with photographs. Bibliography. Index.

IONESCO, EUGENE
Present Past Past Present: A Personal Memoir
Grove, 1971. 192pp. $5.95. Translated by Helen R. Lane, this memoir ranges in time from Ionesco's childhood in Rumania to his life in wartime France.

WULBERN, JULIAN H.
Brecht and Ionesco: Commitment in Context
See Page 538

Mallarme, Stephane

COOPERMAN, HASYE
The Aesthetics of Stephane Mallarme
Russell & Russell, 1971. 305pp. $24.00. Originally published in 1933 and now reissued, this study traces the evolution of Mallarme's text and of his images. An extensive Bibliography is provided.

Sartre, Jean–Paul

LAING, R.D. and D.G. COOPER
Reason and Violence: A Decade of Sartre's Philosophy 1950–1960
Random House, 1971. 184pp. Paper $1.95. Originally published in 1964 and now reissued, this is an introduction to the thought of Sartre by two British psychoanalysts. The authors focus their study on three basic works of Sartre's later years: "Saint Genet," "Questions de Methode," and "Critique de la Raison Dialectique." Foreword by Jean-Paul Sartre. Index.

McCALL, DOROTHY
The Theatre of Jean-Paul Sartre
Columbia, 1971. 195pp. Paper $2.95. Originally published in 1969 and now reissued, this is an exploration of the discrepancy between Sartre's "Project" and the plays as they finally exist. The author relies extensively on Sartre's non-dramatic writings insofar as they elucidate what the playwright is doing in the theatre. All nine of the published plays are discussed. Notes. Selected Bibliography. Index.

POLLMANN, LEO
Sartre & Camus: Literature of Existence
Ungar, 1970. 253pp. $9.95. Originally published in Germany in 1967 and now translated by Helen and Gregor Sebba and issued in the U.S., this is a chronological analysis of the development of the two French writers. The author explains their strong similarities as well as their differences. Illustrated with diagrams. Notes. Index.

GERMANY

Histories and Critiques

GROPIUS, WALTER – Editor
The Theatre of the Bauhaus
See Page 588

SHAW, LEROY R.
The Playwright & Historical Change
University of Wisconsin, 1970. 183pp. $6.50. The author deals with dramas by four of the leading playwrights of the modern German theatre—Brecht, Hauptmann, Kaiser, and Wedekind. He presents the use of dramatic situation on the part of each author as a strategy for coping with reality in a time of shifting historical events. Bibliography. Index.

Studies of Playwrights

Brecht, Bertolt

ESSLIN, MARTIN
Brecht: The Man and His Work
Doubleday, 1971. 379pp. Paper $1.95. Originally published in 1959 and now revised, this was one of the first surveys of Brecht's work. The new edition incorporates recently released letters and documents and unpublished works. The Bibliography has also been brought up to date. Indices.

WULBERN, JULIAN H.
Brecht and Ionesco: Commitment in Context
University of Illinois, 1971. 250pp. $8.95. The author is concerned with the extent to which political commitment (or the lack of it) influences drama. He examines the polemics, dramatic theory, and theoretical practice of Brecht and Ionesco to put the special form of commitment adopted by each author into the context of his creative works. Focusing on the later works of each man, Wulbern analyzes Ionesco's "Rhinoceros" and Brecht's "The Measures Taken," then examines other works. Bibliography. Index.

Goethe, Johann Wolfgang von

GRIMM, HERMAN
The Life and Times of Goethe
Books for Libraries, 1971. 559pp. $26.25. Translated by Sarah Holland Adams, this biography of Goethe was originally published in 1880. The translator writes in her Introduction "These lectures are not intended to give a biography of Goethe, but to show in what sense he was at once the most real, as well as the most ideal, man and poet that ever lived." Chronological Table. Index.

SALM, PETER
The Poem as Plant: A Biological View of Goethe's Faust
Case Western Reserve University, 1971. 149pp. $5.95. An interpretation of Goethe's "Faust" which analogizes Goethe's scientific imagination – the typical plant – on the one hand, and "Faust" on the other. The author begins with a discussion of Goethe's theories of color and plant morphology and shows how the drama embodies a grammar of organic nature. Bibliography. Index.

Grabbe, Christian Dietrich

NICHOLLS, ROGER A.
The Dramas of Christian Dietrich Grabbe
Mouton, 1969. 268pp. $14.95. Professor Nicholls surveys the life of the nineteenth century playwright and discusses in detail each of his plays. The author attempts to show that Grabbe used and adapted the dramatic modes of his time and was not able to break free from the dominating force of dramatic traditions. Bibliography.

Grass, Gunter

WILLSON, A. LESLIE – Editor
A Gunter Grass Symposium
University of Texas, 1971. 95pp. $6.50. A collection of five lectures originally given at the Annual Symposium of the Department of Germanic Languages at the University of Texas. The authors—literary and dramatic critics, scholars, and translators — have contributed their views in five essays on the drama, prose, and poetry of Gunter Grass. The editor of the volume offers an essay that seeks to orient the reader to the aesthetics of Gunter Grass. Bibliography. Index of Names and Titles.

Lessing, Gotthold Ephraim

BROWN, F. ANDREW
Gotthold Ephraim Lessing
Twayne, 1971. 205pp. $5.50. A study of the influential German critic/dramatist/theologian. The author

offers detailed analyses of Lessing's principal dramas and of his pioneering efforts in the realm of literary and artistic criticism. The volume also includes a selection of Notes and References. Selected Bibliography. Index.

Lohenstein, Daniel Casper von

GILLESPIE, GERALD ERNEST PAUL
Daniel Casper von Lohenstein's Historical Tragedies
Ohio State University, 1965. 183pp. $6.25. A study of the seventeenth century German dramatist in which the author suggests that Lohenstein's dramas represent a significant early groping for a modern tragic formula in German literature. Mr. Gillespie concentrates on individual plays in an effort to search out the fundamental conception of each as a means of understanding its style and form. Notes. Bibliography. Index.

GREAT BRITAIN
(Including England, Scotland, and Wales)

General Histories and Critiques

CHANCELLOR, EDWIN BERESFORD
The Pleasure Haunts of London During Four Centuries
Blom, 1971. 466pp. $12.50. Originally published in 1925 and now reissued in a facsimile edition, this is a study of the places where Londoners were entertained and the types of entertainment offered from Tudor London to the early 1900's. Illustrated. Index.

DONALDSON, FRANCES
The Actor-Managers
Regnery, 1971. 195pp. $6.50. The author provides portraits of some theatrical innovators of the nineteenth and early twentieth centuries. Lady Donaldson shows how the "star-system," new standards of production, and well-chosen plays brought about a change in the attitudes toward theatre-going. The actor-managers included are Sir Squire and Lady Bancroft, Sir Henry Irving, Sir George Alexander, Sir Johnston Forbes-Robertson, Sir Herbert Beerbohm Tree, and Sir Gerald du Maurier. Illustrated. Bibliography. Index.

DONOHUE, JR., JOSEPH W. – Editor
The Theatrical Manager in England and America
Princeton, 1971. 216pp. $9.95. Essays examine five theatrical managers, spanning four centuries of the English-speaking stage, in order to evaluate the contributions of each to the drama of his time. Examined are Philip Henslowe, Tate Wilkinson, Stephen Price, Edwin Booth, and Charles Wyndham. An essay by the editor, "The Theatrical Manager and the Uses of Theatrical Research," introduces the volume. Illustrated with sixteen pages of portraits, reproductions of playbills, and other illustrations.

GREIN, J. T.
Premieres of the Year
Blom, 1971. 275pp. $12.50. Originally published in 1900 and now reissued, this is a volume of critiques of productions which appeared on the London stage from May, 1899 to July, 1900. Among the productions reviewed are Sarah Bernhardt's "Hamlet," the first English production of Ibsen's "When Awake from Death," and the first performance of Shaw's "Candida."

LAWSON, ROBB
The Story of the Scots Stage
Blom, 1971. 303pp. $13.75. Originally published in 1917 and now reissued in a facsimile edition, this is a history of the stage in Scotland from the earliest manifestations of the drama in the minstrels and mystery plays through its origin in Edinburgh and Glasgow to the nineteenth century. Illustrated. Bibliography. Index.

LEYSON, PETER
London Theatres: A Short History and Guide
Apollo, 1970. 72pp. Paper $1.75. A guide to and history of eighty theatres and places of interest associated with the theatre in and around London. Illustrated with drawings.

PENLEY, BELVILLE S.
The Bath Stage
Blom, 1971. 180pp. $13.50. Originally published in 1892 and now reissued in a facsimile edition, this is a history of dramatic performances in Bath, England. Chapters detail the visits of prominent actors through the ages including Mrs. Siddons, John Philip Kemble, Master Betty, Edmund Kean, and Ellen Terry. Illustrated.

RICKS, CHRISTOPHER – Editor
History of Literature in the English Language: English Drama to 1710
Sphere, 1971. 422pp. Paper $2.50. Published in England, this is a critical survey of English drama from 1495 to 1710. The volume is intended to give the reader a sense of the many contexts within which drama exists. Contributors include Glynne Wickham, Brian Morris, Ian Donaldson, Richard Proudfoot, and Philip Brockbank. Chronological Table. Notes. Bibliography. Index.

TREWIN, J.C.
London's Theatreland
Pitkin, 1971. 24pp. Paper $1.25. A short history of London's West End theatres. Illustrated with photographs and reproductions of paintings.

WARD, ADOLPHUS WILLIAM
A History of English Dramatic Literature to the Death of Queen Anne
Ungar, 1970. Volume One: 576pp. Volume Two: 767pp. Volume Three: 599pp. Three volume set: $17.50. Republished from the second edition of 1899, this survey begins with the origin of drama in England. After an account of Shakespeare's predecessors, there is a long section on Shakespeare including a discussion of the dramatist's early influence on the Continent, especially in Germany. Volume II also covers Jonson and the later Elizabethans, concluding with a study of the works of Beaumont and Fletcher. Volume III concludes the work with an examination of the later Stuart drama and the decay of tragedy. The third volume also includes an Index.

Chronological Periods: Beginnings to 1485

HELM, ALEX
The Chapbook Mummers' Plays: A Study of the Printed Versions of the North-West of England
Guizer Press, 1969. 54pp. Paper $1.65. A publication which discusses all known chapbook versions of the Folk Play. All versions are summarized, and there is discussion of dating, illustrations, provenance, the source of the texts, and the result of publication. Two complete texts are included. The volume is illustrated with period line drawings. Check List of Known Play Chapbooks.

Chronological Periods: Tudor, Elizabethan, and Stuart (1485-1660)

HISTORIES AND CRITIQUES

BOAS, FREDERICK S.
Shakespeare and the Universities
See Page 530

BOAS, FREDERICK S.
University Drama in the Tudor Age
Blom, 1971. 414pp. $12.50. Originally published in 1914 and now reissued in a facsimile edition, this is a history of the individual plays written and performed at Oxford and Cambridge Universities and a discussion of the general relations between the academic and the professional stage, as well as the attitude to drama of the university authorities in the sixteenth century. Appendices include excerpts from manuscripts, a list of university plays of the Tudor period, and some actor lists. Illustrated. Index.

BRODWIN, LEONORA LEET
Elizabethan Love Tragedy
New York University, 1971. 404pp. $12.50. The author defines the genre of "love tragedy" and traces its historical development. She illustrates the various types of love tragedy and attempts to shed light on the work of the major Elizabethan dramatists, particularly Shakespeare, Marston, Heywood, Beaumont and Fletcher, and Middleton. Notes. Index.

CRAIK, T.W.
The Tudor Interlude
Leicester University, 1967. 158pp. $5.25. Published in England, this is a study of Tudor "interludes," short plays having a moral purpose and personifying vices and virtues as contemporary social types. The conventions belonging to the interludes are displayed, and the links with the theatre of Shakespeare are emphasized. Two representative interludes are analyzed in detail: "Enough Is as Good as a Feast" and "Liberality and Prodigality." Illustrated with twelve pages of plates. Notes. Bibliography. Index.

GALLOWAY, DAVID – Editor
The Elizabethan Theatre: Volume One
Archon, 1970. 130pp. $7.50. A collection of essays on the Elizabethan theatre. The emphasis is on the structure of certain theatres, but all of the essays show an awareness of the physical conditions in which Shakespeare and the other dramatists of the age worked. Among the scholars who have contributed to the volume are: Terence Hawkes, Richard Hosley, Clifford Leech, T. J. B. Spencer, and Glynne Wickham. Illustrated. Index.

GALLOWAY, DAVID – Editor
The Elizabethan Theatre: Volume Two
Archon, 1970. 148pp. $8.00. The main concern of this volume is with the dramatic companies and their personnel during the Elizabethan period. Among the contributors are: S. Schoenbaum, R. A. Foakes, J. A. Lavin, and Bernard Beckerman. Illustrated. Index.

GREENFIELD, THELMA N.
The Induction in Elizabethan Drama
University of Oregon, 1969. 173pp. $6.00. The author studies the Elizabethan dramatists' use of the device of pointing openly to the gulf between make-believe and actuality. Dr. Greenfield studies the dumb show, pantomime, spoken dialogue, and frame plays. She classifies and analyzes the form and comments on modern criticism. Appendices include a list of plays with inductions. Index.

HUSSEY, MAURICE
The World of Shakespeare and His Contemporaries
Heinemann, 1971. 136pp. $10.95. Paper $4.95. Published in England, this book attempts to throw light on the whole background of Elizabethan literature, especially the plays of Shakespeare, Marlowe, and

Jonson. Through text and illustration, the author shows the images that would have come to the minds of the contemporary audiences as they heard the speeches in the various plays. The illustrations have been drawn from many sources to present the physical world of the period and the philosophical assumptions which underlie the themes, characters, and language of the Elizabethan dramatists. Book List. Index.

KING, T. J.
Shakespearean Staging: 1599 – 1642
See Page 530

LEVIN, RICHARD
The Multiple Plot in English Renaissance Drama
University of Chicago, 1971. 277pp. $12.65. This study deals with the period from the beginnings of the English secular theatre in the 1560's to its demise in 1642, drawing most heavily from the two decades of its greatest achievement, coinciding roughly with Shakespeare's professional career. The author concentrates on the detailed analysis of thirty examples of the multiple plot play, including works by Marlowe, Jonson, Middleton, Ford, and Shakespeare, among others. Appendices. Bibliography. Index.

MINER, EARL
Seventeenth Century Imagery
University of California, 1971. 202pp. $10.00. Essays on the use of figurative language from Donne to Farquhar by leading scholars from five countries. The essays stress the major writers of the period and explore a variety of critical approaches in preference to any single methodology. Among the subjects are John Donne's poems and sermons, Ben Jonson's play "The Alchemist," Milton's prose imagery, the imagery of Restoration comedy, particularly in Farquhar's "Beaux Strategem." Index.

REED, ROBERT R.
The Occult on the Tudor and Stuart Stage
Chistopher Publishing, 1965. 284pp. $6.50. A critical study of the use of occult phenomena on the Tudor and Stuart stage. Making use of ninety plays, the author analyzes the factors behind the rise, the popularity, and the decline of each of several occult characters as important figures of the stage. The more significant problems of the ninety plays are discussed. Notes. Bibliography. Index.

RIGGS, DAVID
Shakespeare's Historical Histories: Henry VI and Its Literary Tradition
See Page 528

ROWSE, A. L.
The Elizabethan Renaissance: The Life of the Society
Scribners, 1971. 336pp. $12.50. The author surveys the life of each class in Elizabethan society to present a portrait of Elizabethan life. Chapters are devoted to food and sanitation, sports and clothing, customs and beliefs, and to the sex life of the age. The book ends with a full discussion of witchcraft and astrology, which exerted a profound influence on the thought and habit of the society. Forty-eight illustrations, including reproductions of art work and photographs, illustrate the volume. Notes. Index.

SCHELLING, FELIX E.
Foreign Influences in Elizabethan Plays
Harper & Row, 1969. 160pp. $16.00. Originally published in 1923 and now reissued in a facsimile edition, the general purpose of this volume is to trace the influences affecting the drama in England during the reign of Henry VIII to the years immediately proceding the restoration of King Charles II. French, Italian, and Spanish influences are considered.

SIBLEY, GERTRUDE MARIAN
The Lost Plays and Masques: 1500 – 1642
Russell & Russell, 1971. 205pp. $16.00. Originally published in 1933 and now reissued, this is an annotated list bringing together all that is known about the lost plays of the period. Each entry gives contemporary references to the plays and scholarly opinions as to the plots or identification. Included is a separate list of English plays known to have been acted in Germany. Index of Playwrights.

SPINGARN, JOEL E.
History of Literary Criticism in the Renaissance
Columbia University, 1958. 257pp. $9.00. A republication of the 1908 edition, this work examines literary criticism in France, Italy, and England. The main emphasis is on the sixteenth century when the critics first developed a complete literary theory.

WELLS, STANLEY
Literature and Drama
See Page 516

STUDIES OF PLAYWRIGHTS

Jonson, Ben

BAMBOROUGH, J. B.
Ben Jonson
Hutchinson, 1970. 191pp. $5.50. Paper $2.50. A comprehensive account of Jonson's work, including chapters on the comedies, the tragedies and the masques, and the poetry and prose. The author treats Jonson's development chronologically to show Jonson's aims. Notes. Bibliography. Index.

BAUM, HELENA WATTS
The Satiric and the Didactic in Ben Jonson's Comedy
Russell & Russell, 1971. 192pp. $16.00. Originally published in 1947 and now reissued, this is a study of Jonson's search for an effective dramatic technique. The relation between the comedies of Jonson and his statements about what a comedy should be and should do is considered from several different points of view. Index.

DESSEN, ALAN C.
Jonson's Moral Comedy
Northwestern University, 1971. 256pp. $10.75. A critical, annotated study of the connection between Ben Jonson's comedies and the morality tradition of the Elizabethan era. Each of the major plays is studied in a separate chapter. Index.

McGLONE, JAMES P.
"Volpone": Notes
Cliff's Notes, 1967. 77pp. Paper $1.00. The author has included a scene-by-scene commentary and summary of the play by Ben Jonson. Also provided are character analyses of the various characters in the play and other essays. Review questions are provided for the student. Selected Bibliography.

Marlowe, Christopher

LEVIN, HARRY
Christopher Marlowe: The Overreacher
Faber & Faber, 1967. 231pp. Paper $2.25. A study of the Elizabethan poet, originally published as "The Overreacher" and now reissued. Appendices. List of Authorities. Index.

NORMAN, CHARLES
Christopher Marlowe: The Muse's Darling
Bobbs-Merrill, 1971. 273pp. $7.50. First published in 1946 and now revised and reissued, this is a biography of "the archetypal Elizabethan" poet and playwright. Notes. Selected Bibliography. Index.

Massinger, Philip

CRUICKSHANK, A.H.
Philip Massinger
Russell & Russell, 1971. 228pp. $17.25. Originally published in 1920 and now reissued, this is a documented study of Massinger's works. Twenty Appendices include a Bibliography, a comparison of passages in Massinger's and Shakespeare's works, and notes on Massinger's use of metre. Illustrated with a portrait of Massinger and reproductions of two documents. Index.

Webster, John

MURRAY, PETER B.
A Study of John Webster
Mouton, 1969. 274pp. $14.00. A critical examination of the works of the Jacobean playwright. The author offers detailed critical readings of Webster's plays including "The White Devil," "The Duchess of Malfi," "A Cure for a Cuckold," and "Appius and Virginia." Appendices. Index.

Chronological Periods: Restoration and Eighteenth Century (1660-1880)

HISTORIES AND CRITIQUES

BARBER, RICHARD
Samuel Pepys Esquire
University of California, 1970. 64pp. $3.95. A study which recreates the sights and surroundings familiar to Pepys during the diary period which began in 1660. Four essays deal with the surviving portraits of Pepys, their history and authenticity, Pepys' part in the Restoration, his relations with the Court, his interest in theaters and spectacles, and a reconstruction of his home. Twenty color plates and sixty black-and-white plates are included. Chronology.

BIRDSALL, VIRGINIA OGDEN
Wild Civility: The English Comic Spirit on the Restoration Stage
Indiana University, 1971. 279pp. $10.50. A study of the eleven plays written by the three major comic dramatists of the English Restoration period—Etherege, Wycherley, and Congreve. The author's purpose is to analyze the plays in the light of their functions as challenges to the establishment. Mrs. Birdsall traces the artistic development and the individual comic focus of each playwright and analyzes the ways in which the heroes and heroines emerge as archetypal comic figures. Notes. Index.

ENGLAND, MARTHA WINBURN
Garrick's Jubilee
Ohio State University, 1964. 273pp. $6.25. This is an account of the three-day festival staged by David Garrick at Stratford-upon-Avon in September 1769 in honor of William Shakespeare. Appendices include a list of some persons who attended the Jubilee and the text of Garrick's "Ode upon dedicating a building and erecting a statue to Shakespeare." Index.

GREG, W.W.
A Bibliography of the English Printed Drama to the Restoration – Volume IV: Introductions, Additions, Corrections, Index of Titles
Scolar Press, 1970. 110 +pp. $27.25. Originally

published in 1959 and now reprinted, this volume provides a 166 page Introduction to the "Bibliography," additions and corrections to the first three volumes, and a Title Index to those pieces that have substantive entries in the previous volumes. Illustrated with a frontispiece.

HUGHES, LEO
The Drama's Patrons: A Study of the Eighteenth Century London Audience
University of Texas, 1971. 209pp. $10.00. The author draws from contemporary accounts to analyze the audiences in eighteenth century London. He illustrates the decline in taste from the sophisticated comedy of the Restoration period to the sentimentalism of later decades and describes the effects of audience demands on managers, playwrights, and players. List of Works Cited. Index.

LATHAM, ROBERT and WILLIAM MATTHEWS — Editors
The Diary of Samuel Pepys
University of California, 1970. Volume One: 349pp. Volume Two: 267pp. Volume Three: 329pp. Three volume set: $28.50. The first three volumes in a new and complete edition of the diary of Samuel Pepys. When complete, the edition will include nine volumes of text and footnotes, a tenth volume of commentary, and an Index as the eleventh volume. Each of the presently available volumes comprises a complete year from 1660 through 1662. The first volume also includes an Introduction to the complete diary by Robert Latham. Each volume includes a Reader's Guide to the Diary, A Select List of Persons, and a Select Glossary.

LATHAM, ROBERT and WILLIAM MATTHEWS — Editors
The Diary of Samuel Pepys
University of California, 1970. Volume Four: 465pp. Volume Five: 386pp. Two volume set: $20.00. An additional two volumes in the projected eleven volume edition. The entries in these two volumes are for the years 1663 and 1664. See entry directly above for further information.

LONSDALE, ROGER — Editor
History of Literature in the English Language: Dryden to Johnson
Sphere, 1971. 445pp. Paper $2.50. Published in England, this is a critical survey of English literature dealing with the major figures and the main developments within the significant genres from 1660 to 1790. Among the genres covered, there is an article on drama from 1710 to 1780 by Ian Donaldson. Chronological Table. Bibliography. Index.

MUIR, KENNETH
The Comedy of Manners
Hutchinson, 1970. 173pp. $5.50. Paper $2.50. Professor Muir distinguishes between the comedy of manners and other types of comedy and traces its origins in English and French literature. He discusses Etherege, Dryden, Wycherley, Congreve, Vanbrugh, Farquhar, the decline of comedy in the eighteenth century, and its revival by Sheridan and, belatedly, by Wilde. Bibliography. Index.

SCHNEIDER, BEN ROSS
The Ethos of Restoration Comedy
University of Illinois, 1971. 201pp. $11.35. This study is based on a survey of 1,127 characters in eighty-three plays. The author contends that the ethical dimension of Restoration comedy derives from the traditional aristocratic notion of generosity. He holds that the genre is satiric in method, mirroring society in such a way as to criticize it. The study includes all the comedies most popular in their own time (1660–1730), all the comedies of Etherege, Wycherley, Congreve, Vanbrugh, and Farquhar, and several plays by other playwrights including Dryden, Cibber, Shadwell, Crowne, and Steele. An intensive examination of Congreve's "Love for Love" illustrates the integration in a single play of the ethical principles considered in the book. Appendix. Index.

STRATMAN, CARL J. and DAVID G. SPENCER, MARY ELIZABETH DEVINE — Editors
Restoration and Eighteenth Century Theatre Research: A Bibliographical Guide, 1900 – 1968
Southern Illinois University, 1971. 811pp. $25.00. A compilation of scholarly works published between 1900 and 1968 on the Restoration and eighteenth century theatre. Books, articles, theses, and dissertations are included among the 6,560 entries. The bibliography is divided into subject headings and arranged alphabetically with more than 400 categories being devoted to specific actors, architects, composers, musicians, playwrights, scene designers, and others involved with theatrical activity. The remaining categories include such topics as acting, audiences, ballet, burlesque, costume, dance, pantomime, periodicals, playbills, scenery, toy theatres, and type categories as well as sections devoted to dramatic activities in England, Scotland, and Ireland. Fourteen contributing editors have helped collect the material for the volume. Index.

WELLS, STARING B. — Editor
A Comparison Between the Two Stages: A Late Restoration Book of the Theatre
Blom, 1971. 206pp. $13.50. This is a facsimile edition of the volume of "theatrical chit-chat" that was originally published in 1702. The work has been attributed to Charles Gildon but the editor does not hold to this belief. The volume discusses contemporary plays and players of the Restoration stage. Textual and explanatory notes and a list of books cited in the notes are provided. Illustrated with a reproduction of the title page of the 1702 edition. Introduction by the editor. Index.

STUDIES OF PLAYWRIGHTS

Congreve, William

NOVAK, MAXIMILLIAN E.
William Congreve
Twayne, 1971. 197pp. $4.95. The author describes Congreve's achievements as a writer—what he did and what he failed to do. Each of the plays is examined in a separate chapter. Chronology. Notes. Selected Bibliography. Index.

Dryden, John

KINSLEY, JAMES and HELEN KINSLEY
Dryden: The Critical Heritage
Routledge & Kegan Paul, 1971. 414pp. $16.75. This volume provides a representative collection of critical comments on Dryden (including his own) from 1663 to 1810. Critics whose work is represented include Pepys, Marvell, Rochester, Swift, Congreve, Pope, and Blake. Excerpts from Sir Walter Scott's critical biography of Dryden are included. The editors have provided an Introduction and notes. An Appendix provides a listing of the early editions of the works of Dryden. Index.

Etherege, George

ROSENFELD, SYBIL – Editor
The Letterbook of Sir George Etherege
Blom, 1971. 445pp. $17.50. First published in London in 1928 and now reissued in a facsimile edition with an Introduction and notes by the editor, this is a collection of the letters of Sir George Etherege, the seventeenth century comic dramatist. Also included in the volume are several letters to the playwright, some verses, a catalogue of some of Etherege's books, and other material. Illustrated with seven plates and a map. Index.

Foote, Sam

TREFMAN, SIMON
Sam. Foote, Comedian
New York University, 1971. 302pp. $10.00. A biography of the eighteenth century actor, playwright, and manager. The author attempts to demonstrate that Foote's comedies are a surer guide to the temper of mid-eighteenth century life than the works of his contemporaries. Illustrated. An Appendix lists Foote's performances on the London Stage. Notes. Bibliography. Index.

Reynolds, Frederick

REYNOLDS, FREDERICK
The Life and Times of Frederick Reynolds
Blom, 1971. 796pp. $25.00. Originally published in two volumes in 1827 and now reissued in a facsimile one volume edition. This autobiography of the late eighteenth century British dramatist details the theatre in London during his lifetime. Illustrated with a frontispiece portrait.

Steele, Richard

KENNY, SHIRLEY STRUM – Editor
The Plays of Richard Steele
Oxford, 1971. 443pp. $20.00. This edition of Richard Steele's four plays provides a reliable old-spelling text following modern bibliographical principles. The editor has written an introduction to each play treating its sources and composition, theatrical history, influence on later drama, history of publication, and textual problems. Full bibliographical data and notes are included.

Chronological Periods: Nineteenth Century

HISTORIES AND CRITIQUES

ALLEN, SHIRLEY S.
Samuel Phelps and Sadler's Wells Theatre
See Page 566

ARCHER, WILLIAM
The Theatrical World of 1894
Blom, 1971. 417pp. $12.50. Originally published in 1895 and now reissued in a facsimile edition, this is a collection of articles and reviews dealing with the plays seen on the London stage in 1894. The volume includes an Introduction by George Bernard Shaw and a Synopsis of Playbills of the Year by Henry George Hibbert. Index.

ARCHER, WILLIAM
The Theatrical World of 1895
Blom, 1971. 445pp. $12.50. Originally published in 1896 and now reissued in a facsimile edition, this is a collection of articles and reviews dealing with the plays seen on the London stage in 1895. The volume

includes a Prefatory Letter by Arthur W. Pinero and a Synopsis of Playbills by Henry G. Hibbert. Index.

ARCHER, WILLIAM
The Theatrical World of 1896
Blom, 1971. 423pp. $13.75. Originally published in 1897 and now reissued in a facsimile edition, this is a collection of reviews of plays and other performances seen in London during the year 1896. Also included are critical articles on acting, actors, pantomime, etc. An Introduction, "On the Need for an Endowed Theatre," by the author is included as is a Synopsis of Playbills of the Year by Henry George Hibbert. Index.

BAYNHAM, WALTER
The Glasgow Stage
Blom, 1971. 230pp. $12.75. Originally published in 1892 and now reissued in a facsimile edition, this is a history of the theatre in Glasgow, Scotland, during the first half of the nineteenth century. There is also some information about the theatres and actors there fron the earliest times. Illustrated with a photograph of the Theatre Royal. Index.

DELGADO, ALAN
Victorian Entertainment
American Heritage Press, 1971. 112pp. $6.95. In text and reproductions of contemporary photographs, drawings, and playbills, the author provides a picture of the various forms of entertainment available in Victorian England. Bibliography. Index.

FITZGERALD, PERCY
Memories of Charles Dickens
Blom, 1971. 383pp. $13.75. First published in London in 1913 and now reissued in a facsimile edition, this is a personal recollection of the English author with approximately fifty letters included. Also provided is an account of the two journals edited by Dickens: "Household Words" and "All the Year Round." Seven illustrations. Appendices. Index.

FITZ-GERALD, S.J. ADAIR
Dickens and the Drama
Blom, 1971. 352pp. $12.50. Originally published in 1910 and now reissued in a facsimile edition, this is "an account of Charles Dickens' connection with the stage and the stage's connection with him." Thirty-two illustrations include portraits and reproductions of playbills. Index.

HOWARD, DIANA
London Theatres and Music Halls: 1850—1950
See Page 376

RHYS, HORTON
A Theatrical Trip for a Wager
Blom, 1971. 140pp. $12.50. Originally published in 1861 and now reissued in a facsimile edition. This is the record of a theatrical tour by an English music hall company through the United States and Canada during the late 1800's. Three illustrations.

RICHARDS, KENNETH and PETER THOMSON—Editors
Nineteenth Century British Theatre
Barnes & Noble, 1971. 195pp. $8.00. A survey of Victorian theatre in the form of a collection of essays on a wide range of subjects by several experts. The papers are grouped under three main headings: The Theatre, The Drama, and Shakespearian Production. The third section provides studies of productions of three of Shakespeare's plays during the nineteenth century. Illustrated.

ROWELL, GEORGE
Victorian Dramatic Criticism
Methuen, 1971. 372pp. $14.25. Paper $6.95. Published in England, this is a selection of articles which characterize the plays of the period in performance rather than as literature. The articles are arranged according to various aspects of the theatrical process and provide a picture of the contemporary theatre at work in the words of its leading commentators. There are selections on actors, the theatre and audiences, various genres of plays, pantomime and music hall, and the critic on his craft.

STUDIES OF PLAYWRIGHTS

Wilde, Oscar

RODITI, EDOUARD
Oscar Wilde
New Directions, 1947. 256pp. $3.00. A critical study of the playwright with detailed analyses of the poetry, plays, novels and critical writings. Mr. Roditi is primarily concerned with the position that Wilde's works and ideas occupied in the thought and art of his day. Illustrated with a portrait of Wilde. Appendices. Index.

Chronological Periods: Twentieth Century

HISTORIES AND CRITIQUES

AGATE, JAMES
First Nights
Blom, 1971. 311pp. $12.50. Originally published in 1934 and now reissued in a facsimile edition, this is a collection of fifty-nine critical reviews of plays seen in London from 1930 to 1934. Index.

AGATE, JAMES
My Theatre Talks
Blom, 1971. 316pp. $12.50. Originally published in 1933 and now reissued, this is a collection of talks about the theatre broadcast in England during a period of years from 1925 to 1932. Among the subjects are George Bernard Shaw, Henrik Ibsen, Ellen Terry, "Journey's End," Noel Coward, Sadler's Wells, and "Should Actors Feel?"

AGATE, JAMES
Their Hour Upon the Stage
Blom, 1971. 120pp. $11.75. Originally published in 1930 and now reissued in a facsimile edition, this is a collection of articles dealing with plays, and primarily with the acting, seen on the London stage 1926–1930.

ANDERSON, MICHAEL and JACQUES GUICHARNAUD et al
Crowell's Handbook of Contemporary Drama
See Page 513

EVERSHED-MARTIN, LESLIE
The Impossible Theatre: The Chichester Festival Theatre Adventure
Phillimore, 1971. 144pp. $10.50. An account of the Chichester Festival Theatre which is world-famous for its physical structure and its productions. Sir Laurence Olivier, the theatre's first director, has provided a Foreword. A thirty-two page pictorial record of the theatre has been included. Appendices include a list of plays and players from 1962 through 1970.

GREIN, J.T.
Dramatic Criticism: 1902 – 1903
Blom, 1971. 305pp. $12.50. A collection of drama reviews, originally published in 1904 and now reissued in a facsimile edition. The author reviews sixty-one plays seen in London during 1902 and 1903 and also offers fourteen essays on actors and miscellaneous subjects.

GREIN, J.T.
Dramatic Criticism: 1903 – 1904
Blom, 1971. 306pp. $12.50. A collection of seventy-two reviews of plays seen in London during the period covered in the title. Also included in the volume are nine papers on actors and acting and miscellaneous subjects. The volume was originally published in 1905 and is now reissued in a facsimile edition.

MacCARTHY, DESMOND
Drama
Blom, 1971. 377pp. $12.75. Originally published in 1940 and now reissued in a facsimile edition, this volume consists of reviews of plays and comments on actors and acting seen on the London stage from 1913 through 1934. Among the subjects discussed are: John Barrymore as Hamlet, John Gielgud as Richard of Bordeaux, Sarah Bernhardt, Eleonore Duse, and plays by Somerset Maugham, Noel Coward, G. B. Shaw, and Shakespeare.

MAROWITZ, CHARLES and TOM MILNE, OWEN HALE – Editors
The Encore Reader
Barnes & Noble, 1971. 308pp. Paper $3.65. Originally published in England in 1965 and now issued in the United States, this is a collection of reviews and theoretical articles printed in "Encore" magazine during the 1950's. It provides a background to the new English drama. Among the contributors are: Tyrone Guthrie, Lindsay Anderson, Peter Brook, Tom Milne, Charles Marowitz, Joseph Losey, and Stuart Hall. Illustrated with twelve photographs. Index.

NATHAN, DAVID
The Laughtermakers: A Quest for Comedy
Peter Owen, 1971. 240pp. $11.75. An exploration of comedy, seen through the eyes of comedians and comic writers by means of interviews, inter-linked description, and script examples. The author outlines the development of post-war comedy in Britain, detailing the new approaches to and forms of humor which have emerged. Eight pages of photographs are included. Index.

PRIESTLEY, J. B.
The Edwardians
Harper & Row, 1970. 302pp. $15.00. A survey of the period in modern history from the accession of King Edward VII in 1901 to the outbreak of the first World War. Priestley discusses every aspect of Edwardian life including the outstanding achievements of such writers as Shaw, the acting of Sarah Bernhardt, the singing of Caruso, and the delights of the music hall. Illustrated with forty-three color plates and more than 100 black-and-white photographs and reproductions of works of art. Select Bibliography. Index.

TAYLOR, JOHN RUSSELL
The Second Wave: British Drama for the Seventies
Hill & Wang, 1971. 236pp. $6.50. Mr. Taylor discusses contemporary playwrights in England during the 1970's. Among those studied at greater length are: Peter Nichols, David Mercer, Charles Wood, Edward Bond, Tom Stoppard, Peter Terson, Joe Orton, and David Storey. Twenty-two others are discussed in less detail. Bibliography of Playscripts.

STUDIES OF PLAYWRIGHTS

Bolt, Robert

ANONYMOUS
Notes on Robert Bolt's "A Man for All Seasons"

Methuen, 1971. 80pp. Paper $1.50. A study guide to Bolt's play with biographical notes on the author, historical notes on the background of the play, a summary and detailed analysis of the plot, an examination of the major characters, and essays on the themes of the play. Also included are suggestions for essays and a Selected Book List.

Eliot, T.S.

AUSTIN, ALLEN
T.S. Eliot: The Literary and Social Criticism
Indiana University, 1971. 101pp. Paper $6.75. The primary concern of this study is with Eliot's theory of poetry, his theory and practice of literary criticism, and his social and religious criticism. The author includes a series of notes, an Annotated Bibliography, and an Index.

ELIOT, T.S.
To Criticize the Critic
Farrar, Straus, 1970. 189pp. Paper $2.65. Originally published in 1965 and now reissued, this volume includes eight essays on literature and education. Among the subjects are: Ezra Pound's poetry, the aims of education, American literature and the American language, Dante, and the literature of politics.

MARTIN, GRAHAM – Editor
Eliot in Perspective: A Symposium
Humanities, 1970. 306pp. $11.75. A collection of essays on the work of T.S. Eliot. The editor has provided an Introduction which combines a synthesis of new trends in Eliot criticism with a statement of personal views. Among the contributors are: F. W. Bateson, Harold F. Brooks, and Richard Wollheim. Notes on Contributors. Index.

SENCOURT, ROBERT
T.S. Eliot: A Memoir
Dodd, Mead, 1971. 266pp. $8.95. Edited by Donald Adamson, this is a record of the author's impressions and recollections of Eliot with much new material gathered from among the poet's relatives both in England and the United States. Sixteen pages of photographs. Notes. Index.

Golding, William

HODSON, LEIGHTON
William Golding
Capricorn, 1971. 116pp. Paper $1.25. In a biographical introduction, the author traces Golding's development, background, and ideas. In the following chapters he elaborates and explains the themes of each of the novels. Golding's play, "The Brass Butterfly," is examined in a separate chapter. Bibliography.

Greene, Graham

GREENE, GRAHAM
A Sort of Life
Simon & Schuster, 1971. 220pp. $6.95. The autobiography of the English novelist/playwright. The author describes his childhood, his years at Oxford, his involvement with the Secret Service, and his apprenticeship as a journalist, as well as his early years as a writer.

VANN, J. DON
Graham Greene: A Checklist of Criticism
Kent State University, 1970. 67pp. $3.75. This compilation of criticism about Graham Greene includes bibliographies, books about Greene, chapters about Greene in books, articles about Greene, and a chronological listing of Greene's novels with reviews.

Maugham, W. Somerset

BROWN, IVOR
W. Somerset Maugham
Morgan Grampian, 1970. 85pp. $3.50. A brief biography for the general reader of the novelist and playwright. Illustrated with photographs in color and black-and-white. A summary of events in the author's life, a list of books and plays published, and a Select Bibliography of works on the author are included.

Osborne, John

ANONYMOUS
Notes on John Osborne's "Luther"
Methuen, 1971. 50pp. Paper $1.50. Published in England, this is a study aid to Osborne's play. Full descriptions of the historical background of the author, the genre, and the work are provided. Also included is a summary and a detailed analysis of the plot, an examination of the major characters, questions for study, and a Selected Book List.

CARTER, ALAN
John Osborne
Barnes & Noble, 1970. 194pp. $9.50. A study of the English playwright. Originally published in England in 1969 and now issued in the United States, the study presents a complete and detailed survey of all

of Osborne's plays including his two latest: "Time Present" and "Hotel in Amsterdam." A biographical account of the playwright is also included. Appendices include a list of first performances of plays. Bibliography. Index.

DENNY, NEVILLE – Editor
Luther: A Play by John Osborne
Faber & Faber, 1971. 171pp. Paper $2.75. The text of Osborne's play with an Introduction, notes, and afterword by Denny. Mr. Denny explains the textual difficulties, including historical references, and explores the wider questions raised by the Reformation, and contemporary revolt against accepted ideas. He discusses early criticisms of the play and considers the merits of the original stage production. Bibliographical Note.

Pinter, Harold

BURKMAN, KATHERINE H.
The Dramatic World of Harold Pinter: Its Basis in Ritual
Ohio State University, 1971. 171pp. $8.00. A study of the work of Harold Pinter. The author contends that the poetic images of Pinter's plays are based in ritual and that Pinter employs ritual in his drama for tragicomic purposes. Notes. Bibliography. Index.

GALE, STEVEN H.
Pinter's "The Homecoming" and Other Works
Monarch, 1971. 106pp. Paper $1.00. A critical guide to appreciation of meaning, form, and style in Harold Pinter's "The Homecoming," "The Room," "The Birthday Party," "The Dumb Waiter," "A Slight Ache," "The Caretaker," "The Collection," "The Lover," and other short works. Included are model text questions and essay answers. Annotated Bibliography.

LAHR, JOHN – Editor
A Casebook on Harold Pinter's The Homecoming
Grove, 1971. 199pp. Paper $2.95. A collection of critical essays on Pinter's play. Included are interviews that elucidate the approach to the play by a director, a designer, and various actors. Illustrated with a photograph of the set for the London production. Bibliography.

SYKES, ARLENE
Harold Pinter
Humanities, 1970. 135pp. $7.65. Paper $4.35. The author covers the whole body of Pinter's dramatic work in print. His plays for stage, radio, and television are analyzed in terms of the media for which they were written. Mrs. Sykes traces the development of both theme and technique in the works. Select Bibliography. Index.

Priestley, J. B.

COOPER, SUSAN
J. B. Priestley: Portrait of an Author
Harper & Row, 1971. 240pp. $7.95. A biography of the playwright with many extracts from his writings. Illustrated with a portrait. List of Works.

Shaw, George Bernard

ADAMS, ELSIE B.
Bernard Shaw and the Aesthetes
Ohio State University, 1971. 193pp. $8.00. An examination of Shaw's plays as the product of a unique artistic temperament at work in an intellectual climate that was shaped by the aesthetic movement of the time. Notes. Bibliography. Index.

CARPENTER, CHARLES A.
Bernard Shaw & the Art of Destroying Ideals: The Early Plays
University of Wisconsin, 1969. 262pp. $10.00. Professor Carpenter examines Shaw's first ten plays. He analyzes each play in terms of the particular ideals it sets out to discredit and the realistic alternatives it recommends. Notes. Selected Bibliography. Index.

DUKORE, BERNARD F.
Bernard Shaw, Director
University of Washington, 1971. 199pp. $7.95. This treatment of Shaw as a director examines Shaw's background and experiences in the theatre before he began to direct plays. The author explores various aspects of Shavian directorial theory and practice and analyzes Shaw's basic concern with the actor. The author makes use of Shaw's own rehearsal notes and his letters to actors. Illustrated with sketches of ground plans and costumes by Shaw. Bibliography. Index.

HUGO, LEON
Bernard Shaw: Playwright and Preacher
Methuen, 1971. 270pp. $11.50. A reappraisal of the literary and dramatic qualities of Shaw's plays, viewed in the light of their relationship to his social and political ideas. Among the plays discussed at length are: "Mrs. Warren's Profession" "Candida," "Caesar and Cleopatra," "Man and Superman," "Major Barbara," "Heartbreak House," and "Saint Joan." Select Bibliography. Index.

WAGENKNECHT, EDWARD
A Guide to Bernard Shaw
Russell & Russell, 1971 128pp. $13.25. Originally published in 1929 and now reissued, this is a discussion of Shaw's plays, novels, and critical works. The author interprets the ideas and theories in their relation to Shaw's philosophy. Appendices. Index.

Thomas, Dylan

JONES, DANIEL – Editor
The Poems of Dylan Thomas
New Directions, 1971. 291pp. $6.00. Dr. Jones has collected all the poems of Dylan Thomas, including twenty-six poems written by Thomas before he was sixteen, and arranged them chronologically. The editor has also provided an Introduction and Notes. Index of Titles and First Lines.

MAUD, RALPH and ALBERT GLOVER
Dylan Thomas in Print: A Bibliographical History
University of Pittsburgh, 1970. 261pp. $15.95. A bibliography of works by and about Thomas. Index.

THOMAS, DYLAN
Collected Poems 1934 – 1952
New Directions, 1971. 203pp. Paper $2.75. This edition of all the poems Thomas wished to have preserved was originally published in 1952 and then revised in 1956 with the addition of the poem: "Elegy."

Wesker, Arnold

LEEMING, GLENDA and SIMON TRUSSLER
The Plays of Arnold Wesker: An Assessment
Gollancz, 1971. 222pp. $7.75. The authors have undertaken a play-by-play analysis of theme, structure, characterization, and language in the works of Arnold Wesker, from "The Kitchen" to "The Friends." The volume also includes a section of Notes and References. Cast Lists of various productions are included. Chronology. Bibliography.

IRELAND

Histories and Critiques

BYRNE, DAWSON
The Story of Ireland's National Theatre: The Abbey Theatre, Dublin
Haskell House, 1971. 196pp. $14.50. Originally published in 1929 and now reissued in a facsimile edition, this is a history of Irish theatre and, particularly, of the Abbey Theatre. One chapter deals with the Abbey Players' first visit to America in 1911. Illustrated with nine plates showing the theatre and some of the leading personalities connected with it. Appendix A presents lists of plays presented by the National Theatre Society of Ireland. Appendix B provides a short summary of the little theatre movement in England and America, with lists of representative little theatres which have sprung from the Abbey.

FAY, W.G. and CATHERINE CARSWELL
The Fays of the Abbey Theatre: An Autobiographical Record
Blom, 1971. 314pp. $12.50. Originally published in 1935 and now reissued in a facsimile edition, this is a record of the first company of Irish players that later became the Irish National Theatre. The organization and development of the company, from 1902 to 1907, is written from an actor's point of view. The volume includes the life story of the Fay brothers, W. G. and Frank, and their theatre experiences. Foreword by James Bridie. Fourteen illustrations are included. List of First Productions. Index.

HOGAN, ROBERT – Editor
Towards a National Theatre: Dramatic Criticism of Frank J. Fay
Dolmen Press, 1970. 111pp. Paper $4.25. Published in Ireland, and edited by Robert Hogan, this is a collection of the dramatic criticism of Frank Fay, actor and teacher at the Abbey Theatre. The criticism is not only a record of events on the Dublin stage between 1899 and 1902 but a statement of Fay's principles. The editor's Introduction sets the pieces in the context of their time.

Studies of Playwrights

Behan, Brendan

O'CONNOR, ULICK
Brendan
Prentice–Hall, 1971. 328pp. $6.95. A biography of the Irish playwright written in close association with his wife, his mother, other members of the Behan family, and friends and associates. Illustrated with twenty-three photographs and a drawing. Selected Bibliography. Index.

Carroll, Paul Vincent

DOYLE, PAUL A.
Paul Vincent Carroll
Bucknell University, 1971. 115pp. $4.50. Paper $1.95. A monograph on the Irish writer who is best known for his play "Shadow and Substance." The study demonstrates that some of Carroll's other realistic plays have been undervalued. Carroll's ability as a writer of satirical comedies is examined. Overall Carroll is seen as a playwright whose works possess a depth and universality of view that carry them beyond their regional Irish and Scottish subject matter. Chronology. Selected Bibliography.

Joyce, James

ANDERSON, CHESTER G.
James Joyce and His World
Viking, 1968. 144pp. $6.95. A biography of the Irish novelist which explores the details of his life from his childhood in Dublin to his self-imposed exile in Europe. The biographical details are related to the substance of four of Joyce's works: "A Portrait of the Artist as a Young Man," "Ulysses," "Finnegans Wake," and "Dubliners." Illustrated with 142 photographs. Chronology. Notes. Index.

BRANDABUR, EDWARD
A Scrupulous Meanness: A Study of Joyce's Early Work
University of Illinois, 1971. 185pp. $6.95. The author combines literary criticism and psychoanalytic perceptions in his analysis of Joyce's early work, particularly "Dubliners" and the only extant play, "Exiles." Bibliography. Index.

O'Casey, Sean

BENSTOCK, BERNARD
Sean O'Casey
Bucknell University, 1970. 123pp. $4.50. Paper $1.95. A monograph which discusses the plot, character, and action of most of the Irish playwright's major works. The author considers O'Casey's autobiographical works and shows how they relate to the playwright's dramatic form. Chronology. Selected Bibliography.

MARGULIES, MARTIN B.
The Early Life of Sean O'Casey
Dolmen Press, 1970. 87pp. $5.95. The author attempts to dispel the mysteries of O'Casey's youth. The characters in the autobiographies are given a basis in a factual documentary which results from extensive research in Dublin.

O'CASEY, EILEEN
Sean: An Intimate Memoir of Sean O'Casey
Coward, McCann, 1971. 319pp. $6.95. Edited and with an Introduction by J. C. Trewin, this memoir of the Irish playwright was written by his wife. Mrs. O'Casey describes their married life and the celerated figures known intimately by the O'Caseys, and includes hitherto unpublished letters written to her by her husband and a series of letters exchanged between O'Casey and Shaw. Illustrated with sixteen pages of photographs. List of O'Casey's Works. Index.

O'CASEY, SEAN
I Knock at the Door
Pan, 1971- 191pp. Paper $1.50. A reissue of the first volume in the playwright's autobiography. In this volume, written in the third person, he recreates the days of his Dublin childhood.

O'Keeffe, John

O'KEEFFE, JOHN
Recollections of the Life of John O'Keeffe
Blom, 1971. 845+pp. $25.00. Originally published in two volumes in 1826 and now reissued in a facsimile one volume edition. This autobiography of the eighteenth century Irish playwright gives a picture of the theatre of the last half century in England and Ireland. Illustrated with a portrait of the playwright. Appendix.

O'Kelly, Seumas

SAUL, GEORGE BRANDON
Seumas O'Kelly
Bucknell University, 1971. 101pp. $4.50. Paper $1.95. A monograph which examines the considerable body of the Irish writer's work including the verse, prose, fiction, and drama. Chronology of Key Dates. Bibliographies.

Synge, John Millington

SADDLEMYER, ANN – Editor
Letters to Molly: John Millington Synge to Maire O'Neill
Harvard, 1971. 330pp. $14.65. A primary source for the study of Synge and the Irish theatre movement, these letters to the actress include poems inspired by her as well as extensive information about the Abbey Theatre. Miss Saddlemyer has provided a biographical introduction, a map, and photographs of both Synge and Miss O'Neill. Index.

SKELTON, ROBIN
J. M. Synge and His World
Viking, 1971. 144pp. $7.95. A biographical study which presents a comprehensive pictorial documentation of Synge's life and environment. Illustrated with 130 photographs and other material. Chronology. Select Bibliography. Index.

SKELTON, ROBIN
The Writings of J. M. Synge
Bobbs–Merrill, 1971. 190pp. $8.00. In this critical study of Synge's writings, the author pays particular attention to newly discovered works. Chronology. Bibliography. Index.

Yeats, William Butler

DONOGHUE, DENIS
William Butler Yeats
Viking, 1971. 160pp. $6.95. Paper $2.50. The author explores Yeat's life and work, pointing out the directions—in criticism, politics, religion, and magic—that his poetry bears upon modern feeling. Biographical Note. Bibliography. Index.

JEFFARES, A. NORMAN
W. B. Yeats
Routledge & Kegan Paul, 1971. 118pp. $3.50. Paper $2.25. An introduction to the work of Yeats. Professor Jeffares outlines the events in Yeats' life which influenced his poetry and explains some of its imagery. Suggestions for Further Reading. Select Bibliography.

MAC LIAMMOIR, MICHEAL and EAVAN BOLAND
W. B. Yeats and His World
Thames & Hudson, 1971. 144pp. $8.95. The authors trace Yeats' career covering his directorship of the Abbey Theatre as well as his poetic activities. They analyze the contradictory qualities of the poet/dramatist and provide illustrations of the poet, the people he knew, and the places with which his work and name are associated. The 138 illustrations include photographs and reproductions of art works. Bibliographical Note. Chronology. Index.

MOORE, JOHN REES
Masks of Love and Death: Yeats as Dramatist
Cornell University, 1971. 361pp. $9.75. An analysis and critical appreciation of all of W. B. Yeats' dramas. The works are examined against the background of Yeats' idea of the theatre, his special conception of the hero, his uses of poetic language, and his attempts to create an Irish theatre. Index.

ITALY

KIRBY, MICHAEL
Futurist Performance
See Page 519

JAPAN

NAKAMURA, YASUO
Noh: The Classical Theater
Lippincott, 1971. 248pp. $5.95. Translated by Don Kenny with an Introduction by Earle Ernst, this is an introduction to Noh drama. The approach is largely a visual one as 161 photographic plates in color and gravure are included to complement the text. The author explains the techniques of Noh Theatre, interprets its aesthetics, and recreates the atmosphere of the theatre in which it is performed. Chronology.

ROME, FLORENCE
The Scarlett Letters
See Page 570

TOSHIO, KAWATAKE
A History of Japanese Theater – II: Banraku and Kabuki
Japan Cultural Society, 1971. 103pp. + plates. Paper $3.00. A guide to the performing arts of Japan, particularly Bunraku and Kabuki. Twenty-eight pages of illustrations are included. Index. See also Volume I listed directly below.

YOSHINOBU, INOURA
A History of Japanese Theater – I: Up to Noh and Kyogen
Japan Cultural Society, 1971. 163pp. + plates. Paper $3.00. A basic guide to the history of Japanese theatre from approximately 600 A. D. through the present day. Among the types of theatre studied are Kagura, Gigaku, Bugaku, Saugaku, and the Noh. Sixteen plates are included. Appendices of various repertoires. Index. See also Volume II listed directly above.

NORWAY

EIKELAND, P. J.
Ibsen Studies
Haskell House, 1971. 178pp. $10.50. Originally published in 1934 and now reissued in a facsimile edition, this volume contains studies of four of Ibsen's plays: "Peer Gynt," "Brand," "The Pretenders," and "The Pillars of Society."

IBSEN, HENRIK
The Oxford Ibsen – Volume One: The Early Plays
Oxford, 1970. 715pp. $25.00. Edited and translated by James Walter McFarlane, this volume includes a critical Introduction, a Bibliography, early draft material, and a commentary on each of the plays as well as the texts of seven of the plays. Appendices describe Ibsen's journalistic and dramatic activities in Christiana in 1850–1851 and his work for the Bergen theatre in 1851–1857. The plays include: "Catiline," "The Burial Mound," "Norma," "St. John's Night," "Lady Inger," "The Feast at Solhoug," and "Olaf Liljekrans."

MCFARLANE, JAMES – Editor
Henrik Ibsen: A Critical Anthology
Penguin, 1970. 476pp. Paper $3.25. A critical anthology of criticism on the playwright. Both contemporary and modern viewpoints are provided. A full selection from the writer on his own art is

also included. The editor has contributed introductions, a Table of Dates, a Bibliography, and a full Glossarial Index.

MEYER, MICHAEL
Henrik Ibsen: The Farewell to Poetry 1864–1882
Hart–Davis, 1971. 344pp. $17.50. The second volume of the projected three volume biography of Henrik Ibsen, published in England. The author discusses Ibsen's abandonment of verse, his natural medium, to lay the foundations of modern prose drama, and the violent controversy which surrounded "A Doll's House" and "Ghosts." Illustrated. Select Bibliography. Index.

MEYER, MICHAEL
Ibsen: A Biography
Doubleday, 1971. 865pp. $12.95. This American one-volume edition of the biography of Henrik Ibsen includes all three sections of the work published in England in three volumes. The author reevaluates Ibsen as man and as writer in the light of new material recently discovered. He portrays the changing theatrical world of Ibsen's time and the impact of his life and his writing on his contemporaries. The biography has been called, by The London Times, "...the model of what a biography of a great writer should be." The volume includes sixty photographs. Bibliography. Index.

RUSSIA

Histories and Critiques

EVREINOV, NIKOLAS
The Theatre in Life
See Page 515

GRAY–PROKOFIEVA, CAMILLA – Introducer
Art in Revolution
World–Wide, 1971. 111pp. Paper $3.95. This is a catalogue of the exhibition at the Hayward Gallery, London, of Soviet art and design since 1917. The exhibition was conceived as an attempt to define the modern art movement of Constructivism. Among the essays included in the catalogue is one by Edward Braun: "Constructivism in the Theatre." There are also several pieces by Vsevelod Meyerhold, the Soviet director. Illustrated with reproductions of the art work exhibited.

MUCHNIC, HELEN
Russian Writers: Notes and Essays
Random House, 1971. 462pp. $10.00. A discussion of Russian writers from Pushkin to Solzhenitsyn. Among the playwrights considered are: Mayakovsky, Chekhov, Gorky, and Solzhenitsyn. Index.

Studies of Playwrights

Chekhov, Anton

BRUFORD, W.H.
Chekhov and His Russia: A Sociological Study
Routledge and Kegan Paul, 1971. 233pp. $9.75. Originally published in 1948 and now reissued, Professor Bruford pieces together, in this volume, Chekhov's sketches to provide a portrait of the playwright and a picture of Russia in the 1880's and 1890's. Bibliography. Index of References to Chekhov's Works. General Index.

PRIESTLEY, J.B.
Anton Chekhov
Morgan Grampian, 1970, 87pp. $3.50. A short biography of the playwright which is intended for the general reader. Illustrated with photographs in color and black-and-white. Also provided are a summary of events in Chekhov's life and a Select Bibliography.

SPEIRS, LOGAN
Tolstoy and Chekhov
Cambridge, 1971. 237pp. $8.00. A study of the literary relationship between Tolstoy and Chekhov. Mr. Speirs provides a detailed examination of "War and Peace" and "Anna Karenina" and then studies the work of Chekhov. A final note shows how the achievement of the two authors opened ways for writers in other countries, particularly D.H. Lawrence who developed their methods for his own purposes.

STYAN, J. L.
Chekhov in Performance
Cambridge, 1971. 341pp. $15.75. Professor Styan shows Chekhov's developing mastery of form and technique by detailed commentaries on each of Chekhov's four major plays. After a brief general Introduction, the book considers each play as a whole and than act-by-act. Each commentary takes the form of a narrative account and discussion of the play in performance, describing the stage action, suggesting character motivation, and estimating audience response. The author comments on modern productions as well as the original productions by Stanislavsky. Illustrated.

Gorky, Maxim

HABERMANN, GERHARD
Maksim Gorki
Ungar, 1971. 105pp. $5.95. Originally published in Germany and now translated by Ernestine Schlant and issued in the U.S., this is a concise introduction to the Russian writer and his works. Chronology. Bibliography. Index.

Nabokov, Vladimir

MOYNAHAN, JULIAN
Vladimir Nabokov
University of Minnesota, 1971. 47pp. Paper $ .95. A study of the work of the novelist/poet/playwright. The author concentrates on Nabokov's fiction. Selected Bibliography.

Solzhenitsyn, Alexander

LABEDZ, LEOPOLD – Editor
Solzhenitsyn: A Documentary Record
Allen Lane, 1970. 182pp. $7.50. Published in England, this is a collection of letters, speeches, and articles by Alexander Solzhenitsyn and by his accusers and defenders. Through the collected works, the editor relates the drama of Solzhenitsyn's courageous fight for creative freedom in the Soviet Union. It is traced from 1956 up to the award of the Nobel Prize for Literature in 1970.

LUKACS, GEORG
Solzhenitsyn
M. I. T. Press, 1971. 88pp. $6.95. Paper $1.45. Originally published in German in 1969 and now translated by William David Graf, this literary criticism does not deal with the writer's dramatic work. The first essay, on "One Day in the Life of Ivan Denisovich," explains the nature of Solzhenitsyn's criticism of the Stalinist period. The novels, "The First Circle" and "Cancer Ward," are studied in the second section of the volume.

Tolstoy, Leo

SPEIRS, LOGAN
Tolstoy and Chekhov
See Page 552

TOLSTOY, ILYA
Tolstoy, My Father: Reminiscences
Cowles, 1971. 322pp. $7.95. Translated from the Russian by Ann Dunnigan, these are the reminiscences of his father by Tolstoy's son. He describes the complex personalities of his father and mother, the homelife at the country estate, provides an account of Tolstoy's withdrawal during his spiritual crisis, the degeneration of his marriage, his dramatic flight from home at eighty-two, and his tragic death. The biography sheds new light on Tolstoy's friendship with Turgenev and on the people who provided for his comforts and perhaps served as models for the characters of his literary works. Included are sixteen pages of photographs. Notes and Comments. Index.

SPAIN

Studies of Playwrights

Lorca, Federico Garcia

TREND, J.B.
Lorca and the Spanish Poetic Tradition
Russell & Russell, 1971. 178pp. $16.00. Originally published in 1956 and now reissued, this is a study of eight Spanish poets: Lorca, Unamuno, Ruben Dario, Alfonso Reyes, Jorge Guillen, Cervantes, Calderon, and Berceo, with a chapter on medieval lyric writers. Index.

Sastre, Alfonso

ANDERSON, FARRIS
Alfonso Sastre
Twayne, 1971. 164pp. $5.50. A study of the critical and dramatic writings of the contemporary Spanish playwright. The author attempts to show the substance of the writings, their evolution, and their importance to today's world. Chronology. Notes. Selected Bibliography. Index.

Vega Carpio, Lope de

FITZMAURICE–KELLY, JAMES
Lope de Vega and the Spanish Drama
Haskell House, 1971. 63pp. $9.25. Originally published in 1902 and now reissued in a facsimile edition, this is a study of Lope's contributions to the Spanish drama.

PARKER, JACK H. and ARTHUR M. FOX – Editors
Lope De Vega Studies 1937 – 1962
University of Toronto, 1964. 210pp. Paper $8.00. A critical survey and annotated bibliography. Entries in the bibliography include editions and studies with title, author, year of publication, publisher, pages, and a short summary.

SWEDEN

CAMPBELL, G.A.
Strindberg
Haskell House, 1971. 144pp. $13.25. A reissue of the 1933 study of Strindberg's life and works. Chronology. Bibliography.

LAMM, MARTIN
August Strindberg
Blom, 1971. 561pp. $17.50. Originally published in Sweden in 1940, revised in 1948, and now translated into English and edited by Harry G. Carlson. The biographical and background details of Strindberg's life are provided and there is in-depth scrutiny of the full range of his works. Professor Carlson has added notes and references throughout the text to clarify the points of Swedish history and literature. He has also provided a Bibliography and a biographical essay to Lamm's book.

REINERT, OTTO – Editor
Strindberg: A Collection of Critical Essays
Prentice–Hall, 1971. 178pp. $5.95. Paper $1.95. A collection of essays by twelve authorities on Strindberg and his major plays. The editor has provided an Introduction which suggests that literary criticism should treat Strindberg's work as the imaginative equivalent of his life. Among the contributors are: Robert Brustein, Eric Bentley, Raymond Williams, Par Lagerkvist, Martin Lamm, and Evert Sprinchorn. Chronology of Important Dates. Notes on the Editor and Contributors. Selected Bibliography.

STRINDBERG, AUGUST
A Madman's Manifesto
Cambridge, 1968. 236pp. $7.50. Paper $3.25. First published in 1895 and now reissued as translated by Anthony Swerling, this is an "unexpurgated" account of Strindberg's marriage to Baroness Siri von Wrangel. Two Prefaces written by Strindberg are included in the volume.

SWERLING, ANTHONY
Strindberg's Impact in France: 1920 – 1960
Trinity Lane Press, 1971. 238pp. $15.35. This is an investigation into Strindberg's influence on French writers. The author utilizes unpublished material, his own interviews and correspondence, available published material, and textual examination and comparison in his study which situates the pre-Freudian Strindberg as the prime force on the seminal avant-garde. Psycho-physiological reactions to the plays are listed, and Strindberg's significance in modern France is chronicled. Five illustrations are included as are Appendices, Bibliographies, and an Index.

UNITED STATES

General Histories and Critiques

DONOHUE, JR., JOSEPH W. – Editor
The Theatrical Manager in England and America
See Page 539

GOHDES, CLARENCE
Literature and Theatre of the States and Regions of the U. S. A.
Duke University, 1967. 276pp. $10.00. A historical bibliography of books, chapters from books, magazine articles, pamphlets, anthologies, and monographs dealing with the history of local theatre, poetry, fiction, and other efforts from earliest time to 1964. The listing is divided by states and principal regions.

NATHAN, GEORGE JEAN
The Entertainment of a Nation
Fairleigh Dickinson University, 1971. 290pp. $10.00. Originally published in 1942 and now reissued, this volume by the drama critic covers the theatre and the whole panorama of the American entertainment scene. Among many topics are comments on playwrights, advice to actors and producers, and what happens at first nights. The author examines the motion picture, circus, cabarets, radio soap operas, strip tease, and burlesque. A new Introduction has been provided by Charles Angoff, friend and confidant of the drama critic.

PALMER, HELEN H. and JANE ANNE DYSON
American Drama Criticism
Shoe String, 1967. 239pp. $8.75. This is a bibliography of American drama criticism published from 1890 to 1965. The arrangement of the work is alphabetical by playwright with dates of first productions, criticisms in books and periodicals, and includes volume number, page, and year. Index.

WILLIAMS, HENRY B. – Introducer
The American Theatre: A Sum of Its Parts
Samuel French, 1971. 431pp. $10.00. This is a collection of the addresses prepared for the symposium, "The American Theatre—A Cultural Process," at the first American College Theatre Festival in Washington, D. C., in 1969. The essays provide a comprehensive look at the American theatre from its beginnings to the present day. Among the contributors are Alan S. Downer on playwriting from 1860 to 1920, Richard Moody and Alan Hewitt on acting from 1700 to 1900, Helen Krich Chinoy and Lawrence Carra on directing from 1860 to 1969, and other essayists on other subjects.

Histories through the Nineteenth Century

BLAKE, CHARLES
An Historical Account of the Providence Stage
Blom, 1971. 297pp. $14.50. Originally published in 1968 and now reissued in a facsimile edition, this is a chronological record, from 1745 to 1860, of theatre activity in Providence, R. I. Appendices include notes and lists of the casts of the plays produced in the various theatres.

DALY, CHARLES P.
First Theatre in America
Burt Franklin, 1970. 115pp. $16.95. Originally published in 1896 and now reissued in a facsimile edition. Subtitled "When was the drama first introduced in America? An inquiry," this is an account of players, playhouses, and plays in America during the eighteenth century. Also included in the volume is "A Consideration of the Objections that Have Been Made to the Stage." Illustrated with a portrait of the author.

HATTON, JOSEPH
Henry Irving's Impressions of America
Blom, 1971. 569pp. $15.75. Originally published in two volumes in 1884 and now reissued in a one volume edition, this "series of sketches, chronicles, and conversations" records the impressions he received during the English actor's tour of America during the late nineteenth century. American theatres and actors are mentioned frequently throughout the book, as are the details of Ellen Terry's first appearance in New York and the first appearance of Irving on the American stage.

HILL, WEST T.
The Theatre in Early Kentucky: 1790 – 1820
University Press of Kentucky, 1971. 205pp. $12.50. A comprehensive and chronological record of theatrical production in the area of America's first frontier. The author has recorded information about theatres, methods of production, actors, circuits, managers, performances, and critical reviews. An Appendix contains production data for the Kentucky circuit as well as Cincinnati and the smaller Kentucky towns. The book is illustrated with reproductions of newspaper announcements and portraits of leading figures. Bibliography. Index.

POWER, TYRONE
Impressions of America During the Years 1833, 1834, and 1835
Blom, 1971. 848pp. $25.00. Originally published in two volumes in 1836 and now reissued in a one volume facsimile edition, this is a record of the English actor's travels in America. A small part of the book is devoted to the theatrical productions Power enjoyed during his travels. Two illustrations.

RHYS, HORTON
A Theatrical Trip for a Wager
See Page 545

Histories of the Twentieth Century

ALTMAN, RICHARD and MERVYN KAUFMAN
The Making of a Musical: Fiddler on the Roof
See Page 570

ANDERSON, MICHAEL and JACQUES GUICHARNAUD et al
Crowell's Handbook of Contemporary Drama
See Page 513

BENTLEY, ERIC
Thirty Years of Treason
Viking, 1971. 991pp. $20.00. Selected and edited by Mr. Bentley, this is a collection of excerpts from hearings before the House Committee on Un-American Activities, 1938–1968. Bentley focuses on HUAC's confrontations with and treatments of artists, intellectuals, and performers because he believes HUAC itself betrayed a theatrical bias. Background material from newspaper and magazine articles which ran concurrently with the hearings is included, and the editor provides explanatory passages to provide the proper context. Personal commentary on the committee's various achievements and contributions to American history are provided in a separate conclusion. Excerpts from the testimony of Hallie Flanagan, Adolphe Menjou, Ronald Reagan, Bertolt Brecht, Larry Parks, Elia Kazan, Lillian Hellman, Clifford Odets, Jerome Robbins, Arthur Miller, Joseph Papp, and many others are included. Appendices. Index.

BIGSBY, C.W.E.
Confrontation and Commitment: A Study of Contemporary American Drama 1959 – 1966
University of Missouri, 1969. 187pp. Paper $2.50. Originally published in 1967, this is a reprint of Dr. Bigsby's study. He takes two meaningful concepts for the modern generation and finds in the frequently disparaging social plays of contemporary America a power and a hope for American drama. Among the playwrights studied are: Arthur Miller, Edward Albee, James Baldwin, LeRoi Jones, and Lorraine Hansberry. Bibliography. Index.

BRUSTEIN, ROBERT
Revolution as Theatre
Liveright, 1971. 170pp. $5.95. Paper $1.95. The Dean of the Yale Drama School comments on campus turmoil, radicalism versus liberalism, the fate of the free university, and the new revolutionary life style. He uses his grasp of theatre as a tool for understanding the new radical style of the young.

CHAGY, GIDEON – Editor
The State of the Arts and Corporate Support
Eriksson, 1971. 184pp. $10.00. A collection of articles illuminating the financial plight of arts organizations. Among the examinations are one on the mutual understanding and mistrust that inhibit the growth of working relationships between businessmen and artist, some of the practical ways in which corporations are beginning to help arts groups function effectively, a study of the finances and management of selected museums, orchestras, and resident theatres, and a report on twenty-seven corporate arts support programs. The eight contributors are: Robert

O. Anderson, G. A. McLellan, Granville Meader, Donald L. Engle, Hy Faine, William Ruder, Gordon Stewart, and the editor. Appendices list members of various advisory groups. Index.

COHN, RUBY
Dialogue in American Drama
See Page 587

CUTLER, BRUCE—Editor
The Arts at the Grass Roots
University of Kansas, 1968. 270pp. Paper $3.95. Based on a conference on the arts held in Wichita, Kansas, in 1966, this volume includes the remarks of the seventy-nine panelists and speakers and the question and answer sessions. The volume is a step-by-step account of suggested ways in which communities can make the arts more effective forces in community life. Music programs, theatre programs, dance and art programs, as well as creative writing programs are explored.

ESTRIN, MARC
ReCreation
Dell, 1971. Unpaged. Paper $2.75. A collection of material which is meant to be a grab bag of ideas and techniques for the use of the actor-writer-director-technician of the theatre-of-the-world-is-a-stage idea as propounded by the author. Estrin believes that we should all help to change the world by our performances in life, and he provides suggestions for projects, etc. Illustrated.

EUSTIS, MORTON
B'way, Inc.!: The Theatre as a Business
See Page 586

FREEDMAN, MORRIS
American Drama in Social Context
Southern Illinois University, 1971. 143pp. $5.95. Mr. Freedman studies the ways in which the plays of O'Neill, Miller, Albee, Kopit, and Jones, among others, reflect the social values of their times. The related questions of the essential qualities of American tragedy and playwriting in general are among other basic issues explored in the volume. Selected Bibliography. Index.

GILDER, ROSAMOND et al—Editors
Theatre I
Drama Book Specialists, 1969. 128pp. Paper $4.95. A collection of essays on the American theatre in 1967—1968. Among the contributors are Arthur Miller, Roger Stevens, Clive Barnes, Brooks Atkinson, Richard Barr, Alan Schneider, Harold Clurman, Harold Prince, Tom O'Horgan, Ellen Stewart, and Paul Green. Prepared by Miss Gilder and the Editorial Board of the International Theatre Institute of the United States, the volume includes a thirty page insert in which the articles are translated into French. Illustrated with photographs and drawings.

GILDER, ROSAMOND et al—Editors
Theatre 3
Scribner, 1970. 176pp. $9.95. Paper $4.95. The third annual volume of essays on the American theatre. Articles and essays deal with off-Broadway, off-off-Broadway, and Broadway, as well as various regional theatre companies in 1969—1970. Contributors include John Lahr, Harold Clurman, Walter Kerr, Peter Brook, Richard Schechner, Clive Barnes, Arthur Ballet, and Dan Sullivan. Illustrated with photographs and drawings. An extensive bibliography of books published during the year is also provided.

GILDER, ROSAMUND et al—Editors
Theatre 4
Scribner, 1972. 208pp. $9.95. Paper $4.95. The latest annual volume of essays on the American theatre. Articles and essays deal with off-Broadway, off-off-Broadway, Broadway, resident and repertory theatres for the year 1970—1971. Among the contributors are Martin Gottfried, Clive Barnes, Arthur Ballet, Arthur Miller, Stacy Keach, and Harold Clurman. Illustrated with photographs. Bibliography.

GREENBERGER, HOWARD
The Off-Broadway Experience
Prentice—Hall, 1971. 207pp. $6.95. This is a collection of interviews with an actor, an actress, a playwright, a director, a producer, a costume designer, a set designer, and others who have worked off-Broadway. Among the interviewees are Theodore Mann, Edward Albee, Alan Schneider, Joseph Papp, Coleen Dewhurst, and Lennox Raphael. A group of critics discuss elements of off-Broadway production since the end of World War II. Illustrated with photographs of personalities and productions.

KERR, WALTER
God on the Gymnasium Floor
Simon and Schuster, 1971. 320pp. $7.95. A collection of Mr. Kerr's commentaries on theatre. Most of the essays appeared originally in "The New York Times." They cover such subjects as the new style in theatrical productions, resident theatre groups, nudity on the stage, Harold Pinter, and reviews of contemporary plays and recent revivals. Index.

KRAFT, HY
On My Way to the Theatre
Macmillan, 1971. 216pp. $6.95. Reminiscenses and anecdotes about the people, places, and times the author knew. He details his association with Theodore Dreiser, his friendships with Oscar Hammerstein II, Paul Robeson, Nunnally Johnson, Elia Kazan, Abe Burrows, and other celebrities. He also provides an account of the McCarthy era in Hollywood. Illustrated with drawings by Al Hirshfeld. Index.

KRASSNER, PAUL
How a Satirical Editor Became a Yippie Conspirator
See Page 519

LEWIS, ARTHUR H.
Carnival
Pocket Books, 1971. 277pp. Paper $1.25. Originally published in 1970 and now reissued, this is a study of the American outdoor entertainment form as it exists today and as it was revealed to the author in his travels along the carnival trail for six months in thirty different cities.

LEWIS, MARIANNA O. and PATRICIA BOWERS – Editors
The Foundation Directory: Edition 4
Columbia University, 1971. 642pp. $15.00. This volume provides detailed information on American foundations which provide private philanthropy. Indexed by state, the entries list names, addresses, establishment date, donors, purpose and activity information, financial data, and officers and trustees. Foundations which contribute grants in the performing arts are included. An Analytical Introduction has been provided by F. Emerson Andrews. Indices.

LITTLE, STUART W. and ARTHUR CANTOR
The Playmakers
Doubleday, 1971. 320pp. Paper $2.95. Originally published in 1970 and now reissued, this is an account of the contemporary Broadway scene. Illustrated. Index.

MARTIN, RALPH G.
Lincoln Center for the Performing Arts
Prentice–Hall, 1971. 192pp. $14.95. A history of the Lincoln Center complex from its inception to the aims for the future. Each of the constituent buildings and their occupants are examined. Lavishly illustrated with photographs in color and black-and-white. Index.

MATHEWS, JANE DE HART
The Federal Theatre, 1935 – 1939: Plays, Relief, and Politics
Princeton, 1971. 342pp. Paper $2.95. Originally published in 1967 and now reissued, this is a study of the WPA Theatre Project during the Roosevelt era. Mrs. Mathews explores the venture from its ambiguous origins through the congressional hearings which occasioned its disbanding. Eight pages of photographs. Bibliography. Index.

NATHAN, GEORGE JEAN
The Morning After the First Night
Fairleigh Dickinson University, 1971. 282pp. $10.00. Originally published in 1938 and now reissued, this volume consists of the drama critic's reflections, set down in the form of afterthoughts to reviews of plays and actors prominent in the middle 1930's. Nathan deals with criticism, acting, playwrights, audiences, and Hollywood. A new Introduction has been provided by Charles Angoff.

SAYLER, OLIVER M.
Our American Theatre
Blom, 1971. 399pp. $12.50. Originally published in 1923 and now reissued, this is a study of the American theatre during the period 1908 through 1923. The playwrights, producers, designers, and critics of the time are discussed by the renowned critic. Illustrated. Appendices include lists of Pulitzer drama prize awards, Harvard prize play awards, the records of the Washington Square Players, the Theatre Guild, and the Provincetown Players. Index.

SHEED, WILFRED
The Morning After: Selected Essays and Reviews
Farrar, Straus, 1971. 304pp. $7.95. A collection of essays on books, theatre, films, sports, and politics. The material has been chosen from among that published since 1963 in such periodicals as "Esquire," "New American Review," "The New York Times and Book Review," "Life," and "Sports Illustrated."

SILVESTRO, CARLO – Editor
The Living Book of the Living Theatre
New York Graphic Society, 1971. Unpaged. $10.00. A book of words and pictures about the performing group, The Living Theatre. Written by all the members of the company, it is supposedly a distillation of their thoughts, social philosophy, their lives on and off the stage, and their reactions to the contemporary world. Richard Schechner has written an introductory essay for the volume. Included are 281 black-and-white illustrations.

WHITE, DAVID MANNING – Editor
Pop Culture in America
See Page 628

The Negro in the American Theatre

BAILEY, PEARL
Talking to Myself
See Page 573

BIGSBY, C. W. E. – Editor
The Black American Writer: Volume One – Fiction
Penguin, 1971. 273pp. Paper $1.45. Originally published in 1969 and now reissued, this is a collection of essays on the Negro literary achievement. Among the contributors are James Baldwin, Ralph Ellison, and Langston Hughes. The volume includes "The Negro in American Culture," the text of an important radio seminar with, among others, Lorraine Hansberry and Nat Hentoff. Index.

BIGSBY, C. W. E. – Editor
The Black American Writer: Volume Two – Poetry and Drama
Penguin, 1971. 253pp. Paper $1.45. Originally published in 1969 and now reissued, this is a second collection of essays on the Negro literary achievement.

Among the figures discussed are Lorraine Hansberry, Ossie Davis, and LeRoi Jones. Jean-Paul Sartre's seminal study, "Black Orpheus," is included. Index.

COLE, MARIA and LOUIS ROBINSON
Nat King Cole: An Intimate Biography
See Page 574

FUNKE, LEWIS
The Curtain Rises: The Story of Ossie Davis
See Page 563

HATCH, JAMES V.
Black Image on the American Stage
Drama Book Specialists, 1970. 162pp. $8.00. A bibliography of plays and musicals dealing with the Negro from 1770 to 1970. More than 2,000 entries are included—full length plays, one acts, musicals, revues, operas, and dance dramas by European, African, Asian, and American playwrights. The entries are listed by author with title of play, genre, date, publisher, and library where script may be found. Bibliography. Title and Author Indices.

McCALL, DAN
The Example of Richard Wright
See Page 560

MERYMAN, RICHARD
Louis Armstrong: A Self-Portrait
See Page 573

O'DANIEL, THERMAN B. – Editor
Langston Hughes – Black Genius
See entry in next column

PIRO, RICHARD
Black Fiddler
See Page 570

RALPH, GEORGE
The American Theater, the Negro and the Freedom Movement
Community Renewal Society, 1964. 29pp. Paper $1.50. This is a bibliography of works on the Negro and the American theatre.

Studies of Playwrights

Cummings, E. E.

FRIEDMAN, NORMAN – Editor
E. E. Cummings: A Collection of Critical Essays
Prentice–Hall, 1972. 185pp. $5.95. A collection of fourteen essays on the life and work of the poet/playwright by such contributors as Allen Tate, R. P. Blackmur, William Carlos Williams, Alfred Kazin, Robert Graves, and others. Introduction by the editor. Chronology of Important Dates. Selected Bibliography.

Green, Paul

KENNY, VINCENT
Paul Green
Twayne, 1971. 170pp. $4.95. A study of the work of Paul Green from the earliest stories and one act plays produced by the Carolina Playmakers to the preparation of an outdoor drama scheduled to be produced in 1971 at an outdoor amphitheatre in Georgia. Chronology. Notes and References. Selected Bibliography. Index.

Hughes, Langston

O'DANIEL, THERMAN B. – Editor
Langston Hughes – Black Genius: A Critical Evaluation
William Morrow, 1971. 245pp. $5.95. A collection of thirteen essays on the work of Langston Hughes. The intention is to "increase the readers' respect and appreciation for the scope, quality, and versatility of Langston Hughes's art and literary genius." A Classified Bibliography lists works by Hughes as well as books and articles about Hughes. Illustrated with a portrait.

James, Henry

JEFFERSON, D. W.
Henry James
Capricorn, 1971. 120pp. Paper $1.25. Originally published in 1960 and now reissued, this is a critical biography of the novelist/playwright. The study includes accounts of the viewpoints of his major critics. Bibliography.

Lowell, Robert

FEIN, RICHARD J.
Robert Lowell
Twayne, 1970. 173pp. $4.95. This study traces the development of Lowell's poetry, discussing the works chronologically. One chapter is devoted to each of the major books. Chronology. Selected Bibliography. Index.

Luce, Clare Booth

SHADEGG, STEPHEN
Clare Booth Luce
Simon and Schuster, 1971. 313pp. $7.95. A biography of the playwright/actress/Congresswoman/Ambassador/etc. The author has used personal letters and documents from Mrs. Luce's own files to detail all facets of her life. Illustrated with photographs. Index.

MacLeish, Archibald

SMITH, GROVER
Archibald MacLeish
University of Minnesota, 1971. 48pp. Paper $ .95. A short study of the American poet/playwright. Selected Bibliography.

Mailer, Norman

LUCID, ROBERT – Editor
Norman Mailer: The Man and His Work
Little, Brown, 1971. 310pp. $6.95. A collection of appraisals, critiques, analyses of specific books, and general views of the American author. The editor has provided an Introduction examining Mailer as a writer. Among the contributors are: Dwight MacDonald, Norman Podhoretz, Gore Vidal, Diana Trilling, Alfred Kazin, Tom Wolfe, Calder Willingham, and James Baldwin. Biographical Chronology. Ckecklist of Published Work.

Miller, Arthur

HAYASHI, TETSUMARO
Arthur Miller Criticism (1930 – 1967)
Scarecrow, 1969. 149pp. $5.75. A bibliography of all the known published and unpublished works of the American playwright. Chronology. Lists of Reference Books Used. List of Newspapers and Periodicals Indexed. Author Index.

WEALES, GERALD – Editor
The Crucible: Text and Criticism
Viking, 1971. 484pp. $6.95. Paper $3.25. A complete text of Arthur Miller's play about the Salem witch trials. The editor has provided an Introduction, a Chronology of Miller's life, and a Bibliography. Also included are criticism and analogues by Brooks Atkinson, Henry Hewes, Eric Bentley, Jean-Paul Sartre, and Budd Schulberg, among others.

Odets, Clifford

WEALES, GERALD
Clifford Odets – Playwright
Pegasus, 1971. 205pp. $6.95. A study of the American playwright in which the author mixes criticism with narrative to provide the social and political context in which the reader can understand the playwright's work. A long chapter on "Awake and Sing" establishes the themes, characters, and language that Odets used in the bulk of his work. The chapters that follow detail the variations used from play to play. Notes on Sources. Bibliographical Note. Index.

O'Neill, Eugene

FRENZ, HORST
Eugene O'Neill
Ungar, 1971. 121pp. $5.95. Paper $1.75. A concise introduction to the American dramatist. Translated from the German by Helen Sebba, the volume includes a Chronology, List of Works, Bibliographical Notes, and an Index.

REAVER, J. RUSSELL – Compiler
An O'Neill Concordance
Gale Research, 1969. 1,846pp. Three volume set: $117.50. This concordance is based on the standard Random House edition of O'Neill and the individual plays by Yale University Press. Twenty-eight plays are covered. The compiler hopes the concordance will aid scholars in examining the varied interests in the works of the playwright.

Stein, Gertrude

STEIN, GERTRUDE
Gertrude Stein: Writings and Lectures 1909 – 1945
Penguin, 1971. 446pp. Paper $2.25. Edited by Patricia Meyerowitz, this is a collection of Miss Stein's most representative achievements. Included in the anthology are most of the major lectures she gave on writing. Two plays, "A List" and "Say It With Flowers," are included. Bibliography.

WEINSTEIN, NORMAN
Gertrude Stein and the Literature of the Modern Consciousness
Ungar, 1970. 150pp. $8.25. The author examines Gertrude Stein's literary production in the light of twentieth century theories of language. One chapter is devoted to Miss Stein's play, "Four Saints in Three Acts." Notes. Bibliography of works by and about Miss Stein. Index.

Wilbur, Richard

FIELD, JOHN P.
Richard Wilbur: A Bibliographical Checklist
Kent State University, 1971. 85pp. $4.50. A bibliographical record of the material written by and about Richard Wilbur. The author provides a chronological ordering of approximately the first thirty years of Wilbur's activity as a writer. Field includes a listing of the criticism of Wilbur's work published in America and England.

Wilder, Thornton

STRESAU, HERMANN
Thornton Wilder
Ungar, 1971. 130pp. $5.95. A concise introduction to the American novelist/playwright. Notes. Chronology. Bibliography. Index.

Williams, Tennessee

MILLER, JORDAN Y. – Editor
Twentieth Century Interpretation of "A Streetcar Named Desire"
Prentice–Hall, 1971. 119pp. $4.95. Paper $1.45. Noted contributors offer analyses of Tennessee Williams' play. The editor has included opening-night reviews and notes by the director, Elia Kazan, as well as an introductory essay on the playwright and the play. Selected Bibliography.

Wolfe, Thomas

KENNEDY, RICHARD S.
The Window of Memory: The Literary Career of Thomas Wolfe
University of North Carolina, 1962. 461pp. Paper $3.45. A detailed study of the mind and art of Thomas Wolfe. Following Wolfe's literary output chronologically, the author provides an analysis of each of the novels and stories and an account of the shaping of each work. Notes. List of Sources and Works Cited. Index.

Wright, Richard

McCALL, DAN
The Example of Richard Wright
Harcourt, Brace, 1971. 202pp. Paper $2.25. Originally published in 1969 and now reissued, this is a critical study of the first major black writer in American literature. Of particular interest is the section comparing Wright's "Native Son" with Genet's "The Blacks." Index.

YIDDISH THEATRE

BECK, EVELYN TORTON
Kafka and the Yiddish Theatre
University of Wisconsin, 1971. 248pp. $12.50. In this comparative study, Mrs. Beck demonstrates that the strong dramatic style Kafka displays in his later works was largely due to his intense involvement with the Yiddish theatre. The author traces parallels between many of Kafka's works and twelve of the fourteen Yiddish plays mentioned in his diaries. Appendices. Bibliography. Index.

BERNARDI, JACK
My Father the Actor
See Page 562

BIOGRAPHIES OF STAGE PERSONALITES

COLLECTED (By Author)

ARMSTRONG, CECIL FERARD
A Century of Great Actors: 1750–1850
Blom, 1971. 412pp. $13.75. Originally published in 1912 and now reissued in a facsimile edition, this volume includes an account of the lives, careers, and art of fourteen actors of the English stage. Among those included are: David Garrick, John Philip Kemble, Edmund Kean, William Charles Macready, Master Betty, Charles Macklin, and Joseph Grimaldi. Illustrated with sixteen portraits.

CLAPP, JOHN BOUVE and EDWIN FRANCIS EDGETT
Players of the Present
Blom, 1971. 423pp. $18.75. Originally published in 1899, 1900, and 1901 and now reissued in a one volume edition, this is a collection of biographical accounts of the lives of actors and actresses of the late nineteenth century. Illustrated with twenty-seven portraits. Index.

CLAPP, JOHN BOUVE and EDWIN FRANCIS EDGETT
Players of the Present
Burt Franklin, 1970. 423pp. $50.00. Originally published in three parts in 1899, 1900, and 1901 and now reissued in a facsimile one volume edition, this is a collection of biographical accounts of the lives of actors and actresses of the late nineteenth century. Illustrated with portraits. Index.

DONALDSON, FRANCES
The Actor–Managers
See Page 539

FITZGERALD, PERCY
The Kembles
Blom, 1971. Volume One: 353pp. Volume Two: 414pp. Two volume set: $25.00. Originally published in 1871 and now reissued, this is an account of the Kemble family, including the lives of Mrs. Siddons and her brother John Philip Kemble. It is a history of one of the most famous families of English actors. Illustrated.

FREEMAN, LUCY – Editor
Celebrities on the Couch
Pocket Books, 1971. 188pp. Paper $ .95. Originally published in 1970 and now reissued, this is a collection of accounts of the problems that sent celebrities into analysis and the progress and results of their treatment. Among the fourteen celebrities are: Sid Ceasar, Patty Duke, William Inge, Josh Logan, Claudia McNeil, Jayne Meadows, Vivian Vance, and Tennessee Williams.

HORST
Salute to the Thirties
Viking, 1971. 192pp. $16.95. With a Foreword by Janet Flanner, this is a commemoration of the artistic vitality of the 1930's. Horst, one of the best-known of the "Vogue Magazine" photographers, and his mentor, George Hoyningen-Heune, show the celebrities of the decade. Horst provides an Introduction and Valentine Lawford contributes brief biographies of the personalities of the literature, art, music, ballet, theatre, opera, and film worlds.

KEESE, WILLIAM L.
A Group of Comedians
Burt Franklin, 1970. 91pp. $16.95. Originally published in 1901 and now reissued in a facsimile edition, this volume includes appreciations of five nineteenth century actors: Henry Placide, William Rufus Blake, John Brougham, George Holland, and Charles Fisher. A portrait of each actor is included.

KRONENBERGER, LOUIS and EMILY MORISON BECK – Editors
Atlantic Brief Lives: A Biographical Companion to the Arts
See Page 513

MC CRINDLE, JOSEPH F. – Editor
Behind the Scenes: Theatre and Film Interviews
Holt, Rinehart, 1971. 341pp. $7.95. Paper $3.45. Each interview is preceded by a biographical sketch and brief description of the setting and all have been published previously in various issues of the "Transatlantic Review." Among the thirty-seven workers in theatre and film are: Fellini, Albee, Tynan, Hochhuth, Kopit, Pinter, Feiffer, Schlesinger, Shaffer, Stoppard, Joan Littlewood and Ellen Stewart.

READ, HERBERT – Introducer
Writers on Themselves
British Broadcasting Corp., 1964. 116pp. $3.50. Thirteen writers recall some parts of their earlier lives that, in retrospect, have proved to have been decisive to their development. Herbert Read has contributed an Introduction to the volume, and there are short biographical notes on the contributors. Included are: John Bowen, Julian Mitchell, David Storey, Rebecca West, Ted Hughes, and Sylvia Plath.

SHAW, DALE
Titans of the American Stage
Westminster Press, 1971. 160pp. $5.95. A history of five generations in three notable theatre families: the Forrests, the Booths, and the O'Neills. Illustrated with twenty-four portraits and reproductions of theatre memorabilia. Bibliography. Index.

SIMPSON, HAROLD and MRS. CHARLES BRAUN
A Century of Famous Actresses: 1750–1850
Blom, 1971. 380pp. $12.50. Originally published in 1913 and now reissued, this volume provides

biographical and character studies of the private and stage life of English actresses during the period covered. Among the actresses sketched are: Peg Woffington, Kitty Clive, Mrs. Siddons, the Kembles, and Helen Faucit. Eighteen pages of illustrations. An Appendix lists some of the chief roles played by stars of the period. Index.

TALESE, GAY
Fame and Obscurity
Bantam, 1971. 340pp. Paper $1.25. Originally published in 1970 and now reissued, this is a gallery of portraits of people. The subjects include Frank Sinatra, Peter O'Toole, Josh Logan, Joe Louis, and others. The author also includes the history of the building of the Verrazano Narrows Bridge and a series of reminiscences about New York City.

TREASE, GEOFFREY
Seven Stages
Vanguard, 1965. 195pp. $3.95. Mr. Trease chronicles the lives of seven figures from the world of the theatre. He provides portraits of Moliere, Christopher Marlowe, Sarah Siddons, Giuseppe Verdi, Jenny Lind, Henry Irving, and Anna Pavlova. Illustrated with eight pages of photographs and reproductions of paintings.

INDIVIDUAL (By Subject)

Adams, Maude

PATTERSON, ADA
Maude Adams: A Biography
Blom, 1971. 109pp. $10.75. Originally published in 1907 and now reissued in a facsimile edition, this account of the career of the actress includes twenty-three portraits. Also provided are complete cast lists of eleven of the productions in which Miss Adams appeared in New York.

Barrymore, John

BARRYMORE, JOHN
Confessions of an Actor
Blom, 1971. Unpaged. $9.75. Originally published in 1926 and now reissued in a facsimile edition, this is the autobiography of the actor. The volume includes reminiscences of Barrymore's youth and early performances and closes with a candid letter from Shaw about the "Hamlet" production in London. Illustrated with thirty-three photographs.

FOWLER, GENE
Good Night, Sweet Prince
Ballantine, 1971. 525pp. Paper $ .95. Originally published in 1943 and now reissued, this is one of the great theatrical biographies of all time—the life of John Barrymore. Sixteen pages of photographs. Index.

Benson, Frank

BENSON, FRANK
My Memoirs
Blom, 1971. 322pp. $12.50. Originally published in 1930 and now reissued, these memoirs, according to the author who was an English actor/manager, try "to draw a picture of stage-life and stage artistry" as he has known them over a period of fifty years. The author describes the personalities of his late nineteenth century theatre associates and of the members of the Benson Company, which he founded and directed. Sixteen plates illustrate the volume.

Bernardi, Berel

BERNARDI, JACK
My Father the Actor
Norton, 1971. 233pp. $6.50. With a Foreword by Herschel Bernardi, this is a biography of Berel Bernardi, a Yiddish actor, from his work in the Yiddish theatre in Eastern Europe to the twenty years of touring he did in the United States. Four pages of photographs.

Bernhardt, Sarah

GELLER, GYULA GASTON
Sarah Bernhardt – Divine Eccentric
Blom, 1971. 308pp. $12.50. Originally published in 1933 as translated from the French by E. S. G. Potter and now reissued in a facsimile edition, this is an account of the eccentricities of the French actress. Illustrated with thirteen portraits. Index.

Betterton, Thomas

LOWE, ROBERT WILLIAM
Thomas Betterton
Blom, 1971. 196pp. $10.75. A facsimile reprint of the 1891 edition of the account of the English actor's career. The author provides an account of the stage in England before and during the Restoration period. List of Characters Played by Betterton. Index.

Booth, Edwin

WATERMEIER, DANIEL J.—Editor
Between Author and Critic: Selected Letters of Edwin Booth and William Winter
Princeton, 1971. 329pp. $10.00. The editor provides, with an Introduction and commentary, a selection of 125 letters reflecting Edwin Booth's life from 1869 to 1890. These letters constitute the fullest day-by-day record of Booth's career. The letters are presented chronologically with annotations, and each is preceded by a headnote which provides an introduction to its content and narrative continuity. Twelve pages of illustrations. Bibliography. Index.

Booth, John Wilkes

CLARKE, ASIA BOOTH
The Unlocked Book
Blom, 1971. 205pp. $12.50. Originally published in 1938, seventy years after it was written, and now reissued in a facsimile edition, this is a memoir of John Wilkes Booth by his sister. The author records the Booth family tragedy and the "strain of darkness" in Booth's personality that foreshadowed it. The volume includes clippings from newspapers found in the locked memoir, and letters of the Booth family. A Foreword by Eleanor Farjeon is also included. Illustrated with sixteen plates showing members of the Booth's family and reproductions of manuscripts.

Casson, Sybil Thorndike

SPRIGGE, ELIZABETH
Sybil Thorndike Casson
Gollancz, 1971. 348pp. $11.95. A biography of the late English actress. Her career on the stage and in films is detailed, including her triumph in Shaw's "Saint Joan." Twenty-one pages of photographs are included, as is a Foreward by the actress.

Clive, Catherine

FITZGERALD, PERCY
The Life of Mrs. Catherine Clive
Blom, 1971. 112pp. $10.75. Originally published in 1888 and now reissued in a facsimile edition. This biography of the eighteenth century English actress includes "an account of her adventures on and off the stage and a round of her characters together with her correspondence." Illustrated with a portrait.

Cooper, Thomas Abthorpe

IRELAND, JOSEPH NORTON
A Memoir of the Professional Life of Thomas Abthorpe Cooper
Burt Franklin, 1970. 102pp. $16.95. Originally published in 1899 and now reissued in a facsimile edition, this is an account of the stage career of the English born actor-manager, known as Tom Cooper, who was very popular with American audiences during the nineteenth century. Illustrated with a portrait and reproductions of playbills. List of Characters Performed. Index.

Daubeny, Peter

DAUBENY, PETER
My World of Theatre
J. Cape, 1971. 350pp. $13.95. The creator and director of the World Theatre season in London describes his twenty-five year career as an impresario. He details his career as an actor in Liverpool before the war; his early London productions of works by Lonsdale, Novello, Maugham, and Coward; and his importation of internationally known ballet, opera, and theatre companies. Illustrated with more than seventy photographs.

Davis, Ossie

FUNKE, LEWIS
The Curtain Rises: The Story of Ossie Davis
Grosset & Dunlap, 1971. 64pp. $2.95. Written for young people, this is the biography of the contemporary black actor. Illustrated with drawings on every page. Index.

Drew, Mrs. John

DREW, MRS. JOHN
Autobiographical Sketch of Mrs. John Drew
Blom, 1971. 200pp. $9.75. Originally published in 1899 and now reissued in a facsimile edition, this volume contains the recollections of Mrs. Drew as written as a memento for her children and grandchildren. The first outstanding member of the Drew-Barrymore acting family records the details of her life and career on the London stage during the nineteenth century. John Drew, her son, has provided an Introduction, and Douglas Taylor has contributed biographical notes. Illustrated with forty-two plates.

Duse, Eleonora

BORDEUX, JEANNE
Eleonora Duse: The Story of Her Life
Blom, 1971. 308pp. $12.50. First published in 1924 and now reissued, this is a biography of the nineteenth century Italian actress. Illustrated with eighteen pages of photographs.

STUBBS, JEAN
Eleonora Duse
Ballantine, 1971. 271pp. Paper $ .95. Originally published in 1970 and now reissued, this is a "documentary novel" about the life of the nineteenth century French actress.

Forbes-Robertson, Johnston

FORBES–ROBERTSON, JOHNSTON
A Player Under Three Reigns
Blom, 1971. 292pp. $12.75. Originally published in 1925 and now reissued, this is an informal autobiography of the late nineteenth and early twentieth century English actor who won notable success in Shakespearean roles. Forbes-Robertson describes his stage experiences, his world tours, his activities as a company manager, and comments on his fellow players. Illustrated. Index.

Garrick, David

GARRICK, DAVID
The Diary of David Garrick: Being a Record of His Memorable Trip to Paris in 1751
Blom, 1971. 117pp. $7.50. Originally published in 1928 and now reprinted, this is a facsimile edition. Edited by Ryllis Clair Alexander, the volume is prefaced with an account of the manuscript and the author with comments and explanations of references made in the diary. Eight illustrations.

Gielgud, John

HAYMAN, RONALD
John Gielgud
Heinemann, 1971. 276pp. $10.00. A biography of the actor/director written with Sir John's full cooperation. Personal papers, letters and scrapbooks, and interviews with actors and directors have been utilized to provide a memoir of Sir John's formative years and early successes. The author analyzes the influences on the actor and the influence that he irradiated. He attempts to throw light on Gielgud's methods of working and the ways in which he built up the key performances of his career. Illustrated with forty-four photographs. Chronological Table of Performances. Index.

Gordon, Ruth

GORDON, RUTH
Myself Among Others
Atheneum, 1971. 389pp. $10.00. The critically acclaimed volume of reminiscences and anecdotes about the life, work, and friends of the author/actress. Included in the cast of characters are such performers, playwrights, and politicians as Alexander Woollcott, Billie Burke, Lunt and Fontanne, Moss Hart, the Barrymores, Franklin Roosevelt, the Gish Sisters, George Bernard Shaw, Thornton Wilder, Fiorello LaGuardia, and Noel Coward.

Gwynn, Nell

CUNNINGHAM, PETER
The Story of Nell Gwynn
Blom, 1971. 194pp. $12.50. Originally published in this edition in 1927 and now reissued in a facsimile edition, this biography of the English Restoration period actress contains thirty-nine illustrations.

Hazlitt, William

WARDLE, RALPH M.
Hazlitt
University of Nebraska, 1971. 530pp. $15.00. A biography of William Hazlitt, English essayist and literary critic (1778–1830). Hazlitt became known for his studies and lectures on contemporary authors and the Elizabethan playwrights. The author takes into account the testimony of the writer's contemporaries, his extensive literary output, and the investigations of recent scholars and critics. Eight pages of illustrations. Index.

Irving, Henry

POLLOCK, WALTER HERRIES
Impression of Henry Irving
Blom, 1971. 140pp. $10.75. Originally published in 1908 and now reissued, this is a volume of

reminiscences of the nineteenth century actor. The actor's son has provided a Preface.

Kean, Edmund

HAWKINS, F.W.
The Life of Edmund Kean
Blom, 1971. 850pp. $27.50. Originally published in London in 1869 in two volumes and now reissued in a one volume edition, this is a biography of the nineteenth century actor. From published accounts and manuscript sources, particularly letters and notes by those who worked with Kean, the author analyzes the qualities that made Kean a tragic, suffering figure on stage and off.

PROCTER, B.W.
The Life of Edmund Kean
Blom, 1971. 496 + pp. $18.75. Originally published in 1835 and now reissued in a facsimile edition, this is a biography of the tragic life and career of the nineteenth century English actor. Illustrated with a portrait.

Kemble, John Philip

BOADEN, JAMES
Memoirs of the Life of John Philip Kemble
Blom, 1971. Volume One: 477pp. Volume Two: 595pp. Two volume set: $27.50. Originally published in 1825 and now reissued in a facsimile edition, this is a detailed account of Kemble's life and career. The study includes a "history of the stage from the time of Garrick to the present period." The volumes record the events at Drury Lane Theatre under his management, the fire at Covent Garden, the actor's most successful roles, the acting of contemporaries of Kemble, and also provide a copy of the actor's will.

Langtry, Lillie

GERSON, NOEL B.
Because I Loved Him: The Life and Loves of Lillie Langtry
Morrow, 1971. 255pp. $5.95. A biography of the nineteenth century actress. The author details her early life in England and the attention she received from the social, political, and artistic celebrities of the time as well as her years in the United States. Illustrated with a portrait. Selective Bibliography. Index.

Lecouvreur, Adrienne

RICHTMAN, JACK
Adrienne Lecouvreur: The Actress and the Age
Prentice—Hall, 1971. 240pp. $7.95. A biography of the eighteenth century French actress whose private life inspired at least three plays, one grand opera, and several novels. The author attempts to provide a solution to the mystery of the actress' death. Illustrated with sixteen pages of plates. Notes. Appendix. Selected Bibliography. Index.

Levant, Oscar (Also See Page 272)

LEVANT, OSCAR
The Memoirs of an Amnesiac
Bantam, 1966. 311pp. Paper $ .95. The autobiography of the performer/composer/entertainer.

Macready, William Charles

ARCHER, WILLIAM
William Charles Macready
Blom, 1971. 224pp. $10.75. Originally published in 1890, this is a study of the career of the English nineteenth century actor. It is based on diaries, letters, press reviews, etc., and has a final chapter on the actor's art and character with quotations from various critical opinions. Index.

Maeder, Clara Fisher

TAYLOR, DOUGLAS — Editor
Autobiography of Clara Fisher Maeder
Burt Franklin, 1970. 138pp. $16.95. Originally published in 1897 and now reissued in a facsimile edition, this is an account of the life of the nineteenth century American actress. Illustrated with portraits and reproductions of playbills. Appendices include appreciations of the actress and reviews of her performances.

Martin, Mary

NEWMAN, SHIRLEE P.
Mary Martin on Stage
Westminster Press, 1971. 127pp. $3.95. A biography of Mary Martin, written for younger readers. Thirty-eight photographs of Miss Martin in her most famous

roles and her private life are included. Selected Bibliography.

Merry, Anne Brunton

DOTY, GRESDNA ANN
The Career of Mrs. Anne Brunton Merry in the American Theatre
Louisiana State University, 1971. 170pp. $10.50. Professor Doty traces the career of the English nineteenth century actress from its beginnings in Bristol in 1785 to its end in 1808. Most of the study concerns her appearances with the Chestnut Street company in Philadelphia where she became the most celebrated actress in the American theatre. Illustrated with nine plates. List of Roles Played. Bibliography. Index.

Modjeska, Helena

ALTEMUS, JAMESON TORR
Helena Modjeska
Blom, 1971. 217pp. $12.50. Originally published in 1883, this is an account of the life and career of the Polish actress. The author provides a critical estimate of the art of the actress in the various roles in which she appeared. He summarizes her debuts in London and in America, and reports on her final performance at Booth's theatre in New York. Reviews of her various appearances, as reported by various critics, are included. Illustrated with two portraits.

Montez, Lola

GOLDBERG, ISAAC
Queen of Hearts: The Passionate Pilgrimage of Lola Montez
Blom, 1971. 308pp. $12.50. Originally published in 1936 and now reissued in a facsimile edition, this is a biography of the nineteenth century dancer and courtesan. Illustrated with a portrait. Bibliography.

Olivier, Laurence

DARLINGTON, W.A.
Laurence Olivier
Morgan Grampian, 1968. 92pp. $3.50. A profile of the actor and a record of his career. Illustrated with photographs in color and black-and-white.

Payne, John Howard

HANSON, WILLIS T.
The Early Life of John Howard Payne
Blom, 1971. 226pp. $12.75. Originally published in 1913 and now reissued in a facsimile edition, this is a biography of the first native American who as an actor or dramatist ever attracted attention in Europe. This volume traces Payne's life up to the year 1813 when he left America to seek his fortune in England. Illustrated.

Phelps, Samuel

ALLEN, SHIRLEY S.
Samuel Phelps and Sadler's Wells Theatre
Wesleyan University, 1971. 354pp. $15.00. A biography of the nineteenth century English actor/manager/director. The author covers the full range of Phelps' half-century career with special emphasis on his decades at Sadler's Wells and his work as performer and producer of Shakespearean drama. Illustrated. Appendices. Notes. Selected Bibliography. Index.

Rehan, Ada

WINTER, WILLIAM
Ada Rehan: A Study
Blom, 1971. 211pp. $9.75. Originally published in 1891 and revised and augmented in 1898, this biography of the Irish-born American actress is now reissued in a facsimile edition. The author provides a critical estimate of the art of the actress in the various roles in which she appeared. A series of Appendices provides a Chronology of Miss Rehan's life, a list of her roles, and samples from various critical reviews. Twenty-five illustrations show the actress in roles from her repertory.

Robeson, Paul

ROBESON, PAUL
Here I Stand
Beacon Press, 1971. 119pp. $5.95. Paper $2.45. First published in 1958 and now reissued with a new preface by Lloyd L. Brown. Mr. Robeson discusses the fight for Negro freedom, how it is related to the cause of peace and liberation throughout the world, and his own viewpoints and the stand he has taken. The Appendices include a reminiscence by Robeson's brother and a statement made in 1963.

Salvini, Tommaso

SALVINI, TOMMASO
Leaves from the Autobiography of Tommaso Salvini
Blom, 1971. 240pp. $12.50. Originally published in 1893 and now reissued in a facsimile edition, these are the memoirs of the early years and stage career of the Italian tragedian of the nineteenth century. Eight illustrations are included.

Siddons, Sarah

MANVELL, ROGER
Sarah Siddons: Portrait of an Actress
Putnam, 1971. 385pp. $7.95. A biography of the great English tragic actress of the eighteenth century. Sixty illustrations. Notes. Appendices. Select Bibliography. Indices.

Taylor, Charles

TAYLOR, DWIGHT
Blood — and — Thunder
Atheneum, 1962. 232pp. $4.50. A biography of Charles Taylor, producer of numerous melodramas which starred the young Laurette Taylor. Dwight Taylor provides a recap of the theatre in early twentieth century America as he recounts his father's life.

Wilson, John Dover

WILSON, JOHN DOVER
Milestones on the Dover Road
Faber & Faber, 1969. 320pp. $8.95. Best known for his achievements as an editor of Shakespeare's work, the author traces his steps and describes the various stages of his career. Illustrated with photographs. List of Published Writings. Index.

Wolfit, Donald

HARWOOD, RONALD
Sir Donald Wolfit: His Life and Work in the Unfashionable Theatre
St. Martin's, 1971. 302pp. $10.00. A biography of the English actor who was acclaimed by many as the greatest of all the performers who played "King Lear." A series of Appendices lists parts played, plays presented, and actors employed by Wolfit. Illustrated with photographs. Index.

MUSICAL THEATRE

REFERENCE WORKS, HISTORIES, AND CRITIQUES

AUBRY, PIERRE
Trouveres and Troubadors
Cooper Square, 1969. 174pp. $7.00. Translated from the French by Claude Aveling and originally published in the United States in 1914 and now reissued, this is a study of Medieval troubadors and their music. Illustrated with musical examples. Bibliography.

BOULEZ, PIERRE
Boulez on Music Today
Harvard, 1971. 144pp. $6.95. Translated by Susan Bradshaw and Richard Rodney Bennett. The noted composer and conductor presents a detailed and systematic exposition of his musical thinking and the kinds of technical procedures to which it leads. Boulez clarifies some basic concepts of the relativity of all musical phenomena, analyzes serialization, and explains compositional techniques. Illustrated with musical examples. Index.

EWEN, DAVID
Composers of Tomorrow's Music
Dodd, Mead, 1971. 176pp. $5.00. An introduction to the new forms of avant-garde music, sketching the lives and theories of ten of its leading exponents: Charles Ives, Arnold Schoenberg, Anton Webern, Pierre Boulez, Edgar Varese, John Cage, and others. Illustrated with photographs of the composers. Index.

GAMMOND, PETER
Your Own, Your Very Own!
Ian Allen, 1971. 96pp. $10.95. A history of the golden years of English Music Hall, circa 1860–1910. The compiler profiles the leading "artistes" in this volume designed in the style of a Victorian scrapbook with over 200 illustrations. Also included is a list of 100 great music hall songs. Bibliography. Discography.

GILMORE, CLIFFORD F. – Editor
Records in Review: 1971 Edition
Scribner, 1971. 526pp. $9.95. The sixteenth annual volume of record reviews from the periodical "High Fidelity." The reviews are of classical and semiclassical music exclusively and include information on corresponding tape releases. The reviewers discuss the composition, performance, and sonic quality and compare new recordings with earlier releases. The reviews are listed alphabetically by composers and, in the case of composers frequently recorded, further subdivided by such categories as Chamber Music, Vocal Music, etc. Index of Performers.

MATTFELD, JULIUS
Variety Music Cavalcade: Musical – Historical Review 1620 – 1969
Prentice–Hall, 1971. 766pp. $15.00. Originally published in 1952, this is the third revised edition of the chronology of music published in the United States. The reference work gives title, composer, lyricist, publisher, and date of copyright, with references to contemporaneous events. Index.

SESSIONS, ROGER
The Musical Experience of Composer, Performer, Listener
Princeton, 1950. 127pp. $5.25. Paper $1.95. This volume includes six lectures originally delivered in 1949 at the Julliard School of Music, New York City. The lectures are: "The Musical Impulse," "The Musical Ear," "The Composer," "The Performer," "The Listener," and "Music in the World Today."

STUCKENSCHMIDT, H.H.
Twentieth Century Composers: Germany and Central Europe
Holt, Rinehart, 1971. 256pp. $10.95. Accounts of the lives and works of twenty-five outstanding composers of Central Europe. Among the composers considered are Richard Strauss, Gustave Mahler, Alban Berg, Carl Orff, Kurt Weill, Hans Werner Henze, Bela Bartok, and Leos Janacek. The volume is illustrated with twenty-four pages of photographs. Index.

THOMSON, VIRGIL
Twentieth Century Composers: American Music Since 1910
Holt, Rinehart, 1971. 204pp. $8.95. A study of America's musical progress since the beginning of this century. The author details the work of such composers as Ives, Ruggles, Copland, Varese, Harris, Piston, Sessions, Gould, Barber, Bernstein, and Rorem. Mr. Thomson's three operas are discussed in a separate chapter and a further chapter highlights the developments in Latin American music. Twenty-four pages of photographs and musical examples in the text illustrate the volume. The final section of the book contains 106 biographies of modern American composers and their achievements. Suggested Reading List. Index.

WHITE, DAVID MANNING – Editor
Pop Culture in America
See Page 628

OPERA AND OPERETTA

ALEXANDER, ALFRED
Operanatomy

Orion, 1971. 190pp. $10.95. The author's object is to further the enjoyment of opera by examining various aspects of its component structure including the arts of the conductor, the instrumentalists, the composer, the singers, the producer, and score reading and criticism. Illustrated with musical examples.

CHISOLM, ERIK
The Operas of Leos Janacek
Pergamon, 1971. 390pp. Paper $6.50. A detailed study of the operas of Janacek including "The House of the Dead" and "The Makropulos Case." Other operas are mentioned in the text, and there is a tribute to Janacek by Erik Chisolm plus an Appendix. Illustrated with photographs and musical examples.

COLEMAN, FRANCIS
The Bluffer's Guide to Opera
Crown, 1971. 64pp. Paper $1.00. Information on the history of opera, its performers, and composers, for people who want to hold their own in conversation with opera buffs. Introduction by David Frost.

CROSS, MILTON and KARL KOHRS
More Stories of the Great Operas
Doubleday, 1971. 752pp. $6.95. The act-by-act, aria-by-aria stories of forty-five classic and contemporary operas. Nearly 600 capsule biographies of the leading singers of yesterday and today are included. Glossary of Opera Terms, a survey of opera today, and a listing of opera associations in America are also provided. Index.

EWEN, DAVID
The New Encyclopedia of the Opera
Hill & Wang, 1971. 759pp. $15.00. Originally published in 1955 and now revised and reorganized. Included among the entries, arranged alphabetically, are synopses of every major opera and hundreds of lesser known works, biographies of composers, librettists, singers, conductors, impresarios, stage directors, critics, and teachers; literary sources of opera; histories of famous opera houses and festivals; definitions of opera terms; and descriptions of important vocal and instrumental passages from operas. Special articles on the history of opera and American operas and composers are provided. This edition has more than 5,000 entries and is completely cross-indexed.

GRUN, BERNARD
Gold and Silver: The Life and Times of Franz Lehar
McKay, 1971. 300pp. $8.95. A biography of the creator of "The Merry Widow" and other operettas. The volume is partially based upon the author's recollections of Lehar, but primarily upon his study of records and unpublished sources made available to him by the Lehar family. Illustrated with twenty-four pages of photographs and with numerous musical examples in the text. Mr. Grun has included a list of Lehar's principal compositions. Index.

HUGHES, SPIKE
Famous Verdi Operas
Chilton, 1968. 544pp. $9.50. A study of twelve of Verdi's best known and most performed operas. The author tells the story of each opera, adding critical comment and observations, and in some cases throwing new light on aspects of works which have been firmly established in the repertoire. The book is illustrated with musical examples and contains an index of Verdi's orchestration. An Appendix includes two Verdi letters never before published. General Index.

LAWRENCE, ROBERT
A Rage for Opera: Its Anatomy as Drawn from Life
Dodd, Mead, 1971. 176pp. $5.95. A survey of the last half century of the operatic experience. The author explores the audience, repertoire, singers, conductors, producers, designers, chorus and ballet, and the impresarios. He discusses the changes that have taken place in audiences and repertoires of the great opera houses going back to the days of the Metropolitan in the 1920's. Sixteen pages of photographs. Index.

MACKINLAY, STERLING
Origin and Development of Light Opera
Blom, 1971. 293pp. $12.50. Originally published in 1927 and now reissued in a facsimile edition, this is a general survey of the growth of comic opera. The author discusses the various phases and art forms from the ancient theatre through the Roman and Grecian eras, up to the Gilbert and Sullivan tradition, and the American light opera of the 1800's. Illustrated. Bibliography. Index.

WORSTHORNE, SIMON TOWNELEY
Venetian Opera in the Seventeenth Century
Oxford, 1968. 194pp. $16.95. A republication of the 1954 study of Venetian opera. The volume is illustrated with plates and with musical examples in the text. Appendices. Bibliographies. Index to Musical Examples. General Index.

GILBERT AND SULLIVAN

BULLA, CLYDE ROBERT
Stories of Gilbert and Sullivan Operas
Crowell, 1968. 247pp. $4.95. Mr. Bulla has retold for young readers the stories of eleven Gilbert and Sullivan operas. The volume is illustrated with drawings by James and Ruth McCrea. The author has included selected lyrics from the operas. Indices.

DUNN, GEORGE E.—Compiler
A Gilbert and Sullivan Dictionary
DaCapo Press, 1971. 175pp. $10.50. An unabridged

republication of the edition published in 1936, this is a glossary of words in the Gilbert and Sullivan libretti which may be obscure. In addition, all the characters are described with the names of their original creators and the successors in the roles, as well as particulars of all the operas themselves with first production dates.

MUSICAL COMEDY

ALTMAN, RICHARD and MERVYN KAUFMAN
The Making of a Musical: Fiddler on the Roof
Crown, 1971. 214pp. $5.95. The authors take readers behind the scenes to reveal, step-by-step, the many stages of production, and to illuminate the many complex personalities who participated in the success of "Fiddler on the Roof." Mr. Altman also provides an account of the many foreign productions of the play and describes the process by which the play was transformed into a film. Illustrated with photographs. Index.

EWEN, DAVID
New Complete Book of the American Musical Theatre
Holt, Rinehart, 1970. 800pp. $15.00. A completely revised guide, originally published in 1958, to more than 500 musical shows from "The Black Crook" in 1866 to "Applause." Included are summaries of the work of some 160 composers, librettists, and lyricists, with plot summaries, production history, stars, and songs. Illustrated with photographs. Appendices. Indices.

EWEN, DAVID
The Story of America's Musical Theatre
Chilton, 1968. 278pp. $5.50. Originally published in 1961 and now revised, this is a history of the musical in America from "Flora," performed in Charleston, S. C., in 1735, to the Broadway productions of today. The revue, the musical comedy, the musical play, the composers, the librettists, the lyricists, the stars, and the songs are all covered. Index.

GREEN, STANLEY
Ring Bells! Sing Songs! Broadway Musicals of the 1930's
Arlington House, 1971. 385pp. $14.95. A history of the Broadway musical comedy stage of the 1930's. Mr. Green focuses on the 175 new productions of the decade and shows how the world beyond Broadway affected this traditionally escapist genre. Brooks Atkinson has provided an Introduction, and the volume is illustrated with almost 200 photographs and reproductions of programs and advertisements of the era. Appendices include a Discography; lists of shows with credits, film versions, London productions; and a Bibliography. Index.

MANDER, RAYMOND and JOE MITCHENSON
Revue: A Story in Pictures
Taplinger, 1971. 56+pp. $10.95. A history in text and pictures of the revue genre of musical comedy. Noel Coward has provided a Foreword. The authors have included 225 photographs illustrating the revue from 1831 through 1970 in England. There are seven Indices including: Revues Illustrated, Authors and Lyricists, Composers, Designers, and Actors.

PIRO, RICHARD
Black Fiddler
Morrow, 1971. 242pp. $5.95. The story of a white teacher's fight to produce a Jewish musical, "Fiddler on the Roof," in a black ghetto school with black and Puerto Rican students. The production was so successful that it was nationally televised. Illustrated with photographs of the production.

ROME, FLORENCE
The Scarlett Letters
Random House, 1971. 209pp. $6.95. An account of the American-Japanese collaboration on the musical production of "Gone with the Wind." Illustrated with photographs.

POPULAR MUSIC

COHN, NIK
Rock from the Beginning
Pocket Books, 1970. 216pp. Paper $ .95. A reissue of the 1969 history of rock music. Among the musicians reported on are: Bill Haley, Elvis Presley, the Beatles, the Rolling Stones, and Bob Dylan. Sixteen pages of photographs. Index.

DANCE, STANLEY
The World of Duke Ellington
Scribners, 1970. 311pp. $8.95. Paper $2.95. A composite portrait of Duke Ellington through interviews with the musician himself and the musicians who have worked with him. The volume is illustrated with more than fifty photographs. Discography. Chronology. Index.

EDITORS OF "ROLLING STONE"
The "Rolling Stone" Interviews
Paperback Library, 1971. 465pp. Paper $1.50. This volume contains seventeen interviews considered by the editors of the music periodical "Rolling Stone" to be the best published from the end of 1967 to the early months of 1971. The musicians interviewed include: Eric Clapton, Ravi Shankar, Jim Morrison, Frank Zappa, Mick Jagger, John Lennon, Bob Dylan, David Crosby, and Grace Slick. An Introduction has been provided by Jann Wenner. Illustrated with photographs of the musicians.

EISEN, JONATHAN – Editor
Twenty-Minute Fandangos and Forever Changes
Vintage, 1971. 271pp. $7.95. Paper $2.95. An anthology of writings on rock music and rock culture. Among the subjects are drugs, sex, the Doors, Iggy Stooge, Andy Warhol, Janis Joplin, and Elvis Presley. Included is a sixteen page section of photographs.

GARLAND, PHYL
The Sound of Soul
Regnery, 1969. 246pp. $5.95. Miss Garland traces the development of soul music from its earliest beginnings to its present position as a million dollar business. Among the artists studied are Aretha Franklin, Chuck Berry, B. B. King, and Mahalia Jackson. Illustrated with photographs. Discography. Index.

GOLDMAN, ALBERT
Freak Show
Atheneum, 1971. 389pp. $10.00. A collection of reviews and essays originally published from 1959 through 1970. The pieces constitute a review of the current pop culture scene including theatre, music, films, and books, but especially rock music. Index.

McCARTHY, ALBERT
The Dance Band Era
Chilton, 1971. 176pp. $10.00. A comprehensive, critical survey of bands and bandleaders from 1900 through the 1940's. The author examines the bands both in musical terms, describing developments in instrumentation and techniques of arrangement, and in their social and economic context, discussing the roles of radio and records, cinemas and hotels, and theatres. The author evaluates the bands' recorded achievements, and each chapter is accompanied by a select list of available recordings. More than 200 photographs illustrate the volume. Discography. Bibliography. Index.

ROXON, LILLIAN
Rock Encyclopedia
Grosset & Dunlap, 1971. 611pp. Paper $3.95. Biographies, discographies, commentary, analysis, and miscellany on over 1,200 personalities and 22,000 songs of the rock idiom. Originally published in a cloth edition in 1969, this edition does not include the photographs from the original edition. Appendices.

RUSSELL, ROSS
Jazz Style in Kansas City and the Southwest
University of California, 1971. 292pp. $12.50. A full-scale history of Kansas City Jazz, tracing the development of southwestern jazz from its grass roots to the style evolved in Kansas City. Musical profiles of the great musicians are included. The author has provided thirty-two pages of photographs, a section of Notes, a Discography, and a Bibliography. Index.

SCHIFFMAN, JACK
Uptown: The Story of Harlem's Apollo Theatre
Cowles, 1971. 210pp. $6.50. A history of the Apollo Theatre from its beginnings in the 1930's. Anecdotes about the black performers who appeared there are included. Sixteen pages of photographs. Index.

SHAW, ARNOLD
The Rock Revolution
Paperback Library, 1971. 254pp. Paper $ .95. A history of rock music from Elvis Presley and rockabilly to the Beatles and on to the latest type of acid rock and soul. Illustrated with thirty-two pages of photographs. Glossary of rock terms. Discography. Index.

SHAW, ARNOLD
The Street that Never Slept
Coward, McCann, 1971. 378pp. $10.00. A history of show business on one block of New York's 52nd Street, between Fifth and Sixth Avenues. Mr. Shaw reports on the jazz musicians, the comics, the singers, the strippers, and the clubs where they worked. Interspersed are interviews with many of the people who gave The Street its character. Illustrated with more than fifty photographs. Index.

SHAW, ARNOLD
The World of Soul
Paperback Library, 1971. 380pp. Paper $1.25. Originally published in 1970 and now reissued, this is a history of the evolution of black American music. Illustrated with photographs. Discography. Index.

SHELTON, ROBERT and BURT GOLDBLATT
The Country Music Story
Arlington House, 1971. 256pp. $7.95. Originally published in 1966 and now reissued, this is a picture history of country and western music over the past forty years. The authors discuss the origins of the music, the varieties, the stars, and the innovators. Hundreds of photographs of musicians and country-music memorabilia. Included is a Selective List of Country and Western LP Recordings. Index.

SIMON, GEORGE T.
Simon Says: The Sights and Sounds of the Swing Era, 1935 – 1955
Arlington House, 1971. 492pp. $19.95. A collection of writings on bands, singers, and musicians of "the golden age of popular music and jazz" selected from "Metronome Magazine." Over 225 photographs illustrate the volume. Index.

WOOD, GRAHAM
An A – Z of Rock and Roll
Studio Vista, 1971. 128pp. Paper $4.95. The author provides short biographies of a hundred rock and roll performers—English and American. Also included in the volume is a listing of million record sellers by rock artists: 1955–1961. Illustrated with photographs.

SONG BOOKS

ALDRIDGE, ALAN – Editor
The Beatles Illustrated Lyrics #2
Delacorte, 1971. 125pp. $5.95. A second collection of illustrated Beatles lyrics in book form. Lyrics for ninety songs are provided and they are illustrated by such internationally famous artists as John Alcorn, Michael English, Etienne Delessert, Peter Vos, and others.

BACHARACH, BURT and HAL DAVID
Bacharach and David: Greatest Hits
Charles Hansen, 1971. 215pp. Spiral bound $5.95. A compilation of 149 songs by Bacharach and David. The music is arranged for piano, organ, guitar, and voice. An appreciation of both the composer and the lyricist is included. Illustrated.

BACHARACH, BURT and HAL DAVID
The Bacharach and David Song Book
Simon & Schuster, 1971. 127pp. Paper $3.95. Originally published in 1970 and now reissued, this song book contains the words and music for thirty-seven of the songs. Introduction by Dionne Warwicke. Music arranged for piano and guitar by Norman Monath.

DYER–BENNET, RICHARD
The Richard Dyer-Bennet Folk Song Book
Simon & Schuster, 1971. 176pp. $9.95. A collection of fifty traditional songs and ballads with guitar accompaniments by Mr. Dyer-Bennet. Piano arrangements are by Harry Rubinstein. The folk-singer has provided an autobiographical note and introductions to each song. Illustrated with drawings by Rodney Shackell. Discography. Index of First Lines.

GRAEME, JOY – Editor
The Irish Songbook
Collier, 1971. 186pp. Paper $2.95. Originally published in 1969 and now reissued, this is a collection of seventy-five songs collected, adapted, written, and sung by the Clancy Brothers and Tommy Makem. The songs are arranged for piano and guitar by Robert DeCormier. Illustrated with drawings and photographs.

LINDSAY, CYNTHIA
The Frank Loesser Song Book
Simon & Schuster, 1971. 223pp. $12.50. A collection of fifty-one songs from films and plays. Each song has been arranged for piano with chord notations for guitarists. Preface by Richard Rodgers. Illustrated by Paul Bacon. Index of First Lines. Index of Titles.

MAKEBA, MIRIAM
The World of African Song
Quadrangle Books, 1971. 119pp. Paper $3.95. A collection of twenty-four songs from Africa. A long Introduction and notes on the songs have been provided by Solomon Mbabi-Katana. Jonas Gwangwa and E. John Miller, Jr., have edited the music. Illustrated by Dean Alexander. Discography of Miriam Makeba. Index of First Lines.

NICHOLAS, A.X. – Editor
The Poetry of Soul
Bantam, 1971. 103pp. Paper $1.00. Lyrics of "soul music" songs by such writers as Nina Simone, Aretha Franklin, Otis Redding, B. B. King, and others. The editor has provided an Introduction. Discography.

RAPOSO, JOE and JEFFREY MOSS
The Sesame Street Song Book
Simon & Schuster, 1971. 127pp. $6.95. A collection of thirty-six songs from the television program, "Sesame Street." The songs have been arranged by Sy Oliver. Loretta Trezzo has provided illustrations for the volume. Index of Songs. Index of First Lines.

VOCAL TRAINING

ROSE, ARNOLD
The Singer and the Voice
Faber & Faber, 1971. 267pp. $11.95. A new and revised edition of the study originally published in England in 1962. This is a detailed analysis of vocal production and training techniques. The author has evolved a new approach to the problems of resonance and positive control of tone color. Diagrams and anatomical drawings. Appendices. Bibliography. Index.

RUSHMORE, ROBERT
The Singing Voice
Dodd, Mead, 1971. 332pp. $10.00. Paper $2.25. An informal survey of various aspects of the singer's art. The author's subject is basically opera singing, but there are also discussions applicable to pop singers. There are descriptions of the various types of voices with anecdotes about some of the greatest opera singers, pop artists, and amateurs. Illustrated with drawings and photographs. Glossary. Bibliography. Index.

URIS, DOROTHY
To Sing In English: A Guide to Improved Diction
Boosey & Hawkes, 1971. 317pp. Paper $6.95. Much of the material included in this text was tested in classrooms at the Mannes College of Music and the Manhattan School of Music where the author taught speech and diction for singers. Included in the volume are sections on: the range of diction; structure, sense, and stress; English, a legato language; the vowel content of American English; the shapes and sounds of the consonants; and a working method of studying the text of a song. Illustrated with musical examples. Appendices include a list of suggested recordings and a Selected Bibliography. Indices.

BIOGRAPHIES

Collected (By Author)

BLESH, RUDI
Combo: USA
Chilton, 1971. 240pp. $6.95. Subtitled "Eight Lives in Jazz," this is a volume of biographical material on, reminisces of, and appreciations of eight great jazz musicians. The musicians included are: Louis Armstrong, Jack Teagarden, Sidney Bechet, Lester Young, Billie Holiday, Gene Krupa, Eubie Blake, and Charlie Christian. Illustrated with eight pages of photographs. Bibliography. Discography. Indices.

CHILTON, JOHN
Who's Who of Jazz: Storyville to Swing Street
Chilton, 1972. 419pp. $7.50. Originally published in England in 1970 and now issued in the United States, this anthology of biographies details the careers of over 1,000 musicians. Illustrated with eighty-eight pages of photograph.

GURALNICK, PETER
Feel Like Going Home
Dutton, 1971. 222pp. $6.95. Paper $2.95. This book of profiles of blues and rock 'n roll artists is intended to show a kind of historical progression of this type of music from its traditional country roots into the early days of rock. Among the artists profiled are: Muddy Waters, Johnny Shines, Skip James, Howlin' Wolf, Jerry Lee Lewis, and Charlie Rich. Illustrated with photographs. Discography. Bibliography.

LYDON, MICHAEL
Rock Folk: Portraits from the Rock 'n' Roll Pantheon
Dial Press, 1971. 200pp. $6.95. A study of seven individual or group figures significant in the rock music world. The artists are placed in their most characteristic settings and their careers, personal styles, and influences are discussed. The artists include: Chuck Berry, Carl Perkins, B. B. King, Smokey Robinson, Janis Joplin, The Grateful Dead, and The Rolling Stones. Illustrated with photographs.

SOMMA, ROBERT – Editor
No One Waved Good-Bye
Outerbridge & Dienstfrey, 1971. 126pp. Paper $1.95. Essays on four of the top figures in contemporary pop music—all of whom have died recently—Brian Epstein, Brian Jones, Janis Joplin, and Jimi Hendrix. Illustrated.

WILMER, VALERIE
Jazz People
Bobbs–Merrill, 1971. 167pp. $5.00. Paper $2.45. Based on interviews, the author provides profiles of fourteen jazz musicians, including Art Farmer, Cecil Taylor, Theonious Monk, Randy Weston, Clark Terry, and Archie Shepp. Illustrated with photographs. Index.

Individual (By Subject)

Amram, David

AMRAM, DAVID
Vibrations
Viking, 1971. 469pp. Paper $3.75. Originally published in 1968 and now reprinted, this is the autobiography of the musician/composer. Illustrated with photographs.

Anderson, Marian

NEWMAN, SHIRLEE P.
Marian Anderson: Lady from Philadelphia
Westminster Press, 1966. 175pp. $4.25. A biography of the first Negro to sing at the Metropolitan Opera. Miss Anderson's famous concert at the Lincoln Memorial in Washington, D. C. in 1939 is described. Illustrated with photographs. Bibliography. Index.

Armstrong, Louis

MERYMAN, RICHARD
Louis Armstrong: A Self-Portrait
Eakins Press, 1971. 59pp. $4.95. Paper $2.95. Based on an interview with Louis Armstrong which originally appeared in "Life Magazine" in 1966, the musician tells in his own words of the "music we lived" in New Orleans, Chicago, New York, Europe, Africa, and Asia. Illustrated with fifteen photographs taken between 1910 and 1966.

PANASSIE, HUGUES
Louis Armstrong
Scribner, 1971. 149pp. $6.95. A biography of the great jazz musician and a close examination of his music by the noted French jazz critic. Illustrated with more than thirty photographs. Selected Discography.

Bailey, Pearl

BAILEY, PEARL
Talking to Myself
Harcourt, Brace, 1971. 233pp. $5.95. Miss Bailey attempts to describe "all the things one can learn and feel across the footlights." She discusses the state of contemporary life including the American family, the generation gap, the entertainment world, and the perils of fame.

Berlin, Irving

JAY, DAVE
The Irving Berlin Songography: 1907 – 1966
Arlington House, 1969. 172pp. Paper $1.00. A listing of Irving Berlin's songs with notes on their introducers. Recordings of songs are listed with the artist and recording number.

Cash, Johnny

CARPOZI, JR., GEORGE
The Johnny Cash Story
Pyramid, 1970. 128pp. Paper $ .75. A biography of country singer Johnny Cash. Included is a sixteen page photograph section.

WREN, CHRISTOPHER S.
Winners Get Scars Too
Dial, 1971. 229pp. $6.95. A biography of performer Johnny Cash. The author traces the musician's career from his boyhood on an Arkansas farm to his current eminence as one of America's most popular entertainers.

Cole, Nat King

COLE, MARIA and LOUIS ROBINSON
Nat King Cole: An Intimate Biography
Morrow, 1971. 184pp. $5.95. A biography of the composer/performer by his wife. A feature of the volume is a complete discography of all of Cole's recordings including information on title, date, and record number. Illustrated with eight pages of photographs.

Ellington, Duke

DANCE, STANLEY
The World of Duke Ellington
See Page 570

Goodman, Benny

CONNOR, D. RUSSELL and WARREN W. HICKS
BG On the Record: A Bio-Discography of Benny Goodman
Arlington House, 1969. 691pp. $10.00. Also available with a two record set of recordings: $20.00. A completely revised version of the discography published in 1958, this volume includes a chronological listing of every recording on which Goodman appears, complete data on the records, and a comprehensive biography of the musician. Illustrated with forty-one photographs. Three Indices. The record set includes twenty-eight performances recorded from 1929 to 1945 never issued before on LP and includes vocalists Fred Astaire, Peggy Lee, Buddy Clark, Dick Haymes, and Helen Ward, among others.

Jones, Tom

JONES, PETER
Tom Jones
Avon, 1971. 176pp. Paper $ .75. Originally published in 1970 and now reissued, this is the biography of the internationally successful singer from Wales. Illustrated with photographs. Discography.

Joplin, Janis

DALTON, DAVID
Janis
Simon & Schuster, 1971. 212pp. $9.95. Paper $4.95. This collection of articles, interviews, reviews, photographs, and songs comprises a biography of Janis Joplin. Included are forty-eight photographs and fourteen songs identified with the singer. Also included is a 33rpm record of Janis singing and talking.

Lennon, John

WENNER, JANN
Lennon Remembers
World, 1971. 191pp. $4.95. This is a re-edited collection of the interviews with John Lennon which were originally published in the periodical, ''Rolling Stone.'' Lennon speaks candidly about the early days of the Beatles, their involvement with the Maharishi, and the disintegration of the group. Illustrated with fifty-six pages of photographs.

McCracken, James and Sandra Warfield

McCRACKEN, JAMES and SANDRA WARFIELD
A Star in the Family
Coward McCann, 1971. 388pp. $6.95. Edited by Robert Daley, this is the tape-recorded diary of one

year in the lives of two internationally known opera singers. Illustrated with sixteen pages of photographs.

Martin, Mary

NEWMAN, SHIRLEE P.
Mary Martin on Stage
See Page 565

Porter, Cole

KIMBALL, ROBERT – Editor
Cole
Holt, Rinehart, 1971. 283pp. $25.00. With a biographical essay by Brendan Gill, this is a collection of almost two hundred of the lyrics of Cole Porter. Hundreds of photographs and reproductions of memorabilia are included showing scenes from the films and plays and moments from the private life of the composer. Also provided are a Chronology of Songs and Productions with credits, a Discography, and an Alphabetical List of Songs.

Sinatra, Frank

LONSTEIN, ALBERT I. and VITO R. MARINO
The Compleat Sinatra
Library Research Assoc., 1970. 388pp. $19.95. The authors document the career of Frank Sinatra. Among the highlights of the volume are a chronological listing of every commercial recording on which Sinatra appears as vocalist and a listing of privately owned tapes and recordings; complete dates, matrix numbers, personnel, arrangers, conductors, alternate takes, unissued sides; complete dates, studio credits, cast, synopsis, songs, running time, and short critique for every film; listing of television, concert, radio, and Paramount Theatre appearances; listing of V-Discs; and a Song Index, Album Index, Concert Index, and an Index of Orchestras, Arrangers, Composers, Soloists, Vocalists, and Vocal Groups. Each section includes biographical information. Also included are more than twenty-five pages of photographs.

Strauss, Richard

DEL MAR, NORMAN
Richard Strauss: A Critical Commentary on His Life and Work
Chilton, 1969. Volume One: 462pp. Volume Two: 452pp. Each volume: $12.50. The first two volumes in a projected three volume work. The author provides a definitive study of the composer. Illustrated with photographs and musical examples in the text. Appendices include a catalogue of early works, a list of works discussed, a Bibliography, and a Chronology. Indices.

Welk, Lawrence

WELK, LAWRENCE and BERNICE McGEEHAN
Wunnerful, Wunnerful!
Prentice–Hall, 1971. 294pp. $7.95. The autobiography of the popular orchestra leader and entertainer. Illustrated with twenty-two photographs.

DANCE

GENERAL HISTORIES, CRITIQUES, AND APPRECIATIONS

ATWATER, CONSTANCE
Tap Dancing: Techniques, Routines, Terminology
Tuttle, 1971. 179pp. $6.50. A guidebook to the art of tap dancing. Basic, intermediate, and advanced steps and routines are described in detail, and information on costumes, recital programs, and the operation of a dance studio is provided. Forty-four photographs and sketches illustrate the text. List of Suppliers. Index.

BEAUMONT, CYRIL – Editor
A Bibliography of the Dance Collection of Doris Niles and Serge Leslie
C.W. Beaumont, Part I: A–K, 1966. Part II: L–Z, 1968. 597pp. Each volume: $11.75. A two volume annotated record of over 2,000 books that have been written about dance, dancers, and dance techniques. Books are arranged in alphabetical order under authors, followed by bibliographic information and a short synopsis of the work. Annotations are by Serge Leslie. Subject Index.

BINNEY, EDWIN
A Century of Austro-German Dance Prints: 1790 – 1890
Dance Perspectives, 1971. 76pp. Paper $2.95. An introduction to and catalogue of dance prints from Germany and Austria. Fifty-two of the prints are reproduced. Bibliography. Index to Theatre Works Cited.

BOORMAN, JOYCE
Creative Dance in the First Three Grades
See Page 581

CAYOU, DOLORES KIRTON
Modern Jazz Dance
National Press, 1971. 148pp. $5.95. Paper $3.95. After a brief section on the origin and history of jazz dance, the author provides material on warm-up and rhythmic exercises, isolations, turns, walks, combinations, and class organization. Content is organized by types of movement, so that the teacher may select from various chapters to build lessons suitable for a particular class. The volume is illustrated with photographs and sequence drawings. List of Recommended Recordings.

DIMONDSTEIN, GERALDINE
Children Dance in the Classroom
See Page 581

ELLFELDT, LOIS and EDWIN CARNES
Dance Production Handbook
National Press, 1971. 220pp. $8.95. Paper $5.95. Elementary information on the production of dance programs from the first decision to produce a performance to the final removal of equipment from the theatre after the performance. Material included: performance space, choosing a date, setting up a budget, musical accompaniment, scene and costume design, lighting design, scenery construction, publicity, technique of rehearsal, and the actual performance. Illustrated with drawings and diagrams. Appendices. Glossary. List of Selected References.

ELLFELDT, LOIS
A Primer for Choreographers
National Press, 1971. 121pp. Paper $2.95. Originally published in 1967 and now reissued, this is an attempt to explain choreography to beginning students. After an introductory chapter on what dance is, the author provides a series of movement experiences which answer the questions of all would-be choreographers. Illustrated with drawings by Sue Powell. Glossary. List of Selected Readings.

GATES, ALICE A.
A New Look at Movement: A Dancer's View
Burgess, 1968. 187pp. Paper $5.75. The author suggests that this volume is "designed to simplify and clarify personal concepts and understandings of it (movement), and to guide and stimulate student teachers to find their own ways and approaches to the teaching of activity." Illustrated with drawings. Bibliography. List of Suggested Supplementary Readings.

LABAN, RUDOLF and LISA ULLMANN
The Mastery of Movement
Plays, Inc., 1971. 190pp. $10.00. This third edition of Laban's work has been revised by Lisa Ullmann. It was originally published in England and is now issued in the United States. The reader is introduced to the basic principles of movement expression and experience and is provided with exercises to practice those principles. The relationship between the inner motivation of movement and the outer functioning of the body is explored. Included are three mime plays and a series of scenes for study. Illustrated with tables. Index.

PERCIVAL, JOHN
Experimental Dance
Universe Books, 1971. 160pp. $7.95. Mr. Percival seeks to illuminate some of the ideas and trends that have resulted from the contemporary dance scene. He writes about the birth and development of modern dance as well as the widening of the scope of the classical ballet over the past seventy years. In many cases, the words of the choreographers, composers, and designers themselves are used to explain their purposes and make their actions clear. Illustrated

with sixty-four pages of photographs. Sources of Quotations. Index.

SHIPLEY, GLENN
Modern Tap Dictionary
Dance Publications, 1963. 39pp. Paper $1.00. This compilation of commonly used tap dancing terms seeks to standardize those terms. Explicit movements. A Bibliography is also provided.

SORELL, WALTER
The Dancer's Image: Points and Counterpoints
Columbia, 1971. 469pp. $16.65. Intended as "my last will for the dancer, my testament to the dance ...," this book is the summing up of the author's lifetime of experience with, and thought about, the dance. Mr. Sorell surveys the panorama of dance and the ways in which it has reflected the search of the artist for the truth about himself and his world. He provides reminiscences of Isadora Duncan, Mary Wigman, Anna Pavlova, Ruth St. Denis, and others as well as a series of chapters exploring the painters, actors, and writers behind the dance. Illustrated. Bibliography. Index.

THORNTON, SAMUEL
Laban's Theory of Movement: A New Perspective
Plays, Inc., 1971. 134pp. $7.95. Originally published in England and now issued in the United States, this volume brings together the philosophy of Rudolf Laban's theories of movement, the principles which derive from it, and the movement principles implicit in Laban's own publications. The author also discusses Laban's life and the influence of his ideas. Illustrated with diagrams. Bibliography. Index.

WILLIS, JOHN
Dance World 1971
Crown, 1971. 229pp. $10.00. The sixth annual volume of the pictorial and statistical record of the dance season in the United States. The present edition covers the 1970–71 season and provides more than 450 photographs of the dancers and productions. The author includes performances in New York, in Brooklyn, at Jacob's Pillow, Connecticut College, Saratoga, and the Ethnic Dance Festival in Barnstable, Mass., as well as performances by regional companies throughout the United States. There is a section of biographical data of dancers and choreographers, an obituary section, and an Index.

TYPES OF DANCE

Ballet

ALEXANDRE, ARSENE
The Decorative Art of Leon Bakst
Blom, 1971. 51pp. + plates. $27.50. First published in 1913 and now reissued with the plates in half-tone, this is an appreciation of the art of the theatre and ballet designer. Appreciation by Arsene Alexandre and notes on the ballets by Jean Cocteau (translated from the French by Harry Melvill). The seventy-seven plates include designs from "L'Apres-Midi d'un Faune," "Scheherazade," and "Salome." This edition is uniform with "The Designs of Leon Bakst for The Sleeping Princess" by Leon Bakst and with "Bakst: The Story of the Artist's Life" by Andre Levinson.

BAILEY, SALLY – Editor
Letters from the Maestro: Enrico Cecchetti to Gisella Caccialanza
Dance Perspectives, 1971. 56pp. Paper $2.95. Letters from the dancer/choreographer/teacher to one of his pupils. Commentary is provided by the editor. Illustrated.

BAKST, LEON
The Designs of Leon Bakst for The Sleeping Princess
Blom, 1971. 18pp. + plates. $27.50. A collection of designs for the Diaghilev production of "The Sleeping Princess" in 1921. The volume was originally published in 1922 and is now reissued. A preface on the ballet and the work of Bakst by Andre Levinson is included. The fifty-four plates show costume and set designs. This edition is uniform with "The Decorative Art of Leon Bakst" by Arsene Alexandre and with "Bakst: The Story of the Artist's Life" by Andre Levinson.

BRINSON, PETER and CLEMENT CRISP
The International Book of Ballet
Stein & Day, 1971. 304pp. $8.95. A guide to 115 major ballets by thirty-eight of the world's great choreographers. Each ballet is described in detail with complete production credits including original dancers, synopsis, and commentary. Provided is an introductory chapter on the historical background of ballet and a note on Soviet ballet. Each choreographer is discussed and a short biography of his life and work is provided. Illustrated. List of Books for Further Reading. Indices.

BUCKLE, RICHARD and VALENTINE GROSS
Nijinsky on Stage
Studio Vista, 1971. 141pp. $10.95. This is a collection of action drawings of Nijinsky and the Diaghilev Ballet made by Valentine Gross in Paris between 1909 and 1913. Mr. Buckle has contributed an Introduction and notes on the drawings, and the volume also includes a Chronology of the life of Valentine Gross as compiled by Jean Hugo.

DE GAMEZ, TANA
Alicia Alonso: At Home and Abroad

Citadel, 1971. 191pp. $10.00. A pictorial biography of the ballerina from her childhood to her present prominence in the National Ballet of Cuba. Lavishly illustrated with photographs.

DOMINIC, ZOE and JOHN S. GILBERT
Frederick Ashton: A Choreographer and His Ballets
Harrap, 1971. 256pp. $16.95. A portrait of the life and art of Sir Frederick. Eighteen of the ballets are discussed and appreciations and critiques of the choreographer's art are provided by the author, Marie Rambert, Cecil Beaton, Robert Helpmann, Margot Fonteyn, Michael Somes, Ninette de Valois, and others. Interviews with Ashton reveal his methods of creating ballets and his views on his dancers and his critics. Miss Dominic has provided about 100 pages of photographs of the ballets and their dancers. A complete list of ballets and other works with original cast credits is included.

GUEST, IVOR
Fanny Elssler
Wesleyan, 1970. 284pp. $15.00. A biography of one of the most brilliant dancers of the Romantic ballet. Eye-witness accounts of the performances, biographic detail of her life, highlights of her travels in Russia and the United States, and a history of her triumph in "Giselle" are included. Thirty-one pages of illustrations are provided. Bibliography. Genealogical Tree of the Elssler Family. Index.

LEVINSON, ANDRE
Bakst: The Story of the Artist's Life
Blom, 1971. 241pp. $27.50. Originally published in 1923 and now reissued, this is a biography and appreciation of Leon Bakst, designer for the Diaghilev ballet company. The volume includes more than sixty half-tone plates plus drawings in the text. The edition is uniform with "The Decorative Art of Leon Bakst" by Arsene Alexandre and with "The Designs of Leon Bakst for The Sleeping Princess" listed under Leon Bakst.

MARKOVA, ALICIA
Giselle and I
Vanguard Press, 1961. 200pp. $5.95. The "prima ballerina assoluta" records her intimate association with the role of "Giselle." She also sheds light on the many great dancers who have been her partners. Illustrated with sixty pages of photographs.

PERCIVAL, JOHN
The World of Diaghilev
Dutton, 1971. 159pp. Paper $2.25. An introduction to the life, work, and world of Serge Diaghilev, the founder of Ballet Russe. Illustrated with photographs and reproductions of drawings and paintings. Provided is a list of productions of the Company with date of premiere, and names of composer, choreographer, scenographer, designer, and principal dancers. Book List.

SLONIMSKY, JURI et al
The Soviet Ballet
DaCapo, 1970. 285pp. $20.00. An unabridged republication of the edition first published in 1947, this is a series of essays on the dance, the dancers, the choreographers, and the companies in Soviet Russia. 103 pages of photographs. Index.

SPARGER, CELIA
Anatomy and Ballet
Theatre Arts, 1971. 96pp. $6.25. The fifth edition, revised, of the handbook originally published in 1949. Miss Sparger explains barre exercises in terms of the body. Photographs, reproductions of X–rays, and drawings show the effect of balletic movements on the physique.

TERRY, WALTER
The Ballet Companion
Dodd, Mead, 1968. 236pp. Paper $2.50. A guide to ballet with information about every aspect of the art. The author discusses the history, the technique, the companies and the productions, the costumes, and the interpretation of roles. Illustrated with drawings and photographs. Glossary. List of Ballets (with production details). Index.

Modern

McDONAGH, DON
The Rise and Fall and Rise of Modern Dance
New American Library, 1971. 303pp. Paper $1.25. Originally published in 1970 and now reissued, this is a guide to modern dance. Through a series of profiles of the new dancer/choreographers, the author provides a view of the aims and achievements of, among others: Paul Taylor, Merce Cunningham, Alwin Nikolais, Meredith Monk, and Twyla Tharp. An introductory chapter traces the development of modern dance. Illustrated with eight pages of photographs. Chronologies of each of the major artists. Index.

MORRIS, MARGARET
My Life in Movement
Peter Owen, 1971. 206pp. $10.50. A reprint of the volume first published in England in 1969. Miss Morris is a pioneer of modern dance techniques. She describes in detail—with her own diagrams—her methods of exercise by dance techniques. She recalls her life and development as a dancer and teacher and some of the well-known people who have attended her schools. Illustrated with diagrams and photographs. Index.

SCHLUNDT, CHRISTENA L.
Into the Mystic with Miss Ruth
Dance Perspectives, 1971. 56pp. Paper $2.95. An

illustrated and annotated study of Ruth St. Denis. The author studies the work and the influence of the dancer/choreographer.

SEROFF, VICTOR
The Real Isadora
Dial, 1971. 441pp. $10.00. A biography of Isadora Duncan which seeks to separate the myths from the facts of the life of the dance pioneer. Illustrated with photographs. Bibliography. Index.

SIEGEL, MARCIA B. – Editor
Nik: A Documentary
Dance Perspectives, 1971. 56pp. Paper $2.95. The latest edition of the periodical examines the work of the choreographer Alwin Nikolais. Profusely illustrated with photographs in both black-and-white and in color.

TURNER, MARGERY J. and RUTH GRAUERT, ARLENE ZALLMAN
New Dance: Approaches to Nonliteral Choreography
University of Pittsburgh, 1971. 128pp. $7.95. The author deals exclusively with developments in modern dance since 1951. There are chapters by musician Arlene Zallman, who discusses a method of instruction in music for the dance, and by Ruth Grauert, who discusses the lighting design for new dance performance. Among the dancers and choreographers discussed are: Alwin Nikolais, Merce Cunningham, Erick Hawkins, Murray Louis, and Paul Taylor. Illustrated with photographs. Appendices include a Bibliography and lists of dance films, recorded music, and lighting equipment. Glossary. Index.

Ethnic

FERGUSSON, ERNA
Dancing Gods: Indian Ceremonials of New Mexico and Arizona
University of New Mexico, 1970. 286pp. $7.50. Paper $2.45. A study of the ceremonies and ceremonial dances of the Pueblo Indians, the Hopis, the Navajos, and the Apaches. Illustrated. Index.

TOGI, MASATARO
Gagaku: Court Music and Dance
Walker/Weatherhill, 1971. 207pp. $5.95. Translated by Don Kenny, this is an introduction to the performing art of Gagaku, a form of the dance which was originally created during the seventh and eighth centuries. 220 illustrations in color and black-and-white. Chronology.

Social

IRVINE, BILL and BOBBIE IRVINE
The Dancing Years
W.H. Allen, 1970. 176pp. $8.95. Published in England, this is a record of the career of the Irvines, a ballroom dancing team. The authors, World Champion Award winners thirteen times, take the reader behind the scenes of the ballroom dancing world. Illustrated with twenty-four pages of photographs.

PARSON, THOMAS E.
How to Dance
Barnes & Noble, 1971. 115pp. Paper $1.50. Originally published in 1947 and now revised and updated, this is a guide to social dancing with step-by-step lessons and illustrations of the basic patterns and variations of favorite dances. There are new sections on Discotheque dances and on Folk and Square dancing. Illustrated with diagrams and drawings.

RUST, FRANCES
Dance in Society
Routledge & Kegan Paul, 1969. 280pp. $9.95. An analysis of the relationship between the social dance and society, in England, from the middle ages to the present day. The book concludes with a sociological survey of young people's habits and attitudes with relation to dancing. Illustrated. Appendices. Notes. Index.

OTHER CATEGORIES OF THEATRE

RELIGIOUS THEATRE

BRANDT, ALVIN G.
Drama Handbook for Churches
Seabury Press, 1964. 176pp. $4.50. This handbook begins with general suggestions for organizing a drama program, then provides specific instructions on all aspects of production. Chapters are included on the use of the small stage or church setting to enhance dramatic productions. Contemporary developments in church drama are also discussed. List of Religious Plays. Index.

COLLINS, FREDA
Children in the Market Place: Stepping Stones to Playmaking
J. Garnet Miller, 1968. 148pp. $4.50. Originally published in 1942 and now revised and updated, this volume includes all aspects of the subject of using drama in the religious education of children. The author provides chapters on dramatization in the classroom and on the actual production of plays. Two short plays are included. Illustrated with drawings and photographs. Bibliography.

EHRENSPERGER, HAROLD
Religious Drama: Means and Ends
Abingdon, 1962. 287pp. $6.00. A study of the structure and form of religious drama, with practical advice for ministers and church organizations interested in staging drama for more significant worship. Sixteen pages of illustrations of productions.

JEEP, ELIZABETH
Classroom Creativity
See Page 581

JOHNSON, ALBERT
Church Plays and How to Stage Them
United Church Press, 1966. 174pp. Paper $3.00. A practical handbook for directors of church drama with discussions of acting and directing techniques, suggestions for costuming, lighting, props, set construction, how to select the right religious play, and three new plays for the church.

LOVE, MARGARET
Let's Dramatise
Chester House, 1968. 96pp. Paper $1.50. The author explains the various forms drama can take in Christian education. The author is particularly interested in impromptu dramatization as opposed to the rehearsing and producing of a prepared script. An Appendix of names and addresses of English organizations is included. Illustrated.

CHILDREN AND THE THEATRE

General Reference Works

CHEIFETZ, DAN
Theater in My Head
Little, Brown, 1971. 178pp. $5.95. The author conducted a free, racially integrated theatre workshop for children, ages eight to eleven, on thirteen successive Saturdays in a New York City church. This book describes what happened and how it happened: what the children said, what they did, and, from the director's point of view, what it seemed to mean. Mr. Cheifetz outlines a practical program for working with young children. Sixteen pages of photographs.

DODD, NIGEL and WINIFRED HICKSON – Editors
Drama and Theatre in Education
Heinemann, 1971. 176pp. $6.50. This book grew out of a conference of teachers and lecturers at all levels of education in Bristol, England, in 1969. The book opens with a survey of drama and theatre in education in England. Contributors explore the fields of improvisation and literature, movement as a preparation for drama, the school play, and the professional theatre in and for schools. Detailed summaries of discussions which followed the presentation of papers at the Conference are provided. Appendices.

HANGER, EUNICE – Editor
Drama for High Schools
See Page 533

McCASLIN, NELLIE
Theatre for Children in the United States: A History
University of Oklahoma, 1971. 317pp. $8.95. This history of children's theatre in the United States is arranged chronologically by decades extending from the Children's Educational Theatre of 1903 to groups active in 1971. Under each section, theatre for children is discussed from the standpoint of sponsorship: national organizations, community centers, schools and colleges, and professional theatre. Miss McCaslin records the important work of the Drama League and the Association of Junior Leagues of America; she describes the work of significant producing groups, both amateur and professional; and points out the trends in theme and subject matter. The author also presents a history of subsidies: federal, state, and private. Illustrated with thirty-two pages of photographs. A nineteen page Bibliography is also included. Index.

PICKERING, KENNETH
Drama Improvised
Coach House Press, 1971. 60pp. Paper $1.75. A source book of ideas for teachers working with children in the field of improvised drama. The volume is illustrated with photographs, and the author has included a Bibliography.

PIRO, RICHARD
Black Fiddler
See Page 570

Drama in the Classroom

GOODRIDGE, JANET
Creative Drama and Improvised Movement for Children
Plays, Inc., 1971. 158pp. $5.95. Originally published in England in 1970 as "Drama in the Primary School" and now published in the United States, this handbook aims to provide some ideas for teachers of drama who are working with young children. The author's approach shows the teacher how to correlate creative dramatics with other related subjects—physical education, arts and crafts, speech, English, and music. The techniques have been tested in schools in England. Each chapter contains suggested scenes and a book list.

JEEP, ELIZABETH
Classroom Creativity
McGraw—Hill, 1970. 148pp. Paper $3.45. An idea book for teachers of religion, this volume contains ideas for classroom activities, designed to draw the student toward an awareness of God, His World, and the dignity of persons. The author offers helpful hints on encouraging self-expression in children through creative participation in art, drama, dance, song, etc., practical suggestions for including these activities in the curriculum, and thoughts on the creative use of audio-visual materials. The volume is illustrated with drawings, and the author has included a Bibliography.

LOWNDES, BETTY
Movement and Creative Drama for Children
See entry in next column

MARTIN, WILLIAM and GORDON VALLINS
Exploration Drama
Evans, 1971. Five volumes: 315pp. $9.50. Published in England, these volumes include a teacher's book and four books for students. The authors explore the nature of dramatic action, the organization of material, and the use of disciplines and techniques in a creative form. The teacher's book contains suggestions on how the material might be approached. "Carnival" contains children's games, stories, and rituals, and simple studies of people in their environment. "Legend" includes a selection of myths, legends, ballads, and folk plays from different parts of the world. "Horizon" is a series of stories of adventure including some historical material and songs. "Routes" includes stories, songs, poems, plays, and documentaries including experiments with magic, dance, and environmental and scientific studies. Each book is illustrated.

TYAS, BILLI
Child Drama in Action
Drama Book Specialists, 1971. 107pp. $6.95. The author intends his book to be used as a manual by teachers actually engaged in doing dramatic work with children from the ages of six to ten. Twenty-two lessons each contain dramatic exercises, situations for discussion and improvisation, practice in role-playing, and a story outline for dramatizing, with full instructions for the teacher. Illustrated with drawings. List of Suggested Recordings. Bibliography.

Music and Movement

BENTLEY, WILLIAM G.
Learning to Move and Moving to Learn
Citation, 1970. 90pp. Paper $2.35. The author presents exercises that boys and girls can perform individually or in groups to improve their skill in body management. Illustrated with photographs. List of Equipment. Selected Bibliography. List of Selected Audio-Visual Materials.

BOORMAN, JOYCE
Creative Dance in the First Three Grades
David McKay, 1969. 121pp. $6.00. An introduction to to the ways of providing learning experiences for young children, based upon the work of Rudolf Laban, in creative dance. Illustrated with photographs, drawings, and diagrams.

DIMONDSTEIN, GERALDINE
Children Dance in the Classroom
Macmillan, 1971. 270pp. $10.50. The premise of Dr. Dimondstein's book is that "one of the major functions of elementary schooling is to develop in children a sense of self-knowledge and self-identification with their own creative abilities." The materials presented have evolved over a twenty year period of teaching music and movement to children. Actual classroom problems and suggested lessons are provided and illustrated with photographs. Lists of records, songs, books, and films are included. Index.

LOWNDES, BETTY
Movement and Creative Drama for Children
Plays, Inc., 1971. 144pp. $5.95. Originally published in England under the title "Movement and Drama in the Primary School " and now issued in the United States. The author begins with a discussion of what movement thinking and creative drama are and how both may be used by the teacher to get children to communicate and learn. Sensory awareness and body awareness activities are covered in separate chapters as are locomotion and mime. Verbal drama improvisations are grouped in five separate

stages. Illustrated with photographs taken during the actual classes. List of Books for Further Reading. Index.

RAPOSO, JOE and JEFFREY MOSS
The Sesame Street Song Book
See Page 572

Films, Television, and Radio

BURKE, RICHARD C. – Editor
Instructional Television
See Page 624

GIBSON, TONY
The Use of E. T. V.: A Handbook for Students and Teachers
See Page 622

GLUCKSMANN, ANDRE
Violence on the Screen
See Page 600

GRIFFITH, BARTON L. and DONALD W. MACLENNAN – Editors
Improvement of Teaching by Television
See Page 624

LARSON, RODGER with ELLEN MEADE
Young Filmmakers
See Page 611

MAYNARD, RICHARD A.
The Celluloid Curriculum
See Page 602

MORRIS, NORMAN S.
Television's Child
See Page 623

RYNEW, ARDEN
Filmmaking for Children
Pflaum, 1971. 159pp. Paper $5.25. The purpose of this book is to stimulate filmmaking in the elementary school. The author hopes it will demonstrate how the medium can be used with ease and simplicity and how to make the educational environment more enriching for children. The book provides information on the author's approach as an art teacher in creating a filmmaking program in an elementary school, and information to those educators who wish to examine the educational potential of filmmaking. The volume includes "Motion Picture Production Handbook," the student's volume described below. Illustrated with drawings, diagrams, and photographs.

RYNEW, ARDEN
Motion Picture Production Handbook
Pflaum, 1971. 64pp. Paper $2.25. This is a handbook for young filmmakers which the author hopes will contain most of the information needed in order to start making films. It is to be used in conjunction with the teacher's volume, "Filmmaking for Children," listed above. Illustrated with drawings. Glossary. Index of Illustrations.

SARSON, EVELYN – Editor
Action for Children's Television
See Page 623

Acting for Children

JOHNSON, ALBERT and BERTHA JOHNSON
Drama for Junior High with Selected Scenes
A.S. Barnes, 1971. 208pp. $6.95. A book about acting for junior high school students. The book also includes nine selected scenes for various combinations of male and female characters. The authors provide a list of additional scenes.

OLFSON, LEWY
You Can Act!
Sterling, 1971. 144pp. $2.95. A book on acting for children. Pantomime, improvised plays, plays from scripts, puppet plays, and acting in chorus are all covered in simple terms. Short plays are provided for the children to act. A teacher's guide is also included. Glossary. Illustrated with drawings. Index.

Production of Plays

CONRAD, EDNA and MARY VAN DYKE
History on the Stage
Van Nostrand, 1971. 128pp. $7.95. A guidebook for teachers wishing to use the medium of improvised plays to instruct their young students. The authors use the subject of American history and include advice on choosing and reading the book, getting the students to derive the script, costuming and making stage sets, casting and directing, rehearsing and performing. Included is a script for "Show Boat" as an example. Illustrated with eighty-nine photographs taken during the course of an actual project. List of Suggested Novels and Reference Books. Index.

COURTNEY, RICHARD
The School Play
See Page 586

JOHN, MALCOLM – Editor
Music Drama in Schools
Cambridge, 1971. 176pp. $15.65. Fifteen contributors show how music and drama can be combined in school

stage productions. They describe successful music drama productions and outline how they conceived the ideas for their productions and how they went about solving the problems they faced. Discussed are: aspects of writing the story, the music and libretto, and casting the production. Illustrated with musical examples. List of Books for Further Reading. Index.

JOHNSON, RICHARD C.
Producing Plays for Children
Richards Rosen Press, 1971. 154pp. $6.96. A volume in "The Theatre Student" series. This is a manual for the production of plays for children. It is directed toward high school drama departments and youth organizations. Among the subjects covered are finding the right play, the backstage work, acting techniques, and touring of the final production. Appendices include examples of a typical production calendar, audition forms, rehearsal schedules, and a selected list of plays and sources of supplies. The volume is illustrated with photographs and drawings. The author has included a Bibliography which provides a selected list of books on theatre, creativity and creative drama, children's theatre, acting and various other aspects of production, and periodicals.

PURDY, SUSAN
Costumes for You to Make
Lippincott, 1971. 121pp. $4.95. Clear and simple directions for making costumes with readily available, low-cost materials. Step-by-step instructions illustrate how to assemble every basic costume part with information on trimming, padding, fastening, and hemming, and other finishing details. Illustrated with color drawings. Index.

Books for Children

Histories of Theatre

BULLA, CLYDE ROBERT
Stories of Gilbert and Sullivan Operas
See Page 569

Biographies

FUNKE, LEWIS
The Curtain Rises: The Story of Ossie Davis
See Page 563

NEWMAN, SHIRLEE P.
Mary Martin on Stage
See Page 565

PUPPETS AND MARIONETTES

General Histories

BOHMER, GUNTER
The Wonderful World of Puppets
Plays, Inc., 1971. 156pp. $8.95. Translated from the German by Gerald Morice, this book is based on the famous Puppet Collection of the City of Munich. Puppets from Europe and Asia are illustrated and discussed. Among the many types presented are hand puppets, rod puppets, shadow puppetry, and paper or toy theatres. Illustrated with sixteen color plates and seventy-six pages of black-and-white photographs and drawings. Index.

COLLIER, JOHN PAYNE
The Dialogue of the Puppet Show
See entry below under CRUIKSHANK

CROTHERS, J. FRANCES
The Puppeteer's Library Guide: The Bibliographic Index to the Literature of the World Puppet Theatre – Volume One: The Historical Background of Puppetry and Its Related Fields
Scarecrow Press, 1971. 474pp. $17.50. The first in a projected six volume series. This volume lists books on the historical background of world puppetry including bibliographies, histories, Punch and Judy material, and international material by country. Also provided are lists of organizations, guilds, and periodicals of puppetry. Publishers' and Booksellers' Addresses. Author Index.

CRUIKSHANK, GEORGE
Punch and Judy
Blom, 1971. 148pp. $12.00. Originally published in 1929 and now reissued in a facsimile edition, this is a history of the Punch and Judy puppet shows. Also included is "The Dialogue of the Puppet-Show, An Account of Its Origin, and of Puppet Plays in England" by John Payne Collier, and a Bibliographical Note by Anne Lyon Haight. Twenty-eight illustrations.

RANSOME, GRACE GREENLEAF
Puppets and Shadows: A Bibliography
Faxon, 1931. 74pp. $2.00. A listing of puppet plays published up to 1930.

Puppets of Various Nations

OBRAZTSOV, SERGEI
The Chinese Puppet Theatre
Faber & Faber, 1961. 55pp. $4.25. The famous Russian puppet-master analyzes the ancient art of puppetry in China. The work has been translated from the Russian by J. T. MacDermott. Illustrated with photographs.

SCOTT–KEMBALL, JEUNE
Javanese Shadow Puppets
Columbia, 1970. 65pp. Paper $1.50. A short study of the art of shadow puppetry in Java. The volume is illustrated with plates of the collection of puppets in the British Museum. Six of the thirty plates are in color. Bibliographical Note. Glossary. Index.

Instruction Books

ALKEMA, CHESTER JAY
Puppet-Making
Sterling, 1971. 48pp. $2.95. A guide for the creation of puppets. Illustrated with black-and-white and color photographs. Index.

CHRISTOPHER, CATHERINE
The Complete Book of Doll Making and Collecting
Dover, 1971. 290pp. Paper $3.00. Originally published in 1949 and now reissued in a revised second edition. The volume tells in non-technical terms how to create all kinds of dolls from soft rag dolls to many of more advanced technique. The author also recounts the history of dolls. Photographs and diagrams illustrate the book. Dictionary of Doll Definitions. Index.

FEATHERSTONE, DONALD
Military Modelling
A.S. Barnes, 1971. 159pp. $6.95. A comprehensive collection of facts and information together with instructions for making model soldiers, military vehicles and buildings, and converting or adapting existing models. Instructions on moulding and casting model soldiers, soldering and gluing, painting, construction of dioramas, etc. Illustrated with photographs.

FRASER, PETER
Puppet Circus
Plays, Inc., 1971. 152pp. $4.95. The author has gathered together instructions for reconstructing original Victorian puppets which may be used in a circus theme. He provides step-by-step diagrams and drawings to make the puppets as close to the originals as possible. Individual sections of the volume cover the painting, plastic modelling, and authentic costuming of the puppets as well as the actual performance of the puppet circus. List of Suppliers. Bibliography.

ROSS, LAURA
Hand Puppets: How to Make and Use Them
World's Work, 1971. 191pp. $5.95. Step-by-step directions and diagrams for making simple hand puppets. The volume includes three puppet plays: "Rumplestiltskin," "Punch and Judy," and "A Visit from Outer Space." Instructions for dressing and handling puppets, setting up a stage, and writing and producing a show are provided. Illustrated with photographs and drawings. Index.

Plays for Puppets

ROSS, LAURA
Puppet Shows Using Poems and Stories
Lothrop, Lee and Shepard, 1971. 192pp. $4.95. A collection of poetry and stories that permits staging of puppet shows with little or no planning, preparation, or rehearsal. Production notes for each of the selections include the technique of the production, the setting, the cast, and the action. Illustrated with drawings.

YEATS, JACK B.
The Collected Plays of Jack B. Yeats
Bobbs–Merrill, 1971. 382pp. $17.50. Edited and with an Introduction by Robin Skelton, this collection of plays by the Irish painter and playwright includes eight plays for the miniature theatre as well as nine plays for the "Larger" theatre. Appendices include an essay by Yeats on how the plays for the miniature theatre were produced. Illustrated with drawings of costume and set designs.

MINIATURE THEATRES

YEATS, JACK B.
The Collected Plays of Jack B. Yeats
See entry directly above.

CLOWNS, CIRCUS, PANTOMIME, COMMEDIA DELL'ARTE

DISHER, M. WILLSON
Greatest Show on Earth
Blom, 1971. 306pp. $12.50. Originally published in 1937 and now reissued in a facsimile edition, this is a history of the nineteenth century circus founded by Philip Astley and performed at his Royal Amphitheatre of Arts in London, England. The author describes the new style of theatrical entertainment—"feats of activity on horseback"—which, he contends, changed the course of English theatre and drama. The volume is illustrated and includes an Index.

GREENWOOD, ISAAC JOHN
The Circus: Its Origin and Growth Prior to 1835
Burt Franklin, 1970. 117pp. $16.95. Originally published in 1898 and now reissued in a facsimile edition, this is an account of the early circus, particularly in England and America, and its famous performers. Included are twelve illustrations.

RENZI, RENZO – Editor
Federico Fellini: I Clowns
See Page 605

MAGIC

BALL, W.W. ROUSE
Fun with String Figures
Dover, 1971. 80pp. Paper $1.00. An unabridged republication of the work first published in England in 1920. The author provides an introduction to the art of making figures with a piece of string. Instructions for making twenty-seven figures are included in text and illustrations. Glossary. Index.

BURSILL, HENRY
More Hand Shadows
Dover, 1971. Unpaged. Paper $1.00. An unabridged republication of the work originally published in 1860. Sixteen shadows are illustrated.

HAWKESWORTH, ERIC
Conjuring
Faber & Faber, 1971. 86pp. $3.75. The author provides instructions on how to make and perform tricks and illusions. They include examples of mindreading, escapology, ventriloquism, and stage illusions. Illustrated with drawings.

MERLINI (CLAYTON RAWSON)
How to Entertain Children with Magic You Can Do
Simon & Schuster, 1971. 175pp. Paper $2.95. Originally published in 1962 and now reissued, this is a guide for parents who wish to keep their children amused. Tricks with matches, coins, ropes, cards, and mind reading stunts are included. Illustrated with photographs.

SCARNE, JOHN
Scarne's Magic Tricks
Crown, 1971. 256pp. $4.95. Originally published in 1951 and now reissued, this is a compendium of 200 magic tricks from the repertoire of the well-known magician. The tricks are performable with simple props and without sleight-of-hand. They are described in the text and illustrated with drawings.

WIT AND HUMOR

FOX, SONNY
Jokes ... and How to Tell Them
Putnam, 1965. 95pp. $4.85. A compendium of jokes with hints on presentation. Comedian Alan King has provided an Introduction to the volume and Bob Gray has provided the drawings.

ORBEN, ROBERT
The Encyclopedia of One-Liner Comedy
Doubleday, 1971. 232pp. $5.95. A collection of 2,000 short comic lines by the writer of television comedy. The jokes are arranged under subjects with an Index.

PART TWO: BOOKS ON TECHNICAL ARTS

PRODUCTION

GENERAL REFERENCE WORKS

BAX, PETER
Stage Management
Blom, 1971. 313pp. $12.50. Originally published in 1936 and now reissued in a facsimile edition, this is a guide for the manager concerned with forming a technical staff and directing its work, preparing a promptbook, arranging for stage decor, costumes, and properties. The author was stage manager of The Theatre Royal, Drury Lane, London, among others. Illustrated. Appendices. Bibliography. Index.

CLARK, BRIAN
Group Theatre
Pitman, 1971. 120pp. $5.75. A guide to the techniques of group interpretation in the theatre, the movement which has produced the productions of "Marat/Sade," "Hair," and The Living Theatre Company. The author describes the qualities needed in a group and its leader and demonstrates with examples how the group can "work in" to an existing text, "work around" a set theme or documentary material, or "work out" a play of their own from the controlled use of improvisation. An Appendix provides primary sense exercises. Reading List. Index.

COURTNEY, RICHARD
Drama for Youth
Pitman, 1964. 172pp. $6.25. A guide to amateur production written with the special needs of schools, youth clubs, and training colleges in mind. The book covers improvised drama as well as the choice and production of conventional plays. The work of the producer, acting techniques, make-up, scenic design, stagecraft, lighting, costume, and stage properties are all dealt with in detail. Illustrated. List of Plays. List of Suppliers. Bibliography. Index.

COURTNEY, RICHARD
The School Play
Cassell, 1966. 215pp. $4.25. A guidebook on the production of plays in schools. Mr. Courtney's experience in England enables him to explain how to choose a play and the principles of acting, decor, properties, lighting, costume, make-up, sound, and business and house management. Illustrated with photographs, drawings and diagrams. Play List. List of Major English Suppliers. List of Recommended Books. Glossary. Index.

CRAMPTON, ESME
A Handbook of the Theatre
Drama Book Specialists, 1972. 264pp. $6.95. Originally published in 1964 and now revised, this is a guide to play production. After an introduction on the nature of drama and the history of theatre, the author describes the activities of each member of the production team: director, stage manager, designer, actor, front of the house personnel, etc. Information has been up-dated; the lighting section has been rewritten and the illustrations replaced; illustrations in the make-up section have been replaced; and additions have been made to the Reading List for the design chapter as well as to the General Reading List. Illustrated with drawings, diagrams, and photographs. Glossary.

CULP, RALPH BORDEN
The Theatre and Its Drama: Principles and Practices
Wm. C. Brown, 1971. 455pp. $11.35. An introductory text for students. The basic elements of theatre are considered; the theatre is examined as a participant in human affairs; and a series of chapters deal with the principles and techniques of creating theatre. These chapters focus collectively on "how a play means." Illustrations of the author's theses are provided by means of a selected play script including: "As You Like It," "Everyman," "Othello," and "Tom Sawyer." Children's theatre and creative dramatics are considered in a separate chapter. Illustrated with drawings and diagrams. Glossary. Index.

DATE, SUSAN and KELVIN WATSON
Come Down Stage: A Practical Guide to Amateur Drama
Pelham Books, 1971. 140pp. $6.95. Published in England, this guidebook provides instructions in how to organize an amateur group's activities in producing a play. Included are suggestions on setting up the production group, choosing and rehearsing a play, the technology of the production, duties of staff members both on and off the stage including the front-of-the-house staff. Illustrated with diagrams and drawings. List of English Suppliers. Bibliography. Index.

DODRILL, CHARLES W.
Theatre Management Selected Bibliography
A. E. T. A., 1966. 10pp. Paper $ .75. This is a mimeographed bibliography of theatre management materials available. These materials deal with front-of-the-house operation and the entries include information on the author, title, and publisher, as well as a short summary of the text.

ELLFELDT, LOIS and EDWIN CARNES
Dance Production Handbook
See Page 576

EUSTIS, MORTON
B'way, Inc.!: The Theatre as a Business
Blom, 1971. 356pp. $12.50. Originally published in 1934 and now reissued in a facsimile edition, this is a factual digest of all the commercial aspects of the theatre, from production to set design for profit, the

financial problems of the acting profession, contracts and unions. Appendices illustrate typical contract forms and list theatrical unions.

GRUVER, BERT
The Stage Manager's Handbook
Drama Book Specialists, 1972. 220pp. $6.95. Originally published in 1953, this manual has become the standard work for stage managers. The work has now been revised and brought up-to-date by Broadway stage manager Frank Hamilton. The guide provides step-by-step procedures for managing a production from the pre-rehearsal period through the run of the show, and touring. Appendices include examples of working prompt scripts and selected union rules. Illustrated with charts and diagrams.

MACLAY, JOANNA HAWKINS
Readers Theatre: Toward a Grammar of Practice
Random House, 1971. 110pp. Paper $3.00. An introduction to this new form of theatre which emphasizes the text of a play as opposed to the total theatrical effect sought by conventional theatre. The author provides suggestions on selection of scripts, casting, and performance. Notes. Index.

YOUNG, JOHN WRAY
Community Theatre: A Manual for Success
Samuel French, 1971. 155pp. Paper $3.00. The author states the philosophical and practical procedures which can lead community theatres to new levels of artistic and economic success. He provides chapters on organizing the community theatre; programming; front-of-the-house problems; the requirements of, and for, a director; technical, business, legal, and budgeting problems. The chapter on the audience charts methods of increasing ticket sales and winning larger audiences.

INDIVIDUAL ASPECTS OF PRODUCTION

PLAYWRITING

BURACK, A.S. – Editor
The Writer's Handbook
The Writer, 1971. 788pp. $10.00. A complete guide to all phases of the craft of writing. One hundred authorities have each written a chapter containing practical instruction in the writing of novels and short stories, articles, verse, humor, juvenile books, plays, and television scripts. Information on the business side of writing (manuscript preparation, agents, copyright, etc.) is also given. A list of markets for the sale of manuscripts gives publishers' editorial requirements, payment rates, addresses, names of editors, etc. Also included is a list of leading American literary agents and organizations for writers.

COHN, RUBY
Dialogue in American Drama
Indiana University, 1971. 340pp. $9.50. Mrs. Cohn analyzes functioning dialogue in major modern American plays. She examines imagery, rhythm, original turn of phrase, fidelity to character, and the theatrical visability of the dialogue of each play. The author discusses plays written by a select group of American novelists and poets including Eugene O'Neill, Arthur Miller, Tennessee Williams, Edward Albee, and others. She concludes her book with a brief exploration of drama and theatre today. Notes. Bibliography. Index.

SMILEY, SAM
Playwriting: The Structure of Action
Prentice–Hall, 1971. 315pp. $10.50. Paper $6.00. A practical description of the techniques needed for the perfection of the art of playwriting. The author dissects the process of writing a play, exploring all principles and methods, including many ideas about selecting and arranging dramatic material. Many examples of outstanding dramas are included. Extensive material on the business and marketing procedure for the finished play is also included. Bibliography. Index.

STILLMAN, FRANCES
The Poet's Manual and Rhyming Dictionary
Crowell, 1965. 387pp. $6.95. Based on "The Improved Rhyming Dictionary" by Jane Shaw Whitfield, this is a complete handbook for poets. The first part provides an up-to-date guide to the techniques of poetic composition; the second comprises an exhaustive rhyming dictionary. The author offers a thorough treatment of the craft of modern poetic forms and the various meters used in English with examples. An Appendix offers advice on achieving publication and supplies a list of periodicals that regularly publish poetry. Index. (Although not a book on playwriting, the volume may be of some value to playwrights.)

WITTENBERG, PHILIP
The Protection of Literary Property
The Writer, 1968. 267pp. $7.95. An exploration of the complex subject of literary property and the law. The author traces the history and development of the concept of literary property and gives detailed information on the United States Copyright Law. He includes sections on international copyright agreements, plagiarism, piracy, infringement, permissions, the right of privacy, etc. A chapter on censorship is a summary of the idea of censorship and its application to today's writings. Index.

WOOD, CLEMENT
Wood's New World Unabridged Rhyming Dictionary
World, 1971. 1,040pp. $12.50. This is the sixteenth edition of the rhyming dictionary. It lists single, double, and triple rhymes with every rhyming sound pronounced, thus providing the phonetic values. The author also provides three explanatory sections: The

Vocabulary of Poetry, The Complete Form-book for Poets, and Versification Self-Taught.

DIRECTING

HODGE, FRANCIS
Play Directing: Analysis, Communication, and Style
Prentice—Hall, 1971. 394pp. $11.95. The author shows, step by step, how to approach a play to discover its dramatic values and how to direct the production with these aims in mind. The reader is guided in ways to communicate ideas to actors and designers and, through intensive discussions of style, the author shows how a director can express himself by conceiving of the individuality of each play and by finding an individual way to produce. Exercises for students are included. Illustrated with drawings and photographs. Bibliography. Index.

WELKER, DAVID
Theatrical Direction: The Basic Techniques
Allyn and Bacon, 1971. 419pp. $13.25. A textbook for the study of directing techniques. Discussion is aimed at the beginning director. Methods and techniques are described in detail, including many examples of specific instructions that can be used in working with the actors. Among the topics discussed are: the role of the director, the director as artist, analysis of the script, auditions and casting, the rehearsal, and training the actors. Illustrated with drawings, diagrams, and photographs. Glossary of Technical Terms. Index.

STAGE AND THEATRE DESIGN

Reference Works and General Histories

ALEXANDRE, ARSENE
The Decorative Art of Leon Bakst
See Page 577

ARNHEIM, RUDOLF
Visual Thinking
University of California, 1971. 345pp. Paper $4.25. Originally published in 1969 and now reissued, in this study Professor Arnheim contends that all thinking is basically perceptual in nature. He shows that the fundamental processes of vision involve mechanisms typical of reasoning and he describes problem-solving in the arts as well as imagery in the thought-models of science. The volume is of immediate interest to the educator for the function of art in education. Students of scenic design will probably find it interesting. Illustrated. Notes. Bibliography. Index.

BABLET, DENIS
La Scene e l'Immagine: Saggio su Josef Svoboda
Speedimpex, 1970. 254pp. $13.00. Published in Italy and written in the Italian language, this is a critical analysis of the work of the Czech scenic and costume designer. A feature of the volume is the collection of 101 photographic illustrations of the work of the designer and the numerous drawings and sketches in the text.

BAKST, LEON
The Designs of Leon Bakst for "The Sleeping Princess"
See Page 577

BERMAN, EUGENE
The Graphic Work of Eugene Berman
Clarkson Potter, 1971. 332pp. $15.00. A collection of the work of the scene designer. Preface and notes on the works by Berman with a Foreword by Russell Lynes. Over 700 black-and-white reproductions are provided but these do NOT include any of the artist's theatre designs.

BURIAN, JARKA
The Scenography of Josef Svoboda
Wesleyan University, 1971. 202pp. $25.00. A study of the theatre designs of the Czechoslovakian "scenographer." A biographical and critical essay on Svoboda provides a background in Czech theatre; then the study is devoted to detailed, professional considerations of some sixty key productions, described largely in Svoboda's own works. More than two hundred black-and-white photographs illustrate the work. Register of Productions. Selected Bibliography.

CHENEY, SHELDON
The New Movement in the Theatre
See Page 518

FOLENA, GIANFRANCO
Disegni Teatrali di Inigo Jones
Speedimpex, 1970. 82pp. Paper $5.00. A catalog of the theatrical designs of Inigo Jones. Thirty-eight illustrations are provided. The accompanying text is, however, in the Italian language.

GROPIUS, WALTER – Editor
The Theatre of the Bauhaus
Wesleyan University, 1971. 109pp. Paper $4.95. Originally published in 1924, translated into English in 1961, and now reissued, this is a collection of articles giving evidence to the Bauhaus approach in the specific field of stage work. Walter Gropius has provided an Introduction and the articles are by Oskar Schlemmer, Laszlo Moholy-Nagy, and Farkas Molnar. Illustrated with drawings and photographs.

LEVINSON, ANDRE
Bakst: The Story of the Artist's Life
See Page 578

MURARO, MARIA TERESA and ELENA POVOLEDO
Disegni Teatrali dei Bibiena
Speedimpex, 1970. 130pp. + plates. Paper $8.00. A study of the architectural designs and drawings of the eighteenth century Italian designer, Galli Bibiena. The volume includes 165 plates; however, the accompanying text is in the Italian language.

SHERINGHAM, GEORGE and JAMES LAVER
Design in the Theatre
Blom, 1971. 157pp. $12.50. Originally published in 1927 and now reissued in a facsimile edition, this collection of articles and essays includes contributions by E. Gordon Craig, Charles B. Cochran, and Nigel Playfair. More than 100 black-and-white illustrations show costume and scenery designs by English and Continental designers. Select Bibliography.

COULIN, CLAUDIUS
Step-by-Step Perspective Drawing
Van Nostrand, 1971. 112pp. $13.95. Originally published in Germany in 1966 and now translated by John H. Yarbrough, and issued in the United States, this is a guidebook for architects, draftsmen, and designers. It begins with a general explanation of drawing instruments and materials, then starts the reader on a course in descriptive geometry, from simple isometric projections through perspective renderings of complicated planes and rounded forms. There are forty-three pages of drawings, and facing each is a page of text that explains the drawings and the methods used to construct them. Each of these units is an exercise for the student and they add up to a complete presentation of technical drawing. Index.

Manuals and Instruction Books

BRYSON, NICHOLAS L.
Thermoplastic Scenery for Theatre
Drama Book Specialists, 1972. 104pp. Spiral bound $7.95. Written for the scene designer and technician, this is a step-by-step guide for producing low cost set pieces using a homemade vacuum forming machine. This first volume in the projected series provides information on the construction and operation of the machine, as well as data on the general considerations and fabrication processes of the art. Illustrated with more than 125 photographs and diagrams.

BURRIS-MEYER, HAROLD and EDWARD C. COLE
Scenery for the Theatre: Revised Edition
Little, Brown, 1971. 518pp. $32.00. The first complete revision of the handbook and guide to theatre scenery since its first edition in 1938. The text has been completely updated with the advice and assistance of several professional experts. The volume features over 1,000 photographs, line drawings, and diagrams, all juxtaposed to the related text; thirty-four tables; an Appendix of mathematical formulas and graphs; a lengthy Bibliography; and eight full-color pages that provide step-by-step instruction in the craft of scene painting. The purpose of the authors is to provide the apprentice or student of theatre production with facts, procedures, principles, and general knowledge on setting the stage. Bibliography. Index.

CAMPBELL, ROBERT and N.H. MAGER – Editors
How to Work with Tools and Wood
Pocket Books, 1971. 488pp. Paper $1.25. Originally published in 1952 and revised and enlarged in 1955, this is a do-it-yourself guide for the beginning carpenter. Illustrated and discussed are the use and care of basic tools, varieties of wood, woodworking joints, and the use of various power tools. Index.

Auditoriums and Stages

MARTIN, RALPH G.
Lincoln Center for the Performing Arts
See Page 557

SCHUBERT, HANNELORE
The Modern Theatre: Architecture, Stage Design, Lighting
Praeger, 1971. 222pp. $35.00. Translated from the German by J. C. Palmes, this book traces the development of theatre building since 1945, particularly in the fields of lighting, scenery changes, seating arrangements, and acoustic effects. Examples of new theatres have been chosen from all over the world including the National Theatre in Brussels, the Folkets Hus in Stockholm, the Lincoln Center complex in New York, and the Alley Theatre in Houston. The author provides floor-plans, sections, and elevations of each of the buildings considered, supplemented by many indoor and outdoor photographs. Technical data for the theatres built after World War II is also provided. Bibliography. Index of Names

Acoustics

SMITH, T. and P. E. O'SULLIVAN, B. OAKES, and R. B. CONN – Editors
Building Acoustics
Oriel Press, 1971. 242pp. $14.35. Based on a seminar organized by the British Acoustical Society, and edited by four leading acoustical experts, this is a practical textbook about modern problems in building acoustics. Subjects covered range from external traffic noise through conduction of sound energy via structural junctions and the airborn sound insulation of glass, walls and floors, to problems of measuring reverberation and predicting the performance of porous fibrous materials.

Illustrated with photographs, drawings, diagrams, charts, and tables, the volume includes notes, references and discussions on the twelve papers presented at the conference and herein reprinted. Index of Authors and Contributors. Subject Index.

Stage Decoration

Architecture

CALLENDER, JOHN HANCOCK – Editor-in-Chief
Time-Saver Standards: A Handbook of Architectural Design
McGraw–Hill, 1966. 1,299pp. $30.00. Originally published in 1946 and reissued with additions in 1950 and 1954, this fourth edition of the handbook is completely revised and expanded. It is intended primarily to meet the needs of those who design buildings and offers essential data in each area of building construction and its allied fields. Each subject has been specially prepared by an outstanding authority. Information on structural design, building materials and components and techniques, environmental control, residential and non-residential design elements, and site planning and recreation. Index.

Furniture

GABRIEL, JURI
Victorian Furniture and Furnishings
Grosset & Dunlap, 1971. 159pp. $3.95. A selective guide to furniture and furnishings of the Victorian era. Included are 260 color illustrations. List of Books to Read. Index.

GOTTSHALL, FRANKLIN H.
Reproducing Antique Furniture
Crown, 1971. 240pp. $9.95. A guide to the construction, hardware, and finishing of antique reproductions. The first section of the book describes the fundamentals of cabinetmaking and the rudiments of woodwork. Forty crafts projects are presented with a bill of materials required, and a running text with explanations of all processes. Illustrated with 600 photographs and drawings. Glossary. Index.

HINCKLEY, F. LEWIS
A Directory of Queen Anne, Early Georgian and Chippendale Furniture
Crown, 1971. 277pp. $10.00. The author presents evidence to show that furniture long considered English in origin was actually designed and produced in Dublin. The volume includes 225 photographic illustrations of 467 examples of such furniture. Index.

HOPE, THOMAS
Household Furniture and Interior Decoration
Dover, 1971. 141pp. Paper $3.50. An unabridged republication (with minor corrections) of the original 1807 edition. Sixty original plates and ten new illustrations show the furniture and decoration of the Regency period. A new Introduction has been written by David Watkin.

O'NEIL, ISABEL
The Art of the Painted Finish for Furniture and Decoration
Morrow, 1971. 382pp. $19.95. A comprehensive course of study, with minutely detailed instructions, on the art of the painted finish. The author has included historical background and explicit instructions concerning methods, tools and materials. The four sections deal with: Glazes, Lacquer, and Casein; Painting, Antiquing, and Distressing; Leafing, Gilding, and Burnishing; and Faux Finishes. Every major type of decorative painted finish is covered in the text and thirty-eight plates and 100 how-to drawings. The book will be of great value to scenic designers. Subject Outline. List of Books for Suggested Reading.

Decorative Arts and Design

ALBERS, ANNI
On Designing
Wesleyan University, 1971. 81pp. Paper $4.95. Originally published in 1959 and now reissued, this is a collection of articles by the textile designer. Illustrated with twelve photographed examples of her art.

BARRETT, CYRIL
An Introduction to Optical Art
Dutton, 1971. 160pp. Paper $2.25. This is an exploration of contemporary "Op Art." The author studies its various forms technically and artistically, he describes and explains the general characteristics, and traces its historical development. Illustrated with over one hundred examples of the art form. Bibliography. Index.

FRANCISCONO, MARCEL
Walter Gropius and the Creation of the Bauhaus in Weimar
University of Illinois, 1971. 336pp. $11.95. A study of the Bauhaus from 1919. The ideals and artistic theories of the founding years are detailed from Walter Gropius' unpublished papers and hitherto unstudied writings. The author describes the contributions which artists in the early Bauhaus made to its formation, analyzes the nature of the earliest work produced, and shows its connection to the later design work. The volume is illustrated with forty-two figures and also includes Appendices, a Bibliography, and an Index.

HILLIER, BEVIS
The World of Art Deco
Dutton, 1971. 224pp. Paper $7.50. This book, a product of the 1971 exhibition at The Minneapolis Institute of Arts, offers a record of the 1930's "Moderne" style. Nearly fifteen hundred objects, ranging from furniture to articles of clothing, have been drawn from private collections, museums, and dealers and these are illustrated in sixteen color plates and over 300 black-and-white illustrations. Bibliography.

KOCH, ROBERT
Louis C. Tiffany's Glass, Bronzes, Lamps
Crown, 1971. 208pp. $8.50. A collector's guide to the objects produced by the artist or those under his supervision. Biographical details of Tiffany's life and facts about the design, the materials, and the processes used in his art are provided. Mr. Koch has added the complete 1906 Tiffany price list of almost 1,500 items and an illustrated 1933 catalogue of eighty-five lamps and shades. Included are 287 photographs and design drawings of the art objects, reproductions of advertisements, and the details of the manufacturing process.

LORRIMAR, BETTY
Creative Papier Mache
Watson—Guptill, 1971. 104pp. $7.95. Miss Lorrimar guides the reader through a discussion of the materials and techniques of molding, using free-form shapes, making and using paper pulp, and decorating the finished objects in this introduction to the art of papier mache. Text and more than 100 illustrations detail the making of simple articles such as bowls, trays, puppets, scenery and stage properties, among other articles. The volume also includes a List of Suppliers and a Bibliography. Index.

Lighting

LIGHTING ASSOCIATES
Lighting Symbol Templates

Scale: ½" = 1"—Section View	$5.95
Scale: ¼" = 1"—Section View	$5.95
Scale: ½" = 1"—Plan View	$2.95.
Scale: ¼" = 1"—Plan View	$2.95

STEIN, DONNA M.
Thomas Wilfred: Lumia—A Retrospective Exhibition
Boston Book and Art Publishers, 1971. 102pp. Paper $8.95. A catalogue of the art works of Thomas Wilfred exhibited at the Corcoran Gallery of Art. Included are technical drawings and photographs illustrating the artist's life. Miss Stein provides an essay/introduction to the artist and his works. Chronology. List of Compositions for the Clavilux. List of Recorded Compositions. List of Major Exhibitions. Bibliography.

WILFRED, THOMAS
Projected Scenery: A Technical Manual
Drama Book Specialists, 1965. 56pp. Spiral bound $3.95. This manual gives explicit instructions for building and operating equipment for projecting settings on a screen or cyclorama as a substitute, or addition to, painted and lighted backdrops. Illustrated. List of Manufacturers of Supplies and Equipment. Glossary of Optical Terms.

COSTUME

General Histories

ALEXANDRE, ARSENE
The Decorative Art of Leon Bakst
See Page 577

BAKST, LEON
The Designs of Leon Bakst for "The Sleeping Princess"
See Page 577

BIGELOW, MARYBELLE S.
Fashion in History: Apparel in the Western World
Burgess, 1970. 342pp. $13.25. A history of costume from the dress of Ancient Egypt to the costumes of the modern age. The author also studies fashion design and fashion illustration. Illustrated with contemporary and period material. Bibliography. Index.

BRADLEY, CAROLYN
A History of World Costume
Peter Owen, 1964. 451pp. $14.50. The author provides a view of the development of dress from primitive times to the present. Presented in an outline form, the volume provides a detailed description of the garments worn by men and women through the ages. Each historic period is treated as a unit with chapters arranged under uniform topics. Short historical sketches and chronologies introduce every chapter. Sixty-two full page plates and maps are included. General Bibliography.

BROGDEN, JOANNE
Fashion Design
Reinhold, 1971. 96pp. $5.50. Paper $2.75. The author attempts to portray the kind of world in which the fashion designer works. She introduces the novice to the practical aspects of design by giving short biographies of the great fashion designers, detailing the training necessary, and providing ideas for sources of fashion. Illustrated.

BROOKE, IRIS
Footwear: A Short History of European and American Shoes

Theatre Arts, 1971. 131pp. $5.50. A survey of shoe fashions beginning with Roman sandals through the recent past. The author shows how footwear was fundamentally shaped by practical needs, by materials available, and by methods of cobbling and manufacture. Illustrated with drawings by the author.

CASSIN-SCOTT, JACK
Costume and Fashion in Color – 1760 – 1920
Macmillan, 1971. 209pp. $4.95. The author has divided 160 years of costume and fashion into eight periods in which certain styles were dominant. Ninety-six color plates trace the evolution of Western fashion from the times of Louis XV to the 1920's. He has also provided sketches in black-and-white to further illustrate the text. Glossary. Index.

GARLAND, MADGE
The Changing Form of Fashion
Praeger, 1970. 130pp. $8.95. Miss Garland discusses the myriad ways in which men and women have embellished, decorated, or disfigured themselves in order to look more attractive. She describes the changing fashion in feminine beauty and contrasts the periods of revelation of female charms with those when discretion was preferred. She also discusses the fashion creators from the couturiers of the sixteenth and seventeenth centuries to the personalities and creators of today. Forty-eight pages of plates illustrate the volume. Index.

HURLOCK, ELIZABETH B.
The Psychology of Dress: An Analysis of Fashion and Its Motive
Blom, 1971. 244pp. $12.50. Originally published in 1929 and now reissued, this is a study of fashion's influence upon society and society's influence on fashion. Illustrated. Bibliography. Index.

LEVINSON, ANDRE
Bakst: The Story of the Artist's Life
See Page 578

MOORE, DORIS LANGLEY
Fashion through Fashion Plates: 1771 – 1970
Clarkson N. Potter, 1971. 192pp. $12.50. A study of fashion over two hundred years. In text and 165 illustrations, the author provides a reference work for students of costume and for designers. Seventy-two of the illustrations are in color and include representative samples of fashion photography from 1901 to the present day. Index.

SANDRE, ANTONIO
Il Costume Nell'Arte
Speedimpex, 1971. 326pp. $45.00. Published in Italy, with the text in the Italian language, this is a history of costume from Ancient Egypt, Mesopotamia and Palestine to the Greek, Ertrurian, and Roman eras, through the Medieval and Renaissance times. The volume is lavishly illustrated with black-and-white and full color photographs and reproductions of works of art. Bibliography.

SCHROEDER, JOSEPH J., – Editor
The Wonderful World of Ladies' Fashions
Follett, 1971. 254pp. Paper $4.95. This is an illustrated history of the evolution of women's fashions covering a period from 1850 to 1920. The fashions are illustrated by means of contemporary woodcuts, steel engravings, and half-tones selected from old books, periodicals, and catalogues. Original descriptive material accompanies most of the illustrations and entire pages of fashions and related advertising are reproduced exactly as they originally appeared decades ago.

SHERINGHAM, GEORGE and JAMES LAVER
Design in the Theatre
See Page 589

British Costume

ARNOLD, JANET
Patterns of Fashion I
Drama Book Specialists, 1972. 72pp. Paper $10.00. Originally published in 1964 and now republished with corrections, this is a practical guide to the construction and cutting of Englishwomen's dresses, circa 1660–1860. Miss Arnold provides a brief history of pattern cutting and dressmaking, a pictorial outline of costumes, and drawings and patterns of dresses, taken from original pattern specimens, with details showing their construction. Illustrated. List of Selected Books and Periodicals.

ARNOLD, JANET
Patterns of Fashion 2
Drama Book Specialist, 1972. 88pp. Paper $10.00. Originally published in 1966 and now republished with corrections, this is a continuation of Miss Arnold's guide to the construction and cutting of Englishwomen's dresses. This volume includes drawings and patterns of dresses, taken from original specimens, from 1860 to 1940. Illustrated. List of Primary Sources. List of Selected Books for Students.

Other National Costumes

CHIBA, REIKO – Editor
Painted Fans of Japan
Tuttle, 1971. 41pp. $4.50. Printed in the form of a fan, this volume, first published in 1962 and now reissued, includes photographic representations of fifteen fans used in representative Noh dramas. Each of the fans is illustrated in color with an appropriate

haiku and identification as to period, title of play, type of play, and character using the fan. The editor also includes an Introduction on fans and the Noh drama.

FAIRSERVIS, JR., WALTER A.
Costumes of the East
Chatham Press, 1971. 160pp. $15.00. The focus of this volume is an area from Scandinavia to the Bering Sea and from the Eastern Mediterranean through Southeast Asia. The costumes are illustrated in drawings and in color photographs of some of the Eurasian collection belonging to the American Museum of Natural History. Bibliography. Index.

GUMMERE, AMELIA MOTT
The Quaker: A Study in Costume
Blom, 1971. 232pp. $12.50. Originally published in 1901 and now reissued, this is a study of the history of the costume of Quakerism. Separate chapters study the coat, the hat, the bonnet, beards, wigs and bands, and the costume of the Quakeress. Included are twenty-nine full page plates and forty illustrations in the text. Index.

McCLELLAN, ELIZABETH
History of American Costume: 1607 – 1870
Tudor, 1969. 655pp. $5.95. Originally published in 1904 and now reissued, this classic work includes nearly 800 illustrations including photographs, portraits, and drawings to provide comprehensive information on men's, women's, and children's wear for all classes, ages, occupations, and occasions. Glossary. Index.

Military Dress, Arms and Armour

AKEHURST, RICHARD
Antique Weapons for Pleasure and Investment
Arco, 1970. 174pp. $5.95. A guide for those interested in collecting antique weapons. Advice on where and how to buy, points that affect values, and hints on restoration are given. Chapters describe types of weapons from many parts of the world and the author has provided 104 black-and-white photographs and color plates. Bibliography. Index.

ANGELO, DOMENICO and HENRY ANGELO
The School of Fencing
Land's End Press, 1971. 113pp. + plates. $5.95. This volume includes facsimiles of three works on fencing by the noted eighteenth century fencing masters. "The School of Fencing" was the first fencing manual to insist on the value of fencing as an exercise. The two works by Henry Angelo are "Hungarian and Highland Broad Sword" and "The Angelo Cutlass Exercises." The volume includes reproduction of etchings and engravings by Thomas Rowlandson.

KINGSLAND, P.W. and SUSAN KEABLE
British Military Uniforms and Equipment: 1788 – 1830 – Volume One
World, 1971. 32pp. + plates. $20.00. This oversized volume (11 – 1/4'' x 16 – 3/4'') was researched by P.W. Kingsland under the supervision of the National Army Museum, London, and drawn by Peter Henville and Malcolm McGregor. Illustrated with drawings and photographs and eight full-page reproductions in color or original paintings. The text tells the history of the units and describes the uniforms.

NORTH, RENE
Military Uniforms: 1686 – 1918
Bantam, 1971. 159pp. Paper $1.45. Originally published in 1970 and now reissued, this is a condensed history of military dress presented under the headings of compaigns. All the illustrations by John Berry are in color. Also included are a list of places to visit, a list of books to read, a Glossary, and an Index.

RANKIN, ROBERT H.
Uniforms of the Sea Services
Arco, 1971. 324pp. $24.50. A history of the uniforms of the United States Navy, Marine Corps, and the Coast Guard from the Revolutionary War to the present. Detailed descriptions of the various uniforms worn during specified periods of history (including the women's services) are given. The author has provided 225 black-and-white or color illustrations of the various uniforms, weapons, and decorations. The volume also includes a series of footnotes, a Bibliography, and an Index.

WILKINSON, FREDERICK
Arms and Armor
Grosset & Dunlap, 1971. 159pp. $3.95. A guide to the development of arms and armor from the Ancient Sumerians and Egyptians to the twentieth century. Described and illustrated with 500 full-color drawings are all manner of weapons including African and Oriental weapons. Glossary. Index.

Instruction and Pattern Books

CUMMINGS, RICHARD
101 Costumes for All Ages, All Occasions
David McKay, 1971. 194pp. $4.95. Instructions for making 101 costumes, with variations on the basic theme, and including a full range of period costumes, Halloween costumes, and costumes from the author's imagination. Basic patterns are provided as are instructions on the selection, cutting and sewing of materials and the making of accessories. The author includes two complete plays and outlines for several costume pageants and tableaux. Illustrated with over seventy-five drawings and diagrams. Bibliography. Index.

MARGOLIS, ADELE P.
The Dressmaking Book
Doubleday, 1967. 294pp. $4.95. The author provides a complete step-by-step course in style and sewing. It is a simplified guide for beginners with illustrations which amplify the text. Index.

PURDY, SUSAN
Costumes for You to Make
See Page 583

Jewelry

FRANKLIN, GEOFFREY
Simple Enamelling
Watson–Guptill, 1971. 103pp. $7.95. An introduction to the basic techniques of the art of enamelling. The author explores the types of enamel available, the types of metal best suited to the work, and the necessary equipment and types of kilns. Detailed sections are provided on all aspects of the art. Sixty-eight illustrations, six in full color, are included. Suppliers List. Bibliography. Index.

MARYON, HERBERT
Metalwork and Enamelling
Dover, 1971. 335pp. Paper $3.50. This fifth edition incorporates revisions from the author's manuscript. Maryon treats every aspect of the craft in detail from basic tools to casting and enamelling. Over 300 figures and thirty-six photographs amplify the discussion of tools, materials and construction. Tables. Appendix. Bibliography. Index.

Masks

ALKEMA, CHESTER JAY
Masks
Sterling, 1971. 48pp. $2.95. How to make masks from easily obtainable materials. Paper masks, papier mache masks, and cardboard masks are all described and pictured in illustrations. Index.

Heraldry

DOWER, JOHN W.
The Elements of Japanese Design
Walker/Weatherhill, 1971. 170pp. $12.50. A handbook of family crests, heraldry, and symbols containing 2,715 examples of the crests divided into 211 different motifs drawn from many aspects of nature and life. The symbolism of the crests is explained in the text and the detailed commentaries that accompany the illustrations. Appendix. Bibliographic Notes. Index.

THE ACTOR AND HIS CRAFT

THEORIES AND HISTORIES OF ACTING

BROWN–AZAROWICZ, MARJORY FRANCES
A Handbook of Creative Choral Speaking
Burgess, 1970. 148pp. Paper $5.25. This text on choral speaking includes material on the background of the art, metrical emphasis, methods of teaching, voice production, and techniques for the advanced choir. Illustrated with diagrams. Bibliography.

CLARK, BRIAN
Group Theatre
See Page 583

FAST, JULIUS
Body Language
Pocket Books, 1971. 183pp. Paper $1.50. Originally published in 1970 and now reissued, this is not a theatre book. The author discusses movements of the body that may amplify or contradict verbal expression. This new science of kinesics may, however, be of value to actors. Selected References.

FINDLATER, RICHARD
The Player Kings
Stein and Day, 1971. 288pp. $7.95. The author discusses some of the great actors of the Shakespearean theatre. Among those whose performances are studied are: David Garrick, John Philip Kemble, Edmund Kean, William Charles Macready, Henry Irving, John Gielgud, Laurence Olivier, and Michael Redgrave. Chronologically the period is from 1600 to 1930. Illustrated with portraits of the actors. Index.

FOOTE, SAMUEL
A Treatise on the Passions
Blom, 1971. 44pp. $6.75. Originally published in 1747 in London and now reissued, this is an eighteenth century book on acting. The author also provides "a critical enquiry into the theatrical merit" of two actors in productions of "Othello" and a third in a production of "King Lear."

GOULD, THOMAS R.
The Tragedian: An Essay on the Histrionic Genius of Junius Brutus Booth
Blom, 1971. 190pp. $12.50. Originally published in 1868 and now reissued, this is a study of some of the roles played by the nineteenth century actor. Illustrated with a photograph of a marble bust of Booth.

GUTHRIE, TYRONE
Tyrone Guthrie on Acting
Viking, 1971. 96pp. $8.95. The author argues the case for a serious professional approach to theatre. After establishing that good acting is a matter of technique and can therefore be taught, Guthrie analyzes the relation between student and teacher as well as methods of teaching. He discusses stagecraft, technique, make-up, movement, and vocal training; he gives advice on how to approach a dramatic role, including the value of improvisation; he comments on straight and character acting, and legitimate theatre as opposed to mass media; and, in conclusion, he views the changes that are constantly occuring. Included is a gallery of forty-one photographs of actors. Index.

HARRIS, JULIE and BARRY TARSHIS
Julie Harris Talks to Young Actors
Lorthrop, Lee & Shepard, 1971. 192pp. $4.95. Miss Harris explores the demands, frustrations, sacrifices, and the joys of acting. The book is a first-hand and personal view of the art, technique, and profession of acting. Illustrated with twenty-five photographs of Miss Harris in some of the roles she has played. Included in the volume are a list of roles played by Miss Harris, a list of colleges and universities offering programs in theatre arts, a list of the leading acting schools in New York City, and a list of books. Index.

HAYMAN, RONALD
Techniques of Acting
Holt, Rinehart, 1971. 188pp. $5.95. Originally published in England in 1969 and now issued in the United States, this is an attempt to describe the different approaches that the actor needs to make to different media—theatre, film, and television—and to show how the art of acting has entered into a new phase of growth. Mr. Hayman looks both at the lessons to be drawn from the theories of directors such as Stanislavsky and Brecht and those to be drawn from some of the great performances of individual actors in our time. Appendices. Index.

HELD, JACK PRESTON
Improvisational Acting
Wadsworth, 1971. 152pp. Paper $3.35. A handbook of exercises for the student actor which the author hopes will lead to self-discovery of the student's potentials in creative acting. The exercises are arranged from solo work to complex ensembles, with sections on characterization and rehearsal and performance techniques. Each category is introduced with a principle and purpose to be achieved and concludes with a set of worksheets for progressive evaluations. Illustrated with diagrams. List of Selected Readings.

HILL, JOHN
The Actor: A Treatise on the Art of Playing
Blom, 1971. 326pp. $18.50. Originally published in 1750 and now reissued in a facsimile edition, this treatise studies the art of acting as applied to the London stage during the eighteenth century.

JOHNSON, ALBERT and BERTHA JOHNSON
Oral Reading: Creative and Interpretive
A. S. Barnes, 1971. 175pp. $6.95. An approach to oral communication. The Johnsons provide a delineation of methods of improving the ability to read aloud for pleasure and profit. Considerations of the physical and psychological aspects of reading are provided; then the authors turn to examples and exercises for stress, kinetics, and movement, gesture, and facial expressions as well as timing. Choric drama, verse choir, and readers' theatre are discussed with a selection of material for reading. Index.

KING, NANCY
Theatre Movement: The Actor and His Space
Drama Book Specialists, 1971. 175pp. $7.50. Paper $3.50. Miss King explains the importance of movement training to the total training of the actor. She includes exercises to help him strengthen his body, improve coordination, aid in relaxation, and heighten awareness of kinesthetic sense, as well as control his non-verbal communication in rehearsal and performance. Illustrated with photographs. Index of Exercises.

LEE, CHARLOTTE I.
Oral Interpretation
Houghton Mifflin, 1971. 518pp. $11.95. First published in 1952, this is a revised fourth edition of the text on oral interpretation. The author lays stress on analysis of organization, structure, style, and the various devices used in prose, drama and poetry. The first four chapters provide basic principles of interpretation of prose, drama and poetry. Appendices provide instructions on how to build and present a program and a brief history of theories of interpretation. Bibliographies. Index.

MAISEL, EDWARD – Editor
The Resurrection of the Body
Dell, 1971. 204pp. Paper $2.45. Originally published in 1969 and now reissued, this is a selection of the writings of F. Matthias Alexander, an Australian, who developed a technique for restoring the body as a means toward better health. His body-mind technique has come into wide use for training actors in the contemporary theatre. Appendices. Bibliographic Note.

OLFSON, LEWY
You Can Act!
See Page 582

PENCE, JAMES HARRY – Compiler
The Magazine and the Drama: An Index
See Page 513

WEAPONS ON STAGE

ANDERSON, BOB
All About Fencing
Stanley Paul, 1970. 94pp. Paper $2.50. The senior fencing coach for the English Olympic team provides an introduction to foil fencing. A feature of the volume is the series of photographs which, when the pages are flipped, seem to move and thus illustrate fencing movements.

BEAUMONT, C–L de
Fencing: Ancient Art and Modern Sport
A. S. Barnes, 1971. 274pp. $8.95. An encyclopedic text for the modern fencer. The author provides chapters covering training, tactics, judging and presiding, and the organization of a club, and material on matches and competitions. Among the weapons discussed are the foil, the epee, and the sabre. Illustrated with drawings and photographs. Glossary of Fencing Terms. Appendices.

PANTOMIME

ALBERTS, DAVID
Pantomime: Elements and Exercises
University of Kansas, 1971. 69pp. $5.50. The author provides an introduction and guide to both the essential elements and the specialized exercises of the art of pantomime. After a discussion of the elements and the philosophical substance of the art, he moves on to its direct application, providing detailed procedures in text and ninety action photographs. In addition, four original mimes written by the author, a Selected Bibliography, and a Filmography are included.

PARDOE, T. EARL
Pantomimes for Stage and Study
Blom, 1971. 395pp. $12.75. Originally published in 1931 and now reissued in a facsimile edition, this textbook, by one of the foremost historians of the art of pantomime, describes hundreds of mimes which offer exercise (and creative work) for the head, torso, and limbs. A selection of scenes for pantomimes from plays by Shakespeare and other authors is provided. The emotional basis of the art, technique for groups and individuals, and the commedia dell'arte are also examined. Indices

SHEPARD, RICHMOND
Mime: The Technique of Silence
Drama Book Specialists, 1971. 143pp. $7.50. Designed for use by an individual or as a classroom text, this is a thirty-lesson course in mime. Louise Sandoval has provided 167 drawings to illustrate the text. A brief history of mime, an explanation of mime make-up, and a biography of the author are included.

MAKE-UP

CORDWELL, MIRIAM and MARION RUDOY
The Complete Book of Hair Styles, Beauty & Fashion
Crown, 1971. 128pp. $3.95. Paper $1.95. A how-to book that coordinates hair styles with all the elements of make-up, color, and dress design to bring out the best in personal appearance. Over 135 drawings and photographs illustrate the volume.

HYMAN, REBECCA
The Complete Guide to Synthetic Hairpieces and Wigs
Grosset & Dunlap, 1971. 96pp. Spiral bound $1.95. Professional advice on the selection, care, shaping, and styling of synthetic hairpieces. Illustrated with photographs and drawings.

LU, STEVE
Face Painting in Chinese Opera
Drama Book Specialists, 1968. 183pp. $35.00. Originally published in Singapore and now distributed in the United States, this volume includes eighty full-page (8½ x 11) color plates of various face designs used in Chinese drama and opera. An introduction to the art and descriptive texts about the plates are included.

NICHOLAS, DENISE
The Denise Nicholas Beauty Book
Cornerstone Library, 1971. 95pp. Paper $1.45. A complete guide to good grooming and feminine beauty from head to toe for the black woman. Illustrated with drawings.

PE–CHIN, CHANG
Chinese Opera and Painted Face
Drama Book Specialists, 1969. 244pp. $30.00. Originally published in Taipei and now distributed in the United States, the first section of this volume traces the origins and development of Chinese opera at different stages in its history, its particular characteristics and functions. The second part of the book reviews in detail the transformation of Chinese opera, and painted faces and their significance. A special feature of the volume is the collection of 1,100 full-color illustrations of specific facial make-up and hair styles. These illustrations also show hats and headgear.

PERAZA, LYDIA
200 Best Hairdos for Every Occasion
Pyramid, 1970. 126pp. Paper $ .75. A guide to the newest of hair styles for women. Illustrated with photographs.

STEVENS, ANGELA
How to Set and Style Your Own Wig
Arco, 1971. 96pp. $4.50. Paper $1.95. A professional hair stylist provides instructions in setting, styling, and care of all kinds of hair pieces with 133 step-by-step photographic illustrations.

TERRY, ELLEN and LYNNE ANDERSON
The Theatre Student: Makeup and Masks
Richards Rosen Press, 1971. 111pp. $6.96. The authors attempt to illustrate some guideposts of basic theatrical cosmetic art. Also treated is the making of masks. Illustrated. Bibliography.

WOODFORDE, JOHN
The Strange Story of False Hair
Routledge & Kegan Paul, 1971. 126pp. $6.50. The social history of false hair since Ancient Egyptian times. Published in England, the volume documents the historical attitudes toward wigs and the various types and styles of wigs prevalent through the ages from Ancient Egypt and Rome to the popularity of wigs in the present day. Illustrated with reproductions of period art. Notes. Index.

CAREER OPPORTUNITIES

FARBER, DONALD C.
Actors' Guide
Drama Book Specialists, 1971. 134pp. $3.50. The author subtitles his book "What You Should Know About the Contracts You Sign." It prepares the actor for contracts under all unions in all media. What the actor is entitled to, and what is expected of him, are both discussed.

LAGOS, POPPY
Geographic Casting Guide for New York City
Lagos Enterprises, 1971. 16pp. Paper $1.75. Over 350 casting contacts for performers in the theatre, motion picture, advertising, television, and modeling fields. Indexed by geographic area with an alphabetic cross-reference index.

MODELING

CARTER, FRED F.
Free and Easy
Peter Glenn, 1971. 128pp. Spiral bound $4.95. A text for models to enable them to perform freely and naturally in front of the camera. Text and photographs illustrate preparatory exercises and sample poses.

DEFORD, FRANK
There She Is: The Life and Times of Miss America
Viking, 1971. 351pp. $10.00. Mr. Deford traces the "Miss America" contest from 1921 to 1971. He studies a typical pageant from the local (Wilson, North Carolina) competition, to the state and national contests, and then tracks the winner home. Illustrated with forty pages of photographs. Appendices of statistics are provided. Index.

FORD, EILEEN
Secrets of the Model's World
Trident, 1971. 222pp. $8.95. The director of the Ford Model Agency reveals the behind-the-scenes secrets of modeling. She describes not only the profession but how to get a job in it. Illustrated with photographs of models.

SCENES AND MONOLOGUES

CHILDRESS, ALICE – Editor
Black Scenes
Doubleday, 1971. 154pp. $3.95. Paper $1.75. Fifteen scenes for actors, directors and students of drama to use as practice material in classrooms or as audition material. Each of the scenes was written by a black author about the black experience. They offer a chance to see the drama in the everyday lives of black people and to learn how to present that drama to others. The editor has provided an Introduction to the volume, short biographies of the playwrights, and a Selected Bibliography. Among the authors included are: Ossie Davis, Ted Shine, Ed Bullins, Julian Mayfield, Lorraine Hansberry, Loften Mitchell, Douglas Turner Ward, and Alice Childress.

FEDYSZYN, STAN
Scenes: For Actors
Wadsworth, 1971. 244pp. Paper $5.25. Twenty scenes in chronological order, each of which discusses at least one of the specific acting problems. Most of the scenes have from two to five characters and two of the excerpts have crowds for group work. Among the playwrights excerpted are: Shakespeare, Sophocles, Racine, Sheridan, Chekhov, Shaw, Giraudoux, and Brecht.

GRUMBACH, JANE and ROBERT EMERSON
Actor's Guide to Monologues
Privately printed, 1971. 35pp. Paper $1.75. A guide to over 700 monologues for men and women from classical and modern plays in print. The monologues are classified as to type. Each entry includes the character's name and age, first line, publisher's edition, and approximate length in time of the monologue.

JOHNSON, ALBERT and BERTHA JOHNSON
Drama for Junior High with Selected Scenes
See Page 582

MARRIOTT, AMBROSE and HILDA TAGGART – Editors
Twelfth Anthology of Poetry, Prose and Play Scenes
Guildhall School, 1971. 292pp. $4.50. Published in England, this anthology contains monologues, short excerpts from long plays, and poetry for use in classroom work.

SPEECH

Training

CAPP, GLENN R.
Basic Oral Communication
Prentice–Hall, 1971. 399pp. Paper $7.95. Originally published in 1961 as "How to Communicate Orally" and now revised and updated under the new title. The author takes the reader through the processes of preparation, composition, and presentation, and applies rhetorical principles to the major types of communication situations of today. Excerpts from historical and contemporary speeches are included. Index.

TURNER, J. CLIFFORD
Voice and Speech in the Theatre
Pitman, 1970. 148pp. $5.95. Originally published in 1950 and now reissued, this is an exposition of the nature of voice and speech in which the author examines each component factor separately. Mr. Turner expounds his view that voice training must be based upon correct physiological usage. Exercises are provided by the author, who is best known for his work with the Royal Academy of Dramatic Art and the London Central School of Speech Training and Dramatic Art. Written primarily for the actor, the book is considered one of the standard textbooks in Great Britain. The volume is illustrated with drawings, diagrams, and musical examples. An Appendix includes a list of speeches for practice use. Index.

URIS, DOROTHY
To Sing in English: A Guide to Improved Diction
See Page 572

Dialects

MATTHEWS, WILLIAM
Cockney Past and Present
Gale Research, 1970. 245pp. $12.65. A facsimile reprint of the 1938 edition, this is a history of the dialect of London from the sixteenth century to the present day. The author includes chapters on Cockney in the music hall, mannerisms and slang, pronunciation and grammar, and the influence of Cockney on standard English. Bibliography. Index.

PART THREE: BOOKS ON MOTION PICTURES, TELEVISION, AND RADIO

MOTION PICTURES

WORLD CINEMA

Histories, Appreciations and Critiques

AMELIO, RALPH J.
Film in the Classroom: Why Use It. How to Use It
Pflaum, 1971. 181pp. Paper $4.50. A development and extension of "The Willowbrook Cinema Study Project" published in 1969. Since that volume was published, a revision of the program has been made. This is a description of a two-semester film study course intended for high school or college teachers interested in setting up a film program. Illustrated with photographs. Appendices include sample project materials, student film reviews, a cinema questionnaire, a list of film books and periodicals used in the course and for background reading, and addresses of major film distributors.

BLUM, DANIEL and JOHN KOBAL
A New Pictorial History of the Talkies
Putnam, 1971. 352pp. Paper $4.95. Originally published in 1958 and completely revised in 1968 by John Kobal, this volume traces the history of the talking picture from 1928 through 1968. Over 4,000 stills from the films illustrate the volume. Index.

BOYUM, JOY GOULD and ADRIENNE SCOTT
Film as Art: Critical Responses to Film Art
Allyn & Bacon, 1971. 397pp. Paper $6.50. The authors explore the theory and criteria for film criticism, then they reprint nearly 100 critical responses to twenty-five modern film classics. Among the critics included are: Bosley Crowther, Hollis Alpert, Andrew Sarris, Dwight MacDonald, Pauline Kael, Judith Crist, Howard Barnes, Archer Winston, and James Agee. Illustrated with photographs. List of Suggested Readings.

CASTY, ALAN
The Dramatic Art of the Film
Harper & Row, 1971. 192pp. Paper $4.65. The nature and possibilities of film as an art are examined in this text. The author approaches the unique visual characteristics of film through its technical elements in a series of chapters and then focuses on the dramatic elements as they are modified by the demands of the form. Illustrated with photographs from films. Indices.

CAVELL, STANLEY
The World Viewed: Reflections on the Ontology of Film
Viking, 1971. 174pp. $5.95. This is a philosophical exploration of the nature of movies. Mr. Cavell examines some of Hollywood's stars, directors, and most famous films, as well as the great European directors, and provides a theory for understanding the art of film.

COWIE, PETER – Editor
A Concise History of the Cinema: Volume One – Before 1940
A. S. Barnes, 1971. 212pp. Paper $3.50. More than thirty contributors, each chosen for his interest in a particular field, provide the basic facts of interest in the history of films before 1940. The volume is divided into sections on various countries (including the United States, Britain, France, Italy, Germany, Scandinavia, Eastern Europe, Japan and elsewhere) and economic trends, and technical developments. Illustrated with photographs from the films under discussion. Select Bibliography. Index to Film Titles.

COWIE, PETER – Editor
A Concise History of the Cinema: Volume Two – Since 1940
A. S. Barnes, 1971. 261pp. Paper $3.50. A continuation of the study listed above. The volume is divided into sections on various countries, on documentary and animated films, economic trends, and technical developments. Illustrated with photographs from the films under discussion. Index to Film Titles.

CROWTHER, BOSLEY
The Great Films: Fifty Golden Years of Motion Pictures
Putnam, 1971. 258pp. Paper $3.95. Originally published in 1967 and now reissued, this is a history of the motion picture as seen through Crowther's choice of the fifty greatest films of all time from all countries. Analytical studies of the fifty films are provided with complete credits and illustrations from the films. There is a supplementary list of a hundred other outstanding films. Bibliography. Index.

CURTIS, DAVID
Experimental Cinema
Universe Books, 1971. 168pp. $6.95. A survey of the development of film experimentation over the past fifty years from the pioneer work of Edwin S. Porter and Norman O. Dawn to the new American cinema of filmmakers Stan Brakhage, Gregory Markopoulos, Ron Rice, Andy Warhol, and others. Filmmakers from all over the world are discussed. Illustrated with photographs. Bibliography. Index.

DICKINSON, THOROLD
A Discovery of Cinema
Oxford, 1971. 164pp. $8.50. Paper $5.00. A personal view of the development of the film medium during its first seventy-five years. The author links the technical innovations, changes in the audiences, and social and political upheavals to the desire for quick profits and details the divergence of interest between the commercial film-makers and those who

have used the film as a vehicle of expression. Almost 150 photographs show scenes from classic films and the leading directors and innovators. Appendices. Bibliography. Indices.

ENSER, A. G. S.
Filmed Books and Plays: 1928–1969
Andre Deutsch, 1971. 509pp. $15.00. A list of books and plays from which films have been made from 1928 to 1967 with a supplementary list for 1968 and 1969. Films, nearly all of which are either English or American, are listed by title and by author in separate lists. Information includes name of maker or distributor, the year of registration, author of original book, and the name of the publisher.

FREDRIK, NATHALIE
The New Hollywood and the Academy Awards
Ace, 1971. 208pp. Paper $1.50. This new edition of "Hollywood and the Academy Awards" covers the entire history of the Academy Awards from 1927 through the awards given for 1970 films. The author provides credits and comments on each "Best Picture" and short biographies of each of the winning actors and actresses. Also included are lists of "Other Nominees" and technical awards. More than 250 photographs are included. Foreword by Bob Hope.

FREULICH, ROMAN and JOAN ABRAMSON
Forty Years in Hollywood
A. S. Barnes, 1971. 201pp. $12.50. A collection of reminiscences and anecdotes of experiences witnessed by or related to the photographer who spent over forty years in the film industry. Nearly 200 photographs, many taken by Freulich, of stars and films illustrate the volume. Index.

FURHAMMAR, LEIF and FOLKE ISAKSSON
Politics and Film
Praeger, 1971. 257pp. $12.50. Originally published in Sweden and now issued in the United States as translated by Kersti French, this is an examination of the relationship between movies and politics. The authors view not only overtly propagandist cinema but also entertainment films with political content and the political pressure exerted on them. The first of the book's three sections deals with the history of politics and film, notably in the United States, Britain, Germany, and Russia. The second section looks in detail at specific films including "Triumph of the Will," "Spanish Earth," "Mrs. Miniver," and "Torn Curtain." The final section examines the principles underlying the relationship of politics and film, including such topics as the aesthetics of propaganda and the depiction of political figures. Illustrated with 150 photographs, many from the actual films. Bibliography. Index.

GIFFORD, DENIS
Science Fiction Film
Dutton, 1971. 160pp. Paper $2.25. The author explores the fantasy film from 1897 to 1970. He divides the genre into three types of films: films of invention, exploration, and prediction. Illustrated with photographs. Index.

GLUCKSMANN, ANDRE
Violence on the Screen
British Film Institute, 1971. 78pp. Paper $1.95. A report on research into the effects on young people of scenes of violence in films and television. The report was originally published in France in 1966 and has now been translated by Susan Bennett. A Foreword discussing the report has been contributed by Paddy Whannel, and Dennis Howitt provides a summary of research since 1966.

GROVE, MARTIN A. and WILLIAM S. RUBEN
The Celluloid Love Feast
Lancer, 1971. 174pp. Paper $1.95. This is a close look at the history of the erotic film and at the makers of these films which show human sexual activity in all its varieties. Illustrated with photographs. Bibliography.

HALLIWELL, LESLIE
The Filmgoer's Companion
Avon, 1971. 1,072pp. Paper $3.95. Originally published in 1966, revised in 1967 and again in 1970, and now reprinted in a paper bound edition, this is an international encyclopedia of film information. The volume contains over 6,000 entries on films, film-makers, themes, and technical terms. Each entry contains biographical or historical notes and a selected list of principal credits for each of the personalities involved. The treatment of leading figures of the silent screen has been extended.

HANSON, GILLIAN
Original Skin
Stacey, 1970. 192pp. $7.75. An account of nudity and sex in cinema and theatre. Miss Hanson chronicles the "outburst" in 1967 to the final crumbling of the censorship bastion. She also investigates the two-way relationship between theatre and cinema and the merits of total freedom in the arts. Illustrated with photographs. Bibliography.

HARDY, FORSYTH – Editor
Grierson on Documentary
Praeger, 1971. 411pp. $10.00. Paper $5.50. Originally published in 1946 and revised in 1966, this collection of writings that guided the development of documentary film-making is now reissued. The writings comprise a history of the documentary film movement and include Grierson's comments on films and directors of the 1930's and an account of how he made his film, "Drifters." Illustrated with twenty-five pages of photographs.

JARVIE, I. C.
Movies and Society

Basic Books, 1970. 394pp. $10.00. The author limits the aims of his study to "...an essay towards...a sociology of the cinema." Jarvie investigates the influence of movies upon our lives. He examines how films are made and how this affects what is shown. He highlights conflicts inherent in the roles of producers, actors, and directors; the requirements of artistic versus industrial success; and the filmmaking histories of various films including Huston's "Red Badge of Courage." Also provided are a discussion of the role of the film critic and a basis for more objective film criticism. An Appendix is titled "Film and the Communication of Values." Bibliography. Indices.

JARVIE, I. C.
Towards a Sociology of the Cinema
Routledge & Kegan Paul, 1970. 394pp. $15.00. Published in England, this work is subtitled "A comparative Essay on the Structure and Functioning of a Major Entertainment Industry." The author attempts to provide a framework for comparative sociological analysis of the cinema. He discusses the main aspects of the sociology and examines the problems which are central to it. Appendix. Annotated Bibliography. Indices.

KAHLE, ROGER and ROBERT E. A. LEE
Popcorn and Parable: A New Look at the Movies
Augsburg Publishing, 1971. 128pp. Paper $2.95. An examination of contemporary filmmaking in which the authors propose to find in feature films a resource for Christian faith and for communication of religious truths. Illustrated with five photographs. List of Books for Further Reading.

KNIGHT, ARTHUR – Introducer
The New York Times Directory of the Film
Arno/Random House, 1971. 1,243pp. $25.00. This reference contains a comprehensive index of performers, directors, producers, cinematographers, and screenwriters and the films they made from 1913 to 1968; an index of major motion picture companies and their films of the same period; a portrait gallery with photographs of more than 2,000 actors and actresses; a year-by-year list of the winners of the Academy Awards, the New York Film Critics awards, and The New York Times Ten Best Films awards. The most important feature of the volume is, however, the actual reviews of all of these award-winning films—over five hundred of them—reproduced in their entirety as they were originally published in the "Times."

LEVIN, G. ROY
Documentary Explorations
Doubleday, 1971. 420pp. $10.00. Paper $4.95. The author has conducted fifteen interviews with eighteen documentary film-makers from England, France, Belgium, and the United States. A range of aesthetic and political considerations are discussed. The book includes a brief history of documentary film as well as filmographies on each director. Twenty-four pages of photographs. Selected Bibliography. Index.

LEYDA, JAY
Films Beget Films
Hill & Wang, 1971. 176pp. Paper $1.95. Originally published in 1964 and now reissued, this is a critical study of the compilation film—the film form that makes use of earlier films for effects ranging from propaganda to drama. The author discusses the first compilation film in 1902, analyzes the work in the Soviet Union in the 1920's, discusses the techniques of the 1930's, and the license sometimes taken with films. Appendices. List of Sources. Index.

LIMBACHER, JAMES L. – Editor
Feature Films on 8mm and 16mm
Bowker, 1971. 269pp. $13.50. This is the third edition of the directory of feature films available for rental, sale and lease in the United States. The films are listed in alphabetical order and each entry contains the title of the film, the releasing company, year of original release, running time, special information, and the code abbreviation of the distributor. List of Addresses of Film Companies and Distributors. List of Film Companies and Distributors by Area. List of Film Reference Works. Index of Directors.

McCARTY, CLIFFORD
Published Screenplays: A Checklist
Kent State University, 1971. 124pp. $6.50. This checklist provides information on screenplays (both complete and excerpts) published in the English language and issued commercially. The scripts are listed alphabetically and information provided includes production company and date, director, author, source, and location of the published work. Included are data for 388 screenplays. Index.

MANVELL, ROGER
Shakespeare and the Film
Praeger, 1971. 172pp. $10.00. The author examines the major films adapted from Shakespeare's plays during the period of the sound film. These range from the Douglas Fairbanks-Mary Pickford "The Taming of the Shrew" in 1929 to the Grigori Kozintsev "King Lear" and the Peter Brook "King Lear"—both made in 1970. Manvell discusses the degree to which Shakespeare's original intentions can be conveyed by substituting the heightened atmosphere of film and its visual imagery for the poetic imagery of the verse. 127 photographs illustrate the set and costume designs and include scenes from twenty-four films. Filmography. Selected Bibliography. Index.

MAST, GERALD
A Short History of the Movies
Bobbs–Merrill, 1971. 463pp. $12.95. Paper $4.95. The author traces the evolution of the motion picture art. He studies the themes, the imaginations,

the techniques, and the visual qualities of film artists from all over the world. The text is heavily illustrated with stills from the films under discussion. An Appendix lists books and films for further reading and viewing. Index.

MATTHEWS, J. H.
Surrealism and Film
University of Michigan, 1971. 198pp. $8.50. The author examines a wide variety of surrealist pronouncements, scripts, and films—from movies made for commercial release to ephemeral short subjects unfamiliar to most movie-goers. He treats the surrealists' unique and demanding approach to the art of the film and shows how they have handled cinematic problems in their own productions and the problems that have been given precedence in theory and practice. Particular attention is paid to the work of Luis Bunuel. Illustrated with sixteen pages of photographs. Notes. Index.

MAYNARD, RICHARD A.
The Celluloid Curriculum
Hayden, 1971. 276pp. $10.60. Subtitled "How to Use Movies in the Classroom," this is a guide for high school and college teachers. The author provides methods of approach and teaching units as well as points on scheduling, funding, and film rental. Two basic teaching approaches are outlined: the first uses the film on the same plane as literature; the second approach uses movies as the primary classroom source to be studied for their intrinsic value as historical and social documents. Eight teaching units are provided for each approach. Bibliographies and Filmographies for student and teacher are included. Illustrated with photographs. Index of Film Titles.

RICHTER, HANS
Hans Richter by Hans Richter
Holt, Rinehart, 1971. 191pp. $27.50. The materials in this volume have been chosen and edited by Cleve Gray to illustrate the work of the film-maker, sculptor, painter, and writer. The personal analyses and anecdotes follow the development and continuing achievements of the contemporary artist. The making of Richter's abstract films and the theories behind them are discussed. Illustrated with over 125 black-and-white illustrations and with sixteen pages in color. Glossary of Names. Notes on the Text. List of Works of Art Illustrated.

SCHEUER, STEVEN H. – Editor
Movies on TV: 1972–73 Edition
Bantam, 1971. 498pp. Paper $1.50. More than 8,000 films are listed in this guide to films now being shown on television. Information provided includes country of origin, year of release, stars, and brief comments on all the films. This edition is completely revised from the previous edition dated 1971–72. The volume includes more than 900 new entries.

SOHN, DAVID A.
Film: The Creative Eye
Pflaum, 1970. 176pp. Paper $3.95. The premise of this book is that visual literacy is becoming increasingly important. The author provides a program to increase observational skills through discussion of a number of short films which, he contends, add to perception and understanding of the environment, and entertain as well as educate. Illustrated with photographs.

TYLER, PARKER
Sex Psyche Etcetera in the Film
Pelican, 1971. 240pp. Paper $1.65. Originally published in 1969 and now reissued, this is a study of sex in the cinema. The author also presents essays on film aesthetics and on "the artist in crisis." Index.

WHYTE, ALISTAIR
New Cinema in Eastern Europe
Dutton, 1971. 159pp. Paper $2.25. A survey of films and filmmakers from Poland, Hungary, Czechoslovakia, Yugoslavia, and other countries in Eastern Europe. Illustrated with photographs. Bibliography. Index.

WLASCHIN, KEN
The Bluffer's Guide to the Cinema
Crown, 1971. 64pp. Paper $1.00. Information on directors, actors, and genres of the film art for people who would like to be able to bluff their way through conversations with film buffs. Introduction by David Frost.

Collected Reviews and Essays

ADLER, RENATA
A Year in the Dark
Berkley, 1971. 383pp. Paper $1.50. Originally published in 1969 and now reissued, this is a collection of approximately 180 reviews and essays from the "New York Times" during 1968–69.

BAZIN, ANDRE
What is Cinema? Volume II
University of California, 1971. 200pp. $6.95. These essays, selected and translated by Hugh Gray, include Bazin's major studies on the Western, on Chaplin, and on neorealism. Also included are essays on stylistic integrity and on the Hays office aesthetic contributions to Howard Hughes' "The Outlaw." The translator's Introduction outlines Bazin's personalist philosophical background. Notes. Index.

COOKE, ALISTAIR – Editor
Garbo and the Night Watchmen
McGraw–Hill, 1971. 285pp. $7.95. First published in 1937 and now reissued, this is a collection of the writings of British and American film critics. Among

the nine contributors are: Graham Greene, Meyer Levin, Otis Ferguson, and Mr. Cooke himself. For this edition Mr. Cooke has provided a new Preface which looks forward and backward, and an Annotated Index which cites technical details of the films discussed in the essays. A feature of the volume is the section in which all nine writers individually discuss Chaplin's film, "Modern Times." Illustrated with 140 black-and-white photographs.

FARBER, MANNY
Negative Space
Praeger, 1971. 288pp. $7.95. A collection of reviews and essays, and film criticism of the past twenty-five years by the writer for "The New Republic," "Film Culture," and "Artforum," among other periodicals. Among the subjects covered are various directors, the New York film festivals of 1967, 1968, and 1969, and the decline of the actor.

FERGUSON, OTIS
The Film Criticism of Otis Ferguson
Temple University, 1971. 475pp. $12.50. Edited and with a Preface by Robert Wilson, and a Foreword by Andrew Sarris, this is a republication of Otis Ferguson's movie reviews. The reviews were originally written from 1934 to 1941 and printed in "The New Republic." Ferguson developed an aesthetic of the sound film that pointed the way to practically all the breakthroughs in film scholarship of the past ten or fifteen years and he anticipated the "auteur" theory in his emphasis on directors. Index of Names. Index of Films and Reviews.

KAEL, PAULINE
Going Steady
Bantam, 1971. 372pp. Paper $1.95. Originally published in 1970 and now reissued, this is a collection of the writings of the film critic for "New Yorker" magazine from 1968 and 1969. The writings are in sequence so that the reader can "follow not only what was evolving in films during a crucial period of social and aesthetic change ... but follow the reviewer's developing responses." Index.

KAUFFMANN, STANLEY
Figures of Light: Film Criticism and Comment
Harper & Row, 1971. 296pp. $8.95. A collection of Kauffmann's important film reviews, covering the years 1967–1970, most of which were written for "The New Republic." Index.

MACDONALD, DWIGHT
On Movies
Berkley, 1971. 544pp. Paper $1.50. Originally published in 1969 and now reissued, this is a collection of essays and reviews which covers approximately forty years. Index.

PECHTER, WILLIAM S.
Twenty-four Times a Second: Films and Film-Makers
Harper & Row, 1971. 324pp. $7.95. A collection of critical essays on films and film-makers and on the theory of film appreciation. The essays cover the years 1960 through 1970. Among the film-makers discussed are: Ford, Renoir, Bunuel, Welles, Hitchcock, Antonioni, Godard, Ray, Capra, and others. Index.

REED, REX
Big Screen, Little Screen
Macmillan, 1971. 433pp. $7.95. A collection of reviews and articles written from 1968 to the present on a variety of subjects but mostly on American movies and television. Index.

SALEM, JAMES M.
A Guide to Critical Reviews: Part IV – The Screenplay from "The Jazz Singer" to "Dr. Strangelove"
Scarecrow Press, 1971. 1,420pp. Two volume set: $35.00. A bibliography of critical reviews of feature length motion pictures released from 1927 through 1963. Approximately 12,000 American and foreign screenplays are included and reviews cited are those which appeared in American or Canadian periodicals. Also provided is a list of Academy Award winners from 1927 to 1962.

SARRIS, ANDREW
Confessions of a Cultist: On the Cinema – 1955/1969
Simon & Schuster, 1971. 480pp. Paper $3.95. Originally published in 1970 and now reissued, this is a collection of film reviews and articles which appeared, mostly in the "Village Voice," from 1955 to 1969. Mr. Sarris offers a chronicle of the cinema in one of the liveliest periods of its history. Index.

SIMON, JOHN
Movies Into Film: Film Criticism 1967 – 1970
Dial Press, 1971. 448pp. $9.95. A collection of Mr. Simon's reviews and essays from "The New Leader" with introductory comments on the direction in which film is moving. Mr. Simon discusses adaptations of plays and novels, politics and society, the youth film, sex, major directors, and festivals and awards among other topics. Index.

SIMON, JOHN
Private Screenings
Berkley, 1971. 352pp. Paper $1.25. Originally published in 1967 and now reissued, this is a collection of reviews originally printed in "The New Leader" from 1963 to 1966. Several essays have been specifically written for this volume including the author's "Critical Credo." Index.

THOMPSON, HOWARD – Editor
The New York Times Guide to Movies on TV
Quadrangle, 1971. 223pp. Paper $1.95. Over 2,000 capsule reviews, with credits and plot synopses, of some of the movies from the 1950's and 1960's now available on television. The reviews are edited

versions of the commentary originally written for "The Times," and the editor includes his own one line capsule comments. Illustrated with photographs from the films reviewed. Introduction by Bosley Crowther.

Annuals

COWIE, PETER – Editor
International Film Guide: 1972
A.S. Barnes, 1971. 512pp. Paper $3.95. The annual guide to movies around the world. The editor includes a survey of world production, sections on directors of the year, festivals, film music, films on 16mm, films for young people, animation, film archives, and film schools. Illustrated. Index.

DENBY, DAVID – Editor
Film 70/71
Simon & Schuster, 1971. 319pp. $7.95. Paper $2.95. This is the fourth anthology of criticism by the National Society of Film Critics. It presents a cross section of critical opinion on some of the most interesting films of the year and includes reflections on trends, genres, and moods. Among the contributors are: Penelope Gilliatt, Richard Schickel, Andrew Sarris, Joseph Morgenstern, Stanley Kauffman, Hollis Alpert, Pauline Kael, John Simon, Arthur Knight, Harold Clurman, and David Denby. Notes on the Contributors. Index.

GERTNER, RICHARD – Editor
International Motion Picture Almanac – 1972
See Page 611

MORGENSTERN, JOSEPH and STEFAN KANFER – Editors
Film 69/70
Simon & Schuster, 1971. 286pp. $7.95. Paper $2.95. A collection of reviews and essays on the most noteworthy films of the year, written by members of the National Society of Film Critics. Detailed discussion of the 1969 annual awards is provided as are articles dealing with the current and future state of motion pictures. Among the contributors are: Pauline Kael, Stanley Kauffmann, Andrew Sarris, Richard Schickel, Arthur Schlesinger, and John Simon. Index.

SPEED, F. MAURICE – Editor
Film Review: 1971 – 1972
A.S. Barnes, 1971. 244pp. $6.95. The new edition of the film annual which covers the cinema year in detail with casts, technical credits, and release dates of all the general releases and Continental films of the period, together with illustrations of most of them. Among the special features is an essay on the treatment of Shakespeare's plays on the screen. Index.

WILLIS, JOHN – Editor
Screen World – 1971
Crown, 1971. 260pp. $8.95. The twenty-second annual volume of the pictorial and statistical record of the movie season. Records in this edition comprise a survey of the 1970 season. The editor has included more than 1,000 photographs. Index.

FILMS OF PARTICULAR COUNTRIES

France

LEPROHON, PIERRE
Jean Renoir
Crown, 1971. 256pp. Paper $3.50. Adapted from the Cinema d'Aujourd'hui series volume published in France in 1967 and now translated into English by Brigid Elson, this is an investigation into the director's films and philosophy. In addition to the essay by Leprohon, the volume includes texts by Renoir on cinema, screenplay excerpts, and a selection of criticism. Illustrated with photographs. Bibliography. Filmography. Index.

Germany

BAXTER, JOHN
The Cinema of Josef von Sternberg
A.S. Barnes, 1971. 192pp. Paper $2.95. An analysis of all of von Sternberg's films and a new interpretation of his career. Illustrated with photographs. Select Bibliography. Filmography.

MANVELL, ROGER and HEINRICH FRAENKEL
The German Cinema
Praeger, 1971. 159pp. $10.00. A survey of German films from the 1920's through the 1960's. The authors detail the origins of the films in the revolutionary theatre of Max Reinhardt and in the Expressionism prevalent in the arts during this period. They provide a detailed account of the use of film as propaganda by the Nazis, an overall analysis of the German cinema after World War II, and a survey of the younger German directors. Illustrated with 100 photographs. Bibliography. Indices.

Great Britain

DURGNAT, RAYMOND
A Mirror for England: British Movies from Austerity to Affluence

Praeger, 1971. 336pp. $11.95. A survey of British films from the mid-1940's to the late 1960's. This reappraisal shows how British films have reflected British predicaments, moods, and myths with an intuitive accuracy. Sixteen pages of photographs. Bibliography. Indices.

GOUGH-YATES, KEVIN – Editor
Michael Powell in Collaboration with Emeric Pressburger
British Film Institute, 1971. 16pp. Paper $ .75. A monograph on the British film director which includes two interviews with Powell, one with his collaborator, Pressburger, an Introduction by the editor, a Filmography, and an article on the use of color in motion pictures by Powell.

India

SETON, MARIE
Portrait of a Director: Satyajit Ray
Indiana University, 1971. 350pp. $8.95. The author examines in detail the work of the Indian film-maker as musician, scenarist, and director. His ancestry, his youth, the films, and his part in the films are all studied. Illustrated with photographs. List of Films. Appendices. Index.

Italy

ARMES, ROY
Patterns of Realism
A.S. Barnes, 1971. 226pp. $12.00. A study of Italian neorealist cinema. The author includes a discussion of the political background to wartime Italian cinema. Among the directors examined are Luchino Visconti, Vittorio De Sica, Roberto Rossellini, Federico Fellini, Pier Paolo Passolini, and the comedy films of Luigi Zampa and others. Illustrated with 250 photographs including scenes from films under discussion. A Filmography provides complete credits and cast lists for forty-five films. Bibliography. Index.

CAMERON, IAN and ROBIN WOOD
Antonioni
Praeger, 1971. 152pp. $5.95. Paper $2.95. Originally published in 1969 and now revised and brought up-to-date to include the film the Italian director made in the United States, "Zabriskie Point." Illustrated with stills from each of the films. Filmography. Bibliography.

HUGHES, EILEEN LANOUETTE
On the Set of "Fellini Satyricon"
Morrow, 1971. 248pp. Paper $2.95. A behind-the-scenes diary of the making of Fellini's film. The author observed the director in action for six months and also interviewed everyone from the director himself to the actors, cameramen, set and costume designers, and the wardrobe mistress. Illustrated with sixteen pages of photographs.

HUSS, ROY – Editor
Focus on Blow-Up
Prentice–Hall, 1971. 171pp. $5.95. Paper $2.45. A collection of reviews, essays, interpretations, and criticism of Antonioni's film, "Blow-Up." Ranging from discussions of the director's style and techniques to examinations of the film's relation to today's youth culture, the material is by such authorities as Arthur Knight, Andrew Sarris, Stanley Kauffmann, and many others. A special section includes the short story by Cortazar that inspired the film, a study of the adaptation, and a short analysis of the film's key scenes. Illustrated with eight pages of photographs. Bibliography. Filmography. Index.

RENZI, RENZO – Editor
Federico Fellini: I Clowns
Cappelli Editore, 1970. 414pp. $47.50. A study of clowns, the art of clowning, and Fellini's film, "The Clowns." The volume includes essays on and appreciations of clowns through the ages. Also included is the script by Fellini for his film. The volume is lavishly illustrated in color and in black-and-white with art works, photographs, and scenes from the film. The complete text of the volume is in the Italian language.

Japan

RICHIE, DONALD
Japanese Cinema
Doubleday, 1971. 261pp. Paper $3.95. This is an extensively revised, expanded, and updated version of "Japanese Movies" published originally in 1961. Mr. Richie provides a history of Japanese film from the beginning through 1970 as well as an exploration of Japanese culture and the Japanese mind. The author relates the films to other art forms and discusses not only the well-known classics of Kurosawa and Mizoguchi but also the popular entertainment films as well. An Appendix lists 16mm films distributed in the United States. Illustrated with forty-eight pages of photographs. Index.

SVENSSON, ARNE
Screen Guide: Japan
A.S. Barnes, 1971. 190pp. Paper $3.50. A guide to the work of the major directors, players, technicians, and other key figures in the Japanese cinema. Brief

biographical sketches and filmographies are provided. Illustrated with photographs. Chronology. Glossary of Terms. Index of 2,000 Film Titles.

Poland

McARTHUR, COLIN – Editor
Andrzej Wajda: Polish Cinema
British Film Institute, 1970. 60pp. Paper $ .75. A study of the cinema of Polish film director Wajda complete with two interviews with the director and a Filmography.

Spain

JODOROWSKY, ALEXANDRO
El Topo: A Book of the Film
See Page 620

Sweden

YOUNG, VERNON
Cinema Borealis: Ingmar Bergman and the Swedish Ethos
David Lewis, 1971. 331pp. $12.50. A study of the films made by the Swedish director. The author analyzes all of the films and offers a critique of the beliefs from which the director's films and plays derive. Illustrated with photographs. Footnotes. Appendices. Selective Bibliography. List of Works for Theatre and Television. Film Chronology. Index.

United States

ALLOWAY, LAWRENCE
Violent America: The Movies 1946 – 1964
New York Graphic Society, 1971. 95pp. $7.95. The author, a well-known art critic, focuses on the American action film to characterize popular genres as they have developed and influenced one another. Mr. Alloway views films in relation to other popular art forms and as part of our entire society, particularly as they contribute to the taste for violence in our society. Included in the volume is an Appendix of credits and program notes for the thirty-five films in the series of showings which Mr. Alloway directed at the Museum of Modern Art in 1969. The study is illustrated with thirty-three pages of photographs and includes a section of Notes.

ANOBILE, RICHARD J. – Editor
Why A Duck?
New York Graphic Society, 1971. 288pp. $7.95. This is a collection of over 600 frame-by-frame blow-ups of scenes from nine of the films the Marx brothers made during the 1930's and 1940's. The actual dialogue from the films is printed with the photographs to present as direct as possible a transition from the film to the printed page. Groucho Marx has written an Introduction to the volume, and Richard Shepard has provided a Preface which tells of his experiences in seeing the films during their first release.

BARBOUR, ALAN G.
A Thousand and One Delights
Macmillan, 1971. 177pp. $7.95. Paper – Collier, $3.95. In text and photographs the author recalls the "fun films" of the 1940's—films which were largely escapist in nature. Among the personalities and genres he includes are the series of films starring Maria Montez and Jon Hall, the Abbott and Costello series, the horror classics, comedy films, the serials, mystery and suspense films, westerns, and John Wayne's series of action films. Illustrated with over 260 photographs.

BARBOUR, ALAN G.
The Thrill of It All
Collier, 1971. 204pp. $7.95. Paper $3.95. A pictorial history of the B-Western from "The Great Train Robbery" to the color films of the genre's last days of glory in the 1950's. Lavishly illustrated with scenes from the films, portraits of the stars, and reproductions of advertising posters.

BAXTER, JOHN
The Cinema of John Ford
A. S. Barnes, 1971. 176pp. Paper $2.95. A study of the director's filmic language and philosophy. The author discusses a wide selection of Ford's films from the early silents through to the films made in the early 1960's. Illustrated with photographs. Filmography. Selected Bibliography.

BENTLEY, ERIC – Editor
Thirty Years of Treason
See Page 555

BERGMAN, ANDREW
We're In the Money
New York University, 1971. 200pp. $7.95. The author examines films against the background of economic and social influences of the 1930's. Mr. Bergman's study traces the assumptions and myths embodied in the movies of the 30's to demonstrate the varied ways they helped the nation's institutions and values survive the decade. The volume is illustrated with sixteen pages of photographs and includes a section of Notes and a Bibliography. Index.

BILLINGS, PAT and ALLEN EYLES
Hollywood Today
A. S. Barnes, 1971. 192pp. Paper $2.95. A guide to the contemporary Hollywood scene through 370 artists who are making significant contributions. Each entry gives a biographical profile mentioning highlights in careers and all films since 1960. Illustrated with scenes from films of many of the artists listed. Index of Film Titles.

CAREY, GARY
Cukor and Co.
N. Y. Graphic Society, 1971. 167pp. Paper $2.95. An assessment of the career of one of Hollywood's outstanding directors, George Cukor, and of the writers and actors who participated in the films. The author provides an account of the making of some fifty films from 1930 through 1969. Illustrated with photographs.

EVERSON, WILLIAM K.
The Films of Hal Roach
Museum of Modern Art, 1971. 96pp. Paper $2.50. A presentation of the films, stars, techniques, and theories associated with Hal Roach, one of the foremost comedy-film pioneers. The text also includes a recent interview with Roach. Illustrated with stills from the films and photographs of the stars and directors of the period. Bibliography.

EVERSON, WILLIAM K.
A Pictorial History of the Western Film
Citadel, 1971. 246pp. Paper $3.95. Originally published in 1969 and now reissued, this is an examination of the whole range of the Western film genre. Everson uses nearly five hundred stills as illustrations to trace Westerns from "The Great Train Robbery" through to the films of the 1960's. Index.

FRENCH, PHILIP
The Movie Moguls
Regnery, 1971. 170pp. $5.95. Originally published in England in 1969 and now issued in the United States, this is an informal history of the Hollywood tycoons. The author considers the backgrounds, characters, and careers of Walter Wanger, Walt Disney, Darryl F. Zanuck, Samuel Goldwyn, Howard Hughes, Louis B. Mayer, David O. Selznick, Harry Cohn, Cecil B. DeMille, and the Warner Brothers. Illustrated with photographs. Biographical Notes. Bibliography. Index.

GEDULD, HARRY M. – Editor
Focus on D. W. Griffith
Prentice–Hall, 1971. 182pp. $5.95. Paper $2.45. A collection of essays on, and commentary by, D. W. Griffith, a pioneer film-maker. Among the contributors are: Griffith's wife, Linda Arvidson, Erich von Stroheim, Jay Leyda, and Ezra Goodman. Illustrated with photographs. Chronology. Filmography. Selected Bibliography. Index.

GIDAL, PETER
Andy Warhol – Films and Paintings
Dutton, 1971. 160pp. Paper $2.25. An analysis of the work of the avant-garde artist, particularly his films. Illustrated with photographs. Chronology. Index.

GOTTESMAN, RONALD – Editor
Focus on "Citizen Kane"
Prentice–Hall, 1971. 178pp. $5.95. Paper $2.45. Analyses of Orson Welles' film and its impact on modern film and culture. Investigations of the relationship between the film and the personality and methods of its director are provided as are studies of the complexities of plot, technique, and stylistic innovations of the film. Included among the contributors are: Arthur Knight, Andrew Sarris, Francois Truffaut, and Jorge Luis Borges. Illustrated with photographs. Plot Synopsis. Content Outline. Script Extract. Filmography. Selected Bibliography. Index.

GOW, GORDON
Hollywood in the Fifties
A. S. Barnes, 1971. 208pp. Paper $2.95. A study of the work of the directors and actors active in the United States in the 1950's. The newest volume in the series which started with "Hollywood in the Twenties" by David Robinson, and continued with "Hollywood in the Thirties" by John Baxter, and "Hollywood in the Forties" by C. Higham and J. Greenberg. Illustrated with photographs. Index.

GREEN, FITZHUGH
The Film Finds Its Tongue
Blom, 1971. 316pp. $13.50. First published in 1929 and now reissued in a facsimile edition, this was one of the first comprehensive accounts of the talking film. Included are chapters on the first great talking actors, and on the actors who couldn't make it in sound films. Illustrated with photographs and other material.

GRIFFITH, RICHARD
The Talkies
Dover, 1971. 360pp. Paper $5.95. An anthology of articles and illustrations from "Photoplay" magazine, 1928–1940. Original ads for classic films, photographs of the stars in their film roles and in their private lives, articles, and gossip about the stars are all included. Foreword by Lawrence J. Quirk. Index.

HAMBLETT, CHARLES
The Hollywood Cage
Hart, 1971. 447pp. Paper $3.95. Originally published in 1969 and now reissued, this is a British magazine writer's observations of Hollywood. Hamblett provides closeups of Marilyn Monroe, Humphrey Bogart, Elizabeth Taylor, Marlon Brando, and many of the other great stars. Lavishly illustrated with photographs. Index.

HARMAN, BOB
Hollywood Panorama
Dutton, 1971. 96pp. Paper $3.95. Thirty color panels depict one-thousand-and-one stars of the silent and sound eras against typical Hollywood backgrounds. An outline key is provided for each of the panels with a short description of each of the players. The panels are designed to be assembled into a wall mural.

HENDERSON, ROBERT M.
D. W. Griffith: The Years at Biograph
Farrar, Straus, 1971. 250pp. Paper $2.95. Originally published in 1970 and now reissued, this is an in-depth exploration of the work of D. W. Griffith during the years between 1908 and 1913 when the director was beginning his directing career at the Biograph Studio in New York. Illustrated with photographs. Appendices. Bibliography. Index.

KAEL, PAULINE
The Citizen Kane Book
Little, Brown, 1971. 440pp. $15.00. Miss Kael's study of the history of the film, "Citizen Kane," is entitled "Raising Kane." She reports on and analyzes the film from conception to completion. The volume also includes the complete shooting script of the film with over eight frames illustrating the text. Notes on the shooting script have been prepared by Gary Carey and a cutting continuity (a record of the completed film) are also provided.

KRAFT, HY
On My Way to the Theater
See Page 556

LAHUE, KALTON C.
Dreams for Sale
A. S. Barnes, 1971. 216pp. $8.50. A history of the Triangle Film Corporation which utilized the talents of D. W. Griffith, Thomas H. Ince, and Mack Sennett during the years 1915–1919. The films and the men and women who made them, are all described. Illustrated with many rare photographs. Index.

LAHUE, KALTON C.
Mack Sennett's Keystone: The Man, the Myth and the Comedies
A. S. Barnes, 1971. 315pp. $10.00. An evaluation of the style of comedy employed by Mack Sennett, the myths that have grown up around it, and the man responsible for it. Mr. Lahue documents in text and 300 illustrations the methods and techniques of production, the actors, and the scripts. Index of Titles. Index of Names.

LATHAM, AARON
Crazy Sundays: F. Scott Fitzgerald in Hollywood
Viking, 1971. 308pp. $7.95. This biography of Fitzgerald covers the years he spent in Hollywood working on the scripts for such films as "Gone With the Wind," "The Women," and "Madame Curie." Mr. Latham was given the opportunity to study all of Fitzgerald's work, and he has also interviewed many of Fitzgerald's friends and colleagues. Notes. Index.

LEE, RAYMOND and B. C. VAN HECKE
Gangsters and Hoodlums
A. S. Barnes, 1971. 264pp. $8.95. A recreation of the screen world of the gangster particularly in the 1930's and 1940's. Nearly 350 photographs depict the stars and the productions including the gangster-comedy and the juvenile delinquent. A brief introductory text by the authors sets the scene for the photographs.

LEVIN, MARTIN – Editor
Hollywood and the Great Fan Magazines
Arbor House, 1971. 224pp. Paper $3.95. Originally published in 1970 and now reissued, this volume is a collection of articles, photographs, and miscellania from the popular film fan magazines of the 1930's.

McCAFFREY, DONALD W. – Editor
Focus on Chaplin
Prentice–Hall, 1971. 174pp. $5.95. Paper $2.45. Articles and criticism on Charles Chaplin's development as an actor and director, his dramatic range, and the universality of his humor. A selection of critical reviews and a section of scenario excerpts are provided. Eight pages of photographs. Filmography. Selected Bibliography. Index.

McCLELLAND, C. KIRK
On Making a Movie: Brewster McCloud
New American Library, 1971. 359pp. Paper $1.50. The day-to-day journal of the on-location filming of the movie, "Brewster McCloud," in Houston, Texas. The volume is complete with the shooting script of the film and the original screenplay by Doran William Cannon. Included are production shots and stills from the film.

MALTIN, LEONARD
The Great Movie Shorts
Crown, 1971. 236pp. $9.95. A nostalgic look at the great movie short subjects of the 1930's and 1940's. Firsthand information and anecdotes are provided by the people who made the films, and the author has included complete data (cast, director, release date, studio, synopsis) of over one-thousand short subjects. Among the subjects and stars included are: The "Our Gang" comedies, Robert Benchley's lectures, "Crime Does Not Pay" series, the Leon Errol bedroom farces, Laurel and Hardy, W. C. Fields, Buster Keaton, Harry Langdon, Edgar Kennedy, Andy Clyde, John Nesbitt, Pete Smith, and Charley Chase. Illustrated with more than 200 photographs. Index.

MORELLA, JOE and EDWARD Z. EPSTEIN
Rebels: The Rebel Hero in Films
Citadel, 1971. 210pp. $9.95. In this volume the authors trace the film career of the rebel hero—the self-tortured non-conformist—both as a character on

screen and in the private lives of the actors who have portrayed the hero on screen. The book ranges from John Garfield's performance in the 1938 film, "Four Daughters," through to the anti-heroes of today: McQueen, Redford, Fonda, Hoffman, Newman, et al. Illustrated with nearly 500 photographs.

MUNDEN, KENNETH W. – Editor
The American Film Institute Catalog of Motion Pictures Produced in the United States: Feature Films, 1921 – 1930
Bowker, 1971. 1,653pp. Two volume set: $55.00. The first volume in this catalog describes United States feature motion pictures released between January 1,1921 and December 31, 1930. The films described are those intended for public showing. Each film of concern is given a separate entry and is arranged by title in alphabetical sequence. The descriptive entry gives production company, distributor, date of release, copyright date, data on audio aspects, color, gauge, length, production and cast credits, and a description of the contents of the film including an indication of genre, the literary source, a summary of the purpose and scope. The accompanying volume is the "Credit and Subject Index." Listed alphabetically in the Credit Index are all personal and institutional or corporate names credited in the preceding volume. The "Subject Index" classifies the films in major categories, and all films are listed under as many subject headings as are deemed necessary to reveal their content.

PARISH, JAMES ROBERT – Editor
The Great Movie Series
A. S. Barnes, 1971. 333pp. $15.00. A comprehensive study of twenty-four of the editor's choice of the greatest sound film series made in Hollywood. Each series of films is discussed in a separate chapter detailing the literary origin, biographies of the leading players, detailed filmographies of each of the episodes, and cast and technical credits. There are over 300 stills illustrating the series which include: Andy Hardy, Blondie, Charlie Chan, Dr. Kildare, Francis the Talking Mule, Maisie, Sherlock Holmes, Tarzan, and the Thin Man series.

RICHIE, DONALD
George Stevens: An American Romantic
New York Graphic Society, 1970. 104pp. Paper $2.50. A monograph on the American film director illustrated with photographs from the films. A Filmography provides complete credits for each of the films. Also included is a list of awards received by Stevens and his films.

ROSENTHAL, ALAN
The New Documentary in Action: A Casebook in Film Making
University of California, 1971. 287pp. $11.95. The author focuses on the nonfiction film-makers: his techniques, his conceptions of his work, his artistic strategies, and his creative and practical problems. A general introduction analyzes recent tendencies in documentary films, discusses relations between fiction and nonfiction forms, and summarizes the effects of television documentary. Film-makers represented in the book have earned recognition in a wide variety of forms and include Allan King, Frederick Wiseman, Albert Maysles, Peter Watkins, Dan Alan Pennebaker, and others. Illustrated. Index.

SENNETT, TED
Warner Brothers Presents
Arlington House, 1971. 428pp. $11.95. A study of the films produced at the Warner Brothers studios during the 1930's and the 1940's and of the personalities and actors who helped to create them. A Filmography lists every film released by the Warner Brothers between January 1,1930 and December 31, 1949—976 in all—with cast, credits, plot line, and an excerpt from a contemporary "New York Times" or "Variety" review. The author includes 168 photographs, a Bibliography, a List of Warner Brothers Awards, and an Index.

SHAVELSON, MELVILLE
How to Make a Jewish Movie
Prentice–Hall, 1971. 244pp. $6.95. A humorous account of the making of the film, "Cast a Giant Shadow," which starred Kirk Douglas, John Wayne, Frank Sinatra, and the Israeli Army. The film was an artistic and commercial flop. Illustrated with photographs.

SILVA, FRED – Editor
Focus on "The Birth of a Nation"
Prentice–Hall, 1971. 184pp. $5.95. Paper $2.45. A collection of reviews, commentaries, and essays on D. W. Griffith's film, "The Birth of a Nation." Introduced by the editor, the volume also includes an appreciation of Griffith by James Agee, cast and production credits, a plot synopsis, and a content outline. Illustrated with eight pages of photographs. Filmography. Bibliography. Index.

SPEARS, JACK
Hollywood: The Golden Era
A. S. Barnes, 1971. 440pp. $12.00. A collection of essays on motion picture history and film personalities. The articles in this volume were originally published by the author in "Films in Review" from 1955 to 1968, but they have been revised, expanded, and updated with new material. They cover the history of Hollywood from the role of films in propagandizing World War I to behind-the-camera glimpses of Mary Pickford and Charlie Chaplin. Illustrated with more than 200 photographs. Appendix. Index of Names. Index of Titles.

STEDMAN, RAYMOND WILLIAM
The Serials: Suspense and Drama by Installment
University of Oklahoma, 1971. 514pp. $9.95. The

author traces the evolution of the serial drama from its origins in magazines and comic strips to the motion picture cliffhangers, to the radio adventure serials, and the "soap-operas" of the 1930's and 1940's, to the television form in the 1950's, 1960's, and 1970's. Mr. Stedman illustrates how such programs have reflected and influenced the times in which they appeared. Illustrated with more than sixty photographs. Appendices. Bibliography. Indices.

TAYLOR, JOHN RUSSELL and ARTHUR JACKSON
The Hollywood Musical
McGraw–Hill, 1971. 279pp. $12.95. Mr. Taylor provides a personalized history and study of musical films made in Hollywood. He provides anecdotes about the singers, dancers, composers, choreographers, designers, and directors of the genre. Mr. Jackson has compiled, for the second half of the volume, an encyclopedic reference guide to 1,443 films. Detailed filmographies are given for 275 of the best known. The authors have provided twelve color and 113 black-and-white photographs. Also included is an extensive biographical index which provides information about more than 1,100 individuals associated with the film musical. Index of Songs. Index of Titles.

THOMAS, BOB
The Heart of Hollywood
Price/Stern/Sloan, 1971. 110pp. $7.95. A fifty year pictorial record of the film capital and of the Motion Picture and Television Relief Fund. The author celebrates the founding and achievements of the Fund to which the leading Hollywood citizens have contributed their time and talents. The photographs are mostly rare candid shots, many of which have never before been published.

WAGENKNECHT, EDWARD
The Movies in the Age of Innocence
Ballantine, 1971. 270pp. Paper $2.95. Originally published in 1962 and now reissued, this is a personal view of silent movies. The author records how the generation for which they were created responded to the first motion pictures, actors, directors, and theatres. Illustrated with photographs. Indices.

WALKER, ALEXANDER
Stanley Kubrick Directs
Harcourt, Brace, 1971. 272pp. $8.95. A pictorial and textual analysis of Kubrick's methods of and thoughts on filmmaking. Discussed in detail are three major films: "Paths to Glory," "2001: A Space Odyssey," and "Dr. Strangelove." More than 300 photographs illustrate the study. Filmography.

WEAVER, JOHN T. – Compiler
Twenty Years of Silents: 1908 – 1928
Scarecrow Press, 1971. 514pp. $29.00. This volume provides a listing of the screen credits of actors, actresses, directors, and producers for the years 1908 to 1928. Also included in the volume is a list of silent film studio corporations and distributors.

WHITE, DAVID MANNING – Editor
Pop Culture in America
See Page 628

WILK, MAX
The Wit and Wisdom of Hollywood
Atheneum, 1971. 330pp. $8.95. Memories and anecdotes and jokes from Hollywood. The wit and humor is provided by many of the personalities of the film business including: Jack Benny, George Burns, Groucho Marx, Nunnally Johnson, Joe Mankiewicz, and others.

WILSON, EARL
The Show Business Nobody Knows
Cowles, 1971. 428pp. $6.95. The popular columnist reveals the intimate lives of the star performers in the entertainment world. He looks into what's behind the nudity revolution and its present popularity and discusses the secret scandals involving the business and private activities of stars, producers, and directors. Illustrated with thirty-two pages of photographs. Index.

OTHER COUNTRIES

DEWEY, LANGDON
Outline of Czechoslovakian Cinema
Informatics, 1971. 122pp. $4.75. This outline traces the course of both Czech and Slovak feature films from 1898 to 1970; shows national characteristics reflected therein; follows the artistic genealogy, and includes directors, technicians, and performers. Illustrated with photographs. Index.

MILNE, TOM
The Cinema of Carl Dreyer
A. S. Barnes, 1971. 192pp. Paper $2.95. A study of fourteen films made by the Danish film director. Illustrated with scenes from the films. Filmography with casts and credits.

TECHNIQUES OF PRODUCTION

General Reference Works

BAYER, WILLIAM
Breaking Through, Selling Out, Dropping Dead and Other Notes on Film-Making
Macmillan, 1971. 227pp. $5.95. According to the

author, this book is a "collection of random, subjective, and often idiosyncratic notes about filmmaking—attitudes, facts, speculations, and suggestions ... intended for and addressed to the young filmmaker who is faced with enormous problems of career development; who is ... embarking upon a first feature; who is exploring ways of financing, organizing, and selling an independent picture; and who is looking for a way to work within that structure called 'the film industry'."

BRANSTON, BRIAN
A Film Maker's Guide
Allen & Unwin, 1967. 205pp. $8.25. Published in England, this is a guide to planning, directing, and shooting films for pleasure and for sale to television. The author provides a manual of instruction and training that includes film, cameras, lights, lenses, sound, editing, dubbing, and the markets for the completed film. An analysis of a 16mm film, "Adventure—Balloon to Serengeti," is included. Illustrated with photographs and diagrams. Glossary of Technical Film Terms. Appendices. Index.

BUTLER, IVAN
The Making of Feature Films — A Guide
Penguin, 1971. 191pp. Paper $1.75. The author provides an account of the processes involved in the making of feature films today, primarily in Britain and the United States. Each chapter in the book deals with a particular job: the producer, director, script writer, actor, continuity girl, editor, distributor, censor, etc. Illustrated with photographs. Index.

CUSHMAN, GEORGE
Movie Making in 18 Lessons
Chilton, 1971. 128pp. $5.95. A step-by-step introduction to movie making. Use of camera, film, lenses, tricks and effects, lighting, continuity, editing, sound, and showmanship are described and illustrated in text and photographs.

GERTNER, RICHARD — Editor
International Motion Picture Almanac — 1972
Quigley, 1971. 716pp. $15.00. The forty-third annual edition of the reference book dealing with the business of motion pictures. Provided are statistics, award and poll winners, a who's who section, a list of features released in the United States from 1955 to 1971, information on corporations, theatre circuits, buyers and bookers, equipment, services, talent and literary agencies, codes, censorship, and the press. Indices.

GOODWIN, NANCY and JAMES N. MANILLA
Make Your Own Professional Movies
Collier, 1971. 209pp. $1.95. A guide to making films with home movie cameras. Six original shooting scripts are included with production crew instructions for the casting director, wardrobe mistress, prop man, set designer, music and sound-effects director, and producer-director-cameraman. Also included are a glossary of terms, descriptions of the functions of each member of the production crew, and ideas for other films.

KUHNS, WILLIAM and THOMAS F. GIARDINO
Behind the Camera
Pflaum, 1971. 178pp. Paper $3.50. The authors provide "a foundation in the techniques of filmmaking." They provide information on cameras, film, how to handle light, sound, script writing, acting, editing, and titling. In addition, they provide a diary of the making of a student film, "Sparrow." The final section of the book is a critique of the 16mm film by two film teachers. Illustrated with photographs. Appendices include an Annotated Bibliography.

LARSON, RODGER with ELLEN MEADE
Young Filmmakers
Avon, 1971. 186pp. Paper $ .95. Originally published in 1969 and now reissued, this book details the basic essentials of the film-making experience to help young film-makers understand how to use the technical means at their command. The authors describe some of the films teenagers are making today and deal with such matters as the nature of film language, the actual shooting of a film beginning with the formulation of an idea and script, including the responsibilities of the film-maker as his own director and cameraman. Illustrated. Glossary. Index.

LEWIS, JERRY
The Total Film-Maker
Random House, 1971. 208pp. $6.95. This is an inside look at the way in which films are made by the comedian/producer/director. The book is distilled from Mr. Lewis' lectures to graduate students at the University of Southern California and includes anecdotes and personal experiences as well as technical details on the producer's job, writing a script, preparing for the day's shooting, actual filming, dealing with actors and the film crew, and the problems of the cutting room and the sound track, as well as distribution and exploitation of the finished film. A concluding section includes essays on comedy and comedians. Eight pages of photographs illustrate the volume.

ROBERTS, KENNETH H. and WIN SHARPLES, JR.
A Primer for Film-Making
Bobbs—Merrill, 1971. 546pp. $15.00. Paper $9.25. Subtitled "A Complete Guide to 16MM and 35MM Film Production," this is a basic, step-by-step guide to the art and craft of contemporary filmmaking which covers all aspects of technique. Such areas as the camera, lighting, editing, the laboratory, opticals and titles, film sound, and budgeting are covered in detail. A comprehensive listing—together with sources of availability—is offered of all necessary production and post-production equipment. Illustrated with line drawings and photographs. Appendices

include a List of Significant Films, A Budget Outline and a Dictionary of American Standard Nomenclature. Bibliography. Index.

RYNEW, ARDEN
Filmmaking for Children
See Page 582

RYNEW, ARDEN
Motion Picture Production Handbook
See Page 582

WYSOTSKY, MICHAEL Z.
Wide-Screen Cinema and Stereophonic Sound
Hastings House, 1971. 282pp. $15.00. Translated from the Russian by A. E. C. York, and edited, annotated, and introduced by Raymond Spotiswoode, this book describes the progress of wide-screen cinema and stereophonic sound throughout the world, paying particular attention to Russian developments in these fields. The fundamentals of the subject as well as the technical details are provided. Illustrated with drawings and diagrams. Bibliography. Index.

Cinematography

HAPPE, L. BERNARD
Basic Motion Picture Technology
Hastings House, 1971. 362pp. $10.00. A comprehensive survey of the technical basis of professional cinematography. Starting with a brief history of cinema, the author shows the developments currently being investigated and, with the help of illustrations, he describes the design and application of cameras and equipment for all film gauges. The mechanics of film, its manufacture, characteristics and usage, other forms of sound and picture recording and transmission, and their applications are all fully covered. Appendices. Bibliography. Glossary. Index.

MALTIN, LEONARD
Behind the Camera
Signet, 1971. 240pp. Paper $1.50. A study of the cinematographer's art. Full-length interviews with five major figures—Arthur C. Miller, Hal Mohr, Hal Rossen, Lucien Ballard, and Conrad Hall—are included as is a long essay on the great American cameramen. Lists of each of the cinematographer's films are included. Illustrated with thirty-two pages of photographs. Index.

Directing

BARE, RICHARD L.
The Film Director
Macmillan, 1971. 243pp. $8.95. A Hollywood film director tells the aspiring film-maker how to direct in a step-by-step handbook. The fundamentals of camera angle, sound synch, lighting, and editing are all covered as well as the director's influence on the performances, the director's requirements and responsibilities, and how to create a job. Illustrated with photographs. Appendices include lists of universities offering film degrees, award winners, and a Glossary. Bibliography. Index.

HIGHAM, CHARLES and JOEL GREENBERG
The Celluloid Muse: Hollywood Directors Speak
Regnery, 1971. 268pp. $7.95. Originally published in England in 1969 and now issued in the United States, this is a series of self-portraits of fifteen American film directors, based on taped interviews. The authors have provided an introduction to each subject, describing the director's milieu and personality. The subjects are: Alfred Hitchcock, Fritz Lang, John Frankenheimer, Billy Wilder, Lewis Milestone, George Cukor, Rouben Mamoulian, King Vidor, Jacques Tourneur, Vincente Minelli, Jean Negulesco, Robert Aldrich, Curtis Bernhardt, Irving Rapper, and Mark Robson. The authors have also provided filmographies of each of the directors and a special preface setting the Hollywood scene. Sixteen page section of photographs. Index.

SARRIS, ANDREW – Editor
Hollywood Voices
Bobbs–Merrill, 1971. 180pp. $7.50. A collection of interviews with film directors. The editor has provided a general introduction, critical notes on the directors, and lists of films of each director. The nine directors interviewed are: George Cukor, Rouben Mamoulian, Otto Preminger, Preston Sturges, John Huston, Joseph Losey, and Nicholas Ray, Abraham Polonsky, and Orson Welles. Among the interviewers are: Mr. Sarris, Ian Cameron, Penelope Houston, John Gillett, and William Pechter. Illustrated with scenes from the directors' films.

Special Effects

CAUNTER, JULIEN
How to Make Movie Magic in Amateur Films
Chilton, 1971. 348pp. $7.95. A guidebook to special effects for the amateur film-maker. The author describes every method of trickery from the simplest illusions to the advanced techniques used by professional movie and television cameramen. Among the effects explained are those achieved by the use of exposure, lenses, focusing, diffusion, distortion, and tricks with camera speeds, reverse action, stop motion, superimpostion, and chemical after-treatment. Illustrated with drawings and diagrams. Indexed Glossary.

Editing

BURDER, JOHN
The Technique of Editing 16MM Films
Hastings House, 1971. 152pp. $10.00. First published in 1958 and now revised to include footage and duration charts and references to the latest film stocks and equipment developments, this is a practical, how-to-do-it guide on the technique of editing films. Illustrated with drawings and diagrams. Glossary of Technical Terms. Index.

Acting

HAYMAN, RONALD
Techniques of Acting
See Page 595

BIOGRAPHIES AND APPRECIATIONS OF SCREEN PERSONALITIES

Collected (By Author)

BEST, MARC
Those Endearing Young Charms
A. S. Barnes, 1971. 279pp. $10.00. This collection of memorabilia presents fifty of the most notable child performers of the screen. The stars are listed alphabetically with information on date and place of birth, education, hobbies, how they were discovered, when and where they made their debuts, and a list of films and television credits. Among those presented are: Freddie Bartholomew, Joan Carroll, Jackie Cooper, Brandon DeWilde, Bobby Driscoll, Edith Fellows, Mitzi Green, Jackie "Butch" Jenkins, Carolyn Lee, Baby Leroy, Roddy McDowall, George "Spanky" McFarland, Dickie Moore, Margaret O'Brien, Mickey Rooney, Shirley Temple, Virginia Weidler, Jane Withers, and Natalie Wood. Over 300 photographs provide a studio portrait and stills of various movie roles for each of the performers.

KANIN, GARSON
Tracy and Hepburn: An Intimate Memoir
Viking, 1971. 307pp. $7.95. Kanin recounts, through personal anecdotes, the lives of Katharine Hepburn and Spencer Tracy throughout their long friendship. The book has been critically acclaimed for its portraits of the two actors.

LAHUE, KALTON C.
Ladies in Distress
A. S. Barnes, 1971. 334pp. $10.00. An appreciation of forty representative heroines of the silent screen era in America. For each of the subjects, Mr. Lahue provides a brief biographical picture of their lives on and off-screen and supplies photographs of the ladies as they appeared in their films. Among the ladies included: Mary Astor, Theda Bara, Marion Davies, Geraldine Farrar, Greta Garbo, Bessie Love, Mary Miles Minter, Arline Pretty, Norma Shearer, and Clara Kimball Young.

McCRINDLE, JOSEPH F. – Editor
Behind the Scenes: Theatre and Film Interviews
See Page 561

PARISH, JAMES ROBERT
The Fox Girls
Arlington House, 1971. 722pp. $14.95. Through the medium of biographies of sixteen of 20th-Century-Fox's actresses, the author provides a history of the motion picture studio. Each of the stars is presented by means of a biography and a detailed filmography with generous selections of portraits, candid photos, and scenes from the films—over 850 photographs. The "girls" included are: Theda Bara, Janet Gaynor, Shirley Temple, Alice Faye, Loretta Young, Sonja Henie, Linda Darnell, Betty Grable, Gene Tierney, Anne Baxter, Carmen Miranda, June Haver, Jeanne Crain, Marilyn Monroe, Sheree North, and Raquel Welch.

Individual (By Subject)

Agee, James

AGEE, JAMES and JAMES HAROLD FLYE
Letters of James Agee to Father Flye
Ballantine, 1971. 271pp. Paper $1.25. Originally published earlier in 1971 and now reissued with a new Preface and previously unpublished letters by Father Flye. The letters chronicle Agee's life from his school days to his years as a script writer in Hollywood, to the culmination of his career. An Introduction by Robert Phelps is included.

LARSEN, ERLING
James Agee
University of Minnesota, 1971. 47pp. Paper $ .95. A study of the poet/critic/novelist/screen writer. The author concentrates on Agee's non-dramatic work. Selected Bibliography.

Astor, Mary

ASTOR, MARY
A Life on Film

Delacorte, 1971. 245pp. $7.50. An autobiography of the film star describing her recollection of forty-five years of life in the film world from the silents to the 1960's. She describes the making of her films, explains the mechanics of movie making, and the special tricks of closeups, make-up, and wardrobe. Illustrated with fifty-nine photographs. A Filmography with complete credits and casts has been compiled by DeWitt Bodeen. Index.

Capra, Frank

CAPRA, FRANK
The Name Above the Title
Macmillan, 1971. 513pp. $12.50. The autobiography of the film director and his forty year career from the rise of the motion picture during the Mack Sennett days through his major successes and many Academy Awards. Anecdotes and memories about the stars he has worked with, plus a portrait of Harry Cohn, advice to young film-makers, an analysis of the great directors, the techniques of photography, and the methods pioneered by Capra provide interesting chapters. Illustrated with photographs. Index.

Chaney, Lon

ANDERSON, ROBERT G.
Faces, Forms, Films: The Artistry of Lon Chaney
A.S. Barnes, 1971. 216pp. $8.50. A biography and study of Lon Chaney, Sr.'s life and career. Mr. Anderson provides a collection of over 150 stills which shows Chaney in all his major characterizations, and in his text he details the means the artist used to create those characterizations. Included is a complete index of Chaney's films with credits and a chronology of his life. Index to Text. Index to Illustrations.

Chaplin, Charles

McDONALD, GERALD D. with MICHAEL CONWAY, and MARK RICCI – Editors
The Films of Charlie Chaplin
Citadel, 1971. 224pp. Paper $3.95. Originally published in 1965 and now reissued, this is a study and record of the film career of the great screen clown. The editors provide biographical material and appreciations of Chaplin as well as details on all of Chaplin's films from 1914 through 1957. Provided are synopses of the plots of the films, extracts from reviews, cast and production credits, and photographs of scenes from the films. Index.

Cooper, Gary

DICKENS, HOMER
The Films of Gary Cooper
Citadel, 1971. 281pp. Paper $3.95. Originally published in 1970 and now reissued, this is a documented pictorial study of the screen star. Included are a biographical study of Cooper, as well as a record of the ninety-two films in which he appeared. Synopses, cast listings, technical credits, and reviews are included. More than 400 photographs from the films are presented as well as many candid shots and studio portraits.

Crawford, Joan

CRAWFORD, JOAN
My Way of Life
Simon and Schuster, 1971. 224pp. $7.50. An autobiography of the actress and a guide for women in which Miss Crawford explains her secrets of how she keeps vital, young, interested, and interesting. She shares her recipes for entertaining, her formula for organizing time and energy, her wardrobe and make-up secrets. Illustrated with eighty-two photographs.

Dwan, Allan

BOGDANOVITCH, PETER
Allan Dwan, The Last Pioneer
Praeger, 1971. 200pp. $6.95. An introduction to the career of, and an interview with, Allan Dwan, who directed Hollywood films from 1911 to 1961. The director discusses his entire career. Illustrated with scenes from the films. Filmography.

Fields, W. C.

FIELDS, W.C.
Fields for President
Dodd, Mead, 1971. 163pp. $5.95. Originally published in 1940 and now reissued with biographical commentary and an Introduction by Michael M. Taylor. Fields' only book, it is an anthology of gags, sketches, comic situations, and views on politics, babies, big business, marriage, physical fitness, and many other subjects. Illustrated with sixty-one photographs, some of which have never been published before.

MONTI, CARLOTTA with CY RICE
W.C. Fields and Me

Prentice–Hall, 1971. 227pp. $6.95. A memoir of W. C. Fields by the woman who lived with him for fourteen years. Anecdotes, reminiscences, and glimpses into his private life are provided. Illustrated with photographs. Index.

Fitzgerald, F. Scott

CROSS, K. G. W.
F. Scott Fitzgerald
Capricorn, 1971. 120pp. Paper $1.25. Originally published in 1964 and now reissued, this is a critical biography of the writer which draws upon his autobiographical works to illuminate his writings. A survey of Fitzgerald criticism is included. Bibliography.

MAYFIELD, SARA
Exiles from Paradise
Delacorte Press, 1971. 309pp. $8.95. A biography of Zelda and Scott Fitzgerald based on personal recollection and on research. Bibliography. Index.

TURNBULL, ANDREW
Scott Fitzgerald
Ballantine, 1971. 372pp. Paper $1.25. Originally published in 1962 and now reissued, this is a biography of the American writer from his childhood in St. Paul to his final days in Hollywood. Critically acclaimed upon its initial publication, the volume includes a sixteen page section of photographs and a chronology of the main events in Fitzgerald's life. Index.

Fitzgerald, Zelda

MILFORD, NANCY
Zelda
Avon, 1971. 511pp. Paper $1.50. Critically acclaimed upon its initial publication in 1970 and now reissued, this is a biography of Scott Fitzgerald's wife. The main portion of the book details the long struggle against recurring mental illness. Sixteen page section of photographs. Index.

Flynn, Errol

THOMAS, TONY with RUDY BEHLMER, CLIFFORD McCARTY
The Films of Errol Flynn
Citadel, 1971. 223pp. Paper $3.95. Originally published in 1969 and now reissued, this is a complete record of the career of the film star. Each of the films from 1933 through 1959 is chronicled in text and photographs with complete casts and production credits. Foreword by Greer Garson.

Gable, Clark

CARPOZI, JR., GEORGE
Clark Gable
Pyramid, 1971. 206pp. Paper $ .95. Originally published in 1961 and now reissued, this is a biography of the late film actor. Thirty-two pages of photographs are included.

Garbo, Greta

BAINBRIDGE, JOHN
Garbo
Holt, Rinehart, 1971. 320pp. $10.95. Originally published in 1955 and now reissued in an entirely new format with revisions to bring it up-to-date, and illustrated with 132 photographs, this is considered to be the definitive biography of the actress and includes a full list of her films with cast and production credits.

SJOLANDER, TURE
Garbo
Harper & Row, 1971. 139pp. $12.00. Nearly two hundred photographs detail the private and public life of Greta Garbo. Most of the photographs are candid shots taken during the off-screen life of the film star.

Garland, Judy

TORME, MEL
The Other Side of the Rainbow
Bantam, 1971. 196pp. Paper $1.25. Originally published in 1970 and now reissued, this is a portrait of Judy Garland during the nine month period when she was the star of her own television series. The author was "music consultant" for the series. Illustrated with photographs.

Head, Edith

HEAD, EDITH and JANE KESNER ARDMORE
The Dress Doctor

Little, Brown, 1959. 249pp. $4.95. The autobiography of the famous designer. Miss Head describes her work for the famous motion picture stars such as Marlene Dietrich, Mae West, Rita Hayworth, and many others. She includes a section on dress for the modern woman. Illustrated with photographs and drawings.

Hepburn, Katharine

DICKENS, HOMER
The Films of Katharine Hepburn
Citadel, 1971. 244pp. $9.95. A tribute to the career of the American actress. Every film in which she appeared is documented with cast, credits, synopses, and reviews. All of the plays in which Miss Hepburn has acted are also included. More than four hundred photographs illustrate the text, including candid shots and studio publicity photographs as well as scenes from the films and plays.

Hughes, Howard

GARRISON, OMAR
Howard Hughes in Las Vegas
Dell, 1971. 255pp. Paper $1.25. A reprint of the book first published in 1970. The author traces the development of the business details which made Hughes the most powerful man in Nevada. This edition does not contain the photographs from the original edition.

KEATS, JOHN
Howard Hughes
Pyramid, 1970. 336pp. Paper $1.25. Originally published in 1966 and now reissued, this is a biography of the controversial figure—including the years in Hollywood, and the Las Vegas empire. Illustrated with photographs.

Huston, John

TOZZI, ROMANO
John Huston: A Pictorial Treasury of His Films
Falcon, 1971. 158pp. $3.95. The author provides a running summary of the film director's life and films. The text is illustrated with photographs from each of the films from 1931 through 1970. The 136 photographs show not only scenes from the films directed by Huston, but also those in which he acted. Also included is a complete list of all the films with cast and production credits.

Ivens, Joris

IVENS, JORIS
The Camera and I
International Publishers, 1969. 280pp. Paper $1.95. This is the autobiography of the documentary film-maker. It is both a history of documentary filmmaking and Ivens' personal story. Illustrated with photographs from Ivens' films. Filmography.

Keaton, Buster

BLESH, RUDI
Keaton
Collier, 1971. 395pp. Paper $2.95. Originally published in a hard cover edition in 1966 and now reissued in a paper bound edition, this is a biography and study of the work of Buster Keaton. All of Keaton's films are evaluated, there is an annotated list of films, and the volume is illustrated with more than one hundred photographs. Index.

Knef, Hildegard

KNEF, HILDEGARD
The Gift Horse
McGraw–Hill, 1971. 384pp. $7.95. Translated from the German by David C. Palastanga, this is the critically acclaimed autobiography of the German actress. She describes her childhood in Berlin in the 1930's, her life in the German army and in a Russian prison camp, as well as her careers in films and on the stage in Germany and the United States.

Lake, Veronica

LAKE, VERONICA and DONALD BAIN
Veronica
Citadel, 1971. 281pp. $6.95. Originally published in England in 1969 and now published in the United States, this is the autobiography of the motion picture actress who walked out on fame and success at the peak of her career. The volume is illustrated with thirty-two photographs. Index.

Lancaster, Burt

VERMILYE, JERRY
Burt Lancaster: A Pictorial Treasury of His Films

Crown, 1971. 159pp. $3.95. A chronicle of the career of the film actor in text and photographs. Complete filmography with cast and production credits is included from 1947 through 1971. Illustrated with at least one scene from each film plus studio portraits and candid photographs.

Lloyd, Harold

LLOYD, HAROLD and WESLEY W. STOUT
An American Comedy
Blom, 1971. 204pp. $8.75. Paper—Dover, 1971. 138pp. $3.00. Originally published in 1928 and now reissued, this is the autobiography of the great comedian's early life and his beginnings in films. He also details the methods and motives behind his screen classics: creating the character with the spectacles, shooting without scripts, evolving visual jokes. He also provides memories and interpretations of other movie greats. The paper edition also includes an Introduction by Richard Griffith, and an interview with Mr. Lloyd by H. I. Cohen. The volume is illustrated with photographs. Index.

March, Fredric

QUIRK, LAWRENCE J.
The Films of Fredric March
Citadel, 1971. 255pp. $9.95. A complete record of the career of the actor. It includes stills from all the films he made, as well as many from his stage and television appearances, and informal and candid photographs from the actor's private collection. Casts, credits, synopses, and critiques of all the films from 1929 to 1970 are provided along with a biographical study.

Mercouri, Melina

MERCOURI, MELINA
I Was Born Greek
Doubleday, 1971. 253pp. $6.96. This is the autobiography of the Greek actress from her childhood in Athens, to her early training in the theatre, to her success in films. Miss Mercouri relates the history of her long relationship with the director, Jules Dassin, and tells of the successful films they have made together. Running through this story of her life is her deeply felt love for her native country and her present fight for its political freedom. Illustrated with fourteen pages of photographs.

Neal, Patricia

FARRELL, BARRY
Pat and Roald
Dell, 1971. 188pp. Paper $ .95. Originally published in 1969 and now reissued, this is the story of Patricia Neal's extraordinary recovery from a series of massive strokes with the faith, help, and love of her husband, Roald Dahl. Although the original edition was illustrated with photographs, they are not included in this edition.

Newman, Paul

QUIRK, LAWRENCE J.
The Films of Paul Newman
Citadel, 1971. 224pp. $9.95. An account of the career of Paul Newman from his beginnings as a stage actor to his current acting and directorial sucesses. Casts, credits, and synopses, as well as reviews of the films are included. More than 400 photographs include scenes from all the films and plays and a gallery of portraits and candid photographs.

Olivier, Laurence

DARLINGTON, W.A.
Laurence Olivier
See Page 566

Poitier, Sidney

HOFFMAN, WILLIAM
Sidney
Lyle Stuart, 1971. 175pp. $5.95. A biography of Sidney Poitier. The actor details his struggles to maintain his integrity as a black man while advancing his career to the point of winning an Academy Award for "Lillies of the Field." Illustrated with sixteen pages of photographs including scenes from the films and candid shots.

Preminger, Otto

PRATLEY, GERALD
The Cinema of Otto Preminger
A. S. Barnes, 1971. 192pp. Paper $2.95. A report on the career of the film director. Each of the films is listed in a Filmography with complete cast and

production credits, a short synopsis, and comments by Preminger. In addition, there is a report on his acting and the stage productions he has directed. Illustrated with photographs.

Presley, Elvis

HOPKINS, JERRY
Elvis: A Biography
Simon & Schuster, 1971. 448pp. $7.95. A biography of singer/film star, Elvis Presley. Illustrated with thirty pages of photographs. A discography and a list of films are included.

Renay, Liz

RENAY, LIZ
My Face for the World to See
Lyle Stuart, 1971. 457pp. $7.95. The biography of the woman who was a "V—girl" during World War II, became a high-fashion model, a stripper, a Mafia moll, and a minor figure in films.

Rogers, Will

BROWN, WILLIAM R.
Imagemaker: Will Rogers and the American Dream
University of Missouri, 1971. 304pp. $10.00. This study, rhetorical rather than historical or biographical, centers upon ideas rather than verbal forms and presents Will Rogers as the embodiment of the American Adam. Through selections from his speeches and newspaper columns, Rogers' humor and philosophy are detailed. The author focuses on social-cultural values in America as bases by which audiences may judge communicators and judges Rogers as "the richest possible elaboration of the American dream." Illustrated. Notes. Bibliography. Index.

Sinatra, Frank

RINGGOLD, GENE and CLIFFORD McCARTY
The Films of Frank Sinatra
Citadel, 1971. 249pp. $9.95. A record of Frank Sinatra's career from his days as a vocalist with the Tommy Dorsey orchestra to his announcement that he was retiring in 1971. The volume covers every film Sinatra made, as well as the concert and television appearances. The authors have also supplied a biographical study of the actor/singer and more than 400 photographs illustrating his career.

Stuart, John

STUART, JOHN
Caught in the Act
The Silent Picture, 1971. 32pp. Paper $1.50. The English actor recaps his career in films, television, and on stage from 1920 to 1970. Illustrated with twenty photographs.

Tracy, Spencer

SWINDELL, LARRY
Spencer Tracy
New American Library, 1971. 280pp. Paper $ .95. Originally published in 1969 and now reissued, this is a biography of the late motion picture actor from his childhood in Milwaukee to the great films he made in the 1940's, 1950's, and 1960's. The volume is illustrated with thirty-two pages of movie stills and other photographs of the actor. The author has also included a complete Filmography and an Index.

Turner, Lana

MORELLA, JOE and EDWARD Z. EPSTEIN
Lana: The Public and Private Lives of Miss Turner
Citadel, 1971. 297pp. $6.95. This "unauthorized" biography purports to be an "unvarnished" portrait of the star stripped of myth or press agentry. The authors follow Miss Turner's career from her discovery at a Hollywood soda fountain to the present day. Illustrated with sixteen pages of photographs.

Ustinov, Peter

THOMAS, TONY
Ustinov in Focus
A.S. Barnes, 1971. 192pp. Paper $2.95. A report on the life and career of English actor/director Peter Ustinov. Each of the films from 1947 to 1969 is included with an essay on the film, complete cast and production credits, and stills from the film. Also included is a list of books and plays by Ustinov and a list of his recordings.

Von Stroheim, Erich

CURTISS, THOMAS QUINN
Von Stroheim
Farrar, Straus, 1971. 357pp. $10.00. A biography of Erich von Stroheim and a study of his work. The author details Stroheim's years of poverty in New York, the roles played in his career by Griffith, Fairbanks, Laemmle, Thalberg, and Mayer, and the story of Greta Garbo's friendship. Foreword by Rene Clair. Included are eighty-eight pages of photographs. Filmography. Bibliography.

Warhol, Andy

WARHOL, ANDY et al – Editors
Andy Warhol
Boston Book and Art, 1971. Unpaged. $7.50. Published on the occasion of the Andy Warhol exhibition at the Modern Museet in Stockholm in 1968, this volume includes reproductions of paintings, photographs taken at the Warhol "factory," scenes from Warhol's films, and candid photographs. More than 600 photographs are included.

Wayne, John

TOMKIES, MIKE
Duke: The Story of John Wayne
Regnery, 1971. 149pp. $5.95. A biography of the film actor, known to his family and friends as "Duke." The author provides the story of the man behind the legends and includes details of all of Wayne's films from 1930 and his "superstardom" from 1939 to the present. The volume is illustrated with sixteen pages of photographs. The author has also provided a Filmography.

Welles, Orson

BESSY, MAURICE
Orson Welles
Crown, 1971. 195pp. Paper $3.50. Translated by Ciba Vaughan, from the Cinema d'Aujourd'hui series volume published in France in 1963, and brought up-to-date, this is an investigation into the films and philosophy of the actor/director. In addition to the essay by Bessy, the volume also includes texts by Welles on cinema, a selection of criticism, and a previously unpublished screenplay — "Salome." Illustrated with photographs. Filmography. Bibliography. Index.

Zanuck, Darryl F.

GUSSOW, MEL
Don't Say Yes Until I Finish Talking
Doubleday, 1971. 318pp. $7.95. A biography of Darryl F. Zanuck, head producer for many years at 20th Century Fox Film Studios.. Illustrated with photographs. Complete Filmography: 1924–1970. Index.

SCREENPLAYS

ANTONIONI, MICHELANGELO
Blow–Up
Simon & Schuster, 1971. 119pp. Paper $2.95. Translated from the Italian by John Mathews, this publication is based on the original screenplay and the dialogue cutting continuity of the final screen version. The volume also includes three interviews with Antonioni, notes on the differences between the original screenplay and the final version, complete cast and production credits, and twenty-four pages of stills from the film.

ANTONIONI, MICHELANGELO
Screenplays of Michelangelo Antonioni
Orion Press, 1971. 361pp. Paper $3.95. This volume includes four screenplays by the Italian director: "Il Grido," "L'Avventura," "L'Eclisse," and "La Notte." Also included is an Introduction by the director. Illustrated with scenes from the films and photographs of the director at work. Production credits are included.

BUNUEL, LUIS
Belle de Jour
Simon & Schuster, 1971. 168pp. Paper $2.95. A translation, by Robert Adkinson, of the film written and directed by Bunuel. Two interviews with Bunuel, an essay on the film by Andrew Sarris and an essay by Elliot Stein are included in the volume with twenty-four pages of stills from the film.

BUNUEL, LUIS
Tristana
Simon & Schuster, 1971. 144pp. Paper $2.95. The screenplay of the film by Luis Bunuel. The volume includes twenty-four pages of photographs from the film and an Introduction to the film by J. Francisco Aranda.

CACOYANNIS, MICHAEL
The Trojan Women
Bantam, 1971. 116pp. Paper $ .95. The screenplay of the film starring Katharine Hepburn is included in this volume with a sixteen page selection of photographs from the film. A feature of the volume is the inclusion of Euripides' play in the Edith Hamilton translation, plus her essay, "A Pacifist

in Periclean Athens." Cacoyannis has provided a special Introduction.

CANNON, DORAN WILLIAM
Brewster McCloud
See Page 608 under McCLELLAND

FEIFFER, JULES
Carnal Knowledge
Farrar, Straus, 1971. 118pp. $4.95. Paper $2.25. The screenplay of the film written by Feiffer and directed by Mike Nichols with Jack Nicholson, Arthur Garfunkel, Candice Bergen and Ann Margret in the leading roles. Fourteen pages of photographs are included.

FELLINI, FEDERICO
The Clowns
See Page 605 under RENZI

FELLINI, FEDERICO
Early Screenplays
Grossman, 1971. 198pp. $6.95. Paper $2.95. This volume presents the first two screenplays Fellini wrote and directed: "Variety Lights" (1950) and "The White Sheik" (1952). Cast and production credits are included for each film, and the volume is illustrated with photographs from the films.

FORMAN, MILOS et al
Taking Off
New American Library, 1971. 220pp. Paper $1.25. The complete screenplay of the first film in the English language by Czech film-maker, Milos Forman. Collaborators on the script were John Guare, Jean-Claude Carriere, and John Klein. In addition to the script, this volume includes an interview with the director and an original article on the making of the film. Illustrated with 150 photographs.

GARDNER, HERB
Who Is Harry Kellerman and Why Is He Saying Those Terrible Things About Me?
New American Library, 1971. 156pp. Paper $1.25. The screenplay of the new film starring Dustin Hoffman. Production and cast credits are included as are lyrics for five songs from the film. Illustrated with stills.

GARRETT, GEORGE P. and O. B. HARDISON, JR., JANE R. GELFMAN – Editors
Film Scripts One
Appleton, 1971. 544pp. Spiral bound $10.50. Film scripts for "Henry V" by Laurence Olivier and Reginald Beck, "The Big Sleep" by William Faulkner, Leigh Brackett, and Jules Furthman, and "A Streetcar Named Desire" by Tennessee Williams, adapted by Oscar Saul. There is a general introduction by the editors, an introduction to each script, an Appendix showing a typical call sheet and a shooting schedule, a Glossary, and a Bibliography.

GARRETT, GEORGE P. and O. B. HARDISON, JR., JANE R. GELFMAN – Editors
Film Scripts Two
Appleton, 1971. 548pp. Spiral bound $10.50. Film scripts for three classic films. The editors have provided a general introduction, an introduction to each script, a Glossary, and a Bibliography. An Appendix shows a typical call sheet and a shooting schedule. Scripts included:

Carl Foreman: High Noon
Reginald Rose: Twelve Angry Men
Nathan E. Douglas and Harold Jacob Smith: The Defiant Ones

GILLIATT, PENELOPE
Sunday Bloody Sunday
Bantam, 1971. 136pp. Paper $ .95. The screenplay of the critically acclaimed film directed by John Schlesinger. Complete credits are included as are sixteen pages of photographs from the film.

HARWOOD, RONALD
The Making of "One Day in the Life of Ivan Denisovich"
Ballantine, 1971. 271pp. Paper $1.25. The screenplay of the critically acclaimed film which starred Tom Courtenay in the leading role. The film was based on the novel by Alexander Solzhenitsyn. The novel is included in the volume in a new translation by Gillon Aitken. An Introduction by Harwood describes the making of the film. Sixteen pages of photographs are included.

JODOROWSKY, ALEXANDRO
El Topo: A Book of the Film
World, 1971. 173pp. $6.95. Paper $3.95. A scene-by-scene, image-by-image narrative of the film by its Spanish writer, director, star, and composer. Also included in the volume is an interview with Jodorowsky in which he talks about the making and the meanings of the film. The volume has been edited by Ross Firestone, and the translation is by Joanne Pottlitzer. Illustrated with photographs from the film and with photographs taken during the interview.

KUROSAWA, AKIRA
The Seven Samurai
Simon & Schuster, 1971. 224pp. Paper $3.45. Introduced and translated by Donald Richie, this is the scenario of the classic Japanese film. This edition is based on the script of the 160 minute version since the 200 minute version was lost before its general release. Complete cast and production credits are provided, and the volume is illustrated with thirty-two pages of photographs from the film.

LELOUCH, CLAUDE
A Man and A Woman
Simon & Schuster, 1971. 116pp. Paper $2.25. Translated, and with a description of the acting, by Nicholas

Fry, this script of the French director's film was built up from a shot-by-shot viewing of the film. An interview with the director and cast and production credits are provided in the volume along with twenty-four pages of photographs.

McCARTY, CLIFFORD
Published Screenplays: A Checklist
See Page 601

MAILER, NORMAN
Maidstone
Signet, 1971. 191pp. Paper $1.50. The script of the film, together with an account of the filming, and an essay on filmmaking. A twelve-page insert includes color photographs from the film.

MANKIEWICZ, HERMAN J. and ORSON WELLES
The Citizen Kane Book
Little, Brown, 1971. 440pp. $15.00. An account, "Raising Kane," by Pauline Kael, of the classic film from conception to completion leads off this volume. Also included is the complete shooting script of the film by Mankiewicz and Welles with a cutting continuity (a record of the completed movie). Notes have been prepared by Gary Carey on the shooting script, and an Appendix lists the credits of Herman J. Mankiewicz. Illustrated with over eight frames from the film. Index.

MENZEL, JIRI and BOHUMIL HRABAL
Closely Watched Trains
Simon & Schuster, 1971. 144pp. Paper $2.95. Translated by Josef Holzbecher, this is the script of the film made by Czech director, Jiri Menzel. The volume includes twenty-four pages of stills from the film, an Introduction by Bohumil Hrabal, and essays by Jan Zalman and John Simon on the film and the director.

NICHOLS, DUDLEY
Stagecoach
Simon & Schuster, 1971. 152pp. Paper $2.95. The script of the film for which the director, John Ford, won the Best Director Award of the New York Film Critics. An essay on the film by Ernest Haycox is included as is a series of notes on the differences between the screenplay and the actual film. Twenty-four pages of stills from the film are included.

PASOLINI, PIER PAOLO
Oedipus Rex
Simon & Schuster, 1971. 150pp. Paper $2.95. Translated by John Mathews, this volume includes the script of Pasolini's film, complete cast and production credits, an essay on the Oedipus myth by Pasolini, a complete cutting continuity section, and twenty-four pages of stills from the film.

PINTER, HAROLD
Five Screenplays
Methuen, 1971. 367pp. $13.75. This collection of screenplays shows how Harold Pinter impresses his own personality on material which is not originally his own. All of the scripts are based on novels by other writers. The screenplays included are: "The Servant," "The Pumpkin Eater," "The Quiller Memorandum," "Accident," and "The Go-Between."

ROBBE–GRILLET, ALAIN
The Immortal One
Calder & Boyars, 1971. 173pp. $9.50. Translated from the French by A. M. Sheridan Smith, this is the scenario for the film made by writer-director Robbe-Grillet. The author provides an introductory note to the screenplay which is set in Istanbul and is the recollection of a love affair of a young Frenchman with a beautiful girl who is seemingly held in terror. Technical directions are simplified, and there are indications of the sound track. Illustrated with forty stills from the film.

TESHIGAHARA, HIROSHI
Woman in the Dunes
Phaedra, 1966. 94pp. Paper $2.95. Script of the classic Japanese film which won first prize at the Cannes Film Festival in 1965. Illustrated with over 100 photographs from the film.

VAJDA, LADISLAUS
Pandora's Box (Lulu)
Simon & Schuster, 1971. 136pp. Paper $2.95. Translated from the German by Christopher Holme, this is the script of the classic German film directed by G. W. Pabst and based on two plays by Frank Wedekind. The volume includes an essay by Louise Brooks, the star of the film, and an essay on the director's work with Miss Brooks by Lotte H. Eisner. Twenty-four pages of stills from the film are included.

WELLES, ORSON
The Trial
Simon & Schuster, 1971. 176pp. Paper $2.95. Nicholas Fry has provided an English translation and description of the action from the French edition of Welles' film of Kafka's novel. Included in the volume are a short interview with Orson Welles and cast and production credits. Illustrated with twenty-four pages of photographs showing scenes from the film.

WILDER, BILLY and I. A. L. DIAMOND
The Apartment and The Fortune Cookie
Praeger, 1971. 191pp. $6.95. Paper $3.45. The scripts of the two original screenplays. Production and cast credits are included. Illustrated with production stills.

TELEVISION

HISTORIES AND CRITIQUES

BARRETT, MARVIN – Editor
The Alfred I. duPont–Columbia University Survey of Broadcast Journalism: 1970 – 1971
Grosset & Dunlap, 1971. 183pp. $5.95. Paper $1.95. Subtitled "A State of Siege," this is a critical assessment of broadcast news coverage and of the running conflict between government and broadcasters. A feature of the volume is the script of "The Selling of the Pentagon" and an analysis of the furor that broadcast caused between government and broadcasting. Index.

BRITISH BROADCASTING CORPORATION
BBC Handbook 1970
BBC, 1970. 303pp. Paper $2.75. A guide to the developing patterns of broadcasting in England in the 1970's. The two English television networks, the growth of color and satellite communications, the radio services, and the BBC's function of broadcasting to the world in forty languages are all discussed. Illustrated with charts, photographs, and maps. Bibliography. Index.

BROWN, LES
Television: The Business Behind the Box
Harcourt, Brace, 1971. 374pp. $8.95. The Television Editor of "Variety" analyzes the business of television in a documentary of a typical year in the television business. He analyzes the differences between the networks, the conflict between the networks and their affiliate stations, and assesses the quality of the men who control the medium. He explains the rating system, the strategies employed to plan a television season, the role of the Federal Communications Commission, and explores "public" television. Index.

CHERINGTON, PAUL W. and LEON V. HIRSCH, ROBERT BRANDWEIN – Editors
Television Station Ownership: A Case Study of Federal Agency Regulation
Hastings House, 1971. 304pp. $12.50. The articles in this report examine the functioning of a key federal regulatory agency, the FCC, by focusing on its operations in the field of television station licensing. Appendices. Illustrated with charts and tables.

CHESTER, GIRAUD and GARNET R. GARRISON, EDGAR E. WILLIS
Television and Radio
Appleton, 1971. 613pp. $15.95. Revised and updated to take into consideration the changes which have occurred in broadcasting since the date of the last edition, 1963, this Fourth Edition of the text covers both the sociological and technical-presentational sides of television and radio and also reviews important foreign systems. Part One deals with television and radio in society, and Part Two covers television and radio in the studio. The authors have included excerpts from actual scripts and commercials to illustrate the text. The volume is also illustrated with photographs, figures and tables. Glossary of Studio Terms. Bibliography. Index.

DIAMANT, LINCOLN
Television's Classic Commercials
Hastings House, 1971. 305pp. $14.50. This is a study of sixty-nine "classic" commercials aired on United States television between 1948 and 1958. The author assesses not only the sales impact of the messages but also their overall marketing and sociological significance. The commercials are arranged chronologically in categories of products. Each is illustrated and transcribed in analytic script form with notes and a critical commentary. The author also includes a general history of American television commercial advertising since the end of World War II. Illustrated. Appendices. Glossary.

GIBSON, TONY
The Use of E. T. V.: A Handbook for Students and Teachers
Hutchinson, 1970. 127pp. $5.00. Paper $2.75. In this guide, published in England, educational television—and in particular closed circuit television—is shown as a flexible, dynamic, teacher-oriented method of overcoming teacher shortages and improving the effectiveness of the teaching process. Illustrated with photographs and diagrams.

GLUCKSMANN, ANDRE
Violence on the Screen
See Page 600

GORDON, GEORGE N.
Educational Television
Center for Applied Research in Education, 1965. 113pp. $9.00. Dr. Gordon has provided a primer of definitions and explanations of terms and concepts of educational television. The history, financial bases, public service aspects, the effects of educational and instructional television, and the future of both, constitute the content of the book. All of the significant experiments in educational television are discussed. Bibliography. Index.

KEELEY, JOSEPH
The Left-Leaning Antenna
Arlington House, 1971. 320pp. $8.95. The author documents his theory that television networks lean towards the political left in their news and commentary. He suggests that the networks are abusing their public trust and offers a program for concerned

citizens who would achieve a better balance of political viewpoints. Appendices include the text of Vice President Agnew's attack on media bias, delivered in 1969, and the Code of the National Association of Broadcasters.

KENNEDY, DONALD
So You Think You Know TV
Ace, 1971. 160pp. Paper $ .75. A collection of quizzes to test the reader's knowledge of television shows and personalities.

LACKMANN, RON
Remember Television
Putnam, 1971. 192pp. $7.95. A collection of early television listings, original scripts, old ads, and photographs from the programs and of the personalities of television from 1947 through 1958. Index.

MORRIS, NORMAN S.
Television's Child
Little, Brown, 1971. 238pp. $6.95. The author probes the impact of television on children under ten. Based upon an extensive series of interviews with clinical psychiatrists and psychologists, educators, television executives, producers, performers, advertisers, parents, and children themselves, the volume analyzes the effect of television on a child's values; the relationship between violence on television to a child's knowledge; and the motives behind television advertising aimed at small children. Morris includes suggestions on methods of controlling harmful television viewing in the home and the improvement of programming. Bibliography.

PECKOLICK, ALAN – Designer
Rowan and Martin's Laugh-In: The Burbank Edition
World, 1969. Unpaged. $2.95. Compiled from scripts of television's "Laugh-In" in 1968 and 1969, this is a print version of the comedy show. Illustrated with reproductions of great art and with photographs, a special feature is the "Playboy"—type fold-out of Ruth Buzzi in color.

ROBINSON, JOHN – Editor
Educational Television and Radio in Britain
British Broadcasting Corp., 1966. 292pp. $4.50. This volume provides a comprehensive picture of developments in the field of educational progress and of the steps that need to be taken to insure the closest cooperation among all the bodies and institutions involved at national and local levels in England. Index of Topics.

SARSON, EVELYN – Editor
Action for Children's Television
Avon, 1971. 127pp. Paper $1.25. This report on the first national symposium on the effect of television programming and advertising on children presents a program of opposition to "exploiters," suggestions on how the medium might be used purposefully, and a list of substitutes for television in the lives of children. Many distinguished authorities have contributed to the report.

SCHRAMM, WILBUR
The Impact of Educational Television
University of Illinois, 1960. 247pp. $5.00. These essays on educational television in the community and the classroom, on the effect of educational television on children, and a proposed theory for the effect of educational television are based on research conducted at leading universities. Bibliography.

SHAMBERG, MICHAEL and RAINDANCE CORPORATION
Guerrilla Television
Holt, Rinehart, 1971. 160pp. $7.95. Paper $3.95. Raindance Corporation is a video-collective of which Michael Shamberg is a member. They make video tapes and develop information tools. It is their contention that television has a stranglehold on the American mind. They point out how lowcost portable video-tape cameras, video cassettes, and cable television can be used to design alternate television networks that favor portability and decentralization. This how-to manual suggests ways to develop a media ecology and effect social change through information tools and tactics. Illustrated with drawings and photographs.

SHAYON, ROBERT LEWIS
Open to Criticism
Beacon Press, 1971. 324pp. $9.95. The television-radio editor of "Saturday Review" defines the role of the critic in contemporary society and sets forth his own views on the principles and techniques of criticism. The author also provides a selection of his own critical articles, among them discussions of the great political telecasts of the last decade, articles on the politics of the television industry and the regulatory agencies, a discussion of a television commercial, and his own reactions on watching an interview with the father of a student killed at Kent State University. Index.

SLOAN COMMISSION ON CABLE COMMUNICATIONS
On the Cable: The Television of Abundance
McGraw-Hill, 1971. 256pp. Paper $2.95. The Sloan Commission was established in June 1970 to assess the possibilities of cable television. The report shows the concern with social and economic consequences of the new technology and how the public interest might best be served by its growth and development. The report includes a summary of major conclusions and recommendations. Appendices.

THOMEY, TEDD
The Glorious Decade
Ace, 1971. 224pp. Paper $ .95. A history of television in the 1950's. Illustrated with photographs of the stars of the period.

WHITE, DAVID MANNING – Editor
Pop Culture in America
See Page 628

YOUNG, BRIAN – Introducer
I. T. V. 1971.
I. T. V., 1971. 240pp. Paper $3.25. A guide to England's Independent Television Network. The first half of the volume deals with the programs on the network. Other sections include how advertising is controlled, technical operations, and information on the companies included in the network. Illustrated with photographs and maps. Bibliography. Index.

TECHNIQUES OF PRODUCTION

General Reference Works

BURKE, RICHARD C. – Editor
Instructional Television
Indiana University, 1971. 145pp. $7.50. A study of the role of television in education, emphasizing its usefulness for making special resources available to a wider audience and for implementing such innovations as team teaching. Among the subjects studied are the roles of the school administrator, the television teacher, the television administrator, and the evaluation of learning from televised instruction. Selected Bibliography. Notes. Index.

CANTOR, MURIEL G.
The Hollywood TV Producer: His Work and His Audience
Basic Books, 1971. 256pp. $7.95. The author explores the work setting and the professional background of television producers and then shows how producers function and how the networks, directors, actors, and free-lance writers influence the selection of content. The work is based on the author's interviews with eighty Hollywood producers over a two-season period. Miss Cantor contends that the critics of television have been correct in suggesting that, to remain in production, a producer must first please the business organization that finances production. Appendices. List of References. Index.

CHESTER, GIRAUD and GARNET R. GARRISON, EDGAR E. WILLIS
Television and Radio
See Page 622

GERTNER, RICHARD – Editor
International Television Almanac – 1972
Quigley, 1971. 684pp. $15.00. The latest edition of the reference book dealing with the business of television. Statistics, who's who, producing corporations, services, and information on programs are provided. Indices.

GLENN, PETER and MAGGE GOLD
Madison Avenue Europe: 1971 – 1972
Peter Glenn, 1971. Unpaged. Paper $6.95. A handbook for the advertising, film fashion, and photograph industries which lists useful information and addresses for firms and individuals in London, Amsterdam, Brussels, Copenhagen, Stockholm, Paris, Barcelona, Madrid, Milan, Rome, Zurich, Geneva, Vienna, and cities in West Germany. Illustrated. Indices.

GLENN, PETER
Madison Avenue Handbook: 1971
Peter Glenn, 1971. 192 + pp. Paper $6.95. The latest edition of the annual directory listing services for the art director. Cities covered include: New York, Atlanta, Boston, Chicago, Detroit, Philadelphia, Washington, and major cities in Florida and Canada. Information includes advertising agencies, talent agencies, photographers, artists, prop sources, rental sources, magazines, restaurants, hotels, etc.

GRIFFITH, BARTON L. and DONALD W. MACLENNAN – Editors
Improvement of Teaching By Television
University of Missouri, 1969. 238pp. Paper $2.50. Originally published in 1964 and now reissued, this is a collection of the papers from the National Conference of the National Association of Educational Broadcasters at the University of Missouri in 1964. The fundamental matters of philosophy, organizations, and relationships are assessed. Index.

JONES, PETER
The Technique of the Television Cameraman
Hastings House, 1971. 243pp. $14.50. Originally published in 1965 and now revised by Edward Thomas, this study introduces, in non-technical terms, studio equipment and the camera. The author deals at length with composition and movement as well as lighting and the special problems of outside or remote broadcasts. Illustrated with drawings and diagrams. Glossary of Technical Terms. Index.

SHARPS, WALLACE S.
Commercial Television
Fountain Press, 1958. 496pp. $5.50. Subtitled "A Manual of Advertising and Production Techniques," this book covers in detail all major techniques for live and film transmission and includes the latest information on presentation, from five-second slides to advertising magazines. The legal section contains information for advertising practicioners. Also included is a dictionary of over 1,200 terms used in advertising, and film and television production. Illustrated. Index.

STURLEY, K. R.
Sound and Television Broadcasting: General Principles
Iliffe, 1961. 382pp. $10.95. Published in England, this is a text on the basic principles of sound and television broadcasting engineering and operations.

The introductory chapter deals with basic physical principles and their application to broadcasting. Other chapters follow on sound and television studios, telecine and telerecording. Among other topics covered are apparatus, techniques and procedures; outside television broadcasting; amplitude and V. H. F. modulated transmitters; the problems of conveying the sound and television program frequencies; and communicating between the various studio centers and transmitting centers. The text is amplified by photographs and over 200 line drawings. Index.

Script Writing

BLISS, EDWARD and JOHN M. PATTERSON
Writing News for Broadcast
Columbia, 1971. 298pp. $15.00. This volume is designed to serve as a text on how to write news for radio and television. Techniques for reporting the increasingly complex issues in the concise language required by the media are explained in detail with examples taken from actual news scripts. The importance of conversational style and its influence on the print media, and writing of leads, bulletins, and material to be voiced over film are covered. An illustrated concluding chapter on "The Evening News" provides a close look at the organization of the network evening news broadcast. In it are reproduced the complete scripts of three major network programs illustrated with photographs of the television image. Foreword by Fred W. Friendly. Bibliography. Index.

HALL, MARK W.
Broadcast Journalism: An Introduction to News Writing
Hastings House, 1971. 159pp. $6.95. Paper $5.65. The author covers the basics of radio-television news writing style as well as providing information and guidelines for handling the major types of stories that a broadcast journalist might be expected to cover during his career. Professor Hall combines the specialized techniques of writing associated with the world of broadcast journalism with some of the more important approaches developed over the years by experienced reporters and writers. Appendices include a style guide, common writing errors, and UPI coverage of the Paris Peace Talks and Apollo Eleven. Index.

WIMER, ARTHUR and DALE BRIX
Workbook for Radio and TV News Editing and Writing
Wm. C. Brown, 1971. 287pp. Spiral bound $9.25. A third edition of the book originally published in 1959. The purpose of the volume is to offer material of professional standards for use in training students to prepare news for the air. Material for the writing and editing exercises was drawn from actual news situations. Appendices.

Acting and Career Opportunities

HAYMAN, RONALD
Techniques of Acting
See Page 595

HYDE, STUART W.
Television and Radio Announcing
Houghton, Mifflin, 1971. 549pp. $13.25. Originally published in 1959 and now revised to include new data, new emphases, and new specializations. All material retained from the first edition of this text was thoroughly reworked and updated including the chapters on voice and diction, the International Phonetic Alphabet, and foreign pronunciation. The volume now presents a realistic picture of the broadcasting industry today, describes the kinds of jobs available to announcers, and discusses the skills and personal characteristics necessary for success in the field.

BIOGRAPHIES OF TELEVISION PERSONALITIES

FRISCHAUER, WILLI
Will You Welcome Now ... David Frost
Hawthorn, 1971. 248pp. $6.95. A biography of the television interviewer and entertainer. The author documents Frost's interviewing methods and his handling of diverse figures from politics and the entertainment industry. Illustrated with sixteen pages of photographs. Bibliography. Index.

REYBURN, WALLACE
Frost: Anatomy of a Success
Macdonald, 1968. 154pp. $4.95. An "in-depth" study of the television interviewer/humorist/author/businessman—David Frost. Sixteen pages of photographs are included.

TELEVISION SCRIPTS

AVERSON, RICHARD and DAVID MANNING WHITE – Editors
Electronic Drama: Television Plays of the Sixties
Beacon Press, 1971. 355pp. $9.95. A collection of nine television plays with a Preface by the editors and an Introduction by Hubbell Robinson. Illustrated with photographs from the productions. Cast and production credits. Biographies of playwrights.

Tad Mosel: That's Where the Town's Going
Sidney Carroll: Big Deal in Laredo
Arnold Perl: Who Do You Kill?
Ernest Kinoy: Blacklist
Sam Peckinpah: Noon Wine
Ellen M. Violett: The Trap of Solid Gold

Loring Mandel: Do Not Go Gentle Into that Good Night
Ellison Carroll: Teacher, Teacher
Richard Levinson and William Link: My Sweet Charlie

CAPOTE, TRUMAN and ELEANOR PERRY
Trilogy
Colier, 1971. 279pp. Paper $2.95. Originally published in 1969, this is a collection of three stories by Truman Capote and the television adaptations of those stories by Capote and Eleanor Perry. Essays by Capote and Frank Perry, and notes on the adaptations complete the volume. Illustrated with photographs. Scripts included: "Miriam," "Among the Paths to Eden," and "A Christmas Memory."

CURTEIS, IAN
Long Voyage Out of War
Calder & Boyars, 1971. 259pp. $7.50. Paper $3.95. A trilogy of television plays about the effects of war on the same protagonist at different times and in different societies. The first play, "The Gentle Invasion," evokes the atmosphere and spirit of a rural community at the outbreak of World War II. "Battle at Tematangi" is set in the Philippines in 1954 and finds the protagonist caught up in a revolutionary war. "The Last Enemy" is set in 1976 and centers on the conflict of the protagonist as an idealist caught between trying to help society as a whole and trying to help a sick individual within it. The trilogy was specially commissioned by B. B. C. Television.

OSBORNE, JOHN
The Right Prospectus
Faber & Faber, 1970. 48pp. $3.95. Paper $1.95. Osborne's new play was written especially for television and concerns a middle-aged couple who enroll as pupils in an English public school.

OSBORNE, JOHN
Very Like A Whale
Faber & Faber, 1971. 54pp. $4.25. Paper $1.95. A television play with a powerful theme of a famous and respected man tearing his life to bits.

RADIO

HISTORIES AND CRITIQUES

BRIDSON, D. G.
Prospero and Ariel: The Rise and Fall of Radio
Gollancz, 1971. 352pp. $10.75. A personal recollection by the writer and producer for BBC Radio. He discusses his own memorable program from 1935 to 1969 and the personalities he has met and with whom he has worked. Eight pages of photographs. Index.

BRIGGS, ASA
The History of Broadcasting in the United Kingdom: The War of Words – Volume III
Oxford, 1970. 766pp. $10.75. This volume covers the period from 1939 to 1945 and is concerned with the impact of the Second World War on the structure, organization, and programs of the BBC. The role of the BBC inside and outside Britain within the context of the general political and military history of the war is examined. Illustrated with twenty-four plates and diagrams and charts in the text. Bibliographical Note. Appendices. Index.

BRITISH BROADCASTING CORPORATION
BBC Handbook 1970
See Page 622

CHESTER, GIRAUD and GARNET R. GARRISON, EDGAR E. WILLIS
Television and Radio
See Page 622

KOCH, HOWARD
The Panic Broadcast
Avon, 1971. 163pp. Paper $ .95. Originally published in 1970 and now reissued, this is a history of Orson Welles' radio show, "Invasion from Mars." Photographs, cartoons, and newspaper articles of the aftermath of the broadcast are included as is the complete script. In an introductory interview, Arthur C. Clarke provides comments on possible life on Mars.

PASSMAN, ARNOLD
The Deejays
Macmillan, 1971. 320pp. $7.95. A history of record players on radio. It is also the history of the countrywide radio stations and the recording companies and their role. Many of the leading disc jockeys are studied in detail including: Al Jarvis, Freddie Robbins, Jazzbo Collins, Alan Freed, Murray Kaufman, and Martin Block. Index.

PERRY, DICK
Not Just a Sound: The Story of WLW
Prentice–Hall, 1971. 242pp. $6.95. A history of the Cincinnati radio station, WLW, the winner of the first George Peabody Award. The volume includes thirty-two pages of photographs. Index.

TECHNIQUES OF PRODUCTION

Script Writing

HALL, MARK W.
Broadcast Journalism: An Introduction to News Writing
See Page 625

Sound Recording and Audio Techniques

BRITISH BROADCASTING CORPORATION
Better Sound: Study Notes
British Broadcasting Corp., 1968. 16pp. Paper $ .60. These notes accompanied six radio programs broadcast in England in 1968 and provide an independent short guide to sound reproduction and recording principles and techniques. The pamphlet is illustrated with diagrams. Book List.

STURLEY, K. R.
Sound and Television Broadcasting: General Principles
See Page 624

Acting

HYDE, STUART W.
Television and Radio Announcing
See Page 625

RADIO SCRIPTS

KOCH, HOWARD
Invasion from Mars
See entry in previous column

REED, HENRY
Hilda Tablet and Others
BBC Publications, 1971. 204pp. $7.75. Originally presented on the Third Programme of the BBC, these four radio plays deal with the researches of Herbert Reeve into the life of the novelist, Richard Shewin. The four pieces are regarded by many critics in England as the funniest and most sustained social comedy written for radio.

REED, HENRY
The Streets of Pompeii and Other Plays for Radio
BBC Publications, 1971. 335pp. $11.50. Six radio plays originally broadcast in England between 1950 and 1955. All have Italian themes and settings.

PART FOUR: THE MASS MEDIA AND THE POPULAR ARTS

GENERAL HISTORIES AND CRITIQUES

ADAMS, ROBERT – Editor
Creativity in Communications
New York Graphic Society, 1971. 152pp. $20.00. A seminar in book form, conducted by experts in the communications industry. Focusing on creative problem-solving in advertising and sales promotion in all media—from film to billboards—the book is illustrated with 270 black-and-white images and with fifteen illustrations in color. The volume also includes a recording, "Understanding Sound." The twenty essays include works on press advertising, research, direct mail advertising, agency relations, etc. Index.

DEVOL, KENNETH S. – Editor
Mass Media and the Supreme Court
Hastings House, 1971. 369pp. $14.50. This work contains fifty-two key discussions of the United States Supreme Court, under the direction of Chief Justice Earl Warren, which involve freedom of expression—the opinions of the Court along with concurrences and dissents. Emphasis is placed on the forty-three major media decisions handed down from 1953 through the "Pentagon Papers" case in 1971. Also included are fifty reprints of important articles on these topics from various journals of law and mass communication. Appendices include amendments to the U.S. Constitution, Justices of the U.S. Supreme Court, a Glossary of Legal Terms used in the text, and a Table of Cases. Index.

WHITE, DAVID MANNING – Editor
Pop Culture in America
Quadrangle, 1970. 280pp. $6.95. Paper $2.45. A collection of articles from "The New York Times" dealing with radio, television, film, theatre, music, art, and books. The editor has provided an Introduction, and other contributors include: Marya Mannes, Howard Taubman, David Karp, Carl Foreman, Tyrone Guthrie, Richard Schickel, John Canaday, and Barnaby Conrad. List of Suggested Reading. Index.

WORKS ON THE ADVERTISING INDUSTRY

DELLA FEMINA, JERRY
From Those Wonderful Folks Who Gave You Pearl Harbor
Pocket Books, 1971. 256pp. Paper $1.25. Originally published in 1970 and now reissued, this is a behind-the-scenes look at the world of advertising agencies.

OGILVY DAVID
Confessions of an Advertising Man
Ballantine, 1971. 152pp. Paper $ .95. Originally published in 1963 and now reissued, this is a discussion of the complex business of advertising. The author describes the management of an advertising agency, and asks the question, "Should advertising be abolished?"

WORKS ON MARSHALL McLUHAN

McLUHAN, MARSHALL
Understanding Media
McGraw–Hill, 1965. 364pp. Paper $1.95. Marshall McLuhan raises two fundamental questions about the modern world in this reprint of the 1964 publication. "What are communications and how do communications affect mankind?" Introduction. Bibliography.

McNAMARA, EUGENE – Editor
The Interior Landscape: The Literary Criticism of Marshall McLuhan
McGraw–Hill, 1971. 239pp. Paper $2.95. Originally published in 1969 and now reissued, this volume contains fourteen essays which attempt to reveal Marshall McLuhan as an outstanding and unique literary critic.

MILLER, JONATHAN
Marshall McLuhan
Viking, 1971. 133pp. $4.95. Paper $1.75. An assessment of the religious, cultural, and intellectual values in McLuhan's life that have most influenced his attitudes. Bibliography. Index.

AUTHOR INDEX

TITLE INDEX

LIST OF PUBLISHERS

A. E. T. A.
See: American Theater Association

AMS Press, Inc.
56 East 13 Street
New York, N. Y. 10003

ASC Holding Corp.
1782 North Orange Drive
Hollywood, Calif. 90028

Abbey Library
See: Murray Sales & Service Co

Abelard—Schuman, Ltd.
257 Park Avenue South
New York, N. Y. 10010

Abingdon Press
201 Eighth Avenue South
Nashville, Tenn. 37202

Abrams (Harry N.), Inc.
110 East 59 Street
New York, N. Y. 10022

Ace Books
1120 Avenue of the Americas
New York, N. Y. 10036

Adams & Dart
40 Gay Street
Bath, Som., England

Addison—Wesley Publishing Co.
Reading, Mass. 01867

Africana Publishing Corp.
101 Fifth Avenue
New York, N. Y. 10003

Ahrens Book Co.
116 West 14 Street
New York, N. Y. 10011

Airmont Publishers
c/o Associated Booksellers
147 Mc Kinley Avenue
Bridgeport, Conn. 06606

Albyn Press
50 Alexandra Road
London SW19, England

Aldine—Atherton, Inc.
529 S. Wabash Avenue
Chicago, Ill. 60605

Aldine Publishing Co.
22 South Audley Street
London W1, England

Alexander (Burt)
810 East 48th Street
Brooklyn, N. Y. 11203

Alfred Music Co,
75 Chane Drive
Port Washington, N. Y. 11050

Allen (George) & Unwin, Ltd.
40 Museum Street
London WC1, England

Allen (Ian), Ltd.
Terminal House
Shepperton, England

Allen (W. H.) & Co., Ltd.
43 Essex Street
London WC2, England

Allograph Press
220 Fifth Avenue
New York, N. Y. 10011

Allyn & Bacon, Inc.
470 Atlantic Avenue
Boston, Mass. 02210

Almqvist & Wiksell
26 Gamla Brogatan
PO Box 63
Stockholm 1, Sweden

American Academy of Dramatic Arts
120 Madison Avenue
New York, N. Y. 10016

American Book Co.
c/o Van Nostrand—Reinhold
450 West 33 Street
New York, N. Y. 10001

American Council on Education
1 Dupont Circle, NW
Washington, D. C. 20036

American Heritage Press
1221 Avenue of the Americas
New York, N. Y. 10020

American Library Association
50 East Huron Street
Chicago, Ill. 60611

American R. D. M. Corp.
148 Lafayette Street
New York, N. Y. 10013

American Scholar Publications
777 Third Avenue
New York, N. Y. 10017

American Society of Cinematographers
Box 2320
Hollywood, Calif. 90028

American Society of Composers, Authors and Publishers
575 Madison Avenue
New York, N.Y. 10022

American Theatre Association
1317 F Street, NW
Washington, D.C. 20004

American TV—Radio Commercials Festival
30 East 60 Street
New York, N.Y. 10022

Amphoto
915 Broadway
New York, N.Y. 10010

Anchorage Press
Cloverlot
Anchorage, Ky. 40223

And (Metin)
Vali Dr. Resit Cad. 19/16
Kavaklidere/Ankara, Turkey

Angus & Robertson, Ltd.
2 Fisher Street
London WC1, England

Antioch Press
c/o Kent State University Press
Kent, Ohio 44242

Apollo
73 Fillebrook Road
London E11, England

Apollo Editions, Inc.
666 Fifth Avenue
New York, N.Y. 10019

Appleton—Century—Crofts
440 Park Avenue South
New York, N.Y. 10016

Arbor House
757 Third Avenue
New York, N.Y. 10017

Arc Books
219 Park Avenue South
New York, N.Y. 10003

Arcadia House
c/o Crown Publishers
419 Park Avenue South
New York, N.Y. 10016

Archer House
c/o Howard Moorepark
444 East 82 Street
New York, N.Y. 10028

Architectural Book Publishing Co.
10 East 40 Street
New York, N.Y. 10016

Archive Press
603 Madison Avenue
New York, N.Y. 10022

Archon Books
Hamden, Conn. 06514

Arco Publications, Ltd.
3 Upper James Street
London W1, England

Arco Publishing Co.
219 Park Avenue South
New York, N.Y. 10003

Argonaut, Inc.
737 N. Michigan Avenue
Chicago, Ill. 60611

Argonaut, Inc.
See: Zeno Publishers

Arlington House, Inc.
81 Centre Avenue
New Rochelle, N.Y. 10801

Arms & Armour Press
2—6 Hampstead High Street
London NW3, England

Arno Press
330 Madison Avenue
New York, N.Y. 10017

Arnold (E.J.) & Son, Ltd.
Butterley Street, Hunslet Lane
Leeds, England

Arnold (Edward), Ltd.
25 Hill Street
London W1, England

Arrow Books, Ltd.
See: Hutchinson Publishing Group

Art Fair, Inc.
80 Fourth Avenue
New York, N.Y. 10003

Artemis Press, Ltd.
Sedgwick Park
Horsham, Sussex, England

Artia, Prague
See: W. Heffer & Sons

Arts Council of Great Britain
105 Piccadilly
London W1, England

Arts, Inc.
667 Madison Avenue
New York, N.Y. 10021

Asia Publishing House
420 Lexington Avenue
New York, N.Y. 10017

Associated Council of the Arts
1564 Broadway
New York, N.Y. 10036

Associated Publishers, Inc.
1538 9 Street, SW
Washington, D.C. 20001

Association for Childhood Education
3615 Wisconsin Avenue NW
Washington, D.C. 20016

Association Press
291 Broadway
New York, N.Y. 10007

Astor–Honor, Inc.
67 Southfield Avenue
Stamford, Conn. 06904

Atheneum Publishers
122 East 42 Street
New York, N.Y. 10017

Athlone Press
See: Humanities Press

Athlone Press
c/o University of London
4 Gower Street
London WC1, England

Atlantic–Little, Brown
See: Little, Brown & Co.

Atlantic Monthly Press
8 Arlington Street
Boston, Mass. 02116

Audel (Theodore) & Co.
4300 West 62 Street
Indianapolis, Ind. 46268

Augsburg Publishing House
426 South Fifth Street
Minneapolis, Minn. 55415

Aurora Publishing, Inc.
170 Fourth Avenue North
Nashville, Tenn. 37219

Avon Books
959 Eighth Avenue
New York, N.Y. 10019

Award Books
See: New American Library

B.B.C. Publications
35 Marylebone High Street
London W1, England

Bailey Bros. & Swinfen, Ltd.
Warner House
Folkestone, Kent, England

Baker (John) Publishers, Ltd.
4, 5, 6 Soho Square
London W1, England

Baker (Walter H.) Co.
100 Chauncy Street
Boston, Mass. 02111

Ballantine Books
101 Fifth Avenue
New York, N.Y. 10003

Bantam Books
666 Fifth Avenue
New York, N.Y. 10019

Barker (Arthur), Ltd.
5 Winsley Street
London W1, England

Barmerlea Book Sales, Ltd.
"Annandale", North End Road
London NW11, England

Barnes (A.S.) & Co.
Forsgate Drive
Cranbury, N.J. 08512

Barnes & Noble Books
10 East 53 Street
New York, N.Y. 10022

Barrie & Jenkins
2 Clement's Inn
London WC2, England

Barrie & Rockliff
See: Barrie & Jenkins

Barron's Educational Series
113 Crossways Park Drive
Woodbury, N.Y. 11797

Bartholomew House
205 East 42 Street
New York, N. Y. 10017

Basic Books
10 East 53 Street
New York, N. Y. 10022

Basic Books
c/o Transatlantic Book Service
51 Weymouth Street
London W1, England

Batsford (B. T.), Ltd.
4 Fitzhardinge Street
London W1, England

Beacon Press
25 Beacon Street
Boston, Mass. 02108

Beaumont (Cyril W.)
68 Bedford Court Mansions
Bedford Avenue
London WC1, England

Beginnings of the American Film
GPO Box 2552
New York, N. Y. 10001

Bell (G.) & Sons, Ltd.
6 Portugal Street
London WC2, England

Belle–Maria, Inc.
130 East 63 Street
New York, N. Y. 10021

Benn (Ernest), Ltd.
154 Fleet Street
London EC4, England

Berkley Publishing Corp.
200 Madison Avenue
New York, N. Y. 10016

Bete (Channing L.) Co.
Box 112
Greenfield, Mass. 01301

Bethany Press
2640 Pine Street
St. Louis, Mo. 63166

Biblo & Tannen Booksellers
63 Fourth Avenue
New York, N. Y. 10003

Binsfords & Mort
2505 SE 11 Avenue
Portland, Oregon 97242

Birks (Reginald)
c/o Empire Civic Theatre
Sunderland, Durham, England

Black (A. & C.), Ltd.
4, 5, 6 Soho Square
London W1, England

Blackie & Sons, Ltd.
Bishopbriggs
Glasgow, Scotland

Blackwell (Basil)
108 Cowley Road
Oxford, England

Blaisdell Publishing Co.
See: Xerox Education Group

Blandford Press, Ltd.
167 High Holborn
London WC1, England

Bles (Geoffrey), Ltd.
59 Brompton Road
London SW3, England

Blom (Benjamin), Inc.
2521 Broadway
New York, N. Y. 10025

Blond (Anthony), Ltd.
See: Holt–Blond, Ltd.

Bloomsbury Bookshop
31–35 Great Ormond St.
London WC1, England

Bobbs–Merrill Co.
4300 West 62 Street
Indianapolis, Ind. 46268

Bodley Head, Ltd
9 Bow Street
London WC2, England

Bonanza Press
Box 2037
Santa Cruz, Calif. 95060

Bond Street Publishers, Ltd.
124 New Bond Street
London W1, England

Bond Wheelwright Co.
Porter's Landing
Freeport, Maine 04032

Book Sales, Inc.
352 Park Avenue South
New York, N. Y. 10010

Books for Libraries
50 Liberty Avenue
Freeport, N.Y. 11520

Boosey & Hawkes, Inc.
Oceanside, N.Y. 11572

Boosey & Hawkes, Music Publishers, Ltd.
295 Regent Street
London W1, England

Borden Publishing Co.
1855 West Main Street
Alhambra, Calif. 91801

Boston Book & Art Publishers
c/o Worldwide Books
1075 Commonwealth Avenue
Boston, Mass. 02215

Bowes & Bowes, Ltd.
9 Bow Street
London WC2, England

Bowker (R. R.) Co.
1180 Avenue of the Americas
New York, N.Y. 10036

Bramante Editions
See: Speedimpex

Bramhall House
See: Bailey Bros. & Winfen, Ltd.

Branch–Smith, Inc.
120 St. Louis Avenue
Fort Worth, Texas 76101

Branden Press
221 Columbus Avenue
Boston, Mass. 02116

Branford (Charles T.) Co.
28 Union Street
Newton Centre, Mass. 02159

Braziller (George), Inc.
1 Park Avenue
New York, N.Y. 10016

Brill (E. J.)
1966 Broadway
New York, N.Y. 10023

British & American Film Press
c/o Cinema/TV Today
142 Wardour Street
London W1, England

British Broadcasting Corporation
See: B. B. C. Publications Corp.

British Film Institute
81 Dean Street
London W1, England

British Information Services
845 Third Avenue
New York, N.Y. 10022

British Standards Institution
2 Park Street
London W1, England

British Universities Film Council
72 Dean Street
London W1, England

Broadcast Music, Inc.
589 Fifth Avenue
New York, N.Y. 10017

Brockhampton Press, Ltd.
Leicester, England

Brodie (James), Ltd.
15 Queen Square
Bath, Som., England

Brown University Press
129 Waterman Street
Providence, R.I. 02912

Brown (William C.) Co.
135 South Locust
Dubuque, Iowa 52001

Bruce Publishing Co.
866 Third Avenue
New York, N.Y. 10022

Brussel & Brussel
80 Fifth Avenue
New York, N.Y. 10011

Buffalo Spectrum Press
See: State Univ. of N.Y. at Buffalo

Burgess Publishing Company
426 South Sixth Street
Minneapolis, Minn. 55415

Burke Publishing Co., Ltd.
14 John Street
London WC1, England

Burns & Oates, Ltd.
25 Ashley Place
London SW1, England

Business Books, Ltd.
103–110 Waterloo Road
London SE1, England

Business Publications, Ltd.
See: Business Books, Ltd.

Butterworth & Co.
88 Kingsway
London WC2, England

Byron (The) Press
Department of English
University of Nottingham
Nottingham, England

C. P. A. S. Publications
Falcon Court
32 Fleet Street
London EC4, England

Caithness Books
21 High Street
Thurso, Caithness, England

Calder & Boyars, Ltd.
18 Brewer Street
London W1, England

Cambridge University Press
32 East 57 Street
New York, N. Y. 10022

Cambridge University Press
200 Euston Road
London NW1, England

Campfield Press
St. Albans, Herts., England

Campton (D.)
35 Liberty Road
Glenfield, Leicester, England

Cape Goliard Press, Ltd.
See: Cape (Jonathan), Ltd.

Cape (Jonathan), Ltd.
30 Bedford Square
London WC1, England

Cappelli Editore
See: Speedimpex

Capricorn Press
705 Anacapa Street
Santa Barbara, Calif. 93101

Carlton Press, Inc.
84 Fifth Avenue
New York, N. Y. 10011

Carnation Press
Box 101
State College, Pa. 16801

Carnegie Institute of Technology
Schenley Park
Pittsburgh, Pa. 15213

Carnegie Institute of Washington
1530 P Street NW
Washington, D. C. 20005

Carson & Comerford, Ltd.
19–21 Tavistock Street
London WC2, England

Case—Western Reserve University
c/o Press of Case Western Reserve Univ.
Cleveland, Ohio 44106

Cass (Frank) & Co., Ltd.
67 Great Russell Street
London WC1, England

Cassell & Co., Ltd.
35 Red Lion Square
London WC1, England

Catholic University of America Press
620 Michigan Avenue NE
Washington, D. C. 20017

Caxton Printers, Ltd.
312 Main Street
Caldwell, Idaho 83605

Celebrity Service, Inc.
171 West 57 Street
New York, N. Y. 10019

Center for American Studies
Brussels, Belgium

Center for Applied Research in Education, Inc.
70 Fifth Avenue
New York, N. Y. 10011

Central Book Company
850 DeKalb Avenue
Brooklyn, N. Y. 11221

Central Books, Ltd.
37 Gray's Inn Road
London WC1, England

Century House, Inc.
Watkins Glen, N. Y. 14891

Chandler Publishing Co.
124 Spear Street
San Francisco, Calif. 94105

Chapman (G. K.), Ltd.
2 Ross Road
London SE25, England

Chappell & Co., Ltd.
50 New Bond Street
London W1, England

Chatham Press, Inc.
15 Wilmont Lane
Riverside, Conn. 06878

Chatto & Windus, Ltd.
40–42 William IV Street
London WC2, England

Chelsea House Publishers
70 West 40 Street
New York, N.Y. 10018

Cherokee Publishing Co.
Box 1081
Covington, Ga. 30209

Chester House Publications
See: Methodist Book Room

Chicorel Library Publishing Corp.
330 West 58 Street
New York, N.Y. 10019

Children's Press, Inc.
1224 West Van Buren Street
Chicago, Illinois 60607

Children's Theatre Press
See: Anchorage Press

Chilton Book Company
401 Walnut Street
Philadelphia, Pa. 19106

Christopher Press
c/o Christopher Publishing House
53 Billings Road
North Quincy, Mass. 02171

Cinefax
Box 151
Kew Gardens, N.Y. 11415

Cine/Graphic Publications
Box 430
Hollywood, Calif. 90028

Cinema/TV Today
142 Wardour Street
London W1, England

Citadel Press
222 Park Avenue South
New York, N.Y. 10003

Citation Press
See: Scholastic Book Services

City Lights Books
1562 Grant Avenue
San Francisco, Calif. 94133

Clark (Arthur H.) Co.
1264 South Central Avenue
Glendale, Calif. 91204

Clark Publishing Co.
500 Hyacinth Avenue
Highland Park, Ill. 60035

Clark Publishing Co.
Pocatello, Idaho 83201

Clarke, Irwin & Co., Ltd.
Clarwin House
701 St. Clair Avenue West
Toronto, Ontario, Canada

Clematis Press, Ltd.
18 Old Church Street
London SW3, England

Cliff's Notes, Inc.
Lincoln, Nebraska 68501

Clifton Books
200 Madison Avenue
New York, N.Y. 10016

Clifton Books
New England House
New England Street
Brighton, England

Clifton Press
Newtown, Montgomery, England

Coach House Press
53 West Jackson Boulevard
Chicago, Illinois 60604

Coleman–Ross
See: Scribners

College & University Press
263 Chapel Street
New Haven, Conn. 06513

College Printing & Typing Company
453 West Gilman Street
Madison, Wisc. 53703

Collier Books
866 Third Avenue
New York, N.Y. 10022

Collier–Macmillan Publishers
35 Red Lion Square
London WC1, England

Collingridge (W.H. & L.), Ltd.
Hamlyn House
42 The Centre
Feltham, England

Collins (Wm.) Sons & Co.
215 Park Avenue South
New York, N.Y. 10003

Collins (William) Sons & Co., Ltd.
14 St. James's Place
London SW1, England

Columbia University Press
562 West 113 Street
New York, N.Y. 10025

Combridge (C.), Ltd.
Wrentham Street
Birmingham, England

Community Renewal Society
116 South Michigan Avenue
Chicago, Illinois 60603

Constable & Co., Ltd.
10 Orange Street
London WC2, England

Cooper Square Publishers
59 Fourth Avenue
New York, N.Y. 10003

Corgi Books, Ltd.
57–59 Uxbridge Road, Ealing
London W5, England

Cornell University Press
124 Roberts Place
Ithaca, N.Y. 14850

Cornerstone Library
630 Fifth Avenue
New York, N.Y. 10020

Country Life Books
c/o Hamlyn Publishing Group
Hamlyn House, 42 The Centre
Feltham, Middlesex, England

Coward, McCann and Geoghegan
200 Madison Avenue
New York, N.Y. 10016

Cowles Book Company
114 West Illinois Street
Chicago, Illinois 60610

Crescendo Publishing Co.
48–50 Melrose Street
Boston, Mass. 02116

Crescent Books
See: Crown Publishers

Cresset Press
See: Barrie & Jenkins

Crest Publishing
210 Fifth Avenue
New York, N.Y. 10010

Criterion Books
257 Park Avenue South
New York, N.Y. 10010

Criterion Music Corp.
150 West 55 Street
New York, N.Y. 10019

Critical Digest
GPO Box 2403
New York, N.Y. 10001

Crogham (A.)
17 Coburgh Mansions
Hander Street
London WC1, England

Crowell (Thomas Y.) Co.
666 Fifth Avenue
New York, N.Y. 10019

Crowell Collier & Macmillan
866 Third Avenue
New York, N.Y. 10022

Crown Publishers
419 Park Avenue South
New York, N.Y. 10016

Curtis Books
Chestnut East Building
Philadelphia, Pa. 19107

Da Capo Press
227 West 17 Street
New York, N.Y. 10011

Dance Horizons
1801 East 26 Street
Brooklyn, N.Y. 11229

Dance Magazine
268 West 47 Street
New York, N.Y. 10036

Dance Perspectives
29 East 9 Street
New York, N.Y. 10003

Dance Publications Co.
See: Borden Publishing Co.

Dance Teachers' Association
See: International Dance Teachers' Assoc.

Dancing Times, Ltd.
18 Hand Court
London WC1, England

Darton, Longman & Todd, Ltd.
85 Gloucester Road
London SW7, England

Darwen Finlayson, Ltd.
50A Bell Street
Henley-on-Thames, England

David & Charles, Ltd.
South Devon House
Railway Station
Newton Abbot, Devon, England

Davies (Peter), Ltd.
15–16 Queen Street, Mayfair
London W1, England

Davis (F. A.) Co.
1915 Arch Street
Philadelphia, Pa. 19103

Davis Publications
229 Park Avenue South
New York, N. Y. 10002

Davis Publishing Co.
250 Potrero Street
Santa Cruz, Calif. 95060

Davis–Poynter, Ltd.
Broadwick House
Broadwick Street
London W1, England

Davis (Rupert Hart)
3 Upper James Street
Golden Square
London W1, England

Dawson (Wm.) & Sons, Ltd.
Cannon House
Folkestone, Kent, England

Dawsons of Pall Mall
Cannon House
Folkestone, Kent, England

Day (John) Co.
257 Park Avenue South
New York, N. Y. 10010

De Graff (John), Inc.
34 Oak Avenue
Tuckahoe, N. Y. 10707

Deane (H. F. W.), Ltd.
31 Museum Street
London WC1, England

Definition Press
39 Grove Street
New York, N. Y. 10014

Delacorte Press
See: Dell Publishing Co.

Dell Publishing Co.
750 Third Avenue
New York, N. Y. 10017

Denison (T. S.) & Co.
5100 West 82 Street
Minneapolis, Minn. 55431

Dent (J. M.) & Sons, Ltd.
10–13 Bedford Street
London WC2, England

Depot Press
See: University of Illinois Press

Deutsch (Andre), Ltd.
105 Great Russell Street
London WC1, England

Dial Press
750 Third Avenue
New York, N. Y. 10017

Dickenson Publishing Co.
16561 Ventura Blvd.
Encino, Calif. 91316

Dillon's University Bookshop, Ltd.
1 Malet Street
London WC1, England

Dobson Books, Ltd.
80 Kensington Church Street
London W8, England

Dodd, Mead & Co.
79 Madison Avenue
New York, N. Y. 10016

Dolmen Press, Ltd.
8 Herbert Place
Dublin 2, Eire, Ireland

Dolphin Book Co., Ltd.
1A Southmoor Road
Oxford, England

Dorrance & Co.
1809 Callowhill Street
Philadelphia, Pa. 19130

Doubleday & Company
277 Park Avenue
New York, N.Y. 10017

Douglas Book Corp.
652 West 163 Street
New York, N.Y. 10032

Dover Publications
180 Varick Street
New York, N.Y. 10014

Drama Book Specialists/Publishers
150 West 52 Street
New York, N.Y. 10019

Dramatic Publishing Co.
86 East Randolph Street
Chicago, Illinois 60601

Dramatists Play Service
440 Park Avenue South
New York, N.Y. 10016

Duchy Press
8 Lancaster Road
Harrogate, Yorkshire
England

Duckworth (Gerald) & Co., Ltd.
43 Gloucester Crescent
London NW1, England

Duell, Sloan & Pearce
1716 Locust Street
Des Moines, Iowa 50336

Duffy (James) & Co., Ltd.
21 Shaw Street
Dublin 2, Eire
Ireland

Dufour Editions
Chester Springs, Pa. 19425

Duke University Press
Box 6697
College Station
Durham, N. Carolina 27708

Dutton (E.P.) & Co.
201 Park Avenue South
New York, N.Y. 10003

Eakins Press
155 East 42 Street
New York, N.Y. 10017

East–West Center Press
535 Ward Avenue
Honolulu, Hawaii 96814

Easton Valley Press
Box 113
Ansonia Station
New York, N.Y. 10023

Edinburgh University Press
22 George Square
Edinburgh, Scotland

Editions du Centre National
de la Recherche Scientifique
15 Quai Anatole–France
Paris V11e, France

Edizione Scientifiche Italiane
Naples, Italy

Edwards Bros.
See: MacIntosh (A.N.)

Eerdmans (Wm. B.) Publishing
255 Jefferson Avenue SE
Grand Rapids, Mich. 49502

Efron (George)
41 West 83 Street
New York, N.Y. 10024

Eldridge Publishing Co.
Franklin, Ohio 45005

Elek (Paul) Books, Ltd.
54–58 Caledonian Road
London N1, England

Elsevier Publishing
52 Vanderbilt Avenue
New York, N.Y. 10017

Elsevier Publishing Co.
61 Pall Mall
London SW1, England

Embassy Theatre Arts
Box 1231
Englewood Cliffs, N. J. 07632

English Folk Dance and Song Society
Cecil Sharp House
2 Regent's Park Road
London NW1, England

English Theatre Guild, Ltd.
Ascot House
52 Dean Street
London W1, England

English Universities Press, Ltd.
St. Paul's House
Warwick Lane
London EC4, England

Epworth Press
27 Marylebone Road
London NW1, England

Eriksson (Paul S.)
119 West 57 Street
New York, N.Y. 10019

European Publishers Representatives
36 West 61 Street
New York, N.Y. 10023

Evans Brothers, Ltd.
Montague House
Russell Square
London WC1, England

Evans (M.) & Co.
216 East 49 Street
New York, N.Y. 10017

Evans Publishing Co.
50 West 57 Street
New York, N.Y. 10019

Evans Publishing Co.
Box 22
Everglades, Florida 33929

Evelyn, Adams & Mackay
c/o Adams & Dart
40 Gay Street
Bath, Som., England

Evelyn (Hugh), Ltd.
9 Fitzroy Square
London W1, England

Exposition Press
50 Jericho Turnpike
Jericho, N.Y. 11753

Expression Company
PO Box 11
Magnolia, Mass. 01930

Eyre & Spottiswoode, Ltd.
11 New Fetter Lane
London EC4, England

Faber & Faber, Ltd.
3 Queen Square
London WC1, England

Fairleigh Dickinson University Press
Rutherford, New Jersey 07070

Falcon Books
c/o C.P.A.S. Publications
32 Fleet Street
London EC4, England

Falcon Enterprises
c/o Crown Publishers
419 Park Avenue South
New York, N.Y. 10016

Fallon (C. J.). Ltd.
43 Parkgate Street
Dublin 8, Eire
Ireland

Farrar, Straus & Giroux
19 Union Square West
New York, N.Y. 10003

Favil Press, Ltd.
152 Kensington Church Street
London W8, England

Fawcett World Library
1 Astor Plaza
New York, N.Y. 10036

Faxon (F.W.) Co.
15 Southwest Park
Westwood, Mass. 02090

Federal Legal Publications
95 Morton Street
New York, N.Y. 10014

Fell (Frederick), Inc.
386 Park Avenue South
New York, N.Y. 10016

Fernhill House
303 Park Avenue South
New York, N.Y. 10010

Ferry Press
177 Green Lane
London SE9, England

Film Culture
GPO Box 1499
New York, N.Y. 10001

Fireside Books
10 South Brentwood Blvd.
St. Louis, Missouri 63105

Fleet Press
156 Fifth Avenue
New York, N.Y. 10010

Florida State University Publications
15 NW 15 Street
Gainesville, Florida 32601

Focal Press
10 East 40 Street
New York, N.Y. 10016

Focal Press, Ltd.
31 Fitzroy Square
London W1, England

Folcroft Library Editions
Box 182
Folcroft, Pa. 19032

Folger Shakespeare Library Publications
See: Cornell University Press

Folklore Society
c/o University College
Gower Street
London WC1, England

Folkways Records
165 West 46 Street
New York, N.Y. 10036

Follett Publishing Co.
1010 West Washington Blvd.
Chicago, Illinois 60607

Fontana Books
c/o Collins (Wm.) Sons & Co.
14 St. James's Place
London SW1, England

Forbes Robertson, Ltd.
34 Melbury Gardens
London SW20, England

Foreign Languages Publishing House
Moscow, Russia

Fortress Press
2900 Queen Lane
Philadelphia, Pa. 19129

Fortune Press
See: Skilton (Charles) Publishing

Foulsham (W.) & Co., Ltd.
Yeovil Road
Slough, Bucks., England

Fountain Press, Ltd.
46–47 Chancery Lane
London WC2, England

Four Continents Book Corp.
156 Fifth Avenue
New York, N.Y. 10010

Four Square Books
See: New English Library, Ltd.

Fox (Sam) Publishing
1540 Broadway
New York, N.Y. 10036

Foyle (W. & G.), Ltd.
119–125 Charing Cross Road
London WC2, England

Franklin (Burt)
235 East 44 Street
New York, N.Y. 10017

Free Press
866 Third Avenue
New York, N.Y. 10022

French & European Publications
610 Fifth Avenue
New York, N.Y. 10020

French Book Guild
101 Fifth Avenue
New York, N.Y. 10003

French (Samuel)
25 West 45 Street
New York, N.Y. 10036

French (Samuel), Ltd.
26 Southampton Street, Strand
London WC2, England

Frewin (Leslie) Publishers, Ltd.
5 Goodwin's Court
St. Martin's Lane
London WC2, England

Friends of the Jewish Theatre
426 West 58 Street
New York, N.Y. 10019

Friendship Press
475 Riverside Drive
New York, N.Y. 10027

Funk & Wagnalls
666 Fifth Avenue
New York, N.Y. 10019

Gabberbocchus Press, Ltd.
42A Formosa Street
London W9, England

Gale Research Co.
Book Tower
Detroit, Michigan 48226

Gallery Press
Seel House
29 Seel Street
Liverpool, England

Garnstone Press, Ltd.
59 Brompton Road
London SW3, England

Gee & Co., Ltd.
151 Strand
London WC2, England

Geis (Bernard) Associates
128 East 56 Street
New York, N.Y. 10022

Gerard Designs
133 West 72 Street
New York, N.Y. 10023

Giles (Paul Kirk)
48–01 42 Street
Sunnyside, N.Y. 11104

Ginn & Company
See: Xerox College Publishing

Glenn (Peter) Publications
19 East 48 Street
New York, N.Y. 10017

Globe Book Co.
175 Fifth Avenue
New York, N.Y. 10010

Golden Press
See: Western Publishing Co.

Golden Quill Press
Francestown, N.H. 03043

Gollancz (Victor), Ltd.
14 Henrietta Street
Covent Garden
London WC2, England

Goodyear Publishing Co.
15115 Sunset Blvd.
Pacific Palisades, Calif. 90272

Gordian Press, Inc.
85 Tompkins Street
Staten Island, N.Y. 10304

Gousha (H.M.) Company
2001 The Alameda
San Jose, Calif. 95150

Grant & Cutler, Ltd.
11 Buckingham Street, Strand
London WC2, England

Green (Warren H.)
10 S. Brentwood Blvd.
St. Louis, Missouri 63105

Greene (Stephen) Press
Box 1000
Brattleboro, Vermont 05301

Greenwood Press
51 Riverside Avenue
Westport, Conn. 06880

Gregg International Publishers
157 South Ridgewood Road
Kentfield, Calif. 94904

Gregg Press, Inc.
70 Lincoln Street
Boston, Mass. 02111

Grosset & Dunlap
51 Madison Avenue
New York, N.Y. 10010

Grossman Publishers
625 Madison Avenue
New York, N.Y. 10022

Grove Press
53 East 11 Street
New York, N.Y. 10003

Guild of Pastoral Psychology
41 Redcliffe Gardens
London SW10, England

Guildhall School of Music & Drama
John Carpenter Street
Victoria Embankment
London EC4, England

Guizer Press
51 Station Road
Ibstock, Leicester, England

Hafner Publishing Co.
866 Third Avenue
New York, N.Y. 10022

Hairdressers Technical Council
39 Grafton Way
London W1, England

Hale (Robert) & Co., Ltd.
63 Old Brompton Road
London SW7, England

Hall (G.K.) & Company
70 Lincoln Street
Boston, Mass. 02111

Hamish Hamilton Ltd.
90 Great Russell Street
London WC1, England

Hamlyn Publishing Group, Ltd.
Hamlyn House
42 The Centre
Feltham, Middlesex, England

Hansen (Charles)
Hansen Educational Music & Books
1860 Broadway
New York, N.Y. 10023

Harcourt Brace Jovanovich
757 Third Avenue
New York, N.Y. 10017

Harper & Row
10 East 53 Street
New York, N.Y. 10022

Harrap (George) & Co., Ltd.
182–184 High Holborn
London WC1, England

Harris–Wolfe & Co.
235 N. Main Street
Jacksonville, Illinois 62650

Hart–Davis (Rupert), Ltd.
3 Upper James Street
London W1, England

Hart Publishing
719 Broadway
New York, N.Y. 10003

Harvard University Press
Kittridge Hall
79 Garden Street
Cambridge, Mass. 02138

Harvey House
5 South Buckhout Street
Irvington-on-Hudson, N.Y. 10533

Harvill Press, Ltd.
30A Pavillion Road
London SW1, England

Haskell House
280 Lafayette Street
New York, N.Y. 10012

Hastings House
10 East 40 Street
New York, N.Y. 10016

Hawthorn Books
70 Fifth Avenue
New York, N.Y. 10011

Hayden Book Co.
116 West 14 Street
New York, N.Y. 10011

Heath (D.C.)
125 Spring Street
Lexington, Mass. 02173

Heather Enterprises
3258 South Wadsworth Blvd.
Denver, Colorado 80277

Heffer (W.) & Sons, Ltd.
20 Trinity Street
Cambridge, England

Heineman (James H.)
475 Park Avenue
New York, N.Y. 10022

Heinemann (William), Ltd.
15–16 Queen Street
London W1, England

Heinman (W.S.)
1966 Broadway
New York, N.Y. 10023

Her Majesty's Stationary Office
London EC1, England

Herald Press
616 Walnut Avenue
Scottdale, Pa. 15683

Herder & Herder
1221 Avenue of the Americas
New York, N.Y. 10019

Herder (B.) Book Co., Ltd.
Billingshurst, Susex, England

Heritage Press
6 East 39 Street
New York, N.Y. 10016

Herzl Press
515 Park Avenue
New York, N.Y. 10022

Hewitt Brothers
7320 Milwaukee Avenue North
Chicago, Illinois 60648

Hilary Press
13 Blithfield Street
London W8, England

Hill & Wang
19 Union Square West
New York, N.Y. 10003

Hillary House
303 Park Avenue South
New York, N.Y. 10010

Hinrichsen Editions, Ltd.
10–12 Baches Street
London N1, England

Hispanic Institute
613 West 155 Street
New York, N.Y. 10032

Hodder & Stoughton, Ltd.
Warwick Lane
London EC4, England

Hogarth Press
Box 6012
Honolulu, Hawaii 96818

Hogarth Press, Ltd.
40–42 William IV Street
London WC2, England

Holiday House
18 East 56 Street
New York, N.Y. 10022

Hollis & Carter, Ltd.
9 Bow Street
London WC2, England

Holt–Blond, Ltd.
120 Golden Lane
London EC1, England

Holt, Rinehart & Winston
383 Madison Avenue
New York, N.Y. 10017

Home & Van Thal
c/o Ernest Benn, Ltd.
154 Fleet Street
London EC4, England

Hooks (Ed)
c/o Seven Lively Arts
853 Seventh Avenue
New York, N.Y. 10019

Hopkinson & Blake
329 Fifth Avenue
New York, N.Y. 10016

Horizon Press
156 Fifth Avenue
New York, N.Y. 10010

Houghton Mifflin Company
2 Park Street
Boston, Mass. 02107

Humanities Press
303 Park Avenue South
New York, N.Y. 10010

Humphries (Bruce)
68 Beacon Street
Somerville, Mass. 02143

Huntington Library Publications
1151 Oxford Road
San Marino, Calif. 91108

Huntington Press
2986 Joaquin Place
Fresno, Calif. 93726

Hurst & Blackett, Ltd.
See: Hutchinson Publishing Group

Hurst (C.) & Co., Ltd.
40A Royal Hill
London SE10, England

Hutchinson Publishing Group, Ltd.
3 Fitzroy Square
London W1, England

Icon Books, Ltd.
9 Down Street
London W1, England

Iliffe
88 Kingsway
London WC2, England

Imperial Society of Teachers of Dancing
70 Gloucester Place
London W1, England

Imported Publications
320 West Ohio Street
Chicago, Illinois 60610

Independent Television Authority
70 Brompton Road
London SW3, England

Indiana University Press
Tenth & Morton Streets
Bloomington, Indiana 47401

Informatics
49 Lordship Lane
London SE22, England

Inkshed Enterprises
11 Acol Road
London NW6, England

Institute for Personal Development
67 Pavillion Road
London SW1, England

Inter–Varsity Press
Downers Grove, Illinois 60515

International Publishers Co.
381 Park Avenue South
New York, N.Y. 10016

International Scholarly Book Services
60A Mill Trading Estate
Acton Lane
London NW10, England

International Textbook Co., Ltd.
Intertext House
Stewarts Road
London SW8, England

Iowa State University Press
Press Building
Ames, Iowa 50010

Irish University Press, Ltd.
60 Russell Square
London WC1, England

Israeli Folk Dance
515 Park Avenue
New York, N.Y. 10022

Jalaluddin Rumi Publications
2 Cowper Road
London W3, England

Japan Cultural Society
See: Japan Publications Trading Co.

Japan Publications Trading Co.
1255 Howard Street
San Francisco, Calif. 94103

Japan Times
See: Japan Publications Trading Co.

Jarrold & Sons, Ltd.
Barrack Street
Norwich, England

Jenkins (Herbert)
See: Barrie & Jenkins

Jenkins Publishing Co.
Box 2085
Austin, Texas 78767

John Day Company
257 Park Avenue South
New York, N.Y. 10010

John Knox Press
801 East Main Street
Richmond, Va. 23209

John Rain Associates
232 Madison Avenue
New York, N.Y. 10016

Johns Hopkins University Press
Baltimore, Md. 21218

Jonathan David Publishers
68–22 Eliot Avenue
Middle Village N.Y. 11379

Jones (Marshall) Co.
Francestown, N.H. 03043

Jordan & Sons, Ltd.
15 Pembroke Road
Bristol, England

Joseph (Michael), Ltd.
Bedford Square
London WC1, England

Judson Press
Valley Forge, Pa. 19481

Kaye & Ward, Ltd.
21 New Street
London EC2, England

Kaye (Nicholas), Ltd.
See: Kaye & Ward, Ltd.

Kemp's Commercial Guides, Ltd.
c/o Kemp's Printing & Publishing Co., Ltd.
299 Gray's Inn Road
London WC1, England

Kenedy (P. J.) & Sons
886 Third Avenue
New York, N.Y. 10022

Kenkyusha, Tokyo
See: Hurst (C.) & Co., Ltd.

Kennikat Press
90 South Bayles Avenue
Box 270
Port Washington, N.Y. 11050

Kent and Sussex Authors' Conclave
11 Woodville Road
Bexhill, Sussex, England

Kent State University Press
Kent, Ohio 44242

Kimber (William) & Co., Ltd.
Godolphin House
22A Queen Anne's Gate
London SW1, England

Kjos (Neil A.) Music Co.
525 Busse Highway
Park Ridge, Illinois 60608

Knopf (Alfred A.)
201 East 50 Street
New York, N.Y. 10022

Kodansha International
599 College Avenue
Palo Alto, Calif. 94306

Kraus Reprint Co.
Route 100
Millwood, N.Y. 10546

KTAV Publishing House
120 East Broadway
New York, N.Y. 10002

Lady Bird Series
See: Wills & Hepworth, Ltd.

Lagos Enterprises
PO Box 149, Radio City Station
New York, N.Y. 10019

Lake House Investments, Ltd.
41 W.A.D., Ramanayake Mawatha
Colombo, Ceylon

Lancer Books
1560 Broadway
New York, N.Y. 10036

Lancet (The)
7 Adam Street, Adelphi
London WC2, England

Lancet (Michael)
128–130 High Street
Esher, Surrey, England

Land's End Press
18 East 12 Street
New York, N.Y. 10003

Lane (Allen)
The Penguin Press
74 Grosvenor Street
London W1, England

Lane (John)
See: Bodley Head, Ltd.

Las Americas Publishing Co.
152 East 23 Street
New York, N.Y. 10010

Latimer New Dimensions, Ltd.
4 Alwyne Villas
London N1, England

Latimer Press
See: Latimer New Dimensions, Ltd.

Laurie (T. Werner), Ltd.
9 Bow Street
London WC2, England

Law–Arts Publishers
453 Greenwich Street
New York, N.Y. 10013

Lawrence & Wishart, Ltd.
46 Bedford Road
London WC1, England

Leisure Arts, Ltd.
18–22 St. Annes Crescent
London SW18, England

Leisure Time Books
c/o Sportshelf
PO Box 634
New Rochelle, N.Y. 10802

Lewis (David), Inc.
216 West 89 Street
New York, N.Y. 10024

Lewis (F.) Publishers, Ltd.
1461 London Road
Leigh-on-Sea, England

Lewis (H.K.) & Co., Ltd.
PO Box 66
136 Gower Street
London WC1, England

Library Association
Ridgemount Street
London WC1, England

Library Research Associates
Box 180G
Monroe, N.Y. 10950

Lippincott (J.B.) Co.
East Washington Square
Philadelphia, Pa. 19105

Little, Brown & Company
34 Beacon Street
Boston, Mass. 02106

Littlefield, Adams & Company
81 Adams Drive
Totowa, New Jersey 07512

Liveright
386 Park Avenue South
New York, N.Y. 10016

Liverpool University Press
123 Grove Street
Liverpool, England

Living Books
11 West 42 Street
New York, N.Y. 10036

Lockwood (Crosby) and Sons, Ltd.
3 Upper James Street
Golden Square
London W1, England

London House & Maxwell, Inc.
c/o British Book Centre
Fairview Park
Elmsford, N.Y. 10523

London Magazine Editions
30 Thurloe Place
London SW7, England

London School of Dramatic Art
Glentworth Street
London, England

Longman Group, Ltd.
Longman House
Burnt Mill, Harlow, Essex, England

Longmans, Green & Co., Ltd.
See: Longman Group, Ltd.

Lorrimer Publishing, Ltd.
47 Dean Street
London W1, England

Los Angeles County Museum of Art
5905 Wilshire Blvd.
Los Angeles, Calif. 90036

Lothrop, Lee & Shephard Co.
105 Madison Avenue
New York, N.Y. 10016

Louisiana State University Press
Hill Memorial Building
Baton Rouge, La. 70803

Loyola University Press
3441 N. Ashland Avenue
Chicago, Illinois 60657

Lucas Bros., Publishers
909 Lowry Street
Columbia, Missouri 65201

Luce (Robert B.)
2000 N Street, NW
Washington, D.C. 20036

Lutterworth Press
Albion House
Woking, Surrey, England

Luzac & Company
PO Box 157
46 Great Russell Street
London WC1, England

M.I.T. Press
28 Carleton Street
Cambridge, Mass. 02142

MacDonald & Co., Ltd.
49 Poland Street
London W1, England

Macdonald & Evans, Ltd.
8 John Street
London WC1, England

MacFadden–Bartell Corp.
205 East 42 Street
New York, N.Y. 10017

Macgibbon & Kee, Ltd.
3 Upper James Street
London W1, England

McGrath Publishing Co.
821 15 Street, NW
Washington, D.C. 20005

McGraw–Hill Book Company
1221 Avenue of the Americas
New York, N.Y. 10020

McKay (David) Company
750 Third Avenue
New York, N.Y. 10017

Maclelland & Stewart, Ltd.
See: Oxford University Press

Macmillan
866 Third Avenue
New York, N.Y. 10022

Macrae Smith Co.
225 South 15 Street
Philadelphia, Pa. 19102

Maestro
See: Speedimpex

Manchester Public Libraries
St. Peter's Square
Manchester, England

Manchester University Press
316 Oxford Road
Manchester, England

Manor Books
329 Fifth Avenue
New York, N.Y. 10016

Marks (Edward B.) Music Corp.
136 West 52 Street
New York, N.Y. 10019

Marquette University Press
131 West Wisconsin Avenue
Milwaukee, Wisconsin 53233

Marshall Cavendish Books, Ltd.
58 Old Compton Street
London W1, England

Martello
See: European Publishers Representatives

Mason (P. J.)
1 Whitney Road
Burton Latimer
Kettering, Northants., England

Massachusetts Inst. of Technology Press
See: M. I. T. Press

Mayflower Books, Ltd.
3 Upper James Street
London W1, England

Melborne University Press
See: Inter. Scholarly Book Services, Inc.

Mercier Press, Ltd.
4 Bridge Street
Cork, Eire, Ireland

Meredith Corp.
1716 Locust Street
Des Moines, Iowa 50336

Merlin Press, Ltd.
11 Fitzroy Square
London W1, England

Merriam (G. & C.)
47 Federal Street
Springfield, Mass. 01101

Merrill (Charles E.) Publishing Co.
1300 Alum Creek Drive
Columbus, Ohio 43216

Merrill (Robert)
6520 Westfield Blvd.
Indianapolis, Indiana 46220

Messner (Julian)
1 West 39 Street
New York, N.Y. 10018

Methodist Book Room
2 Chester House, Pages Lane
London N10, England

Methuen & Co., Ltd.
11 New Fetter Lane
London EC4, England

Michigan State University Press
Box 550
East Lansing, Michigan 48823

Miller (J. Garnet), Ltd.
1–5 Portpool Lane
London EC1, England

Miller (Marvin) Associates
Box 4105
Covina, Calif. 91722

Mills & Boon, Ltd.
17–19 Foley Street
London W1, England

Mitre Press
52 Lincoln's Inns Fields
London WC2, England

Modern Library, Inc.
See: Random House

Monarch Press
See: Simon & Schuster

Morgan & Morgan, Inc.
400 Warburton Avenue
Hastings-on-Hudson, N.Y. 10706

Morgan–Grampian Books, Ltd.
Summit House
Glebe Way
West Wickham, England

Morrow (William) & Co.
105 Madison Avenue
New York, N.Y. 10016

Mouton & Co.
PO Box 1132
The Hague, Netherlands

Mowbray (A. R.) & Co., Ltd.
The Alden Press
Osney Mead
Oxford, England

Muller (Frederick), Ltd.
Ludgate House
110 Fleet Street
London EC4, England

Murray (John) Publishers, Ltd.
50 Albemarle Street
London W1, England

Murrays Sales & Service Co.
Cresta House
146 Holloway Road
London N7, England

Museum of Modern Art
11 West 53 Street
New York, N.Y. 10019

Museum Press, Ltd.
39 Parker Street
London WC2, England

National Christian Education Council
Robert Denholm House
Nutfield, Redhill, Surrey, England

National Contemporary Theatre Conference
See: National Theatre Arts Conference

National Council of Teachers of English
1111 Kenyon Road
Urbana, Illinois 61801

National Press Books
850 Hansen Way
Palo Alto, Calif. 94304

National Press, Inc.
128 C Street, NE
Washington, D.C. 20002

National Theatre Arts Conference
3333 Chippewa Street
Columbus, Ohio 43204

National Theatre Conference
University of Wisconsin
Madison, Wisconsin 53706

Naylor Company
1015 Culebra Avenue
San Antonio, Texas 78201

Negro Universities Press
See: Greenwood Press

Nelson (Thomas), Inc.
Copewood & Davis Streets
Camden, New Jersey 08103

Nelson (Thomas) and Sons, Ltd.
36 Park Street
London W1, England

Nether Press
25 Whitehall Park
London N19, England

New American Library
1301 Avenue of the Americas
New York, N.Y. 10019

New Directions Publishing Corp.
333 Avenue of the Americas
New York, N.Y. 10014

New English Library, Ltd.
Barnard's Inn, Holborn
London EC1, England

New Era Books
See: Central Books

New Era Printing
Box 265
Deep River, Conn. 06417

New York Graphic Society, Ltd.
140 Greenwich Avenue
Greenwich, Conn. 06830

New York Public Library
Fifth Avenue & 42 Street
New York, N.Y. 10018

New York University Press
Washington Square
New York, N.Y. 10003

Newgate Press
See: National Christian Education Council

Newnes Educational Publishing Co., Ltd.
See: Butterworth & Co.

Nicholson (Ivor) & Watson, Ltd.
49 Brighton Road
Redhill, Surrey, England

Nijhoff (Martinus), Ltd.
Lange Voorhout 9–11
PO Box 269
The Hague, Netherlands

Nisbet (James) & Co., Ltd.
Digswell Place
Welwyn, Herts., England

Noble & Noble
750 Third Avenue
New York, N.Y. 10017

Noonday Press
See: Farrar Strauss & Giroux

Normal Press
25 Vicarage Lane
Upper Hale
Farnham, Surrey, England

Northwestern University Press
1735 Benson Avenue
Evanston, Illinois 60201

Norton (W.W.) & Co.
55 Fifth Avenue
New York, N.Y. 10003

Norwich Public Libraries
Bethel Street
Norwich, England

Novello & Co., Ltd.
Borough Green
Sevenoaks, Kent, England

Oak Publications
33 West 60 Street
New York, N.Y. 10023

Obolensky (Ivan) Inc.
1326 Madison Avenue
New York, N.Y. 10028

Octagon Books
See: Farrar Straus & Giroux

October House
160 Avenue of the Americas
New York, N.Y. 10013

Odhams Books, Ltd.
Hamlyn House
42 The Centre
Feltham, Middlesex, England

Odyssey Press
See: Bobbs Merrill

Ohio State University Press
2070 Neil Avenue
Columbus, Ohio 43210

Ohio University Press
Administrative Annex
Athens, Ohio 47501

Oldbourne Press
See: Macdonald & Co., Ltd.

Oliver & Boyd
Tweeddale Court
14 High Street
Edinburgh, Scotland

Oriel Press, Ltd.
32 Ridley Place
Newcastle-upon-Tyne, England

Orion Press
125A East 19 Street
New York, N.Y. 10003

Outerbridge & Dienstfry
See: Outerbridge & Lazard

Outerbridge & Lazard
200 West 72 Street
New York, N.Y. 10023

Owen (Peter) Ltd.
12 Kendrick Mews
Kendrick Place
London SW7, England

Oxford University Press
200 Madison Avenue
New York, N.Y. 10016

Oxford University Press
Ely House
37 Dover Street
London W1, England

Pacific Books
Box 558
Palo Alto, Calif. 94302

Package Publicity Service
1564 Broadway
New York, N.Y. 10036

Pagent—Poseidon
644 Pacific Street
Brooklyn, N.Y. 11213

Pan Books, Ltd.
33 Tothill Street
London SW1, England

Panther Books, Ltd.
3 Upper James Street
Golden Square
London W1, England

Paperback Library
315 Park Avenue South
New York, N.Y. 10010

Parents' Magazine Press
52 Vanderbilt Avenue
New York, N.Y. 10017

Parrish (Max) & Co., Ltd.
See: Macdonald & Co., Ltd.

Patterson Blick, Ltd.
Britannia House
100 Drayton Park
London N5, England

Paul (Stanley) & Co., Ltd.
See: Hutchinson Publishing Group, Ltd.

Paulist/Newman Press
400 Sette Drive
Paramus, New Jersey 07652

Peak Press
8 Highfield Close
Davenport, Stockport, England

Pegasus Publishing
4300 West 62 Street
Indianapolis, Indiana 46268

Pelham Books, Ltd.
52 Bedford Square
London WC1, England

Pelican
c/o Penguin Books, Inc.
Baltimore, Md. 21207

Penguin Books, Inc.
7110 Ambassador Road
Baltimore, Md. 21207

Penguin Books, Ltd.
Harmondsworth, England

Pennsylvania State University Press
215 Wagner Building
University Park, Pa. 16802

Pergamon Press
Maxwell House, Fairview Park
Elmsford, N.Y. 10523

Pergamon Press, Ltd.
Headington Hill Hall
Oxford, England

Personality Posters
74 Fifth Avenue
New York, N.Y. 10011

Peter Glenn
See: Glenn (Peter)

Pflaum/Standard
38 West Fifth Street
Dayton, Ohio 45402

Phaedra, Inc.
49 Park Avenue
New York, N.Y. 10016

Phaidon Press, Ltd.
5 Cromwell Place
London SW7, England

Phillimore & Co., Ltd.
Shopwyke Hall
Chichester, Sussex, England

Phillip (George) & Son, Ltd.
12–14 Longacre
London WC2, England

Philosophical Library
15 East 40 Street
New York, N.Y. 10016

Phoenix House Publications
See: Dent (J.M.) & Sons, Ltd.

Pilgrim Press
See: United Church Press

Pilgrim Press
See: National Christian Education Council

Pioneer Press
103 Borough High Street
London SE1, England

Pirandello Society
c/o Mrs. M. Smith
Fosse Beck, Bewerley
Pateley Bridge, England

Pitkin Pictorials, Ltd.
11 Wyfold Road
London SW6, England

Pitman Publishing Corp.
6 East 43 Street
New York, N.Y. 10017

Pitman (Sir Issac) & Sons, Ltd.
Pitman House
Parker Street, Kingsway
London WC2, England

Pittsburgh Playhouse Press
See: Coach House Press

Plays, Inc.
8 Arlington Street
Boston, Mass. 02116

Pocket Books
630 Fifth Avenue
New York, N.Y. 10020

Popular Library, Inc.
355 Lexington Avenue
New York, N.Y. 10017

Pordes (Henry)
529B Finchley Road
London NW3, England

Potter (Clarkson N.), Inc.
419 Park Avenue South
New York, N.Y. 10016

Praeger Publishers, Inc.
111 Fourth Avenue
New York, N.Y. 10003

Premier Press
PO Box 4428
Berkeley, Calif. 94704

Premier Press, Ltd.
30 Osborne Street
London E1, England

Prentice–Hall, Inc.
Englewood Cliffs, N. J. 07632

Press of Case Western Reserve University
The Quail Building
Cleveland, Ohio 44106

Price/Stern/Sloan, Inc.
410 N. La Cienega Blvd.
Los Angeles, Calif. 90048

Primestyle
21 Highfield Avenue
St. Austell, Cornwall, England

Princeton University Press
Princeton, New Jersey 08540

Principia Press, Inc.
5743 Kimbark Avenue
Chicago, Illinois 60637

Probsthain (Arthur)
41 Great Russell Street
London WC1, England

Progress House, Ltd.
270 North Circular Rd.
Dublin, Eire, Ireland

Progress Publishers
See: Imported Publications

Proscenium Press
Box 361
Newark, Delaware 19711

Public Affairs Committee
381 Park Avenue South
New York, N. Y. 10016

Public Affairs Press
419 New Jersey Avenue, SE
Washington, D. C. 20003

Purdue University Studies
South Campus Cts.
Purdue University
Lafayette, Indiana 47907

Purnell & Sons, Ltd.
49 Poland Street
London W1, England

G. P. Putnam's Sons
200 Madison Avenue
New York, N. Y. 10016

Pyramid Communications, Inc.
919 Third Avenue
New York, N. Y. 10022

Pyramid Press
820 Kentucky Home Life Bldg.
Louisville, Kentucky 40202

Pyramid Press
407 Industrial Park
Palm Springs, Calif. 92262

Pyramid Publications
See: Pyramid Communications, Inc.

Quadrangle Books, Inc.
330 Madison Avenue
New York, N. Y. 10017

Queen Anne Press, Ltd.
See: Macdonald & Co., Ltd.

Queens University of Belfast
Institute of Irish Studies
Belfast, Ireland

Quigley Publishing Co.
1270 Avenue of the Americas
New York, N. Y. 10020

Rainbird Publishing Group, Ltd.
44 Edgware Road
London W2, England

Rand–McNally & Co.
8255 Central Park Avenue
Skokie, Illinois 60076

Random House, Inc.
201 East 50 Street
New York, N. Y. 10022

Rapp & Whiting, Ltd.
105 Great Russell Street
London WC1, England

Rebel Press, Ltd.
2 Derby Street
London W1, England

Recipes for Starving Actors
c/o Victor Izay
2316 West Verdugo Avenue
Burbank, Calif. 91506

Redman (Alvin), Ltd.
See: Bailey Bros. & Swinfen, Ltd.

Regency Press, Ltd.
43 New Oxford Street
London WC1, England

Regnery (Henry) Co.
114 West Illinois Street
Chicago, Illinois 60610

Reinhardt (Max), Ltd.
9 Bow Street
London WC2, England

Reinhold
See: Van Nostrand Reinhold

Religious Theatre
c/o Wichita State University
Wichita, Kansas 67208

Revell (Fleming H.) Co.
Old Tappan, New Jersey 07675

Reynal
See: Trans-Atlantic Book Service

Rinehart Press
See: Holt, Rinehart & Winston

Rockliff Publishing Corp.
See: Barrie & Jenkins

Rodale Books, Inc.
33 East Minor Street
Emmaus, Pa. 18049

Rodney Books, Ltd.
9–11 Monmouth Street
London WC2, England

Ronald Press Co.
79 Madison Avenue
New York, N.Y. 10016

Rosen (Richards) Press
29 East 21 Street
New York, N.Y. 10010

Ross (Alan), Ltd.
See: London Magazine Editions

Routledge & Kegan Paul, Ltd.
68–74 Carter Lane
London EC4, England

Roy Publishers
30 East 74 Street
New York, N.Y. 10021

Russell & Russell
122 East 42 Street
New York, N.Y. 10017

Rutgers University Press
30 College Avenue
New Brunswick, New Jersey 08903

Ryerson Music Publishers
71 West 23 Street
New York, N.Y. 10010

S.C.M. Press
See: Student Christian Movement Press

S.P.C.K.
See: Society for Promoting Christian Knowledge

Saifer (Albert)
Box 56, Town Center
West Orange, New Jersey 07052

St. John's University Press
Grand Central & Utopia Parkways
Jamaica, N.Y. 11432

St. Martin's Press
175 Fifth Avenue
New York, N.Y. 10010

Scarecrow Press, Inc.
52 Liberty Street
Metuchen, New Jersey 08840

Schenkman Publishing Co.
3 Mt. Auburn Place, Harvard Square
Cambridge, Mass. 02138

Schirmer (G.), Inc.
609 Fifth Avenue
New York, N.Y. 10017

Schocken Books, Inc.
200 Madison Avenue
New York, N.Y. 10016

Schofield & Sims, Ltd.
35 St. John's Road
Huddersfield, England

Scholarly Press
22929 Industrial Drive East
St. Clair Shores, Mich. 48080

Scholars' Facsimiles & Reprints
Box 344
Delmar, N.Y. 12054

Scholastic Book Services
50 West 44 Street
New York, N.Y. 10036

Schott & Co., Ltd.
48 Great Marlborough Street
London W1, England

Scolar Press, Ltd.
20 Main Street
Menston, England

Scorpion Press
Pakefield Street
Lowestoft, Suffolk, England

Scott (Bertie) Foundation
c/o Campbell Allen
188 Goldhurst Terrace
London NW6, England

Scott Foresman & Co.
1900 East Lake Avenue
Glenview, Illinois 60025

Scribner's (Charles) Sons
597 Fifth Avenue
New York, N.Y. 10017

Seabury Press, Inc.
815 Second Avenue
New York, N.Y. 10017

Secker (Martin) & Warburg, Ltd.
14 Carlisle Street
London W1, England

Sheed & Ward
64 University Place
New York, N.Y. 10003

Sherbourne Press
1640 South La Cienega Blvd.
Los Angeles, Calif. 90035

Sheridan House, Inc.
Box 254, South Station
Yonkers, N.Y. 10705

Sherratt (John) & Son, Ltd.
The Saint Ann's Press
Park Road
Altrincham, Chesire, England

Shire (H.M.)
2 Bilstrode Gardens
Cambridge, England

Shire Publications
12B Temple Square
Aylesbury, Bucks., England

Shoe String Press
995 Sherman Avenue
Hamden, Conn. 06514

Shorewood Publishers
724 Fifth Avenue
New York, N.Y. 10019

Shull (Leo) Publications
136 West 44 Street
New York, N.Y. 10036

Sidgwick & Jackson, Ltd.
1 Tavistock Chambers, Bloomsbury
London WC1, England

Signet
See: New American Library

Silent Picture (The)
613 Harrow Road
London W10, England

Silverhill Academic Enterprises
See: Kent & Sussex Authors' Conclave

Simon & Schuster, Inc.
630 Fifth Avenue
New York, N.Y. 10020

Simon's Directory
See: Package Publicity Service

Skilton (Charles), Ltd.
50 Alexandra Road
London SW19, England

Peter Smith
6 Lexington Avenue
Gloucester, Mass. 01930

Soccer Associates
Box 634
New Rochelle, N.Y. 10802

Society for Promoting Christian Knowledge
Holy Trinity Church
Marylebone Road
London NW1, England

Society for Theatre Research
14 Woronzow Road
London NW8, England

Society of Motion Picture
& Television Engineers
9 East 41 Street
New York, N.Y. 10017

Something Else Press
Elm Street
Millerton, N.Y. 12546

Southern Illinois University Press
Box 697
Carbondale, Illinois 62901

Southern Methodist University Press
Dallas, Texas 75222

Souvenir Press, Ltd.
95 Mortimer Street
London W1, England

Speedimpex U. S. A., Inc.
23–16 40th Avenue
Long Island City, N. Y. 11101

Speller (Robert) & Sons
10 East 23 Street
New York, N. Y. 10010

Sphere Books, Ltd.
30–32 Grays Inn Road
London WC1, England

Sport Shelf & Soccer Assoc.
PO Box 634
New Rochelle, N. Y. 10802

Spring Books
See: Hamlyn Publishing Group

Stacey (J. W.), Inc.
2575 Hanover Street
Palo Alto, Calif. 94304

Stacey Publications
1 Hawthorndene Road
Hayes, Bromley
England

Stage Guild
50 South La Salle Street
Chicago, Illinois 60603

Stanford University Press
Stanford, Calif. 94305

Stanwix House, Inc.
3020 Chartiers Avenue
Pittsburgh, Pa. 15204

Stanyan/Cheval Books
8721 Sunset Blvd.
Hollywood, Calif. 90069

State University of New York Press
99 Washington Avenue
Albany, N. Y. 12201

State University of New York at Buffalo
Buffalo, N. Y. 14214

Steck–Vaughn Company
Box 2028
Austin, Texas 78767

Steele Enterprises
306 West 4 Street
New York, N. Y. 10014

Stein & Day
7 East 48 Street
New York, N. Y. 10017

Steiner (Rudolf) School Trust, Ltd.
38 Clinton Road
Edinburgh, Scotland

Stephens (Patrick), Ltd.
9 Ely Place
London EC1, England

Sterling Publishing Co.
419 Park Avenue South
New York, N. Y. 10016

Stipes Publishing Co.
10–12 Chester Street
Champaign, Illinois 61820

Stockwell (Arthur H.), Ltd.
Ilfracombe, Devon, England

Stuart (Lyle), Inc.
120 Enterprise Avenue
Secaucus, New Jersey 07094

Stubs Publications
246 West 44 Street
New York, N. Y. 10036

Student Christian Movement Press
56–58 Bloomsbury Street
London WC1, England

Student Outlines Co.
295 Huntington Avenue
Boston, Mass. 02115

Studio Vista Publishers
Blue Star House, Highgate Hill
London N19, England

Study Master, Inc.
311 Crossways Park Drive
Woodbury, N. Y. 11797

Swallow Press, Inc.
1139 South Wabash Avenue
Chicago, Illinois 60605

Syracuse University Press
Box 8, University Station
Syracuse, N. Y. 13210

TAB Books
Blue Ridge Summit, Pa. 17214

Talbot Press, Ltd.
89 Talbot Street
Dublin, Eire, Ireland

Tanager Press
153 South Bradford Street
Dover, Delaware 19901

Tantivy Press
108 New Bond Street
London W1, England

Taplinger Publishing Co.
200 Park Avenue South
New York, N.Y. 10003

Tarcher (J.P.), Inc.
9110 Sunset Blvd.
Los Angeles, Calif. 90069

Tavistock Publications, Ltd.
11 New Fetter Lane
London EC4, England

Teachers College Press
Columbia University
1234 Amsterdam Avenue
New York, N.Y. 10027

Temple University Press
Philadelphia, Pa. 19122

Texas Western Press
University of Texas
El Paso, Texas 79968

Thab Publishers
43 Richmond Road
West Wimbeldon
London SW20, England

Thames & Hudson, Ltd.
30 Bloomsbury Street
London WC1, England

Theatre Arts Books
333 Avenue of the Americas
New York, N.Y. 10014

Theatrical Variety Publications
Box 9745
N. Hollywood, Calif. 91609

Toastmaster International
2200 N. Grand Avenue
Santa Ana, Calif. 92711

Toucan Press (The)
Mount Durand
St. Peter Port, Gurnsey
England

Transatlantic Arts, Inc.
North Village Green
Levittown, N.Y. 11756

Trans–Atlantic Book Service, Ltd.
51 Weymouth Street
London W1, England

Transworld Publishers, Ltd.
Cavendish House
57–59 Uxbridge Road, Ealing
London W5, England

Traylen (Charles W.)
Castle House
49–50 Quarry Street
Guildford, Surrey, England

Trident Press
630 Fifth Avenue
New York, N.Y. 10020

Trinity Lane Press
2 Covent Garden
Cambridge, England

Trinity University Press
715 Stadium Drive
San Antonio, Texas 78284

Tri–Ocean Books
62 Townsend Street
San Francisco, Calif. 94107

Triton Publishing Co., Ltd.
1A Montague Mews North
London W1, England

Troubador Press
126 Folsom Street
San Francisco, Calif. 94105

Tudor Publishing Co.
221 Park Avenue South
New York, N.Y. 10003

Tulane University
Publications Dept.
New Orleans, La. 70118

Tuttle (Charles E.) Company
28 South Main Street
Rutland, Vermont 05701

Twayne Publishers
31 Union Square West
New York, N.Y. 10003

Twentieth Century Fund
41 East 70 Street
New York, N.Y. 10021

Twentieth Century Press
320 South Jefferson Street
Chicago, Illinois 60606

Tyndale House
336 Gundersen Drive
Wheaton, Illinois 60187

Tyndale Press
39 Bedford Square
London WC1, England

UNESCO Publications Center
See: Unipub, Inc.

Unger (Frederick) Publishing Co.
250 Park Avenue South
New York, N.Y. 10003

Unipub, Inc.
Box 433
New York, N.Y. 10016

United Church Press
1505 Race Street
Philadelphia, Pa. 19102

United Synagogue Book Service
218 East 70 Street
New York, N.Y. 10021

Universal Publishing & Distributing
235 East 45 Street
New York, N.Y. 10017

Universe Books
381 Park Avenue South
New York, N.Y. 10016

University of Alabama Press
Drawer 2877
University, Alabama 35486

University of Arizona Press
Box 3398
Tucson, Arizona 85722

University of Birmingham Press
PO Box 363
Birmingham
England

University of California Press
2223 Fulton Street
Berkeley, Calif. 94720

University of Chicago Press
5801 Ellis Avenue
Chicago, Illinois 60637

University of Florida Press
15 NW 15 Street
Gainesville, Florida 32601

University of Georgia Press
Athens, Georgia 30601

University of Hawaii Press
See: University Press of Hawaii

University of Hull
The Library
Hull, England

University of Illinois Press
Urbana, Illinois 61801

University of Kansas
The Libraries
Lawrence, Kansas 66044

University of Kentucky Press
See: University Press of Kentucky

University of London
Institute of Germanic Studies
29 Russell Square
London WC1, England

University of London Press
St. Paul's House
Warwick Lane
London EC4, England

University of Maine Press
Orono, Maine 04473

University of Massachusetts Press
Munson Hall
Amherst, Mass. 01002

University of Miami Press
Box 9088
Coral Gables, Florida 33124

University of Michigan Press
615 East University
Ann Arbor, Michigan 48106

University of Minnesota Press
2037 University Avenue, SE
Minneapolis, Minn. 55455

University of Missouri Press
107 Swallow Hall
Columbia, Missouri 65201

University of Nebraska Press
901 North 17 Street
Lincoln, Nebraska 68508

University of New Mexico Press
Albuquerque, New Mexico 87106

University of North Carolina Press
Box 2288
Chapel Hill, North Carolina 27514

University of North Dakota Press
Box 8006, University Station
Grand Forks, North Dakota 58202

University of Notre Dame Press
Notre Dame, Indiana 46556

University of Oklahoma Press
1005 Asp Avenue
Norman, Oklahoma 73069

University of Oregon Books
Eugene, Oregon 94703

University of Pennsylvania Press
3933 Walnut Street
Philadelphia, Pa. 19104

University of Pittsburgh Press
127 N. Bellefield Avenue
Pittsburgh, Pa. 15213

University of Queensland
St. Lucia, Queensland
Australia

University of Tennessee Press
Communications Building
Knoxville, Tenn. 37916

University of Texas Press
Box 7819, University Station
Austin, Texas 78712

University of Toronto Press
Front Campus
Toronto, Ontario, Canada

University of Washington Press
Seattle, Washington 98105

University of Wisconsin Press
Box 1379
Madison, Wisconsin 53701

University Press at Buffalo
Box F
State University of New York
Buffalo, N.Y. 14214

University Press of Hawaii
535 Ward Avenue
Honolulu, Hawaii 96814

University Press of Virginia
Box 3608, University Station
Charlottesville, Virginia 22903

University Publishers
130 Babson Street
Mattapan, Mass. 02126

University Publishing Co.
1126 Q Street
Lincoln, Nebraska 68501

University Tutorial Press, Ltd.
9–10 Great Sutton Street
London EC1, England

Vallentine, Mitchell & Co., Ltd.
67 Great Russell Street
London WC1, England

Van Nostrand Reinhold Co.
450 West 33 Street
New York, N.Y. 10001

Vanderbilt University Press
Nashville, Tenn. 37325

Vane (Nicholas), Ltd.
c/o Kaye & Ward, Ltd.
21 New Street
London EC2, England

Vanguard Press
424 Madison Avenue
New York, N.Y. 10017

Vanous (Arthur) Co.
20 Banta Place
Hackensack, New Jersey 07601

Vantage Press, Inc.
516 West 34 Street
New York, N.Y. 10001

Vernon & Yates
26 Old Brompton Road
London SW7, England

Verry (Lawrence), Inc.
16 Holmes Street
Mystic, Conn. 06355

Victoria & Albert Museum
Exhibition Road
London SW7, England

Viking Press, Inc.
625 Madison Avenue
New York, N.Y. 10022

Vintage
See: Random House

Vision Press, Ltd.
157 Knightsbridge
London SW1, England

Wace & Co., Ltd.
3–11 Eyre St. Hill
London EC1, England

Wadsworth Publishing Co.
Belmont, Calif. 94002

Walck (Henry Z.), Inc.
19 Union Square West
New York, N.Y. 10003

Walker & Co.
720 Fifth Avenue
New York, N.Y. 10019

Walker/Weatherhill
See: Walker & Co.

Ward (Edmund), Ltd.
See: Kaye & Ward

Ward Lock, Ltd.
116 Baker Street
London W1, England

Warne (Frederick) & Co., Ltd.
40 Bedford Square
London WC1, England

Washburn (Ives), Inc.
750 Third Avenue
New York, N.Y. 10017

Washington Square Press
630 Fifth Avenue
New York, N.Y. 10020

Watson—Guptill Publications
165 West 46 Street
New York, N.Y. 10036

Watts (Franklin), Inc.
845 Third Avenue
New York, N.Y. 10022

Wayne State University Press
5980 Cass Avenue
Detroit, Michigan 48202

Wayside Press
1501 Washington Road
Mendota, Illinois 61342

Wehman Bros.
158 Main Street
Hackensack, New Jersey 07601

Weidenfeld (George) & Nicolson, Ltd.
5 Winsley Street
London W1, England

Weinberger (Josef), Ltd.
10—16 Rathbone Street
London W1, England

Wells Gardner, Darton & Co., Ltd.
Faygate
Horsham, Sussex, England

Wesleyan University Press
100 Riverview Center
Middletown, Conn. 06457

Western Publishing Co.
1220 Mound Avenue
Racine, Wisconsin 53404

Western Reserve University
See: Press of Case Western Reserve Univ.

Westminster Press
Witherspoon Building
Philadelphia, Pa. 19107

Westminster Productions, Ltd.
Westminster Theatre
Buckingham Palace Road
London SW1, England

Weybright & Talley, Inc.
750 Third Avenue
New York, N.Y. 10017

Wheaton (A) & Co.
Headington Hill Hall
Oxford, England

Wheelwright (Bond) Co.
Porters Landing
Freeport, Maine 04032

Wheelwright Press
975 SW Temple
Salt Lake City, Utah 84101

Whitaker (J.) & Sons, Ltd.
13 Bedford Square
London WC1, England

Wiley (John) & Sons, Inc.
605 Third Avenue
New York, N.Y. 10016

William—Frederick Press
55 East 86 Street
New York, N.Y. 10028

Willis Music
440 Main Street
Cincinnati, Ohio 45202

Wills & Hepworth
Ladybird Books
Box No. 12
Derby Square
Loughborough, England

Wilshire Book Co.
12015 Sherman Road
N. Hollywood, Calif. 91605

Wilson (G. F.) & Co., Ltd.
Eastgate Printing Works
Town Quay
Southampton, England

Wilson (H. W.) Co.
950 University Avenue
Bronx, N. Y. 10452

Winsor & Newton
555 Winsor Drive
Secaucus, New Jersey 07094

Wisconsin Film Society Press
1312 West Johnson Street
Madison, Wisconsin 53715

Witherby (H. F. & G.), Ltd.
15 Nicholas Lane
London EC4, England

Wolfe Publishing, Ltd.
10 Earlham Street
London WC2, England

Wolff (Oswald), Ltd.
52 Manchester Street
London W1, England

World Publishing Co.
110 East 59 Street
New York, N. Y. 10022

World Wide Books
250 West 57 Street
New York, N. Y. 10019

World's Work, Ltd.
The Windmill Press
Tadworth, Surrey, England

Writer, Inc. (The)
8 Arlington Street
Boston, Mass. 02116

Xerox College Publishing
191 Spring Street
Lexington, Mass. 02173

Xerox Education Group
1200 High Ridge Road
Stamford, Conn. 06905

Yale University Press
149 York Street
New Haven, Conn. 06511

Yennadon Plays
Heatherdene
Dousland
Yelverton
England

Yoseloff (Thomas), Ltd.
18 Charing Cross Road
London WC2
England

Zeno Publishers
6 Denmark Street
London WC2
England

Zondervan Publishing House
1415 Lake Drive SE
Grand Rapids, Michigan 49506

Zwemmer (A.), Ltd.
24 Litchfield Street
London WC2
England

About the editor:

RALPH NEWMAN SCHOOLCRAFT was educated in theatre at Columbia University. He has been employed as a director, stage manager, lighting technician, and costume assistant. Mr. Schoolcraft has appeared as an actor on Broadway, off-Broadway, and off-off-Broadway, as well as appearing in national touring companies in most of the other forty-nine states. Currently he is marking his twenty-third year as an actor with the Traveling Playhouse, a children's theatre company. His work as a specialist in the research of performing arts literature began at The Drama Book Shop in 1965.